Payroll Answer Book
2017 Edition

by Deborah Ellis Timberlake, Esq., CPP

Payroll Answer Book gives payroll professionals guidance on the steps they need to take to comply with the laws and regulations governing payroll. From both a legal and practical standpoint, broad and deep coverage is given to the payroll implications of the wage and hour law and how to handle the federal employment taxation of benefits offered to employees. Detailed information is provided on computing and paying payroll taxes, how to handle garnishments and other deductions, how to determine whether workers are employees or independent contractors, what records must be kept, what the benefits and disadvantages of direct deposit of employees' wages are, how to treat sick pay, how to handle a merger or acquisition, what to ask when employees work abroad, and how the payroll department can protect employees' data. In addition to answering the full range of payroll questions, the *Payroll Answer Book* contains abundant examples that illustrate necessary calculations.

Highlights of the 2017 Edition

The 2017 Edition of *Payroll Answer Book* brings the payroll professional up to date on the latest federal law and regulatory changes. Highlights include:

- How to complete the 2017 W-2 Form (see Qs 4:89 and 9:466).

- Safe harbor rule for *de minimis* errors (see Q 4:111).

- Revised due dates for forms (see Table 1-1).

- Additional analysis about the method of acquisition of a predecessor's property being material (see Q 12:40).

- The same-day Automated Clearing House (ACH) rule enters Phase 2 (see Qs 5:23-5:29).

- An example illustrating withholding for a 2017 levy (see Q 7:68).

- The trends and additional requirements for states and localities to report sick pay (see Q 10:33).

- Reporting deadlines for returns under the Affordable Care Act (see Q 1:45).

- 2017 examples of the annualized wages method (see Q 2:85).

 Wolters Kluwer

- The FUTA credit reduction for 2016 for California and the Virgin Islands, down from four states the previous year (see Q 3:42).

- Electronic Income Withholding Order (e-IWO) Program to submit a lump sum payment and receive a one-time lump sum e-IWO (see Q 7:32).

- The increased penalty for failure to furnish a correct W-2 (see Q 4:110).

- The IRS and 37 states sharing tax examination results (see Q 4:134).

- Changes in states' data breach requirements for employers to quantify and report (see Qs 14:52 and 14:54).

- Changes around misclassification of workers as independent contractors vs. employees (see Q 6:39).

- Examples of how states protect their rights to taxes due in an M&A event (see Q 12:93).

- Explanation about new forms that employers must provide to employees and submit to the IRS (see Q 1:45).

- The date when the 2017 exemption from federal income tax withholding will expire (see Q 2:66).

- The 2017 limit on the amount of income and unearned income a dependent can earn and still claim exemption from withholding (see Q 2:66).

- The threshold for withholding income tax on distributions of Indian gaming profits to tribal members (see Q 2:112).

- Due dates for filing 2017 Form 941 (see Q 4:46).

- Maximum amount of adoption expenses excludable for 2017 and income limitations (see Qs 9:49 and 9:51).

- Update on rates to use for imputing income for employer-provided aircraft (see Q 9:111).

- Updated information on the limits for leased vehicles used by employees (see Q 9:116).

- Tax credit for increasing research activities reported on Schedule B of Form 941 (see Q 4:45).

- Guidelines for substitute Forms W-2, W-2c, W-3, and W-3c (see Q 4:93).

- Updates on state regulations around pay cards (see Qs 5:42 and 5:53).

- Additional requirements from the Consumer Financial Protection Bureau (CFPB) (see Q 5:44).

- Exemption amounts for wages paid to domestic workers in 2017 (see Q 6:25).

- 2017 federal employment tax rates and wage bases (see Q 2:2).

- List of holidays for 2017 (see Q 4:20).

- 2017 qualified transportation exclusion limits for parking and transit with parity in effect (see Q 9:454).

- Withholding allowances for each pay period for 2017 (see Q 2:83).

- 2017 personal exemption and standard deduction amounts needed to compute exemption from tax levies (see Table 7-4).

- 2017 figures used to withhold federal income tax from wages paid to nonresident aliens (see Q 2:118).

- Rate for imputing the cents-per-mile valuation method (see Q 9:176).

- Updated state directories for labor (see Appendix A), income tax withholding (see Appendix B), and employment security agencies (see Appendix C).

- Guidelines for use of mobile payments (see Qs 5:56–5:58).

- New Form I-9 released in November 2016, replacing the old form, changing some of the information reported, and making several other improvements (see Q 1:6).

- Updated tables for federal income tax withholding (see Q 2:77).

- New limit for Social Security is $127,200 for 2017 (see Q 2:2).

- U.S. Department of Labor issued Unemployment Insurance Program Letter No. 02-17 North American Industry Classification Codes for Calendar Year 2017 (see Q 3:10).

- New guidelines for Form 8809, Application—Extension of Time to File Information Returns for W-2, 1042-S, 1099, 1094-C, 1095-B, and 1095-C (see Q 4:39).

- IRS has created two new forms—8879-EMP and 8453-EMP—for employees to file electronically (see Q 4:49).

- Several states (Massachusetts, Oregon, Rhode Island) have accelerated the deadline to January 31 for filing State Form W-2 (see Q 4:77).

- Now 31 states have signed MOU with the IRS under the Questionable Employment Tax Practice (QETP) (see Q 6:21).

- State legislative and court updates on worker classifications (see Q 6:69).

- Handling wage repayments of an overpayment in the same year and thereafter (see Q 1:33).

- Final Rule on Delivering the Exceptions for Executive, Administrative, Professional, Outside Sales, and Computer Employees under FLSA on May 18, 2016; threshold raised to $913 (equivalent of $47,476 annually) from $455 (see Q 8:46).

- U.S. Court of Appeals—Eastern District Texas signed injunction, placing the required implementation of the Final Rule on hold (see Q 8:46).

- Courts are split on whether overtime rules apply to Native American organization (see Q 8:30).

- Wage and Hour Division confirms broad definition of joint employment (see Q 8:37).

- Ride-sharing services such as Uber have been challenged by drivers wishing to be classified as employees (see Q 8:99).

- Changes in sick pay rules in 2017 (see Q 10:33).

- Significant change on data privacy from the European Commission and the United States (see Q 14:95).

- State notification requirements for data breach (see Q 14:52).

- Certain states are now removing encrypted data from safe harbor exceptions (see Q 14:52).

- Three states do not have data privacy requirement (see Q 14:52).

- New rule, General Data Protection Regulation (GDPR), establishes new standards for data privacy (see Q 14:95).

- New information on data privacy rules for Asia Pacific (APAC) (see Q 14:97).

- Requirements for cell phone provided by employer to be a working condition fringe benefit (see Q 9:105).

- Cents-per-mile valuation method decreases to $0.535 for 2017, down from $0.54 for 2016, and the FMV for 2017 is $17,800 for a truck or van (see Q 9:121).

- High-low per diem rates for high-cost and other cities increased to $282 and $189 respectively (see Q 9:174).

5/17

For questions concerning this shipment, billing, or other customer service matters, call our Customer Service Department at 1-800-234-1660.

For toll-free ordering, please call 1-800-638-8437.

Payroll
Answer Book

2017 Edition

Deborah Ellis Timberlake, Esq., CPP

This publication is designed to provide accurate and authoritative information in regard to the subject matter covered. It is sold with the understanding that the publisher and the author(s) are not engaged in rendering legal, accounting, or other professional services. If legal advice or other professional assistance is required, the services of a competent professional should be sought.

—From a *Declaration of Principles* jointly adopted by
a Committee of the American Bar Association and
a Committee of Publishers and Associations

Published by Wolters Kluwer in New York.

Wolters Kluwer Legal & Regulatory U.S. serves customers worldwide with CCH, Aspen Publishers and Kluwer Law International products.

Printed in the United States of America

ISBN 978-1-4548-8354-8

ISSN 1540-6490

1 2 3 4 5 6 7 8 9 0

About Wolters Kluwer Legal & Regulatory U.S.

Wolters Kluwer Legal & Regulatory U.S. delivers expert content and solutions in the areas of law, corporate compliance, health compliance, reimbursement, and legal education. Its practical solutions help customers successfully navigate the demands of a changing environment to drive their daily activities, enhance decision quality and inspire confident outcomes.

Serving customers worldwide, its legal and regulatory portfolio includes products under the Aspen Publishers, CCH Incorporated, Kluwer Law International, ftwilliam.com and MediRegs names. They are regarded as exceptional and trusted resources for general legal and practice-specific knowledge, compliance and risk management, dynamic workflow solutions, and expert commentary.

WOLTERS KLUWER SUPPLEMENT NOTICE

This product is updated on a periodic basis with supplements and/or new editions to reflect important changes in the subject matter.

If you would like information about enrolling this product in the update service, or wish to receive updates billed separately with a 30-day examination review, please contact our Customer Service Department at 1-800-234-1660 or email us at: *customer.service@wolterskluwer.com*. You can also contact us at:

Wolters Kluwer
Distribution Center
7201 McKinney Circle
Frederick, MD 21704

Important Contact Information

- To order any title, go to *www.wklawbusiness.com* or call 1-800-638-8437.

- To reinstate your manual update service, call 1-800-638-8437.

- To contact Customer Service, e-mail *customer.service@wolters kluwer.com*, call 1-800-234-1660, fax 1-800-901-9075, or mail correspondence to: Order Department—Wolters Kluwer, PO Box 990, Frederick, MD 21705.

- To review your account history or pay an invoice online, visit *www.WKLawBusiness.com/payinvoices*.

Preface

Federal and state rules regarding payroll administration have become increasingly complex, as well as increasingly interrelated with other areas of expertise. Today's employers must implement and maintain accurate payroll procedures while coping with new qualifications for exempt employees, taxation of benefits, worker classifications, deposit rules, tax reporting requirements, recordkeeping stipulations, and other requirements. Omissions and errors can result in costly penalties.

At the same time, many payroll practitioners report they are being asked to become more specialized, particularly for short-term projects. Recognizing this need, we have included examples and depth to our answers in an attempt to anticipate payroll practitioners' needs.

To that end, *Payroll Answer Book*, 2017 Edition, is designed to give concise, accurate, and up-to-date answers to the questions that most concern payroll administrators, employers, human resources directors, accountants, tax preparers, and professional advisors. This comprehensive manual covers over 1,700 commonly asked questions about the payroll function in clear, accessible language. Keep informed (and prepare for the certified payroll professional exam or the fundamental payroll certification exam) with answers to the following questions:

- What information must be included on the employee's paycheck and/or pay stub?

- How is the required new-hire reporting implemented?

- How are FICA taxes computed on cash and noncash compensation?

- What are the state tax laws that apply to direct deposit for payment of wages?

- What criteria do the IRS apply in determining whether a worker is an independent contractor?

- What are the consequences when an employer misclassifies a worker?

- What are the penalties for violation of the equal pay provisions of the Fair Labor Standards Act (FLSA)?

- When is a worker exempt from FLSA's minimum wage and overtime requirements?

- Who are expatriates?

- How does the employer determine the value of a taxable fringe benefit to be included in the employee's wages?

- How are benefits provided to domestic partners treated for employment tax purposes?

- What are the nondiscrimination requirements that apply to cafeteria plans, and how are disqualified benefits taxed and reported?

- How are garnishments and voluntary creditor payments handled?

- How are benefits taxed and reported?

- Are any employers exempt from the payment of federal unemployment taxes?

- How does the state unemployment tax credit work?

- What are the general rules for depositing taxes?

- What is the trust fund recovery penalty?

- How are outplacement services treated for payroll tax purposes?

- When are sick pay benefits not subject to FICA and FUTA taxes?

- What are the most common methods used to calculate state income tax withholding?

- When may an employer pay employees less than the state minimum wage?

- What penalties can be imposed for improperly maintained payroll records?

- What are the payroll implications of a merger or an acquisition?

- How are benefits reported on the Form W-2?

- May an employer pay FITW, FICA, and FUTA taxes using a credit card?

- What are the requirements for surviving corporations filing Form 941 in the event of a statutory merger or consolidation?

- Are there special payroll rules that make the application of the successor employer rules to disregarded entities more difficult?

- May Forms I-9 be stored electronically?

- What are the potential problems associated with pay cards?

- What concerns are there around data security?

To further assist subscribers in handling complex payroll functions, *Payroll Answer Book*, 2017 Edition, also offers the following indispensable features:

- Payroll consequences of a merger, acquisition, divestiture, or other business restructuring.

- State-by-state requirements for pay frequency.

- Federal and state retention requirements for various types of payroll records.

- Detailed instructions on how to complete Form W-2, Form 940, Form 941, and other essential forms.

- IRS filing deadlines.

- Directories of state labor departments and state agencies related to payroll administration.

Payroll Answer Book includes a chapter on global payroll, which will help payroll professionals determine the type of questions to ask when launching a payroll in a new country. With the continued globalization of American corporations, this should prove a valuable resource.

The 2017 Edition also includes a chapter that reviews data privacy from a payroll practitioner's perspective and outlines areas to establish procedures and controls.

Payroll Answer Book uses simple, straightforward language wherever possible and offers a number of useful features to aid the reader.

Format. The question-and-answer format breaks down complex subject areas into concise units. Introductory text provides an overview of the subject to be covered in each chapter. Extensive cross-referencing facilitates locating information. The questions are numbered consecutively within each chapter (e.g., Q 1:1, Q 1:2, Q 1:3).

List of Questions. The detailed List of Questions that follows the Table of Contents helps the reader to locate areas of immediate interest. A series of subheadings helps to organize questions by topic within each chapter.

Examples. Throughout each chapter, specific examples help to simplify complex concepts. Sample calculations of taxes and other deductions are provided as well.

Appendices. For the reader's convenience, supplementary reference materials related to payroll administration are contained within the appendices that appear at the end of the book. These useful resources include addresses, phone numbers, and websites for state labor departments, state agencies dealing with income tax withholding, and state employment security agencies.

Index. At the end of *Payroll Answer Book* is an index, provided as a further aid to locating specific information. All references in the index are to question numbers rather than page numbers.

Acronyms and Abbreviations. Because of the breadth of subject area, a number of terms and statutory references are abbreviated throughout *Payroll Answer Book*, 2017 Edition. Among the most common of these shorthand references are:

- Code or I.R.C.—The Internal Revenue Code of 1986.

- ERISA—The Employee Retirement Income Security Act of 1974, as amended.

- IRS—The Internal Revenue Service.

- DOL—The U.S. Department of Labor.

- FICA—The Federal Insurance Contributions Act.

- FLSA—The Fair Labor Standards Act.

- FUTA—The Federal Unemployment Tax Act.

The detailed explanations and convenient resource material presented in *Payroll Answer Book*, 2017 Edition, should provide an essential guide to all aspects of payroll administration.

May 2017

About the Author

Deborah Ellis Timberlake, Esq., CPP, is Vice President, Global Payroll for Arrow Electronics. At Arrow, Ms. Timberlake will deploy the global strategic blueprint for this industry leader in 85 countries. Prior to joining Arrow Electronics, Ms. Timberlake spent the last eight years as the Principal of Timberlake and Associates.

Ms. Timberlake has over 30 years' experience in payroll, tax, accounting, and human resources. She has been a pioneer in business process outsourcing, with extensive experience in the global arena, where she provided global strategic and transformation services. She has developed plans for business process improvements, measuring performance, organization resizing, coaching, and training.

Ms. Timberlake has been an executive in several Fortune 500 companies and has managed dozens of payrolls of Fortune 500 companies as a service provider. From sales and solutions to transformation and operations, Ms. Timberlake has experience in most vertical markets and has successfully transformed many organizations.

She has served on the Board of Directors for the American Payroll Association (APA) and several APA task forces and committees, including Best Practices, Global, Certified Payroll Professional (CPP) Certification, and Data Privacy. Ms. Timberlake is a regular speaker at APA, Bloomberg BNA, and Webster Buchanan conferences and has published articles and white papers on various payroll topics. She is a CPP and holds the Global Payroll Management Certificate.

Ms. Timberlake also authored the 2016, 2015, 2014, 2013, 2012, and 2011 Editions of *Payroll Answer Book*. Ms. Timberlake holds a B.S. in Accounting from Hunter College and a J.D. from Brooklyn Law School.

Ms. Timberlake is the author of Chapters 1, 2, 3, 4, 5, 6, 8, 9, 10, 11, 12, and 14.

Contributors

Amorette (Amy) Nelson Bryant has worked in the payroll profession since 1982—as a payroll manager for 17 years and since 1999 as a garnishment consultant, author, and speaker. Her client assignments include software documentation, staff training, developing garnishment procedures, to comply with legal requirements. She has also managed software conversions. Ms. Bryant's first contract involved developing training materials and a book for the federal Office of Child Support Enforcement (OCSE), following passage of new federal and state laws in 1996. As a volunteer she also worked with the OCSE to design the standardized withholding order and changes to subsequent versions. She is a member of the committee that developed criteria for a standardized electronic withholding order. Ms. Bryant acted as an observer to the Uniform Law Commission on Uniform State Laws (ULC) when the Uniform Interstate Family Support Act of 1996 (UIFSA) was written. In 2011, Ms. Bryant was also involved with the Uniform Wage Garnishment Act. Her book, *Complete Guide to Federal and State Garnishment*, was used to document the numerous state laws and the need to standardize those laws. She served on two committees with the Texas Attorney General's Office, Division of Child Support Enforcement, as an employer representative.

Ms. Bryant is active in the payroll community. As a long-time member of the APA, she twice served as Chair of (and continues to serve on) the APA GRTF Subcommittee for Child Support and Other Garnishments and is a member of the APA Hotline committee. She was co-founder of the Portland, Oregon, APA Chapter and the Texas Payroll Conference.

Ms. Bryant is the author of *Complete Guide to Federal and State Garnishment*. For several years, Ms. Bryant has updated the garnishment Chapters in the *California Payroll Guide* and the *Payroll Answer Book* (all published by Wolters Kluwer). She also conducts webinars for various companies.

Ms. Bryant is the author of Chapter 7.

Michele M. Honomichl is the Founder, Executive Chairman, and Chief Strategy Officer of Celergo, a leading Global Payroll Service Provider managing local, offshore, and expat payrolls in over 120 countries for clients predominantly in the financial services, business services, technology, and oil and gas industries. As the single point of contact for all global payroll needs, Celergo manages changes, calculations, compliance, funding and reporting through standardized global payroll processes that ensure visibility and compliance. Celergo supports it clients through its Centers of Excellence in Chicago, Bogota, Budapest, and Singapore.

As the CSO, Ms. Honomichl's responsibilities include thought leadership and setting the strategic direction for Celergo's services, technologies, and market expansion. She is passionate about creating innovative and integrated technologies that simplify processes and enhance the user experience.

Previously, Ms. Honomichl was a founder of GPSLink and chief architect of the virtual relocation management model—a revolutionary web-based technology to help manage expatriate administration. She also worked at Ford Motor Company, where she supported the creation of a world-class expatriate administration center and launched a global expatriate management system. She holds a

B.S. in Finance from Michigan State University and an M.B.A. from the Kelley School of Business at Indiana University.

Ms. Honomichl has presented at APA, SHRM, the Conference Board, and many other entrepreneurial and relocation venues on a variety of global payroll, HR, expatriate, business and technology topics.

Ms. Honomichl is the author of Chapter 13

Contents

Contents

CHAPTER 6
Employees and Independent Contractors 6-1

Contents

CHAPTER 10

Sick Pay 10-1

CHAPTER 11

Required Recordkeeping and Record Retention 11-1

CHAPTER 12

Mergers, Acquisitions, Divestitures, and Other
Business Restructurings 12-1

List of Questions

Wage-Bracket Method

Percentage Method

Annualized Wages Method

Part-Year Employment Method

Cumulative Wages Method

Average Estimated Wages Method

Additional Withholding Requirements

Supplemental Wage Payments

Controlling Unemployment Costs

Title XII Loan

Paying FUTA Taxes

Form 940: Employer's Annual Federal Unemployment (FUTA) Tax Return

Penalties

Financing State Benefits

Chapter 5 Direct Deposit

Chapter 6 Employees and Independent Contractors

Section 530 of the Revenue Act of 1978

Classification Settlement Program

Voluntary Classification Settlement Program

Tax Court Review

Assistants of Independent Contractors

Temporary Workers

Benefit Plans

Professional Employer Organizations

Chapter 7 Garnishment and Other Deductions

Medical and Spousal Support

Fair Labor Standards Act

Chapter 8 The Fair Labor Standards Act

Coverage—Jurisdiction

Overview

Enterprise Coverage

Exemptions

Exemptions from Payment of Minimum Wage and Overtime

White-Collar Exemptions

Executive Exemption

Contract Work Hours and Safety Standards Act (CWHSSA)

Other Laws Affecting Employer-Employee Relationship

Public Employers: Federal, State, County, and City Governments

Chapter 9 Benefits Treated as Compensation

Interviewee Expenses

Jury Pay

Leave Sharing

Legal (Group) Benefits

Life Insurance (Non-Group-Term Insurance and Split-Dollar Insurance)

Long-Term Care Benefits

Outplacement Services

Pension and Profit Sharing Plans

Annuities and Pensions

Benefits Under a Qualified Plan

Participant Loans

Reporting of Plan Distributions

FICA and FUTA Taxability of Pension Benefits

Hardship and Other Distributions

ESOPs

401(k) Plans

Early Distributions Tax—Pensions

Scholarships and Fellowships

Severance Pay

Spousal Travel

Stock and Stock Options

Chapter 10 Sick Pay

Federal Income Tax Withholding

FICA and FUTA Taxes

Forms W-2 and W-3

Chapter 11 Required Recordkeeping and Record Retention

Summary of Retention Requirements

Employee Privacy Concerns in Recordkeeping

Disposal of Records

Chapter 12 Mergers, Acquisitions, Divestitures, and Other Business Restructurings

Overview

Federal Payroll Rules for Statutory Mergers, Consolidations, and Other Section 381 Transactions Involving Corporations

Matters to Be Resolved in Filing a Final Form 941 under Current Rules

Impact of Mid-Quarter Effective Dates

More about Schedule D (Form 941)

Statutory Mergers and Consolidations: Employee Forms W-4

Year-End Filing in Statutory Mergers and Consolidations: W-2

Federal Successor Employer Rules

Federal Income and FICA Tax Compliance under the Successor Employer Rules

Standard Procedure

Standard Rules for Form 941

Filing Forms W-2 under the Standard Procedure

Forms W-4 under the Standard Procedure

Alternate Procedure

Alternate Requirements for Forms 941

Physical Security

Data Life Cycle Management

Technology Considerations

Chapter 1

Overview

Payroll is a dynamic function in every organization today. The fast-changing statutory framework that supports processing timely and accurate payrolls combined with an increasingly global economy require a thorough understanding of every phase and process that underlies the payroll and employment tax functions. Increased enforcement of these requirements by federal, state, and local taxing authorities has also served to elevate the focus on the compliance aspects of payroll administration, making it a material consideration for internal audit and risk management purposes. Over the past few years, many tax benefits were set to expire and have received a reprise at the last minute. For example, under the Obama Administration, significant changes to tax policy and health care have occurred and further changes to worker classification and the funding of unemployment, as well as changes in our social systems (e.g., Social Security reform) are proposed that will further challenge payroll and employment tax professionals.

This chapter presents a broad view of the key federal requirements that commonly fall within the scope of the payroll and employment tax functions. *The Payroll Answer Book* is designed to provide answers to frequently asked payroll and employment tax questions, with reference to statutory, administrative, or other citations. The subject areas included in this chapter are explored in greater depth in subsequent chapters.

Overview

Q 1:1 How does the employer and employee relationship affect the payroll process?

The initial step in the payroll process is to determine whether a worker is an independent contractor or an employee. In making that determination, it is necessary to determine if an employment relationship exists between the employer and worker. This process is not arbitrary, but rather is governed by specific legal definitions and the subjective scrutiny of certain relevant facts within the work arrangement. A worker is not necessarily an employee. Some workers may be lawfully classified as independent contractors and others may be considered the employees of a third party, as in the case of temporary agency referrals and leased employees. Further, work may be performed by U.S. and non-U.S. employees both within and outside the United States or the employer may be a U.S. or foreign entity engaged in performing services within the United States. When a U.S. employer pays compensation to its employees, that compensation may be subject to federal, state, local, and international withholding and employment tax. By contrast, payments to valid independent contractors are generally not subject to these requirements. Because worker classification errors have an impact on federal and state revenues, in particular, unemployment insurance, FICA, and benefits, the Internal Revenue Service (IRS) and a number of states are taking additional measures to uncover worker misclassification and/or impose stiffer fines on employers for such errors. This enforcement trend is causing businesses to study more carefully the federal and state guidelines that govern when a worker must be classified as an employee. The subject of worker classification is covered in greater detail in chapter 6.

Q 1:2 What is the importance of accurate wage and employment tax reporting?

The primary means for the U.S. Treasury to collect income taxes is through the income tax withholding requirements of the Internal Revenue Code (I.R.C.). Many states and localities similarly collect income taxes through the withholding process. In addition, an individual's eligibility for Social Security, Medicare, disability, unemployment, and similar benefits is tied to the proper collection and reporting of Federal Insurance Contributions Act (FICA) and disability/unemployment insurance taxes. Thus, federal, state, and local taxing authorities closely monitor employers' tax deposits and reports to ensure accurate and timely collection of these revenues, and interest and penalties can be levied on employers or "responsible parties" when such payments are not accurately and timely paid. Government agencies (state and federal) and workers rely on information statements and returns and other employment-related forms (such as Forms W-2, Wage and Tax Statement; and Form 941, Employer's QUARTERLY Federal Tax Return) in determining tax liabilities and benefits (such as Social Security, unemployment, and disability). Errors made in the withholding and reporting process can have a direct impact on the employee and employer.

Further, responsible parties can be held personally liable for failure to deposit withholding and employment taxes accurately and on time.

Q 1:3   Do payroll withholding and reporting requirements for states follow the rules for the federal employment taxes?

Generally, yes. However, each state that imposes a state or local income tax (nine states do not) establishes its own set of rules for what constitutes taxable compensation and for collection and reporting of withholding and employment taxes. In many states, the rules for determining what constitutes taxable wages closely follow the treatment of such payments for federal employment tax purposes. This publication focuses primarily on the federal withholding and employment tax requirements, with some focus on state differences (e.g., Section 125 plans).

Q 1:4   When are withheld taxes and the most common tax forms due?

Table 1-1 provides a summary of forms, payroll definitions, and due dates. Note that the due dates shown are the dates by which the form must be filed. Employers will meet the "file" or "furnish" requirement if the form is properly addressed and mailed first class on or before the due date. If any date shown falls on a Saturday, Sunday, or legal holiday (as defined in 5 U.S.C. § 6103), the next business day becomes the due date.

Table 1-1. Due Dates for Commonly Filed Tax Forms

Form	Explanation	Due Date
Form 940	Employer's Annual Federal Unemployment (FUTA) Tax Return. FUTA is paid on the first $7,000 of earnings per employee. The taxes due for each calendar quarter are deposited by the end of the following month.	Filed annually and due on the last day of the month following the end of the calendar year (January 31). If all taxes were timely paid and for the full amount, there is an automatic 10-day extension on the due date.
Form 941	Employer's QUARTERLY Federal Tax Return. Used to report the amount of federal income tax withholding, Social Security, and Medicare taxes owed to the IRS.	Last day of the month following the end of a calendar quarter: January 31, April 30, July 31, October 31. If all taxes were timely paid and for the full amount, there is an automatic 10-day extension on the due date.

Table 1-1.   Due Dates for Commonly Filed Tax Forms (*cont'd*)

Form	*Explanation*	*Due Date*
Form 943	Employer's Annual Federal Tax Return for Agricultural Employees. Annual reporting by agricultural employers.	Filed annually and due on the last day of the month following the end of the calendar year (January 31). If all taxes were timely paid and for the full amount, there is an automatic 10-day extension on the due date.
Form 944	Employer's ANNUAL Federal Tax Return. Small employers report federal income tax withholding, Social Security, and Medicare taxes.	Filed annually and due on January 31. If all taxes were timely paid and for the full amount, there is an automatic 10-day extension on the due date.
Form 945	Annual Return of Withheld Federal Income Tax. Used to report nonpayroll withholding.	Filed annually and due on the last day of the month following the end of the calendar year (January 31). If all taxes were timely paid and for the full amount, there is an automatic 10-day extension on the due date.
Form 1042-S/ 1042	Foreign Person's U.S. Source Income Subject to Withholding.	Form 1042-S due to recipients and the IRS with annual transmittal (Form 1042) no later than March 15.
Form 1094-B	Transmittal of Health Coverage Information Returns.	Due to the IRS on February 28 (March 31, if filed electronically).
Form 1095-B	Health Coverage return to report employee's health coverage.	Due to the employee by March 2.
Form 1094-C	Transmittal of Employer-Provided Health Insurance Offer and Coverage Information Returns.	Due to the IRS on February 28 (March 31, if filed electronically).
Form 1095-C	Employer-Provided Health Insurance Offer and Coverage.	Due to the employee by March 2.

Table 1-1. Due Dates for Commonly Filed Tax Forms (*cont'd*)

Form	Explanation	Due Date
Form 1096	Annual Summary and Transmittal of U.S. Information Returns. Sent to the IRS processing center for the employer's area.	Due to the IRS on January 31 of each year with copy A of Forms 1099-MISC.
Forms 1099	Different 1099 forms are used to report various types of earnings and distributions at the end of a calendar year, including Form 1099-R, Distributions From Pensions, Annuities, Retirement or Profit-Sharing Plans, IRAs, Insurance Contracts, etc., and Form 1099-MISC, Miscellaneous Income.	Due to the recipient by January 31 of each year. Due to IRS on January 31 (if filed on paper or electronically and if reporting amounts in Box 7 nonemployee compensation).
Form W-2	Wage and Tax Statement. Used to report certain earnings and deductions for the calendar year.	Due to the employee and Social Security Administration by January 31 of each year starting with 2016 returns for both paper and electronic forms.
Form W-3	Transmittal of Wage and Tax Statements. Used to transmit copy A of Forms W-2.	Due to the SSA on January 31 with Forms W-2 whether filed on paper or electronically.
Form W-4	Employee's Withholding Allowance Certificate. Used to determine the proper withholding allowances to which the employee is entitled.	Required for newly hired employees on day of hire and when an employee's withholding elections change (a new W-4 must be filed within 10 days if the number of allowances decreases). Employers must make the changes included on the Form W-4 no later than the first payroll period ending on or after the 30th day from the date they received it from the employee.

Employers deposit their federal payroll and withholding tax liabilities on either a monthly or semiweekly basis. There are two exceptions to this general rule. First, certain very small employers may be able to pay their accumulated taxes with their quarterly or annual returns (e.g., Forms 943 and 944). These are employers that accumulate less than $2,500 in total tax liabilities in the quarter or the year. The second exception accelerates deposits for any employer that accumulates $100,000 or more in tax liabilities in a deposit period; for these employers, the deposit must be on the business day following the day that accumulated liabilities reach $100,000 or more.

Status as either a semiweekly or monthly depositor is based on the employer's aggregate liability for federal income tax withholding and FICA taxes over the "lookback" period. The lookback period is the 12-month period ending on June 30 of the prior calendar year. Employers reporting a total of $50,000 or less in tax liabilities during their lookback period are monthly depositors. Larger total deposits in the lookback period make the employer a semiweekly depositor. New employers are treated as monthly depositors. See chapter 4 for additional information on deposits of federal withholding of income taxes and FICA taxes, and chapter 3 for federal unemployment insurance (FUTA) taxes.

New Employees

Q 1:5 Which federal employment forms are required of a new employee?

Form W-4 (Employee's Withholding Allowance Certificate)

An employer must ask each new employee (including non-U.S. citizens and residents) to complete and sign a Form W-4 that includes the employee's name and Social Security number (SSN) from the Social Security card. Any employee who does not have a Social Security card must apply for one and demonstrate to the employer that such application has been made. Call 1-800-772-1213 for information on this filing. [Pub. No. 15]

 If the Form W-4 is not completed, the employer must withhold based on a single marital status with zero allowances. See chapter 2.

Form I-9 (Employment Eligibility Verification)

Under the Immigration Reform and Control Act of 1986 (IRCA), all employers are required to collect and retain certain information on each worker's identity and eligibility for U.S. employment. Specifically, each employer is required to:

1. Verify the identity of a worker and the eligibility of each employee to work in the United States (verification is accomplished through examination of specific documents to be presented by the employee);

2. Attest that it has seen the required employment verification documents; and

3. Maintain records of each worker's employment verification.

The form used for these purposes is the I-9. Employers must use the Form I-9 (Rev. Mar. 08, 2013). See Q 1:6 for more information.

Q 1:6   What are the current requirements for Form I-9?

All U.S. employers are responsible for the proper completion and retention of a Form I-9 for each individual, whether U.S. citizen or non-U.S. citizen, they hire for employment in the United States. In addition to English, the I-9 is available in Spanish. The I-9 is not filed with any governmental agency, but must be retained by the employer until the later of either (1) three years after the date of hire, or (2) one year after employment is terminated. The form must be retained in such a way that it is available for timely inspection, if requested by the authorized governmental agency.

On November 14, 2016, the U.S. Citizenship and Immigration Services (USCIS) published a revised Form I-9, Employment Eligibility Verification that will expire on August 31, 2019. The form was updated to included embedded instructions, drop down lists, and calendars to facilitate completion of the form. Some additional changes include: provide last names only; provide I-94 number only; and a new Citizenship/Immigration Status. Employers had until January 21, 2017 to begin to use the new form.

The employer must record on the form the documents employees present to verify their identity and employment eligibility (see Q 1:7). Exceptions to having a valid Form I-9 on file apply when:

- The individual was hired before November 7, 1986, and has been continuously employed by the same employer.
- The individual provides domestic services in a private household that are sporadic, irregular, or intermittent.
- The individual provides services for the employer as a valid independent contractor.
- The individual provides services for the employer, under a contract, subcontract, or exchange entered into after November 6, 1986. However, the contractor (e.g., professional leasing company or temporary employment agency) is required to perform the responsibilities associated with the I-9 process.

Record retention: Form I-9 records may be stored at the worksite of the workers to whom they relate, at a company's headquarters, or at another location, as long as the storage location makes it possible for the documents to be transmitted to the worksite within three days of an official request for the documents for inspection. The I-9 may be stored electronically.

Completion of Form I-9: A new employee must complete Section 1 of Form I-9 at the time employment begins. Within three business days of the employee's beginning work, the employer must examine the employee's identity and employment eligibility documents (see Q 1:7) and record them in Section 2 of the Form I-9. The employer is responsible for reviewing the documentation presented by the employee and recording that document information in Section 1. In the examination process, the employer is required to review the documentation provided by the employee and make a reasonable determination that the documents so provided appear to be genuine for the individual who presented them. The employer is then required to certify under penalty of perjury that the documents appear to be genuine for the employee and that, to the best of the employer's knowledge, the employee is eligible to work in the United States.

Requesting additional or different documentation in an attempt to block employment of the individual is prohibited and may constitute an unfair immigration-related employment practice. The employer should not recommend nor suggest any specific documentation to complete Form I-9. When the documentation presented by an individual does not reasonably appear to be genuine or relate to the employee who presents it, the employer is required to reject that documentation and ask for other documentation from the list of acceptable documents contained in Form I-9. An employer should not continue to employ an employee who cannot present documentation that meets the Form I-9 requirements. (Note that the I-9 verification process can be completed electronically through the E-Verify program. See Q 1:8 for more information.)

Section 3 should be completed and signed by an employer if an employee is updating his or her information or is reverifying employment eligibility. Reverification must be performed by the expiration date of the document as shown in Section 1.

Photocopies of documents: An employer may not review photocopies of identity or employment eligibility documents to fulfill I-9 requirements. Only original documents issued by the appropriate issuing authority may be used in the employment verification. A single exception to this requirement for original documents permits a certified photocopy of a birth certificate. An employer is also permitted to make a photocopy of the documentation submitted by the individual to satisfy Form I-9 recordkeeping requirements and to maintain copies of that documentation in its files. However, keeping photocopies of such documentation is not required. When it is the employer's practice to make copies of documents, that practice must be consistently applied to every employee, without regard to citizenship or national origin.

Employees at Distant Locations

At times an employer may hire a new employee who does not physically come to that employer's offices to complete paperwork. With such employees, the employer's I-9 responsibility must be properly delegated to an agent who can (and does) perform the required employment verification process. Authorized agents include, but are not limited to, notaries, public accountants, attorneys, personnel officers, and foremen. Because copies of documents may not be used to fulfill the initial I-9 verification process, an employer may not rely on documents that are faxed in by a new employee. If an employer uses the services of a professional employer organization (PEO) (i.e., an employee leasing company), both the employer and the PEO must maintain copies of the Form I-9.

Q 1:7 What documents are acceptable for Form I-9 employment eligibility verification purposes?

Form I-9, which was revised November 14, 2016, provides a list of documents which may be used to substantiate an employee's identity and eligibility to work in the United States. The documents in List A provide both identity and employment eligibility; the documents in List B substantiate only the employee's identity; and the documents in List C substantiate only work eligibility. An employee who provides a document from List A meets the I-9 substantiation requirement. However, an employee who does not provide a document from List A is required to provide a document from both List B and List C.

LIST A—Documents that Establish Both Identity and Employment Eligibility

- U.S. Passport or U.S. Passport Card.
- Permanent Resident Card or Alien Registration Receipt Card (Form I-551).
- Foreign passport that contains a temporary I-551 stamp or temporary I-551 printed notation on a machine-readable immigrant visa.
- Employment Authorization Document that contains a photograph (Form I-776).
- In the case of a nonimmigrant alien authorized to work for a specific employer incident to status, a foreign passport with Form I-94 or Form I-94A bearing the same name as the passport and containing an endorsement of the alien's nonimmigrant status, as long as the period of endorsement has not yet expired and the proposed employment is not in conflict with any restrictions or limitations identified on the form.
- Passport from the Federated States of Micronesia (FSM) or the Republic of Marshall Islands (RMI) with Form I-94 or Form I-94A indicating nonimmigrant admission under the Compact of Free Association Between the United States and the FSM or RMI.

LIST B—Documents that Establish Identity

- Driver's license or ID card issued by a state or outlying possession of the United States, provided it contains a photograph or information such as name, date of birth, gender, height, eye color, and address.
- ID card issued by federal, state, or local government agencies or entities, provided it contains a photograph or information such as name, date of birth, gender, height, eye color, and address.
- School ID card with a photograph.
- Voter's registration card.
- U.S. Military card or draft record.
- Military dependent's ID card.
- U.S. Coast Guard Merchant Mariner Card.
- Native American tribal document.
- Driver's license issued by a Canadian government authority.

- For persons under age 18 who are unable to present a document listed above: School record or report card; clinic, doctor, or hospital record; or day-care or nursery school record.

LIST C—Documents that Establish Employment Eligibility

- Social Security Account Number card unless the card has one of the following restrictions: not valid for employment; valid for work only with INS authorization; or valid for work only with DHS authorization.
- Certification of Birth Abroad issued by the Department of State (Form FS-545).
- Certification of Report of Birth issued by the Department of State (DS-1350).
- Original or certified copy of a birth certificate issued by a state, county, municipal authority or territory of the United States bearing an official seal.
- Native American tribal document.
- U.S. Citizen ID Card (Form I-197).
- Identification Card for Use of Resident Citizen in the United States (Form I-179).
- Employment authorization document issued by the Department of Homeland Security.

Q 1:8   What is E-Verify?

E-Verify is an electronic employment eligibility verification system, which is free to all employers. Participating employers complete the Form I-9 for each new hire and then submit an electronic query that includes information from Sections 1 and 2 of the Form I-9. The employer then receives an automated response regarding the U.S. employment eligibility of the new employee. E-Verify is a joint program of the Social Security Administration (SSA) and the U.S. Department of Homeland Security, U.S. Citizenship and Immigration Services. Therefore, by participating in the E-Verify program, employees' U.S. work eligibility is verified at the same time that their names and SSNs are validated by the SSA.

 For more information, go to www.uscis.gov/e-verify or call 1-888-464-4218.

Q 1:9   Is E-Verify mandatory?

Contractors and subcontractors of the U.S. federal government are required to use E-Verify effective September 8, 2009. [Executive Order 12989, as amended by President George W. Bush on June 6, 2008]

Businesses should be certain to check the state requirements governing E-Verify. A number of states (Alabama, Arizona, Mississippi, South Carolina, and Utah) have passed laws making E-Verify mandatory for employers to use for all employees. Other states require use of E-Verify for various purposes (e.g., for contractors and subcontractors of the state government). For example, Colorado and Minnesota require employers to use E-Verify for contractors only.

Q 1:10   How often must an employee complete a Form W-4 claiming exemption from federal income tax withholding?

An employee must submit a new Form W-4 for each year he or she claims to be exempt from federal income tax withholding. The form should be submitted by the employee by February 15. If the employee does not submit a new Form W-4, the employer should withhold based on the previous Form W-4 that did not claim exemption from withholding. If such a Form W-4 does not exist, the employer should compute federal income tax withholding as if the employee had claimed single with zero withholding allowances. [Pub. No. 15; Pub. No. 505] For 2017, employees can claim exemption from withholding if they expect a refund of all federal income tax withheld in 2017 because they have no federal income tax liability and had a right to a refund of all federal income tax withheld for 2016 because they had no federal income tax liability.

Q 1:11   What is new-hire reporting?

Under federal law, each state is mandated to require that employers report certain information about their newly hired employees. Federal law requires new hire reporting as a means to assist in the issuance of child support withholding orders, and, in some states, to detect unemployment insurance fraud. With respect to child support enforcement, new hire reporting allows an individual with liability for child support in that state to be tracked on a national basis when the employee moves and becomes employed in another state. New-hire reporting also assists agencies in more promptly issuing wage withholding orders to employers.

State laws concerning the required data elements of a new hire report vary by state. However, under federal law, the minimum data required includes: (1) the employer's name, address, and Federal Employer Identification Number and (2) the new employee's full name, SSN, date of hire, and current residential address. Employers generally submit information on every new hire within 20 days of the date of hire, unless the submission is made electronically or magnetically. When an employer reports electronically or with magnetic media, the submission must be made at least twice a month, 12 to 16 days apart. If an employer has employees in two or more states, it may either report the workers in the state where they work, following the new-hire reporting requirements for that state; or if it files magnetically or electronically, it may select one of the states where the employees work and report all new hires to that state's designated new-hire reporting office. An employer that selects the second option must notify the federal Department of Health and Human Services as to which state it has designated to receive all its new-hire information. See chapter 7 for more information.

Q 1:12   What are the employer's basic responsibilities regarding verification of an employee's SSN?

Employers must obtain each employee's name and SSN, which are then reported on the annual wage and tax statement, Form W-2. This requirement applies to all U.S. employees, including U.S. citizens, U.S. residents, and nonresident aliens. Employers may ask employees, for payroll purposes, to show their Social Security card, but the law does not require that employees show their Social Security card to the employer.

Penalties can be imposed by federal, state, and local taxing authorities for reporting an invalid SSN, or a name and SSN that do not match SSA's records. To avoid such penalties, employers should ensure that the name and SSN on the employee's Social Security card match the name and SSN as contained in the payroll system. (See Q 1:15 for more information.)

An employee who is legally eligible to work in the United States may obtain a Social Security card by completing Form SS-5, Application for a Social Security Card, and providing the proper documentation to the SSA. This form is available at SSA offices, can be obtained by calling 1-800-772-1213, or can be downloaded and printed from www.socialsecurity.gov/online/ss-5.html. If an employee has applied for an SSN but does not have it by the time the employer must file Form W-2, the employer should enter "Applied For" on a paper form. If the employer files the Forms W-2 electronically, it should enter all zeroes (000-00-0000) in the Social Security number field. When the employee receives the SSN, Form W-2c, Corrected Wage and Tax Statement, must be filed for only the most current year to show the employee's correct SSN and amounts previously reported.

If employees are given a new Social Security card reflecting a different name (e.g., due to marriage or divorce), employers should update their payroll records so that the name as revised on the Social Security card is reflected on the Form W-2. A W-2c should be filed for the most recent tax year. It is not necessary to correct the previous years' Forms W-2 to reflect a change in name. [Pub. No. 15]

Q 1:13   May the employer make and keep a photocopy of the employee's Social Security card?

Yes, to be able to properly report an employee's name and SSN on a Form W-2, an employer may copy an employee's Social Security card if the employee presents it; however, see Q 1:14.

Q 1:14   Are there risks in asking employees to show their Social Security card to the employer?

Employers must be certain if asking for a copy of an employee's Social Security card that the request is being made for tax reporting purposes and not for I-9 verification purposes. Under the Immigration Reform and Control Act of 1986, employees have the choice of providing one of a number of documents for I-9 verification (see Q 1:7). It is a violation subject to penalty to require that the

Social Security card be one of those documents. [Illegal Immigration Reform and Immigrant Responsibility Act of 1996, Pub. L. No. 104-208, 110 Stat. 3009]

Q 1:15   How can an employer verify a worker's SSN?

The Social Security Administration established the SSN Verification Service to allow employers to validate SSNs. Validating SSNs can reduce the errors of filing Forms W-2 and avoid penalties for incorrect statements. Filing Forms W-2 with the correct SSNs ensures that employees will receive the proper credit toward their future Social Security benefits.

- *Business Services Online:* Employers may verify the matching of employees' names and SSNs through the SSA's Social Security Number Verification Service (SSNVS), which renders immediate results through SSA's Business Services Online (BSO). To utilize the online service, an employer must complete an application and receive an access and activation code. Once the employer receives that code, the online service can be used. SSNVS lets an employer manually enter up to 10 names per screen and SSNs in each session, with unlimited sessions allowed. If there is a mismatch, SSNVS will advise if the name or number is recorded as a person who is deceased, or invalid for some other reason. BSO is available at http://www.ssa.gov/bso/bsowelcome.htm.

  Note. Through BSO, an employer may also upload electronic files of up to 250,000 names and SSNs and receive the results usually the next day. Instructions for formatting the file are available at http://www.ssa.gov/bso/bsowelcome.htm.

- *Nonelectronic:* Employers may submit a request of up to 50 names and numbers to the local Social Security office to be verified. Requests for up to 300 names and numbers may be submitted to the SSA's Wilkes-Barre Date Operations Center after registering.

Q 1:16   Why is it important that an employee's name and SSN match?

From an employee's point of view, the name and the SSN that appear on an employee's Form W-2 need to match the name and SSN on the employee's Social Security card for the employee's wages to be properly credited for Social Security benefit purposes.

For an employer, the name and SSN must match so that the employer is not subject to Form W-2 reporting penalties. Also, the employer can save processing costs and reduce the number of W-2cs.

Q 1:17   What steps must an employer take if it is informed that there is a mismatch of an employee's name and SSN?

If an employer is notified that an employee's SSN and name do not match, the SSA advises the employer to do the following:

1. Compare the failed SSN matches to the employment records to see if a typographical error was made in the employer's records. If so, the employer should correct the data or records and resend only the corrected data to the SSA.

2. If the error was not a typographical one, the employer should ask to see the employee's Social Security card (or ask the employee to examine it) to ensure that the SSN and name are correctly shown on the Form W-4. If an error was made on the Form W-4, the employee should correct the Form W-4. The employer then corrects its records and resends only the corrected data to the SSA.

3. If the Social Security card and employer's records match, the employer should refer the employee to a Social Security office to determine and correct the problem. Once the mismatch is resolved, the employee should inform the employer of the resolution.

4. If the employee is unable to give the employer a valid SSN, the employer must document its efforts to obtain the corrected information. This documentation must be retained by the employer for four years.

5. If the employee has terminated, the employer should make an effort to obtain the corrected information from the former employee and submit corrected information, if available, to the SSA on Form W-2c.

Q 1:18　How can an employee verify that Social Security payments are properly credited?

Employees can and should verify the accuracy of information recorded by the SSA. The agency maintains a year-by-year and cumulative total of wages that have been subject to Social Security wage reporting. The SSA no longer sends individuals age 25 and older a Social Security benefits and earnings statement that shows a year-by-year listing of the employee's earnings that were subject to Social Security tax, an estimate of the employee's retirement earnings, estimates of disability and survivor benefits, and the number of credits the employee has earned and will need to earn to be entitled to the benefits. However, individuals may get a personalized estimate of their Social Security benefits by using the SSA's Benefit Calculator. It is important for employees to verify the accuracy of information about their reported wages because a General Accounting Office study showed that 25 percent of certain groups of workers had a loss of $15 per month in benefits, and 1 percent had no coverage because of Form W-2 wages that were not properly posted to employees' correct social security accounts.

Q 1:19　Are SSNs required for individuals who are exempt from all employment taxes?

Yes. The SSN must be reported by payers on the Form W-2 or Form 1099 (for independent contractors).

Q 1:20   What is the purpose of an adoption taxpayer identification number?

An adoption taxpayer identification number (ATIN) is a tax processing number issued by the IRS as a temporary taxpayer identification number for a child who is in the domestic adoption process and who will not be eligible for an SSN by the time the Form 1040 on which he or she is claimed as a dependent is due. An ATIN is not a permanent identification number and is intended only for temporary use. Upon finalization of the adoption process, an SSN for the child must be obtained by the legal parent(s). The individual or individuals adopting the child may use the ATIN to claim the child as a dependent and to claim the child and dependent care credit, child tax credit, and adoption credit on Form 1040. An ATIN cannot be used to claim the earned income tax credit (EITC) for the child being adopted. An amended return claiming the EITC may be filed once the adoption is complete and an SSN is assigned. [Form W-7A]

Q 1:21   How can an individual obtain an ATIN for a child?

A taxpayer must complete Form W-7A, Application for Taxpayer Identification Number for Pending U.S. Adoptions, to obtain an ATIN. The W-7A is an application form and requires copies of documents validating the fact that the child was placed in the taxpayer's home for adoption (rather than foster care) by an authorized placement agency. The Form W-7A and copies of the original documentation must be mailed to Department of the Treasury; Internal Revenue Service; Austin, TX 73301-0066. If a child is not a U.S. citizen or resident alien, a W-7 application for IRS Individual Tax Identification Number can be obtained for the child in order to secure deductions for the child.

Wages

Q 1:22   Are all wages generally subject to federal withholding and federal employment taxes?

All wages are subject to federal withholding and federal employment taxes unless the payments are specifically exempted from one or more of the taxes under the I.R.C. and/or Treasury regulations. I.R.C. Section 3401(a) contains the definition of wages and exemptions for federal income tax (FIT) withholding purposes. I.R.C. Section 3121(a) contains the definition of wages and exemptions for FICA tax purposes. I.R.C. Section 3306(b) provides the same information for FUTA tax purposes.

Wages include all compensation given to an employee for services performed. The compensation may be in cash or in other forms, and it includes salaries, vacation allowances, bonuses, commissions, and certain fringe benefits. It does not matter how the employer measures or makes payments (e.g., completion of the project or a percentage of profits). If the cash or noncash payment is for services rendered, it is generally subject to federal withholding and employment taxes. In addition, compensation paid to a former employee for services performed while the individual was employed constitutes wages subject to withholding and employment taxes. The I.R.C. exempts certain payments from taxation and sometimes sets either maximum or minimum limitations for application of these taxes. [I.R.C. §§ 61(a), 3121(a), 3306(b), 3401(a); Pub. No. 15]

Q 1:23 Are wages not paid in cash subject to federal withholding and employment taxes?

Generally, yes. When a trade or business pays employees in a medium that is neither cash nor a readily negotiable instrument, such as a check, the employer is said to be making payments "in kind." Payments in kind may be in the form of goods, lodging, food, clothing, or services provided to the employee by the employer, unless specifically exempt by the I.R.C. Generally, the fair market value of such payments at the time they are provided is subject to federal income tax, federal income tax withholding and Social Security, Medicare, and FUTA taxes. However, certain noncash payments, such as for household work, agricultural labor, and service not in the employer's trade or business, are specifically exempt from Social Security, Medicare, and FUTA taxes. Employers generally are required to withhold federal income tax on the value of in-kind payments only if the employer and the employee agree to do so; however, noncash payments for agricultural labor, such as commodity wages, are treated as cash payments subject to federal withholding and employment taxes if the substance of the transaction is a cash payment. [I.R.C. §§ 61(a), 3121(a), 3306(b), 3401(a), 3402; Pub. No. 15]

Q 1:24 What is the doctrine of constructive receipt?

The I.R.C. states that an individual is in *constructive receipt of wages* when the employee has a right to accept the wages without substantial limitation. An individual cannot elect to delay the taxation of income and postpone constructive receipt of that income by merely not accepting a check or by asking to be paid in a later pay period. [I.R.C. § 451; Treas. Reg. § 1.451-2]

The determination of whether a wage payment has been constructively received is not an easy task: Conditions may apply to the payment that could delay the income taxation of such payment, even though it is currently subject to Social Security and Medicare taxes. That is so for certain nonqualified deferred compensation programs established for management-level employees, and is subject to strict rules under I.R.C. § 3121(v) and the I.R.C. Section 409A (see chapter 9).

Example 1. Paul is on a month-long vacation, and his paycheck for the payday occurring during that vacation is held in the payroll office until he returns. Paul is treated as having received the pay on the normal payday—even though he did not physically have possession of the check, it was available to him—and the pay is subject to withholding and other employment taxes for the normal pay period.

Example 2. Rain Spring Company's pay period ends December 27, and the payday for that period is January 2. Employees are in constructive receipt of that pay on January 2, the normal payday, and the pay is subject to income tax withholding and other employment taxes for January, even though the payment is for work performed in the previous year.

Example 3. Venus, a sales rep for AmpiPower Electronics, participates in a nonqualified deferred compensation plan. In 2017, she elects to forgo $10,000 of income that will be contributed to the nonqualified deferred compensation plan. Assuming the amount is not subject to substantial risk of forfeiture, that contribution will be wages for FICA tax purposes but not currently subject to income tax withholding. [Treas. Reg. § 1.451-2]

Note that the doctrine of constructive receipt does not apply to salary reductions under a cafeteria plan or salary deferred under a 401(k) plan.

Q 1:25   What is the impact of backdating and postdating paychecks?

Wages are considered paid when wages are constructively received. Regardless of the date printed on a paycheck, the date that the employee has taken constructive receipt determines the date of the employer's withholding and employment tax deposit obligations. [Treas. Reg. §§ 1.451-2, 31.3121(a)-2, 31.3301-4]

Some employers attempt to achieve a more favorable tax situation, either for themselves or their employees, by backdating and postdating paychecks. According to the IRS, the date of the check is irrelevant; wages are taxable when they are actually or constructively received. The latter is the date that establishes the requirements for withholding federal payroll taxes and timely payment and reporting.

Q 1:26   When must wages be paid?

The Fair Labor Standards Act (FLSA) does not require that wages be paid within a certain length of time after the employee renders services. Federal courts have ruled that wages are "unpaid" unless they are paid on the employee's regular payday. Payments not made on the regular payday violate the FLSA's minimum wage and overtime pay requirements. State laws generally impose time limits on when an employee must be paid following the close of the pay period.

Q 1:27   How often must an employer pay an employee?

Neither the FLSA nor the I.R.C. regulates how often an employer must pay employees or how soon after performing services the employee must be paid, as long as it is reasonable. Most states, however, impose specific requirements that control the frequency of paychecks and how soon after the pay period a paycheck must be produced.

Table 1-2 provides a state-by-state summary of requirements for wage payment frequency.

Table 1-2.   Payment Frequency

State	Wage Payment Requirements	Exceptions
AL	Biweekly or semimonthly. (Note: Law applies only to public service corporations engaged in transportation and employing 50 or more workers.)	—
AK	Semimonthly or monthly at employee's election.	—
AZ	Regular intervals not to exceed 16 days.	Compensation may be paid monthly to professionals, administrators, executives, and outside salespersons of out-of-state employers.
AR	Semimonthly for salespersons, mechanics, laborers, and certain other employees. In 24 equal semimonthly installments for court reporters and case coordinators.	Large businesses may pay qualified management and executive employees monthly if they are paid more than $25,000 per year.
CA	Semimonthly. Wages earned between the 1st and 15th of a month must be paid between the 16th and 26th of the month; wages earned between the 16th and the end of the month must be paid between the 1st and 10th of the following month.	Qualified executive, administrative, or professional employees; employees who work on commission at vehicle dealerships; public employees; and agricultural and domestic workers who board and lodge with employer may be paid monthly by the 26th.
CO	Monthly, unless another agreement is in effect.	—
CT	Weekly, with an 8-day holdover permitted.	The labor commissioner may grant exceptions.
DE	Monthly.	State employees and specified railroad employees must be paid biweekly.
DC	Semimonthly.	Executives, administrators, and professionals; U.S. and D.C. governments; and employers subject to the Railway Labor Act. Employers may continue to pay employees monthly if that was their prior custom.

Table 1-2. Payment Frequency (*cont'd*)

State	Wage Payment Requirements	Exceptions
FL	—	
GA	Semimonthly.	Agricultural, sawmill, and turpentine workers; officials, heads, and subheads of departments.
HI	Semimonthly.	Employers may receive exemptions from the director of labor.
ID	Monthly.	—
IL	Semimonthly.	State and federal employees. Executive, administrative, and professional employees and employees on commission may be paid once a month.
IN	Semimonthly or biweekly, at employee's request.	Agricultural and certain salaried employees. Specified types of employers may pay employees biweekly. Certain institutional public school employees may have different agreement.
IA	Monthly, semimonthly, or biweekly.	Certain agricultural laborers.
KS	Monthly.	—
KY	Semimonthly.	Executive, administrative, and professional employees; outside salespersons and outside collectors.
LA	Semimonthly if not otherwise designated. Manufacturing, mining, and oil employees of businesses employing at least 10 workers and public service corporation employees must be paid biweekly or semimonthly.	Executive, administrative, professional, and supervisory employees. Certain public service corporation employees as provided by statute. Clerical force and salespersons.
ME	At regular intervals not to exceed 16 days. Weekly for specified employers and municipalities.	—
MD	Semimonthly or biweekly.	Administrative, executive, and professional employees.

Table 1-2. Payment Frequency (*cont'd*)

State	Wage Payment Requirements	Exceptions
MA	Weekly or biweekly.	Qualified railroad and hospital employees; agricultural and executive, administrative, and professional employees. Casual employees must be paid within 7 days after end of work period.
MI	Semimonthly; wages earned during the first 15 days of a month must be paid on or before the first day of the succeeding month. Wages earned from the 16th to the last day of a month must be paid by the 15th day of the succeeding month.	Certain agricultural employees. Employers may also set up weekly, biweekly, or monthly pay schedules and will be in compliance if statutory guidelines are followed.
MN	Every 31 days.	Public service corporation employees must be paid semimonthly. Transitory employees must be paid every 15 days.
MS	Public service corporations and employers engaged in manufacturing that employ 50 or more workers must pay employees semimonthly or biweekly.	Executive, administrative, and professional employees.
MO	All corporations, factories, and all railroad industry employers must pay employees semimonthly.	Executive, administrative, and professional employees; sales employees; and employees compensated on a commission basis.
MT	Within 10 days of the time wages become due and payable. Employees who fail to submit timesheets by established deadline may be paid at the next pay period. If there is not an established time when wages are due and payable, the pay period is presumed to be semimonthly.	Professional, supervisory, agricultural, and technical employees may be paid monthly.
NE	Established regular payday.	Certain independent employees.

Table 1-2.   Payment Frequency (*cont'd*)

State	*Wage Payment Requirements*	*Exceptions*
NV	Semimonthly. For work done before the first day of a month, wages must be paid by 8:00 a.m. on the 15th of the month. For work done before the 16th day of the month, wages must be paid by 8:00 a.m. on the last day of the month.	Specified executive, administrative, and professional employees; supervisors; and outside salespersons.
NH	Weekly, within 8 days after the week in which the work was performed.	Certain domestic employees and agricultural laborers. Upon petition to commissioner, who may permit less frequent payment (but at least monthly).
NJ	Semimonthly.	Executive, supervisory, and railroad employees.
NM	Semimonthly.	Professional, administrative, and executive employees and outside salespersons may be paid monthly unless their salaries are subject to provisions of a collective bargaining agreement.
NY	Weekly for manual and railroad workers. Monthly for salespersons working on commission. Semimonthly on regular paydays for clerical and other workers.	Large employers may pay manual workers semimonthly. Certain executive, administrative, and professional employees are exempt.
NC	Regular payday, which may be daily, weekly, biweekly, semimonthly, or monthly.	—
ND	Monthly.	Railroads must pay at least semimonthly.
OH	Semimonthly.	Trades, professions, or occupations where the custom is otherwise or by written contract.
OK	Semimonthly.	Management-level employees. Government workers may be paid monthly.
OR	At least every 35 days.	Specified piecework and forest production employees must be paid monthly.

Table 1-2. Payment Frequency (*cont'd*)

State	*Wage Payment Requirements*	*Exceptions*
PA	Semimonthly.	Railroad employees.
RI	Weekly, except for employees whose compensation is fixed at a biweekly, semimonthly, monthly, or yearly rate.	Government employees and employees of religious, charitable, and literary institutions may be paid at other intervals. Labor director may allow less frequent payment upon written petition.
SC	Regular payday.	Employers with fewer than 5 employees in the preceding 12 months and domestic laborers in private homes.
SD	Monthly.	—
TN	Semimonthly. All wages earned prior to the first day of the month must be paid by the 20th day of the month. Wages earned by the 16th of the month must be paid by the 5th day of the succeeding month.	Employers with fewer than 5 employees.
TX	Semimonthly.	Employees who are exempt under the overtime provisions of the FLSA may be paid monthly.
UT	Semimonthly.	Government, agricultural, and domestic workers.
VT	Weekly.	Biweekly or semimonthly if employer gives written notice.
VA	Salaried employees must be paid monthly. Hourly employees must be paid biweekly or semimonthly, except that those earning over 150 percent of the average weekly wage may agree to be paid monthly.	Students employed by their school and executive personnel.
WA	Monthly; semimonthly for state employees.	—
WV	Semimonthly no more than 19 days apart, unless agreed.	Semimonthly for railroad employees.

Table 1-2.   Payment Frequency (*cont'd*)

State	Wage Payment Requirements	Exceptions
WI	Monthly.	School employees (public and private). Quarterly for employees engaged in logging operations and farm labor. Migrant agricultural workers and traveling sales crews must be paid at least semimonthly on regularly established paydays.
WY	On regular paydays. Manufacturing, railroad, mine, refinery, oil and gas, and other factory employees must be paid semimonthly.	Agricultural employees.

Source: 2017 Multistate Payroll Guide (2017, CCH Incorporated).

Q 1:28   What methods of payment are permitted?

Federal law does not specify the media (e.g., cash or a check) that must be used to pay an employee, although the FLSA does restrict certain in-kind payments. Most states have enacted laws regulating payment by check or cash. Both federal and state laws generally control direct deposit of an employee's pay. Lately, more states have allowed employers to impose mandatory direct deposit, but with restrictions. Some states have also added provisions governing pay cards (see chapter 5).

Payment by check or cash is generally permitted in all 50 states (the states either require these forms of payment or have no law). A few states require that when payment is made by check, the employer must make arrangements for employees to be able to cash the pay checks with or without cost to the employee.

A few states permit employers to pay employees in the form of scrip or tokens. These states require that the scrip or tokens be converted into cash on the employer's payday. The Department of Labor has issued regulations on the use of scrip, tokens, and vouchers. These regulations permit the use of vouchers to document wages earned. Vouchers cannot be used as a form of payment. [29 C.F.R. § 531.34]

Q 1:29   May an employer require an employee to accept direct deposit as a condition of employment?

State laws vary. Employers unsure about how state law may affect their direct deposit program can contact the NACHA or a Federal Reserve bank or seek legal counsel. (See Table 5-1 in chapter 5 for state direct deposit rules.)

Q 1:30   What information must be provided on the employee's paycheck, pay stub, or both?

Federal law is silent concerning the specific information to be provided on an employee's paycheck. Most employers provide sufficient information to permit an employee to verify gross wages and to reconcile the specific deductions to the employee's net pay. Most states require that the paycheck or pay stub show the employee's gross wages, tax withholdings and other deductions, the employer's payday, and the date. In some states and for certain industries, the employer may be required to separate regular wages from overtime pay. When a third-party provider is utilized to process payroll, the employer must ensure that state requirements are met when producing paychecks.

Q 1:31   How does an employer handle unpaid wages of a deceased employee?

State laws generally dictate when and to whom the wages of a deceased employee are paid. For the income tax withholding and employment tax treatment of wages and taxable fringe benefits paid to a deceased employee, see chapter 9. [I.R.C. § 691(a)(1); Rev. Rul. 71-525, 1971-2 C.B. 356]

The taxation of these wages also depends on when the wages are paid, as follows:

- Paid before death, but occurs before check is cashed—reissue to estate or beneficiary.
- Paid after death, in same calendar year—FIT withholding is reported on Form 1099, and FICA withholding is reported on Form W-2.
- Paid after death, in next calendar year—FIT withholding is reported on Form 1099. There is no FICA tax withheld in the year after death.

Q 1:32   What happens when a paycheck is unclaimed?

Under most state laws, an unclaimed paycheck is treated as abandoned property and must be paid over to a state authority after the paycheck remains unclaimed for a specified period of time. A state's escheat laws generally control abandoned property.

Q 1:33   How are wage repayments handled?

When wages are paid to employees that later must be repaid (e.g., as required under a relocation agreement and salary overpayments), the manner in which the repayment is treated for withholding and employment tax purposes depends on the tax year of the repayment according to the claim-of-right doctrine, as follows:

- *Repayment in the year of the overpayment.* The amount repaid by the employee is treated similar to a pretax deduction—the repayment reduces federal income, Social Security, Medicare and federal unemployment insurance taxable wages in the payroll period of the repayment.

- *Repayment in year(s) subsequent to overpayment.* Under the claim-of-right doctrine, the amount repaid is treated as an aftertax deduction that is posted to an employee receivable account so that current-year taxable wages, withholding, and employment taxes are not affected by the repayment. The repayment is generally equal to the overpayment less FICA tax withholding. The alternative is for the employer to repay the gross overpayment and, the employer issues a refund of FICA tax on the amount of the wages repaid. In such situations, employees must certify they have not and will not claim a FICA tax refund on their personal tax returns [I.R.C. §§ 1341, 67(b)(10); Pub. No. 525]

Q 1:34   May an employee avoid taxation by returning wages that have been paid?

The IRS held that the return of a portion of a president's salary that was required to capitalize the corporation did not reduce either the president's or the corporation's employment tax liability on the wages originally paid. The IRS also said that the refund did not entitle either the president or the corporation to a credit for future taxes. In another case, a federal employee received a lump-sum payment for annual leave upon leaving the employment of one agency and repaid the money upon being hired by another federal agency to restore his annual leave. The IRS held that the employee was entitled to adjust his gross income and the amount subject to FIT withholding to reflect the repayment. Notice that if the return of the wages occurs in a year subsequent to the initial payment by the employer, the claim-of-right doctrine applies. See Q 1:33 [Rev. Rul. 71-289, 1971-2 C.B. 399; Rev. Rul. 75-531, 1975-2 C.B. 21]

Q 1:35   May an employee avoid income tax withholding and other employment taxes by having wages paid to another party?

No, although when wages are paid for certain benefit purposes, they are not treated as being "paid to another party" and receive tax-free treatment, subject to certain nondiscrimination rules as discussed more fully in chapter 9. The I.R.C. and Treasury regulations treat as income all wages that are "actually or constructively" paid to the individual. Thus, any payment to which the worker is entitled is subject to FIT withholding and Social Security and Medicare taxes even if the employee elects not to receive the payment. This is called the doctrine of constructive receipt. [Treas. Reg. §§ 1.145-2, 31.3121(a)-2, 31.3301-4]

There are exceptions to this general rule under various provisions of the I.R.C. relating to employee benefits: I.R.C. Section 125 for cafeteria plans, which permits the employee to select between a taxable and nontaxable benefit; and I.R.C. Sections 403, 401(k), and 457(b) and/or (f) for elective contributions to tax-qualified saving arrangements. The I.R.C. also allows delayed payment of benefits to which the individual is entitled without current taxation, as long as those benefits remain subject to a substantial risk of forfeiture, as in a nonqualified deferred compensation plan for a select group of management employees. See chapter 9 for additional information on these arrangements. [Treas. Reg. § 1.451-2]

Example. Jesse is a celebrity who regularly contributes to a charity. Jesse cannot avoid income tax withholding or FICA and FUTA taxation on payments under a contract to appear at a local civic center by having those payments made to the charity. He is in constructive receipt of the income, which is subject to federal tax withholding and FICA and FUTA taxes.

Note. The IRS has issued guidance to establish a plan under which employees can donate their leave to co-workers who have been adversely affected by a major disaster. The leave is included as wages of the employee who receives the leave (recipient) rather than the employee who donates the leave (donor). [Notice 2006-59, 2006-28 I.R.B. 60; Notice 2012-69, 2012-51 I.R.B. 712]

Deposits

Q 1:36   Are federal income tax and FICA tax withholding deposited separately or together?

Federal income and FICA taxes are deposited together through the Electronic Federal Tax Payment System (EFTPS). Form 8109 is no longer accepted for payroll tax deposits. See chapter 4 for deposit requirements.

Q 1:37   When are employers required to withhold and deposit federal income tax withholding and employment taxes?

Employers are required to withhold federal income and FICA taxes when they pay employees for services rendered. In the case of independent contractors, backup tax withholding may be required under certain circumstances. Before an employer can determine if federal income tax withholding will be required, it must review the service relationship between itself and the person providing services. The individual performing the services may fall within any one of the following categories: (1) independent contractor; (2) common-law employee; (3) statutory employee; and (4) statutory nonemployee; federal income tax withholding is not required in all of these categories. See chapter 6 for a discussion of nonemployee relationships. [Pub. No. 15-A; Rev. Rul. 90-93, 1990-45 I.R.B. 4]

Q 1:38   When are employers required to deposit withholding taxes electronically?

An employer must use EFTPS for all federal withholding and employment taxes that must be deposited. An alternative to the EFTPS is to arrange with a banker service provider to make the deposit on behalf of the employer.

Employers use EFTPS to deposit taxes reported on any of the following tax forms:

Form 720	Quarterly Federal Excise Tax Return
Form 940	Employer's Annual Federal Unemployment (FUTA) Tax Return
Form 941	Employer's QUARTERLY Federal Tax Return
Form 943	Employer's Annual Federal Tax Return for Agricultural Employees
Form 944	Employer's ANNUAL Federal Tax Return
Form 945	Annual Return of Withheld Federal Income Tax
Form 990-C	Farmers' Cooperative Association Income Tax Return
Form 990-PF	Return of Private Foundation or Section 4947(a)(1) Nonexempt Charitable Trust Treated as a Private Foundation
Form 990-T	Exempt Organization Business Income Tax Return
Form 1042	Annual Withholding Tax Return for U.S. Source Income of Foreign Persons
Form 1120	U.S. Corporation Income Tax Return
Form CT-1	Employer's Annual Railroad Retirement Tax Return

Employers that are required to make deposits by EFTPS and fail to do so may be subject to a failure to deposit penalty up to 10 percent. This penalty is in addition to the failure to file Form 941, Form 944, or Form 945. [Treas. Reg. § 31.6302-1(h)(2)(ii); Pub. No. 15; I.R.S. News Release 98-287; Notice 99-20, 1999-17 I.R.B. 16]

Other Depositors

Q 1:39   What is a common paymaster?

The term *common paymaster* is used to describe a means for paying and withholding employment taxes for an employee who works for two or more related employers. If two or more related corporations (see Q 1:40) employ the same individual at the same time and pay this individual through a common paymaster, which is one of the corporations, the corporations are considered a single employer for federal employment tax purposes. When a common pay-master is used, the two employers may pay less in Social Security and FUTA taxes. They have to pay and withhold FICA tax on no more in Social Security wages than a single employer would ($127,200 for 2017). That is, the employee's pay from both corporations is aggregated in determining caps on Social Security ($127,200 for 2017) and FUTA ($7,000 for 2017) taxes.

Each corporation must pay its own part of the employment taxes and may deduct only its own part of the wages. The deductions will not be allowed unless the other corporation reimburses the common paymaster for the wage and tax payments. [Treas. Reg. § 31.3121(s)-1; Pub. No. 15-A]

Q 1:40 When are corporations considered related for purposes of using common paymaster rules?

Related employers that employ the same employee may use a common paymaster to avoid overpayment of Social Security and FUTA taxes. A business qualifies as a common paymaster only when it is a member of two or more related corporations that meet one of the following tests at any time during the year:

1. The corporation is a member of a group of corporations in which 50 percent of the stock of one corporation is owned by one or more of the other corporations;

2. At least 50 percent of one corporation's officers are concurrently officers of the other corporation;

3. If no stock is issued by a corporation, 50 percent or more of the members of one corporation's board of directors are members of the other corporation's board of directors or the members of one corporation's board hold 50 percent or more of the voting power in the other corporation; or

4. At least 30 percent of one corporation's employees are concurrently employed by the other corporation.

[I.R.C. §§ 3121(a), 3306(p); Treas. Reg. § 31.3306]

Q 1:41 Are third-party payers required to withhold income and employment taxes?

Any lender, surety, or other third party that pays wages (or supplies funds specifically to pay wages) directly to the employees of an employer, or to the employee's agent, is responsible for any required withholding on those wages. This includes the withholding of federal income tax (FIT) (the withholding of FIT on third-party disability payments is required only if the employee completes a Form W-4S) and Social Security, Medicare, and railroad retirement taxes. The third party is also liable for any interest and penalties accruing on these taxes. [Pub. No. 15-A]

Q 1:42   How do agents become authorized to pay wages and report withheld employment taxes?

The tax reporting of third-party payments is made under an agreement between the employer and the third party. An employer that wants to request approval to have an agent file and make payments of employment and withholding taxes must file Form 2678, Employer/Payer Appointment of Agent.

Guidance

Q 1:43   How can an employee or employer receive tax help and forms from the IRS?

There are a number of ways to reach the IRS or obtain information on current tax laws:

1. *Online.* Access the IRS's website at www.irs.gov to do the following:

   - Get answers to frequently asked tax questions
   - Obtain blank forms and instructions
   - Complete tax forms online ("fill-in forms")
   - Search publications by topic or keyword
   - Calculate the number of federal income tax withholding allowances an employee can claim ("W-4 calculator")
   - Obtain publications
   - Obtain comments and help via e-mail
   - Learn about current tax issues and news

2. *By mail.* Request tax products by sending an order to: Internal Revenue Service, 1201 N. Mitsubishi Motorway, Bloomington, IL 61705-6613.

3. *By phone.* Order forms, instructions, and publications by calling 800-TAX-FORM (800-829-3676).

[Pub. No. 15]

Q 1:44   Is there a hotline that may be used to contact the IRS Taxpayer Advocate Service?

The IRS opened a 24-hour hotline—1-877-777-4778—to the IRS National Taxpayer Advocate Service. A list of Taxpayer Advocate Service offices can also be found in IRS Publication 1546, The Taxpayer Advocate Service of the IRS—How to Get Help With Unresolved Tax Problems. The Taxpayer Advocate Service should be used only if an initial attempt to solve the problem through the general help number—1-800-829-1040—is unsuccessful.

Latest Developments

Q 1:45 How does the new health care legislation affect Payroll?

The Patient Protection and Affordable Care Act (PPACA), signed into law by President Obama on March 23, 2010, continues to have the following significant employment tax and information reporting implications. [H.R. 3590; Pub. L. No. 111-148] Since then there have been postponements for implementing many of the changes.

Insurer health insurance coverage reporting requirement. Effective in 2014, insurers (including employers that self insure) that provide minimum essential health coverage during a calendar year must report certain health coverage information to both the insured and the IRS. The reporting requirement was extended to apply for 2015 for large employers and 2016 for mid-size employers. The IRS encouraged voluntary compliance without imposing any penalties for employers that filed before these dates.

There are two forms that must be provided to employees. Form 1095-B, Health Coverage, confirms that the employee is covered under the employer's health insurance plan. Form 1095-C, Employer-Provided Health Insurance Offer and Coverage, provides the employee with the supporting documentation to establish eligibility for premium tax credits. To meet these reporting requirements, employers with 100 or more full-time equivalent employees will have to accumulate data on a monthly basis and report annually to the IRS. The data points will involve the payroll and possibly the time reporting systems and must be coordinated with Human Resources, Benefits, and all third-party providers. The data elements include:

- Social Security numbers
- Name and employer ID
- Number of full-time employees for each calendar month
- Total number of employees (FTE) for each calendar month
- Employees' share of the lowest cost monthly premium for self-only, minimum value coverage for each calendar month
- Safe Harbor 4980H
- 4980H transition relief indicators for each month

The transmittal forms to be submitted with the filing of Forms 1095-B and Forms 1095-C are Forms 1094-B and 1094-C respectively. The due date for providing employees with Forms 1095-C is March 2, 2017 and to the IRS, February 28, 2017 (March 31, 2017, if filed electronically). [IRS Notice 2016-04, Dec. 28, 2015] To complete these forms accurately, the Benefits and Payroll departments have to collaborate on collecting the necessary data and incorporating the data for the reports.

Penalty for failure to provide health coverage to certain employees. There are two potential penalties:

1. The larger penalty is assessed if a large employer does not offer minimal essential coverage to at least 95 percent in 2017.

2. Employers that do not offer coverage for all full-time employees and their dependents, offer minimum essential coverage that is unaffordable, or minimum essential coverage that consists of a plan under which the plan's share of the total allowed cost of benefits is less than 60 percent are required to pay a penalty for full-time employees who have certified to the employer as having purchased health insurance through a state exchange with respect to which a tax credit or cost-sharing reduction is allowed or paid to the employee.

These penalties are effective in 2017.

In 2017, President Donald Trump signed an Executive Order directing the Department of Health and Human Services (HHS) to exercise all authority and direction to waive, defer, grant exemption from, or delay the implementation of any pressure or requirement of the Act that would impose a fiscal burden on either the states or families. His order also directs the HHS to provide greater flexibility to states and cooperate with them to implement health programs and encourage the development of a free and open market in interstate commerce.

Chapter 2

Computing Tax Withholding

With limited exceptions, wages paid by employers are generally subject to the requirement to withhold federal income, Social Security and Medicare tax (as well as state and local tax). The collection of taxes in this way is based on a belief by Congress that collecting income and employment taxes at the "source" of payment—from the workers' wages—creates a more efficient tax administration system and ensures that a greater percentage of taxes owed is paid.

The U.S. Treasury and the IRS have devised a set of procedural rules to facilitate the orderly collection and reporting of wages and taxes by employers. Moreover, to ensure that employers comply with these requirements, the law provides for penalties and other adverse consequences for businesses that fail to fulfill these obligations.

This chapter explains the rules governing federal withholding and employment tax and the reporting requirements that apply. Wages that are excluded from withholding and/or employment tax are discussed in chapter 9 and the deposit requirements are explained in chapter 4.

Overview

Q 2:1   What are the general rules that apply to the collection of federal income and employment taxes?

Generally, employers must withhold federal income tax (FITW) and Social Security/Medicare (FICA) tax and pay FICA and federal unemployment insurance tax (FUTA) on covered wages paid to employees. Federal withholding and employment tax must be deposited and reported on a timely basis or one or more penalties can be imposed in addition to interest. Certain payments to an employee may be subject to one federal employment tax (or withholding), but not another. [Pub. No. 15]

Note that FUTA is paid only by the employer and, under the Fair Labor Standards Act, cannot be deducted from employees' wages.

Q 2:2   What are the federal employment tax rates and wage bases for 2017?

Employers are subject to Social Security tax of 6.2 percent. The employee's share for 2017 is 6.2 percent of covered wages up to the annual wage limit. The Social Security wage base for 2017 is $127,200. Employers and employees are not required to pay Social Security tax on wages in excess of the specified annual wage limit. If an employee works for more than one employer and those employers have different employer identification numbers, each employer is required to withhold and pay Social Security tax on all wages paid to the employee up to the annual wage limit. If the combined Social Security tax for all employers exceeds the annual maximum, the employee (but not the employers) may claim a refund of the excess when filing the federal individual income tax return.

Employers and employees are also subject to Medicare tax of 1.45 percent of covered wages. There is no annual wage limit. In addition to withholding the 1.45 percent of covered wages, each employer must withhold an additional 0.9

percent Medicare taxes on wages in excess of $200,000 paid to an employee as a result of the Patient Protection and Affordable Care Act. This Additional Medicare Tax must be withheld in the pay period that the employee wages exceed $200,000 and continues until the end of the calendar year. Final Regulations were issued in late 2013 to provide guidance to employers. [T.D. 9645, 2013-51 I.R.B. 738] The Additional Medicare Tax is an employee tax and is not matched by employers.

Employers are required to pay FUTA tax of 6.0 percent of covered wages up to the first $7,000 of taxable wages. Employers eligible for the maximum FUTA credit of 5.4 percent pay an effective FUTA tax rate of 0.6 percent (0.006) of the first $7,000 of covered wages paid to each employee. FUTA tax may not be deducted from employees' wages. [I.R.C. §§ 3101(a), 3111(a), 3301; Pub. No. 15]

Q 2:3 What federal laws control the collection and reporting of federal income and employment taxes?

The current requirements for withholding, paying, and reporting federal income and employment taxes are derived from laws enacted by Congress and found in Subtitle C (Chapters 21 to 25, inclusive) of the Internal Revenue Code (Code) of 1986, as amended. Those laws have been further clarified and amplified in regulations. The tax laws under Chapters 21 to 25 are subdivided as shown below.

Tax	Chapter of Code	Section of Code
Federal Insurance Contributions Act	21	3101–3128
Railroad Retirement Tax Act	22	3201–3241
Federal Unemployment Tax Act	23	3301–3311
Railroad Unemployment Repayment Act	23A	3321–3322
Federal Income Tax Withholding	24	3401–3406
General Provisions Relating to Employment Taxes	25	3501–3510

The related regulations are preceded by a section symbol and the numeral 31, which refers to Part 31 of Title 26 of the Code of Federal Regulations.

Employer Responsibilities

Q 2:4 Who is responsible for the withholding of federal income and employment taxes?

The employer is responsible for withholding federal income, Social Security, and Medicare taxes. In certain situations, liability for withholding, depositing, and reporting for disability and sick-pay payments may be transferred to the third party.

Q 2:5 What are the general requirements when hiring a new employee?

When hiring an employee, an employer must generally:

1. Verify an individual's identity and eligibility to work in the United States (using Form I-9, Employment Eligibility Verification; frequently the responsibility of the human resources department);

2. Capture for wage and tax reporting purposes the employee's name and Social Security number (SSN) as they appear on the employee's Social Security card; and

3. Require that employees complete and sign Form W-4, Employee's Withholding Allowance Certificate.

When wages are paid, the employer must generally:

1. Withhold federal income tax based on each employee's Form W-4;

2. Withhold Social Security and Medicare taxes; and

3. Withhold all authorized voluntary and involuntary deductions.

Q 2:6 Who is the employer for purposes of withholding federal income, Social Security, and Medicare taxes?

The term *employer*, as it applies to FITW and FICA, is any person or entity for which an individual performs or has performed any service as an employee. If the entity or organization for which the services are performed does not have legal control of the payment of wages, the term *employer* refers to any person or entity that has control over those payments. [I.R.C. § 3401(d)]

An employer can be an individual, a corporation, a partnership, a trust, an estate, a joint-stock company, a syndicate, an association, a government entity, or an unincorporated organization. It does not matter whether the person or entity is engaged in a trade or business or is a tax-exempt organization or a government unit. The term *employer* can also refer to the person or entity making supplemental unemployment benefit payments that are considered wages. (See chapter 6 for a discussion of the employment relationship.) [Treas. Reg. §§ 31.3401(a)-1(b)(14), 31.3401(d)-1; I.R.C. § 3401(d); Rev. Rul. 62-60, 1962-1 C.B. 186]

Q 2:7 Are all employers required to withhold and report employment taxes on wages paid to employees?

Generally, yes. All employers that make payments to individuals for services rendered as employees are subject to the federal withholding and employment tax requirements. Wages paid by state and local government employers are generally subject to FITW and FICA, but FUTA tax does not apply. Certain exceptions to one or more of the federal employment taxes apply to payments made to certain workers in specific industries; those exceptions frequently are conditioned on the employee or employer meeting certain requirements of the I.R.C. or regulations.

Q 2:8   Are there any exceptions to the rule that an employer must withhold and pay employment taxes?

Yes. There are two exceptions to the general rule that an employer must withhold and pay employment taxes. First, when the person or entity that receives the services of an employee does not have control of the payment of wages for such services, the entity having control of the payment of such wages is considered the employer rather than the person or entity for whom the services are performed. Second, a U.S. person or entity that pays wages on behalf of an individual who is a nonresident alien or an entity that is a foreign partnership or foreign corporation not engaged in a trade or business within the United States is considered an employer rather than the foreign service recipient. [I.R.C. § 3401(d)]

Q 2:9   What is a taxpayer identification number?

A taxpayer identification number (TIN) is an account number assigned to a taxpayer (individual or business) by either the IRS or the Social Security Administration (SSA). A TIN may consist of any one of the following:

1. *Social Security number (SSN).* This TIN is for individuals. All employees paid wages by a U.S. employer are required to obtain an SSN. An SSN is obtained by filing Form SS-5, Application for a Social Security Card, with the Social Security Administration (SSA). The SSA issues an SSN to individuals who present the required documentation, including documents showing that they are eligible to work in the United States. The SSN is a nine-digit number in the following format: 000-00-0000.

2. *Employer identification number (EIN).* All businesses with a federal tax or filing obligation are required to obtain an EIN by filing SS-4, Application for Employer Identification Number. The EIN is shown on all federal employment tax returns and information returns. The EIN is a nine-digit number in the following format: 00-0000000.

3. *IRS individual taxpayer identification number (ITIN).* This TIN is for individuals who are not eligible for an SSN but require a taxpayer identification number in order to comply with U.S. tax payment or filing obligations. An ITIN is obtained by filing Form W-7, Application for IRS Individual Taxpayer Identification Number.

Note that an ITIN should generally not be used for federal employment tax reporting purposes. If nonresident aliens do not have SSNs because they are waiting for the SSA to issue them, employers are instructed to enter "applied for" in the SSN field of paper Forms W-2, or zeros in the SSN field of electronically filed Forms W-2.

Q 2:10   What is the significance of the payroll period?

The *payroll period* is the regular interval at which employers pay wages. The payroll period is generally daily, weekly, biweekly, semimonthly, or monthly. The federal income tax withholding calculations take into account both the payroll period and information as provided on employees' Forms W-4. Payroll period is not to be confused with "workweek." (See Q 2:11.) [Pub. No. 15]

Q 2:11   What is a workweek?

A workweek is seven consecutive days, 168 consecutive hours, and is relevant in determining the overtime pay calculation. [29 C.F.R. §§ 778.103–778.106]

Q 2:12   What frequency is used for calculating federal income tax withholding when wages are not paid in regular intervals?

When an employer does not have a set payroll period, the employer must withhold federal income tax as if it paid wages over a daily or miscellaneous payroll period (see Q 2:81). In using the daily or miscellaneous withholding tables, first determine the number of days (including Sundays and holidays) in the period covered by the wage payment. If the wages are unrelated to a specific length of time (e.g., commissions paid on completion of a sale), count back the number of days from the payment period to the latest of (1) the last wage payment made during the same calendar year; (2) the date employment began if it began during the same calendar year; or (3) January 1 of the same year.

When an employer pays an employee for a period of less than one week and the employee signs a statement under penalty of perjury that he or she is not working for any other employer during the same week for wages subject to withholding, the employer should figure withholding based on a weekly payroll period. If the employee later begins to work for another employer and is paid wages subject to withholding, he or she must notify the employer within 10 days and the employer should compute federal income tax withholding on a daily or miscellaneous period. There is no federal labor law requiring that employees be paid at a certain frequency; however, many states do impose such requirements. [29 C.F.R. § 778.114; Pub. No. 15]

Federal Insurance Contributions Act

Q 2:13   What is FICA?

The Federal Insurance Contributions Act (FICA) provides for a federal system of old age, survivors, and disability insurance (OASDI) and hospital insurance (HI). The first three benefits are financed by the Social Security tax; the HI (for persons 65 or older) is financed by the Medicare tax. Because the Social Security tax has a wage base limit and the Medicare tax does not, each is withheld and reported separately. Social Security and Medicare tax are also referred to as "FICA." The Medicare tax now has two components, effective January 1, 2013 as a result of the health care legislation, the Patient Protection and Affordable Care Act (ACA). All wages are subject to the 1.45 percent Medicare tax and wages that exceed $200,000 are subject to withholding of the Additional Medicare Tax of 0.9 percent.

Both the employer and the employee pay FICA (unless an exemption applies to the worker or the wage payment). FICA is deposited and reported at the same time, and in the same manner, as federal income tax withholding (FITW).

Note. The Additional Medicare Tax is not matched by the employer.

Covered wages are subject to FICA regardless of the age of employees and whether or not they are receiving Social Security benefits. [Treas. Reg. §§ 31.3101-3, 31.3102-2, 31.3111-3; Pub. No. 15]

Q 2:14   How is FICA computed?

FICA is computed as shown below (see Q 2:2). [I.R.C. § 3101; Pub. No. 15]

	Employee Rate (2017)	Employer Rate (2017)	Wage Base (2017)
Social Security tax	6.20%	6.20%	$127,200
Medicare wages up to $200,000	1.45%	1.45%	No cap
Medicare wages over $200,000	2.35%	1.45%	No cap

Self-employed individuals pay both the employee and employer taxes shown above under the Self-Employment Contributions Act (SECA). [I.R.C. §§ 1401, 1402]

Q 2:15   May an employer apply rounding in the calculations that determine the amount of FICA to withhold?

Yes. An employer may determine the amount of FICA to withhold (as well as its share of these taxes) by rounding fractional amounts to the nearest cent ($0.01). Rounding to the nearest dollar is permitted for withholding of FICA for domestic employees. [Treas. Reg. § 31.3102-1(c)]

Q 2:16   Who is the employer for purposes of withholding and paying FICA?

For purposes of withholding and paying FICA, an employer is any person or entity that employs one or more employees. The number of employees, how the employer classifies the workers, the period during which they are employed, and the nature of the employer's trade or business are immaterial in the determination of whether an employer is subject to the FICA tax requirements. An employer may be an individual, sole proprietorship, corporation, partnership, trust, estate, joint-stock company, association, syndicate, or tax-exempt organization. Generally, an employer subject to the FICA tax requirements is any person or entity that can control the work of an individual performing services and has the sole power to hire, fire, and supervise the worker. In certain cases, the employer might not be the party paying the wages. [I.R.C. § 3401(d); Treas. Reg. §§ 31.3121(d)-2, 31.3401(d)-1; Rev. Rul. 62-60, 1962-1 C.B. 186; Rev. Rul. 54-31, 1954-1 C.B. 212]

Q 2:17   Can a surety taking over the payroll payments of a contractor be held liable for unpaid FICA?

Yes. This liability was confirmed in a Tax Court case. The court held that a surety that takes over making payroll payments for a contractor is responsible for paying the employer's FICA. A federal district court held that I.R.C. Section 3401(d) defines the employer as a "person for whom an individual performs or performed any service, of whatever nature, as the employee of such person." However, when the "person for whom the individual performed the services does not have control of the payment of wages for such services," the person having control of the payment of such wages is treated as the employer. [Reliance Ins. Co. v. United States, 82 A.F.T.R.2d 98-5116 (1998); Field Serv. Advice (dated and released Aug. 17, 1992)]

Q 2:18   Can an employment agency be held liable for employment taxes of a contractor placed with a third party?

Yes. When the employment agency controls the payment to the contractor (the individual providing the service), that agency can be held liable for nonpayment of employment taxes. This could occur when the contractor has been incorrectly classified as an independent contractor and is later reclassified during a payroll audit. The determination of whether a contractor in any factual situation is an employee or an independent contractor is based on whether the "employer" has the right to control not only the result of the services performed but also the means by which these services are performed. In the case of a highly trained or highly skilled worker, this determination may be based on whether the worker (1) has a significant investment in the business; (2) incurs unreimbursed business expenses; and (3) offers his or her services to the general public. When these factors point to the fact that the worker is not an employee but an independent contractor, the payer does not withhold or pay FICA. Rather, the worker pays self-employment tax, on his or her self-employment income, to account for both portions of Social Security and Medicare tax. The payer is required to report the amounts paid to an independent contractor on Form 1099-MISC, Miscellaneous Income, when total payments from a single source equal or exceed $600 for the calendar year. Form W-2 reporting does not apply to independent contractors, with the exception of workers who qualify as statutory employees under I.R.C. Section 3121(d)(3). Statutory employees are classified as independent contractors for federal income tax purposes, but are employees for FICA purposes. Refer to the "Statutory Classifications" subsection of chapter 6 for additional information.

In Private Letter Ruling 9825009, the IRS determined that a placement firm's client and a nurse provided by the placement firm had entered into an employer–employee relationship and the nurse was not an independent contractor. The nurse's pay was found to be wages subject to FICA and federal income tax withholding. However, under I.R.C. Section 3401(d), when the entity for whom the worker performs services does not control the payment of wages, the party liable for withholding and employment tax is the entity that does control the payment. As a result, the placement firm was liable for withholding and paying the nurse's FICA.

It should be noted that a contractor may also take the place of an employer for the purpose of providing employee benefits, but not in all cases. (See Q 9:401.)

Q 2:19   What is the successor employer exception to the FICA coverage rules?

Despite the rule that employers do not receive credit for the FICA paid by other employers, certain successor employers may take credit for the FICA wages on which the predecessor employer withheld and paid FICA. That is, the successor may include, in determining if the Social Security wage base has been met, the FICA wages paid by the predecessor employer to those employees hired by the successor in the same calendar year. A successor employer for this purpose must satisfy three conditions: (1) it is a corporation that, during the calendar year, acquired substantially all the property used in the trade or business, or used in a separate unit of a trade or business, of the predecessor; (2) the affected employees were employed in the acquired trade or business (or in the trade or business of which the acquired unit was a part) immediately before the acquisition, and are employed in the successor's trade or business (but not necessarily in the acquired trade or business) immediately after the acquisition; and (3) the wages paid before the acquisition were paid during the same calendar year as the acquisition. The form of the acquisition of the assets of a trade or business is immaterial for purposes of this rule. [I.R.C. § 3121(a)(1); Treas. Reg. § 31.3121(a)(1)-1; Priv. Ltr. Rul. 9843019]

-See chapter 12 for more information about predecessor and successor employers.

Example. In April 2017, Gramercy acquired all the assets of Brighton, Inc. Sydney, who had been employed by Brighton and whose year-to-date Social Security wages through April 2017 were $106,800 immediately before the purchase, continues to work for Gramercy after the sale. Sydney is subject to Social Security taxes on the first $20,400 ($127,200 less $106,800) of wages Gramercy pays him during the rest of the calendar year and to 1.45 percent Medicare taxes on all wages paid by Gramercy during the rest of the calendar year. [Pub. No. 15; I.R.C. §§ 3121(a)(1), 3306(b)(1); Priv. Ltr. Rul. 9843019]

Q 2:20   Is the FICA tax obligation of the employer or employee reduced by the amount of FICA withheld and paid by a previous employer in the calendar year?

No. Outside of the exception for a successor employer discussed in Q 2:19, the amount of FICA withheld and paid by an employer is unrelated to the amount of FICA withheld and paid by another employer of the employee having a different EIN. If an employee working for more than one employer in a calendar year pays FICA in excess of the FICA wage limit ($118,500 for 2016), that employee may claim a refund of the excess FICA payment on his or her personal income tax return. Employers are not entitled to a refund of the FICA that they pay.

Note. Employees working for more than one employer and who expect to pay FICA in excess of the wage limit may be able to take into account the FICA overpayment when having their federal income tax withholding calculated by making an adjustment to their Form W-4.

Q 2:21   Are certain types of remuneration exempt from FICA?

Yes. Certain types of remuneration paid to employees may be exempt from FICA under various sections of the I.R.C. (e.g., I.R.C. Section 117—a qualified scholarship; I.R.C. Section 119—payment for meals or lodging furnished for the convenience of the employer; I.R.C. Section 127—payment for educational assistance; I.R.C. Section 129—payment for dependent care assistance; or I.R.C. Section 132—qualified fringe benefits). Additionally, a moving expense reimbursement is not subject to FICA if, at the time the payment is made, it is reasonable to believe that the employee is entitled to a corresponding moving expense deduction under I.R.C. Section 217.

Also exempt from FICA (and FITW and FUTA) are noncash wages paid to employees for services not in the course of the employer's trade or business, regardless of the value of the wages. *De minimis* cash wages paid for services not in the course of the employer's trade or business are also exempt from all FICA; that is, such wages paid for services not in the course of the employer's trade or business are exempt from FICA if they total less than $100 during the year, regardless of whether the employee is regularly employed by the employer (see Q 2:36). [I.R.C. §§ 3401(a)(4), 3401(a)(11)]

Note. The exemptions identified above are generally subject to a variety of conditions, which are more fully described in chapter 9.

Q 2:22   Are employer-provided retirement benefits from a qualified plan subject to FICA?

Generally, no. Neither employer contributions to nor benefits paid from a tax-qualified retirement plan (e.g., stock bonus, pension, profit sharing, 401(k)) meeting the requirements of I.R.C. Section 401(a) are subject to FICA. Employee elective deferrals contributed to a 401(k) plan are, however, subject to FICA when contributed. A special rule applies to benefits paid under a nonquali-fied deferred compensation plan: The value of benefits provided under a nonqualified plan is subject to FICA when the amounts deferred are no longer subject to a substantial risk of forfeiture (e.g., vested). If FICA was not withheld or paid at the time of the vesting, the full amount of the deferral is subject to FICA (and FUTA) when the benefits are distributed. [I.R.C. §§ 3121(v)(2), 3306(v)(2)]

Q 2:23   Is vacation pay subject to FICA?

Yes. Vacation pay is treated as a regular wage payment.

Q 2:24   How are back-pay awards taxed for FICA purposes?

FICA applies to awards of back pay based on the period in which they are paid, not the period for which the awards relate. Thus, a payment in 2017 for back pay relating to any prior year is subject to FICA at the rates and wage base in effect for 2017. [Treas. Reg. § 31.3101-3]

A judge's award of back pay is subject to FICA when received, not when the wages would have been earned, a federal district court decided. Benefit credit for Social Security purposes may be given for periods to which the back pay relates. [Social Sec. Bd. v. Nierotko, 327 U.S. 358 (1946) (as to benefit credit); Bowman v. United States, 824 F.2d 528 (6th Cir. 1987); Mazur v. Commissioner, 1997 U.S. Dist. LEXIS 18924 (W.D.N.Y. Nov. 14, 1997)]

Other types of back-pay awards have been challenged in the courts. Two circuit courts agreed with the government that the full settlements were taxable in cases involving back pay for pension benefits.

Q 2:25   Must employers withhold and pay FICA on wages paid to family members who are their employees?

Wages paid to family members might not be subject to FICA (or FUTA). Specifically exempted are wages paid to a child under age 18 in the employ of his or her parents regardless of whether the child's services are performed in the course of a trade or business. Similarly, wages paid to a child over age 17 but under age 21 in the employ of his or her parents are exempt from FICA if the services are not performed in the course of a trade or business. Wages paid for services performed by a spouse for a spouse or by a parent for a child are not subject to FICA if such services are not performed in the course of the recipient's trade or business. There is also a limited exception contained in I.R.C. Section 3121(b)(3)(B) relating to domestic services provided for certain family members.

Q 2:26　Are the wages paid to children by a family business subject to FICA?

Generally, no. Payments for the services of a child under the age of 18 who works for his or her parents in a trade or business (i.e., a sole proprietorship or a partnership in which each partner is a parent of the child) are not subject to FICA. If the services are for work other than in a trade or business, such as domestic work in the parent's private home, the child is not subject to FICA until he or she reaches age 21. These rules apply even if the child is paid regular wages. [I.R.C. § 3121(b)(3); Pub. No. 15]

Q 2:27　Are wages paid to an individual who is employed by his or her spouse in an unincorporated business subject to FICA?

Generally, yes. Wages for the services of an individual who works for his or her spouse in an unincorporated trade or business owned by the spouse (i.e., a sole proprietorship) are subject to FICA. Wages paid for services of one spouse employed by another in other than a trade or business, such as domestic services performed in a private home, are not subject to FICA, however. [I.R.C. § 3121(b)(3); Pub. No. 15]

Q 2:28　Are wages paid to family members employed by a corporation owned by a spouse or parent, or employed by a partnership in which a spouse or parent is a partner, subject to FICA?

Yes. Wages for the services of a child or spouse are subject to FICA and FUTA if he or she works for (1) a corporation in which the parent or spouse has an ownership interest, even if it is controlled by the child's parent or the individual's spouse; (2) a partnership in which the parent or spouse has an ownership interest, even if the child's parent is a partner, unless each partner is a parent of the child; (3) a partnership in which the parent or spouse has an ownership interest, even if the individual's spouse is a partner; or (4) an estate of a deceased parent or spouse. [Pub. No. 15]

Q 2:29　Are wages of a parent who works for a child subject to FICA?

Wages for the services of a parent employed by his or her child in a trade or business (including a partnership with spouse or nonspouse partners or a corporation) are subject to FICA; however, FICA does not apply to wages paid to a parent for services that are not related to a trade or business.

FICA applies to wages for domestic services (i.e., not a trade or business) when two conditions are met: (1) the parent cares for a child under age 18 who lives with a son or daughter, or the child requires adult supervision for at least four continuous weeks in a calendar quarter because of a mental or physical condition, and (2) the son or daughter is a widow or widower, divorced, or married to a person who, because of a physical or mental condition, cannot care for the child during such period. [I.R.C. § 3121(b)(31)]

Q 2:30   Are there any exemptions from FICA for wages paid to students?

Yes. Wages paid to certain students who are working at a school, college, or university at which they are enrolled and regularly attending classes are exempt from FICA. Similarly, wages paid to such students by private foundations, as defined under I.R.C. Section 509(a)(3) that are operated as schools, colleges, or universities are also exempt from FICA.

The IRS issued Revenue Procedure 2005-11 and final regulations to clarify who qualifies for the student exemption (see Q 2:31).

Q 2:31   How can students' wages qualify for the FICA exemption?

The IRS has issued a final regulation and a revenue procedure to determine whether students who work for a school, college, or university (SCU) are eligible for the exemption from FICA. The guidance distinguishes between career employees who take classes and students who work on campus.

For the exemption to apply, the SCU must primarily provide formal instruction, have a regular faculty and curriculum, and have a regularly enrolled body of students attending the place where the educational activities are carried on.

An employee is considered to be enrolled at the SCU if the employee is registered for a course or courses creditable toward an educational credential, such as a degree or certificate, and is regularly attending classes. These classes are defined as instructional activities led by faculty members or other qualified individuals hired by the SCU. "Other qualified individuals" was added to the final regulation to include adjuncts and other faculty who are not considered regular faculty members. Research activities under the supervision of a faculty advisor necessary to complete a Ph.D. count as instructional activities. The frequency of traditional classroom activities and other activities is considered when determining if the student attends regular classes.

To be eligible for the FICA exemption, the educational aspect must outweigh the service or work that the student performs. The student's work must be incident to and for the purpose of pursuing a course of study. All the relevant facts and circumstances must be evaluated to determine whether the student or the employee aspect is predominant. This determination is made each term.

Full-time employees are not eligible for the exemption. An employee who normally works 40 hours a week is considered full-time. However, working 40 hours per week during academic breaks does not disqualify the student. For employees who are not considered full-time, their normal work schedule and actual hours worked per week are relevant in determining whether the service aspect or the educational aspect is predominant. When determining the employee's normal work schedule, it does not matter that the work has an educational, instructional, or training aspect—it is considered work and not educational. As an employee's normal work hours approach 40 in a week, it is more likely that the worker is predominantly an employee rather than a student.

The educational aspect of an employee depends on the employee's course workload. This is evaluated relative to the full-time course workload at the SCU.

An employee who has the status of a professional employee suggests that the service aspect of the employee's relationship with the employer is predominant. Professional employees are defined as employees whose work requires knowledge of an advanced type in a field of science or learning; requires the consistent exercise of discretion and judgment; and is predominantly intellectual and varied in character. If an employee is licensed as a professional, the licensing further suggests that the service aspect predominates rather than the educational aspect. Professional employees, such as graduate assistants, may be exempt based on facts and circumstances.

Whether an employee is eligible to receive employment benefits is a relevant factor in evaluating the service aspect of an employee's relationship with the employer. Although the receipt of employment benefits no longer automatically disqualifies a student from the exemption, the following employment benefits suggest that the service aspect of an employee's relationship with the employer is predominant: vacation pay, sick leave, or paid holiday benefits; eligibility to participate in a retirement plan; reduced tuition; life insurance; qualified educational assistance; dependent care assistance; and adoption assistance. Eligibility to receive health insurance is not considered in determining whether the service aspect is predominant. State-mandated benefits are given less weight in determining if the work is predominant. [Rev. Proc. 2005-11, 2005-2 I.R.B. 307; T.D. 9167, 2005-2 I.R.B. 261]

In 2009, the Eighth Circuit Court of Appeals, considering the appeal of two U.S. District Court decisions, ruled that medical residents are disqualified from the FICA student exception. In doing so, the court upheld the validity of Treasury Regulations Section 31.3121(b)(10)-2(b)-(d), the amended regulation deemed invalid by the district court. This case combines the appeal of *Mayo Foundation for Medical Education & Research v. United States, and Regents of the University of Minnesota v. United States*. [568 F.3d 675 (8th Cir. 2009)] Specifically, the Eighth Circuit Court of Appeals did not rule that medical residents are not considered students, enrolled or regularly attending classes for any other purpose, but only that the full-time employee provision of the regulation is an acceptable interpretation of the student exception to the FICA coverage rule. The court then decided it was unnecessary to determine if Mayo's primary function "is education and [it] is thus a school, college, or university" within the meaning of I.R.C. Section 3121(b)(10) because Mayo's medical residents clearly do not fall into the student exception as amended. For the same reason, the court also found it unnecessary to determine if the residents were employed by Mayo or the independent hospitals.

In the meantime, the IRS issued Announcement IR-2010-25, which notified employers that filed protective claims for periods prior to April 1, 2005 that it would process the claims for refunds. The IRS would contact these hospitals, universities, and medical residents with more information and procedures for perfecting FICA refund claims. The IRS explained that it made this determination because the new regulations governing the student FICA exception were not effective until April 1, 2005.

With the conflict between the circuits, the Supreme Court heard arguments from the parties as Mayo petitioned the court to review the Court of Appeals ruling. The Supreme Court held that the Treasury's regulation provides that full-time employees working 40 hours or more "are not incident to or for the purpose of pursuing a course of study." Therefore, the medical students were not eligible for the FICA exemption. [Mayo Found. for Med. Educ. & Research, v. United States, 131 S. Ct. 704 (2011)]

Q 2:32   Is there an exemption from FICA for certain wages paid to a student's spouse?

No. Wages paid by an educational institution to the spouse of a student who is enrolled and regularly attending classes are not exempt from FICA unless another exemption applies. In certain cases, such wages may be exempt from FUTA (see chapter 3). [I.R.C. § 3121(b)(10)]

Q 2:33   Is there an exemption from FICA for wages paid to a student nurse?

Yes. Wages paid to student nurses in the employ of a hospital or nurses' training school, who are enrolled and regularly attending classes in a nurses' training school chartered or approved under state law, are exempt from FICA (and FUTA) (see chapter 3). [I.R.C. §§ 3121(b)(13), 3306(c)(13)] Also exempt from FICA are wages paid to certain interns, student nurses, and other students employed in hospitals of the federal government, other than medical or dental interns and residents. [I.R.C. § 3121(b)(6)(B)]

Q 2:34   Are the wages of election workers subject to FICA?

Sometimes. Wages of an election worker are not subject to FICA if the worker is paid less than $1,700 for services performed during 2017. The amount is adjusted for cost-of-living increases under Section 218(c)(8)(B) of the Social Security Act. When wages exceed the current threshold, all wages are subject to FICA.

Q 2:35   What is the difference between a household employee and a homeworker?

A *homeworker* is an individual who performs services for a trade or business in his or her own home. A *household worker* performs household chores in another individual's home.

Q 2:36   Does FICA apply to homeworkers' wages?

Yes. Generally, FICA applies to wages paid to homeworkers; however, cash wages of less than $100 paid in any calendar year to a homeworker who provides services according to the employer's specifications with materials or goods that are furnished by the employer and required to be returned to the employer are exempt from FICA. A homeworker is an individual who produces a product or service for the employer at the worker's home, where services are directed by the employer as described in I.R.C. Section 3121(d)(3)(C). [I.R.C. § 3121(a)(10)]

Q 2:37   When does a household worker become an employee for FICA purposes?

A household worker is an individual paid to provide services for work done in or around another's home (e.g., babysitters, nannies, health aides, private nurses, maids, caretakers, yard workers, and similar domestic workers). A person who provides child care services in his or her own home, for example, is not a household worker.

A household worker becomes an employee subject to FICA when the employer can control not only what work is done, but also how it is done. It does not matter whether the work is full-time or part-time, or that the worker was hired through an agency or from a list provided by an agency or association. It also does not matter whether the worker is paid on an hourly, daily, or weekly basis, or by the job.

When the worker controls how the work is done, the worker is not the payer's employee but is self-employed and subject to self-employment (SECA) tax. A self-employed worker usually provides his or her own tools and offers services to the general public in an independent business. If an agency provides the worker and controls what work is done and how it is done, but the worker is paid by the party at whose home the services are performed, the worker is not the payer's employee. [Pub. No. 926]

Q 2:38   Can wages paid to a homeworker who is not classified as a common-law employee for federal income tax withholding be subject to FICA?

Yes. The IRS held in Field Service Advice (FSA) 1999-611 that wages paid to a computer operator working for her husband's and another business were not subject to federal income tax withholding or FUTA, but were subject to FICA. Note the marital relationship had no bearing on this guidance.

The facts of this FSA appear similar to those in Revenue Ruling 64-280 [1964-2 C.B. 384] and Revenue Ruling 70-340 [1970-1 C.B. 202]. In those revenue rulings, the IRS concluded that a corporation did not exercise, or have the -right to exercise, the degree of direction and control necessary to establish an employer–employee relationship under the usual common-law rules for FUTA and income tax withholding purposes. However, for FICA purposes, the

IRS concluded in both revenue rulings that the workers were employees within the meaning of I.R.C. Section 3121(d)(3)(C). In Revenue Ruling 64-280, the worker performed typing services in her home, and in Revenue Ruling 70-340, the workers were transcribers performing services for a court reporter. [*See also* Priv. Ltr. Rul. 8451004 (Aug. 1, 1984) (where the transcribers used home computers)]

I.R.C. Section 3121(d)(3)(C) provides that for purposes of FICA, the term employee includes any individual (other than an individual who is an employee or officer of a corporation) who performs services for remuneration for any person as a homeworker if the services are (1) performed according to specifications furnished by the person for whom the services are performed; (2) performed on materials or goods that are furnished by such person and required to be returned to such person or to a person designated by him or her; and (3) performed when the contract of service contemplates that substantially all of such services are to be performed personally by such individual. An exception applies to the last condition when the individual has a substantial investment in facilities used in connection with the performance of such services or if the services are in the nature of a single transaction not part of a continuing relationship with the person for whom the services are performed; then the individual will generally not be treated as an employee. [Field Serv. Adv. 1999-611]

Q 2:39   When an employer pays a household worker's portion of FICA, is the tax payment also subject to federal withholding and employment tax?

Yes. When an employer pays the employee's FICA withholding for a household worker employed in a private home without deducting that amount from the worker's wages, the tax payments constitute additional compensation for federal income and federal income tax withholding purposes. This additional compensation is not subject to FICA (or FUTA). [I.R.C. § 3121(a)(6)(A)]

Q 2:40   Are there special rules for withholding and paying FICA on wages paid to household workers?

Yes. Generally, cash wages paid to household workers are subject to FICA unless the services are provided in the private home of an employer for remuneration of less than $2,000 in a calendar year (2017 limit). Noncash wages (e.g., value of food, lodging, clothing) paid to household workers who perform services in private homes are not subject to FICA. If, however, noncash wages are paid to domestic workers in a local college club or local chapter of a college fraternity or sorority, those wages will be subject to FICA, unless an exemption applies. Both cash and noncash wages are exempt from FICA if the household worker is a student worker, that is, an individual enrolled and regularly attending classes at an educational institution. Note that a $1,000 threshold applies for FUTA tax purposes and is based on total cash wages paid for all household employees in a calendar quarter of the current or prior year. [I.R.C. § 3306(c)(2); Pub. No. 926]

None of the following payments to household employees is treated as Social Security or Medicare wages, even when the total wages are equal to more than $2,000 during 2017:

1. Payments to the employer's spouse.
2. Payments to the employer's child who is under age 21.
3. Payment to the employer's parent. Exception: These wage payments count if both of the following conditions apply:
   a. The employer's parent cares for a child of the employer who lives with the employer and either is under age 18 or has a physical or mental condition that requires the personal care of an adult for at least four continuous weeks in a calendar quarter.
   b. The employer is divorced and has not remarried, or is a widow or widower, or is living with a spouse whose physical or mental condition prevents him or her from caring for the employer's child for at least four continuous weeks in a calendar quarter.
4. Payments to an employee who is under age 18 at any time during the year. However, this exception is not available if providing household services is the employee's principal occupation. An employee who is a student and who provides household services is not considered to be working in his or her principal occupation.

Q 2:41   What payments to a household worker are considered cash wages?

Cash wages include wages paid by check, money order, or similar means but do not include the value of food, lodging, clothing, or other noncash items an employer gives to a household employee. However, cash an employer gives to an employee in lieu of these items is treated as cash wages.

Transit passes given to an employee or reimbursements for the amount paid for transit passes (not more than $255 per month for 2017) used to commute to the employer's home do not count as wages if the expenses are substantiated. A transit pass includes any pass, token, fare card, voucher, or similar item entitling a person to ride on mass transit, such as a bus or train. An employer may also provide parking or reimburse the employee for parking at or near the home or at or near a location from which the employer's employee commutes to the home, without those payments being treated as wages. [Pub. L. No. 111-5; Pub. No. 926]

Q 2:42   Are wages paid to agricultural employees subject to FICA?

Sometimes. Wages of agricultural workers, like those of household workers, receive special treatment and in certain situations may be exempt. I.R.C. Section 3121(g) defines agricultural labor for purposes of FICA.

Cash payments made to agricultural workers are taxable wages subject to FICA; however, FICA applies only when cash payments in the calendar year exceed $150 (the so-called cash pay test) or when an employer pays more than $2,500 to all employees for agricultural labor in the calendar year. Noncash items such as food, lodging, transportation, tokens, farm products, or other goods or commodities are not considered FICA wages.

Also exempt from FICA are wages of nonmigrant hand harvest laborers paid on a piece-rate basis when the workers are employed in agriculture for less than 13 weeks during the preceding calendar year. [I.R.C. § 3121(a)(8)] Further, wages of agricultural laborers employed by owners or lessors of land who produce agricultural or horticultural commodities on the land are exempt from FICA if the commodities or proceeds therefrom are shared with the laborers and the laborers' share depends on the amount of commodities produced. Also exempt from FICA tax are wages paid to seasonal agricultural workers who commute daily from his or her permanent home to the farm and earn less than $150 annually. [I.R.C. §§ 3121(a)(8), 3121(b)(1), 3121(b)(16), 3121(g), 3121(o); Treas. Reg. §§ 31.3121(b)(1)-1, 31.3121(g)-1; Pub. No. 225]

When an employer pays an agricultural laborer's portion of FICA or a portion of the laborer's state unemployment taxes (or both) without deducting those taxes from the worker's wages, the tax payments constitute additional compensation. That additional compensation is not subject to FICA. [I.R.C. § 3121(a)(6)]

Q 2:43 Do special FICA rules apply to foreign agricultural workers?

To a limited extent, yes. There is a FICA exemption for foreign workers who perform services under contracts entered into under the Agricultural Act of 1949 or who are lawfully admitted to the United States from the Bahamas, Jamaica, or the British West Indies. There are also exemptions for certain individuals from any foreign country who enter the United States on a temporary basis to perform agricultural labor. [I.R.C. § 3121(b)(1)]

Q 2:44 Are wages paid to nonresident alien employees subject to FICA?

In general, wages paid to nonresident aliens are subject to FICA unless otherwise exempt, just as they would be for U.S. citizens. However, if there is a totalization agreement between the United States and the nonresident alien's country and the U.S. nonresident alien obtains a certificate of coverage from that other country, the U.S. employer is not required to withhold or pay FICA. Note that totalization agreements are generally in effect for only five years. See the Social Security Administration's website for more information on totalization agreements. See IRS Publication No. 515, Withholding of Tax on Nonresident Aliens and Foreign Entities, and IRS Publication No. 519, U.S. Tax Guide for Aliens, detail exceptions to those general rules. [Treas. Reg. § 1.871-1; Pub. No. 15; Pub. No. 515]

Q 2:45   Are wages paid to U.S. resident alien employees subject to FICA?

Yes. However, if there is a totalization agreement between the United States and the resident alien's country and the U.S. resident alien obtains a certificate of coverage from that other country, the U.S. employer is not required to withhold or pay FICA. Note that totalization agreements are generally in effect for only five years. See the Social Security Administration's website for more information on totalization agreements. IRS Publication No. 515, Withholding of Tax on Nonresident Aliens and Foreign Entities, and IRS Publication No. 519, U.S. Tax Guide for Aliens, detail exceptions to those general rules. [Treas. Reg. § 1.871-1; Pub. No. 15; Pub. No. 515]

Q 2:46   Are there special FICA rules for wages paid by tax-exempt organizations and by hospitals (both profit and nonprofit)?

Yes. A few exemptions from FICA apply to wages paid by nonprofit entities and hospitals. Wages of less than $100 per employee paid during a calendar year by an organization that is itself exempt from income tax under I.R.C. Section 503(a) (other than a Section 401(a) organization) or under I.R.C. Section 521 are exempt from FICA. [I.R.C. § 3121(a)(16)]

Q 2:47   Are religious organizations and churches exempt from federal and state unemployment taxes?

Yes. In 1998 this exemption was challenged in the courts and appealed to the U.S. Supreme Court. The Court has refused to hear the case, upholding the exemption of religious organizations and churches from federal and state unemployment tax coverage. [Rojas v. Fitch, 127 F.3d 184 (1st Cir. 1997), cert. denied, 1998 WL 130833 (U.S. June 22, 1998)] Employers must be a religious organization or church, and not simply affiliated with such an organization, to rely on this exemption. Contrast this with not-for-profit organizations, which are exempt only from FUTA, not from state unemployment taxes.

Example. The Roman Catholic Diocese of an area has many affiliated organizations, including an entity entitled "Catholic Charities." Catholic Charities, although affiliated with the Roman Catholic Diocese, does not perform the work of a religious organization or church, but rather assists certain individuals in need. Catholic Charities would not be exempt from federal, only from state, unemployment taxes, as its tax-exempt status does not come from being a religious organization, but rather from performing charitable acts.

Q 2:48   Are services of members of religious orders of churches exempt from FICA?

For services performed after 1984, an employee of a "church" or "qualified church-controlled organization" who fits a narrow definition may be exempt from FICA if an election is made under I.R.C. Section 3121(w). Specifically, such an exemption applies to services "in the exercise of his ministry" or by a member of a religious order "in the exercise of duties required by such order." To qualify, an organization must file Form 8274, Certification by Churches and Qualified Church-Controlled Organizations Electing Exemption From Employer Social Security and Medicare Taxes, before the first date on which the first quarterly return is due. [I.R.C. §§ 3121(b)(8)(A), 3121(w)]

Q 2:49 When are services of ministers deemed to be an exercise of their ministry?

Under Treasury regulations, a minister is performing services that are exempt from FICA if the minister is performing religious worship services or sacerdotal functions. Also, a minister's services in the control, conduct, or maintenance of a religious organization will be deemed services in the exercise of the ministry if such services are for an organization that is an integral agency of the religious organization. If a minister performs services for an organization that is not a religious organization or integral agency of the organization, such services will not be considered ministerial unless they are performed pursuant to an assignment or designation by a religious body constituting the minister's church. [I.R.C. § 3121(b)(8); Treas. Reg. § 31.3121(b)(8)-1(b)]

The Additional Medicare Tax

Q 2:50 What wages and compensation are subject to the Additional Medicare Tax?

Compensation that is subject to the 1.45 percent Medicare tax is also subject to the Additional Medicare Tax. Wages subject to the RRTA taxes are also subject to the Additional Medicare Tax

Q 2:51 Is an employer required to withhold the Additional Medicare Tax from an employee?

Yes. If the employee's wages are in excess of $200,000, the employer is obligated to withhold and remit the Additional Medicare Tax of 0.009 percent.

Q 2:52 What if an employer fails to withhold the Additional Medicare Tax?

The employer is responsible for withholding the required income tax, Social Security and Medicare taxes from employees. If the employer fails to withhold the tax, penalties for failure to withhold, deposit, and report such amounts could apply even if the employee separately pays the tax.

Q 2:53   If an employee is expected to earn more than $200,000 in Medicare wages, is the employer required to withhold the Additional Medicare Tax from the beginning of the year?

No. The Additional Medicare Tax applies once the total compensation exceeds $200,000 per year. The tax applies to both cash compensation and imputed income from group-term life insurance and other noncash fringe benefits an employee may receive.

Q 2:54   Are tips subject to the Additional Medicare Tax?

Yes. Tips are subject to the Additional Medicare Tax, if, when combined with other wages, the tips exceed the $200,000 withholding threshold.

Q 2:55   Will noncash fringe benefits be included in the calculation to determine if the threshold of $200,000 has been met?

Noncash fringe benefits are included in compensation and subject to the Additional Medicare Tax when the total Medicare-taxable compensation exceeds $200,000. The value of noncash fringe benefits is added to regular wages to determine if the $200,000 threshold is met. The guidelines on how to withhold tax on taxable noncash benefits are available in IRS Pub. No. 15 and Pub. No. 15-B.

Q 2:56   Must an employer withhold the Additional Medicare Tax of a former employee with imputed income on group-term life insurance that exceeds $200,000?

A former employee (or retiree) with imputed income on group-term life insurance that exceeds $200,000 may be subject to the Additional Medicare Tax. However, the Additional Medicare Tax will be paid by the former employee on his or her personal income tax return. The employer does not collect the Additional Medicare Tax in this situation.

The Social Security tax, Medicare tax and Additional Medicare Tax will be paid by the former employee on his or her personal income tax return. The employer will report on Form 941 the Social Security and all Medicare taxes.

Q 2:57   What should an employer do if it overwithholds the Additional Medicare Tax?

If the overwithholding of the Additional Medicare Tax is discovered in the same calendar year, the employer must repay or reimburse the overwithheld amount to the employee prior to the end of the calendar year in which it paid the wages. (The employer would also make an interest-free adjustment on Form 941.) If the employer does not discover the overwithholding error until a subsequent year, the employer should not reimburse the employee. The Additional Medicare Tax should be reported on the employee's Form W-2 and the employee will receive credit for the tax withheld when filing his or her personal income tax return.

Federal Income Tax Withholding

Q 2:58   Is there any major legislation that impacts federal income tax withholding rates for 2017?

The income tax withholding rates for 2017 are slightly higher as a result of the American Taxpayer Relief Act (ATRA), which extended, for most taxpayers, the income tax rates that were lowered by the Economic Growth and Tax Relief Reconciliation Act of 2001 (EGTRRA). In addition to making permanent the income tax rates of 10, 15, 25, 28, 33, and 35 percent, ATRA set a new top income tax rate of 39.6 percent. [Pub. L. No. 112-240] The federal income tax withholding rates mirror the income tax rates.

Q 2:59   What are the general federal income tax withholding rules that apply to wages?

Federal income tax is withheld from taxable wages at the time they are actually or constructively received (see Q 1:24). The amount of federal income tax withholding (FITW) is based on the following:

1. Federal taxable wages paid in the period;
2. The method for determining the amount to withhold (e.g., wage-bracket, percentage method, etc.);
3. The pay frequency; and
4. The employee's marital status and personal allowances as reported on Form W-4, Employee's Withholding Allowance Certificate.

[I.R.C. §§ 3401, 3402]

Q 2:60   Are the wages of all employees subject to federal income tax withholding?

Generally, yes. However, there are several groups of workers who are classified as employees under the common-law classification but whose wages are nonetheless exempt from FITW by statute. In addition, certain benefits are exempt from FITW. Those workers and tax-free benefits include the following:

- Active military personnel entitled to combat pay [I.R.C. § 3401(a)(1)]
- Agricultural laborers whose work is not subject to FICA taxation [I.R.C. § 3401(a)(2)]
- Household workers in a private home, local college, or local chapter of a college fraternity or sorority [I.R.C. § 3401(a)(3)]

- Employees who perform services for an employer not in the course of the employer's trade or business (conditioned on an employee's not earning more than $50 in any calendar quarter) [I.R.C. § 3401(a)(4)]

- Citizens or residents of the United States who perform services for a foreign government or international organization outside of the U.S. [I.R.C. § 3401(a)(5)]

- Nonresident aliens who perform certain services [I.R.C. § 3401(a)(6)]

- Duly ordained, commissioned, or licensed ministers of a church [I.R.C. § 3401(a)(9)]

- Newspaper delivery persons under age 18 (as long as they deliver the newspapers to ultimate consumers) [I.R.C. § 3401(a)(10)]

- Newspaper and magazine distributors working under an arrangement in which they agree to sell newspapers and magazines to ultimate consumers at a fixed price and they are allowed to retain the difference between the fixed sales price and the amount charged to them for the items [I.R.C. § 3401(a)(10)]

- Persons who perform services not in the course of an employer's trade or business for which they are paid in any medium other than cash [I.R.C. § 3401(a)(11)]

- Persons who receive a pension or death benefit from a qualified plan under I.R.C. Section 401(a), or from an annuity plan under I.R.C. Section 403(b) [I.R.C. § 3401(a)(12)]

- Employer-paid insurance premiums on group-term life insurance on the life of the employee for the first $50,000 of coverage, provided it is paid under a nondiscriminatory plan [I.R.C. § 3401(a)(14)]

- Persons who receive tips paid in a medium other than cash or cash tips of less than $20 in any calendar month [I.R.C. § 3401(a)(16)]

- Persons who receive tax-free fringe benefits under I.R.C. Sections 127, 129, 74(c), 117, 132, 217, and 105(h)(6) (conditioned on meeting certain requirements) [I.R.C. §§ 3401(a)(15), 3401(a)(18), 3401(a)(19), 3401(a)(20)]. Employer contributions to a Health Savings Account (HSA), whether direct or via pretax salary reductions, are generally excludable from an employee's taxable gross income. If the employer reasonably believes the employee will be able to exclude the HSA contribution from income, the employee and employer contributions are not subject to federal income tax withholding, FICA, or FUTA. In addition, the HSA must be included as part of an I.R.C. Section 125 cafeteria plan arrangement.

- Peace Corps volunteers (with a few exceptions) [I.R.C. § 3401(a)(13)]

Also exempt from FITW is the value of certain facilities or privileges (e.g., entertainment, medical services, discounts on purchases) furnished to employees when these are of relatively small value and are offered occasionally and merely as a means of promoting the health, good will, contentment, or efficiency of the employees. [Treas. Reg. § 31.3401(a)-1(b)(10)]

Q 2:61   Is vacation pay subject to federal income tax withholding?

Yes. Vacation pay is considered a regular wage payment and is subject to FITW. When vacation pay is in addition to regular wages for the vacation period, it may be treated as a supplemental wage payment. If the vacation pay is for a time longer than the employer's usual payroll period, it should be spread over the pay periods for which the employer makes the payment in determining the amount of FITW. Thus, a single payment covering three payroll periods may be treated as having been paid in thirds over three payroll periods for FITW calculation purposes. [Treas. Reg. § 31.3402(g)-1; Pub. No. 15]

Q 2:62   How does an employer determine the federal income tax withholding on regular wages?

The two most common methods are the wage-bracket method (see Qs 2:78–2:81) and the percentage method (see Qs 2:82–2:83). The amount of FITW is based on the applicable pay frequency, the taxable wages paid in the payroll period, marital status, and number of personal allowances as designated on the employee's Form W-4, Employee's Withholding Allowance Certificate.

When the employer makes additional payments, the amount of FITW that applies may be determined by applying a flat rate for supplemental wages (see Qs 2:91–2:96).

Q 2:63   Must an individual who employs a household worker withhold federal income taxes?

Wages paid to a household worker are not subject to FITW; however, if the employee so requests, the employer may choose to withhold federal income tax. Note that an individual who employs a household employee may be required to pay or collect state employment taxes or carry workers' compensation insurance. [I.R.C. §§ 3121(a), 3121(b), 3306(b), 3306(c); Pub. No. 926]

Form W-4

Q 2:64   What is the purpose of Form W-4?

The employer must obtain from every new employee a signed Form W-4, Employee's Withholding Allowance Certificate, indicating the employee's marital status and number of allowances. If the employee fails to furnish a Form W-4, the employer is required to withhold as if the employee were a single taxpayer claiming no allowances. [I.R.C. § 3401(e)]

The rules regarding Form W-4 and withholding allowances are contained in Treasury Regulations Section 31.3402(f)(2)-1. The initial Form W-4 becomes effective for the payroll period in which it is received by the employer. The employee may amend the Form W-4 at any time, and must amend it if a change in circumstances means he or she is actually entitled to fewer allowances than claimed. The employer is not required to implement an amended Form W-4 until the payroll period ending on or after the 30th day after the day on which the employer receives the amended form. However, the employer may choose to put the amended form into effect during an earlier payroll period.

Example. Champion, Inc. pays its employees on the 5th and 20th of the month. One of its employees amends his W-4 and gives it to Payroll on February 5. Payroll must implement the revised W-4 by the March 20 payday. However, Payroll may put the revised W-4 into effect with the February 20 or March 5 payday.

Employers are encouraged to recommend that all employees verify the accuracy of their own Form W-4 at least annually (the IRS suggests each December 1).

A Form W-4 that makes a change for the next calendar year will not take effect in the current calendar year. [I.R.C. § 3402(f)(3)(b)(iii), Treas. Reg. § 31.3402(f)(3)-1(c); Pub. No. 15]

Note. Employers are not permitted to honor any employee-developed substitute Forms W-4. An employee who submits an employee-developed Form W-4 is treated as failing to furnish a valid Form W-4. Employers should continue to honor any valid employee-developed forms they accepted before October 11, 2007. [Treas. Reg. § 31.3402(f)(5)-1 as amended by T.D. 9337, 2007-35 I.R.B. 455]

Q 2:65 When must an employer submit the Form W-4 to the IRS?

The IRS no longer requires employers to automatically send copies of potentially questionable Forms W-4 to the IRS; regulations eliminated this requirement effective April 14, 2005. Previously, an employer had to submit a copy of a W-4 to the IRS when the employee (1) claimed more than 10 withholding allowances or (2) claimed exemption from withholding when wages would normally be more than $200 per week.

Under the new Withholding Compliance Program, the IRS will step up its withholding compliance by making more effective use of information reported on Forms W-2 to ensure that employees have enough federal income tax withheld from their pay. Forms W-4 will still be subject to review by the IRS and the IRS may send a written notice to an employer directing it to submit a Form W-4.

Furthermore, if the IRS determines that federal income tax is substantially underwithheld for a certain employee, the IRS may issue a lock-in letter to the employer specifying the maximum number of withholding allowances the employee may claim.

If the IRS identifies what it believes to be serious underwithholding problems, it may request an employer to submit or make available for examination specified original Forms W-4. If an employer receives a letter from the IRS requiring the submission of Form W-4 for one or more named employees, it should send the requested copies to the IRS at the address provided and in the manner directed by the letter.

After submitting the requested copies of Form W-4 to the IRS, an employer should continue to withhold federal income tax based on that Form W-4 if it is valid. A W-4 is rendered invalid by any change or addition to its wording or if the employee indicates to the employer that the form is in any way inaccurate. A form is also invalid if unsigned or incorrectly filled out.

After examining the submitted Form W-4, the IRS may notify the employer in writing that the employee is not entitled to claim exemption from withholding or that a claimed number of withholding allowances will not be allowed, in which case the employer must withhold federal income tax based on the effective date and maximum number of withholding allowances specified in the IRS notice. These notices are referred to as *lock-in letters*.

Upon receipt of an IRS lock-in letter, the employer has very specific responsibilities. The employer must furnish a copy of the lock-in letter to the affected employee immediately on receipt. It must then impose the new withholding restriction 60 days after the date on the original letter and maintain that restriction. The employer is also required to fax a signed note on company letterhead to the IRS stating that the employee is no longer employed by the business, if that is the case. Such a note must be faxed to the service's Lowell, Mass., office at 1-978-474-1326.

The employer is required to continue the lock-in withholding process for any employee hired as the result of a merger or acquisition based on the transferred W-4 and lock-in letter from the predecessor employer, and must ensure safeguards are in place to prevent employees from increasing their allowances electronically. The employer must also maintain the withholding amount specified in the lock-in letter unless otherwise directed by the IRS or risk being held liable for the amount of tax that should have been withheld. Finally, the employer must remind employees that the notice they received tells them how to contact the IRS if they want to change the withholding status and allowances stipulated.

Employees who wish to protest a lock-in letter need to call or write the IRS with the following information: Form W-4 and its worksheets; their most current pay stub for each job; the number of allowances claimed on current Forms W-4, and the SSNs and dates of birth for any children and proof of any deductions they want to use to claim additional withholding allowances. Employers should not make any changes unless directed by IRS.

If after the employer receives a lock-in letter the employee provides a new W-4 that does not claim exemption from federal income tax withholding and claims fewer allowances than the number shown in the lock-in letter (resulting in more withholding), the employer should withhold based on the subsequent Form W-4 if it is valid. Otherwise, any subsequent Forms W-4 provided by the employee should be disregarded and withholding based on the lock-in letter. To avoid lock-in letters, employees who have a pattern of owing taxes on their personal returns each year should consider increasing the amount of tax withheld from their wages. An employee can decrease the number of allowances to have more taxes withheld.

Q 2:66   Who must complete a Form W-4?

All employees must complete and sign a Form W-4. This form must be completed even if the employee does not believe he or she will owe taxes at the end of the year. When an employee claims exempt status, he or she must complete lines 1, 2, 3, 4, and 7 and insert the word exempt for the filing status on line 7. Forms W-4 claiming exempt status are valid for a single calendar year and a new Form W-4 must be completed each year by February 15. An exemption for 2017 expires February 15, 2018. For 2017, an exemption from federal income tax withholding is not available if (1) the individual's income exceeds $1,050 and includes more than $350 of unearned income (e.g., dividends and interest) and (2) another person can claim the employee as a dependent. [Form W-4 instructions] The employer is not responsible for determining the validity of any employee's Form W-4.

An employer may continue to apply a W-4 for an individual claiming an exemption from federal income tax for 45 days (until February 15) of the next calendar year. If a new W-4 is not filed by then, the employer subsequently treats the employee as single with no allowances. It applies the marital status and number of allowances as shown on a valid W-4 when one is filed.

Q 2:67   May an employer utilize an electronic Form W-4?

Yes. In general, an employer may establish a system for its employees to file withholding allowances certificates electronically. The electronic system must ensure that the information received is the information the employee sent and must document all occasions of employee access to the system that result in the filing of a Form W-4. In addition, the design and operation of the electronic system, including access procedures, must make it reasonably certain that the person accessing the system and filing the Form W-4 is the employee identified on the form.

The electronic filing must provide the employer with exactly the same information as the paper Form W-4 and must be signed by the employee under penalties of perjury. The perjury statement—a statement that certifies the employee is signing the form under penalty of perjury for false statements—must contain the language that appears on the paper Form W-4. The instructions and the language of the perjury statement—sometimes called the jurat—must immediately follow the employee's income tax withholding selections and immediately precede the employee's electronic signature. The jurat on the Form W-4 provides that the employee, under penalty of perjury, declares to have examined the certificate and confirms that it is true, correct, and complete to the best of the employee's knowledge.

The electronic signature must identify the employee filing the electronic Form W-4 and *authenticate* and *verify* the filing. For this purpose, the terms *authenticate* and *verify* have the same meanings as they do when applied to a written signature on a paper Form W-4. An electronic signature can be in any form that satisfies the foregoing requirements. The electronic signature must be the final entry in the employee's Form W-4 submission.

The employer must, upon request by the IRS, supply a hard-copy printout of the electronic Form W-4 and a statement that, to the best of the employer's knowledge, the electronic Form W-4 was filed by the named employee. The hard copy of the electronic Form W-4 must provide exactly the same information as, but need not be a facsimile of, the paper Form W-4. The recordkeeping requirements for electronic W-4s are the same as for the paper form. [Treas. Reg. § 31.3402(f)(5)-1(c)]

The following forms may also be submitted in an electronic format, following the same requirements as those stated above:

- Form W-4P, Withholding Certificate for Pension or Annuity Payments [Ann. 99-6, 1999-4 I.R.B. 24]
- Form W-4S, Request for Federal Income Tax Withholding From Sick Pay [Ann. 99-6, 1999-4 I.R.B. 24]
- Form W-4V, Voluntary Withholding Request. [Ann. 99-6, 1999-4 I.R.B. 24]

Q 2:68   Can an employer pay an individual who has not submitted a Form W-4?

Yes; however, federal income tax withholding is computed as though the employee were single with no allowances.

Q 2:69   Who is responsible for determining the validity of a Form W-4?

The employer is not responsible for the truthfulness or accuracy of the information reported on Form W-4. A penalty of $500 may be assessed on any employee who files a false Form W-4, and both conditions apply:

- The employee makes statements or claims withholding allowances on his or her Form W-4 that reduce the amount of tax withheld.
- The employee has no reasonable basis for those statements or allowances at the time he or she prepares the Form W-4.

Q 2:70   When must an employer reject a Form W-4?

An employer is required to reject a Form W-4 when any one of the following conditions is met:

1. The employee informs the employer that the information being submitted is false.

2. The employee adds or deletes information from the form.

3. The employee does not sign, date, or otherwise complete the form.

4. The form has been modified (e.g., language has been removed).

When a Form W-4 is rejected and there was no prior valid W-4 submitted, federal income tax is computed as if the individual were single with no allowances. If a prior valid W-4 is available, federal income tax should be computed using the prior valid Form W-4. [Treas. Reg. § 31.3402(f)(5)-1]

Also, employers are not permitted to honor any employee-developed substitute Forms W-4. An employee who submits an employee-developed Form W-4 will be treated as failing to furnish a Form W-4. [Treas. Reg. § 31.3402(f)(5)-1 as amended by T.D. 9337, 2007-35 I.R.B. 455] See Q 2:64.

Q 2:71   Are employees allowed to request a flat dollar amount of withholding?

No. Employees may want to have a fixed dollar amount or percentage of wages withheld, but they are limited to using the W-4 instructions and worksheets, on which they choose a marital status, figure how many allowances they are entitled to claim, and can opt, if desired, to have a certain additional amount withheld. When the employer withholds using the flat 25 or 39.6 percent rate for supplemental wages for 2017, the percentage may not be adjusted.

While employees have historically been unable to elect a flat withholding amount or a fixed withholding percentage on Form W-4, employers have often had difficulty in convincing employees of this fact. To assist employers in this regard, the 2017 Form W-4 instructions advise employees that withholding is based on the allowances they claim and "may not be a flat amount or percentage of wages."

Q 2:72   How long must Form W-4 be retained?

Form W-4 must be retained for at least four years from its last effective date.

Q 2:73   When may an employee claim to be exempt from federal income tax withholding?

An employee may claim exemption from federal income tax withholding only if he or she had no federal income tax liability in the previous year and expects to owe no federal income tax in the current year. (The exemption may not apply to dependents with unearned income of more than $350 if their income exceeds $1,050 for 2017.) This exemption is claimed on Form W-4. However, the employee's wages may be subject to FICA and FUTA. [Pub. No. 15, Form W-4 Instructions]

Employees who claim a full exemption from federal income tax in 2017 will have to file a new form to maintain the exemption, as the exemption expires on February 15, 2018. If no new form is filed, employers must begin withholding as if the employee was single claiming no withholding allowances until the employee submits a new Form W-4.

Q 2:74   When an employee revises his or her Form W-4, is a retroactive correction required?

No. When an employer receives a new Form W-4, no adjustment in withholding is required for pay periods before the effective date of the new form; that is, withholding does not have to be adjusted for payments already made. Also, employers should not accept any funds or estimated tax payments from employees that are in addition to withholding based on their Form W-4. Employees who want a larger amount withheld should submit a new Form W-4, and if necessary, pay estimated income tax by filing Form 1040-ES, Estimated Tax for Individuals. [Pub. No. 15]

Q 2:75   Can an employee request that amounts be withheld in excess of what would be withheld given the number of allowances claimed?

Yes. An employee may request additional withholding on line 6 of the Form W-4. The employer is required to withhold the additional amount to the extent that the amount does not exceed wages remaining after deducting all amounts required to be withheld under federal, state, or local law. Additional withholding amounts are considered for all purposes of the I.R.C. as tax required to be withheld, and thus an employer may be subject to liability, penalty, or both for failure to properly withhold such additional amounts. Employees may claim fewer withholding allowances than they are entitled to claim. They may do this to ensure that they have enough withholding or to offset other sources of taxable income that are not subject to withholding. [Treas. Reg. § 31.3402(i)-2]

Q 2:76   How should federal income tax withholding be computed if an employee's Form W-4 is invalid?

The employer should not base withholding on an invalid Form W-4 that it receives from an employee. Instead, the employer must tell the employee that the Form W-4 is invalid and ask for a new one. If the employee does not furnish a new Form W-4, the employer must withhold federal income taxes as if the employee were single with no withholding allowances. However, if the employee has a prior valid Form W-4 on file, the prior valid Form W-4 is used. [Pub. No. 15]

Withholding Methods

Q 2:77   Is there more than one withholding method?

Yes. An employer may elect from several different withholding methods. Moreover, an employer may use different methods with respect to different groups of employees. [Treas. Reg. § 31.3402(a)-1(a)]

Wage-Bracket Method

Q 2:78   What is the wage-bracket method?

Most employers that manually determine the amount of withholding use the wage-bracket method. Under this method, the amount of federal income tax to withhold is taken directly from wage-bracket tables issued by the IRS in Publication No. 15, Circular E, Employer's Tax Guide. There are two tables for each of the payroll periods found in the publication: one for single persons and one for married persons. The tables can be used for weekly, biweekly, semi-monthly, monthly, and daily or miscellaneous pay periods. For pay periods not listed in the tables, see Q 2:81. [I.R.C. § 3402(c); Treas. Reg. § 31.3402(c)-1; Pub. No. 15]

Q 2:79   How are the wage-bracket tables used?

To use the wage-bracket tables, an employer follows these simple steps:

1. Locate the table that corresponds to the employee's payroll period and the employee's marital status.

2. Calculate the employee's wages subject to federal income tax withholding by reducing the employee's gross wages by any pretax deductions (i.e., Section 125 or 401(k) contributions).

3. Locate the wage bracket that contains the employee's wages that are subject to federal income taxes.

4. Identify the amount to be withheld based on the number of withholding allowances on the employee's Form W-4.

5. Add any extra dollar amount of withholding indicated by the employee on line 6 of the Form W-4.

Wage payments above the maximum table amount. Each of the wage-bracket tables has a maximum wage payment amount. The table cannot be used when the employee's wages subject to federal income tax withholding exceed these maximum amounts. For wage payments equaling or exceeding the maximum amount, the percentage method of withholding must be used (see Q 2:83).

Wage payments that equal a wage-bracket amount. When an employee's wage payment is equal to the higher amount in a wage bracket, the next highest wage bracket must be used to calculate the withholding.

Example. Sarah claims married and one allowance on her Form W-4. She is paid a biweekly salary of $840. In the married persons' biweekly payroll period table there are wage brackets of $820-840 and $840-860. Sarah's withholding must be calculated using the $840-860 wage bracket.

Q 2:80 What are the wage-bracket percentage method tables (for automated payroll systems) used for?

The wage-bracket percentage method tables (for automated payroll systems) show the gross wage brackets that apply to each withholding percentage rate for employees with up to nine withholding allowances. These tables also show the computation factors for each number of withholding allowances and the applicable wage bracket. The computation factors are used to figure the amount of withholding tax by a percentage method. [Pub. No. 15-A]

Q 2:81 What are daily or miscellaneous payroll period tables?

The wage-bracket tables for a daily or miscellaneous payroll period may be used for wages that are paid for a period other than a payroll period found in the tables. The withholding amount is determined as follows:

1. Identify the number of days in the payroll period. A nonregular pay period will include Saturdays, Sundays, and holidays that fall in the pay period. When wages are paid without regard to any set pay period, the miscellaneous period begins on the latest of the last wage payment date, January 1, or the date of hire.

2. Divide the current wage payment that is subject to federal income taxes by the number in step 1 to get a daily wage rate.

3. Use the daily or miscellaneous payroll period wage-bracket tables to determine the amount of federal income tax to be withheld.

4. Multiply the amount in step 3 (daily withholding rate) by the number in step 1 (days since last wage payment) to calculate the amount to withhold from the employee's current wage payment.

Percentage Method

Q 2:82 What is the percentage method?

The percentage method of withholding federal income tax is typically used by employers with automated payroll systems and service providers that process payrolls for many employers. The percentage method is more flexible than the wage-bracket method. There are eight percentage method tables covering the various pay periods to calculate withholding. The tables can be used to calculate withholding for quarterly, semiannual, annual, and other unusual pay periods. The percentage method tables are also found in Circular E, Pub. No. 15.

Q 2:83   How is federal income tax withholding calculated under the percentage method?

Steps to be taken in calculating the amount of federal income tax to withhold under the percentage method are as follows:

1. Identify the number of withholding allowances claimed on line 5 of the employee's Form W-4.

2. Identify the employee's payroll period to obtain the value of one withholding allowance for the payroll period, then multiply this amount by the number of allowances claimed (see Table 2-1, adapted from Pub. No. 15).

3. Determine the employee's wages subject to federal income tax withholding by reducing the employee's gross wages by any pretax deductions (e.g., Section 125 or 401(k) contributions).

4. Subtract the value of the withholding allowances (from step 2) from the employee's wages subject to federal income tax (from step 3).

5. Identify the percentage method withholding table for the employee's payroll period and marital status (see Tables 2-2 through 2-4 for samples). For most wage amounts and pay periods, the tables identify an amount to be subtracted before the percentage is applied. In some cases, more complicated steps are required.

6. Use the formula in the table to calculate the withholding tax.

7. Add any extra dollar amount of withholding from line 6 of the employee's Form W-4.

[I.R.C. § 3402(b); Treas. Reg. § 31.3402(b)-1; Pub. No. 15]

Table 2-1.   Withholding Allowance Amounts for 2017

Payroll Period	One Allowance[1]
Weekly	$ 77.90
Biweekly	155.80
Semimonthly	168.80
Monthly	337.50
Quarterly	1,012.50
Semiannually	2,025.00
Annually	4,050.00
Daily or miscellaneous	15.60

---

[1] If more than one, multiply these amounts by the number of withholding allowances.

Table 2-2.   Biweekly Payroll Period

Single Person (including head of household)

If the amount of wages (after subtracting withholding allowances) is:		*The amount of income tax to withhold is:*	
Not over $88		$0	
Over—	*But not over*		*Of excess over*
$ 88	$ 447	$0.00 plus 10%	$ 88
$ 447	$ 1,548	$35.90 plus 15%	$ 447
$ 1,548	$ 3,623	$201.05 plus 25%	$ 1,548
$ 3,623	$ 7,460	$719.80 plus 28%	$ 3,623
$ 7,460	$16,115	$1,794.16 plus 33%	$ 7,460
$16,115	$16,181	$4,650.31 plus 35%	$16,115
$16,181		$4,673.41 plus 39.6%	$16,181

Table 2-3.   Semimonthly Payroll Period

Married Person

If the amount of wages (after subtracting withholding allowances) is:		*The amount of income tax to withhold is:*	
Not over $360		$0	
Over—	*But not over—*		*Of excess over—*
$ 360	$ 1,138	$0.00 plus 10%	$ 360
$ 1,138	$ 3,523	$77.80 plus 15%	$ 1,138
$ 3,523	$ 6,740	$435.55 plus 25%	$ 3,523
$ 6,740	$10,083	$1,239.80 plus 28%	$ 6,740
$10,083	$17,723	$2,175.84 plus 33%	$10,083
$17,723	$19,973	$4,697.04 plus 35%	$17,723
$19,973		$5,484.54 plus 39.6%	$19,973

Table 2-4. Annual Payroll Period

Married Person

If the amount of wages (after subtracting withholding allowances) is:		*The amount of income tax to withhold is:*	
Not over $8,550		$0	
Over—	But not over—		Of excess over—
$ 8,650	$ 27,300	$0.00 plus 10%	$ 8,650
$ 27,300	$ 84,550	$1,865.00 plus 15%	$ 27,300
$ 84,550	$161,750	$10,452.50 plus 25%	$ 84,550
$ 161,750	$242,000	$29,752.50 plus 28%	$161,750
$ 242,000	$425,350	$52,222.50 plus 33%	$242,000
$ 425,350	$479,350	$112,728.00 plus 35%	$425,350
$ 479,350		$131,628.00 plus 39.6%	$479,350

Example. In 2017, Joan is paid biweekly wages of $3,730, which are subject to federal income tax. On Form W-4 she claims married with two allowances and contributes $390 each pay period to her employer's 401(k) plan. She has requested that an additional $60 be withheld because of a gain she expects to have on the sale of stock. Her withholding is calculated using the percentage method, as follows:

Gross wages	$3,730.00
401(k) contribution	390.00
Taxable wages	$3,340.00
Allowance value ($155.80 × 2)	311.60
Wages subject to withholding (after allowances)	$3,028.40
Percentage method table formula (married, biweekly) for wages over $1,050 but not over $3,252; $71.70 plus 15% of excess over $1,050; $3,028.40 – $1,050 = $1,978.40 × 0.15 + $71.70	$ 368.46
Amount of additional withholding	60.00
Total to withhold	$ 428.46

Q 2:84   How do the wage-bracket and the percentage method tables differ?

Each of the two sets of tables includes tables for married and single persons for weekly, biweekly, semimonthly, monthly, and daily or miscellaneous payroll periods.

The basic difference between the two sets of tables is that the percentage method tables allow the amounts to be withheld to be computed easily on a data processing system and the wage-bracket method tables allow an individual to easily look up the amount to be withheld (no computation is necessary). The amount to be withheld under one method will generally be within a dollar or two of the amount to be withheld under the other method.

Employers may use the table that best suits their payroll system needs. The tables for computing income tax withholding from wages exceeding the allowance amount can be used in the systems that separately subtract the allowance amount. The reduction factors in these tables do not include the allowance amount that is automatically subtracted before the table factors are applied to the calculation. For other systems that do not separately subtract the allowance amount, employers will generally use the tables for computing income tax withholding from gross wages.

When employers use the percentage method table, the tax for the period may be rounded to the nearest dollar (it is already rounded to the nearest dollar in the wage-bracket tables). If rounding is applied, it must be used consistently. Withheld tax amounts should be rounded to the nearest whole dollar by (1) dropping amounts under 50 cents and (2) increasing amounts from 50 to 99 cents to the next higher dollar. Such rounding will be deemed to meet the tolerances under I.R.C. Sections 3402(b)(4) and 3402(c)(5). [Pub. No. 15-A]

Annualized Wages Method

Q 2:85 What is the annualized wages method?

Under the annualized wages method, federal income tax withholding is calculated based on an annual payroll period and then divided among the actual payroll periods using the following steps:

1. Multiply the employee's federal income taxable wages for a payroll period by the number of payroll periods in the calendar year (e.g., if weekly, multiply by 52).

2. Determine the amount of annual wages that are subject to withholding after subtracting out the total annual withholding allowance for the number of exemptions on the employee's Form W-4.

3. Determine the amount of federal income tax that would be required to be withheld from the result in step 2 based on an annual payroll period using the percentage method (see Qs 2:82, 2:83).

4. Divide the total amount of withholding determined in step 3 by the number of payroll periods used in step 1 to obtain the withholding amount for each payroll period.

[I.R.C. § 3402(h)(2); Treas. Reg. § 31.3402(h)(2)-1]

Example. In 2017, Stanley is paid wages subject to federal income tax withholding of $5,556 semimonthly. He is married with three withholding allowances claimed on his Form W-4. The amount to withhold for federal income tax for each semimonthly period would be determined under the annualized wages method, as follows:

Annual taxable wages = $5,556 × 24 payroll periods	$133,344
Withholding using percentage method	
Taxable wages	$133,344
Allowance value ($4,050 × 3)	(12,150)
Wages subject to withholding (after allowances)	$121,194
Percentage method formula (married, annual) for wages over $84,550 but not over $161,750: 25% of excess over $84,550 ($121,194 − $84,550)	$36,644
Rate percentage	× 0.25
Subtotal	$9,161.00
Plus	$10,452.50
Tax to withhold—percentage method	$19,613.50
Withholding per payroll period	
$19,613.50 ÷ 24	$817.23

Part-Year Employment Method

Q 2:86 Is there a tax withholding method that can benefit an employee who works for only a portion of the year?

Yes. An employee who works for only a portion of the calendar year may ask the employer to withhold federal income tax under the part-year employment method. The effect of this election is to reduce the amount of income taxes withheld each pay period. The request must be in writing and must contain the following information:

1. The employee's last day of any employment during the calendar year with any prior employer;

2. A statement that the employee uses the "calendar year accounting period"; and

3. A statement that the employee reasonably anticipates he or she will be employed for a total of no more than 245 days (for any employer) during the current calendar year.

Employers determine the amount of income tax withholding under the part-year employment method as follows:

1. Add the wages to be paid to the employee for the current payroll period to any wages the employer has already paid the employee in the current term of continuous employment.

2. Add the number of payroll periods used in step 1 to the number of payroll periods between the employee's last employment and current employment. To find the number of periods between the last employment and current employment, divide (a) the number of calendar days between the employee's last day of earlier employment (or the previous December 31 if later) and the first day of current employment by (b) the number of calendar days in the current payroll period.

3. Divide the step 1 amount by the total number of payroll periods from step 2 to determine the average wages per payroll period since the employee's last employment.

4. Calculate the amount to withhold in the withholding tables on the step 3 amount. Be sure to use the correct payroll period table and to take into account the employee's withholding allowances.

5. Multiply the total number of payroll periods from step 2 by the step 4 amount.

6. Subtract from the step 5 amount the total tax already withheld during the current term of continuous employment. Any excess is the amount to withhold for the current payroll period.

Note. This method is available only when the employee states in writing that he or she is not employed by any employer for more than 245 days in the calendar year—a period defined in the regulations as a "term of continuous employment." A term of continuous employment may be a single term or two or more subsequent terms of employment with the same employer. A continuous term includes holidays, regular days off (e.g., Saturday and Sunday), and days off for illness or vacation. A continuous term begins on the first day an employee works for the employer and earns pay. It ends on the earlier of (1) the employee's last day of work for the employer or (2) if the employee performs no services for more than 30 calendar days, the last workday before the 30-day period. When an employment relationship (e.g., a contract for a specific period) is ended, the term of continuous employment is ended, even if a new employment relationship is established with the same employer within 30 days. [Treas. Reg. § 31.3402(h)(4)-1; Pub. No. 15-A]

Cumulative Wages Method

Q 2:87   How is the cumulative wages method used to compute taxes?

The cumulative wages method is typically used for employees whose wage payments vary from pay period to pay period. This method allows the employer to level the withholding when an employee's wages change dramatically in the pay period. For that reason, it is especially popular with employers of commissioned salespeople. It is attractive to employees who receive a large bonus payment and where treatment as supplemental wages would not be useful. [I.R.C. § 3402(h)(3); Treas. Reg. § 31.3402(h)(3)-1]

To use this method, two conditions apply: (1) the employee must request it in writing and (2) the employee must have been paid at the same frequency since the beginning of the calendar year. The request remains in effect until revoked by the employee. A revocation must be put into effect by the employer no later than the first payroll period ending 30 days after the notice of revocation. The steps to be followed in using the cumulative wages method are as follows:

1. Total the employee's wages subject to federal income tax withholding paid in the calendar year, including wages to be paid for the current payroll period.

2. Divide the total in step 1 by the number of payroll periods in the calendar year, including the current payroll period. This develops an average wage payment for each payroll period.

3. Determine the amount of withholding that would have applied to each average wage payment in step 2 using the percentage method of withholding (see Qs 2:82, 2:83).

4. Multiply the amount in step 3 by the number of payroll periods in the calendar year to date, including the current period.

5. Subtract the total amounts previously withheld from the employee's wages in the calendar year from the total in step 4. The difference, if any, is the amount that must be withheld from the employee's current wages.

Example. In 2017, employee Sheldon is paid wages subject to federal income tax withholding of $6,400 semimonthly. He is married with 3 withholding allowances. He generally has $1,154.80 withheld from each paycheck under the percentage method. Sheldon receives a $14,000 bonus with his second April paycheck (in the 8th payroll period of the year). Sheldon asks his employer in writing to begin withholding under the cumulative wages method in the pay period when he first receives the bonus, believing that this will result in less withholding. The federal income tax withholding for the second pay period in April would be calculated as follows:

Total taxable wages through April 30 ((8 × $6,400) + $14,000)	$65,200
Average wage payment ($65,200 ÷ 8)	8,150
Withholding on $8,150 (percentage method)	1,492.81
$1,492.81 × 8 payroll periods (total under cumulative method)	11,942.48
Less amount withheld through April 15 ($1,154.80 × 7)	(8,083.60)
Withholding amount on second paycheck in April ($11,942.48 − $8,083.60)	$3,858.88

Had Sheldon not elected to change to the cumulative wages method, his withholding on the $14,000 bonus and $6,400 in pay would have been $5,726.75 (assuming the salary and bonus were taxed as a single wage payment and the amount of each was not separately identified) (see Q 2:93). Therefore, the amount withheld from Sheldon's pay in the second pay period in May has decreased by $660.43 using the cumulative wages method.

Average Estimated Wages Method

Q 2:88   What is the average estimated wages method?

Under the average estimated wages method, employers may withhold based on an employee's estimated wages during a quarter. This method may be used only when the employer makes adjustments each quarter to bring the withholding on the estimated wages in line with the amount required to be withheld on wages actually paid. The steps in using this method are as follows:

1. Estimate the employee's total federal income taxable earnings for the quarter using any reasonable method that is documented in the employer's records.

2. Divide the result in step 1 by the number of payroll periods during the quarter to determine the estimated average wage for the employee.

3. Calculate the federal income tax to be withheld from each estimated average wage payment as if the amount in step 2 were actually paid and withhold the amount from the employee's actual wage payments.

Employers may use the average estimated wages method for tipped employees when the tips and withholding on tips are estimated. The required withholding adjustments may be made no later than 30 days after the end of the quarter and are made by additional withholding on the tipped employee's regular wages. [I.R.C. § 3402(h)(1); Treas. Reg. § 31.3402(h)(1)-1]

Additional Withholding Requirements

Q 2:89   How is the withholding amount determined for employees who claim more than 10 allowances?

Each wage-bracket table has columns for up to 10 withholding allowances. When an employee claims more than 10 allowances, the employer must use one of the following methods for determining the amount to withhold:

1. Treat the employee as if he or she is claiming only 10 allowances and thus increase the employee's intended withholdings.

2. Adjust the employee's wages under the wage-bracket method for the withholding allowances above 10 using these steps:

   a. Multiply the number of withholding allowances exceeding 10 by the value of one allowance for the applicable payroll period.

   b. Subtract the result of the calculation in step 2(a) from the employee's wages that are subject to federal income tax withholding.

c. Use this adjusted wage amount in step 2(b) and the appropriate column in the wage-bracket tables for 10 allowances to calculate the amount to withhold.

3. Use the percentage method or alternative method described in Pub. No. 15-A.

Q 2:90   May an employer use another method for determining income tax withholding?

Yes. The employer may use any other method and tables for withholding taxes as long as the amount of tax withheld is about the same (i.e., meets tolerances described in Table 2-5 below) as it would be under the percentage method. When an employer develops an alternative method or table, the full range of wages and allowances for all employees should be tested to be sure that the withholding amounts do not exceed the tolerances contained in Treasury Regulations Section 31.3402(h)(4)-1.

Table 2-5.   Withholding Tolerances

If the tax required to be withheld under the annual percentage rate (Circular E) is	The annual tax withheld by the employer's method may not differ by more than
Less than $10	$9.99
$10 or more but under $100	$10 plus 10% of the excess over $10
$100 or more but under $1,000	$19 plus 3% of the excess over $100
$1,000 or more	$46 plus 1% of the excess over $1,000

[Pub. No. 15-A]

Supplemental Wage Payments

Q 2:91   What are supplemental wage payments?

When employees receive payments from an employer that are not part of their ordinary wages, the payments are referred to as supplemental wages. These may be paid at the same time as regular wages or at any other time. Supplemental wages include the following types of payments:

- Bonuses, prizes, and awards
- Commissions
- Back-pay awards
- Retroactive pay
- Overtime pay
- Severance or dismissal pay

- Payments for unused annual leave
- Tips
- Payments for working during vacation
- Reimbursements for nonqualified moving expenses
- Reimbursements for business expenses under a nonaccountable plan
- Retirement incentive pay
- Lump-sum payment for unused accumulated annual and/or sick leave

Q 2:92 What is the supplemental withholding rate?

For 2016, there are two possible flat withholding rates: 25 percent and 39.6 percent. The American Jobs Creation Act of 2004 increased the supplemental withholding rate to the highest income tax rate for supplemental payments in excess of $1 million. [Pub. No. 15] The American Taxpayer Relief Act set a new highest rate of 39.6 percent beginning in 2013. [Pub. L. No. 112-240] Therefore, the supplemental withholding rate for supplemental payments in excess of $1 million is 39.6 percent in 2017.

Example. In addition to her salary, the board will award CFO Janice a bonus of $2.6 million at the end of 2017. (She has no other supplemental wages for 2016.) The amount to withhold for federal income tax is:

25% × $1,000,000	=	$250,000
39.6% × $1.6 million	=	$633,600
Total		$883,600

The IRS issued regulations that clarify the definition of "supplemental wages." In determining the threshold, an employer would count supplemental wage payments such as nonqualified deferred compensation, nonstatutory stock options, and noncash fringe benefits. When issuing a net bonus, an employer must include the grossed-up amount (rather than the amount of the net bonus) to compute the $1 million. The regulations provide examples of other kinds of supplemental wages.

The regulations also specify that for purposes of the 39.6 percent rate, the amount of regular wages and the method of withholding on the regular wages are irrelevant. [RIN 1545-BD96, 70 Fed. Reg. 767]

Q 2:93 How is withholding determined when supplemental wages are combined with regular wages?

If supplemental wages are paid with regular wages but the amount of each is not specified, federal income tax is withheld as if the total were a single payment for a regular payroll period. [Treas. Reg. § 31.3402(g)-1(a)(2); Rev. Rul. 82-200, 1982-2 C.B. 239]

Q 2:94   How is federal income tax withholding calculated when supplemental wages are paid separately from regular wages?

If supplemental wages are paid separately, or combined with regular wages in a single payment and the amount of each is specified, the income tax withholding method depends partly on whether income tax is withheld from the employee's regular wages in the current or previous calendar year:

1. If income tax is withheld from an employee's regular wages in the current or previous calendar year, one of the following methods may be used for the supplemental wages:

   a. Withhold the flat supplemental withholding rate; or

   b. Add the supplemental and regular wages for the most recent payroll period in the year, then figure the income tax withholding as if the total were a single payment. Subtract the tax already withheld from the regular wages. Withhold the remaining tax from the supplemental wages.

2. If income tax was not withheld from the employee's regular wages in the current or previous calendar year, method 1b above is used. This would occur, for example, when the value of the employee's withholding allowances claimed on Form W-4, Employee's Withholding Allowance Certificate, is more than the wages.

Regardless of the method used to withhold income tax on supplemental wages, they are subject to FICA and FUTA. [Treas. Reg. § 31.3402(g)-1(a)(2); Pub. No. 15]

Q 2:95   How does an employer determine the federal income tax withholding on supplemental wages?

Special rules exist for withholding from supplemental wages, such as bonuses, commissions, and overtime pay. The employer must withhold federal income taxes using either the supplemental flat tax rate or the aggregate method of withholding. The employer may withhold a flat 25 percent on supplemental wages (39.6 percent on supplemental wages in excess of $1 million), which is not reduced by withholding allowances. Alternatively, an employer may elect to aggregate supplemental wages with regular wages paid either during the current payroll period or during the last preceding payroll period (if the payroll periods occur in the same calendar year). With either approach, the aggregate amounts are applied to the normal withholding tables under the percentage method or the wage-bracket method to determine the total amount to be withheld from all wages paid during the period. If the wages paid during the last preceding payroll period are used for computation purposes, the amount to be withheld from the supplemental wages is the aggregate amount to be withheld under the percentage method less the amount actually withheld on the wages in the preceding period. [Treas. Reg. § 31.3402(g)-1(a)(2); Rev. Rul. 82-200, 1982-2 C.B. 239; Rev. Rul. 2008-29, 2008-24 I.R.B. 1149]

Final Treasury regulations released in 2006 provide additional guidance in implementing the requirement to withhold income tax at a flat rate (currently 39.6 percent) for supplemental pay exceeding $1 million in a year. [71 Fed. Reg. 42049-01, 2006-37 I.R.B. 423] The final regulations allow payments to qualify as supplemental wages even though no regular wages have been paid to the employee. The rules also state that the optional flat rate withholding on payments below the $1 million threshold only can be taken if income tax has been withheld on regular wages.

In addition, the regulation provides employers the flexibility to treat tips and overtime pay as regular wages and treat amounts not subject to withholding but includible in Box 1 of Form W-2 as supplemental wages, and requires that commissions always be considered supplemental wages.

The rules do not treat income from disqualifying dispositions of shares of stock acquired pursuant to the exercise of statutory stock options as supplemental wages, but allow employers to treat an entire payment that results in an employee exceeding the $1 million threshold as subject to the mandatory higher flat rate, and permit the deduction of qualified salary deferral amounts to ascertain the net taxable pay for threshold purposes.

The Treasury maintains that payments made by agents of an employer must be considered for determining supplemental pay subject to the mandated flat rate withholding. However, an agent or an employer will be able to apply a *de minimis* rule to exclude less than $100,000 in such payments from the overall calculation in any calendar year. An anti-abuse rule eliminates the *de minimis* option when it is recognized that an employer has created an arrangement with five or more agents to somehow defeat the intent of the mandate, however.

The Treasury denied requests to allow exceptions for foreign tax credit situations or personal deductions.

Q 2:96 How does the employer determine withholding on vacation pay treated as supplemental wages?

Vacation pay normally is subject to federal income tax withholding as if it were a regular wage payment. However, when vacation pay is paid in addition to regular wages (e.g., vacation pay in lieu of vacation or paid in a lump sum on separation from service), it should be treated as a supplemental wage payment and the rules on supplemental wage withholding should be followed. If the vacation pay is for a time longer than the employer's payroll period, the amount of withholding on the vacation pay is determined by spreading it over the payroll periods for which it is paid. [Treas. Reg. § 31.3402(g)-2(c); Rev. Rul. 2008-29, 2008-24 I.R.B. 1149]

Q 2:97   When may the employer use the combined tables for determining income tax withholding and Social Security and Medicare taxes?

If the employer wants to withhold a single amount for income tax, employee Social Security tax, and employee Medicare tax, a deviation of the wage-bracket method—the combined tables—may be used. These tables can be used only if wages for income tax withholding and Social Security tax are identical and if the employee's annual compensation is less than the Social Security wage base ($127,200 for 2017).

The payroll period and marital status of the employee determine which table to use. Combined withholding tables are available for single and married taxpayers for weekly, biweekly, semimonthly, monthly, and daily payroll periods.

If wages are greater than the highest wage bracket in the applicable table, an employer has to use one of the other methods for figuring income tax withholding described in Qs 2:82–2:90 or in IRS Publication No. 15-A. For wages paid in 2017 that do not exceed $127,200, the combined Social Security tax rate and Medicare tax rate is 7.65 percent for the employee and 7.65 percent for the employer.

Employers that use the combined withholding tables should follow these steps to determine the amounts to report on Form 941, Employer's QUARTERLY Federal Tax Return:

1. To determine the employee Social Security tax withheld on the form, multiply the wages by 6.2 percent.

2. To determine the employee Medicare tax withheld on the form, multiply the wages by 1.45 percent.

3. For wages in excess of $200,000, determine the Additional Medicare Tax, multiply the wages in excess of $200,000 by 0.9 percent.

4. To determine the income tax withheld on the form, subtract the amounts from steps 1, 2 and 3 from the total tax withheld.

Employers can figure the amounts to be shown on each employee's Form W-2, Wage and Tax Statement, in the same way. [Pub. No. 15-A]

Q 2:98   Are tips treated as supplemental wages if reported with regular wages?

Yes. If federal income taxes have not been withheld from regular wages, tips should be added to regular wages to determine the amount to withhold. If federal income taxes were withheld from regular wages, you can either:

a. Withhold tax at the supplemental rate; or

b. Combine tips and wages, figure the withholding tax on the combined amount, and subtract the withholding tax for the regular wages to determine the amount to withhold on the tips.

Wage Payments to Family Members

Q 2:99   Must employers withhold federal income taxes from wages paid to family members?

Yes. There is no specific exemption from federal income tax withholding for wages paid to family members who provide services to a trade or business owned by another family member; thus, such wages are subject to federal income tax withholding.

Q 2:100   Are wages paid to children in a family business subject to federal income tax withholding if exempt from FICA?

Yes. Payments to children in a family business are subject to federal income tax withholding even if they are exempt from FICA and FUTA. There is no specific exemption from income tax withholding available for children who are employed in a family business.

Q 2:101   Are wages paid to a spouse who is employed by another spouse in an unincorporated business subject to federal income tax withholding?

Generally, yes. Wages for the services of an individual who works for his or her spouse in an unincorporated trade or business owned by the spouse (i.e., a sole proprietorship) are subject to federal income tax withholding.

Q 2:102   Are wages paid to family members employed by a corporation owned by a spouse or parent, or employed by a partnership in which a spouse or parent is a partner, subject to federal income tax withholding?

Yes. Wages for the services of a child or spouse are subject to federal income tax withholding if he or she works for (1) a corporation in which the parent or spouse has an ownership interest, even if it is controlled by the child's parent or the individual's spouse; (2) a partnership in which the parent or spouse has an ownership interest, even if the child's parent is a partner, unless each partner is a parent of the child; (3) a partnership in which the parent or spouse has an ownership interest, even if the individual's spouse is a partner; or (4) an estate of a deceased parent or spouse. [Pub. No. 15]

Q 2:103   Does federal income tax withholding apply to the wages of a parent who works for a child?

Yes. Wages for the services of a parent employed by his or her child in a trade or business are subject to federal income tax withholding.

Q 2:104　Are there any exemptions from federal income tax withholding for wages paid to students?

No. Wages paid to students who are working at a school, college, or university at which they are enrolled and regularly attending classes are not exempt from federal income tax withholding unless another exemption applies. Wages paid to such students by private foundations, as defined under I.R.C. Section 509(a)(3), that are operated as schools, colleges, or universities are also not exempt from federal income tax withholding. Wages paid to full-time students performing services that constitute an integral part of their academic program in a nonprofit or public educational institution that normally maintains a regular faculty and curriculum and normally has a body of students attending are also subject to federal income tax withholding, as are wages paid to full-time students by an organized camp. [I.R.C. § 3401(a)]

Q 2:105　Is there an exemption from federal income tax withholding for wages paid to a student's spouse?

No. Wages paid by an educational institution to the spouse of a student who is enrolled and regularly attending classes are subject to federal income tax withholding.

Q 2:106　Is there an exemption from federal income tax withholding for wages paid to a student nurse?

No. Wages paid to student nurses performing part-time service for nominal earnings at a hospital as an incidental part of training are subject to federal income tax withholding. [Pub. No. 15]

Q 2:107　Are the wages of election workers subject to federal income tax withholding?

No. Wages paid to election workers are not subject to federal income tax withholding. Such amounts are deemed to be "in the nature of fees paid to public officials." [I.R.C. § 3401(a); Treas. Reg. § 31.3401(a)-2(b)]

Q 2:108　Are there special rules for federal income tax withholding on wages paid to household workers?

Yes. The cash wages of domestic workers in a private home, local college club, or local chapter of a college fraternity or sorority are not subject to federal income tax withholding. Noncash wages paid to a household worker in a private home and noncash wages paid to a domestic worker in a local college club or local chapter of a college fraternity or sorority are also exempt from wage withholding. Cash wages of a student performing household services for a local college club or local chapter of a college fraternity or sorority are exempt from income tax withholding, regardless of the amount, if the student is enrolled and regularly attending classes at an educational institution.

If an employer pays the employee FICA, employee state unemployment taxes, or both for a household worker employed in a private home without deducting these taxes from the worker's wages, the tax payments constitute additional compensation for federal income tax purposes. (As noted earlier, all compensation paid to a domestic worker in a private home is exempt from wage withholding.)

Example. Jeff hires a household employee (who is an unrelated individual over age 18) to care for his child and agrees to pay cash wages of $370 every Friday. He expects to pay his employee $2,000 or more in 2017 and decides to pay the employee's share of Social Security and Medicare taxes from his own funds. Jeff does not withhold any Social Security or Medicare taxes. For each wage payment, Jeff will pay $55.08 when he pays the taxes—$28.31 ($22.94 for Social Security tax, which is 6.2% × $370, plus $5.37, which is 1.45% × $370 for Medicare tax for the employee's share) added to $28.31 (the employer match for Social Security and Medicare taxes for Jeff's share.) For income tax withholding purposes, the employee's wages each payday are $398.31 ($370 plus the $28.31 that Jeff will pay to cover his employee's share of Social Security and Medicare taxes). [Pub. No. 926]

Q 2:109 Do special federal income tax withholding rules apply to employees of tax-exempt organizations?

No. These wages are generally subject to federal income tax withholding on the same basis as wages paid in a trade or business. A FICA or FUTA exemption may apply.

Q 2:110 Are wages paid to agricultural laborers subject to any special federal income tax withholding rules?

For purposes of income tax withholding, I.R.C. Section 3121(g) defines agricultural labor.

Wages paid to agricultural workers are subject to special federal income tax withholding rules that generally do not apply to other employees: Only FICA covered wages are subject to federal income tax withholding. In general, if a cash payment triggers FICA coverage for an agricultural laborer, federal income tax withholding will also apply to all cash wages paid, up to the FICA wage base. Noncash benefits, such as food and lodging, are exempt from FICA and, as a result, are also exempt from federal income tax withholding for farm workers receiving noncash benefits, even if otherwise subject to federal income tax withholding. [I.R.C. § 3401(a)(2)]

Noncash benefits received by agricultural laborers (e.g., food and lodging) are exempt from federal income tax withholding (and FICA and FUTA) as long as they are not paid in lieu of wages. Cash wages of agricultural laborers are exempt from federal income tax withholding (and FICA) if the wages are less than $150 per employee in the calendar year (or more than $150 as long as the employer's expenditures for agricultural labor, cash and noncash, in such year are less than $2,500). These rules are referred to as the minimum cash pay rules for agricultural employees.

Also exempt from federal income tax withholding (and FICA) are wages of nonmigrant hand harvest laborers paid on a piece-rate basis when the workers are employed in agriculture for less than 13 weeks during the preceding calendar year. [I.R.C. § 3121(a)(8); Pub. No. 51]

Indians and Gaming Profits

Q 2:111   Are the wages of American Indians subject to federal employment tax and withholding?

Yes. There is well-established case law holding that Indians are subject to all the federal employment taxes unless specifically exempted by a federal statute or treaty. [Squire v. Capoeman, 351 U.S. 1, 6 (1956); Dillon v. United States, 792 F.2d 849 (9th Cir. 1986), aff'g Cross v. Commissioner, 83 T.C. 561 (1984); Karmun v. Commissioner, 749 F.2d 567 (9th Cir. 1984), aff'g 82 T.C. 201 (1984); Jourdain v. Commissioner, 71 T.C. 980 (1979)]

Q 2:112   When are distributions of Indian gaming profits subject to federal income tax withholding?

Entities that make certain payments to Indian tribal members from gaming profits must withhold federal income tax if:

1. The total payment to a member for the year is over $10,400 for 2017; and
2. The payment is from the net revenues of class II or class III gaming activities (classified by the Indian Gaming Regulatory Act) conducted or licensed by the tribes.

A class I gaming activity is not subject to the withholding requirement. Class I activities are social games solely for prizes of minimal value or traditional forms of Indian gaming engaged in as part of tribal ceremonies or celebrations. Class II gaming activities include (1) bingo and similar games, such as pull tabs, punch boards, tip jars, lotto, and instant bingo, and (2) card games that are authorized by the state or that are not explicitly prohibited by the state and are played at a location within the state. A Class III gaming activity is any gaming that is not class I or class II. Class III includes horse racing, dog racing, jai alai, casino gaming, and slot machines. [I.R.C. § 3402(q); Pub. No. 15-A]

Q 2:113   How is federal income tax withholding determined for gaming profits distributed to tribal members?

The amount of tax to withhold for each payment of gaming profits is figured by using a table in IRS Publication No. 15-A, Employer's Supplemental Tax Guide, for the period for which the payment is made. For example, if the payment is made weekly, Table 1 should be used; if the payment is made semimonthly, Table 3 should be used. If the total payments to an individual for the year are $10,400 or less, no withholding is required.

Example. The monthly payment of gaming profits to Eagle Pathfinder, a tribal member, is $3,500, and Eagle Pathfinder will receive more than $10,400 in 2017. The tax to be withheld, per Table 4 (Monthly Distribution Period), is computed as follows:

1. Payment	$3,500
2. Tax to withhold from Table 4:	
a. $3,500 − $1,644 = $1,856	
$1,856 × 0.15 = $278.40 + $77.70	
b. Total tax	$ 356.10

Eagle Pathfinder has $356.10 withheld from his monthly payment.

Q 2:114 When is federal income tax withheld from gaming profits distributed to tribal members reported and deposited?

Withholding on Indian gaming profits is reported on Form 945, Annual Return of Withheld Federal Income Tax. The amount paid, as well as the withholding, for the tribal members is reported on Form 1099-MISC. The entity making the distribution combines the Indian gaming withholding with all other nonpayroll withholding. Generally, the entity must deposit the amounts withheld by EFTPS. [Pub. No. 15, Pub. No. 15-A]

Special Employer Classifications

Q 2:115 What types of employment are exempt from Social Security and Medicare?

Payments for certain types of employment are exempt from FICA. [I.R.C. § 3121(b)] A partial list of services exempt from FICA follows:

- Services provided by temporary foreign agricultural workers [Treas. Reg. § 31.3121(b)(1)-1]

- Domestic services provided by students for certain college organizations [Treas. Reg. § 31.3121(b)(2)-1]

- Services performed by an individual in the employ of his or her spouse [Treas. Reg. § 31.3121(b)(3)-1]

- Services performed by a child under age 21 for his or her parents outside of a trade or business [Treas. Reg. § 31.3121(b)(3)-1]

- Services on a foreign ship or aircraft outside the United States by non-U.S. citizens for a non-U.S. employer [Treas. Reg. § 31.3121(b)(4)-1]

- Services provided to a U.S. government instrumentality, state, or its subdivision employer that is exempt from FICA taxation (there are exemptions for specific services performed and geographic areas) [Treas. Reg. §§ 31.3121(b)(5)-1, 31.3121(b)(6)-1, 31.3121(b)(7)-1]

- Services provided by an inmate of a penal institution [Treas. Reg. § 31.3121(b)(6)-1(d)(3)]

- Services performed by a minister of a church or religious organization [Treas. Reg. § 31.3121(b)(8)-1]

- Services provided by certain employees or representatives of the railroad industry [Treas. Reg. § 31.3121(b)(9)-1]

- Payments of less than $50 for a calendar quarter from certain nonprofit organizations [Treas. Reg. § 31.3121(b)(10)-1]

- Services provided by students who are enrolled and regularly attending classes at the school for which they provide services and who are not classified as "career employees" of the school (this exemption is not available if the school is a public educational institution that has opted for FICA coverage of student employees) [Treas. Reg. § 31.3121(b)(10)-2]

- Services provided by student nurses [Treas. Reg. § 31.3121(b)(13)-1]

- Services provided to a foreign government, an international organization, or an instrumentality of a foreign government [Treas. Reg. §§ 31.3121(b)(11)-1, 31.3121(b)(12)-1, 31.3121(b)(15)-1]

- Services in delivery or distribution of newspapers, shopping news, or magazines [Treas. Reg. § 31.3121(b)(14)-1]

- Services provided under a share-farming arrangement [Treas. Reg. § 31.3121(b)(16)-1]

- Services provided to a communist organization [Treas. Reg. § 31.3121(b)(17)-1]

- Certain services provided on Guam for the Republic of Philippines [Treas. Reg. § 31.3121(b)(18)-1]

- Services performed by nonresident aliens under an F, J, M, or Q visa [Treas. Reg. § 31.3121(b)(19)-1]

- Services performed by small fishing boat crews (normally fewer than 10 individuals) who receive a share of the catch (or the proceeds from the catch) and less than $100 cash compensation per trip for each crew member [Treas. Reg. § 31.3121(b)(20)-1]

In addition to these specific exemptions applicable to workers of certain employers, Treasury Regulations Section 31.3121(c)-1 provides exemptions for certain types of services.

Q 2:116   What types of employer payments are exempt from FICA?

In general, all compensation paid by an employer to an employee is subject to FICA unless specifically exempted under the I.R.C. [I.R.C. § 3121(a)] Exempt payments include:

- Payments from the employer's qualified pension plan, profit-sharing plan, or annuity [31.3121(a)(3)-1, 31.3121(a)(5)-1]
- Value of excludable employee length-of-service and safety achievement awards, fellowships and scholarships, and nontaxable benefits under I.R.C. §§ 132, 3121(a)(20)
- Sick or disability benefits paid to or on behalf of an employee more than six calendar months after the last month the employee provided services to the employer [Treas. Reg. § 31.3121(a)(4)-1]
- Sickness or injury payments made under a state workers' compensation law [Treas. Reg. § 31.3121(a)(2)-1]
- Noncash payments to an employee for work done outside the employer's trade or business (i.e., nontrade or business activities) or for domestic service in the employer's home [Treas. Reg. § 31.3121(a)(7)-1]
- Cash payments to an employee for domestic service totaling less than $1,900 for 2015 (indexed for inflation) [Treas. Reg. § 31.3121(a)(7)-1(c)]
- Noncash payments to agricultural workers that are not paid in lieu of wages [Treas. Reg. § 31.3121(a)(8)-1]
- Cash payments to agricultural workers if the amount paid to the employee totals less than $150 for the year and the employer's total cash payments to all agricultural workers for the year are less than $2,500 [Treas. Reg. § 31.3121(a)(8)-1]
- Cash payments to employees for periods when the employer provides no services (not including vacation pay and sick pay) [Treas. Reg. § 31.3121(a)(9)-1]
- Cash payments totaling less than $100 for the year made to a home-worker who can be classified as a statutory employee [Treas. Reg. § 31.3121(a)(10)-1]
- Qualified moving expense reimbursements that the employer expects the employee to deduct [Treas. Reg. § 31.3121(a)(11)-1]
- Cash tips totaling less than $20 in a month and noncash tips [Treas. Reg. § 31.3121(a)(12)-1]
- Death or disability retirement benefits paid under an employer plan [Treas. Reg. § 31.3121(a)(13)-1]
- Wages paid to an employee's beneficiary after the year of the employee's death [Treas. Reg. § 31.3121(a)(14)-1]
- Payments made by an employer to a disabled former employee [Treas. Reg. § 31.3121(a)(15)-1]
- Benefit payments made under a nonqualified deferred compensation plan (to the extent these were either grandfathered as not being subject to FICA

or were reported when vested), unless such payments were made to a 401(k) plan

- Elective contributions made under a Section 125 flexible benefits plan (i.e., cafeteria plan) [I.R.C. § 125(a)]

- Cash payments to an employee for work done outside the employer's trade or business totaling less than $100 for the year [I.R.C. § 3121(a)(7)]

- Employer contributions to an HSA, whether direct or via pretax salary reductions, are generally excludable from an employee's taxable gross income. If the employer reasonably believes the employee will be able to exclude the HSA contribution from income, the employee and employer contributions are not subject to federal income tax withholding, FICA, or FUTA. In addition, the HSA must be included as part of an I.R.C. Section 125 cafeteria plan arrangement.

Q 2:117   Are the wages of part-time workers subject to special federal income tax withholding rules?

No. Federal income tax withholding applies to both part-time workers and full-time workers under the same rules. Thus, there is no difference in the treatment of full-time employees, part-time employees, and employees hired for short periods. Nevertheless, it might be more advantageous to withhold federal income taxes under the part-year employment method (see Q 2:86). [Pub. No. 15]

Q 2:118   How is federal income tax withholding calculated for wages paid to nonresident aliens?

In general, employers that pay wages to nonresident aliens must withhold federal income tax (unless excepted by regulations) subject to a special calculation in addition to the regular withholding tax tables that apply to all employees. Nonresident aliens who are not residents of Canada, Mexico, or South Korea may claim no more than one withholding allowance. [I.R.C. § 3402(f)(6); Treas. Reg. § 31.3402(f)(6)-1] Wages paid to nonresident alien employees that are subject to federal income tax withholding and/or FICA are reported on Form W-2, Wage and Tax Statement, and filed with the nonresident alien and the SSA. Wages that are exempt from federal income tax withholding under a treaty are reported on Form 1042-S.

To provide for withholding on wages paid to nonresident aliens that more closely approximates their income tax liability, the IRS issued Notice 2005-76. [2005-46 I.R.B. 947] According to the Notice, nonresident alien employees are required to complete Form W-4 as follows:

1. Not claim exemption from withholding;
2. Request withholding as if they are single, regardless of the actual marital status;

3. Claim only one allowance (if the nonresident alien is a resident of Canada, Mexico, or South Korea more than one allowance may be claimed); and

4. Write "Nonresident Alien" or "NRA" above the dotted line on line 6 of Form W-4.

Nonresident aliens are no longer required to request an additional withholding amount.

Furthermore, Notice 2005-76 provided a procedure for the employer's calculation of withholding of wages of nonresident alien employees. Under this procedure, the employer added an amount (see the chart below) based on the payroll period to the wages of the nonresident alien employee solely for purposes of calculating the income tax withholding for each payroll period.

Under IRS Notice 1036, and included in Publication 15, Employer's Tax Guide, are instructions on how to determine how much to withhold from NRA employees. Employers must first add an amount, based on the payroll period, to wages before determining the amount to withhold under the wage-bracket or percentage method to offset the standard deduction built into the withholding tables (see the chart below). Employers must then determine the income tax withholding using the withholding tables that apply to all employees. For 2017, the amount to add is as follows:

Payroll Period	Add Additional
Weekly	$ 44.20
Biweekly	$ 88.50
Semimonthly	$ 95.80
Monthly	$ 191.70
Quarterly	$ 575.00
Semiannually	$1,150.00
Annually	$2,300.00
Daily or Miscellaneous	$ 8.80

The amounts added are solely for calculating income tax withholding on the wages of the nonresident alien employee and should not be included in any box of the employee's Form W-2. The amount does not increase the income tax liability of the employee. This does not affect Social Security, Medicare, or FUTA tax liability of the employee or employer. Note that this procedure does not apply to wages paid to nonresident alien students and business apprentices from India.

For additional information, refer to Notice 1036 and IRS Publication Nos. 15 (Circular E, Employer's Tax Guide), 515 (Withholding of Tax on Nonresident Aliens and Foreign Entities), and 519 (U.S. Tax Guide for Aliens). See also IRS Notice 1392 for answers to such questions as who is an NRA employee, how residency is determined, what compensation is subject to U.S. income tax withholding, and whether NRA employees must file a U.S. federal personal income tax return.

Q 2:119   What are the withholding and reporting requirements that apply to election workers?

Election workers are individuals who are generally employed to perform services for state and local governments (governments) at election booths in connection with national, state, or local elections. Governments typically pay election workers a set fee for each day of work. Election workers' wages are includible in gross income as compensation for services. An individual employed as an election worker may also perform services for the government in another capacity. [I.R.C. § 61(a)(1)]

These individuals are usually exempt from FICA; however, the state and the SSA may agree to extend Social Security coverage to services of employees of the state or its political subdivisions under a Section 218 agreement, which may cover the services of election workers. If so, the Section 218 agreement may specify the level of fees the election workers must receive to be entitled to coverage. Information about a state's Section 218 agreement can be obtained from the state's Social Security administrator.

When a state and the SSA agree to cover election workers under a Section 218 agreement, I.R.C. Section 3121(b)(7)(F)(iv) provides that the services of an election worker are not treated as employment for FICA purposes if the worker's remuneration is less than $1,700 for the calendar year 2017. This amount is indexed for inflation. The Section 218 agreement may specify a lower threshold for FICA purposes.

Amounts paid to precinct workers for services performed at election booths are "in the nature of fees paid to public officials" and not subject to income tax withholding. [Treas. Reg. § 31.3401(a)-2(b)(2)]

Payments of wages not subject to federal income tax withholding must be reported on Form W-2 if the total of those payments plus the amount of the employee's wages subject to federal income tax withholding, if any, is $600 or more in a calendar year. For example, if a payment of $700 was made to an employee and $500 thereof represents wages subject to federal income tax withholding under I.R.C. Section 3402 and the remaining $200 represents compensation not subject to federal income tax withholding, such wages and compensation must both be reported on Form W-2. If the employee has no wages subject to federal income tax withholding and payments to that employee equal $600 or more in a calendar year, the employer is required to file Form W-2 for that employee. [Treas. Reg. § 1.6041-2(a)(1)]

The employer may elect to report components of income required to be reported on Form W-2 under the above rule on more than one Form W-2. Thus, the amounts paid to an individual for services as an election worker may be reported on one W-2 and amounts paid to the individual for service in another capacity may be reported on another W-2, even though the amounts are aggregated to determine whether reporting applies. [Treas. Reg. § 1.6041-2(a)(1)]

When an election worker's compensation is not subject to FICA, the payment of services is reported on Form W-2 subject to the $600 reporting threshold. Compensation subject to federal income tax withholding is taken into account in determining whether the $600 reporting requirement applies. [Treas. Reg. § 1.6041-2(a)(1)]

I.R.C. Section 6051(a) requires reporting of compensation subject to either FICA or federal income tax withholding. No reporting is required for items of income that are not subject to federal income tax withholding. If an election worker's compensation is subject to FICA, Form W-2 reporting is required, regardless of the amount of compensation. [Rev. Rul. 2000-6, 2000-6 I.R.B. 512]

Q 2:120   When is compensation paid to a U.S. citizen for services performed in a U.S. possession not subject to federal income tax withholding?

The IRS has advised in a 1993 FSA that compensation for services performed by U.S. citizens in a U.S. possession is not subject to U.S. federal income tax withholding under I.R.C. Section 3402 when the compensation is subject to income tax withholding by the possession. This exemption does not apply to employees of the U.S. government or a U.S. agency. [I.R.C. § 3401(a)(8)(A)(ii); Field Serv. Adv. 1999-787]

Tipped Employees

Q 2:121   When are tips paid by a customer to an employee subject to employment taxes?

Cash tips that total $20 or more in a calendar month and are reported to the employer are considered wages subject to federal income tax withholding, FICA, and FUTA. Note that noncash tips and cash tips not meeting the $20 threshold are taxable and included on the employee's Form 1040, but are not subject to FICA or FUTA. Ordinary wages paid to tipped employees are subject to federal employment taxes and withholding in the same manner as wages paid to other employees.

A tip is a voluntary payment from a customer. A payment that is called a "tip" but is established by the employer (e.g., a fixed service charge) and paid to the employer and then distributed to the employee is treated as wages. A tip that is added by the customer and paid to the employer (e.g., added to a charge) is treated as a tip for employment tax purposes when the tip is paid to the employee. However, when the employer requires employees to turn over all tips to the employer and the employer then allocates and distributes the tips among all the employees, the payments are wages, not tips.

When the employer guarantees its servers a fixed hourly rate consisting of wages paid by the employer and tips paid by customers, the tips paid by customers are treated as tip income. [Treas. Reg. §§ 31.3102-3(b), 31.3121(a)(12)-1, 31.3402(k)-1(b), Rev. Rul. 2002-18, I.R.B. 2012-261032]

Q 2:122 What are the employee reporting requirements for tips?

Employees must report to their employer the amount of their tip income for any calendar month in which they receive $20 or more in tips. The $20 threshold is applied to each employer for whom the employee works in the calendar month. The report must be in writing and must be submitted by the tenth day of the month following any month when the employee's tips meet the $20 threshold. When the reporting date falls on a Saturday, Sunday, or legal holiday, the report is due on the next day that is not a Saturday, Sunday, or legal holiday. [Treas. Reg. §§ 31.3121(a)(12)-1, 31.3402(k)-1, 31.6053-4]

Q 2:123 How does an employee report cash tips paid into a pool that is shared with other employees?

Employees are required to report only the amount of tips they actually receive and keep. Thus, when the employee shares his or her tips with other employees, the amount shared is not reported to the employer, but may have to be reported by the other individuals.

Example. A waitress receives $280 in tips in one month and gives the busboy one-fourth. The waitress must report $210 in tips and the busboy must report $70.

[Treas. Reg. §§ 31.6053-1(c), 31.6053-3(j)(13)]

Q 2:124 How do employees report cash tips?

Employees may use IRS Form 4070 to satisfy the written requirement for reporting tips to employers. However, any other format is acceptable as long as it contains the following information: (1) name, address, and SSN of the employee; (2) name and address of the employer; (3) calendar month or other period covered by the report; and (4) total amount of tips received by the employee during the reporting period. The statement should be signed and dated by the employee. [Treas. Reg. §§ 31.6053-1(c), 31.6053-4; Form 4070 instructions]

When an employee terminates his or her employment in a calendar month after the employee has received at least $20 in tips, the employee must report tip income on the earlier of the day on which the last wage payment is made or the tenth day of the following month. [Treas. Reg. § 31.3402(k)-1; Pub. No. 1244]

Q 2:125 When are tips treated as paid to the employee?

It is critical that the employer understand when tips are treated as paid to the employee because that date is the date that any employment tax liabilities arise. The following rules apply: Reported tips are treated as paid when reported. Unreported tips are treated as paid in the month in which they were received. Underreported tips are generally determined following an IRS audit of the employer's tax reporting.

As a result, an employee who receives more than $20 in December of one year but does not report the tips until January of the next year (January 10 is the due date for reporting) is treated as having received the tips in January. If the employee reports a portion in December, only the amount reported in December is treated as paid in December. The employer's obligation to report and pay employment taxes on the tips is based on the same treatment. The employer includes in its quarterly return only the employee tips reported during that quarter, even if the employee may have been paid a portion in the prior quarter. [Treas. Reg. §§ 31.3121(a)(12)-1, 31.3401(f)-1] The same rules apply for determining the employee's wage base threshold for FICA and FUTA taxes.

The IRS released guidance on its pilot Attributed Tip Income Program (ATIP) for employers in the food and beverage industry in 2006. ATIP offered benefits to employers similar to those provided under previous tip reporting agreements but had some significant additional advantages, according to the IRS release. [I.R.S. News Release IR-2006-118]

The details and requirements for participation in ATIP for employers and employees were set out in Revenue Procedure 2006-30. [2006-2 C.B. 110 (updated by Rev. Proc. 2009-53); 2009-49 I.R.B. 746] In general, employers annually elected to participate in ATIP and use the prescribed methodology for reporting tips. At least 20 percent of the gross receipts of participating employers had to be derived from credit-card payments including charged tips. In addition, at least 75 percent of a participating employer's tipped employees had to agree to participate in the program, and participating employers had to report attributed tips on employees' Forms W-2 and pay taxes using the formula tip rate.

The ATIP pilot program was extended for two years, through December 31, 2011 under Revenue Procedure 2009-53. The IRS announced on August 8, 2011 that the ATIP was being discontinued after December 31, 2011. The program drew very few participants. Employers that wish to continue in a voluntary program have the options of the Tip Reporting Determination Agreement or the Tip Reporting Alternative Commitment programs. Additional information is available in IRS Publications 3144 and 3148.

Q 2:126   Is the employer liable for unpaid FICA and FUTA on unreported tips?

The employer is not liable for unpaid FICA and FUTA on unreported tips unless the IRS provides a notice and demand for the taxes under I.R.C. Section 3121(q). This typically follows an audit of the employer's reporting. The employer is only liable for the employer share of FICA on the unreported tips as determined by the IRS.

Employees are liable for the employee share of FICA due on the unreported tips. These amounts are paid with the employee's Form 1040, which will include Form 4137, Social Security and Medicare Tax on Unreported Tip Income. [Treas. Reg. § 31.3121(q)-1]

Q 2:127 How does the employer of a food and beverage establishment obtain a credit for a portion of the FICA it pays on tips?

I.R.C. Section 45B provides a business tax credit for a part of the employer's portion of FICA tax paid on employee tips.

The credit is available for the "excess employer Social Security tax" paid or incurred by the taxpayer. The excess employer Social Security tax is any FICA tax paid by an employer with respect to tips received by an employee during any month, to the extent those tips (1) are deemed to have been paid by the employer to an employee and subject to FICA (without regard to whether the tips are reported) and (2) exceed the amount by which wages (excluding tips) paid by the employer to the employee during that month are less than the total amount that would be payable (with respect to that employment) at the minimum wage rate applicable under the Fair Labor Standards Act (FLSA). The credit has the effect of limiting the employer's employment tax liability to the amount that would be due if the employee received only the minimum wage and not the wages and full tips reported. The employee's earnings record and individual income tax liability are unaffected by the credit.

Only tips that have been received from customers in connection with the providing, delivering, or serving of food or beverages for consumption can be counted in determining this credit, and only if the tipping of employees delivering or serving food or beverages by customers is customary. A taxpayer may elect not to claim the credit for any taxable year.

The IRS has ruled that such credits are available for wages paid by a tax-exempt employer if the employer has nonexempt business activities subject to federal income tax. [Priv. Ltr. Rul. 199931041]

Q 2:128 When are employers required to report tip income and allocated tips electronically?

Any person, corporation, partnership, individual, estate, or trust that is required to file 250 or more information returns (i.e., Forms 8027, 1099, 1098, 5498, W-2G, W-2, and 1042-S) must file such returns electronically.

The filing requirements apply separately to both original and corrected returns. Even though an employer may submit as many as 250 corrections on paper, the IRS encourages electronically submitted corrections. Once the 250 threshold has been met, filers are required to submit any additional returns electronically.

Under certain limited hardship situations, the employer can request relief from these requirements by submitting Form 8508, Request for Waiver From Filing Information Returns Electronically, to IRS. [Rev. Proc. 99-46, 1999-49 I.R.B. 605, Rev. Proc. 2000-49, 2000-47 I.R.B. 491]

The IRS updated the specifications for the electronic filing of employers' information returns of employees' tip income in Revenue Procedure 2006-29. [2006-27 I.R.B. 13] The updated specifications relate to Form 8027, Employer's

Annual Information Return of Tip Income and Allocated Tips. Form 8027 is used by large food or beverage establishments in making annual reports to the IRS on receipts from food or beverage operations and tips reported by employees. The changes made to the old revenue procedure included four new fields and an increase in record length to accommodate the new fields.

Q 2:129   What is the penalty for failure to report tips electronically?

When an employer is required to file electronically but fails to do so and does not have an approved waiver on record, the employer will be subject to a penalty of $100 per return in excess of 250. [Rev. Proc. 99-46, 1999-49 I.R.B. 605]

Independent Contractors

Q 2:130   Must an employer withhold federal income tax on payments to an independent contractor?

No. Payments of $600 or more to valid independent contractors are reported on Form 1099. These forms are filed each calendar year and identify the payee by his or her TIN or SSN and the amount of the payment. The IRS has a TIN matching program that will allow payers to confirm numbers provided by payees before a Form 1099 is filed. Some independent contractors may be subject to backup withholding, however; see Q 2:132.

Q 2:131   Is there any way to confirm with the IRS that no withholding of federal employment taxes is required for a specific independent contractor?

Yes. The Treasury has provided Form SS-8, Determination of Worker Status for Purposes of Federal Employment Taxes and Income Tax Withholding, for this purpose. Either the employer or the payer completes the form and submits it to the IRS for review. Although this form will confirm whether the worker is to be treated as an employee for withholding purposes, it does not establish whether the worker is a common-law employee for other purposes (see chapter 6). Employers are instructed to treat workers as employees subject to FIT, FITW, FICA, and FUTA until such time as the IRS issues a determination that they are independent contractors. (See chapter 6.)

Backup Withholding

Q 2:132   What is backup withholding?

Backup withholding is an alternate method for determining how much must be withheld from nonpayroll payments when an individual fails to provide certain taxpayer information. Businesses generally must withhold 28 percent for 2017 for backup withholding purposes on certain taxable payments. [Treas. Reg. §§ 31.3406(d)-5(d), 31.3406(d)-5(e)]

Q 2:133 When is backup withholding required?

Backup withholding is required (1) when payments for the year are $600 or more and the payee fails to furnish a TIN; (2) when the TIN is incorrect; (3) when the IRS notifies the employer that a payee has understated either interest or dividend income; or (4) when the payee fails to certify that the payee is not subject to withholding for failing to report interest and dividend income. [I.R.C. § 3406; Treas. Reg. § 31.3406(d)-5]

Q 2:134 What payments are subject to backup withholding?

Payments subject to backup withholding include interest, dividends, patronage dividends, rents, royalties, commissions, nonemployee compensation, and certain other payments an employer makes in the course of its trade or business. In addition, transactions by brokers and barter exchanges and certain payments made by fishing boat operators are subject to backup withholding. Backup withholding does not apply to wages and nonpayroll payments from pensions, annuities, Individual Retirement Accounts (IRAs), or real estate transactions. Individuals may elect to have federal income tax withheld from certain pension and annuity payments. [I.R.C. § 3406(h)(10); Treas. Reg. § 35a.9999-3]

Q 2:135 When is Form W-9 used?

Employers can use Form W-9, Request for Taxpayer Identification Number and Certification, to ask payees to furnish a TIN (generally not used for employees) and to certify that the number furnished is correct. Employers can also use Form W-9 to get certifications from payees that they are not subject to backup withholding or that they are exempt from backup withholding. The instructions for Form W-9 include a list of typical payees who are exempt from backup withholding. [Treas. Reg. §§ 35a.9999-1 to 35a.9999-5, 31.3406(h)-3(a)]

Earned Income Credit

Q 2:136 What is the earned income credit?

The earned income credit (EIC) is a payment to certain individuals who earn less than a threshold dollar amount set by the IRS each year. The payment is paid as a credit against income taxes due to the IRS. When the credit exceeds the amount of income taxes due, the individual receives a check from the U.S. Treasury. The amount of the credit is based on the individual's total earned income, whether the individual has a dependent child, and the number of dependent children. When the individual's compensation exceeds the annual threshold based on the number of qualified children, the amount of the credit is reduced and the credit will eventually be eliminated. The maximum EIC for 2017 is $6,318 for a qualified employee with three or more qualifying children.

Q 2:137   What was the advance earned income credit?

Prior to 2011, the I.R.C. permitted certain individuals who were eligible for the EIC and who had at least one child to receive a portion of the credit each pay period, rather than waiting until they filed their tax returns at the beginning of the following year. This portion of the EIC was known as the advance earned income credit (AEIC) and was paid each pay cycle for those who had filed Form W-5, Earned Income Credit Advance Payment Certificate. Note that individuals eligible for the EIC were not automatically eligible to receive the AEIC. The option to receive AEIC expired on December 31, 2010. The EIC is still in place and individuals are able to claim the credit on their Form 1040.

Q 2:138   Who can be classified as a qualifying child for purposes of the EIC?

For purposes of qualifying for the EIC, a qualifying child is the employee's son, daughter, adopted child, stepchild, foster child, or grandchild (or a brother, sister, stepbrother, stepsister, or a descendant of one of the above) who satisfies two criteria. First, the child must be classified as one of the following: (1) under age 19; (2) a full-time student who has not attained age 24 at the end of the tax year; or (3) permanently and totally disabled (there is no age requirement). Second, the child must reside with the employee for more than half of the tax year (or for all of the tax year if a foster child). A child who either is born or dies during the tax year and who resided with the employee during the entire time he or she was alive is treated as having resided with the employee all year.

An otherwise qualifying child who is married by the end of the tax year can be treated as a qualifying child only when the employee may claim the child as a dependent on his or her Form 1040. An exception to this rule permits such treatment for a custodial parent who would be eligible to claim the child as a dependent except for the fact that the noncustodial parent claims the child as a dependent because of (1) a release statement agreement specifying that the employee not claim the child or (2) a pre-1985 divorce decree or separation agreement that allows the noncustodial parent to claim the child. To satisfy this criterion, the noncustodial parent must provide at least $600 for support of the child in the tax year.

Only one party can claim a qualifying child when two parents are eligible. There is a tie-breaker rule. (It is no longer automatic that the parent with the higher adjusted gross income (AGI) will claim the child.) If more than one person claims the EIC using the same child and only one of the persons is the child's parent, the parent can treat the child as a qualifying child. If both parties are the child's parents and they do not file a joint return together, the parent with whom the child lived the longest during the year can treat the child as a qualifying child. If the child lived with both parents the same amount of time during the year and the parents do not file a joint return together, then the parent with the higher AGI can treat the child as a qualifying child. If none of the persons is the child's parent, the person with the highest AGI can treat the child as a qualifying child. [Pub. No. 596]

Q 2:139   What is considered earned income for the EIC?

The definition of earned income for purposes of determining an individual's qualification and amount of EIC includes all wages, salaries, tips, bonuses, and any form of compensation paid for services rendered if the compensation is includible in gross income for the taxable year. Both cash and noncash forms of compensation, such as meals or housing, are included.

If an individual is self-employed, the individual's "net" self-employment income is included in determining the individual's earned income. (Note that although net self-employment income of $400 or less is exempt from self-employment income, it must be included in earned income for EIC purposes.) Earned income does not include employee compensation that is not taxable. The definition of earned income for EIC purposes excludes payments of welfare benefits, pensions, veterans' benefits, Social Security benefits, workers' compensation, unemployment compensation, and interest, dividends, or royalties. The American Taxpayer Relief Act of 2012 extends the earned income credit to December 31, 2017.

Q 2:140   Does the employer have any responsibility to notify employees of eligibility for EIC payments?

Yes. The employer must notify employees who have no income tax withheld that they may be able to claim a tax refund because of the EIC. Although employers do not have to notify employees who claim exemption from withholding on Form W-4, Employee's Withholding Allowance Certificate, the employer is encouraged to notify any employees whose wages for 2017 are less than $39,617 ($45,207 if married filing jointly) if there is one qualifying child $48,340 ($53,930) for three or more qualifying children; that they may be eligible to claim the credit for 2017. This is because eligible employees may receive a refund of the amount of EIC that is more than the tax they owe.

Copy B of the 2017 Form W-2, Wage and Tax Statement, which is the copy filed with the employee's federal tax return, has a statement about the EIC on the back. If the employer gives employees that copy by January 31, 2018, the employer does not have to give the employee any other notice about the EIC.

An employer must give a household employee a notice about the EIC only if the employer agrees to withhold federal income tax from the employee's wages but the income tax withholding tables show that no tax should be withheld.

If an employer does not give the employee copy B of the Form W-2, a notice about the EIC can instead be any of the following items:

1. A substitute Form W-2 with the same EIC information on the back of the employee's copy; that is, on copy B of the Form W-2;

2. Notice 797, Possible Federal Tax Refund Due to the Earned Income Credit (EIC) (required within one week of the receipt of the Form W-2); or

3. A written statement with the same wording as in Notice 797 (required within one week of the receipt of the Form W-2).

If Form W-2 is required but is not given on time, the employer must give the employee Notice 797 or a written statement about the 2017 EIC by January 31, 2018. If Form W-2 is not required, the employer must notify the employee by January 31, 2018. The notice may be mailed to the individual by first-class mail. The notice cannot merely be posted for all employees to see. If a substitute Form W-2 is given on time but does not have the required statement, the employer must notify the employee within one week of the date the substitute Form W-2 is given. [I.R.C. § 3507(f); Treas. Reg. § 31.6051-1(h); Pub. No. 15]

Q 2:141   Is military pay eligible for the EIC?

Yes. Furthermore, U.S. military personnel stationed on duty in a foreign country are treated as having lived in the United States. Thus, their income becomes eligible for the EIC. [I.R.C. § 32(c)(4)]

The Common Paymaster

Q 2:142   What is a common paymaster?

A common paymaster is any member of a related group of corporations that disburses wages to employees of two or more of the corporations in the group and that is responsible for keeping books and records for the payroll with respect to those employees. The common paymaster may pay concurrently employed individuals (see Q 2:143) by one combined paycheck drawn on a single bank account, or by separate paychecks drawn by the common paymaster on the accounts of one or more employing corporations. Additionally, a related group of corporations may use multiple common paymasters. For instance, a group may use a different common paymaster for certain classes of employees. [Treas. Reg. §§ 31.3121(s)-1(b)(2), 31.3306(p)-1]

Q 2:143   What is the advantage of using a common paymaster?

Using a common paymaster allows certain related corporations to avoid overpayment of FICA and FUTA. [I.R.C. §§ 3121(s), 3306(p); Treas. Reg. §§ 31.3121(s)-1(a), 31.3306(p)-1(a)]

Generally, employers cannot consider the wages paid by other employers during the calendar year for purposes of establishing if the FICA and FUTA taxable wages bases have been reached for the calendar year. "Related" corporations that "concurrently" employ an employee, however, may aggregate the wages paid to the employee for purposes of establishing the FICA and FUTA taxable wage bases if the employees of the related corporations are paid by a common paymaster. Two corporations are considered related during the calendar year if in any given calendar quarter they satisfy one of the following four conditions:

1. *Stock ownership test.* The corporations are members of a controlled group—either a parent-subsidiary group or a brother-sister group—as defined under I.R.C. Section 1563(a); or would be members of a controlled group under I.R.C. Section 1563(a) but for the exceptions relating to entities that may not be included on a consolidated return (e.g., insurance companies, foreign corporations, and exempt organizations if the "at least 80 percent" ownership requirement in I.R.C. Section 1563(a) was replaced with "more than 50 percent").

2. *Common directors test.* In the case of one corporation that does not issue stock, either 50 percent or more of the board members of one corporation are members of the other corporation's board, or the holders of 50 percent or more of the voting power to select members are concurrently the holders of more than 50 percent of that power with respect to the other corporation.

3. *Common officers test.* Fifty percent or more of one corporation's officers are concurrently officers of the other corporation.

4. *Common employees test.* Thirty percent or more of one corporation's employees are concurrently employees of the other corporation.

[Treas. Reg. §§ 31.3121(s)-1(b)(1), 31.3306(p)-1]

Concurrent employment is defined as a contemporaneous employment relationship, which is not exempt from FICA, between an individual and two or more corporations. The regulations provide that an employee must have a concurrent relationship with two or more related corporations under which he or she has agreed to provide services for the benefit of each corporation in exchange for wages that, if deductible for purposes of federal income tax, would be deductible by the employing corporation. [Treas. Reg. § 31.3121(s)-1(b)(3)]

Example 1. Steele Corporation employs individuals A, B, D, E, G, and H. Alloy Corporation employs individuals A, B, C, X, and Y. Flatiron Corporation employs individuals A, C, I, J, L, and M. Flatiron Corporation is the paymaster for all 13 individuals. The corporations have no officers or stockholders in common.

Steele Corporation and Alloy Corporation are related corporations for common paymaster purposes because at least 30 percent of Alloy's employees (i.e., A and B) are also employees of Steele's. Alloy and Flatiron are related corporations because at least 30 percent of Alloy's employees (i.e., A and C) are also employees of Flatiron. Steele and Flatiron are not related corporations, because neither corporation has 30 percent of its employees concurrently employed by the other corporation and they do not meet any of the other tests for classification as related corporations. Only A is employed by both Steele and Flatiron.

For purposes of determining the amount of the tax liability for wages paid by the common paymaster, B is treated as having one employer. C has two employers for determining Social Security taxes because, although Alloy and Flatiron are related corporations for these purposes, C is not employed by Flatiron, the common paymaster. A is also treated as having two employers because Steele and Flatiron cannot be treated as related corporations. D, E, G, H, I, J, L, M, X, and Y are not concurrently employed by two or more corporations; accordingly, common paymaster treatment for purposes of determining Social Security taxes is inapplicable to them. [Treas. Reg. § 31.3121(s)]

Example 2. Corporations Bowl, Shaker, and Roll meet the definition of related corporations for the first time on April 5, 2017 and cease to meet it on October 5, 2017. Sami is concurrently employed by Bowl, Shaker, and Roll throughout 2017. In each of the four calendar quarters of 2017, Sami's remuneration from Bowl, Shaker, and Roll is $50,000, $60,000, and $110,000, respectively. All of the remuneration to Sami from Bowl, Shaker, and Roll for the year is disbursed by Bowl, the common paymaster. Under these circumstances, the amount of wages subject to I.R.C. Sections 3102 and 3111 is as follows:

Wages Paid by Related Employers
(Wage base is $127,200 for 2017)

Calendar Quarter 2017	Bowl Inc.	Shaker Inc.	Roll Inc.
First quarter	$50,000	$60,000	$110,000
Second quarter	$50,000	$60,000	$110,000
Third quarter	$50,000	$60,000	$110,000
Fourth quarter	$50,000	$60,000	$110,000

Employer's Portion of Social Security Wages

Calendar Quarter 2017	Bowl Inc.	Shaker Inc.	Roll Inc.
First quarter	$50,000	$60,000	$110,000
Second quarter	$77,200[1]	0	0
Third quarter	0	0	0
Fourth quarter	0	$60,000[2]	$17,200[3]

---

[1] The $50,000 paid by Bowl in the first quarter is treated as being paid under a common paymaster for the second quarter. The combined wages paid in the second quarter for Bowl, Shaker, and Roll exceed the Social Security wage base. Therefore, only $77,200 ($127,200 − $50,000) is subject to Social Security tax in the second quarter.

[2] For the second and third quarters, Shaker is not liable for Social Security tax, because the tax is paid by the common paymaster. Because Shaker is not a related corporation in the fourth quarter, Shaker must pay Social Security tax on wages paid in the fourth quarter.

[3] For the second and third quarters, Roll is not liable for Social Security tax, because the tax is paid by the common paymaster. Because Roll is not a related corporation in the fourth quarter, Roll must pay Social Security tax on wages paid in the fourth quarter—up to the Social Security wage base. Roll had already paid tax on wages of $110,000 in the first quarter, so it must only include wages of $17,200 in the fourth quarter ($127,200 − $110,000).

Similar allocations apply in determining the total employer allocation for all employment taxes.

Q 2:144   Who is liable when the common paymaster does not remit the correct amount of FICA or FUTA?

If the common paymaster fails to remit FICA or FUTA (in whole or in part), it remains liable for the full amount of the unpaid portion of these taxes. In addition, each of the other related corporations using the common paymaster is jointly and severally liable for its appropriate share of these taxes. That share is determined under a formula that is based on the lesser of (1) the amount of the tax liability of the common paymaster for the employees' portion of FICA and FUTA, after taking into account any tax payments that were made, or (2) the amount of the liability for the employees' and employer's FICA and FUTA that would have existed for wages paid to the employees from the related corporation (reduced by an allocable portion of any taxes previously paid by the common paymaster for wages paid by the related corporation).

For purposes of determining the portion of taxes paid by the common paymaster to be allocated to each related employer, the amount of taxes paid is multiplied by a fraction, the numerator of which is the portion of total liability of the common paymaster under I.R.C. Section 3121(s) that is allocable to the related employer and the denominator of which is the total amount of the common paymaster's liability under Section 3121(s). The amount of these liabilities is determined by disregarding any prior tax payments. These rules apply whether or not the tax on employees was withheld from the employees' wages. [Treas. Reg. § 31.3121(s)-1(c)(2)]

Q 2:145   Can an unincorporated entity be part of a common paymaster?

No. Employees providing services to partnerships and sole proprietorships cannot be paid through a common paymaster.

Q 2:146   How are an employee's wages and taxes paid through a common paymaster reported for purposes of Form W-2?

The common paymaster (using its EIN) reports the combined wages to the SSA and the employee on one Form W-2. If a Form W-3 is sent to the SSA, the common paymaster indicates in Box h (Other EIN used this year) any other EIN it used to report wages. In addition, the common paymaster should note on Form W-3 that the wages reported are governed by Treasury Regulations Section 31.3121(s)-1.

Q 2:147   How is the liability for Social Security taxes on wages paid by a common paymaster allocated to the related employers?

Two methods of allocation are permitted under the regulations, depending on whether the related employer maintains a record of the wages paid to its employees by the common paymaster.

When the related employer maintains a record of the wages paid to its employees, the "remuneration-based allocation rules" are used; if such records are not maintained, the allocation is based on the "group-wide allocation rules." Presumably, all employers would be maintaining appropriate records. In either case, the allocations must be made with respect to each payment of wages. Employers will also follow these rules in determining the income tax deductions for employment taxes paid by the related employer. [Treas. Reg. § 31.3121(s)-1(c)(2)]

Note that when an employer is no longer treated as a related employer, no credit is given for the FICA and FUTA paid by the common paymaster unless the employer is the common paymaster. [Treas. Reg. § 31.3121(s)-1(c)(1), ex. 3]

Remuneration-based allocation rules. Under the remuneration-based method of allocation, each related employer that pays through a common paymaster is allocated a tax liability under the following formula:

$$\text{Portion of wages paid for the services provided to the related employer} \times \frac{\text{Employee's and employer's portion of Social Security taxes with respect to wages paid by common paymaster in pay period}}{\text{Total wage payment for wages paid for all related corporations using a common paymaster}}$$

The IRS may adjust the payments under this formula if the wages are inappropriate for the corporation following the principles of Treasury Regulations Section 1.482-2(b). Thus, a group of related employers may not use the common paymaster to artificially pay wages from an employer when few or no services have been provided by an individual. [Treas. Reg. § 31.3121(s)-1(c)(2)(ii)]

Group-wide allocation rules. Under the group-wide method of allocation, the IRS District Director may allocate the employee's and employer's Social Security taxes in "an appropriate manner" to a related corporation when the common paymaster fails to remit the taxes to the IRS. Allocation of liabilities in an appropriate manner varies according to the circumstances. It may be based on sales, property, corporate payroll, or any other basis that reflects the distribution of the services performed by the employee, or a combination of the foregoing bases. To the extent practicable, the IRS District Director may use the principles of Treasury Regulations Section 1.482-2(b) in making the allocations. [Treas. Reg. § 31.3121(s)-1(c)(2)(iii)]

Taxation and Reporting for the Deceased

Q 2:148   How are wages of a deceased employee treated for withholding and other employment taxes?

The federal income tax withholding, FICA, and FUTA requirements for wages paid to a deceased employee will vary depending on when the wages were paid in relation to the employee's death.

If the employee dies after receiving the paycheck but before cashing it, the employer should reissue the paycheck to the employee's beneficiary or estate. The amounts paid and taxes withheld will not change. These amounts are included in the employee's final Form W-2, Wage and Tax Statement.

If the employee dies before the wages are paid, and if the wages are paid in the calendar year of the employee's death, they are not subject to federal income tax withholding but they are subject to FICA and FUTA. The Social Security and Medicare wages are included in the deceased employee's final Form W-2, Boxes 3–6. The amount of wages subject to federal income tax is reported in Box 3 of Form 1099-MISC, Miscellaneous Income, in the name of the beneficiary of the payment.

If wages are paid after the date of death and in the calendar year following the calendar year of death, the wages are not subject to federal income tax withholding, Social Security, Medicare, or FUTA. These amounts are reported in Box 3 of Form 1099-MISC in the name of the beneficiary of the payment. [I.R.C. §§ 691(a)(1), 3121(a)(14), 3306(b)(15); Rev. Rul. 86-109, 1986-2 C.B. 196; Rev. Rul. 71-525, 1971-2 C.B. 356]

Penalty Assessment

Q 2:149   What are the penalties for failing to withhold income tax?

An employer that fails to withhold income tax is liable for the amount that it should have withheld. Additionally, the employer may be subject to a 20 percent penalty under I.R.C. Section 6662 on the income tax that should have been withheld and reported on Form 941, Employer's QUARTERLY Federal Tax Return, or Form 944, Employer's ANNUAL Federal Tax Return. I.R.C. Section 6672 imposes a 100 percent penalty on persons who are required to collect, truthfully account for, and pay over wage withholding and employment taxes and willfully fail to do so. This penalty applies to "responsible persons," that is, persons who have control over the collection and deposit of payroll taxes, such as corporate officers and agents designated by the employer.

Disregarded Entities

Q 2:150   Who is responsible for the employment tax obligations related to employees providing services to a qualified Subchapter S subsidiary or to another disregarded entity?

A qualified Subchapter S subsidiary (Qsub) is a domestic corporation that is owned 100 percent by an S corporation that elects to treat the subsidiary as a Qsub. In general, a corporation for which a Qsub election has been made is not treated as a separate corporation for federal tax purposes. It is basically disregarded; all assets, liabilities, and items of income, deduction, and credit of the Qsub are treated as assets, liabilities, and items of income, deduction, and credit of the parent S corporation. Similar rules apply to a qualified real estate investment trust subsidiary under I.R.C. Section 856(i) and to a business entity that has a single owner and is not a corporation under Treasury Regulations Section 301.7701-2(b). Such a business entity is disregarded as an entity separate from its owner for all federal tax purposes.

When a disregarded entity has employees, a question arises as to who is responsible for withholding, depositing, and reporting of federal employment taxes. In 1999, the IRS issued Notice 99-6 [1999-1 C.B. 321] stating that employment taxes for employees of a Qsub, or an entity disregarded as an entity separate from its owner under Treas. Reg. § 301.7701-2(c)(2), may be reported and paid either:

1. By the owner (as if the employees of the disregarded entity are employed directly by the owner) using the owner's name and taxpayer identification number (TIN), or

2. By each entity recognized as a separate entity under state law using the entity's own name and TIN. Under this method, the owner retains responsibility for the employment tax obligations of the disregarded entity.

On August 16, 2007, the IRS issued final regulations eliminating disregarded entity status for purposes of federal employment taxes [T.D. 9356]. The regulations require a disregarded entity to be treated as a corporation for employment tax purposes, and, accordingly, to be liable for employment taxes on wages paid to employees of the disregarded entity. Furthermore, the disregarded entity is responsible for satisfying other employment tax obligations (e.g., making timely deposits of employment taxes, filing returns, and providing wage statements to employees on Forms W-2). The owner of the disregarded entity is no longer liable for employment taxes or satisfying other employment tax obligations with respect to the employees of the disregarded entity. The disregarded entity continues to be disregarded for other federal tax purposes. The final regulations apply to wages paid on or after January 1, 2009.

For wages paid prior to January 1, 2009, the owners of disregarded entities may continue to use the procedures permitted by Notice 99-6. Notice 99-6 generally requires an employer using method 1) to continue to use method 1) unless and until otherwise permitted by the IRS. However, Notice 99-6 is modified with respect to wages paid after August 16, 2007, and before January 1, 2009, so that a taxpayer may switch from method 1) to method 2) without seeking approval from the IRS.

The final regulations also clarify that an owner of a disregarded entity treated as a sole proprietorship is subject to taxes under the Self-Employment Contributions Act (SECA) and retain the example that an individual owner of a disregarded entity continues to be treated as self-employed for SECA taxes and not as an employee of a disregarded entity for employment tax purposes. The IRS released additional guidance through Treasury Decision 9554 that clarifies the applicability of the exceptions under I.R.C. 3121(b)(3) for employers of disregarded entities.

Getting IRS Assistance

Q 2:151 How may an employer obtain additional information from the IRS on employment tax withholding?

Recorded tax information is available from Tele-Tax, a service that provides information on many personal and business federal tax topics. Callers can listen to up to three topics on each call made. Touch-tone service is available 24 hours a day, seven days a week.

Table 2-6 lists employment tax topics under this service. Select, by number, the desired topic; then call 1-800-829-4477 for recorded tax information. For the directory of topics, listen to topic 123.

Table 2-6. Tele-Tax Topics

Topic No.	Subject
751	Social Security and Medicare Withholding Rates
752	Form W-2—Where, When, and How to File
753	Form W-4—Employee's Withholding Allowance Certificate
755	Employer Identification Number (EIN)—How to Apply
756	Employment Taxes for Household Employees
757	Form 941 and Form 944—Deposit Requirements
758	Form 941—Employer's QUARTERLY Federal Tax Return and Form 944—Employer's ANNUAL Federal Tax Return
759	Form 940—Employer's Annual FUTA Tax Return—Filing and Deposit Requirements

Table 2-6.   Tele-Tax Topics (*cont'd*)

Topic No.	Subject
760	Form 943—Reporting and Deposit Requirements for Agricultural Employer
761	Tips—Withholding and Reporting
762	Independent Contractor vs. Employee
763	The Affordable Care Act
803	Waivers and Exceptions

[Pub. No. 15]

Employers can obtain 2017 information returns and employer products (e.g., Forms W-2, 940, 941, 944, 945, 1099-MISC; Publications 15 (Circular E, Employer's Tax Guide), 15-A (Employer's Supplemental Tax Guide), and 15-B (Employer's Tax Guide to Fringe Benefits)) online at www.irs.gov/businesses. Select "Online Ordering of Information Returns and Employer Returns." Employers may also request these returns and employer products via mail by completing Form 7018, Employer's Order Blank. A PDF version of Form 7018 is available at www.irs.gov, Forms and Publications. Employers can also contact their local IRS office or the national information line at 1-800-829-3676.

Other publications employers may want to obtain include: Circular A, Agricultural Employer's Tax Guide (Publication 51); IRS Publication No. 509, Tax Calendars for 2015 (or IRS Publication 1518, IRS Tax Calendar for Small Businesses and Self-Employed); IRS Publication No. 515, Withholding of Tax on Nonresident Aliens and Foreign Entities; IRS Publication No. 535, Business Expenses; IRS Publication No. 583, Starting a Business and Keeping Records; and IRS Publication No. 1635, Understanding Your EIN.

For information on tax withholding, an employer should obtain IRS Publication No. 505, Tax Withholding and Estimated Tax. Along with Form W-4, Employee's Withholding Allowance Certificate.

If you have problems that you cannot resolve with the IRS, you can reach out to the Taxpayer Advocate Service at 877-777-4778. The Taxpayer Bill of Rights outlines the rights of taxpayers. Information can be obtained at http://www.irs.gov/Advocate and irs.gov/sams.

Chapter 3

Federal Unemployment Insurance

The Federal Unemployment Tax Act (FUTA) is generally designed to coordinate with state unemployment insurance laws to provide limited benefits to employees who have lost their jobs through no fault of their own and are actively seeking employment with a new employer.

Although the employment tax laws generally classify taxable wages paid to employees in the same way for federal income tax withholding (FITW), Federal Insurance Contributions Act (FICA) taxation, and FUTA taxation, the reporting requirements for FUTA taxes differ from those for FITW and FICA. This chapter addresses the reporting and deposit rules that apply to FUTA taxes, and provides an overview of some of the variables that exist under the state unemployment insurance rules. Chapter 4 addresses reporting and deposit rules that apply to FICA taxes.

Overview

Q 3:1   What are Federal Unemployment Tax Act contributions?

The Federal Unemployment Tax Act (FUTA) taxes paid by liable private employers are used to maintain a federal program for the payment of unemployment compensation to eligible employees who have lost their jobs, or, in the case of workshare programs, have experienced a significant reduction in their hours due to the economic necessity of the employer. Government agencies and certain nonprofit organizations are exempt from FUTA tax, but are not exempt from state unemployment insurance tax. (See Q 3:18.)

The FUTA system coordinates with state unemployment systems to provide these benefits. Under the Act, the federal government pays no direct benefit payments to claimants; benefits are payable to claimants only under the unemployment compensation laws of the various states and territories. The amount of the FUTA tax due on each employee's wage is based on covered wages (up to the taxable wage limit, currently $7,000) for covered employment. Unlike the tax on a state level, the FUTA tax rate generally is a set rate of 6.0 percent, minus a 5.4 percent credit for timely paid state taxes, for a net FUTA tax rate of 0.6 percent.

Note. An exception to the 0.6 percent net rate applies to employers doing businesses within a state that has borrowed funds from the federal government in order to pay unemployment benefits and has failed to repay that loan balance by the due date. These states are referred to as credit reduction states. (See Qs 3:42–3:45 for more details.)

The requirements for payment of FUTA taxes are separate and apart from the requirements applicable to FICA (Medicare and Social Security), state unemployment, or state disability insurance taxes. [I.R.C. § 3301; Pub. No. 15]

Q 3:2   Do both the employer and employee pay FUTA taxes?

No. FUTA taxes are imposed on employers only. Under the Fair Labor Standards Act, it is unlawful for an employer to collect these taxes from employees or to withhold FUTA taxes from an employee's wages. (Note that, in some states, an employee may be required to make state unemployment insurance contributions.) FUTA taxes are imposed on any employer that during the current calendar year or preceding calendar year (1) paid wages aggregating at least $1,500 in any calendar quarter or (2) employed at least one employee for at least one day in 20 different calendar weeks. (State guidelines may vary—for example, in California, it is only necessary to have paid in excess of $100 in total wages in a calendar quarter to one or more employees to be considered an employer liable for state unemployment insurance coverage.)

Special rules apply to employers that employ agricultural labor or domestic labor (see Qs 3:21, 3:22).

Q 3:3   What is the function of the federal unemployment tax?

The FUTA tax is used to cover all of the federal and some of the state administrative costs incurred to operate the unemployment insurance system, and partially funds extended federal benefits when applicable. It does not directly fund unemployment benefit payments to claimants except in times of extreme economic hardship. State unemployment insurance contributions that are collected by the states from employers are used to pay weekly benefits.

Q 3:4   In what ways do unemployment taxes resemble insurance?

Unemployment insurance is intended to be a social insurance program—paid for by a tax on employers and, in some states, a tax on employees. To be eligible for unemployment benefits, unemployed individuals must have worked in employment covered by unemployment insurance for a specified period of time, have lost their jobs through no fault of their own (with limited exception as provided for under state law), and, with limited exception, be searching for full-time employment.

If losses (unemployment claims that are paid to employees as compensation and charged to an employer's account), including claims filed by qualified individuals who are no longer employed by the company, increase, so must payments collected to pay for them. The employer's cost may be affected by the total unemployment picture as well as by the employer's own experience (i.e., contributions paid in and benefits paid out).

Q 3:5   What are state unemployment insurance taxes?

State unemployment insurance (SUI) taxes are used solely by the state employment security agencies to pay cash benefits to eligible unemployed individuals. State employer unemployment taxes are computed as the employer's assigned tax rate times the wages paid to employees up to a "taxable wage base." The state taxable wage base varies from state to state and is established by state law either as a set amount that at least matches the federal taxable wage base of $7,000 (e.g., California at $7,000), or an amount that changes each year based on certain variables (e.g., North Carolina, calculated at $23,100 for 2017 and New York at $10,900). Washington increased the wage base to $45,000, the highest wage base of all states. State employer unemployment tax rates vary from state to state, year to year, and employer to employer, generally based on two factors: (1) the overall fiscal condition of the state's unemployment trust fund balance and (2) the employer's individual experience (benefits charged to the employer's account vs. the employer's taxable payroll for a specified period). In a few states (e.g., Alaska, New Jersey, Pennsylvania), employees also pay into the state unemployment insurance system.

Note. Practitioners frequently refer to state unemployment insurance tax using the term SUI or SUTA tax and federal unemployment insurance taxes as FUTA tax.

Employers Defined

Q 3:6   How are employers defined for purposes of paying FUTA taxes?

The definition of *employer* for FUTA tax purposes is similar to the definition for federal income tax withholding, Social Security, and Medicare taxes. The nature of the employer's business generally does not affect whether the employer must pay FUTA tax. An employer for FUTA tax purposes may be an individual, a corporation, a partnership, a trust, an estate, a joint-stock company, an association, a syndicate, joint venture, or other unincorporated organization, or a tax-exempt organization (an exception is a 501(c)(3) non-profit organization).

Each of the following employers is required to pay FUTA taxes:

1.   A nonagricultural employer that paid $1,500 or more in wages during any calendar quarter of the current calendar or preceding calendar year.

2.   A nonagricultural employer that employed at least one employee for at least part of one day in at least 20 different calendar weeks during the current calendar or preceding calendar year.

3.   An agricultural employer that during any calendar quarter in the current or preceding calendar year paid wages totaling $20,000 or more for agricultural labor.

4.   An agricultural employer that employed at least 10 employees for some part of a day in at least 20 calendar weeks in the current or preceding calendar year.

5.   An employer that paid a domestic employee at least $1,000 during any calendar quarter in the current or preceding calendar year for domestic work provided at a private home, a local college club, or a local chapter of a college fraternity or sorority. [I.R.C. § 3306(a)]

Q 3:7   What is the "1-in-20" test that is used to determine if a person or entity is an employer for FUTA tax purposes?

A person or entity is an employer under the 1-in-20 test and liable for the payment of FUTA taxes if the person or entity employs at least one individual for some portion of the day in 20 different calendar weeks. This test is applied to the current or preceding calendar year and the calendar weeks do not have to be consecutive. The test is not contingent on the employee being the same worker in each of the 20 weeks. Individuals who are on sick leave or vacation are counted as employees for this test for each week of the leave.

A *calendar week* for purposes of this test is the seven-day period beginning on Sunday and ending on Saturday, except that short weeks at the beginning and end of the calendar year are treated as full calendar weeks. A *day* is the 24 hours of a calendar day. [Rev. Rul. 91-373, 1991-2 C.B. 348; I.R.C. § 3306(a)(1); Treas. Reg. § 31.3306(a)-1; Rev. Rul. 71-87, 1971-1 C.B. 290; Rev. Rul. 71-88, 1971-1 C.B. 291]

Wages Subject to FUTA Tax

Q 3:8   Are all payments subject to FUTA tax?

In general, all payments to an employee are subject to FUTA tax unless specifically exempted under the Internal Revenue Code (I.R.C.). [I.R.C. § 3306(b); Treas. Reg. §§ 31.3306(b)(2)-1 to 31.3306(b)(10)-1] A partial listing of exemptions follows:

- Tips that are not required to be reported by an employee to an employer (generally limited to tips of less than $20 a month) [Treas. Reg. § 31.3306(b)];

- The value of group-term life insurance coverage [I.R.C. § 3306(b)(2)(C)];

- Generally, a fringe benefit meeting the requirements of I.R.C. Sections 117 and 132. [Temp. Treas. Reg. § 31.3306(b)-1T] (The basic rule is that all fringe benefits are treated as taxable compensation, unless specifically excluded from wages under I.R.C. Sections 3306(b)(1) through (b)(16).);

- Expense reimbursements meeting the requirements of I.R.C. Section 62(c) that are substantiated and paid from an accountable plan [Treas. Reg. § 31.3306(b)-2];

- Salary reductions to purchase benefits made under a Section 125 flexible benefits plan (i.e., cafeteria plan), other than elective deferrals that were used to fund a deferred compensation plan (e.g., 401(k) plan) or are to be used for adoption assistance [Treas. Reg. § 31.3306(b)(2)-1];

- Payments made to an employee by an employer on account of the employee's retirement [Treas. Reg. § 31.3306(b)(3)-1];

- Sick or disability benefits paid after a date that is more than six calendar months after the last month the employee provided services to the employer [Treas. Reg. § 31.3306(b)(4)-1];

- Payments from a qualified retirement plan [Treas. Reg. § 31.3306(b)(5)-1];

- Sickness or injury payments made under a state workers' compensation law [I.R.C. § 3306(b)(2)(A)];

- The value of excludable meals and lodging provided by the employer [Section 3306(b)(14)];

- Payment by an employer of the employee's FICA taxes [Treas. Reg. § 31.3306(b)(6)-1];

- Noncash payments to an employee for work done outside the employer's trade or business [Treas. Reg. § 31.3306(b)(7)-1];

- Payments made by an employer to an employee after the calendar month in which the employee attains age 65 and when two conditions are met: (1) the employee does no work for the employer (e.g., is on a standby basis); and (2) an employer–employee relationship exists during the period when the payment is made [Treas. Reg. § 31.3306(b)(8)-1];

- Qualified moving expense reimbursements that the employer expects the employee to deduct [Treas. Reg. § 31.3306(b)(9)-1];

- Death benefits paid to a beneficiary or retirement disability benefits paid from a retirement plan to a terminated employee. These are basically payments that would not have been paid had the employee not terminated employment [Treas. Reg. § 31.3306(b)(10)-1];

- Reimbursement for or provision of either excluded educational benefits or dependent care assistance [Treas. Reg. §§ 31.3306(b)-1(h), 31.3306(b)-2, 31.3306(b)(13)-1];

- Services of a household employee in a private home [Treas. Reg. § 31.3306(c)(2)-1(a)];

- Payment for services of a household nature performed by an employee in or about the facilities of a college club, fraternity, or sorority that do not exceed $1,000 in any calendar quarter (e.g., cooks, gardeners, housekeepers, maids, handymen) [Treas. Reg. §§ 31.3306(c)(2)-1(b), 31.3306(c)(10)-2];

- Cash payments to employees that do not exceed $50 in any calendar quarter [Treas. Reg. § 31.3306(c)(3)-1];

- Services performed by an inmate of a penal institution [I.R.C. § 3306(c)(21)];

- Noncash payments to agricultural workers [Treas. Reg. § 31.3306(k)-1(e)];

- Benefit payments made under a deferred compensation plan to the extent that the benefits were grandfathered as being exempt or were reported when vested [Treas. Reg. § 31.3306(r)(2)-1]; and

- Wages paid to a beneficiary after the calendar year of an employee's death.

In addition to the payments for services provided to an employer listed earlier, certain types of employment are exempt from FUTA tax. A partial listing is shown below. [I.R.C. §§ 3306(c), 3306(s), 3309(b), 3508; Treas. Reg. §§ 31.3306(c)(1)-1 to 31.3306(c)(18)-1]

- Services provided on a foreign ship outside the United States [Treas. Reg. § 31.3306(c)(4)-1];

- Services performed by an individual for his or her spouse in a trade or business [Treas. Reg. § 31.3306(c)(5)-1(a)(1)];

- Services provided by a father or mother in the employ of his or her child [Treas. Reg. § 31.3306(c)(5)-1(a)(2)];

- Services provided by a child under age 21 for his or her parents [Treas. Reg. § 31.3306(c)(5)-1(a)(3)];

- Services performed for a federal, state, or local government employer, including political subdivisions [Treas. Reg. §§ 31.3306(c)(6)-1, 31.3306(c)(7)-1];

- Services provided to religious, charitable, educational, and certain other nonprofit employers [Treas. Reg. §§ 31.3306(c)(8)-1, 31.3306(c)(10)-1];

- Services provided by a railroad employee for the railroad industry [Treas. Reg. § 31.3306(c)(9)-1];

- Services provided by full-time students for the school where they attend classes or for an organized camp [Treas. Reg. § 31.3306(c)(10)-2];

- Services provided by full-time students performing service for academic credit, combining instruction with work experience as an integral part of the program (unless the program was established for or on behalf of an employer or group of employers) [I.R.C. § 3306(c)(10)(C)];

- Services provided for a foreign government or an international organization (e.g., UNESCO, the United Nations) [Treas. Reg. §§ 31.3306(c)(11)-1, 31.3306(c)(16)-1, 31.3306(c)(12)-1];

- Services provided as student nurses or hospital interns [Treas. Reg. § 31.3306(c)(13)-1];

- Payments to insurance agents who receive only commissions [Treas. Reg. § 31.3306(c)(14)-1];

- Newspaper deliverers under age 18 who deliver directly to customers [Treas. Reg. § 31.3306(c)(15)-1];

- Services provided by individuals on small fishing vessels [Treas. Reg. § 31.3306(c)(17)-1];

- Services provided by certain nonresident aliens working as nonimmigrants under F, J, M, or Q visas [Treas. Reg. § 31.3306(c)(18)-1];

- Services provided by alien agricultural workers under an H-2a visa [Treas. Reg. § 31.3306(k)-1(e)];

- Services provided by an election worker [Pub. No. 15]; and

- Services provided by statutory nonemployees (direct sellers, certain newspaper deliverers of any age, and real estate agents) [I.R.C. §§ 3508(a) and 3508(b)].

Q 3:9   Is vacation or leave pay subject to FUTA tax?

Yes, vacation pay and leave pay are subject to FUTA tax at the time of payment as if they were a regular wage payment.

Special Classes of Employment

Q 3:10   Are the wages of all employees subject to FUTA tax?

No. There are several groups of workers who are classified as employees under the common-law test but whose wages nonetheless are exempt from FUTA taxation under I.R.C. Section 3306(b). In general, these include:

1. Wages paid by an employer that exceed $7,000 in the calendar year. [I.R.C. § 3306(b)(1)]

2. Certain medical payments on account of an employee's sickness or disability. [I.R.C. § 3306(b)(2)]

3. Workers' compensation benefits. [I.R.C. § 3306(b)(2)]

4. Disability payments that are made more than six months after the last calendar month the employee worked for the employer. [I.R.C. § 3306(b)(4)]

5. Benefit payments from a qualified pension or profit-sharing plan under I.R.C. Section 401(a) or from an annuity plan under I.R.C. Section 403(b). [I.R.C. § 3306(b)(5)]

6. Employer payment of the employee's portion of FICA taxes. [I.R.C. § 3306(b)(6)]

7. Noncash remuneration paid to an employee not in the course of the employer's trade or business. [I.R.C. § 3306(b)(7)]

8. Noncash remuneration paid to agricultural workers. [I.R.C. § 3306(b)(11)]

9. Benefits exempt from income taxation under I.R.C. Section 74(c), 117, 119, 127, 129, 132, or 217. [I.R.C. §§ 3302(b)(12)–3302(b)(16), 3306(b)(9)]

10. Services provided for certain federal government employees. [I.R.C. § 3306(c)(6)]

11. Services provided by employees of state governments, political subdivisions, and instrumentalities of states and political subdivisions. [I.R.C. § 3306(c)(7)]

12. Services provided by a duly ordained, commissioned, or licensed minister of a church. [I.R.C. § 3306(c)(8)]

13. Services provided by a student nurse in the employ of a hospital where the nurse is enrolled in a course of nursing study, and services provided by a medical intern who has completed four years of study at a medical school. [I.R.C. § 3306(c)(13)]

14. Services performed as an insurance agent if payment is solely through commissions. [I.R.C. § 3306(c)(14)]

15. Newspaper delivery persons under age 18 (as long as they deliver the newspapers to ultimate consumers). [I.R.C. § 3306(c)(15)]

16. Newspaper and magazine distributors working under an arrangement in which they agree to sell newspapers and magazines to ultimate consumers at a fixed price and are allowed to retain the difference between the fixed sales price and the amount charged to them for the items. [I.R.C. § 3306(c)(15)]

17. Services performed for an international organization. [I.R.C. § 3306(c)(16)]

18. Crew members on fishing boats that normally contain fewer than 10 individuals. The exemption is allowed to the extent that the crew members' remuneration is based on a prearranged percentage of the boat's catch or proceeds therefrom. [I.R.C. § 3306(c)(18)]

19. Persons engaged in catching, taking, harvesting, cultivating, or farming any kind of aquatic form of animal or vegetable life. The exemption does not apply to persons engaged in catching or taking salmon or halibut for commercial purposes or to persons employed in connection with a vessel of more than 10 net tons. [I.R.C. § 3306(c)(17)]

20. Services performed by a full-time student or the employee of an organized summer camp. [I.R.C. § 3306(c)(20)]

21. Wages paid to a member of a Native American tribe relating to income derived by Native Americans from exercise of fishing rights. [I.R.C. § 7873]

22. Employer contributions to a Health Savings Account (which is part of an I.R.C. Section 125 cafeteria plan arrangement), whether direct or via pretax salary reductions if the employer reasonably believes the employee will be able to exclude the HSA contribution from income, the employee and employer contributions are not subject to federal income tax withholding, FICA, or FUTA taxes.

On November 17, 2016, the U.S. Department of Labor issued Unemployment Insurance Program Letter No. 02-17, containing changes to the North American Industry Classification Codes for Calendar Year 2017, for use by state workforce agencies that have a potential effect of unemployment insurance benefits.

Q 3:11   Are wages paid to a child by his or her parent subject to FUTA tax?

Payments for the services of a child under the age of 21 working for his or her parent, whether or not in a trade or business, are not subject to FUTA tax. These rules apply even if the child is paid regular wages. Note that although these wages are not subject to FUTA tax, other taxes may apply, such as federal and state income tax withholding.

Q 3:12   Are wages paid to an individual who is employed by his or her spouse subject to FUTA tax?

No. Wages for the services of an individual who works for his or her spouse in a trade or business are not subject to FUTA tax. Also, the services of an individual employed by his or her spouse in other than a trade or business, such as for domestic service in a private home, are not subject to FUTA tax. [Pub. No. 15]

Q 3:13   Are wages paid to family members ever subject to FUTA tax?

Wages for the services of a child or spouse are subject to FUTA tax if he or she works for (1) a corporation, even if it is controlled by his or her parent or spouse; (2) a partnership, even if the child's parent is a partner, unless each partner is a parent of the child; (3) a partnership, even if the individual's spouse is a partner; or (4) an estate of a deceased parent. [Pub. No. 15]

Q 3:14　Are there any exemptions from FUTA tax for wages paid to students?

Wages paid to students who are working at a school, college, or university at which they are enrolled and regularly attending classes are exempt from FUTA tax. Wages paid to students, scholars, trainees, teachers, etc. who qualify as nonimmigrant aliens under Section 101(a)(15)(F), (J), (M), or (Q) of the Immigration and Nationality Act (holding F-1, J-1, M-1, or Q-1 visas) are also exempt from FUTA tax. (FUTA tax may apply, however, if the employee becomes a resident alien.) Also, services provided by full-time students performing service for academic credit, combining instruction with work experience as an integral part of the program, are exempt from FUTA tax unless the program was established for or on behalf of an employer or group of employers.

Q 3:15　Is there an exemption from FUTA tax for wages paid to a student's spouse?

Wages paid by an educational institution to the spouse of a student who is enrolled and regularly attending classes at the institution are exempt from FUTA tax if the spouse/employee is advised at the time services are performed that the employment relates to a program to provide financial assistance to the student/spouse and the employment is not covered by any unemployment insurance.

Q 3:16　Is there an exemption from FUTA tax for wages paid by an organized camp to full-time students?

Wages paid by an organized camp to full-time students employed for fewer than 13 calendar weeks by the camp are exempt from FUTA tax if the camp (1) did not operate for more than seven months in the current or preceding calendar year or (2) had average gross receipts for any six months in the preceding calendar year that were not more than 33³/₁ percent of its average gross receipts for the other six months. [I.R.C. § 3306(c)(20)]

Q 3:17　Is there an exemption from FUTA tax for wages paid to a student nurse?

Wages paid to student nurses in the employ of a hospital or nurses' training school, who are enrolled and regularly attending classes at a nurses' training school chartered or approved under state law, are exempt from FUTA tax. [I.R.C. §§ 3121(b)(13), 3306(c)(13)]

Q 3:18　What special rules apply to the FUTA tax coverage of employees of religious organizations?

Some religious organizations, such as I.R.C. Section 501(c)(3) organizations, are exempt from FUTA tax. Note, however, these organizations are not exempt from SUI tax. Section 501(c)(3) organizations may choose to pay SUI tax in the same manner as private employers or may elect instead to reimburse the state unemployment trust fund dollar-for-dollar for the unemployment benefits paid to former employees.

Q 3:19   Are there special FUTA tax rules for wages paid to patients by hospitals (both profit and nonprofit)?

Wages paid by hospitals to patients are exempt from FUTA tax (regardless of whether the hospital is a nonprofit institution).

Q 3:20   Does FUTA tax apply to wages paid to nonresident aliens?

In general, wages paid to nonresident aliens who are performing services within the United States are subject to FUTA tax. See IRS Publication No. 515, Withholding of Tax on Nonresident Aliens and Foreign Entities, and IRS Publication No. 519, U.S. Tax Guide for Aliens, for exceptions to this general rule. [Pub. No. 15]

Q 3:21   Are wages paid to agricultural employees subject to FUTA tax?

The definition of agricultural labor that appears in the FICA coverage rules of the I.R.C. applies for FUTA tax coverage as well.

Noncash wages of agricultural laborers are exempt from FUTA tax. The cash wages of an agricultural laborer are exempt from FUTA tax if (1) the employer paid cash remuneration of less than $20,000 collectively to agricultural laborers during every calendar quarter in the current and preceding calendar years and (2) the employer did not employ 10 or more agricultural laborers during at least one day in 20 different weeks during the current and preceding calendar years.

When an employer pays the employee's portion of Social Security and Medicare taxes and/or the employee's portion of state unemployment taxes (in the few states that require employees to pay SUI tax) for an agricultural laborer without deducting these taxes from the worker's wages, the tax payments constitute additional compensation. However, this additional compensation is not subject to FUTA tax.

Special rules apply to wages of certain agricultural workers that are subject to FUTA tax that generally do not apply to other employees; only those wages subject to Social Security and Medicare taxes are subject to FUTA tax. In general, that means that if a cash payment triggers Social Security and Medicare coverage for agricultural labor, it will be subject to FUTA tax. FUTA tax applies to cash wages paid to agricultural employees, provided the employer meets minimum coverage thresholds.

Q 3:22   Are there special rules for FUTA tax on wages paid to household workers?

Yes. Noncash wages paid to a household worker in a private home are not subject to FUTA tax. Noncash wages paid to a household worker in a local college club or local chapter of a college fraternity or sorority are not exempt from FUTA tax unless another exemption applies. An employer need not pay FUTA tax on the cash wages of household workers in a private home, local college club, or local chapter of a college fraternity or sorority unless the employer paid cash wages of $1,000 or more to individuals performing such work in any calendar quarter during the current or preceding calendar year. Cash wages of a student performing household services for a local college club or local chapter of a college fraternity or sorority are exempt from FUTA tax regardless of the amount if the student is enrolled and regularly attending classes at the educational institution. However, cash wages paid to all other household workers are subject to FUTA tax if equal to or more than $1,000 in any calendar quarter of the current and preceding calendar years. (The $1,000 limitation was indexed beginning in 1996, but has not since increased.)

If an employer pays the employee's FICA and/or employee's SUI tax (employees pay a SUI tax in Alaska, New Jersey, and Pennsylvania) for a household worker employed in a private home without deducting these taxes from the worker's wages, the tax payments constitute additional compensation. [I.R.C. § 3121(a)(6); Pub. No. 926]

See Q 3:61 for reporting requirements for FUTA taxes paid on household employees' wages.

Calculating FUTA Tax

Q 3:23   How is FUTA tax determined?

FUTA tax is computed by applying a 6.0 percent rate to the taxable wage base of $7,000 and deducting any allowable credits; however, the credits cannot reduce the effective tax rate below 0.6 percent of the taxable wage base. Thus, the maximum annual FUTA tax liability with respect to an employee who is paid at least $7,000 during the year is $420, and the minimum liability is $42. (The taxable wage base does not include accrued but unpaid wages.)

Q 3:24   How does the FUTA tax credit work?

The FUTA tax credit is calculated in two parts. The first is based on the difference between the rate the employer pays to the state and the federal maximum credit rate of 5.4 percent, and the second is based on dollar amounts paid to the state on a timely basis. A 100 percent credit is allowed on the taxes paid by the due date of the federal unemployment tax form (see Q 3:56) up to the 5.4 percent maximum allowable credit. A 90 percent credit is allowed on the taxes paid after the due date. [I.R.C. § 3302(a)(3)]

Example 1. Brackman Book's SUI tax rate for 2017 is 5.4 percent, and its state unemployment tax liability for 2017 is $175,000. Brackman Book pays $148,750 (85 percent) by February 1, 2018 and $26,250 a week later.

Brackman Book's credit against its FUTA tax liability for 2017 is 100 percent of the amounts deposited by January 31, 2018 and 90 percent of the amounts deposited after January 31: (100% × $148,750 + (90% × $26,250)), or $172,375.

Note that when an employer pays SUI tax at a rate of less than 5.4 percent, an additional credit is given for the difference between what the employer pays and the 5.4 percent FUTA tax credit.

Example 2. Starburst, Inc. employs 725 employees and pays SUI at a tax rate of 4.2 percent for 2017. Starburst, Inc. is given an additional FUTA tax credit of 1.2 percent (5.4 percent less 4.2 percent). This additional credit is available regardless of the timeliness of the state deposits. If Starburst, Inc.'s payroll subject to federal unemployment tax is $880,000, the potential additional credit is $10,560 ($880,000 × 1.2%).

Starburst, Inc. pays 80 percent of its 2017 state unemployment tax obligation by January 31, 2018 and the remaining 20 percent after February 1 but prior to the filing of its Form 940. Starburst, Inc.'s state tax liability for 2017 is $36,960 ($880,000 × 4.2%). Starburst, Inc.'s FUTA tax liability is calculated as follows:

Total FUTA tax liability ($880,000 × 6.0%)	$52,800
Credit for difference in federal and state rates (5.4% – 4.2% = 1.2% × $880,000)	$10,560
Credit for State unemployment taxes:	
Paid by February 1, 2017 ($880,000 × 80% × 4.2% = $29,568 × 100%)	29,568
Paid after February 1, 2017, but before the filing of Form 940 ($880,000 × 20% × 4.2% = $7,392 × 90%)	6,652.80
Total credit	46,780.80
Total FUTA taxes due	$6,019.20

If Starburst, Inc. had paid 100 percent of its SUI contributions on time, the FUTA tax due would have been $5,280 ($880,000 × 0.006). However, since $7,392 ($880,000 × 20% × 4.2%) was not paid timely, the FUTA tax credit is reduced by $739.20 ($7,392 – ($7,392 × 90%)). Consequently, Starburst, Inc.'s FUTA tax liability is $6,019.20 ($5,280 + $739.20) instead of $5,280.

An employer will also lose all or a portion of its FUTA tax credit if any or all of its federal taxable wages were not considered taxable by state law. See Q 3:34 for more details.

Also, in order for employers within a particular state to receive the full 5.4 percent credit, the state: (1) must meet certain certification requirements (e.g., state law must provide for a maximum computed SUI tax rate of at least 5.4 percent), and (2) must have repaid any outstanding federal unemployment loan within two years. For example, for calendar year 2016 there were two jurisdictions in which employers received a credit reduction because those states failed to timely repay their federal loans. (See Qs 3:27 and 3:42 for more details.)

Q 3:25   Is the FUTA tax credit available to employers that elect state coverage?

An employer that is not subject to a state's unemployment law can elect to become subject to it under certain conditions. Once an employer elects to be subject, the required contributions it pays to the state unemployment insurance fund can be credited against FUTA tax. [Rev. Rul. 72-185, 1972-1 C.B. 327; Rev. Rul. 69-356, 1969-1 C.B. 270]

Q 3:26   Is a FUTA tax credit available for SUI tax paid by employees?

No. Only a few states (i.e., Alaska, New Jersey, and Pennsylvania) currently require that employees pay SUI tax. FUTA tax cannot be charged to the employee, and there is no FUTA tax credit available to the employer for any SUI tax paid by employees.

Q 3:27   What are the requirements to receive a FUTA tax credit for SUI tax payments?

An employer may receive up to a 5.4 percent FUTA tax credit for taxes paid to state unemployment funds if:

1. The employer submits all required forms and pays all state unemployment compensation taxes by the Form 940 deadline;

2. The state unemployment compensation program is certified by the federal government; and

3. The state has repaid any unemployment loans or interest owed to the federal government within two years.

Employers that pay their state unemployment taxes on time can receive a 90 percent offset credit on the permanent portion of the federal rate (i.e., 6.0% × 0.9 = 5.4%). In short, employers typically pay the federal system $42 per employee (0.6 percent times the $7,000 wage base). An employer is allowed to take the full 5.4 percent credit for the first three FUTA tax deposits of the year. Adjustments, if necessary, are made with the final fourth quarter FUTA tax deposit or with the annual Form 940 (see Q 3:54). Most employers do not pay the full 6.0 or 6.2 percent because they receive a credit of up to 5.4 percent for the full and timely payment of SUI contributions. Note that only the first $7,000 of wages is subject to FUTA tax. States may impose SUI tax on a larger amount. Companies often make the error of directly transferring state taxable payroll figures to Form 940, Employer's Annual Federal Unemployment (FUTA) Tax Return. This effectively over-reports the taxable payroll for FUTA tax purposes if the state has a SUI taxable wage base in excess of the $7,000 federal limit. When this occurs, the employer can apply for a credit or refund of the FUTA overpayment, but only for as far back as three years. [I.R.C. § 3302(a); Treas. Reg. § 31.3302(a)-1]

Example. During the calendar year 2017, Hanson Electric, Inc. employs Jeff in the State of Washington and pays him a salary of $78,000 a year. The 2017 taxable wage base in Washington is $45,000, and Hanson Electric's 2017 state unemployment tax rate is 4.2 percent. Hanson Electric will report $45,000 of Jeff's salary to the State of Washington as taxable wages and pay state unemployment taxes on these wages of $1,890. Hanson Electric will report $7,000 of Jeff's salary as FUTA taxable wages and pay FUTA taxes of $42. (Jeff's wages will exceed $7,000 in first quarter at a net FUTA tax rate of 0.6 percent (6.0% − 5.4% FUTA tax credit).)

Q 3:28   How does the credit against FUTA tax apply if the employer is exempt from state unemployment insurance?

There is no credit available for FUTA tax when the employer is exempt from state unemployment insurance. Such an employer pays the full 6.0 percent of each employee's compensation up to $7,000. [I.R.C. § 3303]

Q 3:29   How do state unemployment taxes differ?

Each state may establish a tax structure, qualification requirements, benefit levels, and disqualification criteria that conform to federal requirements. Federal law generally requires states to:

1. Deposit collected taxes into the unemployment trust fund of the U.S. Treasury upon receipt;

2. Maintain an account in the Unemployment Trust Fund; and

3. Allow reduced rates to employers based on their unemployment experience.

State laws generally differ in the way they apply to the following concerns:

1. Definition of employer (e.g., nonprofit and government);

2. Definition of worker (e.g., domestic or agricultural);

3. Minimum number of workers/amount of wages that establishes liability;

4. The computation method for contribution rates and taxable wage base (meeting basic federal requirements);

5. When an unemployed individual may become eligible for benefits;

6. The level of benefits and how long they are payable; and

7. Events that may result in disqualification of eligibility for benefits.

[For detailed information, see *2017 Multistate Payroll Guide* (Wolters Kluwer, 2017).]

Q 3:30　May an employer reduce its FUTA tax liability by paying into a state unemployment fund?

Yes. An employer may reduce its FUTA tax liability by obtaining a credit equal to taxes paid to a state unemployment fund. If an employer pays the state taxes by the last day for filing its annual federal unemployment tax return (generally January 31 of the succeeding calendar year, or February 10 if the employer timely deposited its full FUTA tax liabilities), the maximum credit allowed is 90 percent of the permanent FUTA tax rate (i.e., 90 percent of the permanent 6.0 percent tax to equal a maximum credit of 5.4 percent). If it pays the state taxes after the due date of the annual federal unemployment tax return, the maximum credit is 90 percent of the credit it would have been entitled to had it paid the taxes by the due date. In certain circumstances an extension to file Form 940 can be requested and granted. Then the due date for paying the state taxes and obtaining the FUTA tax credit is the extended due date. [Treas. Reg. §§ 31.3302(a)-1(c)(2), 31.3302(a)-1(c)(3); I.R.C. § 3302(a)(3)]

Q 3:31　Is the $7,000 FUTA taxable wage limit applied to each employer of the employee?

Yes. If an employee works for two or more employers in the same calendar year, each employer will be required to pay FUTA tax on the first $7,000 it pays to the employee.

However, when the employers are related, the employer may establish a common paymaster agreement. With a common paymaster, one employer makes the payroll for employees who work for two or more related employers. In this way, the $7,000 federal wage cap is applied only once. (Note that strict requirements apply in using the common paymaster approach.) [I.R.C. § 3306(p); Treas. Reg. § 31.3306(p)-1]

Note. While some states may follow federal guidelines when it comes to common paymaster situations, others do not recognize the common paymaster as the sole employer for SUI tax purposes. If the state does not recognize the common paymaster arrangement, each employer that is part of the common paymaster arrangement must pay SUI tax on the wages paid by that employer up to the state's SUI taxable wage base.

See chapter 12 for details about how the annual wage cap is applied when a merger or acquisition takes place.

Q 3:32　What is a successor employer for FUTA tax purposes?

A successor employer is an employer that acquired a unit of an employer's trade or business or all or most of the property used in the trade or business of another employer, and immediately after the acquisition employs one or more individuals who were employed by the previous owner immediately before the acquisition.

A successor employer may be eligible for a credit based on the federal and state unemployment contributions paid by the previous employer.

See Q 3:33 and chapter 12 for more details.

Q 3:33   May a successor employer use state unemployment tax credits of a prior employer?

For FUTA tax credit purposes (see Q 3:34), the SUI contributions paid by the predecessor employer may be claimed by the successor employer in the calendar year that it acquired substantially all of the property used in a trade or business of the predecessor employer, or that was used in a separately identifiable segment of the business of the predecessor employer. Additionally, the successor employer must, immediately after the acquisition, employ in its trade or business one or more individuals who immediately before the acquisition were employed in the trade or business of the predecessor employer. If, however, the predecessor employer paid wages that are subject to SUI tax to any employee who was not employed by the successor employer immediately after the acquisition, the successor is permitted only a ratable portion of the predecessor's credit. Moreover, the predecessor employer must not be subject to FUTA tax for any employee for the calendar year after the acquisition. [Treas. Reg. § 31.3306(b)-1(b); Rev. Rul. 54-313, 1954-2 C.B. 371]

See chapter 12 for more details.

Q 3:34   Does the FUTA tax credit apply against wages exempt from SUI tax, but not exempt from FUTA tax?

No. An employer will lose the FUTA tax credit for the portion of federal taxable wages that were not considered taxable by state law. For example, if the state's unemployment law excludes from the definition of wages those payments made to a company's corporate officers, the federal unemployment taxes associated with these wages are not eligible for the 5.4 percent credit because payments to corporate officers were exempt from SUI tax. In this case, the employer must pay FUTA tax at the full 6.0 percent on the corporate officer's wages.

Q 3:35   To which state is SUI tax paid?

In general, SUI tax is paid to the state in which the employee works. Therefore, if an employee lives and works in different states, SUI tax is paid to the work state and not the resident state.

If an employee works in more than one state, four factors are used to determine which state has jurisdiction over the employee for SUI tax purposes:

1. *Localized services.* An employee whose services are localized within one state is subject to the unemployment insurance laws of that state.

An employee's services are localized within one state when the employee performs services outside the state that are incidental to the services performed in the state.

2. *Base of operations.* An employee whose services are not localized within one state generally comes under the jurisdiction of the state that contains the base of operations for the employee. A base of operations typically is the location where the employee reports to work; has an office; receives mail, phone messages, and supplies; or receives instructions from the employer.

3. *Base of direction or control.* If the first two factors do not determine which state has jurisdiction for unemployment insurance purposes, the employer's "place of direction or control" will be the jurisdiction for determining taxes. An employer's place of direction or control exists in the state where the employer exercises, or has the right to exert, control over the services performed by the employee.

4. *Employee's state of residence.* Where none of the first three factors applies, the state where the employee has a permanent residence has jurisdiction over the employee for unemployment insurance purposes if the employee works in that state.

[Rev. Rul. 79-391, 1979-2 C.B. 352]

Controlling Unemployment Costs

Q 3:36   What can an employer do to control its unemployment costs?

There are several recommended ways to control unemployment tax costs:

1. Submit the quarterly SUI contribution and wage reports and pay the associated taxes in a timely manner. Failure to do so may result in the assessment of penalties and interest, loss of unemployment tax credit to the employer's account, and in many states the assignment of a "penalty rate," which is often the highest assignable SUI tax rate for the calendar year.

2. Respond to any unemployment benefit claim notice or request for separation information timely and fully. Be sure to report all payments made to employees upon separation from employment, such as vacation pay, severance pay, retirement or pension payments, etc. Failure to provide full and accurate information regarding an individual's separation from employment on a timely basis may result in unwarranted benefits charged against the employer's account, and the potential for an increase in the future SUI tax rate.

3. If the individual's separation from employment was due to misconduct, or the individual voluntarily resigned, respond to any unemployment claim notice with complete details regarding the reason for separation.

Provide documentation, such as copies of written warnings, letters of resignation, etc. Be prepared to attend an appeal hearing to present factual information and evidence. A company representative with first-hand knowledge of the reason the individual separated from employment should attend the hearing.

4. Offer job openings to qualified ex-employees in good standing with the company. Should an ex-employee refuse a job offer, report the refusal to the appropriate state employment security office.

5. Thoroughly review UI benefit charge statements, usually issued by state employment security agencies on a quarterly basis, for accuracy. Protest any discrepancies within the time limits provided for in state law or regulations.

6. Review annual SUI tax rate notices for accuracy. Protest any discrepancies within the time limits provided for in state law or regulations.

There also are three common methods to reduce an employer's unemployment tax rate that are permitted by various states. These are voluntary contributions (26 states follow this approach), joint or common rate accounts (12 states use this method), and transfers of experience (this may be mandatory or optional depending on the state). For more details on these methods, see Qs 3:37–3:40.

Q 3:37 How does paying voluntary contributions work to lower the SUI tax rate?

Twenty-six states allow employers, generally within 30 days of when the SUI tax rates are released each year, to make direct payments into their SUI tax reserve accounts (or, in a few benefit ratio states, reduce state unemployment insurance benefit charges) in addition to their ordinary tax payments. This has the effect of increasing the ratio of reserves to payroll, and can instantaneously lower the company's SUI tax rate.

Generally, such payments are warranted only when the company's ratio of reserves to payroll is near the threshold of the next lower rate bracket on the rating schedule, and then only when the company's payroll is expected to remain relatively stable or to increase. Thus, the additional contributions can serve to move the employer's ratio to a point where a lower rate applies. This approach should be carefully examined because such contributions may not always be desirable. The additional contributions may exceed the benefit of the lower rate. Caution should be taken in calculating the voluntary contribution amount and profitability. In many states, the voluntary contribution is considered to be "irrevocable," meaning that once the state receives the employer's check, the payment is nonrefundable—even if the desired rate reduction is not achieved.

In states using the benefit ratio method, voluntary contributions can be a benefit where payrolls are increasing.

The 26 states that currently have provisions for voluntary contributions are Arizona, Arkansas, Colorado, Georgia, Indiana, Kansas, Kentucky, Louisiana, Maine, Massachusetts, Michigan, Minnesota, Missouri, Nebraska, New Jersey, New Mexico, New York, North Carolina, North Dakota, Ohio, Pennsylvania, South Dakota, Texas, Washington, West Virginia, and Wisconsin. California permits voluntary contributions if Schedule E or F is not in effect. Schedule F + is in effect for 2017. Consequently, California voluntary SUI contributions are not permitted for 2017.

Q 3:38   Does the FUTA tax credit apply to voluntary contributions?

No, employers should not include voluntary contributions when calculating the FUTA tax credit employers receive for timely paid state unemployment taxes. An employer receives credit for federal unemployment tax purposes only for those state unemployment taxes (often referred to as contributions) that are required to be paid into the state's unemployment trust fund. This does not include:

- Any unemployment taxes withheld from employees (e.g., in the states of Alaska, New Jersey, and Pennsylvania);
- Penalties or interest charges;
- Voluntary contributions generally made by the employer to reduce its assigned unemployment tax rate; or
- Special surcharges, administrative taxes, or other amounts at times paid with the state quarterly unemployment taxes, but used for purposes other than to pay for unemployment benefits (usually shown separately on the quarterly tax return).

Q 3:39   How may an employer's SUI tax rate be lowered through joint accounts?

Some states give employers the option to establish joint accounts. Under this technique, experience-rated employers can potentially lower their SUI tax rates by merging their individual accounts, for rating purposes only, into a single account. This method can benefit related employers where some have a high SUI tax rate and others have a significantly lower SUI tax rate, but should be elected as an option only when the average SUI tax rate for the combined group is reduced.

When possible, the particular grouping of entities should be examined at the expiration of the applicable joint account election (e.g., at the close of the calendar year) because the process may not always be or always continue to be advantageous. If, for example, one of the grouped entities has had a catastrophic claims year, it would be prudent to exclude it from the grouping for the subsequent joint account election period. As previously alluded to, not all states allow for a single-year joint account election, and this should be taken into account before making a joint account election. For instance, if the state requires that the grouping remain in place for a period of longer than one year, the risk in keeping the accounts linked may be too great to justify any savings in the early period of the election. For all of these reasons, a careful review of a particular state's joint rating requirements should be evaluated, including who can form a joint account, how long the account must be maintained, when withdrawals are permitted, and which accounts should be linked.

Currently 12 states permit joint accounts: Arizona, Arkansas, California, Connecticut, Delaware, Hawaii, Missouri, New Jersey, New York, Ohio, South Carolina, and West Virginia.

Q 3:40   Are there other incentives for employers to make voluntary contributions?

Several states have implemented legislation that addresses the employers' negative account balances. In Arkansas, for example, a surtax imposed on employers with a negative account balance is reduced when the employers make voluntary contributions. In New York, the negative balance is involuntarily eliminated when in excess of 21 percent, while Pennsylvania allows the employers to elect to reduce the negative balance when voluntary contributions are made.

Employers in Kansas with a negative account balance are assigned a maximum rate of 5.4 percent and will be subject to a surcharge from 0.2 percent to a maximum of 2.2 percent. For 2017 the range for an employer with a negative balance could reach 5.6 percent to 7.6 percent.

Q 3:41   How do transfers of experience operate to lower an employer's unemployment tax rate?

State unemployment laws and regulations vary in their treatment of an acquisition of part or substantially all of one company (the predecessor) by another unrelated company (the successor). In some states, the successor employer is required to assume the SUI rating experience of the predecessor employer, whether or not that transfer of experience is beneficial to the successor. In other states, the successor employer may have the option to decline the transfer of the predecessor's SUI rating experience. In the case of an already liable successor employer assigned a low SUI experience rate, choosing not to transfer the predecessor's SUI rating experience may prove to be the best option. However, a newly liable successor employer may decide to request the transfer of experience from the predecessor's account rather than be assigned a higher rate that applies to new employers in the state. In some states, a partial transfer of experience is not allowed, while a total transfer of experience may be allowed (or required). Careful consideration must be made before requesting a transfer of experience in the optional states—once the successor employer requests the transfer of experience, the transfer typically cannot be rescinded.

A successor employer that makes an acquisition mid-year must also consider the SUI taxable wages already reported by the predecessor to the SUI agency for the predecessor's employees. Typically, if the predecessor's experience is transferred to the successor, the successor employer may carry over the transferring employees' SUI taxable wages that were already reported for the year, thereby avoiding starting over on the calculation of the acquired employees' SUI taxable wages. However, if a transfer of experience does not occur, the successor employer must typically pay SUI tax on all SUI taxable wages it pays to the transferred employees after the date of acquisition.

The SUTA Dumping Prevention Act of 2004 required states to amend their unemployment laws by January 1, 2006 and create regulations to require a transfer of experience, whether partial or total, when "common ownership" exists between the predecessor and successor employers. This was to eliminate a practice known as "SUTA dumping," also referred to as state unemployment tax avoidance. SUTA dumping is a tax evasion scheme involving the manipulation of an employer's SUI tax rate to achieve a lower rate, and thereby pay less SUI tax. SUTA dumping could be accomplished through a variety of methods, such as transfers of workforce and payroll, restructuring, acquisitions, mergers, and shell transactions, all decided with the primary purpose of lowering the SUI tax rate. Great care should be taken with mergers and acquisition. See discussions in chapter 12 on SUTA Dumping.

Title XII Loan

Q 3:42 What is the FUTA credit reduction for Title XII loan repayments?

The Title XII loan program provides that the federal government can lend to states' funds to continue their unemployment programs when they are experiencing financial difficulties as defined under Title XII of the Social Security Act. These loans are to be used to continue payment of state unemployment benefits after a state's funds have been exhausted. If a state defaults on the repayment of the federal loan, the 5.4 percent credit available to employers in that state is reduced, thereby increasing the employer's FUTA tax liability. The extra FUTA taxes paid by the employers in the credit reduction state go toward reducing the state's outstanding Title XII loan balance.

The FUTA tax credit reduction that applies to employers in a Title XII loan default state is equal to 0.3 percent of the FUTA taxable wages for that state paid beginning with the second consecutive January 1 in which the federal loan has not been repaid. For each succeeding year in which there is an unpaid balance, the credit is reduced by an additional 0.3 percent. The credit reduction for each state appears on Form 940. An additional credit reduction for a taxable year beginning with the third or fourth consecutive year in which advances have not been repaid can be applied. The amount of the reduction is determined by multiplying the wages paid by the employer in the state by the average employer contribution rate for that state in the immediately preceding tax year that exceeds 2.7 percent. On the fifth or any succeeding consecutive January 1 in which there remains an outstanding balance, additional credit reductions, called the BCR add-on, equal to 0.5 percent, may be assessed. A state may apply for a waiver of the BCR add-on.

States with outstanding Title XII loans may qualify for a limit or cap on their credit reduction if the state fund meets certain solvency requirements to be determined by the U.S. Department of Labor.

As of November 10, 2016, two jurisdictions had not repaid their outstanding loans to the federal government. The credit reduction jurisdictions for 2016 whose employers had to pay a FUTA tax of 1.8 percent were California and Virgin Islands. Employers in the credit reduction states, as well as employers that are required to pay state unemployment taxes in multiple states, are required to complete Schedule A of Form 940.

Q 3:43 What is the impact of interest on federal loans to states and employers?

The states are charged interest on federal loans. The rate of interest charged in any year is the same as that paid by the federal government on balances in state unemployment trust funds for the quarter ending December 31 of the preceding year but not greater than 10 percent annually. If a state repays its federal loan by September 30 of the calendar year in which the loan was received, there is no interest charged. The only condition attached to the no-interest charge is that no additional advances be received during the period remaining in the calendar year following the repayment. Interest, if any, is payable on the last day of the fiscal year in which the state took receipt of the federal loan.

In order to pay the interest owed to the federal government, the state will levy against its employers an additional assessment or surcharge for each calendar year that the state continues to owe on the federal loan. The annual assessment is typically calculated as a percentage of the employers' SUI taxable wages.

Q 3:44 What happens if there is a failure to pay interest when due?

States are required to pay interest when due. If interest is not paid when due, federal unemployment compensation is withheld and the state's unemployment compensation is not certified; this will result in employers in that state losing their eligibility for the full 5.4 percent FUTA tax credit. This is a rare occurrence.

Q 3:45 Is the FUTA tax credit available if the employer pays state unemployment taxes to the wrong state?

Yes. As long as the employer makes a timely payment of its SUI contributions, the credit is available. As a result, if it is later found that the employer made a SUI tax payment to the wrong state, the federal credit is still available to the extent the correct amount of tax was paid to the wrong state. [Treas. Reg. § 31.3302(a)-1(c)(4)]

Paying FUTA Taxes

Q 3:46　How is the amount of FUTA tax to deposit during the calendar year computed?

For deposit purposes, FUTA tax is figured quarterly. The FUTA tax liability is computed by multiplying the amount of FUTA taxable wages paid during the quarter by the applicable FUTA rate. This computation is used only on the first $7,000 of taxable wages per employee for that calendar year. Once an employee's wages exceed $7,000 from a single employer, those wages in excess of $7,000 are not subject to FUTA tax.

If an employer's FUTA tax liability for the quarter is $500 or less, the employer does not have to make a FUTA tax deposit. Instead, the liability is carried over to the next quarter for purposes of determining if the $500 threshold has been exceeded and a payment requirement applies. If at the end of the first, second, or third quarter, the unpaid annual FUTA tax liability is $500 or less, a deposit need not be made. The balance as of December 31 must be paid no later than January 31 of the following year. Total annual liabilities of $500 or less can be paid with the Form 940. [I.R.C. § 7503; Treas. Reg. §§ 31.6071(c)-1, 31.6302(c)-3; Pub. No. 15]

Q 3:47　How is FUTA tax deposited?

FUTA tax is deposited through the EFTPS. The Federal Tax Deposit Coupon, Form 8109 is no longer accepted. See Q 3:50 [Treas. Reg. Section 31.6302(c)-3(b)]

Q 3:48　How do you pay the balance due for Form 940 that exceeds $500?

A balance due for Form 940 that is greater than $500 must be electronically deposited. If the balance due were $500 or less, the employer may pay the balance due by credit or debit card or by check. [Pub. No. 15]

Q 3:49　To whom is the check or money order made out when FUTA tax is paid?

On balance due payments of $500 or less made with Form 940, employers make the check or money order payable to the United States Treasury. Employers should write their EIN, "Form 940," and the tax year to which the payment applies on the check or money order enclosed with the Form 940-V. This helps ensure proper crediting of the employer's account. Employers should enter the amount of the payment on the Form 940-V payment voucher included with the Form 940. If the employer information is not preprinted on the payment voucher, employers should enter the requested information. [Rev. Rul. 72-1, 1972-1 C.B. 327; Rev. Rul. 69-356, 1969-1 C.B. 270; Pub. No. 15]

Q 3:50   When is electronic deposit of FUTA tax required?

An employer's total deposits for Social Security, Medicare, railroad retirement, withheld income taxes, excise tax, and corporate income tax must be paid by electronic funds transfer for all such payments. Form 8109 and 8109-B, Federal Tax Deposit Coupon, was discontinued after December 31, 2010. Employers have the option of enrolling in the EFTPS, Electronic Federal Tax Payment Service or using their financial institution, service provider or trusted third-party to make the transmission. There is no charge to use EFPTS but financial institutions, service providers, and third-party providers generally will charge a fee.

The Electronic Federal Tax Payment System (EFTPS) offers various options including the option to make same day payments. If the employer was required to make deposits by electronic funds transfer and failed to do so, the employer may be subject to a 10 percent penalty. Employers not required to make electronic deposits may voluntarily participate in EFTPS. For information on EFTPS, call 1-800-945-8400 or 1-800-555-4477. (These numbers are for EFTPS information only.) [Treas. Reg. § 31.6302-1(h)]

Q 3:51   May an employer pay FUTA tax using a credit or debit card?

Yes. Employers filing Form 940 with a balance due of $500 or less are allowed to pay the amount owed on the return by credit card over the phone or via the Internet. A credit or debit card payment can be made for the balance on the current return that is due. Credit and debit card payments can be made through designated third-party service providers that will obtain credit authorization during the transaction and provide a confirmation number as proof of payment. The service providers charge a convenience fee based on the amount of the payment. Payments are effective on the date the charge is authorized. Note, however, that federal tax deposits cannot be made by credit or debit card (amounts not properly deposited may be subject to a 10 percent penalty).

Q 3:52   May an employer pay FUTA tax electronically?

Yes.Employers filing the Form 940 electronically also have the option of using the electronic fund withdrawal (EFW) payment method. For additional information, go to http://www.irs.gov/uac/Pay-Taxes-by-Electronic-Funds-Withdrawal. Employers also have the option to use the same-day wire payment method using the Federal Tax Collection Service (FTCS). This option must be arranged with your financial institution in advance and may be subject to additional transaction fees. Visit http://irs.gov/payments for the Same-Day

Taxpayer Worksheet form to provide to your financial institution. The U.S. Treasury is also reviewing the recent Same-Day ACH program.

Q 3:53   When are FUTA tax payments due?

FUTA tax is generally paid on a quarterly basis for accumulated liabilities in excess of $500. [I.R.C. § 6157] FUTA tax balances in excess of $500 at the end of quarter are due on the following dates (note that all FUTA tax must be paid no later than January 31):

Calendar Quarter	Due Date of Tax
January 1–March 31	April 30
April 1–June 30	July 31
July 1–September 30	October 31
October 1–December 31	January 31

If the due date falls on a Saturday, Sunday, or legal holiday, the deposit is due on the next business day.

Note. A legal holiday is defined as a legal holiday in the District of Columbia. See Q 4:20.

When an entity first becomes an employer during the calendar year, it begins paying FUTA tax in the calendar quarter in which it began paying wages. An exception exists for situations where the FUTA tax accrued within a calendar quarter, plus any FUTA tax accrued in other quarters but not paid, does not exceed $500. If the unpaid accrued amount in any calendar quarter is $500 or less, a deposit need not be made during that quarter. The liability is carried over to the next quarter. [Treas. Reg. § 31.6302(c)-3(a)(1)]

FUTA tax for the fourth calendar quarter must be deposited by January 31 of the next calendar year, unless the amount due is $500 or less. If the amount due is $500 or less, the remaining tax may be paid with the Form 940 by the due date of the return, or January 31. [Treas. Reg. § 31.6302(c)-3(a)(3)]

If the employer is unable to pay its SUI contributions by January 31, it can preserve its right to the maximum allowable FUTA tax credit by securing a filing extension for the Form 940. If the extension is granted, the employer will receive full credit for SUI contributions that are paid by the extended due date for the Form 940. (Note, however, that an extension granted to file Form 940 does not extend the due date for paying the federal unemployment tax due—interest and late-payment penalties will apply if FUTA taxes are paid after the applicable due date.) [Treas. Reg. § 31.3302(a)-1]

Form 940: Employer's Annual Federal Unemployment (FUTA) Tax Return

Q 3:54 What are the filing requirements with respect to FUTA taxes?

Employers must report FUTA tax and wages annually on Form 940, Employer's Annual Federal Unemployment (FUTA) Tax Return.

Q 3:55 How do employers receive a Form 940?

The IRS no longer mails preaddressed Forms 940 to employers. Employers must download the form from the IRS website at http://www.irs.gov.

Q 3:56 When is Form 940 filed?

Form 940 should be filed by January 31st following the end of the calendar year. However, if all FUTA tax was timely paid and for the full amount, the employer has 10 additional days (i.e., until February 10th) to file the return. The form is deemed to be timely filed if it is properly addressed and postmarked no later than the due date.

Q 3:57 Where is Form 940 filed?

Form 940 is sent to the IRS for the region that covers the employer's state. The employer's state is the state where the employer's legal residence, principal place of business, office, or agency is located. See the Form 940 instructions for the correct mailing address.

Note. The addresses for sending Forms 940 with a payment are different from those without a payment. The addresses for returns with payment include a P.O. Box number. The returns are filed based on your state, and the specific address can be found in the instructions for Form 940.

If an employer does not have a principal place of business, office, agency, or a legal residence in any IRS district, then the return should be filed at one of the following addresses:

Without a Payment: Internal Revenue Service, P.O. Box 409101, Ogden, UT 84409

With a Payment: Internal Revenue Service, P.O. Box 37940, Hartford, CT 07176-7940

	Without a Payment	With a Payment
Connecticut, Delaware, District of Columbia, Florida, Georgia, Illinois, Indiana, Kentucky, Maine, Maryland, Massachusetts, Michigan, New Hampshire, New Jersey, New York, North Carolina, Ohio, Pennsylvania, Rhode Island, South Carolina, Tennessee, Vermont, Virginia, West Virginia, Wisconsin	Department of the Treasury Internal Revenue Service Cincinnati, OH 45999-004	Internal Revenue Service P.O. Box 804521 Cincinnati, OH 45280-4521
Alabama, Alaska, Arizona, Arkansas, California, Colorado, Hawaii, Idaho, Iowa, Kansas, Louisiana, Minnesota, Mississippi, Missouri, Montana, Nebraska, Nevada, New Mexico, North Dakota, Oklahoma, Oregon, South Dakota, Texas, Utah, Washington, Wyoming	Department of the Treasury Internal Revenue Service Ogden, UT 84201-0046	Internal Revenue Service P.O. Box 37940 Hartford, CT 06176-7940

Form 940 may also be filed electronically. See the IRS website at http://www.irs.gov and look under "e-file."

If you are filing an amended return, mail the return to the "address without payment" address.

Q 3:58   How is the Form 940 completed?

Detailed instructions for completing Form 940 follow:

Questions a through d

These questions help the IRS understand what type of return is being filed; for instance, is it an amended return, is the return being filed by a successor employer, were there no payments made to employees in the calendar year, and is it a final return?

Amended returns

When it is necessary to file an amended Form 940, check the amended return box "a." Employers file the amended return with the IRS Center where they would have filed the original return without payment. Do not mail an amended Form 940 to a P.O. Box, even if it includes a payment. The amended filing is made by completing and signing a new paper Form 940 with the correct amounts for the tax year of the correction. Attach a statement describing the reason for filing an amended return. If the amended return is for an aggregate Form 940, attach Schedule R (Form 940) only for the employers that have adjustments on the amended Form 940. A Form 843, Claim for Refund and Request for Abatement, is not used to claim a refund or request an abatement of penalty.

Final return (general rule)

Employers that will not have to file returns in the future should check the box "d" and then complete and sign the return. If the employer starts paying wages subject to FUTA taxes in the future, the employer resumes filing the Form 940.

Part 1

This section requires the employer to identify the state in which it is required to pay SUI tax. Note that if the employer has employees in more than one state, the employer must check the box on Line 1b and complete Schedule A. Also, an employer in a credit reduction state, a state identified as not timely repaying money borrowed from the federal government to pay unemployment benefits, must check the box on Line 2 and complete Schedule A.

Part 2

This section requires the employer to determine its FUTA tax liability before adjustments. Specifically:

Line 3: Total payments to all employees.

Line 4: Payments exempt from FUTA taxes. Check the boxes that apply, 4a Fringe benefits, 4b Group-term life insurance, 4c Retirement/Pension, 4d Dependent care, and 4e Other.

Line 5: Total of payments made to each employee in excess of $7,000.

Line 6: The sum of lines 4 and 5.

Line 7: Total taxable FUTA wages.

Line 8: FUTA tax before adjustments. Line 7 × .006 = Line 8

Part 3

This section determines any adjustments. If a line does not apply, it is to be left blank.

Line 9: If all of the taxable FUTA wages were excluded from state unemployment tax, line 7 is multiplied by 0.054. If Line 9 applies to your company, Line 10 and Line 11 should be left blank.

Line 10: If some of the taxable FUTA wages paid were excluded from state unemployment tax, or if the employer paid any state unemployment tax late, complete the worksheet in the Instructions. Enter the amount from line 7 of the worksheet on this line 10.

Line 11: If a credit reduction applies, it is entered here (from the Total Credit Reduction line of Schedule A).

Part 4

This section determines the FUTA tax liability and balance due or overpayment. If any line does not apply here, it is to be left blank.

Line 12: The total FUTA tax after adjustments (lines 8 + 9 + 10 + 11 = line 12).

Line 13: The FUTA tax deposited for the year, including any overpayment applied from a prior year.

Line 14: The balance due. If more than $500, the FUTA tax must be deposited; if it is $500 or less, it may be paid by check, money order, credit or debit card, electronic funds withdrawal (if Form 940 is filed electronically), with Form 940, or deposited.

Line 15: If line 13 is more than line 12, the overpayment amount is entered here. The appropriate box must be checked to instruct the IRS to either apply the overpayment to the next return or send a refund.

Part 5

This section is used to report FUTA tax liability by quarter only if Line 12 is more than $500.

Line 16 (including a through d for each quarter): Reports the total amount of liability (if line 12 is more than $500), not the amount deposited. Skip line 16 if the amount on line 12 is $500 or less. The line is to be left blank if there is no liability for the applicable quarter.

Line 17: The total tax liability for the year, and must equal line 12.

Part 6

In this section, the IRS asks if it may speak with a third-party designee, if applicable. In addition to the designee's name and phone number, a five-digit Personal Identification Number, designated by the employer, is included here for identification when talking to the IRS.

Part 7

This section includes the signature line, where a contact phone number must be included.

The form also has a box for paid preparers only, and asks for identification information including the preparer's PTIN, along with name and address, date, firm's name, phone number, and EIN.

Form 940-V is a separate page. This is a payment voucher, and must be cut away from the page. Use Form 940-V if you plan to pay FUTA taxes of $500 or less with the Form 940. Do not staple the check or money order to Form 940-V.

Schedule A is for multistate employers and provides credit reduction information (if applicable). It must be completed, as noted earlier, if the employer paid SUI contributions to more than one state, or if wages were paid in any state that was subject to a credit reduction.

On Schedule A for 2016, there are 53 boxes, listing the postal abbreviations of states and the District of Columbia, Puerto Rico, and the U.S. Virgin Islands, the FUTA taxable wages, the reduction rate, and the total credit reduction, if applicable. Employers must place an "X" in the box of every state in which state unemployment taxes were required, even if employers in that state were not subject to a credit reduction. Employers that paid wages in states with a credit reduction must enter their FUTA taxable wages and then multiply them by the reduction rate to get the amount of the credit reduction.

The sum of the credit reductions for each applicable state represents the total credit reduction. In addition to the bottom of Schedule A, it is placed on Line 11 on Form 940.

Q 3:59   Were any significant changes made to Form 940 for 2016?

No. Form 940 is basically the same for 2016 as it was in 2015. Schedule A was modified to include the credit reduction rates for the two jurisdictions that must report the credit reduction for 2016.

Q 3:60   Are payments to household employees reported on Form 940?

Generally, no. See Q 3:61.

Q 3:61   How is FUTA tax reported for household employees?

Household employers file a FUTA tax return (Schedule H or Form 940) only if they paid cash wages of $1,000 or more (for all household employees) in any calendar quarter in the prior year or current year for household work in a private home, local college club, or a local chapter of a college fraternity or sorority. In addition, individuals, estates, and trusts that owe FUTA tax for household work in a private home, in most cases, must file Schedule H (Form 1040) instead of Form 940. (See the instructions for Schedule H.) Generally, employers of household employees must file Schedule H (Form 1040), Household Employ-ment Taxes, instead of Form 940. However, when employers employ both household employees and other employees, the employer has the option to report Social Security, Medicare, and withheld federal income taxes for the household employees on Form 941, 943, or 944 instead of on Schedule H. Employers that report a household employee's wages on Form 941, 943, or 944 must use Form 940 to report FUTA tax. [Form 940 instructions]

If an employer pays household employees cash wages totaling $1,000 or more in any calendar quarter of 2016, the first $7,000 of cash wages paid to each household employee in 2017 and 2018 is FUTA taxable wages. (A calendar quarter is January through March, April through June, July through September, or October through December.) If an employee's cash wages reach $7,000 during the year, do not figure the FUTA tax on any wages paid that employee during the rest of the year.

If the cash wages are less than $1,000 in each calendar quarter of 2017, but the employer had a household employee in 2016, the cash wages it paid in 2017 may still be FUTA taxable wages. They are FUTA taxable wages if the cash wages paid to household employees in any calendar quarter of 2016 totaled $1,000 or more. [Pub. No. 926]

Employers should not count wages paid to any of the following individuals as FUTA taxable wages:

1. Their spouse.
2. Their children who are under age 21 as of December 31 of the tax year.
3. Their parent.

Example. You hired a household employee (who is not related to you) on February 13, 2017 and agreed to pay cash wages of $260 every Friday. During February and March, you paid the employee cash wages of $1,820. Because you paid cash wages of $1,000 or more in a calendar quarter of 2017, the first $7,000 of cash wages you pay the employee (or any other employee) in 2017 or 2018 is FUTA taxable wages. The FUTA taxable wages paid may also be subject to state unemployment tax.

During 2017, you pay your household employee cash wages of $11,960. Your FUTA tax for 2017 is $42 ($7,000 × 0.006). (Note that employers may pay more in FUTA taxes for the calendar year 2017 if their state has a FUTA tax credit reduction due to unpaid federal loans.)

Q 3:62   How is FUTA tax for agricultural workers reported?

Employers that employ agricultural workers subject to FUTA tax file Form 940 when either of the following applies: Cash wages of $20,000 or more were paid to farm workers during any calendar quarter in the prior year or current year, or 10 or more farm workers were employed during some part of a day (whether or not at the same time) for at least one day during any 20 different weeks in the current or preceding year.

Wages paid to nonresident aliens admitted on a temporary basis to the United States to perform farm work, also known as workers with H-2A visas, count in meeting this threshold. However, wages paid to H-2A visa workers are not subject to FUTA tax.

Penalties

Q 3:63   What is the penalty for failure to file a FUTA tax return?

A penalty of 5 percent per month of the unpaid tax due is imposed on a taxpayer for failure to file a FUTA tax return on time. If the actual FUTA tax liability is less than the amount shown on the Form 940, the penalty is computed based on the actual FUTA tax liability. However, if the amount required to be shown on the Form 940 is greater than the amount actually shown, the penalty applies to the amount actually shown on the return. Thus, if an employer timely files Form 940 reporting FUTA tax that it has timely paid and the IRS subsequently determines that the FUTA tax reported is less than the FUTA tax that should have been reported, the employer will not be liable for a failure to pay penalty. [I.R.C. § 6651(a)(2)]

Q 3:64   What is the penalty for failure to make timely FUTA tax deposits?

The penalty is a percentage that varies based on the length of time the FUTA tax deposits are delinquent. The percentage to be used is as follows:

1. 2 percent of the undeposited amount if it is paid within five days of the due date;
2. 5 percent of the undeposited amount if it is paid within six to 15 days of the due date.
3. 10 percent of the undeposited amount if it is paid more than 15 days after the due date or amount is paid within 10 days of the date of the first notice the IRS sent asking for the tax due;
4. 10 percent if the deposit amount is paid directly to the IRS or paid with the tax return; or
5. 15 percent of the undeposited amount if it is not paid within 10 days after the employer receives its first IRS delinquency notice or on the same day a notice and demand for immediate payment is received, whichever is earlier. [I.R.C. § 6656(b)]

Late deposit penalty amounts are determined using calendar days, starting from the due date of the liability.

Q 3:65   How may the penalty for late filing be mitigated if Form 940 is delinquent?

An automatic extension to February 10 or the next business day is available for employers that have timely and correctly paid all of their FUTA tax. Two additional provisions can mitigate or eliminate a late filing penalty. First, in computing the penalty, "the amount required to be shown on the return" is reduced by any FUTA tax actually paid in by the due date of the payment. Therefore, if all the FUTA tax was timely deposited, a failure to timely file Form 940 may not produce a late filing penalty. Second, the penalty may be waived if reasonable cause for the failure to file can be shown and a valid extension is requested by the due date. The extension is requested by sending a letter detailing the reason for the extension to the same address at which Form 940 is filed. [Treas. Reg. §§ 31.6071(a)-1(c), 301.7503-1]

Financing State Benefits

Q 3:66   Is an employer's SUI tax rate based on the unemployment benefits paid to that employer's former employees?

Yes, state unemployment laws have this feature, which is often referred to as *experience rating*. Thus, employers with lower benefit charges generally pay a lower experience rate (other factors also apply). Monitoring this rating requires constant attention to a variety of factors that companies tend to overlook.

Although it is common practice to split the administration of unemployment benefits between the company's personnel and finance functions, erroneous charges or invalid claims can be overlooked, and as a result raise the employer's state unemployment tax rate. It is important to monitor all unemployment claims and charges to ensure proper administration of an account method (see Q 3:68).

Q 3:67   Do all employers pay SUI tax in order to fund unemployment benefit claims?

No. There are two methods for the employer funding of unemployment benefits: one method applies to nonprofit employers (e.g., hospitals and private schools) and government entities, and the other method applies to for-profit employers. The key element to both is that they are paid for by the employing company. Only a few states allow payroll deductions from an employee's pay for unemployment benefit funding purposes, and the percentage withheld is relatively small in those cases.

Nonprofit organizations (such as 501(c)(3) organizations, as provided for under that section of the I.R.C.) and governmental entities (and Indian tribes) are allowed two options for funding unemployment benefits. The first option is to make SUI contributions using the same method as applies to for-profit employers. The second is referred to as the reimbursing method. Under the reimbursing method, instead of paying SUI tax on the SUI taxable wages of employees, nonprofit and governmental entities elect to "reimburse" the state agency dollar-for-dollar for the amount of unemployment benefits charged against their accounts. For example, if employee Howard files an unemployment claim and collects $3,000 in unemployment benefits during the first quarter of the year, his nonprofit employer would pay $3,000 to the state agency for the quarter. For an organization with few unemployment benefit charges, the reimbursement option can result in significant unemployment cost savings.

Q 3:68   What methods do states apply in the development of the employer's SUI tax rate for unemployment insurance?

Four experience-rating methods are used currently in the United States for the purpose of financing state unemployment benefits. Furthermore, all these methods are based on a position that past experience is a rough forecast of benefits to be paid in the future; it is in this way that the unemployment system most resembles an insurance plan.

The four methods for determining employer state unemployment tax rates are known as (1) the reserve ratio formula, (2) the benefit wage ratio method, (3) the benefit ratio formula, and (4) the payroll variation (stabilization) method. Two states (Michigan and Pennsylvania) use a combination of the reserve ratio and benefit ratio methods. These four methods are detailed in Qs 3:69–3:75.

Q 3:69   What are the components of the reserve ratio formula?

Under the reserve ratio formula method (which is used by most states), each employer paying unemployment taxes has a reserve account. That is a theoretical account of the employer from which benefits will be paid to its former employees and into which the state unemployment taxes paid by the employer are credited. The amount in each company's reserve account is divided by the company's average taxable payroll (i.e., the average of all employees' pay up to the state's wage base) for a set period of time (generally three fiscal years). The result is a ratio. This ratio is then applied to a table of rates to determine the amount needed to maintain that reserve. The larger the payroll in relation to the reserves, the larger will be the future contributions to the reserve—higher state unemployment taxes. Contributions increase the reserve, and benefit payments to former employees are charged against the reserve. If benefits decrease in relation to the company's average payroll, the company's tax rate should decrease. In effect, unemployment benefits paid to former employees directly reduce those reserves and can, where payroll levels are stable, require an almost dollar-for-dollar increase in payment.

Q 3:70   Where is the reserve ratio system presently used?

Thirty-five states and territories use the reserve ratio method to determine unemployment taxes: Arizona, Arkansas, California, Colorado, District of Columbia, Georgia, Hawaii, Idaho, Indiana, Kansas, Kentucky, Louisiana, Maine, Maryland, Massachusetts, Missouri, Montana, Nebraska, Nevada, New Hampshire, New Jersey, New Mexico, New York, North Carolina, North Dakota, Ohio, Puerto Rico, Rhode Island, South Dakota, Tennessee, Virgin Islands, West Virginia, and Wisconsin. Michigan and Pennsylvania use a combination of the reserve ratio and benefit ratio methods.

Q 3:71   What are the components of the benefit wage ratio method?

In the benefit wage ratio method, the amount charged against a base period employer is equal to the wages the employer paid the individual during that individual's base period (generally the first four of the last five calendar quarters) rather than the actual unemployment benefits paid by the state to the individual. The amount of benefit wages charged against the employer is generally limited to the state's taxable wage base. Typically, three years of benefit wages are divided by three years of taxable payroll to equal the benefit wage ratio, which is used to determine the unemployment tax rate assigned to the employer for the year.

The states using the benefit wage ratio method provide what is referred to as "rehire credits" to an employer that rehires a former employee during the individual's benefit year (the 52-week period following the initial filing of an unemployment claim). Once the employer notifies the state in writing of the rehire, the state will reduce the amount of the benefit wages charged against the employer by a percentage generally determined by how much is left of the individual's benefit entitlement at the time of rehire.

Q 3:72   In what states is the benefit wage ratio method currently in effect?

Currently the benefit wage ratio method is used in only two states: Delaware and Oklahoma.

Q 3:73   What are the components of the benefit ratio formula method?

Under the benefit ratio method of rate computation, benefit charges are directly related to taxable wages. The benefits charged against an employer's account for a specified period of time (generally three to five fiscal years) are divided by the employer's taxable payroll for the same period of time to equal a benefit ratio. Depending on the state, the benefit ratio is either the employer's assigned tax rate, or a component of the employer's tax rate.

Q 3:74   In what states is the benefit ratio method in effect?

Currently, 18 states use the benefit ratio method to determine unemployment taxes: Alabama, Connecticut, Florida, Illinois, Iowa, Maryland, Michigan (uses a combination of reserve ratio and benefit ratio methods), Minnesota, Mississippi, Oregon, Pennsylvania (uses a combination of reserve ratio and benefit ratio methods), South Carolina, Texas, Utah, Vermont, Virginia, Washington, and Wyoming.

Q 3:75   What are the components of the payroll variation method or stabilization method?

This is the most unusual of the four methods used to determine SUI tax rates, and only Alaska uses it. Under this method, Alaska simply examines an employer's total payroll to see if it is rising or dropping (i.e., the amount of stabilization or variation). That is, if total payroll declines, the experience rate will increase; if payroll is constant or increasing, a more favorable rate will follow. It is unique because the payment of benefits to former employees is not a factor in the experience rating equation. Basically, there is no direct benefit to an employer in reducing unemployment benefits paid to former employees.

Q 3:76   How does an employer report and pay state unemployment taxes?

SUI tax is paid to the state employment security agency on a quarterly basis. Employers must file a quarterly return, generally due at the end of the month following the end of the quarter (e.g., April 30 is the deadline to file the report for the first quarter of the year). The quarterly return is made up of two parts, the contribution report and the wage report. The contribution report is a summary of the total (or gross) wages paid to a company's employees for the quarter, less the excess wages paid over the state's taxable wage base to each employee (e.g., for Washington, $45,000 per employee), to equal the taxable payroll for the quarter. The SUI taxable wages are multiplied by the SUI tax rate assigned to the employer for the calendar (or in some states, fiscal) year to arrive at that quarter's SUI tax liability. The quarterly wage report lists each individual employed for the quarter by Social Security number, name, and the total wages paid to each employee for the quarter. Some states ask for additional information, such as the number of weeks the individual was employed for the quarter. The information on the wage report is used for benefit eligibility. Employers may be required by the state to provide this information in a magnetic media or electronic format. Likewise, employers may be required to pay the quarterly unemployment taxes electronically.

Q 3:77   How do I determine the amount of wages on which to pay SUI tax?

Each state establishes by law the wage limit at which an employer stops paying SUI tax for each employee for the year. This threshold is referred to as the "SUI taxable wage base." The state's SUI taxable wage base must at minimum be equal to the federal unemployment taxable wage base of $7,000. For example, in New Jersey the first $33,500, up from $32,600 for 2016, paid to an employee by an employer during a calendar year constitutes "SUI taxable wages." Any wages paid over the $9,000 SUI taxable wage base in Ohio are considered "excess wages" and are not used to compute SUI tax for the rest of the calendar year. The range of SUI taxable wage bases throughout the United States varies greatly, from those states that provide for the federal annual limit of $7,000, to states such as Washington where the SUI taxable wage base varies each year ($45,000 for 2017).

An employer cannot consider wages paid by another employer to the employee during the calendar year in arriving at the SUI taxable wage base limit unless the employer is a successor to the employer, and transfer of experience is applicable. Employers may be able to transfer the SUI taxable wage base for an employee who has been transferred by the same employer during the calendar year from one state to another. See Q 3:32 through Q 3:33 for more information.

Q 3:78   Do all states assign SUI tax rates on a calendar-year basis?

For most states, SUI tax rates are assigned to employers on a calendar-year (January 1 through December 31) basis. However, there are states (including

Delaware, Montana, New Hampshire, New Jersey, Tennessee, Vermont, and Virginia), where SUI tax rates are assigned to employers on a state fiscal year basis (e.g., July 1 through June 30).

Q 3:79   How is the SUI tax rate of a new employer determined?

Each state's unemployment law generally provides for a new employer rate at which an employer newly liable in the state pays until it has established SUI experience, usually anywhere between one to three years after the date the employer began employment in the state. (A newly liable successor employer that has acquired the experience of a predecessor would not typically start at the new employer rate.) For example, in Alabama, newly liable employers pay at a starting rate of 2.7 percent until they have had employment in the state for a sufficient period of time to qualify for experience rating.

Benefit Eligibility

Q 3:80   Who is eligible for benefits under a state's unemployment insurance laws?

It is important to understand that the state's decisions to award or deny unemployment benefits are based on eligibility, not financial conditions or need. It is equally important to realize that, although the state seeks information from employers in making its eligibility decisions, it has its own set of guidelines mandating how it uses this information in making these decisions. Failure to understand these guidelines and how they work can be a major source of frustration to employers attempting to control their unemployment costs.

With some limited exceptions, the intent of unemployment insurance is to provide temporary wage replacement payments to people unemployed through no fault of their own. The state must generally decide which party was at fault in causing the unemployment. The same principle applies to both quit and discharge situations.

Q 3:81   How is unemployment benefit eligibility generally determined?

To be eligible for benefits, claimants in all states must meet certain standards. The claimant must:

1. Have earned a certain amount of wages in the base period (generally the first four of the last five calendar quarters preceding loss of employment);
2. Be totally or partially unemployed through no fault of his or her own;
3. File a claim;
4. Be physically or mentally able to work;
5. Register for work through the state unemployment office;

6. Seek suitable work and be available to work (benefits will not be denied to a claimant who is on jury duty or in a state-approved training program); and

7. Satisfy state waiting periods where applicable (generally a one-week period).

Q 3:82 What conditions permit benefits to be paid when the separation has been determined to be a discharge?

Benefits are generally available when an employer discharges an employee. In most states, employees who are terminated for misconduct connected with the work can be denied benefits. Here, the state laws generally look for some type of conduct that is detrimental to the employer's best interests. Employers must provide proper documentation of the situation. If the charge of misconduct is supported, the state can deny benefits.

A common source of confusion about eligibility for unemployment insurance arises from a failure to distinguish between a discharge for cause and a discharge for misconduct. The two are not the same.

An example of a discharge for cause where unemployment benefits may not be awarded by the state is a probationary employee who cannot keep pace with the job and is terminated. This is a discharge for cause, or good reason, but it is not misconduct on the employee's part (it is not the employee's fault that he or she could not meet the job's requirements).

Under certain cases, such as theft of company property, a discharge may be for good cause and misconduct. Most states permit an employer to contest a former employee's claim for benefits for a discharge where misconduct is documented.

Q 3:83 Are unemployment benefits available when there has been a voluntary quit?

Sometimes. Employers may be surprised to learn that an individual who quits under many circumstances is just as eligible for unemployment benefits as someone who is laid off because of a plant shutdown.

Most states pay unemployment benefits to workers who terminated their employment for "good cause." The issue in determining whether benefits are to be paid in such cases is generally not whether the employer had good cause for its actions, but whether the employee had good cause for leaving the job. In general, if no reasonable alternative existed and the individual pursued all remedies available before quitting, the separation may be deemed to be for good cause.

Q 3:84   Can separation for a non–work-related cause result in the payment of unemployment benefits that are charged to the employer's account?

Yes, events that lead to a quit for which benefits could be paid need not be work-related to provide good cause for leaving employment. Non-work-related situations such as transportation problems or child care requirements, as well as uncompensated or excessive overtime requirements (work-related), can provide good cause for quitting when no reasonable alternative is available to the person facing them. Under these situations, the employee who quits could be eligible for benefits depending on state law, and those benefits could be chargeable to the employer.

Some states have amended their laws to allow for the payment of unemployment benefits to employees who voluntarily quit their jobs due to domestic violence, personal or family illness, or to follow a spouse who is transferred out of the area. Generally, benefits awarded under these circumstances are not charged against employer accounts.

Q 3:85   When is an employee's discharge deemed to be a discharge for cause?

A termination for cause or misconduct for unemployment insurance purposes generally exists when four elements are present:

1. The existence of a reasonable company rule;
2. Knowledge by the employee of that rule;
3. A willful breach of the rule that directly leads to the discharge; and
4. Actual or potential harm to the company's interests.

Employers that contest a claim for unemployment benefits from a former employee because of misconduct need to document these four elements with the understanding that the state is required to assume that the employee was terminated through no fault of his or her own. This leaves employers with the burden of proof in asserting otherwise. Thus, each of the elements above must generally be present in order to successfully challenge a claim that has been made against the employer's account. If one or more of these elements is missing from the employer's documentation, or is impossible to prove, the state may decide that the discharge was for reasons other than misconduct, leaving the benefits as chargeable to the employer's account.

Q 3:86   How can an employer establish that the employee had knowledge of the rule that he or she failed to follow?

This can be one of the more difficult aspects of demonstrating that a discharge was for misconduct. A good way to demonstrate that employees knew of the rules they broke is to distribute handbooks of the organization's complete set of rules at the time of hire. The last page of an ideal handbook should have an acknowledgment that states, "I have read and understood this handbook," with a space for the employee's signature. This page, dated and signed, should be kept in the employee's personnel file. The handbook should remain with the employee. The employer should also be sure to keep a copy of the handbook and each revision. If and when a change to the handbook is made, the employer should be able to document evidence that each employee received the updated version (e.g., signed employee notices and company copies of general employee notices).

Alternatively, particularly where individual department regulations are concerned, employers may post the rules prominently on bulletin boards, sign-in stations, and other areas. A record of the posting and the rules stated should be maintained in personnel records. An effective general rule is that the more unusual or department specific a particular rule is, the harder it is to show that employees were informed of it. Another method for demonstrating the employee's knowledge of the rule violated is to issue a warning to him or her (see Q 3:87).

Q 3:87   How can it be established that a willful breaking or breach of the rule led directly to discharge?

Showing or proving that an employee was discharged for misconduct because of a willful act is not easy. The state assumes the employee's action leading to the discharge was not willful unless the employer states otherwise. Generally, in these contested cases, the former employee will rarely acknowledge that his or her misconduct was willful. With some exceptions, the best evidence that an employee has acted in a willful and intentional manner to disregard company rules is the recurrence of the problem or similar situation, and that the individual was issued warnings about the misconduct. The existence of warnings, both verbal and written, is a key component to establishing misconduct connected with the employee.

Although there is nothing wrong with a verbal warning, it can be difficult to document that type of warning many months later. Warnings therefore should also be written. Written warnings overcome the presumption that the infractions are judgmental errors, or "good-faith" mistakes, neither of which are treated as misconduct.

Warnings may not be necessary where the conduct is extreme, such as theft, or activities that are harmful to the employee or other workers' health (e.g., intoxication on the job). However, warnings are essential where the violations are connected to the more usual infractions, such as excessive absence from work or tardiness.

Q 3:88   What additional considerations may be involved in a discharge for misconduct?

A discharge for misconduct is best documented when the infraction leads directly to an immediate discharge. The greater the time lapse between the infraction and the discharge, the harder it will be to convince the state that the infraction caused the discharge.

Q 3:89   May an employee's eligibility to receive unemployment benefits be based on a voluntary quit due to a reduction in compensation?

Yes, it may in some states, if the employee has also had a reduction in hours worked and if state law so provides for such benefits. Federal law permits a state to pay partial benefits for periods of partial "unemployment" when an employee works less than regular full-time hours for his or her employer. [UIPL Letter No. 8-98 (Jan. 12, 1998)]

Some states offer what is called a workshare program as an alternative to an employer laying off skilled employees when the employer is experiencing a slowdown. An employer can reduce employees' hours (up to 60 percent in the state of Massachusetts), and qualified workers may receive partial unemployment benefits to replace a portion of their lost wages. For example, if an employee's workweek is reduced by 20 percent (or eight hours), the employee may be eligible to receive 20 percent of his or her unemployment insurance weekly benefit entitlement, in addition to the 32 hours of earnings from his employer. The employer must voluntarily sign up for this program in the states that offer it.

Q 3:90   What are the dos and don'ts regarding documentation at the time of separation?

To limit exposure to unwarranted benefits, it is necessary to document promptly all facts concerning the discharge—the elements of misconduct.

Regardless of the type of separation, there are some dos and don'ts in dealing with a discharge.

Do:

1. Document facts directly related to the discharge, not opinions or conclusions.

2. Complete the documentation as soon as possible after the infraction, verbal warning, or discharge is complete. It can be astonishing how quickly participants' and witnesses' memories fade.

3. Communicate in clear terms to the employee why the action is being taken and document that communication.

Don't:

1. Do not try to build a case for the purpose of unemployment insurance or any other proceeding you may anticipate with the individual. Remember, the purpose of documentation is to record facts and behavior, not to speculate about motivation.

2. Do not use vague terms or conclusory statements in any documentation.

3. Do not delay in acting on the events leading to the discharge.

Q 3:91 What documentation should be associated with a voluntary quit?

State laws vary on benefit eligibility, but in most states the employee must establish good cause attributable to the employer to qualify for unemployment benefits under a voluntary-quit scenario. Employers should document the reasons leading to a voluntary quit. Here are a few suggestions:

1. Conduct an exit interview if possible. Make this a priority at the time an employee separates from employment.

2. Obtain a signed resignation statement from the employee detailing his or her reason for leaving the company. This statement should be completed by the employee with no assistance from the company supervisor. If the employee refuses to provide a specific reason, note this in the documentation.

3. Avoid accepting vague reasons such as "for personal reasons" or "family illness." Ask for more specific information. Again, if there is a refusal to comply with these requests, make the refusal to provide that information a part of the separation record.

4. If the company needs and wants the employee to remain, ask the employee to consider working in a different capacity.

5. Allow the employee to work out his or her notice period unless there are very strong reasons to do otherwise. If there are reasons for a more rapid termination, consider paying the employee through his or her notice period. If an employee does not work until the end of the notice period, document precisely what was done.

Q 3:92 How should a discharge be documented?

There are no specific requirements, but here are some suggestions:

1. Be specific and factual in the written documentation. If certain facts leading to the discharge are unclear or open to dispute, resolve these before discharging the employee.

2. Begin with the last act or omission on the employee's part that led to the discharge decision, and work back to prior warnings for similar instances, if any.

Although it may be impossible to cover all the reasons for discharge, and the ways to document a discharge may vary from case to case, in general an employer will want to consider the following:

1. As the seriousness of the offense increases, the degree and amount of documentary support prepared should increase.

2. Exercise special diligence when the employee denies having done the act for which he or she is being discharged. It is important in such cases to be certain that the act can be proven "beyond a reasonable doubt." This typically requires additional witnesses, documented acts, and more.

3. The employee should be told the exact reason for the discharge, and the employer should note whether the employee agrees with the reasons for the discharge.

4. Be especially careful where the discharge results from a "general review" of the individual's performance or record over a period of time, rather than from some specific act or omission on the employee's part. It is difficult, if not impossible, to establish misconduct in these cases.

Q 3:93 Who is the "moving party" in a claim for unemployment benefits?

In most cases, the states look at who made the decision about the employee's last day of work. In general, but not always, if the employee chose the day, the employee has voluntarily quit. If the employer made the choice, it is a discharge. This approach helps resolve complications that can arise and is a good test to apply whenever there is a question of discharge or quit.

Example. Jessica, a Payroll Analyst with Environ Industries, gives notice that she has obtained another job and will be leaving the company next month to work for a competitor. Concerned that she will take confidential information to her new employer, Environ Industries tells Jessica to leave the next day, terminating her pay as of her last day of work.

Jessica was discharged and did not quit for unemployment benefit purposes. The company chose her last day of work. The company's reasons for doing so do not ordinarily matter for unemployment benefit purposes. The company could have continued Jessica's salary through the end of her original notice, even though she physically left the premises. Then her termination would have been a quit. (Note that, in some states, the employer would be liable for benefit charges only for the period between the date of termination and the employee's notice of termination date.)

A discharged employee who is given two weeks' notice but decides to terminate employment at a date earlier than the discharge date is generally classified as a quit.

Q 3:94 What management procedures can limit the cost of unemployment benefits?

The largest portion of an employer's overall unemployment insurance expense is paid to the state. The state unemployment insurance system imposes employer contributions that vary based on the employer's experience, generally assigning higher SUI tax rates to employers with a greater number of unemployment claims filed against them by former employees. The greater the amount of benefit charges levied against the employer's account, the greater the SUI contributions it pays. Employers should monitor all unemployment claims filed by former employees and, where applicable, contest invalid claims within the time limits imposed under state law.

An employer may contest an unemployment claim filed by a former employee who does not qualify for benefits under state law (e.g., employees who are terminated because they stole from the employer may not be entitled to benefits). When an employer does not respond to a state notice of a claim filed or does not contest a claim, the benefits paid generally are charged against the employer's account. Most states have specific rules on how and when to contest a claim that, if not followed, eliminates the employer's right to appeal the payment of benefits later found to be paid in error.

Payments made to employees at the time of discharge, often referred to as wages in lieu of notice, dismissal pay, and wage continuation pay, should also be taken into consideration, as these payments may delay the payment of unemployment benefits. The employer should notify the state agency in its response to the unemployment claim notice that the individual has received such a payment.

Q 3:95   Does an employer have any recourse with regard to a state's decision to pay unemployment benefits?

Most states, but not all, notify the employer of a claim for unemployment benefits. This notice generally consists of copies of both the application for benefits and the written decision allowing or denying them. The state then decides whether benefits are due and, if so, permits the employer to appeal the finding.

In most states, an employer or employee may make further appeal to an unemployment insurance appeals board, a final step in the administrative process. This is typically a mere review of the appeal hearing, and no further appearance or evidence is allowed, except under very unusual circumstances.

Q 3:96   What recent legislative and administrative changes affect unemployment taxes?

The President's Budget Proposal for 2017 includes recommendations for the Unemployment Insurance system to (a) extend the Unemployment Insurance program to those who may lose their job; (b) provide protection for those who take a pay cut in order to get back to work; and (c) ensure that state programs have the resources to protect workers in the midst of a recession.

There has been a trend in recent years of employers using contingent workers. The definition of a "contingent employee" may involve an independent contractor relationship or a strict employer/employee relationship. This is an area that will be addressed on both the state and federal levels.

Chapter 4

Depositing and Reporting Federal Income and FICA Taxes

Withheld federal income and employment taxes are required to be deposited with the federal government and reported by the employer on a periodic basis. The due date of these deposits is based, in part, on the amount of the taxes to be deposited (or that have been deposited historically). This chapter discusses the deposit and reporting requirements for withheld federal income taxes and Social Security and Medicare taxes withheld and paid by the employer.

Overview

Q 4:1   How are withheld income taxes and FICA taxes deposited?

In general, the employer must deposit federal income tax withheld and both the employer and employee shares of Social Security and Medicare taxes remitting electronically through the Electronic Federal Tax Payment Service

(EFTPS). Prior to 2011, employers that were not required to file electronically could remit payments by check with the Form 8109, Federal Tax Deposit Coupon. Now, only in limited situations will payment by check be available. A balance due with the Form 941 and Form 944 may be paid by credit or debit card. [Pub. No. 15]

Q 4:2   Are businesses required to notify the IRS of an address change?

Yes, employers notify the Internal Revenue Service (IRS) of a new business mailing address or business location by filing Form 8822-B, Change of Address. [Pub. No. 15]

Employer Identification Number

Q 4:3   What is the purpose of an employer identification number?

An employer identification number (EIN) is used by the federal government to identify each employer for a multitude of federal reporting requirements. For employment tax purposes, the EIN is used to report employment taxes and is included in the tax returns filed with the IRS and in the information statements given to employees or annuitants.

The EIN is a nine-digit number issued by the IRS. The digits are arranged as follows: 00-0000000. This number is used to identify the federal tax account of employers and certain entities that have no employees. Employers use their EINs on all the returns and payments sent to the IRS, Social Security Administration (SSA), and certain other federal agencies. Some states may also use the EIN for various state tax reporting and payment purposes. [I.R.C. § 6109; Treas. Reg. § 301.6109-1]

Q 4:4   How can an employer obtain an EIN?

Employers can apply for an EIN online, by telephone, fax, or mail. Note. The IRS limits the issuance to one EIN per responsible party per day.

Online. The preferred method is online. This method is free of charge. To apply online, go to the IRS website at www.irs.gov and click on *Apply for an Employer Identification Number (EIN) Online.* The online application process is available:

Monday–Friday 6:00 a.m. to 12:30 a.m. Eastern Time

Saturday 6:00 a.m. to 9:00 p.m. Eastern Time

Sunday 7:00 p.m. to 12:00 a.m. Eastern Time

If a third-party designee (TPD) is completing the online application on behalf of the employer, the employer must authorize the third party to apply for and receive the EIN on the employer's behalf.

Once the application is completed, the employer will receive its EIN immediately.

Fax. Under the Fax-TIN program, an employer can receive its EIN by fax within four business days. The employer should fax Form SS-4 (see mail option below) to the Fax-TIN number listed for your state under "Where to Apply" in Publication 1635. The state to select is the state where the employer's principal business, office, or agency, or legal residence (in the case of an individual) is located. Fax-TIN is available 24 hours a day, seven days a week.

Mail. An employer can receive its EIN by mail in about four weeks. Employers should complete Form SS-4. "Form SS-4" and "Instructions for Form SS-4" can be obtained from the IRS website at www.irs.gov and clicking *Forms and Publications*. Employers should ensure that the Form SS-4 contains all of the required information. The application should be mailed to the address listed on page 2 of the Instructions for Form SS-4. The state to select is the state where the taxpayer's principal business, office or agency, or legal residence (in the case of an individual) is located.

Telephone. Only international applicants may apply for an EIN by phone by calling 267-941-1099.

For additional information about EINs, the employer should refer to Publication 1635, Understanding Your EIN. Publication 1635 can be obtained from the IRS website at www.irs.gov and clicking *Forms and Publications*.

If the employer does not have Internet access, the employer can order Form SS-4, Instructions for Form SS-4, and Publication 1635 from the IRS by calling 1-800-TAX-FORM (1-800-829-3676).

An EIN should be requested before paying wages to employees; however, the application for an EIN must be sent no later than seven days after the employer first pays wages. [Treas. Reg. § 31.6011(b)-1(a)(2)]

Q 4:5   Can an employer have more than one EIN?

No, an employer should have only one EIN. An employer with more than one EIN should check with the IRS Service Center (1-800-829-4933) where it files its federal returns to verify which EIN it should use. The IRS Service Center phone numbers are included in the Form SS-4 instructions.

However, when a single employer consists of multiple corporations, each corporation should have a separate EIN for each entity for which it is required to file federal returns and/or make federal tax payments. [Rev. Rul. 73-526, 1973-2 C.B. 404] See chapter 12 for information on EINs in the event of a merger or acquisition.

Q 4:6　What if the EIN has not been received by the due date of the first federal return and/or tax payment?

If an employer has not yet received its EIN before the due date of a deposit or return, the employer should write "Applied for" in the space provided for the EIN and also note the date it applied for the EIN. [Treas. Reg. § 31.6302-1(i)(4); Form SS-4 instructions; Pub. No. 15]

Q 4:7　Can a new employer make a deposit without an EIN?

The IRS recommends that an employer obtain an EIN through the online application process in order to receive an EIN the same day. In addition, all federal employment tax deposits made after December 31, 2010 must be made electronically. [Pub. No. 15]

Deposit Schedules and Deadlines

Q 4:8　When are employers required to deposit federal income and employment taxes?

In general, employers are required to deposit withheld federal income taxes and Social Security and Medicare (FICA) taxes along with the employer's share of FICA taxes throughout the year on either a monthly or semiweekly basis. The payment schedule that applies is based on the amount of taxes that were paid in the lookback period. See chapter 3 for depositing Federal Unemployment Tax Act (FUTA) taxes.

An employer's federal income tax withholding and FICA payment schedule for the current calendar year is determined based on the total federal income tax withholding and FICA liability (as reported on Form 941, Employer's QUARTERLY Federal Tax Return) for the 12-month period ending on June 30 of the prior year. (For example, the determination, or "lookback," period for 2017 is July 1, 2015 through June 30, 2016.) When the employer's federal income tax withholding and FICA liability during the lookback period is $50,000 or less, the employer is categorized as a monthly depositor, whose deposits are due on the 15th day of each month following the month in which the liability was incurred. When the employer's combined federal income tax withholding and FICA liability is greater than $50,000 during the lookback period, the employer is designated as a semiweekly depositor, whose deposits are due within three business days after the end of any semiweekly period in which the employer incurs a liability. Employment tax liabilities incurred on Wednesday through Friday must be deposited on the next Wednesday, and liabilities incurred on Saturday through Tuesday must be deposited on the next Friday. Note that liabilities are generally incurred on the date that wages were paid or made available to employees without substantial limitation. [Treas. Reg. § 31.3602-1(b)]

Note that two exceptions apply to the semiweekly and monthly deposit schedule: one for very small employers and another for very large payments. (For a summary of deposit rules, see Table 4-1.)

Table 4-1.   Summary of Deposit Rules for Social Security and Medicare Taxes and Withheld Federal Income Tax

Deposit Requirement	Deposit Threshold	Deposit Due Date
Quarterly or Annual Rule (employment tax payment is made with returns filed by small employers)	If your tax liability is less than $2,500 for the current quarter or the preceding quarter, and you did not incur a next-day deposit obligation during the current quarter.	Employers may pay the taxes to the IRS with the quarterly Form 941 or the annual Form 943/944. For Form 945, the period to determine the liability is annual.
Monthly Rule	If the total tax liability during the lookback period was $50,000 or less	Employers must deposit the taxes accumulated in any month by the 15th* of the month following the month in which the liability was incurred, so long as the total tax liability is not more than $100,000 (see the next-day rule below).
Semiweekly Rule	If the total tax liability during the lookback period was more than $50,000	Employers must deposit employment taxes on Wednesday (if the liability was incurred on the previous Wednesday, Thursday, or Friday) or on Friday (if the liability was incurred on the previous Saturday, Sunday, Monday, or Tuesday), so long as the total tax liability is not more than $100,000.
Next-Day Rule (for large employers)	If the employer accumulates $100,000 or more in total tax liability at any time	The entire amount is due the business day following the day the accumulated liability is $100,000 or more.

---

* Deposits that fall on a non-business day are due on the next business day.

In making the determination as to the deposit schedule, only the tax liability as originally reported on Form 941 is used in ascertaining whether the $50,000 threshold has been reached during the lookback period. Adjustments made on Form 941-X or 944-X do not affect the amount of the tax liability for previous periods for purposes of the lookback rule. [Treas. Reg. § 31.6302-1(b)(5)]

Example 1. For the 12-month period from July 1, 2015 to June 30, 2016, an employer reports $83,650 in federal income tax withholding and FICA liabilities on its quarterly Forms 941. This employer becomes a semiweekly depositor for 2017. The company pays wages on Friday and incurs a liability of $9,667 for federal income tax withholding and FICA taxes. This employer must deposit the entire $9,667 on or before the following Wednesday.

Example 2. A semiweekly depositor for 2017 accumulates a federal income tax withholding and FICA liability of $104,466 on Monday, March 13. These taxes must be deposited no later than Tuesday, March 14. This employer remains a semiweekly depositor for 2017. The employer then incurs a $2,787 liability on Wednesday, March 15. These taxes are to be deposited by the following Wednesday, March 22.

Example 3. Monthly and Semiweekly Schedules: Palisade, Inc. reported Form 941 taxes as follows:

2016 Lookback Period*		2017 Lookback Period*	
3rd Quarter 2014	$11,300	3rd Quarter 2015	$15,500
4th Quarter 2014	$14,100	4th Quarter 2015	$15,800
1st Quarter 2015	$14,300	1st Quarter 2016	$16,100
2nd Quarter 2015	$12,600	2nd Quarter 2016	$16,500
	$52,300		$63,900

* The lookback period is the 12-month period ending on the June 30 of the prior year.

Palisade, Inc. is a monthly schedule depositor for 2016 because its tax liability for the four quarters in its lookback period (third quarter 2014 through second quarter 2015) was not more than $50,000. However, for 2017, Palisade, Inc. must follow the semiweekly deposit schedule because the total taxes exceeded $50,000 for the four quarters in its lookback period (third quarter 2015 through second quarter 2016).

Q 4:9 What are the general rules for depositing taxes?

In general, an employer must deposit income tax withheld and both the employer's and employee's portion of the Social Security and Medicare taxes electronically through the Electronic Federal Tax Payment System (EFTPS; see Q 4:33).

The monthly deposit rule may be used for the entire calendar year unless the next-day deposit rule is triggered (e.g., the accumulated liability reaches

$100,000 or more). If the next-day deposit rule is triggered, the employer becomes a semiweekly depositor for the remainder of the current calendar year and the next calendar year.

Q 4:10   Are deposit dates based on when or how often an employer pays its employees?

No. The terms *monthly depositor* and *semiweekly depositor* do not refer to how often a business pays its employees. Rather, these terms describe the federal tax deposit schedule an employer must follow when employment tax liabilities arise. The due date of an employer's federal tax payment depends on the date that wages are paid, the deposit schedule that applies based on the lookback period for that employer, and whether or not accumulated tax liabilities reach or exceed $100,000 within a deposit period.

> **Example 1.** Baldwin Corp. is a monthly schedule depositor for 2017 with seasonal employees. It paid wages each Friday during March but did not pay any wages during April. Under the monthly schedule, Baldwin Corp. must deposit the combined tax liabilities for wages paid in March no later than April 15. Baldwin Corp. does not have a deposit requirement for April that would be due by May 15 because no wages were paid; therefore, it does not have a tax liability for the month.

> **Example 2.** Echo, Inc., which has a semiweekly deposit schedule, pays wages once each month on the last Tuesday of the month. Although Echo has a semiweekly deposit schedule, it will deposit just once a month because it pays wages only once a month. The deposit, however, will be made under the semiweekly deposit schedule as follows: Echo's tax liability for the April 18, 2017 (Tuesday) payday must be deposited by April 21, 2017 (Friday). Under the semiweekly deposit schedule, liabilities for wages paid on Saturday through Tuesday must be deposited by the following Friday.

Q 4:11   Are there any exceptions to the deposit schedule based on the lookback period?

Two general exceptions may cause an employer to deviate from the monthly and semiweekly deposit schedules: (1) the next-day deposit rule and (2) the quarterly deposit rule.

Next-day deposit rule. Under the next-day deposit rule, an employer that accumulates a liability of $100,000 or more at any time during a deposit period must make its federal income tax withholding and FICA deposit on the first business day following the date that the accumulated tax liability reaches or exceeds $100,000.

Quarterly deposit rule. When an employer scheduled as a monthly or semiweekly depositor has an accumulated liability of less than $2,500 for the current quarter or the preceding quarter, and did not incur a $100,000 next-day deposit obligation during the current quarter, the employer may pay its federal income tax withholding and FICA taxes at the end of month following the close of the quarter (i.e., due date, without extension, for filing Form 941). Employers should be cautious in using the quarterly deposit rule. For example, if the accumulated liability for the current quarter is $2,500 or more (and the accumulated liability for the preceding quarter was $2,500 or more), a late deposit penalty will generally be assessed based on the employer's normal deposit schedule (e.g., semiweekly or monthly). [Treas. Reg. § 31.6302-1(f)(4)]

Example. An employer that is a semiweekly depositor withheld $1,810 on March 24 and does not expect to pay any other wages until January. This employer has elected to report and deposit the amount at the end of the month following the close of the calendar quarter. On December 8, it pays an unexpected bonus, resulting in a federal employment tax liability of $700. This employer is no longer eligible for the quarterly deposit rule; therefore, the March 24 payroll was not timely deposited under the semiweekly deposit schedule and the deposit made under the quarterly deposit rule is delinquent and subject to late deposit penalties plus interest.

Q 4:12   Under what schedule does a new employer deposit its federal income tax withholding and FICA liability?

A new employer is automatically categorized as a monthly depositor until it has a lookback period (July 1 through June 30) to use in determining its deposit frequency. However, when any employer (even a new employer) triggers the next-day deposit rule, it becomes a semiweekly depositor for the remainder of the current calendar year. Such an employer continues to file as a semiweekly depositor for the following calendar year. [Treas. Reg. § 31.6302-1(b)(4)]

The lookback period applies regardless of when the employer begins its operation or employs workers and incurs federal income tax withholding and FICA liabilities. For example, an employer that commences operation on March 17, 2017 will have its deposit schedule for the 2018 calendar year based on its federal income tax withholding and FICA liability for the four-month period from March 17, 2017 to June 30, 2017. This employer will be classified as a semiweekly employer for the 2018 calendar year only if its reported liability for the four-month period exceeds $50,000. There is no proration of that threshold. This assumes that the employer's deposits do not trigger the next-day deposit rule in 2017.

Q 4:13   How does the quarterly deposit rule apply?

When any employer accumulates a federal income tax withholding and FICA liability of less than $2,500 for the current quarter or the preceding quarter, and did not incur a $100,000 next-day deposit obligation during the current quarter, it may pay its tax liability at the end of the month following the close of the calendar quarter (e.g., the due date of the Form 941, Employer's QUARTERLY Federal Tax Return). The $2,500 threshold is measured starting with the first deposit period of a calendar quarter in which the employer incurs a liability of less than $2,500. This threshold is cumulative for that quarter.

Example. A monthly depositor incurs a federal income tax withholding and FICA liability of $590 during April 2017, $630 in May 2017, and $710 in June 2017. The employer did not accumulate a tax liability of $2,500 or more during the preceding quarter and did not incur a $100,000 next-day deposit obligation during the current quarter. The employer may skip its monthly deposits for April, May, and June and include a check or money order for $1,930 with its Form 941 due on July 31, 2017.

Q 4:14   When is a payroll tax deposit allowed to be made with the return?

An employer may make a payment with Form 941 instead of depositing if:

1. The employer accumulates employment taxes of less than a $2,500 during the quarter; or

2. The employer is a monthly schedule depositor and is making a payment in accordance with the Accuracy of Deposits Rule.

[Treas. Reg. § 31.6302-1(f)(4)]

Under the Accuracy of Deposits Rule, employers are required to deposit 100 percent of their tax liability on or before the deposit due date. However, penalties will not be applied for depositing less than 100 percent if *both* of the following conditions are met:

1. Any deposit shortfall does not exceed the greater of $100 or 2 percent of the amount of taxes otherwise required to be deposited; and

2. The deposit shortfall is paid or deposited by the shortfall makeup date.

For monthly schedule depositors. Deposit the shortfall or pay it with your return by the due date of the Form 941 for the quarter in which the shortfall occurred. You may pay the shortfall with Form 941 even if the amount is $2,500 or more.

For semiweekly schedule depositors. Deposit by the earlier of the first Wednesday or Friday that falls on or after the 15th of the month following the month in which the shortfall occurred or, if earlier, the due date of Form 941. For example, if a semiweekly schedule depositor has a deposit shortfall during May 2017, the shortfall makeup date is June 14, 2017 (Wednesday). However, if the shortfall occurred on the required April 5 (Wednesday) deposit date for a March 31, 2017 (Friday) pay date, the return due date for the quarter ending March 31 (May 1) would come before the May 17 (Wednesday) shortfall makeup date. In this case, the shortfall must be deposited by May 1. [Treas. Reg. §§ 1.468B-5(b)(1), 31.6302-1(f); Pub. No. 15]

Q 4:15   What deposit deadlines apply to a monthly depositor?

Monthly depositors are employers that reported a total federal income tax withholding and FICA liability of $50,000 or less during their lookback period. A monthly depositor must deposit federal income tax withholding and FICA liabilities accumulated during the calendar month no later than the 15th day of the following calendar month. If the 15th day is a legal holiday, the deposit is due on the next business day. [Treas. Reg. § 31.6302-1(c)]

Note that when a monthly depositor is required to make a next-day deposit because its liability during the month is $100,000 or more, it becomes a semiweekly depositor for the remainder of the current calendar year and all of the following calendar year.

Q 4:16 Can a semiweekly depositor become a monthly depositor during the calendar year?

No. However, when the employer's tax liability is less than $50,000 in the lookback period, it will become a monthly depositor for the following applicable calendar year.

Q 4:17 How does the next-day deposit rule apply?

An employer is required to make a deposit under the next-day deposit rule whenever the undeposited accumulated federal employment tax liability reaches or exceeds $100,000 during a deposit period. Such deposit must be made by the next business day regardless of whether the employer has been classified as a monthly or a semiweekly depositor. [Treas. Reg. § 31.6302-1(c)(3)]

Note that when a monthly depositor is required to make a next-day deposit because the $100,000 liability threshold has been reached, it becomes a semi-weekly depositor for the remainder of the current calendar year and the following calendar year. [Treas. Reg. § 31.6302-1(b)(2)(ii)]

Q 4:18 How is the $100,000 tax liability threshold measured?

The $100,000 tax liability threshold is determined on an employer-by-employer basis, not by division or other subclassification. It is the accumulated undeposited federal employment tax liability that has not been deposited at any time in the deposit period.

Example 1. Halo Bright, Inc. started its business on February 15, 2017. On April 14, 2017, it paid wages for the first time and accumulated a federal employment tax liability of $67,000. On April 28, 2017, Halo Bright, Inc. paid wages and accumulated a federal employment tax liability of $60,000, bringing its undeposited accumulated federal employment tax liability to $127,000. Because this was the first year of its business, the federal employment tax liability for its lookback period is considered to be zero, and Halo Bright, Inc. would normally be subject to the monthly deposit schedule based on the lookback rules. However, because Halo Bright, Inc.'s undeposited accumulated employment tax liability was $127,000 on April 28, 2017, it is now subject to the semiweekly deposit schedule for the remainder of 2017 and for 2018. Halo Bright, Inc. is required to deposit the $127,000 by May 1

(Monday), the next business day. [Treas. Reg. § 31.6302-1(c)(3); Pub. No. 15]

For purposes of the $100,000 deposit rule, an employer does not continue accumulating its undeposited employment tax liability after the end of a deposit period.

Example 2. QualFour Engineering, Inc., a semiweekly schedule depositor, had an undeposited accumulated employment tax liability of $56,000 on a Tuesday (of a Saturday-through-Tuesday deposit period) and an undeposited accumulated liability of $61,000 on Wednesday, the first day of the next deposit period. The $100,000 next-day rule does not apply. Thus, QualFour Engineering, Inc. makes deposits using the semiweekly deposit schedule and deposits $56,000 by Friday and $61,000 by the following Wednesday. [Treas. Reg. § 31.6302-1(c)(3)]

In addition, once an employer accumulates at least $100,000 in a deposit period, it stops accumulating its employment tax liabilities at the end of that day and begins accumulating undeposited liability on the next day.

Example 3. Breakfront, Inc. is a semiweekly schedule depositor. On Monday, Breakfront, Inc. has an undeposited accumulated employment tax liability of $118,888 and must deposit this amount on Tuesday, the next business day. On Tuesday, Breakfront, Inc. accumulates an additional undeposited employment tax liability of $62,220. Because the $62,220 is not added to the previous $118,888 and the $62,220 is less than $100,000, Breakfront, Inc. must deposit the $62,220 by the following Friday. [Pub. No. 15]

Q 4:19   What is meant by business legal holidays?

For the deposit of federal employment taxes, legal holidays are days when federal tax deposits are not considered due. Legal holidays are defined as any legal holiday in the District of Columbia. This is the term used for deposits. For 2017, there are 12 holidays, including the District of Columbia's Emancipation Day, April 16 (observed April 17, 2017). Prior to 2011, the term "banking holidays" was used and, as a result, due dates were postponed when banks were closed for national, state, or local holidays. Now that all employers are required to deposit federal employment taxes electronically, the fact that a bank is closed for a state holiday is not relevant. When an employer's deposit is due on a day designated as a legal holiday, the employer's deposits are due on the next business day. Business days generally exclude Saturdays and Sundays, even if a financial institution is open for certain limited services. [Treas. Reg. § 31.6302-1(c)(4)] (See Q 4:20 for a list of legal holidays.)

For example, semiweekly depositors have three business days to make a deposit after the end of the semiweekly period. If any of the three weekdays after the end of a semiweekly period is a legal holiday, the employer has one additional business day to make its deposit. [Treas. Reg. § 31.6302-1(c)(2)(iii)] Table 4-2 offers helpful guidelines.

Table 4-2.   Semiweekly Deposit Due Dates Changed by Legal Holidays

If the Deposit Period Ends on:	And a Legal Holidays Falls on Any One of These Days . . .	The Deposit Is Delayed Until . . .
Tuesday	Wednesday, Thursday, Friday	The following Monday
Friday	Monday, Tuesday, Wednesday	The following Thursday

Example. A semiweekly depositor has an accumulated undeposited federal employment tax liability of $19,100 on Friday, May 26, 2017. The normal deposit due date is Wednesday, May 31. However, because Monday, May 29, is a holiday in the District of Columbia, the deposit is due no later than Thursday, June 1, 2017, and not Wednesday, May 31, 2017.

When a deposit due date is extended because it falls on a legal holiday, a transfer made as an automated clearing house (ACH) transfer must be initiated on the business day before the legal holiday so that it will be timely transferred on the day following the legal holiday.

Q 4:20   What are the legal holidays?

Table 4-3 lists the federal holidays for 2017, which are considered business holidays for purposes of an ACH transfer. Note that this list does not include state holidays for which there are bank closures within the state or other unscheduled federal holidays (such as a national day of mourning or Inauguration Day.)

Table 4-3.   Legal Holidays 2017

Holiday	Day Observed
New Year's Day (Jan. 1)	Monday Jan. 2 (Observed)
Birthday of Martin Luther King, Jr. (Third Monday in January)	Monday, Jan. 16
Inauguration Day (Jan. 20)	Friday, Jan. 20
Washington's Birthday (Third Monday in February)	Monday, Feb. 20
District of Columbia Emancipation Day (April 16)	Monday, April 17 (Observed)
Memorial Day (Last Monday in May)	Monday, May 29
Independence Day (July 4)	Tuesday, July 4
Labor Day (First Monday in September)	Monday, Sept. 4
Columbus Day (Second Monday in October)	Monday, Oct. 9
Veterans' Day (November 11)	Friday, Nov. 10 (Observed)
Thanksgiving Day (Fourth Thursday in November)	Thursday, Nov. 23
Christmas Day (December 25)	Monday, Dec. 25

Q 4:21   What is the shortfall makeup date?

An employer that timely deposits either 98 percent of its actual federal employment tax liability or is within $100 of the actual deposit obligation can avoid a penalty for an underpayment if the additional amount is deposited by the shortfall makeup date. For semiweekly depositors and employers subject to the one-day rule, the shortfall makeup date is on or before the earlier of the first Wednesday or first Friday on or after the 15th day of the month following the month for which the deposit was required to be made.

Q 4:22   What does a semiweekly depositor do when a deposit period bridges two calendar quarters?

A semiweekly deposit period can cross two calendar quarters. When this occurs, the close of the quarter marks the end of the semiweekly deposit period with the remainder of the semiweekly deposit period ending in the subsequent quarter, thereby creating two smaller semiweekly deposit periods. [Treas. Reg. § 31.6302-1(c)(2)(ii)]

Q 4:23   How are withheld income taxes and FICA taxes deposited?

The IRS requires deposits of withheld income taxes and FICA taxes to be remitted electronically through the EFTPS, Electronic Federal Tax Payment System.

Q 4:24   Can deposits be made to a Federal Reserve bank?

No. Federal Reserve banks are no longer authorized depositaries for federal tax deposits. [Temp. Treas. Reg. § 301.6302-1T]

Q 4:25   What is a Section 3121(q) Notice and Demand?

The Section 3121(q) Notice and Demand is given to an employer when the IRS determines that tipped employees have underreported their tipped income. This may be the result of an audit or information reported on Form 4137, Social Security and Medicare Tax on Unreported Tip Income. The notice must include the words "Notice and Demand" and "Section 3121(q)." The date of the notice establishes the date of the employer liability for the FICA taxes shown in the notice.

Q 4:26   How is the employer's share of underreported FICA taxes reported?

An employer that receives a Section 3121(q) Notice and Demand is liable for the employer's share of Social Security and Medicare taxes on the employee's underreported tips. A line, Section 3121(q) Notice and Demand—Tax due on unreported tips (currently Line 5f), is included on Form 941 to report the employer liability. The employer will deposit the required taxes based on the employer's deposit schedule to avoid deposit penalties. The employer liability must be recorded on Part 2 of Form 941 for a monthly schedule depositor or Schedule B (Form 941) for a semiweekly schedule depositor.

Q 4:27   When are separate deposits required for nonpayroll tax liabilities?

An employer's deposit schedule for nonpayroll withholding (e.g., reportable payments subject to backup withholding; retirement payments for service in the Armed Forces; pensions, annuities, or other deferred compensation) is determined separate and apart from deposits for payroll taxes. Whether an employer is a monthly or semiweekly depositor for nonpayroll deposits is based on whether the total liability for nonpayroll taxes in the lookback period exceeds $50,000. Once the schedule is determined, deposits for nonpayroll withholding follow the rules for depositing payroll taxes.

Separate deposits are required for nonpayroll income tax withholding, and these are reported on Form 945, Annual Return of Withheld Federal Income Tax. These payments include pensions, annuities, gambling winnings, and other items subject to backup withholding. Do not combine deposits that are reported on Form 941. The deposit due dates are basically the same as the deposit dates for payroll tax withholding although the lookback period is the second preceding calendar-year liabilities for the Form 945 deposit requirements. [Pub. No. 15]

Q 4:28   How are overpayments of federal withholding and FICA payments credited?

Deposits of FICA taxes that result in overpayment of liabilities will be credited first to satisfy any underdeposits within the same return period, with the oldest underdeposit being satisfied first. An overpayment at the end of the return period becomes an overpayment of the tax liability on the last day prescribed for payment of the tax. The IRS normally will credit the overpayment amount at that time. However, an employer may elect to apply any overpayment of federal employment taxes from one return period to the first succeeding return period, using Form 941. In such a case, that amount will be credited to the employer's account as of the date of the overdeposit resulting in the overpayment. Form 843, Claim for Refund and Request for Abatement, is not used to apply for a refund for income, FICA or FUTA taxes. [Treas. Reg. §§ 31.6402(a)-2, 31.6413(a)-2]

Q 4:29   What is the order in which payments are credited for late payments?

Tax deposits are applied first to satisfy any past due underdeposits for the quarter, with the oldest underdeposit satisfied first. However, the employer may designate the period to which the deposit applies if the employer receives a penalty notice.

Example. Locust Corp. is required to make deposits of $2,222 per month. It makes timely deposits by January 15 and February 15, 2017. It does not make the deposit by March 15, 2017. On April 16, Locust Corp. deposits $3,100, assuming that it will pay its April deposit in full and apply $878 to the late March deposit. However, because deposits are applied first to past due underdeposits in due date order, $2,222 of the April 16 deposit is applied to the late March deposit. The remaining $878 is applied to the April 16 liability. Therefore, in addition to an underdeposit of $2,222 for March, Locust Corp. has an underdeposit for April 16 of $1,344. Penalties will be applied to both underdeposits. [Rev. Proc. 99-10, 1999-1 C.B. 272; Pub. No. 15]

Q 4:30   Can adjustments to prior periods affect the lookback rule?

Employers base their deposit due dates on the four quarters in the lookback period and their tax liability as originally reported on the corresponding Forms 941. If adjustments are made to correct errors on previously filed employment tax returns, these adjustments do not affect the amount of tax liability for purposes of the lookback rule. If the employer filed Form 941-X, Adjusted Employer's QUARTERLY Federal Tax Return or Claim for Refund, to claim a refund for a prior period overpayment, its tax liability does not change for either the prior period or the current period for purposes of the lookback rule.

Example. An employer originally reported a tax liability of $46,000 for the four quarters in the lookback period ending June 30, 2016. The employer discovered during January 2016 that the tax during one of the lookback period quarters was understated by $7,000 and corrected this error by filing a Form 941-X during the first quarter of 2016. This employer is a monthly schedule depositor for 2017 because the lookback-period tax liabilities are based on the amounts originally reported. In this instance, they were less than $50,000. The $7,000 adjustment is part of the 2017 first-quarter tax liability. [Pub. No. 15]

Q 4:31   Can the taxpayer designate the application of a federal tax deposit?

Yes. According to an IRS Chief Counsel Advice (CCA 199931038), a taxpayer may designate the application of a federal tax deposit, provided the designation includes specific, written instructions regarding the type of tax and the period to which the deposit should apply.

Q 4:32   Will small underpayments of federal income tax withholding and FICA liabilities always result in a penalty?

No. An employer is allowed an underpayment (referred to as a deposit shortfall) without being deemed a delinquent depositor. The underpayment may not exceed the greater of $100 or 2 percent of the amount of liability that is otherwise due for a deposit period. Such deposits must be corrected within a specified period to be classified as a deposit shortfall. Shortfall makeup dates are set based on the employer's deposit schedule:

- For monthly depositors, the shortfall must be deposited by the due date of the Form 941 for the period in which the shortfall occurs. For instance, a shortfall that related to a July deposit must be paid no later than October 31, the due date of the Form 941 for the third calendar quarter.

- For semiweekly depositors or employers subject to the one-business-day rule, the shortfall must be deposited on or before the first Wednesday or Friday, whichever is earlier, falling on or after the 15th of the month following the month in which the deposit was required to have been made. [Treas. Reg. § 31.6302-1(f)]

Example. A semiweekly depositor pays wages and incurs a federal income tax withholding and FICA liability on February 5, 2017. A deposit of $13,100 was made on February 10, 2017. The liability was actually $13,300, resulting in a shortfall of $200. The amount of the shortfall is less than the greater of $100 or 2 percent of $13,300. The deposit is deemed timely as long as the $200 shortfall is deposited by the first deposit date (Wednesday or Friday) on or after the 15th day of March (in this example, Wednesday, March 15, 2017).

When the shortfall threshold (the greater of $100 or 2 percent of the liability) is exceeded, the deposit will be deemed to have been made late and the employer will face a failure-to-deposit penalty (see Q 4:105).

Electronic Deposits

Q 4:33 When must depositors begin depositing payroll taxes electronically?

Since there is no longer an option to deposit payroll taxes by paper coupon, an employer must use the Electronic Federal Tax Payment System (EFTPS) to make deposits unless the employer is eligible to make a payment with the quarterly or annual return.

Q 4:34 How does an employer enroll in EFTPS?

It depends. The IRS offers an EFTPS Express Enrollment for New Businesses [IR 2004-10, 1/15/04]. Employers that receive a new EIN are automatically pre-enrolled in EFTPS. Pre-enrolled employers will receive in the mail an EFTPS personal identification number (PIN) and instructions on how to activate the enrollment. To activate the enrollment, an employer must call a toll-free number, enter its banking information, and complete an authorization for EFTPS to transfer funds from the employer's account to the Treasury's account for tax payments according to the employer's instructions. For more information, an employer may call EFTPS Customer Service at 1-800-555-4477 or 1-800-945-8400.

Alternatively, an employer may enroll in EFTPS online at www.eftps.gov.

Information about EFTPS, including downloadable EFTPS publications, is also available on the IRS website at http://www.irs.gov/uac/EFTPS-The-Electronic-Federal-Tax-Payment-System.

Q 4:35   Which taxes are deposited via EFTPS?

An employer subject to EFTPS will pay all taxes for the following reports electronically:

- Form 720, Quarterly Federal Excise Return
- Form 940, Employer's Annual Federal Unemployment Tax (FUTA) Return
- Form 941, Employer's QUARTERLY Federal Tax Return
- Form 943, Employer's Annual Tax Return for Agricultural Workers
- Form 944, Employer's ANNUAL Federal Tax Return
- Form 945, Annual Return of Withheld Federal Income Tax
- Form 990-C, Farmer's Cooperative Association Income Tax Return
- Form 990-PF, Return of Private Foundation or Section 4947(a)(1) Nonexempt Charitable Trust Treated as a Private Foundation
- Form 990-T, Exempt Organization Business Income Tax Return (and proxy tax under Code Section 6033(e))
- Form 1041, U.S. Income Tax Return for Estates and Trusts
- Form 1042, Annual Withholding Tax Return for U.S. Sources of Income of Foreign Persons
- Form 1120, U.S. Corporation Income Tax Return
- Form CT-1, Employer's Annual Railroad Retirement Tax Return

Q 4:36   How do employers make a payment under EFTPS?

An electronic deposit can be made through either EFTPS-Direct (ACH Debit) or EFTPS-Through a Financial Institution (ACH Credit), or both. Under the direct method, the employer indicates the date on which the EFTPS can initiate the collection of the taxes directly from the financial institution that has the tax payment account(s). When EFTPS is through a financial institution, the employer initiates the direct transfer from the financial institution to the EFTPS. EFTPS payments can be initiated through most computer systems.

The EFTPS is administered through two financial institutions referred to as the TFAs: The Bank of America and Bank One. An employer will utilize the TFA assigned to the state where it makes its federal deposits.

An enhanced version of the EFTPS batch provider software is available for download. The program introduced in 2006 allows tax professionals to register through the software and send up to 1,000 enrollments and 5,000 payments in one transmission. Users can synchronize enrollments and payment history between the software and the EFTPS database in real time. The program is said by the IRS to be "very user-friendly and easy to install," with a complete user's manual and Quick Start Guide also available for download.

Q 4:37   Can an employer initiate a same-day electronic payment?

Yes. Employers required to deposit using EFTPS that have missed the deadline of one day prior to the tax due date under EFTPS-Direct or EFTPS-Through a Financial Institution may use a same-day payment method. Employers must check with their financial institutions as to the fees and procedures involved. This option requires an "enrollment" so it is recommended that employers have the enrollment completed in advance in case this option is required.

With the implementation of same-day ACH, the Treasury is contemplating allowing employers to make same-day ACH transfers for employment taxes.

Q 4:38   What are the penalties for not utilizing EFTPS when required?

This requirement to make electronically initiated deposits for federal taxes includes not only employment taxes but also taxes reported on Forms 1120, 720, 990-C, 990-PF, and 990-T. Employers will be subject to a 10 percent penalty based on the amount of the deposit when the required deposit is not made electronically. In addition, late or delinquent deposits that are made electronically will be subject to late payment penalties and interest as would any other late tax payment. [Rev. Proc. 98-32, § 21, 1998-1 C.B. 935]

Filing Requirements

Q 4:39   What are the federal information statement requirements when a business has paid wages subject to withholding and employment tax?

An employer must prepare a Form W-2, Wage and Tax Statement, for each employee for whom it is required to withhold taxes and must furnish copies of Form W-2 to employees by January 31 of the year following the calendar year in which the wages were paid and taxes withheld. Beginning with the 2016 W-2, the Protecting Americans from Tax Hikes (PATH) Act requires employers to file Forms W-2 with the SSA by January 31 of the year following the calendar year in which the wages were paid and taxes were withheld. This is the same date that employers must furnish Form W-2 to employees. Previously, the due date to file with the SSA was the last day of February (March 31 if electronically filed). Forms W-2 must be accompanied by a Form W-3, Transmittal of Wage and Tax Statements. Additionally, if an employee's employment is terminated during a calendar year, the employer must, if requested by the former employee, provide the former employee with a copy of his or her Form W-2 within 30 days of receipt of a written request.

An employer may file for an extension in the event there has been a disaster or catastrophe. Form 8809, Application for Extension of Time to File Information Returns for W-2, 1042-S, 1099, 1094-C, 1095-B, and 1095-C must be submitted to the IRS. In the case of Form W-2, the request for an extension of up to 30 days is not automatic, must be in writing and must be filed by the transmitter or the party who is authorized to sign a return.

A Form W-2 must contain the following information: name and address of employer, name and address of employee, employer and employee federal taxpayer identification numbers, and, for the calendar year, amount of wages paid, amount of federal income tax withheld, Social Security and Medicare wages, Social Security and Medicare tax withheld, amount of elective deferrals (within the meaning of I.R.C. Section 402(g)(3); i.e., 401(k) salary deferrals) and compensation deferred under I.R.C. Section 457, and amount incurred for dependent care assistance with respect to the employee under a plan described in I.R.C. Section 129(d). Finally, special information is required to be reported in Boxes 10, 11, 12, 13, and 14.

Q 4:40   What are the information return requirements for employers that have paid wages subject to employment tax and withholding?

An employer must file a federal employment tax return. Most employers file the Form 941, Employer's QUARTERLY Federal Tax Return, to report federal income tax withheld from wages and FICA taxes. Some employers may be required to file an annual return (e.g., Form 943 or 944). Form 941 (or its equivalent) is used to report federal and FICA taxable wages, federal income tax withheld, FICA tax, and reductions in the employment tax liability for credits that apply for COBRA premium assistance. Generally, the wage and tax reported on Form 941 agrees with those reported on Form W-2. Certain household employers that employ only domestic workers file Schedule H, Form 1040, in lieu of Form 941 or 944.

The due dates of the federal employment returns are based on calendar quarters. For the specific due dates that apply, see Q 4:46.

If the Form 941 due date falls on a Saturday, Sunday, or legal holiday, the return is due on the next business day.[I.R.C. § 7503; Treas. Reg. § 301.7503-1(b); Pub. No. 509]

A Form 941 is considered timely filed if the date of U.S. Postal Service postmark is the second day before the due date and the proper amount of postage has been paid. [I.R.C. § 7502] The IRS has proposed a rule that a certified or registered mail receipt would establish timeliness of mailing. [REG-138176-02, 2004-43 I.R.B. 710] Alternatively, the IRS recognizes dates of registration for the following private delivery services effective May 6, 2015:

- *Federal Express (FedEx):* FedEx Priority Overnight, FedEx Standard Overnight, FedEx 2 Day, FedEx International Priority, FedEx First Overnight,

FedEx International Next FlightOut, FedEx International Economy, and FedEx International First.

- *United Parcel Service (UPS):* UPS Next Day Air Early A.M., UPS Next Day Air, UPS Next Day Air Saver, UPS 2nd Day Air, UPS 2nd Day Air A.M., UPS Worldwide Express Plus, and UPS Worldwide Express.

- *DHL:* DHL Express 9:00, DHL Express 10:30, DHL Express 12:00, DHL Express Worldwide, DHL Express Envelope, DHL Import Express 10:30, DHL Import Express 12:00, and DHL Import Express Worldwide.

[Notice 2016-30, 2016-16 I.R.B.; Notice 2015-38, 2015-21 I.R.B.]

Q 4:41　Other than the U.S. Postal Service, what means may be used by employers to document a timely filing?

Only specific nonpostal delivery services (see Q 4:40) provided by DHL, Federal Express and United Parcel Service qualify as timely mailed when sent (as opposed to when received). The private delivery service can provide written proof of the mailing date. [Notice 2016-30, 2016-18 I.R.B.; Notice 2015-38, 2015-21 I.R.B.]

Q 4:42　How does the employee report wages paid in error in a prior year?

Wages paid to an employee that are subject to repayment in a subsequent calendar year are subject to the claim-of-right doctrine. Under this rule the employer is prohibited from correcting federal taxable wages that were paid in a previous year or in refunding federal income tax withheld on those wages. Instead, when wages are repaid in a year subsequent to the original payment, the employer issues a Form W-2c for the year of the original repayment showing a reduction in Social Security and Medicare wages. The employer refunds FICA tax due on the reduction in wages if the employee certifies according to the Form 941-X instructions that it did not and will not file a request for refund from the IRS. For adjustment to federal income tax, the employee must follow the instructions as contained in IRS Publication 525, Taxable and Nontaxable Income. [Pub. No. 15]

Q 4:43　How are Social Security and Medicare taxes that are voluntarily withheld from a minister's wages reported?

These amounts are reported as federal income tax withheld on the Form W-2 (Box 2). Ministers can then apply any overpaid federal income tax to their self-employment tax liability on the Form 1040, U.S. Individual Income Tax Return.

Form 941

Q 4:44   What is the Form 941 designed to do?

The stated purpose of the form is to report (1) income taxes withheld from wages, including tips, supplemental unemployment compensation benefits, and third-party payments of sick pay; and (2) Social Security and Medicare taxes both withheld and paid by the employer.

Each quarter, all employers that pay wages subject to income tax withholding (including withholding on sick pay and supplemental unemployment benefits) or Social Security and Medicare taxes must file Form 941, Employer's QUAR-TERLY Federal Tax Return. However, special exceptions apply to employers that file the annual Form 944, those that pay certain seasonal employees, agricultural employees, household employees, and employees located in certain U.S. territories. [Pub. No. 15]

Note. Small employers have the option of filing the annual Form 944 (see Q 4:54).

All employers that pay wages subject to federal income tax withholding and/or Social Security/Medicare tax must file a quarterly Form 941 or its equivalent (e.g., Form 943 or 944).

Q 4:45   What changes have occurred to the Form 941?

The 2017 version of Form 941 no longer includes lines for COBRA premium assistance payments or number of individuals provided these payments. The Form 941 changed in 2013 with the addition of a line (line 5d) to report taxable wages and tips subject to Additional Medicare Tax withholding. The Form 941 and Schedule B were significantly revised in January 2005 and a new Schedule D, Report of Discrepancies Caused by Acquisitions, Statutory Mergers, or Consolidations, was created for filing by applicable employers to explain certain wage, tax, and payment discrepancies between Form 941 and Forms W-2 that were caused by the transfer of wages and taxes pursuant to an acquisition, statutory merger, or consolidation. (See chapter 12 for more details.)

FICA liability for unreported tips. Form 941 continues to include Section 3121(q) Notice and Demand Tax Due on Unreported Tips reported on Line 5f, which was added to Form 941 in 2011 to report the employer FICA liability for unreported tips. Current quarter adjustments for fraction of cents are made on Line 7 and current quarter adjustments for sick pay are made on Line 8. Current quarter adjustments for tips and group-term life insurance are made on Line 9.

Small employers. An employer can pay the amount due with a timely filed Form 941 if its accumulated tax liability is less than $2,500 for the current quarter or the preceding quarter, and the employer did not incur a $100,000 next-day deposit obligation during the current quarter.

Agent reporting. Schedule R, Allocation Schedule for Aggregate Form 941 Filers, was created for agents approved by the IRS under Internal Revenue Code Section 3504 to file a single Form 941, using the agent's own employer identification number, which aggregately reports the Form 941 information of all clients that it represents. See Q 4:120 for additional information.

Employers can now claim a payroll tax credit for increasing research activities by adjusting their tax liability on Form 941 or 941-SS when reporting liabilities on Schedule B.

Q 4:46 What is the due date for filing the Form 941?

The Form 941 is filed starting with the first quarter in which the employer is required to withhold income tax or pay wages subject to Social Security and Medicare taxes. Thus, returns are filed under the schedule shown in Table 4-4.

Table 4-4. Form 941 Filing Schedule

Quarter	Quarter End Date	Due Date of Form 941	Extended Due Date*
Jan., Feb., Mar.	Mar. 31	April 30, 2017	May 10
Apr., May, June	June 30	July 31, 2017	Aug. 10
July, Aug., Sept.	Sept. 30	October 31, 2017	Nov. 13
Oct., Nov., Dec.	Dec. 31	January 31, 2018	Feb. 10

* Employers that deposit all taxes when due for a quarter have 10 additional days after the due date to file the Form 941 without it being treated as delinquent. If the due date for filing a return falls on a Saturday, Sunday, or legal holiday, the employer may file the return on the next business day. [Pub. No. 509; I.R.C. § 7503]

> **Note.** The regulations do not provide an extension for filing Form 941. There is a 10-day extended due date for filing Form 941, provided 100 percent of the tax amount has been timely deposited. Otherwise, penalties will be assessed for late filing. The request is submitted using Letter 0279C, providing the basis for the request.

Q 4:47 How is the Form 941 filed?

Employers have a couple of options for filing the Form 941. The traditional method is to file a paper form by mail or private delivery service (see Q 4:41) to the IRS. The specific IRS address for mailing the return depends on the state where the employer is located as well as whether a payment is included with the Form 941.

The IRS encourages employers to file the Form 941 electronically. One option available to employers with computers and web-based Internet access is to file the Form 941 online through an authorized third-party transmitter. The 941 e-file program is used with a commercial tax preparation software. Information can be obtained at www.irs.gov/efile or call 1-866-255-0654. Employers that use a reporting agent (i.e., a payroll service provider) may utilize the IRS's e-file program.

Employers no longer have the option to file via 941 TeleFile by dialing a toll-free number from a touch-tone phone. The IRS also no longer accepts Form 941 via magnetic media.

Q 4:48   Where is the paper Form 941 filed?

The IRS address for mailing the Form 941 is determined by the employer's legal residence, principal place of business, office, or agency. Send the return to the IRS at the address listed in the Form 941 instructions for that location. Note that there is generally no street address for the IRS. A different IRS mailing address applies if a payment is submitted with the Form 941.

If you have no legal residence or principal place of business in any state, mail all returns without a payment to P.O. Box 409101, Ogden, UT 84409. Mail returns with payment to P.O. Box 105273, Atlanta, GA 30348-5273.

Q 4:49   Can an employer file Form 941 electronically?

IRS has created two new forms to facilitate the filing of employment returns electronically. Forms 8879-EMP and 8453-EMP provide signature authorization to file electronically.

Q 4:50   Are any attachments required to be included with the Form 941?

Yes. Employers that have made deposits under the next-day deposit rule or that are semiweekly depositors must attach Schedule B, Report of Tax Liability. Employers that were involved in a recent acquisition, merger, or consolidation should attach Schedule D, Report of Discrepancies Caused by Acquisitions, Statutory Mergers, or Consolidations. (See chapter 12 for more information.)

Previously, employers had to send with Form 941 copies of any Forms W-4, Employee's Withholding Allowance Certificate, received during the quarter from employees claiming either (1) more than 10 withholding allowances, or (2) an exemption from income tax withholding when the employee's wages were normally more than $200 a week. This is no longer an automatic requirement. Instead, employers separately mail to the IRS only those Forms W-4 specifically requested by the IRS.

Q 4:51 Should any amounts reported on Form 941 be reconciled to other filed reports?

Yes. Certain amounts reported on the Forms 941, Employer's QUARTERLY Federal Tax Return, for the calendar year must agree with the Form W-2, Wage and Tax Statement, and Form W-3, Transmittal of Wage and Tax Statements, filed for the same year. The amounts that should agree are: federal taxable wages, federal income tax withheld, Social Security wages, Social Security tips, and Medicare wages and tips. If these totals do not agree, the IRS will require a full explanation of any differences and correction of any errors. Amounts reported on W-2, W-3, and Forms 941/944/943 may not agree for valid reasons. If they do not match, the employer must determine that the reasons are valid and keep the reconciliation in case there are inquiries from the IRS or the SSA.

Note. Schedule D will explain the differences between Forms 941/943/944 that are due to a merger, acquisition, or consolidation. (See chapter 12 for more information.)

Q 4:52 Are there any processing recommendations for the Form 941 preparer?

The IRS has recommended that filers follow certain procedures to enable accurate scanning and processing. The Form 941 preparer should:

- Omit dollar signs and decimal points. Commas are optional. Report dollars to the left of the preprinted decimal point and cents to the right of it.
- Enter negative amounts using a minus sign (if possible). Otherwise, use parentheses.
- Use 10-point Courier font (if possible) for all entries that are typed or input on the computer. If not, print data entries.
- Leave blank any data field (except lines 1, 2, and 10) with a value of zero.
- Enter the business name and EIN on all pages and attachments.
- Staple multiple sheets in the upper left corner when filing.

Q 4:53 What are the Form 941 filing requirements when a business terminates?

If an employer goes out of business or stops paying wages, a final Form 941 must be filed and the box on line 15 must be checked and the date final wages were paid must be entered. A statement should be attached showing the name of the person keeping the payroll records and the address where those records will be kept. Note that in the case of a business or trade that goes out of business, the employer is required to provide W-2s to employees by the due date of the final return. The W-2s must be filed with SSA by the last day of the month following the due date of the final return.

See chapter 12 for information about a business terminations pursuant to reorganization.

Q 4:54   May smaller employers file a Form 944?

Yes. Employers are able to file once a year on Form 944, Employer's ANNUAL Federal Tax Return, if their estimated annual employment tax liability is $1,000 or less, and they have received notification from the IRS to file Form 944.

Note. An employer required to file Form 944, Employer's ANNUAL Federal Tax Return, can request from the IRS to file quarterly if notification is received from the IRS to file annually. If the employer prefers to file Form 941, Employer's QUARTERLY Federal Tax Return, the employer must make the request to the IRS to change the filing requirement. Form 944 is due the last day of the month following the end of the calendar year. Revenue Procedure 2009-51 is available at http://www.irs.gov/pub/irs-irbs/irb09-45.pdf.

New employers that expect to have an employment tax liability of $1,000 or less and wish to file an annual Form 944 rather than a quarterly Form 941 can check the box on Line 14 on Form SS-4 to indicate so.

Forms 944-SS, 944-PR, and 944-AS have been discontinued and employers previously filing those forms can file Form 944. Alternatively, these employers can request to file Form 941.

Q 4:55   How do seasonal employers that have no wages comply with 941 filings?

Employers must alert the IRS that they will not have to file a return for one or more quarters during the year for which no wages are paid by checking the Seasonal Employer Box on line 16 on Form 941. Employers also should be sure to check the box on the top of Form 941 that corresponds to the quarter reported. The IRS will generally not inquire about unfiled returns if at least one taxable return is filed each year. However, the employer must mark the Seasonal Employer Box on every quarterly return that is filed. Otherwise, the IRS will expect a return to be filed for each quarter. [Pub. No. 15]

Q 4:56   How is Form 941 completed?

The following instructions supply line-by-line assistance in completing Form 941.

Employers must complete their EIN, name, trade name (if any), and address.

Report for This Quarter: Employers must check the box that applies to the quarter for which they are filing.

Part 1: Answer these questions for this quarter.

Line 1, Number of employees who received wages, tips, or other compensation for the pay period including: Mar. 12 (Quarter 1), June 12 (Quarter 2), Sept. 12 (Quarter 3), Dec. 12 (Quarter 4): Enter the number of employees included in the employer's payroll during the pay period that includes March 12, June 12, Sept. 12, or Dec. 12, depending on which quarter the Form 941 applies to. Line 1 must be completed each quarter. Do not include household employees, persons who received no pay during the pay period, farm employees, pensioners, or active members of the Armed Forces. An entry of 250 or more on line 1 indicates a need to file Forms W-2 electronically. Employers may contact the SSA at 1-800-772-6270 or access the SSA Employer Reporting Instructions and Information website at www.socialsecurity.gov/employer for more information.

Line 2, Wages, tips, and other compensation: Enter the total of all wages paid, tips reported, taxable fringe benefits provided, and other compensation paid to the employees that would also be included in box 1 of the employees' Forms W-2. Employers that receive a timely notice from an insurance carrier concerning the amount of third-party sick pay they paid to employees will include the sick pay on line 2.

Line 3, Income tax withheld from wages, tips, and other compensation: Enter the income tax withheld on wages, tips, taxable fringe benefits, and supplemental unemployment compensation benefits. Also include any excise taxes that were required to be withheld on golden parachute payments. An insurance company acting as a third-party payer that is reporting sick pay should enter the income tax it withheld on third-party sick pay here.

Line 4, If no wages, tips, and other compensation are subject to social security or Medicare tax: Check the box on line 4 and skip to line 6 if no wages, tips, and compensation on line 2 are subject to Social Security and Medicare taxes (e.g., certain governmental employers). Leave the box blank if it does not apply.

Line 5a, Taxable social security wages: On line 5a, Column 1, report the total wages, sick pay, or fringe benefits subject to Social Security taxes that you paid to your employees during the quarter. Include payments made by an insurance company to the employees for which the employer received timely notice from the insurance company. Multiply this amount by 0.124 and enter the result in Column 2.

Note. The total Social Security wages plus tips reported for 2017 cannot exceed $127,200. There is no limit on the amount of Medicare wages subject to 1.45 percent. Beginning in January 1, 2013, an Additional Medicare Tax of 0.9 percent on compensation in excess of $200,000 applies.

Line 5b, Taxable social security tips: In Column 1 of line 5b, enter all the tips reported to the employer by the employees during the quarter.

Note. This amount plus the wages reported for 2017 cannot exceed $127,200.

Allocated tips are not included on this line. Multiply the tips reported in Column 1 by 0.124 and enter the result in Column 2.

Line 5c, Taxable Medicare wages & tips: On line 5c, Column 1, enter all wages, tips, sick pay, and taxable fringe benefits that are subject to Medicare tax. Multiply this amount by 0.029 and enter the result in Column 2.

Line 5d, Taxable wages & tips subject to Additional Medicare Tax withholding: On line 5d, Column 1, enter all wages, tips, sick pay, and taxable fringe benefits that are subject to Medicare tax and exceed $200,000 for an employee. Multiply this amount by 0.009 and enter the result in Column 2.

Line 5e: On line 5e, total the Social Security and Medicare taxes by adding Column 2 of lines 5a, 5b, 5c, and 5d.

Line 5f, Section 3121(q) Notice and Demand: On line 5f, enter Section 3121(q) Notice and Demand tax due for unreported tips.

Line 6, Total taxes before adjustments: Add the total federal income tax withheld from wages, tips, and other compensation (line 3), the total Social Security and Medicare taxes before adjustments (line 5e), and the Section 3121(q) Notice and Demand tax on unreported tips (line 5f). Enter the result in line 6.

CURRENT QUARTER'S ADJUSTMENTS: The Form 941 has separate lines for the various current quarter adjustments. Negative numbers should be indicated with a minus sign if possible. The adjustments include the following:

Line 7, Current quarter's adjustments for fractions of cents: Adjustments for fractions of cents (due to rounding) of the employee share of Social Security and Medicare taxes withheld must be entered on line 7.

Line 8, Current quarter's adjustment for sick pay: An employer must enter the adjustment for the employee share of Social Security and Medicare taxes that were withheld by the third-party sick pay payer on line 8.

Line 9, Current quarter's adjustments for tips and group-term life insurance: On line 9, the employer must enter adjustments for any uncollected employee share of Social Security and Medicare taxes on tips and the uncollected employee share of Social Security and Medicare taxes on group-term life insurance premium paid for former employees.

Line 10, Total taxes after adjustment: Employers must add the amounts on lines 6 through 9 and enter the result on line 10.

Line 11, Qualified small business payroll tax credit: On this new line, enter the amount of the qualified small business payroll tax credit. Attach Form 8974.

Line 12, Total taxes after adjustments and credits: Subtract line 11 from line 10.

Line 13, Total deposits, including prior quarter overpayments: On line 13, employers should enter their deposits for the quarter including any overpayment applied from filing Form 941-X or Form 944-X in the current quarter. If line 12 is more than line 13, the employer reports the balance due on line 14. Also include any overpayment from a previous period that was applied to this return.

Line 14, Balance due: The employer should have a balance due only if the net tax liability—for the current quarter or preceding quarter is less than $2,500, and it did not incur a $100,000 next-day deposit obligation during the current quarter. However, amounts may also be due under the accuracy of deposits rule. If line 12 is $2,500 or more and all taxes have been deposited when due, the amount shown on line 14 (balance due) should be zero. When the employer failed to make deposits as required and has amounts due with the return, the employer may be subject to a penalty. Payment may be made using EFTPS, a credit or debit card, a check or money order, or electronic funds withdrawal (EFW). Do not use a credit or debit card or electronic funds withdrawal (EFW) to pay taxes that were required to be deposited.

Line 15, Overpayment: When deposits and/or credits exceed the taxes paid or deposited for a quarter, an employer can have the overpayment refunded or applied to the next quarterly return by checking the appropriate box. If a box is not checked, the overpayment will be applied to your account. The IRS may also apply the overpayment to any past-due tax account that exists under the filer's EIN. If line 15 is under $1.00, the IRS will send a refund or apply it to the next return only on written request.

Part 2: Tell us about your deposit schedule and tax liability for this quarter.

Line 16, Check one: The employer must indicate what type of depositor by checking the appropriate box: if line 12 is less than $2,500 or line 12 on its preceding quarterly return was less than $2,500, and the employer did not incur a $100,000 next-day deposit obligation during the current quarter; if it reported $50,000 or less in taxes during the lookback period, it is a monthly schedule depositor (unless the next-day deposit rule applied); or if it reported more than $50,000 of taxes for the lookback period, it is a semiweekly schedule depositor. If you meet the *de minimis* exception based on the prior quarter and Line 12 for the current quarter is $100,000 or more, you must provide a record of your federal tax liability.

Semiweekly depositors must complete Schedule B. Monthly depositors must indicate their tax liability (not the amount of the deposits) for each month of the quarter on line 16. If the tax liability for any month is negative, enter zero for that month and subtract that negative amount from the tax liability for the following month.

Part 3: Tell us about your business. If a question does NOT apply to your business, leave it blank.

Line 17, If your business has closed or you stopped paying wages: Check the box on line 17 and enter the final wage payment date if the employer goes out of business or stops paying wages. (See Q 4:53 for additional information.)

Line 18, If you are a seasonal employer and you do not have to file a return for every quarter of the year: The employer must check the box on line 18 if it has employees only seasonally (e.g., summer only). This box must be checked for each quarterly Form 941 even when there are no wages to report. (See Q 4:55 for additional information.)

Part 4: May we speak with your third-party designee?

Employers may indicate if they want an employee, a paid tax preparer, or another person to discuss their Form 941 with the IRS by either checking the "Yes" or "No" box. Employers that check the "Yes" box to allow a third-party designee must provide the name, phone number, and a five-digit PIN of the specific person to contact. By designating a third party, the employer authorizes the IRS to call the person with any questions when processing the Form 941. The designee may be authorized to give the IRS missing information, call the IRS about information about processing the Form 941, and respond to certain IRS notices about math errors and return preparation. The IRS will not send notices to the designee. The designee is not authorized to bind the employer to additional tax liability or represent the employer before the IRS. The authorization of the designee will automatically expire one year from the due date of the Form 941.

Part 5: Sign here. You MUST complete both pages of Form 941 and SIGN it.

The Form 941 must be signed by the individual who owns the business if the employer is a sole proprietorship; the president, vice president, or other principal officer if the employer is a corporation (including a limited liability company [LLC] treated as a corporation); a responsible and duly authorized member or officer having knowledge of the employer's affairs if the employer is a partnership (including a LLC treated as a partnership) or unincorporated organization; the owner of the limited liability company if the employer is a single-member LLC treated as a disregarded entity; or the fiduciary of a trust or estate. Corporate officers or duly authorized agents may sign Form 941 by rubber stamp, mechanical device, or computer software program.

Paid Preparer's Use Only

In the "Paid Preparer's Use Only" section of Part 5, a paid preparer must enter his or her name and address and provide a signature and PTIN (Preparer Tax Identification Number) in the spaces provided. If the preparer works for a firm, the firm's name and EIN must be entered too. This section should not be completed by employees of the entity that they are filing for or by reporting agents with a valid Form 8655, unless the reporting agent is offering legal advice.

Q 4:57   How is the Schedule B for Form 941 completed?

The purpose of Schedule B is to report your tax liability for each day of the quarter. This will include the federal income tax you withheld from your employees' pay and the employee and employer Social Security and Medicare tax. Schedule B is provided for semiweekly depositors and should tie in to what was reported on Form 941. See Q 4:8, Table 4-1 for guidance in determining if you are a semiweekly depositor.

Q 4:58 What are the Form 941 filing requirements for sole proprietors with household employees?

If an employer is a sole proprietor and files Form 941, Employer's QUARTERLY Federal Tax Return, for business employees, it may include taxes for household employees on Form 941. Otherwise, report federal income tax, Social Security and Medicare withholding and employment tax for household employees on Schedule H (Form 1040), Household Employment Taxes. [Pub. No. 15]

Q 4:59 What are the Form 941 filing requirements for employers paying wages in U.S. territories?

Special rules apply to employers reporting wages for employees in American Samoa, Guam, the Commonwealth of the Northern Mariana Islands, the U.S. Virgin Islands, or Puerto Rico. If these employees are not subject to U.S. income tax withholding, use Form 941-SS, Employer's Quarterly Federal Tax Return. Employers in Puerto Rico use Form 941-PR, Employer's Quarterly Federal Tax Return. [Pub. No. 15]

Q 4:60 When an employer has two locations, are two Forms 941 filed each quarter?

No. Employers with multiple locations or divisions must file only one Form 941, Employer's QUARTERLY Federal Tax Return, per quarter. Filing more than one return may result in processing delays and may require correspondence between the employer and the IRS. Also, do not report more than one calendar quarter on a return. [Pub. No. 15]

Corrections to Form 941

Q 4:61 How does an employer file an original return for a prior quarter or prior year (i.e., a late filing)?

Employers that file an original return for a quarter in a prior year should use the form for that particular year. There will be penalties and interest assessed for the late filing.

Check the revision date (found under the form number at the top of the form) to identify the year for which the form was developed.

A form for a particular year can generally be used without modification for any quarter within that year. For example, a form with any 2016 revision date (e.g., January 2016) can generally be used without modification for any quarter of 2016.

In all cases, however, the filer should be sure to correctly fill out the "Report for this Quarter" section at the top of the form. If the filer is modifying a form with preprinted information, change the date. Cross out any inapplicable tax rate(s) shown on the form and write in the rate from Table 4-5.

Table 4-5.   Tax Rates

Calendar Year	Wage Base (Each Employee)	Tax Rate on Taxable Wages and Tips*
2017—Social Security	$127,200	12.4%
2017—Medicare	All Wages	2.9%
2016—Social Security	$118,500	12.4%
2016—Medicare	All Wages	2.9%
2015—Social Security	$118,500	12.4%
2015—Medicare	All Wages	2.9%
2015—Additional Medicare Tax	$200,000 and above	0.9%
2014—Social Security	$117,000	12.4%
2014—Medicare	All Wages	2.9%
2014—Additional Medicare Tax	$200,000 and above	0.9%
2013—Social Security	$113,700	12.4%
2013—Medicare	All Wages	2.9%
2012—Social Security	$110,100	10.4%
2012—Medicare	All Wages	2.9%
2011—Social Security	$106,800	10.4%
2011—Medicare	All Wages	2.9%

Q 4:62   How are adjustments or corrections to prior Form 941 filings made?

There are two types of adjustments, and each is corrected in a different manner: current quarter's adjustments and adjustments to correct errors on prior period returns. Current quarter adjustments are made using Form 941; adjustments to correct errors on prior period returns are made using Form 941-X. These adjustments are corrected in the following manner:

Current quarter's adjustments, third-party payer reconciliation. In certain cases, amounts reported as Social Security and Medicare taxes in column 2 of lines 5a–5d of Form 941 must be adjusted to arrive at the employer's correct tax liability (e.g., excluding amounts withheld by a third-party payer or amounts the employer was not required to withhold). Current quarter adjustments are reported on lines 7 through 9 of Form 941 and include the following:

- *Adjustment of tax on tips:* If, by the 10th of the month after the month an employee reported his or her tips, the employer does not have enough employee funds available to withhold the employee's share of Social Security and Medicare taxes, the employer is no longer required to collect the taxes. Employers report the entire amount of these tips on lines 5b

(Social Security tips), 5c (Medicare wages and tips), and, if applicable, 5d (taxable wages and tips subject to Additional Medicare Tax withholding). Include as an adjustment on line 9 the total uncollected employee share of the Social Security and Medicare taxes using Form 941.

- *Adjustment of group-term life insurance premiums paid for former employee where employee has no income from which to withhold:* A former employee's share of Social Security and Medicare taxes on group-term life insurance over $50,000 is paid by the former employee with his or her tax return and cannot be collected by the employer. The value of that benefit that is considered gross wages is determined under regulations and will vary with some group-term insurance contracts. This valuation should be provided by the insurance company. However, include all Social Security and Medicare taxes for such coverage on lines 5a and 5c (Social Security and Medicare taxes), and deduct the amount of the employee share of these taxes as an adjustment on line 9 of Form 941.

- *Adjustment of tax on third-party sick pay:* Report both the employer and employee shares of Social Security and Medicare taxes for sick pay on lines 5a and 5c of Form 941. Deduct on line 8 the Social Security and Medicare taxes on third-party sick pay for which the employer is not responsible. No additional statement for this adjustment is required.

- *Fractions-of-cents adjustment:* If there is a small difference between the computation of the employee share of Social Security and Medicare taxes and the amount actually withheld and this difference is caused by adding or dropping fractions of cents in collecting the tax (rounding), report the difference on line 7 of Form 941. No additional statement for this adjustment is required.

Example. Hampden Auto was entitled to the following current period adjustments for Form 941:

- *Third-party sick pay:* It included Social Security and Medicare taxes of $19,000 for sick pay on lines 5a and 5c. However, the third-party payer of the sick pay withheld and paid to the IRS the employee share ($9,500) of these taxes. Hampden Auto is entitled to a $9,500 sick-pay adjustment (negative) on line 8.

- *Fractions of cents:* Hampden Auto determined that the amounts calculated and deposited for Social Security and Medicare taxes during the quarter were a net $0.42 more than the amount figured on line 5e (Social Security and Medicare taxes including the Additional Medicare Tax). This difference was caused by adding or dropping fractions of cents when figuring employment taxes for each wage payment. It must report a $0.42 fractions-of-cents adjustment (positive) on line 7.

- *Group Life insurance premiums:* Hampden Auto paid group-term life insurance premiums for policies in excess of $50,000 for former employees. The former employees must pay the employee share of the Social Security and Medicare taxes ($215) on the portion of the life insurance coverage over $50,000. However, Hampden Auto must include the employee's share of these taxes with the Social Security, Medicare taxes, and additional Medicare tax reported on lines 5a, 5c, and 5d of Form 941. It is entitled to a $215 adjustment (negative) on line 9.

- *Prior period adjustments.* The correction of underreported and overreported amounts for the same tax period should be reported on a single Form 941-X, Adjusted Employer's QUARTERLY Federal Tax Return or Claim for Refund, unless a refund is requested. If a refund is requested, and the employer is correcting both underreported and overreported amounts, a separate Form 941-X should be filed to correct the underreported amounts only and a second Form 941-X should be filed to correct the overreported amounts. In general, a separate Form 941-X should be filed for each Form 941 that is being corrected and Form 941-X should not be filed with Form 941. Current quarter adjustments for fractions of cents, third-party sick pay, tips, and group-term life insurance continue to be reported on Form 941.

Note. Form 941-X is used to request a refund of federal withholding and employment tax, rather than Form 843. Form 843 is now used only to request an abatement of penalty and interest in certain situations.

Q 4:63   How are errors in prior period reporting of federal tax liability reported?

If an error was made in reporting liabilities in a prior period, the employer can notify the IRS of the error through the Taxpayer Advocate's office or simply respond to the IRS notice that is generated as a result of the discrepancy between tax payments and liabilities.

Q 4:64   How are corrections of income tax withholding reported?

Correct prior quarter income tax withholding errors by making the corrections on Form 941-X, Adjusted Employer's QUARTERLY Federal Tax Return or Claim for Refund, when the error is discovered.

The employer may make an adjustment to correct income tax withholding errors only for quarters during the same calendar year. This is because the employee uses the amount shown on Form W-2 as a credit when filing the income tax return (Form 1040, etc.).

The employer cannot adjust amounts reported as income tax withheld in a prior calendar year unless it is to correct an administrative error. An administrative error occurs when the amount entered on Form 941 is not the amount the employer actually withheld. For example, if the total income tax actually withheld was incorrectly reported on Form 941 due to a mathematical or transposition error, this would be an administrative error. The administrative error adjustment corrects the amount reported on Form 941 to agree with the amount actually withheld from employees. For example, assume that a bonus payment was made from which federal income tax was withheld; however, neither the bonus nor the withholding taxes were reflected on Forms 941 and

W-2. A Form W-2c and 941-X may be filed to report the wages and the taxes withheld pursuant to the bonus. [Instructions for Form 941]

Q 4:65   How are errors in reporting Social Security and Medicare taxes reported?

Correct prior period Social Security and Medicare tax errors by making the appropriate adjustments on lines 8-10 on Form 941-X, Adjusted Employer's QUARTERLY Federal Tax Return or Claim for Refund for the quarter during which the error was discovered. (See Q 4:67 for additional information.)

Q 4:66   What was the purpose of Form 941c, which is now obsolete?

Prior to 2009, Form 941c Supporting Statement to Correct Information, was not a return but rather was attached to a return to provide supporting adjustments to income, Social Security, and Medicare taxes reported on Form 941, 941-M, 941-SS, 943, or 945. Form 941c was filed with the tax return on which the employer was claiming the adjustment (Form 941, 943, 945, etc.). Employers could use Form 941c even though an original return was filed on magnetic media. Form 941c could not be used as a supporting statement for current period adjustments (e.g., adjustment for uncollected employee share of Social Security and Medicare taxes on tips). No supporting statement was required for the fractions-of-cents and third-party sick-pay adjustments. As of January 1, 2009, Form 941c is obsolete and errors discovered on a previously filed Form 941 after December 31, 2008 are required to be corrected using Form 941-X.

Q 4:67   What is the purpose of Form 941-X?

Effective January 1, 2009, errors discovered on a previously filed Form 941 are corrected using Form 941-X, Adjusted Employer's QUARTERLY Federal Tax Return or Claim for Refund. Form 941c is obsolete. In April 2017, a new Form 941 will be released.

Unlike with Form 941c, Form 941-X is not filed with Form 941. Rather, Form 941-X is a dual-purpose standalone form. Also, employers can file Form 941-X as soon as they discover an error, rather than having to wait to file it with the next Form 941. (Note that there is a comparable Form 944-X to correct previously filed Form 944; Form 943-X to correctly previously filed Form 943, etc.) Form 843, Claim for Refund and Request for Abatement, is used just to request abatement for interest and penalties.

Form 941-X is used to make adjustments and claim refunds of income and FICA tax overpayments. The option to make an adjustment or claim a refund will be impacted if Form 941-X is filed within 90 days of the "period of limitations" (see Q 4:68). If an employer is correcting an overpayment reported on a previously filed Form 941, the employer is able to apply the overpayment to the next Form 941 (i.e., make an adjustment) or claim a refund. If an adjustment is made, the amount of the overpayment will be applied as a credit to the quarter in which the Form 941-X is filed. Employers correcting underpayments of employment taxes that result in a balance due can pay using EFTPS, credit card, debit card or by attaching a check or money order to the Form 941-X regardless of the amount of the overpayment. The IRS will make both the tax and wage corrections to the actual period being corrected. A separate Form 941-X is required to be filed for each Form 941 being corrected (i.e., each quarter that is being corrected).

Claims for refund of federal withholding or FICA taxes or abatement previously made on Form 843 are made on the appropriate "X" form (e.g., Form 941-X, Form 944-X).

Q 4:68   What is the due date for filing 941-X?

The due date for filing Form 941-X is determined by the quarter in which the error was discovered and whether there was underreported tax or overreported tax. If the filing is to correct an error for overreported tax, the due date will be the later of three years from the date the Form 941 was filed or two years from the date the tax liability was reported on the form. The due date for a calendar year Form 941 will be deemed April 15 of the following year provided the return was filed before that date. For underreported tax, the deadline for filing Form 941-X and paying the tax is the last day of the month following the quarter the error was discovered. These timeframes are called period of limitations.

Q 4:69   What procedures apply for overwithholding of payroll taxes?

If the employer withheld more than the correct amount of income, Social Security, or Medicare taxes from wages paid, the employee is entitled to claim a refund of the excess, provided the employer has refunded to employees the overwithholding, as applicable, and the certification requirements have been met as contained in Part 2 of Form 941-X and as explained in the Form 941-X instructions. Note that refunds of income tax withheld must be made by the end of the calendar year in which the overwithholding error occurred. Employers should keep records documenting employees' certification as well as records substantiating the refund claim.

Q 4:70   What procedures are followed for underwithholding of payroll taxes?

If the employer withheld insufficient federal income, Social Security, or Medicare taxes from an employee's wages, it can make up the amount from later wage payments, subject to the current calendar year requirement for federal income tax. Note that the employer is liable for any underwithholding, whether or not it was collected from employees' wage payments, and reimbursement for such amounts paid on behalf of employees by the employer is a settlement issue between the employer and its employees. Also note that taxes paid on behalf of employees by their employer are considered wages subject to federal income and FICA tax withholding and a gross up is required to the extent employees have not reimbursed the employer for the tax payments. There are special rules for collecting underwithheld taxes on tips and group-term life insurance. See Publication 15 and the instructions for Forms 941 and W-2. [Treas. Reg. §§ 31.6205-1(b)(1), 31.6205-1(c)(1); Pub. No. 15]

Q 4:71   How does an employer file a claim for refund of overreported prior period liabilities?

If, after December 31, 2008, an employer discovers an error on a prior period federal employment tax return (e.g., Form 941) resulting in a tax overpayment, it should file Form 941-X, Adjusted Employer's QUARTERLY Federal Tax Return or Claim for Refund, for a refund. [I.R.C. §§ 6511(a), 6513(c); Treas. Reg. § 31.6413(a)-1(a); Instructions for Form 941; Pub. No. 15]

Q 4:72   How does an employer make interest-free adjustments?

IRS final regulations modify the process for making interest-free adjustments for both underpayments and overpayments of FICA and federal income tax withholding, effective for any error ascertained on or after January 1, 2009. [T.D. 9405, 2008-32 I.R.B. 293] IRS Revenue Ruling 2009-39 also provides guidance to employers on how to correct employment tax reporting errors using the interest-free adjustment and refund claim processes for errors ascertained on or after January 1, 2009. [Rev. Rul. 2009-39, 2009-52 I.R.B. 951]

Per the regulations, if a return is filed (e.g., Form 941) with less than the correct amount of employee or employer portions of FICA tax reported, and the employer discovers the error after filing the return, the employer is required to adjust the resulting underpayment of tax by reporting the additional amount due on an adjusted return (e.g., Form 941-X) for the return period in which the wages or compensation was paid. The adjustment must be made by the due date of the return period in which the error is ascertained and the amount of the underpayment must be paid by the time the adjustment is made, or interest will begin to accrue from that date.

For underpayments of federal income tax withholding when the incorrect amount was withheld, an adjustment may only generally be made for errors ascertained during the calendar year in which the wages were paid.

With regard to overpayments of FICA tax, the employer is generally required to repay or reimburse its employees the amount of overcollected FICA tax prior to the expiration of the statute of limitations for the applicable period. Once the employer repays or reimburses employees to the extent required, the employer may report both the employee and employer portions of FICA tax as an overpayment on an adjusted return (e.g., 941-X). The employer must certify on the adjusted return that it has repaid or reimbursed its employees to the extent required. (See Part 2 of Form 941-X and the Form 941-X instructions for the certification requirements.)

Note that unlike the previous rules, the Form 941-X is due at the end of the month following the quarter in which the error is discovered. Previously, the amended return was due based on the day (rather than the quarter) the error was discovered. The new procedures are far more lenient in this regard as employers could potentially have a much longer time in which to pay tax underpayments. Further, the underpayment can be paid by check or money order at the time the Form 941-X is filed, regardless of the amount of the underpayment and regardless of the employer's deposit schedule (e.g., monthly or semiweekly) and electronic payment of the underpayment is not required.

Q 4:73   How do I file Form 941-X when there is an amount due?

When completing Form 941-X and Line 20 indicates an amount you owe, payment must accompany the filing of the return. The payment may be made electronically through EFTPS, credit or debit card, or a check or money order. If you are filing Form 941-X after the due date for the Form 941 for the quarter in which the error was discovered, an amended Schedule B of Form 941 must be filed with Form 941-X. See instructions for Form 941-X. Also, if you are also filing a Form 941-X for the same period and you are entitled to a credit, you may not use that credit for the Form 941-X that has a balance due.

Q 4:74   What if a Form 941 was never filed for a particular quarter?

If a quarterly return was never filed, do not use Form 941-X to report tax liabilities and tax deposits. Instead, file Form 941 for each quarter that you have not filed. If Form 941 was not filed because workers were treated as independent contractors instead of employees, complete Form 941-X to adjust your liabilities following the instructions on Line 22 of the form.

Form 943

Q 4:75   What is the purpose of Form 943?

Form 943, Employer's Annual Tax Return for Agricultural Employees, is used to report income tax withheld and employer and employee Social Security and Medicare taxes on wages paid to farm workers. If an employer has household employees working in his or her private home or on a farm operated for profit, those employees are considered farm employees. To report Social Security, Medicare, and income tax withholding on the wages of household employees, the employer may either:

1. File Schedule H (Form 1040), Household Employment Taxes, with the employer's individual income tax return; or
2. Include the wages with other farm employee wages on Form 943.

If the employer paid wages to a household employee in a home that is not on a for-profit farm, the employer must report the taxes on Schedule H. If the wages were paid to nonfarm workers, they are not reported on Form 943. Report them on Form 941, Employer's QUARTERLY Federal Tax Return.

Q 4:76   Are there special rules applicable to agricultural employees?

An agricultural employer reports wages paid to farm workers annually on Form 943, Employer's Annual Tax Return for Agricultural Employees, rather than on quarterly Form 941; however, it must still deposit employment taxes on either a monthly or semiweekly schedule. In applying the rules outlined above, an agricultural employer is a monthly depositor if, during the second calendar year preceding the current calendar year, it accumulated "employment taxes" of $50,000 or less; otherwise, it is a semiweekly depositor.

W-2 Forms

Q 4:77   When must an employer provide a Form W-2?

Employers must file Form W-2 for each employee from whom federal income taxes, Social Security taxes, or Medicare taxes have been withheld. A Form W-2 is also required if federal income taxes, Social Security taxes, or Medicare taxes were not withheld but would have been if the employee had claimed no more than one withholding allowance or had not claimed exemption from withholding on Form W-4, Employee's Withholding Allowance Certificate.

Every employer engaged in a trade or business that pays remuneration for services performed by an employee, including noncash payments, must furnish a Form W-2 to each employee. This applies to any employee even if the employee is related to the employer. An employer must furnish its employees with Form W-2 by January 31 of the year following the calendar year to which the form relates. Many states have accelerated the deadline for filing: Massachusetts, Oregon, and Rhode Island, to name a few. [Treas. Reg. § 31.6071(a)-1(a)(3)(ii)]

Q 4:78   Are employers required to use the official IRS Form W-2?

No. Employers have the option of using "substitute" forms. These substitute W-2 forms must meet the specifications set forth by the IRS in Publication 1141, General Rules and Specifications for Substitute Forms W-2 and W-3. [Rev. Proc. 2016-54, 2016-54 I.R.B. 685; Rev. Proc. 2016-20, 2016-13 I.R.B. 499]

Q 4:79   How are multiple Forms W-2 handled?

If necessary, more than one Form W-2 can be issued to an employee. For example, the employer may need to report more than four coded items in Box 12 on a paper copy of the 2017 W-2. If the employer issues a second Form W-2, Boxes a, b, c, d, e, and f must be completed with the same information as that reported on the first Form W-2. Show any additional items that were not included on the first Form W-2 in the appropriate boxes on the second Form W-2. Do not report the same federal tax data to the SSA on more than one Copy A.

Q 4:80   Where and when is the Form W-2 filed?

Employers file Copy A of the 2017 Form W-2 (along with the entire first page of Form W-3, Transmittal of Wage and Tax Statement) with the SSA by January 31 whether the filing is by paper or electronically. In prior years the due date was the last day of February of the year following the calendar year to which the form relates. (Electronic filers used to have an additional month to file.) The instructions with the form indicate that employers should not staple or tape the Forms W-2 together and should not staple or tape the Forms W-2 to Form W-3.

An employer may request an extension of the due date by sending Form 8809, Application for Extension of Time to File Information Returns, to the address shown on that form. The extension of the filing due date must be requested before the due date and provide a detailed explanation of why the additional time is required. An automatic extension is no longer available. The extension is for 30 days. Note, however, that any extension for filing Copy A and Form W-3 does not extend the date when the Form W-2 is to be provided to employees (see below). Employers are still required to furnish Form W-2 to employees by January 31. Form 8809 may also be filed electronically. If an employer needs to request an extension of time to file Forms W-2, the IRS encourages the employer to complete the request online via the FIRE (Filing Information Returns Electronically) system at http://fire.irs.gov in lieu of the paper Form 8809. File paper Copy A of Form W-2 with the entire first page of Form W-3 at the following address:

Social Security Administration
Data Operations Center
Wilkes-Barre, PA 18769-0001

When the forms are sent by certified mail, the ZIP code should be changed to 18769-0002. For IRS-approved private delivery services, add "ATTN: W-2 PROCESS, 1150 E. Mountain Dr." to the address and change the ZIP code to 18702-7997.

Copy 1 of Form W-2 is mailed to the state or local taxing districts, if applicable. Copies B, C, and 2 of Form W-2 are furnished to the employees, generally by January 31. To meet this requirement, it is not necessary that the forms be received by the January 31 date, only that the forms be properly addressed and mailed on or before the due date.

Extension to furnish Forms W-2 to employees. An employer may request an extension of time to provide Forms W-2 to employees by sending a letter to:

Internal Revenue Service
Information Returns Branch, Mail Stop 4360,
Attn: Extension of Time Coordinator,
240 Murall Drive,
Kearneysville, WV 25430

The letter should be mailed on or before the due date (generally January 31) for furnishing Forms W-2 to employees and contain: the employer's name and address, employer identification number (EIN), statement indicating that an extension of time to furnish Forms W-2 to employees is being requested, the reason for the delay, and the employer's (or authorized agent's) signature.

Q 4:81   What do employers do with undeliverable Forms W-2?

Employers are required to keep undeliverable Forms W-2 for four years. However, undelivered employee copies of the Forms W-2 do not need to be kept by employers if the undelivered Forms W-2 can be produced electronically through April 15th of the fourth year after the year of issue. An undeliverable form is one that the employer tried to deliver but could not. It is generally determined that a reasonable effort has been made when the employer mails the W-2 to the last known address of the employee.

Q 4:82   How is a lost Form W-2 handled?

If an employee loses a Form W-2 and another W-2 is prepared, write "Reissued statement" on the new copy and give it to the employee. Do not send Copy A of the reissued Form W-2 to the SSA. Note that an employer may reissue a Form W-2 to an employee on the IRS official form or on a privately printed substitute form.

Q 4:83   What rules control the issuance of the Form W-2 to an employee who terminates during the year?

An employer may prepare and distribute a Form W-2 before January 31 for employees who terminate employment before December 31. An employer may give copies at any time after employment ends, but no later than January 31. If an employee asks for Form W-2, give him or her the completed copies within 30 days of the request or the final wage payment, whichever is later. (However, see Q 4:84 for what to do when an employer goes out of business.)

Q 4:84   When are W-2s due when an employer goes out of business?

If an employer terminates a business, Forms W-2 must be provided to the employees for the calendar year of termination by the due date of the final Form 941. The employer must also file Forms W-2 with the SSA by the last day of the month that follows the due date of the final Form 941. However, if any of the employer's employees are immediately employed by a successor employer, see Revenue Procedure 2004-53. [2004-34 I.R.B. 320] Also see Revenue Procedure 96-57 [1996-2 C.B. 389], for information on automatic extensions for furnishing Forms W-2 to employees and filing Forms W-2 with the SSA. (See chapter 12 for more information concerning the procedures that apply pursuant to a restructuring.)

Q 4:85   When must an employer file Forms W-2 electronically?

If the employer is required to file 250 or more Forms W-2, the employer must file these forms electronically unless the IRS grants a waiver. If a waiver is not granted, the employer may be charged a penalty for failure to file electronically when required to do so.

Note. The number of forms may not be the same as the number of employees. An employer may request a waiver on Form 8508, Request for Waiver From Filing Information Returns Electronically. Submit Form 8508 to the IRS at least 45 days before the due date of the return. See Form 8508 for filing information.

The reporting specifications for Forms W-2 and W-3 are in SSA Publication EFW2, Specifications for Filing Forms W-2 Electronically. Publication EFW2 can be downloaded from the SSA Employer Reporting Instructions and Information website at www.socialsecurity.gov/employer. Employers can also get these specifications by calling SSA's Employer Reporting Branch at 800-772-6270.

Reporting instructions for electronic filing may differ from the paper reporting instructions. For example, electronic filers may enter more than four items in Box 12 of the 2017 W-2 in one individual's wage report, but paper filers are limited to four entries in Box 12 on Copy A of the 2017 W-2.

Q 4:86   Do employers get any additional time to file if they file electronically?

The Internal Revenue Service Restructuring and Reform Act of 1998 extended the general due date for all employers (not just those with 250 or more W-2s) to file Forms W-2 with the SSA electronically until the last day of March, instead of the last day of February (the due date for W-2s filed on paper) up through the 2015 Forms W-2. For the 2017 Forms W-2 the deadline will be January 31 for both paper and electronic W-2s.

Directions for electronic filing can be found in Specifications for Filing Forms W-2 Electronically (EFW2), Publication 42-007.

Q 4:87   Can an employer file some Forms W-2 electronically and some on paper?

Yes. An employer that files W-2s electronically but maintains a separate payroll not compatible with electronic filing may file up to 249 Forms W-2 in the paper format. This is sometimes done for executive payrolls and for certain reported reimbursements.

Q 4:88   What are the W-2 electronic filing requirements for U.S. possessions?

Regulations extend the standard rule for the reporting requirements for Form W-2 for U.S. employers to employers in U.S. territories and possessions.

Electronic filing requirements apply to any employer filing 250 or more of any one of the following forms: Forms 499R-2/W-2PR, Withholding Statement (Puerto Rico); W-2VI, U.S. Virgin Islands Wage and Tax Statement; W-2GU, Guam Wage and Tax Statement; and W-2AS, American Samoa Wage and Tax Statement. [63 Fed. Reg. 35,517 (June 30, 1998)]

Q 4:89   How is the 2017 Form W-2 completed?

The following are detailed instructions for the completion of Form W-2 for 2017.

General instructions. All entries on Form W-2 should be made in black ink (in 12-point Courier font if possible) and should not be typed in script, italics, or dual case alpha characters. Entries in any boxes should not cross any vertical or horizontal lines in the form. No entry should be erased, crossed out, or struck over. If necessary, void the form and make an additional form. The paper copy of Form W-2 should be filed in either Social Security number (SSN) order or alphabetically by last name of employee.

Dollar amounts. Dollar amounts should be entered without commas or dollar signs, but should include decimals. Example: Enter 15000.00, not $15,000.00.

Hyphenation. The employee's SSN and the employer's EIN should be reported with hyphens. Use the following format: SSN XXX-XX-XXXX, EIN XX-XXXXXXX. [Ann. 92-11, 1992-4 I.R.B. 34]

Hyphens in names should follow these guidelines:

- Compound names no longer require a hyphen. Connect parts of a compound name with either a hyphen or a blank space. Example: ERIC TRIDAS-QUINONNES or ERIC TRIDAS QUINONNES.

- Single-letter prefixes such as O or L must not be separated from the rest of the surname by a blank. The single letter prefix should be connected with an apostrophe adjoined to the rest of the surname. Example: Use O'DELL or ODELL, not O DELL.

- The Social Security computers recognize the common prefixes listed below and do not require a hyphen for the prefixes to be linked to the surname. However, a hyphen may be used. The recognized prefixes are the following: D, L, O, Di, Do, Du, El, La, Le, Li, Lo, Mc, St, Bon, Der, Las, Los, Mac, Mte, San, Sta, Van, Von, Dela, Vander, Vonde.

Professional designation. Do not show professional or other designations such as Mr., Mrs., Dr., or Ph.D.

"Void" Box. This box is checked when an error is made on Form W-2 and this W-2 is being replaced with another complete Form W-2 or no Form W-2 is to be provided for this individual. Be careful not to include any amounts shown on "voided" forms in the totals entered on Form W-3.

Box a: "Employee's Social Security number." Enter the number shown on the employee's Social Security card. If the employee does not have a card, he or she should apply for one by completing Form SS-5, Application for a Social Security Card. If the employee has applied for a Social Security card but the number has not been received in time for filing, enter "Applied for" in Box a on paper Forms W-2 or enter zeros if filing electronically. When the employee receives the card, correct the previous Form W-2 by filing Form W-2c showing the employee's SSN. The SSA allows employers to verify employee's name and SSN online or by telephone. An employee can change his or her name shown on the card by contacting the SSA at 1-800-772-1213. If you do not provide the correct employee name and SSN on Form W-2, you may owe a penalty unless there is a reasonable cause.

Box b: "Employer identification number (EIN)." Show the EIN assigned to the employer by the IRS in this format: 00-0000000. This should be the same number that is used on the employer's federal employment tax returns (Form 941, 943, 944, or CT-1). If the employer does not have an EIN at the time of filing the Forms W-2, enter "Applied for" in Box b, not the SSN of one of the employees or stockholders. To obtain an EIN, file Form SS-4, Application for Employer Identification Number. Form SS-4 may be filed online and received the same day. The request for an EIN may be made by telephone or by mailing the Form SS-4.

Box c: Employer's "name", "address", and "ZIP code". This entry should be the same as shown on the employer's Form 941, 944, 943, CT-1, or Schedule H (Form 1040).

Box d: "Control number." Employers may use this box to identify individual Forms W-2; it has no SSA use. This box does not have to be used.

Box e: "Employee's first name and initial, Last name." Enter the name as shown on the employee's Social Security card (first, middle initial, last). If the name does not fit, the employer may show first initial, middle initial, and last name. Only enter the suffix if it appears on the employee's Social Security card. If the name has changed and the employee has not requested a corrected card from any SSA office, use the name on the original card until the employee receives a corrected card. Do not show titles or academic degrees at the end of the employee's name. Beginning in 2014, third-party payers of sick pay must file Form 8922 with the IRS. This replaces the Third Party W-2 Recap and Third Party W-3 Recap. Form 8922 is filed with the IRS instead of the SSA and should not be filed electronically. Third-party payers of sick pay should not put employee's SSN in Box a.

Box f: "Employee's address and ZIP code (Copy A)." Enter the employee's last known address. Include in the address the number, street, and apartment or suite number, or P.O. box number if mail is not delivered to a street address. For a foreign address, give the information in the following order: city, province or state, and the name of the country. Follow the country's practice for entering the postal code. Do not abbreviate the name of the country.

Box 1: "Wages, tips, other compensation." Show the total wages, tips, and other compensation, before any payroll deductions, paid to the employee during the year. Do not include elective deferrals to a Section 401(k) plan, Section

403(b) arrangement, Section 125 plan, or a Section 457 plan that are exempt from federal income taxes. Where applicable, do include Section 501(c)(18) contributions. Include the following in the total for Box 1:

1. Total wages, bonuses (including signing bonuses), prizes, and taxable awards paid to employees during the year. For example, if the employee worked from December 31, 2016 through January 13, 2017, and the wages for that period were paid on January 16, 2017, include all the wages for this pay period on the 2017 Form W-2, not the W-2 for 2016.

2. Total noncash payments and certain fringe benefits.

3. Total tips reported by employee to employer (not allocated tips).

4. Certain employee business expense reimbursements that are not exempt (i.e., paid from an unaccountable plan).

5. The cost of accident and health insurance premiums for 2 percent or more shareholder-employees paid by an S corporation.

6. Taxable benefits from a Section 125 (cafeteria) plan (i.e., employee chooses cash).

7. Employee contributions to an Archer MSA.

8. Employer contributions to an Archer MSA if includible in the income of the employee.

9. Employer contributions for qualified long-term care services to the extent that such coverage is provided through a flexible spending or similar arrangement.

10. Taxable cost of group-term life insurance in excess of $50,000.

11. Payments for non-job-related educational expenses or for payments under a nonaccountable plan, unless excludable as explained under educational assistance programs. See Publication 970.

12. The amount includible as wages because the employer paid the employee's share of taxes.

13. Designated Roth contributions made under a Section 401(k) plan or under a Section 403(b) salary reduction agreement.

14. Distributions to an employee or former employee from a nonqualified deferred compensation plan (including a rabbi trust) or a nongovernmental Section 457 plan.

15. Amounts includible in income under Section 457(f) because the amounts are no longer subject to substantial risk of forfeiture.

16. Payments to statutory employees who are subject to Social Security and Medicare taxes but not subject to federal income tax withholding must be shown in Box 1 as other compensation. See Box 13, Statutory employee.

17. Cost of current insurance protection under a compensatory split-dollar life insurance arrangement.

18. Employee contributions to a Health Savings Account (HSA).

19. Employer contributions to an HSA if includible in the employee's income.

20. Amounts includible in income under a nonqualified deferred compensation plan because of Section 409A.

21. Payments made to former employees while they are on active duty (for 30 days) in the Armed Forces or other uniformed services.

22. All other compensation, including certain scholarship and fellowship grants. Other compensation includes taxable amounts paid to an employee from which federal income tax is not withheld. Employers may show other compensation on a separate Form W-2.

Box 2: "Federal income tax withheld." Show the amount of federal income tax withheld from the employee's wages for the year. Also include the 20 percent excise tax withheld on excess parachute payments.

Box 3: "Social Security wages." Show the total wages paid (before payroll deductions) subject to employee Social Security tax but not including Social Security tips and allocated tips. (See instructions for Box 7 and Box 8.) Generally, noncash payments are considered wages. Include employee business expense reimbursements reported in Box 1. Employers that paid the employee's portion of Social Security and Medicare taxes rather than deducting them from wages will report these as wages. The total of Boxes 3 and 7 should not be more than the Social Security wage base ($127,200 for 2017).

Also, include elective deferrals (i.e., employee contributions that are exempt from federal income taxes) to certain qualified cash-or-deferred compensation arrangements and to retirement arrangements described in Box 12, Codes D, E, F, G, and S, even though the deferrals are not includible in Box 1. Where applicable, amounts deferred under a nonqualified or Section 457 plan must be included in Boxes 3 and/or 5 as Social Security and/or Medicare wages as of the later of (1) when the services giving rise to the deferral are performed or (2) when there is no substantial risk of forfeiture of the rights to the deferred amount. Include elective and nonelective deferrals (i.e., mandatory employee contributions) to Section 457 plans. Moreover, report designated Roth contributions made under a Section 401(k) plan or under a Section 403(b) salary reduction agreement described in Box 12 (Codes AA–BB, and EE).

Also include in Box 3: (1) taxable cost of group-term life insurance over $50,000 included in Box 1; (2) cost of accident and health insurance premiums for 2 percent or more shareholder-employees paid by an S corporation, but only if not excludable under Section 3121(a)(2)(8); (3) if applicable, employee and nonexcludable employer contributions to an MSA; (4) employee contributions to a savings incentive match plan for employees (SIMPLE) retirement account; (5) adoption assistance benefits; and (6) signing bonuses an employer pays for signing or ratifying an employment contract.

Clergy and religious workers. For certain members of the clergy and religious workers who are not subject to Social Security and Medicare taxes as employees, Boxes 3 and 5 should be left blank. For information on the rules that apply to ministers and certain other religious workers, see IRS Publication 517, Social

Security and Other Information for Members of the Clergy and Religious Workers, and Section 4 (Religious Exemptions) of IRS Publication 15-A, Employer's Supplemental Tax Guide.

Box 4: "Social Security tax withheld." Show the total employee Social Security tax (only the employee's share) withheld, including Social Security tax on tips and the employer's payment of the employee's share. The amount reported in this box should not exceed $7,886.40 ($127,200 × 6.2%). Include only taxes withheld (or paid by the employer for the employee) for 2017 wages and tips.

Box 5: "Medicare wages and tips." The wages and tips subject to Medicare tax are the same as those subject to Social Security tax (Boxes 3 and 7), except that there is no wage base limit for Medicare tax. Enter the total Medicare wages and tips in Box 5. Enter tips the employee reported even if the employer did not have sufficient employee funds to collect the Medicare tax for those tips.

A federal, state, or local agency with employees paying only the Medicare tax, (both the 1.45% and the Additional Medicare Tax of 0.9 percent) will enter the Medicare wages in this box.

Example. An employer paid an employee $184,000 in FICA-taxable wages in 2017. Enter 127,200 in Box 3 for Social Security wages, but enter $184,000 in Box 5 for Medicare wages and tips. There is no limit on the amount reported in Box 5. If the amount of wages paid was $127,200 or less, the amounts entered in Boxes 3 and 5 would be the same.

Box 6: "Medicare tax withheld." Enter the total employee Medicare tax (not the employer's share) withheld. Include only taxes withheld for 2017 wages. The total Medicare tax equals the Medicare wages taxed at 1.45 percent plus the Additional Medicare Tax of 0.9 percent on wages in excess of $200,000.

Box 7: "Social Security tips." Employers show the amount the employee reported even if the employer did not have enough employee funds to collect the Social Security tax for the tips. The total of Boxes 3 and 7 should not be more than $127,200 (the maximum Social Security wage base for 2017). Report all tips in Box 1 along with wages and other compensation. Include any tips reported in Box 7 in Box 5 also.

Box 8: "Allocated tips." For a large food or beverage establishment, show the amount of tips allocated to the employee. (See the Instructions for Form 8027, Employer's Annual Information Return of Tip Income and Allocated Tips.) Do not include this amount in Box 1, 3, 5, or 7.

Box 9: Verification Code.

Box 10: "Dependent care benefits." Show the total amount of dependent care benefits under a dependent care assistance program (i.e., benefits under Section 129) paid or incurred for the employees. Include the fair market value of employer-provided or employer-sponsored day-care facilities and amounts paid or incurred in a Section 125 (cafeteria) plan. Report all amounts paid or incurred, including those in excess of the $5,000 exclusion permitted under

Section 129. This amount will include (1) the fair market value of benefits provided in kind by the employer; (2) an amount paid directly to a day-care facility by the employer or reimbursed to the employee to subsidize the benefit; or (3) benefits from the pretax contributions made by the employee to a Section 125 dependent care flexible spending account. Include any amounts over $5,000 in Boxes 1, 3, and 5. See IRS Publication No. 15-B, Employer's Tax Guide to Fringe Benefits, for additional information.

Box 11: "Nonqualified plans." The amounts shown here can affect an individual's Social Security benefits if he or she collects Social Security benefits and current year earnings exceed certain limits. The purpose of Box 11 is to allow the SSA to determine if any portion of the amount reported in Box 1 or Boxes 3 and/or 5 was earned in a prior year. The SSA uses this information to determine if a Social Security recipient's benefits have exceeded the earnings limit. Show the amount of distributions paid to an employee or former employee from a nonqualified plan or a nongovernmental Section 457(b) plan in Box 11 and also in Box 1. Make only one entry in this box. Distributions from governmental Section 457(b) plans must be reported on Form 1099-R, Distribution From Pensions, Annuities, Retirement or Profit-Sharing Plans, IRAs, Insurance Contracts, etc., not in Box 1 of Form W-2.

If no distributions were made in the year, show the amount of deferrals (plus earnings or less losses) under a nonqualified plan or Section 457(b) plan that became taxable for Social Security and Medicare taxes during the year (but were for prior year services) because the deferred amounts were no longer subject to a substantial risk of forfeiture (i.e., the benefits became vested). Do not report in Box 11 current year salary deferrals that are included in Boxes 3 and/or 5 for current year services.

If distributions were made and deferrals occurred for the employee in the same year and the deferrals are reported in Boxes 3 and 5, do not complete Box 11. See IRS Publication 957, Reporting Back Pay and Special Wage Payments to the Social Security Administration, and Form SSA-131, Employer Report of Special Wage Payments, for additional instructions on reporting these and other kinds of compensation earned in prior years. Do not file Form SSA-131 if contributions and distributions occur in the same year and the employee will not be age 62 or older by the end of that year. Often the employee is requesting this form in the process of applying for Social Security benefits.

Report distributions from nonqualified or Section 457 plans to beneficiaries of deceased employees on Form 1099-R, Distributions From Pensions, Annuities, Retirement or Profit-Sharing Plans, IRAs, Insurance Contracts, etc., not on Form W-2.

Do not report accumulated sick pay or vacation pay in Box 11.

Military employers must report military retirement payments on Form 1099-R.

Box 12: Complete and code the entries for this box for the items described below. Do not report in Box 12 any items that are not listed as Codes A through

EE. Employers do not report in Box 12 any Code Section 414(h)(2) contributions (relating to certain state or local government plans). Instead, employers use Box 14 for these items and any other information they wish to give their employee. For example, union dues and uniform payments that are not taxable to the employee may be reported in Box 14.

Note. Employers should not enter more than four items in Box 12 on each paper Copy A of Form W-2. If more than four items need to be reported in Box 12, use a separate Form W-2 to report the additional items. On all other copies of Form W-2, employers may enter more than four items in Box 12.

Use the IRS code designated below for the item entered followed by the dollar amount for that item. The IRS code designated for each item must be shown even if there is only one amount in this box. Enter the code using a capital letter. Use decimal points but not dollar signs or commas. For example, if $6,400 is being reported for a Section 401(k) plan elective contribution (i.e., salary deferrals), the entry in Box 12 would be: D 6400.00 and not A 6400.00, even though it is the first or only entry to go in this box. Report the IRS code to the left of the vertical line in Boxes 12a through d and the money amount to the right of the vertical line.

Reference Guide for Box 12 Codes

Code A: Uncollected Social Security or Railroad Retirement Tax Act (RRTA) tax on tips. Show the employee Social Security tax on all of the employee's tips that could not be collected because the employee did not have enough funds from which to deduct those taxes. Do not include this amount in Box 4.

Code B: Uncollected Medicare tax on tips. Show the employee Medicare tax or RRTA Medicare tax on tips that could not be collected because the employee did not have enough funds from which to deduct those taxes. Do not include this amount in Box 6.

Code C: Cost of group-term life insurance over $50,000. Show the taxable amount of the cost of group-term life insurance coverage over $50,000 provided to employees (including a former employee). Also, include it in Boxes 1, 3, and 5.

Codes D through H and S, Y, AA, BB, and EE: Use these codes to show the amount of elective deferrals made to the plans listed below. The amount reported as elective deferrals and designated Roth contributions is the portion of the employee's salary (or other compensation) that he or she did not receive because of the deferral. Only elective deferrals and designated Roth contributions should be reported in Box 12 for all coded plans, except, when using Code G for Section 457(b) plans, include both elective and nonelective deferrals. When reporting catch-up contributions for employees who were 50 years of age or older at any time during the year, report the elective deferrals and/or designated Roth catch up and the elective catch up deferrals as a single sum in Box 12.

The following are not elective deferrals and may be reported in Box 14 but not in Box 12: (1) nonelective contributions by an employer (e.g., pension or profit sharing contributions) on behalf of an employee; (2) aftertax employee contributions that are not designated Roth contributions, such as voluntary contributions to a pension plan that are deducted from an employee's pay after all other deductions and taxes; (3) required employee contributions (e.g., certain pension plans require the participant to make aftertax employee contributions); and (4) employer matching contributions.

Note. If any elective deferrals, salary reduction amounts, or nonelective contributions to a Section 457(b) plan during the year are makeup amounts under the Uniformed Services Employment and Reemployment Rights Act of 1994 (USERRA) for a prior year, enter the prior year contributions separately. Enter the codes, the year to which they apply, and the amount. For example, elective deferrals to a Section 401(k) plan of $3,500.00 for 2015 and $2,600.00 for 2016 are reported in Box 12 as follows: D 13 3500.00, D 14 2600.00. The 2017 contribution does not require a year designation; enter a 2017 contribution of $9,500 as D 9500.00.

Code D: Elective deferrals to a Section 401(k) cash or deferred arrangement. Also show the amount deferred under a SIMPLE retirement account that is part of a Section 401(k) arrangement rather than a SIMPLE IRA (see Code S).

Code E: Elective deferrals under a Section 403(b) salary reduction agreement.

Code F: Elective deferrals under a Section 408(k)(6) salary reduction simplified employee pension plan (SEP).

Code G: Elective deferrals and employer contributions (including nonelective deferrals) to any governmental or nongovernmental Section 457(b) deferred compensation plan. Do not report Section 457(f) amounts or amounts deferred under Section 457(b) that are subject to a substantial risk of forfeiture (e.g., amounts not vested).

Code H: Elective deferrals to a Section 501(c)(18)(D) tax-exempt organization plan. Include this amount in Box 1 as wages. The employee will deduct the amount on his or her Form 1040.

Example. For 2017, Vaughan, who is age 49, elected to defer $18,600 to a Section 401(k) plan, made a designated Roth contribution of $1,500 to the plan, and made a voluntary (non-Roth) aftertax contribution of $700. In addition, the employer, on Vaughan's behalf, made a qualified nonelective contribution of $3,200 to the plan and a nonelective profit sharing employer contribution of $4,000.

The total elective deferral of $18,600 would be reported in Box 12 with Code D (D 18600), even though the 2017 elective deferral limit would be $18,000. The employer must report the total amount of a deferral in Box 12 if it exceeds the threshold. The excess is not reported in Box 1.

Note. Excess deferrals and earnings are reported on Form 1099-R. For more information, go to http://www.irs.gov/pub/irs-pdf/i1099r.pdf and download the instructions for Form 1099-R.

The employer may, but is not required to, report the $700 voluntary (aftertax) contribution to the employee in Box 14. The $3,200 nonelective contribution and the $4,000 nonelective profit sharing contribution made by the employer are not reported on Form W-2 unless, like the voluntary aftertax contribution, the employer wants to furnish this to the employee. If so, these are reported in Box 14.

Code J: Nontaxable sick pay. Show any sick pay that was paid by a third party and was not includible in income because the employee contributed to the sick-pay plan. Do not include nontaxable disability payments made directly by a state.

Code K: 20 percent excise tax on excess golden parachute payments. Golden parachute payments made to certain key corporate employees are subject to a 20 percent excise tax. Report the excise tax withheld on these payments in Box 12 using Code K. If the excess payments are considered wages, also report the 20 percent excise tax as income tax withheld in Box 2.

Code L: Substantiated employee business expense reimbursements. Report only the amount treated as substantiated, that is, the nontaxable portion. Use this code only (1) for reimbursements to an employee for employee business expenses using a per diem or mileage allowance in excess of the allowable federal rates, and (2) if the amount reimbursed exceeds the amount treated as substantiated under IRS rules. Include the portion of the reimbursement that is more than the amount treated as substantiated under IRS rules.

Do not include any per diem or mileage allowance reimbursements for employee business expenses in Box 12 if the total reimbursement is less than or equal to the amount treated as substantiated.

Reimbursements to an employee under an accountable plan are not reported.

Code M: Uncollected Social Security or RRTA tax on the cost of group-term life insurance coverage over $50,000 for former employees. If former employees (including retirees) were provided with more than $50,000 of group-term life insurance coverage after the employment relationship ended, the value of the coverage is subject to Social Security taxes. Enter the amount of uncollected Social Security tax on the coverage in Box 12.

Code N: Uncollected Medicare tax on the cost of group-term life insurance coverage over $50,000 for former employees. If former employees (including retirees) were provided with more than $50,000 of group-term life insurance coverage for periods after the employment relationship ended, the value of those benefits is subject to Medicare taxes. Enter the amount of uncollected Medicare tax on the coverage in Box 12.

Code P: Excludable moving expense reimbursements paid directly to an employee. Enter here the excludable moving expenses that are not included in the employee's income because they were qualified moving expenses.

Note. Excludable payments made directly to a third party are not included in Box 12.

Code Q: Nontaxable combat pay. Military employers must report any non-taxable combat pay in Box 12.

Code R: Employer contributions to an Archer MSA. Employers that make contributions to an Archer MSA for their employees show the employer contributions in Box 12 with Code R.

Code S: Employee salary reduction contributions to a Section 408(p) SIMPLE IRA. Show the amount deferred under a Section 408(p) salary reduction SIMPLE individual retirement account (IRA). Note that if the SIMPLE contribution is part of a Section 401(k) arrangement, use Code D. When reporting prior year contributions under USERRA, see the Note under Codes D through H and S above.

Code T: Adoption benefits. Show the total amount paid or reimbursed by an employer for qualified adoption expenses furnished to an employee under an adoption assistance program. Also include adoption benefits paid or reimbursed from the pretax contributions made by the employee to a Section 125 (cafeteria) plan. However, do not include adoption benefits forfeited from a Section 125 (cafeteria) plan. Report all amounts, including those in excess of the $13,570 exclusion for 2017.

Code V: Income from exercise of nonstatutory stock option(s). Employers must show the spread (i.e., fair market value of stock over the exercise price of options(s) granted to the employee with respect to that stock) from the employee's or former employee's exercise of nonstatutory stock options. The amount is included in Boxes 1, 3, and 5. The reporting requirement does not apply to the exercise of a statutory stock option, or the sale or disposition of stock acquired pursuant to the exercise of a statutory stock option.

Code W: Employer contribution to an HSA. Employer contributions to an HSA (including amounts the employee elected to contribute using a Section 125 cafeteria plan) are reported using Code W.

Code Y: Deferrals under a Section 409A nonqualified deferred compensation plan. Employers may, but are not required to, include current year deferrals under a Section 409A nonqualified deferred compensation plan. Any earnings during the year on current year and prior year deferrals may also, but are not required to, be reported using Code Y. For more information, see Notice 2008-115, available at www.irs.gov/irb/2008-52_IRB/index.html, and Notice 2010-6 1/5/10 § IV(A)(2), I.R.B. 2010-3, Jan 19, 2010.

Code Z: Income under Section 409A on a nonqualified deferred compensation plan. Employers must show any income under Section 409A on a nonqualified deferred compensation plan that was included in Box 1. This income is also subject to an additional tax reported on the employee's Form 1040. For correcting Section 409A errors and related reporting, see Notice 2008-13, Notice 2010-6, and Notice 2010-80.

Code AA: Designated Roth contributions to a Section 401(k) plan.

Code BB: Designated Roth contributions under a Section 403(b) salary reduction agreement.

Code DD: Cost of employer-sponsored health coverage. The amount reported with Code DD is not taxable.

Code EE: Designated Roth contributions under a governmental Section 457(b) plan. This amount does not apply to contributions under a tax-exempt organization Section 457(b) plan.

Code FF: Permitted benefits under a qualified small employer health reimbursement arrangement.

Box 13. Checkboxes: The employer is required to check the boxes that apply.

"Statutory employee." Check this box for statutory employees whose earnings are subject to Social Security and Medicare taxes but not subject to federal income tax withholding. Do not check this box for common-law employees. These workers, who are independent contractors under the common-law rules, are treated by statute (i.e., the I.R.C.) as employees. There are four categories:

1. A driver who distributes beverages (other than milk), or meat, vegetable, fruit, or bakery products, or who picks up and delivers laundry or dry cleaning when the driver is the employer's agent or is paid on commission.

2. A full-time life insurance sales agent whose principal business activity is selling life insurance or annuity contracts, or both, primarily for one life insurance company.

3. An individual who works at home on materials or goods that the employer supplies and that must be returned to the employer or to a person the employer names, when the employer also furnishes specifications for the work to be done.

4. A full-time traveling or city salesperson who works on behalf of the employer and turns in orders from wholesalers, retailers, contractors, or operators of hotels, restaurants, or other similar establishments. The goods sold must be merchandise for resale or supplies for use in the buyer's business operation. The work performed for the employer must be the salesperson's principal business activity.

See chapter 6 for details on statutory employees and common-law employees.

"Retirement plan." Check this box if the employee was an "active participant" (for any part of the year) in any of the following:

1. A qualified pension, profit sharing, or stock-bonus plan described in Section 401(a) (including a Section 401(k) plan).

2. An annuity plan described in Section 403(a).

3. An annuity contract or custodial account described in Section 403(b).

4. A simplified employee pension (SEP) plan described in Section 408(k).

5. A SIMPLE retirement account described in Section 408(p).

6. A trust described in Section 501(c)(18).

7. A plan for federal, state, or local government employees or for an agency or instrumentality thereof (other than a Section 457 plan).

See chapter 9 for a description of who qualifies as an active participant. Do not check this box solely for contributions made to a nonqualified plan or Section 457(b) plan. [Notice 87-16, 1987-1 C.B. 446, modified by Notice 98-49, I.R.B. 1998-38, Sept. 21, 1998]

"Third-party sick pay." Check this box only if you are a third-party sick-pay payer filing a Form W-2 for an insured employee or are an employer reporting sick pay payments made by a third party.

Box 14: Other. If 100% of the lease value of a vehicle provided to an employee is reported in Box 1, the lease value must be reported here or on a separate statement to your employee. Otherwise, the employer may use this box for any other information to be given to the employees. Label each item. Examples include state disability insurance taxes withheld, uniform payments, union dues, health insurance premiums deducted, nontaxable income, educational assistance payments, and a member of the clergy's parsonage allowance and utilities. In addition, employers may enter the following contributions to a pension plan: (a) nonelective employer contributions made on behalf of an employee, (b) voluntary aftertax contributions that are deducted from an employee's pay, (c) required employee contributions, and (d) employer matching contributions. When the employer is reporting prior year contributions under USERRA, the employer may report in Box 14 makeup amounts for nonelective employer contributions, voluntary aftertax contributions, required employee contributions, and employer matching contributions. Report such amounts separately for each year.

Boxes 15 through 20: State and local income tax information. Use these boxes to report state and local income tax information. Enter the two-letter abbreviation of the name of the state. The employer's state ID numbers are assigned by the individual states. The state and local information boxes can be used to report wages and taxes for two states and two localities. Keep each state's and locality's information separated by the broken line. If additional space is required to report information on more than two states or localities, file a second Form W-2.

Q 4:90 How are employee business expense reimbursements handled on Form W-2?

An employer's reimbursements to an employee for business expenses are reported in two ways based on whether or not the payments are from an accountable plan (see chapter 9). Generally, payments made under an accountable plan are excluded from the employee's gross income and are not required to be reported on Form W-2. However, if employees are paid a per diem or mileage allowance, and the amount paid exceeds the amount treated as substantiated under IRS rules (the amount exceeds the federal per diem and mileage rates), a portion of the payment is reported. Employers must report as wages on Form W-2 the amount in excess of the amount treated as substantiated. The excess amount is subject to income tax withholding and Social Security and Medicare taxes. Report the amount treated as substantiated (i.e., the nontaxable portion) in Box 12 using Code L if paid from a per diem or mileage allowance plan.

Payments made under a nonaccountable plan are reportable as wages on Form W-2 (Boxes 1, 3, and 5) and are subject to income tax withholding and Social Security and Medicare taxes.

Q 4:91   How are employer-provided benefits reported on Form W-2?

The following is a list of the most common benefits provided, with a description of the reporting requirements that apply (see chapter 9 for a more detailed discussion):

Group-term life insurance. Employers that paid for group-term life insurance in excess of $50,000 for an employee or a former employee must report the amount determined by using the table in IRS Publication 15-B, Employer's Tax Guide to Fringe Benefits. This amount is included in Boxes 1, 3, and 5 of Form W-2 and also in Box 12 with Code C. Employers must withhold Social Security and Medicare taxes for active employees, but not federal income tax. Former employees must pay the employee part of Social Security and Medicare taxes on premiums for group-term life insurance over $50,000 on Form 1040. Employers are not required to collect those taxes. However, the employer must report the uncollected Social Security tax with Code M and the uncollected Medicare tax with Code N in Box 12 of Form W-2. Employers are responsible to pay the employer share.

Archer MSA. An employer's contribution to an employee's Archer MSA is not subject to federal income tax withholding or Social Security, Medicare, or railroad retirement taxes if it is reasonable to believe at the time of the payment that the contribution will be excludable from the employee's income. If it is not reasonable to believe at the time of payment that the contribution will be excludable from the employee's income, employer contributions are subject to income tax withholding and Social Security and Medicare taxes (or railroad retirement tax if applicable), and must be reported in Boxes 1, 3, and 5.

Employers must report all employer contributions to an Archer MSA in Box 12 of Form W-2. See the instructions for Box 12, Code R. Employer contributions to an Archer MSA that are not excludable from the income of the employee also must be reported in Boxes 1, 3, and 5.

An employee's contributions to an Archer MSA are includible in income as wages and are subject to income tax withholding and Social Security and Medicare taxes (or railroad retirement tax, if applicable). Employee contributions are, however, deductible, within limits, on the employee's Form 1040.

See Notice 96-53, 1996-2 C.B. 219, and IRS Publication 969, Health Savings Accounts and Other Tax-Favored Health Plans, for more information on MSAs.

SIMPLE (IRA) retirement account. An employee's salary reduction contributions to a SIMPLE retirement account (an IRA program) are not subject to income tax withholding but are subject to Social Security, Medicare, and railroad retirement taxes. Do not include an employee's contribution in Box 1, but do include it in Boxes 3 and 5. An employee's total contribution must also be included in Box 12 with Code D or S.

An employer's matching or nonelective contribution to an employee's SIMPLE IRA account is not subject to income tax withholding or Social Security, Medicare, or railroad retirement taxes and is not to be shown on Form W-2.

See Notice 98-4 [1998-1 C.B. 269] for more information on SIMPLE retirement accounts.

Adoption benefits. Amounts paid or expenses incurred by an employer for qualified adoption expenses under an adoption assistance program are not subject to income tax withholding and are not reportable in Box 1. However, these amounts (including adoption benefits paid from a Section 125 cafeteria plan, but not including adoption benefits forfeited from a cafeteria plan) are subject to Social Security, Medicare, and railroad retirement taxes and must be reported in Boxes 3 and 5. Also, the total amount must be reported in Box 12 with Code T.

See Notice 97-9 [1997-1 C.B. 365] for more information on adoption benefits.

Sick pay. Employers of employees who received *sick pay* in 2017 from an insurance company or other third-party payer and were notified by the third party of the amount of sick pay involved are generally required to report the information on the employees' Forms W-2. See Sick Pay Reporting in IRS Publication 15-A, Employer's Supplemental Tax Guide, for additional instructions.

Scholarship and fellowship grants. Employers give a Form W-2 to each recipient of a scholarship or fellowship grant only if they are reporting amounts includible in income under Section 117(c). That is, the payments relate to teaching, research, or other services required as a condition for receiving the qualified scholarship. (See IRS Publication 15-A, Employer's Supplemental Tax Guide, and Publication 970 for additional information.) Such amounts are subject to income tax withholding. However, their taxability for Social Security and Medicare taxes depends on the nature of the employment and the status of the organization. See "Students" in Section 15 of Circular E, IRS Publication 15.

Fringe benefits. Employers include all taxable fringe benefits in Box 1 of Form W-2 as wages, tips, and other compensation and, if applicable, in Boxes 3 and 5 as Social Security and Medicare wages. If the employer provided the employee with a vehicle and included 100 percent of its annual lease value in the employee's income, the employer must separately report this value to the employee in Box 14 or on a separate statement. The employee can then determine the value of any business use of the vehicle and report it on Form 2106, Employee Business Expenses. See IRS Publication 15-B, Employer's Tax Guide to Fringe Benefits, for additional information.

> **Note.** Employers that use the commuting rule or the vehicle cents-per-mile rule to value the personal use of the vehicle cannot include 100 percent of the value of the use of the vehicle in the employee's income.

Golden parachute payments. Employers include these payments in Boxes 1, 3, and 5. Employers generally withhold income, Social Security, and Medicare taxes and report these taxes in Boxes 2, 4, and 6, respectively. Excess payments are also subject to a 20 percent excise tax. If the excess payments are considered wages, withhold the 20 percent excise tax and include it in Box 2 as income tax withholding. Also report it in Box 12 with Code K. For additional information, see Sections 280G and 4999.

Q 4:92   Is the information reported on the Form W-2 available to anyone outside the IRS and SSA?

Generally, no. The information on Forms W-2 and W-3 is used to implement the internal revenue laws of the United States and to determine retirement, disability, and survivor insurance benefits under the Social Security Act. I.R.C. Section 6051 requires that employers furnish wage and tax statements to employees and to the SSA. Routine uses of this information include providing it to the Department of Justice for civil and criminal litigation, and to cities, states, and the District of Columbia for use in administering their tax laws. Generally, information returns and statements are confidential, as required by Section 6103.

Q 4:93   Does the IRS allow an employer to use substitute forms to file Form 941?

Employers may use substitute forms to report employment taxes. IRS has provided the guidelines for Form 941 and Schedules B, D, and R. [Rev. Proc. 2016-16, 2016-10, I.R.B. 394]

Tip Reporting for Large Food or Beverage Establishments

Q 4:94   What are the special filing requirements for "large food or beverage establishments"?

Any establishment that provides food or beverages for consumption on the premises may have special annual reporting requirements in addition to its quarterly Forms 941. These special rules apply if the establishment normally employed more than 10 employees on a typical business day during the preceding calendar year and customers customarily tip its food or beverage employees. (Such an employer is referred to as a "large food or beverage establishment.")

When employees of a large food or beverage establishment report in the aggregate tips of less than 8 percent of the establishment's gross receipts, the employer must attribute tip income to employees classified as "directly tipped employees." The amount reported is the amount that, when added to reported tips, equals 8 percent of gross receipts. Each business location of a multiple-location business is considered one establishment for purposes of this rule. Thus, the reported tips from multiple business locations are not aggregated. Gross receipts attributable to carryout sales and to services with respect to which a service charge of 10 percent or more was added are excluded from this computation. Employees are classified as directly tipped employees when they receive tips directly from customers. Waiters, waitresses, and bartenders are treated as directly tipped employees, even when the employee turns all tips over to a tip pool. [I.R.C. § 6503(c); Treas. Reg. § 31.6503-3]

Q 4:95   When is a food or beverage establishment treated as having more than 10 employees?

A food or beverage establishment is considered to have normally employed more than 10 employees on a typical business day during a calendar year when one-half of the sum of (1) the average number of employee hours worked per business day during the calendar month with the largest aggregate gross receipts from food or beverage operations, plus (2) the average number of employee hours worked per business day during the calendar month with the least aggregate gross receipts from food or beverage operations, is greater than 80 hours. The average number of employee hours worked per business day during a month is computed by (1) dividing the total number of hours worked during the month by all employees of the employer working in the food or beverage operation by (2) the total number of days during the month that the food or beverage operation was open for business. Employees who work in both a food or beverage operation and a nonfood or beverage operation (or in more than one food or beverage operation) are credited with hours worked in the food or beverage operation based on a good-faith estimate by the employer. [I.R.C. § 6503(c); Treas. Reg. § 31.6503-3] Additional information can be found in Publications 531 and 1239 to assist in complying with reporting tips.

Q 4:96   How are tips allocated for a large food and beverage establishment?

A large food and beverage establishment meeting the 10-employee threshold can choose among three methods to allocate tips among directly tipped employees. First, it can apply an allocation method that is contained in a good-faith written agreement with at least two-thirds of each occupational category of tipped employees (e.g., busboys, waiters, and hostesses). The agreement must be adopted at a time when there are tipped employees employed in each occupational category of tipped employees established by the employer. The employees must have the right to prospectively revoke the agreement by obtaining the consent of at least two-thirds of the tipped employees in each category. This agreement is effective beginning with the first day of a payroll period that begins after the date of adoption of the allocation method. [Treas. Reg. § 31.6053-3(e)]

An employer without a written agreement on tip allocation must allocate tips with respect to each payroll period pursuant to one of two allocation methods. The gross receipts method uses a multistep formula (described in Treasury Regulations Section 31.6053-3(f)) as follows:

Step 1: Multiply the establishment's gross receipts (less the receipts attributable to carryout sales and sales where more than a 10 percent service charge was added to the bill) from the payroll period by 8 percent.

Step 2: Determine the aggregate amount of tips reported for the payroll period by "indirectly tipped employees," that is, employees who do not customarily receive tips directly from customers, such as busboys and cooks.

Step 3: Subtract from the amount determined under Step 2 the amount determined under Step 1. The resulting excess is the directly tipped employees' aggregate share of 8 percent of the gross receipts of the establishment for the payroll period.

Step 4: For each directly tipped employee, multiply the amount determined under Step 3 by a fraction, the numerator of which is the amount of gross receipts of the establishment for the payroll period that is attributable to the employee, and the denominator of which is the aggregate amount of gross receipts for the payroll period that is attributable to all directly tipped employees.

Step 5: For each directly tipped employee, subtract the amount of tips reported by the employee from the amount determined under Step 4 with respect to the employee. Any excess amount is known as the employee's shortfall for the payroll period.

Step 6: Subtract the aggregate amount of tips reported by all directly and indirectly tipped employees for the payroll period from the amount determined under Step 1. The excess is the amount to be allocated as tips among directly tipped employees who had a shortfall for the payroll period under Step 5.

Step 7: For each directly tipped employee who had a shortfall for the payroll period, multiply the amount determined under Step 6 by a fraction, the numerator of which is the amount of such employee's shortfall as determined in Step 5 and the denominator of which is the aggregate of all shortfalls for the payroll period for all directly tipped employees. The product is the employee's I.R.C. Section 6053(c) allocation for the payroll period.

The third method, hours-worked method, follows the same steps as the gross receipts method above. However, if the average number of employee hours worked per business day during a payroll period is less than 200, then the employer may multiply the amount determined under Step 4 by a fraction, the numerator of which is the number of hours worked by the directly tipped employee during the payroll period and the denominator of which is the number of hours worked by all directly tipped employees during the payroll period.

Q 4:97   How does an employer report an employee's tip allocation under I.R.C. Section 6053(c) to the IRS?

Large food or beverage establishments must file Form 8027 on or before the last day of February for the preceding calendar year, unless the employer files electronically, then the due date is March 31. The return must include the following information: (1) the employer's name, address, and EIN; (2) the establishment's name, address, and identification number; (3) the aggregate gross receipts (less receipts attributable to carryout sales and sales where more than a 10 percent service charge was added to the bill) of the establishment from the provision of food or beverages; (4) the aggregate amount of charge receipts (less receipts attributable to carryout sales and sales where more than a 10 percent service charge was added to the bill) on which there were charged tips; (5) the aggregate amount of charged tips shown on such charge receipts; (6) the aggregate amount of tips reported by the employees during the calendar year; and (7) the aggregate amount of wages the employer is required to report on Forms W-2, Wage and Tax Statement, under I.R.C. Section 6051.

The IRS has decided not to continue its pilot Attributed Tip Income Program (ATIP), which allowed participating employers to report employee tip income based on a formula using a percentage of gross receipts attributed among employees based on restaurant practices. ATIP did not require employers to meet with the IRS to determine tip rates or eligibility, for example, or to sign an agreement with the IRS to participate. It significantly simplified tip reporting requirements. The IRS would not initiate a tip examination during the period in which the employer and employee participate in the program.

Q 4:98   Who is the employer for purposes of determining FICA liabilities for unreported tips after a corporate reorganization?

A 1993 IRS Field Service Advice (FSA) concluded that the IRS will generally follow a principle that the liability for unpaid taxes attaches to the predecessor employer for unreported tips. I.R.C. Section 3121(q) provides that for purposes of determining an employer's liability for payment of employment taxes, tips received by the employee in the course of employment are considered remuneration (and that remuneration is deemed to have been paid by the employer). The timing of this remuneration and the liability for any related employment taxes are conditioned on whether the tips are reported as required under I.R.C. Section 6053(a). Where the tips are reported to the employer, the tips are treated as wages subject to FICA taxation for the period in which the tips are reported. Where tips are not reported, the tips are treated as wages and subject to FICA taxation on the date that the IRS serves notice and demand for such taxes.

The regulations generally contemplate that the employer for purposes of assessing liability for underreported FICA taxes on tips is the same entity when the notice and demand is served and when the tips were paid. Thus the liability generally falls on the employer at the time of the notice and demand. When a corporate reorganization results in a different party who did not have knowledge of the underreporting, the IRS has offered four possible scenarios on how that liability should apply:

1. Basically, the IRS determined that a predecessor is the employer for purposes of making notice and demands under Section 3121(q) for unpaid FICA taxes following a sale of all corporate assets.

2. However, during a reorganization that resulted in a merger under state law, the successor is deemed to be the predecessor employer and liable.

3. When the reorganization resulted in the successor purchasing all the shares of the predecessor, the successor is liable.

4. In a more complex reorganization, the liability can be split.

[Rev. Proc. 96-60, 1996-2, C.B. 399, superseded by Rev. Proc. 2004-53, 2004-34 I.R.B. 320; Field Serv. Adv. (June 4, 1993, released Apr. 30, 1998)] See chapter 12 for more information concerning the employment tax requirements pursuant to a restructuring.

Corrections to Form W-2

Q 4:99　How are corrections to Form W-2 handled?

Form W-2c, Corrected Wage and Tax Statement, is used to correct errors (such as incorrect name, SSN, or amount) on a previously filed Form W-2. These Forms W-2c are sent with Form W-3c, Transmittal of Corrected Wage and Tax Statements, unless the only correction is in the employee's address.

If an error on Form W-2 is discovered after it has been issued to an employee but before the forms are sent to the SSA, mark the "Void" box at the top of the form on Copy A. Prepare a new Copy A with the correct information and send it to SSA. Do not write "Corrected" on Copy A of Form W-2. Write "Corrected" on the new employee's copies (B, C, and 2), and furnish those copies to the employee. If the "Void" Form W-2 is on a page with a correct Form W-2, send the entire page to the SSA. The "Void" form will not be processed. If the void Form W-2 is not on a page with a correct form W-2, do not send the void Form W-2.

When adjustments are made to correct Social Security and Medicare wages or taxes for a prior year, the employer must file Form 941-X, Adjusted Employer's QUARTERLY Federal Tax Return or Claim for Refund, or Form 943-X, for the return period when the error is discovered. The employer must also issue the employee a Form W-2c for the prior year. If you are making corrections to a previously filed Schedule H (Form 1040), see Publication 926. Form W-2c along with Form W-3, Transmittal of Wage and Tax Statements, are filed with the SSA.

The Consolidated Appropriations Act of 2016 accelerated the filing deadline for W-2s. The IRS has eased requirements for issuing corrected forms with minor errors, beginning in 2017. [Pub. L. No. 114-113]

Q 4:100   What steps should be taken to correct a wrong address on a W-2?

Corrections concerning amounts reported on the form are generally made with a Form W-2c, Corrected Wage and Tax Statement. If the wages and other financial information are correct but the employee's address was incorrect, it is not necessary to file Form W-2c with the SSA to show the correct address. Employers may, in lieu of filing Form W-2c, provide a corrected Form W-2 to the employee. Employers may do one of the following: (1) issue a new Form W-2 containing all correct information, including the new address; (2) issue a Form W-2c showing the correct address in Box i; or (3) mail the Form W-2 with the incorrect address to the employee in an envelope showing the correct address, or otherwise deliver it to the employee. If the employee is provided with a corrected W-2, indicate "Reissued statement" on the new copy; do not send Copy A of the corrected W-2 to the SSA.

Q 4:101   Does use of a reporting agent or other third-party payroll service provider relieve the employer of a responsibility to file returns and deposit taxes?

The use of a reporting agent or other third-party payroll service provider does not relieve an employer of the responsibility to ensure that tax returns are filed and all taxes are paid or deposited correctly and on time. [I.R.C. § 3403; Pub. No. 15]

An employer may, under certain circumstances, transfer liability for withholding and reporting for payments of sick pay to a party who is not an agent of the employer and who makes payments to the employees. (See Q 4:121 and chapter 10.)

Form W-3

Q 4:102   How is a Form W-3 completed?

The IRS has combined the instructions for completing Form W-3, Transmittal of Wage and Tax Statements, with the instructions for the Form W-2. Form W-3 is the transmittal form for all W-2s filed under an Employer Identification Number (EIN). The sum of each box reporting wages or taxes for all Forms W-2 under each EIN should equal the amount reported on Form W-3. It is also important that the total of all wages and taxes reported on Forms 941, 943, and 944 agrees with the amounts reported on Form W-3. If there are differences, the IRS and SSA may contact you to explain the discrepancy. The reconciliation is an important part of the year-end process.

The boxes that must be completed on Form W-3 include the following:

Box a: Control number. This is an optional box that may be used for numbering the transmittal.

Box b: Kind of Payer. An employer must check the box that designates which type of payer the employer is. Only one box may be checked. If an employer has more than one type of W-2, send each type with a separate W-3. The kinds of payers are:

- 941 or 941-SS_
- Military (provides W-2 forms for members of the uniformed services)
- 943 (an agricultural employer)
- 944 or 944(SP) and no other category applies
- CT-1 (a railroad employer that provides W-2s for employees covered under RRTA). Do not show employee RRTA in boxes 3 through 7. Those boxes are for social security and Medicare information.
- Household employer (provides Forms W-2 for household employees but does not file Form 941, 941-SS, 943 or 944)
- Medicare government employer

Box b: Kind of Employer. Check only one box unless third-party sick pay also applies. The boxes for kinds of employer include:

- None apply (if none of the other checkboxes apply)
- 501c non-government (non-governmental organizations, such as private foundations, public charities, social and recreational clubs, and veterans organizations)
- State/local non 501c (state or local government or instrumentality)
- State/local 501c (a state or local government or instrumentality and have received a determination letter from IRS that you are also a tax exempt organization under 501(c)(3))
- Federal govt. (federal government entity or instrumentality)

Box b: Third-party sick pay. Check this box if you are a third-party sick payer (or reporting sick pay payments made by a third party) that has checked the "Third-party sick pay" box in Box 13 on Form W-2. File a single Form W-3 for the regular and "Third-party sick pay" Forms W-2.

Box c: Total number of Forms W-2. Show the number of completed individual Forms W-2 that you are transmitting with the Form W-3. Do not count "Void" Forms W-2.

Box d: Establishment number. This box may be used to identify separate establishments in your business. An employer can file a separate Form W-3, with Forms W-2 for each establishment even if the establishments have the same EIN. Alternatively, an employer may use a single Form W-3 for all Forms W-2 of the same type.

Box e: Employer identification number (EIN). An employer must enter the nine-digit EIN assigned by the IRS. The number should be the same as that used on Form 941, Form 941-SS,_943, 944, Form CT-1, or Schedule H (Form 1040). If an employer does not have an EIN when filing Form W-3, enter "Applied For" in the box, not your Social Security number. See Q 4:6.

Box f: Employer's name. Enter the same name as shown on Form 941, Form 941-SS, 943, 944, Form CT-1.

Box g: Employer's address and ZIP code. Enter the address.

Box h: Other EIN used this year. If another EIN was used, enter the number here.

Contact person, telephone number, fax number, and email address. Provide this information in the event that the SSA has any questions during the processing.

Boxes 1 through 8. These boxes correspond to the boxes on the Form W-2 so enter the totals reported in boxes 1 through 8 on Forms W-2.

Box 9: This box is grayed out on the 2017 Form W-3 so do not enter an amount in this box.

Box 10: Dependent care benefits. This box is not applicable to Forms W-2AS, W-2GU, W-2VI. Enter the total reported in box 10 of Forms W-2.

Box 11: Nonqualified plans. Enter the total reported in box 11 on Forms W-2.

Box 12a: Deferred compensation. Enter the total of all amounts reported in Codes D through H, S, Y, AA, BB, and EE in box 12a. Do not enter a code.

Note. The total of Form W-2 Box 12 amounts with Codes A through C, J through R, T through W, Z and DD is not reported on Form W-3.

Box 13: For third-party sick pay use only. Leave this box blank. See Form 8922.

Box 14: Income tax withheld by payer of third-party sick pay. This box should be completed only by an employer with employees who had federal income tax withheld on third-party payments of sick pay. Show the total income tax withheld by third-party payers on payments to all of your employees. Although the tax is included in the box 2 total, it must be separately shown here.

Box 15: State/Employer's state ID number. Enter the two-letter abbreviation for the name of the state or territory (for Forms W-2AS, W-2GU, and W-2VI) being reported on Form(s) W-2. Also enter the state- or territory-assigned ID number. If the Forms W-2 being submitted with this Form W-3 contain wage and income tax information from more than one state or territory, enter an "X" under "State" and do not enter any state or territory ID number.

Box 16 through 19. Enter the total of state/local wages and income tax shown in their corresponding boxes on the Forms W-2 included with this Form W-3. If the Forms W-2 show amounts from more than one state or locality, report them as one sum in the appropriate box on Form W-3. Verify that the amount reported in each box is an accurate total of the Forms W-2. The wage and tax information is not applicable to Forms W-2AS, W-2GU, and W-2VI.

Q 4:103   Is a reconciliation required when filing the Form W-3 with the Forms W-2?

Yes. The amounts in Boxes 2, 3, 5, and 7 from 2017 Form W-3 must reconcile with their respective amounts from the 2017 yearly totals from the quarterly Forms 941 or 941-SS or annual Form 943, Form 944, Form CT-1 (box 2 only), and Schedule H (Form 1040).

Q 4:104   Is it possible that a Form W-3 might not reconcile with the quarterly or annual employment tax return?

Yes. There could be several reasons that might create discrepancies with what is filed on the quarterly or annual returns and with the W-3 totals. For example:

- Manual adjustments may have been reported on an individual employee record but these adjustments did not get accounted for in the tax remittances and filings
- Third party sick pay tax deposit remitted by third party but not included in employees' Forms W-2
- Imputed income on noncash compensation reported on W-2 but taxes were not remitted
- Stock or deferred compensation transactions were completed with third party and were included in employees' Forms W-2 but the related taxes were not remitted.

Penalties

Q 4:105   What are the penalties for failing to deposit payroll taxes?

An employer that fails to deposit payroll taxes (wage withholding, employee FICA, and employer FICA) is subject to penalty under I.R.C. Section 6656. If the deposit is made within five days of its due date, the penalty is 2 percent of the late deposit amount. If the deposit is made more than five days after, but within 15 days of the due date, the penalty is 5 percent of the late deposit amount. If the deposit is made more than 15 days after the due date, the penalty is 10 percent of the late deposit amount. Finally, if the amount due is not paid within 10 days of the first delinquency notice sent to the taxpayer, the penalty is 15 percent of the late deposit amount.

This penalty applies only if the employer actually withheld income taxes and failed to deposit them; it does not apply to an employer that failed to withhold income taxes. [Rev. Rul. 75-191, 1975-1 C.B. 376] However, even where the employer failed to withhold payroll taxes, the penalty would still apply to the employer's portion of FICA taxes required to be deposited. The IRS will waive the failure-to-deposit penalty if the employer can show reasonable cause for not depositing the taxes. [I.R.C. §§ 6656(a), 6656(b)]

Q 4:106   Must the IRS base its determination as to the underreporting of tips on a factual evaluation of the employer?

The IRS may assess an employer's liability for FICA taxes on the aggregate unreported tips of a taxpayer's employees without first determining the extent to which any individual employee actually reported or underreported tips. In *Bubble Room, Inc. v. United States*, the IRS based its determination of the amount of underreported tips on a standard formula that did not take into account whether or not the tips were reported. The IRS failed to recognize a credit normally available for tipped employees when their tips are properly reported. The employer's underreporting liability was based on the gross receipts of the restaurant.

The circuit court agreed with the IRS and found that I.R.C. Section 3121(q) imposes a separate and distinct liability on employers to pay FICA tax independently of the employees' obligation. [Bubble Room, Inc. v. United States, 159 F.3d 553 (Fed. Cir. 1998)]

In the case of *United States v. Fior D'Italia*, the court held that the IRS's method of aggregation was permissible. This ruling was affirmed by the Ninth Circuit and the Supreme Court reversed the opinion and held that the IRS had the authority to assess the restaurant's FICA tax based on the aggregation method. [536 U.S. 288 (2002)]

Q 4:107   What are the penalties for failure to timely pay employer FICA taxes?

A penalty of 0.5 percent per month is imposed on a taxpayer for failure to timely pay employer FICA taxes. This penalty applies only to the amount shown on a Form 941, whether filed timely or not. If the actual liability is less than the amount shown on the return, the penalty is computed based on the actual liability. However, if the amount required to be shown on the return is greater than the amount shown, the penalty will apply only to the amount actually shown on the return. Thus, if an employer timely files a Form 941 reporting an amount of FICA taxes that it has timely paid, it will not be liable for a failure to pay penalty if the IRS subsequently determines that the amount reported is less than the amount that should have been reported. [I.R.C. § 6651(a)(2)]

Q 4:108   What additional procedures may apply when employment tax deposits are not made on taxes withheld?

Separate accounting may be required if an employer does not pay over withheld employee Social Security, Medicare, or income taxes; deposit required taxes; make required payments; or file tax returns. In this case, an employer would receive written notice from the district director requiring it to deposit taxes in a special trust account for the U.S. government. [Pub. No. 15]

Q 4:109   What are the penalties for failure to timely file Form 941?

A penalty of 5 percent per month is imposed on a taxpayer for failure to timely file a Form 941. [I.R.C. § 6651(a)(1)] This penalty is computed on the amount required to be shown on the form (reduced by the amount of tax that was timely paid) and runs until the date the form is filed. However, the aggregate penalty is limited to 25 percent of the tax required to be shown on the return. Also, for each whole month or part of a month in which the tax is paid late (disregarding any extensions of the payment deadline), a penalty of 0.5 percent of the amount of tax generally applies. The maximum for this penalty is also 25 percent. The penalties will not be charged if there is an acceptable reason for failing to file or pay. [Pub. No. 15]

The late filing penalty can be mitigated or eliminated in two ways. First, in computing the penalty, the "amount required to be shown on the return" is reduced by any payroll taxes actually paid by the due date of the payment. Therefore, if all of the payroll taxes had been timely deposited, then a failure to file Form 941 would not produce a late payment penalty. Second, the penalty may be waived if reasonable cause for the failure to file can be shown. [I.R.C. § 6651]

Q 4:110   What are the penalties for failing to file or furnish a correct Form W-2?

The following penalties generally apply to the person required to file Form W-2. The penalties apply to paper filers as well as electronic filers.

Note. Use of a reporting agent or other third-party payroll service provider does not relieve an employer of the responsibility to ensure that Forms W-2 are furnished to employees and filed correctly and on time.

An employer that fails to file a correct Form W-2 by the due date and cannot show reasonable cause may be subject to a penalty. Penalties can apply if the employer (1) fails to file timely, (2) fails to include all information required to be shown on Form W-2, (3) includes incorrect information on Form W-2, (4) files on paper when required to e-file, (5) reports an incorrect taxpayer identification number (TIN), (6) fails to report a TIN, or (7) fails to file paper Forms W-2 that are machine readable.

Note. The IRS may enforce the penalty for mismatched names and SSNs reported on Forms W-2. To avoid the penalty, make a good faith effort to confirm an employee's name and SSN. If there is a mismatch, ask the employee for the correct information and document the solicitation.

The amount of the penalty, which is based on when the correct Form W-2 is filed, has increased as follows:

- $50 per Form W-2 (if the employer correctly files within 30 days; i.e., by March 30) with a maximum penalty of $536,000 per year ($187,500 for certain small businesses).

- $100 per Form W-2 (if the employer correctly files more than 30 days after the due date but no later than August 1) with a maximum penalty of $1,609,000 per year ($536,000 for certain small businesses).

- $260 per Form W-2 (if the employer files after August 1 or does not file the required Forms W-2) with a maximum penalty of $3,218,500 per year ($1,072,500 for certain small businesses).

For purposes of the lower maximum penalties, an employer is a small business if the average annual gross receipts for the three most recent tax years (or for the period the business was in existence, if shorter) ending before the calendar year in which the Forms W-2 were due are $5 million or less.

An employer that meets either of the following exceptions can avoid liability for these penalties: (1) the failure to file was due to reasonable cause and not to willful neglect or (2) the failure to file Form W-2 correctly was attributable to an inconsequential error or omission. An inconsequential error is an error or omission that does not prevent or hinder the IRS from processing the Form W-2 for the purpose that was intended. Errors and omissions that are never inconsequential are those relating to (1) a TIN, (2) a payee's surname, and (3) any money amounts.

A certain *de minimis* rule applies to permit abatement of a penalty for failure to file correct Forms W-2. Under this rule, a full penalty will not apply if the employer: (1) filed the Forms W-2 on or before the required filing date, (2) either failed to include all the information required on the form or included incorrect information, and (3) filed corrections by August 1, 2017 for 2016 Forms W-2.

Employers that satisfy all three conditions will be subject to a lower penalty. The penalty for filing incorrect Forms W-2 (but not for filing late) will not apply to the greater of 10 Forms W-2 or one-half of 1 percent of the total number of Forms W-2 the employer was required to file for the calendar year.

An employer that fails to file a correct Form W-2 due to intentional disregard of the filing requirements or an intentional disregard of the correct information requirements is subject to a penalty of at least $530 per Form W-2 with no maximum penalty for 2017.

Employers that fail to provide correct payee statements (Forms W-2) to their employees and cannot show reasonable cause may be subject to a separate penalty. The penalty applies if the employer: (1) fails to provide the 2016 statement by February 1, 2017. (2) fails to include all information required to be shown on the statement, or (3) includes incorrect information on the statement.

The penalty for failure to furnish correct payee statements is based on when the employer furnishes the payee statement. It is an additional penalty that is applied in the same manner as the failure to file the correct information return by the due date.

An inconsequential error or omission is not considered a failure to include correct information. An inconsequential error or omission cannot reasonably be expected to prevent or hinder the payee from timely receiving correct information and reporting it on his or her income tax return or from otherwise putting the statement to its intended use. Errors and omissions that are never inconsequential are those relating to (1) a dollar amount, (2) a significant item in a payee's address, and (3) the appropriate form for the information provided (i.e., whether the form is an acceptable substitute for the official IRS form).

Any failure to provide a correct payee statement (Form W-2) that is due to an intentional disregard of the requirements to furnish a correct payee statement is subject to a penalty of at least $530 per Form W-2 with no maximum penalty for 2017.

Employers that willfully file a fraudulent Form W-2 for payments they claim were made to another person may be subjected to damages if sued. [I.R.C. § 6721(a)]

Q 4:111   Is there a safe harbor for *de minimis* errors?

Yes. The Protecting Americans from Tax Hikes (PATH) Act added an exception from the penalties for failure to file correct returns and failure to provide a correct Form W-2 to an employee for *de minimis* errors. If a Form W-2 is otherwise correctly filed, these penalties will not apply if the error for a single amount reported on the Form W-2 does not exceed $100 or the amount reported as withheld does not exceed $25. The *de minimis* error safe harbor will apply to Forms W-2 furnished after December 31, 2017. However, if an employee requests a corrected Form W-2, the *de minimis* safe harbor will not apply.

Q 4:112   Will an employee avoid liability for federal income taxes when the employer fails to withhold federal income taxes from payments?

No. The tax court ruled on just such a position in *Lucas v. Commissioner* [T.C. Memo. 2000-14] and *Groom v. Commissioner* [T.C. Memo. 1992-291].

Misclassification of an employee as an independent contractor does not relieve the employee of liability for filing a tax return and paying federal income tax on payments received for services.

Q 4:113   What is the trust fund recovery penalty?

It is a penalty for underpayment of income tax withholding, Social Security taxes, and Medicare taxes. When income, Social Security, and Medicare taxes that must be withheld and/or paid are not withheld or are not deposited or paid to the IRS, the trust fund recovery penalty may apply. The penalty is the full amount of the unpaid trust fund tax. This penalty may apply if these unpaid taxes cannot be immediately collected from the employer or business. [Pub. No. 15]

Q 4:114   When is a company officer personally liable for underpaid payroll taxes?

I.R.C. Section 6672 holds an individual liable for a 100 percent penalty if he or she is responsible for the payment of withholding taxes and willfully fails to have the company remit them. In expanding this concept over the years, the IRS has held that when the liability resulted because the executive had knowledge that the company was not paying the withheld taxes and had the authority to make its payments, that executive became personally liable. Agreeing with this interpretation, the Second Circuit held that a company CFO was personally responsible for its failure to remit withholding taxes. The court imposed this liability on the officer because the officer had "control" over the company's finances. [United States v. Landau, 155 F.3d 93 (2d Cir. 1998)]

The courts addressed this issue in a decision where a company director who had some power over the financial operations (including the power to write checks at the command of the president) did not have the requisite control to become liable for unpaid taxes. The court found that the "crucial inquiry is whether the person had the effective power to pay the taxes owed." This individual had no authority to make decisions with regard to which bills to pay or not pay, including tax bills, said the court. [McGlaughlin v. United States, No. S 98-3819 (D. Md. Jan. 6, 2000)]

The district court ruled that a majority stockholder of a company was liable for the unpaid taxes because he was a responsible person, as defined under Section 6672, and he was not prevented from participating in the company activities. The court held that he had the authority to change the board of directors, which in turn could have changed the management structure of the company. The court concluded, "he chose not to exercise his authority as the primary shareholder." As a result, "he had the effective power to ensure that federal taxes were paid." The court noted that this result may not always be true. A majority shareholder will not always be a responsible person. In this case, the majority shareholder provided the primary funding for the company's operations. [Larson & Larson v. United States, 76 F. Supp. 2d 1092 (E.D. Wash. 2000)] A shareholder who held various executive positions within a company was held liable for payroll taxes by the Fourth Circuit. [Erwin v. United States, 591 F.3d 313 (4th Cir. 2010)]

Q 4:115   Who is liable for the trust fund recovery penalty?

The trust fund recovery penalty may be imposed on all persons who are determined by the IRS to be responsible for collecting, accounting for, and paying over income, Social Security, and Medicare taxes, and who acted willfully in not doing so.

A responsible person can be:

- An officer or an employee of a corporation
- A member or an employee of a partnership
- A corporate director or a shareholder

- A member of a board of trustees of a nonprofit organization
- Another person with authority and control over funds to direct their disbursement
- Another corporation or third-party payer
- Payroll Service Providers (PSP) or responsible parties within a PSP
- Professional Employer Organizations (PEO) or responsible parties within a PEO, or
- Responsible parties within the common law employer (client of PSP/PEO).

"Willfully" means voluntarily, consciously, and intentionally. A responsible person acts willfully if the person must have been or should have been aware of the outstanding taxes and either intentionally disregarded the law or was plainly indifferent to its requirement. No evil intent or bad motive is required. [Notice 784 (Rev. 3-2016); Pub. No. 15]

Q 4:116   Will the IRS ever waive the penalty for failure to accurately and timely file?

The IRS will waive the penalty if the employer can establish that the failure to timely and accurately file was due to reasonable cause. Reasonable cause exists if the failure arose from events beyond the employer's control, such as incorrect information being given by employees, accidental destruction of business records, and so on. Reasonable cause also exists even if the failure was not due to events beyond the employer's control if significant mitigating factors are present, such as a change in reporting requirements from prior years, or a history of compliance. The IRS may accept or reject a reasonable cause excuse at its discretion. [Treas. Reg. § 301.6724-1]

Q 4:117   Are there additional penalties for intentional disregard of the filing requirements?

The normal penalties under Section 6721(a) apply to an employer's unintentional mistakes. In contrast, the penalty for intentional disregard of the requirements to file timely and accurate Forms W-2 is the greater of $530 or 10 percent of the amount required to be reported correctly. There is no maximum dollar amount. Therefore, when an employer purposely underreports the amount of wages paid to an employee, the employer may be liable for a penalty of 10 percent of the amount not reported or reported incorrectly.

Q 4:118   What are the most common errors found on Forms W-2, W-3, 941, 943, 944, CT-1, and Schedule H (Form 1040)?

Employers should check Forms W-2, W-3, 941, 943, 944, CT-1, and Schedule H (Form 1040) to avoid the following common errors:

1. Not reporting bonuses as wages and as Social Security and Medicare wages on Forms W-2 and 941.

2. Not reporting both Social Security and Medicare wages and taxes separately on Forms W-2, W-3, and 941, 944, CT-1, and Schedule H (Form 1040).

3. Not reporting Social Security taxes on Form W-2 in the box for Social Security tax withheld, not misreporting them as Social Security wages.

4. Not reporting Medicare taxes on Form W-2 in the box for Medicare tax withheld, not misreporting them as Medicare wages.

5. Making sure Social Security wage amounts for each employee do not exceed the annual Social Security wage base.

6. Reporting noncash wages that are not subject to Social Security or Medicare taxes as Social Security or Medicare wages.

7. Using an EIN on any quarterly Form 941 for the year (or annual Forms 943, 944, CT-1, and Schedule H (Form 1040)) that is different from the EIN reported on Form W-3 without entering the other EIN on Form W-3 in the box for "Other EIN used this year."

8. Not reconciling the amounts on Form W-3 to the total amounts from Form W-2.

9. Not reconciling Form W-3 with the four quarterly Forms 941 (or annual Forms 943, 944, CT-1, and Schedule H (Form 1040)) for (1) income tax withholding, and (2) Social Security wages, Social Security tips, and Medicare wages and tips. Form W-3 should include Form 941(or annual Forms 943, 944, CT-1, and Schedule H (Form 1040) adjustments only for the current year (i.e., do not report those prior year adjustments on the current year Forms W-2 and W-3). [Form 941, Employer's QUARTERLY Federal Tax Return (or annual Forms 943, 944, CT-1, and Schedule H (Form 1040)); Pub. No. 15]

Third Party Payer Arrangements

The growth of outsourced payroll arrangements for some or all of federal employment tax withholding, reporting, and payment obligations will require employers to consider the obligations under such arrangements. Some of the common third-party arrangements may be:

- Payroll service provider
- Reporting agent
- Agent with approved 2678
- Payer designated under section 3504
- Certified Professional Employer Organization

Q 4:119   How do agents report wages paid?

Generally, in order for an agent to file taxes and make deposits, Form 2678, Employer/Payer Appointment of Agent, must be submitted to IRS for approval.

The agent should enter his or her name as the employer in Box c of Form W-2 and file one Form W-2. However, if the agent (1) is acting as an agent for two or more employers or is an employer and is acting as an agent for another employer and (2) pays Social Security wages in excess of the wage base to an individual, special reporting for payments to that individual is needed.

If an agent meets the requirements in items (1) and (2) above, the agent must file separate Forms W-2 reflecting the wages paid by each employer. On each Form W-2 filed as an agent, the agent should enter the following in Box c:

(Name of agent) Agent for (name of employer) (Address of agent)

As a result of an initiative led by the IRS Office of Taxpayer Burden Reduction, Form 2678 was redesigned to make it clearer and more user-friendly. All versions of Form 2678 prior to the June 2011 (or newer) form are now obsolete. In addition, the IRS has also updated requirements for reporting agents in Revenue Procedure 2007-38 about which transactions they can complete for the taxpayer with a signed Form 8655, Reporting Agent Authorization. The form allows a taxpayer to designate a reporting agent (e.g., accounting service, franchiser, bank, service bureau, etc.) to perform certain acts. Initially, the reporting agent could make deposits and file returns on behalf of a taxpayer. [Rev. Proc. 2007-38, 2007-35 I.R.B. 1442] In August 2012, Revenue Procedure 2012-32 modified the prior revenue procedure and imposed three major changes. [Rev. Proc. 2012-32, 2012-34 I.R.B. 267] First, a reporting agent must use the EFTPS regardless of whether the taxpayer is required to do so or not. Second, at least quarterly, the reporting agent must inform the taxpayer that the authorization (Form 8655) provided to the reporting agent does not change the fact that the taxpayer is responsible for remitting and filing tax returns. And third, any new form 8655 will only increase or decrease the authority of the preceding form. The authority includes, but is not limited to: signing and electronically filing Forms 940, 941, or 944; making federal tax deposits; and receiving duplicate copies of official notices, correspondence, etc.

Q 4:120   What special forms must reporting agents file with the Form 941?

Designated reporting agents are required to include Schedule R, Allocation Schedule for Aggregate Form 941 Filers, with the Form 941, Employer's QUARTERLY Federal Tax Return, if their clients' wages and taxes are included on the Form 941 being filed. The requirement also applies to business that, under the common pay agent option, report on behalf of multiple related companies under a single Form 941.

An entity can receive approval from the IRS to act as an agent of the employer (as defined under I.R.C. Section 3504) for its clients or related employers within a corporate group by filing Form 2678, Employer/Payer Appointment of Agent. Once approved, the agent includes the wages and taxes of all of its clients under its EIN for employment tax deposit and Forms 941/W-2 reporting purposes. This procedure is frequently used by companies that have multiple employer identification numbers (EINs) because only one of the related entities that is designated as the "common pay agent" makes federal employment tax deposits and files wage and tax information in the aggregate under its EIN, thereby eliminating the need for each of the related companies to makes these deposits and file these returns. Many state revenue departments allow for agent reporting for withholding tax and Form W-2 reporting purposes if the returns are filed with the IRS under the common pay agent method. (Note that separate entity reporting has been required for federal and state unemployment insurance purposes for several years.)

Schedule R is used to allocate certain information to each EIN included on the Form 941 (including information pertaining to the agents' employees, if any).

On Schedule R, reporting agents are required to provide the following information:

Column (a): Client's EIN

Column (b): Wages, tips, and other compensation (line 2 of Form 941)

Column (c): Total income tax withheld from wages, tips, and other compensation (line 3 of Form 941)

Column (d): Total social security and Medicare taxes (line 5e of Form 941)

Column (e): Section 3121(q) Notice of Demand—Tax Due on Unreported Tips allocated to the listed client EIN (Line 5f of Form 941)

Column (f): Total taxes after adjustments allocated to the listed client EIN (Line 10 of Form 941)

Column (g): Total deposits plus any other payments allocated to the listed client EIN, e.g., overpayments from previous quarters (Line 11, Form 941)

If the information on Form 941 includes wages and taxes for employees of the reporting agent, the allocated portion relating to the reporting agent's employees are included on Schedule R, line 18. If there are more than 15 clients included on the Form 941, the Schedule R continuation sheet is used.

Q 4:121   Does the Payroll Department have a role in filing Form 1099-MISC?

While W-2s are the typical statement provided to employees, there are situations where Payroll must be involved in issuing a 1099-MISC. This may be because a contractor is paid out of the payroll system, payments are made to a deceased employee, or director fees are paid to an employee-director.

Q 4:122   How are a deceased employee's wages reported?

When an employee dies during the year, the employer must report the accrued wages, vacation pay, and other compensation paid after the date of death in the following manner:

If the payment was made to the employee before death, the wages are taxable, subject to withholding and reported in Box 1 (total wages) of the employee's W-2, subject to Social Security and reported in Box 3 of the employee's W-2, and subject to Medicare and reported in Box 5 of the employee's W-2. These wages are also subject to FUTA taxes.

If the payment of wages was made after the employee's death and in the same year, the earnings are then taxable income to the beneficiary (or estate) to whom they are paid. The earnings are not subject to federal income tax withholding. The earnings would be subject to FICA and FUTA if paid to the beneficiary in the year of death. The employer must report the Social Security and Medicare wages and the corresponding amounts withheld on the deceased employee's W-2 in Boxes 3-6. The amount of taxable income would be reported in Box 3 (Other income) of Form 1099-MISC in the name of the beneficiary (or estate) receiving the payment.

If the payment of wages was made after the employee's death and in a subsequent year, the earnings are then taxable income to the beneficiary (or estate) to whom they are paid. The earnings are not subject to federal income tax, FICA, and FUTA and should be reported only in Box 3 (Other income) of Form 1099-MISC in the name of the beneficiary (or estate) receiving the payment.

If the earnings are paid in a subsequent year to the year of death, they are exempt from federal income tax, FICA, and FUTA taxes.

Example. Before her death on March 12, 2016, Shane was employed by Marigold, Inc. and received $32,200 in wages, on which federal income tax of $4,110 was withheld. When Shane died, Marigold, Inc. owed her $2,460 in wages and $1,230 in accrued vacation pay. The total of $3,690 was paid to Shane's estate on March 17, 2016. Because Marigold, Inc. made the payment during the year of death, it must withhold Social Security and Medicare taxes on the $3,690 and must complete Form W-2 as follows:

Box d	Shane's SSN
Box e	Shane's full name and address
Box 1	32,200 (not including the $3,690 of accrued wages and vacation pay)
Box 2	4,110
Box 3	35,890 (includes the $3,690 of accrued wages and vacation pay)
Box 4	2,225.18 (6.2 percent of the amount in Box 3)
Box 5	35,890 (includes the $3,690 accrued wages and vacation pay)
Box 6	520.41 (1.45 percent of the amount in Box 5)

Marigold, Inc. also must complete F orm 1099-MISC as follows:

Boxes recipient's address, and TIN	Use the estate's name, address, and TIN
Box 3	3,690 (even though amounts were withheld for Social Security and Medicare taxes, the gross amount of the deceased employee's wages is reported)

The full $3,690 amount is required to be reported in Box 3, even though the actual check amount the estate receives is $3,407.71 ($3,690 − (7.65% × $3,690)). The 7.65 percent rate comprises the Social Security tax rate of 6.2 percent plus the Medicare tax rate of 1.45 percent.

If Marigold, Inc. made the payment after the year of death, the $3,690 would not be subject to Social Security and Medicare taxes and would not be shown on Form W-2. However, Marigold, Inc. would still be required to file a Form 1099-MISC, reporting the $3,690 amount in Box 3. [W-2 instructions]

Q 4:123   Is an employer (or other creditor) required to file Form 1099 when a debt is canceled or forgiven?

Cancellation of a debt will result in the debtor realizing income equal to the amount forgiven. I.R.C. Section 6041 does not require a creditor to file a Form 1099 reporting cancellation of indebtedness. This section permits a creditor to report the forgiving of the debt. There is, however, no requirement. This was discussed in an IRS Field Service Advice. Apparently some creditors use the filing of this form as a threat to initiate payment, and some debtors have tried to prevent this type of coercion. Note that this exemption does not directly apply to situations where the debtor and creditor are employee and employer. Such forgiveness between an employer and employee would constitute wages and require reporting on Form W-2 and payment of employment taxes. [Field Serv. Adv. (Aug. 25, 1992, released Apr. 30, 1998)]

Q 4:124   How is the overpayment of wages repaid to employers reported?

When an employee repays an employer for wages received in error, these repayments cannot be used as an offset against current year wages unless the repayments are for amounts received in error in the current year. Repayments made in the current year, but related to wages paid in a prior year or years, require special tax treatment by employees in certain cases. Basically, the repaid wages remain taxable in the year they were paid, and the employee is allowed a deduction for the amount of the repayment in the year he or she makes the repayment. Wages paid in error in a prior year remain taxable to the employee for that year. Because the employee received and had use of those funds during that year, they are fully taxable in the year paid. The employee is not entitled to file an amended return (Form 1040X) to recover the income tax on these wages.

The employee is entitled to a deduction (or a credit, in some cases) for the repaid wages on his or her Form 1040 for the year of repayment.

If the repayment is for wages paid in error in a prior year, Form W-2c must be filed with the SSA to correct the employee's reported Social Security and Medicare wages and taxes. The repaid wages are not reflected in a corrected W-2. Therefore, the employer should not correct wages subject to federal income tax (Box 1) on Form W-2c for the amount paid in error. For repayments that occur after December 31, 2008, the employer is required to file a Form 941-X, Adjusted Employer's QUARTERLY Federal Tax Return or Claim for Refund, in the quarter the repayment occurred. The employer may use the *adjustment process*, by checking the box on line 1 of Form 941-X to apply any credit (negative amount) from line 20 to Form 941 for the quarter in which the Form 941-X is filed. Alternatively, the employer may use the *claim process*, by checking the box on line 2 of Form 941-X to request a refund or abatement of the amount shown on line 20.

Q 4:125 How do state and local government employers report wages of employees?

Federal, state, and local agencies have two options for reporting employees' wages that are only subject to the Medicare taxes for part of the year and full Social Security and Medicare taxes for part of the year. They can either: (1) file a single Form W-2 with the Medicare-only wages and the Social Security and Medicare wages combined (which SSA prefers) or (2) file two Forms W-2 and two Forms W-3. If the first option is selected, the Form W-3 must have the "941" box marked in Box b. If the second option is used, file one Form W-2 for wages subject only to Medicare tax. The employer will also check the "Medicare govt. emp." box in Box b of Form W-3. File the second Form W-2 for wages subject to both Social Security and Medicare taxes with the "941" box checked in Box b of Form W-3.

Q 4:126 How are wages of railroad employees reported?

Railroad employers must file Form W-2 to report their employees' wages and income tax withholding. Reporting electronically may be required; see Q 4:85 on electronic reporting.

If an employee is covered by Social Security and Medicare, Form W-2 must show the Social Security and Medicare wages and the amounts withheld for Social Security and Medicare taxes. The Form W-3 used to transmit these Forms W-2 must have the "941" box marked in Box b.

The employer must report the Tier 1 and Tier 2 taxes withheld in Box 14 of Form W-2. They should be labeled "Tier 1 tax" and "Tier 2 tax." (An employer's contribution to an employee's MSA is not subject to railroad retirement taxes if it is reasonable to believe at the time of payment that the contribution will be excludable from the employee's gross income.) Boxes 3, 4, 5, 6, and 7 apply only to covered Social Security and Medicare employees and are not to be used to report railroad retirement taxes. The Form W-3 used to transmit these Forms W-2 must have the "CT-1" box checked in Box b.

Q 4:127 Is the leasing company that supplies leased employees to a worksite employer the employer for purposes of determining liability for federal employment taxes?

There is no formal guidance from the IRS nor a statute that directly addresses this question. However, in a Field Service Advice (FSA), the IRS agreed that it was the worksite employer and not the leasing company that was responsible for withholding and paying employment taxes.

The FSA hinged on whether the leasing company met all the requirements for being classified as the common-law employer. The term *employer* means the person for whom an individual performs any service, of whatever nature, as the employee of such person. A common-law employment relationship generally exists when the person for whom the services are performed has the right to control and direct the individual who performs the services not only as to the result to be accomplished by the worker but also as to the details and means by which that result is accomplished. That is, an employee is subject to the will and control of the employer not only as to what shall be done but as to how it shall be done. It is not necessary that the employer actually direct or control the manner in which the services are performed; it is sufficient if it has the right to do so. In the FSA, the leasing company argued that under existing precedent it was not the common-law employer because it simply acted as an administrative agent hired for the purpose of facilitating preparation of payroll and Forms 941 and obtaining employee benefits at a discounted cost to the client by taking advantage of economies of scale.

The IRS stated, "Pursuant to Section 3401(d)(1), however, if the person or entity for whom the workers perform the services as employees does not have control for the payment of the wages for such services, the term 'employer' means the person having control of the payment of such wages. Thus, a person other than the common law employer will be treated as an employer for employment tax purposes if: (1) the common law employer does not have control of the payment of the wages, and (2) the third party has control of the payment of the wages."

The leasing company argued that Section 3401(d)(1) did not apply in establishing tax liabilities in this case because the client companies designated payroll frequency and submitted funds to the taxpayer to enable the taxpayer to make the required payrolls. [In re Earthmovers, Inc., 199 B.R. 62 (Bankr. M.D. Fla. 1992)] Assuming this is correct, the IRS agreed with the taxpayer that Code Section 3401(d)(1) did not apply in this case. Thus, the worksite employer was fully liable for unpaid taxes.

Q 4:128　How are wages and employment taxes reported for domestic employees?

Use Schedule H (Form 1040), Household Employment Taxes, to report household employment taxes if paid for any of the following wages to a household employee:

1. Social Security and Medicare wages of $2,000 or more for 2017.

2. FUTA wages.

3. Wages from which federal income tax was withheld.

The employer of a household employee files Schedule H with his or her federal income tax return. An extension to file Form 1040 will also apply to Schedule H.

When no Form 1040 is required, the employer of a household employee has two options: (1) file Schedule H by itself (see the Schedule H instructions for details), or (2) if, besides the household employee, the taxpayer has other employees for whom employment taxes are reported on Form 941 or Form 943 and on Form 940 include the taxes for the household employee on those forms.

Do not use Schedule H (Form 1040) for employment taxes for household employees paid with business or farm employment taxes. Instead, include the Social Security, Medicare, and withheld federal income taxes for the employee on the Form 941, Employer's QUARTERLY Federal Tax Return, that is filed for the business or on the Form 943, Employer's Annual Tax Return for Agricultural Employees. Include the FUTA tax for the employee on Form 940, Employer's Annual Federal Unemployment (FUTA) Tax Return. [Pub. No. 926]

Q 4:129　Do special deposit requirements apply to agricultural employers?

Yes. An agricultural employer reports wages paid to "farm workers" annually on Form 943, Employer's Annual Tax Return for Agricultural Employees, and reports wages paid to nonfarm workers quarterly on Form 941, Employer's QUARTERLY Federal Tax Return. In addition to separate reporting, separate deposit rules apply. An agricultural employer must treat employment taxes reportable on Form 943 separate from nonagricultural wages reportable on Form 941 when determining under what schedule wages reported on Form 943 must be deposited. That is, Form 943 taxes and Form 941 taxes are not combined for purposes of determining whether a deposit of either is due, whether the next-day rule ($100,000 of taxes) applies, or whether any safe harbor is applicable. Separate federal tax deposits must be made for Form 943 taxes and Form 941 taxes. The agricultural employer with taxes reported on Form 941 will follow the deposit schedules for those taxes without regard to taxes to be reported on Form 943. The determination of whether an agricultural employer is a monthly or semiweekly depositor of Form 943 taxes is made according to the following rules:

Monthly depositor. An agricultural employer is a monthly depositor of Form 943 taxes for a calendar year if the amount of Form 943 taxes accumulated in the lookback period (see below) is $50,000 or less. An agricultural employer ceases to be a monthly depositor of Form 943 taxes on the first day after the employer is subject to the next-day rule. At that time, the agricultural employer immediately becomes a semiweekly depositor of Form 943 taxes for the remainder of the calendar year and the succeeding calendar year.

Semiweekly depositor. An agricultural employer is a semiweekly depositor of Form 943 taxes for a calendar year if the amount of Form 943 taxes accumulated in the lookback period (see below) exceeds $50,000.

Lookback period (agricultural employers with farm workers). The lookback period for Form 943 taxes is the second calendar year preceding the current calendar year. For example, the lookback period for calendar year 2016 is calendar year 2014. [Treas. Reg. § 31.6302-1(g)]

Example. Green Harvest Foods, an agricultural employer, employs both farm workers and nonfarm workers (employees in its administrative offices). Green Harvest Foods' depositor status for calendar year 2017 for Form 941 taxes will be based on its employment tax liabilities reported on Forms 941 for the third and fourth quarters of 2015 and the first and second quarters of 2016 (the period July 1, 2015 to June 30, 2016). Green Harvest Foods' 2017 depositor status for Form 943 taxes will be based on its employment tax liability reported on its annual Form 943 for calendar year 2015.

Q 4:130   What return information is required when an employer goes out of business?

If an employer goes out of business, it must file a final return for the last quarter in which wages are paid. If that employer continues to pay wages or other compensation for quarters following termination of business, it must file returns for those quarters. If you are required to file a final Form 941, you are also required to furnish Form W-2 to the employees by the due date of the final Form 941. File Forms W-2 with the SSA by the last day of the month that follows the due date of your final Form 941. [Pub. No. 15]

Q 4:131   Are wage and payroll payments advanced to a payroll processing firm subject to the below-market loan provisions of I.R.C. Section 7872?

No, unless the transfer is designed with the sole purpose of avoiding tax. That was the IRS position in Private Letter Ruling 9852047. [(Dec. 24, 1998)]

When an advance or loan is made from one taxpayer to another taxpayer at below-market interest—in the Private Letter Ruling no interest was paid to the lender—the former is treated as having received compensation equal to the difference in the interest rate charged and the current market interest rate on the date the loan is made. [I.R.C. § 7872(b)]

An advance made to a payroll company of payroll and taxes with no interest being paid to the transferor is a below-market loan; however, the compensation imputed under this rule would have no significant impact on either party's tax liability and, as a result, is exempt under Treasury Regulations Section 1.7872-5T.

Q 4:132   What reporting forms are used for nonpayroll payments such as pension annuities and gambling winnings?

Nonpayroll withholding must be reported on Form 945, Annual Return of Withheld Federal Income Tax. Income tax withholding that is required to be reported on Forms 1099 (e.g., Forms 1099-R), information returns for nonemployee payments, or W-2G, certain gambling winnings, must be reported on Form 945. Only taxes and withholding properly reported on Form W-2 should be reported on Form 941. [Pub. No. 15]

Q 4:133   How are payments to an employee that are not subject to federal payroll taxes reported when the individual also receives wages as an employee from the same party?

Such payments are rare; however, where the employee receives both wages subject and not subject to federal income tax withholding, FICA taxes, or both, the combined amounts are reported on Form W-2. Two Forms W-2 may be used. See Q 2:119 for a revenue ruling on this issue as it applied to election workers.

Q 4:134   Do the IRS and states exchange employment tax examination results?

The Questionable Employment Tax Practice (QETP) initiative is a collaborative, nationwide program seeking to identify illegal practices and increase voluntary compliance with employment tax rules and regulations. A primary QETP focus is for the IRS and state employment officials to exchange data in order to leverage resources and encourage businesses to comply with federal and state employment tax requirements.

The IRS and 37 states have entered into agreements to share employment tax examination results. They are: Arizona, Arkansas, California, Colorado, Connecticut, Florida, Hawaii, Idaho, Iowa, Kansas, Kentucky, Louisiana, Maine, Maryland, Massachusetts, Michigan, Minnesota, Mississippi, Missouri, Nebraska, New Hampshire, New Jersey, New York, North Dakota, Ohio, Oklahoma, Oregon, Pennsylvania, Rhode Island, South Carolina, South Dakota, Texas, Utah, Vermont, Virginia, Washington, and Wisconsin.

A primary benefit of the initiative is that the IRS and participating state workforce agencies can exchange audit reports and audit plans, and participate in side-by-side examinations, when appropriate.

Chapter 5

Direct Deposit

A popular way to pay employees is through direct deposit, a type of electronic funds transfer allowing deposits to be transferred directly to an employee's designated bank or financial institution. In fact, the ability to transfer an employee's pay directly to a financial institution of choice has grown as the primary way to pay employees. When available to employees, three out of four choose the option to have their pay sent directly to their bank account. Many companies offer employees the option to have their pay directed to two or more accounts, encouraging employees to save. In 2015, the ACH network processed nearly 24 billion transactions totaling $41.6 trillion. Electronic payments have become a way of life for many individuals who have elected to use smart devices in connection with electronic payments.

The advantages to both the employer and employee should provide enough incentive for strong participation in direct deposit. An increasing number of direct deposit programs make use of a nationwide network of interregional clearinghouse associations that make payroll deposits into employee accounts at almost every financial institution in the country. While many have embraced direct deposit as an alternative to paying employees with paper checks, there are large businesses that have not offered direct deposit as an option because they have not evaluated the benefits that may be obtained. The next generation of change is making funds available as quickly as possible. Keeping with the demand for faster access to financial transactions, same-day ACH transactions were introduced in three phases beginning in 2016.

A growing trend is paying employees via pay cards. This method of payment is a viable alternative to direct deposit for employees who do not have a bank account. There are also many employees with bank accounts who chose pay cards as a tool for managing their money. Pay cards are even considered as an alternative method of payment when disaster strikes. Companies are using pay cards instead of offcycle checks, practically eliminating paper checks. In 2010, the Federal Reserve Board extended Regulation E to include pay cards. Guidelines around whether an employer can offer pay cards are based on state law. The use of pay cards continues to rise as more states permit them and, in some cases, allow employers to mandate payment to employees by either direct deposit or pay cards. A few more states have approved the use of pay cards in 2016, while others still struggle to put the appropriate laws in place.

This chapter covers the various laws affecting electronic payments (including pay cards) and the steps to implement and maintain electronic payment processing, including employee authorizations, procedures to validate bank and account information, and transfers across the ACH (automated clearing house) network.

Overview

Q 5:1   What are the benefits of direct deposit of an employee's pay?

Direct deposit of pay allows employees to have their employer automatically deposit pay directly into a checking account, savings account, or money market account at a financial institution. Financial institutions include banks, savings and loans, credit unions, and other financial service companies. The transfer of wages directly to a financial institution avoids the need for the employer to mail the check and the need for the employee to visit the bank or check-cashing facility. Direct deposit improves both the timeliness and security of the payment of wages to employees.

Direct deposit provides convenience and immediate access to funds for employees and eliminates the dangers of stolen or lost paychecks. Employees do not have to be at work to receive their pay and will receive their pay on a timely basis regardless of whether they are traveling for business, out sick, or otherwise absent from work on payday. The employer benefits from issuing fewer paper checks include lower costs of paper and MICR ink, as well as, a reduction of the carbon footprint. There is also a savings to the employer of a reduction in the time spent reconciling accounts when outstanding checks are cleared and returned. The employer also gains through increased staff productivity because employees do not have to take time off to deposit their paychecks. Direct deposit also reduces opportunities for fraud through tampered or counterfeit checks.

Q 5:2   Are there any drawbacks to direct deposit of payroll?

Direct deposit of payroll has a number of potential drawbacks. First, it requires additional work. Employers must continuously update their master file of information on direct deposit account numbers and must carefully monitor electronic payments to ensure that they do not continue to be made to the account of terminated employees. The latter may cause companies with high turnover rates to believe that a direct deposit program is too burdensome to maintain.

Next, direct deposit is not a paperless system. Employers must process employee authorization forms and prepare the nonnegotiable "pay information statements" in lieu of paychecks. Additionally, it is easier to order a stop payment for an erroneously issued paycheck than to retrieve funds resulting from an incorrect electronic transfer.

Further, the employer loses the "float" on payroll funds. With traditional checks, employee funds remained in the employer's account until the check deposit cycled through the banking system. The employer was able to earn interest for the period between when the check was issued and when it actually was cleared by the employee's bank. In addition, with direct deposit, the time available for processing payroll may be shortened because of the minimum two-day processing time typically required for direct deposit. Scheduling for holidays becomes even more complicated under a shortened processing period.

Finally, a segment of the workforce may not be eligible for (e.g., poor credit history) or simply may not desire to have their pay deposited with a financial institution. In recent years, pay cards have made electronic payments available to employees who were otherwise not eligible for checking accounts, to receive their pay electronically. Some states severely restrict the use of pay cards while others continue to prohibit employer-imposed direct deposit programs.

Q 5:3   Which federal agency is charged with regulating electronic transfers?

Regulations governing electronic funds transfer (EFT) are established by the Board of Governors of the Federal Reserve System under Title IX, the Electronic Funds Transfer Act, of the Consumer Credit Protection Act. [Pub. L. No. 95-630, 92 Stat. 3641; 15 U.S.C. § 1693] NACHA, a nonprofit banking trade association in Herndon, Virginia, develops the rules and guidelines that are contractually adhered to by ACH operators that in turn establish agreements with participating Depository Financial Institutions (DFIs).

The federal government and state governments share regulatory authority over the direct deposit of an employee's pay.

Q 5:4   What rules and regulations govern direct deposit of payroll?

Direct deposit programs are subject to numerous rules and statutes at both the federal and state levels. At the federal level, the Federal Reserve Board Regulation E [12 C.F.R. part 205] sets forth certain consumer protection rights that apply to EFTs. Direct deposit programs are also subject to certain requirements under the Electronic Funds Transfer Act. [Pub. L. No. 95-630, 92 Stat. 3641; 15 U.S.C. §§ 1693e, 1693k]. Through NACHA, financial institutions adhere to the NACHA Operating Rules that also plays a part in direct deposit of payrolls.

The Dodd-Frank Wall Street Reform and Consumer Protection Act of 2010 created the Consumer Financial Protection Bureau (CFPB) to protect consumers through enforcement of federal consumer financial laws and abusive practices. The CFPB oversees compliance with Regulation E and provides additional guidance.

Each state regulates the payment of wages and, as a result, can establish restrictions on the manner and place at which employees can be paid their wages. Common requirements governing employers in their use of direct deposit include that they: (1) obtain employees' written, voluntary consent, (2) give employees the choice of financial institution, and (3) ensure employees are entitled to a free withdrawal of their wages.

Q 5:5   What is required under the Electronic Funds Transfer Act?

Sections 907 and 913 of the Act apply to direct deposit of payroll. Under Section 907, employers must obtain an employee's advance authorization to transfer funds from the employee's accounts. The authorization to start the deposit no longer has to be in writing.

Under Section 913, an employer may not require an employee to establish an account for receipt of electronic transfers with an employer-selected financial institution as a condition of employment. [Pub. L. No. 95-630, 92 Stat. 3641; 15 U.S.C. §§ 1693c, 1693k]

Q 5:6   What is involved in direct deposits of payroll?

The term electronic funds transfer refers to a process that makes commercial payment electronically rather than through the processing of paper instruments, such as checks or drafts.

EFTs use special sets of computer-generated files to transfer funds between various accounts. The employer creates an electronic file that is formatted as an ASCII file of net pay records for employees who are to receive direct deposits. This file is sent via transmission, CD-ROM, or diskette to the originating depository financial institution (ODFI), typically the bank where the employer maintains business accounts. The ODFI confirms that the file is correct and then processes the transfers through the ACH network. The employee is given a proper confirmation of the deposit. These paperless transactions tell a financial institution to make payment of a specified dollar amount to a specified account.

Q 5:7   What is an originating depository financial institution?

An originating depository financial institution (ODFI) is the financial institution that initiates and warrants direct deposit transactions through the ACH network on behalf of the employer.

Q 5:8   What is an automated clearinghouse?

An Automated Clearinghouse (ACH) Operator facilitates the exchange of commercial electronic payments between banks, savings and loan associations, and credit unions. Under Article 14 of the 2008 *NACHA Operating Rules*, an ACH Operator is defined as a Federal Reserve Bank, or other entity that executes an annual agreement with NACHA to provide clearing, delivery, and settlement services for ACH entities between participating Depository Financial Institutions (DFIs) and exchange transactions with other ACH Operators.

Q 5:9   What is a receiving depository financial institution?

A receiving depository financial institution (RDFI) is the financial institution that provides depository account services to employers and employees and accepts direct deposit payments to those accounts. The RDFI is the institution that the employee designates to receive the direct deposit of his or her wages. Generally, the RDFI is where each employee maintains his or her checking, savings, or money market accounts.

Processing Direct Deposit

Q 5:10   What is required to participate in a direct deposit program?

There are four primary requirements to participate in the EFT process:

1. The employer must offer its employees the benefit of direct deposit;
2. The employee must authorize the employer to begin direct deposit;
3. Both the ODFI (the employer's bank) and the RDFI (the employee's choice of bank, credit union, or savings and loan association) must be part of the ACH network; and
4. The employer must authorize the transfer in sufficient time to make the deposit.

Q 5:11   How is a direct deposit processed?

At the start, an employer collects each employee's personal checking and/or savings account numbers, as well as "bank transit" identification for the employee's bank or financial institution. Transfers made to credit unions or brokerage accounts sometimes require additional preparation. This information is required to create the file transferred each pay period.

The typical direct deposit process begins two days before the employer's payday or pay effective date. On that date, the employer delivers its direct deposit file, which must be in electronic media (i.e., CD, flash drive, or electronic transmission) to the ODFI, that is, to the bank or financial institution maintaining the employer's payroll account. The ODFI typically receives the file on the same day. It identifies the accounts of employees that are maintained at the institution and then transmits the remainder of the employee payroll information through the ACH network one or two days before the direct deposit day. Employers may also work with their ODFI to arrange for a one-day processing schedule. Under this arrangement, the employer delivers the direct deposit file to the ODFI one day prior to the direct deposit day.

On or before the employer's payday the employer's financial institution credits the employees' accounts for the amount of the direct deposit. Employers typically provide employees with paper or electronic statements that have the same information that would have appeared on a pay stub (e.g., gross wages; authorized deductions; and deductions for federal, state, and local tax withholding).

With the increase of electronic payments as the primary method of transmitting funds, NACHA solicited comments about a proposed same-day ACH. Under the proposal, RFDIs would be required to accept ACH files and make payments available the same day. The same-day ACH rule would apply to payrolls as well as other debit and credit payments. (See Qs 5:23-5:29.)

Q 5:12   What types of employee authorizations are required?

If required by state law, an employer must obtain each employee's written authorization before it transfers pay to employees' accounts. When an error occurs, whereby the electronic payment made to the employee is incorrect, the employer is permitted to recover the money without the specific authorization of the employee if certain requirements are met. The entire amount must be reversed within five days of the original payment settlement. The employee must be notified prior to the posting date of the reversing entry. There may be state regulations that require written permission or do not allow a reversal under any circumstance. An ODFI or RDFI can request a copy of an employee's authorization, which the employer must provide. Exhibit 5-1 provides a sample direct deposit authorization agreement. [NACHA Operating Rules art. 2 Section 2]

Exhibit 5-1. Sample Direct Deposit Authorization Agreement

EMPLOYEE NAME: _____

EMPLOYEE NUMBER: _____

I hereby authorize (insert company name) to initiate credit entries and to initiate, if necessary, debit entries and adjustments for any credit entries in error to my account or accounts listed below.

Direct Deposit 1

_____ New _____ Change _____ Terminate

1. Bank or Credit Union Name: _____ Account Number: _____ Routing Number (contact your bank for this number): _____ Account Type:_____ Checking _____ Savings _____ Money Market*

   *If Money Market, your bank will have to advise as to whether it will accept the dollars as _____ Checking or _____ Savings

   Amount of Deposit _____ or _____ Partial Balance (place check mark here), _____ "All" (place check mark here) Attach a voided check or deposit slip for account.

Direct Deposit 2

_____ New _____ Change _____ Terminate

2. Bank or Credit Union Name: _____ Account Number: _____ Routing Number (contact your bank for this number): _____ Account Type: _____ Checking _____ Savings _____ Money Market*

   *If Money Market, your bank will have to advise as to whether it will accept the dollars as _____ Checking or _____ Savings

   Amount of Deposit _____ or _____ "All" (place check mark here) Attach a voided check or deposit slip for account.

Direct Deposit 3

_____ New _____ Change _____ Terminate

3. Bank or Credit Union Name: _____ Account Number: _____ Routing Number (contact your bank for this number): _____ Account Type: _____ Checking _____ Savings _____ Money Market*

   *If Money Market, your bank will have to advise as to whether it will accept the dollars as _____ Checking or _____ Savings

   Amount of Deposit _____ or _____ "All" (place check mark here) Attach a voided check or deposit slip for account.

This authorization agreement is to remain in effect until (insert company name) has received written notification from me on its termination in such time and in such manner as to afford (insert company name) a reasonable opportunity to act on it.

I understand that with my request to terminate my direct deposit, all credits and debits to my account will become effective as practical after the receipt of this form.

I understand that this authorization may not apply to final wages due upon termination of employment.

Signature: _____   Date: _____

Q 5:13   Once an employee gives authorization to the employer for depositing money into his or her account, can the employer take money out of the same account?

Yes, under certain circumstances. An employer may initiate a "reversing entry" for the total amount of the initial credit entry provided (a) the dollar amount is incorrect, (b) the account is the wrong account, or (c) there is a duplicate entry. The reversal must be initiated within five business days of the settlement of the original entry. The reversal cannot be for a portion of the original payment. In addition, the employee must be notified by the settlement date of the reversing entry. No authorization is required if these conditions are met. Another alternative is for the employer to initiate a stop payment for the direct deposit. It is important to determine the state rules for electronic payments in order to ensure compliance. [NACHA Operating Rules, art. 2, Section 2.5]

Q 5:14   What information is required to put direct deposit into effect?

Most direct deposit authorizations must include the employee's name and account number and the transit number and name of the financial institution where the employee maintains his or her account. State law may also require that the employee's spouse sign the authorization when a joint account is designated for the direct deposit.

Most employers ask the employee to submit a blank and voided check or a deposit slip with his or her direct deposit authorization. This ensures that the information contained on the authorization is correct.

Q 5:15   Are there requirements for ensuring that the information transmitted on the files is secure?

As with any payroll data, proper security should be in place to ensure that data is encrypted and protected through transmissions to financial institutions. In the past, the rules around those transactions were based on the SEC (Standard Entry Class) Codes. Since December 4, 2012, NACHA amended the 2012 *NACHA Operating Rules*, creating the ACH Security Framework to protect the security and integrity of certain ACH data throughout the lifecycle. The framework establishes minimum data security obligations around "protected information" transmitted by a non-consumer Depository Financial Institution (DFI), third-party service provider, and third-party sender. This increased security requirement reflects the increased risks of data breach that NACHA seeks to minimize. Originators are required to ensure that policies, procedures, and systems are in place that will conform and comply with the security framework. Protected information pertains to financial information and non-financial account information, such as name and account-related information used to distinguish account holders. The rule became effective September 20, 2013. [2012 *NACHA Operating Rules*, Supplement #2-2012, Dec. 4, 2012]

To further reduce risk to the account holder (employee), NACHA has introduced an amendment to the NACHA Operating Rules that prohibits originators, third-party service providers, and ODFIs from sharing certain customer information. This rule went into effect on March 15, 2013. [2012 *NACHA Operating Rules Supplement* #1-2012, Apr. 27, 2012]

Q 5:16   What is a bank transit number?

A bank transit number is the nine-digit routing number that identifies a financial institution.

Q 5:17   Where does the employee find his or her checking or savings account number and bank transit identification?

The bank transit number and the checking or savings account number are usually encoded in machine-readable ink beginning at the lower left corner of a check or deposit slip. The first group of digits (up to nine digits) is the bank transit number, and it is usually separated from the other numbers by a colon. The second group of digits is the account number. The last group of digits is typically the check sequence number and is irrelevant for direct deposit processing. Rejection of direct deposit transactions frequently occurs when the check sequence numbers and bank transit numbers are confused.

Q 5:18   Do direct deposits to a credit union or brokerage account require special handling?

Special handling of direct deposits to a credit union or brokerage account is sometimes necessary, depending on the routing information provided. The account information on credit union and brokerage account checks and deposit slips is frequently invalid for ACH transactions. Employees who wish to arrange direct deposit to these types of accounts should contact their credit union or investment company for transit and account numbers that are valid for ACH transactions. Credit unions and brokerage firms frequently have special direct deposit forms for their depositors to use.

Q 5:19 How does an employer confirm the validity of transit and account numbers?

Employers have the option of verifying the information through a process of prenotification (commonly known as a prenote). The purpose of a prenote is to test the accuracy of the direct deposit information before funds are transferred from one banking institution to another. The prenote is generally sent in sufficient time to receive notification that the account is valid. Effective September 19, 2014, NACHA has modified the Operating Rules from six banking days to three banking days to receive notification. A minimal amount of information is provided, such as the employee's name, transit number, account number, and "zero dollars and cents or a small amount (e.g., $0.05)." [2014 NACHA Operating Rules, Article Two, Section 2.6.2]

The prenote process ensures that the direct deposit of employee wages is properly routed. The disadvantage of not sending a prenote is that if an error has occurred and the transaction cannot be processed, the funds are sent back to the originating bank. This leaves the employees with no wages and no access to the funds that should be available to them. There are software applications that validate routing numbers for banks listed that can reduce errors around incorrect routing numbers. A failure by the employer to properly complete a direct deposit of wages could lead to a violation of state laws regarding the frequency of payment of wages.

Q 5:20 What steps are required when a direct deposit is not processed?

Even if you use prenotification for a new or changed direct deposit, the transaction may be rejected. While there are many causes for a direct deposit to fail, one common error is an invalid or incorrect routing or account number. The transaction can be resubmitted and is treated as an original transmitted, and not a reinstated entry that could be rejected. [NACHA Operating Rules, effective Aug. 18, 2016]

Q 5:21 What is the time period for processing direct deposit of payroll?

The time period for processing a direct deposit is generally established by the ODFI, which sets a cutoff time for the employer to submit its direct deposit file (typically by 9:00 a.m., two full business days before the effective date of payroll unless a one-day processing schedule has been arranged in advance with the ODFI). Many states require an employee to be paid by 9:00 a.m. on payday. After receiving the employer's direct deposit file, the ODFI will "extract" the accounts it maintains for employees.

Q 5:22 What is an intrabank transfer?

An intrabank transfer is a direct deposit that is made outside of the ACH network. These transfers occur when the employer limits direct deposit to employee accounts maintained with the institution holding the employer's payroll account. This avoids a problem frequently cited by employers as a reason for not using direct deposit: the time constraints imposed by the direct deposit process. Employers may find it difficult or impossible to have the necessary transaction files prepared and submitted to the bank two days before payday. For this reason, the employer may choose to limit direct deposit to employee accounts at the financial institution where the employer maintains its payroll account (if this practice is not prohibited by state law). These direct deposit programs involve only intrabank transfers of funds, permitting the employer to submit the direct deposit information to the bank one day before payday.

Same-Day ACH

On March 19, 2015, the Electronics Payments Association amended the NACHA Operating Rules to permit same-day ACH transactions. The rule requires the Receiving Depository Financial Institutions (RDFI) to receive same-day transactions and provide faster availability to customers. The rule will be rolled out in three phases; the start date was September 23, 2016. The rule creates two transmission periods: transactions initiated by 10:30 a.m. ET must be settled by 1 p.m. ET, and transactions submitted by 2:45 p.m. ET must be settled by 5 p.m. ET. The RDFIs will still have until the end of their processing day to credit the account for Phases 1 and 2. By Phase 3, the RDFI must credit the accounts by 5 p.m. RDFI local time.

There are many situations in Payroll where the use of the same-day ACH option would be beneficial. For example, in the case of termination pay, some states require terminated employees to receive their final pay on the day of termination or shortly thereafter. The same-day ACH option can allow the Payroll department to complete termination requests in a timely manner and avoid costs of extending the termination date or the cost of manual checks. The same-day ACH option can be used for a late or missed payroll or for a single payment to an employee.

Q 5:23   What are the three phases?

The first phase was effective starting September 23, 2016. In the first wave, same-day ACH credit transactions were eligible for same-day processing and will include payroll as well as P2P (person to person) transactions. The RDFIs are required to process these transactions by the end of their processing day. The second wave, which must be implemented by September 15, 2017, will require RDFIs to process both credit and debit transaction by the end of the RDFIs' processing day. There will be two cut-off times for same-day processing. The third and final phase will require both ACH credits and debits and must be implemented no later than March 16, 2018 by 5 p.m. of the RDFI's local time zone. In addition, ATM withdrawals and teller window transactions must be available to the customer by Phase 3 within those timelines.

Q 5:24   What constitutes local time RDFIs?

There is not a simple answer. The RDFIs' local time can be defined as:

- Geographic footprint if in a single time zone
- Based on branches where specific accounts are opened
- Where platforms are hosted
- Based on the client.

The key is that local time should be consistent with the spirit of providing access to funds.

Q 5:25   Are there any transactions that are not subject to the same-day ACH rule?

Yes. Transactions in excess of $25,000 are not subject to the same-day ACH rule, nor are international transactions. A customer cannot create multiple transactions to circumvent the $25,000 threshold. The eligible transactions for same-day ACH represent 99 percent of current ACH network transactions/ volume.

Q 5:26   Does the same-day ACH rule apply to all financial institutions?

All RDFIs must settle eligible transactions. RDFIs can establish the guidelines and fee structures with FIs based on the regulation allowing 5.2 cents entry fee per transaction as a means to help RDFIs recover some of their costs for enabling and supporting mandatory receipt of same-day ACH transactions. Your financial institution will also charge a fee and may have additional requirements for processing same-day ACH transactions.

Q 5:27   What steps should the payroll department take to utilize same-day ACH transactions?

First, talk to your Treasury department and share the circumstances where same-day ACH transactions would be valuable to your organization. Examples of circumstances in which this option is valuable are: to cover an hourly or daily payroll, off cycle payment that is timely, and payments to government agencies or payments on their behalf. It will also be important to compare other options such as wire transfers. There may also be new submission requirements or timelines.

Q 5:28   Can a transaction with a stale or invalid effective date be a same-day ACH entry?

Yes. A transaction that contains a stale or invalid effective date can be transmitted and honored as a same-day ACH transaction. [Supplement for the NACHA Operating Rules, Oct. 2016]

Q 5:29   Will federal and state government agencies participate in the Same-Day ACH program?

The U.S. Treasury has proposed to amend its regulations governing the use of the ACH network by federal agencies. The proposed regulation adopts, with some exceptions, the NACHA Operating Rules as the rules governing the use of the ACH Network by federal agencies and targets August 31, 2017 to begin receiving same-day ACH credits. [81 Fed. Reg. 86302]

ACH participants may originate or receive same-day ACH entries to and from a state government agency.

State Laws and Regulations

Q 5:30   What state laws apply to direct deposit of payroll?

Most states have adopted rules concerning the electronic transfer of payroll funds directly to employee accounts. A number of states have codified their rules concerning direct deposit. Others maintain an official position as a guideline, and some state governments have no laws or regulations. Table 5-1 summarizes state rules and positions regulating the direct deposit of payroll funds. Pay cards are covered by Regulation E; however, some states have treated them different from direct deposit. (See Qs 5:42–5:54.)

Table 5-1.   Permissible Methods of Wage Payment

State	Cash	Check	Direct Deposit
AL	—	—	—
AK	Yes.	Yes.	Yes. Direct deposit must be voluntarily authorized by an employee and made to the financial institution of the employee's choice.
AZ	Yes.	Yes.	Yes. Direct deposit requires the written consent of the employee to a financial institution of the employee's choice. The employee must be allowed one free withdrawal for each deposit. No employee may be discharged or applicant denied employment for refusal to consent to direct deposits. Employee can opt out at any time.

5-13

Table 5-1. Permissible Methods of Wage Payment (*cont'd*)

State	Cash	Check	Direct Deposit
AR	Yes. The employee may demand payment in currency if any check from the employer has been returned for insufficient funds.	Yes. The employee may elect to be paid by check.	Yes. The employee may opt out of direct deposit by providing a written statement.
CA	Yes.	Yes.	Yes. The employee must voluntarily authorize direct deposits, and the employer must deposit the funds in the financial institution of the employee's choice.
CO	Yes.	Yes.	Yes. Direct deposit must be voluntarily authorized by the employee and made to the financial institution of the employee's choice.
CT	Yes.	Yes.	Yes. Employee's written authorization required. Employee may choose financial institution.
DE	Yes.	Yes. Checks must be payable at a place convenient to the place of employment.	Yes. Employee must provide written request and designate financial institution.
DC	Yes.	Yes.	Yes for DC public employees who designate account.
FL	—	Yes.	Yes. Employee must give written authorization and designate the financial institution. An employer may not terminate an employee solely for the employee's refusal to authorize direct deposit. Direct deposit is generally mandatory for state employees.

Table 5-1. Permissible Methods of Wage Payment (*cont'd*)

State	Cash	Check	Direct Deposit
GA	Yes.	Yes.	Yes. Employee must give prior consent and choose the financial institution.
HI	Yes.	Yes.	Yes for state employees.
ID	Yes.	Yes.	Yes. Direct deposit is permitted if the employee has voluntarily authorized direct deposit and chosen a financial institution.
IL	Yes.	Yes.	Yes. When employee designates a financial institution.
IN	Yes.	Yes.	Yes. Direct deposit must be made to financial institution of employee's choice.
IA	Yes.	Yes.	Yes. Employees hired on or after July 1, 2005 may be required to receive wages via direct deposit into financial institution of their choice.
KS	Yes.	Yes. The check must be negotiable in the community of employment.	Yes. The state secretary of labor may approve employer's wage payment by direct deposit.
KY	Yes.	Yes.	State employers must pay wages by electronic funds transfer to employees who make a written request for such to the employing state agency.
LA	—	Yes.	Yes. Mandatory for state employees.
ME	Yes.	Yes.	Yes.
MD	Yes.	Yes.	Yes with employee's authorization.
MA	Yes.	Yes.	Yes for state employees. Direct deposit may be made with the employee's authorization.

Table 5-1.   Permissible Methods of Wage Payment (*cont'd*)

State	Cash	Check	Direct Deposit
MI	Yes.	Yes.	Yes. An employer may mandate wage payment by direct deposit or payroll debit card with proper notice and disclosure.
MN	Yes.	Yes.	Yes. An employer may pay wages by direct deposit to a bank of the employee's choice unless the employee objects in writing.
MS	—	Yes.	—
MO	Yes.	Yes.	—
MT	Yes.	Yes.	Yes. Wages may be paid by direct deposit if the employee consents in writing; the employee may also consent electronically, but the employer must then retain a record of that consent. Direct deposit may not be mandatory.
NE	—	—	Yes for state employees.
NV	Yes.	Yes.	Yes. An employee may agree, in writing, to another disposition of wages. Electronic payment systems may be used.
NH	Yes.	Yes. Checks must be payable at banks convenient to the place of employment.	Yes. An employer may pay wages by direct deposit, with employee's written consent, to bank of employee's choice.
NJ	Yes.	Yes.	Yes. An employer may pay wages by direct deposit to a bank where the employee has an account. An employee may, with timely notice to the employer, elect not to have wages directly deposited.

Table 5-1. Permissible Methods of Wage Payment (*cont'd*)

State	*Cash*	*Check*	*Direct Deposit*
NM	Yes.	Yes.	Yes. An employer may pay wages by direct deposit with the voluntary authorization of the employee, employer, and financial institution.
NY	Yes.	Yes.	Yes. Wages may be paid by direct deposit with the advance written consent of the employee. Consent is not required for executive, administrative, or professional employees earning over $900 per week, or to employees working on a farm, but not working in a factory.
NC	Yes.	Yes.	Yes, with consent of employee.
ND	Yes.	Yes. Checks must be payable at a place convenient to the place of employment.	Yes. Employers may pay wages by direct deposit into the financial institution of the employee's choice.
OH	—	—	Wages to state employees may be paid by direct deposit with the prior written authorization of the employee.
OK	Yes.	Yes.	Yes for state employees who choose the financial institution and have no cost. Direct deposit is permissible for the private sector and may be mandatory if the employee may choose the financial institution.
OR	Yes.	Yes. Checks must be payable in the county where issued.	Yes. An employer and an employee may agree to authorize direct deposit without discount in the financial institution of the employee's choice in Oregon.

Table 5-1.   Permissible Methods of Wage Payment (*cont'd*)

State	Cash	Check	Direct Deposit
PA	Yes.	Yes.	Yes. Written consent of the employee is required for direct deposit. The written agreement must set forth all conditions of the direct deposit and methods by which the employee may terminate the authorization. An employer must provide the employee with a separate written record of each transfer at or prior to the time of the transfer.
RI	Yes.	Yes.	Yes. An employer may pay wages by direct deposit, at the written request of the employee, in the financial institution of the employee's choice.
SC	Yes.	Yes.	Yes. An employer may pay wages by direct deposit in a financial institution in South Carolina. The employee must be furnished a statement of earnings and withholdings. The direct deposit plan must permit the employee to make at least one withdrawal for each deposit, free of charge.
SD	Yes.	Yes.	Yes.
TN	Yes.	Yes.	Yes. The state must implement a direct deposit plan for state employees; direct deposit is permissible for other employers.
TX	Yes	Yes	Yes. An employer may elect to pay wages by direct deposit, but it must give employees at least 60 days' notice before adopting a direct deposit plan.

Table 5-1.   Permissible Methods of Wage Payment (*cont'd*)

State	Cash	Check	Direct Deposit
UT	Yes.	Yes.	Yes. An employee may decline direct deposit by filing a written request with the employer, unless the employer's federal employment tax deposits were $250,000 or more in the preceding calendar year and at least two-thirds of the employees have their wages deposited electronically. Employer may not designate a particular depository institution for exclusive deposit of wages.
VT	Yes.	Yes.	Yes. With the written authorization of the employee, wages may be paid by direct deposit to the financial institution of the employee's choice, in state or out of state.
VA	Yes.	Yes.	Yes. With the written authorization of the employee, payment may be made by direct deposit at a financial institution designated by the employee.
WA	Yes.	Yes.	State employers may, on written request of 25 or more employees, implement a direct deposit system. Employers may not require direct deposit of wages.
WV	Yes.	Yes.	Yes. An employer may pay wages by direct deposit if agreed upon in writing between the employer and the employee.

Table 5-1.   Permissible Methods of Wage Payment (*cont'd*)

State	Cash	Check	Direct Deposit
WI	Yes.	Yes, when payable at a place of business in the county of employment, at the employer's location, or at any bank within the state.	Yes. Direct deposit may be mandated as long as the employee can collect wages at an in-state bank and does not incur additional charges to retrieve the wages. Note. Migrant workers and traveling sales crews must be paid in cash or by check/draft.
WY	Yes.	Yes.	Yes, when authorized by the employee.

Source: 2017 Multistate Payroll Guide (CCH Incorporated, 2017).

Q 5:31   Are there requirements for remittance to state agencies and other parties?

The current process for remitting payments to state revenue agencies has been impacted by the increased volume of payments. It is necessary to have the correct information regarding the third party remitting the payment as well as the taxpayer on whose behalf the payment is made. NACHA has issued guidelines outlined in ACH Operations Bulletin #2-2012 that create a Third-Party Tax Payment (TPP) banking convention for payments remitted to a state taxing agency. The current convention TXP was intended for payments made directly by the taxpayer.

As the increase of third-party payments for garnishment and other types of payments rose, the ability to properly credit payments and perform research has diminished dramatically. The TPP conventions should apply in the following situations:

- Payroll service providers making quarterly employment tax payments on behalf of employers;
- Income withholding payments made by pass-through entities on behalf of nonresident partners;
- The Federation of Tax Administrator, on behalf of its state revenue department members;
- Consumer taxpayer wage garnishments; and
- Other consumer taxpayer levies.

While the TPP convention is optional for employers, state agencies receiving the payments may make it a requirement to use the TPP convention. There is an increase in the number of states establishing guidelines for submitting TPP payments. Colorado, Oregon, and Wisconsin participate using the CCD + format.

Common Concerns for Employers and Employees

Q 5:32 Once the employer has selected a bank, what should the employer's next step be?

A written agreement between the employer and the bank should be prepared. The following items should be included in a typical ACH processing agreement:

1. The employer's obligation regarding prenotification transactions;
2. The bank's base price for each file submitted, cost per credit entry, cost per prenotification, and cost for adjustments and forms;
3. Daily reporting of incomplete processing;
4. A timetable for actions such as reversals, corrections, or changes by the employer;
5. Arrangements for providing the file to the bank (format, timing);
6. The extent of responsibility for delays by the ACH or bank;
7. Indemnification of receiving banks and the ACH by the originating bank for losses from unauthorized or erroneous payments; and
8. Conditions for terminating the agreement.

Q 5:33 What happens if the employee's direct deposit is rejected?

The employer should receive a notification from its bank that the funds paid to an employee through the direct deposit arrangement are being returned with an abbreviated code that represents an explanation of the reason. After receipt of such notice, the employer must issue a payment directly to the employee for the wages owed. The employee and employer must work together to determine what information was incorrect or missing in the direct deposit process. If the account number or bank transit number was incorrect and must be changed, the employer may choose to have a prenotification completed to ensure that the new information is correct and the transaction will be completed.

In some cases, the bank account number is incorrect yet the RDFI can locate the employer/customer name and will credit the payment to the proper account. The RDFI notifies the ODFI, which in turn, notifies the employer with the correct number requesting that the file be updated for future transmissions.

Q 5:34   Once the employer decides to participate in direct deposit, how long will it take before a live payment can be transmitted to the employee's bank account?

Once an employer decides to offer direct deposit as an option to its employees, a 60-day implementation plan is typically required for processing the initial direct deposit. To successfully implement the direct deposit, the employer must do the following:

1. Announce the program to the department managers and staff;

2. Meet with employees to provide the necessary paperwork and information;

3. Establish a process to receive bank notification of problem transmissions, notification of employees of problem transmissions, and replacement of unpaid wages;

4. Submit prenotification transactions for the new participants;

5. Send the "live" information for the payroll if all has gone well to this point; and

6. Make sure the employee receives a statement or pay stub showing the net amount that was sent to his or her bank.

See Q 5:11 for NACHA's proposed change to three banking day prenotification.

Q 5:35   Do state laws permit mandatory direct deposit?

Some states allow mandatory direct deposit. Of these states, many require that the employee be given the choice of financial institutions. Some states also require that employees not incur any additional costs to participate in the direct deposit (i.e., the employee must not be subject to any additional fees for the direct deposit or to access his or her wages). Under Federal Reserve Board Regulation E, an employer can require an employee to choose payment by direct deposit, check, or cash. [Supplement 1 to 12 C.F.R. § 205.10(e)(2)] Under federal rules, the employer cannot require an employee to accept direct deposit at a particular financial institution, even as a condition of employment. [15 U.S.C. § 1693(k); 12 C.F.R. § 205.10(e)(2)]

An employer that has any questions on direct deposit restrictions in its state may contact its state's labor department at the numbers listed in appendix A.

Q 5:36   Once an employee starts direct deposit, can it be stopped?

Yes. Usually the employer provides, on the same authorization form that initiates direct deposit, a section that the employee must sign to terminate direct deposit. The employer should process the termination request based on timelines to implement the changes as quickly as possible.

Q 5:37   What preparations should the employer make when a banking holiday occurs during the payroll processing period?

When the payday is on a holiday and employers want to ensure delivery of payroll by the normal payroll processing date, employers frequently shorten their payroll processing by one day. When the holiday occurs just before the payday, a similar shortening of the payroll processing ensures that the ACH transfer is completed during the normal pay period. For example, consider a Friday payday during the Thanksgiving weekend. Thursday is a banking holiday. If the normal delivery for ACH processing is scheduled for Wednesday, the employer will want to complete the ACH transfer by Monday.

Employers should identify the banking holidays at the start of the calendar year by contacting and coordinating with the bank that will receive the ACH file. By working with the bank that will complete the direct deposit process, the employer can schedule the submission and processing of each payroll to meet the intended goal for delivering payroll.

Q 5:38   What kind of changes warrant another prenotification or authorization by the employee?

Certain changes in the employee's information may require a new authorization or prenotification to ensure that the employee properly receives his or her pay through direct deposit. For example, whenever the employee submits a change of the account number or the bank transit number is changed, the employee will receive a negotiable payroll check until a new authorization form with the correct routing information is submitted and processed. On the other hand, the dollar amount of a direct deposit can be changed as often as the employee would like without requiring the submission of new information. Most employers issue a prenotification for new employees or for account changes but not for increases in the current account. Employees should be advised about a need to make a direct deposit change in sufficient time to process the prenotification.

Q 5:39   What if the employee does not want his or her entire pay sent by direct deposit?

Most payroll systems can accommodate distributing an employer's pay—to more than one account. It becomes a policy issue whether the company wants to reduce paper checks and not allow a "net check" or give the employee as much flexibility as possible. For multiple direct deposits, the employee can choose the banks and accounts and can designate how much money should be sent to each account. Usually a dollar amount must be designated for two of three accounts, and the remaining balance is assigned to the third account or a net check, if permitted.

Example. Jason nets $1,200 per bi-weekly pay period and wants to have $110 deposited into one savings account and $50 into a different savings account to save for his next vacation. He wants the balance to go into his checking account. Jason's designations would look like this:

Bank #1 (savings)	$110.00
Bank #2 (savings)	$50.00
Bank #3 (checking)	Net pay ($1,040—would have a code for the balance with no dollar amount)

If a dollar amount were listed for Bank #3 and that amount were less than the difference between the net pay and the sum of the Bank #1 and Bank #2 amounts, Jason would receive a check for the balance.

Note. To ensure complete electronic election, some companies require that to choose direct deposit, all of the pay must be deposited electronically without a net paper check.

Q 5:40   If an employee uses direct deposit, does his or her personal banking confidentiality become compromised?

No. In fact, direct deposit is one of the most confidential methods of processing a paycheck. Checks processed via traditional payroll methods can be handled by as many as 12 people before reaching the employee's bank account.

Q 5:41   Are there any transfer requirements associated with a direct deposit?

The RDFI must credit an employee's account at the opening of the business day on payday.

Pay Cards

Following a ruling issued by the Superior Court of Pennsylvania permitting the use of a voluntary payroll debit card, legislation was passed to permit payroll cards effective March 3, 2017. [S.B. 1265, L2016] Key aspects of the new legislation provided that: (1) use of a payroll card cannot be a condition of employment; (2) a financial institution insured by the FDIC must be used; (3) at least one withdrawal by the employee is allowed per pay period for any amount; and (4) there must be no fees for the application.

Q 5:42   Are there any options for employees who don't have a bank account?

Yes, a pay card is similar to a debit or automated teller machine (ATM) card. Pay cards are becoming more popular for employees who do not have a bank account and also for underbanked employees. An underbanked employee is one who has a traditional bank account but also uses services from non-financial institutions. For both unbanked and underbanked employees, pay cards offer many of the benefits enjoyed by employees who use direct deposit for their pay. Each payday, the employer deposits money onto the card. The employee is then able to retrieve the funds at a point-of-sale (POS) network participant (such as a member of the Visa or MasterCard network) or at an ATM. Some pay card vendors offer employees a few paper checks with the service to give employees the option to be able to make payments by writing a check.

Q 5:43 Is there any protection for employees' money held in pay card accounts?

Generally, deposits at financial institutions are protected under the Federal Deposit Insurance Corporation (FDIC) as the deposits represent assets and hard earnings entrusted to a bank. [FDIC v. Philadelphia Gear Corp. 106 S. Ct 1931 (1986)] The term "deposit" has been extended to "stored value cards," a term that preceded "access devices" in the General Counsel Memorandum of 1996. Now holders of pay cards have the same protection for their deposits as any other account holder. [General Counsel's Opinion No. 8 (GC8); 74 Fed. Reg. 67155, Nov. 13, 2008]

In the case of theft or fraud, the cardholder's liability would be limited to $50 provided notice is given to the financial institution within two business days. Failure to timely notify the financial institution could result in an increased liability.

Q 5:44 Is there any federal regulation of pay cards?

Pay cards are covered under Federal Regulations E by the Electronic Funds Transfer Act. The term, "payroll card account" is defined as an account directly or indirectly established by an employer, which transfers the consumer's wages, salary, or other compensation on a recurring basis. These transfers may be made through the employer, a third-party payroll processor, a depository institution, or any other person. The card itself is called "an access device" and covers gift cards, debit cards, and pay cards. The Consumer Financial Protection Bureau was created by the Dodd-Frank Wall Street Reform and Consumer Act of 2010 to ensure compliance with Regulation E. [Section 205.12; Supplement 1 to Part 205—Official Staff Interpretations]

On October 5, 2016, the Consumer Financial Protection Bureau (CFPB) issued the Prepaid Rule amending Regulations E and Z to create comprehensive protections for prepaid accounts, including payroll card accounts. There are additional disclosure requirements on the card itself, including notice requirements that must be posted on the financial institution's website. With increased competition in the pay card industry, some financial institutions have expanded the features to include limited credit in overdraft situations. The CFPB requires pay cards to be subject to Regulation Z and its credit card rules.

Q 5:45   Can an employer require its employees to accept their wages via pay cards?

The method of the payment of wages to employees is set by state law. Some states prohibit pay cards while others require that this method of payment may be made with the employee's consent and that, at least with respect to the first withdrawal of the payroll period, there be no cost to the employee. In other words, there can be no transaction fee from the POS network participant or to use the ATM card, or if there is such a fee, the employer incurs that cost.

Q 5:46   Is an employer subject to the requirements imposed on financial institutions that offer payroll card accounts?

Transactions occurring through pay card accounts are considered open loop transactions and follow the rules outlined in Regulation E. Open loop devices allow replenishing the accounts, such as debit cards sold under the Visa and MasterCard logo. Financial institutions are defined as having the ability to hold funds and transactions. An employer or third-party service provider is not considered a financial institution and therefore is not subject to these requirements unless they hold deposit funds and make such transfers.

Q 5:47   Are all payments made by an employer to an employee on a payroll card that are not considered to be subject to Regulation E?

Yes, in addition to compensation for hours worked, an employee may receive from an employer a taxable payment (such as a one-time bonus) that would not be considered a payment under a payroll card account that is subject to Regulation E because it is not regular compensation, the main component of an employee's pay. However, payments of commissions, such as those based on sales, would be considered paid through a payroll card account since commissions typically are part of a basic compensation package.

Q 5:48   How does a deposit onto a pay card differ from a direct deposit into a bank account?

Deposits onto a pay card may be more limited than deposits into a bank account. An employee with a bank account can typically deposit money from other sources into the bank account and may be able to write checks against the account. An employee whose pay is deposited onto a payroll card generally does not have these options. However, employers may opt for additional services for the pay cards. Some vendors offer the option to write checks. Note that all pay cards provide the employee with the ability to use the pay cards for POS (Point of Sale) transactions and receive cash back where available, at practically any vendor carrying the Visa or MasterCard logo.

While the process to set up direct deposit is typically handled within a payroll organization, pay cards are generally managed by a service provider who can offer your employees a wide range of services and options.

Q 5:49   May an employer retrieve an incorrect transfer to the employee's pay card account?

In the event an incorrect amount is transferred to the employee's pay card account, the employer can recover the funds. There is a provision within the regulations that allows the employer to initiate a reversal for the incorrect amount in the same manner a reversal is done for a direct deposit. A reversal must be initiated for the total amount within five days of the original transmission. For a reversal to be permitted, one of the following conditions must have occurred: an incorrect amount was transmitted, the transmission was to the wrong person, or the transmission was to the wrong account.

Q 5:50   What are the potential problems associated with pay cards?

Pay cards are regulated by state laws and some states are restricting their use. For example, Michigan does not allow the employer to pass along to the employee the cost or fees associated with the payroll card. Vermont does not allow wages to be paid via a debit card. A potential problem is an employee's inability to access the funds without a charge. For example, only one transaction at an ATM may be free. Also, amounts from an ATM may only be accessed in set dollar amounts, such as $10 or $20 increments. An employee whose pay is not a multiple of $20 might not be able to access his or her entire net pay through the ATM. Many states also specifically prohibit coercion, which may include requiring that wages be paid by direct deposit or pay card or that the wage payments be mailed to an employee's home on payday.

Q 5:51   Are there requirements to provide the employee statements of activities of the account that the salary has been transmitted to?

The rule to provide statements applies to financial institutions so it does not apply to an employer or third-party provider, unless either of these parties holds the funds in their accounts and distributes the funds to employees. Otherwise the banking institutions are deemed the financial institutions covered by the rule. The statements are not required if the financial institution provides employees access to their financial information under certain alternatives. Those alternatives are to provide balance information available through a readily available telephone line, make available an electronic history of the transactions that covers at least 60 days preceding the date the consumer electronically accessed the account, and provide promptly (upon request) a written history of the consumer's transactions, covering at least 60 days preceding the date the financial institution received the request.

In November 2014, the Consumer Financial Protection Bureau (CFPB) announced the proposal to extend the current 60-day rule for the history of account history to 18 months.

Q 5:52   Are there other requirements imposed on employers that pay via payroll cards?

No. However, the financial institution must provide statements of activities as required under Regulation E, to disclose all fees upon the opening of a payroll cared account or before the first transfer. A proposal coming from the Consumer Financial Protection Bureau (CFPB) would all require the financial institution to provide two forms of disclosure, a short form and a long form, as well emphasize the requirement to accommodate inquiries for resolution of errors and respond to those inquiries within 60 days.

Q 5:53   Are there state guidelines regarding pay cards?

In addition to the federal guidelines, states have the authority for managing the type and frequency of payments to employees. Most states have enacted some form of legislation for pay cards. Some states rally toward allowing employers to offer pay cards, while others do not allow pay cards at all. There has been progress in 2016, advancing the use of pay cards.

Although there has been positive movement for the acceptance of pay cards by several states, there are some states where employers are finding challenges. Connecticut has tried several times to pass legislation, and finally succeeded with S.B. 211, signed by Governor Malloy on June 7, 2016. [Public Act No. 16-125] The law requires voluntary participation, connection to an ATM network, unlimited electronic balance inquiries, and no charge for first two declined transactions per month. In addition, payments under the card cannot be attached by creditors. In September 2016, the New York Department of Labor issued final regulations that became effective in March 2017. The final regulations have stringent requirements for employers, including: (a) employer must obtain consent from employees seven days before the first payment; (b) employees must have access to free ATMs to receive the entire pay for the pay period as well as the entire balance on the card; and (c) employees cannot be charged any fees, such as fees for loading the pay card or fees for using the pay card.

In Pennsylvania, a bill signed into law permits pay cards effective May 3, 2017. The legislation followed the Superior Court of Pennsylvania rule allowing pay card as a voluntary form of wage payment. Key requirements of the law are: (a) institutions must have FDIC-insured funds; (b) use of pay cards cannot be a condition of employment; (c) at least one withdrawal per pay period without a charge must be allowed; and (d) notices must be provided to employees as outlined in the law.

Q 5:54   Does Regulation E supersede state regulations?

The Consumer Financial Protection Bureau is granted preemptive rights over state legislation to the extent that there are inconsistencies between Regulation E and state legislation or administrative rules. The exception is if the state rules are more favorable to employees.

Mobile ACH Payments

The growth of smartphones and other smart devices, along with more mobile solution options for making payments, have increased the demand for additional methods of conducting financial transactions.

Q 5:55   How are mobile ACH payments handled?

NACHA Operating Rules include transactions involving mobile payments. The rule treats mobile payment transactions similar to Internet-based transactions. The transactions are classified by Standard Entry Class (SEC) codes and the new rule extends WEB code, Internet-initiated entries, to mobile payments. The new rule addresses three areas: authorization, risk management, and data security measures. In these three areas, NACHA will develop guidelines for how mobile payments should be accepted over the network and how to ensure security of transaction to thwart fraud. The incorporation of mobile payments with Internet transactions is logical and eliminates the need to create additional codes.

Q 5:56   What should an employer consider for initiating mobile payments?

There are several benefits of using mobile ACH payments, as well as challenges. It is important for the employer to consider all aspects. Some of the benefits of mobile ACH payments are:

- Reduce costs by replacing checks and card payments
- Receive additional authentication and security through mobile devices
- Add another option for unbanked and underbanked populations
- Increase opportunities for smaller employees
- Obtain initiation or approval by Treasury staff even if out of the office.

Some of the challenges are:

- Variety of device functionality and features, including battery life
- Mobile coverage could impact completion of transaction
- Security risks related to user or payment application
- Limitations of mobile device due to screen size and key functionality.

Q 5:57   Are there any additional rules specific to mobile ACH payments?

Some additional requirements include complying with the Telephone Consumer Act to have prior express consent before sending SMS/text messages and federal and state privacy laws (including the Children's Online Privacy Protection Act).

Q 5:58   What are the guidelines for initiating transactions through mobile devices?

NACHA recognizes the growth in mobile payments and its new rule is the beginning of defining how mobile payment transactions will be regulated. As mobile payments are initiated, they are considered to be similar to Internet-initiated payments and are handled the same. Leveraging the current practices for obtaining authorization and reducing the risk of fraud are key benefits to the new rule. The next phase will most likely address business models and technology. Ultimately, additional codes may be required but the initial plan calls for using the current WEB code.

International Payments

Q 5:59   What special rules apply to international ACH transactions?

Since September 18, 2009, NACHA Operating Rules require that all payments funded internationally or sent to another country via the ACH Network be identified as International ACH Transactions using a new Standard Entry Class (SEC) Code—IAT. These rules also require that IAT payments include specific data elements defined by the Bank Secrecy Act's (BSA) "Travel Rule." These transactions differ from international wire transactions.

Note. With the rise in the global network of companies, the payroll professional may be unknowingly involved in an international transaction. If the company is a U.S. subsidiary of a foreign company and there is a portion of an ACH transaction that involves a foreign financial institution, the transaction is most likely an International ACH transaction (IAT).

Q 5:60   What payments are classified as IAT?

The determination of whether a payment is classified as an International ACH Transaction (IAT) depends on where the financial agency that handles the payment transaction (movement of the funds) is located. If the financial agency is outside the United States, then the payment is classified as an IAT. (For this purpose, financial agency means an entity that is authorized by applicable law to accept deposits or is in the business of issuing money orders or transferring funds.) For IAT classification purposes, it does not matter where any other party to the transaction (e.g., the originator or receiver) is located. Therefore, certain transactions that are currently sent as domestic PPDs or CCDs would be categorized as international transactions and must be sent as IATs. The rule governs both inbound and outbound transactions.

Some examples that would be considered an IAT and therefore subject to these rules are:

- A U.S. company originates a payment via U.S. ACH network to U.S. receivers but informs the OFDI that the transfer will come from a foreign account.

- A U.S. subsidiary sends payroll payment instructions for U.S. resident employees to its European bank on behalf of the U.S. subsidiary.

- A U.S. subsidiary sends the payroll file to the foreign parent company. The European company debits the parent company and then sends a SWIFT message to the New York bank. The account in the New York bank is credited on behalf of the U.S. subsidiary.

- An offshore bank provides a service for companies in United States to send funds to offshore banks who have correspondent accounts in the United States for the benefit of employees domiciled in those offshore countries.

Q 5:61   What is the IAT format?

The Office of Foreign Assets Control (OFAC) requires financial institutions and regulators to readily identify all parties to an international transaction and supply certain information for cross-border payments. For this reason, the IAT format includes the following mandatory fields to carry the information needed for a regulatory review:

- Receiver's Account Number
- Receiver's DFI Identification Number
- Payment Amount
- Reason for Payment
- Receiver's Name
- Receiver's Street Address (not P.O. Box)
- Receiver's City, State or Province, and Postal Code
- Originator's Name and Identification Number
- Originator's Street Address (not P.O. Box)
- Originator's City, State or Province, and Postal Code
- ISO destination country code (or at least destination country)
- Receiving bank (name, identification, qualifier, branch country code)
- Amount of entry and FX arrangements
- Transaction type code (reason for payment)

NACHA has approved modifications and refinements that became effective March 21, 2014. The Gateway has an obligation to identify the ultimate foreign beneficiary of an inbound IAT. The rule requires an adjustment of the data that must be included in the entry. The required data are name, address, city, state/province, postal code, and ISO Country Code to comply with the new changes. This information takes priority over remittance data that may have used the same fields. In addition, country names must use the 2-digit alphabetic ISO country code in all relevant fields.

A recent amendment, effective August 16, 2016, clarifies that the Originator's DFI may be from a U.S. or non-U.S. source of funding (for example, a Canadian bank with a U.S. subsidiary).

Q 5:62   When is the IAT format required?

There are several questions to consider when determining if the IAT requirements apply to your company. If there is a positive response to any of the following questions, the IAT format will likely be required.

- Is your company a subsidiary of a multinational company?
- Does your company have foreign subsidiaries?
- Does your company buy or sell to individuals or countries outside the territorial jurisdiction of the United States?
- Does your company send payroll or pension or benefit payments via the ACH Network to individuals that have permanent resident addresses outside the territorial jurisdiction of the United States?

Q 5:63   What are the consequences for failure to comply with the IAT format requirements?

NACHA is responding to a request from the Office of Foreign Assets Control (OFAC) to be able to adequately identify transactions that are international in scope. The agreements that corporate originators sign with their financial institutions state that they will be in compliance with the NACHA Operating Rules and U.S. law. Effective September 18, 2009, the IAT SEC code requires participants to identify international transactions and to code those entries as IAT transactions. If a corporate originator does not comply and the transactions are identified or reported by other financial institutions, ACH Rules Violations can be filed against the Originating Depository Financial Institution (ODFI). If the problem is not resolved, the ODFI may be fined for a rules violation.

U.S. corporations are also required to comply with OFAC obligations and the penalties for ignoring those obligations can be both criminal and civil and include both jail time and fines ranging between $10,000 and $10,000,000 per occurrence depending on the sanctions program that is violated. If the corporate originator has been educated by its financial institution on its IAT requirements and the corporate originator ignores the requirements, in the event of a problem with a transaction, it is very likely that any fines or jail time would be levied against the corporation and not its financial institution. Fines levied for OFAC violations are property of the U.S. government and levied by the OFAC, not the financial institutions. It is also likely that, if a financial institution receives a fine due to noncompliance by a corporate originator of ACH transactions, the financial institution will pass those fines back to the customer. This issue should be covered in the legal agreement between the financial institution and the corporate originator.

Q 5:64   Are pay cards subject to the IAT requirements?

Payroll cards are a growing tool used to pay employees within the United States (see Qs 5:42–5:54). As with funding U.S. employees through an ACH transaction that may be initiated from a foreign financial institution, a pay card that is funded from a financial institution outside the United States must be treated as an IAT.

Q 5:65   Do IAT transactions qualify for Same-Day ACH processing?

No. In the current three-phase rollout of Same-Day ACH processing, IAT transactions are specifically excluded. There is a trend to expand the current capabilities beyond the United States.

Chapter 6

Employees and Independent Contractors

It is an employer's responsibility to determine whether an individual is an employee or an independent contractor for employment tax and reporting purposes. Not all workers are employees. When a worker is an employee, the employer is responsible for certain employment-related obligations, such as withholding and payment of employment taxes, funding workers' compensation and unemployment benefits, and compliance with the Fair Labor Standards Act. When workers provide services as independent contractors, those who pay for those services are, for the most part, exempt from such requirements.

The decision to treat a worker as an employee or as an independent contractor is based on various federal, state, and local guidelines and is not generally at the discretion of the employer. A worker's status is dictated by the relationship that exists between the worker and the employer. Misclassification of a worker as an independent contractor can result in significant employer exposure for unwithheld payroll taxes, backpay, and failure to file appropriate returns, just to name a few. This chapter discusses the factors that help determine whether a worker is an employee or an independent contractor. The consequences for worker misclassification are addressed as well.

In recent years, the landscape has changed dramatically, with businesses using different models for the labor needs of their businesses. As the way companies do business evolves, we are seeing terms used to refer to labor and methods such as *contingent workers*, *contract labor*, *franchising*, *shared economy*, and *low-road outsourcing*. Whichever form of labor a company engages as workers, the rules have been laid out and the employer must be vigilant to ensure that it is in compliance. With all the changes, on the federal government side, President Obama has directed the Department of Labor to actively ensure that workers who are misclassified are identified and employers are held accountable.

It should be noted that this chapter uses the term *employer* to describe any individual or entity that pays workers who provide services (e.g., employees or independent contractors). When the term is used in connection with independent contractors, it does not have the same connotation as it does when used to describe an employer–employee relationship. When used in reference to an independent contractor, *employer* merely refers to the party engaging and paying the contractor.

Overview

Q 6:1 What are the general IRS rules for determining the employment status of a worker?

It is up to the employer, not the Internal Revenue Service (IRS), to correctly determine whether the individual providing services is an employee or an independent contractor. There is no black-and-white definition in the Internal Revenue Code (I.R.C.) that may be used to determine whether a worker is an employee for withholding of employment taxes; such a determination must be made on a case-by-case basis. The analysis includes the employer's right to exert control over an individual and the individual's degree of independence. This is called the common-law definition of employee. There are, however, a limited number of federal statutes and regulations that classify specific workers as either employees or nonemployees for employment tax purposes. When a particular statute or regulation affecting an employee or the employment relationship contains a definition of the term *employee and/or employer,* that definition will apply only to that statute or regulation. For example, under the Fair Labor Standards Act [29 U.S.C. §§ 201 *et seq.*], which governs employment and pay practices, the term *employee* is defined more broadly than under the IRS common-law definition.

It is important to understand that the common-law definition of *employee* generally is determinative of the employee classification for withholding of employment taxes. If the term *employee* is used in a federal rule absent a specific definition for that rule, it is presumed that the term is intended to denote the traditional master–servant relationship as understood by the common-law agency doctrine (see Q 6:15). [Nationwide Mut. Ins. Co. v. Darden, 503 U.S. 318 (1992); Community for Non-Violence v. Reid, 490 U.S. 730, 751 (1989)]

Q 6:2   What are the employment tax implications of employee status?

Compensation paid to an employee is considered wages and subject to the withholding of (1) federal income tax, (2) state and local income tax (if applicable), and (3) Social Security and Medicare taxes. Employers are also required to pay the employer's portion of Social Security and Medicare taxes, Federal Unemployment Tax Act (FUTA) tax, and various state and local taxes including state unemployment insurance. In addition to these tax liabilities, the employer must provide certain statutory benefits for employees. Compensation paid to independent contractors generally is not subject to these requirements.

The Federal Insurance Contributions Act (FICA) imposes an employment tax on the wages paid to *employees*, not on compensation paid to an independent contractor. The tax is imposed in part on the employer [I.R.C. § 3101(a)] and in part on the employee. [I.R.C. § 3102(a)] The employer is required to withhold the employee's share of the FICA tax and pay it over to the IRS. [I.R.C. § 3102(a)] In addition, the I.R.C. imposes unemployment insurance tax on an employer with respect to wages paid to an employee. [I.R.C. § 3301] Penalty provisions apply for failure to properly collect, pay, and report such taxes. [I.R.C. § 6672]

Wages paid to employees must be reported on various information statements and returns that are filed by the employer. Those returns include, but are not limited to, Form 940, Employer's Annual Federal Unemployment Tax Return; Form 941, Employer's QUARTERLY Federal Tax Return; Form 943, Employer's Annual Tax Return for Agricultural Employees; Form 944, Employer's ANNUAL Federal Tax Return; Form W-2, Wage and Tax Statement; and for certain foreign persons working in the U.S., Form 1042-S, Foreign Person's U.S. Source Income Subject to Withholding.

Independent Contractors

Q 6:3   Who, for federal employment tax purposes, can be classified as an independent contractor?

As a general matter, an individual providing services is an independent contractor if the person paying for the services has the right to control or direct only the result of the work, but not the means and methods of accomplishing that result. This is the common-law test for determining whether a worker is an employee or independent contractor. When one party retains the *right to control* the means and methods of a worker's performance, that party generally meets the definition of employer and the worker is likely considered an employee. An independent contractor classification typically applies to individuals such as lawyers, contractors, subcontractors, and auctioneers who offer their services to the public. In general, employees cannot also be independent contractors, nor can independent contractors also be employees of the same payer. (Exceptions can apply to this rule. See, for instance, Rev. Rul. 70-338. [1970-1 C.B. 200]) The determination of whether an individual is an employee or an independent contractor depends on the facts in each case.

Independent contractors have been described as those individuals who are "self-employed and organized as sole proprietorships, partnerships, or corporations, and provide services without the employer's direct control." [Committee on Gov't Operations, Tax Administration Problems Involving Independent Contractors, H.R. Rep. No. 101-979, 101st Cong., 2d Sess. 2 (1990); Pub. No. 15-A] However, the mere existence of a corporation or partnership does not guarantee that the services are being provided through the partnership/corporation. For instance, an individual who formed a corporation for the purpose of providing crop-dusting services was considered an employee of the employer for whom he provided crop-dusting services because he used the equipment of the employer to provide those services. [Rev. Rul. 68-583, 1968-2 C.B. 459]

Q 6:4   What are the federal employment tax implications of independent contractor status?

An unincorporated independent contractor who is engaged in a trade or business is not subject to FICA tax, but instead is subject to a similar tax under the Self-Employment Contributions Act (SECA)—the so-called self-employment tax. SECA imposes a tax on net earnings from self-employment over $400. [I.R.C. § 1401; Treas. Reg. § 1.1402(a)-1] Self-employment tax is reported by an individual on Schedule SE, Self-Employment Tax, of Form 1040, U.S. Individual Income Tax Return. When an independent contractor is incorporated; however, that corporation will treat the contractor as an employee with wages subject to federal income tax withholding, FICA, and FUTA.

SECA taxes are paid directly by the independent contractor; that is, the party paying the independent contractor does not withhold these taxes. Although SECA taxes are nearly equal in amount to the total of the employer and employee portions of FICA tax, their calculation is more complex. A self-employed individual deducts one-half of the self-employment tax from the independent contractor's income as a business expense. [I.R.C. § 164(f)] Special rules apply to the exclusions from taxable income and determination of self-employment earnings. They are set forth in I.R.C. Section 1402.

There are few differences between SECA and FICA tax, but in some cases those differences can be significant. For example, the gross taxable wage base generally is the same under both tax calculations; however, certain items that reduce FICA wages generally do not reduce SECA income unless those items are deductible on the individual's Schedule C, Profit or Loss from Business, of Form 1040 (e.g., certain payments for health insurance and Keogh plan contributions).

Q 6:5   Is federal income tax withholding required from payments made to independent contractors?

No. Independent contractors are treated as self-employed and are themselves responsible for any income or employment taxes that are due. These taxes are paid by self-employed independent contractors either as quarterly estimated payments or paid with the Form 1040, U.S. Individual Income Tax Return. [I.R.C. § 1401; Treas. Reg. § 1.1401-1(a)] However, backup income tax withholding may be required in those instances where independent contractors fail to furnish their taxpayer identification numbers to the payer. See instructions for Form W-9, Request for Taxpayer Identification Number and Certification.

Q 6:6   How are payments to an independent contractor reported to the IRS by the payer?

A party that pays service fees to an independent contractor reports these payments on Form 1099-MISC, Miscellaneous Income, but only when those payments equal or exceed $600 in the calendar year. The payments reported on Form 1099-MISC include any payments to the independent contractor that are reimbursements for materials. Generally, Form 1099-MISC reporting is currently not required when the payment is made to a corporation, the payment is not made by a business (e.g., a payment by a homeowner to a plumber), or when fees to a service provider do not exceed $600 in the calendar year. [I.R.C. § 6041; Treas. Reg. §§ 1.6041-1, 1.6041-3]

A penalty of $100 may be assessed upon the payer for each unfiled Form 1099-MISC. The 1099 failure-to-file penalty for multiple unfiled Forms 1099-MISC is capped at $1,500,000 per year. The IRS, as part of its enforcement activities, may compare each Form 1099-MISC filed by the employer with the Form 1040 filed by the independent contractor. [I.R.C. §§ 6041A, 6721]

Q 6:7   Are the FICA tax withholding obligations reduced when the employee also has self-employment income subject to SECA taxes?

No. When a self-employed individual also works as an employee for an employer (presumably not the party also engaging the individual as an independent contractor), the individual's self-employment income that is subject to SECA taxes will be deemed to consist only of the difference (if any) between his or her wages as an employee and the Social Security taxable wage base. There is no adjustment in the amount of FICA or FUTA that is due on the wages earned as an employee. That is, an employer's obligation to withhold and pay FICA and FUTA is not affected by any SECA taxes that may have been paid by independent contractors on their self-employment income. [I.R.C. § 1402(b)] FICA tax withholding and the employer's matching FICA tax consist of Medicare and Social Security. Employee and employer contributions are made up to the applicable Social Security wage limit for the year ($127,200 for 2017). Note that there is no wage limit for Medicare tax. The Social Security wage limit applies to each separate employer. If, due to work performed for multiple employers, an individual pays Social Security tax in excess of the annual limit, a refund is not made by any of the employers. Instead, the employee claims the excess of the Social Security tax overpayment as additional taxes paid and applied to any taxes due when filing the Form 1040, U.S. Individual Income Tax Return.

Note. An individual cannot generally be an independent contractor and an employee for the same employer. Exceptions do apply, however; therefore, each work relationship must be reviewed on a case-by-case basis.

Worker Classification

Q 6:8   What are the federal income tax implications of classifying a worker as an employee or as an independent contractor?

According to the I.R.C., income derived from self-employment or paid as wages to an employee is taxable compensation for services. Thus, whether a worker is classified as an employee or as an independent contractor, that worker's gross income is subject to federal income tax. However, federal income tax withholding only applies to wages paid to an employee. The availability of certain tax-favored fringe benefits may be dependent upon a worker's classification. An employer can provide tax-free medical insurance for an employee. If, however, these benefits are provided to an independent contractor, the payments are not fully deductible by the independent contractor. Also, a self-employed individual can deduct from taxable income business-related expenses that cannot be fully deducted by an employee when they are not reimbursed by the employer. [I.R.C. § 161]

Expenses that are both ordinary and necessary and that are incurred while carrying on a trade or business of an independent contractor are generally deductible by the contractor (e.g., a vehicle to transport necessary tools, the tools, or insurance on both). [I.R.C. § 162] An employee's deductions for similar business expenses may in some cases be permitted; however, they are treated as miscellaneous itemized deductions and are not fully deductible (i.e., they are a Schedule A, Form 1040, deduction) when not reimbursed by the employer. Generally, employees may deduct employee business expenses only to the extent that the expenses exceed the first 2 percent of adjusted gross income, and that deduction is phased out on reaching certain income levels. [I.R.C. §§ 62, 67] An independent contractor generally may deduct the expenses incurred in conducting his or her trade or business without limit. That has led some workers to seek independent contractor status even when their employer classifies them as employees. [Ware v. United States, 67 F.3d 574 (6th Cir. 1995); Butts v. Commissioner, 49 F.3d 713 (11th Cir. 1995)]

Independent contractors can establish qualified retirement plans based on their self-employment income and may generally contribute the lesser of 25 percent of their "net income" from self-employment or $54,000 for 2017. (Contributions to a SEP are limited to 15 percent of pay up to $270,000 for 2017.) An employee is limited to the retirement plan benefits established by his or her employer. [I.R.C. §§ 401(c), 401(f)] In addition, an independent contractor may find it possible to take a deduction attributable to the use of a portion of a residence as a home office. An employee is generally allowed a home office deduction only when working from home for the convenience of the employer, unless the home office deduction can be taken against self-employment income that was earned in addition to the wages. [I.R.C. § 280A]

Some tax laws favor employees. An employer may deduct the amount paid for the health insurance of its employees, and the employee is not required to include the value of that employer-provided coverage in his or her gross income. [I.R.C. §§ 106, 162; Treas. Reg. § 1.162-10] The Small Business Jobs Act permitted an independent contractor to deduct a portion of his or her premium payment for health insurance against their self-employment tax for 2010. Since 2010, there is no deduction against self-employment tax for premiums paid by independent contractors. However, under certain circumstances, independent contractors may deduct the premiums they pay for health insurance as a business expense. [I.R.C. § 162(l)]

Q 6:9 Does classification as an independent contractor require that an individual have the opportunity for profit or loss?

There is a general requirement that an individual classified as an independent contractor must have the opportunity for profit or loss within the work relationship (although other factors will affect the determination of the individual's status). The IRS ruled in a Technical Advice Memorandum (TAM) that members of a university medical group that was controlled and directed by a plan were employees when they had no investment in the plan and no opportunity for profit or loss. This TAM revoked an earlier TAM that held the workers to be independent contractors. [Tech. Adv. Mem. 9808001]

Q 6:10 Is there any IRS guidance on the determination of employee status versus independent contractor status?

An employer may base its determination on Treasury regulations and rulings that address various worker relationships. Other guidance is available in IRS Publication 1779, Independent Contractor or Employee Brochure; IRS Publication 1976, Do You Qualify for Relief Under Section 530; and IRS Publication 15-A, Employer's Supplemental Tax Guide. All of these publications are available for downloading at http://www.irs.gov. In addition, the IRS has a training materials manual for use by its audit staff, Independent Contractor or Employee Training Materials [Mar. 4, 1997], which is available to the public. The manual, although not official guidance and not as simply written as the previously mentioned IRS publications, can provide insight on specific questions.

Q 6:11 Can an employer request that the IRS confirm a worker's employment status?

Yes. An employer (or an individual) may ask the IRS to determine whether a worker's duties result in the worker being classified as an employee by filing Form SS-8, Determination of Worker Status for Purposes of Federal Employment Taxes and Income Tax Withholding, with the IRS. Such filing allows an employer to obtain a ruling for a newly hired worker whose employment status is in question. It also permits the ruling on a single worker to be extended to a class of workers when the individual is representative of the worker group. Form SS-8 contains an exhaustive series of questions designed to determine the employer's control over the worker, and includes sections addressing behavioral control, financial control, and the relationship of the worker to the entity receiving the services.

The IRS will generally issue a formal determination to the entity receiving the services and will send a copy of the determination letter to the worker. The determination letter is binding on the IRS and only applies to the worker (or class of workers) that is the subject of the letter.

Note. Unless an employer has a reasonable basis for not treating a worker as an employee (in compliance with Section 530 of the 1978 Revenue Act), an employer that submits a Form SS-8 to confirm the status of a worker as an independent contractor should withhold and pay employment taxes on the worker's wages until the IRS ruling is received. Typically, a ruling may be issued anywhere from six weeks to eight months after the filing of the SS-8. If the worker is later determined by the IRS to be an independent contractor, no refund is permitted for the employment taxes previously paid by the employer.

Q 6:12 Can more than one entity be the employer of an employee with regard to the same services?

Yes. Under common law a "person may be the servant of two masters . . . at one time as to one act, if the service to one does not involve abandonment of the service to the other." [This statement is contained in the Restatement (Second) of Agency § 226 (1958) of the official manual establishing operational procedures for the IRS.] Two entities may control different aspects of the employment relationship. For example, an employee leasing company or a professional employer organization may have control over the wages of a leased employee and the right to hire and fire, and the recipient entity (i.e., the worksite employer) will generally control the methods and means of a worker's production. In such circumstances, it may not be clear which entity is the common-law employer, and under such an arrangement dual employment may exist. It should be noted, however, that the IRS infrequently determines that dual employment exists. Indeed, dual employment may be irrelevant for employment tax purposes. The entity that controls the payment of wages to the employee can be treated as the "statutory employer" for employment tax purposes, even if it controls no other aspect of the employment relationship. That party and the worksite employer are both liable for withholding and payment of employment taxes. Effectively, dual employment status becomes relevant when, for whatever reason, one of the employers does not properly withhold and pay tax and/or file the correct return. In this case, the IRS frequently makes an assessment against the secondary employer when the first will not or cannot pay (e.g., bankruptcy). It should also be noted that the determination of who is the common-law employer may be relevant for certain fringe benefit purposes where employer-sponsored benefit plans cover only employees of the employer (or former employees and their beneficiaries). [Tech. Adv. Mem. 8617008]

Q 6:13   May a worker incorporate to avoid being classified as an employee?

No. The common-law test of an employment relationship focuses on the relationship between the individual performing the services and the service recipient. That relationship cannot be changed by merely incorporating the individual providing the services. [Darreal Harris Inc. v. United States, 770 F. Supp. 1492 (W.D. Okla. 1991); Levell v. Commissioner, 104 T.C. 140 (1995); Rev. Rul. 87-41, 1987-1 C.B. 296; Rev. Rul. 74-330, 1974-2 C.B. 278]

Employee Status

Q 6:14   When is a worker an employee for federal employment taxes?

Under a common-law definition, anyone who performs services for an entity or individual is an employee if the entity or individual can control what will be done and how it will be done. An employee classification applies even when an employer gives the employee freedom of action in the way he or she provides the services. What is essential in classifying the relationship as employee–employer is whether the employer has the *right* to control the details of how the services are performed, not whether the employer *actually controls* such details.

There is no uniform definition of *employee* that applies to all federal payroll tax regulations. The IRS generally applies the common-law test to determine whether a worker is an employee or an independent contractor (see Q 6:15). It is the substance of the relationship, not the label that governs the worker's status. In fact, the mere existence of an agreement between the service provider and the service recipient stipulating that the contractor is not an employee is not, in and of itself, determinative of the worker's status. For example, an individual cannot be classified as an independent contractor merely because both the payer and the individual want the classification, or because the individual is employed part time or works under an erratic time schedule. What the parties desire makes no difference in determining whether an employment relationship exists.

Regardless of the common-law definition, certain workers are classified by law as "statutory employees" and others as "statutory nonemployees." For example, certain drivers, full-time life insurance sales agents, and traveling salespeople that meet certain criteria are classified as employees by statute (i.e., they are statutory employees) for employment tax purposes. Likewise, direct sellers, licensed real estate agents, and companion sitters that meet certain criteria are treated as self-employed by statute (i.e., they are statutory nonemployees). Those classifications apply without reference to the common law.

Under the common-law definition as applied by the IRS, superintendents, managers, and other supervisory personnel are generally employees. An officer of a corporation is also generally an employee; however, an officer who performs no services or only minor services and neither receives nor is entitled to receive any pay is not considered an employee. A director of a corporation is not an employee unless the director also provides other services as an employee. [Treas. Reg. 31.3401(c)-1(f)]

Q 6:15   What are the common-law factors used to define an employment relationship?

Under the common-law doctrine of agency, an employer–employee relationship is not capable of exact definition. To determine whether an individual is an employee or an independent contractor, the relationship of the worker and the business must be examined, especially the amount of control the business has over the worker. That is true whether or not the business actually exercises the control, provided the business retains the right to exercise such control. Under common law, this is referred to as the right to control the means and methods of a worker's performance. [Bartels v. Birmingham, 332 U.S. 126 (1947)] Several factors are cited in the *Restatement of Agency* as relevant in determining whether the employer reserves the requisite control to establish a common-law employment relationship.

The common-law factors that will generally determine the degree of control exercised by an employer are as follows:

1. *Custom.* It is appropriate to look to the custom of the community as to the control ordinarily exercised in a particular occupation.

2. *Skill required.* The skill required to perform a particular trade is considered to be an indication of employment status. Independent contractors are likely to be engaged in more highly skilled professions; employees generally perform tasks requiring less skill.

3. *Furnishing of tools.* When an employer supplies equipment or tools necessary to accomplish the work, an employment relationship is indicated.

4. *Control over premises.* When the work is to be performed on the employer's premises or in a specific area or over a fixed route, the worker is more likely to be an employee.

5. *Length of time employed.* Employment over a considerable period with regular hours and the fact of full-time employment with a single employer indicates an employment relationship.

6. *Method of payment.* Payment per unit of time, such as per hour or month, indicates employee status, whereas payment per job indicates independent contractor status.

7. *Nature of occupation.* If the work performed is part of the regular business of the employer, the worker is more likely to be an employee.

8. *Intent.* Although not determinative as to the status of a relationship, the intent of the parties in entering into a relationship and their resulting assumptions as to control is one factor to consider.

[Restatement (Second) of Agency (1958)]

Also relevant in determining employment status are the following factors: whether the hiring party has the right to assign additional projects to the hired party; the extent of the hired party's discretion over when and how long to work, the hired party's role in hiring and paying assistants, whether the hiring party is in business, the provision of employee benefits, and the tax treatment of the hired party. [Nationwide Mut. Ins. Co. v. Darden, 503 U.S. 318 (1992); Community for Creative Non-Violence v. Reid, 490 U.S. 730 (1989)]

Q 6:16   What criteria does the IRS apply in determining whether a worker is an employee or an independent contractor?

The IRS makes clear that the main factor in determining whether an individual is an employee or independent contractor is "the degree of control the business has over its worker." [I.R.S. Fact Sheet 2006-21] Although it offers no "bright-line" test to determine whether a worker is an employee or an independent contractor, the IRS takes the position that the more control the business has over the worker, the more likely it is that the worker is an employee rather than an independent contractor. [I.R.S. Fact Sheet 2006-21]

The distinction between the two classifications focuses on who has control over what must be done and how the work is to be done. Merely calling oneself an employer will not automatically indicate that the worker is an employee; it will, however, be one factor in that determination. An IRS training manual discusses control under the following three criteria and tends to deemphasize the use of its previously applied 20 factors (see Q 6:17).

1. *Behavioral control.* Behavioral factors—including the training and instructions given to the worker—show whether the payer has a right to direct and control how the worker does the task for which the worker was hired. The following are factors considered under this test:

   a. *Instructions given to the worker.* An employee is generally subject to the employer's instructions about when, where, and how to work. Even when no instructions are given, sufficient behavioral control may exist if the employer has the *right to control* how the results of the work are achieved and merely does not exercise that right.

   b. *Training given to the worker.* An employee may be trained to perform services in a particular manner. Independent contractors ordinarily use their own methods.

2. *Financial control.* Financial factors that show whether the payer has a right to control the business aspects of the worker's job generally fall into five categories:

   a. *The extent to which the worker has unreimbursed business expenses.* Independent contractors are more likely than employees to have unreimbursed expenses relating to the work. The fact that the worker has fixed ongoing costs regardless of whether work is currently being performed (e.g., truck operating expenses) tends to indicate the worker is an independent contractor. Employees may also incur unreimbursed expenses in connection with the services they perform for their employer; they are generally lesser amounts than those incurred by an independent contractor.

   b. *The extent of the worker's investment in equipment and supplies.* An independent contractor often has a significant investment in the equipment and facilities he or she uses in performing services for someone else. However, a significant investment is not required for a worker to be classified as an independent contractor.

   c. *The extent to which the worker makes services available to the relevant market.* An independent contractor is generally free to work with others in the market. An independent contractor also often advertises and maintains a visible business location. Offering the same services to several businesses is indicative of an independent contractor.

   d. *How the business pays the worker.* An employee is usually guaranteed a regular wage for an hourly, weekly, or other period of time. An independent contractor is usually paid by the job; however, it is common in some professions (e.g., the law) to pay independent contractors on an hourly basis.

   e. *The extent to which the worker can realize a profit or incur a loss.* Generally, an independent contractor can make a profit or incur a loss with respect to the services provided.

3. *Type of relationship.* The distinction between employee and independent contractor can often be determined by the relationship between worker and payer:

    a. *Written contracts.* Contracts reduced to writing describe the business relationship that the parties intended to create. If the contract describes the relationship between the parties as that of independent contractor--payer, it will likely assist in confirming that classification.

    b. *Employer benefits.* If the payer provides a worker with benefits typically only available to employees (e.g., medical insurance, pension plan, vacation pay, sick pay), an employer–employee relationship is generally indicated.

    c. *Permanency of the relationship.* If the payer engages a worker with the expectation that the relationship will continue indefinitely, rather than for a specific project or period, that is generally considered evidence that the intent was to create an employer–employee relationship.

    d. *The extent to which services performed by the worker are a key aspect of the regular business of the payer.* If a worker provides services that are a key aspect of the regular business activities of the payer, it is more likely that the business will have the right to direct and control the worker's activities and, accordingly, it would indicate an employer–employee relationship. For example, if a law firm hires an attorney, it is likely that it will present the attorney's work as its own and would have the right to control or direct that work.

[Independent Contractor or Employee Training Materials (Mar. 4, 1997); Pub. No. 15-A; Pub. No. 1779]

Q 6:17   What are the 20 factors the IRS has used to measure control in the past?

Before the IRS issued its training manual, Independent Contractor or Employee Training Materials, in 1997 (see Q 6:16), it identified 20 factors to be weighed in determining whether sufficient control was present to establish an employer–employee relationship for employment tax purposes. [Rev. Rul. 87-41, 1987-1 C.B. 296] This was commonly referred to as the IRS 20-factor test.

The 20-factor test is no longer strictly applied by the IRS; however, it can still help in determining whether an individual is an employee or an independent contractor. The guidance is based on a common-law determination. The degree of importance to be attributed to each of the 20 factors varies with the worker's occupation and the circumstances under which the services are performed. It should be noted that specific work arrangements formalistically contrived to achieve a particular status will not govern the employment status determination. The ultimate determination will be based on whether a sufficient degree of control is present to conclude that an employer–employee relationship exists.

	Factors Indicating an Employer–Employee Relationship	Factors Indicating Independent Contractor Status
1. *Instructions.*	If a worker is or may be required to comply with instructions issued by others regarding when, where, and how to work, the worker is more likely to be an employee. Instruction may be oral or written. Employment manuals and company policies or procedures may be used as evidence of control, indicating an employment relationship.	The worker is given instructions only on which services are to be provided. The worker is not typically instructed when, where, and how to perform the services.
2. *Training.*	The presence of a training mechanism is generally an indication that the person for whom services are performed seeks to have the services performed in a particular manner. Training may involve an experienced worker working with a new worker, correspondence, required attendance at meetings, or other methods. The IRS views training periodically or at frequent intervals as a stronger indication of employee status. [IRS Manual 4646: Exhibit 4640-1]	An independent contractor tends to be a skilled worker and is provided with little employer training.
3. *Integration.*	When the success or continuation of a business depends in large part on the integration of workers' services into the business operations, the workers are viewed as subject to a certain degree of control by the business owner and are generally considered employees.	An independent contractor tends to provide specific services for a limited period of time that are not integral to the employer's long-term operation.

	Factors Indicating an Employer–Employee Relationship	Factors Indicating Independent Contractor Status
4. *Services rendered personally.*	If the services must be rendered by a specific individual, employee status is indicated—it is assumed that the person for whom services are performed is interested in the methods used to accomplish the work as well as the results.	The services of an independent contractor generally may be provided by another individual selected by the contractor.
5. *Hiring, supervising, paying assistants.*	Control over workers is generally evidenced when the person for whom services are performed hires, supervises, and pays for the worker's assistants.	When a worker agrees to provide materials and labor pursuant to a contract under which the worker is responsible only for the result and, consequently, the worker hires, supervises, and pays assistants, this factor indicates an independent contractor status.
6. *Continuing relationship.*	A continuing relationship between the worker and the person for whom services are performed indicates employee status. A continuing relationship may exist even though work is performed at frequently recurring, although irregular, intervals.	An independent contractor's services are generally only provided for a limited period of time.
7. *Set hours of work.*	The establishment of set hours of work by the person for whom services are performed is a factor indicating control.	An independent contractor is generally free to perform the services under a schedule he or she sets.
8. *Full time required.*	Control over the amount of time spent working is demonstrated when the worker must devote substantially full time to the business of the person for whom the services are performed and is therefore unable to engage in other gainful work.	An independent contractor is generally free to work when and for whom he or she chooses.

	Factors Indicating an Employer–Employee Relationship	*Factors Indicating Independent Contractor Status*
9. *Performing work on employer's premises.*	Control is indicated when the work is performed on the premises of the person for whom the services are performed, particularly if the work can be performed elsewhere. Evaluation of this factor depends on the nature of the service. Control over the place of work is evidenced where the worker is required to travel a designated route or to work at specific places.	Work performed off the premises indicates some freedom from control.
10. *Order or sequence set.*	If a worker is or may be required to perform services in the order or sequence set by the person or persons for whom the services are performed, this factor shows that the worker is not free to follow his or her own pattern of work.	If a worker can determine the sequence of services to be provided, lack of control is indicated, suggesting an independent contractor relationship.
11. *Oral or written reports.*	A requirement that a worker submit regular reports indicates a degree of control.	An independent contractor generally does not prepare progress reports.
12. *Payment by hour, week, or month.*	Payment by the hour, week, or month generally points to employee status. Payment by commission with some minimal payment guaranteed generally indicates employee status.	Payment made by the job or on a straight commission generally indicates that the worker is an independent contractor.
13. *Payment of business and/ or traveling expenses.*	Generally, if the person for whom the services are performed pays the worker's business or traveling expenses (or both), the worker is an employee. By doing so, the employer generally retains the right to regulate and direct the business activities.	The nature and extent of business expenses of an independent contractor are generally not controlled by the party to whom the services are provided.

	Factors Indicating an Employer–Employee Relationship	Factors Indicating Independent Contractor Status
14. *Furnishing of tools and materials.*	Where significant tools, materials, and other equipment are furnished by the person for whom the services are performed, employment status is suggested.	Where tools and materials are provided by the worker, independent contractor status is indicated.
15. *Significant investment.*	Lack of investment in facilities (e.g., office space rented at fair market value or ownership of a truck) indicates dependence on the person for whom the services are performed and thus indicates employee status.	If the worker invests in facilities (e.g., office space rented at fair market value or ownership of a truck) that are used by the worker in performing services and that are not typically maintained by employees, this factor indicates an independent contractor relationship.
16. *Realization of profit or loss.*	The risk that a worker will not receive payment for services is common to both independent contractors and employees and does not necessarily constitute a sufficient economic risk to indicate treatment as an independent contractor.	A worker who can realize a profit or suffer a loss as a result of the worker's services is generally an independent contractor. Where a worker is subject to a real risk of economic loss because of significant investments or liabilities for expenses (e.g., salary payments to unrelated employees), this factor indicates an independent contractor relationship.
17. *Working for more than one firm at a time.*	A worker who performs services for more than one person *may* be an employee of each of the persons. Having two employers does not necessarily indicate that the worker is an independent contractor.	If a worker performs more than *de minimis* services for a series of unrelated persons or firms at the same time, that factor generally indicates that the worker is an independent contractor.
18. *Making services available to the general public.*	An employee generally provides his or her services to or is only paid by one entity (e.g., an employee does not bill customers for his or her services).	Making services available to the general public on a regular basis indicates independent contractor status.

Factors Indicating an Employer–Employee Relationship	Factors Indicating Independent Contractor Status
19. *Employer's right to discharge.*	The right to discharge a worker indicates employee status. An employer exercises such control through the threat of dismissal, which causes the worker to obey the employer's instructions.	An independent contractor cannot generally be "fired" or the contract terminated so long as the result produced meets the contract specifications.
20. *Worker's right to terminate.*	If the worker has the right to end his or her relationship with the person for whom the services are performed at any time and without incurring liability, that factor indicates employee status.	The terms of the contract indicate when an independent contractor may cease providing services.

[Rev. Rul. 87-41, 1987-1 C.B. 296]

Q 6:18 Have any other IRS tests been used to determine employment status?

Yes, but they no longer apply. In the late 1940s the U.S. Supreme Court fashioned an additional test to supplement the control test, termed the *economic reality test.* In two distinct cases [United States v. Silk, 331 U.S. 704 (1947); Bartels v. Birmingham, 332 U.S. 126 (1947)], the Supreme Court found that workers should be classified as employees when they are, as a matter of economic reality, dependent on the business to which they render service. The Court concluded that the employer must look to the "total situation" in coming to its conclusion about whether workers were employees for purposes of the Social Security Act (SSA), including the risk undertaken, the control exercised, the opportunity for profit, and whether these workers were of the group that the Act was intended to aid.

The economic reality test was rejected by an act of Congress [Gearhart Resolution, H.R.J. Res. 296, 80th Cong., 2d Sess. ch. 468, Pub. L. No. 80-642, 62 Stat. 438 (1948)] passed over presidential veto [1948 U.S. Code Cong. Serv. 2501, 2502] out of concern that the test was too nebulous. As Congress pointed out, every service worker is dependent as a matter of economic reality on another entity, and such an application would include too many workers under FICA, thereby dissipating the Social Security trust. [S. Rep. No. 1255, 80th Cong., 2d Sess., *reprinted at* 1948 U.S. Code Cong. Serv. 1752, 1759, 1762] A focus on agency common law and the control test was later reaffirmed by the Supreme Court. [Nationwide Mut. Ins. Co. v. Darden, 503 U.S. 318 (1992)]

Since that time, the "economic reality test" has been promulgated by the Department of Labor as well as by many state courts. The Department of Labor, in determining issues around minimum wage infractions, requires that the individual in question be an employee in order for the FLSA to apply. To that point, the economic reality test or other factors are taken into consideration. They include (a) the extent to which the work performed is an integral part of the business, (b) how the managerial skills will impact the profit or loss to be received, (c) investments in facilities or equipment for the individual and the employer, and (d) a worker's skill and permanency to the project. If these factors can be substantiated, the individual may be treated as an employee. Some other courts have addressed the economic reality test as well. The Eleventh Circuit reviewed *Solis v. A + Nursetemps* [No.5:07-ov-182-06-10RLL 2013WL 1395863 (M.D. Fla. Apr. 5, 2013)] and held that the workers were employees. In Washington, that state's Supreme Court has also held that the economic realities test used under the FLSA applies in a case involving FedEx Ground drivers. The drivers had contracts, but argued that they were employees. [Anfinson v. FedEx Ground Package Sys., No. 85949-3 (Wash. July 19, 2012)]

Q 6:19   How does the control mandated by external regulation affect a determination of a worker's status for federal employment tax purposes?

The IRS views the rules and requirements of outside regulatory bodies as neutral factors in determining the degree of control that exists in the employment relationship. [Tech. Adv. Mem. 9330007] The Restatement (Second) of Agency (1958), prepared by the Department of the Treasury, attempted to clarify worker-status determinations by providing that even if a statute, regulation, or industry rule dictates a degree of control over a worker, an employer–employee relationship generally exists only if the relationship exists in substance. [Restatement (Second) of Agency § 220] That is, when a factor otherwise indicating control is present only as a result of external regulation (such as the procurement of license plates for trucks pursuant to Interstate Commerce Commission regulation), that factor is ordinarily insufficient to show an employer–employee relationship. [United States v. Mutual Trucking Co., 141 F.2d 655 (6th Cir. 1944)] If, however, an employer exercises control to assure itself that external rules and regulations are being fulfilled (such as by adopting and incorporating external rules into a company manual or its written policies), that constitutes control and may be sufficient to indicate an employer–employee relationship. It is immaterial for the control test that the motivation for the control is based on rules and regulations. [Tech. Adv. Mem. 9330007] In addition, when the employer and workers anticipate or intend that external regulations will be enforced by the employer, that expectation will tend to indicate employment status. [Rev. Rul. 76-138, 1976-1 C.B. 315]

In its guidelines for determining employment status, the IRS's current training manual discusses these issues using an example of a barbershop with union employees. In the example, the shop owner does not control the hours or set the prices for barbershop services, nor does the owner control the level of cleanliness of the shop. The union controls hours of operation and sets prices, and the State Barber Board of Examiners controls the cleanliness of the shop.

The IRS's training manual states that those factors should not be given weight in determining whether an employer–employee relationship exists between the shop owner and the union workers. Instead, the element of control that is present or absent between the shop owner and the workers should be considered together with the reason for its presence or absence. [I.R.S. Manual 4600; Exhibit 4646-1]

Q 6:20   What steps can an employer take to ensure that its independent contractors will not be reclassified as employees by the IRS?

Of primary importance is the employer's own careful evaluation of the factors relied on by the IRS in determining whether an employment relationship exists. (See Qs 6:16 and 6:17.) Although none of the following guarantees that the individual is safe from being reclassified from independent contractor to employee, employers also should consider taking the following steps:

1. Use an independent contractor agreement;
2. Obtain the independent contractor's taxpayer identification number;
3. File all required Forms 1099;
4. Request that the independent contractor issue invoices for payment;
5. Allow the independent contractor to determine where and how to complete the work; and
6. Use contractors who are incorporated.

Q 6:21   What can trigger an audit of your employee and independent contractor classification by the IRS?

Although employers can never eliminate the possibility of an IRS audit, they can reduce the chances that the IRS will examine whether they have properly classified workers as independent contractors. As an initial matter, it is important to note that many audits are triggered by mistakes made on tax returns, not by fraudulent practices. Accordingly, employers should take preventive measures to be sure that individuals are treated and classified correctly, and that compensation paid to independent contractors is not included as employee wages on the employer's tax returns. If there is any question regarding the proper classification of a worker, employers should consult a qualified tax advisor.

In addition to simple mistakes, changes in classification for groups of individuals from year to year may trigger an IRS audit. Further, if an employer has a large group of independent contractors but very few (if any) employees, this also may cause the IRS to conduct an employment tax audit. Additionally, any unusual, unexplained, or excessive entries suggesting an employer may be affirmatively misclassifying individuals to avoid paying employment taxes may also trigger an IRS audit.

The IRS has instituted the following programs that will further assist it in identifying worker classification errors.

(1) Form 8919, Uncollected Social Security and Medicare Tax on Wages, and Form 4137:

In 2007, the IRS issued Form 8919, Uncollected Social Security and Medicare Tax on Wages, for workers who were misclassified as independent contractors by an employer. The form is used by employees to report their share of uncollected Social Security and Medicare taxes owed on the wages paid to them. Form 8919 replaces Form 4137 that was previously used for this purpose with the exception that tipped employees continue to use Form 4137 to report Social Security and Medicare taxes on allocated tips and tips not reported to their employers. [IR-2007-203, Dec. 20, 2007]

A Form 8919 (or, with respect to tipped employees, Form 4137), is filed only in the event that the worker:

- Filed Form SS-8, Determination of Worker Status for Purposes of Federal Employment Taxes and Income Tax Withholding, and received a determination letter from the IRS stating he or she is an employee of the firm;
- Was designated as a Section 530 employee by his or her employer or by the IRS before January 1, 1997;
- Received other correspondence from the IRS that states he or she is an employee;
- Was previously treated as an employee by the firm and he or she is performing services in a similar capacity and under similar direction and control;
- Worked with others who performed similar services under similar direction and control and are treated as employees;
- Worked with others performing similar services under similar direction and control and filed Form SS-8 for the firm and received a determination that they were employees; or
- Has filed Form SS-8 with the IRS and has not yet received a reply.

(2) Questionable Employment Tax Practice (QETP):

Historically, the IRS has had agreements to share information with the states. Typically, the information flowed from the IRS to the states in the form of federal audit adjustments, both corporate and individual. However, as part of its strategy to reduce the tax gap, the IRS has committed to enhancing coordination with the states to share information and compliance strategies.

In keeping with that goal, the IRS together with several states announced in 2007 the launch of the Questionable Employment Tax Practice (QETP) initiative. Under QETP, the IRS and more than two dozen state workforce agencies have entered into agreements to share the results of employment tax examinations. [IR-2007-184, Nov. 6, 2007; FS-2007-25, Nov. 2007] The agreements that form part of the QETP initiative are intended to provide a centralized, uniform means for the IRS and state employment officials to exchange data, thereby leveraging resources and encouraging businesses to comply with federal and state employment tax requirements.

The QETP initiative is a nationwide program that seeks to identify employment tax schemes and illegal practices and increase voluntary compliance with
employment tax rules and regulations. The IRS, the National Association of
State Workforce Agencies, the U.S. Department of Labor, the Federation of Tax
Administrators, and the state workforce agencies of California, Michigan, New
Jersey, New York, and North Carolina worked together to develop the QETP
initiative and endorse the memorandum of understanding (MOU) as a tool to
help increase employment tax compliance at the federal and state levels.
Moreover, the QETP is part of the IRS's efforts to increase enforcement focus on
employment taxes, which constitute an estimated 17 percent of the total tax gap.

The MOU allows the IRS and state workforce agencies to exchange audit
reports and audit plans, and to participate in side-by-side examinations, when
appropriate. The MOU also seeks to:

- Increase compliance with federal and state employment tax filing and
  payment regulations;
- Increase compliance with Form 1099 and Form W-2 filing;
- Increase collection of federal and state employment/unemployment tax
  debts;
- Enhance efforts to reduce the tax gap at the federal and state levels and
  ensure that businesses are all operating on a competitive level playing field
  by ensuring that everyone pays his or her proper share of employment
  taxes; and
- Leverage IRS, state, and other federal agency resources to improve compliance with employment tax laws.

The following 31 states have signed an MOU with the IRS:

Arizona, Arkansas, California, Colorado, Connecticut, Hawaii, Idaho, Kentucky, Louisiana, Maine, Massachusetts, Michigan, Minnesota, Missouri, Nebraska, New Hampshire, New Jersey, New York, North Dakota, Ohio,
Oklahoma, Pennsylvania, Rhode Island, South Carolina, South Dakota, Texas,
Utah, Vermont, Virginia, Washington, and Wisconsin.

The MOUs are the first result of the QETP initiative. The results of this
initiative are intended to be used to find new opportunities for collaboration and
to work toward improved employment tax compliance.

Q 6:22   What should a company do if it is audited by the IRS regarding
its employee and independent contractor classifications?

If the IRS questions or audits an employer regarding whether it has improperly classified individuals as independent contractors, the employer should
understand that the inquiry could have potentially serious financial
consequences. (See Q 6:21.) As an initial matter, the company should gather and
preserve all potentially relevant documentation, including any independent
contractor agreements and invoices, and it should determine how and why it
initially made the classification in question. Although it is generally required to

cooperate fully with the IRS, it should also consider immediately retaining a tax attorney or accountant to represent it during the inquiry, and before making any disclosures.

Specific Occupations and Industries

Q 6:23   Has the IRS provided examples of common employee and independent contractor determinations?

Yes. Several examples of employee and independent contractor determinations appear in IRS Publication 15-A, Employer's Supplemental Tax Guide.

Example 1. *Home remodeler:*

Facts: Jerry Jones has an agreement with Wilma White to supervise the remodeling of her house. Wilma does not advance funds to Jerry to carry out the work. She makes direct payments to the suppliers for all necessary materials. Wilma carries liability and workers' compensation insurance covering Jerry and others he engaged to assist him. Wilma pays Jerry and the assistants an hourly rate and exercises almost constant supervision over the work. Jerry is not free to transfer his assistants to other jobs. He may not work on other jobs while working for Wilma. He assumes no responsibility to complete the work and will incur no contractual liability if he fails to do so.

Determination: Jerry and his assistants perform personal services for hourly wages. They are all employees.

Example 2. *Construction worker:*

Facts: Milton, an experienced tile setter, orally agreed with Home Builders, Inc., a corporation, to perform full-time services at construction sites. He uses his own tools and performs services in the order designated by Home Builders and according to its specifications. Home Builders supplies all materials, makes frequent inspections of Milton's work, pays him on a piecework basis, and carries workers' compensation insurance on him. Milton does not have a place of business and does not hold himself out to perform similar services for others. Either party can end the services at any time.

Determination: Milton is an employee of Home Builders, Inc.

Example 3. *Construction group:*

Facts: Wallace agreed with the Sawdust Co. to supply the construction labor for a group of houses. Sawdust Co. agreed to pay all construction costs. Wallace supplies all the tools and equipment. He performs personal services as a carpenter and mechanic for an hourly wage. He also acts as superintendent and foreman and engages other individuals to assist him. Sawdust Co. has the right to select, approve, or discharge any of Wallace's helpers. A company representative makes frequent inspections of the construction site. When a house is finished, Wallace is paid a certain percentage of its costs. He is not responsible for faults, defects of construction, or wasteful operation. At the end of each week, he presents Sawdust Co. with a statement of the amount he has spent, including the payroll. Sawdust Co. gives him a check for that amount, from which he pays the assistants, although he is not personally liable for their wages.

Determination: Wallace is an employee of Sawdust Co., as are his assistants.

Example 4. *Home roofer:*

Facts: Bill Plum entered into an agreement with Elm Corporation to complete the roofing on a housing complex. A signed contract established a flat amount for the services rendered by Bill, who is a licensed roofer and carries workers' compensation and liability insurance under the business name Plum Roofing. Bill hires his own roofers, who are treated as Bill's employees for federal employment tax purposes. If there is a problem with the roofing work, Plum Roofing is responsible for paying for any repairs.

Determination: Bill, doing business as Plum Roofing, is an independent contractor.

Example 5. *Electrical contractor:*

Facts: Vera, an electrician, submitted a job estimate to a housing complex for electrical work at $16 per hour for 400 hours (i.e., $6,400). She is to receive $1,280 every two weeks for the next 10 weeks; that is not considered payment by the hour. Even if Vera works more or less than 400 hours to complete the work, she will receive $6,400. Vera also performs additional electrical installations under contracts with other companies, which she obtained through advertisements.

Determination: Vera is an independent contractor.

Example 6. *Delivery services:*

Facts: Rose Trucking contracts to deliver material for Forest, Inc. at $140 per ton. Rose Trucking is not paid for any articles that are not delivered. At times, Jan, who operates as Rose Trucking, may lease another truck and engage a driver to complete the contract. Jan pays all operating expenses, including insurance coverage. Jan owns or rents all equipment, and she is responsible for all maintenance. None of the drivers is provided by Forest, Inc.

Determination: Jan, operating as Rose Trucking, is an independent contractor.

Example 7. *Former employee:*

Facts: Steve, a computer programmer, is laid off when Megabyte, Inc. downsizes. Megabyte agrees to pay Steve a flat amount to complete a one-time project to create a certain product. It is not clear how long it will take to complete the project, and Steve is not guaranteed any minimum payment for the hours spent on the program. Megabyte provides Steve with no instructions beyond the specifications for the product itself. Steve and Megabyte have a written contract that provides that Steve is considered to be an independent contractor, that he is required to pay federal and state taxes, and that he receives no benefits from Megabyte. The company will file a Form 1099-MISC. Steve does the work on a new high-end computer, which cost him $7,000. He works at home and is not expected or allowed to attend meetings of the software development group.

Determination: Steve is an independent contractor.

Example 8. *In-store salesperson:*

Facts: Donna is a salesperson employed on a full-time basis by Bob Blue, an auto dealer. Donna works six days a week and is on duty in Bob's showroom on certain assigned days and at certain times. She appraises trade-ins, but her appraisals are subject to the sales manager's approval. Lists of prospective customers belong to the dealer. Donna has to develop leads and report results to the sales manager. Because of her experience, she requires only minimal assistance in closing and financing sales and in other phases of her work. Donna is paid a commission and is eligible for prizes and bonuses offered by Bob, who also pays the cost of health insurance and group-term life insurance for Donna.

Determination: Donna is an employee.

Example 9. *Auto repair services:*

Facts: Sam performs auto repair services in the repair department of an auto sales company. He works regular hours and is paid on a percentage basis. He has no investment in the repair department. The sales company supplies all facilities, repair parts, and supplies; issues instructions on the amounts to be charged, parts to be used, and the time for completion of each job; and checks all estimates and repair orders.

Determination: Sam is an employee.

Example 10. *Auto repair services:*

Facts: An auto sales agency furnishes space for Helen to perform auto repair services. She provides her own tools, equipment, and supplies. She seeks out business from insurance adjusters and other individuals and does all the body and paint work that comes to the agency. Helen hires and discharges her own helpers, determines her own and her helpers' working hours, quotes prices for repair work, makes all necessary adjustments, assumes all losses from uncollectible accounts, and receives, as compensation for her services, a large percentage of the gross collections from the auto repair shop.

Determination: Helen is an independent contractor with her own employees.

Example 11. *Attorney:*

Facts: Michelle, an attorney, is a sole practitioner who rents office space and pays for the following items: telephone, computer, online legal research linkup, fax machine, and photocopier. She buys office supplies and pays bar dues and membership dues for three other professional organizations. Michelle has a part-time receptionist, who also does the bookkeeping. She pays the receptionist, withholds and pays federal and state employment taxes on the receptionist's wages, and files a Form W-2 for the receptionist each year. For the past two years, Michelle has had only three clients, corporations with whom she has had longstanding relationships. She charges the corporations an hourly rate for her services, sending monthly bills detailing the work performed for the previous month. The bills include charges for long-distance calls, online research time, faxes, photocopies, mailing costs, and travel—costs for which the corporations have agreed to reimburse her.

Determination: Michelle is an independent contractor who has an employee.

Example 12. *Cabdriver:*

Facts: Tom rents a cab from Taft Cab Co. for $150 per day. He pays the costs of maintaining and operating the cab. He keeps all fares he receives from customers. Although Tom receives the benefit of Taft's two-way radio communication equipment, dispatcher, and advertising, those items benefit both Taft Cab Co. and Tom.

Determination: Tom is an independent contractor.

Q 6:24 Is a partner an employee under the I.R.C.?

No. A partner is not deemed to be an employee. Partners are self-employed individuals with respect to partnership income. Thus, partnership payments to a partner are not considered wages subject to employment tax. A partner reports a portion of the net income of the partnership on his or her individual tax return. That income, net of certain adjustments, is subject to SECA taxes. [I.R.C. § 1401]

Q 6:25 Do special federal employment classification rules apply to domestic workers?

Yes. Under the Social Security Domestic Employment Reform Act of 1994 [Pub. L. No. 103-387, 108 Stat. 4071], domestic workers are generally treated as employees of the payer for employment tax purposes. When they are not part of the payer's trade or business, however, they are not treated as employees for benefit coverage and other tax laws. Employers of domestic workers (including domestic farm workers) must report any FICA (employee and employer portions) obligations on cash wages paid to such employees above an annual amount of $2,000 for 2017. Household workers under age 18 (babysitters) are exempt, unless their principal occupation is household employment. Employers of domestic workers report and pay FICA taxes on Schedule H of Form 1040. Employers of domestic workers must withhold pay, and report federal income taxes if requested to do so. [I.R.C. §§ 3121(a)(7), 3510; Notice 95-18, 1995-18 I.R.B. 13; Notice 95-54, 1995-44 I.R.B. 21; Notice 2003-70, 2003-43 I.R.B. 916; Pub. No. 15]

Q 6:26   What IRS rules apply to domestic workers employed by agencies?

Domestic workers hired by an agency that is in the business of furnishing domestic services, and that establishes the compensation of the workers to perform domestic services for the agency's clients, are treated as the agency's employees for employment tax purposes. [Rev. Rul. 56-502, 1956-2 C.B. 688, *modified by* Rev. Rul. 80-365, 1980-2 C.B. 300] An agency that is a mere employment agency—that allows the ultimate client and the worker to negotiate the terms and conditions of employment—is not the domestic worker's employer; however, the ultimate customer would be. [Tech. Adv. Mem. 9344003]

Q 6:27   Are telecommuters employees or independent contractors?

A telecommuter is like any other worker. Whether the telecommuter is an employee or independent contractor depends on the employment relationship with the person or entity for whom the worker performs services while at home. A telecommuter's relationship with a payer may be more difficult to determine because, unlike a typical employee, the worker performs services at a location other than the premises of the employer. Thus, it may be hard to determine whether an employer retains the right to control the means or methods by which services are performed by a telecommuter. Note that when a telecommuter is not treated as an employee, the telecommuter may not participate in medical and retirement benefits of the payer.

Q 6:28   Is any industry-specific guidance available from the IRS?

Yes. The Market Segment Specialization Program (MSSP) is an IRS audit program. Under the MSSP, the IRS develops audit techniques and handbooks focusing on tax compliance issues of specific industries. Several of these handbooks—for example, those covering the entertainment industry and the trucking industry—address worker classification issues in specific industries. Guides have also been prepared for auto body and repair, pizza restaurants, beauty and barbershops, garment contractors, the reforestation industry, and ministers. The guides are available at http://www.irs.gov/Businesses/Small-Businesses-&-Self-Employed/Audit-Techniques-Guides-ATGs. In addition to audit handbooks, the IRS has developed a Market Segment Understanding (MSU) Program to help taxpayers and the IRS reach a mutual understanding of tax compliance issues that arise in particular industries. The MSU Program is intended to produce guidance in the form of MSU Guidelines or MSU Program Pro Forma Accords. Only a few MSU Guidelines have been produced to date; two of them address worker classification issues:

1. Classifying Certain Van Operators in the Moving Industry, irs.gov/pub/irs-utl/van-ops.pdf; and

2. Classification of Workers Within the Limousine Industry, irs.gov/pub/irs-utl/limo.pdf.

For more information about the IRS MSU Program, go to http://www.irs.gov/Businesses/Small-Businesses-&-Self-Employed/Market-Segment-Understandings-MSU.

Q 6:29   Does the IRS offer any specific worker classification guidelines for the entertainment industry?

Yes. The IRS has guidance on worker classification in the television commercial production and professional video communication industry. The guidance does not address feature film or network television production. It is not binding on the industry but lays out guidelines on the degree of control over workers that could lead to a classification as an employee. It also sets forth standards for measuring such control. [Classification of Workers Within the Television Commercial Production and Professional Video Communication Industries, Doc. No. 94-4856 (May 16, 1995)]

The guidance focuses on three specific factors to determine whether a worker is an independent contractor for a particular project:

1. *Training.* A worker is deemed to be an employee when the payer provides training at the employer's expense.

2. *Continuous employment.* The trend in the entertainment industry is to change workers from project to project. Workers hired for an indefinite period (i.e., a period that will extend beyond the completion date of a project) are generally employees. Workers hired for a period covering only the completion of a specific project *may be* independent contractors.

3. *Guild or union payments.* When the employer contributes to a guild or union benefit plan on behalf of a worker (e.g., when the worker is provided through a "loan-out" corporation), the worker is an employee. The IRS generally takes the position that when such a worker is classified as an employee, the worker cannot participate in a plan of the loan-out corporation or in a Keogh plan established by an individual as a self-employed individual. A plan can get official guidance on this question by filing for a determination letter from the IRS.

If these three criteria do not establish the worker as an employee, four additional factors must generally be met to find that a worker is an independent contractor:

1. The worker has established a business presence (e.g., the worker has an agent, an employer identification number, an office away from home, or maintains business and accounting records);

2. The worker's services are provided with a potential for loss (e.g., the worker bears certain expenses that are not reimbursed by the employer);

3. The employer does not control the worker's activities; and

4. The employer does not provide instructions to the worker on how to carry out the services to be provided.

Q 6:30   Does the IRS offer special tests for determining the employment status of professional workers?

Yes. The employment tax regulations provide that unincorporated physicians, lawyers, dentists, veterinarians, contractors, subcontractors, and others who practice in an independent trade, business, or profession in which they offer their services to the public are generally independent contractors and not employees. They may, however, be employees of a medical practice that provides such services. [Treas. Reg. § 31.3401(c)-1(c)] Because of the high degree of skill required to be a physician, attorney, or other professional and because their methods of work are prescribed by the techniques and standards of their profession, it is generally agreed that the lay person for whom the services are to be performed will not ordinarily supervise or instruct the professional in the performance of services. Nonetheless, a professional may be hired as an employee (e.g., an in-house attorney or accountant for a corporation) despite the fact that control over the manner in which a professional conducts his or her duties will necessarily be more tenuous and general than control over nonprofessional employees. [James v. Commissioner, 25 T.C. 1296 (1956)]

Both the IRS and courts have found it acceptable to consider control over the "business" or nonprofessional aspects of the relationship between the hiring party and the professional. When sufficient control exists over aspects of the relationship that are separate from the professional aspects of the practice, that control may render the professional an employee. For example, many legal decisions examine the relationship between a hospital-based physician and the hospital to determine whether the physician is an employee. [Azad v. United States, 388 F.2d 74 (8th Cir. 1968); Cowing v. Commissioner, T.C. Memo. 1969-135, 28 T.C.M. (CCH) 696 (1969)]

Requisite control may be determined in accordance with the following criteria:

1. The degree to which the professional has become integrated into the organization of the person or entity for whom services are performed (this includes the manner in which the professional is paid for services, as in a percentage, salary, or percentage with minimum guaranteed salary; whether the professional employs assistants; and whether the professional may engage in services for the public in addition to the work for the payer);

2. The substantial nature, regularity, and continuity of the work, such as where a schedule of definite and fixed hours is set for performance of services;

3. The authority vested in the person for whom services are performed to require compliance with general policies, including whether the professional is answerable to superiors; and

4. The degree to which the professional has been accorded the rights and privileges of employees of the person for whom services are performed, including vacation and holiday pay, sick pay, and insurance benefits.

Thus, when the person for whom services are rendered does not give instruction or training to a professional employee or maintain control over the manner of performance as well as the result, those factors do not necessarily weigh against a finding of employment status in the case of a professional, and the other factors are weighed accordingly. [Rev. Rul. 66-274, 1966-2 C.B. 446; Rev. Rul. 73-417, 1973-2 C.B. 332; Priv. Ltr. Rul. 9416022 (Jan. 14, 1994)]

Statutory Classifications

Q 6:31   What are the special statutory classification rules that govern the status of certain workers under the I.R.C.?

Some categories of workers are specifically designated by the I.R.C. as employees or nonemployees for withholding and employment tax purposes. Thus, a worker in a particular occupation may be statutorily designated as an employee for purposes of income tax withholding or employment taxes, but could potentially be an independent contractor under common-law rules for other purposes, such as employment discrimination laws. [See Rev. Rul. 90-93, 1990-2 C.B. 33 (full-time life insurance salesman considered an employee for FICA purposes but not for purposes of I.R.C. §§ 62 and 67).]

Q 6:32   What is the difference between a statutory employee and a common-law employee for federal employment tax purposes?

Being classified as a statutory employee can have a significant tax advantage over being classified as a common-law employee. Statutory employees retain the tax benefits of a common-law employee (e.g., they may participate in the company's health, retirement, and other fringe benefits), but they can deduct their business expenses on a Schedule C. Business expenses of a common-law employee are deductible as an itemized deduction on Schedule A of the employee's Form 1040 and are subject to a 2 percent of adjusted gross income (AGI) limitation.

An individual who loses the statutory classification must treat any participation in the company's health, pension, or other benefits as taxable income. Such an individual, through payment of SECA taxes, is essentially required to pay both the employee's and employer's portion of FICA taxes.

Q 6:33   What are the statutory employee and nonemployee categories under IRS guidelines?

The following categories describe the employment tax application for workers classified as statutory employees or statutory nonemployees:

1. *Statutory Employees for Purposes of FICA but not for FUTA or Income Tax Withholding*—Full-time commissioned life insurance salespersons whose entire or principal business activity is selling life insurance or annuity contracts or both, primarily for one life insurance company. [I.R.C. § 3121(d)(3)(B)] Also, individuals who work from home on materials or goods (a) that an employer supplies, and (b) that must be returned to the employer (or a person the employer names) if the employer also furnishes specifications for the work to be done. [I.R.C. § 3121(d)(3)(C); Pub. No. 15-A]

2. *Statutory Employees for Purposes of Both FICA and FUTA but Not for Income Tax Withholding*—Full-time traveling or city salespersons who work on an employer's behalf and submit orders to the employer from wholesalers, retailers, contractors, operators of hotels, restaurants, or other similar establishments. The goods sold must be for resale or used in the buyer's business. This work must be the salesperson's principal business activity. [I.R.C. §§ 3121(d)(3)(D), 3306(i)] Also, certain agent-drivers or commission drivers who distribute beverages (other than milk), meat, vegetables, fruit, or bakery products or who pick up and deliver laundry or dry cleaning, when the driver is an agent of the distribution firm and is paid on commission. [I.R.C. §§ 3121(d)(3)(A), 3306(i)]

3. *Statutory Employees for FICA, FUTA, and Income Tax Withholding*—Officers of a corporation. [I.R.C. §§ 3121(d)(1), 3306(i), 3401(c)]

4. *Statutory Nonemployees, No Requirement for FICA, FUTA, and Income Tax Withholding*—Qualified real estate agents and direct sellers, as long as (1) substantially all payments for their services are directly related to the sales or other output (rather than hours worked), and (2) their services are performed under a written contract providing that they will not be treated as employees for federal tax purposes. [I.R.C. § 3508]

5. *Statutory Employees for FICA and Income Tax Withholding but Statutory Nonemployees for FUTA*—Government officers, employees, or elected officials. [I.R.C. §§ 3121, 3401(c), 3306(c)(6), 3306(c)(7)]

Table 6-1 summarizes tax treatment of the five categories just identified.

Table 6-1.   Classification of Employees for Tax Withholding Purposes

Statutory Classifications	Income Tax Withholding	FICA Withholding	FICA Payment	FUTA Payment
Category 1		X	X	
Category 2		X	X	X
Category 3	X	X	X	X
Category 4				
Category 5	X	X	X	

Q 6:34   What are the federal reporting requirements for a statutory employee?

Employers must furnish a Form W-2 to a statutory employee and check "statutory employee" in Box 13 for statutory employees who are subject to FICA but not to federal income tax withholding. Payments to the employee are shown as other compensation in Box 1 of Form W-2. Also, Social Security wages are shown in Box 3, Social Security tax withheld in Box 4, Medicare wages in Box 5, and Medicare tax withheld in Box 6 of Form W-2.

A statutory employee can deduct his or her trade or business expenses from the payments shown on Form W-2 when he or she files Form 1040. Unlike a common-law employee, the statutory employee (identified in Box 13 on the W-2) reports earnings as a statutory employee on line 1 of Schedule C or C-EZ (Form 1040). (A statutory employee's business expenses are not subject to the Schedule A reduction by 2 percent of his or her AGI. That limitation applies to the employee business expenses of common-law employees.) [Pub. No. 15-A]

Q 6:35   When must an employer withhold FICA taxes for statutory employees?

An employer must withhold FICA taxes from statutory employees' wages if all three of the following conditions apply:

1. The service contract states or implies that substantially all the services are to be performed personally by the statutory employees;

2. The employees do not have a substantial investment in the equipment, such as a car or truck, and property used to perform the services (other than an investment in transportation facilities); and

3. The services of the employees are performed on a continuing basis for the same payer.

[Treas. Reg. § 31.3121(d)-1(d)(4)]

Q 6:36   Are real estate sellers and direct sellers statutory nonemployees under the IRS definition?

Yes, but only if they meet the requirements set forth by the IRS. Licensed real estate agents and direct sellers are two categories of statutory nonemployees. These individuals are treated as self-employed for all federal income tax and employment tax purposes. As a result, the employer does not withhold income or other payroll taxes on wages paid to these individuals.

An individual is classified as a statutory nonemployee only if:

1. Substantially all payments for his or her services as a direct seller or real estate agent are directly related to sales or other output, rather than to the number of hours worked; and

2. The services are performed under a written contract providing that the individual will not be treated as an employee for federal tax purposes.

[Pub. No. 15-A]

Q 6:37   Who is a "direct seller" for federal employment tax purposes?

A direct seller is one type of statutory nonemployee. Direct sellers include anyone falling into any of the following groups:

1. Persons engaged in selling (or soliciting the sale of) consumer products in the home or place of business other than in a permanent retail establishment;

2. Persons engaged in selling (or soliciting the sale of) consumer products to any buyer on a buy-sell basis, a deposit-commission basis, or any similar basis prescribed by regulations for resale in the home or at a place of business other than in a permanent retail establishment; or

3. Persons engaged in the trade or business of the delivery or distribution of newspapers or shopping news (including any services directly related to such delivery or distribution).

Also included are individuals involved in direct selling who attempt to increase direct sales activities of their direct sellers and who earn income based on the productivity of their direct sellers. Such activities include providing motivation and encouragement; imparting skills, knowledge, or experience; and recruiting. [Pub. No. 15-A]

Q 6:38   What is the IRS safe harbor for agencies that refer companion sitters?

The IRS defines companion sitters as individuals who are engaged to provide personal attendance, companionship, or household care services to children or to individuals who are elderly or disabled. A safe harbor exists for agencies that refer companion sitters to persons who wish to employ them, called companion placement services. The companion placement agency is not considered the employer and the companion sitter is treated as self-employed for all federal taxes. [Pub. 15-A]

I.R.C. Section 3506 provides that when a business refers sitters to clients, it shall not be treated as the employer of the sitters for purposes of federal employment taxes. In addition, the provision states that the sitter shall not be treated as an employee of the sitter referral business and treated as self-employed for all federal tax purposes.

The safe harbor applies only if the following requirements are met:

1. The business does not pay or receive the compensation paid the sitter; and

2. The business is compensated by the sitter or by the person who engages the sitter on a fee basis.

In Revenue Ruling 80-365 [1980-2 C.B. 300], the IRS emphasized the importance of the first requirement by concluding that an agency that was paid by a client and in turn paid the sitter did not qualify. An agency that received its fee from the sitter and received no payment directly from the client did qualify, however.

Note. Section 3506 relief does not apply to the relationship between the sitter and the client for whom the services are actually performed. Thus, a sitter could be deemed an employee of the client to which he or she is referred notwithstanding the application of I.R.C. Section 3506.

Misclassification of Workers

The workforce has changed over the years, and with those changes come new worker categories. As the old models of the traditional workforce transition to current business models, there are changes in social behavior as well. The "shared economy" is growing, and along with that growth new options have arisen, such as franchising and low-road outsourcing.

Q 6:39   What are the federal withholding and employment tax consequences when an employer misclassifies a worker as an independent contractor?

Although the classification of workers as independent contractors is appropriate in many instances, the IRS has increasingly become concerned with deliberate attempts by employers to misclassify workers as independent contractors for the purpose of avoiding payment of FICA and FUTA taxes and the withholding of federal income tax. When an individual is treated as an independent contractor but is later reclassified by the IRS as an employee, the employer generally becomes liable for payment of delinquent FICA and FUTA taxes. In addition, the employer may become liable for federal income and FICA taxes that were neither withheld from the individual's wages nor paid by the worker to the government. Those liabilities usually include payment of interest due on such taxes. Penalties may also be assessed for unintentional failure to withhold income tax that would have been subject to withholding had the worker been properly treated as an employee and for a portion of the worker's share of the unpaid FICA tax. [I.R.C. § 3509] The misclassified worker ("independent contractor") continues to be responsible in full for his or her federal income tax and share of FICA tax. [Rev. Rul. 86-111, 1986-2 C.B. 176] Uncollected FICA taxes on wages are reported on Form 8919, Form 4137 for tips. The assessments made for large numbers of employees over many years of misclassification can be devastating. [Treas. Reg. § 31.3102(c)-1]

In some cases, FICA and income tax withholding assessments have been made against an employer for amounts that were directly paid by misclassified independent contractors as their own income and self-employment taxes. In other cases, the IRS has allowed an income tax and FICA-SECA offset of employer liability when the worker paid these taxes directly. [I.R.C. § 6521] For assessments resulting in overpayment, the IRS suggests that the individuals who were incorrectly classified as independent contractors (and who paid the SECA tax) file a Form 1040X to obtain a refund of those taxes. Further relief from penalty for misclassification may be available to employers under Section 530 of the Revenue Act of 1978 (see Qs 6:45–6:56). [Independent Contractor or Employee Training Materials (Mar. 4, 1997)]

In addition to the penalties for failure to withhold income tax, there are several penalties that could apply. A sample of those penalties are:

- Failure to file employment returns with a 5 percent per month penalty up to a maximum of 25 percent for the amount of tax
- Failure to make timely deposits of 10 percent for more than 15 days (with lower percentages for shorter periods, 2 percent up to five days and 5 percent up to 15 days)
- Accuracy-related penalty of 20 percent of underpayment of tax or under-statement of tax
- Failure to file a correct return (1099-MISC) of $50 per return
- Failure to provide payee statement (1099-MISC) of $50 per return.

If there is a determination of fraud, the penalties would be substantially higher. The proper classification of a worker, whether a contingent worker, franchiser, or one of the many newer labels, is paramount for employers in order to avoid the pitfall of misclassification of workers.

Q 6:40   What other penalties may apply if a worker is misclassified as an independent contractor?

In addition to liability for the amount of delinquent taxes due as the result of misclassification (see Q 6:39), other penalties may apply.

The penalty for not withholding federal income taxes is 1.5 percent of the employee's federal income tax liability. The penalty for not withholding the employee's share of FICA taxes is 20 percent of the employee's share of FICA. If no Form 1099-MISC has been filed, the amount of liability for income tax withholding is increased to 3 percent, and the liability for the employee's share of FICA taxes increases to 40 percent. The employee remains fully liable for his or her share of the FICA taxes that are due; that is, there is no offset for the 20 percent or 40 percent penalty paid by the employer. The law permits a penalty of up to 100 percent of the employee's share of FICA taxes and the full amount of the federal income taxes that should have been withheld. [I.R.C. § 3509(c)]

Specific relief from penalties may be available under Section 530 of the Revenue Act of 1978 (see Qs 6:45–6:56). When that relief is not available, employers may be able to claim Section 3509 relief. I.R.C. Section 3509 provides for reduced employment tax liability for failure to withhold federal income and FICA tax. Such relief is conditioned on the employer having properly filed Form 1099-MISC for the worker. If an employer uses Section 3509 relief, it cannot use the other relief available under I.R.C. Sections 3402(d) and 6521. Section 3509 does not relieve an employer from its FUTA tax obligations or from penalties that may be imposed by the IRS for failure to file information returns.

I.R.C. Section 3402(d) allows an employer to obtain relief from a retroactive assessment of liability if it can demonstrate that the worker reported the income on his or her Form 1040. This can be demonstrated by a worker completing and signing Form 4669, Statement of Payments Received. Forms 4669 are filed by the employer with the IRS using Form 4670, Request for Relief from Payment of Income Tax Withholding. I.R.C. Section 6521 allows an employer to obtain a credit for its share of FICA tax when the statute of limitations has expired and prevents the worker from obtaining a refund of self-employment tax. [I.R.C. §§ 3509(a), 3509(b); Prop. Treas. Reg. §§ 31.3509-1(a), 31.3509-1(b), 31.3509-1(c)]

Q 6:41   May an employer obtain a refund of FICA taxes it paid on a worker's wages following a determination by the IRS that the worker was in fact an independent contractor?

No, the FICA taxes are forfeited.

Q 6:42   Are there nonpayroll issues relating to misclassification of a worker?

Yes. The status of a worker misclassified as an independent contractor may trigger liability of the employer to third parties for the actions of the individual later found to be an employee. Such liability arises as a result of various state and federal statutes as well as the common-law theory that a master is subject to liability for the torts of his or her servants committed while the servants are acting in the scope of their employment. [Restatement (Second) of Agency § 219 (1958)]

Also, an independent contractor who is later found to be an employee will have a right to claim certain protections under a multitude of federal laws (e.g., the Americans with Disabilities Act and the Family and Medical Leave Act). Further, an independent contractor who is reclassified upon audit as an employee may be entitled to the past accruals of pension and other benefits. [Kenny v. Commissioner, T.C. Memo. 1995-431, 70 T.C.M. (CCH) 614 (1995)] In addition, under the Fair Labor Standards Act and similar state labor laws, individuals who are later found to be employees may be entitled to recoup unpaid minimum wages and overtime, including interest, penalties, and attorneys' fees.

Q 6:43   How can an employer avoid liability for its failure to withhold federal income taxes following a payroll audit?

In the case of intentional disregard, an employer is liable for the entire amount of federal income tax that should have been withheld from an employee's wages unless the employer can show that the employee paid federal income tax on those wages.

Form 4670 (See Q 6:40) will not relieve an employer of liability for related penalties and additions to tax, nor any liabilities imposed under I.R.C. Section 3509. Thus, if an employer mischaracterizes employees as independent contractors and is liable for 1.5 percent of wages paid, it cannot obtain a reduction in the penalty for any income taxes actually paid by its employees. [I.R.C. § 3509(d)(1)(C)]

Q 6:44   Is an intern considered an employee?

An unpaid intern is not considered an employee under the Second Circuit Court of Appeals in two decisions, *Glatt v. Fox Searchlight Pictures, Inc.* [791 F.3d 376 (2d Cir. 2015)] and *Wang v. Hearst* [617 F. App'x 35 (2d Cir. 2015)], where a new test was established. The plaintiffs in *Glatt* looked for compensation under the FLSA and New York labor law using the DOL's six-point test. The court disagreed and established its own criteria in a seven-point "primary beneficiary test." The seven points are as follows:

1. Clear understanding there was no expectation of compensation.
2. Internship provides training that would be similar to an educational environment.
3. Is the internship tied to a formal educational program?
4. Does the internship accommodate the intern's academic commitments corresponding to the academic calendar?
5. The duration is limited to the period that provides the intern with beneficial learning.
6. The intern's work complements, and not displaces, the work of paid employees.
7. The internship is conducted without entitlement of a paid job when the internship is completed.

These decisions affect the Second Circuit only, but provide some indication of what courts may decide on this issue. Employers should be careful about internship programs, ensuring that there is an education component with specific educational development in order to avoid unpaid interns being classified as employees.

Section 530 of the Revenue Act of 1978

Q 6:45   What does Section 530 of the Revenue Act of 1978 offer?

Section 530 of the Revenue Act of 1978 [Pub. L. No. 95-600, 82 Stat. 2763, as amended by § 269(c) of the Tax Equity and Fiscal Responsibility Act of 1982 (TEFRA)] provides certain relief from penalties and payment of employment taxes due as a result of a prior misclassification of an employee as an independent contractor. It is a safe harbor under which an employer may, with a degree of certainty, treat an individual as an independent contractor for employment tax purposes. If its requirements are met, a later reclassification by the IRS will not lead to penalties or liability for unpaid taxes. Its protection extends only to the payer and not to the employee. As a result, the IRS can assess a liability on the employee for his or her portion of FICA taxes on the compensation received from the employer.

To take advantage of the safe harbor, a payer must meet the following criteria:

1. The worker classification has been made on a reasonable basis;
2. There is substantive consistency in the treatment of workers; and
3. The employer reports payments to the independent contractor on Form 1099-MISC.

The relief provided by Section 530 is available for payments made to workers after December 31, 1978. To successfully qualify for such relief, both the "reporting consistency rule" and the "substantive consistency rule" must be satisfied and there must be no reasonable basis not to report the worker as an employee. [Rev. Proc. 85-18, 1985-1 C.B. 518]

Section 530 also prohibits the IRS from promulgating regulations or issuing revenue rulings with respect to worker status for employment tax purposes, until such time as a law is enacted that clarifies worker status. Section 530 was initially intended as a temporary provision, but was made permanent in 1982. [Revenue Act of 1978 § 530]

Note. Section 530 protections apply only to FICA and FUTA taxes, *not to federal income taxes*. As a result, the payments may be treated as employee wages and become included in the employer's qualified retirement plan calculations.

Q 6:46   What effect does Section 530 have on a worker's actual status as an employee?

None. Although Section 530 of the Revenue Act of 1978 may provide an employer with relief from liability for income taxes and withholding responsibility for federal employment taxes for certain misclassification of workers as independent contractors, it does not affect the status of an individual who truly is an employee. *Employees do not become characterized as self-employed independent contractors as a result of Section 530 relief.* Workers who incorrectly pay a self-employment tax may be entitled to a refund of that tax on reclassification to employee status, although any refund will be offset by the employee's share of FICA taxes. The employer may be relieved from its share of employment tax (when an offset is permitted), but the employee remains fully liable for his or her share of such taxes. [Rev. Rul. 85-18, 1985-1 C.B. 518]

Q 6:47   What is considered a "reasonable basis" under Section 530 for not treating a worker as an employee?

Under Section 530 of the Revenue Act of 1978, an employer has a reasonable basis for treating an individual as other than an employee if the employer, in making the determination, reasonably relied on (a) judicial and regulatory precedent, (b) a prior audit, or (c) industry practice.

Judicial and regulatory precedent. This includes court cases, published rulings, and technical advice from the IRS with respect to the employer's workers (e.g., a letter ruling issued to that particular employer). Some courts have also interpreted technical advice to include advice to an employer from tax professionals, such as certified public accountants or tax attorneys. [*E.g.,* Hospital Res. Pers. v. United States, 860 F. Supp. 1557 (S.D. Ga. 1994); J&J Cab Serv., Inc. v. United States, 1995 U.S. Dist. LEXIS 482 (W.D.N.C. 1995)] It is important to note, however, that the IRS determined that an employer was *not entitled* to Section 530 relief when the employer relied on a written statement issued by an IRS examiner after a compliance interview. In short, the IRS concluded that the written statement did not constitute a technical advice memorandum, letter ruling, or determination letter. [Tech. Adv. Mem. 8846015]

Prior audit. For periods after December 31, 1996, the audit relied upon must specifically address the employment classification of workers. (Previously, *prior audit* referred to a past IRS audit of the employer in which there was no assessment for employment taxes attributable to the treatment of independent contractors holding positions substantially similar to the position held by the individual at issue.) The past audit need not have been conducted for employment tax purposes, however. [Rev. Proc. 85-18, 1985-1 C.B. 518] This safe haven is not satisfied when an audit results in an employment tax assessment that is offset by an employer's other claims or refunds.

The IRS generally asserts that the term *substantially similar* here refers to a position in an industry or the type of work performed by a worker. There is authority, however, for the proposition that an employer may alternatively look to the structure of the relationship between the worker and the employer and rely on a prior audit involving workers holding substantially similar positions albeit doing different types of work in different industries. The Fifth Circuit ruled that a taxpayer can reasonably rely on a prior IRS audit to determine the status of workers who were hired at a later date and who hold substantially similar positions in a different industry. [Lambert's Nursery & Landscaping, Inc. v. United States, 894 F.2d 154 (5th Cir. 1990)]

> **Note.** A corporation may use an audit of its predecessor as a reasonable basis for continuing to treat a worker as an independent contractor. [Rev. Rul. 83-152, 1983-2 C.B. 172]

Industry practice. This generally refers to a longstanding, recognized practice of a significant segment of the industry in which the individual performed services. The determination of what constitutes an industry is highly factual, and is determined on a case-by-case basis. The Ninth Circuit has determined that the term *industry* need not encompass nationwide practices in the industry, but may legitimately consist of a discrete local industry practice. [General Inv. Corp. v. United States, 823 F.2d 337 (9th Cir. 1987)] Similarly, the IRS has ruled that small geographic areas generally provide the most appropriate basis for evaluating an industry. Specifically, the IRS determined that the relevant geographic area was the area of competition for customers, not of competition for qualified workers. [Tech. Adv. Mem. 8733004]

The industry practice safe haven does not require that the treatment of workers be uniform throughout the entire industry. It merely requires that the practice be recognized as "the" practice of the industry, meaning that nearly all employers in a significant segment of the industry treat workers accordingly. [Tech. Adv. Mem. 8733004] If an employer has no competitors, there is no industry practice on which an employer may rely. [Priv. Ltr. Rul. 9420002]

Q 6:48 How have the courts applied the reasonable basis test of Section 530?

In enacting Section 530 of the Revenue Act of 1978, Congress left open the possibility that courts could establish a reasonable basis for finding a worker to be other than an employee, even if not expressly set forth under the three alternative safe harbor rules. [Joint Comm. on Taxation, General Explanation of the Revenue Act of 1978, H.R. Rep. No. 13511, 95th Cong., 2d Sess. 302–03 (1978); H.R. Rep. No. 1748, 95th Cong., 2d Sess. 5 (1978)] The House Committee on Government Operations interpreted Section 530 relief to apply in this manner: "If a company cannot claim protection under one of the safe harbor provisions, then the IRS is free to scrutinize the employer's classification decision against 20 'common law' factors." [H.R. Rep. No. 979, 101st Cong., 2d Sess. 4, 14 (1990)]

Various courts have applied the safe harbors in a nonexclusive manner. For example, the Tax Court stated that "[t]he 'reasonable basis' requirement of Section 530 may be satisfied either on general evidence or by meeting any one of three statutory standards which constitute 'safe havens.'" In *Joseph M. Grey, Public Accountant v. Commissioner of the Internal Revenue* [119 C. No.5 Sept. 16, 2002], the Tax Court did not find that Section 530 applied when it was determined that the individual was an employee. In *Peno Trucking v. Commissioner* [102 A.F.T.R.2d Paragraph, 2006-5360] drivers were misclassified as independent contractors when they should have been employees. The Sixth Circuit reversed the Tax Court's decision that relief was not available under Section 530. The Claims Court found a reasonable basis for treatment of workers outside the confines of the safe harbor rules by application of the common-law factors to the factual context involving the workers at issue. [Ridgewell's v. United States, 655 F.2d 1098 (Ct. Cl. 1981)] A district court in Michigan held that "disqualification from the safe harbor protections of the Act does not, by any stretch of the imagination, automatically direct a finding of employee status; it just means that the workers are not automatically independent contractors. Bottom line, an analysis of the common law factors is necessary." [Apollo Drywall v. United States, 71 A.F.T.R.2d (RIA) 931,689 (W.D. Mich. 1993); *see also* Critical Care Register Nursing v. United States, 776 F. Supp. 1025 (E.D. Pa. 1991), *nonacq* (Aug. 4, 1994); Sanderson v. United States, 862 F. Supp. 196 (N.D. Ohio 1994); Fuller v. United States, 1994 U.S. Dist. LEXIS 14676 (D. Mass. 1994); Rev. Proc. 78-35, 1978-2 C.B. 536, *superseded by* Rev. Proc. 81-43, 1981-2 C.B. 616, *superseded by* Rev. Proc. 85-18, 1985-1 C.B. 518; Rev. Proc. 85-18, 1985-1 C.B. 518]

Q 6:49   What is the reporting consistency rule of Section 530?

One requirement for Section 530 relief under the Revenue Act of 1978 is consistency in reporting of payments to independent contractors. This is met when the employer files all federal tax returns required with respect to the worker for the period after December 31, 1978, on a basis consistent with treatment of the individual as an independent contractor; that is, the payments are reported on Form 1099-MISC. A good-faith filing of the wrong form does not mean that the employer failed to file returns consistent with the treatment of an individual as an independent contractor, however. For example, no reporting consistency exists when an independent contractor has erroneously received a W-2 for service rendered to the employer or when an independent contractor accidentally completed a W-4. Thus, an error in filing the correct form will not necessarily block Section 530 relief. [Rev. Rul. 81-224, 1981-2 C.B. 197]

The consistency requirement also applies when a taxpayer fails to file all the required forms in one year but, in a subsequent year, files all required forms and treats the workers as independent contractors, then the taxpayer may qualify for Section 530 relief. [General Investment Corp. v. United States, 823 F.2d 337 (9th Cir. 1987); Rev. Proc. 85-18, 1985-1 C.B. 518]

Q 6:50   What is the substantive consistency rule of Section 530?

One requirement for Section 530 relief under the Revenue Act of 1978 is "substantive consistency" in the treatment of workers. That requirement is met when neither the employer nor any predecessor treated any individual holding a substantially similar position as an employee for purposes of employment taxes after December 31, 1977. Such treatment would include withholding of income or FICA taxes, whether or not actually paid to the government; filing employer tax returns on Form 940, 941, 944, or 943; or issuing Form W-2 statements regarding the individual. Whether an employee holds a position substantially similar to that held by an individual who might otherwise be treated as an independent contractor is based on an analysis of the facts and circumstances at issue. Such a determination would examine the activities, functions, and the type of work performed by the individuals. [Rev. Rul. 87-41, 1987-1 C.B. 296; Institute for Res. Mgmt. v. United States, 22 Cl. Ct. 114 (1990); Lowen Corp. v. United States, 785 F. Supp. 913 (D. Kan. 1992)]

Filing late or amended employer tax returns in compliance with IRS mandates after the misclassification of a worker or workers is identified, however, does not constitute past treatment as an employee. [Rev. Proc. 85-18, 1985-1 C.B. 518] Furthermore, an IRS audit finding that workers are employees does not constitute treatment as an employee by the employer for prior periods; however, subsequent filing of employment tax returns on those same workers will be considered treatment of the workers as employees by the employer.

Q 6:51   Can an employer unintentionally violate the consistency-of-treatment requirement of Section 530?

Yes. The unintentional violation of the consistency requirement of Section 530 of the Revenue Act of 1978 can result in harsh results for unsuspecting employers. For example, when an employer filed a Form 941 and paid FICA tax for one of 57 individuals engaged as roofing applicators, the IRS found that for all periods after 1978, Section 530 relief was unavailable for all of the remaining 56 roofing applicators. [Tech. Adv. Mem. 8127010] Similarly, *Institute for Resource Management v. United States* [22 Cl. Ct. 114 (1990)] involved an employer in the business of locating temporary workers for public utility customers. The employer treated all workers as independent contractors for 12 years until one customer requested that its workers be treated as employees of the employer. The employer agreed to so treat those distinct individuals pursuant to a contract with the isolated customer. That treatment was sufficient to disqualify all workers of the employer from the scope of Section 530.

Q 6:52   May an employer reincorporate and reclassify employees as independent contractors under Section 530?

No. The substantive consistency rules are intended to prevent an employer from changing the way it treats workers to obtain relief under Section 530 of the Revenue Act of 1978. In particular, employers are prohibited from reincorporating and simultaneously reclassifying employees as independent contractors. [H.R. Rep. No. 1748, 95th Cong., 2d Sess. 6 (1978), *reprinted in* 1978-3 C.B. 629, 634; Rev. Proc. 85-18, 1985-1 C.B. 518]

Q 6:53   Does Section 530 offer any penalty relief to any independent contractors who have been misclassified?

No. An independent contractor who does not pay SECA taxes or estimated income taxes has no relief from penalty under Section 530. Application of Section 530 would relieve an employer of its employment tax liabilities, but if the worker is ultimately characterized as an employee, the worker remains liable for his or her share of FICA taxes. [Rev. Proc. 85-18, 1985-1 C.B. 518; Tech. Adv. Mem. 9410005 (Nov. 23, 1993)]

Q 6:54   Is Section 530 relief available to employees?

No. In a claim for underreported FICA taxes, the Eighth Circuit ruled that employees are not entitled to relief under Section 530 of the Revenue Act of 1978, and that the section is available only to employers. In this case, the University of Minnesota did not pay or withhold FICA taxes on stipends awarded to a group of medical students because it believed these students could be treated similarly to other workers who were exempt from FICA taxes under an agreement with the SSA (meeting a requirement for Section 530). The employees claimed relief under Section 530 for underpaid taxes, and the Court ruled that the relief is available only to employers. [Ahmed v. United States, 147 F.3d 791 (8th Cir. 1998)]

Q 6:55   What legislative changes have been made to the application of Section 530 relief?

The Small Business Job Protection Act of 1996 (SBJPA) clarified the application of the reasonable basis criterion of Section 530 and limited the IRS's ability to impose unreasonable requirements on employers that use Section 530 of the Revenue Act of 1978. The changes codify certain court decisions and apply for periods after December 31, 1996.

The specific changes imposed by SBJPA are as follows:

1. Audits of the employer that do not raise the issue of employee status classification may no longer be relied on as a reasonable basis *unless the audit specifically addresses the employment classification of a worker or a similarly situated worker.* In the past, any audit by the IRS that did not question the employment status could be used as a reasonable basis.

2. An employer that reclassifies an independent contractor as an employee under audit is permitted to claim Section 530 relief for the period before the change.

3. When determining whether an employer has a "longstanding practice" of treating workers as independent contractors, the IRS can no longer require that the employer demonstrate that the practice has been in effect for more than 10 years or that the practice was in existence before 1978. This requirement part of the substantive consistency criterion of Section 530 has been referred to as a "longstanding recognized practice" determination.

4. The IRS, on audit, can no longer require that the employer demonstrate that at least 25 percent of the employer's industry treated similarly situated workers as independent contractors.

5. An IRS determination that two workers hold "similarly situated positions" (a part of Section 530's substantive consistency requirement) must take into account the relationship between the employer and employee.

6. Once the employer has complied with all information requests from the IRS and provides sufficient proof that it had a reasonable basis for a worker's classification as an independent contractor, the burden of proving that the worker is an employee shifts to the IRS.

Beginning in 1997, the IRS must inform employers that are being audited for payroll that Section 530 relief may be available. This is typically provided by a form notice, such as IRS Publication No. 1976, Do You Qualify for Relief Under Section 530?.

Q 6:56   What legislative change to Section 530 relief was made with respect to technical service specialists?

The Section 530 safe harbor for independent contractor status no longer applies with respect to technical service specialists, such as engineers, designers, drafters, computer programmers, systems analysts, or other similarly skilled individuals engaged in a similar line of work who provide services for third-party clients pursuant to arrangements between the individuals and the enlisting employers or firms. This change was part of the Small Business Job Protection Act of 1996 (SBJPA), which amended Section 530(d) to the Revenue Tax Act of 1978. The IRS has emphasized, however, that this does not automatically classify such workers as employees or independent contractors; it only affects Section 530 relief. [Revenue Act of 1978 § 530(d), as amended by SBJPA § 1122; Rev. Rul. 87-19, 1987-1 C.B. 455; Rev. Rul. 87-41, 1987-1 C.B. 296]

Q 6:57   What other legislative and regulatory change to Section 530 relief is occurring?

The Obama administration is increasing the challenges for misclassification of workers through a directive to the Department of Labor as well as seeking change in the extent of the use of Section 530 relief. The DOL released the Administrator's Interpretation No. 2015-1 regarding the misclassification of workers, providing additional guidance on what constitutes an employee. On the state level, many jurisdictions have addressed the question of whether Section 530 relief is afforded employers on the state level. In addition to the MOU signed by the DOL, the IRS, and 20 states, the DOL has signed separate agreements with numerous states. Although the IRS and DOL follow two distinct legislative paths, employers should ensure that they are complying on both sides. Another area that has added complexity is the Affordable Care Act as it relates to the requirement to offer benefits to employees. If there is a worker misclassification issue, there may be penalties assessed.

Classification Settlement Program

Q 6:58   What is the Classification Settlement Program?

Employers that have misclassified employees as independent contractors can avoid certain penalties under the IRS Classification Settlement Program (CSP). CSP is an optional settlement program designed to allow IRS field agents and taxpayers to resolve worker classification disputes using standard audit closing agreements with employers. The program is also designed to ensure that the taxpayer has full access to the penalty relief provisions of Section 530 of the Revenue Act of 1978.

The CSP attempts to address three types of worker classification scenarios:

1. The employer has treated the workers in question as independent contractors and has met all of the requirements for relief from retroactive reclassification under Section 530 of the Revenue Act of 1978. In such a

case, no employment tax assessments will be made. Moreover, if the taxpayer wishes to treat the workers as employees prospectively, and the IRS agent agrees with that reclassification, the closing agreement will provide for such prospective treatment, and the taxpayer will not waive its claim to Section 530 relief for prior years.

2. The employer has treated the workers in question as independent contractors but has not met all of the requirements for Section 530 relief. In such cases, a series of graduated settlement offers will be available. The amount of the proposed assessments will depend on which requirements of Section 530 were not met.

3. The employer has treated the workers in question as employees in some respects, but failed to fully carry out its employment tax obligations on that basis (where such failure was in part the result of a belief that the workers were independent contractors for employment tax purposes). In such cases, the closing agreement would not only provide for an employment tax assessment for the years in question, but would also contain an agreement as to the proper classification of the workers for those years and prospectively.

Q 6:59   Is the CSP available for all employment tax issues?

No. The CSP may not be available for cases when the identity of the employer is in question, for example, when the worker is "leased" to the taxpayer by a leasing company or a professional employer organization. The CSP can apply in such situations, however, when the issue of who is the relevant employer is raised at the examination level. [Rev. Rul. 87-41, 1987-1 C.B. 296]

Q 6:60   How can an employer appeal an IRS ruling under the CSP?

Revenue Procedure 99-28 (1999-29 I.R.B. 109) describes a process through which a taxpayer can request referral to the Appeals branch of the IRS for any issue not agreed upon (subject to certain restrictions). Issues that can be referred to Appeals include:

1. Whether a worker is an employee or independent contractor under the common-law test;
2. Whether relief under Section 530 of the Revenue Act of 1978 is available;
3. Whether a worker is a statutory employee or statutory nonemployee;
4. Whether I.R.C. Section 3509 rates are appropriate;
5. Whether the taxpayer qualifies for an interest-free adjustment;
6. Whether certain payments are excepted from the definition of "wages" (e.g., a fringe benefit that would be excludable from gross income under I.R.C. Section 132); and
7. Whether certain payments are excepted from the definition of "employment."

[Rev. Proc. 99-28, 1999-29 I.R.B. 109, superseding Rev. Proc. 96-9, 1996-1 C.B. 575]

Voluntary Classification Settlement Program

Q 6:61   What is the Voluntary Classification Settlement Program?

On September 21, 2011, the IRS introduced its Voluntary Classification Settlement Program (VCSP) to enable employers to voluntarily reclassify their workers as employees for federal employment tax purposes prospectively and obtain relief similar to the Classification Settlement Program (see Q 6:58). The relief under this program allows the employer to pay 10 percent of the employment tax liability that may have been due on compensation paid to the workers for the most recent tax year. Employers will not be liable for any interest or penalties. [IR-2011-95, Sept. 21, 2011; Ann. 2011-64, 2011-41 I.R.B. 503]

Note. Announcement 2011-64 was modified and superseded (see Q 6:62).

Q 6:62   What are the eligibility requirements for the VCSP?

An employer that wishes to participate in the VCSP must meet the following criteria:

- Want to voluntarily reclassify certain workers as employees for federal income tax withholding, Federal Insurance Contribution Act (FICA), and Federal Unemployment Tax Act (FUTA) tax purposes for future periods.

- Have consistently treated the workers as nonemployees.

- Have satisfied any Form 1099 requirements for each of the workers for the preceding three calendar years ending before the Form 8952 was filed. A Temporary Eligibility Expansion (TEE) was made available to employers through June 13, 2013 that allowed an employer to participate in the VCSP even if Form 1099 requirements were not met for the three preceding years. The TEE was not extended beyond its original June 13, 2013 deadline.

- Is not currently under audit by the IRS or by the Department of Labor or a state government agency for the classification of workers. Employers that were audited in the past must have complied with the results of prior examinations.

On December 17, 2012, Announcement 2012-45 was released (superseding Announcement 2011-64) and provides for additional consideration for employers to apply for the VCSP. The VCSP has been modified to: (1) permit a taxpayer under IRS audit, other than an employment tax audit, to be eligible to participate in the VCSP; (2) clarify the current eligibility requirement that a taxpayer that is a member of an affiliated group within the meaning of Section 1504(a) is not eligible to participate in the VCSP if any member of the affiliated group is under employment tax audit; (3) clarify that a taxpayer is not eligible to participate in the VCSP if the taxpayer is contesting in court the classification of the class or classes of workers from a previous audit by the IRS or the Department of Labor; and (4) eliminate the requirement that a taxpayer agree to extend the period of limitations on assessment of employment taxes as part of the VCSP closing agreement with the IRS.

[Ann. 2012-45, 2012-51 I.R.B. 724]

Q 6:63   How may an employer participate in the VCSP?

To participate in the VCSP program, an employer must file Form 8952, Application for Voluntary Classification Settlement Program, at least 60 days before the date the employer wants to treat the workers as employees.

Q 6:64   Are exempt organizations and government entities eligible to participate in VCSP?

Yes, exempt organizations and government entities may participate in VCSP provided that they meet all of the eligibility requirements. However, state and local workers covered under Section 218 agreements are not eligible to participate in the VCSP.

Q 6:65   What information is required on Form 8952?

An employer that intends to file Form 8952 must provide:

a. The total number of all employees of a particular class or classes who will be treated as employees.

b. The beginning date of the employment tax period for which these individuals will be treated as employees.

c. A description of the class or classes for these workers to be reclassified.

In addition, the employer must report the total compensation paid for the entire prior calendar year by employee. The amount that exceeds the applicable FICA limit, $118,500 for 2015 and 2016 and $127,200 for 2017 will be multiplied by 10 percent. That total is the amount that the employer will have to remit to the IRS if the application is accepted. The money should not be submitted with the return.

Q 6:66   What are the conditions for the VCSP agreement?

If the application is accepted, the employer agrees to treat the individuals as employees for future tax periods and:

- Pay 10 percent of the employment tax liability that would have been due on compensation paid to the workers for the most recent tax year, determined under the reduced rates of I.R.C. section 3509(a). See VCSP FAQ 15, for information on how payment under the VCSP is calculated. Also see Instructions to Form 8952;

- Not be liable for any interest and penalties on the amount; and

- Not be subject to an employment tax audit with respect to the worker classification of the workers being reclassified under the VCSP for prior years.

Q 6:67   Have other government agencies impacted by the worker classification issue taken steps to affect compliance?

The Department of Labor (DOL) has entered into a memorandum of understanding (MOU) with the IRS and with 37 states to share information and coordinate law enforcement efforts targeting worker misclassification. The participating states are Alabama, Alaska, Arkansas California, Colorado, Connecticut, Florida, Hawaii, Idaho, Illinois, Iowa, Kentucky, Louisiana, Maryland, Massachusetts, Minnesota, Missouri, Montana, Nebraska, New Hampshire, New Mexico, New York, North Carolina, North Dakota, Oklahoma, Oregon, Pennsylvania, Rhode Island, South Dakota, Tennessee, Texas, Utah, Vermont, Virginia, Washington, Wisconsin, and Wyoming. Under the MOU, the signatories agree to share information and collaborate on enforcement efforts targeting companies that misclassify workers as independent contractors.

Q 6:68   Are states becoming more involved in worker classification issues?

Due to growing concern that worker misclassification impacts both state revenue and benefits that are applicable to employees (but not independent contractors), many states are taking action to define the employee/employer relationship.

In fact, several states currently have such legislation, which impacts employers in those states. In New York, the Construction Industry Fair Play Act presumes certain construction workers are employees unless the worker meets the following three criteria:

1. Performs the job free from control and direction, both under contract and in fact;

2. Performs services outside of the usual course of business for the company; and

3. Engages in an independently established trade, occupation, or business that is similar to the service he or she performs.

In California, the law subjects companies and individuals to penalties of up to $25,000 per violation for misclassification, creates employer liability for fees and deductions imposed on misclassified contractors, and makes consultants and others who advise businesses on independent contractor issues subject to liability. Under the law, "willful misclassification" means avoiding employee status for an individual by voluntarily and knowingly misclassifying that individual as an independent contractor. [Cal. Labor Code §§ 226.8, 2753]

Arizona has enacted legislation, Public Bill 2114, that allows an employer to obtain a signed declaration from the worker of the independent contractor status. Sample language provided in the bill includes statements that the worker:

- Is an independent contractor, not an employee of the company, and, therefore, is not entitled to unemployment or other benefits afforded to employees.
- Is not covered under the company's workers' compensation insurance.
- Is permitted to accept work from other businesses.
- Is responsible for supplying his or her own tools and complying with licensing requirements.
- Is responsible for paying business-related expenses and income taxes.
- Is authorized to determine the days and time the work is performed—but the company may impose quality standards and performance deadlines.

Other states, such as Pennsylvania, have addressed the classification issue through legislation and guidance created for employers to assist them in properly classifying workers. In *Universal Am-Can, Ltd. v. W.C.A.B. (Minteer)* [563 Pa. 480, 762 A.2d 331 (2000)], which revolved around a workers' compensation claim hinging on whether the claimant was an employee, the Supreme Court of Pennsylvania decided that the case should be determined on a fact-based test and on whether the motor company had any influence over the operation of the equipment. The court also addressed that, even though carriers must comply with ICC and PennDOT regulations, that does not determine whether an employment relation exists. In outlining three principles for the employee versus independent contractor debate, the court:

1. Endorsed the common law test of master-servant.
2. Held that compliance with government regulations cannot be used to prove the master-servant relationship.
3. Held that placing the manufacturer's logo on the operator's vehicle does not create a presumption that the master-servant relationship exists.

Tax Court Review

Q 6:69 How does an employer petition the Tax Court to review a worker classification dispute with the IRS?

The Taxpayer Relief Act of 1997 enacted I.R.C. Section 7436 to expand the Tax Court's jurisdiction over employee–independent contractor disputes. In 1998, the IRS also released Notice 98-43, which describes the procedure an employer will follow in petitioning the court for such a review. Under Notice 98-43, an employer can petition the Tax Court for review of an IRS audit reclassification of a group of workers as employees for employment tax purposes. The employer may also ask for review of an IRS disallowance of the relief provision of Section 530 of the Revenue Act of 1978. No review is available for an IRS determination that was previously decided through a private letter ruling.

The notice requires that a business that is entitled to such a petition receive a notice of determination from the IRS following a payroll audit. A notice of determination is generally sent only after the business declines to respond to an IRS "30-day letter." The notice of determination will list the individuals found to be misclassified as independent contractors and will advise the business on how to petition the Tax Court for review. The preliminary calculation of the taxes at issue will be identified on the notice. A special simplified procedure is available when the employment taxes in dispute are $50,000 or less for each quarter involved. As a general matter, any petition request must be mailed by the 91st day following the date the notice of determination was mailed by the IRS. The IRS is then precluded from assessing the taxes attributable to the worker classification or Section 530 issue until the Tax Court's decision is final.

In 2002, IRS issued Notice 2002-5 that modifies and supersedes Notice 98-43 prospectively as well as for cases pending as of August 5, 1997, giving the Tax Court the authority to also determine the amount of the liability. [Notice 2002-5, 2002-1 C.B. 320]

Assistants of Independent Contractors

Q 6:70   Who is responsible for the employment taxes of assistants employed by an independent contractor?

There is no bright-line test for whether a payer of the independent contractor or the independent contractor is responsible for collection and payment of employment taxes for assistants hired by the independent contractor. The following factors should be considered in determining who is the employer of such assistants for employment tax purposes:

1. *Who hired the assistant.* Employment classification may hinge on whether the person who hired the assistant is an employee or an independent contractor under the common-law test. When the individual hiring the assistant is an employee of the employer, the assistant is probably an employee of that same employer. If the hiring party is an independent contractor, the assistant *may be* an employee of the independent contractor.

2. *Industry practice.* Where the industry practice is for the payer that engages the independent contractor to hire assistants and the original payer knew about the hiring of helpers by the independent contractor, the helpers would ordinarily be deemed to be employees of the original payer.

3. *Payment of the assistant.* When the original payer that engaged the independent contractor pays the assistants (or furnishes funds to the independent contractor for the assistants' payment), the assistants will usually be considered employees of the original payer.

Several IRS revenue rulings have analyzed the employee status of helpers and assistants.

- A courier (and vehicle) provided by an unincorporated courier service to a company is an employee of the courier service where the delivery service can recall the operator at any time. [Rev. Rul. 69-348, 1969-1 C.B. 260]

- Physicians hired by the director of a hospital pathology department who are paid out of the director's percentage of the department's income are employees of the director. The director is treated as the employer of the physicians. [Rev. Rul. 72-203, 1972-1 C.B. 324]

- An individual hired to perform some of an executor's official duties in connection with the administration of an estate who is paid out of the executor's account is an employee of the executor. [Rev. Rul. 70-487, 1970-2 C.B. 218]

- Individuals hired by a service company to supply sales clerks to retail stores during peak demand periods are treated as employees of the service company when the service company trains the clerks and supplies its own supervisors to ensure that the clerks conform to the stores' rules. [Rev. Rul. 70-630, 1970-2 C.B. 229]

- Supervisory personnel hired by a contractor to construct a project for the U.S. Navy who approved their hiring but did not direct their work, were employees of the contractors. [Rev. Rul. 71-356, 1971-2 C.B. 350]

- Individuals hired by a contractor that contracts to provide manufactured articles for jobbers are employees of the contractor when the contractor furnishes the machines and tools and directs the work. [Rev. Rul. 70-417, 1970-2 C.B. 207]

- Waiters and chefs hired by a catering service for specific engagements are employees of the catering service when the catering service requires the workers to appear on time, to serve properly, and to safeguard the catering service's equipment. [Rev. Rul. 69-624, 1969-2 C.B. 187]

- Workers hired by a real estate management company as agents of a building owner and paid out of funds from a separate bank account in the building owner's name are employees of the building owner. [Rev. Rul. 70-267, 1970-1 C.B. 205]

- Helpers hired by the drivers of a freight carrier to load or unload shipments who are paid in cash are employees of the carrier for all employment tax purposes (i.e., federal income tax withholding and FICA and FUTA taxes). [Rev. Rul. 55-543, 1955-2 C.B. 400]

- Assistants hired by a mail carrier under contract with the U.S. Postal Service (USPS) are employees of the contract carrier and not the USPS. [Rev. Rul. 69-362, 1969-1 C.B. 254]

Temporary Workers

Q 6:71   How are temporary work employees treated for federal employment tax purposes?

The term *temporary work employees* generally applies to temporary workers who are supplied under a contract with a temporary employment agency. The primary liability for withholding of federal income taxes and withholding and payment of federal employment taxes for such employees resides with the agency. If, however, the temporary employment agency fails to make those payments—it goes out of business—the liability for the taxes resides with the entity for whom the temporary worker provided the services. [I.R.C. § 3401(a)(1)]

Q 6:72   Can the employer avoid treating workers as employees for pension purposes by transferring the workers to a temporary agency?

Probably not. In a key court case involving the pension participation status of temporary workers, freelancers reclassified as employees and then transferred to temporary employment agencies retained their common-law treatment after the transfer. This treatment applies for purposes of establishing eligibility and benefit accruals under an employee stock purchase plan. This employee lawsuit arose following an IRS payroll audit that led to a reclassification of the independent contractors as employees and a requirement under Section 530 of the Revenue Act of 1978 that the employer recognize the workers' status for employment tax purposes. [Vizcaino v. Microsoft Corp., No. C93-178D (Wash. 1998)]

Benefit Plans

Q 6:73   How does the status of a worker affect eligibility for an employer's qualified retirement plan?

The status of an individual as an employee or an independent contractor will be important to an employer in terms of ensuring that its qualified employee pension or profit sharing plan complies with strict regulatory requirements. For example, the IRS requires that qualified pension plans be established and maintained for the exclusive benefit of employees. [I.R.C. § 401(a)] Thus, an independent contractor may not participate in the qualified plan of the person for whom services are performed. It follows that employers may not take deductions for contributions to qualified retirement plans with respect to independent contractors. The Employee Retirement Income Security Act of 1974 (ERISA) provides numerous protections relating to retirement plans established by an employer. These protections are generally not available to independent contractors who establish a Keogh retirement plan.

Note. Under certain circumstances, an employer and an independent contractor may cosponsor a qualified retirement plan, thereby permitting participation by the independent contractor. [I.R.C. § 413(c)] Such a plan is a multiple-employer plan and is not common because of the complexity of the applicable regulations.

Another requirement of both ERISA and the I.R.C. for employer-sponsored retirement plans is minimum coverage. That requirement is met only when an employer demonstrates that the retirement benefits provided to various classes of employees meet certain mathematical tests, based on worker coverage. All employees of the employer are included in such testing. Excluding independent contractors who are in fact employees may cause a plan to fail to satisfy those minimum coverage tests. As well, some independent contractors who have been reclassified as employees might be able to persuade a court that they were entitled to benefits provided to the employer's common-law employees. [Vizcaino v. Microsoft, 97 F.3d 1187 (9th Cir. 1996)] Some employers are attempting to address the *Microsoft* case by including language in contracts with independent contractors that even if they are later reclassified by IRS as employees, they would not be entitled to participate in any benefit plans. However, the minimum coverage tests also generally require that leased employees be covered by either the employer's plan or a similar plan. [I.R.C. §§ 401(a)(4), 410(b), 414(m), 414(n), 414(o)]

Q 6:74   Can an employer's 403(b) plan be made available to an independent contractor?

No. Participation in a Section 403(b) arrangement is limited to certain categories of religious, charitable, scientific, educational, or like employers for their *employees*. Thus, independent contractors who themselves do not qualify as employers eligible to establish a 403(b) plan are ineligible for such benefits. [Rev. Rul. 66-274, 1966-2 C.B. 446; Azad v. United States, 388 F.2d 74 (8th Cir. 1968)]

Q 6:75   How does the status of a worker affect an employer's nonqualified retirement plan?

The law permits an independent contractor (or an employee) to be included in an employer's nonqualified retirement plan when the individual constitutes management or is a highly compensated employee. A deduction may be taken by the employer for certain contributions to or benefit payments from a nonqualified deferred compensation plan for the year that the independent contractor recognizes the contributions or benefits as income for federal income tax purposes. Payments from the nonqualified deferred compensation plan to the independent contractor are not subject to FICA taxes. [I.R.C. § 404(d)]

Q 6:76   Are the courts applying a uniform set of rules to worker classification for retirement plan coverage?

No. In *Ware v. United States* [67 F.3d 574 (6th Cir. 1995)], the Sixth Circuit, upholding a district court's determination that an individual was an independent contractor, stated in dicta that the application of the 20-factor test for classifying workers might differ depending on the context. As an example, the court stated that "control and supervision" may be less important in analyzing the classification of a worker for employee benefit plan purposes. Private Letter Ruling 9546018 [(Aug. 18, 1995)], however, appeared to take the position that employment classification applied for all purposes. In that ruling, which is being reconsidered, the IRS took the unusual step of allowing an employer to rescind participation in a company's retirement plan for workers who were incorrectly classified as employees. In *Vizcaino v. Microsoft* [97 F.3d 1187 (9th Cir. 1997)], independent contractors were successful in demonstrating to one court that the wording in the employer's plan document did not exclude them from coverage in a stock bonus plan when they were reclassified as employees for payroll tax purposes.

Q 6:77   How does the status of a worker affect an employer's fringe benefit plans?

For the most part, tax-free elements of an employer's fringe benefit package are available only to workers classified as employees. Those benefits may include certain insurance coverage, including workers' compensation insurance to cover injury incurred on the job; liability insurance for accidents an employee may cause while on the job; and medical, dental, and disability insurance for employees. Cafeteria plans and tax-free group-term life insurance (up to $50,000) coverage can be made available only to employees. [I.R.C. §§ 79, 125]

The tax consequences of medical and dental insurance payments when the employer pays the premiums differ drastically for employees and independent contractors. For employees, medical benefits paid pursuant to such a plan are tax free; for an independent contractor, such coverage would be taxable to the extent that the worker did not pay the premiums (see Table 6-2). [I.R.C. § 105(g)]

In many states, coverage of an independent contractor under the employer's health care plan causes the plan to be treated as a multiple employer welfare arrangement (MEWA), which is subject to stringent regulations. The Patient Protection and Affordable Care Act (ACA) strengthened enforcement action by giving the Secretary of Labor authority to issue cease and desist orders. An unregistered and illegal MEWA can result in criminal and civil penalties to the sponsor. Those penalties can be extreme when the health care coverage for the independent contractor is from a self-insured plan (i.e., one not fully insured) that is not registered as a MEWA.

Table 6-2. Tax-Favored Benefits Available to Employees and Independent Contractors

Tax-Favored Benefits	To Employee in Employer's Plan	_Availability_ To Independent Contractor in Client's Plan	To Independent Contractor in Own Plan (Unincorporated)
Employee achievement awards[a]	Available		
Group-term life insurance[b]	Available		
Accident and health insurance[c]	Available	Limited exclusion only	Limited, unless incorporated
Tuition assistance[d]	Available		
Meals and lodging[e]	Available		Limited
Group legal services[f]	Available	Available	
Cafeteria plans[g]	Available		
Educational assistance[h]	Available		Available
Dependent care assistance[i]	Available		Available
No-additional-cost fringes[j]	Available		Available
Qualified employee discounts[k]	Available		Available
Working condition fringes[l]	Available	Available	Available
De minimis fringes[m]	Available	Available	Available
Qualified transportation fringes[n]	Available		
On-premises athletic facilities[o]	Available		Available
New-product testing[p]	Available		
Qualified pensions and annuities[q]	Available		Available
Tax-sheltered annuities[r]	Available		
Qualified incentive stock options[s]	Available		

Table 6-2. Tax-Favored Benefits Available to Employees and Independent Contractors (*cont'd*)

		Availability	
Tax-Favored Benefits	*To Employee in Employer's Plan*	*To Independent Contractor in Client's Plan*	*To Independent Contractor in Own Plan (Unincorporated)*
Employee stock purchase plans[t]	Available		
VEBAs[u]	Available		
Nonqualified deferred compensation[v]	Available	Available in limited cases	Generally not available to an unincorporated employer

Notes:

[a] I.R.C. §§ 74(c), 274(j)(3)(B).

[b] I.R.C. § 79(d); Treas. Reg. § 1.79-0(b).

[c] I.R.C. §§ 105(g), 106, 162(l)(1); Treas. Reg. § 1.105-1(a). Coverage and discrimination requirements might apply if the plan is self-funded. I.R.C. § 105(h). Coverage of an independent contractor under his or her client's plan is possible if the coverage is treated as a working condition fringe to the extent of the deduction under I.R.C. Section 162.

[d] I.R.C. § 117(d)(2)(A).

[e] I.R.C. § 119.

[f] I.R.C. §§ 120(c)(1), 120(c)(2), 120(d)(1).

[g] I.R.C. §§ 125(b)(1), 125(d)(1)(A); Prop. Treas. Reg. § 1.125-1, Q&A-4.

[h] I.R.C. §§ 127(b)(2), 127(c)(2); Treas. Reg. § 1.127-2(h)(1)(iii).

[i] I.R.C. §§ 129(d)(2), 129(d)(3), 129(d)(8), 129(e)(3).

[j] I.R.C. §§ 132(b), 132(j)(1); Treas. Reg. § 1.132-1(b)(1).

[k] I.R.C. §§ 132(c), 132(j)(1); Treas. Reg. § 1.132-1(b)(1).

[l] I.R.C. § 132(d); Treas. Reg. § 1.132-1(b)(2).

[m] I.R.C. § 132(e); Treas. Reg. § 1.132-1(b)(4). Certain nondiscrimination rules apply to eating facilities, however.

(n) I.R.C. § 132(f).

(o) I.R.C. § 132(j)(4); Treas. Reg. §§ 1.132-1(b)(1), 1.132-1(b)(3).

(p) Treas. Reg. §§ 1.132-1(b)(2) (flush language), 1.132-5(n).

(q) I.R.C. §§ 401(a)(4), 401(c), 410(b); Treas. Reg. §§ 1.172-17(a), 1.401-0(b).

(r) I.R.C. § 403(b); Treas. Reg. § 1.403(b)-1(a)(1).

(s) I.R.C. §§ 421, 422; Treas. Reg. § 1.421-7(h).

(t) I.R.C. § 423; Treas. Reg. § 1.423-2(e)(2).

(u) I.R.C. § 501(c)(9); Treas. Reg. § 1.501(c)(9)-2(b).

(v) I.R.C. § 404(d).

Professional Employer Organizations

Q 6:78   What is a leased employee?

A *leased employee* is an employee of one employer, called an employee leasing company or a professional employer organization (PEO), whose services are leased to another employer, the recipient or worksite client. The employee leasing company or PEO typically enters into contracts with the worksite client to provide workers, and a fee is paid for each individual furnished. The employee leasing company or PEO often has the right to control and direct the worker's services for the recipient, including the right to discharge or reassign the worker. In reality, however, the work of the leased employee is usually under the supervision of the worksite client.

With respect to PEOs, most arrangements involve them hiring (or "co-employing") the existing employees at the worksite client's location when the contracted arrangement starts. A PEO may hire new workers (who are generally selected by the worksite client), control the payment of their wages, provide unemployment insurance and other benefits, and become the employer for employment tax purposes. Although the PEO typically retains the rights to hire and fire in its contract with the worksite employer, in practice those rights are generally never exercised.

The PEO is required to withhold federal income taxes and FICA and FUTA taxes for leased employees that it employs at a client's worksite. If, however, the PEO does not make those payments (e.g., it goes out of business), the worksite client is fully liable for the taxes. [I.R.C. § 3401(d)(1); Treas. Reg. § 31.3401(d)-1(b); General Motors Corp. v. United States, No. 89-CV-73046-DT (E.D. Mich. 1990)]

Note. For state unemployment insurance (SUI) purposes, some states do not recognize the PEO as the employer, and instead require that the PEO report wages and pay state unemployment taxes under the individual account number of the client employer. Employers should carefully review state law in this regard, as some states can take adverse action against employers that fail to separately report and pay SUI taxes on the compensation paid by their PEO.

Q 6:79 Why do employers use employee leasing companies?

Employers engage the services of an employee leasing company for three basic reasons: (1) to lower costs of payroll processing and workers' compensation insurance, (2) to gain access to broader benefit administration services, and (3) to better manage their human resource obligations. In general, the employee leasing company can provide welfare and retirement plan services at lower costs. In addition, the technical and professional expertise of the employee leasing company is better suited to comply with federal and state employment regulations.

At one time, employers considered leasing as a means to deny a worker access to benefits. With the passage of I.R.C. Sections 414(m), (n), and (o), that practice is not generally possible.

Q 6:80 Are leased employees the employees of the PEO or the recipient client?

There is no definitive answer to that question. That uncertainty is attributable largely to the application of I.R.C. Section 3401(d)(1), the "control of the payment" exception. Section 3401(d)(1) provides that if one entity qualifies as the common-law employer with respect to a worker but a separate entity has control of the payment of wages to the worker, the employer for federal employment tax purposes is the entity with control over the payment of wages. That payer may not necessarily be the common-law employer. In addition, the application of Section 3401(d)(1) to classify the PEO as the employer does not apply to other areas of the law that rely on the common-law definition of *employer,* such as the pension laws under I.R.C. Section 401(a), or to other federal laws (e.g., Fair Labor Standards Act and ERISA).

The leasing firm could nonetheless qualify as the "employer" for federal employment tax purposes, so long as it has control of the payment of wages to the worker. That determination will depend on the contractual relationship between the recipient client and the PEO. The initial assumption might be that the PEO qualifies as having control of the payment of wages to a worker. In practice, however, that is seldom the case. In most reported court decisions that have considered the issue, the leasing firm has been held *not* to have control of the payment of wages to a leased worker. Instead, they were seen as reimbursements of client expenses.

The courts generally demand much more than that the PEO operate merely as a payroll service for a client company. Significant factors that weigh in favor of a leasing firm having control over the payment of wages include (1) the leasing firm being obligated to pay wages to the worker even if it does not receive its fees from the client company and (2) the fee paid by the client company not specifically itemized to show how much of the fee is actually paid by the leasing firm to cover workers' wages.

A leading case in which a leasing firm structured its arrangement with the leased workers so that the leasing firm had control of the payment of wages is *General Motors Corp. v. United States*. [No. 89-CV-73046-DT (E.D. Mich. 1990)] By contrast, cases in which a leasing firm was held *not* to have control of the payment of wages include *In re Professional Security Services, Inc.* [94-1 U.S. Tax Cas. (CCH) 50,148 (Bankr. M.D. Fla. 1993)], and *In re Earthmovers, Inc.* [96-2 U.S. Tax Cas. (CCH) 50,549 (Bankr. M.D. Fla. 1996)].

Q 6:81   What is a CPEO?

The Tax Increase Prevention Act of 2014, enacted on December 19, 2014, required the IRS to set up a certification program for Professional Service Organizations. New I.R.C. Sections 3511, responsibilities for employment tax and reporting, and 7705, defining a CPEO, were added to outline the requirements for PEOs to be certified and maintain their certification. Under I.R.C. 7705, the CPEO is the employer for the purposes of employment taxes, provided there is a contract between the CPEO and the client for wages and other compensation paid by the CPEO. The establishment of the CPEO will better define the relationship and responsibilities between the CPEO and the client.

Q 6:82   What are the requirements to become a CPEO?

To become a CPEO, the PEO must meet the following requirements:

1. Must be a business entity;
2. Have at least one location in the United States;
3. Should have a history of federal, state, and local tax compliance, financial responsibility, and organizational integrity;
4. Should be managed by individuals (a majority of whom are U.S. citizens or residents) who have knowledge or experience regarding federal and state employment tax compliance and business practice relation to these compliance requirements.

Additional information is available at irs.gov; enter CPEO in search. The application for certification as a CPEO requires an application fee of $1,000 and the applicant must:

1. Meet established guidelines of the Secretary related to tax status, background, experience, business, location, and annual financial audits;
2. Secure bond and independent financial review;

3. Meet reporting requirements, including use of the accrual method of accounting.

The application process includes (a) an Individual Identity Verification, (b) Responsible Individual Personal Attestation, and (c) CPEO application.

[REG-127561-15 2016-21 I.R.B.]

Q 6:83   Are there ongoing requirements to maintain CPEO status?

Yes. There is an annual certification that requires the CPEOs to ensure that they have maintained the initial requirements of submitting audited financial statements, maintaining bond, submitting to a background and tax compliance check, and rendering payment of the annual fee of $1,000.

Q 6:84   To which entity—the leasing company or the client/employer—does the 50 percent deduction disallowance apply when a leased employee's meal and entertainment expenses are reimbursed?

Under Section 274 of the I.R.C., a taxpayer's business meal and entertainment deductions are limited to 50 percent of the substantiated cost. This deduction disallowance applies to employers, when employees are reimbursed for their business expenses. The IRS has concluded that when leased employees incur business expenses and are reimbursed, the deduction disallowance applies either to the person who makes the expenditure or to the person who actually bears the expense, but not both. For example, if a leasing agreement states that the client employer is responsible to cover leased employees' expenses, the deduction disallowance will apply to the client employer because the client employer is the person who bears the expense. [Treas. Reg. § 1.274-2(f)(2)(iv)(D)(1)]

Q 6:85   What are the IRS's audit activities in the employee leasing field?

The IRS and the Treasury Department have warned taxpayers that they will be examining certain offshore deferred compensation arrangements involving domestic and foreign employee leasing companies. Under such a typical arrangement, an employee (such as a doctor) would resign from the current employer or professional corporation and sign an employment contract with an offshore employee leasing company, which would lease the former employee's services back to the original employer using one or more intermediaries. These arrangements resulted in the avoidance and evasion of employment taxes as well as individual and corporate income taxes. [I.R.S. News Release IR-2003-45 (Apr. 4, 2003); Notice 2003-22, 2003-18 I.R.B. 851]

Q 6:86   How does the U.S. Department of Labor determine whether a worker is an employee or an independent contractor?

In its attempt to ensure that employers cannot circumvent the minimum wage and overtime requirements of the law, the Fair Labor Standards Act has a much broader view of the employee definition that, upon application, can include more workers than might otherwise be included for IRS purposes. The U.S. Supreme Court held that the following five factors are significant in determining if a worker is an independent contractor or an employee and refers to this as the economic realities test:

1. The extent to which the services are an integral part of the employer's business;

2. The permanency of the work relationship;

3. The amount of an alleged contractor's investment in facilities and equipment;

4. The nature and degree of control by the business using the worker's services; and

5. The amount of initiative, judgment, or foresight used in open-market competition with others that is required for the success of the claimed independent enterprise. [Rutherford Food Corp. v. McComb, 331 U.S. 722 (1947); affirming position in Atlantic Coast Masonry v. Commissioner, TC Memo 2012-283, 104 T.C.M. 189 (Aug. 13, 2012)]

The U.S. Department of Labor relies on the following six factors in determining the classification of a worker:

1. The extent to which the services are integral to the employer's business;

2. The permanency of the work relationship;

3. The amount of the alleged contractor's investment in facilities and equipment;

4. The nature and degree of control by the principal;

5. The alleged contractor's opportunities for profit and loss; and

6. The amount of initiative, judgment, and foresight in open-market competition with others required for the success of the claimed independent enterprise. [WH Publication 1297, Employment Relationship Under the Fair Labor Standards Act]

President Obama directed the Department of Labor to diligently pursue employers in the area of worker misclassification. Workers have brought a variety of situations to the attention of the DOL regarding having to sign contracts, incorporate as a business, and otherwise have the same work responsibilities as employees without the benefits. New classification of workers as contingent, franchisee, contract, low-road outsourcing, and many more will be a challenge for both the IRS and the DOL to determine what satisfies the definition of *employee* under the IRS regulations, FLSA, FMLA, and others.

Chapter 7

Garnishment and Other Deductions

One of the more complex regulatory areas of payroll administration is the processing of voluntary and involuntary payroll deductions. Federal and state laws mesh to produce a complicated set of rules that must be followed before a portion of the employee's pay can be diverted to another party. For example, federal and state laws regulate the maximum amount of an employee's wages that may be garnished by a court order to pay an employee's creditor. Federal and state laws also restrict an employer from terminating employees solely because they are the subject of garnishments. Adding to the complexity of processing a garnishment is the possibility that the court order may not comply with federal and state laws, or there may be a conflict between federal and state law, forcing tough legal decisions by the employer. In such a situation, the employer may need to respond to the court, agency or attorney before processing the order.

This chapter addresses the federal laws that control garnishments and provides a brief overview of state laws that apply.

Overview of Federal Garnishment Law

Q 7:1   What is a garnishment?

A *garnishment*, sometimes referred to as a *levy or wage attachment*, is an involuntary order to withhold and pay a portion of an employee's wages to satisfy creditor, nontax federal and state debts, and support obligations. A garnishment may arise from a support order, general creditor debts, delinquent student loans, overpayments of state or federal benefits, or criminal restitution. Debts are collected through a garnishment that is either issued in a court of law (judicial law) or by a state or federal agency that has been granted the right to collect debt by state or federal law (administrative garnishment). [15 U.S.C. § 1671] Federal law provides the maximum percentage that may be garnished for ordinary garnishment, and for support. State laws can provide the same or greater protections to earnings. The federal Consumer Credit Protection Act (CCPA) excludes voluntary wage assignments, bankruptcy, and tax levies from earnings protections provided for in the CCPA. Federal and state laws provide requirements for tax levies. The Federal Trade Commission provides guidance regarding voluntary wage assignments, and state laws generally provide direction. The United States Bankruptcy Code (title 11, United States Code) provides regulations for discontinuing and or withholding for debts when an individual files for bankruptcy. In many instances, an employer may not make deductions from an employee's pay unless the deduction meets certain requirements. For example, New York State once prevented employers from making deductions from an employee's pay for an overpayment; however, a recent amendment allows employers to recapture overpayments for clerical or mathematical errors with the written consent of the employee. [Labor Law Section 193; Op. Ltr. No. RO-09-0152, N.Y. State Dep't of Labor (Jan. 21, 2010)]

Q 7:2   What is the Federal Garnishment Law?

The Federal Garnishment Law (Title III of the Consumer Credit Protection Act (CCPA)) protects the consumer from unfair or harsh collection practices. Title III of the CCPA limits the amount of an employee's wages that may be withheld for payment of ordinary garnishments such as creditor debts, student loans, or federal and state non-tax debts. The CCPA also places restrictions on the amount that can be withheld from wages for family support, and it protects an employee from being discharged due to a single debt within a 12-month period. The Federal Garnishment Law defines the following:

- Earnings
- Deductions required by law
- Disposable earnings
- Amount of disposable earnings that must be reached to allow withholding for an ordinary garnishment
- Withholding limits for ordinary garnishment and support

All ordinary wage garnishments and support are subject to the provisions of the CCPA. In addition, garnishments for child support payments, student loans, and nonfederal tax debts are also subject to special rules under other federal laws. The provisions of the CCPA are enforced by the U.S. Department of Labor, Wage and Hour Division. [CCPA §§ 301–307; 29 C.F.R. pt. 870]

Bona fide tips, except amounts used to satisfy minimum wage (tip credit), are not considered earnings for purposes of the wage garnishment law. A bona fide tip is paid directly to the employee by a customer, including gratuities transferred free and clear to an employee at the direction of credit customers who add tips to the bill. Tips are considered to be a gift to the person providing the service. Service charges or forced gratuities that are added to the bill by employers are not considered bona fide tips and are included in "earnings" for purposes of garnishment. [U.S. Dep't of Labor, Field Operations Handbook; Fact Sheet #30]

The CCPA does not protect wages for persons whose wages are garnished for federal, state, or local tax levies; bankruptcy; or voluntary wage assignments. Restrictions on those involuntary deductions may be found under applicable federal or state law.

For limits on the amounts that can be garnished, see Q 7:10.

Q 7:3   Do federal garnishment laws override state laws?

As in other areas regulated by both federal and state law, states may impose additional restrictions or place a lower limit on the maximum wage garnishment. Then, state law will generally control. The federal wage garnishment law establishes minimum standards for state garnishment laws. The law that is more generous to the employee, in this case the one that would withhold less money, generally prevails. [CCPA § 307, 15 U.S.C. § 1677]

Q 7:4   What other federal laws apply to garnishments?

In addition to the CCPA, portions of the Child Support Enforcement Amendments of 1984, Personal Responsibility and Work Opportunity Reconciliation Act of 1996 (PRWORA) and the Uniform Interstate Family Support Act of 2008, apply to family support garnishments. The Higher Education Act, as amended in 1991, permits administrative garnishment for student loans. The Federal Debt Collection Improvement Act of 1996 allows administrative wage garnishment (AWG) for all federal nontax debt. In addition, the Internal Revenue Code (I.R.C.) imposes the requirements for tax levies that result in a garnishment of wages. Similar tax levy and other civil garnishment proceedings apply at the state and local level.

Q 7:5   What types of garnishments are subject to the Federal Garnishment Law that is a part of the CCPA?

The Federal Garnishment Law under CCPA applies to the following types of garnishments:

1. Support payments, both current and arrears (more than 12 weeks old), for alimony, children, and cash medical support or the cost of health premiums to cover the child(ren);
2. Creditor debt;
3. Student loan defaults;
4. Federal administrative wage deductions (nontax debts); and
5. State nontax garnishments.

CCPA does *not* regulate deductions related to the following:

1. Federal tax levies (these are regulated by the I.R.C. and Treasury regulations);
2. State and local tax levies; and
3. Bankruptcy orders under the Bankruptcy Act.

Garnishments that are not governed by CCPA may be subject to state and local laws and regulations.

Q 7:6   Do other federal laws impose any restrictions on the amount of garnishments that may be imposed on an employee?

Yes. In addition to the limits imposed by the CCPA, separate federal laws limit the application of certain types of garnishments (e.g., tax levies, student loans, and federal nontax debts). For example:

- Federal law exempts from tax levies a pay period portion (daily, weekly, biweekly, semi-monthly, or monthly) net pay. The exemption is based on the employee's tax filing status, one allowance for himself or herself, and the names and relationship to the debtor of individuals the debtor claims as exemptions. The exempt amount is subtracted from the employee's net pay and the amount that remains must be sent to the Internal Revenue Service (IRS) until the levy is satisfied and released. [I.R.C. § 6332(a); Pub. No. 1494, Table for Figuring Amount Exempt from Levy on Wages, Salary, and Other Income]

- Garnishments for payment of a delinquent guaranteed student loan issued under provisions of the Higher Education Act cannot exceed more than 15 percent (an aggregate of 25 percent when there are multiple debts) of the employee's disposable income when issued by a state guarantee agency.

- Garnishments for federal nontax debts, including delinquent student loans issued by the U.S. Department of Education (DOE) [20 U.S.C. § 1095a] that are issued under provisions of the Debt Collection Improvement Act of 1996 (DCIA), cannot, exceed more than 15 percent of the employee's disposable earnings (an aggregate of 25 percent when there are multiple debts) when issued by a federal agency or collection partner. All deductions for the employees' health insurance must be subtracted before calculating disposable earnings.

Involuntary deductions that are the subject of a bankruptcy filing are not subject to any limitation on the amount of disposable earnings that may be paid to satisfy a court order. Bankruptcy orders issued under the Bankruptcy Act take priority over any other garnishments with the exception of support.

Q 7:7   How does the CCPA address an employer's ability to discharge an employee who has been served with a garnishment?

The CCPA prohibits an employer from discharging an employee because he or she is the subject of a garnishment because of a single indebtedness (see Q 7:8). The protection against discharge applies to tax levies and bankruptcy. Employers violating this provision are subject to criminal penalties. These penalties include a fine of $1,000, imprisonment of up to one year, or both. [15 U.S.C. § 1674(b)]

Other federal laws extend this prohibition to multiple orders relating to family support orders, student loans, and other federal administrative wage garnishments. States may raise the single indebtedness threshold and prohibit an employer from discharging an employee after two or more wage garnishments. [Wage & Hour Op. Ltr. No.WH-31 (Apr. 28, 1970); Wage & Hour Op. Ltr. No.WH-38 (June 5, 1970); Wage & Hour Op. Ltr. No. WH-57 (July 21, 1970)]

Q 7:8   What is meant by a "single indebtedness"?

The term *single indebtedness* refers to one specific debt owed regardless of the number of orders that are issued to collect the same debt. For example, a number of states limit the time period in which wages may be garnished. If the debt is not paid in full during that time, a second garnishment must be issued to collect remaining amounts. The number of orders is immaterial when subsequent garnishments are issued to collect the same debt. The Wage and Hour Division has held that multiple garnishment proceedings over the same debt are also a single debt. Note that when an employee is served with multiple garnishments and the employee obtains a release from all but one garnishment, termination is also prohibited. Earnings are only treated as garnished when a payment is actually withheld from employees' wages.

The Wage and Hour Administrator has also stated that when an employee changes jobs, the employee is given a fresh start. This means that a prior garnishment is ignored. A fresh start is always given when 12 months have elapsed since the last wage garnishment. [Wage & Hour Op. Ltr. No.WH-38 (June 5, 1970); Donovan v. Southern Cal. Gas Co., 715 F.2d 1405 (9th Cir. 1983); Wage & Hour Op. Ltr. No.WH-15 (June 12, 1969); Wage & Hour Op. Ltr. No. WH-116 (Jan. 19, 1971)]

Q 7:9   Are all employees subject to garnishments?

Generally, yes. However, certain employees of government entities (federal, state, and local government) may be exempt from garnishments under the principle of "sovereign immunity." This principle generally prohibits an individual employed by a government entity from being served with a court order or being sued. Most states have enacted laws that affect garnishments of government workers. These employees are always subject to child support orders, student loans, and other federal administrative wage garnishment. They are generally subject to ordinary garnishment for personal debt.

Federal employees are generally subject to garnishments in the same manner as other employees. The Hatch Act Reform Amendments of 1993 included provisions allowing the wages of federal employees to be garnished for the same purposes as other individuals. The garnishment of a federal employee's wages is subject to the provisions of Section 303 of the CCPA, in the same manner and to the same extent as if the agency were a private person.

Postal employees are subject to garnishments following the U.S. Postal Service's reorganization into an independent agency. Some states permit the garnishment of a state employee's wages; however, the state laws may place conditions on the types of garnishments allowed as well as specify exceptions for employees who might be subject to harassment because of their public position (e.g., elected officials and clerks of the court). [42 U.S.C. § 659; Wage & Hour Op. Ltr. No. WH-58 (July 22, 1970)]

Q 7:10   What is the federal limit on the amount of pay that may be garnished?

In the case of a garnishment for child support, the CCPA limits the maximum amount that may be withheld from an employee's earnings to:

1. 50 percent of the employee's "disposable earnings" if the employee is supporting another spouse and/or children; or

2. 60 percent of the employee's "disposable earnings" if the employee is not supporting another spouse and/or children.

When the employee is more than 12 weeks in arrears in support payments, these amounts increase to 55 percent and 65 percent, respectively. Note that state laws may impose a lower percentage. [CCPA § 303(b), 15 U.S.C. § 1673(b); 29 C.F.R. § 870.11(b)]

General creditor garnishments are limited under CCPA to the lesser of 25 percent of disposable earnings or the amount of the employee's disposable earnings that exceeds 30 times the federal minimum wage, whichever is less. [CCPA § 303(a); 29 C.F.R. § 870.10(a)] No deduction can be taken if disposable earnings are less than 30 times federal minimum wage.

Delinquent student loans are limited to 15 percent under the Higher Education Act (HEA), with an aggregated limit of 25 percent under the HEA, following federal CCPA. No deduction can be taken if disposable earnings are less than 30 times federal minimum wage. A federal Administrative Wage Garnishment (AWG) under the Debt Collection Improvement Act of 1996 is limited to

15 percent, with an aggregated limit of 25 percent. No deduction can be taken if disposable earnings are less than 30 times federal minimum wage.

A federal tax levy is also subject to certain limits based on "take-home" pay. These are discussed in Q 7:66. [I.R.C. § 6331]

Q 7:11 What is meant by "disposable earnings" for CCPA purposes?

An employee's disposable earnings for purposes of determining limits on garnishments under the CCPA are equal to the employee's pay period earnings less "deductions required by law." [CCPA § 302, 15 U.S.C. § 1672]

The Department of Labor, in Fact Sheet 30 issued in November 2016, defines *earnings* as **compensation for personal services**, which includes wages, salaries, commissions, bonuses, or other compensation, including periodic payments from a pension or retirement program, or payments from an employment-based disability payment program. Earnings may include payments received in lump sums. For employees who receive tips, the cash wages paid directly by the employer and the amount of the tip credit claimed, if any, by the employer are earnings for the purposes of the wage garnishment law. Tips received in excess of the tip credit amount or in excess of the wages paid directly by the employer (if no tip credit is claimed or allowed) are not earnings for purposes of the CCPA.

[Fact Sheet 30 revised Nov. 2016; Wage & Hour Op. Ltr. No. WH-95 (Dec. 15, 1970); FOH 16a04, 16a05]

Disposable earnings are remaining earnings after deductions mandated by state and federal laws such as withholding for federal and state income taxes, Social Security and Medicare, and state disability and unemployment taxes. Deductions from gross income must also include required employee contributions to a retirement system mandated by state law or under the Railroad Retirement Act. State law generally controls treatment of these deductions. For purposes of determining the amount of federal income tax withholding to be credited as a deduction, the employer applies the number of withholding exemptions *claimed* by the employee on his or her W-4, and not the number to which the employee might be entitled.

Under the CCPA, the calculation of disposable earnings does not include deductions for the following: union dues and initiation fees (not required as a condition of employment); employee contributions to health and welfare insurance premiums (this applies to private and public sector employees); repayments of credit union loans; I.R.C. Section 401(k) contributions; and cafeteria plan contributions. Wage assignments, child support, bankruptcy orders, and tax levies do not reduce disposable earnings. However, the amount deducted for any garnishment with priority must be subtracted from the allowable disposable earnings for garnishments with lesser priority to determine how much, if any, can be deducted for the garnishment with lesser priority. For example, if the employee has both a student loan garnishment and a creditor garnishment, the garnishment which is served first has priority. If the employee has disposable earnings of $400, an aggregate amount of $100 is available for ordinary garnishment. In this case, the student loan of 15 percent was served first, then followed by a creditor garnishment for 25 percent. The employer would deduct $60 for the student loan and then only be able to deduct $40 for the creditor garnishment.

Various opinion letters by the Wage and Hour Division have clarified the following:

- Sick pay and vacation pay are treated as earnings.
- Cash tips paid directly to a service employee are not included in earnings; however, tips identified as a tip credit towards minimum wage are considered earnings. Mandatory tips controlled by the employer or service charges imposed by the employer and then distributed to the employee are also considered earnings. [Wage & Hour Op. Ltr. No. WH-95 (Dec. 15, 1970); Wage & Hour Op. Ltr. No. WH-97 (Feb. 1, 1973)]

When complying with a garnishment order for an employee, employers must be sensitive to any changes in an employee's earnings. Disposable earnings must be recalculated every pay period. Even a slight change to pay, such as the absence or addition of a shift premium payment or a change in tax withholding due to a change in a pretax deduction, impacts the amount that can be deducted for a garnishment based on a percentage of disposable earnings. It could even reduce the amount that can be deducted for support.

Table 7-1 provides an example of a disposable pay calculation. (Note that the exemption from tax levies is determined on the basis of take-home pay. See Q 7:66.)

Table 7-1.   Computing Disposable Pay Under the CCPA

	Pay Before Garnishment	Disposable Pay Calculation
Gross biweekly wages	$1,400.00	$1,400.00
Less:		
Federal income tax withholding	143.14	143.14
State income tax withholding	42.00	42.00
Social Security	81.72	81.72
Medicare	19.11	19.11
Section 401(k) 4%	56.00	N/A
Credit union payment for auto loan*	80.00	N/A
Medical premium pre tax*	40.00	N/A
Net pay	$938.03	
Disposable earnings*		$1114.03

* These payments are made through a voluntary assignment of the employee's wages for payment of a debt, but are currently subject to garnishment and are not treated as a deduction to disposable income.

Q 7:12   **How is the 30 times federal minimum wage limit adjusted for nonweekly pay?**

The federal garnishment limit for general creditor claims that is set at 30 times the federal minimum wage (currently $7.25 an hour) is based on the workweek as defined under the Fair Labor Standards Act (FLSA). That is, a workweek consists of a fixed and regularly recurring period of 168 hours, consisting of seven consecutive 24-hour periods. To determine the equivalent limit for pay made at different intervals, such as biweekly, semimonthly, etc., multiply the weekly amount (30 × $7.25), or $217.50 times 52 and divide by the number of payrolls paid in the calendar year.

Note. A person paid on a daily basis must be protected by the weekly exemption.

An example of how this cap is calculated is shown in Table 7-2.

**Table 7-2. Calculation of Federal Garnishment Limit
(Based on Federal Minimum Wage—$7.25 per Hour)**

	Weekly	Biweekly	Semimonthly	Monthly
		Pay Period:		
Disposable income is equal to or less than:	$217.50	$435.00	$471.25	$942.50
Amount subject to garnishment:	None	None	None	None
Disposable income is more than:	$217.50	$435.00	$471.25	$942.50
But less than:	$290.00	$580.00	$628.33	$1,256.67
Subject to garnishment:	Amount above $217.50	Amount above $435.00	Amount above $471.25	Amount above $942.50
Disposable income of:	$290.00 or more	$580.00 or more	$628.33 or more	$1,256.67 or more
Subject to garnishment:	Maximum at 25% of disposable earnings	Maximum at 25% of disposable earnings	Maximum at 25% of disposable earnings	Maximum at 25% of disposable earnings

See Forms 668-W, 668-W(c), and 668-W(c)(DO), Notice of Levy on Wages, Salary, and Other Income, for a schedule by exemptions and pay periods.

The following examples provide additional illustrations.

Example 1. In February 2017, Bob earns $665.00 per week. His disposable pay, after all federal and state deductions, is $563.75. The maximum garnishment that may be applied is calculated as the lesser of (a) or (b):

a. The federal minimum wage is $7.25 an hour. 30 × $7.25 = $217.50. Disposable earnings less $217.50: $563.75 – $217.50 = $346.25.

b. 25 percent of disposable pay: $563.75 × 0.25 = $140.94. The maximum garnishment per pay period is $140.94 (the lesser of $346.25 or $140.94).

Example 2. In March 2017, Stephanie earns $15 per hour and works 40 hours per workweek. Her weekly wage is $600, and her disposable earnings are $476.30. The maximum garnishment that can be applied is calculated as the lesser of (a) or (b):

a. The federal minimum wage is $7.25 an hour. 30 × $7.25 = $217.50. Disposable earnings less $217.50: $476.30 – $217.50 = $258.80.

b. 25 percent of disposable pay: $476.30 × 0.25 = $119.08. The amount subject to garnishment is $119.08 (the lesser of $258.80 or $119.08).

Example 3. For a week in March 2017, Belinda earns $10 per hour but only works 23 hours in that week. Her weekly wage is $230.00, and her disposable earnings are $213.40. Belinda's disposable earnings are less than the protected amount required by the CCPA as demonstrated in (a):

a. The federal minimum wage is $7.25 an hour. 30 × $7.25 = $217.50. Disposable earnings less $217.50: $213.40 – $217.50 = $4.25.

[29 C.F.R. § 870.10(a)]

Q 7:13   What penalties can be imposed on the employer for failure to follow a garnishment order?

With creditor garnishment, depending upon state law an employer could be subject to as little as the amount that should have been withheld or up to 100 percent of the debt. The employer may also be subject to legal fees, court costs, and other punitive damages.

For child support, must states require the amount not withheld. Illinois, however, has a penalty of $100 a day, for each day past the deadline when funds should have been remitted.

For any garnishment or tax levy, the employer could be required to pay all amounts that were not deducted.

In the case of a tax levy, an employer can be held liable for as little as the required garnishment payment if the order is not followed or as much as 50 percent of the original amount due. Additionally, the courts may impose legal fees, court costs, and other punitive damages on the employer. [I.R.C. § 6332(d)(2)]

Q 7:14   How do state garnishment laws differ from federal laws?

State garnishment laws may differ from federal law by providing greater protection to low-wage earners. The state laws may include the following provisions to benefit employees:

1. Additional deductions to subtract before calculating disposable earnings;
2. A different method to calculate the statutory exemption which results in a higher minimum exemption;
3. A smaller withholding percentage that is applied to disposable earnings;
4. Restrictions as to the number of creditor garnishments that can be deducted at the same time;
5. Additional restrictions on when an employee may be discharged because of a garnishment or different disciplinary procedures relating to a wage garnishment; and
6. Different conditions governing when the garnishment may be applied.

When state law is more favorable to the employee than federal law, the state law will supersede.

There are a number of ways in which state laws protect a greater amount of earnings than does federal law. Those include replacing the federal minimum wage with the state minimum wage, or replacing 30 hours with a higher multiplier (e.g., 35, 40, or 50 hours). California now requires the lesser of federal, state, or local minimum wage in the equation. A few of the more common qualifying conditions follow:

- In Alaska, the exemptions that apply to a portion of an employee's wages, following state law, apply only when the employee is a resident. If the employee is a nonresident, the federal limits apply.

- Some states establish additional exemptions or reduce the withholding percentage if the debtor qualifies as head of household. In Florida, a qualifying Head of Household is entitled to a $750 weekly exemption and must agree to allow his or her wages to be garnished. Exemptions for dependent children living at home could reduce the amount collected, but how the exemption is applied differs among states.

- California requires the greater of federal, state, or local minimum wage in the equation. California also reduces the disposable earnings calculation by 50 percent. As a result, an employee earning $12 who works 40 hours a week and is paid weekly must have disposable earnings greater than $960 before wages can be garnished.

Q 7:15   What steps are recommended for an employer to take in processing a claim for an employee's wages?

Employers are required by state law to comply with various types of wage withholding orders and notices. Failure to comply with these may result in a variety of penalties, ranging from court-ordered appearances, having a Marshall enter the place of business and take all the money from the cash register; to the employer's arrest. These laws generally require that the claims be handled accurately and timely to avoid liability and penalties. Employers should understand that when they withhold and remit earnings in excess of legal limits or on invalid claims, they may be held liable to the employee for the lost wage payment.

Organizations must withhold from payments to contractors for child support. Many states now require that a garnishment or state levy be honored and money withheld from the contractor's pay.

As a result, employers should establish procedures to handle the garnishments received by the organization. Such procedures should include:

1. Determining if the person named in the order is an employee, a former employee, was never employed by the organization, or is an independent contractor;

2. Confirming that the court order or notice is valid under state law and all required documents were delivered;

3. Verifying the amount of the claim to be paid under the notice;

4. Determining whether the garnished amount is within the legal limits of the state;

5. Ranking multiple garnishments for an employee according to priority;

6. Completing all answers or interrogatories including answers for persons who are terminated or were never employed by the employer;

7. Determining, as soon as possible, the correct amount to be withheld; and

8. Reconciling all documents received against those processed or responded to.

Some states require the employer to give the employee documents sent with the garnishment. A copy of all out-of-state income withholding orders for support must be given to the employee. (Some states identify support orders that must be provided to the employee regardless if the orders were issued within or outside the state.) As a policy, many employers notify their employees that their wages will be garnished and the amount or percentage that will be withheld.

A notice of garnishment or assignment normally includes the following information:

1. When wage withholding must begin;

2. If certain documents must be delivered to the employee;

3. The amount or percentage to be withheld;

4. When the withheld amount must be remitted and to whom;

5. When to answer and file interrogatories;

6. How and to whom payment is to be made;

7. The total amount to be garnished under the order;

8. The conditions for stopping wage withholding; and

9. Applicable federal or state laws that must be followed.

Child Support Orders

Q 7:16   What are the federal laws that apply to child support orders?

The following federal laws also regulate support requirements and may set minimum requirements states must include when establishing child support laws that include wage garnishments:

1. The Child Support Enforcement Amendments of 1984 required states to adopt laws governing garnishments resulting from delinquent child support payments.

2. The Family Support Act of 1988 provided for immediate wage garnishment for all support orders enforced through the child support enforcement (CSE) program or through a private attorney.

3. The Personal Responsibility and Work Opportunity Reconciliation Act of 1996 (PRWORA) required employers to report new hires, imposed the minimum number of days in which the employer must begin withholding and remit payments following the deduction, established a central place in each state where support payments must be sent—State Disbursement Unit (SDU), permitted states to define "income," required all states to adopt the Uniform Interstate Family Support Act as written, and required the Office of Child Support Enforcement (OCSE) to develop a standardized withholding order.

4. The Consumer Credit Protection Act (CCPA) limits the amount of disposable earnings that is subject to withholding for child support payments.

The basic federal requirements imposed on states include the following:

1. State laws must provide a method to allocate money to all orders for current support first when the full amount for all support orders cannot be collected.

2. State laws must prioritize the various categories of support, e.g., current, arrears, medical support premiums. Current support must be given first priority. Note. A few states grant priority to medical support premiums, which are considered to be current.

3. State laws must provide procedures for processing child support orders for custodial parents in other states.

4. State laws must require the employer to remit payments within seven business days of the employee's pay date.

5. Withholding for support must continue until the agency or court issues an Income Withholding Order (IWO) to the employer to stop withholding or to make changes to the order.

6. An employer that fails to withhold in accordance with federal or state child support orders can be held liable for the amounts that should have been deducted, plus applicable penalties, interest, and other sanctions.

7. The employer must notify the state CSE agency when an employee whose wages are being garnished terminates employment. In addition, employers must provide the agency with the employee's last known home address and, if known, the new employer's name and address.

8. The employer must begin withholding no later than the first pay period that occurs after 14 working days following the date the withholding notice was mailed.

9. Health insurance must be made available to a child (or stepchild) who does not reside with the employee if the employee is eligible for dependent medical coverage under an employer's plan and a medical support order is sent to the employer. The child is treated like any other employee's child, and the employee pays for the coverage as if the child resided with the employee.

10. Spousal support may be included in the CSE program if a child resides in the spouse's household. A spousal support garnishment is applied simultaneously with the child support garnishment.

11. Employers may not refuse to hire an applicant because of wage garnishment for child support.

[CCPA § 303(b); 42 U.S.C. §§ 651–669]

The federal law is not imposed directly on an employer but requires each state to implement minimum standards that apply to all employers with operations in their state. The federal legislation also provides financial and administrative assistance to states in implementing these requirements. [42 U.S.C. §§ 654(5), 666(a)(8)]

The federal legislation imposes certain mandates but gives the states a degree of latitude in establishing administrative rules to implement the mandated program. [42 U.S.C. §§ 652(a)(10)(c), 652(a)(10)(d)]

Q 7:17   What is the Personal Responsibility and Work Opportunity Reconciliation Act of 1996?

The Personal Responsibility and Work Opportunity Reconciliation Act of 1996 (PRWORA) was enacted to speed and streamline state recovery of delinquent support payments through income withholding. Under this federal law, states must require employers to remit garnished wages to a state disbursement agency within seven business days after the date the payments would have been made to the employee responsible for the child support. The Act also required states and U.S. territories to develop new-hire reporting programs to assist in locating individuals who are delinquent in meeting the payment requirements of a child support order. State laws vary on how these requirements are implemented.

The Uniform Interstate Family Support Act of 1996 was adopted by PRWORA. As a result, employers are required to accept income withholding orders issued by all states, U.S. territories, and Indian tribes.

The Act required the U.S. Department of Health and Human Services to develop a uniform wage withholding order form (Income Withholding Order (IWO)) to be used by employers in all states in processing these withholdings.

Q 7:18 What does the Family Support Act of 1988 require?

All states were required under the Family Support Act of 1988 to establish a comprehensive system providing for the exchange of information and payment of child support orders through electronic funds transfer/electronic data interchange (EFT/EDI). In addition, the federal law generally permits states to:

1. Establish penalties and fines that may be imposed on employers for discharging or disciplining an employee or refusing to hire a worker because of child support claims.

2. Establish laws permitting employers to charge the employee an administrative fee for processing a child support payment as a payroll deduction. The fee may not be deducted from the child support payment but is added to the child support payment in determining whether any of the limitations on the amount of garnishment are exceeded. (Note that the federal Office of Child Support Enforcement takes the position that the employer should deduct the administrative fee from the support payment when there is insufficient disposable pay to cover both the support amount and the administrative fee. The amount deducted for the administrative fee becomes part of the support arrearage that is later paid by the employee.)

3. Establish laws that determine allocation of the support payment when there is more than one support order.

[42 U.S.C. § 654(24)]

Q 7:19 What is the Uniform Interstate Family Support Act?

The Uniform Interstate Family Support Act (UIFSA) was enacted to facilitate the processing of interstate orders. The Act contains model laws that the states must adopt to facilitate interstate support orders. All of the states have adopted these model laws. The Act contains a provision that relieves employers of civil liability for following the UIFSA requirements on a withholding order issued in another state. UIFSA requires all employers to accept orders from any state or U.S. territory provided they are "regular on their face" (appear to be a valid order) and to follow certain components of the order based on the law of the state where the order was issued such as the amount(s) to deduct, and where to send the payments. However, many of the processes, e.g., calculation of disposable earnings, withholding limit(s), employer fee, etc., must follow the law of the state in which the employee works (Principal Place of Employment). This allows for standardized processing requirements when an employee has orders for more than one family issued by different states.

Q 7:20   Does the Federal Office of Child Support Enforcement (OCSE) control child support garnishments?

OCSE has responsibility to monitor the activities of states to ensure the state agencies follow federal requirements. OCSE cannot initiate rules for the states to follow, but rather it does interpret and provide guidance in understanding regulations. Federal law requires each state to establish standards and adopt rules governing the locating of a noncustodial parent and imposing wage withholding to collect delinquent child support. The federal government operates the Federal Parent Locator Service to coordinate this function (and when child support payments are more than $5,000 in arrears, the government may revoke the individual's passport). The states are generally free to establish their own standards for the fees employers in the state may impose, as well as fines and penalties for violations, based on the federal requirements. [42 U.S.C. §§ 652(a)(10), 653] OCSE provides for the National Portal for Electronic Income Withholding Orders (e-IWO). For employers not enrolled in the e-IWO program, OCSE offers the Employer Services Web Application program. The ESWA program allows employers to electronically report future lump-sum payments, to report termination of an employee for whom support was being withheld, and to report that the person named in an income withholding order is not employed.

Q 7:21   Is there a standardized withholding order for child support?

Yes, the federal Office of Child Support Enforcement (OCSE) developed an Income Withholding Order for Support (IWO), approved by the Office of Management and Budget (OMB). That order must be used by all state support agencies and courts. The purpose of the federal form is to provide all the information the employer/payer needs in order to withhold and remit the funds. The order is clearly identified as either being issued by a court/agency or a third party. To help employers, the children's names and dates of birth appear on the front of the order. To ensure conformity, the IWO, which was revised in May 2011, requires an employer/payer to return to the sender any IWO issued or modified on or after May 31, 2012 that is not issued on the standardized federal form. The IWO form is revised every three years. The most current form was issued on July 31, 2014 and expires on July 31, 2017. Comments have been received for revisions to a new IWO form anticipated to be available July 31, 2017 for a period of three years.

Q 7:22   Does wage withholding for child support apply to all employees?

Yes. Two possible conditions may block withholding of a noncustodial parent's wages for child support payments. The employee, employer, or another party may demonstrate to the court that there is good cause not to impose the withholding. The federal law directs states to establish policies to implement these proceedings. [42 U.S.C. §§ 666(a), 666(b)(1)]

Another component of the federal law limits the amount of wages that can be paid to satisfy court- or agency-ordered child support to a percentage of an individual's disposable earnings. Where the individual's permitted amount of disposable wages is less than the amount in the court order, the lesser amount is paid. This limitation is part of the CCPA. [CCPA § 303(b), 15 U.S.C. § 1673; 29 C.F.R. § 870.11(b)]

Q 7:23   What are wages for the purposes of enforcing a child support order?

States are permitted to define the types of income from which child support payments may be withheld. Whereas federal law requires that child support be withheld only from earnings for personal services and retirement income, states have the option of requiring withholding from other forms of income such as dividends, workers' compensation, disability insurance, unemployment, and sale of stock. [42 U.S.C. § 666(b)(8)] States may also allow certain deductions to be taken into account in the disposable pay calculation (e.g., mandatory union dues). When an IWO is served on the payor of non-employee income, the payor must withhold support from the pay.

Q 7:24   How are pretax deductions and imputed income treated for purposes of computing disposable wages for a family support order?

According to the federal Office of Child Support Enforcement's (OCSE) website, pretax deductions should not reduce disposable earnings for family support withholding purposes. Therefore, when calculating disposable income for family support, pretax deductions are added to the employee's taxable wages before determining the employee's allowable disposable income. OCSE provides the following example:

Gross Pay	$1,000
Deduct Section 401(k) contribution pretax deduction	(100)
Taxable earnings	$ 900
Deduct mandatory deductions	(250)
Net pay	$ 650
Add back pretax deduction	$ 100
Disposable earnings:	$ 750

OCSE explains that imputed income (e.g., personal use of company car) is not considered additional income for purposes of calculating disposable income for family support purposes. OCSE provides the following example:

Gross Pay	$ 1,200
Add imputed income of take-home vehicle	$ 275
Taxable earnings	$ 1,475
Deduct mandatory deductions	(320)
Net pay	$ 1,155
Subtract imputed income from net pay	(275)
Disposable earnings:	$ 880

Q 7:25   What are the federal requirements for remitting the amounts withheld under a child support order?

Federal law imposes a seven business-day deadline for submitting the withheld wages to the state agency. That mandated delivery date is measured from the payday on which the amounts were withheld. State law may require a shortened time frame for remitting the withheld amount. Employers are permitted to make a single payment that combines all child support deductions for its employees for a pay period to each state. Such a payment requires that the employer provide an itemization (by employee and date paid) of the amount included. All states, except South Carolina, permit the employer's deposit to be made as an automated clearinghouse (ACH) transfer. There are a number of states that have established a web-based payment service to facilitate electronic payments. [42 U.S.C. § 654B; 45 C.F.R. § 303.100(e)(1)(ii)]

Any income withholding order that does not direct that the payment be made to an SDU must be returned to the issuing party. The only exception to this requirement is South Carolina until such time as a state SDU is established. An IWO that does not direct payment to the SDU is not considered to be "regular on its face." Employers should return an order that is not regular on its face.

Q 7:26   Can the employer combine payments for more than one Income Withholding Order for remittance to the appropriate state agency?

Yes, every state must accept a combined remittance, but the employer must follow the states requirements as to how to identify the employee, case identifier(s), and the amount remitted.

Q 7:27   What procedures apply when an employee has a wage garnishment in addition to a child support order?

Child support payments take priority over any other garnishments or other involuntary deductions under state or federal law with one exception. Exception: When the employee is also subject to a preexisting federal tax levy, the levy has priority if the support was established after the levy was issued.

Note. The date the obligation for support was incurred determines if the support would have priority over a previously served federal tax levy. When support has priority over a federal levy, the levy can still be implemented and if net pay exceeds the amount from levy, money will be deducted for the IRS.

When the employee is subject to support and another attachment such as a creditor garnishment, student loan, etc., the rule of aggregation must be applied. In most states, if the amount deducted for support is less than 25 percent of disposable earnings, the difference generally can be applied to the other attachment. If support is 25 percent or more of disposable earnings, no deduction can be made for the other attachment.

A number of states allow support and a state tax levy to be deducted concurrently. State levies are not subject to CCPA limitations.

When two families initiate two separate child support orders, the state law of the state where the employee works will determine the allocation of support among the families when the total of the orders exceeds allowable disposable earnings.

Q 7:28 How does an employer handle an order issued in another state?

Orders from different states to withhold child support from one employee are delivered directly to an employer. Federal legislation required all states to adopt the provisions of the UIFSA that require employers to honor out-of-state child support withholding orders. Under UIFSA, the order is served directly on an employer without first registering the order with the employer's state. An employer served with an order from another state applies the rules of the state where the employee works in determining the process for implementing the order (e.g., timing of withholding and deadlines for remittance, maximum withholding, and imposition of an administrative fee etc.). [42 U.S.C. § 666(b)(6)]

Q 7:29 How long must the employer continue to apply an order for wage withholding?

The employer must continue the required withholding until the employer is notified by the issuing agency. [45 C.F.R. § 303.100(e)(iv)] Should the employee question the order, the employer must continue to withhold and advise the employee to contact the state agency or, in some circumstances, the issuing county court. When a modification must be made, the agency or court will send the employer an IWO. Generally, the IWO will be marked as amended. If an employee is terminated, but continues to receive separation pay, support must continue to be withheld. Termination of employment does not always end the employer's obligation to withhold if the noncustodial parent is later rehired. The federal Office of Child Support Enforcement (OCSE) provides a matrix on its website titled State/Employer Contact and Program Information: State Income Withholding. The matrix identifies requirements for each state, which include the requirement of how long the employer must retain the order in an active status and implement it if the employee returns to work before the requirement ends.

Q 7:30   How does an administrative charge affect the maximum amount that may be paid under a child support order?

The OCSE states that any administrative charges imposed by the employer are included with the garnishment payment and medical support premiums in determining the withholding limit that applies to that employee. Under federal law, the administrative charge cannot reduce the payment made to the agency; however, collection of a fee could reduce the amount deducted for the support. Colorado and Washington State require the full amount of support to be deducted before the employer can deduct its fee. The administrative fee is to be withheld from the employee's other wages unless the amount of the garnishment and the fee exceed the total amount that may be withheld under state or federal law. Thus the fee could have the effect of reducing the current payment due for support; that amount becomes an arrearage that is due from later payments. [42 U.S.C. § 666(b)(6)(A)(i); 45 C.F.R. § 303.100(e)(1)]. Collection of a fee cannot reduce the employee's hourly income below the federal minimum wage.

States are free to establish rules to permit the collection of an administrative fee each time a child support payment is withheld. [42 U.S.C. § 666]

Q 7:31   Does federal law permit a noncustodial parent served with a child support order to negotiate an alternative method of payment?

Yes. Even though the federal laws mandate states to implement laws for imposing immediate withholding of wages for child support payments, employees subject to such withholding are generally permitted to negotiate an alternative form of payment. This generally requires a written agreement with the party initiating the support order, and the alternative must be negotiated within a short waiting period. Where such an agreement has been negotiated, states are to implement procedures that require automatic withholding if any payment under the agreement is more than a month late.

States are encouraged to establish procedures for an employee who is not currently subject to wage withholding for child support (i.e., to request the individual's employer to withhold support payments). [42 U.S.C. §§ 652(a)(1), 666(a)(3), 666(a)(8)]

Q 7:32   Are there any additional duties when an employee who is subject to child support withholding receives a bonus, back-pay award, or other lump-sum payment?

Generally, if an employer withholds the required amount for child support from an employee's regular wages, it is not necessary to withhold the normal pay period deduction from these extra payrolls unless the deduction for support was not made from the regular payroll run. However, about 16 states have laws that require an employer to notify the state that issued the IWO for support before an employee who is subject to the order is paid a bonus, back-pay award, or other lump-sum payment. The purpose of these laws is to collect delinquent support.

Laws vary as to threshold limits, amount of time the agency has to return information to the employer, and other requirements. Generally, if a deduction must be taken, the agency will send either an IWO with the box for lump sum marked or some other form. The amount to withhold is subject to the withholding limit that applies for the employee in the state in which he or she works. The amount to withhold from the lump-sum payment is the lesser of the total amount of arrears owed or the withholding limit. For example, if an employee owes $3,675 in arrears and has disposable earnings of $6,155 with a withholding limit of 55 percent, the deduction is $3,385.25. Several states claim they are entitled to 100 percent of the bonus, but the DOL's inclusion of lump-sum payments, in their definition/examples of earnings, should make it easier for employers to defend withholding based on the CCPA limits.

A feature of the e-IWO program allows employers to electronically report lump-sum payment information and to receive a one-time lump-sum e-IWO. The OCSE has developed an Employer Services Web Application program (ESWA) to report bonus payments to a number of states. Employers not enrolled in the e-IWO program can streamline the number of notices they currently send to agencies by using the ESWA program. As of January 2017, all but five states (Delaware, Michigan, Rhode Island, Vermont, and Wisconsin) accept lump sum information through ESWA. In Colorado, for example, employers must report lump-sum payments and withhold in the same manner and the same timeframe as other child support. [14-14-111.5 (4)(k5) Co Revised Statutes]

Q 7:33   How should an employer handle an employee's voluntary withholding for payment of child support?

Even though there are no federal restrictions on an employee's asking an employer to withhold and make payments for child support to another party, state laws may establish requirements for such voluntary assignments. In addition, state laws must require immediate wage withholding for all child support, whether or not there are arrears, unless both parents agree otherwise. When a voluntary assignment by the employee arises, the employee should be referred to the state agency in charge of child support. Employers should never withhold more than the withholding limit that should be applied to the individual.

Q 7:34   Are there notification requirements that apply when an employee who is subject to a child support order terminates employment?

Yes. State laws vary; however, employers are generally required to promptly notify the agency that provided the notice when the employee terminates employment. Employers are generally required to provide the last known address of the employee and, if known, the new employer's name and address. [45 C.F.R. § 303.100(d)(1)(X)] The Income Withholding Order also asks for the date and amount of the last payment made to the SDU or tribal CSE agency. For those employers enrolled in the e-IWO program, terminations may be reported through the federal portal to participating states (all states except South Carolina). For employers not enrolled in the e-IWO program, the ESWA program may be used to report termination information to all but four states (Mississippi, Nevada, Rhode Island, and Vermont). Some states have developed a website for online reporting of terminations. Electronic methods ensure that the termination information is received faster and delivered to the correct processing center.

Q 7:35   What notification requirements apply when the employee is not terminated but has no wages that may be attached?

Where the employee either receives no wages from the employer or the full amount of the IWO cannot be withheld, the employer has no liability for full or partial payment under the order. The IWO must be processed every pay period to ensure that available wages are withheld. When an employee who was classified as inactive is reactivated, the withholding must promptly begin again.

In some cases, a disabled employee may be receiving sick pay from some party other than the employer (such as from disability insurance policies). Under these circumstances, the employer is relieved of any liability for withholding and, in most cases, the employer is under no obligation to notify the third-party provider. The employer is generally required to notify the agency of the third-party payer's name and address. The employer would, of course, withhold from the employee's pay as soon as the employee received wages from the employer.

The e-IWO federal portal now accepts electronic notifications to report that an employee is not receiving pay because of various conditions. This tool is available for both new IWOs that are received and orders already established.

Q 7:36   Are there electronic options to receive and respond to notices from the state?

Yes. The most cost-effective method of receiving Income Withholding Orders (IWOs) and responding to or reporting information to state child support agencies is by participating in the electronic income withholding order (e-IWO) program sponsored by OCSE. Both the employer and the state agency must participate for an e-IWO to be effective. The Preventing Sex Trafficking and Strengthening Families Act, which was enacted on September 29, 2014, required that, by October 1, 2015, every state, U.S. territory, and the District of Columbia have the capability of issuing electronic income withholding orders (e-IWOs). As of January 2017, South Carolina is the only state that has not implemented the e-IWO.

All orders sent for an organization are bundled and delivered in one transmission daily to the employer. The employer can choose from three formats: flat file, XML, or PDF. The PDF looks exactly like the document received through the mail. Most employers choose either the spreadsheet or PDF format because there is no programming involved. Not only can a participating employer receive documents electronically, but also the employer can send information electronically through the portal to the participating states. For example, when an IWO is received for a person who is terminated or inactive, the relevant information can be returned in a spreadsheet that is sent with the PDFs. When an employer needs to report that deductions for child support are no longer being made, the employer would select the appropriate code for the reason replying to the state through the portal. Reporting for lump-sum payments may also be handled through the portal.

Employers that use e-IWO report a significant cost savings in the reduction of time in reporting events such as terminations and receipt of workers' comp or disability insurance by employees, and save money by eliminating the cost of postage to send printed letters, notices, copies of forms, etc. Employers are also able to integrate these electronic documents into their management and work-flow tools.

Q 7:37 What penalties can be imposed on an employer that does not comply with a child support withholding order?

An employer that fails to comply with a withholding order for child support becomes liable, to the state, for the entire amount that was required to be withheld but was not. States may also impose penalties and fines on the employer for failure to withhold and/or failure to remit by the required number of days. [42 U.S.C. §§ 666(b)(6)(B), 666(b)(6)(D); 45 C.F.R. § 303.100(f)(1)]

Q 7:38 May an employer terminate an employee because of a child support order?

No. Employers may neither refuse to hire an applicant nor discipline (e.g., terminate) an employee because of a wage withholding order for child support. State law may establish fines that may be imposed on employers for discharging or disciplining an employee or refusing to hire a worker because of child support claims. [42 U.S.C. § 666(b)(6)(D); 45 C.F.R. § 303.100(f)(1)]

Medical and Spousal Support

Q 7:39   May a child support order require that the noncustodial parent's employer provide health insurance?

Yes. Health plans of noncustodial parents' employers must honor judgments or orders that are qualified medical child support orders (QMCSOs); the National Medical Support Notice (NMSN) meets those requirements. Health coverage must be provided under the same terms and conditions that apply to the dependents of other employees. However, the employer must treat the dependent of the noncustodial parent covered under a NMSN as a new dependent and as immediately eligible for coverage if the employee/noncustodial parent is enrolled in a plan or is eligible for insurance. The states must include health insurance as part of the child support orders process when private health insurance is available to noncustodial parents at a reasonable cost.

The employee will pay for the dependent coverage under the same terms as the other employees. If the employer pays for the full cost of dependent coverage, the employer will pay for the NMSN. States must modify their insurance regulations to prohibit an insurer from denying coverage to a noncustodial parent's child. [OBRA '93 § 13623]. Any increase to the employee's premium as a result of adding children as a result of an NMSN is a component of support and must be factored in when calculating support withheld against the allowable limit of the employee.

Q 7:40   Is there a standardized order to withhold for medical support?

Yes, the National Medical Support Notice (NMSN) was developed by the Department of Health and Human Services to make it easier for employers and health plans to comply with orders to withhold medical support. The standardized order includes: Part A, Notice to Withhold for Health Care Coverage; and Part B, Medical Support Notice to Plan Administrator. The NMSN is recognized as a Qualified Medical Child Support Notice. Part A and Part B are separate documents so they can be sent independently to notify the appropriate department and plan administrator to provide coverage. Tribal IV-D agencies are not required to use this form.

Q 7:41   May spousal support be included as part of the child support order?

Spousal support of a custodial parent may be included as a part of wages withheld under a child support order. For a spouse to be eligible to have his or her support withheld through the CSE program, he or she must be living in the same household as the child. Any spousal support is drawn simultaneously with child support. [42 U.S.C. § 666(a)(15)(B)]

An order issued for spousal support only may be paid to the recipient if so ordered. The form used to notify the employer to withhold may be different than the e-IWO.

Q 7:42   How does the Affordable Care Act impact medical coverage for children?

The implementation of the Affordable Care Act requirements will extend to how the states will navigate establishing procedures and regulations to meet the mandate to provide health care coverage; at the time of publication no decisions were made. The options open to employees who may not currently be eligible for company coverage and participate in a Health Exchange will make the process of satisfying medical support orders even more complicated. The payroll professional will have to stay abreast with not only what the federal government will require to comply with this law but how the states may implement guidelines that vary from state to state.

New-Hire Reporting

Q 7:43   Why must employers report newly hired employees?

There are several reasons. Congress passed the Personal Responsibility and Work Opportunity Reconciliation Act of 1996 [Pub. L. No. 104-193, 110 Stat. 2105] as part of its effort to reform the nation's welfare system. A key purpose behind this law was to identify noncustodial parents of children receiving welfare benefits. The Department of Health and Human Services estimates that over 30 percent of child support cases involve parents who do not live in the same state as their children. New-hire reporting is imposed under rules estab-lished by each state, with minimum standards set under federal law. The federal government also provides economic and administrative assistance to states for carrying out these programs.

This program allows states to match new-hire data with child support participant information on a nationwide basis through state CSE agencies. The OCSE is then able to assist states in locating parents who are living in other states and to impose mandatory withholding of wages to collect support payments. This system of federal and state coordination allows the OCSE to distribute employ-ment information on an out-of-contact parent. Upon receipt of new-hire informa-tion from other states, state CSE agencies will take the steps necessary to establish paternity, initiate a child support order, enforce an existing order, or all three.

New-hire reporting also is a means to reduce unemployment fraud at the state level. With reporting of new hires directly to the state, employed individu-als who have fraudulently claimed or continued to claim unemployment benefits can be promptly identified.

Q 7:44   How is new-hire reporting implemented?

An employer must promptly file a report with a state agency for each newly hired employee. The exact reporting requirements are established under state law and vary from state to state. Under federal law, every state, at minimum, requires specific information on both employer and employee (i.e., employer's name, address, and federal employer identification number (EIN) and the employee's name, address, and Social Security number, date of hire and, rehire if the length of separation is greater than 60 days). States may also require additional information on the employee and on the employer's dependent health insurance.

Q 7:45 What are the basic reporting requirements?

Under the federal guidelines, a report (i.e., a copy of Form W-4, Employee's Withholding Allowance Certificate, or its state equivalent) is to be filed within 20 days of the employee's date of hire; states may require a shorter time frame for reporting. States may also establish their own specific requirements for the format for reporting. Under the federal guidelines, when employers elect to report new-hire information magnetically or electronically, those reports must be transmitted at least twice a month; no fewer than 12 days nor more than 16 days apart. A multiple-state employer that reports on a semimonthly basis must report a new hire no later than the next semimonthly reporting date. In addition, an employer operating in many states may choose one state in which to report all new hires.

Although the federal law refers to Form W-4 as being used to report new hires, the Form W-4 does not contain the employee's date of hire or date of rehire, which are now required by federal law, or other additional information that may be required under state law. A federal law prohibits making notations to add this information to the form (i.e., no defacing of the Form W-4 is allowed). As a result, states that require additional information will generally require a specific format or form for the reporting.

State laws dictate how the reports are to be delivered by the employer (e.g., on paper, by first-class mail, via fax, or electronically).

Q 7:46 How do employers that operate on a multistate basis report new hires?

An employer with workers employed in more than one state may designate one state in which it has an employee to receive all of its new-hire reports. Such filing must be made magnetically or electronically (depending on state law). The employer must notify both the state and the U.S. Department of Health and Human Services of its election to report to one state. Employers may use the federal reporting form, *Multistate Employer Notification Form for New Hire Reporting* (Optional Form) available online at https://www.acf.hhs.gov/sites/default/files/programs/css/mse_form.pdf. The completed form may be mailed to:

Department of Health and Human Services
Office of Child Support Enforcement
Multistate Employer Registration
P.O. Box 509
Randallstown, MD 21133

Or Fax to: Multistate Employer Notification Fax:

410-277-9325

Or E-mail to: msedb@acf.hhs.gov If your company merges with or acquires another company, or has other changes that may affect the new hire reporting requirement, OCSE instructs you to send a revised form with the new or updated information.

Alternatively, employers can register or update information online at https://ocsp.acf.hhs.gov/ocse/.

Reporting must include the employer's name, address, and telephone number; the employer's federal EIN; the identity of the state selected for reporting purposes; the other states in which the employer has employees; and the name and telephone extension of a corporate contact.

Q 7:47 What types of entities satisfy the definition of *employer* for new-hire reporting purposes?

The federal definition of the term *employer* for new-hire reporting purposes is the same as the definition for federal income tax purposes (found in I.R.C. Section 3401(d)). That definition includes government entities and labor organizations. At a minimum, in any case in which an employer is required to give an individual a Form W-2 showing the amount of taxes withheld, the employer must meet the new-hire reporting requirements.

Q 7:48 Which workers satisfy the definition of *employee* for new-hire reporting purposes?

The federal guidelines generally require that new-hire reporting be applied for any individual who satisfies the I.R.C. definition of an employee for purposes of federal income tax withholding from wages. Certain employees of a federal or state agency who perform intelligence or counterintelligence functions, however, are not considered employees for new-hire reporting if the agency determines that reporting would endanger the safety of the individual or compromise an investigation. (Private employers are not entitled to this exemption.) [Pub. L. No. 104-193, 110 Stat. 2105]

Q 7:49 What is deemed to be the employee's date of hire?

An employee's date of hire is the first day the individual performs services for wages. An employee who is laid off and rehired is treated as a new hire if he or she is separated from employment for more than 60 days, and the employee must be reported as a new hire using the date he or she returned to work. [42 U.S.C. § 653a]

Q 7:50   Is new-hire reporting required for independent contractors (or subcontractors) who provide services?

It can be required by state law. Under the federal guidelines, if an individual is a bona fide independent contractor (or subcontractor), no reporting is required. However, an employer that misclassifies as an independent contractor an individual who would otherwise be classified as an employee will be considered in violation of the new-hire reporting requirements. A bona fide independent contractor (or subcontractor) who hires individuals as employees will be responsible for the new-hire reporting of those employees. In cases in which the IRS finds that such an independent contractor is misclassified, and is, in reality, an employee, the employer is responsible for new-hire reporting of the misclassified individual and of his or her employees. [42 U.S.C. § 654A]

Q 7:51   How does a temporary employment agency report new hires?

A temporary agency that is paying wages to an individual must submit a new-hire report. The individual needs to be reported only once, even though his or her work with the agency may be intermittent. When there is a break in service from the agency for more than 60 days, the person must be reported as a new hire.

An agency that simply refers workers for employment and does not pay salaries is not generally responsible for reporting. The employer is responsible for new-hire reporting when the worker is hired and paid wages regardless of whether on a full- or part-time basis.

Q 7:52   Is an employer required to report a new hire who terminates before the employee paydate?

Yes. New-hire reporting is required for any individual who is classified as an employee for federal income tax withholding purposes. Even though the noncustodial parent (NCP) does not work long enough to have support deducted from wages, the support agency will obtain current information it may not have. It is not unusual that an agency does not even know the state in which the NCP currently resides. [42 U.S.C. §§ 653A(a)–653A(c)]

Q 7:53   What are the penalties for failing to report a new hire?

Penalties are established by each state for a delinquent or late reporting of new hires. The federal guidelines generally set the maximum fine at $25 per violation and $500 per violation that is the result of a conspiracy between the employer and the employee. [42 U.S.C. § 653A(d)]

Multiple Garnishments

Q 7:54   What happens when an employer receives multiple garnishments for a single employee?

Federal and state laws vary, but as a general rule a support order has priority over any other creditor garnishment. When a federal tax levy was served first and the date of the support obligation is after the levy, the federal levy takes priority. For all other garnishments, date of service is generally the controlling factor. In some states, a state tax levy or garnishment for a debt to a state agency has priority over a creditor garnishment. Bankruptcy will generally stop all deductions for debt except for support, which must continue. Just because a garnishment has a lower priority than another type of garnishment, withholding may still occur if the aggregate of what was withheld for the order with priority does not exceed 25 percent of disposable earnings or a lesser amount required by state law.

When two or more child support orders are received for a single employee, an employer must deduct some money for each order of current support when the total of the current support exceeds the allowable disposable earnings for that employee. State law governs the allocation method (pro rata or equal distribution) that determines how much to allocate for each support order. Current support must be deducted first, but any remaining money must be allocated to the next type of support based on the priority of support types based on each states' laws. [42 U.S.C. § 653A]

Student Loans

Q 7:55   What garnishment rules apply to delinquent student loans?

In 2010, student loans made through the Federal Family Education Loan Program (FFEL; formerly the Guaranteed Student Loan Program) were discontinued. However, outstanding debts must still be collected. Those loans are subject to special wage garnishment rules found in the Higher Education Act. The U.S. Department of Education authorizes "guaranty agencies" to issue wage withholding orders when a borrower fails to meet the loan payment agreements that are a part of the FFEL loan. Basically, these agencies are authorized to recover delinquent debts owed for student loans. When such a garnishment is issued by the guaranty agency (many of which have now merged), the amount of the garnishment is capped at 15 percent of the employee's disposable pay for one order, up to an aggregate of 25 percent when more than one garnishment is issued. The employee may agree in writing to a larger amount as part of an agreement with the agency or the contractor. These garnishment orders require a 30-day notice period during which the agency states its intent to garnish the employee's wages. The employee is also advised in this period of his or her rights to appeal, to inspect records, and to enter into a written agreement on a repayment schedule as an alternative to garnishment. Federal law prohibits an employer from taking disciplinary action against an employee as a result of such a garnishment order (e.g., the employer may not discharge employees or refuse to hire them as a result of such a garnishment order). [20 U.S.C. § 1095a(a); 31 U.S.C. § 3720D]

Since 2002, the Department of Education issues delinquent student loans through the Administrative Wage Garnishment (AWG) provisions of the Debt Collection Improvement Act of 1996 (DCIA). The DCIA legislation allows all federal agencies to issue AWGs for nontax debt.

Q 7:56   How are student loan garnishments handled for employees who return to work after termination?

A special rule applies to employees who are subject to a student loan garnishment and who involuntarily terminate employment after the garnishment order is served. If the employee returns to employment within 12 months of having been involuntarily terminated from employment, the employee is permitted a grace period of 12 consecutive months of reemployment before the wages may be garnished to repay a delinquent student loan. [20 U.S.C. § 1095a(a)(7)]

Administrative Wage Garnishment (AWG)

Q 7:57   What garnishment rules apply to Federal Administrative Wage Garnishments?

Collection of student loans proved to be so successful that Congress passed the Debt Collection Improvement Act of 1996 (DCIA). The DCIA allows every federal agency to establish collection of nontax debts utilizing an administrative wage garnishment. All federal agencies that are owed nontax debts are required to issue an Administrative Wage Garnishment to collect for qualifying debts. The withholding calculation is slightly different than for student loans garnished using the Higher Education Act rules. The DCIA legislation requires that the employee's health insurance premiums—such as medical, dental, and vision—reduce disposable earnings.

Pay Periods

Q 7:58   Can a valid garnishment order require that an employer alter its normal pay period?

No. For example, a garnishment order cannot force an employer that pays on a monthly basis to process the garnishment on a weekly basis.

Q 7:59   Can the exempt amount that applies to an ordinary garnishment (creditor garnishment, student loan, federal nontax debt) be prorated for an employee who is paid daily?

No. Employees must have disposable earnings of at least 30 times the federal minimum wage per week. That cannot be broken down into a lesser amount such as six times the federal minimum wage per day. Employees do not have to work a full week to have wages garnished as long as their disposable earnings are greater than 30 times the federal minimum wage for the week.

Federal Tax Levies

Q 7:60   How are federal tax levies handled?

The IRS imposes a garnishment of an employee's wages generally through the mailing of Form 668-W, Notice of Levy on Wages, Salary, and Other Income. The form notifies the employer of the amount of the levy and of the employer's obligation to withhold and pay the levied amount. Parts 2 through 5 of the form are provided to the employee for his or her record and for the employee to provide information regarding his or her federal income tax filing status. The employee completes and returns to the employer Parts 3 and 4 with the information requested. Part 3 is then returned to the IRS and Part 4 is retained by the employer.

The amount of the garnishment to be applied to the employee's wages is determined based on his or her statement of exemptions and tax filing status as reported in Parts 3 and 4 of the form [Form 668-W instructions] (*not* on the tax filing status or number of exemptions from the Form W-4), net pay, based on deductions at the time the levy is filed, and the employee's payroll cycle, and the amount of any excluded payments. [I.R.C. § 6334(a); Treas. Reg. § 301.6334-1]

Q 7:61   Do federal tax levies have priority over other wage garnishments?

Generally, no, unless the levy is served prior to another garnishment. Even a support order served after a levy is served may have priority, depending on when the support obligation was incurred. When a bankruptcy is served, withholding for a levy must stop.

Q 7:62   Are any earnings exempt from federal tax levies?

Yes. There are six basic payments to an employee that are exempt from garnishment for a federal tax levy:

1. Workers' compensation benefits under a state program;
2. Unemployment compensation benefits;

3. Certain annuity and retirement benefits paid to certain armed services personnel and under the Railroad Retirement Act;

4. Judgments for support of minor children under a court order that occurred before the tax levy;

5. Certain armed-services-related disability payments; and

6. Certain payments that are part of a public assistance program.

[I.R.C. §§ 6334(a), 6334(h); Treas. Reg. § 301.6334-1]

An additional exemption equal to a pro rata share of the employee's standard deduction (as determined by filing of the Form 1040) and valid personal exemptions is available to the employee on completion of Parts 3 and 4 of Form 668-W. [I.R.C. § 6334(d); Treas. Reg. §§ 301.6334-3, 301.6334-4]

Note. IRS publication 1494 provides the pro rata amounts.

Q 7:63 What is Form 668-W?

Form 668-W(ICS) or 668-W(c)(DO), the Notice of Levy on Wages, Salary, and Other Income, instructs the employer to withhold after deducting the exempt amount from the employee's earnings. When the employer receives this form, the employer is to give Parts 2, 3, 4, and 5 to the employee immediately. The employee is to return to the employer Parts 3 and 4 within three workdays. When the employer submits the payment, Part 3 is to be attached to the check. If an employee fails to complete and return Parts 3 and 4, the employer must consider the employee as Married Filing a Joint Return claiming one exemption.

Q 7:64 Does the employer have any responsibility for reviewing the validity of information provided by the employee on Parts 3 and 4 of Form 668-W?

No. The amount of withholding for payment of a federal tax levy should be based on the information provided by the employee in Parts 3 and 4 of Form 668-W, Notice of Levy on Wages, Salary, and Other Income, regardless of whether the employer suspects that the information is incorrect. The employer must, however, make sure the Social Security number is listed for every dependent over the age of six months and that the document is signed and dated.

Q 7:65 May an employer rely on the employee's previously completed W-4 in calculating the exemptions from federal tax levies?

No. The employer must base the amount of an exemption attributable to personal exemptions and standard deductions listed on Parts 3 and 4 of Form 668-W. When the federal tax levy cannot be collected in a single calendar year, the same exemption table must be used. The employee may complete new Parts 3 and 4 of Form 668-W to reflect changes in tax status and personal exemptions. The employee may wish to complete a new Form 668-W Parts 3 and 4 for a new calendar year to take advantage of a change in the new year's tax tables. [Treas. Reg. § 301.6334-3(e)]

Q 7:66   How do the limits on wages available to pay a garnishment differ under the CCPA and I.R.C. (which governs federal tax levies)?

These two federal laws affecting garnishments differ in many ways. First, the limits on wages available for garnishment under the CCPA are based on the concept of a percentage of disposable earnings. Earnings available for a federal tax levy are determined under guidelines specified in IRS Form 668-W and Publication 1494, Tables for Figuring Amount Exempt from Levy on Wages, Salary, and Other Income. Next, the amount of any garnishment that may be paid from disposable income under CCPA is subject to both a limit based on the current minimum wage and a maximum garnishment amount. The CCPA does not provide protection from wages when withholding for a state or federal tax levy. A federal tax levy must attach the full amount of an individual's available net pay after (1) specific exemptions, (2) an allowance for personal exemptions, and (3) a prorated standard deduction (based on the employee's Form 1040 filing status).

Table 7-3 offers a concise comparison of deductions and exceptions under CCPA and the I.R.C.

Table 7-3.   Listing of Deductions and Exceptions Under CCPA and the I.R.C.

Wages That Are Included in Earnings Subject to Garnishment	CCPA (Included in Gross Earnings)	Federal Tax Levy (Included in Gross Earnings)
Applies to all components of an employee's wages and payroll deductions (wages, compensation, commissions)	Yes	Yes
Tips paid directly to employee	No	No
Service charge added to the customer's bill	Yes	Yes
Imputed income (GTLI, personal use of automobile)	No	No

Typical Payroll Deductions	Deductions to Disposable Earnings for CCPA	Exempt from Federal Tax Levy Garnishment
Federal income tax withholding	Yes	Yes
State and local tax withholding	Yes	Yes

Typical Payroll Deductions	Deductions to Disposable Earnings for CCPA	Exempt from Federal Tax Levy Garnishment
FICA (Social Security and Medicare paid by employee)	Yes	Yes
State unemployment tax paid by employee	Yes	Yes
Deduction required for state employer's retirement system	Yes	Yes
Section 125 salary reductions to obtain benefits	No	Yes[1]
401(k) salary deferrals	No	Yes[1]
Payment of required premium on employer-provided health insurance	No	Yes[1]
United Way contribution	No	Yes[1]
Payment of credit union loan	No	Yes
Contribution to savings account not made under direct deposit	No	Yes[2]
Contribution to savings account made under direct deposit	No	No[2]

---

[1] These items are considered exempt when they are in effect prior to the federal tax levy or when imposed (or raised) as a condition of employment.

[2] The federal laws differentiate between regular savings deposits that are made by an employer that distributes a net check and one that is providing direct deposit. This distinction prevents the entire proceeds of an employee's check from being excluded from a federal tax levy where the net check amount is made to a savings account, as opposed to a checking account.

Q 7:67   How is the maximum garnishment determined for payment of a federal tax lien?

The maximum garnishment for a federal tax lien is determined in two steps: First, subtract the exemptions that are available, and second, subtract the sum of pro rata allowance for personal exemptions and standard deductions as reflected by the employee on Parts 3 and 4 of Form 668-W. The IRS provides Publication 1494 to assist in the application of the second component of this calculation. The calculations for 2017 are shown in Table 7-4 in Q 7:71.

Q 7:68   Can an employee's earnings subject to a federal tax levy decrease because of a change in payroll deductions?

Generally, no. However, certain changes in payroll deductions that are not under the control of the employee may serve to reduce the employee's wages subject to a federal tax levy. Such increases in payroll deductions include but are not limited to an increase in the premium an employee must pay for medical insurance, and an increase in contributions to a 401(k) plan (or payment of other benefits) if the contribution is based on a percentage of earnings and the earnings have increased. Note that for these deductions to apply at all, they must have been in effect before the federal tax levy. In addition, changes in involuntary deductions that are required as a condition of employment may serve to reduce the amount available to pay the tax levy.

Example. In 2017, Susan earns $1,850.00 semimonthly. She is paid by check rather than by direct deposit. Of that amount, $125 is paid as a car loan to a local credit union, $92.50 represents her contribution of 5 percent to the company's Section 401(k) plan, and $110 is paid for Section 125 cafeteria plan health insurance. Susan is single and claims one exemption. She files her tax return as a single person. The maximum garnishment for a federal levy is calculated as follows:

Gross wages	$1,850.00
Less:	
Federal taxes	263.30
Sec 125 cafeteria plan health insurance premium	110.00
401(k) plan contribution	92.50
Contribution to a credit union to pay loan	125.00
Susan's net pay	1,259.20
Exempt from levy (paid to employee)	433.33*
	$ 825.87 (paid to IRS)

* This exemption is based on IRS Publication 1494.

IRS Publication 1494, Tables for Figuring Amount Exempt from Levy on Wages, Salary, and Other Income, provides tables that show the amount of an individual's income that is exempt from a notice of levy used to collect delinquent taxes. Susan completed Parts 3 & 4 of Form 668W, in which she claimed her tax filing status as Single. She is entitled to one exemption for herself. In the preceding example, Susan would receive $433.33, and the IRS would receive $825.87. If Susan had identified that she was eligible for additional exemptions when completing Parts 3 & 4 (e.g., if Susan were over age 65), the amount of $64.58 would be added to the $433.33. Additional exemptions may be claimed for an individual or his or her spouse if over age 65 and/or blind, for up to a total of four additional exemptions.

Q 7:69   What is the effect of changing an existing benefit election on the amount of a federal tax levy?

The instructions to Form 668-W, Notice of Levy on Wages, Salary, and Other Income, tell an employer to "allow no new payroll deductions once the [federal tax] levy is received." Except for payroll deductions that are outside the control of the employee, any change in payroll deductions relating to a benefit election is ignored. Thus, although the employee is generally permitted under the Health Insurance Portability and Accountability Act to add health coverage for a newly born child or adopted child, any increase in employee payroll deductions must be approved by the IRS before the additional premium can reduce the amount sent to the IRS. The IRS should be consulted to find out if additional costs for court-ordered medical coverage for a noncustodial child resulting in additional premiums that are received after the federal tax levy may be deducted before the levy is calculated. [42 U.S.C. § 668(b)(7); 11 U.S.C. §§ 507(a)(7), 523(15)]

Q 7:70 How are cafeteria plan elections and 401(k) plan contributions made pursuant to a calendar-year election treated when wages are garnished?

The basic rules applicable to garnishments of federal tax levies treat contribution elections made before receipt of a notice of levy as being excluded from wages available to pay the levy. Thus, although the employer's plan may permit an employee to revise his or her benefit election or to include new deductions in coverage, any changes that result in additional payroll deductions are ignored for purposes of calculating the maximum garnishment amount. A change in the tax year to reduce the employee's payroll contribution would result in additional amounts being paid toward the levy.

Issues relating to a tax levy that spans more than one calendar year are less clear. IRS representatives have generally indicated that even though a plan may require, under the I.R.C., that a benefit election be effective for a single 12-month period, the election (and related payroll deductions) will be treated as being unchanged if the same election continues for a new calendar or plan year. [Pub. No. 1494, Tables for Figuring Amount Exempt from Levy on Wages, Salary, and Other Income]

Q 7:71 Can the IRS rule that an exceptionally large payroll contribution to a savings account not be excluded from wages available to pay a tax levy?

Yes. The employer; however, is not responsible for making the determination as to whether an employee's payroll deduction should be ignored for purposes of calculating the amount payable to the IRS pursuant to the levy. An exception applies only with respect to credit union or other savings contributions that are structured such that the employee's net pay is calculated as the credit union or savings deposit. In this case, the payroll deduction is treated no differently than a direct deposit and is ignored when computing the amount to remit to the IRS. Generally, if the IRS believes that the amounts being remitted in payment of the levy obligation are insufficient, it reserves the right to review the employees' payroll deductions with the employer and to disallow some or all of them in future calculations of the levy deduction.

Table 7-4. Personal Exemptions and Standard Deductions

	2017
Personal exemption:	$ 4,050
Standard deduction:	
Single taxpayer	6,350
Head of household	9,350
Married filing separately	6,350
Married filing jointly	12,700
Surviving spouse	12,700

Q 7:72 What penalties can apply when an employer fails to comply with an IRS Notice of Levy?

An employer that fails to withhold wages that are subject to an IRS Notice of Levy is personally liable for 100 percent of the amount not withheld. The employer may also be subject to an additional penalty of 50 percent, unless the failure is subject to a "reasonable cause." [Treas. Reg. § 301.6332-1(b)(2)]

The employer will not be held liable for failing to withhold on a federal tax levy in the following situations:

1. There are no wages; or
2. The wages are already fully subject to a preexisting levy that has priority over the federal tax levy (e.g., a garnishment for a child support order received before the federal tax levy).

[I.R.C. § 6332(d); Treas. Reg. § 301.6332-1(b)]

Q 7:73 How should the employer handle a Notice of Levy when the employee claims the notice is wrong?

Regardless of any assertions made by the employee, the employer must comply with the Notice of Levy and withhold payments. An employee with a valid assertion that the IRS levy has been satisfied may obtain from the IRS Form 668-D, Release of Levy. The employer is bound by the terms of the levy. The employer has no responsibility to contact the IRS. As a matter of fact, IRS regulations do not allow agents to talk to the employer about the levy.

Voluntary Wage Assignments

Q 7:74 What is a voluntary wage assignment?

An employee may agree with a creditor to have a portion of his or her pay deducted and paid directly to the creditor. The CCPA does not cover voluntary wage assignments.

Q 7:75   When is an assignment of wages deemed to be voluntary?

This is not a payroll issue that is addressed under any federal law, although the Federal Trade Commission (FTC) has established standards for voluntary assignment. As a result, voluntary wage assignments are governed by state law, or in the absence of any state law on voluntary assignment of an employee's wages, by the general principles of contract law. Contract law generally requires that parties to the contract be competent, that the assignment be by mutual consent, that consideration be provided, and that the assignment be legal under state law. An assignment is considered voidable when there is a mistake in the assignment, the assignment is the result of fraud, the assignment was subject to duress or undue influence, or the employee is ruled to be mentally incompetent.

A voluntary assignment differs from a garnishment in that a creditor generally does not go to court to collect under the assignment. However, state laws may require conditions that can limit the creditor's ability to collect under a voluntary assignment. Employers are not generally obligated to begin withholding amounts on a valid assignment unless they are required to do so under state law. In some states, an employer's failure to follow the assignment may result in court action by the creditor.

Q 7:76   What are the basic federal requirements that apply to voluntary assignments?

The FTC issued rules in 1985 that bar lenders or retail installment sellers from directly, or indirectly, using assignment of wages or other earnings as payment for an obligation unless the assignment:

1. Is revocable at any time by the employee debtor;
2. Applies only to wages or other earnings that are already earned at the time the assignment is executed (i.e., it cannot obligate future wages); and
3. Is made through a periodic payroll deduction or preauthorized payment plan.

When a wage assignment leads to a judgment with a garnishment order, federal garnishment law applies to its execution. [16 C.F.R. § 4442(a)]

Q 7:77   What are the basic state laws that apply to a voluntary assignment?

State laws differ widely on how and when a voluntary wage assignment can be enforced. Some states have no restrictions on voluntary assignments. Others have banned them entirely. Where state laws do apply, they generally limit the amounts that can be withheld from an employee's wages and place restrictions on the period over which an employee's wages may be assigned.

In general, the laws of the state in which the employee is employed will determine if the employee has the right to assign and what restrictions apply. [Haberman v. American Sheet & Tin Plate Co., 285 Ill. App. 542, 2 N.E.2d 349 (1936)]

Q 7:78   Are there additional considerations that apply to garnishments and wage assignments?

A garnishment policy should be reasonable and well known to the workers. Although rules specifying "two times and out" have been upheld, many arbiters seem to favor withholding the discharge penalty until the third garnishment. This puts the employee on notice and provides an opportunity to warn the worker that future financial involvement of this kind will lead to discharge.

The rule must be applied in an even-handed manner, with no employee treated in a discriminatory fashion. Application of the policy must be regular and predictable. Additionally, the policy must be lawful and reasonable.

Employers will want to assess the impact of state and federal employment laws, which prohibit discrimination in employment, before terminating employees for incurring wage garnishments. Certain types of employees may be disparately impacted by a wage garnishment policy and this pattern of termination may be found to be discriminatory. Employers that discharge employees who are subject to wage garnishments should document that the discharge was based on job performance and not the garnishments.

The policy should include information as to whether the employer deducts the administrative fee allowed by the employee work state. If the employer does not honor voluntary assignments or other deductions not sponsored by the employer, that information should be made known as well. Employers should review relevant provisions of any applicable labor contracts to determine whether they have any impact on wage garnishments.

Payday Loans

Q 7:79   Is a notice from a payday lender treated the same as a wage assignment?

To manage their finances, employees are increasingly relying on payday loans, which typically carry a high interest rate. Based on the structure of the underlying loan agreements, employees can easily find themselves with outstanding debt that can become an obligation subject to collection.

Payday loans have become a challenge for payroll departments as the lenders attempt to collect the loan by garnishing employees' wages. However, these types of arrangements are typically voluntary assignments and do not qualify as creditor garnishments.

States continue to pass legislation and issue regulations to address payday loans. Illinois, for example, requires the document for a payday loan to state on the face of the agreement "wage assignment" and be signed by the employee. Some states may also require that the default must be greater than 40 days and provide an explanation of how the outstanding debt can be cancelled.

Fair Labor Standards Act

Q 7:80   What limitations are imposed under the Fair Labor Standards Act for wage garnishments?

The FLSA generally treats wage garnishments that are subject to the CCPA limitations and are paid to a creditor as wages paid to the employee for minimum wage and overtime pay compliance. An administrative charge permitted under state law and charged by an employer generally cannot cause the individual's wage to be below the FLSA minimum. [29 C.F.R. §§ 531.39, 531.40]

Q 7:81   How are voluntary payroll deductions handled under the FLSA?

The FLSA imposes certain prohibitions on voluntary payroll deductions. These include, but are not limited to, the following:

- No portion of an employee's wages can be withheld to pay any liability the employer is liable to pay (e.g., federal unemployment or the employer's portion of FICA payments due on the employee's wages). [29 C.F.R. §§ 531.39, 531.40]
- The employer may not impose any involuntary deductions (e.g., uniform charge) that would cause the net employee payment to be less than the FLSA minimum wage or full payment for overtime. [29 C.F.R. § 778.307]

Q 7:82   What types of employer deductions cannot be imposed if the charges would reduce the employee's wage below the FLSA's minimum wage and overtime requirements?

There is no specific listing of which types of payment would violate the FLSA's minimum wage and overtime requirements; however, they are generally deductions deemed to be for the benefit of the employer. Here is a short list of items that would generally be treated as reducing an employee's wages for FLSA purposes:

- A weekly charge for a uniform that must be worn at work. Similarly, the employer's cost to purchase a uniform to be worn at work that is subtracted from wages reduces the employee's minimum wage and overtime pay in the period during which the employee purchased the uniform.
- Reduction in lost time made as a penalty for being late beyond the missed time (there is no requirement to pay for lost time of a salaried employee).
- Deductions for cash shortages or for embezzlements that are imposed on the employee's last paycheck. An employer may not deduct alleged embezzled payments until the claim is validated in a court of law.

- Deductions in a current period for overpayment in a prior period. The employer can make an adjustment for an overpayment; the employer cannot impose a correction that results in an employee receiving less than the minimum wage or full overtime pay.
- Deductions that represent repayment of a debt owed to the employer for an advance or loan to the extent the employee's next payment is below the FLSA's minimum wage and overtime requirements.

[29 C.F.R. § 778.307; Wage & Hour Op. Ltr. No. 239 (Oct. 1, 1973)]

Chapter 8

The Fair Labor Standards Act

Following President Obama's directive to modify and modernize the overtime rule under the Fair Labor Standards Act of 1938 (FLSA), the Department of Labor responded. On May 18, 2016, the Department of Labor issued the Final Rule on Defining the Exceptions for Executive, Administrative, Professional, Outside Sales, and Computer Employees under the FLSA. The "Overtime Rule" or "Final Rule" updates the salary level required for the executive, administrative, and professional ("white collar") exemption to meet the objective to provide overtime protections and simplify the identification of overtime-exempt employees.

The plan raises the salary level from its previous amount of $455 per week (the equivalent of $23,660 per year) to a new level of $913 per week (the equivalent of $47,476 per year). Salaried employees below the new level would typically be entitled to overtime. The Final Rule also raises the compensation level for highly compensated employees from $100,000 to $134,004 annually. The changes were to take effect on December 1, 2016. Employers reviewed their current employees' roles and job descriptions to analyze how the rule would be apply. On November 22, 2016, a preliminary injunction from the U.S. Court of Appeals, Eastern District of Texas, placed the Final Rule on hold. At publication, no new developments have occurred.

The FLSA imposes a minimum wage ($7.25 an hour effective July 24, 2009), a requirement for overtime pay (generally when a nonexempt employee works more than 40 hours in a workweek), restrictions on child labor, recordkeeping obligations, and equal pay requirements for employees covered under the Act.

This chapter identifies which employers (generally referred to as *enterprises*) or individual employees are covered for purposes of the Act, and then discusses the employees to which exemptions apply. It includes an explanation of the white-collar regulations. The chapter also describes the Act's child labor and equal pay provisions. Recordkeeping obligations under the FLSA are addressed in chapter 11. Answers are supported with citations to regulatory guidance and, where applicable, to the Department of Labor's (DOL) Field Operations Handbook. Note that the Field Operations Handbook (FOH) contains the agency's interpretations of the law and its enforcement positions. While the level of deference the FOH receives from the courts will vary depending on the circumstances, it is at a minimum considered informed guidance. It may also provide a good faith defense against the imposition of liquidated damages and even back wages in some circumstances. Employers should consult with experienced counsel concerning reliance on FOH positions.

The Fair Labor Standards Act

Coverage—Jurisdiction

Overview

Q 8:1   What is the Fair Labor Standards Act?

The FLSA is a federal law enacted in 1938 in response to employment conditions existing at the time of the Great Depression. This law has been amended a number of times. The FLSA, with its subsequent amendments, is one of the most important federal laws governing employee wages and working hours. The Act covers a broad range of employment practices:

- It sets the minimum wage and overtime rates covered, nonexempt employees must be paid.

- It places restrictions on the types of work children can perform and the hours they can work.

- It defines certain recordkeeping requirements and mandates equal pay for equal work.

Note that some states and localities impose additional or more stringent wage-hour standards. Since the FLSA does not preempt stricter state and local standards, it is important to note that employers must generally comply with the law that is more beneficial to the employee.

Many employment practices are not regulated under the FLSA. For example, the FLSA does not require that an employee be provided with vacation, holiday, or sick leave, and it does not mandate rest periods or set the maximum number of hours that an employee who is age 16 or older may work. In many regions of the country, employment-related activities not regulated by the FLSA may, however, be subject to state and other federal laws. An employee is covered under the Act if he or she meets the requirements for "individual coverage" or if the employer meets the requirements for "enterprise coverage."

Q 8:2   Does the FLSA coverage apply to the employer or the employee?

Both. The FLSA governs how employers pay employees. When an employer is covered as a covered enterprise, the protections of coverage run to all the employees, unless they are exempt. Employees who are engaged in interstate commerce or the production of goods for interstate commerce are covered individually by the Act.

Q 8:3   Are all employees covered under the FLSA?

No; however, the vast majority of employees are covered. Enterprise coverage applies to all of an employer's workers when the employer is an enterprise engaged in commerce (in this context "commerce" refers to interstate commerce or activities closely related to or directly essential to interstate commerce (commerce between two or more states or a state and a foreign country)). To be an enterprise engaged in commerce, the employer must meet certain tests. It must have two or more employees engaged in commerce or in the production of goods for commerce, or at least two employees handling, selling, or otherwise working on goods or materials that have been moved in or produced for commerce by any person. [29 U.S.C. § 203(s)(1)(A)(i)] The Act also sets a minimum threshold, based on the enterprise's annual dollar volume of sales made or business done (basically at $500,000) for enterprise coverage. However, when an enterprise's revenue falls below the threshold, and enterprise coverage does not apply, individual coverage often applies. Note also that the level of involvement in commerce varies between the two types of coverage. For enterprise coverage, all the involvement in interstate commerce that is necessary is that two or more employees handle, sell, or otherwise work on something that has at some time been moved in interstate commerce. An individual, to whom individual coverage applies, on the other hand, must have regular and continuous involvement in interstate commerce, as opposed to occasional involvement.

The FLSA also specifies that governmental employers, hospitals, nursing homes, elementary and secondary schools, and colleges constitute covered enterprises even if they do not meet the monetary threshold. Note, though, that when an employer's workers are covered under the FLSA, certain workers may be excluded from the minimum wage and/or overtime requirements under FLSA exemptions.

Q 8:4   What types of employees are not covered by the minimum wage and overtime provisions of the FLSA?

Employees of small employers (that do not meet the sales-volume threshold for enterprise coverage, or do not have at least two employees), who are not directly engaged in the activities of interstate commerce, are not covered by the minimum wage and overtime provisions of the FLSA. This would be true, for example, of the sole employee who sweeps up the floor at a barber shop that operates as a sole proprietorship. However, this employee would be covered if, in addition to the chore of cleaning up, he or she were required, on a regular basis, to order supplies from an out-of-state distributor. The FLSA also contains certain exemptions from the minimum wage and overtime requirements.

Q 8:5   Who is an employer under the FLSA?

The FLSA defines an employer as any person or entity "acting directly or indirectly in the interest of an employer in relation to an employee." This definition includes individuals, corporations, partnerships, sole proprietorships, associations, and other groups or entities, such as agents or managers, who act for or are authorized to act for an employer. In some instances the FLSA requires that employers with related activities or unified operations be treated as a single enterprise for purposes of application of the coverage requirements. [29 U.S.C. § 203(d)]

Q 8:6   Does the FLSA apply to all employers located within the United States and its territories?

Generally, yes. The FLSA applies to employers and workers in all 50 states, the District of Columbia, Puerto Rico, the Virgin Islands, and territories or possessions of the United States (including American Samoa, Eriwetok Atoll, Kwajalein Atoll, Guam, Wake Island, the Outer Continental Shelf Islands, and Johnston Island). Coverage of these workers depends on whether either the enterprise or the individual requirements of the FLSA are met. [29 U.S.C. § 213(f)]

Enterprise Coverage

Q 8:7   What is enterprise coverage under the FLSA?

When enterprise coverage applies, all the workers of the enterprise are covered, regardless of their specific activities. (Even if the workers are covered by the FLSA, it is important to note that they may be "exempt" from minimum wage and/or overtime requirements under the Act.) An employer constitutes an enterprise when (1) it has two or more employees who are engaged in commerce or in the production of goods for interstate commerce or who handle, sell, or otherwise work with goods or materials that have been moved or produced for interstate commerce; and (2) the employer meets the sales-volume test ($500,000 or more a year). [29 U.S.C. § 203(s)(1); 29 C.F.R. § 776.21]

Certain employers are deemed to be enterprises engaged in commerce and are covered without regard to their sales volume. These include hospitals, businesses providing medical or nursing care for residents, schools and pre-schools, and governmental agencies. [29 U.S.C. §§ 203(s)(1)(B), 213]

Note. Even if the employer does not meet the enterprise thresholds stated here, the employee is likely covered by the individual coverage provisions of the Act (see Q 8:22).

Q 8:8   How does the gross-receipts threshold affect enterprise coverage under the FLSA?

The $500,000 sales volume threshold acts to remove many small firms from enterprise coverage. Generally, an entity must have annual gross receipts of at least $500,000 before it is subject to enterprise coverage—assuming that the entity also satisfies the other criteria for such classification.

Some small employers are automatically subject to enterprise coverage without regard to the gross-receipts threshold—as long as the employer employs at least two workers. These employers, regardless of size, include:

- Hospitals, nursing homes, and institutions that care for the sick, aged, mentally ill, or disabled;
- Preschools, elementary and secondary schools, and schools for mentally or physically handicapped or gifted and talented children; and
- Public agencies.

[29 U.S.C. §§ 203(s)(1)(B), 203(s)(1)(C)]

Q 8:9   What types of income are included in gross receipts for purposes of the enterprise coverage gross-receipts threshold?

The $500,000 gross-receipts threshold for enterprise coverage includes all of a firm's receipts from all sales made and "business done" during a 12-month period. This revenue includes all interstate and intrastate sales, as well as any other "business done." The phrase "business done," as included in the FLSA, indicates that a firm's sales volume is not limited to sales under a strict accounting interpretation.

An enterprise's annual business volume includes:

- Total sales made by the subject enterprise and its FLSA-exempt units (e.g., separate units that do not satisfy the requirements for FLSA coverage and, as a result, are not covered).
- Gross sales of leased departments (e.g., a leased jewelry department in a department store) that are integral parts of the enterprise.

- Gross income from credit or similar charges.
- Gross sales before any reductions for trade-in allowances, as well as amounts from sales of trade-in merchandise.
- Excise taxes at the retail level that are not separately identified in the price charged to the customer (e.g., certain fuels).
- Rental receipts from apartments.

The following sales-related items may be excluded from an enterprise's annual business-volume computations:

- Credits for returned or exchanged goods
- Rebates
- Discounts
- Sales by family-owned businesses that employ only immediate family members
- Excise taxes charged at the retail level that are separately identified in the price charged to the customer

Excise taxes that may be excluded in the business-volume computation include, but are not limited to:

- State, county, and municipal sales taxes and federal and state excise taxes on gasoline.
- Excise taxes on jewelry, furs, toilet preparations, and luggage.
- Excise taxes on liquid fuel used in diesel-powered highway vehicles.
- Excise taxes on benzene and liquefied petroleum gas used as motor fuel.

[29 C.F.R. §§ 779.259–779.264]

Q 8:10   How is the business-volume threshold calculated under the rolling-quarters method?

The "rolling-quarters method" allows an employer to determine whether the business-volume threshold has been met on a quarter-by-quarter basis. Federal courts have affirmed this method as a valid way of making business-volume computations. [29 C.F.R. § 779.266]

The rolling-quarters method divides the year into quarters (calendar or fiscal). Business volume is determined for the most recently completed quarter, and that amount is added to the business volume for the three preceding quarters. If that amount equals $500,000 or more, the FLSA coverage applies for the subsequent quarter (assuming that other criteria for this classification are met). Once this method is adopted, it must be used for making all subsequent calculations.

Example. Chevy Chair Inc., is calculating whether it is subject to FLSA enterprise coverage for the quarter beginning April 1, 2017.

Quarter	Business Volume
Quarter just ended:	
March 31, 2017	$242,000
Prior three quarters:	
December 31, 2016	$208,000
September 30, 2016	$140,000
June 30, 2016	$150,000

Chevy Chair Inc.'s, total business volume for the previous four quarters equals $740,000—an amount that exceeds the $500,000 business-volume threshold. Assuming that Chevy Chair Inc., satisfies the other enterprise requirements of the FLSA, it must pay the minimum wage and overtime for the quarter beginning April 1, 2017.

Note that regardless of this classification, an employee of Chevy Chair Inc., who is otherwise covered under the individual requirements (not enterprise) must be paid overtime and a minimum wage.

Q 8:11   Must a new business have actual revenues of $500,000 before the FLSA's enterprise coverage applies?

No. Certain businesses (typically new businesses) are treated as having met the $500,000 sales volume threshold from day one, even if their revenues are less than this amount, if it is reasonable to assume that the firm's annual business volume will meet the $500,000 threshold. For example, it is reasonable to assume that a newly opened large department store will meet the threshold. Although the determination of what constitutes a new business depends on the facts and circumstances, the employer must be able to document the basis for its determination not to apply enterprise coverage to its employees.

As a guide to this determination, the business-volume threshold for a new business may be estimated by reviewing actual receipts, on a quarter-by-quarter basis, and annualizing those amounts. This is done by multiplying the business's first-quarter receipts by four, the sum of first- and second-quarter receipts of the new business by two, and the sum of first-, second-, and third-quarter receipts of the new business by one and one-third. After the fourth quarter of operation, the employer would apply the rolling method of computing business volume. [29 C.F.R. § 779.269]

Q 8:12   How is the two-employee threshold determined under the FLSA's enterprise coverage test?

An enterprise must have at least two employees (part-time or full-time) before it can be subject to FLSA enterprise coverage. The determination of whether two or more employees of an employer are engaged in interstate commerce and/or are handling, selling, or working on something that has moved in interstate commerce is made without regard to the employees' exempt status. [29 C.F.R. § 776.22a] Thus, an enterprise may exist when the only two employees who are engaged in interstate commerce are two exempt supervisors. For example, an employer is considered to have two employees for purposes of enterprise coverage even when the employer's only employees are exempt executives. [DOL Field Operations Handbook § 12b01]

Q 8:13 May two or more divisions of a single business or commonly controlled employer be treated as separate enterprises for purposes of the FLSA?

Yes, but it would be uncommon. The courts have generally found that all the activities of a single company constitute an enterprise. The FLSA defines an enterprise as "the related activities performed (either through unified operation or common control) by any person or persons for a common business purpose. . . . " Enterprise coverage applies to all related activities performed by one or more of these persons, including corporate units or other divisions or departments of an organization. Thus, this broad definition tends to have the effect of treating separate operations of related employers as a single enterprise. For example, the Fifth Circuit Court of Appeals held a bank's management of the building where it had its offices to be related to the bank's activities, and thus the building management was a covered enterprise. [29 U.S.C. § 203(r)(1); Wirtz v. Savannah Bank & Trust Co., 362 F.2d 857 (5th Cir. 1966)]

The Tenth Circuit Court of Appeals found in *Hodgson v. University Club Tower, Inc.* [466 F.2d 745 (10th Cir. 1972)] that despite the control that existed over a group of apartments, a motel, and certain business establishments, the entities were not a single enterprise. These entities had separate locations, unrelated management and operations, different services, and different customers. Also, the United States District Court for the Northern District of Iowa, in *Nelson v. Longlines Ltd.* [335 F. Supp. 2d 944 (N.D. Iowa 2004)], found that a holding company and a resort in which the holding company was the sole shareholder and for which the holding company handled the payroll, were not a single enterprise for purposes of the FLSA, even though they were under a common control, in as much as they were not involved in related activities and did not share a common business purpose. However, it should be noted that the FLSA is considered remedial social legislation, and courts are to construe coverage as broadly as possible. [A.H. Phillips, Inc. v. Walling, 324 U.S. 490, 493, 65 S. Ct. 807, 808, 89 L. Ed. 1095 (1945) (recognizing that FLSA must be interpreted broadly to effectuate its "humanitarian and remedial" purpose)]

Q 8:14 Can two separate entities become a single enterprise for purposes of FLSA coverage?

Yes. Two separate corporations (or other entities) are treated as a single enterprise under the FLSA when the entities comprise a series of related activities performed through "unified operations" or under "common control" and have a common business purpose. For example, the Fifth Circuit held that three separate companies performing maintenance, trash removal, and pest control were a single enterprise because they were held out to be a single entity to the public. They also shared the same office space, phone system, and employees. [Donovan v. Janitorial Servs., Inc., 672 F.2d 528 (5th Cir. 1982)]

The Sixth Circuit Court of Appeals found in *Dunlap v. Lourub Pharmacy, Inc.* [525 F.2d 235 (6th Cir. 1975)] that a liquor store and a pharmacy constituted a single enterprise even though the gross receipts of the liquor store and pharmacy operation were owned by the state of Ohio, which also regulated the business. The two stores were located in the same building, had the same employees, and were operated under one management group.

Likewise, the Fifth Circuit Court of Appeals found in *Reich v. Bay, Inc.* [23 F.3d 110 (5th Cir. 1994)] that a general contractor and subcontractor constituted a single enterprise for just over 14 months. During this period of time, the subcontractor provided employees to the general contractor, and both companies paid the employees. Both companies also shared the same principal office and place of business, and one person was responsible for maintaining the business records for both companies.

The FLSA's definition of related activities can cause two separate entities to be treated as a single enterprise. In general, the FLSA does not permit separate enterprise classification of the following related business activities:

- **Auxiliary or service activities.** An employer's auxiliary or service activities are those activities that are related to a firm's principal or "line" activities. These are treated under the FLSA as a single enterprise. [29 C.F.R. § 779.206; Dole v. Odd Fellows Home Endowment Bd., 912 F.2d 689 (4th Cir. 1990); Wirtz v. Savannah Bank & Trust Co., 362 F.2d 857 (5th Cir. 1966)] Examples of auxiliary activities include the operation of employee or customer parking lots, credit rating services for customers, security guard or other protective services at the employer's work location, training services, and administration of the employer's employee benefit and insurance plans.

- **Vertical business structures.** Activities that make up a vertical business structure are aggregated in a single enterprise when the activities are performed in an integrated or interdependent manner for a common business purpose. [Wirtz v. Barnes Grocery Co., 398 F.2d 718 (8th Cir. 1968)] The FLSA prevents integrated activities from being treated as two or more separate enterprises. An example of a vertical business structure would be a company that manufactures, wholesales, and retails a specific brand of merchandise. These three activities constitute a single enterprise, as the ultimate business goal is to distribute the manufactured goods through the retail stores. However, if the manufacturing facility is only indirectly used to manufacture a single component of the products sold in the retail stores, the two related activities might not be treated as a vertical business structure. In such a case these business entities could constitute separate enterprises, even if the operations were under common ownership.

- **Leased departments.** Leased departments within a retail store are generally considered to be related activities of the retail store in which they are located. For example, a retail department store may lease an electronics department to an unrelated corporation rather than staff and operate the electronics department itself. In this example, the leased department is treated as part of the department store for purposes of FLSA enterprise coverage, unless the facts and circumstances indicate otherwise. It does not matter that the two activities are not under common control.

- **Certain incidental or adjunct activities.** Certain other activities that are significantly different from a business's principal activities may be classified as "incidental or adjunct" activities. However, these activities may be considered related if they frequently arise in the course of a business's operations. For example, the services of a bank and an insurance firm might be considered related activities if the bank's employees often perform claims administration or solicitation of insurance sales in conjunction with the bank's financial planning services. [29 C.F.R. §§ 779.215, 779.225]

Q 8:15 When are two employers considered to be under common control, and therefore a single enterprise?

"Control" of a business does not follow the formal controlled group rules of I.R.C. Sections 414(b) and 414(c) that generally apply to coverage of benefits. Rather, for the FLSA, control exists when one entity has the "power to control" another entity.

The essence of the definition of control under the FLSA is a case-specific determination of whether the employer or a group of employers under common control constitutes a single covered enterprise. [Marshall v. Frozen Assets, 513 F. Supp. 591 (E.D. Mo. 1981); Marshall v. Realty Maint., Inc., 23 Wage & Hour Cas. (BNA) 454 (D.N.J. 1977); Marshall v. San Francisco Hosts, 24 Wage & Hour Cas. (BNA) 945 (W.D. Cal. 1979)]. In general, "the word 'control' may be defined as the act of controlling; power or authority to control; directing or restraining; domination." [29 C.F.R. § 779.211] Majority ownership is always construed by DOL as creating control. Control may also be exercised where there is no ownership at all.

Q 8:16 What are the FLSA's conglomerate coverage rules?

Conglomerate coverage is established under a special set of rules that is used to determine enterprise coverage for certain employers. Under these rules, separate retail, service, or agricultural establishments that are under common control with another establishment, with unrelated activities, but that support the activities of the establishment's employees (a "conglomerate") are subject to special FLSA coverage rules when the conglomerate's annual sales or business volume exceeds $10 million. These rules may lead to FLSA coverage when an entity fails to meet the normal sales volume test for enterprise coverage but has employment-related activities with another employer under common control. [29 U.S.C. § 213(g); Fact Sheet 14: Coverage Under Fair Labor Standards Act (FLSA)]

Q 8:17   Are the services of independent contractors considered part of the employer's related activities?

No. The services provided by a bona fide independent contractor are not considered part of an enterprise's related activities. Hence, an independent contractor that provides services for a covered enterprise does not become covered. However, the determination of whether an individual is an employee or an independent contractor can be quite difficult.

Examples of services provided by an independent contractor to a business that are not related activities include, but are not limited to, accounting, legal, or advertising services provided by an independent firm. Note that when these activities are provided by employees, coverage is required. [29 U.S.C. § 203(r)(1)]

For example, a museum that leased county property was found to be an independent contractor under the FLSA. [Powell v. Tucson Air Museum, 771 F.2d 1309 (9th Cir. 1985)] On the other hand, nurses working on a referral basis for hospitals and nursing homes were held not to be independent contractors. [Brock v. Superior Care, Inc., 840 F.2d 1054 (2d Cir. 1988)]

Q 8:18   Are there special enterprise coverage rules for franchises and co-ops?

Yes. An organization that franchises retail or service operations is generally treated as being independent from each separate franchise's operations, provided that they are each under independent ownership. That is, enterprise coverage of one entity will not automatically extend to the other entity (i.e., franchiser to franchisee or franchisee to another franchisee). In most cases the franchisee has merely agreed to use a specific brand name, sell only the goods or products of a certain manufacturer, and engage in cooperative marketing efforts. Similarly, independent businesses may join buying or advertising cooperatives without being treated as part of a larger enterprise for the FLSA coverage. [Stevens v. Welcome Wagon Int'l, Inc., 390 F.2d 75 (3d Cir. 1968); 29 U.S.C. § 203(r); 29 C.F.R. § 779.226]

Q 8:19   Are any employers excluded from FLSA enterprise coverage?

Yes. Regardless of business sales volume or the fact of the business being engaged in interstate commerce, three types of employers are exempt from the FLSA's enterprise coverage: (1) a business in which the only regular employees are members of the owner's immediate family, (2) employees of the legislative branches of state and local governments who are not subject to a public employer's civil service laws, and (3) elected public officials and their appointed staffs. [29 U.S.C. § 203(s)(2)]

Q 8:20   Are family businesses exempt from the FLSA enterprise coverage?

Generally, yes. If certain rules are met, a family business may be excluded from FLSA enterprise coverage. A family business, for FLSA purposes, is defined as a business or service entity whose only employees are family members (i.e., the entity's owner, the owner's spouse, children, parents, or other immediate family members). The following are not immediate family members under the Act: brother, sister, aunt, uncle, nephew, or in-laws. A family business may be a corporation owned by only members of the family, a partnership of family members, or a sole proprietorship. It is important to note that when a family business is exempt from FLSA enterprise coverage, it may lose the exemption when it regularly or frequently employs nonfamily workers. [29 U.S.C. § 203(s)(2)] This is determined on a case-by-case basis.

Q 8:21   When is an enterprise covered under the FLSA's "grandfather" coverage?

The FLSA is periodically amended, and these amendments generally update the coverage requirements. The "grandfather clause" states that any business that was previously covered before the inception of the new standards will continue to be covered by the minimum wage, overtime, and child labor provisions in effect before the effective date of the amendments. For example, the FLSA amendments of 1989 were effective in April 1990 and increased the coverage threshold from $362,500 to $500,000 for certain businesses. Businesses that were covered under the old provision continued to be covered even if they did not gross $500,000. [29 U.S.C. § 203(s)]

Individual Coverage

Q 8:22   How does individual coverage differ from enterprise coverage?

In practical terms (though not historically), the first test usually applied in determining coverage is for enterprise coverage. If enterprise coverage applies, all of the enterprise's employees are covered. If enterprise coverage does not apply, then employees may still be protected by the FLSA if they are "individually covered." This is also known as "traditional" coverage, and it focuses on the individual employee's activities and not the employer's—although it is difficult for an employer to avoid individual coverage if it is involved in interstate commerce activities.

The DOL Field Operations Handbook provides a description of more than 100 specific occupations and gives factors to assist in determining whether employees are engaged in commerce and are entitled to individual coverage. [Field Operations Handbook §§ 11a00–11w13]

Q 8:23   When does the FLSA's individual coverage apply to workers?

In general, individual workers are covered under the individual coverage test in workweeks in which:

1. The employees are engaged directly in interstate commerce;

2. The employees are engaged in the production of goods for interstate commerce;

3. The employees are employed in any process, activity, or occupation that is closely related and directly essential to the production of goods for interstate commerce; or

4. The employees are engaged in activities so closely related to interstate commerce that, as a practical matter, the activities should be considered part of it, as for example, when they work at an instrumentality of interstate commerce, such as an airport.

Under individual coverage criteria, workers are covered even if only a small percentage of their duties or work hours are devoted to interstate commerce so long as the employees' activities are regular and recurring. Individual coverage does not impose a sales volume test. [29 U.S.C. §§ 206(a), 207(a)]

Employees who otherwise satisfy the FLSA's individual coverage criteria and are engaged in both covered and noncovered work during any given week are considered covered and therefore are entitled to FLSA protection for the entire workweek. [29 U.S.C. §§ 206(a), 206(a)]

However, an individual who is infrequently involved in interstate commerce (e.g., makes one or two interstate shipments of equipment over a two-year period) is not generally treated as being involved in interstate commerce. [29 U.S.C. §§ 206(a), 207(a); Remmers v. Egan, 332 F.2d 103 (2d Cir. 1964); 29 C.F.R. § 776.0]

Q 8:24   What is interstate commerce for purposes of the FLSA?

The FLSA defines interstate commerce (referred to in the Act as "commerce") to mean, "trade, commerce, transportation, transmission, or communication among the several States or between any State and any place outside thereof." [29 U.S.C. § 203(b)] A state is defined as "any State of the United States, the District of Columbia or any Territory or possession of the United States." Thus, all trade between entities in two or more states, as well as foreign export or import, is treated as interstate commerce. Therefore, whenever one business or service entity buys from or sells to a business or service entity in a second state, both are involved in interstate commerce. For example, when a law firm buys software directly from an out-of-state vendor, the law firm is involved in interstate commerce. It is important to note that this term is generally construed to be very broad.

Note. The terms *commerce* and *interstate commerce* are used in this chapter to mean interstate commerce as defined under 29 U.S.C. Section 203(b).

The courts have expanded the application of the FLSA by interpreting commerce and interstate commerce more and more broadly. For example, the U.S. Supreme Court established criteria to be used in determining whether an employee or an enterprise is engaged in interstate commerce. According to the Court, this determination is based on whether the employee's activities are "directly and vitally" related to the functioning of an interstate facility that is more a part of interstate commerce than an isolated local activity. [Walling v. Jacksonville Paper Co., 317 U.S. 564 (1978)] The Court has even held that employees who used the telephone to receive out-of-state calls were involved in interstate commerce. [Martin v. Universal Alarm Sys., Inc., No. 91-6372 (E.D. Pa. 1992)]

Q 8:25   Does the FLSA define any specific activities as constituting interstate commerce?

Yes. Other than general commercial activities between entities in two states, the FLSA links certain noncommercial activities that involve "instrumentalities of commerce" as being interstate in nature. Instrumentalities of commerce include fixed or movable facilities on which commerce depends, such as railroads, highways, city streets, pipelines, telephone lines, electrical transmission lines, rivers, streams, or other waterways over which interstate commerce more or less regularly moves; airports; railroad, truck, or steamship terminals; telephone exchanges and radio or television stations; post offices and express offices; bridges and ferries carrying traffic moving in interstate commerce; bays, harbors, piers, wharves, and docks used for interstate shipping; dams, dikes, revetments, and levees that directly facilitate shipping navigation; warehouses or distribution depots devoted to the receipt and shipment of goods in interstate commerce; and ships, vehicles, and aircraft regularly used in transportation of persons or goods in commerce. [29 C.F.R. § 776.11]

Workers are entitled to the protections of the FLSA (under individual coverage) when they work in industries or firms that move goods or are associated with interstate commerce. The FLSA refers to these as "channels" of interstate commerce. Examples of individuals included in channels of interstate commerce include those employed by shipping, transportation, Internet, telephone, television, or radio companies. However, employees whose services are unrelated to such activities are also covered if their work is considered an "essential part of the stream of interstate commerce." Thus, workers whose activities involve the receipt or distribution of goods across state lines (e.g., warehouse employees) and employees who regularly handle credit card purchases for banks are also covered by the FLSA. Goods are considered to be in movement for purposes of this criterion until they reach the ultimate consumer. [29 C.F.R. § 776.8]

Bank and insurance company employees typically are covered because their activities involve the regular and recurring use of channels of commerce to send and receive contracts, orders, receipts, deposits, securities, and other goods.

Q 8:26   Must the employee or the enterprise be engaged in interstate commerce each day of the workweek to be covered under the FLSA?

No. An employee or enterprise is treated as being engaged in interstate commerce if the employee or enterprise engages in any aspect of commerce for any period within a workweek. [29 U.S.C. § 207]

However, note that the interstate commerce requirements for individual coverage under the Act differ somewhat from the requirements for enterprise coverage. For individual coverage, the employee must be engaged in interstate commerce on more than an occasional basis.

Q 8:27   Can janitors or bookkeepers be involved in interstate commerce?

Yes. The regulations provide examples of work or jobs that normally are covered under the "closely related" and "directly essential" standards of interstate commerce. In this context, according to wage-hour guidelines, jobs are closely related and directly essential if they "may reasonably be considered close, as distinguished from remote or tenuous." In other words, if the work of the employee directly benefits production in a realistic sense and contributes to the process of producing goods, it is considered closely related and directly essential. Such jobs include those of janitors, stockroom and warehouse workers, messengers, employees who deliver supplies or equipment, and employees who remove waste materials; such individuals are also covered if they work at facilities involved in interstate commerce. In addition, the following jobs are the types of nonmanual jobs that may be covered under the "related and essential" standard: bookkeepers; clerks; internal auditors; payroll clerks; personnel and human resources employees; advertising, promotion, and public relations employees; draftspersons; inspectors; work instructors; and industrial safety employees. [29 C.F.R. § 776.19(b)]

Note. The employees of independent firms that provide these services to an entity involved in the production of goods for interstate commerce may also be covered. For instance, employees of a small (i.e., with gross revenues of less than $500,000 per year) janitorial service who clean in a factory producing goods for interstate commerce are individually covered in the workweeks in which they do such cleaning, because their activities are closely related and directly essential to the production of goods for interstate commerce. [29 C.F.R. § 776.19]

Q 8:28   Is an employee who commutes across state lines deemed to be involved in interstate commerce?

Not necessarily. Employees who cross state lines to commute to and from work would not be subject to the FLSA unless their work is involved in interstate commerce. Employees are covered under the FLSA's engaged-in-commerce standard when they regularly travel across state lines or international boundaries in the course of their work activities. In addition, employees generally do not become subject to the FLSA because they cross state or international boundaries in certain isolated instances in the course of otherwise local activities. [29 C.F.R. § 776.12]

Q 8:29   Does the FLSA apply to employees who work in a foreign country?

No. Employees working in a foreign country or foreign location that may be subject to U.S. jurisdiction are not covered by the FLSA, even if they are working for an American-based employer. [29 U.S.C. § 213(f)]

Q 8:30   Does the FLSA apply to employees who work for a Native American organization?

The courts are split on this question. In the Ninth Circuit, the Court of Appeals held that overtime provisions of FLSA apply to a retail business owned by Indian tribal members and located on the Puyallup Indian Reservation in Washington State. [Solis v. Matheson, 563 F.3d 425 (9th Cir. 2009)] Factors that may afford a different outcome relate to examples when the employees are tribal officers. [Reich v. Great Lakes Indian Fish & Wildlife Comm'n, 4 F.3d 490 (7th Cir. 1993)]

The FLSA's minimum wage and overtime provisions do apply to a tribal business operating in the commercial workplace that hires both non-Native Americans and Native Americans. A Native American organization that employs only Native Americans for tribal business is not covered. [Donovan v. Coeur d'Alene Tribal Farm, 751 F.2d 1113 (9th Cir. 1985); Martin v. Great Lakes Indian Fish & Wildlife Comm'n, 1 Wage & Hour Cas. 2d (BNA) 58 (W.D. Wis. 1992)]

Q 8:31   Are employees who are required to relocate to another state involved in interstate commerce?

No. An individual who is required by his or her employer to relocate to another state in the course of performing an essentially local trade or occupation is not treated as being engaged in interstate commerce. [29 C.F.R. § 776.12]

Employment Relationship

Q 8:32　How does the FLSA define employment?

The FLSA's definition of employment is quite broad. To employ is to "suffer or permit an individual to work." [29 U.S.C. § 203(g)]

If an employer knows about or tolerates work, this is sufficient to establish an employment relationship with the worker. [29 C.F.R. § 785.11] The mere recognition that an individual is providing services is also likely sufficient to establish an employment relationship under the FLSA. The courts have expanded this definition to include constructive knowledge of work if exercise of reasonable diligence would have given the employer such knowledge. [Reich v. Department of Conservation & Natural Res., 28 F.3d 1076 (11th Cir. 1994)]

The FLSA does not require a contract for an employment relationship to exist.

Q 8:33　Who is an employee under the FLSA?

The FLSA broadly defines employee as "any individual employed by an employer." Even though the FLSA generally requires coverage for any arrangements in which one party "suffers or permits" another person to work, certain individuals who meet this general definition may not qualify as covered employees. [29 U.S.C. § 203(e)] See chapter 6 for a discussion of the common-law determination of the employee–employer relationship. [29 C.F.R. § 525.3(g)]

Q 8:34　Are payments to independent contractors subject to the provisions of the FLSA?

No. The FLSA only applies when an employment relationship exists, and individuals who qualify as independent contractors are not considered employees. However, the FLSA lacks any specific guidance that may be applied in determining whether an individual is an employee or an independent contractor. That determination is based on the facts and circumstances of the working relationship. An employer may not avoid coverage under the FLSA merely by reclassifying a common-law employee as an independent contractor. It is important to note that an individual who is paid as an independent contractor, but in reality is an employee, will be treated as an employee for purposes of FLSA coverage. [Rutherford Food Corp. v. McComb, 331 U.S. 722 (1947)]

Q 8:35　Can a worker be the employee of two employers for the same work?

Yes. Some employment relationships between two (or more) employers are so interrelated that an individual can be "jointly employed" by the employers. Under such circumstances, the FLSA generally applies to the combined working hours for all "joint employers" during the given workweek. [29 C.F.R.§§ 791.2(a), 791.2(b)]

Q 8:36   How does the FLSA coverage apply when an employee works for two or more employers?

Generally, an employee working for two or more unrelated (and not "joint") employers is treated as being covered for services provided to either of the employers, provided the employee meets the FLSA's coverage requirements for each employer. That is, each employer is treated separately for the purposes of FLSA coverage, as long as the employers operate independently of one another (i.e., the employers are separate and distinct). When two employers jointly employ the employee, the time worked for each employer during a given workweek must be totaled for purposes of computing overtime. However, an employee who works 36 hours for one employer and 34 hours for an unrelated (and not "joint") employer in the same workweek is not entitled to overtime pay from either employer. [29 C.F.R. § 791.2; 29 U.S.C. § 203(s)(1)]

Q 8:37   What does the term *joint employment relationship* mean for FLSA purposes?

The determination of whether "joint employment" exists is a case-by-case determination and depends on all the facts and circumstances. An employee is generally considered to be jointly employed, however, if: (1) two or more employers have an arrangement to share an employee's services, (2) one employer is acting directly or indirectly in the interest of the other employer (or employers) in relation to the employee, or (3) the employers share control of the employee because one employer controls the other employer or the two employers are under common control. A joint employment relationship of unrelated employers could occur, for example, when an employee of an electronics store that leases space in a department store performs duties for the department store or is under the direction of the department store's personnel. [29 C.F.R. § 791.2]

In an April 11, 2005, opinion letter, the U.S. Department of Labor's Wage and Hour Division examined whether a Licensed Practical Nurse (LPN) who worked for an acute care hospital during the week and a nursing home on the weekend was jointly employed by both. In this case, both were part of a large health system owned by a single nonprofit holding company. Each facility had its own human resources department, employee handbook, payroll system, retirement plan, and employer identification number (EIN). Further, although this LPN worked for two of the entities, there was no regular interchange of employees. In this case, the Division found that both entities were ultimately under common control of the holding company, and that some of the directors and officers were shared. Further, in examining the relationship between the companies, it appeared that they provided certain human resources support to the other, when needed, and that—although separate—many of the employment policies were identical. In addition, the Division found that job opportunities in one facility were often posted in the other. Accordingly, after examining all the facts and circumstances, the Division found that the hospital and nursing home were joint employers.

On the other hand, the Kansas District Court in *Burnison v. Memorial Hospital, Inc.* [820 F. Supp. 549 (D. Kan. 1993)] held that a joint employer relationship was not created between the City of McPherson, Kansas and Memorial Hospital. In this case, the Hospital operated an emergency medical service pursuant to a formal agreement with the City, which stated that the drivers and attendants (emergency medical technicians and paramedics) were the employees, agents, and servants of the hospital. The hospital had the sole authority to hire and fire the employees and set their work schedules. The hospital also maintained their employment records, trained them, fixed their salaries, provided health and disability insurance, and set and enforced disciplinary rules.

On January 20, 2016, the Wage and Hour Division (Administrator's Interpretation No. 2016-1) confirmed that definition covers joint employment relationships by extending the definition of "employ" to be as broad as possible.

Note that the DOL will find joint employment in almost every situation involving "leased employees" or employees of "temporary help" firms when the company using the leased or temporary employees directs and controls their work.

Q 8:38 Are prisoners who are required to work for the government covered under the FLSA?

Prisoners (inmates) who are required to work while serving a sentence in prison are not employees under the FLSA when the work is within the confines of the prison, on prison farms, in road gangs, and in other areas directly associated with the incarceration program. However, if the inmate is contracted out by an institution to a private company or individual, an employee–employer relationship may be created between the prisoner and the nongovernment entity. In such cases, the inmate may be covered under either the enterprise or individual coverage provisions of the FLSA. It is the DOL's contention that the employment relationship exists even if the nongovernment work is performed on prison property. [DOL Field Operations Handbook § 10b03, 10b27; Henthorn v. Department of Navy, 29 F.3d 682, 686 (D.C. Cir. 1994); Vanskike v. Peters, 974 F.2d 806 (7th Cir. 1992)]

The courts have not necessarily agreed with this position and have held in some cases that prisoners are not employees even when they are contracted out to private parties. This conclusion is based on the fact that the private party lacks the control required of an employment relationship. [Carter v. Dutchess Cmty. Coll., 735 F.2d 8 (2d Cir. 1984)]

Q 8:39 What are the FLSA implications for a telecommuter worker?

The DOL does not distinguish telecommuters from other employees. Telecommuters are covered under the FLSA in the same way as other employees, and the same exemptions apply to them. Employers should consider creating an established policy to cover telecommuting workers.

Q 8:40 Can an employer avoid FLSA coverage through the use of leased employees?

No. The FLSA generally treats leased employees as the employees of both the leasing company and the client company. [29 U.S.C. § 203(r)(1)] See Q 8:37.

Q 8:41 Will a worker with substantial investment in tools be exempt from the FLSA?

The general FLSA requirements that lead to classification of a worker as an employee, and therefore, eligible for overtime and minimum wage, focus on the "economic realities" of the work relationship. When a worker is economically dependent on the business, that fact generally leads to treatment under the FLSA as an employee. In applying the economic reality test, the courts generally look at seven factors (see DOL/WH "Fact Sheet No.13"):

1. The degree of control exerted by the "employer" over the worker
2. The worker's opportunity for profit or loss
3. The permanence of the working relationship
4. The worker's investment in equipment or materials needed to perform the job
5. The degree of skill required to perform the work
6. The extent to which the work is an integral part of the "employer's" business.
7. The degree of independent business organization and operation.

Investment in tools or equipment is only one factor in determining the existence of an employment relationship. Thus, when the only substantial difference between one worker and another is the fact that one worker has a large investment in equipment, this fact alone does not alter the realities of the working relationship. This principle was tested in a lawsuit brought by rig welders in the natural gas pipeline construction industry. The courts found the welders to be employees covered under the FLSA and they were therefore entitled to overtime compensation. [Baker v. Flint Eng'g & Constr. Co., 137 F.3d 1436 (10th Cir. 1998)]

Q 8:42   When are hours worked for one employer treated as hours worked for another employer for purposes of determining overtime under the FLSA?

A single individual may stand in the relationship of an employee to two or more employers at the same time under the FLSA. No provision in the FLSA prevents an individual who is employed by one employer from also entering into an employment relationship with a different employer. A determination of whether the employment by the employers is to be considered "joint employment" or "separate and distinct employments" for purposes of the FLSA depends on all the facts in the particular case. An employee will be employed jointly by two or more employers when employment by one employer is not completely disassociated from employment by the other employer(s). In such a situation, each joint employer is responsible, both individually and jointly, for compliance with all the applicable provisions of the FLSA, including the overtime pay provisions, with respect to the entire employment for the particular workweek.

This issue was addressed in a Wage and Hour Opinion Letter in which an employee worked for a vendor, stocking shelves in the stores where the employee normally worked, and also worked for the vendor at another store owned by the employee's primary employer. The DOL found that the two employers had a "joint employment" relationship with respect to services provided by a single employee. Both employers were responsible for compliance with all the applicable provisions of the FLSA, including the overtime provisions.

However, if such an employee also worked for the vendor in stores not owned by the owner of the store where the employee was regularly employed, no joint employment relationship would exist. [Wage & Hour Op. Ltr., Jan. 27, 1998]

> **Example.** Howard works for LockChain, Inc., full time and for two companies that are not owned by the same stockholders (i.e., are not part of a controlled group). Howard also works for Fan Train, Inc. on a part-time basis selling audio accessories for cars. If he works with Fan Train, Inc. to sell smartphones at LockChain, Inc., that employment would be considered joint employment by LockChain, Inc. and Fan Train, Inc.

Exemptions

Exemptions from Payment of Minimum Wage and Overtime

Q 8:43   What individual exemptions are available under the FLSA?

Numerous exemptions are available under the FLSA. In some cases, an exemption can be quite broad (i.e., a worker is exempt from all FLSA requirements); in others, a worker may be exempt only from the minimum wage or overtime requirements. Some exemptions apply to employees who meet the criteria listed in the FLSA, regardless of the type of business in which they are employed. The most important of these is the exemption for bona fide executive, administrative, and professional employees, and outside sales employees.

Specific exemptions also apply on an industry basis (e.g., transportation, agriculture, seasonal recreation, and entertainment) and to elected public officials. Each of these is subject to a separate set of tests and conditions, as set forth in the FLSA.

Determining when and how an exemption applies can be difficult. The Supreme Court has ruled that the FLSA exemptions are available only when employers and establishments plainly and unmistakably meet the letter, as well as, the spirit, of the law. As a result, employers should assume the employees are nonexempt unless they can clearly document a right to an exemption. Note also that nothing prevents an employer from paying the FLSA minimum wage and overtime even if an employee is exempt from such requirements.

If any one of the conditions of a statutory exemption is not met, the exemption does not apply.

Note that the tests that must be met for the executive, administrative, and professional employee exemption changed in 2004. The tests focus primarily on specific duties and responsibilities of the individual (duties test), rather than his or her job title, and typically require employees to exceed a minimum salary and be paid on a salary basis. [29 U.S.C. § 213]

Q 8:44   Does an employer have much latitude in interpreting the exemptions under the FLSA?

No. The DOL and the courts have generally applied a very narrow interpretation of the exemptions available under the FLSA. An employer can only use the exemptions to avoid minimum wage and overtime when the employee "plainly and unmistakably come within the statute['s] terms and spirit." It is the employer's burden to prove affirmatively that an exemption applies to a specific employee. [Corning Glass Works, Inc. v. Brennan, 417 U.S. 188, 196–97 (1974); Arnold v. Ben Kanowsky, Inc., 361 U.S. 388, 392 (1960); Donovan v. Fragg Bros., Inc., 678 F.2d 1116 (3d Cir. 1982)]

Q 8:45   If an employee is exempt from the provisions of the FLSA, is the employee also exempt from state minimum wage and overtime requirements?

Not necessarily. State laws may have broader coverage and may be more rigorous than the federal law. Under such circumstances, the employer must comply with the law that is most beneficial to the employee.

White-Collar Exemptions

Q 8:46   What are the latest changes in the white-collar exemptions?

Prior to 2004, the white-collar exemptions had been fairly stable for many years, with a salary test of $155 or $170 per week for the "long test" and $250 for the "short test." In 2004, the DOL issued final regulations amending the white-collar exemptions. Among other changes, the two-tier salary level test was eliminated, and the minimum salary for exemption was increased to $455 a week ($23,660 a year), with a separate test for "highly compensated employees" set at $100,000. There were changes to the duties test as explained below. Those final regulations became effective August 23, 2004.

On March 13, 2014, President Obama signed a Presidential Memorandum directing the Department of Labor to review the white-collar exemption and other FLSA provisions to produce regulations in 2015. On June 30, 2015, the DOL issued proposed regulations that include raising the executive, administrative, or professional employee from $455 a week ($23,660 a year) to $921 a week ($47,892 a year), based on 2013 data that would be adjusted for 2016 to $970 per week ($50,440).

There were no recommendations to change the duties under the administrative, executive, professional, or outside sales employees, although the DOL will seek comments on whether these duties should be updated. There was a recommendation to increase the salary for highly compensated employees to $122,148.

On May 18, 2016, the Department of Labor issued the Final Rule on Defining the Exceptions for Executive, Administrative, Professional, Outside Sales, and Computer Employees under the FLSA. The "Overtime Rule" or "Final Rule" updates the salary level required for the executive, administrative, and professional ("white collar") exemption to meet the objective to provide overtime protections and simplify the identification of overtime-exempt employees.

The plan raises the salary level from its previous amount of $455 per week (the equivalent of $23,660 per year) to a new level of $913 per week (the equivalent of $47,476 per year). Salaried employees below the new level would typically be entitled to overtime. The Final Rule also raises the compensation level for highly compensated employees from $100,000 to $134,004 annually. The changes were to take effect on December 1, 2016. On November 22, 2016, a preliminary injunction from the U.S. Court of Appeals, Eastern District of Texas, placed the Final Rule on hold.

Executive Exemption

Q 8:47   Which executives are exempt under the regulations?

To be exempt as an "executive" employee under the current regulations, the individual must:

- Be paid on a salary basis at a level of at least $913 per week not including board, lodging, or other facilities;
- Have a primary duty of managing the enterprise in which the employee is employed, or managing a department or subdivision of the enterprise;
- Customarily and regularly direct the work of two or more full-time employees; and
- Have the authority to hire or fire other employees or be able to suggest or recommend the hiring, firing, advancement, promotion, or other change of status of employees and have the recommendation be given particular weight. [29 C.F.R. § 541.100]

Note. Unlike under the former regulations, the current regulations no longer have a "long test" or "short test.".

Q 8:48   What activities constitute "management" under the executive exemption?

"Management" activities include, but are not limited to, interviewing, selecting, and training employees; setting and adjusting their rates of pay and hours of work; directing the work of employees; maintaining production or sales records for use in supervision or control; appraising employees' productivity and efficiency to be able to recommend promotions or other changes in status; handling employee complaints and grievances; disciplining employees; planning the work; determining the techniques to be used; apportioning the work among employees; determining the type of material, supplies, machinery, equipment or tools to be used or merchandise to be bought, stocked, and sold; controlling the flow and distribution of materials or merchandise and supplies; providing for employees' or the property's safety and security; planning and controlling the budget; and monitoring or implementing legal compliance measures. [29 C.F.R. § 541.102]

Q 8:49   To qualify for the executive exemption, must the department or subdivision that is managed be consistently located in one place?

Not necessarily. A customarily recognized department or subdivision must have a permanent status and a continuing function. However, the department or subdivision need not be physically within the employer's establishment and may move from place to place. In addition, the people supervised may change. For example, an exempt executive may draw and supervise employees from a pool, or supervise a team of workers drawn from other recognized units, if other factors are present that indicate that the employee is in charge of a recognized unit with a continuing function. [29 C.F.R. § 541.103]

Q 8:50   Do part-time employees count toward the requirement that executive employees "direct the work of two or more employees"?

Yes. To qualify for the executive exemption, an employee must direct the work of two full-time employees or their equivalent. Accordingly, this requirement is satisfied if the employee directs the work of one full-time and two half-time employees, four half-time employees, or any other combination of full-time and/or part-time employees that is equivalent to two full-time employees. [29 C.F.R. § 541.104]

Q 8:51   Under the executive exemption, do employees need to have the final word to have their suggestions and recommendations hold particular weight?

No. An employee's suggestions and recommendations may be given "particular weight" even if a higher level manager's recommendation has more importance and even if the employee does not have authority to make the ultimate decision. Factors in making this determination include, but are not limited to, whether it is part of the employee's job duties to make such recommendations, and the frequency with which such recommendations are made, requested, and relied on. Further, such recommendations must pertain to employees the executive customarily and regularly supervises. It does not include occasional suggestions. [29 C.F.R. § 541.105]

Q 8:52   Will executives automatically be disqualified if they perform nonexempt work in addition to their exempt work?

No. As long as employees primarily perform exempt work, they will not be disqualified from the executive exemption if they also perform some nonexempt work. Generally, exempt executives decide when to perform nonexempt duties and remain responsible for the success or failure of business operations under their management while performing the nonexempt work. In contrast, a non-exempt employee generally is directed by a supervisor to perform exempt work for a specified time period. For example, an assistant restaurant manager may serve customers or cook the food but still have the primary duty of management. On the other hand, a relief supervisor or a working supervisor whose primary duty is performing nonexempt work on the production line of a manufacturer is not considered exempt merely because the nonexempt production line employee occasionally has some responsibility for directing the work of other nonexempt production line employees when the exempt supervisor is not available. An electrician is not exempt by just directing the work of other employees on the job site, ordering parts and materials for the job, and handling requests from the prime contractor. [29 C.F.R. § 541.106]

Q 8:53 Can a business owner be automatically exempt as an executive?

Yes. Any employee who owns at least a bona fide 20 percent equity interest in the enterprise and is actively engaged in its management can be considered to be employed in a bona fide executive capacity, therefore meeting the white-collar exemption test as an executive. These owners do not need to meet the salary tests discussed below. [29 C.F.R. § 541.101]

Administrative Exemption

Q 8:54 Which employees qualify for the "administrative" exemption under the FLSA?

Under the current regulations, "an employee employed in a bona fide administrative capacity" is defined as an employee:

- Who is paid on a salary basis at a rate of at least $913 per week (the equivalent of $47,476 per year);
- Whose primary duty is to perform office or nonmanual work directly related to the management or general business operations of the employer or its customers; and
- Whose primary duty includes the exercise of discretion and independent judgment with respect to matters of significance. [29 C.F.R. § 541.200]

Q 8:55 What type of work is "directly related to the management or general business operations" of a company?

To meet the "directly related to management or general business operations" requirement of the administrative exemption, an employee must perform work directly related to assisting with the running or servicing of the business as opposed to, for example, working on a manufacturing production line or selling a product in a retail or service establishment. The regulations give the following examples of work directly related to the management or general business operations of a company: tax, finance, accounting, budgeting, auditing, insurance, quality control, purchasing, procurement, advertising, marketing, research, safety and health, personnel management, human resources, employee benefits, labor relations, public relations, government relations, computer network, Internet and database administration, legal and regulatory compliance, and similar activities. An employee who is an adviser or consultant to the employer's clients or customers may also be exempt. [29 C.F.R. § 541.201]

Q 8:56 What qualifies as exercising "discretion and independent judgment" under the administrative exemption?

Generally, the exercise of discretion and independent judgment involves the comparison and evaluation of possible courses of conduct and acting or making a decision after the various possibilities have been considered. Factors include:

whether an employee has authority to formulate, affect, interpret, or implement management policies or operating practices; whether the employee carries out major assignments in conducting the business; whether the employee performs work that affects business operations to a substantial degree (even if the employee's assignments are related to the operation of a particular segment of the business); whether the employee can commit the employer in significant financial matters; whether the employee has authority to waive or deviate from established policies and procedures with prior approval; whether the employee has authority to negotiate and bind the company on significant matters; whether the employee provides consultation or expert advice to management; whether the employee is involved in planning long- or short-term business objectives; whether the employee investigates and resolves matters of significance on behalf of management; and whether the employee represents the company in handling complaints, arbitrating disputes, or resolving grievances. The term must be applied in light of all the facts involved in the employee's particular employment situation, and generally implies that the employee has the authority to make an independent choice, free from immediate direction or supervision.

An employee can still exercise discretion and independent judgment even though the employee does not have the final word because his or her decisions are reviewed at a higher level. It is irrelevant how many employees are performing identical or similar work; they can all be exercising discretion and independent judgment.

Note. The exercise of discretion and independent judgment does not include clerical or secretarial work, recording or tabulating data, or performing other mechanical, repetitive, recurrent, or routine work—even if the employee is called a statistician. [29 C.F.R. § 541.202]

Q 8:57 How does the administrative exemption apply to educational institutions?

To be eligible as employees employed in a bona fide administrative capacity in an educational establishment under the current regulations, employees must:

• Be paid on a salary or fee basis at a rate of at least $913 per week not including board, lodging, or other facilities or be paid a salary that at least equals the entrance salary for teachers in the educational establishment where employed; and

• Perform administrative functions directly related to academic instruction or training in an educational establishment or department or subdivision as their primary duty. [29 C.F.R. § 541.204]

In the regulations, the term *educational institution* refers to an elementary or secondary school system, an institution of higher education, or other educational institution. For an employee to be exempt, the administrative work at the educational institution must directly relate to academic instruction or training rather than to the general business operations. Employees who are considered to be engaged in academic instruction or training include the superintendent or other head of an elementary or secondary school system, and any assistants, responsible for curriculum, quality, and method of instructing, measuring, and testing the learning potential and achievement of students, establishing and maintaining academic and grading standards, and other aspects of the teaching program; the principal and any vice principals responsible for the operation of an elementary or secondary school; department heads in institutions of higher education; and academic counselors. Examples of duties that block the exemption include dining hall duty; building maintenance; and administrative positions related to student health, guidance, and dietitian services. These employees might qualify as administrative employees under the FLSA general administrative exemptions. [29 C.F.R. § 541.214]

Q 8:58 What are some examples of employees who fall under the administrative exemption?

The DOL lists the following employees as typically within the administrative exemption under the regulations:

1. Insurance claims adjusters, as long as their duties include activities such as interviewing insured individuals, witnesses, and physicians; inspecting property damage; evaluating and making recommendations regarding coverage of claims; determining liability and total value of a claim; negotiating settlements; and making recommendations regarding litigation;

2. An employee who leads a team of other employees assigned to complete major projects for the employer (such as purchasing, selling, or closing all or part of a business; negotiating a real estate transaction or collective bargaining agreement; or designing productivity improvements);

3. An executive assistant or administrative assistant to a business owner or senior executive of a large business but only if the employee, without specific instructions or prescribed procedures, has been delegated authority regarding matters of significance; and

4. Human resources managers who formulate, interpret, or implement employment policies.

5. Purchasing agents with authority to make significant purchases qualify even if the agents need consultation for unusually large commitments.

[29 C.F.R. § 541.203]

Employers often request the DOL's opinion regarding whether certain employees meet the requirements of the administrative exemption. For example, in a September 8, 2006, opinion letter, the DOL found that a loss prevention manager (LPM) of a large retail business satisfied the administrative exemption. In this case, the LPM's primary responsibility was the effective implementation of a loss prevention and shortage control program for the store at which the LPM was employed. This is an important part of the store's management, is often an essential ingredient in determining the profitability of the store, and can even determine the success or failure of the store. Among other things, the LPM analyzes inventory shortage results, allocates store loss prevention resources to successfully reduce inventory shortage, focuses prevention activities on high shortage departments, identifies paperwork control weaknesses and implements procedures to correct them, conducts audits for compliance and ensures store follow-up on price accuracy initiatives, and sells and partners with store management to implement the plan. The LPM also investigates causes of inventory shortage (e.g., complex "paperwork" problem or theft) and then selects appropriate steps to solve the problem. Once the appropriate course of action is selected, the LPM pursues that course of action to a successful completion. In developing cash shortage controls and programs to manage and reduce loss, the LPM develops an appropriate training and awareness program to reduce error, reviews cash discrepancies to keep the store within allowable guidelines, and identifies cash registers with unacceptable shortages. Accordingly, the DOL found that the LPM satisfied the administrative exemption.

Professional Exemption

Q 8:59   Do the white-collar exemptions apply to professionals?

Yes. Professional employees may be exempt under four "professional" exemptions: learned professionals, creative professionals, teachers in educational institutions, and data processing professionals. Under all of these categories, employees must be paid at least $913 per week on a salary or fee basis. [29 C.F.R. § 541.214] (There is an exception to the compensation requirements for doctors, lawyers, and teachers, who have no compensation requirements, and a limited exception for data processing professionals.)

Q 8:60   What is the duties test for an employee to qualify for the learned professional exemption?

To qualify as a learned professional, an employee's primary duty must be the performance of work requiring advanced knowledge in a field of science or learning customarily acquired by a prolonged course of specialized intellectual instruction. The current regulations clarify that advanced knowledge cannot be attained at the high school level. Employees use their advanced knowledge to analyze, interpret, or make deductions from varying facts or circumstances. The fields of science or learning include law, medicine, theology, accounting, actuarial computation, engineering, architecture, teaching, various types of physical, chemical, and biological sciences, pharmacy, and other professions. Although the learned professional generally has an academic degree, the current regulations include the word "customarily" before "acquired by a prolonged course of specialized intellectual instruction" to allow the exemption to apply to the occasional lawyer who has not gone to law school, or the occasional chemist who does not have a degree in chemistry. [29 C.F.R. § 541.301]

Q 8:61 What is the duties test for an employee to qualify for the creative professional exemption?

To qualify as a creative professional, an employee's primary duty must be work that requires invention, imagination, originality, or talent in a recognized field of artistic or creative endeavor as opposed to routine mental, manual, mechanical, or physical work. Recognized fields of artistic or creative endeavors include music, writing, acting, and the graphic arts. Because the duties of creative professionals can vary greatly, the determination of a creative professional is made on a case-by-case basis. Generally the following are considered creative professionals: actors, musicians, composers, conductors, and soloists; painters who at most are given the subject matter of their painting; cartoonists who are merely told the title or underlying concept of a cartoon and must rely on their own creative ability to express the concept; essayists, novelists, short-story writers, and screenplay writers who choose their own subjects and hand in a finished piece of work; and higher level ad writers. Generally, copyists, animators, or retouchers of photographs do not qualify as creative professionals. [29 C.F.R. § 541.302]

Q 8:62 Are teachers considered exempt as professional employees?

Yes. Employees whose primary duty is teaching, tutoring, instructing, or lecturing to impart knowledge and who teach in an educational establishment are considered employed in a bona fide professional capacity and are therefore exempt from minimum wage and overtime requirements. Teachers who spend a considerable amount of time in extracurricular activities such as coaching or moderating clubs are engaged in teaching. Teachers who are employed as such even though they are not certified may still be exempt. [29 C.F.R. § 541.303]

Computer Employees

Q 8:63 Is there a special exemption for employees who work with computers?

Yes. The regulations classify certain highly skilled employees working as computer systems analysts, computer programmers, software engineers, or other similarly skilled workers as exempt from the FLSA's minimum wage and overtime requirements under a special category of professional employee. The exemption is not available for employees engaged in the manufacture or repair of computer hardware and related equipment. Nor is the exemption available to employees (such as engineers or drafters) whose work is highly dependent on or facilitated by the use of computers and computer software programs. Because job titles vary widely and change quickly in the computer industry, they are not determinative of the applicability of the exemption. To qualify for the computer-related exemption, employees must meet a duties test specific to this exemption and a special compensation test. [29 C.F.R. §§ 541.400, 541.401]

Q 8:64   What is the salary test for computer employees?

To be eligible for the exemption, computer employees must earn, either on a salary or fee basis, $455 per week (not including board, lodging, or other facilities) or, if paid on an hourly basis, at least $27.63 per hour. [29 C.F.R.§ 541.400]

Q 8:65   What is the duties test for employees to be exempt as computer professionals?

To be exempt, the computer employee's primary duty/duties must be:

* The application of systems analysis techniques and procedures, including consulting with users to determine hardware, software, or system specifications;

* The design, development, documentation, analysis, creation, testing, or modification of computer systems or programs including prototypes based on and related to user or system design specifications;

* The design, documentation, creation, testing, or modification of computer programs related to a machine operating system; or

* A combination of these duties requiring the same level of skill. [29 C.F.R.§ 541.400]

It is important to note that, even if an employee does not qualify for the computer professional exemption, he or she may still qualify as exempt under the executive or administrative exemption (provided the employee meets all of the respective requirements). [29 C.F.R. § 541.402]

Outside Salespeople

Q 8:66   Are any of the FLSA exemptions available for outside salespersons?

Yes. The regulations provide an exemption from the minimum wage and overtime requirements for outside sales employees whose primary duty is making sales, obtaining orders or contracts for services, or for the use of facilities for which consideration is paid by the customer and these services are customarily and regularly away from the employer's place of business. Writing sales reports, updating or revising the employee's sales or display catalogs, planning itineraries, attending sales conferences, and making incidental deliveries and collections can be considered as part of the outside salesperson's primary duties. [29 U.S.C. § 213(a)(1); 29 C.F.R. § 541.500]

It should be noted that there is no salary or compensation requirement of any kind for outside salespersons.

The U.S. Supreme Court recently addressed whether "detailers" in the pharmaceutical industry meet the definition of outside salespersons. The job of a detailer or pharmaceutical sales rep is to communicate with doctors to explain the pharmaceutical company's medications in hopes that the doctors would prescribe the medication to their patients. The detailers do not actually sell the medications. The Department of Labor argued that the detailers were entitled to overtime because they did not meet the definition of outside salespeople. The U.S. Supreme Court disagreed and held that pharmaceutical reps are considered outside salespeople who are exempt from overtime. [Christopher v. SmithKline Beecham (dba GlaxcoSmithKline), 132 S. Ct. 2156 (2012)]

Salary Requirements

Q 8:67   Are there any special provisions for highly paid executives, administrators, or professionals?

Yes. Highly compensated employees performing office or nonmanual work and paid total annual compensation of $134,004 or more are exempt from the FLSA if they customarily and regularly perform at least one of the duties of the exempt executive, administrative, or professional employee, as set forth in the FLSA exemptions. In addition, to qualify for this exemption, the highly compensated employee must be paid at least $913 (or the equivalent) per week on a salary or fee basis. If the employee's compensation doesn't equal $134,004 as of December 1, 2016, the employer can make an additional payment within one month of year end, and count that payment toward the $134,004. (The payment would count toward the threshold of the prior year, not the current year.)

In figuring the total annual compensation, commissions, nondiscretionary bonuses, and other nondiscretionary compensation earned during the year are included. However, board, lodging, and other facilities as well as payments for medical or life insurance, contributions to retirement plans, and the cost of other fringe benefits are not included.

An employer may prorate the $134,004 for employees who do not work a full year.

The highly compensated employee exemption does not apply to nonmanagement production-line workers and employees in maintenance, construction, and similar occupations, such as carpenters, electricians, mechanics, plumbers, iron workers, craftsmen, operating engineers, longshoremen, construction workers, laborers, and other employees who perform work involving repetitive operations with their hands. [29 C.F.R. § 541.601]

Q 8:68   How does an employer determine whether a white-collar employee meets the salary test if the employee is not paid a weekly salary?

The $913 per week may be translated into equivalent amounts for various pay periods. For example, employees meet the salary test if they are paid $1,826 per biweekly pay period, $1,978.17 per semimonthly pay period, or $3,956.33 per month. [29 C.F.R. § 541.600(b)]

Q 8:69   How is the salary test applied if exempt employees don't work a full year?

If an otherwise exempt employee starts a job midyear or terminates a job before the end of a year, the employer may prorate the salary test based on the number of weeks of employment. Similar to highly compensated employees (see Q 8:67), employers may make one final payment within one month after the end of employment to meet the threshold. [29 C.F.R. § 541.601(b)(3)]

An employer may use any 52-week period (rather than the calendar year) to apply the salary test. [29 C.F.R. § 541.601(b)(4)]

Q 8:70   Does the $913 salary requirement apply to all exempt employees?

No. The following professional employees do not need to meet a salary test to be exempt: teachers; licensed, practicing lawyers or doctors; and medical interns or residents. The salary exemption for medical practitioners does not extend to pharmacists, nurses, therapists, technologists, sanitarians, dietitians, social workers, psychologists, psychometrists, or other members of other professions that service the medical profession. [29 C.F.R. § 541.600(e)]

Alternative salary tests exist for academic administrative employees and computer employees (see Q 8:57 and Q 8:64). [29 C.F.R. §§ 541.600(c), 541.600(d)]

Q 8:71   Must an executive, administrative, or professional employee be paid on a salary or fee basis to be treated as exempt?

Yes. To be exempt, executive, administrative, and professional employees must be paid on a "salary or fee basis." To be paid "on a salary basis," they must generally receive a full week's pay when they perform any work during the week. This is true regardless of the number of days or hours worked, and regardless of the quality of work. The employee's weekly pay cannot generally be reduced for absences of less than a full day for any purpose (except absences under the Family Medical Leave Act—see below), and it cannot be reduced if the lack of work results in a short workweek. Under limited circumstances, the FLSA does permit days off without pay for leave taken for personal reasons, sickness, and certain disciplinary actions. [29 C.F.R. § 541.602(a)]

Q 8:72   May an employer dock an exempt employee's pay and have that employee remain exempt?

Generally, no. If an employer docks an exempt employee's pay, the employee's exempt status may be lost during the period when pay reductions are made, and the reductions may even preclude exempt status for the employee. If an exempt worker's pay is reduced because of a lack of work, those actions are an indication that the employer had no intention of paying the employee on a salary basis. [29 C.F.R. § 541.602(a)] The DOL regulations limit the circumstances when an employer can make deductions to an exempt employee's salary without jeopardizing the employee's exempt status. The permitted deductions include those made for:

- Absences of a full day or more for personal reasons;
- Absences of a full day or more for illness or accident if the employee is covered under a bona fide plan (or insurance policy) that provides sick pay, and has either not yet qualified for or has exhausted such sick pay;
- Disciplinary suspensions of one or more full days for infractions of workplace conduct rules (under very limited circumstances set forth in the regulations); and
- Discipline for a significant safety violation, such as one relating to the prevention of serious danger to the plant or other employees.

[29 C.F.R. § 541.602(b)]

Note. There are also exceptions for family and medical leave taken on an intermittent basis. One of those exceptions is for an FMLA non-qualifying absence when the employee has exhausted paid leave. [29 C.F.R. § 825.220]

In an opinion letter dated March 10, 2006, the DOL examined whether an employer could deduct from the salary of exempt employees or require them to reimburse the employer for damage to or loss of company equipment without jeopardizing the employees' exempt status. In short, the DOL found that such deductions or reimbursements would violate the salary basis requirements under the FLSA, and the employees would no longer be exempt.

Q 8:73   Will paying additional compensation to an otherwise exempt employee cause the worker to become nonexempt?

Probably not. An employer may provide an exempt employee with additional compensation without losing the exemption or violating the salary basis requirement if the employment arrangement also includes a guarantee of at least the minimum weekly required amount paid on a salary basis. The courts have also addressed this issue. In a 1997 Ninth Circuit ruling, a group of engineers (a group classified as professional employees and therefore exempt from the minimum wage and overtime provisions of the FLSA) were paid by Boeing Company under a collective bargaining agreement. The agreement required the engineers to receive a salary based on a 40-hour workweek. The contract also provided for an hourly premium pay rate when their weekly working hours exceeded 48 hours. The premium pay for this additional time was equal to the rate of straight pay plus $6.50 per hour. [Boykin v. Boeing Co., 128 F.3d 1279 (9th Cir. 1997)]

The court's decision followed a 1995 opinion letter holding that payment of additional compensation to exempt employees for hours worked beyond their standard workweek does not cause the workers to lose their exempt status. [Wage & Hour Op. Ltr. Nos. 1737 and 1738 (Apr. 5, 1995)] As this decision has evolved, the DOL now recognizes that exempt employees may be paid additional compensation, including a flat sum, a bonus payment, time and one-half, or a shift differential, without jeopardizing the exempt status of the employee. [Wage & Hour Op. Ltr. No. 2005-20 (Aug. 19, 2005)]

Q 8:74 May an employer dock an exempt employee's salary for unpaid leave?

Generally, no. The DOL generally holds that an employee is to be paid a week's salary for any week in which the employee provided any services. [29 C.F.R. § 541.602(a)] This rule is also subject to the general rule that an employer does not need to pay an exempt employee for any week in which the employee performs no work. However, see the exceptions in Q 8:72.

An exempt employee's pay cannot be reduced for a cash shortage. [Belcher & Shoney's, Inc., 20 F. Supp. 2d 1010 (M.D. Tenn. 1998)]

Q 8:75 May an employer dock exempt employees' wages for absences due to jury duty?

No. Partial-week deductions from pay generally are not permitted for exempt employees' absence from work because they serve on a jury or attend court as a witness. An employer may, however, offset any amounts received by the employee as jury or witness fees against the salary due for the week. [29 C.F.R. § 541.602(b)(3)]

Q 8:76 May an employer dock the wages of employees who are on temporary military leave and therefore do not work a full week?

No. Exempt employees who do not work a full week due to temporary military duty may not be paid less than their full salary. However, an employer can offset any amounts received by an employee for military pay for a particular week against the salary due for that particular week without losing the exemption. [29 C.F.R. § 541.602(b)(3)]

Q 8:77 Can an employer penalize exempt employees for violating safety rules by reducing their pay?

Yes, but only under certain circumstances. An employer can dock the pay of exempt workers to penalize them for violating safety rules only when such rules are "major." According to an opinion letter dated December 5, 1997, docking the pay of exempt employees for "nonmajor" safety violations may cause the exempt employees to lose their exempt status. Usually, unlawful deductions from an exempt employee's salary will cause the worker to lose his or her exempt status. However, the law permits deductions imposed to penalize employees "in good faith for infractions of safety rules of major significance," such as rules to prevent serious danger in the workplace or to other employees (e.g., prohibiting smoking in explosive plants, oil refineries, and coal mines). [29 C.F.R. § 541.602(b)(4); Wage & Hour Op. Ltr. (Dec. 5, 1997)]

Q 8:78   Can an employer suspend an employee for violating other workplace rules?

Yes. Regulations also permit docking an employee's salary for unpaid disciplinary suspensions of one or more full days for violation of workplace conduct rules. Examples of workplace conduct rules are sexual harassment and workplace violence rules.

Q 8:79   Must an executive, administrative, or professional employee work full-time to remain exempt?

No. As long as the employee earns at least $913 per week on a salary basis and his/her primary duty is exempt work, the employee qualifies for the exemption. [Wage & Hour Op. Ltr., FLSA 2006-10NA (June 1, 2006)]

Q 8:80   Will deducting leave from an exempt employee's accumulated leave on an hourly basis cause the white-collar exemption to be lost?

Generally, no. If an employer has a bona fide benefits plan, it is permissible to substitute or reduce the accrued leave in the plan for the time an employee is absent from work, even if it is less than a full day, without affecting the salary basis of payment, if by reducing the leave the employee receives in payment an amount equal to his or her guaranteed salary. [29 C.F.R. § 541.602]

Q 8:81   If an employer requires a white-collar exempt employee to work more than 40 hours per week, or if the employer requires white-collar exempt employees to make up time missed, will the exemption be lost?

No. In an opinion letter dated March 10, 2006, the DOL examined whether the following job requirements would result in a loss of the exemption: (1) requiring exempt employees to work either 45 or 50 hours per week; and (2) requiring, at its option, that exempt employees make up time lost due to personal absences of less than a day. The DOL stated that, as long as the employer did not dock the salary of the exempt employee, the work rules would not destroy the exemption. [Wage & Hour Op. Ltr. No. 2006-6 (Mar. 10, 2006)]

Q 8:82 May an employer pay an exempt employee extra wages for working hours in excess of a set level without causing the employee to be treated as a nonexempt employee?

Yes, under most circumstances. The salary basis test described in the regulations [29 C.F.R. § 541.604] specifically allows the payment of additional compensation beyond the exempt employee's salary.

An employer may provide an exempt employee with additional compensation without losing the exemption or violating the salary basis requirement, if the employment arrangement also includes a guarantee of at least the minimum weekly required amount paid on a salary basis. [Wage & Hour Op. Ltr. No. 2005-20 (Aug. 19, 2005)]

Authority that supports the use of overtime and/or compensatory time for exempt employees is found also under Section 22b01 of the DOL's Field Operations Handbook:

> Extra Compensation Paid for OT. Extra compensation may be paid for overtime to an exempt employee on any basis. The OT payment need not be at time and one-half, but may be at straight time, or flat sum, or on any other basis.

An otherwise exempt employee's status may be lost when the employer indicates that an employee's pay is based on hours worked. This generally would not occur if the employer has a policy of paying exempt employees at straight time for hours worked in excess of 40 hours in a workweek (or if the employees' pay stubs indicate compensation based on "hours worked," or if exempt employees receive "overtime" pay for "hours worked"). However, if the employees were to work fewer than 40 hours and their pay was docked at an hourly rate, the exemption would be lost.

Q 8:83 Are the docking rules different for public employers?

Yes. Different docking rules apply for public employees due to the principle of public accountability—civil servants should not be paid for time they do not work, unless the time off is charged as paid leave. Public employees who are otherwise exempt will not lose the exemption because they are paid under a system established by statute, ordinance, or regulation, or by a policy or practice established pursuant to the principles of public accountability, which requires the public employee's pay to be reduced if the employee is placed on unpaid leave for absences for personal reasons or because of illness or injury of less than one workday when accrued leave is not used by the employee because: permission for its use was not sought or was denied, accrued leave has been exhausted, or the employee chooses to use leave without pay. [29 C.F.R. § 541.710]

Previously, the Ninth Circuit Court of Appeals found in *Abshire v. County of Kern* [908 F.2d 483 (9th Cir. 1990)] that battalion chiefs were not paid on a salary basis because they received overtime pay or compensatory time for time worked outside their normal schedules. However, the U.S. Supreme Court came to a different conclusion in *Auer v. Robbins* [519 U.S. 452 (1997)], for a single or infrequent adjustment in an exempt employee's pay.

Regulations permit public employers to deduct for partial absences without loss of exempt status. [*See also* Barner v. City of Novato, 17 F.3d 1256 (9th Cir. 1994)] Such adjustments in pay without loss of exempt status are permitted for public sector employees who otherwise meet all the FLSA exemption requirements, but due to a statute, ordinance, regulation, or by policy and practice are required to report for their time not worked. Many government employees are paid under a system based on the principle that government employees are publicly accountable for the expenditure of funds and should not be paid for time not worked, and thus are permitted this exception to the salary-basis requirement under the FLSA. Deductions for absences of less than a full day without loss of exemption status are permitted when the employee receives accrued personal or sick pay. The pay plan must require that the exempt employee's pay be reduced (or permit the employee to be placed on leave without pay in lieu of using accrued leave) for absences of less than one day when the following conditions are met: (1) the leave is due to personal reasons or illness or injury; and (2) when permission for use of accrued leave was not requested or was denied, accrued leave has been exhausted, or the employee chooses to use leave without pay.

When the pay of otherwise exempt public employees has been reduced as a result of a budget-required furlough, the employees will lose their exempt status only in the workweek in which the furlough occurs and their pay has been reduced. [29 C.F.R. § 541.710]

Q 8:84   Can an employer adjust an exempt employee's leave to account for hours not worked during the work period under the FLSA?

Generally, yes. In most cases, the FLSA does not restrict adjustments in an employer's sick leave or vacation policies for an exempt employee as long as all the other requirements of the FLSA are met (e.g., the employee receives a full day of pay for any day on which the employee works any time). Sick and personal leave accounts from which leave is determined are not governed by either the FLSA or its implementing regulations. As long as the employee for whom the exemption is sought is always paid a salary in compliance with 29 C.F.R. Section 541.602, the additions to and deductions from the employee's leave accounts in less than a full day's amount (e.g., hourly adjustments) are permissible without jeopardizing the exempt status of the employee. Therefore, deductions from and additions to an employee's leave accounts for hour absences are permissible so long as the employee's salary was maintained. [Barner v. City of Novato, 17 F.3d 1256 (9th Cir. 1994); Graziano v. Society of N.Y. Hosp., 1997 U.S. Dist. LEXIS 15926; York v. City of Wichita Falls, 944 F.2d 236 (5th Cir. 1991)]

Thus, an employer can adjust an exempt employee's accrued leave account for partial-day absences under a bona fide leave program. The exempt employee would receive a full day's pay for the day when the partial-day absence occurred; however, his or her leave account would be reduced for the hours of absence that are the result of an employee-controlled event. [Wage & Hour Op. Ltr. No. 2005-4 (Jan. 7, 2005)]

Q 8:85 Can an employer reduce the pay of an exempt worker for bona fide reasons due to poor economic conditions without violating the FLSA?

Yes. The DOL has held that a bona fide reduction in pay is not a violation of the FLSA's salary-basis requirement. A fixed reduction in salary effective during a period when a company operates a shortened workweek due to economic conditions would be a bona fide reduction not designed to circumvent the salary-basis payment. Employees are considered to be paid on a salary basis when they "regularly receive a predetermined amount constituting all or a part of their compensation which is not subject to reduction because of variations in the hours worked or in the quantity or quality of the work performed," the DOL explained. When a worker's status is changed from exempt to nonexempt because of a reduction in pay or change of duties, the DOL explained that the loss of status will not be retroactive, but will be effective only as of the change. Further, the exemption may be reinstated once the worker performed the requisite duties and met the salary test. [Wage & Hour Op. Ltr. (Feb. 23, 1998)] In another case, a court also agreed that a reduction is permissible so long as the exempt employee receives at least $455 per week and the reduction is done in good faith. [Archuleta v. Wal-Mart Stores, Inc., 395 F.3d 1177 (10th Cir. 2005)]

Q 8:86 May an employer establish a predetermined (but varying) amount of pay prior to each workweek for exempt employees?

Generally, no. Exempt employees must be paid on a salary basis regardless of hours worked. The term salary basis is defined under the FLSA to mean that the employee regularly receives each pay period (e.g., weekly, or a less frequent basis) a predetermined amount constituting all or part of his or her compensation, which is not subject to reduction because of variations in the quality or quantity of the work performed. [29 C.F.R. § 541.602(a)] There may be circumstances where an employer could make occasional prospective reductions in salary in response to business needs. The regulations do not require that the salary set for one period continue to another. [Archuleta v. Wal-Mart Stores, Inc., 395 F.3d 1177 (10th Cir. 2005)]

Note that an employer can avoid certain penalties under the "corrective action" defense. An employer that inadvertently deducts pay from an employee may correct the problem by reimbursing the pay and promising not to make the same mistake in the future. [29 C.F.R. § 541.603]

Special considerations for reduced workweek arrangements. The regulations make no distinction between full and part time employees when it comes to salaried exempt status. That is, employees whom an employer chooses to consider "part time" may still be exempt as long as both the salary and duties tests are met. The employer may then require that the exempt employees work any number of hours, and even though they are labeled part time, no additional compensation is required. For economic reasons, employers may choose to reduce full-time exempt employees to part-time exempt employees, reduce their salaries proportionately (but to no less than $913 per week), and still require them to work many hours. Some employers may even take this approach, but try to give additional compensation to the exempt employees when they work many hours. This can be done, but great care must be taken. The Wage and Hour Division will closely examine any pay plan where the employees are allegedly guaranteed a predetermined amount of money, but where that amount seems to go up and down in proportion to hours. A more sensible approach might be to guarantee a salary of not less than $913 per week and then pay an hourly bonus for hours worked (or, where applicable, hours billed) beyond a certain number.

Q 8:87 How do the provisions of the Family and Medical Leave Act apply to the white-collar exemption?

An exception to the basic salary requirement of the FLSA (i.e., no partial-day reductions) is permitted for white-collar employees who take unpaid leave under the Family and Medical Leave Act (FMLA). [29 C.F.R. § 541.602] The FMLA, which generally applies to employers with 50 or more employees, requires those employers to provide up to 12 weeks of unpaid leave a year for childbirth, adoption, foster care, the employee's serious illness, or the serious illness of a family member. (The FMLA was amended in 2008 to add "military contingency" leave for certain family members of members of the Armed Forces who are called to active duty. The family members can take leave to assist the soldier/sailor/marine/airman with many contingencies associated with the call to active duty. In addition, certain family members can take FMLA leave to care for members of the Armed Forces who are injured on active duty.) This unpaid leave may be on a continuous or intermittent basis. The leave may also be applied through a reduced work schedule. The FLSA allows FMLA-covered employers to provide unpaid leave of less than a day to salaried managerial and professional employees without loss of the FLSA's white-collar exemption. [29 C.F.R. § 825.206]

Q 8:88 Will an otherwise exempt employee be treated as covered if an unintentional error has been made in his or her pay?

Yes. Loss of the white-collar exemption will not occur when improper deductions from the employee's salary are isolated or inadvertent and the employer reimburses the employee for the pay reduction. An employer should correct the error promptly. [29 C.F.R. § 541.603(c)]

Q 8:89   What is the window of correction under the FLSA?

An employer that has violated the FLSA and, as a result, caused an otherwise exempt employee to be a nonexempt employee and subject to overtime may be able to retroactively restore the employee's exempt status under what some courts have referred to as the "window of correction." An employee's exempt status is restored when the employer corrects any payments or nonpayments made in violation of the FLSA. The regulations provide that:

"Improper deductions that are either isolated or inadvertent will not result in loss of the exemption for any employees subject to such improper deductions, if the employer reimburses the employees for such improper deductions." [29 C.F.R. § 541.603(c)]

Seamen and Fishermen

Q 8:90   Which FLSA exemptions are available to seamen and fishermen?

Seamen may be exempt from some or all of the provisions of the FLSA, depending on whether the vessel on which they serve is of U.S. or foreign registry. Seamen on non-U.S. vessels are exempt from the minimum wage and overtime pay provisions of the FLSA. Seamen on U.S. vessels are exempt only from the overtime pay provisions of the FLSA.

A seaman is defined as any member of the crew (but not concessionaires or their employees), or an individual who is the "master" or one subject to the authority, direction, and control of the master on board a vessel operating on navigable waters and who renders services in operating the vessel as a means of transportation.

Also, individuals engaged in offshore fishing operations, including the catching, harvesting, or farming of any kind of fish or other aquatic forms of animal or vegetable life, or in the first processing, loading or unloading, or canning or packing of such products at sea, also are exempt from the minimum wage and overtime pay provisions of the FLSA. [29 U.S.C. §§ 213(a)(3), 213(a)(5), 213(b)(4)]

Casual Babysitters

Q 8:91   Are babysitters exempt from the FLSA's minimum wage and overtime pay requirements?

In general, domestic workers are covered by the Act. Casual babysitters, however, are exempt from the FLSA's minimum wage and overtime provisions. Casual babysitters are defined in wage-hour regulations as individuals who provide babysitting services on an irregular and intermittent basis rather than as a vocation. On the other hand, workers who provide babysitting functions as a full-time occupation are subject to the FLSA's minimum wage and overtime provisions. Casual babysitters will not lose their exemption by performing minimal household work—for example, washing dishes or doing laundry—as long as these duties do not exceed 20 percent of the total hours in the particular babysitting assignment. [29 U.S.C. § 213(a)(15), 29 C.F.R. § 552.5]

Agricultural Workers

Q 8:92   Are agricultural workers exempt from the minimum wage and overtime provisions of the FLSA?

The FLSA contains two agricultural exemptions. The FLSA exempts from both its minimum wage and overtime pay provisions any employee or agricultural worker whose employer did not use more than 500 man-days of agricultural labor in any calendar quarter of the prior calendar year—the so called "small farm" exemption—or who is principally engaged in the range production of livestock. A man-day for purposes of this exemption means "any day during which an employee (excluding members of the farmer's immediate family) performs agricultural labor for not less than one hour." [DOL Field Operations Handbook § 25j01(c); Lopez v. Bergen, 563 F. Supp. 316 (N.D. Tex. 1983); 29 U.S.C. § 213(a)(4)]

There is also a more general exemption from overtime only (although the FLSA's minimum wage requirements apply) for any worker employed in either "primary" or "secondary" agriculture. Primary agriculture includes growing, producing, or harvesting any agricultural or horticultural commodities [29 U.S.C. § 213(b)(13)], as well as the following activities:

- Cultivation and tillage of the soil [29 U.S.C. § 203]
- Outside buying of poultry, eggs, cream, or milk in their raw or natural state [29 U.S.C. § 213(b)(5); DOL Field Operations Handbook §§ 20c01–20c03]
- Transporting "just harvested" goods to market or storage [29 U.S.C. § 213(b)(6)]
- Care and feeding of livestock for substantial periods before slaughter [29 C.F.R. § 516.13]
- Operations relating to grain elevators with five or fewer employees [29 U.S.C. § 213(a)(14)]
- Dairying [29 C.F.R. § 570.123(b)]
- Forestry or lumbering operations [29 U.S.C. § 213(b)(28); 29 C.F.R. § 570.123(b)]
- Raising livestock, bees, fur-bearing animals, or poultry [29 U.S.C. § 203(f)]
- Processing maple sap into sugar (but not refined sugar) or into syrup [29 U.S.C. § 213(b)-(15); 29 C.F.R. § 570.123(b)]
- Canning, packing, or processing of "self-grown" fruit and vegetables. This exemption requires that the employee be primarily employed in agriculture during the workweek and that the employee receive a minimum wage [29 U.S.C. § 213(b)(13); 29 C.F.R. §§ 780.600–780.621]
- Care and feeding of show horses

Special rules apply to each of these agricultural exemptions. [29 C.F.R. §§ 780.400, 780.409]

Employees who are not eligible for an agricultural overtime exemption include the following:

- Employees of a farmer's cooperative;
- Employees of industrialized farming operations;
- Employees of livestock brokers; and
- Employees engaged in office, maintenance, or clerical duties.

[29 C.F.R. § 780.133(a)]

The overtime exemption also applies to employees engaged in "secondary agriculture," which is defined as any activity performed on a farm or by a farmer in conjunction with that farm's farming activities. [29 C.F.R. § 780.128–780.148]

Q 8:93   What exemptions are available to agricultural workers who are commuting pieceworkers?

Agricultural workers who can be classified as commuting pieceworkers are exempt from the FLSA's minimum wage, overtime, and equal pay requirements under certain conditions. A commuting pieceworker is a temporary worker, employed in the hand-harvesting of a crop, who commutes daily from his or her permanent residence. The exemption applies only when the worker:

1. Is employed as a hand harvester;
2. Commutes daily from his or her permanent residence;
3. Is paid on a piece-rate basis; and
4. Was employed in agriculture (including work for all employers) in the preceding calendar year for fewer than 13 weeks. [29 U.S.C. § 213(b)(4)(C)]

Q 8:94   What is a man-day, and what is its significance to agricultural employers?

A man-day is defined as any day in which an employee performs agricultural labor for at least one hour. Members of the farmer's immediate family are excluded from this calculation. Agricultural establishments with more than 500 man-days of agricultural labor during any calendar quarter in the preceding calendar year are subject to the minimum wage as well as additional record-keeping requirements. The employer's records for each agricultural worker must include the following additional information:

- Time of day and day of the week in which the workweek begins;
- Basis on which wages are paid to the workers (e.g., $1.90 per bushel or $3.50 per hour);

- Hours worked each workday and total hours worked each workweek;
- Total daily or weekly earnings;
- Total additions to or deductions from wages paid each pay period, with supporting documentation;
- Total wages paid each pay period; and
- Date of payment and pay period covered by that payment.

Seasonal Employees

Q 8:95   What exemptions are available for seasonal employees?

The FLSA provides an exemption from minimum wage and overtime pay for certain employees employed by an establishment that is primarily a recreational or amusement establishment, "recreational establishment organized camp," or religious or nonprofit education center. The exemption generally requires that the establishment for which the employee works be recreational or amusement in character, or be a religious or nonprofit educational conference center, or organized camp, and that it be seasonal. Such establishments are seasonal if either of two criteria is met: (1) the employer does not operate for more than seven months in any calendar year or (2) the employer's receipts during any six months of a prior calendar year were not more than 33 1/3 percent of the receipts during the other six months of the same year. [29 U.S.C. § 213(a)(3)]

The exemption from the FLSA's minimum wage and overtime pay does not apply to any employer (other than a private entity operating a skiing facility) that, under a contract with the Secretary of Interior or Agriculture, provides services in a national park or national forest or in the National Wildlife Refuge System. [29 U.S.C. § 213(a)-(3)] However, note that an overtime pay exemption is provided under Section 213(b)(29) for employees (seasonal or full-time) who perform services for a private establishment located in a national park, national forest, or wildlife refuge under contract with the Secretary of Interior or Agriculture if the employee receives compensation for employment in excess of 56 hours in any workweek at a rate of one and one-half times the employee's regular rate. [29 U.S.C. § 213(b)(29)]

Exemptions from Payment of Overtime Only

Motor Carriers

Q 8:96   Are passenger bus and truck drivers exempt from the FLSA's provisions?

Certain employees of "motor carriers" that are covered by the Motor Carrier Act are exempt from the FLSA's overtime provision but not from the minimum wage provision. The exemption is available depending on both the employer's classification and the classification of the work performed by the employee.

In general, the motor carrier exemption is available to employees meeting the following three conditions:

- The employees are employed by a "motor carrier."
- The carrier must be engaged in interstate commerce as defined under the Motor Carrier Act.
- The excluded employees must be involved in activities that directly affect the safety of operation of motor vehicles under Section 204 of the Motor Carrier Act.

These requirements are not easily applied. First, there are three types of carriers—common, contract, and private—and the exemption is applied somewhat differently to each. In addition, the Motor Carrier Act designates drivers, drivers' helpers, loaders, and mechanics as the only employees whose work directly affects motor vehicle safety. Thus, only employees within these four categories are eligible for the motor carrier exemption. Finally, the Motor Carrier Act defines interstate commerce more narrowly than does the FLSA. For example, drivers, drivers' helpers, loaders, and mechanics working within a single state are almost always considered to be engaged in interstate commerce under the FLSA. However, employees who engage in strictly intrastate work are not covered by the Motor Carrier Act. Thus, motor carriers with workers engaged in only intrastate activities are not eligible for the motor carrier exemption and must pay overtime under the FLSA. [29 U.S.C. § 213(b)(1); 29 C.F.R. §§ 782.2–782.6] It should be noted, however, that employees of carriers who affect highway safety can be exempt even if they do not leave the state if their intrastate activities are part of a continuous movement of property in interstate commerce.

Airline Employees

Q 8:97   Are employees of airlines exempt from any FLSA provisions?

Some are. Employees of air carriers covered by Title II of the Railway Labor Act are exempt from the overtime pay requirements of the FLSA, but not from its minimum wage requirements. This exemption applies only to employees' activities if they have a reasonably close relationship to an airline's actual carrier activities. It is not applicable, for instance, to the employees of an airline who operate a computerized reservation system. In addition, an airline's airport and flight personnel will not be exempt from overtime pay requirements if they devote more than 20 percent of their time to activities that are not related to the activities of the carrier that bring it under the terms of the Railway Labor Act, i.e., air transportation activities. [29 U.S.C. § 213(b)(3); 29 C.F.R. § 786.1]

Taxicab Drivers

Q 8:98   Are taxicab drivers exempt from the FLSA's overtime pay requirements?

Taxicab drivers are exempt from the FLSA's overtime pay requirements but are subject to the FLSA's minimum wage and equal pay provisions. The exemption, which applies to "any driver employed by an employer engaged in the business of operating taxicabs," is sufficiently broad to apply to drivers of non-taxi vehicles that are a functional part of the employer's taxicab business.

Covered non-driver employees of taxicab companies are not exempt from the FLSA. When a driver performs duties in addition to driving, the driver's overtime pay exemption is lost when the other duties constitute more than 20 percent of the hours worked in any given workweek. [29 U.S.C. § 213(b)(17); 29 C.F.R. § 786.200; DOL Field Operations Handbook § 24h03]

Ride-Hailing Services

Q 8:99   Are ride-hailing services (e.g., Uber/Lyft) drivers exempt from the FLSA overtime requirements?

There have been several cases involving drivers who challenged Uber Technologies, Inc. to classify them as employees entitled to overtime instead of as independent contractors. In two cases in California and Massachusetts, the parties settled for $100 million for the drivers in 2015. The settlement did not change the status of the drivers, and they would continue as independent contractors. In 2016, the judge of the Northern District of California denied approval of the agreement, stating that settlement was not fair, adequate, or reasonable. [O'Connor v. Uber Techs., Inc., et al., C13-03826 EMC (N.D. Cal. 2016); Yucesoy v. Uber Techs., Inc., Case No. 15-cv-00262-EMC (N.D. Cal. Aug. 18, 2016)] In *Berwick v. Uber Technologies, Inc.* [CGC-15-546378 (June 6, 2015)], the California Labor Commission decided that one Uber driver must be classified as an employee and was entitled to the reimbursement of expenses.

Domestic Workers

Q 8:100   Do the FLSA's minimum wage and overtime pay provisions apply to domestic employees?

Domestic employees are generally covered by the FLSA's minimum wage and overtime requirements when they are employed in one or more homes for more than eight hours in any workweek, or if they earn "wages" of at least $50 in any calendar quarter. The term *domestic employees* refers to persons who provide household services at the home of the person who employs them. However, companions for the aged or infirm and casual babysitters are exempt from the law's minimum wage and overtime rules.

Section 2(a) of the FLSA generally holds that "employment of persons in domestic service in households affects commerce" and that the domestics can be entitled to minimum wage and overtime pay. Minimum wage and overtime pay provisions apply when a domestic employee receives wages subject to Social Security taxation (i.e., cash remuneration equals or exceeds $2,000 in 2016) or the employee was employed in domestic work by one or more employers for more than eight hours a day. However, certain exemptions may apply. [29 U.S.C. § 213(b)(21); 29 C.F.R. §§ 552.2(b), 552.2(c), 592.102]

Live-in domestics are exempt from the FLSA's overtime provisions. Note that even though live-in domestics do not have to be paid overtime, they are entitled to the minimum wage. Therefore, employers must maintain records of hours worked by live-in domestics.

However, final regulations, which become effective January 1, 2015, limit the overtime exemption to live-in domestic workers who are employed solely by an individual, family, or household. Live-in domestic workers who are employed by third parties, such as home care or staffing agencies, will be entitled to overtime pay when they work longer than 40 hours in one workweek. [29 C.F.R. § 552.109(c)]

Q 8:101   Are any domestic workers exempt from the FLSA's overtime provisions?

Yes. Three groups of domestic workers (i.e., workers who perform services of a household nature in or about a private home of the individual who hires the worker) are exempt from the FLSA's overtime requirements: (1) casual babysitters, (2) domestic workers who primarily provide companionship services for individuals who are incapable of caring for themselves, and (3) domestic service workers who reside in the household in which they work. [29 C.F.R. § 552.2(a)]. As noted above, casual babysitters and companions are also exempt from minimum wage.

The "companionship services" exemption under Section 13(a)15 of the FLSA means "being with someone to help them with their extreme needs." There are two conditions for this exemption. First, the services provided cannot be those provided by trained medical personnel, such as RNs, LVNs, and LPNs. In addition, there is a 20 percent work tolerance test. The exemption does not apply when the companion spends more than 20 percent of his or her time in general housekeeping duties. [29 C.F.R. § 552.6]

Under final regulations, beginning January 1, 2015, the exemption for companionship services has been narrowed, and will not apply to certified nursing assistants, home health aides, personal care aides, and other caregivers (i.e., direct care workers) who are employed by third parties, such as home care or staffing agencies, or jointly by third parties and families. These employees will be entitled to minimum wages and overtime if they work longer than 40 hours in one workweek. Individuals employed solely by an individual, family, or household remain exempt.

The final regulations define excluded "companionship services" as the provision of fellowship and protection. Companionship services may also include providing care to an elderly person or a person with illness, injury, or disability, under the following circumstances:

1. The care is provided attendant to and in conjunction with the provision of fellowship and protection.

2. The care is limited to assistance with activities of daily living (ADLs) (such as dressing, grooming, feeding, bathing, toileting, and transferring) and instrumental activities of daily living (IADLs), which are tasks that enable a person to live independently at home (such as meal preparation, driving, light housework, managing finances, assistance with the physical taking of medications, and arranging medical care).

3. The time spent providing care does not exceed 20 percent of the total hours worked per person and per workweek.

"Fellowship" means to engage the person receiving the services in social, physical, and mental activities. "Protection" means to be present with the person receiving services in his or her home or to accompany the person outside of the home to monitor the person's safety and well-being. Examples of fellowship and protection may include conversation; reading; games; crafts; and accompanying the person on walks, on errands, to appointments, or to social events. [29 C.F.R. § 552.6]

Small-Town Television and Radio Station Workers

Q 8:102   Are employees of small-town radio and television stations exempt?

Some of these employees are exempt from the FLSA's overtime requirements. The exemption applies to certain employees at radio and television stations in small communities when two conditions are met:

1. The employee must work as an announcer, news editor, or chief engineer at the major studio of a radio or television station.

2. That office must be located in a city or town with a population of 100,000 or less as determined by the most recent census figure of the Bureau of the Census. The test is not met when the city is within a standard metropolitan area with a population greater than 100,000. A city or town with a population of 25,000 or less may satisfy this requirement if located within a metropolitan area with a population of more than 100,000 as long as that city or town is at least 40 "airline miles" from the principal city in such area. [29 U.S.C. § 213(b)(9)]

Commissioned Salespersons

Q 8:103   When are salespeople deemed to be compensated principally on a commission basis?

Commissioned employees may be exempt from overtime under FLSA Section 7(i). To qualify under this exemption, the commissioned employee must be working for a "retail or service establishment." This phrase refers to a business that derives at least 75 percent of its annual dollar sales volume from goods or services that are recognized as retail (i.e., not for resale).

Employees are compensated principally on a commission basis if more than one-half of their compensation comes from commissions. This calculation requires measurement over a representative period of at least a month. For some employees with substantial monthly variations in commissions, the length of the representative period may have to be as long as a year; for other employees of the employer, a month may be sufficient. The employer's records must reflect the employee's representative period for this determination.

A special rule applies to determining whether new employees are paid primarily by commissions. A representative period for a new commissioned salesperson is determined under one of three requirements:

1. The new employee is hired to fill a specific job. In this case, if the job was previously occupied by another employee, the predecessor employee's representative period may be applied to the new employee. This option is available only when it is reasonable to expect similar sales activity from the new employee.

2. The new employee becomes part of a sales group. In this case, the representative period for the group may be applied to the new employee. This option is available only when the employee's experience makes it reasonable to expect that his or her commissions will be proportionate to those of the other group members.

3. When it is not reasonable to expect any commission under either of the first two options, the new employee's earnings experience for a period of not less than one month may be used. A shorter period may be used only until the employer computes the new employee's commissions over the full representative period applicable to other employees.

[29 C.F.R. §§ 779.410–779.421]

Q 8:104   Are commissioned retail salespersons exempt from the FLSA?

Generally, no, but retail salespersons who are compensated principally from commissions are exempt from the FLSA's overtime provisions (but not minimum wage) when the following three conditions are satisfied:

1. More than half the employee's compensation for a representative period (at least one month) is derived from commissions on sales of goods or services;

2. The employee receives an average regular rate in excess of one and one-half times the federal minimum wage in each workweek; and

3. 75 percent of the retail or service establishment's annual dollar volume of sales is retail and not for resale.

A salesperson's regular rate must satisfy the FLSA's minimum wage requirements, but for the exemption to apply, the regular rate must be more than one and one-half times the minimum wage.

The regular rate is determined by dividing the salesperson's total weekly compensation by the number of hours worked in that workweek. Total compensation may consist of a base salary and commissions, plus any part of a draw or guarantee that exceeds commissions. This calculation also includes any supplemental payments made by the employer to increase the employee's earnings to an amount exceeding one and one-half times the minimum wage. Salespeople meeting this exemption must receive overtime pay in any week in which their pay is less than the rate required for the exemption. [29 U.S.C. § 207(i); 29 C.F.R. §§ 279.410–279.421]. See Q 8:184 and the following questions for more information about determining employees' regular rates.

There is another exemption from the payment of overtime for "any salesman, partsman or mechanic primarily engaged in selling or servicing automobiles, trucks or farm implements if he is employed by a nonmanufacturing establishment primarily engaged in the business of selling such vehicles or implements to ultimate purchasers." This exemption is not available to individuals who sell finance contracts, insurance, or other products (though such employees may qualify for the commissioned sales exemption—see Opinion Letter dated March 17, 2003). [29 U.S.C. § 213(b)(10)(A)]

Q 8:105 How is an employee's regular pay rate determined when the employee is paid on a commission basis?

An employee's regular rate is an hourly rate. When an employee is paid on a piece-rate, salary, commission, or other nonhourly basis, the employee's regular rate is computed by totaling the employee's pay for the workweek and dividing the total by the number of hours worked during the workweek. In general, commissions are included in the regular rate regardless of whether the commission is the sole source of income or is paid in addition to a base salary or hourly rate. This is true regardless of the type of formula used to compute the commission. [29 C.F.R. § 778.109]

Q 8:106 How are commissions related to the employee's regular rate of pay?

An employer must add any commissions earned during the workweek to the employee's other earnings to determine the regular rate for overtime purposes. In short, when commissions are earned, they are added to the employee's other earnings and divided by the hours worked in the workweek to determine the regular rate. When commission payments are delayed to a later pay period, the employer must apportion the employee's commissions over the workweek in which they were earned.

Example. Taylor, a sales rep, earned $595.70 in commissions for a month. His employer pays commissions monthly. The amount of the commission allocable to any single week is $137.47 ($595.70 × 12 = $7,148.40 ÷ 52 = $137.47). During the second week of the monthly commission period, Taylor worked a total of 46 hours. Allocating $137.47 of the commission to that week raises his regular hourly rate by $2.99 ($137.47 ÷ 46 = $2.99).

Q 8:107   Does the FLSA's exemption for commissioned retail salespeople apply to other store employees?

Generally, no. For example, the exemption for commissioned retail salespeople does not apply to assistant store managers who direct the salespeople (unless these managers are also paid primarily on a commission basis and meet the other requirements for the exemption). Store managers may meet the criteria for the FLSA's executive exemption and be exempt from the minimum wage and overtime pay provisions on that basis regardless of whether they meet the criteria for the exemption for commissioned retail salespeople.

Commissioned retail salespersons who do not qualify for the sales exemption from the FLSA's overtime provisions must be paid overtime for hours in excess of 40 per week. Their overtime rate is generally 1.5 times their regular rate of pay. [29 U.S.C. § 207(h)(2)(i)]

It should also be noted that employees of retail establishments who meet the requirements of the 7(i) exemption need not be engaged in selling to be exempt. Courts have determined, for example, that banquet waiters and automobile repair technicians paid via commissions are exempt. [Mechmet v. Four Seasons Hotels, Ltd., 825 F.2d 1173 (7th Cir. 1987); Yi v. Sterling Collision Ctrs., Inc., 480 F.3d 505 (7th Cir. 2007)] A recent Seventh Court case provided that window washers receive "points" based on complexity of jobs, and when services were contracted for, deemed this arrangement to be commission-based compensation exempt from FLSA under the retail exception. [Ramon Alvarado, et al. v. Corporate Cleaning Servs., Inc., et al., No. 13-3818 (7th Cir. Apr. 1, 2015)]

Partial Overtime Exemptions

Hospitals and Nursing Home Workers

Q 8:108   Are hospital workers exempt from the FLSA's overtime provisions?

If hospital workers do not fall into any of the exemptions, no. However, hospitals and residential care facilities may use an optional method to compute overtime pay for any or all of their employees. The optional method, also known as the "8/80 rule," permits overtime to be computed using a designated work period of 14 consecutive days in lieu of the traditional seven-day workweek. Otherwise, the FLSA fully applies. Under this rule, employees must be paid time and one-half their regular rate for employment in excess of eight hours in any workday or in excess of 80 hours in any 14-day period, whichever is the greater number of hours. This method is subject to an additional requirement, in that the overtime computation method must be embodied in a collective bargaining agreement or otherwise consented to by the employees to whom it applies. [29 U.S.C. § 207(j)]

Q 8:109   Does the 40-hour threshold for overtime pay apply to hospital workers?

Yes. However, some hospitals or medical care facilities may opt to use the special 80-hour, 14-day rule. Under this rule, workers in hospitals that care for the sick, aged, or mentally ill receive overtime pay when they work in excess of eight hours in any workday or work in excess of 80 hours in a designated 14-day work period, whichever totals the greatest number of overtime hours. [29 U.S.C. § 207(j); 29 C.F.R. § 778.103]

Exemptions by Occupation

Q 8:110   Do the regulations give specific references to FLSA exemptions by occupation?

Yes. The regulations contain specific references to the occupations listed in Table 8-1.

Table 8-1.   29 C.F.R. Part 541 Occupational Index

Note. This index lists, for ease of reference, the sections of this part of the regulations that refer to job titles. The user should note, however, that when job titles do appear in the illustrations in the text, they should not be construed to mean that employees holding such titles are either exempt or nonexempt or that they meet any one of the specific requirements for exemption.

Occupation	CFR Reference
Accountant	541.301(e)(5)
Accounting clerk	541.301(e)(5)
Actor	541.302(c)
Animator	541.302(c)
Announcer, radio	541.302(d)
Announcer, television	541.302(d)
Artist	541.302(c)
Assistant, administrative	541.203(d)
Assistant, executive	541.203(d)
Athletic trainer	541.301(e)(8)
Bookkeeper	541.301(e)(5)
Cartoonist	541.302(c)
Certified public accountant	541.301(e)(5)

Table 8-1. 29 C.F.R. Part 541 Occupational Index *(cont'd)*

Occupation	CFR Reference
Chef	541.301(e)(6)
Claims adjuster	541.203(a)
Clerk, accounting	541.301(e)(5)
Coach	541.303(b)
Columnist	541.302(d)
Comparison shopper	541.203(i)
Composer	541.302(c)
Computer operator	541.400
Computer programmer	541.400
Conductor	541.302(c)
Cook	541.301(e)(6)
Delivery man	541.504
Dental hygienist	541.301(e)(3)
Dentist	541.304
Dietitian	541.204(c)(2)
Doctor	541.304
Driver salesman	541.504
Embalmer	541.301(e)(9)
Essayist	541.302(c)
Examiner	541.203(h)
Executive secretary	541.203(c)
Financial services employee	541.203(b)
Funeral director	541.301(e)(9)
Group leader	541.203(c)
Grader	541.203(h)
Human resource manager	541.203(e)
Inspector	541.203(g)
Inspector, public sector	541.203(j)
Insurance claims adjuster	541.203(a)
Intern	541.304(a)(2), (c)
Journalist	541.302(d)
Lawyer	541.302, 541.304
Lumber grader	541.203(h)
Medical technologist	541.301(e)(1)
Moderator, club	541.303(b)
Musician	541.302(c)

Table 8-1. 29 C.F.R. Part 541 Occupational Index (*cont'd*)

Occupation	CFR Reference
Newspaper reporter	541.302(c)
Newspaper writer	541.302(c)
Novelist	541.302(c)
Nurse	541.301(e)(2)
Optometrist	541.304
Owner	541.101
Painter	541.302(c)
Paralegal	541.301(e)(7)
Personnel clerk	541.203(e)
Physician	541.304
Physician assistant	541.301(e)(4)
Physician, general practitioner	541.304
Physician, intern	541.304
Physician, osteopathic	541.304
Physician, resident	541.304
Podiatrist	541.304
Programmer, computer	541.400
Psychologist	541.204(c)(2)
Purchasing agent	541.203(f)
Radio announcer	541.302(d)
Registered nurse	541.301(e)(2)
Reporter	541.302(d)
Retoucher, photographic	541.302(c)
Route driver	541.504(c)
Salesperson	541.500
Salesperson, driver	541.504
School building manager	541.204(c)
School department head	541.204(c)(1)
School lunch room manager	541.204(c)(2)
School maintenance person	541.204(c)(2)
School principal	541.204(c)(1)
School superintendent	541.204(c)(1)
School vice principal	541.204(c)(1)
Secretary	541.203(d)
Secretary, executive	541.203(d)
Singer	541.302(c)

Table 8-1. 29 C.F.R. Part 541 Occupational Index (*cont'd*)

Occupation	CFR Reference
Social worker, school	541.203(c)(2)
Soloist	541.302(c)
Superintendent, school	541.204(c)(1)
Teacher	541.303
Team leader	541.203(c)
Technologist	541.301(e)(1)
Television worker	541.302(d)
Working foreman	541.106
Working supervisor	541.106
Writer, fiction	541.302
Writer, newspaper	541.302(d)
Writer, screenplay	541.302(c)
Writer, short story	541.302(c)

How to Achieve Compliance

Q 8:111 Are employers required to notify employees of the FLSA's requirements?

Yes. Employers with employees covered under the FLSA are required to display a special poster describing the FLSA's minimum wage, overtime, child labor, and recordkeeping requirements. Copies of the poster are available from the Wage and Hour Division or its regional offices. [29 C.F.R. § 516.4]

Minimum Wage

Q 8:112 What are the minimum wage requirements of the FLSA?

The FLSA requires that each covered employee receive a wage that is equal to the amount established under 29 U.S.C. Section 206(a), currently $7.25 an hour. In general, the FLSA permits an employer to determine whether the hourly rate of an employee meets these requirements for each workweek by averaging pay from all sources during that week.

It is important to note that many states have established minimum wage levels higher than the FLSA. Under such circumstances, employers must comply with the law that is most beneficial to the employee; that is, state law in these cases.

Q 8:113 Does the FLSA require an employer to calculate a covered employee's pay on an hourly basis?

No. Employers may choose to pay a covered employee on a salary, commission, or other basis, as long as the employee's average hourly wage for any given workweek is at least equal to the minimum wage for the hours worked. For example, an employer may pay a base rate plus a piece rate as long as the employee receives at least the minimum wage (and, if applicable, overtime pay) for the hours worked in each workweek.

Q 8:114 May the cost of employer-provided board and lodging be credited toward an employee's minimum wage?

Yes, under certain conditions. An employer may apply the reasonable cost of employer-provided lodging, meals, and "other facilities" customarily furnished to employees against an employer's minimum wage obligations. A cost is "reasonable" when it does not exceed the employer's actual cost. That is, the employer or any affiliate may not profit from the facility that is provided. In addition, the facility must be primarily for the benefit of the employee, not the employer. [29 C.F.R. §§ 531.29, 531.3]

Q 8:115 What are "other facilities" for purposes of the minimum wage credit?

The regulations define facilities to include meals, lodging, and the following:

- Transportation provided to employees between their homes and work, when the travel does not constitute hours worked under the FLSA and the transportation is not essential to the employee's work duties.
- General merchandise provided at company stores and commissaries (including food, clothing, and household effects).
- Fuel (including coal, kerosene, and firewood), electricity, water, and gas provided for the personal use of employees.

Shares of company stock that are issued to an employee do not constitute "facilities" for these purposes. [29 C.F.R. § 531.32]

Q 8:116 What conditions are placed on employer-provided facilities that are credited toward an employee's minimum wage?

The facilities provided by the employer primarily for the benefit or convenience of the employer must not be treated as wages. Employees must be able to accept the facilities voluntarily and be given the option of declining the facilities and receiving the full wage in cash. Facilities may not be credited as wages when they are furnished for the employees' commercial use and are required as a part of the employees' job duties.

Employer-provided lodging generally can be treated as wages only when it is provided primarily for the employee's benefit, such as where the lodging is used for the employee's permanent residence or for an extended period of time. Thus, lodging provided to firefighters or hospital workers for use only during their shifts does not qualify as wages. Such facilities are necessary for the employer's operation, are provided primarily for the benefit of the employer, and do not constitute permanent lodging.

The cost of employer-provided meals may generally be considered part of an employee's noncash "wages" even when the circumstances surrounding an employee's duties do not permit the worker to obtain meals elsewhere. [29 C.F.R. § 531.32(c)]

Q 8:117   Which employer-provided facilities cannot be credited toward an employee's minimum wage?

An employer may not credit the reasonable cost of certain facilities toward the employee's minimum wage when they are provided for the employer's benefit. These facilities typically include:

- Tools and other materials (or services) incidental to carrying on the employer's business.
- Transportation, if it is essential to the employee's duties.
- Membership dues to business (e.g., chambers of commerce) or professional groups that employees join because of their employment.
- Rental charges for a uniform required by the employer.
- Employer-provided medical services and hospitalization required under workers' compensation laws or similar state or local laws.
- Taxes and insurance on the employer's buildings, which are not used for lodgings furnished to the employee.
- The cost of any construction by and for the employer.
- The cost of uniforms and their laundering, where the nature of the business requires the employee to wear a uniform.
- Safety caps, explosives, and miners lamps (in the mining industry).
- Electric power (used for commercial production in the interest of the employer).
- Company police and guard protection.

Note that the cost of employer-provided board, lodging, and similar facilities provided under a collective bargaining agreement may not be considered as part of an employee's wages if the contract excludes such payment from the employee's wages. [29 C.F.R. § 531.32]

Q 8:118   How does an employer determine the reasonable cost of facilities provided to an employee?

The regulations permit an employer to use generally accepted accounting practices to determine the reasonable cost to the employer of facilities provided to an employee. The rules also permit the employer to add adequate depreciation to the actual cost of operating and maintaining the facility, plus a reasonable allowance—up to 5.5 percent—for interest on the depreciated amount of capital invested by the employer. However, if the amount computed under this formula is greater than the fair rental value—or the fair price of commodities or facilities offered for sale—the employer would be limited to fair rental value or fair price as the "reasonable cost" of the facility. [29 C.F.R. §§ 531.3, 531.33]

Q 8:119 Can the cost of uniforms be treated as part of an employee's minimum wage?

Generally, no. The cost of uniforms and their maintenance may not be credited toward an employee's minimum wage in industries in which employers require their employees to wear uniforms. Employees may be provided uniforms due to the nature of the business or because the law requires the wearing of uniforms in their industry. In these cases, the cost of the uniform is a business expense that the employer has no right to require the employee to bear. That cost cannot reduce the employee's wage below the minimum wage or cut into overtime compensation required by the FLSA. [29 C.F.R. §§ 531.3, 531.32, 531.36; W-H Fact Sheet No. 16]

Example. Stephanie works in a restaurant and is subject to the statutory minimum wage of $7.25 an hour. She is paid an hourly wage of $8.80 an hour and regularly works 28 hours a week. Stephanie's employer may legally deduct no more than $41.85 a week ($8.80 – $7.25 = $1.55; $1.55 × 27 hours = $41.85).

Q 8:120 May laundry costs to maintain an employer-required uniform be credited toward an employee's minimum wage?

No. These costs, like the cost to obtain the uniform, not only cannot be credited toward the minimum wage, they actually cannot cause employees' wages to fall below the FLSA's minimum wage. In other words, when an employer is paying an amount at or slightly above the applicable minimum wage, the employer will end up reimbursing employees all or a portion of their laundry and maintenance costs to prevent such costs from cutting into employees' minimum wage or overtime pay required by the FLSA. [29 C.F.R. §§ 531.3, 531.32, 531.36]

Note. An employee's laundry costs generally do not have to be reimbursed if the uniforms are of a "wash-and-wear" material requiring only machine washing and drying. If they can be laundered with other personal garments, a uniform maintenance reimbursement would not be required to keep wages above the minimum wage. Uniforms that require daily or special laundering due to heavy soilage or use, or that require ironing, dry cleaning, or patching and repairs due to the nature of the work, generally require a uniform maintenance reimbursement when those costs would cut into the employee's minimum wage and overtime pay. [W-H Pub. No. 1428] Also see Marshall v. S.F. of Ohio [25 Wage & Hour Cas. (BNA) 227 (S.D. Ohio 1980)]

Q 8:121   Does the FLSA prohibit an employer from requiring the employee to purchase a uniform?

No. The FLSA does not prohibit an employer from requiring a prospective employee to purchase or maintain a uniform as a condition of employment, as long as the cost of the uniform does not effectively reduce the employee's wages below the minimum wage or cut into any overtime pay that is due. If it does, the employer must reimburse the employee no later than the next regular payday to the extent that the cost of the uniform cuts into the minimum wage or overtime compensation required by the FLSA for that pay period. The employer may not spread the reimbursement over several pay periods or the life of the garment.

Example. Jessica is a plumber's assistant who is required to purchase a uniform costing $85 when the minimum wage is $7.25. During her first workweek of 40 hours she is paid $8.90 per hour. Because she was not reimbursed for the cost of the uniform, her wages are below the minimum wage (($356 − $85 = $271) ÷ 40 = $6.78). Her employer must reimburse Jessica $19 to bring her pay up to minimum ($7.25 × 40 = $290 − $271 = $19).

Q 8:122   Does the FLSA prohibit the use of employee "kickbacks," or limit deductions from an employee's pay?

Yes. Any payment by the employee or deduction from the employee's wages, except as noted in Qs 8:114–8:121, that is directly or indirectly returned to the employer or to another person for the employer's benefit is treated as a kickback and is prohibited. Also, the regulations prohibit deductions from the employee's pay that reduce the employee's wages below the minimum wage or cut into overtime pay that are not covered under the exceptions noted in Qs 8:114–8:121. An employer that requires employees to provide certain tools of the trade is prohibited from deducting the cost of these tools from the employees' pay if the cost of the tools purchased by employees cuts into their minimum required wages. [29 C.F.R. §§ 531.35, 531.40]

The term deductions under this restriction applies to payments for such articles as tools, theft, damaged equipment, and other items that do not constitute "board, lodging, or other facilities."

Thus, even though the reasonable cost of lodging, meals, and facilities can effectively lower the employee's wages below the minimum wage, the cost of uniforms or other employer-required articles may not. [29 C.F.R. § 531.36(b)] The employer also cannot require that the employee purchase specific items at a retail store maintained by the employer.

Q 8:123   How do payroll deductions affect the determination of an employee's minimum wage or overtime pay?

The FLSA permits the employer to deduct certain types of payments from an employee's pay without those deductions affecting the determination of the employee's minimum wage. This includes taxes, court-ordered payments, certain employer-provided facilities, and payments to an employee's assignees. [29 C.F.R. §§ 531.38, 531.39, 531.40]

Deductions are permitted for amounts that the employee has directed to be paid by the employer to third parties. These include, but are not limited to, payments on behalf of the employee for U.S. savings bonds, IRAs, Section 401(k) plans, union dues, insurance premiums, and contributions to churches and charitable organizations. [29 C.F.R. § 531.40] The FLSA also allows employers to make payroll deductions for certain court-ordered payments to an employee's creditors, trustees, or other third parties arising out of garnishment, bankruptcy proceedings, trustee process, or wage attachment proceedings. Employers or parties acting on the employer's behalf may not derive any profit or benefit from making such deductions. [29 C.F.R. § 531.39]

Employers can deduct taxes (e.g., income taxes and an employee's share of Social Security and Medicare) from an employee's wages even when the remaining wages fall below the federal minimum wage. However, no deduction may be made for any tax or share of tax required to be paid by the employer. [29 C.F.R. § 531.38]

As an enforcement position, the DOL permits employers to recover the amount of loans or cash advances of wages to employees without limit (but any interest to the employer cannot cut into minimum wage and overtime due).

Tipped Employees

Q 8:124　What is the significance of being classified as a tipped employee for FLSA purposes?

Employees who are classified as "tipped employees" are subject to special minimum wage and overtime requirements. The FLSA permits the employer to pay a tipped employee an hourly rate that is lower than the minimum wage if tips paid to the employee are sufficient to raise the worker's regular rate to at least the minimum wage. If tips are insufficient to increase the employee's wages to the minimum wage, the employer must make up the difference. Tipped employees are entitled to overtime pay when their hours exceed 40 per week. Note that a tipped employee's overtime rate is based on one and one-half times the full minimum wage. An employee qualifies as a tipped employee if he or she "customarily and regularly" receives more than $30 per month in tips and is engaged in a serving occupation. Employees who share in a "tip pool" or other tip-sharing arrangement are also treated as tipped employees if they satisfy the same $30-per-month tip threshold and work in serving positions.

The regulations define customarily and regularly as "a frequency which must be greater than occasional, but which may be less than constant." [29 C.F.R. § 531.58] Wage and hour rules identify employees in such occupations as waiters, bartenders, bus persons, bellhops, taxicab drivers, and barbers as employees who typically meet the classification of customarily and regularly receiving more than $30 per month in tips. [29 C.F.R. § 531.57]

Q 8:125   Must the $30 tip threshold be met each month to classify an employee as a tipped employee?

No. An employee's occasional failure to receive $30 in any month because of sickness, vacation, or seasonal fluctuations will not disqualify the employee as a tipped employee. [29 C.F.R. § 531.57]

Q 8:126   When may an employer credit tips as part of the employee's minimum wage?

An employer may credit tips of up to $5.12 an hour to an employee who is classified as a tipped employee. As a result, the employer of a tipped employee can pay as little as $2.13 an hour, as long as the employee's total pay (wages plus tips) measured on an hours-worked basis satisfies the FLSA's minimum wage requirements. An employer must notify the employees of the statutory tip credit provision and permit employees to retain all tips received (with the exception of contributions to a bona fide tip pool). When tips are required to be turned over to the employer as part of an employer's gross receipts, the tip credit cannot be taken and the employer must pay the applicable minimum wage in full. Employers cannot use a different tip credit during overtime hours than they use during straight-time hours. [29 U.S.C. § 203(m); 29 C.F.R. §§ 531.50, 531.55]

> **Example.** Kathy, a waitress who works 40 hours per week, is paid $2.35 an hour in cash wages plus tips. During one week, she earns $465 in tips, or an average of $11.63 per hour in tip income. Kathy's employer takes a tip credit of $4.90 ($7.25 – $2.35) an hour against the tips Kathy received toward meeting the minimum wage of $7.25. Kathy's wages, including the tips, are at least equal to $7.25 per hour and, therefore, satisfy the FLSA minimum wage requirement.
>
> However, the following week, Kathy works a different shift and earns only $185 in tips for 40 hours, or an average of $4.62 an hour. That, combined with her hourly wage of $2.25, is only $6.87, which is less than the minimum wage of $7.25. Kathy's employer must pay an additional $0.38 an hour, or $15.20 for the week, to meet the FLSA minimum wage requirements.

Q 8:127   What records are required for tipped employees?

Employers electing to credit tips of tipped employees toward the FLSA-required minimum wage must identify the pay records of employees whose minimum wages are determined in part by tips. The employer must maintain weekly or monthly records of tips reported by the employees (employers may use reports made by the employees on IRS Form 4070, Employee's Report of Tips to Employer, or any other report with similar information). These forms must identify the amount of tips that have been credited toward each employee's wages, not to exceed $5.12 per hour.

The employer's tip records must identify the employee's hours worked each workday when the employee performs duties that customarily and regularly elicit tips and the total daily straight-time payment for such hours. The records must also identify the employee's hours worked each workday when the employee performs duties that do not customarily and regularly elicit tips and the daily straight-time earnings for such hours.

Employers must retain records relating to tipped employees for a minimum of two years. [29 C.F.R. § 516.28]

Q 8:128 Are cafeteria-style restaurants entitled to a special tip-reporting exemption?

The IRS ruled that there is no special exemption from tip reporting in cafeteria-style restaurants unless there is, in fact, no tipping. The employer that was subject to the ruling had attempted to apply a general tip-reporting exemption available under Treasury Regulations Section 31.6053-3(j)(7)(ii) for large food or beverage establishments, which applies only to cafeteria-style restaurants in which tipping is not customary. To obtain the exemption, the employer has to demonstrate that the patrons do not, in fact, tip. The taxpayer in this ruling was a restaurant where patrons could choose to order from a table (where they would be waited on by a server) or use a buffet line. Individuals who ordered from the buffet would be provided bread and other incidentals. Tipping at these types of restaurants is customary. Thus, the IRS ruled that the exemption did not apply. [Tech. Adv. Mem. 9834001]

Q 8:129 Which employee funds may be used for the payment of payroll taxes when an employee receives tips?

The employer must collect federal income tax, Social Security tax, and Medicare tax on the employee's tip income. These amounts can be collected from the employee's wages or from other funds he or she makes available. [Pub. No. 15]

Q 8:130 How are tip credits that are used by an employer to meet its minimum wage requirement handled in the pay rate determination?

Only tip credits taken by an employer to meet the FLSA minimum wage requirements are included in a tipped employee's regular pay rate. Rules on tip credits allow an employer to count customer tips paid to employees as covering up to $5.12 of one hour's wages. [29 C.F.R. § 531.60]

Example. Trevor, a waiter, receives $5.65 an hour in cash wages, plus tips. During one week Trevor works 48 hours and reports $165 in tips. Trevor's employer takes a credit against his tips in the amount of $1.60 for each hour to make up the remaining amount of the minimum wage. The eight hours of overtime are paid at an hourly rate of $9.28 (($7.25 × 1.5) – $1.60).

(Overtime must be based on one and one-half times the minimum wage.) Therefore, Trevor will receive $226 for the first 40 hours (40 × $5.65), plus $74.24 ($9.28 × 8) for the eight hours of overtime, plus $165 in tips, or a total of $465.24. Remember, the employer must take the same tip credit in an overtime hour as in a straight-time hour.

If Trevor's tips were under $1.60 an hour ($7.25 minimum wage – $5.65 cash wage), Trevor's employer would have to make up the difference on all hours.

Q 8:131 May an employer use tips from a tip-pooling arrangement as a credit toward a tipped employee's minimum wage pay?

Yes. The FLSA's requirement that a tipped employee be permitted to keep all tips is not invalidated by a tip-pooling or tip-sharing arrangement. These arrangements may operate in a variety of ways and still qualify under the FLSA as tips. The principal characteristic of these arrangements is that a portion of the tips given to an employee is diverted to one or more coworkers. For example, certain employees (e.g., bus persons and bartenders) may share in a percentage of tips received by waiters and waitresses. [29 C.F.R. § 531.54] This percentage must be customary and reasonable. For enforcement purposes, the DOL accepts 15 percent of tips as customary and reasonable. Also, only serving employees can participate in a tip pool, not cooks, managers, etc.

Certain other types of tip sharing cannot be credited toward the FLSA minimum wage requirements. These are sometimes referred to as "tip-back" arrangements. They are characterized by a requirement that the employees turn over their tips to their employer to be treated as gross receipts for the employer. Such amounts are not treated as tips for purposes of the FLSA. When such agreements are in place, employers must pay employees the full hourly minimum wage. No tip credit can be given for such tips. [29 C.F.R. § 531.59]

Q 8:132 Who can be included in the tip pool?

An appeals court held that salad preparers working solely in the kitchen could not be treated as tipped employees "because the salad preparers abstained from any direct intercourse with diners, worked entirely outside the view of restaurant patrons, and solely performed duties traditionally classified as food preparation or kitchen support work." [Myers v. Copper Cellar Corp., 192 F.3d 546 (6th Cir. 1999)]

In an opposing position, the Court held that hosts at Outback were included with those who were tip-sharing because they actually engaged with customers and regularly would receive tips. [Igore v Outback Steakhouse of Florida, 106 F.3d 299 (6 Cir. 1998)] Another example where the tip-sharing policy applied was for bartenders who poured or mixed drinks for customers brought to their tables. [Budrow v. Dave & Busters of California, Inc., 90 Cal. Rptr. 3d 239 (Cal. Ct. App. 2d Dist. 2009)]

Q 8:133   When must employers pay tips charged on a credit card?

Employers must pay the tips charged on a credit card to the employee no later than the next regular payday. Employers may not wait until they are reimbursed by the credit card company. The employer may recover tips that have been paid to an employee when a credit card charge becomes uncollectible. The recovery may be made through an out-of-pocket payment by the employee or through payroll deductions. However, that recovery cannot cause the employee's wage for the pay period in which the correction is made to be less than the minimum wage. The employer should thoroughly document these recovery steps.

The employer can deduct from the credit card tips paid to the servers the amount of the administrative fee charged by the credit card company, but no more.

Q 8:134   How are tipped employees paid when they perform other duties for the employer?

A tipped employee who customarily and regularly earns at least $30 a month in tips but also performs other nontipped duties for the employer may be treated as holding a dual job for the employer. When such dual jobs consist of "distinguishable occupations," an employer must treat the worker as a tipped employee only with respect to the hours he or she works in the tipped occupation. [29 C.F.R. § 531.56]

Example 1. Ruth, a hotel maid, also serves as a worker in the hotel's restaurant. She regularly earns $70 in tips as a waitress, which is clearly distinguishable from her maid occupation. She occasionally receives a tip for maid services. The hotel must treat Ruth's as a dual-job employee and may credit tips toward her wages during the hours she works as a waitress. She will be paid the full minimum wage while performing her maid duties.

The hotel does not have to treat an employee as having dual jobs simply because the employee performs duties that do not produce tips, as long as they are reasonably related to the tipped job. The hotel may credit the employee's tip wages when he or she performs these "nontipped duties" because these duties do not constitute a separate occupation.

Example 2. Ruth (from Example 1) leaves her maid duties and now splits her working hours between setting tables, filling sugar, salt, and pepper dispensers, and making coffee, and waitressing. She is considered a tipped employee for all duties.

Q 8:135   Does a tip-out program covering hosts, hostesses, bus persons, and bartenders violate the FLSA's minimum wage requirements?

It can; however, if properly structured, it is permitted. The Sixth Circuit ruled in 1998 that a restaurant's policy requiring servers to contribute a percentage of their total sales (the tip-out) to a tip pool for hosts, hostesses, bus persons, and bartenders did not violate the FLSA. A steakhouse required its servers to contribute three percent of their total gross sales (the tip-out) during each shift to a tip pool. This fund was distributed by the steakhouse management to the hosts, hostesses, bus persons, and bartenders. The servers and bus persons were paid $2.13 an hour, not including tips, and the company credited the tip-out allocation to these workers to satisfy its minimum wage obligation. The hostesses also had their tip allocations credited toward their minimum wage requirements. At issue was whether hostesses and bus persons were treated as tipped employees and eligible for the tip credit.

The court held that the hosts and hostesses qualified under the FLSA as tipped employees and, as a result, could have their tip allocations credited toward their minimum wage requirement. This credit is generally available to employees who receive more than $30 a month in tips. [29 U.S.C. § 203(t)] A valid tip-out program in which the employer credits allocated tips toward the worker's minimum wage must include a written notice that outlines the tip credit and tip-pooling arrangement. [Kilgore v. Outback Steakhouse of Fla., Inc., 160 F.3d 294 (6th Cir. 1998)]

Q 8:136   How is overtime determined for servers when a banquet hall imposes an additional charge for tips?

Nondiscretionary "tips" are to be included in the employees' regular pay rate when determining the employees' overtime pay. When the establishment imposes a service charge on each sale and tipping is not customary, such charges do not have the character of tips. These service charges, when paid to the employees, are compensation under the control of the employer and so are included in the employees' regular pay rate for purposes of determining overtime pay. Tip credit rules do not apply to such payments.

The DOL has ruled that restaurant or hotel employees may be qualified under the FLSA exemption applicable to "commissioned" workers, and not be eligible for overtime payment. Service charges added to customer bills in lieu of tips will generally be classified as commissions.

An employee of a service or retail establishment may be exempt from the FLSA's overtime provisions only when the worker's pay satisfies two criteria: (1) the regular pay rate is more than one and one-half times the minimum wage and (2) more than half of the employee's compensation for a representative period (not less than a month) represents commissions on goods or services. Service charges, such as those charged by a banquet hall, constitute commissions. [29 U.S.C. § 207(i)]

Hours Worked

Q 8:137   How are an employee's hours worked determined?

Generally, employees must be paid for all time that an employer "suffers or permits" them to work. An employer cannot use estimates or arbitrary formulas to compute how much time an employee works.

Q 8:138   Which hours of work are required to be compensated under the FLSA?

Employees must be paid for all hours that they are "suffered or permitted" to work. Hours of work have been defined through the courts to include:

- Hours that an employer requires an employee to be on duty, including waiting time if it is primarily for the benefit of the employer. [Armour & Co. v. Wantock, 4 Wage & Hour Cas. (BNA) 862 (1944); Halferty v. Pulse Drug Co., 864 F.2d 1185 (5th Cir. 1989)]

- Time spent in "physical or mental exertion controlled or required by the employer and pursued necessarily and primarily for the benefit of the employer." [Tennessee Coal Co. v. Muscoda Local No. 123, 4 Wage & Hour Cas. (BNA) 294 (1944)]

- Time when an employee is required to be on the employer's premises, on duty, or at a prescribed worksite. [Anderson v. Mt. Clemens Pottery Co., 6 Wage & Hour Cas. (BNA) 83 (1946)]

Q 8:139   What time is not considered "working hours" under the FLSA?

The following is not considered "work time" under the FLSA: sick leave; annual leave; holidays; funerals; weather-related absences; changing clothes, washing up; failing to supply sufficient work; athletic contest achievement as a participant, official, or scorer, even if the contest is sponsored by the employer; and charitable work done by an employee outside of work hours. [29 U.S.C. § 203(o); 29 C.F.R. pt. 785; 29 C.F.R. § 778.218; DOL Field Operations Handbook §§ 31g01–31b13]

Q 8:140   What types of activities before or after an employee's normal workweek hours must be compensated under the FLSA?

In general, an employer must pay the FLSA minimum wage and overtime pay for preparatory and other incidental duties that are an integral part of an employee's principal employment duties. [29 C.F.R. pt. 785] These compensable hours include, but are not limited to:

- Caring for tools that are used by the employee at work (e.g., time spent by firefighters to clean fire hoses). Even though these are additional activities, they are considered part of the worker's "principal activity," and the time spent must be counted as hours worked. [Cooley v. United States, 26 Wage & Hour Cas. (BNA) 50 (Fed. Cir. 1983)]

- Time spent before the start of the normal work hours to prepare the worksite if the employee is required to be there. [Lindon v. United States, 738 F.2d 1057 (9th Cir. 1984)]

- Standby time during short plant shutdowns. [29 C.F.R. § 785.15]

- Traveling from one worksite to another or traveling out of town during business hours. [29 C.F.R. §§ 785.38, 785.39]

For example, time spent by poultry workers putting on or taking off required protective gear that is integral and indispensable to the employee's work will be considered as hours worked. In addition, time spent walking to the production area after putting on such protective gear and walking away before taking it off also will be considered hours worked. [IBP v. Alvarez, 545 U.S. 1161 (2005)].

Q 8:141   Does the FLSA require the use of time clocks?

No. The FLSA does not prescribe a particular time-keeping method. Regardless which time-keeping method an employer chooses, the FLSA requires employers to accurately and completely record all of its employees' "work hours."

Q 8:142   Must workers be compensated for waiting time?

The "hours worked" status of time spent waiting on the job generally depends on whether the worker has been engaged to wait or is waiting to be engaged. For example, an employee with no assigned duties or working hours for the day who reports to a trucking company hoping he will be hired to unload any trucks when they arrive is waiting to be engaged. On the other hand, if an employee is told to report at a certain time and be ready to unload a truck as soon as it arrives, he is engaged to wait and is working even as he waits for the truck.

Once an employee begins the workday, however, all time spent waiting constitutes hours worked for purposes of the FLSA minimum wage and overtime pay provisions. This applies even when an on-duty employee is allowed to leave the worksite or the employer's premises. Examples of compensable waiting time include a delivery worker's time spent waiting for the delivery van to be loaded or waiting for the next assignment.

Off-duty waiting time is not compensable under the following conditions:

- Employees are completely relieved of their duties.
- The waiting period is long enough for workers to effectively use the time for their own purposes.
- Such workers have been told that they can leave their jobs and that they will not have to resume working until a specified time. For example, a bus driver assigned to a Chicago-to-Milwaukee run, who is completely relieved of duty for six hours before making a return trip, is not treated as working during the idle time.

[29 C.F.R. §§ 785.14–785.17]

Q 8:143   Does an employee have to receive the FLSA minimum wage and overtime pay for time spent waiting in a paycheck line or time spent waiting to check in or check out?

No. The FLSA does not require that an employee be paid minimum wage and overtime pay for time spent waiting in a paycheck line, checking in or out of work, or waiting to start work at a designated time. These activities generally are not considered to be an integral part of the employee's principal activity.

The FLSA also does not require an employer to pay for time recorded on a punch clock or other device that reflects an employee's early arrival or delayed departure, as long as the employee does not perform any work-related duties during this time. [29 C.F.R. § 790.7(g)] However, care should be taken to minimize time between when employees punch in and when they begin to work and so begin to be paid. The more time punched in but not paid, the more likely the DOL will suspect employees are not being paid for all hours worked.

Q 8:144   Must employees be paid for time they are on call?

It depends. Time spent on call is compensable when the employee's activities while on call are so severely restricted that the employee cannot use the time for his or her own purposes. If, however, the employee can effectively use the on-call time for personal use, the time spent on call is not treated as hours worked. For example, on-call employees who do not have to remain on an employer's premises, but are required only to leave word or a telephone number where they can be reached, need not be paid for the on-call time. Also, employees are not required to be paid simply because they are required to wear a pager or carry a cell phone.

However, employees who are required to remain on call on the employer's premises and cannot use the time for their own purposes are working while on call and must be paid for the time spent waiting. [29 C.F.R. §§ 785.14–785.17]

One court examined a case in which an employer required its computer technicians to monitor building alarms weekdays from 4:30 p.m. to 7:30 a.m. and 24 hours a day on weekends. The employees received three to five alarms per shift and had to respond to an alarm within 10 to 15 minutes. The court required the employer to pay back pay for 15 hours each weekday and 24 hours each weekend day because of the employer-imposed requirements and the frequency of interruptions resulted in the employees being unable to use the on-call time primarily for their own benefit. [Pabst v. Oklahoma Gas & Elec. Co., 228 F.3d 1128 (10th Cir. 2000)]

Q 8:145   Does the FLSA require any rest periods or coffee breaks?

No. The FLSA does not require employers to give workers any rest breaks during the workday. Such breaks may, however, be required under state law. [29 C.F.R. § 785.18]

Q 8:146   Must the employer compensate a nonexempt employee for rest breaks of 20 minutes or less?

Yes. The "practice or policy of granting nonexempt employees a 20-minute (or less) uncompensated rest/break period each workday would" violate the minimum wage and overtime provisions of the FLSA.

The employer must generally pay employees for break periods of 20 minutes or less a day, even when they are required to sign out and are completely relieved from duty and able to use the time away from work for their own personal purposes.

Regulations note that rest periods of short duration, running from 5 to about 20 minutes, promote the efficiency of employees and are customarily paid for as working time.

When a regular rest/break period is longer than 20 minutes and the employees are free to go where they please, these periods are not considered hours worked. [29 C.F.R. § 785.19] This is true even if employees are not permitted to leave the premises.

Q 8:147   Does an employee have to receive minimum wage and overtime pay for rest periods during the employee's normal workweek?

Although the FLSA does not require that an employee be provided with a specific rest period during the workday, the FLSA does require that when an employer grants rest periods of short duration (generally 20 minutes or less), that time must be counted as hours worked and compensated accordingly. Such rest periods are generally deemed to be for the benefit of the employer because they promote the efficiency of workers. [Mitchell v. Greatens, 13 Wage & Hour Cas. (BNA) 3 (10th Cir. 1956)]

Q 8:148   Must maintenance workers who are subject to callbacks be paid for 30-minute meal break periods?

In some cases, yes, if the employer's requirements result in the meal break being predominantly for the benefit of the employer. The Fifth Circuit ruled that maintenance workers must be paid for 30-minute meal breaks if they are subject to interruptions and occasional callbacks and are otherwise not free to leave the premises. In general, employees are entitled to wages and overtime compensation if they are not completely relieved from duty for the purpose of eating meals. In this case, the mealtime was used "predominantly" for the benefit of the employer instead of the employees. A key factor in the court's decision was that the employees were required to wear their radios and tools during lunch and remain in radio contact. [Bernard v. IBP, Inc. of Neb., 154 F.3d 259 (5th Cir. 1998)]

Q 8:149   Are meal periods treated as time worked?

Generally, no. Bona fide lunch or meal periods do not have to be counted as time worked for purposes of the FLSA minimum wage and overtime pay requirements. A meal period is treated as bona fide when it ordinarily lasts for at least 30 minutes and workers are uninterrupted and completely relieved from all their job duties during that time. This means that if office or factory workers are required to eat at their desks or machines, then the time spent must be treated as hours worked. Employees who must answer the phone during the meal period must be paid for the meal period. The DOL has ruled that when an employee voluntarily chooses to remain at his or her desk or workstation during a meal period, the individual must be compensated unless he or she is completely relieved of all duties while at the desk or workstation (e.g., he or she cannot be required to answer the phone). [29 C.F.R. § 785.19; Hernandez v. Ethyl Corp., 83 So. 2d 150 (La. Ct. App. 1955)]

When an employee uses a punch clock or other device to record his or her hours, it is not necessary for the employee to check in and out for a mealtime break for the meal period to be uncompensated, as long as the break is regularly scheduled and no work-related activities are required during that break. [29 C.F.R. §§ 785.19, 785.42]

A meal period shorter than 30 minutes is generally treated as hours worked. Time allowed for snacks or coffee breaks cannot be treated as a bona fide meal period, and such breaks are compensable rest periods. Workers placed on a standby status for a possible duty call are entitled to pay for their mealtime. The possibility that employees might have to respond to an emergency during a meal period ordinarily does not transform a bona fide meal period into hours worked. [29 C.F.R. §§ 785.18, 785.19]

Q 8:150   Do employees have to be compensated under the FLSA for time spent sleeping on the job?

Perhaps. A determination about whether an employee must be compensated for on-the-job time spent sleeping (or engaging in other personal business) will depend on the employee's work schedule.

Employees who are required to be on duty for a work schedule of fewer than 24 hours and who are permitted to sleep (or engage in other personal activities when not busy) must be compensated for that time during their required work schedule.

However, when an employee's required work schedule is 24 hours or more, the employer and worker may agree to exclude sleeping time of not more than 8 hours. This exemption applies on the conditions that: (1) the sleeping time is scheduled; (2) there are adequate sleeping facilities; and (3) it is reasonable to assume that the employee can sleep during that time.

The employee must be compensated for the full sleep period if he or she is interrupted for a prolonged period during the scheduled sleep period to perform job duties and cannot get at least five hours of sleep. [29 C.F.R. §§ 785.20–785.23]

Q 8:151   Do employees have to be paid minimum wage and overtime pay while in training classes?

Yes. As a general rule, on-the-job training of employees counts as compensable work time under the FLSA. This includes basic training for newly hired employees. There is, however, an exception to this general rule for meetings and training periods that satisfy four requirements:

1. The training period or meetings are held outside regular working hours.
2. Attendance is fully voluntary (i.e., there must be no implied requirement by the employer).
3. The training program or meeting is not directly related to the employee's job. (Training is job-related if it teaches employees how to perform their current job more effectively but does not train them for a new job.)
4. The employee does not perform any productive work while attending the course or meeting.

The regulations also hold that time for certain training that is job-related is not compensable hours worked if the training is performed by a bona fide educational institution independent of the employer. [29 C.F.R. § 785.31] The following scenarios would fail one or more of the requirements, and the training time would be compensable if:

- Attendance is required by the employer; or
- Employees are led to believe that their working conditions or employment situations will be adversely affected if they do not attend. [29 C.F.R. §§ 516.34, 785.27–785.32]

The courts have generally held that time spent studying at home is not compensable under the FLSA overtime provisions if the study allowed or will allow the employee to qualify for a new position. [Price v. Tampa Elec. Co., 806 F.2d 1551 (11th Cir. 1987)]

Q 8:152   Must employees be paid for time attending employer-mandated training?

Yes, employer-mandated training is compensable time. The right to be paid for such training cannot be negotiated away under a collective bargaining agreement. A county law enforcement agency sought (unsuccessfully) to increase a normal workweek to 43 hours by adding three hours of medical training. The agency sought to treat those three hours as personal time for which no compensation was to be paid. [29 C.F.R. § 785.27]

Q 8:153 Must an employer compensate nonexempt employees for testing time to maintain a state-required license?

Generally, the FLSA does not require employers to pay nonexempt employees for training and testing time to obtain and maintain state-required agent licenses or to meet continuing education requirements under certain conditions. Attendance at training programs is discussed in DOL regulations at 29 C.F.R. Sections 785.27 through 785.32. Under these regulations, attendance at training programs does not have to be counted as working time if the following four criteria are met:

1. Attendance is outside of the employee's regular working hours.
2. Attendance is in fact voluntary.
3. The course, lecture, or meeting is not directly related to the employee's job.
4. The employee does not perform any productive work during such attendance.

No payments are required for training when the training is taken at (or when it corresponds to) courses offered by independent bona fide institutions of learning and the training is voluntarily attended by an employee outside of normal working hours. [29 C.F.R. § 785.27]

In some cases, employees with licenses issued by the state are required by their employers to keep such licenses current. For example, a paramedic employed by a hospital may be required by the hospital to keep the license current, which means the paramedic has to attend certain training courses. While this would appear to fail both the second and third requirements listed above, the DOL has held that such training is not hours worked if the requirement for the training is imposed by the state and not the hospital, and if the license is "portable"—that is, the employee can go to work for another employer and the license is still valid.

Q 8:154 How does the FLSA treat preemployment training with respect to minimum wage and overtime pay?

Employer-provided training for prehire trainees or other individuals who have not been hired may not count as hours worked, but each situation must be examined carefully. Preemployment training is not hours worked when four conditions are met:

1. The training is primarily for the benefit of the trainees, rather than for the benefit of the employer.
2. The trainees, once employed, do not replace regular workers.
3. The trainees are not entitled to a job at the end of the training.
4. The employer and the trainees agree at the beginning that no wages will be paid during the program.

Note. This exemption applies only to individuals who have not been hired. The fact that an individual has been hired but does not begin work until after the training causes the hours to be compensable. Also, to be primarily for the benefit of the trainees, the training must be more general rather than specific to the employer. The Field Operations Handbook (FOH) says that the training must be similar to that which would be given in a vocational school. [FOH 10b11(b)(1)]

Q 8:155 Is an employer required to compensate an employee for travel from the employee's home to the worksite?

Generally, no. The Portal-to-Portal Act, which amended the FLSA, provides that an employer is not required to pay an employee for ordinary time spent traveling to and from work, whether the employee works at a fixed job location or various job sites. The Act excludes from working time certain travel and walking time and other similar "preliminary" and "postliminary" activities performed prior to, or right after, the workday, unless such activities are compensable by contract, custom, or practice. [29 C.F.R. § 785.35]

The DOL regulations provide that "normal travel" between home and the assigned place of work is not compensable unless the payment is expressly recognized by contract or policy. "Normal travel" is generally interpreted as "time spent by a specific worker traveling to work." The term does not specify an objective standard for how long the employee commutes or may be expected to commute.

In 1999, a district court ruled on a repairman's travel from home to his first worksite and from his last worksite to his home. An employer is not required to pay a worker for such activities as "walking, riding, or traveling to and from" the actual place of work. The court held that nothing in the FLSA or its regulations, as currently written, required the company to compensate the repairman for the commute to and from his home, regardless of the extensive travel, when such travel was usual for the employee. The district court's decision was affirmed by the appeals court. [Kavanagh v. Grand Union Co., 192 F.3d 269 (2d Cir. 1999)]. If the employee had regularly worked at a set location, and had been assigned to travel to and from a distant location in the same day, the result might have been different. See 29 C.F.R. Section 785.37, which holds that travel to another city by an employee who normally works at a fixed location " . . . cannot be regarded as ordinary home-to-work travel occasioned merely by the fact of employment. It was performed for the employer's benefit and at his special request to meet the needs of the particular and unusual assignment." On the other hand, see the *Imada* case discussed below in Q 8:156.

Q 8:156 Does the FLSA require compensation for an employee's travel to offsite training?

Compensation for an employee's commuting to offsite training may not be required. Federal law does not require payment for travel time to a site where "an employee is to perform essential parts of the activities the employee has been hired to perform," the Ninth Circuit Court of Appeals has ruled. For example, the FLSA does not require that an employee be compensated for travel between home and worksite, regardless of whether the employee's work location is fixed or changes. The Act generally defines the worksite to be where an employee performs essential parts of the activities the employee was hired to perform.

The 1999 appeals court decision regarding travel by California law enforcement officers who were required to attend a minimum of 24 hours of approved training every two years confirmed this exemption. Two to three times a year, the training occurred in other cities, requiring travel. One officer stayed overnight and sought to be compensated, alleging that the travel fell under a FLSA exception whereby travel to another city for a special or unusual one-day assignment performed primarily for the employer's benefit is compensable. [29 C.F.R. § 785.37] The court held that approved training cannot be characterized as either "special" or "unusual" when it is a normal requirement of the position, contemplated—and in fact mandated—by the officer's employment. In addition, the requirement was described in the collective bargaining agreement. The court stated that the FLSA requires compensation for travel only when the travel occurs during the normal workday or on corresponding hours on nonworking days. [Imada v. City of Hercules, 138 F.3d 1294 (9th Cir. 1998)]

Q 8:157   Does the FLSA require minimum wage and overtime pay for overnight travel?

Yes, under certain circumstances. When the overnight travel time is during the employee's normal working hours, it is compensable. This requirement applies to travel hours on Saturdays, Sundays, and holidays that correspond to an employee's normal working hours on other days of the week. Overnight travel can be hours on a trip taken by car, train, or other public transportation that keeps an employee away from home overnight. Travel at other hours that keeps an employee away from home is generally not compensable and, as with normal working schedules, bona fide meal periods during the overnight travel may be excluded. [29 C.F.R. §§ 785.39, 785.41; Boll v. Federal Reserve Bank, 365 F. Supp. 637 (E.D. Mo. 1973)]

One-day trips are also compensable. These are special assignments lasting for one day that require an employee to travel to another city. Time spent in such one-day assignments for employees who normally work at one location counts as time worked. Again, bona fide meal periods and the time spent traveling between the worker's home and point of departure (e.g., an airport or rail station) are not treated as time worked. [29 C.F.R. § 785.37]

Q 8:158   Must an employer pay employees for time spent commuting in company cars?

Generally, no. As a result of a 1996 amendment to the FLSA, time spent in home-to-work travel by an employee in an employer-provided vehicle, or in activities performed by the employee that are incidental to the use of the vehicle for commuting, is not "hours worked" and, therefore, does not have to be paid. This provision applies only if the travel is within the normal commuting area for the employer's business and the use of the vehicle is subject to an agreement between the employer and the employee. [Employment Standards Admin. Fact Sheet No. 96-13]

If the employer requires workers to commute in employer-provided vehicles from the employer's pickup location to the job site, the employees would be paid for such travel time.

Q 8:159   Must the employer include commuting time in determining hours worked?

Generally, no. The Portal-to-Portal Act of 1947 generally excludes from FLSA minimum wage and overtime pay for the time during which an employee is "walking, riding, or traveling to and from the actual place of performance of the principal activity or activities," unless these activities are compensable under the terms of a contract, or payment for these hours is an industry practice. The 1947 Act also excludes time when activities are "preliminary to" or "postliminary to" the employee's principal work activities. [29 C.F.R. § 785.50]

However, if the employee is required to report to a meeting place where he or she is to pick up other employees or to receive instructions before traveling to work, the travel is compensable after the first stop. [29 C.F.R. § 785.35; Marshall v. R&M Erectors, Inc., 429 F. Supp. 771 (D. Del. 1977)]

Q 8:160   Does an employee have to receive minimum wage and overtime pay for time spent representing the employer at an after-hours sports, charitable, or civic activity?

Generally, yes. However, time spent by an employee after hours at a social, charitable, or civic activity is not considered hours worked under the FLSA as long as that attendance is voluntary and not a condition of employment. This exemption applies even when the event is sponsored by the employer. [DOL Field Operations Handbook § 31b05]

Q 8:161   When do employees have to receive minimum wage and overtime pay for charitable work requested by their employer?

When an employer orders or requests an employee to work for a public or charitable cause, that time is treated as hours worked and is compensable. Such activities also count as hours worked if they are performed while the worker is required to be on the employer's premises. When the employer directs those activities on the worksite, employees must also be compensated under the FLSA. [29 C.F.R. § 785.44] Finally, when the employee volunteers for activities that are the same or similar to those that the employee is hired to perform, the time is included as hours worked. [DOL Field Operations Handbook § 10b03(c)] However, if the volunteer activity is not similar to the employee's regular duties and is voluntarily performed outside normal working hours, the activity will not be considered hours worked. [Wage & Hour Op. Ltr. Nos. 2005-33 (Sept. 16, 2005) and 2006-4 (Jan. 27, 2006)]

Q 8:162   Must an employee receive minimum wage and overtime pay for time spent receiving medical care?

Generally, no. However, if the medical care is provided on the employer's premises during working hours, or if the worker receives the medical care off the premises at the employer's direction, those hours are subject to the FLSA wage and overtime pay provisions.

An employee is compensated under the FLSA for time spent to obtain a health certificate from a company doctor on the employer's premises when the examination is during the employee's normal work schedule. Employees who are required to take a physical examination as a condition of their employment must be paid for the exam time, regardless of whether the exam occurs on or off the employer's premises. [29 C.F.R. § 785.43]

Q 8:163   Must an employer compensate employees for time required to complete an employer drug test or required physical?

Yes. An employer must compensate an employee for time that is required for drug testing and physical examinations required by the employer as a condition of employment. The time spent is compensable whether the exam occurs on or off the employer's premises. This time falls under the FLSA requirement that employee attendance at a meeting, whether during or outside of working hours, for the purpose of submitting to a mandatory drug test imposed by the employer constitutes hours worked. [Wage & Hour Op. Ltr. (Sept. 15, 1997)]

Q 8:164   How does the "rounding off" method for start and stop times work?

An employer may identify the employee's starting or stopping times to the nearest five minutes, one-tenth, or quarter of an hour. To take advantage of this method, the amount of time rounded should average out over time so the employee is compensated for all hours worked. [29 C.F.R. § 785.48(b)]

Q 8:165   How does the *de minimis* rule work?

An employer can disregard insubstantial or insignificant periods of time beyond a worker's scheduled hours when "as a practical administrative matter" that disregarded time is small. In this case, small means "only where there are uncertain and indefinite periods of time involved of a few seconds or minutes duration, and where the failure to count such time is due to considerations justified by industrial realities." The courts generally have considered intervals of 10 minutes or less to be *de minimis*; other courts have held that periods of time resulting in pay of less than $1 are not *de minimis*. It is important to note, however, that an "employer may not arbitrarily fail to count as hours worked any part, however small, of the employee's fixed or regular working time or practically ascertainable period of time he is regularly required to spend on duties assigned to him." [29 C.F.R. § 785.47] Employers should be very cautious before excluding "hours worked" under the *de minimis* rule.

Q 8:166 Are any activities associated with an employee's normal work duties excluded from compensable working time?

Generally, no. The FLSA minimum wage and overtime pay requirements apply to any time spent on activities that are "closely related" to the worker's principal activities, even if those tasks are performed before or after an employee's regularly scheduled workweek. The DOL regulations contain one exception to this general rule. Time spent changing clothes or washing up at the beginning or end of a workday can be excluded from compensable time under the terms of a collective bargaining agreement or pursuant to an industry custom or practice under such a contract. [29 C.F.R. § 785.24(c)] However, if the clothes changing or washing is integral and indispensable to the worker's principal activities, the time is hours worked. [Steiner v. Mitchell, 350 U.S. 247, 256 (1956)]

Q 8:167 How does the FLSA apply to changes in daylight saving time?

Hourly employees may work an additional hour on the date that daylight saving is terminated. When most of the nation's clocks are moved backward one hour to mark the end of daylight saving time, some employees who normally work an eight-hour schedule spanning midnight may work nine hours. These workers must be paid for all nine hours, and the additional hour worked must be counted in determining the number of hours worked during that week for overtime purposes.

When daylight saving time begins in the spring, some employees who normally work an eight-hour schedule will work only seven hours during their shift. The FLSA does not require payment for this missed hour. If the employer pays the employee for an eight-hour period over the seven-hour period, the additional hour's pay does not raise the employee's regular rate of pay for this period. [29 C.F.R. § 785.11]

Q 8:168 Must an employer compensate an employee for unauthorized work before or after an employee's normal work schedule?

Yes. The FLSA requires payment of minimum wage and overtime pay for unauthorized work that, although unauthorized or even prohibited, is performed with the knowledge and acquiescence of management. If, for example, a worker voluntarily continues a duty beyond the end of a normal work schedule and a supervisor or manager knows or has reason to believe that the work is occurring, the employee is entitled to be paid for that work. This rule applies even when an employer's rules or formal policy forbids unauthorized work.

Note that this pay-for-unauthorized work rule applies to work performed by employees at home or elsewhere off the premises. When management knows or has reason to believe that an employee is performing such work, the time must be treated as compensable hours worked. [29 C.F.R. §§ 785.11–785.13]

Even though employers are obligated to compensate employees for such work, it is important to note that they may still enforce company policy by disciplining such employees, if appropriate under the circumstances.

Q 8:169   Must an employer pay minimum wage and overtime pay for time spent changing clothes or washing up?

Yes, if the time spent by employees to change clothes or wash up at the beginning or end of the work schedule is considered part of their "principal activities" because of the nature of the workers' duties. This same rule applies when such activities are required by an employer's rules, statute, or ordinance. No pay is required if employees elect to do the required changing or washing at home. The FLSA authorizes contractual provisions under union-negotiated contracts that exclude such time from compensable time. [29 U.S.C. § 203(o); 29 C.F.R. §§ 785.24–785.26, 790.8; IBP, Inc. v. Alvarez, 546 U.S. 21 (2005)]

Unionized steelworkers who were required to don protective clothing and gear, including flame-retardant jackets, pants, and hoods; hard hats; "snoods"; "wristlets"; work gloves; leggings; "metatarsal" boots; safety glasses; earplugs; and respirators did not have to be paid for their changing time because the items were considered clothes, which fell under the FLSA Section 203(o) exception allowing employees covered under a collective bargaining agreement to waive otherwise compensable changing time. [Sandifer v. United States Steel Corp., 134 S. Ct. 870 (2014)]

Q 8:170   What is show-up pay?

Union contracts frequently provide payments to compensate workers for the inconvenience of reporting to work when there is not sufficient work or returning to work after regular hours because of emergency work. This time can be classified as "show-up" or "callback" pay. [29 C.F.R. §§ 778.220, 778.221] Certain state laws may require employers to pay employees a minimum amount of money under such circumstances, but the FLSA does not.

Overtime

Q 8:171   What are the basic requirements for payment of overtime?

The FLSA requires employers to pay nonexempt employees for hours worked in excess of 40 during any given workweek at a rate one and one-half times their regular pay rate. Unlike some state laws, the FLSA does not require employers to pay overtime for hours worked in excess of any daily maximum, nor does it require overtime pay for work performed on Saturdays, Sundays, or holidays. The workweek is the basis for computing an employee's overtime. Under the FLSA, each workweek stands alone for purposes of calculating overtime.

Q 8:172   How is an employee's overtime rate determined?

When an employee is entitled to overtime pay, it must equal at least one and one-half times his or her "regular rate" for each hour (or fraction thereof) of overtime. The regular rate includes all compensation received by the employee in the workweek with a few statutory exclusions. Overtime pay is based on hours worked in excess of 40 hours during a given workweek. [29 U.S.C. § 207(b)(1)]

Q 8:173   When must overtime be paid?

The FLSA generally requires that overtime be paid on the payday covering the period in which the overtime was worked. If the amount of overtime wages that are due cannot be determined by this date, the employer may pay the overtime portion of wages as soon as it is calculable after the regular payday. However, overtime payments must be made no later than the payday following the date on which the overtime pay can be determined.

When errors resulting in overpayment are made in the overtime computations, a correction may be made by deducting the amount of the overpayment in the next pay period. [29 C.F.R. § 778.106] Before making such deductions, however, an employer should be sure it complies with the state laws regarding deductions from wages. Some states will not allow a deduction even when the employee consents to the deduction to recover payment.

Q 8:174   Can employees waive their right to receive overtime or other compensation?

No. It is clear that, absent court or DOL approval, an employee cannot waive the right to receive overtime. For example, the Fifth Circuit ruled in Bernard v. IBP, Inc. of Nebraska [154 F.3d 259 (5th Cir. 1998)] that nonexempt workers may not waive their rights to overtime. It is also clear that the right to overtime cannot be waived through a union contract.

Q 8:175   Can an employer avoid paying for overtime in one week by reducing an employee's bonus in a subsequent workweek?

No. Such an arrangement would violate the overtime pay requirements of the FLSA for nonexempt employees. The FLSA does not permit the averaging of hours over a two-week period. A nonexempt employee must be paid overtime for all hours worked in excess of 40 in a workweek. [29 C.F.R. § 778.104]

Q 8:176   Does the FLSA permit the payment of employees on a per-call basis?

Yes, but the employees must still be paid overtime based on their regular rate, unless some exemption applies.

Define Workweek

Q 8:177   What is the employer's workweek for purposes of the FLSA?

The FLSA requires an employer to be in compliance each workweek. The term workweek generally refers to a fixed, recurring, 168-hour period consisting of seven consecutive 24-hour periods. Compliance with the FLSA's minimum wage and overtime pay requirements is based on hours worked in the workweek. [29 C.F.R. § 778.105] The FLSA does not permit averaging of hours worked over two or more workweeks, but does permit a longer "work period" for purposes of determining overtime pay for public sector law enforcement and fire protection personnel. [29 U.S.C. § 207(k); 29 C.F.R. § 553.200] The FLSA also permits an alternative method of determining overtime hours for certain hospital workers providing for overtime based on eight hours per day or 80 hours in a 14-day period. [29 U.S.C. § 207(j)]

Q 8:178   Does the FLSA permit the employer to select which seven-day period to use as its workweek?

Yes. The employer determines its workweek based on its specific needs. The workweek need not coincide with the calendar week and may begin on any day and at any hour of the day. Once the beginning time of the workweek is established, it remains fixed. According to the regulation, "The beginning of the workweek may be changed if the change is intended to be permanent and is not designed to evade the overtime requirements of the Act." [29 C.F.R. § 778.105]

Q 8:179   Must the employer's workweek be the same as the employer's pay period?

No. The fact that FLSA compliance is measured on a workweek basis does not restrict an employer from paying its employees on a daily, weekly, biweekly, semimonthly, monthly, or piecework basis. However, the workweek remains the basis for computing overtime even if a different pay period is used. [29 C.F.R. § 778.104]

Q 8:180　Which of the FLSA requirements are applied on a workweek basis?

Almost all of them. The employer must comply with the FLSA overtime pay and minimum wage requirements for each workweek. These workweek requirements also apply when employees are paid on a basis other than an hourly rate. That is, an employer may not generally average hours worked over two or more workweeks to avoid paying overtime or minimum wage. For example, an employer may not base the compliance on any 168-hour period other than the workweek, or an average of two workweeks, even if both weeks happen to fall within one pay period. [29 C.F.R. § 778.104]

Q 8:181　May the employer change its workweek?

The employer's selected workweek must generally be a fixed period that does not vary from one pay period to another. However, the workweek may be changed when the change is designed to be permanent. Employers cannot make such change to avoid paying overtime. [29 C.F.R. § 778.105]

Q 8:182　What calculations are required when a workweek changes?

When a seven-day workweek is changed, there will generally be an overlap in days and hours worked. An employee is generally given the benefit of overtime calculated under the old workweek or the new workweek. That is, the employee is given the higher amount, but is not paid double for any overlapped days.

Thus, an employee is paid on a seven-day workweek beginning on Sunday, June 5. The employer changes the seven-day workweek to begin on Friday, June 10. Hours worked on Friday, June 10 and Saturday, June 11 will be included in both workweeks. The employer includes the overlapping days in the old workweek and determines overtime for Sunday, June 5, to Saturday, June 11. Then the employer calculates pay for Friday, June 10, to Thursday, June 16. The employee gets the greater of the two calculations. [29 C.F.R. §§ 778.301, 778.302]

Example. During the week of June 5-11, Phillip works eight hours on Monday, Tuesday, Wednesday, Thursday, Friday, and Saturday for a total of 48 hours. Phillip then works eight hours on the following Monday, Tuesday, and Wednesday. Phillip does not work Thursday or Friday. Since Phillip's employer changed workweeks, Phillip must be paid in the most favorable manner. For the week June 5-11, Phillip worked 48 hours. For the new workweek June 10-16, Phillip worked 40 hours. Phillip must be paid 8 hours overtime for the workweek June 5-11.

Q 8:183   Can the number of hours during two workweeks ever be averaged for purposes of overtime payment?

No. The FLSA [29 U.S.C. § 207(f)] does provide a limited exemption for certain jobs that, by necessity, require irregular work hours from week to week. In addition, the Wage and Hour Division has approved certain pay plans that "balance" overtime in one week against "undertime" worked in another week. These plans are frequently described as "time-off" or "prepayment" plans and apply to hourly rated employees. Such a plan permits an employee to be paid a constant wage from workweek to workweek or from pay period to pay period. These plans must be structured under rules set in regulations and generally require that time off be for one and one-half the overtime hours. [29 C.F.R. §§ 778.402–778.414] These plans are of limited usefulness, however, and are generally more trouble than they are worth.

Regular Rate

Q 8:184   What is the significance of an employee's regular rate?

A nonexempt employee must receive a regular rate that equals or exceeds the minimum wage under the FLSA, and that worker's overtime pay must be at least one and one-half of the employee's regular rate. [29 U.S.C. §§ 206, 207]

The regular rate of pay is determined by dividing the total compensation (with limited exceptions) in the workweek (not including overtime pay) by the total hours worked. **Example.** Brent, a line mechanic, earns $17 an hour working for Noble Enterprises, Inc., a manufacturer. When Brent works the night shift, he receives an additional $3 an hour as a shift differential.

In a week that Brent works 36 hours during the day shift and 19 hours on the night shift, his regular rate of pay is determined as follows:

36 hours @ $17 an hour	$612.00
19 hours @ $20.00 an hour	$380.00
Total wages in week	$992.00 for 55 hours of work

Brent's regular rate of pay is $992 ÷ 55 hours = $18.04

Brent's overtime for 15 hours is 0.50 × 15 × $18.04 = $135.30

Brent's pay for the week is $992.00 + $135.30 = $1,127.30

Q 8:185   How is an employee's regular pay rate determined when the employee works at two or more rates in a single week?

When an employee performs two tasks in a single workweek for which he or she is entitled to two pay rates, the employee's normal pay rate is determined under a weighted average. The employer may, under specific circumstances, pay overtime at the rate in effect when overtime is worked (see 29 C.F.R. § 778.415).

Example. Tess works for Seaview Heights, Inc. at a job paying $12 an hour for 28 hours and at a job paying $15 an hour for 22 hours. Her regular pay rate for the workweek is [($12 × 28) + ($15 × 22)] ÷ 50 = $13.32. She is entitled to overtime pay of $6.66 (or 0.5 × $13.32) for 10 hours. She is eligible for an additional payment of $66.60 ($6.66 × 10). [29 C.F.R. § 778.115]

Q 8:186　How is the overtime rate determined when an employee works at two different jobs and receives premium pay for one of the jobs?

An employee's pay for overtime hours worked is based on the employee's regular pay rate. That pay rate is generally determined based on all pay received by the employee during the workweek. However, the FLSA permits certain amounts of premium pay (i.e., overtime premiums) to be disregarded in this determination. In other words, employers need not pay overtime on overtime. There are three types of overtime premium which need not be included in the employee's regular rate. These are premiums paid for: (1) hours in excess of eight in a day or 40 in a week or in excess of the employee's normal working hours [29 U.S.C. § 207(e)(5)]; (2) hours on Saturdays, Sundays, and other special days [29 U.S.C. § 207(e)(6)]; or (3) hours outside of the hours established by agreement or contract as the basic workday or workweek. [29 U.S.C. § 207(e)(7)] [See also 29 C.F.R. §§ 778.201–778.203.] The exclusion applies to any premium paid for working hours in excess of eight in a day or 40 in a week or in excess of the employee's normal working hours. For hours on Saturdays, Sundays, and other special days or hours outside of the hours established by agreement or contract as the basic workday or workweek, to be excluded, the premium must be at least one and one-half times the employee's regular rate.

An employer inquired whether premium pay for the "secondary" job could be disregarded in the determination of a regular pay rate. Employees were paid at one and one-half times the rate of their primary job (which was the rate for the secondary job) when they worked more than 40 hours, regardless of which job they performed.

When an employee works at two jobs for which different levels of pay exist, the employer may not adjust the determination of the worker's regular pay rate for the secondary job, which pays a premium, unless it is paid only for one of the reasons stated earlier. The DOL found that time worked on the "secondary" job would not qualify under any of the exceptions specified in 29 U.S.C. Sections 207(e)(5), (6), or (7) because the employer does not pay premium pay for overtime hours on other than a 40-hour workweek basis and the hours on the "secondary" job are not necessarily "overtime" hours. Some of the hours an employee works on his or her regular job could result in the employee working more than 40 hours. [29 C.F.R. § 778.115]

Q 8:187   Do employer awards become a part of the regular rate calculation?

Most awards are included in the determination of an employee's regular rate. They include prizes won by employees for quality, quantity, or efficiency in the performance of their customary duties that are performed during an employee's regular working hours. The value of the prize is allocated over the period in which it is earned. If merchandise is awarded, the employer allocates the cost of the merchandise.

A new employee referral award need not be included in an employee's regular rate of pay if: (1) participation in the referral program is voluntary; (2) the employee's efforts do not involve a significant amount of time; and (3) the activity is limited to after-work hours. If any of these conditions are not met, the value of the award must be included in the employee's regular rate of pay. [Wage & Hour Administrative Op. Ltr. WH-941]

Awards granted to employees under a bona fide suggestion plan award program may or may not be considered remuneration for employment. The award, based on the value of the suggestion and not related to the employee's earnings, is generally excludable from the employee's regular rate determination. [29 C.F.R. §§ 778.332, 778.333]

Q 8:188   Are discretionary bonuses included in the calculation of an employee's normal pay rate for overtime payments?

Generally, no, but only if the bonuses are truly discretionary. A bonus paid to an employee at the employer's discretion is not included in an employee's regular rate. For a bonus to be treated as discretionary, however, it must not be based on hours worked, units produced, or work quality; nor can the payment be under any agreement, promise, or previously announced plan to pay the bonus. Both the fact that the bonus is to be paid, and the amount of the bonus, are only determined at or near the end of the bonus period.

Example. Tumbleweed Lumber, Inc. announces that it will institute a semiannual bonus program that is based on the number of items sold. The bonus will be paid only if Tumbleweed Lumber, Inc. has the cash flow to do so. A bonus paid under such a program is not discretionary, even though the company retains discretion, because the program was announced and is production-based. The bonus would be included in the employee's normal pay rate for determining the rate of overtime pay. [29 C.F.R. § 778.211]

Q 8:189   Are percentage-of-earnings bonuses included in the calculation of an employee's normal pay rate for overtime payments?

No. Where an employer's bonus payments are calculated as a percentage multiplied by the employee's total earnings (straight time plus any overtime pay), the bonus payment does not have to be included in the regular rate calculation. [29 C.F.R. § 778.210] For example, in a Wage and Hour Opinion

Letter dated February 17, 2006, the employer paid a monthly bonus to its nonexempt employees who met certain attendance standards. The bonus was calculated as a percentage multiplied by the employee's total earnings (straight time plus overtime pay). The DOL found that the bonus payment need not be included in the regular rate calculation. [Wage & Hour Op. Ltr. No. 2006-4 NA (Feb. 17, 2006)]

Q 8:190   Are stay or retention bonuses included in the calculation of an employee's normal pay rate for overtime payments?

Yes. In a November 4, 2005 opinion letter, the DOL examined whether a stay or retention bonus paid to nonexempt employees should be included when calculating the regular rate for overtime purposes. According to the employer requesting the opinion, the retention benefits were offered to encourage employees to remain at a facility for a certain length of time. The employees were offered three options for the payout of the stay bonus, including: (1) full payment of the stay bonus on a particular date; (2) deferred payment of the stay bonus until a future date, accruing interest at 4 percent; or (3) continuous equal monthly payment of the stay bonus until it is fully paid. The DOL found this bonus was nondiscretionary, regardless of how it was paid, and that it must be included in the calculation of the regular rate for the purposes of calculating overtime payments. [Wage & Hour Op. Ltr. No. 2005-47 (Nov. 4, 2005)]

Q 8:191   Are benefits provided under certain employee benefit plans included in the determination of an employee's normal pay rate?

No. Payments an employer makes to, or benefits provided under, a bona fide profit sharing, thrift, savings, retirement, life insurance, or medical plan are excluded from an employee's regular rate. However, different rules must be satisfied depending on the type of plan to which the employer contribution is made.

DOL rules are not identical to the Internal Revenue Code. In general, however, pension or welfare plans that meet I.R.C. requirements will also qualify for the exclusion from the regular rate. Note that employee contributions to such plans (e.g., a Section 401(k) salary deferral) are treated as part of an employee's normal pay-rate pay, even if the contributions are made under a tax-exempt plan (e.g., a Section 401(k) or cafeteria plan under I.R.C. Section 125).

Q 8:192   Is the value of tax-free benefits purchased under a cafeteria plan included in the employee's regular wages for purposes of determining pay for overtime?

Yes, in some cases. Under I.R.C. Section 125 cafeteria plans, an employee is permitted to select between tax-free and taxable benefits (e.g., cash). Under such a plan, the value of the tax-free benefits that could have been selected as a taxable benefit is included in the employee's regular rate of pay.

Under the FLSA regulations, a plan qualifies as a bona fide plan and the value of benefits is excludable only if the plan does "not give an employee the option to receive any part of the employer's contribution in cash instead of the benefits under the plan." [29 C.F.R. § 778.215(a)] When a plan offers cash as an option (as in a salary reduction plan), the amount available as cash is includible in the employee's regular rate of pay.

Q 8:193   May an employer that, under a contract, voluntarily pays for idle time exclude these payments from the determination of an employee's normal pay rate?

Generally, yes. Although the FLSA does not require employers to make idle-time payments, many employers do so because of industry practice or a contractual agreement. This pay is made to employees when they are kept off the job by unusual circumstances. Such idle-time payments may be excluded from an employee's regular pay rate only when the payment is sporadic in nature and infrequent. Idle-time pay must be approximately equivalent to the amount the employee would normally have earned had the employee worked for the same time period.

Idle-time payments generally include payments for:

- A failure by the employer to provide sufficient work for employees;
- An inability of employees to reach the workplace because of weather;
- Machinery breakdowns; or
- Emergency conditions outside the control of the employer.

[29 C.F.R. § 778.218]

Q 8:194   How are show-up pay and callback pay treated for minimum wage and overtime purposes?

A collective bargaining agreement typically provides a guarantee of a minimum number of hours of work or pay when the employee is asked to return to work after normal business hours (callback pay). Callback pay is treated in a manner similar to show-up pay. Premium rates for hours actually worked may be excluded from the employee's regular rate and credited toward overtime compensation due the employee. Straight-time rates and premium rates for hours not actually worked are excluded from the employee's regular rates and are not creditable toward any overtime pay that may be due.

A show-up clause in a collective bargaining agreement typically guarantees workers a minimum number of hours of work or pay when they are required to report for work. The portion of the show-up guarantee that is compensation for hours actually worked (if any) is included in the employee's regular rate for purposes of computing overtime compensation. The portion of the show-up guarantee that is payment for time not actually worked is not included in the employee's regular rate, nor may it be credited toward any overtime pay. When a premium rate (i.e., a rate at least one and one-half times the regular rate) is paid for show-up work, the premium for time actually worked is excluded from an employee's regular rate, but can be credited against the overtime compensation due the employee. [29 C.F.R. § 778.220]

Q 8:195   Is the compensation derived from exercise of a stock option considered part of a nonexempt employee's regular rate of pay for purposes of overtime under the FLSA?

Generally, no. This issue was first addressed in a February 12, 1999, Wage and Hour Opinion Letter, in which the DOL held that the additional compensation received from the exercise of a stock option earned by a nonexempt employee should be treated as part of the employee's regular rate of pay for purposes of determining the employee's wages for overtime. After public outcry, the DOL withdrew its opinion, and in 2000, the Worker Economic Opportunity Act amended the FLSA to exclude such value from the determination of an employee's regular rate of pay.

Q 8:196   How is a nonexempt salaried employee's pay rate determined?

In general, a salaried employee who is not exempt under the FLSA must receive minimum wage for all hours worked (i.e., the "regular rate" of pay must equal or exceed the minimum wage) and overtime for all hours worked over 40 in the workweek. There are generally two categories of salaries for nonexempt employees. Some employees are paid a salary intended to compensate a specified number of hours, usually 40. Other employees are paid their salaries as their straight-time pay for all hours worked, many or few.

When nonexempt employees are paid a salary intended to compensate them for 40 hours, their regular rate is determined by dividing the salary by the number of hours for which the pay is intended to compensate the employee during the given workweek. [29 C.F.R. § 778.113]

Example. Aaron is paid an annual salary of $42,000 or $807.69 per week, intended to compensate him for 40 hours per week. During one week he works 52 hours. Aaron's regular rate is determined by dividing his weekly salary by 40 hours, which in this case equals $20.19 per hour. Since his salary is intended to compensate only 40 hours, he has been paid nothing for the overtime hours, neither straight time nor overtime. He is entitled to full time and one-half, or $30.29 per hour, for the 12 overtime hours, which comes to $363.48. His total pay is $807.69 + 363.48 = 1,171.17.

Note that when a nonexempt employee is paid on an annual salaried basis intended to compensate for 40 hours per week, one must divide the annual salary by the total projected annual hours, using a 52-week year, or 2,080 hours for a 40-hour expected workweek, to compute the regular rate of pay.

Q 8:197 Under what conditions can an employee be paid on a fluctuating workweek basis?

To use the fluctuating workweek method to pay overtime to salaried nonexempt employees, there must be a clear mutual understanding between employer and employee that the salary is the employee's straight-time pay for all hours worked, whether many or few. This means that although the employee is paid a fixed base amount for all hours worked, the employee is entitled to his or her base salary whether he or she works 1 hour or 40 hours, and the employee must be paid overtime when he or she works more than 40 hours in a workweek. [29 C.F.R. § 778.114] Employers should take care to be sure that they are complying with all of the technical requirements set forth in the regulations, when implementing a fluctuating workweek method of payment. Before implementing this method, they should consult their attorney to ensure that all such requirements are being met.

The fluctuating workweek method is often the issue of litigation. For example, in *Griffin v. Wake County* [142 F.3d 712 (4th Cir. 1998)], the Court examined whether Wake County, North Carolina, properly paid a class of emergency medical technicians (EMTs) a half-time overtime premium according to the fluctuating workweek pay plan rather than standard time-and-a-half overtime compensation. In this case, the EMTs had a preset written schedule working 24 hours on, 24 hours off, 24 hours on, 24 hours off, 24 hours on, and then 96 hours (four days) off. Under the pay plan, the EMTs were paid a flat weekly salary as straight-time pay for the hours they work each week, whether 48, 72, or some other number. In addition, they were paid an overtime premium of one-half their regular hourly rate for hours worked in excess of 40 per week. The Court found that the County's pay plan complied with the fluctuating workweek requirements under the regulations and dismissed the EMTs claims. Among other things, the Court held that the fluctuation in hours did not have to be unpredictable and that the EMTs understood—and did not have to consent to—the plan.

In an August 31, 1999, opinion letter, the DOL's Wage and Hour Division also considered whether an employer's pay plan complied with the fluctuating workweek requirements. In this case, the client paid its employees a salary that reflected an agreed-on amount for the first 40 hours in each workweek, plus 10 additional hours of "overtime pay"—essentially a guaranteed salary for 50 hours each week. Regardless of how much the employees worked, they received this salary. Even though the lump-sum salary was based on a hypothetical 50-hour week, the Division found that it did not comply with the regulations. In particular, the Division noted that the fluctuating workweek regulations require an employer to pay overtime premium pay for each hour worked over 40 in a workweek. In this case, the lump sum did not constitute an overtime premium, even though it was based on 50 hours. In short, the Division found that the employer could not shortcut the regulations, and was required to pay the overtime premium per hour over and above the agreed-on salary.

Q 8:198   How is a salaried nonexempt employee's normal pay rate determined when the employee works on a fluctuating workweek?

When salaried nonexempt employees are paid a fixed pay rate regardless of hours worked in any week (there must be a clear mutual understanding that the salary is the straight time payment for all hours worked, whether many or few), the employee is entitled to overtime when those hours exceed 40 hours in any workweek. Such an employee's regular pay rate will change each week based on the actual number of hours worked in the workweek. The regular pay rate is determined by dividing the fixed payment by the hours worked in the workweek. These calculations will affect the calculation of overtime pay. The employer must ensure that the applicable minimum wage is paid for each hour worked. [29 C.F.R. § 778.114]

Note that employees paid under this method get only half of their regular rate for overtime hours. This still complies with the requirement that employees get time and one-half for overtime hours because the salary is the straight-time component of employees' pay for all hours, including the overtime hours. Since the straight time has already been paid, all that remains to be paid is the additional half time for each overtime hour.

Example 1. Jesse is paid $810 a week for all hours worked. He works 44 hours in one week and 45 hours during the next week. His regular rate during the first week is $18.41 ($810 ÷ 44) and $18.00 ($810 ÷ 45) in the second. He is due half-time totaling $36.82 ($18.41 × 0.5 × 4) for the 4 hours of overtime in the first week and $46.03 ($18.41 × 0.5 × 5) for 5 hours of overtime in the second workweek.

Example 2. Ted is a nonexempt assistant manager at a fast food restaurant. He and his employer have agreed that he will receive a fixed salary of $530 per week. Due to a scheduling problem, Ted works 80 hours one week when the minimum wage is $7.25. In this case, his regular rate for the week is $6.63 ($530 ÷ 80 hours). Ted's employer will have to pay him an additional $49.60 ($7.25 minimum wage − $6.63 = $0.62 × 80 hours) straight time to bring him up to minimum wage. In addition, Ted is entitled to $145.00 overtime premium ($7.25 × 0.5 × 40 overtime hours) for a total weekly pay of $724.60 ($530 fixed salary + $49.60 additional straight time + $145.00 overtime premium).

Q 8:199   How is an employee's regular pay rate determined when the employee is paid on a biweekly, monthly, or semimonthly basis under a fluctuating workweek?

An employee's regular pay rate is always determined based on the hours worked in a single workweek. If the employee is paid a fixed amount for a biweekly, semimonthly, or monthly period, those amounts are first converted to a weekly pay amount. Then the employee's regular pay rate is determined by dividing that weekly pay by the hours worked.

A biweekly salary is converted to a weekly equivalent by multiplying the biweekly amount by 26 and then dividing by 52. [29 C.F.R. § 778.114]

Example 1. Zach a nonexempt employee, is paid a biweekly salary of $1,630 for a fluctuating workweek. In one week, Zach works 66 hours. Zach 's pay is first annualized (26 × $1,630 = $42,380). That amount is divided by 52 to determine his weekly salary equivalent of $815. Zach's weekly pay is divided by the number of hours actually worked to get his regular pay rate. Zach's regular rate for the week is $12.35 ($815 ÷ 66 hours). He is entitled to $160.55 of additional overtime pay for the 26 hours ($12.35 × 0.5 × 26 = $160.55).

Note. A semimonthly salary is converted to a weekly equivalent by multiplying by 24 and dividing by 52.

Example 2. Mary is paid a semimonthly salary of $1,850 for a fluctuating workweek. In one week, Mary works 46 hours. Her annualized pay is $44,400 ($1,850 × 24). Her weekly pay equivalent is $853.85 ($44,400 ÷ 52). Her regular pay rate is $853.85 ÷ 46 = $18.56. She is entitled to additional overtime pay of $55.68 for 6 hours ($18.56 × 0.5 × 6).

Note. A monthly salary is converted to a weekly equivalent by multiplying the monthly salary by 12 and dividing by 52.

Example 3. Harry is paid a monthly salary of $5,200 and works a *fixed workweek* of 40 hours. Harry's pay is first annualized (12 × $5,200 = $62,400). That amount is divided by 52 to produce $1,200. His regular rate is $30.00 ($1,200 ÷ 40 hours).

Q 8:200 How is the regular pay rate determined for employees paid on a piecework basis?

An employee classified as a "pieceworker" or as a "piece-rate worker" is generally paid on the number of units he or she produces. Pieceworkers are generally paid overtime compensation based on their regular pay rate. The FLSA also permits workers and employers to agree that overtime will be paid on the basis of a "piece and one-half" rate.

A pieceworker's regular pay rate starts with the total weekly earnings from piece rates and all other sources (e.g., a production bonus or base pay). This total is divided by the number of hours worked by the employee during the week to obtain the regular pay rate. This amount may not be less than the FLSA minimum wage. The individual's overtime pay rate must be at least one and one-half times the regular rate for hours worked in excess of 40 per week. [29 C.F.R. § 778.111]

Example 1.   Estella is a pieceworker who is paid $1.60 for each finished unit. She is entitled to a production bonus of $45 when she completes more than 45 units in the workday. One workweek, Estella works 48 hours, during which she produces 41 units the first day (for piece-rate earnings of $1.60), 64 units the following three days ($2.30 each) ($45 ÷ 64 = $0.70 plus $1.60), and 44 units the final day ($1.60 each). Estella's weekly earnings total $577.60, which include three $45 bonus payments for the days in which she produced more than 45 units. Her total earnings of $577.60 divided by 48 hours, produces a regular pay rate of $12.03. Estella is entitled to additional pay of $48.12 ($12.03 × 0.5 × 8 hours).

Example 2.   Evan sews jeans at the rate of $5.75 each. During one week when the minimum wage was $7.25, Evan produced 38 jeans in 40 hours for piecework earnings of $218.50 (38 pieces × $5.75 each). Evan's employer must pay him an additional $71.50 for a total of $290 in order to bring his wages up to the minimum wage (40 hours × $7.25).

When a pieceworker's rate is coupled with a minimum hourly guarantee, the regular pay rate is the greater of the amount determined above or the minimum pay rate. [29 C.F.R. § 778.111]

Q 8:201   Are payments for vacation, holiday, illness, or retirement compensation included in the calculation of an employee's regular rate for overtime?

No. [29 C.F.R. § 778.200]

Q 8:202   When may an employer use a day-rate plan to calculate overtime?

Employers can utilize a daily-pay plan, but continue to be required to keep accurate records of the hours worked by their nonexempt employees, and comply with the minimum wage and overtime provisions of the FLSA. Under a daily-rate plan, the employees are paid a fixed amount for any day in which they do any work at all. At the end of the workweek, the employer divides the total payments by the number of hours worked to determine the regular rate. The regular rate is then divided by two to get the additional half-time premium, which in turn is multiplied by the number of overtime hours worked.

Example.   Roger is paid $145 per day. On Monday, he works 12 hours. He works 8 hours per day on Tuesday, Wednesday, Thursday, and Saturday. He works 9 hours on Friday. His basic compensation is: 6 days × $145 = $870. He worked 54 hours. His regular rate is: $870 ÷ 54 = $16.11. His overtime premium is $16.11 ÷ 2 = $8.06. Total overtime is 14 × $8.06 = $112.84. Total pay is $870 + $112.84 = $982.84.

Q 8:203   When a union contract provides for overtime pay for less than 40 hours, are these payments a part of the employee's pay rate?

Generally, no. Some collective bargaining agreements establish a premium rate when the employee works more than a designated daily and/or weekly maximum (e.g., eight hours a day or 36 hours per week). If an employee working under such a contract works more than 40 hours in the workweek, the employee is entitled to overtime pay under the FLSA. The FLSA also allows the employer to exclude the additional payments under the union contract (i.e., in the case of the employee mentioned earlier, for hours above 36) from the determination of an employee's regular rate. The FLSA also allows the employer to credit these payments toward any FLSA overtime compensation due the employee when his or her hours exceed 40. [29 C.F.R. § 778.202]

Q 8:204   May an employer treat premium pay as part of its minimum wage and overtime requirements?

Generally, no. The term premium pay generally relates to additional pay under a contractual or other agreement for work. Work on days when an employee might otherwise be off (e.g., Saturdays, Sundays, holidays, the sixth or seventh day of the workweek, or other "days of rest") fit this category. This pay is generally excluded from an employee's regular rate and can be credited against overtime compensation due under the FLSA. This treatment is generally available only when the premium pay is at one and one-half times the employee's regular pay rate. [29 C.F.R. § 778.203]

Q 8:205   May employers establish length-of-service thresholds before an employee is eligible for holiday pay?

Yes. Nothing in the FLSA prevents an employer from establishing thresholds of minimum service before an employee is eligible for holiday pay, as long as all the other requirements of the FLSA are met. Employers frequently establish higher hourly rates (e.g., double hourly rates) for employees who work on holidays (i.e., Christmas, Easter, Fourth of July), and limit such payments to employees who have been employed for at least 90 to 120 days. This avoids having to pay a seasonal employee (who does not meet the required service threshold) more than regular or overtime pay. Such provisions are permitted under the FLSA.

Note that when an employee who is receiving the higher holiday hourly wages is also subject to overtime, the holiday pay is not part of the employee's regular rate for determining the overtime pay.

Special Payment Plans: Time Off, Prepayment, and Belo

Time-Off Plan

Q 8:206   May an employer accumulate overtime hours and offer a compensatory time-off plan?

Not in the private sector, unless an exemption applies. An employer may offer what appears to be compensatory time off in the same pay period for hours worked in excess of 40 hours in one workweek of the pay period—this is the so-called "time off plan," discussed below. [Wage & Hour Release (Mar. 8, 1950)] In the public sector, however, comp time for overtime is permitted under certain circumstances.

Q 8:207   What is a time-off plan for purposes of overtime pay?

A time-off plan is a plan that is intended to keep employees' pay constant by giving them time off (at one and one-half times the overtime hours) in the pay period for overtime worked earlier in the same pay period. A time-off plan differs from a "prepayment plan" and a "compensatory time-off plan." These plans are difficult to administer without violating the FLSA. [Wage & Hour Op. Ltr. (May 5, 1994); DOL Field Operations Handbook § 32j16b]

Such a plan is available only when the pay period covers at least two workweeks. Under such a plan, the employee's hours in the second workweek are reduced by one and one-half times the number of hours worked in the first week. The employees are actually paid all the straight time and overtime they are due.

Such a plan might be applied when the employer wants to pay (or budget) a set amount each pay period for an employee who may work overtime in one week. There are no regulations discussing prepayment and time-off plans, although there are several opinion letters describing how such plans may comply with the FLSA. In many cases, employers that attempt to apply these plans eventually violate the law. An employer contemplating such a program should have it reviewed by their attorney or the Wage and Hour Division.

Example 1. Phil is hired at a rate of $15 an hour and receives a paycheck every two weeks. He is scheduled to work a 40-hour workweek. Pursuant to the company's time-off pay plan, he is paid $600 every week. During the first week of the two-week pay period he works 44 hours, and during the second workweek of that pay period his employer limits his hours to 36 hours (so the four hours at the one and one-half-time rate can be taken into account). Under the time-off plan, he is given credit for 6 hours in the second week for the four hours of overtime in the first week of the pay period. This plan complies as a time-off plan. Note that this is not a compensatory time-off plan. Phil is normally paid $15 × 80 = $1,200 every two weeks. In this case, he gets (40 × $15) + (4 × $22.00), or $688.00 for the first week, and (36 × $15), or $540.00, in the second week, for a total of $1,228.00.

This type of pay plan would not allow an employer to carry forward the overtime obligation to be available to be used as compensatory time in a subsequent pay period. Also, this type of plan is not available if the actual overtime work occurs in the second week of the two-week pay period.

Prepayment Plan

Q 8:208   What is a "prepayment" plan for purposes of overtime calculation?

A prepayment plan is available only for hourly workers. It involves the payment of overtime to employees before the period in which the overtime is earned. A prepayment plan requires that the company pay an employee more than the employee's earnings for the particular workweek or pay period. The difference between the amount paid and the actual earnings is treated as an advance or loan against overtime to be worked by the employee in a later workweek or pay period. Under a valid prepayment plan, an employer can never owe the employee money beyond the payday when the wages or overtime are due. A prepayment plan does not allow an employer to avoid the payment of wages that are otherwise subject to overtime pay. A prepayment plan must satisfy the following three conditions:

1. Employees participating in the plan must be paid on an hourly basis at fixed hourly pay rates.

2. Time-off adjustments are made in the ratio of one and one-half hours off for each overtime hour worked, and this adjustment must be made within the pay period.

3. Regular (and overtime at one and one-half of the regular pay) compensation for the hours actually worked during each workweek of the pay period must be computed at the established hourly rates. That compensation must be paid at the end of each period, without regard to the hours actually worked or earnings in any other pay period.

Example. Harold is employed under a prepayment plan that pays him for a full 40 hours of work for any workweek in which he works less than 40 hours. Harold is paid $15 per hour and works 36, 43, 37, and 48 hours over four weeks. He is paid biweekly.

In the first week, Harold works only 36 hours, but receives $600 pay. The company has a credit of $60, which it has overpaid (4 × $15).

In the second week, Harold earns $667.50 ($15 × 43 = $645, plus $15 × 0.5 × 3), but he receives only $600. Deducting the $67.50 from the $60 credit, the company has a debit of $7.50 in Harold's account. Since the employer owes Harold $7.50, it cannot carry this amount forward, but must include the $7.50 in his pay for this pay period.

In the third week, Harold works 37 hours but gets $600 in pay. The company has a credit of $45 (3 × $15).

In the fourth week, Harold works 48 hours, for which he is owed $780 (48 × $15 = $720, plus $15 × 0.5 × 8 = $60). He is paid $600, and the company's credit of $45 is wiped out. In addition, the company must pay Harold an additional $135 to avoid violating the FLSA's overtime pay provisions.

Note. The advance payment that is credited to the employee in week two does not alter the employee's regular rate of pay. These types of plans are rarely used and will invite close scrutiny in an audit by the Wage and Hour Division [Wage & Hour Op. Ltr. No. 2005-3 (Jan. 7, 2005)]

Belo Plan

Q 8:209   What are Belo, or guaranteed wage, plans?

A Belo pay plan is named after a United States Supreme Court decision and involves Section 7(f) of the FLSA.

This provision of the FLSA provides a narrow exception to the usual method of calculating overtime. When an employee's normal weekly hours vary above and below 40 hours, the employer and employee (or union) may agree to a guaranteed pay rate that will be paid for any number of hours worked in a week, up to a specified number of hours. The purpose of this exception is to provide a stable income to an employee whose pay would otherwise fluctuate significantly from week to week. The provision also allows an employer to predict and control labor costs. [29 C.F.R. §§ 778.404–778.414; Walling v. A.H. Belo Corp., 316 U.S. 624 (1942); Wage & Hour Op. Ltr. No 2009-3NA, Jan. 16, 2009]

Q 8:210   How does a Belo wage plan work?

A Belo wage plan requires the employee and employer to agree to payment for a specific number of hours a week. Under a Belo plan, the employee's pay is generally based on more than 40 hours of work in the week, whereas a prepayment plan is generally based on 40 hours a week. The number of hours of work specified in the agreement should reflect a reasonable estimate of the number of hours the employee can be expected to work over several periods. Under the agreement, the employer need not pay the maximum number of hours the employee is expected to work in any one week. The FLSA caps the number of hours under the agreement at no more than 60 hours a week. [29 C.F.R. § 778.411]

The pay rate for the hours under the agreement must be based on an agreed-on regular hourly rate; when the employee's hours under the agreement exceed 40 hours in the week, overtime must be paid. The agreed-on regular pay rate cannot be less than the statutory minimum wage, and the overtime rate must be at least one and one-half times the agreed-on regular pay rate. The agreement prevents an employer from seeking the protections of a Belo plan when the plan violates the FLSA overtime pay requirements.

Example. Taylor is under a Belo plan in which she is paid for 55 hours. Taylor's regular rate is $24 an hour, and her additional overtime rate is $12 an hour. The $1,500 guarantee is based on $1,320 for 55 hours ($24 × 55) plus an additional $180 representing the half-time overtime pay ($12 × 15).

In some cases, an employer will pay an employee covered under a Belo plan hourly rates that are lower than the hourly rate that would be paid without the Belo agreement. The pay rate under the Belo plan cannot be less than the statutory minimum wage.

A Belo plan must be a bona fide agreement between the employee (or union) and employer and must specify the regular rate and overtime rate. The plan must specify the amount of pay under the plan that is guaranteed, not merely a minimum number of hours of work guaranteed. The agreement need not be in writing; however, most employers document the agreement in writing.

Q 8:211   Which employees may be covered under a Belo wage plan?

A Belo wage guarantee plan may be offered only to employees whose normal working hours in any workweek are irregular. The fluctuation in hours worked each week must be due to the nature of the work, not to actions of the employer or employee. The variation in hours worked in the week must be above and below 40 in a week. Examples of the types of job duties that may necessitate irregular hours include on-call service workers, newspaper reporters, and insurance adjusters. Although office workers generally do not qualify for a Belo plan, certain job responsibilities, such as copy editing, may qualify for such a plan. [29 C.F.R. § 778.405]

Q 8:212   How is pay handled under a Belo wage plan?

A Belo plan guarantees a weekly payment. The employee must be paid the full guaranteed amount for any week in which he or she works. Thus, the employer may not deduct for leaves of absences due to sickness or personal reasons unless the absence is for the full workweek. The FLSA does permit the guarantee of weekly pay to be reduced or prorated when a partial-week absence is the result of the employee being hired or terminated midweek or being subjected to a disciplinary penalty involving a leave of absence. [29 C.F.R.§ 778.410]

Q 8:213   Can a Belo plan be offered to individuals who are paid commissions?

Generally, no. A Belo plan must pay a guaranteed hourly rate, which is the employee's regular rate. When commissions, bonuses, or other compensation is paid, the regular rate changes. This is inconsistent with the Belo requirement of a guaranteed regular rate, which means that Belo employees cannot be paid any additional compensation. [29 C.F.R. § 778.408(c)]

Q 8:214   May an employee under a Belo plan be paid on other than a weekly basis?

Yes. However, the amount guaranteed under the Belo plan must be a weekly amount based on the workweek. The pay period for that guaranteed payment may be biweekly, semimonthly, and so on. [29 C.F.R. § 778.410]

Caution. A Belo payment plan is very difficult to implement properly. Employees must maintain very accurate records of hours worked. It is recommended you have any proposed Belo plan reviewed by legal counsel.

Child Labor

Q 8:215   What child labor restrictions are contained in the FLSA?

The FLSA prohibits any "oppressive child labor" in connection with interstate commerce (i.e., between states or for import or export). The FLSA also prohibits the transport of any goods produced by an establishment that used oppressive child labor within 30 days of the initial date of shipment.

As used in the FLSA the phrase "oppressive child labor" means the employment of any child under the age of 18 that violates the child labor restrictions of the FLSA. [29 U.S.C. §§ 212, 213(c)]

Q 8:216   Does the FLSA regulate the employment of minors under 18 years of age?

Yes. The FLSA generally prohibits any minor under the age of 18 from working in certain hazardous occupations (HOs). There are 17 occupations that have been deemed "hazardous." The prohibition on working in hazardous occupations is the only limitation for minors aged 16 and 17. Minors between the ages of 14 and 16 are permitted to work in an occupation not deemed to be hazardous by the DOL, when that employment does not interfere with the minor's education and well-being. Also, there are a number of additional occupations prohibited for such minors. In addition, the work schedule of minors who are 14 and 15 years old is limited regarding the number of hours that may be worked in the workweek. These hours are limited to nonschool time. Children under the age of 14 generally cannot be employed. An exception is permitted for jobs in the performing arts, delivering newspapers, certain agricultural work, or working for their parents.

In addition to the FLSA, most states have laws regulating minimum ages, types of employment, and hours of work, as well as requiring notices and work permits for employed minors. When state laws are more restrictive than the FLSA, the state laws apply. [29 C.F.R. §§ 570.2(a), 570.31, see also 29 U.S.C. § 213(c)]

Q 8:217   What working-hour restrictions apply to 14- and 15-year-olds?

A minor who is 14 or 15 years old may be employed in nonagricultural work for a limited number of hours based on whether school is in session. The minor may not work more than three hours on any school day, and not more than eight hours on a nonschool day. In addition, these minors may not work more than 18 hours in any school week, and not more than 40 hours in a nonschool week. These minors may be employed only in hours outside of normal school hours. However, as described below, minors enrolled in an approved work training program may be employed during school hours in an approved program.

A minor aged 14 or 15 must work only during the hours between 7 a.m. and 7 p.m. These hours are extended during the summer (June 1 through Labor Day), when the minor may work until 9 p.m.

The FLSA permits minors 14 and 15 years old to be employed in Work Experience and Career Exploration Programs (WECEP) that coincide with school hours when certain conditions are met, such as:

- The Wage and Hour Division must approve the program.
- The students must receive school credit for on-the-job experience.
- The program must be school-supervised and school-administered.
- The employment must not be in manufacturing, mining, or other hazardous occupations.
- The students may not be employed for more than 23 hours in any week while school is in session, nor for more than 3 hours on any school day.

[29 C.F.R. §§ 570.35, 570.35(a)]

Q 8:218   What hours-of-work restrictions apply to minors hired in agriculture?

Several general rules apply to minors employed in agriculture. These are generally applied based on the minor's age. Other than a restriction on working in hazardous occupations and on hours of work, there are no federal child labor restrictions on employing individuals aged 16 and older in agriculture. Children under the age of 16 may not work during school hours unless in an approved school program. Minors under the age of 17 who are enrolled in certain vocational or training programs or who are employed on a farm owned or operated by their parents may be employed under certain conditions to perform a limited number of hazardous duties.

Children 14 and 15 years old may work on a farm in any capacity except where the duties would involve occupations deemed to be hazardous. Children under the age of 14 may be employed only in nonhazardous agricultural jobs and only with written parental consent.

Minors who are employed on a farm owned or operated by a parent or a person acting as the minor's guardian are permitted to engage in hazardous work at any time. They may also work during school hours. [29 C.F.R. §§ 570.1–570.2, 570.70–570.123]

Q 8:219   What jobs in a retail or service establishment can a 14- or 15-year-old perform?

A minor aged 14 or 15 may be employed in any of the following occupations:

- Office and clerical work
- Bagging and delivering customer orders
- Price marking, assembling orders, shelving, and packing
- Errand and delivery by foot, bicycle, or public transportation
- Cashiering, selling, modeling, work in advertising, and window trimming
- Cleanup by hand or with a vacuum cleaner and maintenance of grounds (not using a power-driven mower or cutter)
- Kitchen work with a limited use of power equipment
- Work in connection with automobiles, trucks, and buses (dispensing fuel, cleaning, and polishing, but not using heavy power equipment)
- Cleaning produce, wrapping, and sealing (away from freezers and meat coolers)

[29 C.F.R. § 570.34(a)]

Q 8:220   Are there any jobs in a retail or service establishment that a 14- or 15-year-old may not perform?

Yes. The FLSA regulations allowing minors 14 and 15 years old to work in retail or service establishments may not be construed to permit the following types of work (in addition to the 17 hazardous occupations):

- Hazardous jobs identified by the Secretary of Labor
- Mining, manufacturing, or processing that requires the performance of any duties where goods are mined, manufactured, or produced
- Work in or about boiler rooms
- Maintenance or repair of the establishment, machines, or equipment
- Outside window washing that involves working from window sills, and all work requiring the use of ladders or scaffolds
- Cooking and baking, except where cooking is accomplished without an open flame or in situations in which deep-frying is required if the equipment utilizes an automatic lowering device
- Activities involving the operation or repair of power-driven food slicers and grinders, food choppers and cutters, and bakery-type mixers
- Work in freezers and meat coolers; preparation of meats for sale (except wrapping, sealing, labeling, weighing, pricing, and stocking when performed in other areas)
- Loading and unloading goods to and from trucks, railroad cars, or conveyors
- All occupations in warehouses except office and clerical work [29 C.F.R. §§ 570.33, 570.34(b)]

- Communications or public utility jobs
- Meat processing and work in areas meat are processed

Q 8:221   What types of occupations are considered hazardous occupations?

The FLSA prohibits minors below the age of 18 from being employed in hazardous occupations. These occupations include:

- Workers in plants that handle or store explosives or any goods containing explosives
- Motor vehicle drivers and outside helpers (however, licensed minors at least 17 may occasionally and incidentally drive a vehicle under certain conditions)
- Workers in logging operations, including operation of any sawmill, lathe mill, shingle mill, or cooperage stock mill
- Workers exposed to radioactive materials
- Workers involved in excavation operations
- Workers involved in wrecking and demolition of buildings or ship breaking
- Workers involved in the manufacturing of brick, tile, or similar products
- Workers involved in slaughtering and meat packing establishments or rendering plants
- Coal mining operations
- Certain occupations involving power-driven hoisting devices
- Operators of power-driven metal forming, punching, and shearing machines and hoisting apparatuses
- Operators of power-driven bakery machines
- Operators of power-driven paper-products machines
- Operators and maintainers of circular and band saws and guillotine shears
- Workers involved in application of weatherproofing materials and substances to roofs of buildings and other structures
- Operation of power-driven woodworking machines
- Mining operations other than coal

[29 C.F.R. §§ 570.50–570.68]

Q 8:222   Is there a specific law regarding teen drivers?

Yes. The Drive for Teen Employment Act sets out specific circumstances in which 17-year-olds may drive (e.g., only during daylight hours, with valid driver's license, the truck or automobile does not exceed 6,000 pounds, and not when towing other vehicles or for route deliveries.) [29 U.S.C. § 213(c)(6)]

Q 8:223   Does the FLSA require employers to obtain a certificate to verify the age of the worker?

No. However, although certificates are not required, the employer is required to maintain proof of age for each minor employed. In addition, compliance with the FLSA's child labor law rests solely with the employer. Employers that routinely hire minors are liable for violations of the FLSA regardless of whether the minor provided a valid or fraudulent certificate. As a result, to protect themselves most employers will want to obtain age certificates from state or federal agencies to verify the age of minors. [29 C.F.R. §§ 570.5–570.12]

Q 8:224   How can an employer obtain verification of the age of a minor?

An employer may request a certificate of age from an appropriate county or state agency. The minor may apply for the certificate. The employer should maintain the certificate while the individual is employed and return it to the issuing agency (or to the minor in agricultural employment) when the minor's employment is ended. Without such evidence of the minor's age, the employer may be subject to prosecution for violation of the FLSA. [29 C.F.R. §§ 570.5– 570.12, 570.121]

Penalties

Violations of Minimum Wage and Overtime

Q 8:225   What penalties can be imposed under the FLSA for failure to comply with its minimum wage and overtime pay requirements?

The DOL's Wage and Hour Division has jurisdiction over administration and enforcement of the FLSA. The Wage and Hour Division can sue an employer to comply with the law and seek damages for violations. [29 C.F.R. §§ 578.1–578.4, 580.1–580.18]

A wage and hour lawsuit may be brought by the Division or an employee to recover unpaid minimum wages and overtime pay, plus an equal amount for damages when there has been willful violation. Employers may also be subject to a $1,100 fine for each violation deemed to be willful or repeated. Officers of an employer who willfully violate the FLSA can be fined and, under very rare circumstances, subjected to imprisonment. Owners of corporations can be fined and also personally named in lawsuits brought by the Division. [29 C.F.R. pt. 578]

Q 8:226   What penalties under the FLSA can be imposed when the employer does not prove to the court that it reasonably believed it was complying with the FLSA?

Liquidated damages (i.e., double damages) will be awarded when an employer does not prove that it acted in good faith and reasonably believed it was acting legally when it failed to pay an employee time and a half for overtime hours worked. [Shea v. Galaxie Lumber & Constr. Co., Ltd., 152 F.3d 729 (7th Cir. 1998)]

Q 8:227   Can an employer rely on a Wage and Hour Division opinion?

When an employer actually relies on an official opinion of the Wage and Hour Division, such reliance can be a defense against back wages. For example, in one case, the employer cited a 1992 written opinion of the Acting Administrator of the DOL Wage and Hour Division that agreed with its position with regard to a payment plan for a group of nurses.

The opinion was consistent with the language of the regulation and therefore met the tests of the Supreme Court, said the appeals court. [Fazekas v. Cleveland Clinic Found. Health Care Ventures, Inc., 204 F.3d 673 (6th Cir. 2000)] The employer must show that it actually relied on the published position of the Wage and Hour Division to obtain a defense against back wages.

Q 8:228   Can the chairman of the board of directors of a company, or a business owner, be deemed the employer and subject to back pay and liquidated damages under the FLSA?

Yes. The chairman of the board of directors of a corporation can be treated as the employer and held personally liable for FLSA violations under the "economic realities" test, which requires meeting four conditions. The alleged employer must (1) have the power to hire and fire employees, (2) supervise and control work schedules, (3) determine the rate and method of payment, and (4) maintain employment records.

This was the finding of an appeals court case in which the chairman did not maintain direct control over the payroll processing and was held liable because of his degree of operational control in all other areas. All major business decisions had to be reviewed by him. [Herman v. RSR Sec. Servs., Ltd., 172 F.3d 132 (2d Cir. 1999)]

In addition, since the statute defines an employer to include anyone who acts in the interest of an employer with respect to employees, an owner of a business may be personally liable for back wages and damages, even if the business is a corporation.

Q 8:229 Can any other representative of a company be subject to personal liability under the FLSA?

In *Lamonica Safe Hurricane Shutters* [2013 U.S. App. LEXIS 4599 (11 Cir. 2013)], the appeals court ruled that any individual with control over an employer's financial affairs who could potentially cause an employer to violate FLSA regulations could be subject to personal liability under the FLSA. Further, the court was not making a distinction between corporate officers and board directors. The one control factor was if there was financial control over making a decision about the corporate assets.

Q 8:230 Do the FLSA anti-retaliation provisions protect employees who are fired for complaining to management over a possible violation?

Yes. The anti-retaliation provisions of the FLSA do protect employees who either complain to their employers or make informal FLSA complaints with the DOL against their employers, the Ninth Circuit has decided. An employee must communicate the substance of the allegations to the employer. [Lambert v. Ackerly, 180 F.3d 997 (9th Cir. 1999)]

Note that an employee who was fired before any lawsuit was filed could not later assert protections under the FLSA's anti-retaliation provisions. [Ball v. Memphis Bar-B-Q Co., 228 F.3d 360 (4th Cir. 2000)]

Q 8:231 Is there a statute of limitations for making a claim for back wages?

The statute of limitations under the FLSA is generally two years. That is, employees may recover unpaid minimum wages and/or overtime compensation during a period extending two years back from the date a lawsuit is file. The statute may be extended to three years in the event of a willful violation. Once a lawsuit is filed, the statute of limitations stops running, but it runs until a lawsuit is filed. This means that employees' claims for back pay can be eroded by the passage of time. Take for example employees who worked for an employer from January 1, 2014 until December 31, 2017. If they file a lawsuit for back wages under the FLSA on January 1, 2018, their potential recovery period is January 1, 2015 to January 1, 2017. If the court ruled that there was a violation, and further ruled that it was willful, the recovery period would extend back to January 1, 2014. However, any violations which occurred in 2014 are not recoverable, since they are barred by the statute of limitations.

The Equal Pay Act (EPA) is actually a section of the FLSA, section 6(d). Therefore, recovery of discriminatory underpayments under the EPA is governed by the same statute of limitations as recovery of unpaid minimum wage and/or overtime compensation.

In response to the U.S. Supreme Court's ruling in the *Ledbetter* decision (Ledbetter v. Goodyear Tire & Rubber Co. 550 U.S. 618 (2007)), on January 29, 2009, President Obama signed into law the Lilly Ledbetter Fair Pay Act (LFPA) of 2009. The Act expressly rejects the previous holdings that required employees to file pay discrimination complaints within 180/300 days of the original pay decision. The LFPA allows employees to go back almost indefinitely to establish the existence of a discriminatory pay practice by establishing that employees may file such complaints within 180/300 days of:

1. When a discriminatory compensation decision or other pay practice is adopted;

2. When an individual becomes subject to a discriminatory compensation decision or other practice; or

3. When an individual's pay is affected by application of a discriminatory compensation decision or other practice, including every time the individual receives pay based on the discriminatory compensation decision or practice.

The LFPA amends not only Title VII, but the Age Discrimination in Employment Act (ADEA), the Americans with Disabilities Act (ADA), and the Rehabilitation Act of 1973. It does not directly affect the Equal Pay Act, which is part of the FLSA. Note that the LFPA does not extend the statute of limitations for making a claim for back wages, but rather extends, almost indefinitely, the period of time that employees have to make such claims.

Violations of Child Labor

Q 8:232   What are the penalties for violation of the child labor laws?

Penalties are assessed on a graduated scale based on the severity of the violation. Maximum penalties of $50,000 per employee who was the subject of a violation where there was death or serious injury could be assessed. Willful violations may also be prosecuted criminally, resulting in fines, imprisonment for up to six months, or both.

The DOL may assess the civil penalty and use the funds to reimburse the government for the cost to prosecute a violation. There is no right to a jury trial to challenge the assessment. Employers have only 15 days after receipt of the DOL penalty assessment to contest the assessment, and appeals are limited. [29 U.S.C. § 216(e); 29 C.F.R. §§ 579.1–579.5]

Federal Government Contracts

Davis-Bacon Act

Q 8:233   What is the Davis-Bacon Act?

Enacted in 1931, the Davis-Bacon Act sets minimum standards for employees of contractors and subcontractors on federally funded construction projects. These standards include the following:

1. Contractors who have contracts of $2,000 or more are required to pay wages and fringe benefits that are comparable to other workers in the same geographic region of the construction project.

2. Contractors who have contracts of $2,000 or more must pay overtime as required under the Contract Work Hours and Safety Standards Act, at one and one-half times the employee's regular rate for any hours in excess of 40 in the workweek.

3. All contractors are prohibited from forcing any employee kickbacks or rebates of hours on the employee's entitled pay.

[40 U.S.C. §§ 314 et seq.]

Service Contract Act

Q 8:234   What is the Service Contract Act?

The McNamara-O'Hara Service Contract Act of 1965 was designed to impose prevailing wage and hour benefit provisions on employers that have contracts of at least $2,500 to provide services to the federal government through the use of service employees. Covered employers must provide the prevailing minimum wage and fringe benefits for similar employment in the localities. These employers may not include the payment of fringe benefits in the employee's wages in determining a covered employee's minimum wage and overtime pay. [41 U.S.C. §§ 351–358]

Walsh-Healey Public Contracts

Q 8:235   What is the Walsh-Healey Public Contracts Act?

The Walsh-Healey Public Contracts Act of 1936 (WHPCA) is a federal law that regulates the wages and hours of employees who work for employers that manufacture or furnish the federal government with materials, supplies, articles, or equipment. The WHPCA applies when such employers have contracts exceeding $10,000 with the federal government. The WHPCA is applied along with the FLSA in most cases. [Walsh-Healey Act, 41 U.S.C. §§ 35 et seq.]

Q 8:236   What requirements does the WHPCA impose on covered employers?

The WHPCA does the following:

1. Sets standards for payment of the prevailing minimum wage for straight-time hours

2. Sets payment of time and one-half for hours worked in excess of 40 hours in one week

3. Prohibits employment of any male under the age of 16 (18 for females) (different standards for male and female employees would be unenforceable under modern jurisprudence)

4. Prohibits employment of prison labor

5. Requires the maintenance of sanitary and nonhazardous working conditions

6. Requires a posting of coverage under the WHPCA in a prominent place

Failure to comply can result in a penalty under the WHPCA, which is similar to that under the FLSA. Employers can also be barred from further government contracts. [Walsh-Healey Act, 41 U.S.C. §§ 35 et seq.]

Q 8:237   How is the WHPCA imposed?

The WHPCA is imposed on employers that manufacture or furnish goods for the federal government when the contract to furnish those goods exceeds $10,000. An employer with two contracts, each for less than $10,000, would not be covered by the provisions of the WHPCA.

Also, several types of contract work are exempt from the WHPCA. These include certain public construction or service contracts; contracts for materials that may be obtained on the open market; contracts for agricultural or farm products processed by the original producer; contracts for furnishing radio, telephone, cable, or telegraph through companies regulated by the Federal Communications Act of 1934; contracts for rental of real or personal property; contracts with publishers or sales agents for the development of periodicals or newspapers of the publisher; and contracts for public utilities.

The WHPCA generally does not apply to subcontractors who are unrelated to an employer that is covered under the WHPCA. [41 U.S.C. §§ 35 et seq.]

Q 8:238   On what basis do the wage-hour rules under the WHPCA apply?

Basically, the wage-hour rules under the WHPCA, as under the FLSA, apply on a workweek basis. A workweek is a 168-consecutive-hour period beginning on the same hour and calendar day of each week. [41 U.S.C. § 35; 41 C.F.R. §§ 50.201–50.206]

Contract Work Hours and Safety Standards Act (CWHSSA)

Q 8:239   What is the Contract Work Hours and Safety Standards Act (CWHSSA)?

The CWHSSA is imposed on employers, either contractors or subcontractors who use laborers and mechanics on projects for the federal government. The regular workweek under CWHSSA is defined as 40 hours and requires overtime to be paid at one and half times the hourly rate. The rule applies to contracts in excess of $100,000. [40 U.S.C. $3701, Pub. L. No. 87-581, 76 Stat. 357]

Other Laws Affecting Employer-Employee Relationship

Public Employers: Federal, State, County, and City Governments

Q 8:240   How do the FLSA's minimum wage and overtime rules apply to employees of federal, state, and local governments?

The FLSA generally applies to government employers as it does to private employers. In addition, though, it provides certain exceptions for government employers that are not available to private employers. For example, the FLSA may exempt individuals who volunteer their services to government agencies. The FLSA also allows governments to use "compensatory time off" (i.e., at least one and one-half hours of time off for each hour of overtime worked) in lieu of overtime compensation. There are also special overtime rules for law enforcement and fire protection workers.

Special exemptions from the FLSA minimum wage and overtime pay requirements are available to legislative branch employees and workers at small law enforcement and firefighting departments, as well as to elected officials, political appointees, and their personal staffs.

The compensatory time-off provision provides additional flexibility for state and local government employers. A government entity may adopt a compensatory time-off plan when the following conditions are met:

- The compensatory time provisions are adopted pursuant to an agreement or understanding between the public agency and the employees' representative, or between the public agency and individual employees where the employees do not have a designated representative prior to the performance of the work. This is a one-time agreement, and can take the form of a condition of employment.

- Compensatory time off must be provided at a rate of at least one and one-half hours for each hour of employment for which overtime pay normally would be required.

- Employees must be allowed to receive cash compensation for unused compensatory time when the employment relationship is terminated.

- The applicable agency must permit employees to use accumulated compensatory time within a reasonable time after an employee makes a request to use such compensatory time, if such use does not unduly disrupt the operation of the agency.

- The applicable agency will pay cash for overtime hours worked that exceed the maximum limits for that group of employees. Employees engaged in public safety, emergency response, or seasonal activities may accrue not more than 480 hours of compensatory time (320 overtime hours actually worked). Employees who work in activities other than the preceding are limited to 240 hours of compensatory time (160 overtime hours actually worked).

- Where the agreement or understanding between the agency and an individual employee takes the form of an express condition of employment, the employee must knowingly agree to the arrangement of compensatory time and be informed of the employee's rights to use, preserve, or cash out accumulated compensatory time.

[29 C.F.R. §§ 553.20–553.27]

Q 8:241   Do the FLSA minimum wage and overtime pay provisions apply to elected public officials?

No. The FLSA expressly states that certain public officials in state or local government who are not subject to the government's civil service laws are not "employees" as that term is used in the Act. Four categories of individuals excluded are:

1. Elected public officials of a state, local government, or agency thereof;
2. Individuals appointed by a state or local elected official to serve at a policy-making level;
3. The personal staff of a state or local elected public official; and
4. Individuals serving as legal advisors with respect to constitutional or legal powers of a state or local elected official.

Under this exemption, elected city council members and mayors are generally exempt from the FLSA minimum wage and overtime pay provisions. [29 U.S.C. § 203(e)(2)(C); 29 C.F.R. § 553.11]

In addition, individuals employed in the legislative branch of a state or local government are generally exempt from the FLSA's minimum wage and overtime pay provisions unless they are covered by the civil service laws of the employing jurisdiction, are employed by a legislative library, or are nonelected school board officials or their appointees. [29 C.F.R. § 553.12]

Q 8:242   Do the FLSA minimum wage and overtime requirements apply to federal employees?

Generally, yes. There are, however, a few exceptions. For example, U.S. military personnel and employees of the U.S. Senate are exempt from the FLSA minimum wage and overtime pay requirements. In addition, government agencies may apply for a certificate from the Wage and Hour Division to employ full-time students and handicapped employees at an hourly rate that is below the minimum wage.

Q 8:243   May a state or local government worker be given compensatory time off in lieu of overtime?

Yes. A state, political subdivision of a state, or an interstate government agency, unlike private employers, may adopt a program that grants employees compensatory time off in lieu of overtime pay (referred to as "comp time" arrangements). A compensatory time-off plan must meet the following conditions:

1. The compensatory time off is to be provided at a rate of at least one and one-half hours for each hour of employment for which overtime would otherwise be due (i.e., work in excess of 40 hours in the workweek).

2. The compensatory time-off arrangement is adopted prior to the performance of work, pursuant to an "agreement or understanding" between the public agency and the employees' representative, or between the public agency and individual employees where the employees do not have a designated representative. The program need not be in writing, but if the agreement or understanding is with an individual employee, a record of its existence must be kept.

3. Where the agreement or understanding between the agency and an individual employee takes the form of an express condition of employment, the employee must knowingly consent to the pay/time-off arrangement and be informed of his or her rights to use, preserve, or cash out the compensatory time that he or she accumulates.

4. The government jurisdiction permits employees to use accumulated compensatory time off within a reasonable period after an employee requests the time off, provided the use does not unduly disrupt the agency's operation.

5. Employees must be entitled to receive cash compensation for unused accumulated compensatory time off when they terminate employment.

6. When the plan has a cap on the maximum accumulation of compensatory time off, the employer must pay cash overtime compensation for any hours of overtime worked above an applicable accumulation maximum. [29 C.F.R. §§ 553.20–553.27]

Special recordkeeping rules apply to these plans. [29 C.F.R. § 533.50]

Q 8:244   What restrictions may be placed on a compensatory time-off plan?

Employers that qualify for a compensatory time-off plan may require the employee to use the compensatory time off at a time when the employee's workload is light, or an employer may specify periods during which the time off may not be taken. In general, the employer may condition the use of compensatory time to periods when it will not unduly disrupt the employer's operation. [29 C.F.R. § 553.25]

This issue was addressed in an appeals court decision. The court stated, "Although employees have a right to use comp time when it would not unduly disrupt the public employer's business, the FLSA does not give employees the right of absolute control over the use of comp time."

Under the facts of the case, a fire district had argued that the issue was not a matter for the courts to decide, because the firefighters' contract contained specific arbitration steps to follow to resolve payroll and related disputes. The appeals court explained, however, that if disputes arise over statutory rights, employees do not have to exhaust the remedies spelled out in a contract. In contrast, noted the court, if the dispute concerns rights arising from the contract itself, then resolution of the dispute must follow the remedies specified in the contract. [Collins v. Lobdell, 188 F.3d 1124 (9th Cir. 1999)] The court then added, the "legislative history and the interpretive regulations suggest that employers and employees should reach agreements concerning the use and preservation of compensatory time."

Another appeals court took an approach less deferential to employers, concluding that the limitation on leave unduly disrupting the employer's operation applied only to disruption to actual governmental operations and not to the fiscal impact of the leave. [Beck v. City of Cleveland, 390 F.3d 912 (6th Cir. 2004)]

Q 8:245　What rules apply to the cashing out of accumulated compensatory time-off hours?

A state or local government employee or an employee of a public agency may cash out his or her accumulated compensatory time-off hours in two ways: a cash-out of accrued compensation time or a cash-out at termination of employment.

1. Cash-out of accrued time. Employers may make payments for accrued compensatory time at any time. The payment shall be at the regular rate earned by the employee at the time the employee receives the payment.

2. Cash-out upon termination of employment. The FLSA requires that an employer fully compensate employees for all compensatory time-off hours they have accumulated when they terminate their employment. In this case, the payment is based on the greater of:

   a. The employee's regular rate earned at the time of termination; or

   b. The employee's average regular rate for the last three years of employment.

[29 C.F.R. § 553.27]

Note. The FLSA does not sanction a plan that gives employees the right to elect when to cash out the accumulated time. Under such a plan, the right to elect to receive the payment would trigger taxation of the right to receive a payment when that right is exercisable, under the doctrine of constructive receipt. [I.R.C. § 83]

Q 8:246　Does the FLSA set a maximum number of compensatory time-off hours that may be accumulated?

Yes. The FLSA limits the amount of compensatory time-off hours that an employee of a public agency or state or local government may accumulate. A maximum limit of 240 hours applies to most public employees; however, a higher maximum of 480 hours applies to employees working in public safety, emergency response, or seasonal activities.

Note. Employees reach the 240-hour compensatory time-off limit after 160 hours of actual overtime.

When employees reach this limit, they must receive cash for any additional hours of overtime worked. Employees may not waive their right to receive cash compensation for additional overtime worked beyond the applicable limit. Employers may establish accumulation limits that are lower than the statutory caps.

The 480-hour compensatory time-off limit (i.e., 320 hours of overtime) applies only to the employees of state and local governments engaged in the following types of activities:

1. Emergency response, including rescue work, ambulance services, and dispatching emergency vehicles and personnel

2. Public safety activities, including law enforcement, firefighting, and security work performed in correctional institutions

3. "Seasonal activities," broadly defined as work occurring during regular and recurring periods of "significantly increased demand." This latter group could include individuals involved in snow removal during a prolonged blizzard, for example.

The actual work performed by the employee, rather than the job classification or designation, controls which limit applies. An employee regularly working in activities included in the 480-hour limit is covered by that limit. An employee who performs activities that are subject to both maximum limits must be treated as being subject to the lower limit when he or she performs duties not eligible for the higher limit. [29 U.S.C. § 207(o); 29 C.F.R. §§ 553.22–553.24]

Example. Zane, who often mows lawns in the summer—subject to the 480-hour cap—sometimes shovels snow in the winter, a job that is subject to a lower cap. If Zane accumulated 300 hours during the summer and later worked overtime shoveling snow, he would have to receive overtime pay when shoveling snow, because 300 hours exceeds the 240-hour cap for nonseasonal work.

Q 8:247   Do the FLSA's white-collar exemptions apply to executives, administrators, and professionals in the public sector?

Generally, yes. However, special rules apply. Executives, administrators, and professionals in the public sector are exempt from the FLSA's minimum wage and overtime pay provisions when certain requirements are met. This exemption generally follows the rules that apply to nonpublic sector employees. The nonpublic sector exemption generally prohibits an exempt employee from having his or her pay reduced for absences of less than a full day from work. The pay of executive, administrative, and professional employees in the public sector may be reduced because of absences of less than a full day due to personal reasons, illness, or injury, and the individual may remain exempt when he or she meets certain regulatory standards. These standards apply to both the employee's duties and his or her compensation. This modification to the full-day-of-pay salary requirement applies only to public employers whose pay system was established by statute, ordinance, regulation, or public policy or practice, and which, due to a public accountability pay system, prohibits payment for time not worked or covered by paid leave. [29 C.F.R. § 541.710]

Q 8:248 Do any exemptions to the white-collar exemption apply to public sector employees?

Yes. Certain public sector employees who meet all the other criteria for the white-collar exemption but, under certain circumstances, are not paid for time not worked during absences of less than one day, can still qualify for the exemption. These individuals are exempt from the no-hourly-pay reduction requirement for salaried employees and can have their salary reduced for time not worked. Such reductions are limited to those required by statute, ordinance, regulation, or by policy or practice that requires government employees to be publicly accountable for the expenditure of funds. The FLSA permits reductions for absences of less than a day without loss of the white-collar exemption if such an employee is placed on leave without pay in lieu of accrued leave for absences of less than a day due to personal reasons or illness or injury. This exemption to the fixed salary requirement is conditioned on the following:

a. The employee is covered under a personal or sick leave plan;

b. Permission for use of accrued leave has not been requested or has been requested and denied;

c. Accrued leave has been exhausted; or

d. The employee chooses to use leave without pay.

Public employees whose pay has been reduced as a result of a budget-required furlough will lose their exempt status only for the workweek in which the furlough occurs and their pay has been reduced. [29 C.F.R. § 541.710]

Q 8:249 Are public sector court reporters subject to a specific overtime exemption?

Yes. The FLSA exempts from the calculation of the regular rate, for overtime purposes, the wages paid to, and hours worked by, a public sector court reporter who is preparing a court transcript when two conditions are met:

1. The work is performed outside the employee's normal working hours; and

2. The employee received a payment for the work on the basis of a per-page rate and this rate equals or exceeds:

    a. the maximum rate established by state or local law;

    b. the maximum rate established by a judicial administrative office; or

c. the rate negotiated between the employee and the party requesting the transcript (other than a presiding judge).

[29 U.S.C. § 207(o)(6)]

Q 8:250   Who are law enforcement employees under the FLSA?

The FLSA defines law enforcement employees as workers who meet three criteria:

1. The individual is a uniformed or plainclothes member of a body of officers established by state statute or local ordinance to maintain "public peace and order and to protect both life and property from accidental or willful injury, and to prevent and detect crimes";

2. The individual has the power to arrest; and

3. The individual received or will receive on-the-job training or instruction in law enforcement principles and techniques.

Employees who satisfy all these criteria are treated as engaged in law enforcement activities regardless of their rank or their status as "trainee," "probationary," or "permanent." An individual classified as a law enforcement employee can also be involved in incidental duties not associated with law enforcement, such as public presentations or equipment maintenance. [29 C.F.R. § 553.211] Note that for exemption purposes, the term "law enforcement personnel" also includes security personnel in correctional institutions.

Q 8:251   Are there any exemptions from the FLSA minimum wage and overtime pay requirements for public safety personnel?

Yes. Many of the FLSA general exemptions regarding minimum wage and overtime pay carry over to public safety personnel. For instance, fire chiefs, police chiefs, police captains, and some criminal investigators may qualify for the executive, administrative, or professional exemption. Sheriffs who are elected (and their personal staffs) who are not part of the civil service may be exempt from the provisions of the FLSA under the special exemption for elected officials and appointees.

Small police and firefighting departments are exempt from the FLSA overtime requirements. Law enforcement and fire protection departments with more than five employees may reduce their overtime liability by establishing "work periods" of 7 to 28 days. Under such a plan, overtime is paid only when an employee's total hours exceed an amount set in the regulations based on the length of the work period.

The FLSA permits public safety and emergency response employees working for agencies with compensatory time-off arrangements to accumulate up to 480 hours of compensatory time off. The FLSA otherwise limits accumulated compensatory time off to 240 hours. [29 U.S.C. §§ 207(k), 207(o), 207(p), 213(b)(20); 29 C.F.R. § 553.201]

Otherwise, the FLSA applies to any nonexempt individuals. Apparently, a growing number of lawsuits are arising in the public sector, where the regular rate of pay for nonexempt firefighters has been improperly calculated.

Q 8:252   What is the small police and fire department exemption from overtime?

The FLSA authorizes an overtime exemption for small law enforcement and fire protection agencies. The exemption is available only to those employees actually engaged in bona fide law enforcement and firefighting activities. In general, the exemption is lost if employees spend more than 20 percent of their working time in the performance of non-law-enforcement or nonfirefighting duties. This exemption applies to small law enforcement or fire protection agencies that employ, during the workweek, fewer than five employees engaged in law enforcement or fire protection activities. Clerical or administrative employees are excluded from the five-employee threshold. In determining whether this exemption is applicable under the five-employee threshold, law enforcement and fire protection personnel are considered separately. [29 C.F.R. §§ 553.200, 553.210–553.212]

Example. A small city has 12 law enforcement employees and only three fire protection employees. The firefighters are exempt from the FLSA's overtime requirements, but the law enforcement employees are not.

Q 8:253   Who are fire protection employees under the FLSA?

Fire protection employees are defined under the FLSA regulations as any employee whose duties satisfy the following requirements:

1. The individual is employed by an organized fire department or fire protection district;

2. The employee receives training as a firefighter to the extent required by state statute or local ordinance;

3. The individual has the "legal authority to engage in the prevention, control, or extinguishment of a fire of any type"; and

4. The individual performs activities that are required for, and directly related to, the prevention, control, or extinguishment of fires. An exempt individual may perform incidental nonfirefighting functions, such as housekeeping, equipment maintenance, lecturing on fire safety, and inspecting homes and schools for fire hazards.

Individuals who are "civilian" employees of fire departments, fire districts, or forestry services, including dispatchers, alarm operators, maintenance workers, and cooks, are not considered under the FLSA to be fire protection workers. The FLSA's definition of fire protection employees includes employees of forest conservation or other public agencies who have forest firefighting responsibilities. [29 C.F.R. § 553.210]

Q 8:254   Has the definition of firefighter for FLSA purposes changed?

Yes. The FLSA was amended in 1999 to clarify which public sector emergency workers are covered by the special overtime rules governing employees engaged in "fire protection activities." Section 3(y) of the FLSA defines an "employee in fire protection activities" as a firefighter, paramedic, emergency medical technician, rescue worker, ambulance worker, or hazardous materials worker who is trained in fire suppression; has the legal authority and responsibility to engage in fire suppression; is employed by a public sector fire department; and is engaged in the prevention, control, and extinguishment of fires or in response to emergency situations where life, property, or the environment is at risk. [29 U.S.C. § 203, Pub. L. No. 106-151, 113 Stat. 1731 (1999)]

Note that this section of the FLSA statutes is not to be construed as reducing compensation standards contained in a collective bargaining agreement that provide for higher pay than that guaranteed under the overtime exemption for public sector employees engaged in fire protection activities.

Q 8:255   Are ambulance and rescue workers considered to be either fire protection or law enforcement employees?

The law and regulations are ambiguous. Prior to the adoption of FLSA Section 3(y) (discussed at Q 8:255), ambulance and rescue employees of a public agency could be treated as individuals engaged in fire protection or law enforcement if a substantial portion of their services was directly related to either law enforcement or firefighting. Ambulance and rescue personnel satisfied this criterion if they received training in the rescue of fire, crime, and accident victims or of firefighters or police injured in the line of duty and they are regularly dispatched to fires, crime scenes, riots, natural disasters, or accidents. [29 C.F.R. § 553.215] Note, however, that the definition in Section 3(y) requires that ambulance and rescue workers are only deemed fire protection employees entitled to the partial overtime exemption when they have been trained to and are responsible for, and (though the courts have split on this) engage in fire suppression activities. So it is clear that ambulance and rescue employees employed by fire departments are not exempt unless they are trained to, responsible for, and (maybe) engage in fire suppression activities.

What remains unclear is how the exemption might apply to ambulance and rescue workers who are not part of the fire department. The ambiguity stems from the fact that 29 C.F.R. Section 553 has not been updated to account for the amended FLSA Section 3(y). One school of thought says that only ambulance and rescue workers employed by a fire department who meet the definition of Section 3(y) can be exempt. Others take the position that 29 C.F.R. Section 553.215 still applies to the extent not superseded by Section 3(y), meaning ambulance and rescue workers employed by a police department or as an independent department could still be exempt. However, such workers would still have to show that a substantial portion of their services was directly related to law enforcement activities, and in many cases the vast majority of ambulance dispatches are for purely medical issues.

Since the area remains unclear, employers should seek guidance from counsel.

Q 8:256   What is the workweek exception to the FLSA's 40-hour overtime rule for law enforcement employees and firefighters?

The FLSA generally requires that overtime be calculated on the basis of a 40-hour workweek. A special exception gives fire protection and law enforcement agencies with five or more employees the option of calculating overtime pay using "work periods" of 7 to 28 consecutive days. Under this exception, the work period can be of any duration not less than 7 and not more than 28 days. The employee is paid overtime when his or her total hours in the work period exceed a scheduled limit found in the regulations. The work period remains fixed once the beginning and ending times are established. The regulations permit the beginning and ending of the work period to be changed, as long as the change is not designed to avoid the payment of overtime and is intended to be permanent. [29 U.S.C. § 207(k); 29 C.F.R. § 553.224]

A district court for Western Virginia ruled that an employer could not assert an exemption under the 28-day schedule when overtime had been determined on another basis. The "mere discussion [of a 28-day work cycle] is insufficient to establish the Section 207(k) exemption." The court stated that an employer can establish a regularly recurring work period by: (1) publicly declaring the intent to adopt a Section 207(k) work period; and (2) implementing a work period that permits employees to work a regular cycle of between 7 and 28 days, even when there is no public declaration. The employer in this case did not use either of these methods to establish a 28-day work period, but continued to pay wages based on the calendar month. An employer may not take advantage of the 207(k) exemption unless the provision has been affirmatively claimed. [Taylor v. Fluvanna County, No. 3:98CV00106 (W.D. Va. Nov. 5, 1999)]

Overtime is due when employees of a law enforcement or fire protection agency work in excess of the hours for the established work period, as shown in Table 8-2.

Table 8-2. Maximum Hours in Work Period Above Which Overtime Pay Is Required Under Section 207(k)

Work Period (Days)	Fire Protection	Law Enforcement
28	212	171
27	204	165
26	197	159
25	189	153
24	182	147
23	174	141

Table 8-2. Maximum Hours in Work Period Above Which Overtime Pay Is Required Under Section 207(k) (cont'd)

Work Period (Days)	Fire Protection	Law Enforcement
22	167	134
21	159	128
20	151	122
19	144	116
18	136	110
17	129	104
16	121	98
15	114	92
14	106	86
13	98	79
12	91	73
11	83	67
10	76	61
9	68	55
8	61	49
7	53	43

Example. A law enforcement agency with six law enforcement employees uses a 14-day work period. During the work period, Josh, a police officer, works 120 hours. He is entitled to overtime compensation for 34 hours in the work period. [29 C.F.R. § 553.230]

The work schedules for police and fire protection employees generally exceed seven days, and the regulations use the term tour of duty to refer to "the period of time during which an employee is considered to be on duty for purposes of determining compensable hours." A common tour of duty may consist of nine days, with six days on the job and three days off. A public agency might use a 9-, 18-, or 27-day work period. This exception to the FLSA's normal overtime requirement is designed to match the agency's pay period with the normal tour of duty for personnel.

In general, an employer would choose the longest work period possible for the tour of duty. A longer work period will permit the employer to control its overtime liability by excusing employees from work following the performance of unscheduled work. [29 C.F.R. § 553.220]

Q 8:257   Are police and fire protection employees entitled to pay for meal periods?

The FLSA's general rules for determining hours worked (including pay for meal periods) apply to firefighters and law enforcement personnel, except when agencies calculate overtime on a "work-period" basis.

If a public agency elects to calculate overtime on a work-period basis, special rules apply to law enforcement employees and firefighters regarding meal periods. In the case of police, the public agency may exclude meal periods from hours worked for tours of duty of 24 hours or less, as long as the employee is "completely relieved from duty" during the meal period. Meal periods during continuous periods of surveillance or while required to remain on call in barracks are compensated because the employee is not completely relieved of duty.

Firefighters who are employed on a work-period basis and are confined to a "duty station" for a tour of duty of 24 hours or less must be paid for meal periods. Meal periods may be excluded from compensable hours for police officers and firefighters who are on a tour of duty of more than 24 hours and where the employer and employee have agreed to exclude mealtime from compensable hours of work. [29 C.F.R. § 553.223]

Q 8:258   Is there an exception for public sector volunteers?

Yes. Individuals who volunteer their services to public agencies generally are not subject to the FLSA minimum wage and overtime pay provisions. (This exemption does not generally extend to private employers.) The volunteer exemption is available to public agencies only when the following conditions are met:

1. The services are offered freely and without pressure or coercion—direct or implied—from the "employer";

2. The individual neither receives nor expects any compensation other than paid expenses, reasonable benefits, or a nominal fee for performing the voluntary services; and

3. The voluntary services differ from any service that the individual is employed (and paid) to perform for the same public agency.

[29 C.F.R.§§ 553.100–553.106]

Example. Vera, an employee of a city who volunteers to help in a city-promoted celebration, is not subject to the FLSA minimum wage and overtime provisions for her volunteer work as long as she does not perform any duties that are similar to the duties that she performs for the city as an employee.

Apprentices, Messengers, Student-Learners, Students, and Handicapped Employees

Q 8:259   May an employer obtain a special certificate from the Wage and Hour Division, permitting it to pay messengers, student-learners, and apprentices less than the minimum wage?

Yes. The Wage and Hour Division of the DOL is authorized to issue special certificates, allowing employers to pay certain categories of workers less than the statutory minimum wage. These workers include messengers, learners (including student-learners), and apprentices.

Employers wishing to employ messengers, student-learners, or apprentices at subminimum wages must apply for authority to do so from the Wage and Hour Division. In actual practice, the Wage and Hour Division issues very few of these certificates.

An employer that pays less than the minimum wage to any of these groups pursuant to a special certificate is subject to additional payroll recordkeeping requirements. [29 U.S.C. § 214(a); 29 C.F.R. §§ 516.30, 520]

Q 8:260   May an educational institution obtain a certificate from the Wage and Hour Division, permitting it to pay students less than the minimum wage?

Yes. An educational institution can pay full-time students who are enrolled at the institution an hourly rate lower than the minimum wage. This exception is only permitted if the institution applies for and receives an exemption from the Wage and Hour Division. Educational institutions that receive an authorizing certificate may pay full-time students 85 percent of the applicable statutory minimum wage. An employer that pays less than the minimum wage to students pursuant to a special certificate is subject to additional payroll recordkeeping requirements. [29 U.S.C. § 214(b); 29 C.F.R. § 516.30]

Q 8:261   May an employer obtain a certificate from the Wage and Hour Division, authorizing the payment of special minimum wages to workers with disabilities?

Yes. Employers that have received a certificate from the Wage and Hour Division may pay special minimum wages to workers who have disabilities, when those disabilities diminish their productivity for the work being performed. Employers must apply for and obtain an authorizing certificate prior to paying special minimum wages to employees who have disabilities for the work being performed. An employer that pays less than the minimum wage to workers with disabilities pursuant to a special certificate is subject to additional payroll recordkeeping requirements. [29 U.S.C. § 214(c); 29 C.F.R. §§ 516.30]

Q 8:262   What conditions apply to students who are employed as sports attendants?

Minors 14 and 15 years old may be employed as attendants at professional sporting events, provided that they work outside of school hours and perform only sports-attending duties. These duties include:

1. Pre- and postgame or practice setup of balls, items, and equipment;

2. Clearing the field or court of debris or moisture during play;

3. Providing ice, drinks, towels, and so on to players during a game; and

4. Running errands for trainers, managers, coaches, and players before, during, and after a sporting event.

[29 C.F.R. § 570.35(c)(2)]

Q 8:263   When are apprentice training hours not compensable under the FLSA?

Training hours in an apprentice training program are generally treated as hours worked and subject to the FLSA minimum wage and overtime pay requirements. However, hours spent in an organized program of related, supplemental instruction by employees in bona fide apprenticeship programs are not treated as hours worked, provided that:

• The apprentice is employed under a written apprenticeship agreement that meets the standards of the Bureau of Apprenticeship and Training of the DOL;

• The training time does not involve any productive work or performance of the apprentice's regular duties; and

• There is no written agreement to treat such time as hours worked.

[29 C.F.R. § 785.32]

Q 8:264   What is the "youth minimum wage"?

Employers may pay employees under 20 years of age any wage rate that is not less than $4.25 per hour for the first 90 consecutive calendar days (not work days) after they are first employed. An employer may not take any action to displace employees (including partial displacements such as a reduction of hours, wages, or benefits) to hire employees at the youth minimum wage. [29 U.S.C. § 206(g)]

Q 8:265   When can employers provide remedial education during the workweek with no overtime pay?

An employer may require that an employee spend up to 10 hours in the aggregate in any workweek in remedial education without payment of overtime compensation for that time. The overtime exemption is limited to employees who lack a high school diploma or educational attainment at the eighth-grade level. The remedial education must be designed to provide reading and other basic skills at an eighth-grade level or below, or to fulfill the requirements of a high school diploma or GED. Such remedial training may not include job-specific training. Employees must be compensated their regular rate of pay for the time spent receiving remedial education. The education must be conducted during specific periods of time set aside for such training, and, to the extent practicable, away from the employee's normal workstation. An employer that relies on this overtime exemption must maintain and preserve records, showing the hours spent each workday and total hours spent each workweek by the employee receiving such education, as well as the compensation received by him or her for such time during the pay period. [29 U.S.C. § 207(q); 29 C.F.R. §§ 516.34, 778.603]

Equal Pay Act

Q 8:266　What provisions does the FLSA contain regarding equal pay for equal work?

The equal-pay provisions of the FLSA prohibit an employer from discriminating against employees on the basis of sex by paying employees of one sex lower wages than employees of the opposite sex for performing equal work—that is, work that requires equal skill, effort, and responsibility, and is performed under similar working conditions. The term wages for purposes of this prohibition includes all payments made to an employee as remuneration for employment, including the employee's wage rate or salary, plus vacation and holiday pay, premium payments, fringe benefits, expense reimbursement, and so on. The Equal Pay Act does not prohibit the payment of different wages to employees of the opposite sex when the difference is due to one of four factors:

- A bona fide seniority system;
- A merit system;
- A system that determines wages based on the quantity or quality of work; or
- Any factor other than sex.

[29 U.S.C. § 206(d); 29 C.F.R. §§ 1620.10–1620.12]

Q 8:267　What agency is responsible for enforcement of the equal-pay provisions of the FLSA?

Administration and enforcement of the equal-pay provisions of the FLSA are the jurisdiction of the Equal Employment Opportunity Commission (EEOC).

Q 8:268   What are the penalties for violation of the equal-pay provisions of the FLSA?

In addition to lost wages, a victim of discrimination under the Equal Pay Act may recover liquidated damages in an amount equal to lost damages. Liquidated damages are not automatic, however. The Equal Pay Act also authorizes an award of attorney's fees to a prevailing plaintiff. "Willful" violations of the Equal Pay Act are subject to criminal penalties (i.e., fines of up to $10,000, imprisonment for up to six months upon a second conviction, or both). The EEOC has jurisdiction over this FLSA section. The EEOC, therefore, may bring a lawsuit against an employer, as can an individual employee. [29 U.S.C. § 216]

WARN Act

Q 8:269   What is the WARN Act?

The Worker Adjustment Retraining and Notification (WARN) Act is a federal law that requires a covered employer to furnish a 60-day written notice prior to a plant closing or mass layoff. The written notice must be sent to the affected employees (and/or their union, if they are represented by one), the state dislocated worker unit, and the chief elected official of the local government where the closing or layoff is to occur.

Q 8:270   When is a WARN notification required?

WARN applies only to "covered employers"; that is, employers that employ (1) 100 or more employees, excluding part-time employees (defined as an employee who is employed for an average of fewer than 20 hours per week or who has been employed for fewer than 6 of the 12 months preceding the date on which the notice is required), or (2) 100 or more employees who (in the aggregate) work at least 4,000 hours per week (not counting overtime).

WARN requires a covered employer to provide written notice at least 60 days in advance of a "plant closing" or "mass layoff" at a single site. A "plant closing" is defined as the permanent or temporary shutdown of a single site of employment (or a facility within a single site), if the shutdown results in an "employment loss" during any 30-day period for 50 or more employees, excluding part-time employees. A "mass layoff" is defined to include a reduction in force that results in an "employment loss" at a single site of employment during any 30-day period for either (1) at least one-third of the employees, totaling at least 50 employees (excluding part-time employees), or (2) at least 500 employees (excluding part-time employees). Notably, the requirements of WARN are only triggered if there is an "employment loss." That term means (1) an employment termination (other than a termination for cause), voluntary departure, or retirement; (2) a layoff exceeding six months; or (3) a reduction in hours of work of more than 50 percent during each month of any six-month period.

An employer that violates WARN is liable to each affected employee for an amount equal to back pay and benefits for the period of the violation (60 days minus the number of days for which the employer had given proper notice). In addition, an employer that fails to provide proper notice is subject to a civil penalty not to exceed $500 for each day of the violation. WARN authorizes the recovery of attorney's fees to the prevailing party in a lawsuit. [29 U.S.C. §§ 2101–2109; 29 C.F.R. § 639]

In addition to the requirement from the Department of Labor, there are requirements at the state level. For example, New York State requires that private businesses with 50 or more employees provide the WARN notice in the case of closing or layoffs of 25 or more, mass layoffs of 250 or more. The notice must be made 90 days prior to the change. The consequences of not complying with the WARN Act can include the payment of wages and benefits to workers and civil penalty.

Q 8:271   What are the requirements to post WARN notice and communicate to the impacted employees?

There are no requirements to post notices or posters within the workplace. There are requirements for notification of representatives of employees and individual employees.

The notice to representatives must include:

- The name and address of the employment site where the plant closing or mass layoff will occur, and the name and telephone number of a company official to contact for further information.
- A statement about whether the planned action is expected to be permanent or temporary and, if the entire plant is to be closed, a statement to that effect.
- The expected date of the first separation and the anticipated schedule for making separations.
- The job titles of positions to be affected and the names of the workers currently holding affected jobs.

The notice to individual employees must include:

- A statement about whether the planned action is expected to be permanent or temporary and, if the entire plant is to be closed, a statement to that effect.
- The expected date when the plant closing or mass layoff will begin, and the expected date when the individual employee will be separated.
- An indication of whether or not bumping rights exist.
- The name and telephone number of a company official to contact for further information.

The notice may include additional information useful to the employees such as information on available dislocated worker assistance, and, if the planned action is expected to be temporary, the estimated duration.

Chapter 9

Benefits Treated as Compensation

The Internal Revenue Code (I.R.C. or Code) generally treats any payment made to an employee (or the fair market value of a benefit provided to an employee) as additional compensation subject to federal income tax withholding, Social Security and Medicare (FICA), and Federal Unemployment Tax Act (FUTA) taxes, unless specifically exempt from tax. [I.R.C. §§ 61(a)(1), 3121(a), 3306(b), 3401] Therefore, unless specifically excluded from wages, all compensation and fringe benefits provided to employees are wages subject to employment tax and withholding. Statute, regulations and other reliable authority offer a multitude of exemptions to this general treatment for certain bona fide wage payments and benefits. Unfortunately, there is no uniform set of rules that can be used to determine whether wage payments and fringe benefits are exempt from the federal withholding and employment taxes. When a fringe benefit is exempt under a section of the I.R.C. from any of these employment taxes, the benefit must generally be provided under a plan meeting certain requirements under that section (e.g., be a written plan or satisfy certain nondiscrimination requirements). In addition, an annual dollar limitation may apply and that dollar limitation may change each year, depending upon the underlying benefit and the corresponding statute.

This chapter describes the most common wage payments and fringe benefits provided by employers to employees and the federal withholding and employment tax treatment that apply.

Fringe and Employee Benefits: General Overview

Q 9:1 Under what circumstances is the value of employer-provided benefits treated as additional compensation?

As a general rule, the I.R.C. requires all remuneration for services performed for an employer by an employee to be treated as wages and to be subject to federal income tax (FIT), federal income tax withholding (FITW), FICA, and FUTA taxes. The traditional definition of wages includes payments made in cash or by check, or in a noncash medium. Thus, hourly wages, annual salaries, commissions, piece rates, bonus payments, and incentive payments are treated as wages. In addition, the value of fringe benefits (generally based on fair market value) and other noncash awards is also treated as wages, unless specifically excluded from FIT, FITW, FICA, and FUTA. Traditional fringe benefits that are not treated as compensation include group medical insurance (a "welfare benefit") and employer-reimbursed business expenses. Nontraditional benefits that are subject to FIT, FITW, FICA, and FUTA include certain permanent cash advances and employee loan agreements under which the unpaid balance is forgiven. [I.R.C. §§ 61(a)(1), 3121(a), 3306(b), 3401(a)] Remember that any payment that is not taxable is the exception, and must be specifically exempt from FIT, FITW, FICA, and FUTA under a reliable authority (e.g., Internal Revenue Code, IRS regulations, IRS revenue rulings, case law, etc.).

The IRS provides updated guidance each year on determining the fair market value (FMV) of select employer-provided benefits and their tax treatment in Publication 15-B, Employer's Tax Guide to Fringe Benefits.

Q 9:2 What are the federal pension benefits limits for 2017?

The limits on qualified pension plan contributions and benefits have been updated for 2017:

Benefit Feature for Pension or Profit Sharing Plans	2016	2017
Pretax employee contributions (i.e., salary deferrals) for 401(k) and SARSEP plans and 403(b) annuities (calendar years)	$18,000	$18,000
SIMPLE IRA and SIMPLE 401(k) pretax employee contribution limit (for calendar years)	$12,500	$12,500
Annual benefit limit for I.R.C. § 415(b)(1)(A) defined benefit pension plans at Social Security retirement age (plan years ending in)	$210,000	$215,000
Combined employer–employee contribution limits for defined contribution plans I.R.C. § 415(c)(1)(A)	$53,000	$54,000
Annual compensation limit for determining benefits and contributions [I.R.C. § 401(a)(17) and I.R.C. § 408(k)(3)(C)] (plan years beginning in)	$265,000	$270,000

Benefit Feature for Pension or Profit Sharing Plans	_2016_	_2017_
Catch-up contributions for 401(k) and 403(b) plans for individuals age 50 by December 31	$6,000	$6,000
Catch-up contributions for SIMPLE IRA and SIMPLE 401(k) plans (for calendar years)	$3,000	$3,000

Q 9:3 What recent changes affect the federal employment tax treatment of employer-provided fringe benefits?

As a result of a United States Supreme Court decision [United States v. Windsor, 133 S. Ct. 2675 (2013)], the IRS now recognizes all legally married same-sex couples as married for federal tax purposes, regardless of whether the couple lives in a jurisdiction that recognizes same-sex marriage or not. [Rev. Rul. 2013-17, 2013-38 I.R.B. 201] This change of policy affects the employment taxability of benefits, such as health insurance, offered to same-sex spouses. See Q 9:147.

The American Taxpayer Relief Act of 2012 (ATRA) was signed into law on January 2, 2013 and addressed a number of tax provisions that expired or were about to expire. In the area of benefits, ATRA permanently extends employer-paid educational expense, employer-provided childcare facilities and services and enhancements in the adoption assistance offered to adoptive parents. ATRA also created parity in the transportation benefits offered to employees. Finally, ATRA extended the American Opportunity Tax Credit through 2017.

The adoption credit was increased under the Patient Protection and Affordable Care Act for 2010 and 2011 and the health care law made the credit refundable. The 2010 Tax Relief Act extended the credit through 2012 but did not extend the option for a refundable credit or the increased credit. As a result, the maximum credit allowed for adoption of a child with special needs was $13,460 for 2016 and $13,570 for 2017.

Fringe Benefits

Q 9:4 What are fringe benefits?

The term "fringe benefit" is not specifically defined in the I.R.C., although the definition of a "welfare benefit" under the Employee Retirement Income Security Act ("ERISA") includes many "fringe benefits" and the I.R.C. governs the tax treatment of these benefits. I.R.C. Section 132 identifies several tax-free fringe benefits, but this is not a complete list of fringe benefits provided to employees. The generally accepted definition of a "fringe benefit" is a benefit that is provided to employees in addition to their base pay. Fringe benefits include health and welfare benefits (medical, dental, vision), transportation fringe benefits, discounts on property or services obtained from the employer, flights on employer-provided airplanes, certain tickets to entertainment or sporting events, qualified tuition credits, dependent care assistance, qualified moving expenses, free parking, employer-provided car or truck use, and working-condition fringes. In addition, some taxable benefits, such as paid vacation, are also classified as fringe benefits. In fact, the term *fringe benefit* tends to be a generic classification that refers to any employer-provided benefit, including accident and health coverage and retirement benefits.

Q 9:5 How are employee fringe benefits treated for federal employment tax purposes?

In general, the FMV of fringe benefits provided to employees or to their family members is treated as compensation and subject to FIT, FITW, FICA, and FUTA. In other words, unless specifically identified by the I.R.C. as exempt from these taxes, any benefit is included in taxable wages. To that end, several categories of fringe benefits have preferential tax treatment under the I.R.C. and are not treated as taxable as long as certain requirements under the I.R.C. or regulations are met. The federal tax treatment of fringe benefits is not uniform. For example, salary deferrals under a 401(k), 403(b), or 457 plan are exempt from FIT and FITW but are subject to FICA and FUTA; however, most other "pretax" or salary reductions used to purchase "qualified" benefits under a Section 125 cafeteria plan are exempt from FIT, FITW, FICA, and FUTA (with the exception of adoption assistance, which is subject to FICA and FUTA but exempt from FIT and FITW). In general, the value of a *taxable benefit* provided to a spouse, domestic partner, and dependents of an employee is treated as additional compensation to the employee. When no specific exemption from federal withholding and employment tax is available, the value of any fringe benefit provided to an employee or family member of the employee is treated as wages and subject to FIT, FITW, FICA, and FUTA.

The amount of a noncash taxable benefit that is included in the employee's wages is generally the FMV of the benefit less the sum of: (1) any amount contributed by the employee toward the cost of the benefit and (2) the amount, if any, specifically excluded from gross income under the I.R.C. Thus, when the employee is required to pay for a portion of the cost of a non-excludable benefit provided by an employer, the employee will only be treated as having additional wages on the taxable value less any amounts paid by the employee. The FMV of a few taxable benefits may be determined by reference to IRS valuation methods rather than the actual cost (e.g., Uniform Premium Table I for group-term insurance in excess of $50,000 or life insurance coverage for employees' dependents).

Taxable benefits include payments for holidays, vacations, cash awards, and the employer's payment of an employee's taxes. [Ann. 85-113, 1985-31 I.R.B. 31; Rev. Rul. 58-113, 1958-1 C.B. 362; Treas. Reg. § 31.3401(a)-1(b)(6)]

Q 9:6 What are IRS audit guidelines for fringe benefits?

The IRS released audit technique guidelines to its website (www.irs.gov) related to executive compensation providing IRS auditors with specialized information on issues involving market segments, which the IRS said "may be an industry such as construction or farming, a profession like ministers, or an issue like passive activity losses." The guidelines cover "examination techniques, common and unique industry issues, business practices, industry terminology and other information to assist examiners in performing examinations." These guidelines are a helpful planning tool in predicting how to avoid problems in the event of an IRS audit.

Included are issues relating to excessive employee remuneration under I.R.C. Section 162(m), stock-based compensation, golden parachutes, nonqualified deferred compensation, transfers of compensatory stock options to related persons, and split-dollar life insurance. The guidelines identify the documents to be reviewed, the questions to be asked and answered, the rules to which different forms of compensation are subject, how and when to issue information document requests (IDRs) and follow up with subpoenas, and other matters related to audits of the specific subjects.

Specifically, the fringe benefit audit guidelines tell examiners to "start with the assumption that its value will be taxable" and delve into topics ranging from awards and bonuses to loans, athletic skyboxes and cultural or entertainment suites, club memberships, corporate credit cards, and executive dining room services. Also discussed are how to account for outplacement services, qualified employee discounts, security-related and standard transportation including chauffeurs and employer-paid parking, spousal and dependent life insurance, transfers of property, employee use of listed property, relocation expenses, noncommercial air travel, employer-paid vacations, spousal or dependent travel, wealth management and qualified retirement planning services, and an employer's payment of the employee's share of Social Security and Medicare taxes.

The guidelines devoted to auditing golden parachutes list a variety of documents to research in determining whether a payment will be subject to a 20 percent excise tax on the recipient as an excess payment and not be deductible to the payer. The guidelines identify nine steps to follow in making the determination, and specific issues to address under each one.

A substantial portion of the audit technique guidelines deals with stock-based compensation. The Stock Based Compensation Audit Techniques Guide reviews whether the stock was actually transferred, if there was a transfer to a related person, whether an election to be taxed when the stock is actually transferred rather than when it vests under Section 83(b) has been made, whether Section 409A applies, and whether lapse and non-lapse restrictions provide a real risk of forfeiture. It also covers same-day sales of different kinds of stocks and "phantom stock," involving the "crediting of shares of stock to a service provider's account without ever issuing the actual shares to the employee," which the IRS said would be considered nonqualified deferred compensation under certain circumstances.

There is also a guide devoted to transfers of compensatory stock options, which identify potential issues ranging from timing of the corporate deduction to promoter expenses, whether employment taxes are due, and whether the family limited partnership may not be a bona fide partnership or may be subject to re-characterization under Treasury Regulations Section 1.701.2.

The guide on nonqualified deferred compensation states that the IRS audit should focus on when the deferred amounts are includible in the employee's gross income and when those amounts are deductible by the employer, and includes changes under I.R.C. Section 409A. The split-dollar life insurance audit technique guide addresses interim valuation and safe harbor rules, as well as how to address any modifications to the life insurance policy, who the policy owner is, whether the employee or his or her beneficiary is entitled to a death benefit or cash surrender under the policy, and changes to the policy made after September 17, 2003.

Each of the rules relating to the specific fringe benefits is dealt with in greater detail herein.

Q 9:7   How does the employer determine the value of a taxable fringe benefit to be included in employees' wages?

The FMV of a noncash fringe benefit is defined under regulations to be "the amount that an individual would have to pay for the particular fringe benefit in an arm's-length transaction." The FMV may not necessarily be the employer's cost to obtain the benefit. For example, volume discounts may be available to an employer resulting in costs that are less than the FMV. That is, the employer's actual cost to provide the benefit cannot be used to establish FMV unless the employer's cost is attributable to an arm's-length transaction. [I.R.C. § 83(b); Treas. Reg. § 1.62-21(b)(2)]

In addition to these general rules, certain fringe benefits are determined by reference to special IRS valuation rules that disregard the actual cost or true FMV of the benefit (e.g., group-term life insurance). Separate IRS guidance specifies how and when a special valuation rule applies. For example, special valuation rules may be used to determine the value of personal use of a company car, personal flights on company aircraft (a special rule applies for air travel of airline employees), taxable meals provided at an employer-operated eating facility, and group-term and non-group-term life insurance. No uniform set of rules applies in determining the value of fringe benefits. For example, the premium table for taxable group-term insurance differs substantially from the premium table used in determining the value of employer-provided split dollar life insurance. (See each relevant section of this chapter for the applicable valuation rules.) [I.R.C. §§ 79, 101(a), 132; Treas. Reg. § 1.61-21(b)]

Q 9:8   When are fringe benefits treated as paid for withholding and reporting purposes?

Under the general rule, wages, including taxable fringe benefits, are considered paid when they are made available to employees without substantial limitation. [I.R.C. § 1.451-2(a)] In certain limited circumstances, the I.R.C. and other administrative guidelines provide for special timing rules or "rules of convenience." Specifically, rules of convenience are available for taxable group-term life insurance, personal use of company cars and planes and transportation fringe benefits.

- *Group-term life insurance.* The value of taxable group-term life insurance may be treated as paid at whatever frequency the employer chooses, so long as the benefit is treated as having been paid no later than the end of the year to which the benefit relates. Notification need not be made to the IRS or to employees concerning the frequency at which taxable group-term life will be recognized as wages subject to employment tax and withholding. [Notice 88-82; Ann. 85-113, 1985-31 I.R.B 31]

- *Transportation fringe benefits.* Transportation fringe benefits, which include transit passes, fare media and employer-provided parking that are in excess of the amounts exempt from wages subject to employment tax and withholding may be treated as paid at whatever frequency the employer chooses so long as the benefit is treated as having been paid no later than the end of the year to which the benefit relates. Notification need not be made to the IRS or to employees concerning the frequency at which excess transportation fringe benefits will be recognized as wages subject to employment tax and withholding. [Treas. Reg. § 1.32-9 (Q&A 22)]

- *Personal use of company cars and planes.* The value of the personal use of company cars and planes may be treated as paid at whatever frequency the employer chooses, so long as the benefit is treated as having been paid no later than the end of the year to which the benefit relates. Notification need not be made to the IRS or to employees concerning the frequency at which taxable personal use of company cars or planes will be recognized as wages subject to employment tax and withholding. Additionally, employers may elect to use the special accounting rule under which the employer treats benefits received in November and December as received in the subsequent calendar year. [Ann. 85-113, 1985-31 I.R.B. 31; Temp Reg. § 31.3401(a)-1(T)] See Q 9:9 for additional information concerning the special accounting rule.

Q 9:9   What is the special accounting rule and what requirements apply?

Because of time needed to collect mileage information and calculate taxable amounts for personal use of cars or jets, the IRS gives employers the option of treating taxable income pursuant to these benefits for November and December as though they were received in the subsequent taxable year. For example, an employee's personal vehicle use for November and December of 2017 can be treated as personal vehicle use incurred in 2018.

The special accounting rule may be applied with respect to one qualifying benefit, and not another. For example, the employer may elect to use the special accounting rule with respect to personal use of company cars but not for purposes of taxing and reporting personal use of the company jet. The IRS need not be notified of the employer's election to use this rule. However, other requirements apply as follows:

1. Employees must be directly notified that the special accounting rule was used no sooner than the last paycheck of the calendar year and no later

than the date on which the employee receives the Form W-2 for the tax year to which the benefit relates (generally, January 31).

2. When the rule is applied with respect to a particular benefit, it must be consistently used for each subsequent year the benefit is made available to employees.

3. The rule must be consistently used for all employees receiving the benefit.

4. Employees must report deductions related to the specific fringe benefit (i.e., automobile or jet) in the same period that the employer reported the taxable income. [Ann. 85-113, 1985-31 I.R.B. 31; Treas. Reg. 1.61-21(c)(7)]

Q 9:10 Can nonemployees (e.g., directors, independent contractors, and partners in a partnership) receive tax-free benefits?

For the most part, nontaxable fringe benefits are only available to employees (and some former employees) and their immediate family members (i.e., spouse and dependents). Directors and independent contractors generally are not considered employees, although a director may also provide services as an employee and receive benefits as an employee. Partners of partnerships are not generally treated as employees of the partnership and usually cannot exclude from earned income many of the tax-free fringe benefits available to the non-partner employees of the partnership; however, both can receive pension benefits and dependent care benefits under I.R.C. Section 129 on a tax-free basis, if the benefit is offered in a manner proven to not discriminate in favor of highly compensated employees (HCEs). An active "member" of a limited liability company (LLC) that elects to be taxed as a partnership is generally treated as a partner and subject to the rules applicable to partnerships. Note that compensation and taxable benefits provided to a partner are not subject to FIT, FITW, FICA, and FUTA. However, the partner's earned income is subject to self-employment taxes, which are similar to FICA taxes. [Rev. Rul. 88-76, 1988-2 C.B. 360]

The rules that treat certain fringe benefits as taxable compensation apply when those benefits are provided to nonemployees such as partners and directors. For example, the value of a director's personal use of a company-provided vehicle is treated as additional compensation subject to FIT. In addition, the FMW of the vehicle use is determined in the same manner as applies to employees—that is, a general valuation standard or safe harbor method is used to determine the value of the personal use of the car. FITW, FICA and FUTA do not apply outside of the employer–employee relationship; therefore, partners and directors are responsible for paying any federal taxes owed on these benefits. For this reason, the IRS generally requires that the value of taxable benefits provided to nonemployees be reported on information returns and statements.

Securities and Exchange Commission disclosure rules for executive compensation must be fulfilled as part of any fringe benefit provided to employees. In addition, other compensation limits may apply. For instance, the Troubled Asset

Relief Program amended I.R.C. Section 162(m), limiting a financial institution's compensation deduction to $500,000, and expanded the definition of "covered employees."

Withholding Requirements: Taxable Fringe Benefits

Q 9:11　How does the employer determine the amount of federal income tax to withhold on a noncash taxable fringe benefit?

Fringe benefits generally meet the IRS definition of "supplemental wages." Accordingly, employers may, at their option, use a flat tax rate instead of the annual or computerized withholding method for computing federal income tax provided federal income tax was withheld from regular wages paid to the employee in the current or preceding tax year and the supplemental wage payment is paid separate from regular wages or is separately identified. For 2017, the federal flat tax rate for supplemental wages is 25 percent. A mandatory rate of 39.6 percent applies to supplemental wages in excess of $1 million in the calendar year. See Qs 2:91–2:93 for more information on supplemental wage payments.

Q 9:12　How are taxable fringe benefit payments to a deceased employee's beneficiaries or a disabled employee treated for Social Security, Medicare, and FUTA taxes?

Certain payments made on account of the death (or disability) of an employee may be exempt from FICA and FUTA. Wage payments and benefits treated as wages that are made to a deceased employee's estate or a beneficiary after the employee dies, but in the calendar year of death, are subject to Medicare, Social Security (to the extent payments are below the Social Security wage base), and FUTA. Wages that are paid before the date of death but not cashed or deposited are subject to the same withholding and employment tax rules as wages paid to a nondeceased employee. Wages paid to a deceased employee's estate or to a beneficiary in the calendar year following the year of death are not subject to FICA or FUTA. [I.R.C. §§ 3121(a)(14), 3306(b)(15); Rev. Rul. 86-109, 1986-2 C.B. 196]

Certain types of benefits may be provided to dependents of deceased employees without the value of those benefits being considered wages of the dependents or the deceased employee (e.g., qualified employee discounts, on-premise athletic facilities). [I.R.C. §§ 132, 3121(a)(20), 3306(b)(16), 3401(a)(2)]

Disability payments under a definite plan or system (as opposed to a one-time payment) paid to a former employee are subject to Medicare, Social Security (to the extent payments are below the Social Security wage base), and FUTA only for the first six full calendar months following the employee's absence from work. However, if the payments would have been paid had the employment relationship not ended (e.g., accrued vacation pay), the amounts paid are subject to Medicare, Social Security (to the extent payments are below the Social Security wage base), and FUTA. Other than certain group-term life insurance benefits provided to a former employee who terminated employment due to permanent disability, the value of fringe benefits provided to a disabled former employee is treated as wages. [I.R.C. §§ 3102(d), 3121(a)(2), 3306(b)(2)]

Wage payments to a disabled employee or former employee made when the employee is entitled to Social Security disability benefits under Section 223(a) of the Social Security Act are not subject to FICA if the employee's entitlement to the Social Security benefits commenced in a prior calendar year. This FICA exemption is contingent on the employee not performing any services for the employer during the period for which the disability payments are made. Note that there is no similar FUTA exemption for these payments. [I.R.C. § 3121(a)(15)]

Most monthly pension and annuity benefits, as well as certain deferred compensation paid at retirement or as a periodic disability benefit, are exempt from Social Security, Medicare, and FUTA.

Q 9:13   What are the employment tax deposit rules that apply to taxable fringe benefits?

The deposit due date that applies to taxable fringe benefits is determined by reference to the date the fringe benefit was provided to the employee (see chapter 4).

Q 9:14   What is the method used for computing federal income tax withholding on the value of taxable noncash fringe benefits?

In order to recognize noncash taxable fringe benefits as wages for tax reporting purposes and withhold the required federal, state, and local taxes, it is necessary to add the amount to a cash wage payment so that the reporting and withholding requirements can be met on the combined amount. This process of adding a noncash amount to cash wage payment only for purposes of recognizing the wage amount for tax and reporting purposes is called imputing and, in this instance, the taxable fringe benefit is referred to as "imputed income."

Payroll systems process imputed income in one of two ways: (1) the imputed income is added to regular wages for purposes of adjusting the total amount subject to withholding and employment tax reporting and is then subtracted on an aftertax basis, or (2) the taxable wages are automatically adjusted for the imputed income amount (in other words, there is no need to deduct the noncash fringe benefit on an after-tax basis). The latter approach is preferable as there is never a risk that the employee will be overpaid by the amount of the imputed income due to a failure to deduct the amount on an after-tax basis. Under both methods, the employee's net pay is reduced by the amount of withholding tax owed on the imputed income.

Example. Employee Jeff has year-to-date wages in the amount of $96,000 and was furnished with a company car, the personal use of which was valued at $460 for the month. His employer treats the noncash fringe benefit as imputed income together with a bonus payment of $6,600. The imputed income is subject to federal income tax, federal income tax withholding, Social Security, and Medicare.

Regular Wages	$6,600.00
Imputed Income	460.00
Total Taxable Wages	7,060.00
Federal income tax withholding at 25%	(1,765.00)
Social Security tax at 6.2%	(437.72)
Medicare tax at 1.45%	(102.37)
Net pay before aftertax deductions	4,754.91
Imputed income	(460.00)
Net pay	4,294.91

Jeff's net pay had he not had imputed income would have been $4,445.10 [$6,600 − 6,600 x (25% + 1.45% + 6.2%)]. The difference between $4,445.10 and $4,294.91 is $150.19, the tax withheld [$460.00 × 32.65% (25% + 6.2% + 1.45%)].

Q 9:15   What are the employer's options for withholding taxes from noncash fringe benefits at the end of the year?

Frequently, it is discovered at the end of the year that an employee has received a noncash taxable benefit that is subject to employment tax and withholding; however, there are no regular wages remaining from which the withholding taxes can be paid. For example, assume that final wages for 2017 are paid on December 26 and on December 30 it is discovered that the employee received a gift card of $150. The value of the gift card, or $150, is considered wages subject to federal income tax, Social Security, Medicare, and federal unemployment tax in 2017.

Additionally, state and local withholding taxes may also apply. How can the employer meet its withholding tax obligations for this payment in 2017, given that the employee will not receive any further wage payments in 2017 from which these taxes can be paid?

There are two options available to the employer for meeting its withholding tax obligations in situations such as this:

(1) Pay withholding tax on behalf of the employee. The employer has the option of paying the employee's withholding tax obligations and not recovering

these taxes from employees. It is essential, however, that with respect to nonagricultural employees, the employer correctly calculate the additional taxable wages that accrue as a result of paying employees' taxes. The I.R.C. provides that all amounts paid to employees, unless specifically exempt, are wages subject to income tax withholding, including taxes that are the obligation of the employee that are paid by the employer. In other words, when the employer pays the employee's federal income, Social Security, and Medicare taxes, these amounts are subject to withholding. This results in a pyramiding effect of the tax on the tax. To simplify the calculation of the wage amount in this scenario, the IRS prescribes a formula, which is generally referred to as "gross-up." [I.R.C. § 3401] See Q 9:447 for more on the gross-up formula.

(2) Advance the employee's taxes. The employer also has the option of paying the employee's withholding tax obligations and recovering the tax advance in the subsequent calendar year. Under this option, the employer includes in its employment tax deposit not only the employer taxes that are owed, but also the withholding tax that was otherwise due from the employee. The amount deposited on behalf of the employee is reported on the current year's Form W-2 in Boxes 2 (federal income tax withheld), 4 (Social Security tax withheld), and 6 (Medicare tax withheld) as though the employee paid the taxes. Under IRS guidelines, the employer must recover this tax advance no later than April 1 of the following tax year. The amount that is not repaid to the employer by April 1 of the subsequent calendar year is deemed wages, subject to gross-up (see Q 9:447) and reported on Form W-2c in the year the tax advance was originally made. [Ann. 85-113, 1985-31 I.R.B. 31]

Note. When the employer recovers the tax advance in the subsequent year, it should not be reflected on the subsequent year's Form W-2. Instead, the tax advance should be treated as an employee receivable that is deducted on an aftertax basis. Finally, businesses subject to Sarbanes-Oxley should be cautious in making tax advances on behalf of corporate officers as restrictions may apply. [Pub. L. No. 107-204]

Reporting of Fringe Benefits

Q 9:16   How are nontaxable fringe benefits reported?

Most *nontaxable* fringe benefits are exempt from the federal employment tax reporting requirements. Exceptions apply when the nontaxable benefit is required to be reported on the employee's Form 1040 (e.g., for dependent care benefits, excludable moving expenses, medical savings account (MSA) contributions, and qualified adoption assistance benefits). Where applicable, these benefits are reported on the employee's Form W-2 (e.g., Boxes 10 and 12). See the relevant sections of this chapter for the specific reporting requirements that apply.

Q 9:17   In general, how are taxable fringe benefits reported on the Form W-2?

When a fringe benefit is taxable, it is reported in Boxes 1 and 5 and, if applicable, Box 3 of Form W-2. Certain taxable fringe benefits may also be subject to additional reporting requirements. For example, dependent care assistance benefits are reported in Box 10; employer reimbursement of employee business expenses from a nonaccountable plan and payments that exceed substantiated amounts are reported in Box 12 with Code L; taxable group-term life insurance is reported with Code C in Box 12. Only four lines of information are allowed in Box 12 on a paper Copy A of Form W-2. If more information is required, an additional Form W-2 is used. See each section of this chapter and chapter 4 for additional guidance for the reporting of fringe benefits on Forms 941 and W-2.

Additional information concerning the reporting requirements that apply to select fringe benefits can be obtained from IRS Publication 15-B, Employer's Tax Guide to Fringe Benefits.

Reimbursements for Business Expenses

Q 9:18   Do the regulations governing reimbursement of an employee's business expenses apply to employees of any type of employer?

Yes. The regulations governing reimbursement of employee business expenses generally apply to all employees, including those working for government employers, nonprofit organizations, and employers in the private sector.

Accountable Business Expense Reimbursement Plans

Q 9:19   What constitutes an "accountable plan"?

The term *accountable plan* refers to an employer's plan that provides reimbursement of expenses that have been properly substantiated (i.e., have adequate and timely supporting documentation as to the essential nature and amount of the expense and the time, place and business purpose). Reimbursements of business expenses made from an accountable plan are not treated as additional compensation of the employee and are not subject to FIT, FITW, FICA, or FUTA. The most common business expenses reimbursed by employers are those incurred for business travel, business/entertainment meals, or business mileage within the metropolitan area.

A business expense reimbursement is treated as being made from an accountable plan if the plan meets all of the following requirements: (1) the expenses have a business connection, (2) the expenses are properly substantiated, and (3) the employee must return payments that exceed substantiated expenses (i.e., excess payments) within a reasonable time period. [Treas. Reg. §§ 1.162-2(c) to 1.162-2(g)]

Q 9:20   What is a nonaccountable expense reimbursement plan?

A nonaccountable expense reimbursement plan is an arrangement that does not require a business connection (e.g., reimbursement of commuting expenses), the appropriate and timely substantiation of a business expense reimbursement or advance, or the return of amounts not used for business. All payments under a nonaccountable plan are treated as wages subject to FIT, FITW, FICA, and FUTA.

An employer's payments are treated as paid under a nonaccountable plan when either of the following two conditions exists:

1. The employee is not required to or does not substantiate expenses to the employer on a timely basis, including providing receipts or other documentation where required; or

2. The employer advances an amount to its employee for business expenses and the employee is not required to, or does not, timely return any amount he or she does not use for business expenses.

Employer payments to an employee for travel and other necessary business expenses under a nonaccountable plan are treated as additional wages and subject to FIT, FITW, FICA, and FUTA at the time the payment is made (or the next regular payroll period occurring after the date the reimbursement is made). The employee may be eligible to deduct a portion of the substantiated expenses on his or her Form 1040 as an itemized business expense deduction.

Substantiation is also required for reimbursements of certain fringe benefits (e.g., adoption assistance benefits, educational assistance, health flexible spending accounts, and dependent care reimbursements), but no business connection requirement applies to health reimbursement accounts, dependent care reimbursements, adoption assistance reimbursement, and some educational assistance plans. However, other requirements may apply if these reimbursements are not to be treated as additional wages. [Rev. Proc. 97-45, 1997-2 C.B. 499; Pub. No. 15]

The IRS Small Business/Self-Employed Division posted to its website field guidance for examiners auditing excess per diem payments. Because the IRS requires that payments made with no mechanism for tracking allowances paid should be treated as made under a nonaccountable plan, such payments would all be treated as subject to employment tax and withholding. The guidance differentiates between payments for taxable periods ending on or before December 31, 2006, and those coming afterward. For the earlier period, "absent egregious circumstances or evidence of intentional noncompliance, the examiner should not treat a plan as entirely nonaccountable solely because excess per diem payments were not treated as wages. Instead, the examiner should treat only the excess amounts over the federal per diem limit as wages." Although the guidance covers all industries, the IRS said the issue "frequently arises in audits of transportation or construction businesses." The guidance also provides criteria for examiners to determine whether plans are nonaccountable, which would render all per diems paid as taxable.

Q 9:21   When does an expense have a "business connection"?

An expense has a "business connection" when it is paid or incurred by an employee in the performance of services as an employee for the employer and the expense would be deductible on the employee's own personal income tax return had it not been reimbursed by the employer. An advance may qualify as a payment with a business connection if the advance is substantiated for a business expense that is deductible by the employee or employer under I.R.C. Sections 161 to 198, and the amount of the advance is computed to closely approximate the business expense to be incurred. [Treas. Reg. § 1.162-2(d)]

Q 9:22   When is a business expense "properly substantiated" under an accountable plan?

A business expense is "properly substantiated" when an employee can document or verify the amount, business nature, and critical elements of the amount paid by the employer through advances, allowances, or reimbursements. The substantiation must occur within a reasonable time period. [Treas. Reg. § 1.162-2(e)]

The term *substantiation* is discussed in I.R.C. Section 274(d). The requirements for substantiation typically include the identification of: (1) the amount of the expense, (2) the time and place of the business activity, (3) the business purpose of the expense, (4) if applicable, the business relationship of the individual to whom the expense relates, and (5) the names of the guests and employees in attendance. [Temp. Treas. Reg. § 1.274-5T; Rev. Proc. 97-45, 1997-2 C.B. 499]

Expenses covered by I.R.C. Section 274(d) are considered substantiated when the employee provides sufficient information to the employer to identify the nature and elements of the expense as sufficient for the employer to conclude that such expenses were attributable to the employer's business activities. These may include specific items such as travel and lodging for a business meeting, food and beverages furnished on the business premises, recreation expenses of employees (other than the highly compensated), and meetings with prospective customers. Substantiation is likely to be deemed inadequate if broad or vague statements such as "misc." are used in explaining the business nature of the expense. However, exceptions apply in the case of expenses that were incurred along the employee's normal tour of duty. For instance, travel to call on customers in a salesperson's assigned territory need not include the names and addresses of each customer called on. [I.R.C. §§ 274(d), 274(e)]

> **Example.** Jim is traveling away from home for his employer. When he returns, he submits for reimbursement a breakfast receipt for three people. Jim must be able to provide information sufficient to substantiate the amount, time, the names, and the business relationship of the two guests, and business purpose of the breakfast.

Reimbursements under a health flexible spending account, dependent care reimbursement plan, and adoption assistance plans must follow these basic requirements and identify the nature of the expense as being consistent with the plan's requirements. Appropriate substantiation is required; for example, an employee must provide the taxpayer identification number of the dependent care provider. This is sometimes problematic, as individual childcare providers often do not report their income. No dependent care reimbursement should be allowed without the dependent care provider's taxpayer identification number (SSN or EIN) having been provided.

Q 9:23 What type of records must an employee keep to substantiate the business purpose of an expense?

An employee is required to keep adequate records to reflect the essential nature of the business purpose of the travel and entertainment expenses incurred as well as documents substantiating medical and dependent care expenses, adoption assistance expenses, certain moving expenses, and the business use of a company car or jet. These records should generally include the amount, time, location, and business purpose of any expense that is to be reimbursed to the employee. In certain cases, safe harbor methods are available that lessen this recordkeeping requirement. These are referred to as "deemed" substantiation methods.

When the I.R.C. or regulations require substantiation of a business expense and related records have not been kept, the employer can be denied a deduction for the reimbursement, the employee can lose an exclusion for the payment from gross income, or both, and both the employer and employee are required to pay tax on the amount. An accountable plan will generally require proper substantiation.

For certain types of reimbursements (e.g., travel allowances) or an employee's business use of company property, both the employer and the employee must separately satisfy the substantiation requirements. See each relevant section of this chapter for specific substantiation requirements. [I.R.C. §§ 162, 274(d); Treas. Reg. § 1.274-5A]

Q 9:24   Can an employer simplify the process of substantiation while complying with the regulations?

In lieu of having employees substantiate the actual amount of a travel expense while on business away from home, an employer may create a reimbursement system that pays fixed amounts (e.g., a per diem) for meals, travel, and transportation away from home. As long as the amount of the per diem does not exceed the rates established by the federal government, the employee is treated as having substantiated the *amount* of the per diem payments. Note that the employee must still substantiate the time, place, and business nature of the mileage or per diem expense.

A per diem allowance plan that reimburses employees for travel expenses while away from home is treated as meeting the requirement for substantiation of the amount of the expense when it satisfies four conditions:

1. The per diem allowance is paid only for ordinary and necessary expenses that are incurred by an employee for meals, lodging, and incidentals while away from home on business.

2. The amounts paid under the per diem allowance do not exceed the federal per diem rate or other IRS-approved rate or are paid under a flat rate or stated schedule adopted as a normal business practice.

3. The amount of the per diem allowance does not exceed the anticipated expenses.

4. The employee must be required to return the portion of the per diem allowances attributable to days that travel expenses were not incurred (or in the case of mileage allowances, miles not attributable to business) in a reasonable time. [Rev. Proc. 98-64, 1998-52 I.R.B. 32; Notice 93-29, 1993-18 I.R.B. 14]

The amount of the per diem allowance is based on the federal per diem rate that applies to the geographical location of the temporary work assignment. The federal per diem rate for travel in the continental United States is a composite of the lodging, meal, and incidental rates.

Employers may provide for either a combined per diem rate for lodging and meals and incidental expenses or only a single per diem rate for meals and incidental expenses, provided the employer reasonably expects that the employee will incur no lodging expenses or lodging is paid directly. See Qs 9:164–9:175. [Rev. Proc. 2009-47, 2009-42 I.R.B. 524]

Q 9:25   May an employer reimburse an employee for business use of a leased auto?

Yes. An employer may use the mileage allowance method to reimburse employees for mileage incurred in using their personal vehicles for the business of the employer. While employees need to furnish receipts to substantiate their mileage expenses, all other substantiation rules continue to apply (e.g., an expense report or trip log showing the time, date, business purpose of the trip, and business miles attributable to the trip). [Treas. Reg. § 1.274-5(g)(3)]

Q 9:26   What type of documentation is required for employee substantiation under an accountable plan?

Employee requests for reimbursement of travel, entertainment and gifts, use of a passenger automobile, or other business expenses must generally be documented with receipts or paid invoices. The employer may treat travel-related expenditures of up to $75 as substantiated without an actual receipt if all other requirements for substantiation are met (e.g., amount of expense, time, date, and nature of business expenses). Actual expenses can be recorded using log and account books, diaries, expense statements, trip sheets, and so on. The employee is responsible for maintaining these records. [Notice 95-50, 1995-2 C.B. 333; Rev. Proc. 97-45, 1997-33 I.R.B. 1; Temp. Treas. Reg. § 1.274-5T(c)(2)]

Q 9:27   Must an employee substantiate travel-related expenses that are $75 or less?

Under the current requirements, employees need not substantiate the amount of expenses that are $75 or less; however, the other substantiation requirements must be met. An arrangement otherwise satisfies the documentation requirement when information is submitted to the payer that establishes the amount, date, place, and essential character of the expense. The rules permit the employer to set a lower threshold at which receipts must be furnished by employees. [Treas. Reg. § 1.274(d); Notice 95-50, 1995-2 C.B. 333]

Q 9:28   Do special business expense substantiation rules apply to federal employees?

Yes. The IRS released guidance that requires certain federal employees to substantiate their business expense reimbursements by keeping an expense log or account record book. Thus, employees no longer have to submit actual expense receipts for expenses that do not exceed $75. Receipts and records for lodging must be kept for four years. This log must identify the amount of the expense and be approved by an official of the employer. The log must be available for review and reflect the amount, time, place, and business purpose of each business expense. The employer must establish a written statement of policy and procedure for reimbursement and be subject to review by an independent government party (e.g., Inspector General). [Rev. Proc. 97-45, 1997-2 C.B. 499]

Q 9:29   Does an accountable plan require the return of excess advances?

Yes. Advances that exceed actual bona fide business expenses must be returned within a reasonable period of time to avoid being treated as additional wages. Although determining the reasonable period for returning amounts in excess of expenses depends on the facts, there are two "safe harbor" methods that may be followed by an employer to ensure compliance: (1) the fixed-date method and (2) the periodic statement method. However, if there exists a pattern of excess reimbursements, the employer may not use the safe harbor methods to avoid treatment of its business expense reimbursements as paid under a nonaccountable plan. [Treas. Reg. § 1.62-2(g)(3)]

Q 9:30   What is a reasonable period of time?

The IRS defines a *reasonable period of time* for substantiation by either of the following two methods:

The fixed-date method:

1. An advance is not paid more than 30 days before the employer anticipates that an expense will be incurred by the employee.

2. An advance made within 30 days of when the expense is incurred is substantiated by the employee within 60 days after the advance was paid or the expense was incurred.

3. The portion of the reimbursement or advance that was not substantiated is returned to the employer within 120 days after the advance was paid or the expense was incurred.

The periodic statement method: Under this method, the employee is given one or more advances. Then, on a periodic basis (at least quarterly), the employer provides a statement to the employee showing amounts for which no substantiation has been provided. The employee substantiates expenses, or returns the portion of the reimbursement or advance that was not substantiated, within 120 days of the date that the employer provides the employee with a statement showing the amount that requires substantiation (e.g., outstanding travel advances). [Treas. Reg. § 1.162-2(g)(2)(i)]

Q 9:31   Does the IRS impose any specific time limits on substantiation and reimbursement of excess amounts?

No. However, an accountable plan must require substantiation of expenses and the return of excess amounts within a reasonable period. An employer may choose to follow either of two safe harbor methods to determine what constitutes a reasonable period: the fixed-date or the periodic statement method. Employers may also elect to apply facts-and-circumstances criteria to establish a reasonable time period for substantiating expenses and returning excess amounts. Permanent advances, that is, standing amounts for which substantiation is not required, are wages at the time they are paid. [I.R.C. § 274(d); Treas. Reg. § 1.162-2(g)]

Example. Amherst Shipping advances $19,000 for the year to its salesperson, Sharon. It has no reasonable basis for expecting an employee's business expenses to exceed $1,000 in any quarter. When Sharon substantiates her expenses each quarter, Amherst Shipping will advance an additional amount equal to the substantiated amount. This creates a permanent advance of $19,000. The amount of this advance has not been determined based on anticipated expenses, and is not made within a reasonable period of the expected expenses to be incurred by the employee. This arrangement is made under a nonaccountable plan. Amherst Shipping must report its entire advance as wages on Sharon's Form W-2, and the advance is subject to federal income tax withholding, and FICA and FUTA taxes when the advance is made. Sharon may deduct, as an employee business expense on her Form 1040 tax return, substantiated expenses related to the advance.

Q 9:32   If an employer's accountable plan complies with the regulations structurally but procedural violations occur, is the plan still treated as an accountable plan?

Generally, yes. However, when an arrangement otherwise satisfies the accountable plan requirements but expenses frequently are not substantiated within a reasonable period of time, or amounts in excess of the substantiated expenses are seldom returned within a reasonable period of time, all payments made from the plan are treated as taxable wages. As noted earlier, the regulations permit the employer to apply a facts-and-circumstances test (rather than adopting one of the safe harbors) (see Q 9:31 for safe-harbor rules on time limits) to determine what constitutes a reasonable time period. As a result, an occasional failure to timely substantiate or return an excess payment should not cause an otherwise accountable plan to be treated as a nonaccountable plan, as long as the employer generally imposes a set of procedures that follow the IRS guidelines. There is no bright-line test for when repeated violations of these requirements result in a plan being treated as nonaccountable. [Treas. Reg. §§ 1.162-2(g)(1), 31.3121(a)-3, 31.3231(e)-3, 31.3306(b)-2, 31.3401(a)-4]

> **Example.** Samuel is given an advance of $5,100 on March 15 for travel and business expenses for a March 26 trip. His employer applies the fixed-date safe harbor for reimbursements. If Samuel returns on April 13 and does not submit his substantiated expenses within 100 days, his employer would be required to treat the entire $5,100 as paid under a nonaccountable plan and consider the advance as wages subject to employment tax and withholding, unless a factual determination by the employer could support a reasonable extension of the period (e.g., Samuel was in a location where it was not possible to submit his receipts and expense statement either electronically or by mail). If Samuel substantiates the expenses after the 100-day period and after they have been included in his gross income, the plan does not fail to be an accountable plan if it otherwise meets the substantiation requirements. Then only the amounts paid under the arrangement in excess of the properly substantiated amounts are treated as paid from a nonaccountable plan. [Treas. Reg. § 1.62-2(h)(2)]

Q 9:33   What are the employer's reporting and withholding responsibilities under an accountable plan?

The employer does not report substantiated business expense payments under an accountable plan in any box on the employee's Form W-2 because these payments are exempt from FIT, FITW, FICA, and FUTA. However, employers that provide a per diem or mileage allowance that exceeds the amount deemed to be substantiated (e.g., the federal rate) must include the excess per diem or mileage allowance in Form W-2, Boxes 1, 3, and 5, and report the amount that is equal to the federal maximum rate in Box 12 with Code L. The portion of a per diem or mileage allowance that is in excess of IRS-approved per diem or mileage allowance plan rates is treated as paid under a nonaccountable plan.

Q 9:34 Are payments made under a nonaccountable plan included in an employee's taxable wages?

Yes. All amounts paid under a nonaccountable plan are included in the employee's taxable wages and are subject to FIT, FITW, FICA, and FUTA. The employer must report payments made under a nonaccountable plan on Form W-2 (Boxes 1, 3, and 5) and withhold and report the associated tax.

An employee who receives taxable compensation for a valid business expense from a nonaccountable plan may be able to deduct the expense as an employee business expense (subject to the 2 percent threshold on adjusted gross income (AGI)) on his or her Form 1040 Schedule A.

Example. Cascade pays its salespeople $610 per day. On days a salesperson travels away from home on business, Cascade designates $150 of the $610 as a reimbursement for travel expenses. Because the payment is $610 per day whether or not the employee is traveling away from home, this payment is not made under an accountable plan; therefore, the full allowance must be reported on the employee's Form W-2 and is subject to federal income tax withholding, FICA, and FUTA. Note that although the full $610 is compensation to the employee, he or she may deduct as an employee business expense the amount of the actual business expense on Schedule A, Form 1040, subject to the 2 percent AGI limitation for such deductions. [Treas. Reg. § 1.162-2(i)]

Q 9:35 Can an employer provide payments from both accountable and nonaccountable plans under the same arrangement?

Payments from both an accountable and nonaccountable plan can be made under the same arrangement (e.g., the arrangement provides for reimbursement of substantiated business and personal nonbusiness expenses) where the payments can be treated as paid from two separate plans.

The part of the arrangement that provides payments for the excludable employee business expenses can be treated as its own separate arrangement when it satisfies the business connection test and otherwise meets the requirements for an accountable plan. The part of any arrangement that provides payments for nonbusiness expenses could then be treated as paid from a separate nonaccountable arrangement. The separation between payments made from the accountable and nonaccountable arrangements of the plan must be clearly identifiable. However, an accountable plan that fails to require that employees properly substantiate expenses and return excess amounts will be treated as a nonaccountable plan; in that case, all payments made from the plan will be treated as additional compensation, including expenses that would otherwise have been treated as paid from an accountable plan. That is, the IRS will not divide a business expense reimbursement plan into two components when it fails to fully follow the requirements for substantiation and taxation and reporting of nonaccountable plan payments.

> **Example.** A major airline pays an expense allowance to its pilots and flight attendants who travel away from their home base airports whether or not they are "away from home" under the tax rules. The employer treats the part of the arrangement that provides allowances for travel away from home as an accountable plan. The employer treats allowances for travel not away from home as being paid from a nonaccountable plan. Thus, the company must report the non-away-from-home allowances as wages on the employees' Forms W-2 and must withhold and pay employment taxes. [Treas. Reg. § 1.62-2(j), ex. 2]

Q 9:36   What are the advantages of nonaccountable plans?

Nonaccountable plans can eliminate the employer's handling of reimbursements and retention of additional supporting records. Under a nonaccountable plan, the employer merely pays a set taxable dollar amount to the employee without regard to the actual business expenses that will be incurred and without requiring substantiation. It is up to the employee to claim a business expense deduction when filing the Form 1040. The drawback to establishing such an arrangement is the potential for employment tax overpayments (e.g., Social Security and Medicare) because both the employer and employee will likely pay FICA on business-related reimbursements that could have been excluded from FICA had they been paid from an accountable plan. In addition, the employee may also pay more federal income tax under this arrangement because nonreimbursed employee business expenses are only deductible to the employee to the extent they exceed 2 percent of the employee's AGI. [Treas. Reg. §§ 1.62-2(c), 1.62-2(d), 1.62-2(h)]

Q 9:37   Must the provisions of the employer's substantiation requirements and deadlines for substantiation be part of a written accountable plan?

A written plan that includes the documentation requirements and deadlines for substantiation and return of excess is implied in the IRS guidelines. Having a written plan that includes these requirements ensures that substantiated expenses will not be treated as paid under a nonaccountable plan and subject to FIT, FITW, FICA, and FUTA. [Treas. Reg. § 1.62-2(e)(1)]

Q 9:38   When must an unsubstantiated expense reimbursement or advance be treated as wages subject to withholding and employment tax?

In general, if expenses are not substantiated to the employer within a reasonable period of time or amounts in excess of those substantiated are not returned, they must be treated as wages subject to FIT, FITW, FICA, and FUTA that are paid no later than the next payroll period following the date on which the reasonable period expired. [Treas. Reg. § 1.62-2(h)(2)]

Example. Employee Foster made travel arrangements through his employer's travel agent on April 15. Foster failed to submit an expense report and other substantiating documentation for this travel. Under the business expense policy, Foster is required to submit an expense report showing the time, place, and business purpose and travel receipts no later than 30 days following the date on which he books a ticket, or May 15. Foster is paid on the 5th and the 20th of the month. Foster's employer is required to include the April 15 travel charge in wages for withholding tax and reporting purposes no later than May 20, which is the next payroll period following May 15.

Per diem and mileage allowances. A per diem or mileage advance that is calculated at a rate that is in excess of the federal rate is treated as wages subject to FIT, FITW, FICA, and FUTA in the payroll period following the employee's substantiation of the advance (assuming, of course, that the substantiation occurred within a reasonable period of time as prescribed under the employer's policy). [Treas. Reg. § 1.62-2(h)(2)(i)(B)(3)]

Achievement Awards

Q 9:39   What is an achievement award?

An achievement award is a statutory classification for property (but not cash) that may be transferred to employees *without* the value of that property being treated as wages subject to FIT, FITW, FICA, and FUTA taxes. The I.R.C. provides for two types of achievement awards: a "length of service award" and a "safety award." Both of these award programs must satisfy certain requirements to be exempt from FIT, FITW, FICA, and FUTA. [I.R.C. § 274(j)]

An employer can exclude from the recipient's wages the FMV of all employee achievement awards provided to an employee during the year that do not exceed $400 for the plan year. A higher per-employee annual limit of $1,600 applies to "qualified plan awards"; however, a maximum average award value of $400 applies to all awards made in the year. An award qualifies as a qualified plan award if the award is made under a written plan that does not discriminate in favor of HCEs (as determined under the I.R.C.'s pension rules, i.e., more than 5 percent owners in the current or prior year or individuals who, for 2015, earned more than $120,000). [I.R.C. § 414(q)] See Q 9:318.

An award cannot be treated as a qualified plan award if the average cost per recipient of all awards in the year under an employer's qualified achievement plan is more than $400. *De minimis* awards are excluded from this average cost calculation. That is, an employer could not average three $5 awards and one $1,585 award to satisfy the $400 average cost threshold for a qualified plan award.

If during the year an employee receives awards made under a qualified safety award plan and receives awards under a qualified length of service award plan, the exclusion for the total cost of all awards to that employee cannot be more than $1,600. In addition, the $400 (nonwritten plan) and $1,600 (written plan) award limits cannot be aggregated to exceed $1,600 for any one employee during the year. IRS guidance specifically does not define the term *year* for purposes of measuring these dollar thresholds; however, the I.R.C. refers to the tax year of the employee (i.e., the calendar year). As a result, the dollar thresholds should be measured based on payments made in the calendar year. [I.R.C. §§ 74, 274(j)(4)]

Example. Bronco, Inc. provides a tablet valued at $900 to Phyllis as part of its length of service awards. For the year, the average cost of all achievement awards was $400. The plan is not a qualified plan award, and the excludable award benefits are limited to $400 per employee. Phyllis has additional compensation of $500 ($900 − $400) for the award.

Health awards not covered. Employers seeking to provide incentive to employees for changing behavior to lower health care costs have considered cash payments for certain activities. These payments cannot be considered achievement awards because they are not directly tied to length of service or safety. In addition, healthcare insurers have been offering cash rewards for healthy behavior; self-insured employers also have been offering such incentives. If the payments come from the health insurer, the insurer will (or should) issue a 1099-MISC to the recipient participant. If the payments come from the employer's self-insured plan, the payments should be included in the employee's Form W-2.

Q 9:40   What is a length of service award?

A length of service award is a noncash employee achievement award given to an employee for no reason other than having completed a specific period of employment with the employer. The exemption from federal income tax withholding, FICA, and FUTA applies to the value of the length of service award when two eligibility conditions are met: (1) the award is given to employees who have at least five years of employment with the employer and (2) the award is given to employees no more frequently than once every five years. Because these are employee achievement awards, the dollar threshold for achievement awards applies (e.g., $400 maximum or $1,600 for a qualified plan award). As with all achievement awards, there must be a ceremonial observance. [I.R.C. §§ 74(a), 274(j); Treas. Reg. § 1.74-1(a)]

Q 9:41   What is a safety award?

A safety award is a noncash employee achievement award given to an employee for meeting any employer-defined safety criteria. An exemption from federal income tax withholding, FICA and FUTA applies to the value of the award when two eligibility criteria are met: The award is not given to (1) more than 10 percent of the workforce in any one year, or to (2) managers, administrators, professional employees, or clerical employees. Because these are employee achievement awards, the dollar threshold for achievement awards applies (e.g., $400 maximum or $1,600 for a qualified plan award). [I.R.C. §§ 74, 274(j)(4)]

Q 9:42   What other requirements must be met for achievement awards to be provided on a tax-free basis?

To be excludable from the employee's wages, the award must be tangible personal property (not cash, travel vouchers, certificates, or securities, but could be a microwave, jewelry, or electronic equipment) given to an employee as either (1) a length of service award or (2) a safety achievement award. Basically, the award must be given as part of a meaningful presentation, and under circumstances that do not indicate that the payment is disguised compensation. That is, an employer cannot avoid federal employment taxes on a bonus by making the bonus a tangible gift under a disguised achievement award program. [I.R.C. §§ 3121(a)(20), 3306(b)(16), 3401(a)(19) I.R.C. 274(j)]

Example. Gwen, an assembly line employee who satisfies her employer's criteria for safety, is given a gaming console costing $400. The value of the award is not treated as taxable wages if it is part of a bona fide safety award program.

Q 9:43   What are the reporting requirements for achievement awards that are excluded from wages?

Achievement awards that are excluded from wages subject to FIT, FITW, FICA, and FUTA are not reported on Forms W-2, 940, or 941. [Pub. No. 15-A]

Q 9:44   What are the reporting requirements for achievement awards that are treated as wages?

An achievement award that does not meet the plan and eligibility requirements for either a safety award, a length of service award, or an award that exceeds the dollar limits, is treated as additional compensation subject to FIT, FITW, FICA, and FUTA as such is reported on Form W-2 in Boxes 1, 3, and 5. [I.R.C. § 61]

Q 9:45   Are not-for-profit employers permitted to implement an achievement award plan?

Yes. The language of I.R.C. Section 74(c) seemingly places a restriction on the ability of nonprofit entities to implement an achievement award, but practically speaking has not prevented not-for-profits from such implementation. Specifically, the statute refers to "amount allowable as a deduction" for permitting achievement awards, and not-for-profits do not utilize tax deductions because they are not subject to income tax. The section has been interpreted by practitioners to be applied to payments made from tax-exempt employers as if the not-for-profit entity was a taxable entity. [I.R.C. § 74(c)(3)]

Q 9:46   Does a special limitation apply to a length of service award for firefighters and emergency medical treatment workers?

Yes. A special tax-free award is available to certain volunteer firefighters and paramedics (or their beneficiaries). A state, political subdivision of a state, any agency or instrumentality of a state or subdivision of a state, and any other organization exempt from tax under I.R.C. Section 457 may provide certain length of service awards for volunteer firefighters, emergency medical service personnel, and ambulance driver personnel of up to $3,000 a year. Certain conditions apply to awards and other taxable payments made to such individuals. [I.R.C. § 457(e)(11)(B)]

Q 9:47   Has the IRS developed any guidelines for the structure of an achievement award?

No; however, the IRS has ruled on various plan designs that were not entitled to an exclusion. These include informal awards to salespeople initiated by a sales manager [Rev. Rul. 60-113, 1960-1 C.B. 382], prizes awarded by the employer to further the company's goals and objectives [Rev. Rul. 86-31, 1986-1 C.B. 75], and awards to employees for suggestions that improve productivity. [Rev. Rul. 70-471, 1970-2 C.B. 199]

Adoption Assistance

Q 9:48   What is an adoption assistance plan?

An adoption assistance plan is an employer-sponsored plan that either pays for, or reimburses employees for, qualified adoption expenses incurred when an employee adopts, or, in some cases, attempts to adopt, a child. Employer payments (even those exceeding the annual dollar threshold) under a "qualified" adoption assistance plan that satisfy I.R.C. Section 137 are exempt from FITW but are subject to FICA and FUTA. Special income and employment tax rules apply to adoption assistance benefits funded with Section 125 salary reductions under a cafeteria plan. No exclusion from FITW is available for more than 2 percent shareholders in a Subchapter S Corporation.

Note that the I.R.C. allows individuals to take a tax credit for certain qualified adoption assistance benefits. An employee may take advantage of both the full tax credit and full exclusion for employer payments as long as these separate tax benefits do not apply to the same expenses. [I.R.C. §§ 127(b)(3), 137(c)(2); Notice 97-9, 1997-2 I.R.B. 35; Pub. No. 968]

Qualified adoption assistance benefits include all reasonable and necessary fees, court costs, attorneys' fees, travel (including meals, lodging, and fare), and other expenses directly related to a legal adoption of a "qualified" child. The tax credit and exclusion from FITW is available for expenses relating to attempted adoption if the child is a citizen or resident of the United States and eventually another child is successfully adopted. The expenses of adopting a foreign child qualify only if they result in an adoption of that child. Also, no exclusion from FITW is provided for the reimbursement of expenses that relate to the adoption of a spouse's child. [I.R.C. §§ 23(d), 137(d)]

Cafeteria plans may include an adoption assistance plan. All of the adoption assistance requirements remain if the plan is included inside the cafeteria plan. See Q 9:49.

Q 9:49   What requirements apply to a qualified adoption assistance plan?

To be exempt from FITW, the plan benefits must meet the following requirements:

1. The benefits must be provided under a written plan.
2. The FITW exclusion for adoption assistance benefits per eligible child may not exceed $13,570 for 2017 (this is a maximum aggregate limit per child, not an annual limit). [Rev. Proc. 2010-40, 2010-46 I.R.B. 663]

   An eligible child is an individual who is under age 18, or who is physically or mentally incapable of caring for himself or herself at the time the assistance is provided. A child with special needs is a child who is a citizen or resident of the United States who cannot be or should not be, as determined by a state (or the District of Columbia), returned to his or her parents, and who is subject to a condition that the state has determined would otherwise impede the adoption without special assistance. Thus, no age limit applies to a child who is physically or mentally handicapped and is incapable of caring for himself or herself. These dollar limits apply to married couples, unmarried couples (who are treated as a single taxpayer), or unmarried individuals who are adopting. [I.R.C. § 23(d)]

   The IRS has proposed a revenue procedure that would establish certain safe harbors to determine the finality of the adoption of a foreign-born child, for purposes of the adoption credit and the exclusion for employer-provided adoption assistance. [Notice 2003-15, 2003-1 C.B. 540]

Note that although a taxpayer's exclusion from income taxes phases out based on annual earnings, employers need not consider the income phaseout for purposes of determining if the benefit is excluded from FITW. The employee should be reminded to file Form 8839, Qualified Adoption Expenses, with his or her personal income tax form to establish the amount of exclusion.

3. The plan cannot: (1) discriminate in favor of HCEs determined under the pension rules (individuals who are more than 5 percent owners in the current or prior year or who earned more than $120,000 for the preceding year); or (2) provide more than 5 percent of the total benefits to more than 5 percent owners. [I.R.C. § 414(q)] The same nondiscrimination rules that apply to educational assistance benefits under I.R.C. Section 127 apply to adoption assistance benefits, per I.R.C. Section 137(c)(2).

Qualified expenses do not include surrogate parenting. The income tax exclusion and the related exemption from FITW for adoption assistance benefits increased with the passage of the Patient Protection and Affordable Care Act and the credit was temporarily made refundable. The American Taxpayer Relief Act of 2012 (ATRA) eliminated the credit as a refundable credit. The credit was also made permanent. [Pub. L. No. 112-240; Pub. L. No. 111-148; Pub. L. No. 107-16; I.R.C. § 137(f); Notice 97-9, 1997-2 I.R.B. 35; Ann. 97-64, 1997-26 I.R.B. 9]

Q 9:50   Can an adoption assistance benefit be provided under a cafeteria plan?

Yes. An adoption assistance benefit is specifically authorized as a permitted benefit under I.R.C. Section 125. [I.R.C. § 137(c)] Thus, a cafeteria plan (a Section 125 plan) may be established that permits an employee to make salary reduction contributions under a cafeteria plan to an adoption assistance flexible spending account (FSA) to obtain reimbursements for qualified expenses. Salary reductions (i.e., pretax deductions) for an adoption assistance benefit under a cafeteria plan are exempt from FITW but are subject to FICA and FUTA. [Notice 97-9, 1997-2 I.R.B. 35; Pub. No. 968]

A cafeteria plan providing for adoption assistance benefits can also permit mid-plan-year changes in the employee's benefit elections upon the commencement or termination of an adoption proceeding. [Prop. Treas. Reg. § 1.125-4(c)(2)(iv)]

Note that the at-risk rules (sometimes referred to as the "use it or lose it" rules) that are imposed under the cafeteria regulations also apply to adoption assistance benefits. These at-risk rules require that any unreimbursed salary deductions be forfeited at the end of the plan year. That is, unused amounts may not be carried forward to a subsequent year. For this reason, adoption assistance FSA participation must be carefully planned. If an expected adoption is not completed during a given plan year, in some circumstances, the participant will forfeit dollars contributed to the FSA. Similarly, although termination of adoption proceedings is a qualified reason to cease contributions to an adoption assistance FSA, funds that have already been contributed may not be returned to the plan participant, except via qualified claims of adoption expense. [Prop. Treas. Reg. § 1.125-1, Q&A 28]

Q 9:51   What is the employment tax treatment of adoption assistance benefits?

An employer excludes from FITW any payments for substantiated and qualified adoption expenses for eligible children. This exclusion from FITW applies even if the employee's AGI is in excess of the income threshold of $203,540 but is completely phased out for taxpayers with modified adjusted gross income of $243,540 or more in 2017. (Note the FITW exclusion limit of adoption assistance benefits of $13,570 (for 2017) applies to each child and is not an annual limit.) Adoption assistance benefits are, however, not exempt from FICA and FUTA. [Prop. Treas. Reg. § 1.125-1, Q&A 28]

Q 9:52   What is the substantiation requirement for adoption assistance benefits?

The employee must provide adequate records (including receipts) (e.g., meet the basic substantiation requirements, except for the business connection requirement) to demonstrate that the reimbursement or payment of adoption assistance benefits is for a qualifying expense. [I.R.C. § 137(c)]

Q 9:53   How are adoption assistance benefits reported?

All adoption assistance benefits (employer-provided benefits and employee pretax contributions to an adoption assistance flexible spending account) are subject to Social Security and Medicare and are reported in Boxes 3 and 5. For 2017, adoption assistance benefits in excess of $13,570 per qualifying adoption ($13,460 for 2016) are included in wages taxable for FIT, FICA, and FUTA and are reported in Form W-2, Boxes 1, 3, and 5. All employer-provided adoption assistance benefits and adoption assistance expenses that were paid or reimbursed from pretax contributions made by an employee pursuant to an adoption assistance flexible spending account are reported in Box 12 with code T. Per the Form W-2 reporting instructions, amounts forfeited from an adoption assistance flexible spending account are not included in the amount reported in Box 12, code T. [Ann. 96-134, 1996-53 I.R.B. 60]

Q 9:54   Are there any reporting requirements that employees receiving adoption assistance benefits should consider?

Employees who receive qualified adoption assistance benefits are required to report those benefits on Form 8839, Qualified Adoption Expenses, when they file their Form 1040. This reporting is used to coordinate the tax credit and tax-free benefit associated with adoption assistance expenses. An employee may not claim a tax credit and an income exclusion for the same expense. [Ann. 96-134, 1996-53 I.R.B. 60]

Advances and Loans

Q 9:55 How are advances and loans to employees treated for employment tax purposes?

Salary advances and draws are treated as wages subject to FIT, FITW, FICA, and FUTA at the time they are paid; however, expense advances paid under an accountable plan are excluded from wages subject to FIT, FITW, FICA, and FUTA. Amounts paid under a bona fide loan arrangement meeting the IRS requirements are not included in wages subject to FIT, FITW, FICA, and FUTA until the day on which the employer can no longer reasonably expect that the loan balance will be repaid.

An employer cannot recharacterize wages as expense advances or loans to delay or evade the FIT, FITW, FICA, or FUTA requirements. [Rev. Rul. 68-239, 1968-1 C.B. 414; Rev. Rul. 68-238, 1968-1 C.B. 420]

Q 9:56 How does the employer handle repayment of an advance that was previously treated as additional compensation?

An employee who repays an advance that was previously treated as wages may not be treated as not having received that additional compensation for federal income taxes based on when the repayment is made. When the advance is repaid in the same calendar year that the advance was treated as additional compensation, an adjustment can be made on the employee's records, and no wages for federal income tax withholding, FICA taxes, and FUTA taxes for the amount of the advance will be reported on the employee's Form W-2.

Federal taxable wages and income tax withholding. If the employee makes the repayment in a subsequent calendar year, no adjustment in reportable wages for federal income taxes reported or withheld is permitted for the year in which the advance was reported. The repaid amount may be taken as a deduction (and in certain situations a credit for tax paid may be available) by the employee on his or her income tax return (Form 1040) subject to the limitations set forth in IRS Publication 525. When repayment is made in a subsequent year, the employer will generally require that the gross amount of the advance be repaid.

Social Security, Medicare wages, and FUTA wages. The FICA treatment of a repayment differs from federal income tax withholding. A repayment or previously reported advance in a subsequent year requires correction of amounts reported to the Social Security Administration (SSA). The employer will be required to file a corrected Form W-2 (Form W-2c) and make an adjustment on the Form 941 for the period of the repayment. The employer may obtain a credit for employer FICA tax paid on the adjustment and a refund of employer FICA withholding taxes if the employee signs a statement that he or she will not request a FICA refund. The employer may also be able to request a credit for FUTA taxes paid in the year the advance was reported as wages. This credit is available only if wages for that year (after subtracting the repaid amount) do not exceed $7,000. [Form W-2 instructions]

These issues frequently arise when the employer makes an advance to an employee with repayment conditioned on the employee's continued employment (e.g., a relocation bonus with a portion that must be repaid if the employee leaves the job within 12 months). This payment is treated as compensation when paid to the employee. A repayment could occur in a subsequent year and a Form W-2c would be required for the tax year the relocation bonus was paid.

Q 9:57 What is the tax limit of a loan balance for a terminated employee?

An outstanding balance of a loan or advance that was not previously treated as wages is generally treated as additional wages for FIT, FITW, FICA, and FUTA purposes when the employee is no longer obligated to repay the amount. As a result, unpaid loan balances generally are treated as wages at the time the employee terminates unless the terminated employee agrees to continue making the installment payments required under the loan agreement or otherwise satisfies the loan balance. When an employer forgives an employee's loan balance, the amount that is forgiven by the employer is treated as wages subject to FIT, FITW, FICA, and FUTA. [Rev. Rul. 68-239, 1968-1 C.B. 414; Rev. Rul. 68-238, 1968-1 C.B. 420]

Q 9:58 Do special reporting rules apply for large employee loans?

Yes. Portions of large employee loans may result in additional wages to the employee even if the employee is liable for the full repayment of the loan. Employee loans that exceed a daily aggregate balance of $10,000 create "imputed interest income" on the value of the interest that was not charged or that was computed at a below-market interest rate. This imputed income results in additional wages to the employee each year equal to the difference between the market interest rate the employee would have paid and the rate that the employee actually pays. These additional wages are subject to FIT, FICA, and FUTA taxes and are reported as wages on the employee's Form W-2, but FITW is not required. Market rate interest is determined based on the "applicable federal rate" made public by the IRS in monthly tables. [I.R.C. §§ 1274(d), 7872]

A special exception to this imputed interest rule applies for certain large relocation loans used to purchase a new home when made to employees because of a job relocation, when the move qualifies for a moving expense deduction. [I.R.C. § 7872-1; Treas. Reg. § 1.7872]

Q 9:59 How is "imputed" interest income calculated on large employee loans?

Imputed interest income is an additional wage payment that arises when employees obtain favorable interest rates—or are not charged any interest—on large loans (more than a $10,000 aggregate daily balance per employee) from their employers. The employee is treated as having additional wages (an amount of interest income is imputed) equal to the difference between interest calculated at the federal interest rate determined on the date the loan was made and the interest the employee actually pays. [I.R.C. § 7872; Temp. Treas. Reg. § 1.7872.L5T]

The federal rate applied to calculate the amount of imputed interest income is determined under the following table:

Term of Loan	Applicable Federal Rate
Not over 3 years	The federal short-term rate
Over 3 years but not over 9 years	The federal mid-term rate
Over 9 years	The federal long-term rate

The federal rates are updated and published each month by the IRS.

Example. Shaun is the general manager of a financial planning firm. On August 1, she is given a $42,000 interest-free loan from her employer payable over a 10-year period. The purpose of the loan is to build an extension on her home (i.e., not related to a job relocation) while providing an incentive for Shaun to stay with her current employer. The loan is to be repaid in quarterly payments after the fourth year and must be repaid upon the earlier of 10 years or when she terminates employment. The federal long-term rate is 1.56 percent on the date the loan is made. Shaun has $655.20 in imputed interest for the first year of the loan ($42,000 × 1.56).

Q 9:60   How are interest-free or below-market loans reported for employment tax purposes?

The additional compensation (i.e., imputed interest) that arises from an interest-free or below-market interest loan is subject to federal income tax, FICA, Medicare, and FUTA, but not to FITW.

Include in Boxes 1, 3, and 5 of the employee's Form W-2 the imputed interest income arising from the loan (or Form 1099-MISC for below-market loans made to an independent contractor; e.g., director). [I.R.C. §§ 3121(a), 3306(b), 7872(f)(9)(B), 7872(b), 7872(c) Reg. § 1.7872-11(d); Pub. No. 535]

Athletic Facilities

Q 9:61   May on-premises employer-provided athletic facilities be treated as a tax-free benefit?

Yes. Under I.R.C. Section 132(j), employees may be given access to and may use certain on-premises athletic facilities without the value of that use being treated as wages subject to FIT, FITW, FICA, and FUTA. Athletic-facility benefits generally include a pool, tennis court, golf course, health club, yoga and other physical fitness instructors, or similar facilities. The use of these facilities by employees is not subject to FIT, FITW, FICA, or FUTA as long as three conditions are met: (1) the facility must be on the employer's premises (although not necessarily the same place where the employee provides services); (2) the facility must be operated by the employer; and (3) substantially all of the use of the facility must be by employees, former employees, and their spouses and dependents.

No exclusion from FIT, FITW, FICA, and FUTA applies to the value of the facility if the athletic facility is available to the general public through the sale of memberships or rental of the facilities. For example, no exclusion from FIT, FITW, FICA, and FUTA is available if the facility is part of a resort that is used by the guests or residents of the resort. Nor is the exclusion available when the employer merely pays the membership fees of employees who join a health or country club; such benefits are treated as additional wages and are subject FIT, FITW, FICA, and FUTA.

Note that there are no nondiscrimination requirements that would cause such benefits offered only to HCEs to be taxable, as long as the other requirements are met. [I.R.C. §§ 132(j)(4), 3121(a)(20), 3306(b)(16), 3401(a)(19); Treas. Reg. §§ 1.132-1(b)(3), 1.132-1(f)(5)]

Q 9:62 Is the value of on-site athletic facilities provided to employees subject to federal employment taxes?

No. As long as access to the facilities meets the requirements of I.R.C. Section 132(j), the value of an employee's use of such facilities is exempt from FIT, FITW, FICA, and FUTA. If the use of the athletic facilities does not qualify as a tax-free fringe benefit under this section, then the FMV of such use is treated as additional wages and is subject to FIT, FITW, FICA, and FUTA. [I.R.C. §§ 132(j)(4), 3121(a)(20), 3306(b)(16)]

Q 9:63 Can an employer pay for or reimburse an employee for an off-site athletic facility as a tax-free fringe benefit?

No. Such benefits will be treated as additional wages and are subject to FIT, FITW, FICA, and FUTA. Even if the employees believe they will make use of the facility membership to conduct business, such membership fees are not a permitted tax-free fringe benefit. However, see Q 9:108 regarding club dues.

Awards, *De Minimis*

Q 9:64 What is a *de minimis* award?

A *de minimis* award is a gift of a service or property (other than cash), the value of which is so small that accounting for it is administratively impractical. The value of these noncash awards can generally be treated as working-condition fringe benefits and is exempt from FIT, FITW, FICA, and FUTA.

A *de minimis* award is generally subject to a frequency condition (i.e., the award or gift must be provided on an infrequent and sporadic basis). A cash or refundable voucher will never qualify as a *de minimis* award. Thus, for example, gift certificates and gift cards are not *de minimis* and are treated as wages subject to FIT, FITW, FICA, and FUTA.

Example. The CFO of Jarama Space, Inc. gave Jenny tickets to a Denver concert because Jenny's performance on a project was exceptional. This could be treated as a *de minimis* award; however, a cash or refundable voucher will never qualify as a *de minimis* award. Accordingly, a debit card given to an employee to pay for those same tickets would be treated as income. [Treas. Reg. § 1.132-6(c)]

Q 9:65 Are awards other than safety or length of service awards subject to employment taxes?

Yes. Any awards, whether paid in cash or another medium, that do not satisfy the requirements of I.R.C. Sections 74 and 274 or that cannot be classified as *de minimis* fringe benefits are treated as additional wages and are subject to FIT, FITW, FICA, and FUTA. [I.R.C. § 61; Prop. Treas. Reg. § 1.74-2] This rule must be strictly applied.

The I.R.C. does permit a special wage withholding exemption for certain noncash sales achievement awards given to commissioned salespersons. Such noncash awards may be excluded from FITW, but are subject to FIT (reported in Form W-2, Box 1), FICA, and FUTA. [I.R.C. § 3402(j); Treas. Reg. § 31.3402(j)-1; Rev. Rul. 96-65, 1996-2 C.B. 6]

Back-Pay Awards

Q 9:66 What are back-pay awards?

Back-pay awards are employer payments that result from an employee's claim for prior underpaid or unpaid wages. These generally arise from a lawsuit or settlement over wages that are the result of an alleged Fair Labor Standards Act (FLSA) or other federal or state labor law violation. In some cases, back pay may also include payment for punitive or emotional distress damages, attorneys' fees, and interest.

Q 9:67 How are back-pay awards treated for employment tax purposes?

In most cases, employers treat back pay as wages for all purposes in the period when the back-pay award is paid. However, back pay is reported and credited for Social Security benefits (and eligibility for benefits) in the year when earned (not paid) if awarded under a state or federal statute (e.g., Age Discrimination in Employment Act, Americans with Disabilities Act, FLSA, state minimum wage laws, and state laws that protect an individual's right to work and right to wages).

Legal fees, punitive damages, and interest awarded by a court are not treated as wages even though they may be subject to federal income taxes. [Rev. Rul. 80-364, 1980-2 C.B. 294; Rev. Rul. 78-336, 1978-2 C.B. 255]

Most damages for back pay are generally subject to FIT, FITW, FICA, and FUTA when paid to an employee. Only damage awards made on or after August 20, 1986, in payment for physical injuries or physical sickness are excludable from FIT, FITW, FICA, and FUTA taxes. [I.R.C. § 104(a)(2)] When no employment relationship exists, some courts have held that amounts paid for any purpose are not FIT, FITW, FICA, or FUTA. This position is generally rejected by the IRS. [Churchill v. Star Enters., 81 A.F.T.R.2d (RIA) 98-703 (E.D. Pa. 1998)]

A payment of back pay should be reported on the Form W-2 in Boxes 1, 3, and 5 for the year when paid. [I.R.C. §§ 3101(a), 3101(b), 3111(a); Rev. Rul. 89-35, 1989-1 C.B. 900; United States v. Cleveland Indians Baseball Co., 532 U.S. 200 (2001)] The IRS requires employers to report payments for punitive and emotional distress on Form 1099-MISC in Box 3.

Q 9:68   How are back-pay awards treated for FICA and FUTA purposes?

Back pay is treated as wages for FICA and FUTA purposes in the period when received, even if for wages owed in a prior period. Thus, the payment is included in Boxes 1, 3, and 5 of the employer's Form W-2 in the year paid, even if the back pay is reportable to the SSA for a prior period. [I.R.C. §§ 3101(a), 3101(b), 3111(a), 3111(b); Rev. Rul. 89-25, 1989-1 C.B. 280; Priv. Ltr. Rul. 9635013 (Aug. 30, 1996); United States v. Cleveland Indians Baseball Co., 532 U.S. 200 (2001)]

Q 9:69   How are back-pay awards under a state or federal statute reported for a prior period?

When back pay is awarded by a court for claims arising under a federal or state (but not local) statute, employers include these payments and related taxes on Form W-2 for the year when paid and not for the year in which the back pay was earned. [Pub. No. 957]

A payment of back pay is treated as awarded under a federal or state statute if the payment is made pursuant to an award or determination approved by a court or the government agency responsible for enforcing the federal or state statute. Back-pay awards can be made pursuant to any of the following laws (this list is not all-inclusive): the Age Discrimination in Employment Act, Equal Pay Act, Civil Rights Act, FLSA, Family and Medical Leave Act (FMLA), or state minimum wage, child labor, or other state law protecting an individual's employment rights.

Back-pay awards that restore an individual's right to work or to past wages that are negotiated out of court are generally not treated as made under a federal or state statute unless approved by a court. For example, back-pay awards that result in retroactive pay increases under a collective bargaining agreement are not treated as paid under a federal or state statute.

Reporting of wages (but not compensatory damages, attorneys' fees, or interest) for Social Security benefits purposes requires that such wages be reported to the SSA for the period when earned. The SSA should be advised of payments made in the current year for back pay awarded under a statute for prior years. The employer sends a statement to the SSA (not Form W-2 or Form W-2c) so that it may update the employee's records. The employer prepares a special report to the SSA that includes the following information: (1) the employer's name, employer identification number (EIN), and address; (2) the name and phone number of a contact person; and (3) a listing of employees who are receiving the back-pay payment showing each employee's name, Social Security number, amount of pay to be reported in each prior period (excluding amounts received as damages), total amount of other wages paid in the periods to which the back pay is being awarded, and amount of any back pay that is subject to Social Security or Medicare taxes.

IRS Publication 957, Reporting Back Pay and Special Wage Payments to the Social Security Administration, has instructions for reporting to the SSA back pay under a statute and other compensation that was paid to employees in a year subsequent to the year earned. The SSA accepts special wage reports on paper using Form 131 (contained in Publication 957) or a paper listing as outlined in Publication 957. The paper listing is filed with the local Social Security office. The SSA's Business Services Online (BSO) can accept special wage payment reports electronically. For questions concerning the electronic filing of special wage payments, employers are asked to contact the regional employer services liaison officer (ESLO). SSA's BSO as well as a directory of the ESLO representatives are available in Publication EFW2 at www.socialsecurity.gov.

Bonus Payments

Q 9:70   How are bonus payments treated for federal employment tax purposes?

Bonus payments are generally subject to FIT, FITW, FICA, and FUTA at the time they are paid. (Exceptions apply to nonqualified deferral compensation. See Q 9:331.) The amount of federal income tax to withhold may be determined by adding the payment to the employee's other wages for the most recent period and applying the appropriate withholding using one of the tables, then subtracting the tax that was already withheld. Alternatively, the employer may withhold a flat 25 percent for payments made in 2015. [Rev. Rul. 66-190, 1966-2 C.B. 457; I.R.C. § 3402(o)]. In 2015, the flat supplemental withholding rate is 39.6 percent for supplemental payments in excess of $1 million (see Q 2:92).

Q 9:71   Are there special rules for retention bonuses?

Yes. There is a special issue with regard to the bankruptcy of the employee. The Bankruptcy Code provides, effective October 17, 2005, that retention bonuses may not be paid and avoid the bankruptcy estate unless the payment is essential to retaining the person because that person has a "bona fide job offer from another business" with equal or greater compensation, and the services provided by that person are "essential to the survival of the business." Furthermore, Section 503(c) places caps on the amounts of such bonuses, limiting retention bonuses for key employees to 10 times the amount of similar payments given to nonmanagement employees for any purpose (during the year in which such payment is made) or if no such similar payments were made, the amount of the retention bonus cannot be greater than an amount equal to 25 percent of the amount of any similar payments made to such insider for any purpose during the previous year in which the payment is made.

Q 9:72   How is a "signing bonus" treated for federal employment tax purposes?

Amounts that an employer pays as bonuses for signing or ratifying a contract in connection with an employer–employee relationship are wages for FIT, FITW, FICA, FUTA. [Rev. Rul. 2004-109, 2004-50 I.R.B. 958] Prior to 2005, when a bonus was for signing a contract, which had no provisions for performance of services at a later date, the payment was not wages subject to federal income tax withholding. [Rev. Rul. 58-145, 1958-1 C.B. 360]

Q 9:73   What is push money?

Push money is a type of incentive payment generally made by a manufacturer to salespeople employed by a retailer. The payment is designed to encourage the salespeople to "push" a specific product. The IRS originally stated in Revenue Ruling 70-337 that when push money is paid by the manufacturer, the payments are treated as being paid by an entity other than an employer and such amounts are not subject to withholding and employment taxes, though they are fully subject to federal income taxes. The IRS also held in this ruling that this same principle can apply when the payment is made through the employer. Under such an arrangement, the manufacturer authorizes the employer to make the push money payments and then reimburses the employer. [Rev. Rul. 70-337, 1970-1 C.B. 191]

Later, in two private letter rulings, the IRS took a different position, holding that push money was paid for services rendered. One ruling focused on self-employment taxation, commenting that push money paid by an automobile manufacturer was not self-employment income because "the payment may be subject to [federal] income tax withholding and [FICA] and [FUTA] taxes." This ruling was made, perhaps, because the large value of the payments was found by the IRS to be for services rendered. [Priv. Ltr. Rul. 9423004, June 10, 1994]

The second ruling focused solely on the FICA taxation of push money payments made by a dealer. The IRS held that the push money was compensation for services rendered and was subject to FICA taxes. Presumably the same treatment would apply to federal income tax withholding and FUTA. [Tech. Adv. Mem. 9525003, Jun. 23, 1995]

In light of this most recent IRS guidance, employers are prudent to treat as imputed income subject to federal income tax, federal income tax withholding, Social Security, Medicare and FUTA all push money that is paid directly to employees by a third party. Alternatively, third-party payers of push money could be asked to make the payments directly to the employer for distribution to employees. Under the latter approach, the employer can withhold federal income, Social Security and Medicare taxes from the push money at the time it is paid to employees.

Cafeteria Plans

Q 9:74   What is a cafeteria plan?

Cafeteria plans (sometimes referred to as flexible benefit plans or Section 125 plans) are employer arrangements that permit participants (employees and some former employees) to choose between cash wages (or a taxable benefit) and certain qualified benefits (i.e., nontaxable benefits). See Q 9:84 for a discussion of benefits permitted to be offered under an I.R.C. Section 125 plan.

The cash election generally involves employees' agreement to reduce their wages to obtain a tax-free benefit. If the employee elects a "qualified benefit" (i.e., tax-free benefit), the employee contributions to the plan in the form of salary reductions ("pretax contributions") are excluded from the employee's wages for FIT, FITW, FICA, and FUTA purposes. (Note that salary deferrals for adoption assistance are subject to FICA and FUTA but excluded from FITW.) This tax benefit is available only when the plan satisfies all the requirements of I.R.C. Section 125 and each benefit provided satisfies the I.R.C. requirements applicable to that benefit.

A cafeteria plan must generally offer a choice between taxable and nontaxable benefits. A plan that merely gives an employee a choice between two nontaxable benefits (e.g., health benefits under either a health maintenance organization [HMO] or a preferred provider organization [PPO]), without also including the element of a reduction of wages, is not a Section 125 plan. This can be a confusing point. When an employee elects to contribute toward the cost of employer-provided health insurance in lieu of receiving the same amount in wages, that employee has chosen a "benefit" rather than "cash." That choice must take place under the provisions of a Section 125 plan for that choice between cash and benefits to be tax preferred. Most Section 125 plans are funded through elective employee contributions—also referred to as salary reductions or pretax contributions. If an employee's salary reduction election satisfies the requirements of I.R.C. Section 125, the dollar amount of the election is exempt from FIT, FITW, FICA, and FUTA (although salary reductions that are made as 401(k) salary deferrals or that are made for adoption assistance benefits are subject to FICA and FUTA taxes). [I.R.C. § 125; Prop. Treas. Reg. § 1.125-1, Q&As 1, 2]

In 2007, IRS published proposed rules on cafeteria plans under I.R.C. Section 125. [72 Fed. Reg. 43938-01, 2007-39 I.R.B. 681] The proposed rules "generally preserve the rules of the existing proposed regulations, while adding clarifications" relating to law changes and guidance issued since the previous rules were issued, according to a news release issued by the IRS and the Treasury Department. The proposed rules would generally be effective for plan years beginning on or after January 1, 2009. The IRS said taxpayers may rely on the proposed rules until final rules are issued. As of late 2008, practitioners are still awaiting the issuance of the final rules, but it is assumed that the proposed rules should continue to be relied upon.

The proposed regulations confirm that the only way a plan sponsor may offer employees a choice between taxable and nontaxable benefits is through a separate written cafeteria plan (consisting of one or more documents) that complies with the requirements of I.R.C. Section 125. The cafeteria plan (or amendments to an existing cafeteria plan) must be adopted and effective on or before the first day of the plan year when choices are permitted (or before the first day an amendment takes effect). The proposed regulations clarify that the plan must contain certain required elements, including a description of the benefits offered through the plan; rules governing participation, employee elections, and contributions; special requirements applicable to any health care, dependent care, or adoption assistance flexible spending account (FSA); and provisions for contributions and distributions to a health savings account (HSA) (if offered). Plans that include health care or dependent care FSAs must also describe any grace period rules that have been adopted.

Failure to meet the written plan rules—or failure to operate according to the terms of the written plan—would mean the plan is not a Section 125 cafeteria plan. As a result, employees would be subject to taxation on the value of the taxable benefit with the greatest value that they could have elected to receive. For example, if written documents that address all the specific items required by the proposed regulations were not in place by January 1, 2010, the premiums paid under a premium conversion plan would be taxable income to covered employees for 2010.

Q 9:75   What fringe benefits or welfare benefits does Section 125 provide?

I.R.C. Section 125 really offers no fringe benefits or welfare benefits itself; it merely serves to block the application of the doctrine of constructive receipt when the employee elects to reduce his or her pay and have it paid to the plan. That is, Section 125 is only the mechanism for making before-tax salary deferrals to obtain certain welfare benefits. However, Section 125 does dictate which employer-sponsored benefits may be offered on a tax-preferred basis, using the Section 125 plan as a vehicle for tax avoidance. In other areas of the I.R.C., an employee's right to receive wages is treated as taxable wages and subject to all federal employment taxes, regardless of whether the wages are taken or used for some other purpose. The typical small cafeteria plan allows an employee to purchase a benefit (e.g., medical insurance) and pay for that benefit through a before-tax salary reduction election. The I.R.C. treats a valid election to forgo wages under a cafeteria plan as a reduction in wages at the time the election is made. Without application of the rules of Section 125, any choice made by an employee would be taxable, even if used for the purchase of benefits that are not taxable as income when paid by an employer. The amount of the election is then exempt from FIT, FITW, FICA and FUTA, unless the benefit provided under the plan is subject to FICA and FUTA (e.g., a 401(k) contribution or adoption assistance benefits). [Prop. Treas. Reg. § 1.125-1, Q&A 4]

Q 9:76   What are the basic requirements for a Section 125 plan?

A Section 125 plan must: (1) be a written plan that is communicated to employees, (2) satisfy certain eligibility and nondiscrimination requirements, (3) provide a choice between cash (or a taxable benefit) and qualified tax-free benefits, and (4) impose certain restrictions on a change of salary reduction elections during the plan year. [I.R.C. § 125]

Q 9:77   What are the eligibility and nondiscrimination requirements that apply to cafeteria plans?

A cafeteria plan must satisfy the following three eligibility and nondiscrimination requirements of I.R.C. Section 125:

1. The plan must not discriminate as to eligibility in favor of "highly compensated individuals" with respect to the plan's participation rules. The term "highly compensated individual" is defined under Section 125(e) and Proposed Treasury Regulations Section 1.125-1, Q&A 13. This definition differs somewhat from that of the group of employees classified as highly compensated employees for pension purposes under I.R.C. Section 414(q);

2. The plan must not discriminate in favor of "highly compensated participants" with respect to contributions and benefits under the plan; and

3. The total value of all benefits provided to "key employees," as defined in I.R.C. Section 416(i)(1), does not exceed 25 percent of the total benefits provided. This test is referred to as the 25 percent concentration test (see Q 9:81). [I.R.C. §§ 125(b), 125(c), 125(e)] Of these three tests, only the 25 percent concentration test has a specific mathematical formula that can be readily applied. Section 125(g)(3)(a) indicates that the nondiscriminatory classification tests for pension plans under Section 410(b) can be applied to determine if the plan's eligibility is nondiscriminatory, as required in

item 1 in the preceding list. This criterion for item 2 is met when all eligibility requirements (e.g., a minimum age and service requirement) for highly compensated individuals also apply to non-highly compensated individuals.

Example. A cafeteria plan offered by a banking firm to its employees permits a new COO, who is a "highly compensated employee" under the regulations, to enter on his date of hire but requires a staff employee to work 90 days. This plan does not satisfy the first requirement listed above. As a result, the tax-free benefits available to the highly compensated individuals in the plan are not excluded from those individuals' wages under Section 125. (The highly compensated individuals' salary reductions are wages subject to all federal employment taxes.) [I.R.C. § 125(b)(1)(A)]

In a situation where the employer wishes to provide a benefit on a more favorable (quicker) timeframe to certain individuals, the employer should offer the benefit on a taxable basis to that individual until he or she has met the standard eligibility requirements for the plan. The preceding example could have a different outcome if the employer permitted the newly hired employee to participate in health coverage, but with aftertax dollars rather than pretax dollars. This has a tax impact on the one individual for a limited period of time, but does not jeopardize all other highly compensated plan participants.

Q 9:78   Who are the "prohibited groups" for nondiscrimination testing of cafeteria plans?

Nondiscrimination testing under Section 125 requires that employers identify four classes of employees in whose favor the plan may not discriminate: highly compensated individuals, highly compensated participants, HCEs, and key employees. These classes are identified as the "prohibited groups" for which the separate nondiscrimination testing of a cafeteria plan must be applied. Each of the Section 125 nondiscrimination tests looks to a separate prohibited group classification. This can be confusing to a person not accustomed to these terms. In many cases, especially for smaller employers, the population in the key employee group is the same as the individuals in the HCE group. It is important to clearly identify which test is being applied to which prohibited group.

A highly compensated individual, for purposes of the Section 125 eligibility test, includes any individual who is (1) an officer, (2) a shareholder owning more than 5 percent of the voting power or value of all classes of stock, (3) an employee who is highly compensated (no guidance is provided on this definition; the determination is based on all the facts and circumstances), or (4) a spouse or dependent of any one of the preceding. [I.R.C. § 125(e); Prop. Treas. Reg. § 1.125-1, Q&A 13] Note that although nondiscrimination in eligibility testing applies to individuals classified in the I.R.C. as "highly compensated individuals," the IRS has said informally that an employer may, in lieu of this term, apply the pension definitions to nondiscrimination testing when no definite rules are available. This testing would demonstrate good-faith compliance with the I.R.C. requirements. However, if the facts and circumstances warrant it, it may be possible to classify a person as "highly compensated" who would not, otherwise, be defined as such for retirement plan testing. For example, the most highly placed administrator in a not-for-profit organization may not meet the highly compensated definition requirements, and yet, may be classified, for testing purposes, as highly compensated.

A "highly compensated participant" is defined as a "highly compensated individual" who is also a participant in the cafeteria plan. The nondiscrimination tests for benefits provided under the plan apply to highly compensated participants.

For the definitions of which individuals constitute HCEs or key employees, see Qs 9:318 and 9:320.

Q 9:79   How is the nondiscrimination in eligibility test satisfied for cafeteria plans?

This nondiscrimination requirement for eligibility under a cafeteria plan under Section 125 looks at the individuals who are eligible to participate in the plan (i.e., are covered). The plan's coverage must satisfy all four of the following requirements:

1. The plan must benefit a classification of employees that is not found by the IRS to discriminate in favor of HCEs. This testing follows both the definition of HCEs and the classification tests for pension plans under Sections 414(q) and 410(b).
2. The plan may not require an employee to complete more than three years of employment with the employer as a condition of participation in the plan.
3. The length of service required for eligibility to participate must be the same for all employees.
4. Employees meeting the plan's service requirements (item 2) must be permitted to participate no later than the first day of the first plan year beginning after that requirement is satisfied. [Prop. Treas. Reg. § 1.125-1, Q&As 9, 10, 19]

Note. The testing for eligibility under a Section 125 plan does not take the place of any eligibility testing that may be required for any plan offered through the cafeteria plan. Accordingly, the failure to test an underlying plan of the cafeteria plan will result in a problem under both of the two plans. For example, the failure to test a dependent care reimbursement plan under a cafeteria plan could result in a highly compensated employee having to pay taxes on the benefit under the dependent care plan; if the cafeteria plan is not tested, the participant may have to pay taxes on all of the other plans thereunder.

Q 9:80   How is the nondiscrimination in benefits test satisfied for cafeteria plans?

The nondiscriminatory benefits or contribution requirements of Section 125(c) are met when the plan's nontaxable and total benefits—or the employer contributions allocable to the purchase of these benefits—do not discriminate in favor of highly compensated participants. There is no specific IRS guidance on how to satisfy this requirement, although employers should attempt to document their having met this requirement.

The IRS does provide a special safe harbor rule for testing employer contributions for discrimination in health benefits under a cafeteria plan. Under this safe harbor, a plan is not discriminatory when the employer's contribution (including salary reductions) on behalf of each participant equals: (1) 100 percent of the health benefit cost for the majority of highly compensated participants who are similarly situated (e.g., have single or family coverage) or (2) 75 percent of the cost of the most expensive health benefit coverage elected by any similarly situated participant. Note that this is only a safe harbor. The safe harbor also offers an exception permitting contributions to exceed either of these two limits as long as the contribution bears a uniform relationship to a participant's compensation. This is not a particularly useful safe harbor, and there is no further guidance on how to apply it. Plans not meeting this safe harbor may, under a facts-and-circumstances review, demonstrate that benefits are not nondiscriminatory in favor of highly compensated participants. [I.R.C. § 125(g)(2)]

In general, this discrimination testing may be too vague to allow for any mathematical testing (and it only applies to health benefits). The sponsor should document that a good-faith attempt was made to show that benefits are not discriminatory in favor of the highly paid or owners.

Q 9:81   How is the 25 percent concentration test for cafeteria plans satisfied?

This is a straightforward mathematical test that compares the total benefits provided to key employees in the current year to the total benefits provided to all employees. A "key employee" has the same definition as in pension laws (see Q 9:320). [I.R.C. § 416(i)(1)]

A cafeteria plan is discriminatory when the total nontaxable benefits provided to key employees exceed 25 percent of the total nontaxable qualified benefits provided for all employees under the plan. When this testing is applied to medical benefits under a self-insured plan, the calculation can be based on the premium value of the coverage provided, rather than on actual benefits or reimbursements received by employees and dependents under a self-funded plan. [I.R.C. § 125(b)(2)]

Note that the 25 percent concentration test is conducted with all of the benefits offered by the plan. Various elements of the cafeteria plan are not tested separately. Also, even though a dependent care assistance benefit has an independent 25 percent test, those benefits are also tested in this overall 25 percent key employee concentration test.

Example. Chamber Spencer LLC. offers employees the ability to contribute toward health insurance premiums on a pretax basis. The company also offers a medical reimbursement FSA and a dependent care assistance FSA. All dollars contributed by plan participants on a pretax basis are tested together. The medical FSA dollars do *not* have a separate 25 percent concentration test, and although the dependent care FSA is subject to independent testing with regard to prohibited groups, those dollars are also used in the overall Section 125 plan testing.

Q 9:82 How would the nondiscrimination tests be changed under the new proposed cafeteria plan rules?

The proposed regulations provide significant new guidance that should alleviate some of the past uncertainty about applying the three basic nondiscrimination tests that apply to cafeteria plans: (i) the eligibility test; (ii) the contributions and benefits test; and (iii) the key employee test. For purposes of the nondiscrimination tests, the proposed regulations offer new definitions of several important terms, including highly compensated individual, five percent shareholder, officer, key employee, highly compensated participant, and compensation. The proposed regulations use a modification of the nondiscriminatory classification rule from the I.R.C. Section 410(b) qualified retirement plans rules to fashion a proposal for the eligibility test. The new guidance on the contributions and benefits test proposes an objective test, reminiscent of the ADP and ACP tests used for 401(k) plans, to determine when the actual election of benefits is discriminatory. Finally, the proposed regulations explain the safe harbor for cafeteria plans providing health benefits and create a safe harbor for premium-only plans that satisfy certain requirements.

The proposed regulations contemplate nondiscrimination tests on the last day of the plan year, taking into account all non-excludable employees and former employees who were employed on any day during the plan year. It is noteworthy that the new cafeteria plan nondiscrimination rules do not replace the nondiscrimination testing requirements that may apply to a component benefit plan under the cafeteria plan (such as a group-term life insurance plan, self-insured medical plan, or a dependent care assistance program).

Q 9:83 How are otherwise tax-free benefits treated when the cafeteria plan is found to be discriminatory?

A cafeteria plan that fails to satisfy the nondiscrimination testing requirements causes highly compensated participants to include in their wages the maximum amount of all taxable benefits (or cash) they could have chosen under the plan, and these amounts are subject to all federal employment taxes. The value of benefits provided to individuals who are not highly compensated participants is not treated as wages.

Example. Frank, the company CFO and a highly compensated participant, has the opportunity to select benefits of up to $1,500 consisting of cash (up to $400) and three tax-free benefits: (1) coverage under a group medical plan (cost of $600), (2) disability benefits (up to $250), and (3) dependent care assistance (up to $200). As long as the plan is qualified, only the cash benefit is taxable if Frank chooses it. Frank chooses $300 cash and tax-free benefits of $1,200 and as a result has additional wages of $300. The plan is later found to be discriminatory because the highly compensated participants enter on their date of hire, whereas other employees must work 30 days. Frank is now responsible for an additional $100 ($400 for the maximum taxable benefits that were available under the plan, less the $300 already taxed) in wages. [Prop. Treas. Reg. § 1.125-1 Q 11]

A plan that violates the key employee 25 percent concentration test of Section 125 causes the key employees to include in wages the maximum amount of taxable benefits they could have chosen (e.g., the total amount of salary reduction), less the value of the taxable benefits that they actually chose. The value of benefits provided to non-key and non-highly compensated participants in a discriminatory plan remains excluded from their wages.

Q 9:84 What are "qualified benefits" under a Section 125 cafeteria plan?

A Section 125 plan may provide the following tax-free benefits (i.e., the qualified benefits): coverage under an accident and health plan (e.g., medical, dental, vision, or disability, but not long-term care), group-term life insurance with a death benefit of up to $50,000, dependent care, and qualified adoption assistance. In addition, a cafeteria plan may permit the purchase or sale of vacation time off by plan participants. A cafeteria plan may not provide the following benefits on a tax-free basis: scholarship and fellowship grants under I.R.C. Section 117, employee fringe benefits under I.R.C. Section 132 (e.g., a transportation benefit), meals and lodging, employer contributions to a MSA, long-term care, and dependent group life insurance. [I.R.C. § 125(f); Prop. Treas. Reg. § 1.125-1, Q&A 5; Temp. Treas. Reg. § 1.125-2T, Q&A 1]

Effective as of the August 6, 2007 date of publication in the *Federal Register*, the proposed regulations for cafeteria plans provide that the amount includible in the employee's gross income on excess group-term life insurance coverage is to be determined solely on the basis of the Table I rates. [72 Fed. Reg. 43938-01, 2007-39 I.R.B. 681] Under this approach, the actual cost of the coverage paid through salary reductions or flex credits is excludable from the employee's gross income.

Although in most cases the tax impact on employees will be relatively minor, this change will require an adjustment in the way employers calculate the additional income to be imputed and reported on Form W-2 for employees who receive group-term life insurance coverage through a cafeteria plan, beginning with the 2007 tax year.

Q 9:85   May employers add a transportation benefit option to their Section 125 cafeteria plan?

No. A Section 125 plan cannot offer a transportation benefit without losing its exemption from FIT, FITW, FICA, and FUTA. However, the Transportation Equity Act for the 21st Century [Pub. L. No. 105-78, 111 Stat. 1467] allows employers to offer employees the option of electing to obtain qualified transportation benefits by reducing their compensation outside of a Section 125 plan. See Qs 9:452 through 9:461 for more information about parking and mass transit reimbursement programs.

An election by an employee to reduce his or her wages and receive certain transportation benefits is exempt from the I.R.C.'s constructive receipt rules under Section 132(f), not Section 125 (see Qs 9:452–9:461). [Treas. Reg. § 1.132-9, Internal Legal Mem. 200018052 (Mar. 10, 2000)]

Q 9:86   How are the benefits under a cafeteria plan purchased?

Benefits under a cafeteria plan may be purchased with employer contributions, employee aftertax contributions, and employee pretax contributions, or a combination of all three. Most cafeteria plans offer some form of pretax salary reduction election by the employee. A pretax employee contribution (generally irrevocable for one year) must be made pursuant to a salary reduction agreement with the employer under which the participant elects to: (1) have his or her salary reduced by a given amount or (2) forgo a salary increase in exchange for a choice of benefits under the cafeteria plan. [Prop. Treas. Reg. § 1.125-1, Q&A 6]

When a cafeteria plan is funded through employer contributions, the employer will typically set aside an amount of money for each employee participant (typically a flat dollar amount), and then the employee will elect how to spend those funds. When the employee elects to take a taxable benefit or cash, only the value of the benefit or amount of cash is treated as additional wages.

Q 9:87   Are cafeteria plans covering union employees subject to special rules?

Yes. A cafeteria plan that covers only union employees is not subject to the nondiscrimination requirements that apply to other Section 125 plans. [I.R.C. § 125(g)(1)]

Q 9:88   Must participation in a cafeteria plan be limited to active employees of the employer?

Proposed regulations state that a cafeteria plan may permit employees and former employees to make elective contributions that select between taxable and nontaxable benefits. A cafeteria plan may not cover individuals classified as self-employed (e.g., partners in a partnership, sole proprietors, or members of an LLC taxed as a partnership). Dependents of employees may receive benefits obtained under a cafeteria plan (e.g., dependent medical care), but are generally precluded from making an election under the plan. [Prop. Treas. Reg. § 1.125-1, Q&A 4]

The IRS ruled that a retiree cannot avoid taxation on benefits paid from a qualified retirement plan by diverting his or her retirement income through a cafeteria plan. [I.R.S. Coordinated Issue Paper on Cafeteria Plans and Qualified Retirement Plan Hybrid Arrangements, UIL 125.05-00, Feb. 1, 2000]

Q 9:89   What salary reduction election requirements apply to a cafeteria plan?

As a general rule, all elections made under a cafeteria plan (i.e., both elections as to benefit options chosen and the amount of salary reduction) must be made prior to the start of the plan year and be irrevocable for the entire plan year. This requirement is part of the proposed regulations under I.R.C. Section 125, not part of the I.R.C. (but strictly followed by the IRS). A failure to comply with these election rules will cause the plan to lose its exclusion from the constructive receipt rules, and all participants will then treat their total salary reduction (or the maximum taxable benefit they could have received) as additional wages, less any amount previously reported as wages. Certain exceptions to the fixed-election requirements do apply if these exceptions are incorporated into the plan document (e.g., change in family status, certain changes in costs, and change in status rules). See Q 9:186. [Prop. Treas. Reg. §§ 1.125-1, Q&A 2, 1.125-2, Q&A 6(a)]

In the case of a new participant who enters during the plan year, the election must be made prior to the date that a new participant enters the plan. With the exception of a permitted enrollment under the Health Insurance Portability and Accountability Act of 1996 (HIPAA), under no circumstances must a Section 125 plan permit a retroactive election or change to election. The proposed regulations, however, would permit a cafeteria plan to provide that an employee's election of coverage made within the first 30 days of employment can be retroactively effective as of the date of hire. Any pretax contributions used to pay for coverage during the retroactive period must be made from compensation that is not yet currently available when the coverage election is made. This special rule eliminates the need to require a new employee to pay for retroactive coverage through aftertax contributions. It should be noted that this rule does not apply to any employee who terminates employment and is rehired within 30 days after termination or who returns to employment following an unpaid leave of absence of less than 30 days.

Q 9:90   When are election changes under a cafeteria plan permitted during the plan year?

A cafeteria plan may be drafted with no permitted election change during the plan year for any reason; if that is the case, then none can be made.

A cafeteria plan may also be drafted to permit a change in election during the plan year for one type of benefit (e.g., health insurance coverage or group-term life insurance) but not permit changes in the plan year for other types of benefits such as FSAs. When a change in election is permitted under regulation, the change in election must be related to an event affecting the employee or dependent.

Changes in medical, disability insurance, or life insurance are permitted when there is a "change in family status" (e.g., marriage, divorce, death of a spouse or dependent, number of dependents, change in residence, birth or adoption of a child, or commencement or termination of a spouse's job). These events could lead to election changes if the benefit coverage under the plan was consistent with the event (e.g., affected by the event). Note that an election change is not permitted unless drafted into the plan document. As a result, questions relating to changes in elections should be answered only after a review of plan document language regarding such changes.

Salary reduction options to obtain other types of benefits, such as adoption assistance and dependent care, may be changed at the occurrence of other events not meeting the definition of changes in status. These events will be identified in the plan document.

The regulations also permit a change in the employee's election when there are significant changes in the cost of the benefits.

Q 9:91 What is a "significant cost increase" for purposes of making an election change under a cafeteria plan?

Regulations permit a Section 125 plan to allow a change in election when there is a significant change in the cost of coverage that would be passed on to the participant during the period of coverage (e.g., increased salary reduction); however, this exception does not apply to an election made to fund a health FSA. A plan may be drafted to have an automatic change in the participant's election when the cost of a qualified benefit increases (or decreases) during a period of coverage and the plan requires that the participant's salary reduction elections be adjusted for the cost change. The guidance does not provide a bright-line test for what is considered "significant"; a reasonable interpretation is required.

When a Section 125 plan contains a provision allowing for a change in election, the employees typically are permitted either to make a corresponding election to obtain new coverage at a lower cost, or to revoke their elections.

For example, if the cost of a group health insurance policy significantly increases during the plan year and that cost or a portion of that cost is passed on to the participant by increasing the salary deferral election, employees who are covered under the option could be permitted to increase their salary reduction election or instead elect to revoke their election for that health care option and if available choose to purchase coverage under another coverage offered by the employer, or elsewhere.

This ability to make an election change because of a significant increase in cost applies in a special way to dependent care benefits. An employee may be permitted to make a change in election because of a cost increase only when a provider who is unrelated to the employee imposes the increase. The I.R.C. defines the term *relative* for this condition under Sections 152(a)(1) through (8), incorporating the rules of Sections 152(b)(1) and (2). [Treas. Reg. § 1.125-4(f)(2)]

Example. Angel participates in a calendar-year cafeteria plan maintained pursuant to a collective bargaining agreement. This cafeteria plan offers various benefits, including indemnity health insurance and a health FSA. As a result of midyear negotiations: (1) premiums for the health insurance program are increased in the middle of the year; (2) insurance co-payments for office visits are reduced under the indemnity plan; and (3) a change in the HMO option is made.

The change in benefits results in a reduction in the cost of insurance premiums. Accordingly, the cafeteria plan may automatically decrease the amount of salary reduction contributions of affected participants by an amount that corresponds to the premium change, if that provision is in the plan document. However, the plan may not permit employees to change their health FSA elections to reflect the midyear change in co-payments under the indemnity plan.

Because of the change of the HMO option to the benefit package, the cafeteria plan may permit affected participants to make an election change to elect the new HMO option. They could opt out of the insurance option and into the HMO and make changes in their salary reduction elections to effect the change. Keep in mind, however, that no change is permitted to be made to the medical FSA election based on a change in cost of benefit.

Q 9:92 May a cafeteria plan permit an election change when the benefit coverage changes?

A change in election option may be drafted into the cafeteria plan for certain coverage changes. When the coverage under a plan is significantly curtailed or ceases entirely during the plan year, the cafeteria plan can, and should, permit affected employees to revoke their elections during the plan year. Where this applies, each affected employee may be permitted to make a new election (on a prospective basis) for coverage under another benefit option providing similar coverage. A special condition applies to such changes for coverage under an accident or health plan. Coverage is treated as significantly curtailed only if there is an overall reduction in coverage provided to participants under the plan (e.g., there is reduced coverage to the full group of participants). For example, if a participant's favorite doctor drops his participation with the health carrier that would probably not be classified as an overall reduction in coverage that affects participants under the plan. However, if one of the only two local hospitals decides to leave participation with the health carrier, that may well be classified as an overall reduction in coverage affecting the full group of participants. [Treas. Reg. § 1.125-4(f)(3)]

Q 9:93   What requirements apply to midyear participant elections for group-term life insurance and health benefits under a cafeteria plan?

A cafeteria plan that provides access to health care and group-term life insurance may incorporate a "change in status" election to permit a participant to revoke a benefit election after the start of the plan year and to make a new election with respect to the remainder of the plan year, if events leading up to the election change meet certain requirements. [Treas. Reg. § 1.125-4(c)]

The following list establishes events that can be classified as a "change in status" event, permitting an election change for group-term life insurance and "health and accident" benefits. The reader will note that the cafeteria plan regulations refer to the term "health and accident" as being benefit coverage under an accident or health plan as defined in regulations under I.R.C. Section 105 (e.g., a group medical plan, an HMO, disability insurance, or a health FSA).

A cafeteria plan may also provide that elections for benefits other than group-term life insurance and health and accident benefits be revised during the plan year under proposed regulations when the plan incorporates a "change in family status" election for those benefits (e.g., dependent care assistance benefits).

Change-in-Status Events

The following events are referred to as "changes in status" for purposes of modifying an election under a cafeteria plan during the plan year for a group-term life insurance benefit or health benefits:

1. *Change of legal marital status.* Events that change an employee's legal marital status include the following: marriage, death of spouse, divorce, legal separation, and annulment.

2. *Number of dependents.* Events that change an employee's number of dependents include the following: birth, death, adoption, and placement for adoption.

3. *Employment status.* These are any of the following events that change the employment status of the employee, the employee's spouse, or the employee's dependent: a termination or commencement of employment; a strike or lockout; a commencement of or return from an unpaid leave of absence; and a change in worksite. In addition, if the eligibility conditions of the cafeteria plan or other benefit plans of the employer for coverage provided to the employee, spouse, or dependent are conditioned on the employment status of that individual and there is a change in that

individual's employment status with the consequence that the individual becomes (or ceases to be) eligible under the plan, then that change constitutes a change in employment and, in turn, a change in status. For example, when a plan only applies to salaried employees and an employee switches from salaried to hourly paid with the consequence that the employee ceases to be eligible for the plan, then that change constitutes a change in employment status.

4. *Dependent's ability to satisfy eligibility requirements.* These are events that cause an employee's dependent to satisfy or cease to satisfy eligibility requirements for coverage on account of attainment of age, student status, or any similar circumstance.

5. *Change of residence.* This includes a change in the place of residence of the employee, spouse, or dependent. [Treas. Reg. § 1.125-4(c)]

The regulations cite certain types of coverage changes that may trigger a change in election to coordinate with a health care mandate. These include changes in health care coverage under COBRA, a medical support order, changes in Medicaid or Medicare eligibility, and special enrollment rights under HIPAA. An event that is classified as a change-in-status event will only permit changes to an election under a cafeteria plan during the plan year when coverage under benefit programs is affected by the event. This is referred to as the "consistency rule."

> **Example.** Sandblast Company provides health coverage and a health FSA for its employees through its cafeteria plan. Before the beginning of the calendar year, James elects employee, spouse, and child health coverage under Sandblast Company's cafeteria plan and also elects to make a salary reduction election to pay for this coverage and to obtain benefits under the health FSA. James's wife, Sherry, obtains employment after being unemployed during the year. Sherry's employer, Swim Fast, offers health coverage to its employees and a healthcare FSA at a lower cost to its employees. James wants to revoke his elections for employee, spouse, and child coverage, and is considering electing employee-only health coverage under Sandblast Company's plan or obtaining family health coverage under Swim Fast's plan. The change in employment status for Sherry is a change in status and, under Sandblast Company's plan, James can become eligible for employee-only coverage. James may elect employee-only health coverage under Sandblast Company's plan to cover just himself, or James may cancel coverage under Sandblast Company's plan if Sherry elects family health coverage under Swim Fast's plan to cover the family. Sandblast Company's cafeteria plan may permit James to make either election change.
>
> The Sandblast Company cafeteria plan may also permit James to reduce his salary reduction contributions to decrease his coverage and thus his contributions under the Sandblast Company health FSA.

Q 9:94   What is the "consistency rule" and how does it apply to changes in election for health coverage or group-term life insurance?

A change in an election under a cafeteria plan for health coverage or group-term life insurance is permitted for certain changes in status as described in Q 9:92. However, the change-in-status event must affect the benefit offered under the plan for the election change to be valid. That is, the change in status must affect eligibility for coverage under an employer's plan to which the election applies. This is referred to as the "consistency rule." This rule also applies to benefit election changes that may be made for other benefits as a result of a "change-in-family status."

For example, a change in status related to an employee's divorce would have a direct effect on the health coverage that has been elected for that spouse and could be an event allowing the employee to drop that coverage and have the salary reduction election reduced. In addition, the regulations confirm that the divorce, legal separation, or death of a spouse would satisfy the consistency rule for coverage under a group life insurance (or even disability coverage) benefit elected by the employee. Thus, the employee could elect to reduce or increase his or her group life insurance under the cafeteria plan following the death of a spouse (or one of the other events identified previously). [Treas. Reg. § 1.125-4(c)(3)]

Q 9:95   May a cafeteria plan be drafted to permit an election change for HIPAA required coverage in the plan year?

Yes, a cafeteria plan may be written to permit an employee to revoke an election for coverage under a group health plan and make a new election that corresponds with the special enrollment rights provided under HIPAA. [I.R.C. § 9801(f); Treas. Reg. § 1.125-4(a)]

Example. Scallop Tree Investing LLC provides health coverage for its employees pursuant to a plan that is subject to the provisions of HIPAA. Under the plan, employees may elect either employee-only coverage or family coverage. Scallop Tree also maintains a calendar-year cafeteria plan under which qualified benefits, including health coverage, may be purchased through a salary reduction election. Scallop Tree's employee, Alice, is married to Tyler and they have a child, Taylor. In accordance with Scallop Tree's cafeteria plan, Alice elects employee-only health coverage before the beginning of the calendar year. During the year, Alice and Tyler adopt a child, Zane. Within 30 days of the adoption, Alice makes an election to change her employee-only health coverage to obtain family health coverage for Tyler, Taylor, and Zane as of the date of Zane's adoption.

Alice satisfies the conditions for special enrollment of an employee with a new dependent under HIPAA; as a result, she may enroll in the family coverage under Scallop Tree's accident or health plan to provide the HIPAA-required coverage effective as of the date of Zane's adoption. [I.R.C. § 9801(f)(2)]

Scallop Tree's Section 125 cafeteria plan may be written to permit Alice to change her salary reduction election to revoke the election for employee-only and make an election to pay for the family coverage when the new coverage goes into effect. Or the cafeteria plan may be written so it does not permit a change in the salary reduction election. Note that Alice's adoption of Zane is classified as a change in status, and the election of family coverage is consistent with that change in status. [Treas. Reg. § 1.125-4(b)]

Q 9:96   May an employee alter his or her cafeteria election to pay for a COBRA election?

In certain situations, yes. For example, when an employee, the employee's spouse, or a dependent becomes eligible for COBRA coverage due to a reduction in the individual's hours of employment (e.g., the covered individual is no longer eligible for the employer's medical plan), this would result in a COBRA-qualifying event. COBRA would then permit the spouse or dependent to obtain continuation coverage. If the plan document permitted, then the employee participating in the cafeteria plan could make an election change to pay for the coverage. That is, the regulations make it clear that a cafeteria plan may be written to permit the employee to elect to increase his or her salary reduction payments under the employer's cafeteria plan at the time of the COBRA election to pay for the continuation coverage of the employee or a dependent covered under the employee's employer-provided health plan. A similar provision may be included in the plan where the state requires similar continuation coverage under an employer's plan. [Treas. Reg. § 1.125-4(c)(3)(iv)]

Note that reimbursements of a COBRA insurance premium (or any insurance premium) of a spouse or dependent would not be permitted under a health FSA. In most cases, there will be no mechanism to reimburse the employee for that expense.

Example. Henry, a single parent, elected family health coverage under a calendar-year cafeteria plan maintained by his employer, Ombram. Henry and his 26-year-old child, Marla, were covered under Ombram's health plan. In 2017, Marla turned 27, and, under the terms of the Ombram health plan, dependents must be under the age of 27 to receive coverage. Henry revoked his election for family health coverage and obtained employee-only coverage under the Ombram cafeteria plan.

Marla's loss of eligibility for coverage under the terms of the health plan was a change in status. A revocation of Henry's election for family coverage under the cafeteria plan and a new election for employee-only coverage corresponded with the change in status.

Marla could then elect COBRA continuation coverage for herself under her father's employer's plan. Henry could pay for that COBRA coverage under the cafeteria plan on behalf of his daughter. [Treas. Reg. § 1.125-4(c)(3)(iv)]

Q 9:97   Can an employee and employer work together to create a "change," to permit a change in election under the plan?

Certain changes in status or other circumstance may permit employees to make a change in election when the change in election is consistent with the change in circumstance. At times, an employee may request his or her employer to assist in creating a scenario wherein the employee could make a change in election. Although an employee could theoretically choose to be divorced merely to make a change in election midyear, such a change is certainly highly unlikely. However, it is not unheard of for an employee to request that his or her employment terminate, then be reinstated, to create an instant "change in status." This is not permitted. [Treas. Reg. § 1.125-4(c)(4), ex. 8]

Example. Before the beginning of the year, Jackie elects to participate in a cafeteria plan maintained by her employer, Shamrock LLC. Jackie does not experience any of the events that are classified as a change in status. Jackie wants to cancel her health care coverage. She arranges with her employer to formally terminate and be rehired a week later, hoping that such a termination will be classified as a change in status.

The Treasury Department states in its regulations that under the facts and circumstances outlined above, a principal purpose of the termination of employment was to alter the cafeteria plan election. The employer had agreed to the reinstatement at the time of termination; accordingly, Jackie does not have a change in status permitting a change in her election under the cafeteria plan.

Note that Jackie's termination of employment could constitute a change in status and permit a cancellation of coverage during the period of unemployment, as long as Jackie's original cafeteria plan election was reinstated on resumption of employment in the plan year.

If, instead, Jackie terminates employment and cancels coverage during a period of unemployment, and then returns to work more than 30 days following her termination of employment, the cafeteria plan may permit Jackie the option of returning to the election in effect prior to termination of employment or making a new election under the plan. In addition, under these circumstances the cafeteria plan may prohibit Jackie from returning to the plan during that plan year. [Treas. Reg. § 1.125-4(c) (exs.)]

Q 9:98   Are there any special rules that apply to elections relating to health care coverage ordered by a judgment, decree, or court order?

Yes. The changes in status regulations for group-term life insurance and health care coverage under a cafeteria plan permit a document to include an election change for any judgment, decree, or order resulting from a divorce, legal separation, annulment, or change in legal custody (including a qualified medical child support order) that requires health coverage for an employee's child or for a foster child who is a dependent of the employee. The cafeteria plan document can provide that the change in the salary reduction election to pay for the cost be automatic where the order requires coverage for the child as a dependent under the employer's plan, or the plan can make the election an option available to employees. The plan may also be drafted to permit the employee to make an election change to cancel coverage for the child if the order requires the spouse, former spouse, or other individual to provide coverage for the child. [ERISA § 609; Treas. Reg. § 1.125-4(d)]

Q 9:99   What are the election changes under a health plan that are permitted when the participant or covered dependent becomes entitled to Medicare or Medicaid?

The final regulations provide that when an employee, spouse, or dependent who is enrolled in an employer's health plan becomes entitled to coverage (i.e., becomes enrolled) under Part A or Part B of Title XVIII of the Social Security Act (Medicare) or Title XIX of the Social Security Act (Medicaid, and for other than coverage consisting solely of benefits for the distribution of pediatric vaccines), a cafeteria plan may be written to permit the employee to make an election change to cancel or reduce coverage of that employee, spouse, or dependent under the health care plan. In addition, if an employee, spouse, or dependent who has been entitled to such coverage under Medicare or Medicaid loses eligibility for such coverage, the cafeteria plan may permit the employee to make an election change to commence or increase coverage of that individual under the health care plan. [Treas. Reg. § 1.125-4(e)]

Q 9:100   How are election changes under a cafeteria plan for other benefits (nonhealth and group-term life insurance) handled?

Basically, the "change-in-family status" rules as described in the 1989 proposed regulations Section 1.125-2 continue to apply to qualified benefits other than group-term life insurance and health benefits.

The circumstances that allow a revocation of an existing election with respect to benefits other than group health plan benefits and group-term life insurance benefits are referred to as "changes in family status." A cafeteria plan may, but is not required to, allow a participant to change his or her election of other benefits "on account of . . . and consistent with a change in family status." Benefit election changes are consistent with a change in family status only if the election change is "necessary and appropriate" as a result of the change in family status. [Prop. Treas. Reg. § 1.125-2, Q&A 6(c)]

The 1989 regulations define a "change in family status" with regard to an election of other benefits as:

1. The marriage or divorce of the employee;
2. The death of the employee's spouse or dependent;
3. The birth or placement for adoption of a child of the employee;

4. The termination or commencement of employment of the employee's spouse;

5. The switching from part-time to full-time employment status, or vice versa, by the employee or the employee's spouse;

6. The taking of an unpaid leave of absence by the employee or the employee's spouse; or

7. A "significant change" in the health coverage of an employee or spouse attributable to the spouse's employment.

If such a change in election is to be permitted, it must be reflected in the plan document. [Prop. Treas. Reg. § 1.125-2, Q&A 6(c)]

An employee who takes qualified leave under FMLA may elect to revoke a benefit during that leave. In addition, an employee returning from FMLA leave must be permitted to reinstate his or her previous election.

Q 9:101   Must an election change for either a "change in status" or a "change-in-family status" be incorporated into the plan document?

Yes. If the employer wishes to permit any election change under a Section 125 plan during the plan year, the procedures for validating the change must be in the plan document.

Q 9:102   May a cafeteria plan permit an employee to buy or sell vacation days?

Yes, and the structure of this plan option varies in design. This option is described in Proposed Treasury Regulations Section 1.125-2, Q&A 5(c). One requirement attached to providing this benefit in a cafeteria plan is that the plan cannot permit an individual to carry over unused days purchased under the plan to another plan year. This rule is applied by requiring that vacation days not purchased under the Section 125 plan be used before the employee uses vacation days that were purchased under the cafeteria plan. In addition, when a plan allows an individual to cash out unused vacation days, the cash must be paid during the plan year.

Example. Rockfall, Inc., an employer, provides employees with three weeks of paid vacation for each calendar year of service and permits them to "purchase" an additional week of vacation (perhaps by giving up certain tax-free benefits). Sean buys three days of additional leave at the start of the plan year. If Sean does not take the full three weeks of regular leave, he cannot use the three days of purchased leave. The plan may permit Sean to cash out his three days' additional leave before the end of the year. The payment for the three days is treated as additional wages and subject to all federal employment taxes. [Prop. Treas. Reg. § 1.125-2, Q&A 5(c), ex. 1]

Q 9:103   How are qualified benefits obtained under a cafeteria plan treated for federal employment tax purposes?

Salary deferrals made under a Section 125 plan, except for contributions to a 401(k) plan, are exempt from all federal employment taxes if the salary deferrals are used to obtain qualified benefits. Most qualified benefits obtained under a cafeteria plan are not subject to FITW, FICA, or FUTA. Adoption assistance benefits paid from an adoption assistance plan are not subject to FITW but are subject to FICA and FUTA. 401(k) salary deferrals made under a cafeteria plan are subject to FICA and FUTA but not FITW. When an employee elects to receive a taxable benefit (or cash) instead of a qualified benefit, the cash (or if a taxable benefit, the value of that benefit) is treated as wages generally subject to FIT, FITW, FICA, and FUTA. Note that although the value of tax-free benefits obtained through a cafeteria plan is not subject to FIT, FITW, or FICA, the value of the benefit may be reportable (e.g., the value of dependent care benefits is reported in Box 10 of the employee's Form W-2). [I.R.C. §§ 3121(a)(4), 3306(c)(3); Pub. No. 535 Ch. 5]

Q 9:104   Are employee contributions to a cafeteria plan subject to ERISA's trust requirements?

In many cases, yes. However, the DOL has specifically stated that it is not enforcing penalties for employers that fail to comply with this requirement. The Employee Retirement Income Security Act (ERISA) generally requires that welfare plan assets (e.g., employee contributions) be transferred to a separate trust, to an insurance company, or to a benefit provider as soon as practical, but no later than 90 days after the pay period contribution has been withheld by the employer. These general rules treat employee contributions under a cafeteria plan and aftertax employee contributions as *plan assets*.

Note that although ERISA requires the transfer of employee contributions to a separate trust, few employers do so. The Department of Labor (DOL) has developed guidance providing an exemption from enforcement of penalties when this transfer is not made.

The DOL has stated that a cafeteria plan used to collect before-tax or aftertax employee contributions for payment of welfare benefits was not, "in itself, a separate welfare benefit plan." [PWBA Op. Ltr. 96-12A (July 17, 1996)] The DOL then went on to conclude, however, that when the cafeteria plan was "part of the Group Health Plan inasmuch as it constitutes a mechanism by which the Group Health Plan, an ERISA welfare benefit plan, is funded with employee contributions, it is part of a welfare plan."

As noted earlier, most employers do not establish a separate trust but merely hold the employee contribution in a general corporate account until the employee contributions are used to pay benefits. Retaining plan assets is a clear violation of ERISA, but has not been the subject of any DOL enforcement programs. Final regulations issued by the DOL on May 17, 1988, and amended on August 7, 1996, defined the date on which participant contributions will be deemed to be plan assets for certain ERISA purposes. In general, those rules require that participant contributions that have become plan assets be transferred to a trust as soon as it is reasonable to segregate these assets from the employer's general assets. But under no circumstances may the employer retain the assets for more than 90 days in the case of a welfare plan. This regulation would therefore appear to require that salary reduction amounts under a cafeteria plan that are used to buy ERISA benefits be transferred to a separate trust within a few days after they are withheld from the employee's paycheck. [29 C.F.R. §§ 2510.3102(a), 2510.3102(c); ERISA § 403(a)]

However, on August 12, 1988, the DOL suspended its enforcement of these trust requirements with respect to all cafeteria plans. The DOL stated that it will not assert a violation caused by "the failure to hold participant contributions to cafeteria plans in trust." Note that this enforcement relief only applies to the requirement to hold assets in a trust. Other fiduciary penalties continue to apply to the misuse of these funds. [ERISA Technical Release No. 88-1 (Aug. 12, 1988)] Thus, for example, the fiduciaries of the welfare plan would be personally responsible for employee contributions lost when a business fails. The technical release was superseded by ERISA Technical Release No. 92-01 [57 Fed. Reg. 23,272 (June 2, 1992)], in which the DOL continued its position. The DOL added that with respect to these kind of plans, it "will not assert a violation in any enforcement proceeding or assess a civil penalty with respect to a cafeteria plan because of a failure to meet the reporting requirements solely as a result of using participant contributions to pay plan benefits or expenses attendant to the provision of benefits." The technical release goes on to add that in the case of a cafeteria plan that satisfies I.R.C. Section 125 but does not have a trust, the reporting exemptions of Technical Release 88-1 continue to be available as long as participant contributions are used within 90 days of receipt to pay premiums. The DOL regulations also allow similar reporting and disclosure exemptions for certain welfare plans that cover fewer than 100 participants and whose benefits are paid solely from the sponsor's general assets, from insurance contracts, or from a combination of the two.

The ultimate impact of these regulations on cafeteria plans is unclear. Employers should be aware that the DOL's decision to suspend enforcement does not preclude participant lawsuits to enforce any trust requirement that might apply to welfare benefits provided under a cafeteria plan, nor does it affect the plan's reporting and disclosure obligations, including possible CPA audits, imposed by the IRS.

Cellular Phones

Q 9:105   Is the value of a cellular phone or other portable handheld device provided to an employee treated as wages?

Cellular phones and other portable or handheld devices or smart devices are not defined as "listed property" under I.R.C. Section 280(F)(d) effective for years beginning after December 31, 2009 as a result of the Small Business Jobs Act of 2010. [Pub. L. No. 111-240] Therefore, the heightened substantiation requirements associated with listed property are no longer required. The IRS has stated that the value of cell phones provided to employees is not includible in income because the benefit is a working condition fringe benefit if there are substantial reasons relating to the employer's business, other than compensation to the employee. Examples of business reasons are: (a) the employee needs to speak to clients located in other time zones outside the employee's normal work day, (b) the employer must be able to reach the employee for work-related emergencies, or (c) the employee must be available to speak with clients at times when the employee is away from the office. The IRS Notice also states that when an employer provides the employee with a cell phone primarily for noncompensatory business reasons, the IRS will treat the value of any personal use of a cell phone as a *de minimis* fringe benefit, which is excludable from the employee's income. [Notice 2011-72, 2011-38 I.R.B. 407 (Sept. 19, 2011)]

Q 9:106   What are the tax implications when an employer has a Bring Your Own Device (BYOD) policy?

Some employers have established policies to answer business questions about "bring your own device" (BYOD), especially because it is common for employees to use their cellular phones and other smart devices for work. Policies vary among employers from completely paying for employees' devices to reimbursing employees a percentage of the employees' bill. In these cases, there is no tax impact to the employee as this falls within the rules around an allowable business expense to the extent that the use is for business purposes. Employers should ensure there is a clear policy about the use and be able to account for the business use.

This is an area that states may also be influencing how BYOD policies may be structured. In *Cochran v. Schwan's Home Service Inc.* [228 Cal. App. 4th 1137 (2014)], the court of appeals ruled that when an employee is required to make business calls on his or her personal phone, there must be a reasonable reimbursement for those calls.

Chauffeur Services

Q 9:107   Is the value of chauffeur services provided by an employer included in an employee's gross income?

The value of chauffeur services that are required for bona fide business reasons (e.g., chauffeur/bodyguard for security purposes) is not included in wages subject to FIT, FITW, FICA, and FUTA. Where there is no bona fide business purpose for the chauffeur services, the employer will include in the employee's wages the value of these services (including the FMV of any waiting time while the chauffeur is on call). The FMV of the chauffeur's services is separate and apart from the FMV of the automobile. Where the chauffeur is an employee of the employer, the FMV of the chauffeur's services may be based on compensation received by the chauffeur. The FMV of the chauffeur's services must take into account special qualifications such as evasive driving skills and the ability of the employee to select a specific driver. Where an employer-paid chauffeur also performs substantial business services for the employer, the FMV of the chauffeur's driving services may be reduced proportionately by the amount of time the chauffeur spends performing other duties. [Treas. Reg. §§ 1.61-21(b)(5), 1.132-5(m)(5)]

Club Dues and Athletic Facilities

Q 9:108   Is the value of employer-paid club dues treated as taxable wages to the employee?

Generally, yes. However, a portion of employer-paid dues or other membership fees to any club organized for business, pleasure, recreation, or other social purpose may qualify as a working-condition fringe benefit that is excluded from wages subject to FIT, FITW, FICA, and FUTA. To qualify as exempt from FIT, FITW, FICA, and FUTA, (1) the employer payments must not be treated by the employer as compensation; (2) the employee's business use must be substantiated; and (3) the payment must qualify as a business expense of the employee if the employee paid the amount. Note that club dues that are excluded from wages as having a business connection are not deductible as a business expense on the employer's federal tax return. Where the club is used for nonbusiness purposes, employer-paid dues are treated as additional wages subject to FIT, FITW, FICA, and FUTA to the extent of the value of the nonbusiness use.

Employer-paid dues for professional or business organizations generally qualify as a tax-free working-condition fringe benefit and are not subject to FIT, FITW, FICA, and FUTA. [Treas. Reg. § 1.132-5(s)]

Q 9:109   Is the value of the use of an employer on-premise facility taxable to the employee?

No. An on-premise athletic facility that is available to an employee, spouse, or dependent children can be excluded from the employee's wages if the facility is primarily for the use of employees. Reimbursements to employees for the use of athletic facilities that are not located on the employer's premise are a taxable benefit, the value of which is includable in wages and subject to FITW, FICA, and FUTA.

Company Aircraft or Vehicles

Q 9:110   How is the fair market value of the personal use of a company aircraft determined?

The value of a personal flight on an employer aircraft is includible in an employee's gross income as wages and is subject to FIT, FITW, FICA, and FUTA; however, the amount may be excluded from FIT, FITW, FICA, and FUTA when the employee reimburses the employer for the FMV of the use. [Treas. Reg. § 1.61-21(a)(3)]

An employer has the option to use the special valuation rule to determine the taxable wages attributable to the personal use of an aircraft for FIT, FITW, FICA, and FUTA purposes as long as the employer uses the same special valuation rule for all of its employees receiving the company aircraft benefit. [Treas. Reg. § 1.61-21(g)(14)(i)] The employer is free to change valuation methods from year to year. The IRS has ruled an employer may use the special valuation rule to determine the FMV of the personal use of a company aircraft provided to an employee regardless of the fact that another employee may choose to use the general valuation rule to reimburse the employer for such use. Using the general valuation method to determine the value of a personal flight generally results in a higher amount than the value determined under the special valuation method. The IRS ruled that permitting employee reimbursement on a basis that differs from the valuation method does not require the employer to lose its ability to use the special valuation rules for such aviation travel. [Priv. Ltr. Rul. 9840015, Oct. 2, 1998]

Q 9:111   How is the value of travel in employer-provided aircraft treated for federal employment tax purposes?

The value of flights in a company-provided aircraft that are for substantial business purposes is excludable from gross income as a working condition fringe benefit. The value of nonbusiness travel (domestic or foreign) in a company-provided aircraft is treated as additional compensation and subject to federal employment taxes. (A special exception as a no-additional-cost service is available to airline employees who fly for nonbusiness reasons on an employer's aircraft.) The value of the personal use of such an aircraft is the price that an individual would pay to lease a similar aircraft (not the value of travel on a commercial aircraft) for a similar flight. Where the airplane travel is other than on a commercial aircraft (i.e., where other passengers purchase tickets for travel), the employer may value the nonbusiness use of a company aircraft under an alternate valuation method. The alternate valuation method applies a series of calculations: (1) determine the number of miles flown, (2) multiply that mileage by the standard industry fare level (SIFL) applicable to the flight (see below), (3) multiply the amount in item 2 by the applicable aircraft multiple based on the aircraft's weight and the status of the employee (control or noncontrol; see below), and (4) add to the amount in item 3 the applicable terminal charge. [Treas. Reg. § 1.61-21(g)(5)]

Following are the SIFL rates (which are revised semiannually):

	SIFL Mileage Charge for Travel Distances		
	Up to 500 Miles	501 to 1,500 Miles	Over 1,500 Miles
1-1-11 to 6-30-11	.2237	.1640	.1706
7-1-11 to 12-31-11	.2395	.1826	.1756
1-1-12 to 6-30-12	.2455	.1872	.1800
7-1-12 to 12-31-12	.2569	.1959	.1884
1-1-13 to 6-30-13	.2655	.2024	.1946
7-1-13 to 12-31-13	.2654	.2024	.1946
1-1-14 to 6-30-14	.2515	.1918	.1844
7-1-14 to 12-31-14	.2530	.1929	.1855
1-1-15 to 6-30-15	.2490	.1898	.1825
7-11-15 to 12-31-15	.2341	.1785	.1716
1-1-16 to 6-30-16	.2144	.1635	.1572
7-1-16 to 12-31-16	.2061	.1572	.1511

Note. For tax purposes, the SIFL is lagged six months.

The Weight Control Factor for Control and Noncontrol Employees	Factor Based on Employee Status	
Maximum Certified Take-Off Weight	Control	Noncontrol
6,000 lbs. or less	62.5%	15.6%
6,001 lbs. to 10,000 lbs.	125%	23.4%
10,001 lbs. to 25,000 lbs.	300%	31.3%
25,001 lbs. or more	400%	31.3%

See Q 9:322 for a description of a control employee.

A special rule permits the value of an employee's personal use of company aircraft to be treated as of no value when at least 50 percent or more of the regular passenger seating capacity is occupied by individuals whose flights are primarily for the employer's business purpose. [Treas. Reg. § 1.61-21(g)(12)] The value of travel by a spouse or other dependent determined under these same rules is treated as additional compensation to the employee unless the 50 percent threshold is met. [Treas. Reg. § 1.61-21(g)(12)(v)] Travel by a dependent under age two is excluded in the valuation. [Treas. Reg. § 1.61-21(g)(1)]

Where the employee combines a personal and business trip on a company-provided aircraft and the primary purpose of the travel is for business, the value of the personal use is determined for the portion of the travel that was personal in nature (i.e., the business portion is disregarded). If the travel is not primarily for business travel, the entire trip is treated as being for personal use. [Treas. Reg. § 1.61-21(g)(4)(iii)]

Q 9:112   Must the employer's business deduction for a company airplane be equal to the amount treated as taxable wages?

The amount reported to an employee as compensation is the *value* of the benefit received. However, the employer may take a deduction equal to the *cost* of the benefit provided. In some cases, the cost may be different from the value. The employer's deduction may not exceed the actual cost incurred, even if the value reportable to the employee as taxable compensation is greater than the actual cost. In the case of business and even nonbusiness (i.e., vacation) flights, the employer is generally not limited to a deduction that equals the amount of compensation reportable to employees, with an important exception:

Note. For company airplane (or other entertainment, amusement, or recreation) expenses on behalf of "specified individuals" that are incurred after October 22, 2004, the deduction by the employer may not exceed the amount treated as compensation by such a "specified individual." This change was made by the American Jobs Creation Act of 2004, which amended I.R.C. Section 274(e)(2). Specified individuals include officers, directors, and owners of more than 10 percent of the company.

Q 9:113   What are the basic rules that apply to an employee's personal use of a company vehicle?

An employee's business use of an employer-provided vehicle is a tax-free fringe benefit, and the value of this use is not included in the employee's wages for FIT, FITW, FICA, and FUTA purposes. When employers allow employees to use a company car for nonbusiness purposes, the value of that usage is generally required to be included as additional compensation and is subject to FIT, FITW, FICA, and FUTA. The employer may elect not to withhold federal income tax on the value of this use. Where the employer does not withhold federal income tax, the employer must provide a notice by January 31 of the year for which the election not to withhold will apply, or within 30 days of the day a vehicle is made available. Employers can choose among several valuation methods in determining the fair market value of the personal use.

When an employer reimburses employees who use their own automobiles (or leased automobiles) for business purposes, the reimbursement will constitute wages subject to FIT, FITW, FICA, and FUTA unless paid under an accountable plan, which includes the requirement to substantiate the business use of the automobile. An employer can simplify these substantiation requirements by using the standard mileage rate or the fixed and variable rate (FAVR) allowance methods.

Exceptions to the personal use valuation rules may apply under the following circumstances: (1) under the fringe benefit rule of I.R.C. Section 132(j)(3) for auto salespersons; (2) I.R.C. Section 132(f) for qualified transportation benefits (e.g., van commuting); (3) personal use of a "qualified nonpersonal use vehicle" (i.e., a company-provided car or truck with markings or fixtures that generally prohibit personal use) [I.R.C. § 274(i)]; and (4) occasional personal usage as a *de minimis* fringe benefit (e.g., using the car to drive to lunch or to run a personal errand between business calls). See related sections in this chapter.

The value of an employee's commute to and from work in a company-provided vehicle constitutes additional wages, except in the case of a nonpersonal use vehicle (e.g., police car, ambulance, etc.) (see Q 9:114).

Q 9:114   When are commuting expenses incurred in an employer-provided vehicle exempt from wages subject to withholding and employment tax?

The I.R.C. excludes commuting expenses incurred in an employer-provided vehicle when such commuting expenses meet the definition of a working condition fringe benefit. [I.R.C. § 132(a)(3)]

Employee use of a qualified nonpersonal use vehicle meets the definition of a working condition fringe benefit if the vehicle will not be used more than a minimal amount for personal purposes (other than commuting) and the vehicle conforms to the requirements set forth in Temporary Treasury Regulations Section 1-274-5T(k). Common examples of nonpersonal use vehicles include fire engines, ambulances, clearly marked police and fire vehicles, flatbed trucks, school buses, etc.

An employee does not have to substantiate the business use of a nonpersonal use vehicle in order to exclude its value from income.

The IRS stipulates that the exclusion of an employee's value of the use of a clearly marked police or fire vehicle applies only to a vehicle that is required to be used for commuting by a police officer or fire fighter who, when not on a regular shift, is on call at all times. Other than commuting, personal use of the vehicle, outside the limit of the police officer's arrest powers or the fire fighter's obligation to respond to an emergency, must be prohibited by the governmental unit. [IRS website, FAQs on nonpersonal use vehicles]

Q 9:115   Is there an exception to the commuting rule for unsafe conditions?

Yes, A company may provide transportation for an employee to commute to and from work, when there are unsafe conditions under the commuting rule for $1.50 for a one-way commute if certain guidelines are followed. The requirements are that the employee would ordinarily walk or use public transportation for commuting, there is a written reimbursement policy for commuting because of unsafe conditions, and the employee only uses the transportation for commuting in unsafe conditions and not for personal use. The requirements must be met on a trip-by-trip basis. The determination if there are unsafe conditions may be based on circumstances that a reasonable person would consider it unsafe to walk or use public transportation. One factor that would indicate unsafe conditions is a history of crime in the geographic area surrounding the workplace or the employee's home at the time of day that the employee commutes. The employee who is being reimbursed must also meet certain criteria. The employee must be a "qualified employee" who is paid hourly, not considered exempt under FLSA, and has not received more than $120,000 in pay during the year. The transportation must be provided by an unrelated party who is paid directly by the employer or, if paid by the employee, is reimbursed under a bona fide reimbursement program.

Q 9:116   How does the employer determine the amount to be included in taxable income for personal use of a company vehicle?

The fair market value (FMV) of employees' personal use of a company car can be determined under the "general valuation method," which values the personal use on what it would cost the employee to obtain the same vehicle use in an arm's-length transaction in the same geographic region. That is, the amount included in wages is based on what it would cost to lease the vehicle for the personal use (the general valuation method). This method tends to produce the highest value and may be, therefore, the least desirable from the employee's standpoint. In addition to the general valuation method, there are several alternative methods to establish the FMV of the personal use: (1) the commuting valuation method, (2) the cents-per-mile valuation method, (3) the annual lease valuation method, and (4) the fixed and variable rate method. An alternative valuation may only be used when one of the following four conditions are met:

1. The employer reports the value of the personal use as additional compensation for calendar years when the vehicle was used.

2. The employee includes the value of the personal use for the year in which the benefit is provided.

3. The employee is not a "control employee" under Treasury Regulations Section 1.61-21(f)(5) or 1.61-21(f)(6). (See Q 9:322.)

4. The employer demonstrates a good-faith effort to treat and report the personal use correctly.

The value of the usage is reported as employee wages for the year of the use and no later than January 31 of the calendar year following the personal use. However, a special accounting rule permits the employer to establish a reporting period that delays reporting the value of an employee's personal use during the months of November and December until the next calendar year. This treatment is to be applied on a consistent basis. Delayed reporting does not affect an employer's use of an alternate valuation method to determine the value of the automobile usage. [Treas. Reg. § 1.61-21(c)(3); Ann. 85-113, 1985-31 I.R.B. 31]

Under the *commuting valuation method*, the personal use of an employer-provided vehicle for commuting purposes is valued at $1.50 each one way ($3.00 per round-trip commute). This method is permitted where the employee commutes to or from work for bona fide noncompensatory business reasons (e.g., uses a company car under unsafe conditions or at an unsafe time). Where more than one employee commutes in the same vehicle, the $1.50 one-way or $3.00 round trip applies to each employee. [Treas. Reg. § 1.61-21(f)]

Under the *annual lease valuation (ALV) method*, the employer must use an IRS table to determine the annual lease value of the car that is based on its FMV on the first day it was made available for personal use to the employee. This method can also be used if the employee uses a company vehicle for less than the entire calendar year. The employee's portion of this annual value is based on the employee's personal use percentage (i.e., the personal miles divided by total miles driven). The FMV of the vehicle is the cost of the vehicle in an arm's-length transaction. The FMV of a leased vehicle can be determined under one of three safe harbor methods. A company with 20 or more qualified vehicles (i.e., regularly used for business purposes) that have an FMV not exceeding $21,100 for a passenger automobile or $23,300 for a truck or van for 2017 and that uses the ALV method may elect instead to use the fleet average valuation method. This method applies the ALV tables to the average FMV of all the vehicles in the fleet. [Treas. Reg. § 1.61-21(d); Notice 2016-12, IRB 2016-6, 312] (See Q 9:119.)

Under the *cents-per-mile valuation method,* a standard mileage rate is multiplied by the total number of miles driven for personal use to determine the employee's taxable compensation. The standard mileage rate is $0.535 for 2017. For 2016, the standard mileage rate was $0.54. If the employer does not provide the fuel, the mileage rate can be reduced up to $0.055 per mile. This method cannot be used if the FMV of the vehicle exceeds $15,900 for a car or $17,800 for a truck for 2017, or if the car is not driven for at least 10,000 miles (including the personal use). [Notice 2014-11, 2014-13 I.R.B. 880; Rev. Proc. 2012-13, 2012-3 I.R.B. 295; Treas. Reg. § 1.61-21(e)] (See Q 9:121.) [Notice 2017-3, Jan. 7, 2017; Rev. Proc. 2017-3, I.R.B. 2017-1, 130; Update Rev. Proc. 2016-3, 2016-1 I.R.B.]

The regulations permit employers to use different valuation methods for each employee; however, if either the ALV or the vehicle cents-per-mile rule is adopted for an employee's valuation, that method must be used for all subsequent years during which the employee uses the vehicle. An exception to this rule permits the employer to switch to the commuting valuation method for any period when the vehicle qualifies for that method. The value of the personal use and the employment tax liability can be applied on a pay period, quarterly, semiannual, annual, or other basis. Personal use and company use must be documented with adequate records, otherwise the IRS may require that the full ALV be treated as additional wages. If the same vehicle is used by two or more employees, all the employees' usage is valued under the same method. [I.R.C. § 61; Treas. Reg. § 1.61-21]

The regulations require that an employer report as additional wages the commuting use or other personal use of a company vehicle when the use is for more than one day a month. [Treas. Reg. § 1.132-6(e)]

Q 9:117   What is the general valuation rule for personal use of company vehicles?

An employer may determine the value of an employee's personal use of a company vehicle by using the FMV an employee would pay in the commercial market for a similar vehicle for the same length of time (e.g., a commercial lease). That valuation must take into consideration any special equipment provided in or on the vehicle if the employee may use the special equipment for personal reasons. This method does not permit a cents-per-mile rate calculation unless commercial rates are available under similar terms. This method generally requires a per diem charge and is generally not as favorable to the employee as the other valuation methods. Most companies will elect to use one of the alternate valuation methods because those methods generally produce a lower value to be treated as wages to the employee. Where an employee fails to meet all of the requirements for an alternate valuation method, the IRS will impose the general valuation methods. [Treas. Reg. § 1.61-21(b)(4)]

Special Valuation Methods

Q 9:118 How is the personal use of a company vehicle valued under the commuting-only valuation method?

For certain noncompensatory purposes, an employer can value an employee's personal use of a company vehicle for commuting to and from work at $1.50 per one-way commute and $3.00 per round trip. This method can only be used when the following conditions are met: (1) the vehicle is owned (or leased) by the company and is not provided to the employee for personal use (i.e., it may not be used in connection with the employer's trade or business); (2) the employer requires the employee, for business reasons, to commute to and from work in the vehicle (e.g., unsafe conditions during the commute require the arrangement); (3) the employee is not a control employee; (4) the employer has a written policy that prohibits reimbursement to pay for the expenses of the employee's personal vehicle; (5) the vehicle must not be available for other personal use (except for certain *de minimis* usage); and (6) the employee must be an individual who qualifies as a nonexempt employee for overtime pay under the FLSA and who is paid on an hourly basis. [Treas. Reg. §§ 1.61-21(f), 1.61-21(k)(6); 5 U.S.C. § 5316]

Q 9:119 How is the annual lease valuation method applied?

The employer may value an employee's personal use of a company vehicle under the ALV method when certain conditions are met. This method computes the value of the employee's usage based on the percentage of personal use by the employee (personal miles/total miles) multiplied by the FMV of an annual auto lease. The lease value is taken from an IRS table, which is based on the FMV of the automobile as of the first day of usage by the employee (see Table 9-1). This is the employer's cost, including sales tax and title fees, for an employer-owned vehicle (but not manufactured by the employer). Where the vehicle is leased by the company, the employer may use one of three safe harbor methods to determine the FMV: (1) the "blue book" value (or other nationally recognized valuation source); (2) the manufacturer's suggested retail price less 8 percent; or (3) the dealer's invoice plus 4 percent (must be an arm's-length transaction). [Treas. Reg. § 1.61-21(d)(5)]

Table 9-1. Annual Lease Value for Automobiles, 2017

Automobile Fair Market Value	Annual Lease Value
$0–999	$ 600
1,000–1,999	850
2,000–2,999	1,100
3,000–3,999	1,350
4,000–4,999	1,600
5,000–5,999	1,850
6,000–6,999	2,100
7,000–7,999	2,350
8,000–8,999	2,600
9,000–9,999	2,850
10,000–10,999	3,100
11,000–11,999	3,350
12,000–12,999	3,600
13,000–13,999	3,850
14,000–14,999	4,100
15,000–15,999	4,350
16,000–16,999	4,600
17,000–17,999	4,850
18,000–18,999	5,100
19,000–19,999	5,350
20,000–20,999	5,600
21,000–21,999	5,850
22,000–22,999	6,100
23,000–23,999	6,350
24,000–24,999	6,600
25,000–25,999	6,850
26,000–27,999	7,250
28,000–29,999	7,750
30,000–31,999	8,250
32,000–33,999	8,750
34,000–35,999	9,250
36,000–37,999	9,750
38,000–39,999	10,250
40,000–41,999	10,750

Table 9-1.   Annual Lease Value for Automobiles, 2017 (*cont'd*)

Automobile Fair Market Value	Annual Lease Value
42,000–43,999	11,250
44,000–45,999	11,750
46,000–47,999	12,250
48,000–49,999	12,750
50,000–51,999	13,250
52,000–53,999	13,750
54,000–55,999	14,250
56,000–57,999	14,750
58,000–59,999	15,250

For automobiles with an FMV greater than $59,999, the annual lease value = (0.25 × FMV) + $500. [Treas. Reg. § 1.61-21(d)(2)(iii)]

When the employer provides the fuel under this method, an additional 5.5 cents per mile ($0.055 per mile in 2017) is added to the employee's wages for personal use of the vehicle.

When the employee uses the vehicle for less than a year but at least 30 days, the employee's personal use for the month is determined by multiplying the percentage of personal use by 1/12 of the annual lease value. If the vehicle is available for personal use for less than 30 days, the value of that availability is determined under the daily lease valuation method. The daily lease valuation method is the ALV multiplied by (1) four and (2) a fraction with the number of days the vehicle was available to the employee divided by 365. Thus, the daily rate can be four times the prorated ALV. For usage of less than 30 days, an employer may elect to apply 1/12 of the ALV instead of the daily lease value for the actual days used.

Example. Shannon's company purchased an automobile for Shannon's business and occasional personal use. The automobile cost $54,100. The ALV for the automobile is $14,250. The monthly lease value is $1,280. Shannon's personal use of the car for the month was 9.5 percent (i.e., she drove 8,400 miles total, which included 800 miles of personal use). She has additional wages of 0.095 × $1,280 or $121.60.

When the employee has use of the vehicle for at least 30 days, but those days span two calendar years, the employer may either (1) elect the special accounting method and treat the employee's personal use during the months of November and December as if leased in the next plan year, or (2) prorate the ALV between the two years. [Treas. Reg. § 1.61-21(d)(4)]

Q 9:120 What fleet valuation rules are available under the annual base value method?

A company that has 20 or more "qualified vehicles" and that uses the ALV method may elect to utilize the fleet valuation method to determine the average ALV for the fleet. Under the fleet valuation method, the employer uses an average FMV of all vehicles in the fleet to determine the ALV of each vehicle. A "qualified vehicle" is a vehicle that is regularly used for company business and that does not have an FMV of more than $21,100 for cars or $23,300 for trucks or vans first placed in use in 2017. The 20-qualified-vehicle threshold must be met by January 1. It is met if the employer has at least 20 vehicles meeting these requirements in the previous calendar year.

The taxable value of fuel provided for personal use of a vehicle under the fleet valuation method is 5.5 cents ($0.055) each mile for 2017, unless the actual value of such fuel can be calculated. That determination may be based on the actual fuel costs per mile driven for at least 10 percent of the vehicles in the fleet or, if less, 20 vehicles. [Treas. Reg. §§ 1.61-21(d)(3), 1.61-21(d)(5); Rev. Proc. 91-30, 1991-1 C.B. 563]

Q 9:121 How is the cents-per-mile valuation method applied?

An employer may determine the FMV of an employee's personal use of a company vehicle under a standard mileage rate (adjusted each year). The rate is charged for all personal usage at $0.535 effective January 1, 2017. The cents-per-mile method can only be used when the following conditions are met: (1) the vehicle must be used for business by employees on a regular basis throughout the year or as long as the vehicle is owned or leased by the employer and must be driven at least 10,000 miles a year; (2) the FMV of the automobile cannot exceed $15,900 for a car or $17,800 for a truck or van for 2017; (3) if the employee pays for all fuel, the mileage rate is reduced by $0.535 per mile in 2017; (4) the vehicle must be primarily used by employees; and (5) the employer reports only personal use of the vehicle on Form W-2, Box 1. The vehicle cannot be used by a control employee, defined in Q 9:322.

Q 9:122 How is the value of the personal use of a company vehicle reported for employment tax purposes?

The FMV of personal use is treated as additional wages and subject to FIT, FITW, FICA, and FUTA. The value is reported in Boxes 1, 3, and 5 of Form W-2. In addition, if 100 percent of the usage is reported as additional compensation to the employee, report the lease value in Box 14 or on a separate statement if sufficient space is not available in Box 14.

Q 9:123   May an employer elect not to withhold federal income taxes from the FMV of an employee's personal use of a company car?

Yes. An employer can choose not to withhold federal income tax on the value of an employee's personal use of a highway motor vehicle the employer provides. This choice does not have to be made for all employees. The employer can withhold federal income tax from FMV of the personal vehicle use of some employees but not others; however, the employer must withhold the applicable FICA and pay FICA and FUTA on the FMV of the personal vehicle use of all employees.

When an employer chooses not to withhold federal income tax for personal use of a company vehicle, the employer must (1) notify the employee that no federal income taxes will be withheld and (2) include the value of the benefits in Boxes 1, 3, and 5 on a timely furnished Form W-2.

The employee notice must be in writing and must be provided to the employee by January 31 of the election year or within 30 days after a vehicle is first provided to the employee, whichever is later. This notice must be provided in a manner reasonably expected to come to the attention of the affected employee. For example, the notice may be mailed to the employee, included with a paycheck, or posted where the employee could reasonably be expected to see it. The employer may also change its election not to withhold federal income tax at any time by notifying affected employees in the same manner. [Pub. No. 15-B; Ann. 85-113, 1985-31 I.R.B. 31]

Q 9:124   What are the special valuation rules for an employee's use of a demonstration vehicle?

The personal use of a demonstration vehicle by a full-time automobile salesperson is excluded from the salesperson's compensation as a working-condition fringe benefit when certain requirements are met. This tax-free treatment is available when the use of the vehicle is limited to only salespersons (not managers), when the vehicle is not used to store personal possessions, and when the vehicle is not used for personal vacation trips in excess of 75 miles from the dealership or the route the salesperson commutes to work.

There are two methods to determine if the value of the personal use by an auto salesperson qualifies as a working-condition fringe benefit: the full exclusion determination or the partial exclusion determination. The IRS also permits a simplified method to value personal usage that does not meet the requirements to be a working-condition fringe benefit.

Full exclusion—simplified determination. The IRS has released safe harbor guidelines that, if followed, may be used to treat the full usage of a demonstration automobile as a working-condition fringe benefit. To satisfy this determination, the following conditions must apply to such usage:

1. The employer establishes a written policy that is communicated to the employees and includes all the following restrictions:

- No personal use of the demonstration vehicle for vacation travel.

- Only salespersons may use the vehicle outside of normal business hours.

- No personal possessions may be stored in the automobile.

2. The maximum personal use outside of normal business hours per day does not exceed the salesperson's commute plus 10 miles.

3. The employer maintains certain records to demonstrate compliance with these guidelines.

An employer may rely on the safe-harbor simplification test for full exclusion of a salesperson's personal use of a demonstration automobile when records are maintained on the personal usage sufficient to calculate this usage. To meet this safe harbor, these records must include (1) an identification of which vehicle was used by which salesperson, (2) records reflecting each salesperson's use outside of normal business hours (including both personal and nonpersonal usage), and (3) a record of the mileage commute for each salesperson. The employer must calculate and retain in its records, at least monthly, the salesperson's total personal usage. [Rev. Proc. 2001-56, 2001-51 I.R.B. 590].

When a full-time salesperson's daily usage exceeds the limit of 10 miles per day plus commute mileage, the employer may use the general valuation method or a simplified valuation method. Under the simplified valuation method, the value of the personal usage by a full-time salesperson is a daily rate based on the value of the demonstration vehicle. That is, if the salesperson's personal use of a demonstration vehicle exceeds the 10-mile-plus-commute-mileage limit, the usage on that day is a daily rate under the following table. (Note that this table may be used when all the conditions below are met.)

Value of Demonstration Automobile	Daily Valuation Rate
0 to $14,999	$ 3
$15,000 to $29,999	6
$30,000 to $44,999	9
$45,000 to $59,999	13
$60,000 to $74,999	17
$75,000 and above	21

Conditions for simplified daily rate. When a full-time salesperson uses a demonstration vehicle for personal purposes in a way that does not meet all the conditions for exclusion as a working-condition fringe benefit, the daily valuation rate may apply. This valuation method is available when:

1. The employer has a written policy limiting personal use of a demonstration vehicle that is communicated to the employee (and based on the safe harbor requirements identified earlier); and

2. The employer must expect that the employees have complied with those requirements.

However, an auto dealer's improper application of the safe harbor valuation method requires valuation under the FMV methods. This was confirmed in a technical advice memorandum (TAM). The IRS denied a taxpayer (an automotive distributor) use of the safe harbor valuation method when it improperly applied that method. As a result, the employer had to value the use of a company-provided car under the general valuation method. [Tech. Adv. Mem. 9816007, Apr. 17, 1998]

Under the applicable regulations, the FMV of an employer-owned vehicle must be based on the employer's cost in an arm's-length transaction. Auto manufacturers and their affiliates must base the valuation on the cost that an individual customer would pay for the vehicle. The regulations require that the safe harbor method be applied properly; otherwise, the FMV of personal use is determined under the general valuation method. That is, the value is determined based on what it would cost to lease the vehicle. [Treas. Reg. §§ 1.61-21(d)(5), 1.274-6]

Substantiation of Business Use

Q 9:125 What are the business substantiation requirements that apply to the use of a company vehicle?

The FMV of an employee's use of a company-provided vehicle is excluded from wages subject to FIT, FITW, FICA, and FUTA to the extent the employer can demonstrate that use of the vehicle was primarily for business purposes. Employers can satisfy this requirement by keeping adequate records or other appropriate evidence (including statements submitted by employees) that all or a portion of the use of the vehicle was for the employer's trade or business. The employer may rely on adequate records maintained by the employee or statements made by the employee and corroborated by adequate records. If the employer relies on the employee's records, the employee must retain the original records and the employer must retain a copy of them. [I.R.C. §§ 162, 274(d); Temp. Treas. Reg. § 1.274-6T]

The employer may elect instead to include the full value of the use of the company vehicle in the employee's wages, using either general valuation or the lease value method. If 100 percent of the vehicle's use is included in wages subject to FIT, FITW, FICA, and FUTA, the employee may be able to deduct substantiated business use as a nonreimbursed employee business expense on Form 1040, subject to any restrictions or limitations that apply. [Temp. Treas. Reg. § 1.274-5T(e)]

Q 9:126 What safe harbor rules apply to the business substantiation requirements?

Employers can satisfy their business substantiation requirements for demonstrating that an employee's use of a company vehicle is solely for business purposes by implementing a written policy that no personal use of a company vehicle is permitted, or only commuting use is permitted. The employer satisfies its substantiation requirement with such a statement when six conditions are met: (1) no employee using the vehicle lives at the business premises, (2) the vehicle is owned or leased by the employer and is provided for business use, (3) the vehicle is kept on business property during nonbusiness hours, (4) only *de minimis* personal use is permitted, (5) the employer has no reason to believe that the vehicle is being used for personal reasons other than commuting, and (6) there must be evidence that the vehicle use satisfies these first five requirements. [Temp. Treas. Reg. § 1.274-6T]

When the employer uses a safe harbor substantiation method that includes a commuting-use-only policy, seven conditions must be met: (1) the employee is required to commute in the company vehicle for noncompensatory business reasons, (2) the vehicle is owned or leased by the employer and is provided for business use, (3) the employer has a formal written policy that no personal use of the vehicle is permitted (other than commuting to and from work and *de minimis* personal use), (4) the employer has no reason to believe that the vehicle is being used for personal reasons beyond commuting, (5) the employer includes in the employee's gross income the appropriate commuting expense ($1.50 one way and $3.00 each round trip), (6) the employee using the automobile is not a control employee, and (7) the employer retains sufficient documentation to demonstrate compliance with the first six requirements. [Temp. Treas. Reg. § 1.274-6T]

Q 9:127   What type of substantiation of business use for a company vehicle is required of an employee?

The employee who uses a company vehicle for personal use must substantiate the business use of the vehicle by maintaining adequate records to demonstrate such use. There are no specific requirements as to the type of documentation that must be kept. Instead, IRS regulations state that "written evidence has considerably more probative value than oral evidence alone." In other words, an employer should not rely on an employee's memory to support an expense contested by the IRS. A contemporaneous log is not required; however, "a recording of the elements of an expenditure or of a business use of [a company vehicle] made at or near the time of the expenditure or use, supported by sufficient documentary evidence has a high degree of credibility not present with respect to a statement prepared subsequent thereto when generally there is a lack of adequate recall." This generally means that the employee should maintain a log or enter on a timely basis in a diary or similar record the time, date, location, business use, and mileage connected to the company vehicle. [Temp. Treas. Reg. § 1.274-5T(c)]

Q 9:128   What are the substantiation requirements for qualified nonpersonal use vehicles?

The substantiation requirements that apply when a company vehicle is available for the personal use of an employee do not apply to a "qualified nonpersonal use vehicle." This exemption is available because a nonpersonal use vehicle is the type of vehicle that does not lend itself to personal use. Examples of nonpersonal use vehicles are found in Regulations Section 1.274-5(k) and include: clearly marked police and fire vehicles, ambulances or hearses used for these purposes, a vehicle carrying a logo and loaded with a gross weight of 14,000 pounds, cement mixers, combines, garbage trucks, forklifts, passenger buses with a capacity of at least 20 passengers, delivery trucks with seating capacity only for the driver (or only the driver and a folding jump seat), dump trucks, flatbed trucks, and unmarked vehicles used by law enforcement officers if the personal use is officially authorized. Special rules apply to police and fire vehicles, moving trucks, specialized entity repair trucks, unmarked law enforcement vehicles, and trucks and vans that have been modified to discourage personal use by employees. [Temp. Treas. Reg. § 1.274-6T(h)]

Q 9:129   Does the exemption from the substantiation requirements for a nonpersonal use vehicle apply to a company's truck or van?

Yes, if one of two conditions are met: (1) the vehicle is one of the 19 types described in Treasury Regulations Section 1.274-5(k)(2) (e.g., a delivery vehicle with only a driver's seat or a driver's seat and a folding jump seat) or (2) the truck or van has been modified to make personal use unlikely. The regulations provide examples: (1) a van that has been modified and has only a front bench seat in which permanent shelving fills most of the cargo area and that is generally loaded with merchandise or equipment and has been specially painted and (2) a pick-up truck 14,000 pounds or less. [Treas. Reg. § 1.274-5(k)(7)]

Q 9:130   Does the fact that a vehicle has a company logo qualify the vehicle as a nonpersonal use vehicle?

No. Substantiation (or deemed substantiation) is required for any company vehicle that is available for personal use. Only certain vehicles classified as nonpersonal use vehicles under the regulations are exempt from any substantiation requirement for business use. These vehicles are generally of the type that makes personal use impractical. [Treas. Reg. § 1.274-5(k)]

Q 9:131   How is the shared use of a company vehicle for nonbusiness reasons treated?

When the employer provides a company vehicle for personal use by more than one employee (e.g., pooled commuting to work in a company vehicle), each employee's compensation must include the employee's proportionate share of the FMV of their personal use. That FMV can be determined under the general valuation method or one of the alternate valuation methods (ALV, commuting-only, or cents per mile). [Treas. Reg. § 1.61-21(c)(2)]

Q 9:132 Does a company vehicle used only for commuting satisfy the business use requirements?

Yes. If the commuting vehicle is used by at least three employees in a commuting pool each business day, it is treated as a business use vehicle even if it is not used for any other business purpose. [Treas. Reg. § 1.61-21(f)(1)(v)]

Q 9:133 May an automobile salesperson use a demonstration vehicle for personal use as a tax-free working-condition fringe benefit?

Generally, yes. As long as certain conditions are met, a "full-time automobile salesperson" may use a "qualified demonstration use" vehicle without the FMV of that use being treated as additional wages to the employee. To be excluded from gross income, there must be substantial restrictions on the personal use of the vehicle.

A full-time automobile salesperson is an individual who: (1) is employed by an automobile dealer, (2) customarily spends at least one-half of a normal business day performing functions of a floor salesperson or sales manager, (3) is directly engaged in substantial promotion and negotiation of rates to customers, (4) customarily works a number of hours that is considered full-time in the industry (at least 1,000 hours in the calendar year), and (5) derives at least 25 percent of his or her gross income from the automobile dealership in negotiating and promoting sales of automobiles. An owner or general manager of an automobile dealership who is not directly involved in sales does not qualify for this exclusion, even if the individual is paid based on sales of automobiles by the dealership's salespeople.

A qualified demonstration use vehicle is a vehicle that is currently in the inventory of the automobile dealership and is available for test-drives by customers during normal business hours.

A demonstration use vehicle is subject to four restrictions on personal use: (1) the demonstration vehicle must not be used by any individual other than the salesperson (i.e., a family member cannot use the vehicle); (2) personal use for a vacation is prohibited; (3) no storage of personal possessions is permitted; and (4) the salesperson's personal use outside of normal business hours is limited. This last requirement is met when the employee is not permitted to drive beyond the immediate geographic area of the dealership (i.e., the greater of 75 miles from the dealership's location or the one-way commute from the salesperson's home to the sales office). [Treas. Reg. § 1.132-5(a)]

Q 9:134   What are the reporting requirements for an employee's nonbusiness use of company automobiles?

When an employee has use of the employer's highway motor vehicle for personal purposes, the FMV of that usage must be included in the employee's wages. That value is included in Boxes 1, 3, and 5 of the employee's Form W-2. If the employer reports 100 percent of the FMV as gross income (i.e., both business and personal miles), the employer must also report that value in Box 14 of Form W-2 or provide a separate statement. [Pub. No. 535]

Dependent Care

Q 9:135   What are dependent care assistance benefits?

Dependent care assistance benefits are employer payments for certain expenses related to the care of an eligible dependent while the employee (and spouse, if married) is at work. These benefits can be either for the care of a dependent by a qualified provider or provided through an employer-operated facility. An eligible dependent is defined as a child under age 13, an aging parent or other dependent who is mentally or physically challenged, or a disabled spouse. For the dependent care benefits to be tax free, the care must enable an employee (and spouse, if married) to be gainfully employed. Thus, benefits are not available when only one individual in a marriage is employed (e.g., where an individual is employed but the spouse only does volunteer work, no tax-free dependent benefits are available). Certain exceptions apply to the gainful employment requirement when a nonworking spouse is in school or is disabled.

A qualifying child for purposes of dependent care assistance is defined by I.R.C. Section 152.

The IRS treats qualifying children of divorced or separated parents as the dependents of both parents under several tax code sections for health and fringe benefits, regardless of whether the custodial parent releases the claim to the exemption.

Although dependent care benefits typically are provided as employer reimbursements to the employee, they may be paid directly to the dependent care provider (e.g., babysitter) or may be directly provided through an employer's onsite day care facility. The I.R.C. requires that a dependent care assistance plan be in writing and that the plan not discriminate in favor of "highly compensated employees" (HCES) as determined under the pension laws. Payments from a discriminatory plan are taxable to the HCEs. [I.R.C. §§ 21(b), 129, 414(q)]

I.R.C. Section 129 permits employers to exclude from an employee's wages the value of dependent care assistance benefits provided by the employer when certain requirements are met. [I.R.C. §§ 129(a)(2)(A), 129(b), 3121(a)(18), 3306(b)(13), 3401(a)(18); Pub. No. 535 Ch. 5]

Q 9:136   Under what conditions can dependent care assistance qualify for an exclusion from wages?

In general, benefits paid from plans not meeting all of the I.R.C. Section 129 requirements are included in wages subject to FIT, FITW, FICA, and FUTA. The Section 129 requirements are:

1. The dependent care assistance must be provided under a written plan document.

2. The plan may not discriminate in favor of individuals classified as HCEs under the pension rules (see Q 9:318). If this is the only violation, only the value of benefits available to the HCEs are included in their compensation.

3. The maximum income exclusion allowed in the calendar year is limited to $5,000 per year ($2,500 each for married taxpayers filing separately), regardless of the number of dependents. This amount is not indexed for inflation.

4. If the employee is married, the spouse must also be gainfully employed, disabled, or attending school.

5. Reimbursement or payment of dependent care expenses by the employer requires substantiation as to the nature and amount of the expense, the date the expense was incurred (only expenses incurred in the plan year, which has been extended by the IRS to include 2 and one half months after the plan year may be reimbursed), and the provider's Social Security or federal identification number (use Form W-10, Dependent Care Provider's Identification and Certification).

In no event may the total exclusion exceed the employee's earned income for the year or, if the employee is married, the lesser of the individual's or spouse's earned income. That is, the amount of the exclusion is limited to the earned income of the individual or spouse, whoever has the least earned income.

Example. Jason and Jennifer pay $4,700 for dependent care for their child; however, Jennifer only earns $4,100, while Jason earns $50,000. Only $4,100 will be excluded from the couple's reporting on Form 1040 for the year. If Jason's or Jennifer's employer benefits are valued at $5,000, only $4,100 is excluded from income on the couple's Form 1040.

The employer also should inform the employee about the dependent care tax credit available and the circumstances under which the credit may be more advantageous than the exclusion. In the event the spouse is a full-time student or incapable of caring for himself or herself, special rules apply to the exclusion allowed. [I.R.C. §§ 129(a)(2)(A), 129(b), 3121(a)(18), 3306(b)(13), 3401(a)(18); Prop. Treas. Reg. § 1.125-2; Pub. No. 535 Ch. 5]

Q 9:137　Can expenses incurred after the plan year be reimbursed without being subject to the I.R.C. Section 125 "use it or lose it" provision?

Yes. Notice 2005-42 [2005-23 I.R.B. 1204], released May 18, 2005, extended the year-end deadline for FSAs by a two and one-half month grace period. The notice, according to the Treasury Department and IRS, permits a grace period immediately following the end of each plan year during which any unused plan benefits or contributions remaining may be paid or reimbursed to plan participants for qualified benefit expenses incurred. It modifies the rule prohibiting the receipt of deferred compensation under I.R.C. Section 125 cafeteria plans (see Qs 9:195–9:199).

Q 9:138　What benefits may be provided under a dependent care assistance plan?

A dependent care assistance plan may make payments directly to a dependent care provider or reimburse an employee for his or her payment of any dependent care provider that is necessary for the employee (and spouse, if married) to be gainfully employed. These payments are limited to dependent care for children under age 13 or other dependents who cannot care for themselves. Payments cannot be made for care that also includes a training or educational component, and the care must be limited to hours when the employee and spouse are employed. Thus, overnight summer camp expenses do not qualify. [I.R.C. §§ 129(e)(1), 21(b)(2)(A)(ii)]

Dependent care expenses are expenses that qualify for the dependent care tax credit under I.R.C. Section 21. In certain cases, household expenses provided with the care qualify as dependent care expenses (e.g., for an elderly parent). No exclusion is available for child care that is paid to a child of the employee under age 19 or child care that is paid to anyone the employee can claim as a dependent. [I.R.C. §§ 129(b), 129(c) Pub. No. 503]

It should be noted that because the Social Security number or taxpayer ID of the dependent care provider must be reported by the taxpayer, dependent care services that are paid improperly "under the table" (meaning appropriate taxes are not withheld and paid over to the taxing authorities), do not qualify for dependent care reimbursement.

Q 9:139　Do nondiscrimination requirements apply to a dependent care assistance plan?

Yes. Benefits provided under an employer-sponsored dependent care plan are not treated as additional wages to HCEs when, among other things, the plan does not discriminate in favor of HCEs as to either (1) eligibility to participate in the plan, or (2) contributions made or benefits provided on behalf of participants. HCEs are defined for pension purposes in Q 9:318. [I.R.C. §§ 129(d)(2), 414(q)]

The eligibility requirement is met when the plan covers a class of employees that the IRS finds does not favor HCEs or their dependents. This requirement is generally considered met when the plan's coverage satisfies the pension non-discrimination classification tests of I.R.C. Section 410(b).

A dependent care benefit plan satisfies the second nondiscrimination requirement (listed above) when two tests are met:

1. No more than one-fourth of the employer-paid benefits for the year are provided to individuals who own more than 5 percent of the stock, capital, or profits interest in the employer (note that stock ownership of one family member can be attributed to certain other family members); and

2. The average benefits provided to non-highly compensated employees (NHCEs) is at least 55 percent of the average benefit provided to HCEs. [I.R.C. §§ 129(d)(4), 129(d)(8)]

Note that for purposes of identifying ownership for the one-fourth limitation noted above, an individual is treated as owning the stock owned by: (1) a spouse; (2) minor children (and adult children and grandchildren if the individual owns more than 50 percent of the employer); and (3) certain partnerships, trusts, and corporations in which the individual has an interest. [I.R.C. §§ 129(e)(5), 1563]

There is some disagreement among professionals on how the 55 percent average benefits test is to be calculated. Most tax practitioners interpret the law to say that the total benefit provided to HCEs is divided by the total number of HCEs eligible to participate and that percentage is compared to the total value of benefits provided to all eligible NHCEs as divided by the number of NHCEs eligible to participate. Others believe the divisor in each of these fractions is limited to only the number of individuals actually participating in the plan (i.e., receiving benefits). Informally, IRS speakers favor the first method, which is generally more difficult to pass.

The employer may disregard certain employees in determining whether a dependent care assistance program satisfies the 55 percent average benefits test. The employer may exclude employees who are younger than 21 years of age, have not completed a year of service, or are covered by a collective bargaining agreement (provided dependent care benefits were a subject of bargaining) from consideration for both the eligibility and benefits nondiscrimination tests. In addition, employees with less than $25,000 in annual compensation may be disregarded when dependent care assistance benefits are provided through salary reductions under a cafeteria plan. [I.R.C. § 129(d)(8)(B); Prop. Treas. Reg. § 1.125-1, Q 18]

It is important to ensure that employers are actually conducting the nondiscrimination test for dependent care. Many payroll practitioners have found that once the plan is adopted, testing is not conducted, putting participants at risk for penalties and interest for underpayment of income taxes.

Q 9:140 How are benefits under a discriminatory dependent care plan treated for employment tax purposes?

A dependent care assistance program that is found to fail the I.R.C.'s nondiscrimination requirements for dependent care benefits results in the value of benefits made available to HCEs (as defined under pension laws) being included in their compensation. That is, all benefits paid to the HCEs are treated as compensation and are subject to federal income tax withholding and FICA and FUTA taxes. [I.R.C. §§ 129(d)(1), 414(q)]

Q 9:141 What is a dependent care flexible spending account?

A dependent care FSA is an employer-sponsored benefit plan that each year establishes a maximum dollar amount of benefit that may be used to reimburse an employee for "qualifying" dependent care expenses. These plans may be funded through employer, employee, or employer and employee contributions. When the plan is funded through employee contributions under a Section 125 cafeteria plan, those contributions are made on a before-tax salary reduction basis (exempt from all federal employment taxes). Those salary reductions and elections must generally remain in place for a full plan year. When dependent care FSAs are funded through a Section 125 plan, unused amounts must be forfeited at the end of the plan year (see Qs 9:195–9:199).

When these plans satisfy certain eligibility and expense substantiation requirements, the reimbursements from the dependent care FSA are not treated as compensation to the employee.

Q 9:142 How is the employment tax exclusion applied to dependent care expenses?

Dependent care benefits of up to $5,000 per year are excluded from wages subject to FIT, FITW, FICA, and FUTA. In most cases, the employer may have no knowledge of factors that affect the maximum dependent care expense deduction of the employee (i.e., whether a spouse is employed, the filing status of an employee and spouse, the spouse's wages). The IRS regulations generally permit the employer to apply a reasonableness test to determine whether the amount of the dependent care expense is excludable from taxable wages. As a result, employers normally treat the first $5,000 of dependent care benefits as excludable whether paid through salary reductions or employer contributions, unless the employee provides information that causes the employer to no longer expect that the employee can claim a federal income tax deduction for all or a portion of the $5,000 benefit. [I.R.C. §§ 3121(a)(18), 3306(b)(13), 3401(a)(18)]

Q 9:143 How are employer-provided dependent care benefits reported?

The total value of the dependent care benefit plan that satisfies I.R.C. Section 129 is reported by the employer on Form W-2, Box 10, but not in Box 1, 3, or 5.

Include in Box 10 amounts that are nontaxable (up to $5,000) and any assistance that exceeds the $5,000 annual limit (or $2,500 for married individuals filing separately). Report in Box 1, 3, or 5 the amount of dependent care assistance that exceeds the $5,000 limit. When the employer is the provider of the dependent care or pays the provider of the care directly, employees receiving benefits should be given a completed Form W-10, Dependent Care Provider's Identification and Certification. Note that the amount reported in Form W-2, Box 10 is the total value of benefits provided, not just the amount of any employee contributions under a cafeteria plan.

Neither the dependent care credit nor the exclusion for employer-provided dependent care assistance benefits can be claimed by the employee unless the dependent care provider is identified by name, address, and (if not an exempt organization) taxpayer identification number. The dependent care recipient should request this information on Form W-10 directly from the provider when those payments are made. [Pub. No. 15-B]

Director Fees

Q 9:144   Are director fees subject to employment taxes and wage withholding?

No. Fees paid to directors of a corporation who are not also employees of the corporation are not wages subject to FITW, FICA, or FUTA. A director is treated as a self-employed individual. The fees paid to the director are fully taxable to the director and are reported by the corporation on Form 1099-MISC, Box 7. Note that in certain cases a director may also be an employee of the corporation (e.g., an officer). Wages paid to a director for services rendered as an employee (e.g., officer) are subject to FIT, FITW, FICA, and FUTA and are reported on Form W-2. [Treas. Reg. §§ 31.3121(e)-1(b), 31.3306(i)-1(e), 31.3401(c)-1(f)]

Disability (Insured) Benefits

Q 9:145   How are benefits paid under a disability insurance policy treated for federal employment taxes?

Disability benefits provided under an insurance policy for which premiums were paid by the employee on an aftertax basis are exempt from FIT, FITW, FICA, and FUTA. When an employer-provided policy is paid by the employer or by the employee on a pretax basis (e.g., with salary deductions under a Section 125 plan), the benefits are subject to FIT, in some instances, FITW, and, unless an exception applies, FICA and FUTA taxes. [I.R.C. § 104] (See chapter 10 for tax savings that can apply by including the employer-paid premium in federal taxable wages subject to federal income tax withholding.) Employer-provided disability benefits are exempt from FICA and FUTA if paid:

1. On or after termination of employment because of retirement due to disability under an employer plan;

2. After the expiration of six calendar months following the last calendar month in which the employee worked for the employer;

3. From a policy that the employee paid for on an aftertax basis;

4. Under a workers' compensation law; or

5. On a basis that relates to period of time absent from work (e.g., for loss of a limb).

[I.R.C. §§ 3121(a)(4), 3121(a)(13), 3121(a)(15), 3306(b)(4), 3306(b)(10); Treas. Reg. § 31.3401(a)-1(b)]

With most short-term disability programs paid by a provider other than the employer, the employer and benefit provider will agree on who withholds the applicable employment taxes and prepares the tax reporting. The agreement between the third-party carrier and the employer as to who withholds the applicable tax and prepares the tax reporting will require some third parties to issue the benefit check, withhold the taxes, and report the taxable wages and withholdings under their own EIN. Under some agreements, a third party will issue the check, withhold the appropriate amount, and then transfer the tax reporting liability to the employer. If this is the case, the third party must supply the employer with a statement of benefits paid by January 15 of the following year (although most carriers will do this more frequently).

If benefits are paid under a third-party insurance policy, the disability pay is subject to federal income tax withholding only when the employee completes a Form W-4S. The portion of the payment that is taxable (i.e., wages) equates to the percentage the employer contributes to the cost of the plan or the employee's contribution with pretax dollars (see chapter 10 for more information).

Domestic Partner Benefits

Q 9:146 How are benefits provided to domestic partners treated for employment tax purposes?

Benefits provided to an employee's domestic partner are treated as additional wages of the employee unless the domestic partner qualifies as a spouse or a dependent under the I.R.C. [Treas. Reg. §§ 31.3121(a)(2)-1, 31.3306(b)(2)-1] It is noted that the Pension Protection Act of 2006 includes a provision that allows for the transfer of an individual's retirement plan benefits to a domestic partner or other nonspouse beneficiary (sibling, parent, child) when the individual dies. Another provision allows retirement plan hardship distributions for same sex couples under similar rules that permit plan participants to draw on their retirement funds in the case of a qualifying medical or financial emergency.

Q 9:147   May a same-sex domestic partner be treated as a spouse for federal employment law purposes?

Yes. The IRS announced that same-sex individuals, regardless of where they reside (in a jurisdiction that recognizes same-sex marriage or in a jurisdiction that does not recognize same-sex marriage), who have legally married in jurisdictions that recognize same-sex marriages, will be treated as married for federal tax purposes. Also, if a domestic partner qualifies as a dependent, his or her benefits qualify as tax-free if they are tax-free to the employee (i.e., health and welfare benefits). [Rev. Rul. 2013-17, 2013-38 I.R.B. 201]

The Supreme Court ruling in *Obergefell v. Hodges* [576 U.S. ___ 135 S. Ct. 2584 (2015)] ruled that same-sex marriage is a right. This decision means that domestic partners may be included for benefits within companies. In addition, the Treasury issued final regulations [§ 301.7701-18, 81 Fed. Reg. 60609, Sept. 2, 2016] that define husband and wife as two individuals legally married to each other. Couples who are legally married, whether same sex or not, are afforded the right to tax-free benefits under their employer plans.

Q 9:148   When may spousal benefits be offered on a tax-free basis to a same-sex domestic partner of an employee?

Although legally married same-sex couples are treated as married for federal tax purposes, this tax treatment does not apply to registered domestic partnerships. In general, the value of spousal benefits provided by an employer to an employee's same-sex domestic partner is treated as the taxable wages of the employee subject to FIT, FITW, FICA, and FUTA; however, the IRS held in a private letter ruling that some same-sex domestic partners may qualify as *dependents* (rather than spouses) when certain criteria are satisfied and as such are not included in the gross income of the employee or the employee's domestic partner. In this ruling, the employer amended its health plan to cover an employee's same-sex domestic partner as a dependent. The program required the employee and his or her partner to complete a "declaration of domestic partnership."

In Private Letter Ruling 9717018 [(Jan. 22, 1997)], an employee's domestic partner was treated as a dependent of the employee when the partner satisfied the definition of dependent under the I.R.C. [I.R.C. § 152(a)(9)] That section imposes the following three conditions on determining whether an individual can be considered a dependent of the employee:

1. The employee provides more than half of the domestic partner's support.
2. The domestic partner has his or her principal residence with the employee and is a member of the employee's household.
3. The relationship between the employee and the domestic partner does not violate state or local law. Unfortunately, the IRS has provided no real guidance on how this last requirement is to be interpreted. [Priv. Ltr. Rul. 9850011 (Sept. 10, 1998)]

When a domestic partner cannot qualify as a dependent, benefits paid under a self-funded plan are tax free only when the employee either (1) pays for the coverage at a rate that is comparable to insurance or (2) the employee picks up that value as taxable income.

Note. Where local laws are not conclusive as to whether a man and woman can cohabit without violating state or local law, the employer should adopt a clear policy regarding the tax treatment of such benefits. In most cases, the domestic partner benefits will be taxable to the employee. The employee then must choose between paying for the coverage or picking up the value of the coverage as additional wages. [Priv. Ltr. Ruls. 9034048 (Aug. 24, 1990), 9231062 (May 7, 1992), 9603011 (Jan. 19, 1996), 9717087; I.R.C. § 152(a)(9)]

Q 9:149 May an employer provide tax-favored group-term life insurance to a domestic partner?

No, unless the domestic partner qualifies as a dependent (or is legally married). The IRS addressed this issue in a private letter ruling that made a slight change as to when employers may provide tax-free benefits to an employee's domestic partner. The ruling was requested to establish the taxability of benefits offered to the domestic partner and, if taxable, how those benefits are valued for inclusion in the employee's income. This employer's inquiry addressed several types of benefits, including group-term life insurance. The request on the life insurance benefits might seem a bit odd because regardless of the status of the domestic partner (e.g., a legal dependent), the value of the employer's group-term life insurance coverage on any dependent is fully taxable to the employee.

A key reason for this ruling was to establish how the taxable value of group-term life insurance benefits provided to domestic partners would be determined. The IRS held that the group-term life insurance of any domestic partner, spouse, or dependent is taxed under the uniform premium table rate of Table I, Treasury Regulations Section 1.79-3(d)(2) [see Table 9-3 in Q 9:225]. This is the same rate table that applies to the taxation of group-term life insurance for the employee that exceeds $50,000. This table is generally less favorable than the table used to determine life insurance benefits that do not qualify as group-term life insurance (i.e., the PS 58 table or actual insurance company rates, if lower). [Priv. Ltr. Rul. 9717018 (Jan. 22, 1997)]

I.R.C. Section 132(a)(4) permits an employer to provide tax-free group-term life insurance to an employee's spouse or dependent as a fringe benefit as long as the face amount does not exceed $2,000. The same coverage may be provided to a domestic partner who satisfies the requirements to be classified as a dependent under the I.R.C. [I.R.C. § 152(a)(9); Treas. Reg. § 1.132-6(e); Priv. Ltr. Rul. 9717018 (Jan. 22, 1997); Notice 89-110, 1989-2 C.B. 447]

Q 9:150   What valuation method has the IRS applied to domestic partner benefits?

The IRS addressed this issue in a private letter ruling, where an employer requested confirmation on the tax treatment of group health benefits provided under a self-funded accident and health plan (i.e., noninsured). The IRS held that where insured benefits are provided to a domestic partner who qualifies as a dependent or spouse, the taxable value of the health coverage is excluded from the employee's compensation.

When the domestic partner does not satisfy the requirements for either the spousal or the dependent classification, the value of the insured coverage included in the employee's compensation is based on the premiums to obtain that coverage. When taxable benefits are provided under a self-funded plan to a domestic partner who does not qualify as a dependent or spouse, the FMV of the coverage (i.e., not the amount of benefits paid) amount is treated as additional wages. [Priv. Ltr. Rul. 200108010 (Feb. 23, 2001); Field Serv. Adv. 199911012 (Dec. 10, 1998)]

This taxation is addressed in I.R.C. Section 61, which requires employees to include in gross wages the excess of the FMV of employer-provided benefits less any payment by the employee or any amounts exempt under the I.R.C. Treasury Regulations Section 1.61-21(b)(2) states that FMV is a facts-and-circumstances determination. The regulation goes on to say that the FMV will generally be the cost for the individual to obtain those benefits in an arm's-length transaction. The IRS initially took the position that the amount to be reported as additional employee wages for a domestic partner's health benefits was the FMV of the coverage as determined by the cost the domestic partner would have to pay for the same coverage on an individual policy basis. The IRS has apparently relaxed that position and is permitting employers to report the FMV of the group medical coverage for the domestic partner who is treated as a dependent. At this time, there is no formal guidance. Note that private letter rulings may not be used to establish a valid basis for another employer's position or similar circumstances. As a result, employers wishing to take advantage of this approach, which will generally result in a lower tax liability to employees, will want to request their own private letter ruling.

Note. The IRS is treating as legally married the same-sex spouses who were married in a jurisdiction that recognizes such marriages.

Q 9:151   Do COBRA continuation coverage and HIPAA notices apply to domestic partners?

COBRA and HIPAA, for the most part, have similar applications to an employee's dependents who are covered under an employer's health plan. But subtle differences exist that affect domestic partners. COBRA regulations specifically identify a qualified dependent as the employee, his or her spouse, or dependent child. Thus, a domestic partner who cannot be classified as a spouse or dependent under state law is generally exempt from COBRA coverage. HIPAA contains no such provision and would appear to apply to any domestic partner who could be classified as a spouse or a dependent when covered under the employer's health plan. [I.R.C. § 4980B(g)(1)(A)]

Q 9:152   May a domestic partner participate in a university's tuition reduction plan that benefits an employee's dependents?

No. A "qualified tuition reduction" plan must follow the requirements of I.R.C. Section 117(d)(2), which limit benefits to individuals who are classified as a spouse or dependent child under I.R.C. Section 132(h). [Priv. Ltr. Rul. 200137041 (Sept. 14, 2001)] Also, the IRS treats qualifying children of divorced or separated parents as the dependents of both parents under several tax code sections for health and fringe benefits, regardless of whether the custodial parent releases the claim to the exemption.

Note. The IRS is treating as legally married the same-sex spouses who were married in a jurisdiction that recognizes such marriages.

Eating Facilities

Q 9:153   When do employer-operated eating facilities qualify as a tax-free fringe benefit?

Meals provided to employees at an employer-operated eating facility can be treated as a tax-free *de minimis* fringe benefit when the following requirements are met: (1) the eating facility is leased (or owned) and operated (directly or indirectly) by the employer, (2) the eating facility is located on or near the business premises of the employer, (3) the meals furnished are provided during or immediately before or after the employee's workday, and (4) the revenue derived from the facility (i.e., price charged the employees) normally equals or exceeds its direct operating costs. Meals refer to food, beverages, and related services provided at the facility. [Treas. Reg. § 1.132-7]

This exclusion from gross income applies to meals provided to HCEs if access to the facility is available on substantially the same terms to a nondiscriminatory group of employees. The employer may not use any conditions or classifications to restrict access that discriminates in favor of HCEs. [I.R.C. § 132(e)(2)]

An HCE is defined in the same way as under the pension laws (see Q 9:318). Note that, unlike the nondiscrimination rules that apply to other no-additional-cost services, these rules do not aggregate discriminatory benefits attributable to an executive-only dining facility with nondiscriminatory eating benefits in a facility that is open to all employees on a nondiscriminatory basis. These nondiscriminatory requirements are applied separately to each eating facility. Meals at one facility can qualify, whereas meals at the other do not. In addition, an employer-provided eating facility can restrict access to such facilities in a manner that discriminates in favor of the highly compensated, without losing the exclusion from gross income, as long as "executive group employees" (the top 1 percent of employees by compensation) do not use the facility on more than a *de minimis* basis. [Treas. Reg. § 1.132-8]

As a result, the existence of an executive dining room would not necessarily mean that the value of meals in the company cafeteria would be included in the income of the executives; however, the FMV of the meals in the discriminatory facility must be included in the income of the HCEs. [Treas. Reg. § 1.132-8(d)(5)]

Q 9:154   May a casino provide tax-free meals to all employees?

Maybe. The IRS has ruled in two situations that the value of meals furnished to casino employees is included in the employees' wages subject to FIT, FITW, FICA, and FUTA. In these situations, the employer failed to demonstrate full compliance with the requirements of I.R.C. Section 119. Both casinos required their hourly employees to remain on the premises during their shifts and to use employee dining rooms where meals were provided at no cost. The casinos did not report the value of the meals as wages subject to FIT, FITW, FICA, and FUTA.

The rulings focused on an I.R.C. requirement that the value of employer-provided meals be included in wages for employment tax purposes unless the meals are provided on the employer's premises for a substantial noncompensatory business reason. An employer may demonstrate compliance with the noncompensatory requirement when the meals meet one of the following four requirements: (1) meals are available in case of emergency; (2) the nature of the business requires short meal periods, during which workers are not allowed to eat elsewhere; (3) workers cannot be expected to eat elsewhere because of a lack of eating facilities nearby; or (4) the workers are employed in a restaurant or other food-service establishment. [I.R.C. § 119]

The IRS found that while the regulations allow for a reasonable interpretation of these rules, the employer must demonstrate substantial compliance with the regulations. Apparently, the casinos merely stated that these conditions applied and made no effort to document the basis for their statements. [Tech. Adv. Mems. 9841001 (Oct. 9, 1998), 9841002 (Oct. 9, 1998)]

However, in a separate case, the appeals court overruled the IRS, holding that an employer could exclude 100 percent of the value of meals provided to its employees when the employer had a policy requiring employees to stay on its premises for breaks. The court said that such a policy was based on noncompensatory reasons. [Boyd Gaming Corp. v. Commissioner, 177 F.3d 1096 (9th Cir. 1999)]

Q 9:155   What is the current status of employer-provided meals in the hospitality industry?

After the IRS lost in *Boyd Gaming Corp.*, the IRS stopped work in its settlement initiative aimed at the tax treatment of meals in the hospitality industry. In August 1998, the IRS released Announcement 98-77, containing draft training materials and a settlement initiative relating to tax issues for employer-provided meals. This guidance was intended to assist employers and IRS auditors in applying current statutes relating to the taxation of employer-provided meals. In IRS Announcement 99-77 [1999-32, I.R.B. 243], IRS stated that it will follow the ruling of the U.S. Circuit Court of Appeals in *Boyd Gaming Corp. v. Commissioner.*

As of 1998, a section of the IRS Restructuring and Reform Act generally provides that all meals provided to employees on the employer's business premise are treated as furnished for the convenience of the employer as long as one-half of the meals provided satisfy the I.R.C. requirements for being provided for the convenience of the employer. When a meal program meets these requirements, the FMV of the meal is not included in the employee's wages.

Q 9:156   How are meals of an employer-operated eating facility valued when they do not qualify as a tax-free fringe benefit?

The fair market value of meals must be included in wages subject to FIT, FITW, FICA, and FUTA if (1) the eating facility is found to be discriminatory in favor of highly compensated employees; (2) the facility fails to meet the convenience of the employer test under I.R.C. Section 119; or (3) the direct operating costs of the facility exceed revenues. In all of these circumstances, the FMV is computed in one of two ways:

(1) *Individual meal subsidy.* The "individual meal subsidy" is determined by multiplying the amount paid by the employee for a particular meal by a fraction, the numerator of which is the total meal value and the denominator of which is the gross receipts of the eating facility for the calendar year, and then subtracting the amount paid by the employee for the meal. The taxable value of meals provided to a particular employee during a calendar year, therefore, is the sum of the individual meal subsidies provided to the employee during the calendar year. This method can be used only if there is a charge for each meal selection and if each employee is charged the same price for any given meal selection.

   Example.   The total direct operating costs for Food Frenzy as of the last 12-month testing period was $6,850. Employee Joseph paid $760 for his meals for the same period. Total cash receipts and the amount cross-charged to business units for deductible meals (business meals, goodwill meals, and food service personnel free meals) was $2,400.

   (a) Direct Operating Costs $6,850

   (b) $6,850 × 150% is $10,275

   (c) Revenues and Deductible Meals $2,400

   (d) $10,275/$2,400 = $4.28

   (e) $760 (employee meal payments) × $4.28 = $3,252.80 total meal value

   (f) Total taxable income to employee is $2,492.80 ($3,252.80 − $760)

(2) *Total meal subsidy.* Instead of using the individual meal subsidy, the employer may allocate the "total meal subsidy" (total meal value less the gross receipts of the facility) among employees in any manner reasonable under the circumstances. The employer can allocate the total meal subsidy on a per-employee basis if the employer has information that would substantiate to the satisfaction of the IRS that each employee was provided approximately the same number of meals at the facility. [Treas. Reg. § 1.61-21(j)]

Q 9:157   Is the value of meals provided at an employer eating facility reported on the employee's W-2?

No. If the meal benefits provided at an employer eating facility qualify under I.R.C. Section 119(a) are furnished for the convenience of the employer under I.R.C. Section 132 as a *de minimis* fringe benefit, or under I.R.C. Section 2741(d) as a business or entertainment expense, the value of the benefit is exempt from FIT, FITW, FICA, and FUTA. However, if (1) the eating facility is found to be discriminatory in favor of HCEs; (2) the facility fails to meet the convenience of the employer test under I.R.C. Section 119; or (3) the direct operating costs of the facility exceed revenues, the FMV of the meals must be included in the amounts reported in Boxes 1, 3, and 5 of the employees' Form W-2. [Treas. Reg. §§ 1.119-1(a), 1.132-8] See Q 9:156 for information on determining the FMV of the meals.

Educational Assistance

Q 9:158   What are educational assistance benefits?

Educational assistance benefits are most commonly characterized as an employer's reimbursement for (or direct payment of) the tuition and fees of an employee who attends certain classes or courses of study. The tax treatment of these benefits varies based on whether the benefits are job related or non-job-related. Where the educational assistance plan is structured to provide reimbursements of employee-paid expenses, the reimbursement must be structured under an "accountable plan" (see Qs 9:19–9:38). [Treas. Reg. § 1.127-2(i)]

Job-related educational benefits may be provided to an employee as a working-condition fringe benefit without the value of the benefits being treated as wages for FIT, FITW, FICA, and FUTA purposes when the course of study meets certain requirements. Reimbursement for travel to and from the course of study may be made as a working-condition fringe benefit only for job-related course work. [I.R.C. § 127; Treas. Reg. § 1.162-5]

Educational assistance benefits may be provided to a current employee, a former employee who retired or was terminated because of a disability, a leased employee who provides services to the employer, or a sole proprietor or a partner.

For non-job-related educational assistance benefits, current law permits an exclusion of up to $5,250 per year for employer-provided benefits. These reimbursements can be used to cover the cost of books, tuition, lab fees, and similar costs (but not travel and lodging) associated with graduate and non-graduate level courses. (This provision was extended by 2010 Tax Relief Act until December 31, 2012. Then the American Taxpayer Relief Act 2012 (ATRA) permanently extended this benefit.) Such benefits are not included in wages subject to FIT, FITW, FICA, or FUTA if the benefits are provided under an educational assistance program that satisfies I.R.C. Section 127(b). The value of benefits not excluded under Section 127 or as a working-condition fringe benefit is treated as additional wages and is subject to FIT, FITW, FICA, and FUTA. [I.R.C. §§ 127, 3121(a)(18), 3306(b)(13), 3401(a)(18)]

Q 9:159   What are job-related educational assistance benefits?

Job-related educational assistance benefits are reimbursements or employer-paid benefits for books, supplies, lab fees, tuition, and certain transportation costs (between the place of work and the educational facility) for courses that are related to the employee's job. These are treated as nontaxable working-condition fringe benefits (i.e., are exempt from FIT, FITW, FICA, and FUTA) when they satisfy the following four conditions:

1. The educational program helps maintain or improve skills that an employee is required to have for his or her employment.

2. The educational course is expressly required by the employer, or is legally required to retain an established employment relationship, status, or rate of compensation.

3. The course of study is not taken to qualify the employee for another type of work.

4. The educational assistance is provided to the employee for the benefit of the employer.

The definition of *employee* for purposes of these benefits includes self-employed individuals and retired, disabled, or laid-off former employees. Note that there is no annual dollar limit on the value of job-related educational assistance benefits that may be excluded from wages subject to FIT, FITW, FICA, and FUTA. [I.R.C. § 127; Treas. Reg. §§ 1.127-1, 1.127-2, 31.3121(a)(18)-1, 31.3306(b)(13)-1, 31.3401(a)(18)-1]

Q 9:160   What type of educational benefits do not qualify as job-related?

Educational courses that are required to meet the minimum educational requirements necessary to qualify for employment, or education that will qualify an employee for a new trade or business, are not deemed to be "job-related." [I.R.C. § 127; Treas. Reg. § 1.162-5]

Example. Shelby, a financial analyst, is enrolled in studies that will lead to qualification as a Certified Public Accountant (CPA). These expenses could qualify Shelby for a new position as a payroll tax accountant, because she is now a CPA, and as a result, the expenses are not job-related. They could qualify as non-job-related educational expenses available under an educational assistance plan structured to comply with the requirements of I.R.C. Section 127 and would be tax-free up to $5,250 per year.

Q 9:161   What are the requirements for a qualified Section 127 educational assistance plan?

The value of non-job-related educational assistance benefits up to $5,250 per year provided by an employer is excluded from wages subject to FIT, FITW, FICA, and FUTA when the benefits are offered under an educational assistance plan that qualifies under I.R.C. Section 127. I.R.C. Section 127 requires the plan to meet certain form and eligibility requirements, which include the following:

1. The educational assistance plan must be formalized in a separate written document and be communicated to the employees. Recordkeeping is crucial.

2. The plan may not discriminate in favor of HCEs (as defined in the pension rules of I.R.C. Section 414(q)).

3. No more than 5 percent of the benefits can be provided in any year to the group of shareholders or owners owning more than 5 percent of the employer. Plans covering union employees, where the educational benefits were part of the collective bargaining agreement, are excluded from this requirement.

4. The plan cannot be part of a cafeteria plan that permits the employee to choose between educational assistance benefits and taxable compensation.

5. The plan cannot pay for any tools or supplies (other than books) that the employee can use after the end of the course nor can the plan pay for meals, lodging, or transportation related to the educational benefits.

6. The employer must retain sufficient records to substantiate the valid nature of the reimbursements.

These restrictions do not prevent an educational assistance plan from conditioning a reimbursement on successful completion of the course of study or attainment of a specific grade level, nor is an employer prevented from basing the maximum reimbursement on the number of hours worked. [I.R.C. § 127(b); Notice 96-41, 1996-45 I.R.B. 4]

Q 9:162   How are educational assistance program benefits treated for federal employment tax purposes?

Non-job-related benefits received from an I.R.C. Section 127 qualified educational assistance plan are excluded from FIT, FITW, FICA, and FUTA. The exclusion for non-job-related educational assistance benefits is limited to $5,250 per employee during a calendar year. The value of benefits that exceed $5,250 or that are paid from a plan that does not meet the requirements of Section 127 are treated as wages subject to FIT, FITW, FICA, and FUTA. All job-related educational expenses are exempt from FIT, FITW, FICA, and FUTA if they meet the working condition fringe benefit definition under Treasury Regulations Section 1.162-5. [Pub. No. 15-A]

Q 9:163   How are nontaxable educational assistance benefits reported?

Educational assistance benefits that are exempt from wages subject to FIT, FITW, FICA, and FUTA, either under I.R.C. Section 127 or as a working condition fringe benefit, are not reported on Form W-2. In addition, Form 5500 is not required for educational assistance benefits provided under I.R.C. Section 127.

Employee Business Expenses

Per Diem

Q 9:164   What is the advantage of using a per diem rate or other fixed allowance reimbursement for lodging, meals, and incidental expenses?

A per diem allowance is a payment made under an accountable plan for lodging, meals, and incidental expenses for business travel away from home that is based on a fixed daily rate. The rate used may either be the federal per diem rate, a flat rate, stated schedule, or other reasonable method that is applied on a reasonable and consistent basis. By using a per diem reimbursement plan that meets certain IRS requirements, the process of maintaining an accountable plan is simplified. A per diem allowance that satisfies certain dollar thresholds and other substantiation requirements for lodging, meals, and incidental expenses will be deemed to have met one component of substantiating a business expense: substantiating the "amount of the expense." Thus, the employee is not required to report and verify the amount of the actual expenses incurred. This requirement of an accountable plan is deemed met when: (1) the allowance (or reimbursement) is made under an accountable plan, (2) the expenses are for business travel away from home on a temporary basis, and (3) the amount of the allowance does not exceed the federal rates for the region where the employee travels or the rate is under the high-low substantiation method, the two IRS-approved methods. The employee must continue to substantiate the period of travel and business nature of the expense. [Treas. Reg. § 1.62-2(f); Rev. Proc. 2011-47, 2011-42 I.R.B. 520]

Q 9:165   Are all employees eligible to receive a per diem or other fixed allowance?

Yes. The employer may establish any policy for reimbursing any employee for business travel. However, an employee who owns more than 10 percent of the employer, or who is a close relative (e.g., spouse, brother, sister, ancestor, or descendant) of such an owner must substantiate the actual expenses for the allowance or reimbursement to be treated as made under an accountable plan. [Rev. Proc. 2003-80, 2003-45 I.R.B. 1037]

Q 9:166   What is the federal per diem rate?

The federal per diem rate sets a maximum dollar threshold that acts as a safe harbor daily rate for travel, meals, and incidental expense reimbursements (or allowances) for an employer-provided plan. Reimbursements of amounts up to these federal per diem rates may be made without regard to the employee's actual expenses. The employer may establish a per diem rate above or below the federal rates, but only the portion of the amounts up to the federal rate are treated as a nontaxable per diem reimbursement. Amounts paid in excess of these rates that are not fully substantiated are treated as amounts paid from a nonaccountable plan and are treated as additional wages that are subject to withholding and employment tax.

The General Services Administration (GSA) establishes the rates for each fiscal year, beginning on October 1, for such expenses based on the location of the employee's travel. The GSA continental U.S. per diem rates are available on the Internet at http://www.gsa.gov/perdiem. The employer may also elect to use the high-low substantiation method (see Q 9:174) rather than the federal rate for each area. The same method must be applied to the same employee for the full year.

The structure of the federal rate is designed to reflect reasonable levels of expense reimbursement for an employee's travel expenses, lessening the substantiation requirements for the employer and employee. Incidental expenses include tips for baggage handlers. The cost of taxis, lodging taxes, and laundry, and telegrams or telephone calls are not included in the federal rates and may be reimbursed separately from the employee's per diem allowance. A full per diem allowance may only be used where the employee travels sufficiently far from home where an overnight stay would ordinarily be necessary. However, a per diem for meals and incidental expenses (M&IE) may be reimbursed in a situation where an employee could, but for personal or business reasons did not, stay overnight. [Rev. Proc. 2003-80, 2003-45 I.R.B. 1037]

Q 9:167   How may an employer establish its per diem allowances?

An employer may establish either a flat per diem rate or utilize a stated schedule designed to reflect the actual expenses incurred. Either must be applied on a uniform and objective basis. Typically, an allowance is tied to the number of substantiated days an employee is traveling away from home, but any method is permitted as long as it is consistently applied and follows reasonable business practice. For example, an employer may establish an hourly payment rate that covers M&IE for an employee traveling away from home. The dollar amount of a reimbursement or allowance under such a method is deemed substantiated as long as the total payment is not expected to exceed the actual cost of the employee's travel. An employer that pays a per diem rate for the employee's M&IE and also reimburses for other meal expenses will not be treated as having a per diem plan and the employee will be required to substantiate the per diem payments for the plan to be treated as an accountable plan. Note that if the employee can reasonably be expected to incur an expense for a meal or lodging, the per diem rate does not have to be reduced if no expense is incurred (e.g., a client pays for the meal). [Rev. Proc. 2003-80, 2003-45 I.R.B. 1037]

Where an employer pays a per diem allowance for M&IE rather than reimbursing the employee's actual expenses, the amount of the expenses is deemed substantiated when the allowance does not exceed the federal M&IE rate. Where a per diem allowance is in effect, an employee may be reimbursed for M&IE only when the following four conditions are met (i.e., an employer may automatically apply a M&IE rate when one of four conditions is met): (1) the employer pays the employee for actual expenses for lodging, (2) the employer provides the lodging in-kind, (3) the employer pays the cost of the lodging directly to the provider of the lodging, and (4) the employer does not have a reasonable belief that lodging expenses were or will be incurred by the employee. [Rev. Proc. 93-50, 1993-2 C.B. 586; Rev. Proc. 2001-47, 2001-42 I.R.B. 332] There has been a modification of the definition of incidental expense under the Federal Travel Regulations. [Notice 2011-81 superseded]

Q 9:168   Does a per diem allowance have to be reasonable?

Yes. A per diem travel allowance that exceeds reasonably expected expenses results in amounts in excess of the applicable federal rate being treated as paid from a nonaccountable plan (and reportable in Box 12 with Code L on the employee's Form W-2). These amounts are treated as additional compensation and are subject to FIT, FITW, FICA, and FUTA. Reimbursements for reasonable travel expenses are excluded from wages subject to FIT, FITW, FICA, and FUTA when paid under an accountable plan. Reasonableness is generally determined based on expenses for similar travel that have been substantiated. Amounts up to the applicable federal rate are deemed reasonable, unless they are compensatory in nature. A contractual agreement between labor and management to set the level of per diem will not automatically meet these requirements, without additional documentation of actual expenses to be incurred. [Treas. Reg. §§ 31.3121(a)-1(h), 31.3401(a)-1(b)(2); American Airlines, Inc. v. United States, 204 F.3d 1103 (Fed. Cir. 2000)]

Q 9:169 How are excess amounts paid above the federal allowable per diem rates reported?

If the employer pays a per diem or M&IE allowance in lieu of reimbursing actual expenses, any additional payment with respect to such expenses is treated as additional wages subject to withholding and federal employment tax. Therefore, the excess amount must be included in Boxes 1, 3, and 5 of the Form W-2 and the tax withheld included in Boxes 2, 4, and 6. In addition, the excess (reimbursement above federal rate or amount substantiated) must be reported in Box 12, with Code L, of the Form W-2. [Form W-2 instructions; Rev. Proc. 2002-63, 2002-41 I.R.B. 691]

Q 9:170 How are per diems for partial days away from home treated?

The federal per diem or M&IE rate is available for a full day of travel from 12:01 a.m. to 12:00 midnight. When travel is for less than a full day, these rates must be prorated. The employer may utilize one of several methods to prorate the per diem. The employer may apply a safe harbor by reducing the applicable federal M&IE rate by 25 percent for each partial day during which the employee is traveling away from home. Or an employer may apply any proration method as long as it is applied on a reasonable and consistent basis. [Rev. Proc. 96-28, 1996-1 C.B. 686; Rev. Proc. 2002-63, 2002-41 I.R.B. 691]

Q 9:171 Do special rules apply to per diem allowances for the transportation industry?

Yes. Employers with employees in the transportation industry are entitled to apply an M&IE per diem allowance of $63 for 2016-2017 for any locality of travel in the continental United States and $68 for 2016-2017 for any travel outside the continental United States in lieu of the otherwise available M&IE allowance. The employer must use one rate for a single employee during the calendar year. In other words, the employer cannot switch from a transportation M&IE rate to the federal rate for travel to cities where the federal rate is higher.

An employee is treated as being in the transportation industry when the employee's work responsibilities (1) are of a type that directly involves moving people or goods by plane, barge, bus, ship, train, or truck; and (2) regularly require the employee to travel away from home during a single trip that typically involves travel to places with different federal M&IE rates. An employer must apply these criteria on a reasonable and consistent basis. [Notice 2014-57, 2014-42 I.R.B. 723; Rev. Proc. 2011-47, 2011-42 I.R.B. 520; Notice 2015 -63, I.R.B. 2015-40, Oct. 5, 2015, Notice 2016-58, 2016-41 I.R.B. Oct. 11, 2016]

Q 9:172 What is the tax treatment of travel expenses incurred by partners of a partnership or a sole proprietor?

Individuals who are treated as self-employed (e.g., partners of a partnership, members of an LLC electing to be treated as a partnership for federal income tax purposes, and sole proprietors) are not entitled to use a per diem allowance plan, but may substantiate any reasonable expense under an accountable plan. They may generally deduct expenses meeting the per diem and M&IE requests equal to 50 percent; however, for sole proprietors in the transportation industry, the deductible amount is increased to 65 percent of the allowable federal M&IE amounts rather than receive an allowance. The amount of such a deduction is deemed substantiated if the amount, time, place, and business purpose of the expenses are substantiated. Note that where this deduction on Form 1040 is taken as an itemized deduction, it is subject to the 2 percent floor on itemized deductions (i.e., an employee business expense). Of course, such individuals may also fully substantiate lodging, meals, and incidental expenses as a business expense subject to any I.R.C. limitations that apply. [I.R.C. § 274(m)]

Q 9:173   What is the tax treatment of travel expenses of nonresident aliens?

Payments made to or on behalf of nonresident aliens as reimbursements for travel and lodging expenses are excluded from wages subject to FIT, FITW, FICA, and FUTA if paid under an accountable plan. The IRS has informally determined that the "accountable plan" and "working-condition fringe benefit" rules also apply to nonresident aliens.

High-Low Per Diem Substantiation

Q 9:174   What is the high-low substantiation method?

When employees travel to a number of different geographic locations, the employer may choose to use an alternate per diem method referred to as the "high-low" substantiation method. This eliminates the need to apply a different per diem rate to each locality of travel. Instead, the high-low substantiation method establishes one federal per diem rate for high-cost localities and another for low-cost localities. Effective October 1, 2016 to September 30, 2017, this method permits allowances of up to $282 a day for high-cost localities or $189 a day for other localities to be deemed substantiated. The election to use the high-low substantiation method rather than other per diems for a specific employee must be applied consistently. [Notice 2014-57, 2014-42 I.R.B. 723; Pub. No. 1542; Notice 2016-58, I.R.B. 2016-41]

The IRS announced that it intended to discontinue the high-low substantiation method. A number of taxpayers requested the IRS to retain the method. [Announcement 2011-42, 2011-32 I.R.B. 138] The IRS continues to authorize the high-low method. The per diem rates will be published annually in a separate Revenue Procedure.

The definition of incidental expenses has the same meaning as in the Federal Travel Regulations. [41 C.F.R. 300-3.1]

Future changes will be announced in the annual notice providing special per diem rates. On September 7, 2011, the GSA published interim (temporary) regulations to fees and tips given to porters, baggage carriers, hotel staff, and staff on ships. Expenses related to transportation between places of lodging or business, and places where meals are taken, and mailing cost of filing travel vouchers and paying employer-sponsored charge card billings are no longer included in incidental expense. If an employee uses the per diem rates, those charges can be deducted separately or reimbursed.

An employer may apply the high-low method when lodging is the only expense that will be incurred or when the employer has reason to believe that the employee will not incur meal and incidental expenses. An employer may use only the M&IE rate when it believes the employee will not incur lodging expenses or when lodging expenses will be paid directly. Where the employer is applying the high-low method for lodging and M&IE, and for certain business travel the employee is only reimbursed for M&IE (rather than lodging and M&IE), the employer must apply the regular federal per diem rates for M&IE. [Rev. Proc. 2009-47, 2009-42 I.R.B. 524] The meal and incidental expense daily allowance for high-cost localities is $65 and $52 for other locations.

There were several changes to the list of high-cost localities. Table 9-2 gives some samples of high-cost localities.

Table 9-2. Sample High-Cost Localities of Travel Effective October 1, 2016

Key City[1]

Sedona, AZ (March 1-April 30)

Napa, CA (October 1–October 31 and May 1–September 30)

Hershey, PA (June 1–August 31)

Denver/Aurora (October 1-November 30 and February 1-September 30)

Grand Lake, CO (December 1–March 31)

Seaside, OR (July 1-August 31)

---

[1] This table only shows the rates for some sample areas (used in the example below).

Example. During March 2017, Victor travels eight days to Denver, CO, a high-cost location. He is reimbursed under the high-low method for this travel. He may receive on a tax-free basis up to $282 (per day) for substantiated travel expenses.

Q 9:175   How does a per diem allowance affect the employer's deduction for lodging, meals, and incidental expenses?

Normally an employer is entitled to deduct, as a business expense, 100 percent of the cost of an employee's substantiated lodging and incidental expenses and 50 percent of the employee's substantiated M&IE (including taxes and tips related to the meal). When the employer uses a per diem allowance for M&IE, a special deduction limitation applies. The M&IE expenses are treated as being entirely for meals and the entire M&IE allowance is subject to this 50 percent deduction limit. If the employer's per diem allowance rate is lower than the combined federal lodging and M&IE rates, the employer may only treat 40 percent of the total M&IE allowance as paid for meals and subject to the lower limitation.

This tax deduction treatment for the employer does not affect the amount that is exempt from withholding and federal employment taxes when a reimbursement is only partially deductible to the employer. The entire reimbursement will be treated as made under an accountable plan and will be tax free to the employee as long as the substantiation requirements are met. [Treas. Reg. § 1.62-2(h)(1)]

Mileage Allowance

Q 9:176   What is a mileage allowance?

An employer may reimburse employees for the cost of using a personal (or employee-leased) automobile for local or away-from-home business travel on a cents-per-mile basis, on a flat-rate schedule, or under a FAVR. See Q 9:178.

A mileage allowance must be made under an accountable plan; must be properly substantiated; and must not exceed certain limits. If the payment is not properly substantiated, it will be treated as paid from a nonaccountable plan and will be subject to withholding and federal employment tax.

The standard mileage rate for business use of a personal automobile (other rates apply to certain nonpersonal use of a personal automobile) is $0.535 for 2017 ($0.54 for 2016). This allowance covers the fixed cost of operating a vehicle (e.g., depreciation, maintenance, tires, gasoline, oil, insurance, and registration fees). Parking fees and tolls attributable to business travel may be reimbursed in addition to the mileage rate. (See Q 9:316 for moving expense mileage rates.) [Rev. Proc. 93-51, 1993-42 I.R.B. 30]

Q 9:177   What is a flat rate or stated schedule allowance for business use of a personal vehicle?

As an alternative to using a mileage allowance, the employer may use a flat rate or a stated schedule. Under this arrangement, the employer typically makes a periodic payment at a fixed rate to cover the fixed costs (including depreciation, insurance, registration and license fees, and personal property taxes) of using a car for business purposes and then applies a cents-per-mile rate allowance to cover the operating costs (including gas, oil, tires, and routine maintenance and repairs). Or the employer may apply a varying allowance based on a stated schedule for the different locations where the employee uses a car for business purposes.

The advantage of using the standard business mileage rate meeting certain IRS requirements is that the allowance may be used to satisfy the dollar amount of the expense requirement for substantiating a business expense. The employee must continue to substantiate the business nature of the expense and the number of miles driven. As long as the amount reimbursed under either a mileage rate or a fixed or standard rate is less than the federal business standard mileage rate multiplied by the number of substantiated business miles, the cost to use the automobile is deemed substantiated. [Rev. Proc. 2004-64, 2004-2 C.B. 898]

FAVR Allowance for Use of Personal Auto

Q 9:178   What is the fixed and variable rate allowance?

A FAVR allowance is a type of mileage allowance, developed under safe harbors established by the IRS, that may be used to reimburse an employee for business use of a personal (or employee-leased) automobile. With a FAVR, an employer may choose to reimburse an employee for expenses related to the business use of a personal automobile according to an allowance that combines periodic fixed and variable rate payments (the so-called FAVR allowance).

Employees do not submit a record of their actual expenses when the employer reimburses under the FAVR method, even though such reimbursement may exceed the federal standard mileage rate. A FAVR allowance is deemed substantiated up to the amount of the allowance less the sum of (1) any portion of a periodic variable payment related to miles exceeding the business-use miles substantiated by the employee (less any amounts for nonbusiness use that the employee returns to the employer); (2) any portion of a fixed periodic payment relating to the period when the employee was not covered by the FAVR allowance (less any amount for such usage that the employee returns to the employer); and (3) any optional high mileage payments. [Rev. Proc. 98-64, 1998-52 I.R.B. 32]

A FAVR allowance has two components: a flat periodic payment and a payment based on an automobile's annual mileage. A flat periodic payment is to cover the employee's fixed costs for use of the automobile (e.g., depreciation, insurance, registration, and license fees for the car). The periodic payment is based on the employee's variable costs to operate the automobile (e.g., gas, oil, tires, and routine maintenance) that relate to the actual miles driven during the calendar year. The fixed and operating costs must be paid at least quarterly, and at least five employees must be covered by a FAVR allowance during the year.

The employer must establish the FAVR allowance based on data derived from the retail prices in the employee's base location, and the allowance must be reasonable and statistically defensible in approximating actual expenses of the employee group receiving the allowance. The FAVR allowance is based on the cost of a standard automobile selected by the employer, and that cost may not exceed 95 percent of the automobile's retail price (plus state and local taxes) or $27,900 for automobiles or $31,300 for trucks and vans for 2017. A periodic fixed payment may be computed by dividing the total projected fixed cost for the standard automobile for all years of the "retention period." The retention period is the period selected by the employer and must be at least two years. [Rev. Proc. 2010-51, 2010-51 I.R.B. 883; Notice 2012-1, 2012-2, I.R.B. 260; Notice 2016-1, 2016-1 I.R.B. 265; I.R.S. Notice 2016-79, 2016-52, I.R.B.]

Q 9:179   What restrictions apply to an allowance based on a fixed and variable rate?

When FAVR is used, the annual business mileage must be at least 6,250 miles in the calendar year or 75 percent of the annual business mileage of the FAVR allowance. When employees are covered by FAVR for less than a full calendar year, these limits may be prorated on a monthly basis. Control employees are not permitted to receive a FAVR allowance (although the IRS applies a more limited definition of *control employee* here). (See Q 9:322.) At no time may a majority of the employees covered by a FAVR allowance be management employees. Additionally, at least five employees of an employer must be covered by one or more FAVR allowances during a calendar year. [Rev. Proc. 93-51, 1993-42 I.R.B. 30, 1993-2 C.B. 593, IRS RPR, Dec. 27, 1993; Rev. Proc. 2010-51, Dec. 20, 2010, I.R.B. 883]

An employee must return any excess allowances under a FAVR for the allowance to be treated as made under an accountable plan. The employee must return any portion of (1) a periodic variable payment received that relates to miles in excess of the substantiated business miles or (2) a periodic fixed payment that relates to a period during which the employee was not covered by the FAVR allowance. [Rev. Proc. 93-51, 1993-42 I.R.B. 30]

Employer Payments to an Employee's Estate

Q 9:180   How are wages paid to a beneficiary of a deceased employee treated for employment tax purposes?

Wages and accumulated leave paid after an employee's death and in the same calendar year are generally paid to the legal representative of the estate. These amounts are subject to FICA and FUTA but are exempt from FITW.

These amounts are included in Boxes 3 and 5 (but not Box 1) of the deceased employee's Form W-2. The related Social Security and Medicare taxes withheld are included in Boxes 4 and 6 of Form W-2. The taxable portion of the wages, which would normally be reported in Box 1 of Form W-2, that are paid to a beneficiary is reported on Form 1099-MISC, Box 3, in the name of the beneficiary who receives the payments. [Treas. Reg. §§ 31.3121(a)-1(g), 31.3306(b)-1(h), 31.3401(a)-1(b)(3); Form 1099-MISC instructions]

Wages paid after the calendar year of death are not subject to FITW, FICA, and FUTA taxes. These payments are reported only on Form 1099-MISC, Box 3, in the name of the estate or beneficiary who receives the payments. [I.R.C. §§ 691(a)(1), 3121(a)(14), 3306(b)(15); Rev. Rul. 86-109, 1986-2 C.B. 196]

Family and Medical Leave Act

Q 9:181   What is the Family and Medical Leave Act?

The Family and Medical Leave Act of 1993 (FMLA) is a federal law that imposes a mandatory leave and benefit protection policy on certain employers. Basically, the law permits a covered employee with a serious illness or an employee with a family member who has a serious illness, or an employee with a newborn or newly adopted child, to take up to 12 weeks of unpaid leave without losing any rights to benefits or other employment-related credits that accrued prior to the leave. The leave does not have to occur on consecutive weeks or days and can be applied on a cumulative basis to partial days of leave. Note that an exempt employee (e.g., salaried employee under the FLSA) may be charged for a partial day's leave under the FMLA without losing his or her exempt status. [FMLA § 104(a)(2); 29 C.F.R. § 825.206]

One FMLA requirement affecting payroll is that the employer must continue to maintain coverage under any "group health plan" while the employee is on FMLA leave, on the same terms and conditions that apply to active employees. This means that if the employer is paying for the full amount of the health coverage, the employer continues to pay for the coverage while the employee is on approved leave. When an employee is required to pay for all or a portion of the coverage, the employee may elect to terminate the health coverage during the FMLA leave, in which case he or she would not be required to pay for any portion of the health care coverage during that period. When an employee elects to terminate coverage during FMLA leave, all health coverage must be restored upon returning to work, with no restrictions that did not exist before the leave. [FMLA § 103; 29 C.F.R. §§ 825.209, 825.210(a)]

The first expansion of the FMLA since its enactment was effective January 28, 2008 by the National Defense and Authorization Act for FY 2008 and provided for protected leaves related to service in the U.S. Armed Forces, including the National Guard and the Reserves. Under the expansion of the law, the FMLA requires businesses to offer up to 26 weeks of unpaid leave to employees who provide care to a close family member (defined as a spouse, son, daughter, parent or next of kin) who suffers from a serious injury or illness incurred while serving in the U.S. Armed Forces. In 2009, President Obama signed the National Defense and Authorization Act for FY 2010 that expanded coverage to qualified veterans. In 2012, proposed regulations were issued to implement the National Defense and Authorization Act for FY 2010. Another law, Airline Flight Crew Technical Corrections Act, changed the way hours worked are calculated: 504 hours in 12 months and 60 minimum number of hours employee was scheduled for airline flight crew members.

In addition, employers will be required to provide 12 weeks of FMLA leave to close family members of the person serving in the Armed Forces who has a "qualifying exigency."

Regulations. The Department of Labor (DOL), in its regulations under the 2008 changes in the law, decided that procedures used when taking military family leave should be the same as those used for other types of FMLA leave whenever possible. Accordingly, the DOL incorporated a discussion of the new military family leave entitlements into the regulatory provisions that concern the taking of FMLA leave for other qualifying reasons. The DOL also created four additional regulations to address specific employee and employer responsibilities for purposes of military family leave. [See 29 U.S.C.A. §§ 825.126, 825.127, 825.309, 825.310.] The DOL decided to incorporate, wherever feasible, the military family leave entitlements into the FMLA regulations governing the taking of job-protected leave for other qualifying reasons. In most cases, these changes are modest technical changes that acknowledge the military leave entitlements in the context of the FMLA. For example, some references to certification in the regulations have been altered to clarify whether they refer only to "medical certifications" of a serious health condition or if they refer also to "certifications" under the military family leave provisions.

Q 9:182 To which employers does the FMLA apply?

Employers with 50 or more employees for each working day during each of 20 calendar workweeks in the current or preceding calendar year are subject to the FMLA. Employees, for purposes of determining whether FMLA applies, include part-time employees and employees on leave or suspension. The 50-employee count applies to all employees of an employer who work within 75 miles of any employer facility. The FMLA applies to an employee of such an employer if the employee has been employed for at least 12 months (not continuous) and the employee worked at least 1,250 hours in the 12-month period prior to the leave.

The FMLA applies to state and municipal government employees as well as nongovernment employees. Public agencies and private schools (elementary and secondary) are covered regardless of the number of employees. An employer will apply the provisions of the FLSA that define the terms "employees" and "hours worked" in meeting these requirements. Note that the FMLA only applies to individuals who are employed in the United States or any of its territories and possessions. [FMLA § 101, 29 U.S.C. § 2611; 29 C.F.R. §§ 812.104, 825.111]

Q 9:183   Can two or more employers be treated as a single employer for purposes of the 50-employee threshold?

Yes. The FMLA applies both an "integrated employer" test and a "joint employment test" in determining whether two or more separate employers can be considered as one employer. Thus an employer that might not otherwise be required to provide FMLA leave could be subject to the FMLA. Two or more employers satisfy the integrated employer definition under the FMLA when their operations are closely interrelated, even when common ownership does not exist. The concept is similar to the single enterprise under the FLSA. Employers are treated as "integrated" when they have the following attributes: common management, interrelated business operations, centralized control of labor relations, and some degree of common ownership or financial control. These are not objective thresholds, thereby giving the DOL significant latitude in grouping employers as a single employer.

In a similar way, employees of two or more employers can be grouped as a single employee group when there is joint control over the work or working conditions of an employee. Thus employees who may not satisfy the requirement of 12 months of service and 1,250 hours worked for a single employer may meet these thresholds for an "integrated employer." When joint employment exists, all of the employee's hours and periods of service are aggregated, and like the integrated employee test, the joint control test is subjective. [29 C.F.R. §§ 823.106(a), 823.106(b)]

Q 9:184   Under what conditions may an employer require an employee on FMLA leave to pay health care and other coverage premiums?

The employer must continue to pay its share of the cost of the health insurance to maintain coverage during the leave unless the employee elects to discontinue the coverage. This requirement does not apply to the cost of other nonmedical benefits requiring employee contributions (e.g., life insurance). However, during the FMLA leave the employer may have to pay the premium for nonhealth benefits to protect the employee's right to that coverage upon returning from leave. This could be required to avoid a loss of the identical coverage when the employee returns to work. In some cases, insurance coverage terminated when a premium is not paid may not be restored by the provider without restrictions that did not exist prior to the FMLA leave (e.g., a preexisting condition may be imposed on life insurance unless the employee passes a physical). Such a condition could prevent the employer from restoring the same coverage and would, as a result, violate the FMLA and subject the employer to severe penalties. Under these circumstances, the employer's responsibility to provide the identical insurance coverage would continue, even though no life insurance company would provide a policy. As a result, the employer may have to pay the full value of the death benefit. [Prop. Treas. Reg. § 1.125-3, Q&A 2]

Q 9:185 What payment methods are permitted under a cafeteria plan for group health coverage when the employee is on approved FMLA leave?

When an employee's health benefits are being purchased through salary reductions under a cafeteria plan (i.e., Section 125 plan), special rules apply to the employee's elective contributions for coverage during the leave. First, the employee cannot generally be required to make payments (either through cash payments or other sources) for health benefits while on unpaid FMLA leave. The regulations permit an employee to retain the coverage and make payments under one of three methods described below. This may be done through a change in the amount of elective contribution to the cafeteria plan. The IRS has released extensive guidance on how employee-paid benefits may continue during FMLA under a cafeteria plan. [Treas. Reg. § 1.125-3]

A cafeteria plan may offer, on a nondiscriminatory basis, one or more of the following payment options to an employee continuing group health coverage while on FMLA leave: (1) prepay prior to the FMLA leave, (2) pay during the FMLA leave ("pay-as-you-go"), or (3) pay after the FMLA leave ("catch-up"). The cafeteria plan document must contain the available options. [Prop. Treas. Reg. § 1.125-3, Q&A 3]

Payments under one of these three methods can be made on a pretax basis out of available taxable compensation, or on an aftertax basis; however, a prepayment cannot be mandated (i.e., be the only option), and any catch-up payments must be agreed on before the FMLA leave is taken. Catch-up can be the only option, but only if it is the only option for individuals on unpaid leave not related to FMLA. If both prepayment and catch-up are offered, then pay-as-you-go must also be offered, but only if it is also offered to other individuals for non-FMLA, unpaid leave. The cafeteria plan document must specify the permitted election options. [Prop. Treas. Reg. § 1.125-3, Q&A 3(b)]

An employee on FMLA leave is also permitted to revoke an existing election of group health plan coverage (including a health FSA) under a cafeteria plan (and thus avoid payment of the benefit while on leave) and have all rights and coverage restored upon return. An employee may also elect not to continue the coverage upon returning from FMLA leave. [Prop. Treas. Reg. § 1.125-3, Q&A 1; 29 C.F.R. § 825.209(e)]

Some employers continue an employee's health care coverage or other benefit purchased under a cafeteria plan and do not seek repayment for any employee contributions the employer makes. This may be done when the employer wants to avoid the possibility that an employee may not be insurable upon return. However, an employer that decides to charge an employee for the employee's required payment for the health coverage maintained during the unpaid FMLA leave may receive payment in any of the following five ways:

1. Ask the employee to pay the coverage at the same time (e.g., each pay period) as if the coverage was being paid by payroll contributions.

2. The employer may seek payment on the same schedule as payments are made under COBRA, but the additional COBRA administration charge may not apply.

3. The employee may, at the employer's option, elect to prepay the coverage pursuant to a revised election under the cafeteria plan.

4. The employer may apply the same policies for payment of coverage that apply to employees on other unpaid leave (except to the extent those employees are required to prepay for any coverage).

5. The payment may be made under any method voluntarily agreed to between the employer and the employee.

Where applicable, the employee may be permitted to change his or her cafeteria election to accommodate the payment method selected. [29 C.F.R. § 825.210(c)]

Q 9:186   Can employees on FMLA leave change a cafeteria plan election?

Yes. An employee on FMLA leave (paid or unpaid) has the right to revoke or change a benefit or salary reduction election under the same terms and conditions that are available to active employees who participate in the cafeteria plan and who are not on FMLA leave. Thus, if an open enrollment period occurs during the FMLA leave, the employee on leave must be given access to all benefits available to active employees. [Prop. Treas. Reg. § 1.125-3, Q&A 1] As noted above, an employee may also alter his or her election to comply with the FMLA payment options permitted in the plan document.

Q 9:187   What is a "serious health condition" under the FMLA?

A serious health condition is an "illness, injury, impairment or physical or mental condition" involving inpatient care in a health facility or continuing treatment by a health care provider. The continuing treatment should involve a period of incapacity (e.g., an inability to perform duties at work) of at least three consecutive calendar days and involve treatment by a licensed health care provider. The three-day requirement does not apply to chronic conditions or incapacity relating to pregnancy or prenatal care.

Merely staying home from work and taking over-the-counter medication will not qualify the individual for FMLA leave. [29 C.F.R. § 825.114]

Q 9:188   How does an employee demonstrate that the requested leave is for a serious health condition?

An employee can be required to provide the employer with a certificate from a health care provider at the time the leave is requested to substantiate that the leave is necessitated by a serious health condition. The certificate can be required to be provided no sooner than 15 days after the employer has requested the certificate. A longer period may apply where practicable, as long as the employee makes a good-faith effort to comply.

The certificate should contain: (1) the date when the serious health condition commenced, (2) the diagnosis of a serious health condition, (3) an estimate of the duration of the serious health condition, (4) a statement of the treatment (including number of medical appointments that may be required and the duration and frequency of those appointments), (5) whether the individual requires hospitalization, and (6) a statement detailing the medical necessity of the leave. [FMLA § 103(b); 29 C.F.R. § 825.306]

An employer can require an additional certificate once every 30 days; where doubt exists, the employer can require, at its own expense, that the employee obtain a second opinion on the health condition and need for FMLA leave. [29 C.F.R. §§ 825.307, 825.308]

Q 9:189 If a husband and a wife both work for the same employer, is the maximum FMLA leave two 12-week periods?

The FMLA permits an employer that employs a husband and wife to limit the total FMLA leave to an aggregated total of 12 weeks for the same event per year. This limitation only applies to the: (1) birth of a child, (2) placement of a child for adoption or foster care (or to care for the child after placement), or (3) care of a sick parent with a serious health condition. [FMLA § 102(f); 29 C.F.R. § 825.202(b)]

This shortened limit does not apply to the total days of unpaid leave taken by an employee under the FMLA to care for a spouse who is on FMLA leave.

Q 9:190 How is the per-year limitation on the 12 weeks of FMLA leave determined?

The employer may select any of the following four 12-month periods, as long as the period is consistently and uniformly applied to all employees. The four alternatives for determining the "12-month period" during which the 12 weeks of FMLA leave entitlement occurs are:

1. The calendar year;
2. Any fixed 12-month period during the calendar year;
3. A 12-month period that starts on the day the employee begins the 12-week FMLA leave, so each employee would have a separate 12-month period; or
4. A rolling 12-month period that is generally measured backward from the date the leave ends.

Under the fourth method, the maximum FMLA leave is the 12 weeks under the FMLA less the number of weeks taken in the last 12 months. [29 C.F.R. §§ 825.200(b), 825.200(c)]

Q 9:191   Must the FMLA leave be taken on a continuous basis?

No. The 12 weeks of FMLA leave need not be taken on a continuous, full-time basis. Under certain conditions the employee may take FMLA leave via an intermittent or reduced work schedule. The intermittent leave may be used for follow-up care and other medical appointments. Leave taken for birth or placement of a child for adoption or foster care cannot be taken intermittently or via a reduced work schedule unless both employer and employee agree to the schedule. FMLA leave taken for the care of a spouse, child, or parent with a serious health condition is permitted via a reduced work schedule or intermittently when that form of leave is "medically necessary." With intermittent leave the hours are totaled and can only be capped for FMLA purposes when the total equals 12 weeks. [29 C.F.R. §§ 823.201, 825.117, 825.203]

When an employee requests leave that will, for the foreseeable future, require an intermittent or reduced work schedule, the employer can require the employee to transfer temporarily to an available alternative position for which the employee is qualified. The transfer must not involve a reduction in pay or benefits and must be designed to better accommodate the employee than does the current work position. [FMLA § 102(b)(2); 29 C.F.R. § 525.204]

Note that special rules apply to teachers who are employees of schools when the reduced work schedule or intermittent leave would cause them to be on leave for more than 20 percent of the total number of working days during the period of leave. Such employees may be required to take the leave for a particular duration or transfer to an alternative position during the leave. Similar restrictions apply to noncontinuous leave taken at the end or beginning of the academic year. [29 C.F.R. §§ 825.600–825.604]

Q 9:192   Are salaried employees permitted to take reduced-work-schedule leave under FMLA without violating the FLSA?

Yes. The FLSA normally requires that an exempt worker—one to whom the FLSA's minimum wage and overtime rules do not apply—not have weekly or daily pay reduced for leave. When an exempt employee's pay is reduced for less than a full day, the exempt status generally is lost under the FLSA. Reductions in pay for unpaid intermittent or reduced FMLA leave do not cause the FLSA exemption from overtime to be lost. Thus an exempt employee whose pay is reduced under the FMLA for intermittent leave does not become eligible for overtime pay upon return. [29 U.S.C. § 2612; 29 C.F.R. § 825.206(b)]

Q 9:193   Can the employer require the employee to use accrued paid leave for the FMLA leave?

Yes. The employer can institute a uniform policy that requires employees to apply all available paid leave (sick leave, personal leave, or vacation leave) toward the 12 weeks of FMLA leave before applying unpaid leave. [29 C.F.R. § 825.207]

If the employer will be substituting the employee's paid leave for unpaid FMLA leave, the employer must notify the employee of its decision. That determination must be made (1) before the leave begins or (2) before an extension of current leave is granted. This requirement is delayed where the employer did not receive sufficient advance notice that the leave would be taken. Note that the employer is permitted to add the unpaid 12 weeks of FMLA leave to any paid leave used first as FMLA leave. An employee who is required to take paid leave cannot alter his or her cafeteria plan election during the period of paid leave. [29 C.F.R. § 825.208]

Q 9:194   How do the benefits and rights restoration provisions under the FMLA apply?

An employee returning from FMLA leave must be entitled to "equivalent benefits" upon his or her return. [29 C.F.R. § 825.214(a)] In other words, the employee must be permitted, upon return, to choose to be reinstated to group health coverage, including coverage under a health FSA. But note that the employee may also choose to elect not to participate after the unpaid FMLA leave. [Prop. Treas. Reg. § 1.125-3, Q&A 1]

For purposes of this requirement, the term *benefits* refers to all benefits provided by the employer to its employees. *Equivalent* generally means that "benefits must be reserved in the same manner and at the same levels as provided when the leave began, and subject to any changes in benefit levels that may have taken place during the period of FMLA leave affecting the entire workforce, unless otherwise elected by the employee." However, an employee returning from FMLA leave has no greater right to benefits for the remainder of the plan year than if he or she had been continuously employed during the FMLA period. [29 C.F.R. § 825.215(d); Prop. Treas. Reg. § 1.125-3, Q&A 1; 29 C.F.R. § 825.312(d)]

Flexible Spending Accounts

Q 9:195   What is a flexible spending account?

A flexible spending account (FSA) is a type of fringe benefit where the employer permits the employee to submit certain personal expenses for reimbursement from an account established for the benefit of the employee. If the plan is properly structured and administered, the reimbursements are not treated as wages for federal income taxation or FICA or FUTA taxes. With many FSAs, the employee makes contributions through a Section 125 plan to establish the fund from which the reimbursements are paid. In other cases, the FSA account is funded in part (or fully) through employer contributions. The FSA account is generally treated by employers as an unfunded plan and merely represents a bookkeeping entry on the employer's books and records. Some employers do establish separate trusts for health FSA accounts. [Treas. Reg. § 1.125-2, Q&A 7(c)]

The most common types of FSAs are (1) health care spending accounts under I.R.C. Section 105, (2) transportation benefits identified in I.R.C. Section 132, (3) dependent care spending accounts under I.R.C. Section 129, and (4) adoption assistance under I.R.C. Section 137. A "premium only" or "premium conversion" arrangement to permit employees to pay toward the cost of health and accident benefits on a pretax basis is most often not accomplished via an FSA. However, a premium payment and reimbursement account could be set up to reimburse an employee for individual health and accident insurance in certain circumstances.

In 2002, the IRS authorized a new type of reimbursement account—a Health Reimbursement Arrangement (HRA)—that is funded only through employer contributions (see Qs 9:238–9:248). The rules for these FSA plans differ significantly from those of health FSAs. Each type of FSA is subject to a different set of rules. For example, dependent care FSAs are generally not subject to the "advance-payment" requirements that apply to health FSAs, and transportation benefits cannot be funded under a Section 125 plan. It should be noted that, in Notice 2005-86 [2005-49 I.R.B. 1075], Treasury and the IRS clarified that coverage by the FSA disqualifies an individual from contributing to a health savings account (has) during the two and one-half month grace period allowed for FSAs, even where the health FSA has reached its annual benefit limit. However, the notice also provided guidance to employers on how they can amend their FSAs to enable covered individuals to contribute to HSAs during the grace period.

(Effective January 1, 2004, the IRS authorized a different type of savings vehicle for payment or reimbursement of medical expense—the HSA under I.R.C. Section 223. This is not classified as an FSA. See Qs 9:257–9:272 for more information on HSAs.) The law imposes restrictions that are applicable to both health and dependent care FSAs. These include:

1. Reimbursements must be for expenses incurred during the plan year, plus two and one-half months (which was effective in 2005), provided that the plan document has been revised.

2. Reimbursement can be made only when the nature of the expense is verified by an independent third party showing the amount of the expense.

3. A written statement must be provided by the participant that the expense has not been reimbursed by, or is not reimbursed under, any other plan coverage. [Prop. Treas. Reg. § 1.125-2, Q&A 7(b)(5)]

4. Except in the case of HRAs, unused amounts at the end of the year must be forfeited, unless the plan document has been revised to allow for reimbursements for expenses incurred during the plan year plus an additional two and one-half months. Where funded through a Section 125 plan, the unused amounts in one type of FSA (e.g., a dependent care FSA) cannot be used to obtain benefits in another type of FSA (e.g., a health FSA).

Each of these FSA benefits is subject to a separate set of requirements (e.g., nondiscrimination) and administrative requirements under I.R.C. Sections 105(h) and 129. [Prop. Treas. Reg. § 1.125-2, Q&As 6(a), 7(b)]

Reimbursements from employers to employees through a credit or debit card for expenses provided under a qualified HRA, FSA, or accident and health plan are not included in gross income and are not taxable to the employee. [Rev. Rul. 2003-43, 2003-21 I.R.B. 935, 2003-1 C.B. 935, IRS RRU, May 06, 2003] Subsequent guidance from the IRS, gave employers more ways to substantiate claimed medical expenses when employees use debit and credit cards in medical reimbursement plans and dependent care assistance programs. [Notice 2006-69, 2006-31 I.R.B. 107; amplified Notice 2006-69 2006-31 I.R.B. 107; Notice 2007-2 2007-2 I.R.B. 254] Employers sponsoring health FSAs or HRAs may provide employees with a payment card, where the payment card processor provides a system of approving and rejecting card transactions using inventory control information, effective for plan years beginning after December 31, 2006. In such a system, the inventory control information compares the purchase with a list of items qualified as medical expenses under I.R.C. Section 213(d). Employers may use cards for dependent care assistance programs, but expenses cannot be reimbursed before they are incurred.

The proposed regulations consolidate previous guidance on how debit cards may be used by health care FSAs. The consolidated rules include special transitional rules for substantiation of medical expenses for health care FSA debit cards used for purchases at supermarkets, grocery stores, discount stores, and wholesale clubs that do not have a medical care merchant category code, and purchases through mail-order and web-based vendors that sell prescription drugs. The proposed regulations would also establish new rules that permit dependent care FSAs to pay or reimburse dependent care expenses through the use of debit cards.

Effective July 1, 2009, FSA debit cards work only at pharmacies or retail locations that have implemented a certified Inventory Information Approval System (IIAS). The IRS requires the implementation of this new technology by the pharmacies. The IIAS technology allows FSA eligible items to be recognized and approved for purchase at checkout at retail locations.

Limited Purpose FSA. A Limited Purpose FSA is a tax savings account that reimburses employees for eligible dental and vision care expenses. The Limited Purpose FSA works the same way as a traditional FSA: employees decide how much money to contribute, and that amount is deducted tax free from their pay. Similar to a traditional FSA, any money remaining in the account at the end of the plan year is forfeited. The difference between a traditional and Limited Purpose FSA is that general medical expenses are not eligible for reimbursement under a Limited Purpose FSA. This type of flexible spending program is designed for consumers who have an HSA and are not permitted to be covered by a traditional FSA while contributing to that HSA.

Qualified reservist distribution. A special rule allows amounts in a health FSA to be distributed to reservists ordered or called to active duty. This rule applies to distributions made after June 17, 2008, if the plan has been amended to allow these distributions. The employer must report the distribution as wages on Form W-2 for the year in which the distribution is made. The distribution is subject to employment taxes and is included in gross income. A qualified reservist distribution is allowed if the employee was, because he or she was in the reserves, ordered or called to active duty for a period of more than 179 days or for an indefinite period, and the distribution is made during the period beginning on the date of the order or call and ending on the last date that reimbursements could otherwise be made for the plan year that includes the date of the order or call.

Q 9:196   Are employee contributions to an FSA under a cafeteria plan subject to federal employment taxes?

Salary reductions that are used to fund a health FSA, adoption assistance FSA, or dependent care FSA are not treated as wages for any federal employment taxes when made under a qualified Section 125 plan. That is also the case for salary reductions outside of a Section 125 plan made to a transportation FSA. The portion of any salary reductions used to obtain a nontaxable benefit (other than a 401(k) contribution) is generally not considered income subject to federal income taxation or FICA or FUTA taxes. Adoption assistance benefits paid from an employer-provided plan (e.g., an FSA) are subject to FICA and FUTA taxes. See Q 9:48.

Salary deferrals to a 401(k) plan made under a cafeteria plan are subject to FICA and FUTA taxation. [I.R.C. §§ 3121(a)(5)(G), 3121(v)(1), 3306(b)(5)(G), 3306(r)(1); Notice 97-9, 1997-2 I.R.B. 35]

Q 9:197   How are elections and benefit payments handled for a dependent care flexible spending account?

When a dependent care reimbursement account is funded through salary reductions under a Section 125 plan, the employee makes his or her pay-period salary reduction election prior to the period when expenses will be reimbursed (generally prior to the first day of the plan year). A plan may permit new participants to enter the plan after the start of the plan year, in which case a new participant may make an election for the remainder of the plan year. The plan must limit reimbursements to expenses incurred after the employee has entered the plan (generally on the first day of the plan year) and prior to the end of the plan year or when participation ends, if earlier.

Once the salary reduction election is made to contribute to the dependent care plan, the election must generally remain in effect for the full plan year; however, where the plan document permits the employee to amend or revoke an election for a "change in family status," a "change-in-status" modification may be made when the change in family status occurs and it affects the benefit being provided (e.g., birth of a child or spouse leaving his or her job) (see Qs 9:74–9:104). A change in the election may also be permitted under the plan document if the dependent care provider increases the fees charged. [Treas. Reg. § 1.125-4(f)]

Example. Conway has one child, Charles. Conway's employer, Chisolm Plumbing, Inc., maintains a calendar-year cafeteria plan that allows employees to elect coverage under a dependent care FSA. Prior to the beginning of the calendar year, Conway elects to reduce his biweekly salary to make 26 payments of $180 ($4,680 for the year) to pay for Charles's dependent care. During the year, Charles has his 13th birthday, and Conway wants to stop making salary reduction contributions for the dependent care FSA benefit.

Such a change is permitted because when Charles turns 13, he ceases to satisfy the definition of a "qualifying individual" under the I.R.C. [I.R.C. §§ 21(b)(1) and 21(b)(2)] Accordingly, on Charles's birthday, there is a change in status that affects Conway's employment-related expenses. Therefore, Conway may make a corresponding change under Chisolm Plumbing, Inc.'s cafeteria plan to cancel coverage under the dependent care FSA if permitted under the plan document. [Prop. Treas. Reg. § 1.125-4(c)(4); Notice 97-9, 1997-2 I.R.B. 35] Some employers, however, have added to their plan documents that a change in the age of the dependent to any age other than when the dependent is no longer eligible to be the subject of the plan is not allowed. In other words, some plan sponsors have reasoned that the birthday during the plan year is known prior to the election, and such a plan change is an administrative inconvenience and therefore not allowed.

Q 9:198 What are the requirements applicable to health, adoption assistance, and dependent care FSAs?

Traditionally, health, adoption assistance, and dependent care FSA benefits funded under a Section 125 plan were subject to certain requirements: (1) only expenses incurred during the plan year may be reimbursed, (2) all payments must be made from an accountable plan, (3) unused portions cannot be carried over to the next year (the "risk-shifting" requirement), and (4) the plan must provide for a period of coverage that is at least 12 months or the entire length of a short plan year.

However, the IRS has loosened the rules. An employer can amend its health or dependent care FSA plan to allow expenses incurred through March 15 to be reimbursed from the previous year's contribution. [Prop. Reg. § 1.125-5] Alternatively, up to $500 of unused amounts remaining in a health FSA may be carried over to the following year. [Notice 2013-71, 2013-47 I.R.B. 532]

A health, adoption assistance, or dependent care FSA may reallocate, on a pro rata or per capita basis, unused balances (forfeited funds) in the employee's FSA accounts to all participants in a subsequent year. The employer may also retain any forfeited amounts and use them to offset administrative expenses of the plan. [Prop. Treas. Reg. § 1.125-2, Q&A 7; ERISA Technical Release 92-01]

Q 9:199   What are the requirements applicable to health FSAs that do not apply to adoption assistance and dependent care FSAs?

There are several, and the requirements are fewer when the health FSA benefits are not funded under a Section 125 plan.

A health FSA (but not dependent care or adoption assistance FSAs) funded under a Section 125 plan (1) must exhibit the risk-shifting and risk-distribution characteristics of insurance for both employer and employee, (2) must reimburse only medical expenses defined under I.R.C. Section 213 or 105(b), and (3) cannot reimburse for participant-paid premiums used to pay for health insurance coverage. Another type of benefit offered under a cafeteria plan is commonly called a "premium only plan" (POP); this kind of plan provision can use pretax salary reductions to pay the premiums for health insurance. [Prop. Treas. Reg. § 1.125-2, Q&A 7(b)(4)]

The IRS has made it clear that the health FSA must exhibit employer risk shifting (not required of dependent care FSAs). This requirement is satisfied when the health FSA provides uniform coverage throughout the year. For example, if the employee's salary reduction is $100 per month, then a full $1,200 must be available to pay benefits at any time throughout the year. Thus an employee who has so far only participated for one month (contributed $100) must be permitted to receive a reimbursement for a full $1,200. Note that although it may be possible, with voluntary cooperation of the former plan participant, to recover excess employer reimbursements that exceed a terminated participant's salary reduction, it is seldom feasible. [Prop. Treas. Reg. § 1.125-2, Q&A 8; see also Prop. Treas. Reg. § 1.125-1, Q&A 17, EE-016-79 (May 7, 1984), for additional rules.]

A health FSA may be subject to continuation coverage under COBRA. Certain COBRA rules apply specifically to Health FSAs. See COBRA Final Regulations Section 54.4980B-2, Q&A 8.

Frequent Flyer Miles

Q 9:200   What is the taxation of frequent flyer miles an employee earns on business travel?

The IRS issued formal guidance on the treatment of an employee's nonbusiness use of frequent flyer miles earned while on business-related travel. [Ann. 2002-18, 2002-10 I.R.B. 621, Feb. 21, 2002] The IRS stated that such use is a tax-free *de minimis* benefit. This exclusion does not apply if the benefits are converted to cash or other circumstances that may be considered a tax avoidance scheme. While this guidance does not answer all the questions, the IRS recognizes that further guidance is required. Any future decision would affect benefits prospectively giving taxpayers some comfort that complying with the current guidance would prevent a future audit.

The personal use of frequent flyer mileage earned on business travel is treated as a *de minimis* fringe benefit because it is unrealistic to account for the value of the benefit. However, where a formal program is in place that tracks the frequent flyer mileage and requires employees to return certificates for future trips or payments for missed or late flights, the exclusion of frequent flyer miles accumulated by employees can continue to be in effect. The IRS released a private letter ruling holding that one employer's policy regarding the value of frequent flyer miles earned on business travel was taxable income received under a nonaccountable plan. The employer had a formal policy that required employees to use any remaining frequent flyer mileage for business travel, but permitted employees to apply any remaining mileage for personal travel. [Priv. Ltr. Rul. 9547001 (Nov. 24, 1995)]

The Tax Court held that an employer's cash reimbursement for the value of business travel taken using an employee's accumulated frequent flyer mileage is taxable income. [Charley v. Commissioner, 1996 U.S. App. LEXIS 18248 (9th Cir. 1996)] It was this case that was the primary impetus for the Announcement described above allowing tax-free nonbusiness use of frequent flyer miles.

While there are still many open questions about how to treat benefits derived from frequent flyer programs, the IRS has clearly stated that an employee can accumulate frequent flyer miles from business travel that is excluded from income. One caveat is that employers that impose restrictions or other requirements related to reporting or turning over the benefits to the employer run the risk of creating a taxable event.

Fringe Benefits

Q 9:201 How are fringe benefits provided by an employer treated for federal employment tax purposes?

I.R.C. Section 132 offers a variety of exclusions from compensation (and related withholding and federal employment taxes) for certain fringe benefits and reimbursement of employee expenses provided to an employee. These fringe benefits are specifically defined under I.R.C. Section 132 and include certain personal use of employer-provided autos, flights on employer-provided aircraft, free or discounted commercial flights, vacations, discounts on property or services, certain business-only memberships in clubs, and other payments or property to an employee that qualify as *de minimis* fringe benefits. If not specifically excluded under the I.R.C., IRS regulations, administrative guidelines, or case law, the value of any fringe benefit provided by an employer to an employee must generally be included in the employee's wages (less any amounts the employee pays for the benefit). The IRS recently addressed wellness credits, a popular employee benefit, that encourages employees to take positive actions around their health. In the IRS Memorandum 201622031 [May 27, 2016 PRESP-118788-15], the IRS stated that an employer must include the payment of cash awards for participating in wellness rewards in the employee's gross income.

Examples of specific fringe benefits permitted under I.R.C. Section 132 that are not treated as wages, when certain conditions are met, include the following:

1. Services provided to employees at no additional cost to the employer.

2. Qualified employee discounts.

3. Working-condition fringes that are property or services the employee could deduct as a business expense if he or she had paid for them (e.g., a company car for business use and subscriptions to business magazines).

4. Minimal-value fringes, generally referred to as *de minimis* fringe benefits (including an occasional cab ride when an employee must work overtime, local transportation benefits provided because of unsafe conditions and unusual circumstances, and meals the employer provides at eating places run for the employees if the meals are not furnished at below cost). Meals furnished at a discount may qualify as *de minimis* fringes, but they cannot be provided without some cost.

5. Qualified transportation fringes subject to specified conditions and dollar limitations (including transportation in a commuter highway vehicle, any transit pass, and qualified parking).

6. Qualified moving expense reimbursements.

7. The use of on-premises athletic facilities if substantially all of the use is by employees, their spouses, and their dependent children.

8. Qualified tuition reduction, which an educational organization provides its employees for education. [For more information on these benefits, see Pub. No. 15-B]

The tax laws relating to certain fringe benefits impose a nondiscrimination requirement on an exclusion from gross income. Fringe benefits subject to a nondiscrimination requirement include (1) no-additional-cost services, (2) qualified employee discounts, (3) meals provided at an employer-operated eating facility, and (4) qualified tuition reductions. The benefit need not be available to all employees, but the group eligible for benefits must constitute a nondiscriminatory classification of the entire employee population (i.e., the plan must cover a broad cross-section of all employees). [I.R.C. §§ 132(a)-132(j), 414(q)]

De Minimis Fringe Benefits

Q 9:202   What is a *de minimis* fringe benefit?

A "*de minimis* fringe benefit" is described in the I.R.C. as any property or service offered to the employee, the value of which is so small as to make accounting for it unreasonable or administratively impractical. This determination is made after taking into account the frequency with which the employer provides similar fringes to the employees. Cash payments are never considered a *de minimis* fringe benefit unless the cash is for meals or transportation fare and specific exemptions governing the meal payment or local transportation fare are met. Special rules also apply to an employer's gift of a cash-equivalent benefit, such as a gift certificate. [I.R.C. § 132(e)(1); Treas. Reg. § 1.132-6(c)]

For example, many employers provide coffee or similar beverages to their employees. Some employers may also provide an occasional meal. The frequency with which these benefits are provided to the employees is a factor to be considered when determining whether the value is *de minimis*. Meals offered to employees once or twice a week probably would not satisfy these requirements, barring unusual considerations.

Examples of *de minimis* benefits include occasional parties and picnics for employees; coffee and doughnuts; occasional tickets to the theater or a sporting event; occasional typing of personal letters or personal use of copying machines; occasional meal money or cab fare when employees are required to work overtime (provided these payments are not based on the number of hours worked); and occasional meals provided at a reduced price when provided at an employer-operated eating facility (i.e., an employer cafeteria). This last *de minimis* benefit is conditioned on the revenues of the eating facility being at least equal to its operating costs. Special rules outside of *de minimis* fringe benefits apply if the eating facility is operated on a full-time basis.

In general, *de minimis* fringe benefits do not have to be provided to employees on a nondiscriminatory basis—they can favor HCEs (e.g., free soft drinks for the officers); however, meals provided at an employer-operated eating facility cannot be discriminatory in favor of HCEs. When a particular dining room or cafeteria is routinely restricted for use by HCEs, those employees must include the FMV of meals obtained in these facilities in their taxable wages. [I.R.C. § 132(e); Treas. Reg. §§ 1.132-1(b), 1.132-6, 1.132-7]

Q 9:203   May the employer offer *de minimis* fringe benefits to nonemployees?

Yes. *De minimis* fringe benefits may generally be provided to anyone associated with the employee without being treated as taxable compensation. For example, "qualified," on-premises athletic facilities may be used without tax consequences by employees, their spouses, and dependent children. Eating facilities may be available to nonemployees on the same terms as they are made available to employers.

Q 9:204   Are occasional meal money and local transportation benefits considered *de minimis* benefits?

Yes, under certain limited conditions. Meals, meal money, or local transportation fare provided to an employee are excluded as a *de minimis* fringe benefit when the amounts paid are reasonable and satisfy the following three conditions: (1) the payments are provided on an occasional basis, (2) the benefits are provided because the employees are working after normal business hours, and (3) in the case of meals or meal money, the payments must be provided to enable the employee to work overtime. [Treas. Reg. § 1.132-6(d)(2)]

A special valuation rule allows an employer to provide commuting expenses when unusual circumstances exist and other transportation is unsafe. In such cases, the employee can exclude the payments to the extent each one-way trip exceeds $1.50. Transit passes and tokens are tax free up to $255 for 2017. [Treas. Reg. §§ 1.132-6(d)(2)(iii), 1.132-9; Rev. Proc. 2006-53, 2006-48 I.R.B. 996; Pub. L. No. 111-5]

Example. Frontier provides Brooke with $3.25 in subway tokens each workday. The aggregate benefit may not be great in value, but it is not a *de minimis* fringe benefit because it does not satisfy the I.R.C. requirement that the payment be infrequent. If the payment is under a qualified transportation plan, the tokens are not additional income. (See Qs 9:452–9:461.) [Pub. No. 15-B]

Q 9:205   Are group meals considered *de minimis* fringe benefits?

Yes. Although the reference to "group meals" is not defined by the IRS, Treasury Regulations Section 1.132-6(e)(1) cites "group meals" as a benefit that meets the requirements for a *de minimis* fringe benefit. Presumably, this would apply to an infrequent gathering of employees where a meal is provided.

Q 9:206   How do employers determine whether cash meal allowances or reimbursements qualify as *de minimis* benefits?

The employer must determine both the frequency with which the benefits are provided and whether the benefits can be considered so small in amount as to make accounting for them administratively impractical. [I.R.C. § 132(e)(1)]

The IRS has taken the position that meals provided on a "routine basis" to employees who work overtime are not *de minimis* fringes because the employee's overtime and emergency work were a part of the company's normal business practice. The employer's consistent practice of providing meal allowances and reimbursements for overtime work failed to be a *de minimis* fringe benefit, resulting in payments that should have been, but were not, treated as taxable wages. [Tech. Adv. Mem. 9148001, Nov. 29, 1991] Thus, an employer must at least consider what is being provided and make a conscious decision about the appropriate tax treatment.

Note that in certain cases meals provided for noncompensatory reasons and for the convenience of the employer may be provided on a regular basis without the value of those benefits being treated as additional compensation. (See Q 9:156.)

Q 9:207   When are cash payments for meals not treated as additional compensation?

No exclusion is available for an employer's cash allowance for meals unless the meals have a business purpose and are substantiated under an accountable plan. Payments not made under an accountable plan are additional compensation and subject to withholding and federal employment tax. [Treas. Reg. §§ 1.119-1(a), 31.3401(a)]

Q 9:208   Is the value of meals regularly provided to an employee a *de minimis* fringe benefit?

No, if the meals are compensatory in nature.

Example. Nu Champions Leadership maintains a summer day camp near several eating facilities. The employees at the camp are provided a free lunch in lieu of compensation. The value of the lunch meals served at the camp for its instructors is not a *de minimis* fringe benefit, nor is it exempt under I.R.C. Section 119.

No-Additional-Cost Services

Q 9:209   What are the most typical fringe benefits that qualify as no-additional-cost services?

The most common no-additional-cost fringe benefits include air travel for employees of an airline, hotel rooms for employees of a hotel, and merchandise discounts for department store workers.

No-additional-cost services are benefits that give an employee free or discounted access to an employer's business services or retail operations at little cost to the employer. The value of a no-additional-cost service or qualified employee discount is also excludable from an employee's wages if offered to the spouse and dependent children of active employees, retired employees, disabled employees, the surviving spouse of an employee, or an orphaned child under age 25 of a deceased employee; however, the employee must be working in (or have formerly worked in) the same line of the employer's business that is providing the service or discount. Special rules apply to certain no-additional-cost services in the airline industry. [Treas. Reg. § 1.61-21] See Q 9:211. While it could be argued that there is economic loss in that goods or airline seats are inventory that may have otherwise been sold at retail, such a debate is not necessary as the IRS has provided clear guidelines.

Q 9:210   When may no-additional-cost services be offered tax free to employees?

An employer may offer no-additional-cost services to its employees without the value of those services being treated as wages subject to FIT, FITW, FICA, and FUTA when those services meet the following four conditions:

1. The service is regularly offered for sale to customers (and not just to employees) as part of the employer's normal business activities. An exception to this rule permits two employers to enter into reciprocal agreements to provide services to each other's employees.

2. The employer bears no substantial cost, including lost revenue or additional labor, in providing these services to the employees. If an employee reimburses the employer for the cost, that reimbursement is ignored in determining whether there was a substantial additional cost. An employer will be deemed to incur substantial costs if a significant amount of time is spent by the employer or its employees in providing the service.

3. The services are provided to employees or former employees who are retired or disabled and their spouses or dependent children (and for certain airline travel by parents of airline employees). A no-additional-cost service can only be provided to employees in the "line of business" that provides the service. Special rules define line of business; special rules also provide that for this purpose, if it is not uncommon for one industry to be operated without the other, both industries will be considered in the same line of business.

4. Substantially the same services are available to a broad group of employees on a nondiscriminatory basis that does not favor HCEs as defined under I.R.C. Section 414(g). HCEs are defined under the pension laws as more than 5 percent owners in the current or prior year or individuals whose gross wages exceeded $120,000 in 2015 (see Q 9:318). Discriminatory benefits for HCEs are subject to federal income tax withholding and all employment taxes. [I.R.C. §§ 132(b), 132(f), 132(h), 132(i); Treas. Reg. §§ 1.132-1(b)(3), 1.132-2, 1.132-4, 1.132-8]

Q 9:211 What are the special requirements that apply to airline travel by airline employees?

The value of air travel provided to employees (and their dependents) of a corporation engaged predominantly in "airline-related services" that is affiliated with an airline carrier may be treated as a no-additional-cost service. Airline-related services include such services as baggage handling, ticketing and reservations, operating an airport coffee shop or gift shop, catering, flight planning, and weather analysis. The definition of a dependent for airline travel includes parents of individuals eligible to receive these services. [I.R.C. § 132(h)(6)]

The value of air transportation provided to employees of a qualified affiliate of an airline (i.e., a member of a group in which another member operates the airline) who are directly engaged in providing airline-related services is excluded from gross income when provided by the airline or affiliate. [Pub. No. 535] Thus, an airline that "code shares" or otherwise partners with the employer airline may provide the same service with no taxable consequences to the employee.

Example. Taylor lives in Bakersville, California, and is a flight attendant for Fly High Airways. Her base is in San Francisco, California. In order to get to San Francisco to work on her appointed Fly High Airways flight, she must take a flight on Cloud Nine Air. Because Cloud Nine Air and Fly High Airways use code-sharing, the value of Taylor's flight is not taxable to her.

Q 9:212   Can an employer require employees to pay an amount for a no-additional-cost service or offer it through a rebate?

Yes. The exclusion from withholding and federal employment tax is available when the service is provided at no cost, at a reduced price, or through a rebate. [Treas. Reg. § 1.132-2(a)(3)]

Q 9:213   Must a no-additional-cost fringe benefit be offered to all employees?

Generally, no; however, the tax exemption may be lost if the plan is discriminatory in favor of HCEs.

The regulations provide that the exclusion from income rules for HCEs (determined under the pension coverage rules) applies if the benefits available to non-highly compensated employees are available to (1) all employees or (2) non-highly compensated employees on substantially the same terms. Benefits may be limited to a group of employees that satisfies the pension coverage rules. [Treas. Reg. § 1.132-8(c)]

Certain employees may be excluded from a tax-free fringe benefit without the plan being deemed discriminatory. In general, employees with less than a year of service, part-time employees working fewer than 17.5 hours per week, part-year employees working no more than six months a year, and employees under age 21 do not have to be considered for nondiscrimination testing purposes. In addition, employees covered by a collective bargaining agreement may be disregarded when determining whether a plan is discriminatory provided the benefit was the subject of good-faith bargaining. [I.R.C. §§ 132(c), 414(q)]

Q 9:214   Who are treated as highly compensated employees under I.R.C. Section 132?

The definition of highly compensated employee (HCE) for fringe benefits follows the definition of an HCE that applies to pension and profit sharing plans. [I.R.C. § 414(q)] See Q 9:318.

Q 9:215   Do reciprocal agreements between unrelated employers regarding access to no-additional-cost services qualify under I.R.C. Section 132?

Yes. The I.R.C. recognizes a reciprocal agreement to provide no-additional-cost services to employees of unrelated employers as long as neither employer incurs substantial additional costs and all other requirements of I.R.C. Section 132 are met. These reciprocal agreements can apply only to no-additional-cost fringe benefits and not to the other fringe benefits permitted under I.R.C. Section 132. [Treas. Reg. § 1.132-2(b)]

Qualified Employee Discounts

Q 9:216   What is a qualified employee discount?

A "qualified employee discount" refers to any employee discount that is available for retail as goods or services offered to the public by the employer. A qualified employee discount must meet one of two conditions to be treated as a nontaxable fringe benefit: (1) in the case of goods, the discount cannot exceed the gross profit percentage of the price at which the goods are being offered by the employer to customers; or (2) in the case of services, the discount cannot exceed 20 percent of the price at which the services are being offered by the employer to customers. The gross profit margin is determined under the following formula:

(total sales – cost of goods sold) ÷ total sales

Qualified goods or services are defined as goods or services that are offered for sale to customers in the line of business in which the employee performs substantial services. Qualified discounts may not be offered on real property or property held for investment, such as securities. [I.R.C. § 132(c)(1)]

Like no-additional-cost services, qualified employee discounts must be (1) provided in a nondiscriminatory manner that does not favor HCEs as defined under the pension laws, and (2) provided on substantially the same terms and conditions to a broad cross-section of employees. [I.R.C. § 132(i)]

Working-Condition Fringe Benefits

Q 9:217   What is a working-condition fringe benefit?

The most common examples of working-condition fringe benefits are employer-paid meals, travel, use of company cars, professional or association dues, uniform allowances, and magazine subscriptions. Special rules define when the personal use of a company car is excludable. The value of home computers and cellular telephones provided by an employer may be excludable when the substantiation requirements are met. [I.R.C. § 274(d)(4)]

Working-condition fringe benefits also include, but are not limited to, such items as a bodyguard provided for security reasons, use of a demonstration automobile by a full-time automobile salesperson, job-related educational classes, and outplacement services (when these job-hunting services are not offered in lieu of severance payments). [I.R.C. § 132(d); Treas. Reg. §§ 1.132-1(b)(2), 1.132-5]

A working-condition fringe benefit is defined as any property or service provided to an employee to the extent that, if the employee paid for such property or service, such payment would be allowable as a deduction under I.R.C. Section 162 or 167. This determination is made without regard to the 2 percent floor that applies to the itemized deductions on the employee's Form 1040. That is, the expense must be one that would be an ordinary and necessary business expense if the employee had purchased the property or service directly. Working condition fringes are not excluded from the nondiscrimination rules.

A working-condition fringe benefit generally must meet four requirements:

1. The benefit can only be offered to a current or former employee, partner, director, or independent contractor performing services for the employer.
2. The employee's use of the property must relate to the employer's trade or business.
3. The employee would be entitled to a business deduction on his or her Form 1040 income tax return if the employee had paid for the property or services directly.
4. The employee is required to maintain records to substantiate the nature and essential elements of the business expense.

A working-condition fringe benefit generally is not available to family members of the employee because such a benefit would not satisfy the requirements that the expense be deductible by the employee as a business expense under I.R.C. Section 162 or 167. [Treas. Reg. § 1.132-5(r)]

Q 9:218   May working-condition fringe benefits be offered to any nonemployees or volunteers?

No. In general, a working-condition fringe benefit may only be provided on a tax-free basis to current employees, partners, directors, or independent contractors performing services for the employer.

Certain volunteer workers may be provided working-condition fringe benefits without the benefits being treated as taxable compensation. These include volunteers working for a tax-exempt organization or a federal, state, or local government unit who may exclude working-condition fringes from their income as long as the value of the benefits they receive is substantially less than the value of the volunteer services they perform. Should the value of the benefits exceed the value of the services provided, the volunteers may also be entitled to an exclusion for working-condition fringes as employees or independent contractors. Typical working-condition fringe benefits offered to volunteers include directors' and officers' liability insurance protection. The value for working-condition fringes is not reported on any Form 1099 the organization might otherwise issue to the volunteer. [I.R.C. § 132(d); Treas. Reg. §§ 1.132-1(b)(2), 1.132-5]

Q 9:219   Can club dues paid by an employer qualify as a working-condition fringe benefit?

Maybe. The I.R.C. generally disallows business deductions by corporations for payments of membership dues paid to a club organized for trade association, pleasure, recreation, or other social purposes. Such payments are generally treated as compensation to the employee whose dues are being paid. That employee may then be entitled to an employee business deduction for a portion of these payments where the membership is used for valid and substantiated business reasons.

Notwithstanding these broad rules, club dues may qualify as a working-condition fringe benefit when three conditions are met: (1) the club dues are not treated as wages, (2) the expenses would be deductible by the employee had the organization not been classified as a "club" under I.R.C. Section 274(a)(3), and (3) the employee provides documentation as to the use of the club being solely for business purposes (otherwise only a portion of the dues may be deductible). [I.R.C. §§ 274(a)(3), 274(e)(4); Treas. Reg. § 1.132-5(s)]

Note that payment of membership dues to certain organizations that are not classified as clubs is permitted without being subject to taxation under Section 274(a)(3). These organizations include business leagues, chambers of commerce, professional organizations, civic or public service organizations, boards of and trade associations. Substantiation of business purpose for these payments is required. [Treas. Reg. §§ 1.132-5(q), 1.132-5(s), 1.132-5(t)]

Gifts to Employees

Q 9:220   How are employer gifts treated for federal employment taxes?

Generally, the value of all gifts or awards made to employees by an employer for services rendered is treated as additional compensation and subject to FIT, FITW, FICA, and FUTA. Gifts (not cash payments) of nominal value may, however, be treated as *de minimis* fringe benefits, and then the value is exempt from FIT, FITW, FICA, and FUTA. A gift is treated as a *de minimis* fringe benefit when it meets all the following requirements: (1) it has a nominal value (no dollar threshold is specified); (2) is made infrequently; (3) accounting would be administratively impractical; and (4) it is furnished for the purpose of promoting health, good will, contentment, or efficiency of employees (i.e., not disguised compensation). A gift certificate or gift card does not qualify as a *de minimis* benefit because it is cash-in-kind. [Treas. Reg. § 1.32-6; TAM 200437030; I.R.C. §§ 3121(a), 3306(b), 3401(a)]

The law does permit the employer to make tax-free awards (not cash) if they meet the requirements of safety or length-of-service achievement awards (see Q 9:40).

Golden Parachutes

Q 9:221   What is a golden parachute?

A golden parachute is an arrangement that pays a significant benefit or compensation (e.g., cash, stock, or deferred compensation) to certain shareholders and key executives (e.g., officers and HCEs under pension rules) of a publicly held company (and certain independent contractors of such entities)—generally referred to as "disqualified individuals"—when there is a change in control or ownership of the employer. The arrangement may consist of a single contract and other arrangements entered into between a corporation and the disqualified individuals. Certain penalties apply to large golden parachutes. [I.R.C. §§ 280G, 4999]

No corporate income tax deduction is allowed for payments classified as "excess parachute" payments. The disqualified individual who receives an excess parachute payment is also subject to a 20 percent nondeductible excise tax to be withheld by the corporation on the parachute payments. These limitations generally apply to payments made under a contract entered into, significantly amended, or renewed after June 14, 1984. Only golden parachute awards that exceed a specific dollar threshold based on the employee's prior compensation are subject to this penalty. A payment (or series of payments) is treated as an excess parachute payment, and is subject to a penalty, if the present value of the payment equals or exceeds three times the "average compensation" of the recipient over the previous five-year period. Once the payment is classified as an excess payment, the full amount of the parachute payments over the individual's average compensation is subject to the 20 percent excise tax and a withholding requirement. [I.R.C. § 280G; Prop. Treas. Reg. § 1.280G-1]

Example. Helene, an officer of a publicly held corporation, receives a golden parachute payment of $3,360,000, all of which is included in her compensation. This is more than five times greater than her average compensation of $475,000 (as measured over the previous five-year period) and thus triggers the golden parachute penalties. The excess parachute payment is $2,885,000 ($3,360,000 − $475,000). The corporation cannot deduct the $2,885,000 and must withhold the excise tax of $577,000 (20 percent of $2,885,000).

Regulations. The Treasury Department filed two rules to implement provisions of the above law. Treasury also issued a revised version of executive compensation guidelines [Treasury Notice 2008-PSSFI] for financial institutions participating in the department's Systemically Significant Failing Institutions program and a list of Frequently Asked Questions about executive compensation requirements under the TARP Capital Purchase Program.

Notice 2008-PSSFI provides guidance in a question and answer format on executive compensation standards for financial institutions participating in Treasury's Systemically Significant Failing Institutions program. Financial institutions may rely on rules in Notice 2008-PSSFI for compliance with Section 111(b) of the Emergency Economic Stabilization Act, the notice said.

These two interim rules were superseded by the Interim Final Rule on TARP Standards for Compensation and Corporate Governance—June 15, 2009, along with the October 2008 Interim Final Rule, and confirm that a TARP recipient cannot deduct compensation in excess of $500,000 for SEOs.

It is important to note that golden parachute payments may be subject to I.R.C. Section 409A (see Q 9:324).

Q 9:222   How are golden parachute payments treated for payroll tax purposes?

Payments under golden parachute contracts, like any termination pay, generally are subject to Social Security, Medicare, federal unemployment taxes, and federal income tax withholding. This basically includes all such payments, regardless of whether payments are subject to the 20 percent excise tax. [I.R.C. § 280G] The amount of income that may be included in pay, and subject to payroll taxes, may be impacted by I.R.C. Section 409A (see Q 9:324).

The IRS released audit technique guides on its website (www.irs.gov) related to executive compensation providing IRS auditors with specialized information on issues involving market segments. Included are issues relating to excessive employee remuneration under I.R.C. Section 162(m), and golden parachutes, among others. Specifically, the fringe benefit audit guidelines tell examiners to "start with the assumption that its value will be taxable" and go on to discuss more specifics. The piece devoted to auditing golden parachutes lists a variety of documents to research in determining whether a payment will be subject to a 20 percent excise tax on the recipient as an excess payment and not be deductible to the payer. It identifies nine steps to follow in making the determination, and specific issues to address under each one.

In an attempt to deal with the financial crisis, legislation directed at assisting financial institutions was passed in 2008. Specifically, provisions under the Troubled Asset Relief Program amended I.R.C. Section 162(m), limiting a financial institution's compensation deduction to $500,000, and expanded the definition of "covered employees." [Pub. L. No. 110-343]

Q 9:223   How are golden parachute payments reported?

The full parachute payment (including the excise tax withheld) is reported on Form W-2 in Boxes 1, 3, and 5. The golden parachute 20 percent excise tax is reported in Box 12 with Code K. The 20 percent excise tax that is withheld is included with other federal income tax withheld in Box 2. Report a golden parachute payment made to an independent contractor on Form 1099-MISC in Box 7 along with all other compensation (nonemployee compensation);

any excess payment to an independent contractor that is subject to the excise tax penalty is reported in Box 13.

Note that certain payments are exempt from treatment as a golden parachute, including (1) amounts treated as reasonable compensation, (2) payments by certain privately held corporations and S corporations, and (3) payments made from a qualified pension or profit sharing plan.

Group-Term Life Insurance

Q 9:224 What is group-term life insurance?

Group-term life insurance is a form of term life insurance that covers all or some employees under a policy negotiated by the employer. Only the first $50,000 of the group-term life insurance can be provided as a tax-free benefit to an employee (and be exempt from FIT, FITW, FICA, and FUTA). The value of any group-term life insurance provided in excess of $50,000 is included in the employee's compensation using Table 1, Uniform Premium Table from Treasury Regulations Section 1.79(d)(2). (See Table 9-3 in Q 9:225.) Many employers pay all or a portion of the premium cost of the basic group-term life policy, often equal to or a factor of the annual salary of the employee, giving employees the option of purchasing additional supplemental coverage. For purposes of identifying if the monthly coverage has been exceeded, the coverage to the employee under all term-life policies that are carried directly or indirectly by the employer may be aggregated. For example, if an employee has $40,000 of coverage available under the basic policy and purchases additional coverage of $20,000, the taxable excess is $10,000 [($40,000 + $20,000) − $50,000], the FMV of which is determined by reference to the age of the employee as of December 31 and the IRS Uniform Premium Table.

Only death benefits provided through group-term insurance that satisfy the requirements of I.R.C. Section 79 are eligible for this exclusion. Thus, individual-term policies or policies with cash value owned by the employer but payable to an employee's beneficiary do not qualify. Group-term life insurance contracts must be owned by the employer or the plan, and the beneficiary must be an individual (or party other than the employer) designated by the employee and not the employer. The $50,000 exclusion and valuation of benefits in excess of the $50,000 for group-term life insurance also is available for a disabled employee who terminated employment in the calendar year.

The exclusion from wages is not available for key employees (as defined by the pension laws under I.R.C. Section 416(i)) if the group-term life insurance benefits discriminate in favor of key employees as to either eligibility to participate or the benefits that are provided. The value of other forms of employer-provided life insurance (e.g., group permanent, individual term policies, or individual cash value policies) is included in wages subject to FIT, FITW, FICA, and FUTA. These life insurance benefits are valued under a different IRS table, and are generally referred to as "PS 58 costs" or, for benefits provided after

2001, Table 2001 (see Table 9-4, Q 9:281). The IRS released guidance in Notice 2002-8 on how to value certain types of employer-provided life insurance benefits that do not meet the definition of group-term life insurance under I.R.C. Section 79. [Treas. Reg. §§ 1.72-8(a), 1.72-16(b)(4)]

Q 9:225   How is the fair market value of taxable group-term life insurance benefits calculated?

An employer calculates the taxable value of group-term insurance in excess of $50,000 (or 100 percent of the value of discriminatory group-term life insurance to HCEs) by utilizing Table I, Uniform Premium Table (see Table 9-3). The table is based on monthly rates per $1,000 of coverage. To determine the monthly taxable value, multiply the number of thousands of dollars of insurance coverage in excess of $50,000 (figured to the nearest 1,000 or 100 percent of the coverage to an HCE under a discriminatory plan) by the appropriate cost per thousand per month in the table. Although the table is a monthly calculation, group-term life may be included in the employee's wages once a year or periodically throughout the year (e.g., every pay period, monthly, quarterly, or at any frequency), as long as it is included at least annually.

The age of the employee on the last day of the current calendar year is used to determine the rate from Table 1. When coverage is started or terminated during the calendar year, the employee is taxed only for months in which coverage existed. If the employer provides group-term life insurance for a period of coverage of less than one month, the employer prorates the monthly cost over that period of coverage. [Treas. Reg. § 1.79-3]

Effective as of the August 6, 2007 date of publication in the *Federal Register,* the proposed regulations for cafeteria plans provide that the amount includible in the employee's gross income on this excess group-term life insurance coverage is to be determined solely on the basis of the Table 1 rates. [72 Fed. Reg. 43,938, 2007-39 I.R.B. 681] Under this new approach, the actual cost of the coverage paid through salary reductions or flex credits is excludable from the employee's wages for withholding and tax purposes.

As a result of this change in the tax treatment of group-term life insurance that is provided under a cafeteria plan and purchased with pretax dollars, there are again tax advantages in offering group-term life insurance under a cafeteria plan and giving employees the option of purchasing the benefit on a pretax basis.

If group-term life insurance is purchased with pretax dollars, care should be taken to ensure that only aftertax contributions are used in computing the net FMV of group-term life insurance in excess of $50,000 but these pretax contributions reduce the wages that are subject to FIT, FITW, FICA, and FUTA.

Table 9-3 gives the current rates charged to individuals with excess group-term life insurance.

Table 9-3. Table 1, Uniform Premiums for $1,000
of Group-Term Life Insurance Protection

	Cost Per Month Per $1,000 of Life Insurance in Excess of $50,000
5-Year Age Brackets	*Current*
Under 25	$0.05
25 to 29	0.06
30 to 34	0.08
35 to 39	0.09
40 to 44	0.10
45 to 49	0.15
50 to 54	$0.23
55 to 59	0.43
60 to 64	0.66
65 to 69	1.27
70 and above	2.06

Example. Buckshot Corp. provides $165,000 of group term life insurance to its three employees (ages 38, 54, 64 as of December 31) who qualify under I.R.C. Section 79. The amount of imputed income pursuant to taxable group-term life insurance is shown below.

A Participant's Monthly Taxable Income for the $115,000
($165,000 Minus $50,000) of Excess Coverage

	Uniform Premium Monthly Rates
Age 38 (115 x $0.09)	$10.35
Age 54 (115 x $0.23)	26.45
Age 64 (115 x $0.66)	75.90

Q 9:226   How is the taxable portion of group-term life insurance benefits calculated when more than $50,000 is purchased by an employee under a cafeteria plan?

Prior to August 7, 2007, the IRS required that when group-term life insurance under I.R.C. Section 79 was offered under a Section 125 cafeteria plan, the FMV of the taxable excess over $50,000 was calculated as: (1) the greater of the employee's contributions toward the purchase of the insurance and employer non-elective contributions ("flex credits") to pay for the group-term life insurance coverage, or (2) the cost as determined by reference to IRS Uniform Premium Table I. [Notice 89-110, 1989-2 C.B. 447; I.R.S. Reg. § 1.79-3(d)(2)]

These previous requirements generally negated any tax benefit of offering group-term life under a cafeteria plan on a pretax basis.

Effective August 7, 2007, the final cafeteria plan regulations reversed previous guidance governing group-term life insurance under a cafeteria plan. Under the revised guidance, the FMV of taxable group-term life insurance is determined by using only the value of the insurance under Table I minus all employee aftertax contributions toward the cost of the group-term life insurance coverage. The revised guidelines also provide that the entire amount of the pretax contributions and employer contributions (flex-credits) for group-term life insurance coverage on the life of the employee is excluded from wages subject to federal income tax, federal income tax withholding, Social Security, Medicare and FUTA taxes. [Preamble to I.R.S. Prop. Reg. § 125; 72 Fed. Reg. 43,938 (Aug. 6, 2007); I.R.S. Prop. Reg. § 1.125-1(k)]

As a result of the cafeteria plan guidelines, employees who contribute more toward the cost of their insurance rather than the Table I value will enjoy a greater tax benefit if their contributions are made on pretax, rather than an aftertax, basis because federal (and FICA) taxable wages are reduced by 100 percent of the pretax contribution for group-term insurance while aftertax dollars are applied only up to the Table I value. Therefore, if an employee contributes, on an aftertax basis, more than the Table I value, the excess contribution does not reduce federal (or FICA) taxable earnings.

Note. An employer cannot arbitrarily decide to change employee contributions from an aftertax to a pretax basis, nor can the pretax option be made available without first amending the cafeteria plan to include group-term life insurance or creating a new cafeteria plan that governs the group-term life insurance benefit. Therefore, employers should consult a qualified Section 125 professional before making the pretax purchase option available for group-term life insurance. (See Q 9:79 for more information on cafeteria plans.)

Q 9:227   Is the exclusion from taxable income for group-term life insurance available to former employees?

Yes. Group-term life insurance may be provided to certain former employees (including retirees) under the same exclusion that is available to active employees. A former employee for this purpose must be an individual with a continuing relationship with the employer (e.g., a retiree). The retiree need not be receiving current wages to have a relationship with the employer. Note that this exclusion is not available for terminated employees. It should be noted that the concept of who is a "retiree" is becoming more difficult as many retirement plans are 401(k) plans with a reduced age, sometimes as low as 55, being used for the definition of "Normal Retirement Age." As the workforce has changed dramatically in recent years, the concept of a "retiree" may have to be expanded for purposes of these rules, but the IRS has not yet changed the standard.

For example, the employer may provide tax-free group-term life insurance on the life of a former employee who has attained the company's retirement age under a pension plan maintained by the employer. Under certain conditions the employer may also provide tax-free group-term life insurance on the life of a former disabled employee, but only if the employee is disabled as defined under I.R.C. Section 72(m)(7). [Treas. Reg. § 1.79-3(b)(2)]

Note that while the coverage in excess of $50,000 provided to a retiree is subject to FICA and FUTA, there may be no source of funds from which the employer may withhold FICA. The former employees will then be required to pay the employee's share of Social Security and Medicare taxes with their income tax returns. The employer reports the taxable amount on Form W-2 by including it in Boxes 1, 3, and 5; the amount of underwithheld Social Security and Medicare taxes owed by the former employee is reported in Box 12, with Codes M and N, respectively, for coverage provided after separation from service; and the amount of this imputed income is reported in Box 12 with Code C. [Pub. No. 15-A] An employee receiving group-term life insurance coverage while an employee and as a retiree, will have imputed income from group-term life insurance and will have FICA taxes withheld for the period as an employee and uncollected FICA once retired.

A special rule also permits an employer to exclude from wages subject to FIT, FITW, FICA, and FUTA the value of coverage provided to certain retired or disabled employees that exceeds $50,000 in the year of termination. This exclusion applies only to coverage provided after the date the employee ceases to be employed by the employer. [Treas. Reg. § 1.79-2(b)(2)]

Q 9:228 When is a group-term life insurance plan considered discriminatory in favor of key employees?

A group-term life insurance plan is considered discriminatory if it favors individuals who are classified as "key" employees (1) as to eligibility to participate in the plan or (2) in the type and level of benefits provided. A key employee is an individual who meets the pension definition of key employee under I.R.C. Section 416(i). (See Q 9:320.)

A group-term life insurance plan meets the nondiscriminatory participation requirements when one of the following coverage requirements is met: (1) the plan benefits 70 percent or more of all employees, (2) at least 85 percent of the participants are not key employees, (3) the plan benefits a classification of employees that the IRS has determined does not discriminate in favor of key employees, and (4) the group-term life insurance benefits are provided under a cafeteria plan. [I.R.C. § 79(d)(3)(A)]

These nondiscrimination requirements are determined by excluding the following employees from the testing: (1) employees with less than three years of service, (2) part-time or seasonal employees (i.e., employees who customarily work 20 hours or less a week or five months or less a year), (3) employees covered by a collective bargaining agreement that provides for life insurance benefits that were the subject of good-faith bargaining, and (4) nonresident aliens who received no U.S. earned income.

In general, a group-term life insurance plan must make the benefits available to key employees also available to all participants. This does not prevent a plan from providing different levels of life insurance coverage for various groups, as long as the coverage bears a uniform relationship to compensation or job classification. [I.R.C. §§ 79, 3121(a)(2)(C), 3306(b)(2)(C); Treas. Reg. §§ 1.79-1, 1.79-3]

Q 9:229   How are benefits under a discriminatory group-term plan treated for employment tax purposes?

When a group-term life insurance plan is found to discriminate in favor of key employees, the cost of the key employee's first $50,000 of life insurance is not excluded from income and is subject to FIT (but not FITW) and FICA (but not FUTA). The taxable value of that income is determined using the larger of the employer's actual cost or the Table I amount. This cost is reported in Box 1, 3, and 5 of the employee's Form W-2. The value of group-term life insurance provided to nonkey employees continues to be excluded from gross income for the first $50,000 of group-term life insurance coverage when a plan is found to be discriminatory. [I.R.C. § 3306(b)(2); Temp. Treas. Reg. § 1.79-4T]

Q 9:230   May an employer provide tax-free group-term benefits to dependents of an employee?

Yes, but not under I.R.C. Section 79. Group-term life insurance of no more than $2,000 each on the lives of a spouse or child can be provided as a tax-free *de minimis* fringe benefit under I.R.C. Section 132. Amounts in excess of this $2,000 threshold cause the entire value of the coverage to be treated as additional compensation to the employee. The value of any taxable coverage is taxed using the table applicable to group-term life insurance (Table 1, Uniform Premium Table [see Table 9-3 in Q 9:225]). If the age of the spouse or dependent is not available, you may use the age of the employee for Table I purposes. [Notice 89-110, 1989-2 C.B. 447; Treas. Reg. §§ 1.61-2(d)(2)(ii)(b), 1.132-6(e)(2), 31.3401(a)(14)-1]

Even if tax free as a *de minimis* benefit, dependent life insurance may not be paid on a pretax basis through a cafeteria (Section 125) plan. [Notice 89-110, 1989-2 C.B. 447.]

Q 9:231   How is the value of taxable group-term life insurance benefits reported on Form W-2?

The value of excess life insurance coverage (i.e., amounts over $50,000) is treated as taxable wages subject to FIT and FICA but not FITW and FUTA. On Form W-2, the value of the excess coverage (i.e., above $50,000) less employee aftertax contributions is included in Boxes 1, 3, and 5; the value of the excess coverage based on Table 1, Uniform Premium Table, is reported in Box 12, Code C. If the employer elected to withhold federal income tax, the amount withheld is included in Box 2. Excess coverage provided to former employees (i.e., the coverage provided after employment was terminated) is reported in the same way, unless the employer cannot collect the former employee's portion of the FICA taxes. In this case, the amount of FICA tax not withheld is reported in Box 12, Code M (Social Security) and Code N (Medicare).

Health Care Benefits

Accident and Health Plans

Q 9:232   What is an accident and health plan?

For employment tax purposes, the term *accident and health plan* can refer to a variety of employer-sponsored plans offering one or more of the following benefits: health insurance, access to an HMO or PPO, disability benefits provided under an insurance contract, an accident insurance plan, or employer reimbursements for medical expenses of the employee. The term can also refer to plans that pay monthly benefits for absences from work or for the loss of a body part such as a foot or finger. The rules for the federal income taxation (and FICA and FUTA taxation) of employer payments for coverage of an employee and dependents and of the benefits paid under an accident and health plan are contained in I.R.C. Sections 104, 105, and 106. Some benefits are fully nontaxable, some are fully taxable, and some condition the tax status of the benefit provided on the plan's meeting certain nondiscrimination requirements that do not favor highly paid employees or business owners. [I.R.C. §§ 105(h), 106(a)]

Effective for plan years beginning after May 21, 2009, the Genetic Information Nondiscrimination Act amends ERISA Section 702 to prohibit enrollment restriction and premium adjustment on the basis of genetic information or genetic services. The law also prevents health plans and insurers from requesting or requiring that an individual take a genetic test. The law applies to all health insurance programs, including those under ERISA, state-regulated plans, and the individual market.

Q 9:233   Is the value of health care coverage provided by an employer taxable to the employee?

Generally, no. Employer contributions to pay for health insurance coverage and accident and health benefits (e.g., health insurance premiums) are not treated as additional compensation for FIT, FICA, and FUTA. Nor does the employer treat as compensation the value of the medical benefits actually provided under a self-insured health plan that meets certain requirements. The law does require that such benefit payments be made under a plan. A plan can be part of a contract, a collectively bargained agreement, a written plan, an insurance contract, or other arrangement communicated to the employee.

[I.R.C. §§ 3121(a)(2), 3306(b)(2)] Employer-provided coverage that makes lump-sum payments, unrelated to an employee's absence from work (e.g., lump-sum payments for the loss of a limb or other body part), may also be excluded from an employee's gross income. Benefits paid to an employee as a workers' compensation benefit are not subject to federal income taxes or FICA or FUTA taxes. [I.R.C. §§ 104(a)(3), 3121(a)(2)(A), 3306(b)(2)(A)]

When the employer makes cash reimbursements to employees for incurred medical expenses or makes payments directly to a health care provider under a valid health plan (as opposed to purchasing an insurance policy to make those payments), the reimbursement is generally not treated as additional compensation when certain requirements are met. Nondiscrimination requirements apply to such payments (i.e., noninsured) received by "highly compensated individuals." The exemption from gross income for direct employer payments of medical expenses is limited to payments for medical expenses identified in I.R.C. Section 213(c)(1) and not paid under any insurance or other plan. [I.R.C. §§ 104, 105, 106]

Q 9:234   Are employer payments made directly to providers (i.e., not from an insurance policy) for medical or hospital expenses of an employee taxable to the employee?

Generally, payments made by an employer to a health care provider (in lieu of, or supplemental to, payments under a medical insurance policy) are not treated as additional compensation when made under a plan that satisfies Section 105. Direct employer payments to a physician or hospital (or reimbursements to an employee) may be taxable to "certain highly compensated individuals" when the plan fails to satisfy the nondiscrimination requirements of Section 105(h). Such a plan is generally referred to as a self-insured, or self-funded, plan because payments are made directly from the employer's operating accounts. A health FSA under a cafeteria plan is a form of self-funded plan. The benefit payments under a self-funded plan may also be paid from a trust to which the employer and sometimes the employees contribute. A self-insured medical plan can generally be identified as a plan for which the employer purchases reinsurance. Reinsurance generally makes payments to the employer when the medical cost for an employee or the employee group exceeds certain established dollar limits. [I.R.C. § 105(h)]

Q 9:235   Is there a minimum number of employees who must participate for an accident and health plan to be considered valid?

No. Regulations provide that an employer-sponsored accident and health plan may cover as few as only one employee. Thus, an employer could pay an employee's premium for an individually owned health insurance policy (a disability insurance policy) without the value of those premiums being included in the individual's compensation. [Treas. Reg. § 1.105-5(a)]

Q 9:236 How are accident and health benefits provided to partners and employees of a partnership (or LLC taxed as a partnership) treated?

All of the exclusions available to common-law employees of a corporation are available to common-law employees of a partnership or an LLC taxed as a partnership. There is no similar exclusion from gross income for a partner (an individual with earned income under I.R.C. Section 401(c)(2)) under Section 106. Such payments by the partnership are treated as guaranteed payments and included in the partner's Schedule K-1 of Form 1065, U.S. Partnership Return of Income. A portion, but not all, of these premiums will generally be deductible by the partner. [Rev. Rul. 91-26, 1991-1 C.B. 184]

Dependent Health Care Coverage

Q 9:237 Is the value of accident and health benefits provided to the dependents of an employee excluded from the employee's compensation?

Yes. The employer may provide accident and health coverage to the dependents of an employee; however, a plan may not be established to cover only the dependents of employees without the value of those benefits being included in the employee's compensation and subject to all federal employment taxes. [I.R.C. §§ 3121(a)(2), 3306(b)(2); Treas. Reg. §§ 31.3121(a)(2)-1, 31.3306(b)(2)-1] This exclusion does not extend to same-sex couples, even where one of the couple declares the other as a dependent.

In addition, a law passed in 2008 guaranteed continued coverage of a dependent child who is a full-time student and over the age of 18 if that child must leave school for medical treatment. [I.R.C. § 9813 as added by Pub. No. L. 110-381] There is an excise tax of $100 per day under I.R.C. Section 4980D for failure to meet this requirement.

The Patient Protection and Affordable Care Act extends dependent coverage of adult children up to the age of 26. [Pub. L. No. 111-148]

Health Reimbursement Arrangements

Q 9:238 What is a health reimbursement arrangement?

The term *health reimbursement arrangement* (HRA), previously used to describe a variety of benefit plans offered by an employer, was given new meaning under Notice 2002-45, which identified a new type of plan. Under the Notice, an employer may establish an account from which it reimburses health care expenses incurred by an employee and the employee's dependents without those reimbursements being included in the employee's wages. If the HRA is properly structured, benefits paid thereunder are excluded from all federal employment taxes.

An HRA is an arrangement that (1) is paid for solely by the employer and not provided pursuant to a salary reduction election under a Section 125 cafeteria plan; (2) reimburses an eligible individual for medical care expenses (as defined by Section 213(d) or excludable under Section 105(b) of the I.R.C.) incurred by the individual or the individual's spouse and dependents (as defined in Section 152); and (3) provides reimbursements up to a maximum dollar amount for a coverage period with any unused portion of the maximum dollar amount at the end of a coverage period carried forward to increase the maximum reimbursement amount in subsequent coverage periods. To the extent that an HRA is an employer-provided accident or health plan, meeting all the requirements of I.R.C. Section 105(h), the value of the coverage and all reimbursements of medical care expenses are excludable from the employee's wages under Section 106 and 105. [Notice 2002-45, 2002-28 I.R.B. 93]

Q 9:239   How does a health reimbursement arrangement differ from a flexible spending account under a cafeteria plan?

Both HRAs and FSAs under a cafeteria plan reimburse an employee (and the employee's dependents) for expenses related to health care. However, HRAs are required to be funded only through employer contributions, whereas FSAs are typically funded with employee contributions—usually through salary reductions under a Section 125 plan (a cafeteria plan). FSAs are subject to numerous I.R.C. requirements, including a "use-it-or-lose-it" requirement at the end of the plan year for unreimbursed amounts. That is, unused accounts may not be carried forward to the next year. This requirement does not apply to HRAs. Because an HRA does not have to conform to the use-it-or-lose-it rules applicable to FSAs, an HRA may accumulate unused amounts to apply to reimbursement in future years. Note that while the federal tax status of an HRA was described in Notice 2002-45, HRAs are welfare plans under ERISA and, as a result, are subject to numerous DOL requirements not discussed in the IRS notice.

An HRA that reimburses a covered individual's medical expenses is not subject to the following restrictions that apply to health FSAs offered under a Section 125 plan: (1) the prohibition against a benefit that defers compensation by permitting employees to carry over unused elective contributions or plan benefits from one plan year to another plan year; (2) the requirement that the maximum amount of reimbursement must be available at all times during the coverage period; (3) the mandatory 12-month period of coverage; and (4) a special exception from the general requirement that medical expense reimbursements must be incurred during the period of coverage.

Note that when an individual participates in both an FSA and an HRA that reimburse the same health care expenses, Notice 2002-45 requires that an ordering rule apply to the payment of eligible medical expenses. A participant must exhaust all the amounts in the HRA before any amounts in the FSA can be used to reimburse a medical expense. However, a Section 125 health FSA will not violate this rule if coverage is provided under both an HRA and a Section 125 health FSA and the FSA reimburses a type of medical care expense that is not reimbursable by the HRA. Thus, where a combination FSA and HRA is provided, the plan structures must take into account the fact that the FSA is subject to a use-it-or-lose-it requirement, and such arrangements could result in the employee not being able to use the amounts accumulated under an FSA funded with salary reductions. [Notice 2002-45, 2002-28 I.R.B. 93]

The IRS provided further clarification by stating that unused amounts from accident and health plans that are disbursed irrespective of medical care expenses are not excludable from gross income under I.R.C. Section 105(b). [Rev. Rul. 2005-24, 2005-16 I.R.B. 892] The Revenue Ruling stated that "Section 106 provides that the gross income of an employee does not include employer-provided coverage under an accident or health plan," but added that Treasury Regulations Section 1.105-2 provides that only amounts paid specifically to reimburse the taxpayer for expenses incurred for prescribed medical care are excludable. Specifically, according to the ruling, "[i]f an employee is not paid specifically to reimburse medical care expenses but is entitled to receive the payment irrespective of whether any medical expenses have been incurred, none of the payments are excludable from gross income under Section 105(b) whether or not the employee has incurred medical expenses during the year." The ruling cited Notice 2002-45 as it related to the tax treatment of HRAs, which it noted is paid solely by the employer and not pursuant to a salary reduction election or otherwise under a Section 125 cafeteria plan. By comparison, HRA reimburses the employee for medical care expenses incurred by the employee and by the employee's spouse and dependents, and provides reimbursements up to a maximum dollar amount with any unused portion of that amount at the end of the coverage period carried forward to subsequent coverage periods. Part II of the notice states that "to qualify for the exclusion from gross income, an HRA may only provide benefits that reimburse expenses for medical care as defined in Section 213(d). An HRA does not qualify for the exclusion under Section 105(b) if any person has the right to receive cash or any other taxable or nontaxable benefit under the arrangement other than the reimbursement of medical care expenses."

The ruling also applies to employer-provided reimbursement arrangements that are limited only to retired employees, as well as to employer-provided arrangements that cover active employees or both active employees and retirees. The ruling addresses only reimbursement arrangements paid for solely by an employer under specified tax code sections. It was effective December 31, 2005.

Q 9:240   What type of health care reimbursement may be provided under a health reimbursement arrangement?

Reimbursements—amounts paid to an employee or dependent—under an HRA must be limited to expenses for medical care as defined in Sections 105(b) and 213(d). Generally, this will be the same expenses that are deductible on an employee's Schedule A, Form 1040, with one important addition. As a medical plan defined by Section 105, an HRA (and FSA) may reimburse for over-the-counter medicines when used to treat a medical condition. *See* Revenue Ruling 2003-102. [2003-2 C.B. 559]

Although an HRA will generally limit the reimbursement to expenses incurred in the year of the reimbursement, an HRA may reimburse an expense incurred in a prior year if the individual was covered under the HRA during the prior year.

Example. Nicole was covered under an HRA in 2016 and 2017. In 2017, a hospital sent a bill for an expense that was not billed in 2016 for care provided in 2016. The HRA may reimburse the expense in 2017 out of funds set aside for 2016; an FSA could not operate in this way unless the bill was received and processed before two and one-half months after the end of 2016 (assuming the FSA plan was not amended to carryover funds).

Each expense submitted for reimbursement must be substantiated (see Substantiation under accountable plan, Q 9:22). An HRA may neither reimburse a medical care expense that is incurred before the date the HRA is in existence nor reimburse a medical care expense that is incurred before the date an employee first becomes enrolled under the HRA. An HRA is permitted to make a reimbursement for health insurance covering medical care, including employee paid for accident or health coverage for current employees, retirees, and COBRA-qualified beneficiaries. However, no reimbursement is permitted for qualified long-term care services. [Notice 2002-45, 2002-28 I.R.B. 93]

Q 9:241   What types of payments are permitted under a health reimbursement arrangement?

Only payments for the medical care that would otherwise qualify as a medical deduction on Schedule A, Form 1040, of the employee, former employee, or a dependent are permitted. After 2010, non-prescription medicines (other than insulin) do not qualify as an expense for HRA purposes unless a doctor provides a prescription for such medicines. An HRA cannot permit any person to receive cash (or any other taxable or nontaxable benefit other than the reimbursement of medical care expenses). If any such right exists, all payments, including amounts paid to reimburse medical care expenses, from the HRA are treated as additional compensation and subject to all federal employment taxes. [Pub. No. 969]

Example 1. Jim participates in an HRA that pays a death benefit of $35,000 that is unrelated to any medical expenses related to Jim's death. Under this HRA, all amounts paid are treated as additional wages. Tax-free death benefits are not permitted under an HRA because they are not included under I.R.C. Section 213(d).

Example 2. Ralph, a manager, participates in an HRA that pays a lump-sum cash payment to retirees, or any terminated participant with at least 10 years of participation in the plan. The amount of the payment is based on the unpaid balance in their HRA accounts at the date of retirement or termination of employment. Under this HRA all amounts paid are treated as additional wages. Retiree benefits may only be paid to staff employees through a qualified pension or profit sharing plan, otherwise the plan is in violation of ERISA. [Notice 2002-45, 2002-28 I.R.B. 93; Notice 2011-5, 2011-3 I.R.B. 314, January 17, 2011 modifies Notice 2010-59; Rev. Rul. 2010-23; Notice 2011 modifies 2010-59 to allow debit cards to be used for prescriptions for over-the-counter drugs]

The total amount of annual payments is subject to a cost-of-living adjustment, announced no later than June 1 of the preceding year.

Q 9:242   Who may be covered under a health reimbursement arrangement?

An HRA can provide health care reimbursement benefits to the following individuals: current and former employees (including retired employees), spouses and dependents of former employees (as defined in Section 152 and modified by the last sentence of Section 105(b)), and the spouses and dependents of deceased employees.

The Working Families Tax Relief Act of 2004 (WFTRA) (effective January 1, 2005) amended the definition of "dependent" under I.R.C. Section 152 (used by I.R.C. Section 105(b)) to add certain relationship, residency, and age requirements. The Act also included a limit on gross income of dependents, but IRS Notice 2004-79 [2004-49 I.R.B. 898, Nov. 17, 2004] (effective January 1, 2005) clarified that an individual's status as a dependent for purposes of Section 105(b) is determined without regard to new Sections 152(b)(1) and 152(b)(2) and 152(d)(1)(B). Also, the IRS treats qualifying children of divorced or separated parents as the dependents of both parents under several tax code sections for health and fringe benefits, regardless of whether the custodial parent releases the claim to the exemption.

Note that a self-employed individual is not considered an "employee" under the I.R.C. and cannot participant in an HRA. For this purpose, a self-employed individual is defined under the pension rules, Section 401(c).

An HRA may continue to reimburse former employees or retired employees for medical care expenses after termination of employment or retirement (even if the employee does not elect COBRA continuation coverage). This reimbursement may be based on a formula that is tied to years of service or may be the unpaid amounts accumulated over the employee's years of participation in the plan. An HRA may also apply a uniform administrative expense to such accounts. [Notice 2002-45, 2002-28 I.R.B. 93]

Example. Karina, a former employee, participated in an HRA prior to retiring from Full Basket Co. Under her plan, she may continue to submit expenses for her medical expenses after retirement up to the unreimbursed portion of her HRA account at her date of retirement. [Notice 2002-45, 2002-28 I.R.B. 93]

Q 9:243 Can a health reimbursement arrangement be part of a Section 125 cafeteria plan?

No. The exclusion from income and federal employment taxes is conditioned on no portion of the HRA benefit being funded with pretax salary reductions under a Section 125 cafeteria plan. [Notice 2002-45, 2002-28 I.R.B. 93; Rev. Rul. 2002-41, 2002-28 I.R.B. 75] Although an HRA may not be part of the array of choices within a cafeteria plan, an employer is permitted to offer both a cafeteria plan and an HRA to eligible employees.

Q 9:244 How could insured medical benefits under a Section 125 plan be structured with a health reimbursement account?

An employer may provide an HRA in conjunction with another accident or health plan, with the accident or health plan being paid for through salary reductions under a Section 125 cafeteria plan, when all the terms of the salary reduction election limit the use of salary reductions to pay only for the specified accident or health plan offered in conjunction with the HRA. Under a facts and circumstances evaluation, the benefits paid from the HRA are not treated as additional income. That is, the mere fact that an employee may participate in the HRA only if the employee participates in a specified accident or health plan that is funded through salary reductions does not necessarily result in the salary reduction being attributed to the HRA. [Rev. Rul. 2002-41, 2002-28 I.R.B. 75]

Q 9:245 Are health reimbursement arrangements subject to COBRA?

Generally, yes. However, based on the level of benefits payable under the HRA, the HRA may be exempt from some of the COBRA requirements. Both Notice 2002-45 and Revenue Ruling 2002-41 provide a description of how COBRA may affect an HRA offered in conjunction with a major medical plan. [Notice 2002-45, 2002-28 I.R.B. 93; Rev. Rul. 2002-41, 2002-28 I.R.B. 75]

Q 9:246 Are the nondiscrimination rules of Section 105(h) applicable to HRAs?

Yes. The nondiscrimination rules under Section 105(h) apply to all non-insured medical expense reimbursement plans. (See the discussion on the nondiscrimination under Health Care Benefits—Self-Funded Health Benefits, Q 9:254.) [Notice 2002-45, 2002-28 I.R.B. 93]

Q 9:247 Does IRS Notice 2002-45, which describes the rules that apply to health reimbursement arrangements (HRAs), identify areas where potential problems with HRAs may arise?

Yes. HRAs are considered accident or health plans under the I.R.C. and are also welfare plans under ERISA. As a result, HRAs are subject to a variety of statutory rules not addressed in Notice 2002-45. I.R.C. issues not addressed include (1) the deduction limitations under I.R.C. Section 419 and 419A (for employer contributions to welfare benefit funds) and under I.R.C. Section 404 (for amounts paid or accrued under plans providing for deferred benefits that are not provided through a welfare benefit fund), and (2) the application of the certificate of creditable coverage and the nondiscrimination requirements under HIPAA. Another concern is the application of any reporting and disclosure requests under ERISA for a welfare plan. [Notice 2002-45, 2002-48 I.R.B. 93]

Q 9:248   What are the federal employment tax reporting requirements that apply to a health reimbursement arrangement?

As long as the HRA meets the requirements of Notice 2002-45 and the nondiscrimination requirements that apply to self-insured plans under I.R.C. Section 105(h), none of the reimbursements made under an HRA are reportable as wages.

Insured Medical Plans

Q 9:249   Do fully insured health plans have to meet any nondiscrimination requirements?

No. Employer premiums for the purchase of accident or health insurance for employees and their dependents are not treated as wages, even when provided in a discriminatory manner, and are not subject to Social Security, Medicare, FUTA, or federal income taxes. Thus, it would be possible for the corporation to pay all of the insurance premiums on the officers, but require other employees to pay for the same coverage. [I.R.C. § 106; Priv. Ltr. Rul. 9603011, Jan. 19, 1996] Note that self-funded plans are possibly subject to different treatment for discrimination, as discussed in Q 9:254 et. seq.

Q 9:250   Are health benefits provided through a prepaid HMO or PSO plan treated as insured plans?

Yes. Employer contributions to a prepaid HMO or PSO are treated as payments to an insurance contract and are not subject to the discrimination requirements of I.R.C. Section 105(h). The benefits provided from a prepaid HMO or PSO are also excluded from wages. [I.R.C. § 106; Treas. Reg. § 1.106-1]

In addition, employer-provided benefits under a prepaid dental maintenance organization (DMO) plan are treated as an insured accident and health plan and are exempt from all federal employment taxes under I.R.C. Section 106.

Q 9:251   Are all employee contributions to an accident or health plan excluded from wages?

No, payroll deductions to pay for medical premiums are made from wages after payment of all federal employment taxes. Employee salary reductions that go to an accident and health benefit plan are excluded from wages and are exempt from all federal employment taxes only when made under a cafeteria plan that satisfies Section 125. Employee payments made through payroll deductions (i.e., aftertax payments outside a Section 125 plan) to pay for an accident and health insurance contract are treated as wages and subject to federal income tax withholding and FICA and FUTA taxes. [I.R.C. §§ 61, 125]

Caution. Employee contributions made under a Section 125 plan may be subject to certain state or local employment taxes.

Q 9:252 May an employer permit an employee to choose between nontaxable health insurance or additional wages?

Yes. An employer may establish a plan permitting an employee to select between being covered under the employer's health plan and receiving additional wages under a cafeteria plan election without the employee being treated as having additional wages when the benefit is selected. However, this election must be made under an I.R.C. Section 125 plan, or the value of the benefits received is treated as additional wages. Only a valid election under a cafeteria plan permits an employee to receive tax-free benefits in lieu of fully taxable compensation. [I.R.C. § 125; Priv. Ltr. Rul. 9406002] Under proposed regulations, the requirement to make this valid election must be made under the authority of a written plan document.

Self-Funded Health Benefits

Q 9:253 What is a self-funded plan?

The term *self-funded plan* (also referred to as *self-insured*) generally refers to a plan where the payment of benefits comes from the employer's operating accounts rather than from an insurance company or under a prepaid HMO program. Benefits under these plans are subject to the nondiscrimination requirements of Section 105(h).

Q 9:254 Are medical and diagnostic benefits paid directly by an employer subject to the Section 105(h) nondiscrimination requirements?

Generally, yes. Employer-provided health benefits paid from a self-insured plan (as opposed to a fully insured plan) must satisfy certain nondiscrimination requirements; however, some diagnostic benefits are exempt from this requirement. The I.R.C. imposes two nondiscrimination requirements on a self-insured plan: It must not discriminate in favor of "highly compensated individuals" as to eligibility and it must not discriminate in favor of "highly compensated individuals" as to the benefits that are available.

Employer-paid physical examinations and other medical diagnostic procedures for employees (but not their dependents) are exempt from the nondiscrimination requirements that apply to self-insured plans. These are exempt under I.R.C. Section 132 as a working-condition fringe benefit. A procedure qualifies as a medical diagnostic procedure when it involves routine examinations and general tests but not treatment, or tests for a known injury or illness. The procedure must be performed at a facility providing only medical and related services (i.e., not in an office of the employer). [Treas. Reg. §§ 1.105-11(g), 1.132-5(a)(iv)]

Q 9:255   Who are highly compensated individuals for self-insured medical benefit purposes?

For purposes of self-insured or noninsured medical plans and benefits, the term "highly compensated individual" is defined under Section 105(h)(5). Although many nondiscrimination rules for fringe benefits follow the pension rules in describing the prohibited group, the nondiscrimination requirements applicable to self-insured medical benefits under I.R.C. Section 105 do not. A highly compensated individual under Section 105 is an individual who, during the current plan year, is: (1) one of the five highest paid officers; (2) a shareholder owning more than 10 percent of the value of the employer's stock; or (3) among the top paid (top 25 percent) of all employees. [I.R.C. § 105(h)(5)]

Q 9:256   How are highly compensated individuals taxed in a discriminatory noninsured health plan?

Benefits provided from a noninsured (generally referred to as self-insured) accident and health plan are subject to nondiscrimination rules. A self-insured medical plan is considered nondiscriminatory as long as the plan's coverage does not favor individuals classified as highly compensated individuals under Section 105(h)(5) as to (1) eligibility to participate in the plan or (2) the type of benefits provided.

Nondiscriminatory participation. A self-insured medical plan meets the Section 105(h) nondiscriminatory participation requirement when the plan satisfies one of the following: (1) it benefits at least 70 percent of all employees of the employer; (2) at least 70 percent of all employees are eligible to participate, and 80 percent or more of those eligible actually benefit under the plan; or (3) the plan benefits a classification of employees that the IRS has determined does not discriminate in favor of "highly compensated individuals." The third criterion is to be determined on a facts-and-circumstances basis. Most practitioners believe that the last test can be met by meeting the nondiscriminatory classification tests that apply under Section 410(b) for qualified retirement plans. Note that the term "benefit under the plan" as used here is not defined. Most practitioners generally presume that it refers to the group of employees who are eligible, not just those who elect the coverage under the plan.

The I.R.C. permits an employer to disregard the following employees in performing these participation tests: (1) employees with fewer than three years of service as of the beginning of the plan year; (2) employees who have not attained age 25 at the beginning of the plan year; (3) part-time or seasonal employees; (4) employees covered by a collective bargaining agreement, when accident and health benefits were a subject of the bargaining; and (5) non-resident aliens who received no U.S. earned income. [I.R.C. § 105(h)(3)]

For purposes of these exclusions, part-time employees are individuals who customarily work fewer than 25 hours a week, or who customarily work up to 35 hours a week if other employees work substantially more hours. Seasonal employees are individuals who customarily work fewer than seven months a year and may include individuals who customarily work up to nine months a year if other employees work for substantially more months. [I.R.C. § 105; Treas. Reg. § 1.105-11]

Nondiscriminatory benefits. The types and levels of benefits provided by a self-funded plan to highly compensated individuals must also be provided to all participants. [I.R.C. § 105; Treas. Reg. § 1.105-11(c)(3)]

Example 1. Livingston Lights offers to pay for all prescription expenses of company officers, but all other employees must pay a $25 co-pay. This is a "self-funded" benefit that discriminates in favor of the officers, who are generally some of the highly compensated individuals. Thus, all prescription payments to the highly compensated individuals are taxable and subject to federal income tax withholding and FICA and FUTA taxes.

Example 2. Edward, the son of the CEO of Livingston Lights, has a unique ailment that generally would not be entitled to payment from the self-insured health plan. The company amends the plan to provide special coverage for that ailment. This plan is found to be discriminatory as to benefits provided because only the company CEO's son can take advantage of the coverage. All payments made on behalf of Stanley for that ailment are treated as additional compensation to the president.

The portion of health benefits paid from a discriminatory self-insured health plan that is treated as additional wages is subject to federal income taxes; however, such taxable benefits are not subject to federal income tax withholding or FICA or FUTA taxes. [I.R.C. §§ 3121(a)(2)(B), 3121(a)(4), 3306(b)(2)(B), 3306(b)(4), 3401(a)(20)]

Health Savings Accounts

Q 9:257 What is a health savings account?

An HSA is a tax-exempt trust or custodial account set up for the purpose of paying (or reimbursing) qualified medical expenses of the account holder. For additional information, the IRS released detailed guidance in question-and-answer format pertaining to tax-favored health savings accounts, addressing a range of issues including eligible individuals, high deductible health plans, contributions, distributions, prohibited transactions, establishing HSAs, and administration of HSAs. [Notice 2008-59, 2008-29 I.R.B. 123]

Q 9:258   Who is eligible to establish an HSA?

An "eligible individual" means, for any given month, a person who is covered only by a "high deductible health plan" (HDHP) on the first day of that month. Eligibility is reestablished each and every month. An eligible individual must not have any health coverage that does not meet the requirements of a HDHP, with certain exceptions. A person enrolled in Medicare will not be an eligible individual, nor will a person who is claimed as a dependent on another person's tax return.

Q 9:259   How is a high deductible health plan defined?

An HDHP must not provide benefits until a certain deductible limit is met, and must cap the insured's expense at a certain out-of-pocket maximum.

For self-only coverage, the 2017 annual deductible must be at least $1,300. The annual out-of-pocket expenses (including deductibles, co-payments, and other amounts, but not premiums) must not exceed $6,550. For family coverage, the deductible must be at least $2,600, and the out-of-pocket limit is $13,100.

Q 9:260   Who may contribute to an HSA?

Any eligible individual may contribute to an HSA. When an employee sets up an HSA, the employee, or the employer, or both may contribute to the HSA. If an employer fails to make comparable contributions to the HSAs of its employees during a calendar year, an excise tax equal to 35 percent of the aggregate amount contributed by the employer to the HSAs of its employees during that calendar year is imposed on the employer, according to proposed regulations.

Comparability rules. The IRS released final regulations providing guidance on employer comparable contributions, effective January 1, 2010. [T.D. 9457, 2009 WL 2849001 (IRS TD), 74 Fed. Reg. 45994-01] Under I.R.C. Section 4980G(d), employers may make larger contributions to the HSAs of non-highly compensated employees (NHCEs) than they make to highly compensated employees (HCEs). The rules provide that employer contributions to the HSAs of NHCEs may be larger than the contributions to HCEs with comparable coverage during a period. On the other hand, employers may not make higher contributions to HCEs than they make for NHCEs during a period.

The IRS said that under the Health Opportunity Patient Empowerment Act of 2006, which was included in the Tax Relief and Health Care Act of 2006 [Pub. L. No. 109-432], those who are eligible individuals as of the first day of the last month of the employees' taxable year may make, or have made on their behalf, the maximum annual HSA contribution based on their high deductible health plan (HDHP) coverage—i.e., self or family coverage—on that date. A portion of that contribution would be included in income and subject to a 10 percent tax if the individual fails to remain an eligible individual for 12 months after the last month of the taxable year, e.g., December 1, 2014 through December 31, 2015.

The final rules state that employers can contribute up to the maximum contribution on behalf of all employees who are eligible individuals on the first day of the last month of the employees' taxable year. The provision includes "mid-year eligible individuals," defined as those who became eligible after January 1 of the calendar year and eligible individuals who were hired after January 1 of the calendar year. The IRS said that employers that make the maximum calendar year HSA contribution, or who contribute more than a pro rata amount, on behalf of mid-year eligible individuals, will still be in compliance with the comparability rules, even though some employees will have received more contributions on a monthly basis than employees who worked the entire calendar year.

If an employer provides more than the monthly pro rata amount, or the employer contributes the maximum amount, for the calendar year to the HSA of one mid-year eligible individual, then the employer must make contributions on an equal and uniform basis to the HSAs of all comparable participating mid-year eligible employees.

The IRS said the final rules stipulate that if an employer offers qualified HSA distributions to any qualified employee covered under any HDHP, the employer must also offer qualified HSA distributions to all eligible individuals covered under any HDHP.

Excise taxes. Excise taxes imposed under I.R.C. Sections 4980B-E and 4980G must be reported on Form 8928, Return of Certain Excise Taxes Under Chapter 43 of the Internal Revenue Code. The excise tax must be paid at the time prescribed for the filing of the excise tax return, with no extensions. I.R.C. Sections 4980E and 4980G impose a 35 percent excise tax penalty on employers that fail to make comparable calendar year contributions to their employees' HSAs. Sections 4980B and 4980D assess an excise tax penalty of $100 a day per beneficiary on group health plans that fail to comply with contribution requirements.

Under I.R.C. Sections 4980B and 4980D, employers and third parties (such as insurers and third party administrators) must file the return on or before the due date for filing a person's federal income tax return, the IRS said. An extension to file the person's income tax return does not extend the date for filing the Form 8928.

Multiemployers and specified multiple employer health plans under I.R.C. 4980B or 4980D must file the excise taxes on or before the last day of the seventh month after the end of the plan year, according to the IRS. The final rules also state that for the excise tax under Section 4980E or 4980G for noncomparable contributions, the tax return is due on or before the 15th day of the fourth month following the calendar year in which the noncomparable contributions were made.

Family coverage issues. According to an IRS Revenue Ruling, an individual can contribute to an HSA even if his or her spouse has family health insurance coverage, as long as that coverage does not include the HSA-holder. [Rev. Rul. 2005-25, 2005-18 I.R.B. 971] The spouse with the HSA may contribute the same amount annually to the HSA as any other individual. The ruling is effective for plan years beginning after December 31, 2005. The Revenue Ruling explained how the eligibility and contribution rules apply to a married individual who has HDHP coverage if the individual's spouse also has non-HDHP family coverage. The ruling said a married individual can contribute to an HSA even though his or her spouse has non-HDHP family coverage, so long as the individual is not covered by the spouse's non-HDHP.

HSA and FSA issue. In Notice 2005-86 [2005-2 C.B. 1075], Treasury and the IRS clarified that coverage by the FSA disqualifies an individual from contributing to an HSA during the two and one-half month grace period afforded FSA users, even where the health FSA has reached its annual benefit limit. However, the notice also provided guidance to employers on how they can amend their FSAs to enable covered individuals to contribute to HSAs during the grace period.

Q 9:261   How much may be contributed to an HSA?

The maximum contribution amount is determined monthly. The maximum monthly contribution for an eligible individual with self-only coverage under an HDHP is 1/12th of the lesser of 100 percent of the annual deductible under the HDHP (a minimum of $1,300 in 2016 and 2017) or $3,350. [Rev. Proc. 2015-30, 2015-20 I.R.B. 970]

For an eligible individual with family coverage under an HDHP, the contribution amount may not exceed 1/12th of the lesser of 100 percent of the annual deductible under the HDHP (a minimum of $2,600 in 2016 and 2017) or $6,750 for 2016 and 2017.

Q 9:262   Is there a catch-up provision for eligible individuals who are age 55 or older?

Yes, eligible individuals who are age 55 or older, but not enrolled in Medicare, may make a catch-up contribution to an HSA. In 2017, as in 2016, the catch-up contribution amount reaches its maximum of $1,000 under the statute, and must remain at the level unless the legislature changes the ceiling.

Q 9:263   May an HSA contribution be paid on a pretax basis through a Section 125 cafeteria plan?

Yes, an eligible individual may set aside funds on a pretax basis to an HSA via an employer-sponsored Section 125 cafeteria plan if the plan allows it.

Q 9:264   How are HSA contributions made by an individual treated for tax purposes?

Contributions made to an HSA by an eligible individual are deductible when determining AGI for personal income tax purposes. If the HSA contribution was made through a Section 125 cafeteria plan, the tax benefit has already been received, and no further tax deduction may be taken on the personal tax return.

Q 9:265 How are HSA contributions made by an employer treated for tax purposes?

Employer contributions to an employee's HSA are treated in the same as employer-provided coverage for medical expenses under an accident or health plan, and are thus excludable from the employee's gross income, and considered to be a deductible expense for the employer.

The employer contributions are not included in wages subject to FIT, FITW, FICA, FUTA, or taxes under the Railroad Retirement Tax Act.

Contributions to an employee's HSA through a cafeteria plan are treated as employer contributions. The employee cannot deduct employer contributions on his or her federal income tax return as HSA contributions or as medical expense deductions under Section 213.

Q 9:266 How is the HSA contribution of an S-corporation owner or partner in a partnership treated for tax purposes?

In January 2005, the IRS released IRS Notice 2005-8 [2005-4 I.R.B. 368], clarifying the tax treatment of HSA contributions by S-corporation owners and partners in a partnership. Although generally, employer contributions to an HSA for a participant are excludable from that person's gross income, an HSA contribution for an S-corporation shareholder or a partner in a partnership is not deductible by the employer, and is includible in the gross income of the shareholder or partner. On the individual tax return of the shareholder or partner, they may take an "above the line" tax deduction, similar to that available to any eligible individual who makes an HSA contribution directly with aftertax funds.

Q 9:267 What happens when HSA contributions exceed the maximum amount that may be deducted or excluded from gross income in a taxable year?

Contributions to an HSA are not deductible to the extent they exceed the permitted limits. Contributions by an employer to an HSA for an employee are included in the gross income of the employee to the extent that they exceed the limits, or if they are made on behalf of an employee who is not an eligible individual. In addition, an excise tax of 6 percent for each taxable year is imposed on the account beneficiary for excess individual and employer contributions.

However, if the excess contributions for a taxable year and the net income attributable to such excess contributions are paid to the account beneficiary before the last day prescribed by law (including extensions) for filing the account beneficiary's federal income tax return for the taxable year, then the net income attributable to the excess contributions is included in the account beneficiary's gross income for the taxable year in which the distribution is received but the excise tax is not imposed on the excess contribution and the distribution of the excess contributions is not taxed.

Q 9:268   When is an individual permitted to receive distributions from an HSA?

An individual is permitted to receive distributions from an HSA at any time. Although contributions to an HSA may be made only while considered to be an "eligible" individual (i.e., covered only by an HDHP), distributions from an HSA do not require such eligibility.

Q 9:269   How are distributions from an HSA taxed?

Distributions from an HSA used exclusively to pay for qualified medical expenses of the account beneficiary, his or her spouse, or dependents are excludable from gross income. In general, amounts in an HSA can be used for qualified medical expenses and will be excludable from gross income even if the individual is not currently eligible for contributions to the HSA.

However, any amount of the distribution not used exclusively to pay for qualified medical expenses of the account beneficiary, spouse, or dependents is includible in gross income of the account beneficiary and is subject to an additional 10 percent tax on the amount includible, except in the case of distributions made after the account beneficiary's death, disability, or attaining age 65.

Q 9:270   Are HSAs subject to ERISA or HIPAA rules?

No, HSAs are not regulated by ERISA or HIPAA.

Q 9:271   How does an eligible individual set up an HSA?

The eligible individual executes an agreement with a custodian who sets up an HSA trust. The IRS has issued model forms for establishing HSAs. They are Form 5305-B, Health Savings Trust Account, and Form 5305-C, Health Savings Custodial Account. These forms are for the account holder and the HSA custodian. They are not meant to be submitted to the IRS.

Q 9:272   Who can be a custodian or trustee of an HSA?

Revised IRS Notice 2004-50 [2004-33 I.R.B. 1], Q&A 72, states that any insurance company or any bank may serve as a qualified HSA trustee or custodian. Also, any other person or entity already approved by the IRS to be a trustee or custodian of IRAs or Archer MSAs is automatically approved to be an HSA custodian or trustee. In a proposed rulemaking (70 Fed. Reg. 50233), the Treasury Department and the IRS incorporated, clarified, and expanded guidance provided in prior Notices, which answered a range of general questions. The proposed rules clarify that any insurance company or bank can be an HSA trustee or custodian.

Idle-Time Payments

Q 9:273　What are idle-time payments?

Idle-time payments are typically made to employees for time when they actually did no work but were required to be available. These are usually made under a guarantee to employees for idle time (i.e., any time during which an hourly employee performs no services and would otherwise receive no wages). These payments are wages for the purposes of federal income tax withholding and FICA and FUTA taxes. [I.R.C. § 61; Pub. No. 15-A]

Income Tax Services

Q 9:274　What type of tax preparation services may be provided to employees as a *de minimis* fringe benefit?

Generally, none. This was discussed in Field Service Advice 200137039 [(June 19, 2001)], in which the IRS ruled that the value of tax preparation services made available to an employee is not excludable from compensation as a working-condition fringe benefit. However, the IRS has stated in a private letter ruling (which is applicable only to the employer requesting the ruling) that the value of tax return preparation services offered to employees and paid by an employer under a Volunteer Income Tax Assistance (VITA) program is not treated as wages. The services under this ruling were provided at the employer's workplace and were established with the assistance of the IRS. Such a program may not pay for the services of a tax preparer who offers similar services to the public. The IRS also confirmed in that private letter ruling that an employer may provide, as a *de minimis* fringe benefit, electronic tax return processing and transmission of an employee's tax returns at a VITA site. [Priv. Ltr. Rul. 9442003]

Q 9:275　May an employer provide tax-free retirement planning services for employees?

Yes. An employer that maintains a "qualified employer plan" may provide to its employees retirement income planning services as a tax-free fringe benefit under I.R.C. Section 132(a)(7). A qualified employer plan is any plan, contract, pension, or account described in I.R.C. Section 219(g)(5). These include profit sharing plans, 401(k) pension plans, 403(a) and 403(b) annuities, SEPs, and SIMPLE plans. Such income planning services are designed to help an individual plan for retirement and may not include tax preparation, accounting, or brokerage services. These services must be available on a nondiscriminatory basis that does not favor HCEs. This exclusion is not subject to any statutory limit on the value of the services that may be provided.

Interviewee Expenses

Q 9:276   How is a reimbursement of interview travel expenses treated for federal employment tax purposes?

A prospective employer may pay for the reasonable travel expenses of a prospective interviewee or reimburse the individual for substantiated travel expense without the value of the travel or reimbursement being treated as compensation. Such payments, if substantiated, would not be reported. [Treas. Reg. §§ 1.62-2, 31.3121(a)-3, 31.3306(b)(2); Rev. Rul. 91-67, 1991-52 I.R.B. 11]

Jury Pay

Q 9:277   What is the employment tax treatment of jury pay?

Individuals who are on jury duty are typically paid a daily rate of pay for their time by the courts. Employers may elect to pay an employee's daily wages for the time the employee is absent from work or the difference between the employee's daily wages and the amount received as jury pay. In either case, only the wages paid by the employer are subject to FIT, FITW, FICA, and FUTA.

Some employers pay the employees their regular daily wages in full and ask that the employee turn the jury pay over to the employer. In this case, only the difference between the employee's daily wages and the jury pay turned over to the employer is subject to FIT, FITW, FICA, and FUTA. [I.R.C. §§ 61(a), 62(a)(13); Treas. Reg. § 1.62-2(a); Rev. Rul. 68-425, 1968-2 C.B. 420]

Leave Sharing

Q 9:278   What are leave-sharing plans?

There are several types of leave sharing plans. The most common plan is set up for an employee to donate a certain number of leave days (or hours) to a group leave account that can then be drawn on by other employees in an emergency. These plans are designed to provide for additional leave when an employee has run out of leave and an emergency occurs. Some plans limit the number of days that an employee may use from the leave-sharing plan over a period of time.

The IRS addressed, in Notice 2001-69 [2001-46 I.R.B. 491, 2001-2 C.B. 491, IRS Not, Oct 25, 2001], the taxation of leave contributed to a charity. Under this guidance, only contributions of leave donated to a charity before January 1, 2003, were not taxed to employees. Employers (but not employees) cannot deduct the payment to a charity under I.R.C. Section 162. Amounts contributed for this purpose are reported in Box 1, 3, and 5 of the W-2.

Q 9:279   How are benefits received under leave-sharing plans treated for payroll tax purposes?

In general, when an employee assigns his or her wages to another employee, for instance, through a leave-sharing program, the amount donated to other employees continues to be treated as wages paid to the donor employee. [I.R.C. § 61; Lucas v. Earl, 281 U.S. 111, 50 S. Ct. 241, 74 L. Ed. 731 (1930); and Helverinq v. Eubank, 311 U.S. 122, 61 S. Ct. 149, 85 L. Ed. 81, 1940-2 C.B. 209 (1940)]

With respect to employer-sponsored leave-sharing plans, there are two exceptions as follows:

- *Bona-fide medical leave sharing arrangements.* When employees who suffer medical emergencies qualify to receive leave surrendered to the employer by other employees to an employer-sponsored leave bank, the amounts paid by the employer to a leave recipient pursuant to the plan are includible in the wages of the recipient and subject to federal income tax, federal income tax withholding, Social Security, Medicare, and FUTA, unless otherwise excluded from wages under another section of the I.R.C. [Rev. Rul. 90-29, 1990-1 C.B. 11; I.R.C. § 61] In this instance, the donor employee (e.g., the employee who surrenders leave to the employer or deposits leave in the leave bank) is not in receipt of wages subject to federal income tax, federal income tax withholding, Social Security, Medicare, or FUTA. In addition, the donor employee cannot claim a deductible expense or loss on his or her federal Form 1040 either upon surrender or deposit of the leave or its use by the recipient employee.

- *Qualified employer-sponsored major disaster leave-sharing plans.* If amounts are donated under a leave-sharing plan to assist employees affected by a major disaster declared by the president of the United States, the recipient employee, rather than the donor employee, is deemed to be in receipt of wages subject to federal income tax, federal income tax withholding, Social Security, Medicare, or FUTA unless the donor employee is also the recipient of the leave. Note that the employer-sponsored leave bank must meet the requirements set forth in IRS Notice 2006-59 in order for the exclusion from the donor-employee's wages to apply. In addition, the donor employee cannot claim a deductible expense or loss on his or her federal Form 1040 either upon surrender or deposit of the leave or its use by the recipient employee. [Notice 2006-59, 2006-28 I.R.B. 60]

Legal (Group) Benefits

Q 9:280   May an employer provide tax-free group legal benefits to employees?

No. The value of any group legal benefits provided by the employer is included in wages subject to FIT, FITW, FICA, and FUTA (less any amounts paid for the benefits by the employee). [I.R.C. §§ 120, 3121(a)(17), 3306(b)(12)]

Life Insurance (Non-Group-Term Insurance and Split-Dollar Insurance)

Q 9:281   Is the value of non-group-term life insurance coverage provided by an employer on the life of an employee treated as additional compensation to the employee?

Yes. The value of the death benefit under an employer-provided life insurance policy that is not excludable under the group-term life insurance provisions of I.R.C. Section 79 (which generally excludes from compensation the value of coverage of up to $50,000) is treated as additional compensation. Whereas only group-term life insurance coverage in excess of $50,000 is treated as additional compensation to the employee, there is no exclusion from federal employment taxes for any coverage provided under non-group-term insurance contracts owned by the employer. The value of all life insurance benefits that do not meet the law's definition for group-term life insurance is determined under an IRS-defined rate schedule, either the "PS 58 Table" or Table 2001 (see Table 9-4). An employer may elect, if certain requirements are met, to use the insurer's published rates for one-year term insurance when those rates are less than the table rates. The PS 58 cost table has been updated.

Beginning in 2002, the value of new non-group-term life insurance provided to an employee must be determined under a new rate table republished in Notice 2002-8 [2002-4 I.R.B. 398], referred to as Table 2001.

Life insurance protection for calendar years after 2001. Notice 2002-8 contains a new rate table, Table 2001, for valuing non-group-term life insurance benefits provided by employers, and has established new methods for recharacterizing transactions in which the employee obtains a right to cash values in policies that are paid by the employer. See Table 9-4.

Reporting requirement. The Pension Protection Act of 2006 added I.R.C. Sections 6039I and 101(j), both of which concern employer-owned life insurance contracts. Section 6039I provides that applicable policyholders owning one or more of these insurance contracts will file returns showing for each year, the contracts are owned number of employees at the end of the year; the number of these employees insured under these contracts at the end of the year; the total amount of insurance under such contracts at the end of the year; the applicable policyholder's name, address, and taxpayer identification number and the type of business in which he or she is engaged; and that the policyholder has valid consent for each insured employee, or the number of insured employees, for whom valid consent was not obtained.

I.R.C. Section 101(j)(1) provides that the amount of death benefits excluded from gross income in such contracts shall not exceed an amount equal to the sum of the premiums and other amounts paid for the contract. I.R.C. Section 101(j)(2) provides exceptions to the previous section's general rule for such contracts when certain notice and consent requirements are met. The exceptions are based on either the status of the insured as an employee within one year of death or as a highly compensated employee or individual, or the extent to which death benefits are paid to a family member, trust, or estate of the insured or used buy an equity interest in the applicable policyholder from any of the three parties.

Regulations adopting proposed rules and removing temporary rules on information reporting on employer-owned life insurance contracts under I.R.C. Section 6039I were released in 2008. In addition, the IRS released Form 8925, Report of Employer-Owned Life Insurance Contracts, for taxpayers to use to comply with the reporting requirements. The rules apply generally to taxpayers engaged in a trade or business who are directly or indirectly beneficiaries of a life insurance contract covering an employee of the trade or business on the date it is issued.

Regulations. The IRS issued final regulations adopting proposed rules and removing temporary rules on information reporting on employer-owned life insurance contracts under I.R.C. Section 6039I. [T.D. 9431, 73 Fed. Reg. 65981-01, 2008 WL 4808819 (F.R.)] The temporary rules provided that the IRS Commissioner could prescribe the form and manner of meeting the reporting requirements under Section 6039I on applicable policyholders who own at least one employer-owned life insurance contract issued after August 17, 2006.

The IRS released Form 8925, Report of Employer-Owned Life Insurance Contracts, on January 24, 2008, for taxpayers to use to comply with the reporting requirements. The rules apply generally to taxpayers engaged in a trade or business who are directly or indirectly beneficiaries of a life insurance contract covering an employee of the trade or business on the date it is issued, the IRS said.

The Pension Protection Act of 2006 [Pub. L. No. 109-280] added to I.R.C. Sections 6039I and 101(j), both of which concern employer-owned life insurance contracts. I.R.C. Section 6039I provides that applicable policyholders owning one or more of these insurance contracts must file returns showing the following for each year the contracts are owned: the applicable policyholder's number of employees at the end of the year; the number of these employees insured under these contracts at the end of the year; the total amount of insurance under such contracts at the end of the year; the applicable policyholder's name, address, and taxpayer identification number, and the type of business in which he or she is engaged; and that the policyholder has valid consent for each insured employee, or the number of insured employees for whom valid consent was not obtained.

I.R.C. Section 101(j)(1) provides that the amount of death benefits excluded from gross income in such contracts shall not exceed an amount equal to the sum of the premiums and other amounts paid for the contract. I.R.C. Section 101(j)(2) provides exceptions to the previous section's general rule for such contracts when certain notice and consent requirements are met.

The exceptions are based on either the status of the insured as an employee within one year of death or as a highly compensated employee or individual, or the extent to which death benefits are paid to a family member, trust, or estate of the insured, or used to buy an equity interest in the applicable policyholder from any of the three parties.

Table 9-4.   Table 2001 Interim Table of One-Year Term Premiums for $1,000 of Life Insurance Protection

Attained Age	Section 79 Extended and Interpolated Annual Rates
0	$0.70
1	$0.41
2	$0.27
3	$0.19
4	$0.13
5	$0.13
6	$0.14
7	$0.15
8	$0.16
9	$0.16
10	$0.16
11	$0.19
12	$0.24
13	$0.28
14	$0.33
15	$0.38
16	$0.52
17	$0.57
18	$0.59
19	$0.61
20	$0.62

Table 9-4.   Table 2001 Interim Table of One-Year Term Premiums for $1,000 of Life Insurance Protection (*cont'd*)

Attained Age	Section 79 Extended and Interpolated Annual Rates
21	$0.62
22	$0.64
23	$0.66
24	$0.68
25	$0.71
26	$0.73
27	$0.76
28	$0.80
29	$0.83
30	$0.87
31	$0.90
32	$0.93
33	$0.96
34	$0.98
35	$0.99
36	$1.01
37	$1.04
38	$1.06
39	$1.07
40	$1.10
41	$1.13
42	$1.20
43	$1.29
44	$1.40
45	$1.53
46	$1.67
47	$1.83
48	$1.98
49	$2.13
50	$2.30
51	$2.52
52	$2.81
53	$3.20

Table 9-4.   Table 2001 Interim Table of One-Year Term Premiums for $1,000 of Life Insurance Protection (*cont'd*)

Attained Age	Section 79 Extended and Interpolated Annual Rates
54	$3.65
55	$4.15
56	$4.68
57	$5.20
58	$5.66
59	$6.06
60	$6.51
61	$7.11
62	$7.96
63	$9.08
64	$10.41
65	$11.90
66	$13.51
67	$15.20
68	$16.92
69	$18.70
70	$20.62
71	$22.72
72	$25.07
73	$27.57
74	$30.18
75	$33.05
76	$36.33
77	$40.17
78	$44.33
79	$49.23
80	$54.56
81	$60.51
82	$66.74
83	$73.07
84	$80.35
85	$88.76
86	$99.16

Table 9-4.   Table 2001 Interim Table of One-Year Term Premiums for $1,000 of Life Insurance Protection (*cont'd*)

Attained Age	Section 79 Extended and Interpolated Annual Rates
87	$110.40
88	$121.85
89	$133.40
90	$144.30
91	$155.80
92	$168.75
93	$186.44
94	$206.70
95	$228.35
96	$250.01
97	$265.09
98	$270.11
99	$281.05

The taxable amounts determined under the table are reduced by any amounts the employee pays toward the death benefit. Where the death benefits of a life insurance policy covering an employee are to be paid to the corporation (e.g., key-man insurance), the value of that coverage is not taxable to the employee. [Treas. Reg. § 1.61-2(d)(2)(ii)]

Q 9:282   What is split-dollar life insurance?

In general, split-dollar life insurance is an arrangement between two or more parties (typically, an employer and employee) to allocate the benefits of a life insurance policy—and, in some cases, the costs of the contract—between the parties. Such an arrangement can be structured in either an equity or nonequity split-dollar form. With a nonequity split-dollar life insurance arrangement, the employee receives life insurance coverage but does not have an interest in the policy cash value (or equity) contract. The employee, not the employer, is the beneficiary of the life insurance protection under the arrangement. Under an equity split-dollar life insurance arrangement, the employer and employee typically share an interest in the policy cash value.

Final regulations released in September 2002 require the employer to choose between two mutually exclusive classifications for taxation of an equity split-dollar life insurance arrangement: a loan classification (i.e., the employee is the owner of the contract), or an economic benefit classification (i.e., the employer is the owner). When the arrangement is characterized as a loan, the employer is treated as loaning the amount of its premium payments to the employee who is the "owner" of the contract. The loan classification generally governs the taxation of split-dollar arrangements described as "collateral assignment" arrangements. The employee will have additional compensation equal to the interest on these loans, unless paid each year.

When the arrangement is characterized as an economic benefit, the employer is the owner of the life insurance contract and is treated as providing economic benefits to the employee (e.g., life insurance protection and a right to some or all of the policy's cash value). The economic benefit classification generally governs the taxation of split-dollar arrangements described as endorsement arrangements. In the case of an equity split-dollar life insurance arrangement where the employer is the owner of the policy, the value of the economic benefits provided to the employee during the taxable year equals (1) the cost of any current life insurance protection provided to the employee, (2) the amount of policy cash value to which the employee has current access (less any amount included in the employee's compensation for a prior taxable year), and (3) the value of any other economic benefits provided to the employee (to the extent not actually taken into account for a prior taxable year).

A split-dollar life insurance arrangement does not include an insurance contract in which the only parties to the arrangement are the policy owner and the life insurance company. For example, under so-called "key man" life insurance arrangements, a company purchases a life insurance contract to insure the life of a "key" employee or shareholder but retains all the rights and benefits of the contract (including the rights to all death benefits and cash value); these are not treated as split-dollar arrangements.

Note. Under Section 402 of the Sarbanes-Oxley Act, public reporting companies may not make extensions of credit to officers and directors in the form of personal loans. This will impact the use of split-dollar life insurance arrangements for directors and officers of public companies. Other companies may not be as affected by this rule.

Q 9:283 What is the tax treatment of a split-dollar life insurance arrangement?

The payroll tax treatment (i.e., whether the value of benefits under the arrangement is included in the employee's compensation) depends on whether the agreement is classified as an economic benefit or a loan. This treatment depends on who is the owner of the contract. If the employee owns the contract, loan treatment applies. If the employer is the owner, treatment as an economic benefit applies. Ownership, as determined under the final regulations, is not necessarily by the individual(s) named on the contract. Note that these are two mutually exclusive classifications: that is, the split-dollar life insurance is classified as either one *or* the other.

A special tax rule applies when ownership of the contract is transferred from the employer to the employee and the arrangement essentially is reclassified from a loan to an economic benefit. In such an instance, no employer payments (before or after the transfer) may be treated as split-dollar loans on or after the date of the transfer. At the time of the transfer, the employee must fully take into account (i.e., report as additional compensation) all economic benefits provided under the split-dollar life insurance arrangement. Thus, the amount of any loan that is not repaid at the time of the transfer is treated as forgiven and constitutes additional compensation to the employee.

In general, when the employer is the owner of the split-dollar policy, but the employee has an economic benefit in the policy's value (e.g., life insurance coverage and/or has access to the policy's cash value), the employer is treated as providing an economic benefit to the employee. The value of those economic benefits, reduced by any consideration paid by the employee to the owner, is includible in compensation.

The value of the benefit constitutes a payment of compensation, unless the employee is a stockholder. Then it may be classified as a distribution or a capital contribution. Basically, when an employer provides an employee with full access to the cash values, the employee is treated as having compensation equal to the cash values that are available (less any amounts paid or included in income in a prior year), even if the employee does not withdraw those values.

When the employee also receives life insurance coverage, the employee has compensation equal to the value of the death benefit as determined using Table 1 (the PS 58 table is no longer available), less any amount paid (see Table 9-3 in Q 9:225).

The value of the economic benefits provided to the employee equals the total amount of policy cash value to which the employee has current "access" (to the extent that such amount was not actually taken into account for a prior taxable year), *or* is inaccessible by the employer or the employer's creditors. An employee has access to policy cash value if the nonowner employee can directly or indirectly make a withdrawal from the policy, borrow from the policy, or effect a total or partial surrender of the policy. Policy cash value is inaccessible to the employer if the employer does not have the full rights to policy cash value normally held by an owner of a life insurance contract. Policy cash value is inaccessible to the employer's general creditors if, under the terms of the split-dollar life insurance arrangement or by operation of law or any contractual undertaking, the creditors cannot, for any reason, effectively reach the policy cash value in the event of the owner's insolvency.

Loan treatment. A split-dollar arrangement is subject to loan treatment when the employee is the owner of the contract, with all or a portion of the life insurance premiums paid by the employer as a loan to the employee. A payment made pursuant to such a split-dollar life insurance arrangement is a split-dollar loan. The employer and employee are treated, respectively, as borrower and lender when three conditions are met: (1) the payment is made either directly or indirectly by the employer to the employee; (2) the payment is a loan under general principles of federal tax law or, if not a loan under general principles of federal tax law, a reasonable person would expect the payment to be repaid in full to the employer (whether with or without interest); and (3) the repayment is to be made from, or is secured by, either the policy's death benefit proceeds or its cash surrender value, or both.

The final regulations also introduce a new concept in this loan treatment. Each payment under a split-dollar life insurance arrangement is treated as a separate loan for federal tax purposes. The employer cannot elect to treat all payments made during a single year (or single calendar quarter) as one loan.

Frequently, the employer imposes no requirement for payment of reasonable interest on these loans. These loans may then be treated as below-market loans. In such an instance, the loan is recharacterized as a loan with interest at the applicable federal rate (AFR), coupled with an imputed transfer by the employer to the employee. The timing, amount, and characterization of the imputed transfers between the lender and borrower will depend on the relationship between the employer and the employee (e.g., the imputed transfer is generally characterized as a compensation payment if the lender is the borrower's employer), and whether the loan is a demand loan or a term loan. See Q 9:60 on below-market loans.

Special rules are provided in the final regulations for split-dollar term loans payable upon the death of an employee and certain split-dollar term loans that are conditioned on the future performance of substantial services by an employee. These split-dollar loans are classified as "split-dollar term loans" for purposes of determining whether the loan provides for sufficient interest. The rate used to determine the amount of forgone interest each year is the AFR based on the term of the loan, determined on the date the split-dollar loan is made, and the rate is not determined annually.

When a split-dollar loan provides for stated interest that is subsequently waived, cancelled, or forgiven, the amount of interest involved is treated as retransferred from the lender to the borrower. In addition, this amount generally is increased by a "deferral charge."

Payments made by the employee to an employer pursuant to a split-dollar life insurance arrangement are applied to the split-dollar loan balance in the following order: first, to accrued but unpaid interest on all outstanding split-dollar loans, in the order the interest accrued; then, to principal on the outstanding split-dollar loans, in the order in which the loans were made; then, to payments of amounts previously paid by the lender pursuant to the split-dollar life insurance arrangement that were not reasonably expected to be repaid; and finally, to any other payment with respect to a split-dollar life insurance arrangement.

The value of the imputed interest or interest not paid is a transfer of property to the employee and results in additional compensation that is subject to FICA and FUTA taxes, but not federal income tax withholding. [I.R.C. § 3306(b); Treas. Reg. §§ 1.7872-15, 1.61-22]

A change to employer-owned life insurance in the Pension Protection Act of 2006 is applicable to split-dollar life insurance plans. Specifically, in the case of an employer-owned life insurance contract, I.R.C. Section 101(j) (added by PPA 2006) limits the amount of death benefits that can be excluded from the gross income of an applicable policyholder to the sum of the premiums and other amounts paid by the policyholder for the contract. The provision was generally effective for life insurance contracts issued after August 17, 2007, but also applies to contracts issued on or before that date if there is a material change in the contract, such as a material increase in the death benefit.

IRS guidance from Notice 2008-42 provides that a modification of a split-dollar life insurance arrangement that does not affect the life insurance contract underlying the arrangement is not a material change in the life insurance contract that would cause it to lose its "grandfathered" status and become subject to I.R.C. Sections 101(j) and 264(f) (denying a deduction for interest expense that is allocable to the unborrowed policy cash value of a life insurance policy or an annuity or endowment contract).

Q 9:284   Who is the "owner" of a split-dollar life insurance contract?

The owner of a split-dollar life insurance contract generally is the person named as the policy owner in the contract. When two or more persons are designated as the policy owners, the final regulations specify that the first-named person generally is treated as the owner of the entire contract.

However, when two or more parties are named as policy owners of a life insurance contract and each party has, at all times, all the incidents of owner-ship with respect to an undivided interest in the contract, those persons are treated as owners of separate contracts. Neither are split-dollar arrangements. An undivided interest in a life insurance contract will consist of an identical fractional or percentage interest or share in each right, benefit, and obligation with respect to the contract. For example, when an employer and an employee own a life insurance contract and share equally in all rights, benefits, and obligations under the contract, they are treated as owning two separate con-tracts, with neither contract treated as part of a split-dollar life insurance arrangement. If, however, the employer and the employee agree to enter into a split-dollar life insurance arrangement with respect to what otherwise would have been treated as the employer's (or the employee's) separate contract, the purported undivided interests will be disregarded, and the entire arrangement will be treated as a split-dollar life insurance arrangement.

Special ownership rules apply when the contract is owned by a member of the employer's controlled group, a "secular trust," a grantor trust treated as owned by the employer (including a rabbi trust), or a welfare benefit fund sponsored by the employer. In such a case the owner is treated as the employee's employer.

The final regulations address the tax treatment of a transfer of the life insurance contract from the employer to the employee. A transfer of a life insurance contract (or an undivided interest in the contract) that is part of a split-dollar life insurance arrangement is treated, for tax purposes, as occurring on the date that the employee becomes the owner of the contract (or an undivided interest in the contract). Only when ownership of the contract is formally changed at the time of the transfer will the employee be treated as the owner for all federal income and employment tax purposes. The FMV of an undivided interest may not be discounted through any other arrangement between the parties.

If, after a transfer of an entire life insurance contract, the employer pays premiums, the payment of those premiums is includible in the employee's gross income unless the payments are split-dollar loans.

Q 9:285 When an S-corporation owns split-dollar policies on several employees, is another class of stock created?

The IRS ruled in Private Letter Ruling 200441023 [(Oct. 8, 2004)] that an S-corporation owning split-dollar policies does not create a second class of stock. The ruling was necessary because S-corporation rules limit the corporation to a single class of stock in which rights to distributions and liquidation are identical.

Q 9:286 What is the effective date of the final split-dollar regulations?

The tax treatment specified in the final regulations applies to any split-dollar life insurance arrangement entered into after September 17, 2003, and to any split-dollar life insurance arrangement entered into on or before September 17, 2003, if the arrangement is materially modified after September 17, 2003. Certain changes in a contract to comply with Section IV, Paragraph 4 of Notice 2002-8 [2002-1 C.B. 398] for contracts entered into prior to January 2, 2002, will not be treated as materially modifying a contract.

These final regulations provide a nonexclusive list of other contract changes that will not result in a material modification for purposes of the effective date.

The final regulations generally treat only one person as the owner of the life insurance contract. Because only the owner of a life insurance contract can have an investment in that contract, a nonowner employee cannot have basis in the contract for any of the costs of current life insurance protection. In addition, such costs should not be included in the nonowner's basis or investment in the contract if and when the nonowner becomes the owner of the contract, because those payments were made for annual life insurance protection, which protection was exhausted prior to the nonowner's acquisition of the contract.

To the extent the employee has neither paid for nor taken into account the current life insurance protection (Table 1), the proceeds paid to the estate or designated beneficiary of the employee constitute a separate transfer of cash not shielded from income tax under I.R.C. Section 101(a). That is, it is fully taxable to the beneficiary as a payment for the benefit of a deceased employee.

Q 9:287   When may an employer value the death benefits under a split-dollar arrangement under the insurer's term rates?

An employer may, under certain circumstances, utilize an insurer's premium rate for determining the value of employer-provided life insurance protection when those rates are less than the rates under Table 2001 (see Table 9-4, Q 9:281). Only an insurer's lower published premium rates that are available to all standard risks for initial issue one-year term insurance can be used subject to the following restrictions. For periods after December 31, 2003, the IRS will not consider an insurer's published premium rates to be available to all standard risks who apply for term insurance unless three conditions are met: (1) the insurer communicates the rates to individuals who apply for term insurance coverage from the insurer, (2) the insurer regularly sells term insurance at these rates to individuals who apply for term insurance coverage through the insurer's normal distribution channels, and (3) the insurer does not "more commonly" sell term insurance at higher premium rates to individuals that the insurer classifies as a standard risk under insurance policies that the insurer applies for the issuance of term insurance. [Notice 2002-8, 2002-4 I.R.B. 398]

Q 9:288   Are life insurance benefits provided under a pension plan subject to employment taxes?

The value of life insurance benefits provided under an employer's pension plan is treated as additional compensation subject to federal income tax but not federal income tax withholding or FICA or FUTA taxes. For years prior to 2002, the value of this insurance is determined using the PS 58 method (see Q 9:281). After 2001, the valuation methods that apply to split-dollar insurance under Notice 2002-8 [2002-4 I.R.B. 398] are to be applied (i.e., Table 2001 rates). For 2001, the employer may use either method. These amounts, less any payments made by the employer, are reported in Box 1 and with a Code 9 in Box 7 on Form 1099-R. When such amounts are included in the employee's gross income, the death benefit related to the life insurance, but not the cash values, is paid to an employee's beneficiary free of any federal income tax and FUTA taxation. In addition, the accumulated PS 58 and Table 2001 costs reported by the participant are not subject to federal income taxes when the pension benefits are paid. These are treated by the participant as basis and when paid are not taxable. [I.R.C. § 72]

Beginning in 2005, any life insurance contract transferred from an employer or a tax-qualified plan to an employee must be taxed at its full FMV. Previously, I.R.C. Section 402(a) and regulations interpreting that section provided that amounts distributed by a retirement plan that is exempt from tax are taxable to the distributee at FMV, or the entire cash value of an annuity or life insurance contract. FMV and entire cash value are not defined under the regulations, leaving ambiguous whether entire cash value includes a reduction for surrender charges.

Q 9:289   When does corporate-owned life insurance trigger taxation to the corporation?

The general rule is that proceeds from corporate owned life insurance (COLI) are not taxable to the business. The Pension Protection Act of 2006, however, requires businesses to treat proceeds from corporate-owned life insurance as income unless the insured was an employee within 12 months of death, or was a director or highly compensated employee or individual at the time the contract was issued, or the proceeds paid to the insured's beneficiary are used to buy back any equity interest owned by the insured at the time of death. [Pub. L. No. 109-280, 120 Stat. 780]

Temporary regulations effective November 13, 2007 were issued simply for the purpose of IRS granting itself the power to issue a form by which employers may report the tax treatment of COLI.

Long-Term Care Benefits

Q 9:290   What are long-term care benefits?

Long-term care (LTC) can include both medical and nonmedical support services that are not associated with an individual's hospitalization. LTC is designed to help individuals who suffer from a chronic long-term physical or mental condition rather than provide for treatment by a physician or hospital relating to an immediate health need.

HIPAA defined "qualified long-term care" as necessary diagnostic, preventive, therapeutic, curing, treating, mitigating, and rehabilitative services, and maintenance or personal care services that are required by a "chronically ill" individual and are provided under a plan of care prescribed by a licensed health care practitioner. [I.R.C. § 7702B(c)(1)]

LTC typically can provide services that help with the following: dressing, eating, bathing, moving from a bed to a chair, maintaining continence, walking, and using the bathroom. These are generally referred to as activities of daily living (ADLs). Thus, LTC can be provided by an adult daycare center, home health care facility, a nursing home, or providers of respite care, which allows the caregiver time for his or her personal business.

Tax-free transfers are not available between annuity contracts without LTC riders and life insurance contracts with LTC riders. The Pension Protection Act of 2006, however, permits LTC riders on annuity contracts and provides special tax treatment for the LTC component of a life insurance or annuity contract, including allowing the cash value of such contracts to pay the LTC benefit, making LTC payments to a reduction in basis, allowing tax-free transfers between annuity contracts even if one has an LTC rider (with similar rules for life insurance contracts), and providing special rules that treat the LTC rider as a separate contract for certain purposes. [Pub. L. No. 109-280, 120 Stat. 780]

Q 9:291   Are long-term care insurance premiums paid by an employer excludable from an employee's wages?

Yes. The I.R.C. generally treats a long-term contract as an accident and health plan. Thus, employer-paid premiums for LTC insurance coverage should not be includible in the wages of the employee. This exclusion from wages is not available to a more than 2 percent shareholder in a Subchapter S corporation. This exclusion from wages is limited to a specific dollar cap that is based on the individual's age at the time premiums are paid; following are the annual caps for 2015, 2016 and 2017.

	2015	*2016*	*2017*
Age 40 or less	$ 380	$ 390	$ 410 (+ 5.1%)
Age 41–50	$ 710	$ 730	$ 770
Age 51–60	$1,430	$1,460	$1,530
Age 61–70	$3,800	$3,900	$4,090
Over age 70	$4,750	$4,870	$5,110 (+ 4.9)

These limits are indexed and are based on the individual's actual age at the end of the calendar year. [I.R.C. §§ 106(a), 213(d)(10)(A), 7702B(a)(3), Rev. Proc. 2015-53, 2015-44 I.R.B. Nov. 2, 2015, Rev. Proc. 2016-55, 26 CFR60-1.602, I.R.B. 2016-45, Nov. 7, 2016]

The value of LTC benefits provided by an employer for employees up to these limits is not subject to federal income tax withholding or FICA or FUTA taxes. [I.R.C. §§ 3121(a)(2)(B), 3306(b)(2)(B), 3306(b)(4), 7702B(a); Ann. 92-16, 1992-5 I.R.B. 53]

Note that LTC insurance benefits may not be provided as a qualified benefit under a cafeteria plan because benefits are payable beyond the current plan year. As a result, an individual may not purchase an LTC contract with before-tax salary reductions under a Section 125 plan. [I.R.C. § 125(f)]

Q 9:292   What is a qualified long-term care insurance contract?

In general, an LTC insurance contract is an insurance policy that meets the definition of a "qualified long-term care insurance contract" under I.R.C. Section 7702B(b). That section requires LTC insurance contracts to contain provisions such as the following:

1. The only insurance protection provided under the contract is coverage of qualified LTC services.

2. The contract does not pay or reimburse expenses incurred for services that are reimbursable under Title XVIII of the Social Security Act (or would be reimbursable but for the application of a deductible or coinsurance amount).

3. The contract is guaranteed renewable.

4. The contract does not provide for a cash surrender value or other money that can be paid, assigned, or pledged as collateral for a loan or borrowed.

5. All premium refunds and dividends under the contract are to be applied as reductions in future premiums or to increase future benefits. An exception to this rule is for a refund made on the death of the insured or on a complete surrender or cancellation of the contract that cannot exceed the aggregate premiums paid. [I.R.C. § 7702B(b)(2)(C)]

6. The contract satisfies certain consumer protection provisions concerning model regulation and model act provisions, disclosure, and nonforfeitability.

7. The contract meets certain provisions of the National Association of Insurance Commissioners' (NAIC) LTC insurance model regulation dealing with such issues as guaranteed renewal or noncancellability, prohibitions on limitations and exclusions, extension of benefits, continuation or conversion of coverage, replacement of policies, unintentional lapse, disclosure, postclaims underwriting, minimum standards, the requirement to offer inflation protection, and the prohibition against preexisting conditions and probationary periods in replacement policies.

8. The contract meets certain provisions of the NAIC LTC insurance model act relating to preexisting conditions and prior hospitalization.

9. The contract contains certain nonforfeiture provisions.

10. The insurer complies with the disclosure requirements of I.R.C. Section 4980C(d).

Q 9:293 What are the long-term care insurance contract disclosure requirements?

The insurer must provide a notice that identifies the specific terms and benefits of the LTC contract. The policy meets the law's disclosure requirements when its issuer provides a contract, outline of coverage, and policy summary. These notices must satisfy certain requirements of the NAIC LTC insurance model act relating to the individual's right to return the policy, the outline of coverage, and the incontestability period. Where a contract is purchased in the workplace, either as an employer-paid benefit or paid by the employee through payroll deduction, the employer will want to ensure that these requirements are met. [I.R.C. §§ 4980C(c), 4980C(d)]

A qualified LTC insurance contract must be delivered to the policyholder within 30 days of the approval date by the insurance company. If a claim is denied, the issuer of the qualified contract must provide a written explanation of the reasons for the denial and make available all information relating to the denial within 60 days of a written request from the policyholder. [I.R.C. §§ 4980C(c)(2), 4980C(c)(3)]

A penalty tax equal to $100 per insured can be assessed on the insurer for each day that any of these requirements are not met for each qualified LTC insurance contract. [I.R.C. § 4980C(b)]

Q 9:294   Who is treated as a chronically ill individual?

The law defines a "chronically ill" individual as a person who has been certified by a licensed health care practitioner as being unable to perform, without substantial assistance, at least two ADLs for at least 90 days. A person may be considered chronically ill when the individual requires substantial supervision to avoid possible threats to his or her health and safety because of a severe cognitive impairment, and the condition has been certified by a licensed health care practitioner within the previous 12 months. [I.R.C. § 7702B(c)(2)(A)]

Activities of daily living are (1) eating, (2) toileting, (3) transferring, (4) bathing, (5) dressing, and (6) continence. An LTC insurance contract is "qualified" when the policy takes into account at least five of these ADLs in determining whether a person is chronically ill. [I.R.C. § 7702B(c)(2)(B)]

Q 9:295   Can a long-term care insurance contract be offered as a qualified benefit under a cafeteria plan?

No. The value of any qualified LTC insurance provided through a Section 125 plan will be included in the employee's gross income. Thus, while the value of employer-paid premiums for LTC insurance is not taxable, and current-year medical expenses for LTC for the employee or dependent can be paid through a health FSA, an employee may not buy LTC insurance using a salary reduction for a cafeteria plan. [I.R.C. §§ 106(c)(1), 125(f)]

Meals and Lodging

Q 9:296   How are employer-provided meals treated for federal employment tax purposes?

The value of meals provided to an employee is treated as additional compensation, except where the I.R.C. provides specific exclusions. These exclusions are generally conditioned on the meals being provided for valid business reasons or as a *de minimis* fringe benefit. That is, the meals other than *de minimis* fringe benefits are provided because of certain job requirements rather than for compensatory reasons. An employer-paid meal is not additional compensation when it falls into one of the following categories:

1. Meals provided for the convenience of the employer, on the employer's premises, and as a condition of employment;
2. Away-from-home meals that are related to a business purpose; or
3. Infrequent and nominal value meals that may be treated as a *de minimis* fringe benefit.

Where meals are disguised compensation, the value of the meal is treated as additional compensation and subject to all federal employment taxes (see Qs 9:153–9:157).

If a client leases employees from a leasing company and the company reimburses the employee for meals and incidental expenses, an IRS ruling determined which party can take the deduction when a leasing company and a client, who are unrelated parties, enter into a written leasing contract under which the leasing company leases drivers to the client to haul products in exchange for the client's periodic payments to the leasing company. [Rev. Rul. 2008-23, 2008-18 I.R.B. 852] Neither the leasing company nor the client deducts the amounts as compensation on its originally filed income tax return and neither treats the meals and incidental expense amounts as wages for purposes of withholding, under the facts described therein.

Employer-Provided Lodging

Q 9:297   How is employer-provided lodging treated?

The value of lodging provided by an employer to an employee is generally treated as additional compensation and subject to FIT, FITW, FICA, and FUTA unless a specific exclusion applies. Employer-provided lodging can be exempt from FIT, FITW, FICA, and FUTA under I.R.C. Section 119. This exemption applies where the lodging is: (1) furnished for the employer's convenience, (2) furnished on the employer's premises, and (3) required as a condition of employment. For example, the value of lodging provided to camp counselors at an overnight summer camp would not be included in the employee's gross income.

Q 9:298   What does "for the convenience of the employer" mean?

The term "for the convenience of the employer" generally means that there is a substantial business purpose for providing lodging other than to provide additional compensation to the employee. [Treas. Reg. § 1.119-1(a)(2)]

Whether lodging is provided for the convenience of the employer depends on all the facts and circumstances of the specific situation. A written statement that lodging is for the employer's convenience is not sufficient to support such a claim. [Treas. Reg. § 1.119-1(a); I.R.C. §§ 3121(a)(19), 3306(b)(14)]

Q 9:299   Do special employer-provided lodging rules apply to educational institutions?

Yes. The value of qualified campus lodging provided to an employee of an educational institution is not treated as additional compensation where the employee pays rent equal to the lesser of (1) 5 percent of the appraised value of the qualified campus lodging or (2) the average rental of similar facilities rented to individuals other than employees or students. Qualified lodging refers to lodging situated on or near the campus. [I.R.C. § 119(d)]

Q 9:300   May hospitals exclude the value of lodging provided to medical residents?

Generally, no, unless the lodging benefits satisfy the requirements of I.R.C. Section 119. The IRS has ruled on lodging provided to residents in a technical advice memorandum. It held that the value of living quarters provided to a worker is provided for compensatory reasons and, therefore, included in the worker's wages under Treasury Regulations Section 1.61-2(d)(3). That section establishes an exception when three conditions are met: (1) the lodging is "furnished for the convenience of the employer" and (2) meets two additional requirements under Section 119: (i) the lodging is on the business premises of the employer, and (ii) accepting the lodging is a condition of employment.

For the lodging to be considered on the employer's premises, it must be provided either at a place where the employees perform a significant portion of their duties or where the employer conducts a significant portion of its business. In the ruling, the IRS found that the employer's lodging program failed to satisfy this criterion, holding that the "convenience of the employer" and "condition of employment" tests are basically applied to all employees in the same position. In this case, the hospital did not require all of the residents to live in hospital-owned housing, and thus this criterion was not a necessary employment requirement. The value of the resident's lodging was subject to FITW, FICA, and FUTA. [Tech. Adv. Mem. 9824001[SMJ40], June 12, 1998]

Q 9:301   What is a parsonage housing allowance?

A parsonage allowance is a cash allowance paid to a "minister of the Gospel" (member of the clergy) to be used to obtain housing. The I.R.C. excludes a parsonage allowance (or the value of lodging made available to a "minister of the Gospel") from all federal employment taxes, even if the parsonage is treated as additional compensation. [I.R.C. § 107; Treas. Reg. § 1.107-1; Rev. Rul. 78-448, 1978-2 C.B. 105]

Q 9:302   When is the rental value of a home furnished to a minister excluded from taxable income?

I.R.C. Section 107 provides that gross income of a "minister of the Gospel" does not include the rental value of a home furnished to the minister as a part of the minister's compensation. Also, rental allowance paid to a minister as part of the minister's compensation is exempt to the extent used by the minister to rent or provide a home. A similar exemption applies to FICA and Self-Employment Contributions Act taxes for services performed by a "duly ordained, commissioned or licensed minister" of a church in the exercise of his ministry. [I.R.C. §§ 1402(c)(4), 3121(b)(8)(A)]

The performance of sacerdotal functions, the conduct of religious worship, the administration and maintenance of religious organizations and their integral agencies, and the performance of teaching and administrative functions at theological seminaries will be considered the duties of a minister under I.R.C. Section 107. [Treas. Reg. § 1-107-1(a); Priv. Ltr. Rul. 199910055 (Dec. 10, 1998)]

Q 9:303   When is temporary housing excluded from an employee's gross compensation?

Under certain conditions, job-related expenses (meals and lodging) for extended periods away from the taxpayer's home may be excluded from an employee's gross income. Only expenses for "temporary travel" of up to one year in duration are eligible for this treatment. If the employer expects the duration of the travel away from home to exceed one year, all reimbursements are treated as additional compensation subject to FIT, FITW, FICA, and FUTA (including the long-term travel expenses for the first 12 months). This treatment of long-term travel expenses as additional compensation occurs from the date it is no longer reasonable to expect that the away from home job assignment will last less than one year. When such payments are considered additional compensation, all amounts are subject to FIT, FITW, FICA, and FUTA. [Notice 93-29, 1993-18 I.R.B. 14; Rev. Rul. 93-86, 1993-2 C.B. 71]

Medical Savings Accounts

Q 9:304   What are medical savings accounts?

Medical savings accounts (MSAs), which were renamed as Archer MSAs by the Consolidated Appropriations Act of 2001, are a type of health and accident plan that combines an IRA-like savings vehicle (i.e., the Archer MSA) with a high deductible health insurance policy. HIPAA enacted Archer MSAs as a pilot program for small employers. Under the program, an employer may make contributions to an employee's Archer MSA that are not treated as additional compensation and are not subject to federal income tax withholding or FICA or FUTA taxes. [I.R.C. § 106(b)(3)] An employee may also make contributions to an Archer MSA that are deductible from the individual's federal income taxes (but are made from compensation subject to federal income withholding and FICA and FUTA taxes). Archer contributions can be made by either the employer (or the spouse's employer) or employee, but not both. [I.R.C. § 220(b)(5); Ann. 2002-90, 2002-40 I.R.B. 684, Ann. 2002-2 C.B. 684, Oct. 7, 2002]

In 2007, the IRS updated instructions for electronic filing of Form 8851 information returns regarding Archer medical savings accounts. The IRS noted that trustees filing more than 250 Forms 8851, Summary of Archer MSAs, are required to use the IRS's File Information Returns Electronically (FIRE) System. Major changes to the return include: renaming the Martinsburg Computing Center as the Enterprise Computing Center-Martinsburg (ECC-MTB); ECC-MTB no longer accepts magnetic media filing for Forms 8851, only filings through the FIRE System are allowed; and filers should call ECC-MTB at 866-455-7438, extension 3, for log-on instructions for the FIRE System. The IRS noted that there have been substantial changes to the FIRE System and said users should carefully review the information provided on the Web.

Note. Although Archer MSAs remain available, the same purpose is served with the newer HSAs, which may have broader appeal. See Qs 9:257–9:272.

Q 9:305   What conditions apply to MSAs?

In addition to working for a small employer, an employee must be covered under an insurance policy that qualifies as a high deductible policy and cannot maintain any other health insurance.

The maximum annual amount that may be contributed to the Archer MSA is directly related to the deductible amount under a high deductible insurance policy and whether the policy coverage is for an individual or a family. The Archer MSA contribution in the calendar year is capped at 65 percent of the deductible for individual coverage and 75 percent of the deductible for family coverage.

For calendar year 2017, the limitation on contributions for an individual with self-only coverage under a high deductible health plan was $3,350. For calendar year 2017, the limitation on contributions for an individual with family coverage under a high deductible health plan is $6,750.

For tax years beginning in 2017, the annual deductible for an Archer MSA high deductible health plan may not be less than $2,250 and not more than $3,350 for single coverage, and not less than $4,500 and not more than $6,750 for family coverage. Also, annual out-of-pocket expenses (exclusive of premiums) cannot exceed $4,500 for single coverage and $8,250 for family coverage.

The health insurance policy cannot pay for any out-of-pocket or other treatment until the employee has met the dollar amount of the deductible. That is, a qualifying policy cannot offer an 80/20 coinsurance, a $15 office visit option, or other payment until the full deductible is met. Beginning after December 31, 2010, nonprescription medicines (other than insulin) no longer qualify as an expense for Archer MSA purposes unless a prescription is provided.

An individual's Archer MSA contribution is only permitted when the employee or covered dependent has no other health insurance. Specialized medical coverage is excluded from this restriction (such as dental insurance, LTC insurance, or vision insurance). [I.R.C. §§ 106(b), 220(b), 220(c)(2)]

Q 9:306   How are employer contributions to an MSA treated for employment tax purposes?

Contributions to the Archer MSA account of eligible employees may either be made by the employer or the employee, but not both. Contributions made by the employer, within specific limits, are not treated as additional compensation. Employer contributions in excess of limits are included in wages subject to FIT,

FITW, FICA, and FUTA. [I.R.C. §§ 106(b), 220(b), 3121(a)(5), 3306(b)(17), 3401(a)(21)]

The amount of the employer contribution is limited to 1/12th of the pro rata portion of the annual contribution (limited to a percentage of the high deductible coverage or the employee's wages from the employer) for each month of coverage. Employer contributions to the Archer MSA accounts need not be made on a monthly basis; they can be accumulated and contributed periodically during the year as long as the monthly limits are met.

Example 1. Spruce Line Inc. provides qualifying high deductible insurance coverage for its employees. The deductible in 2017 is $3,500 for individuals and $7,000 for family coverage. Sheldon is single and covered under the plan. His employer is entitled to contribute $2,275 (65 percent of $3,500) to Sheldon's MSA at $189.58 each month. Spruce Line decides to contribute 85 percent of the maximum for each employee, or $2,975 annually (or $247.92 each month) for Sheldon. Sheldon is only covered under the high deductible policy for 10 months. His maximum MSA account, if funded by the employer, is 10 × $247.92 or $2,479.20 for the year. The contribution that exceeds the limit of 65 percent of the maximum deductible is income subject to FITW, FICA, and FUTA. The law places conditions on employee MSA contributions. The contribution for all employees in all MSA accounts of the employer must be based on the same percentage of the deductible under the plan or a flat dollar amount that does not exceed compensation. An excise tax penalty of 35 percent can be levied on employers that make payments to plans that fail to meet this requirement. [I.R.C. § 4980E]

Example 2. The employer maintains two HDHPs for two groups of employees in separate locations. The policies differ in the limit of the deductible for individual and family coverage. If an employer's MSA contributions for each location are an equal percentage of the deductible under the two high deductible insurance plans, the plan qualifies as an MSA. If the two plans have employer contributions of 80 percent and 90 percent, respectively, the MSA contributions are subject to a penalty of 35 percent of the total contribution. Note that an exception to this general rule applies to part-time employees who may be subject to a different employer contribution amount or percentage. [I.R.C. § 4980E]

Q 9:307   Is an MSA a qualified benefit under a cafeteria plan?

No; thus, an employee cannot use tax-free salary reductions to fund an Archer MSA. An employer may offer the HDHP as an option under the cafeteria plan. As a result, that insurance can be paid with salary reductions that are exempt from FIT, FITW, FICA, and FUTA. An employee who selects the high deductible insurance would then make contributions to an MSA account outside of the cafeteria plan. The employee's MSA contribution cannot be part of the cafeteria plan and must be made out of wages that were subject to FITW, FICA, and FUTA. [I.R.C. § 125(f); Notice 96-53, 1996-51 I.R.B. 5]

Q 9:308　Can employees use the funds in their MSA to pay COBRA health insurance premiums?

Yes. This is an exception to the rule that Archer MSA accounts cannot be used to pay medical insurance. Where an individual is eligible for COBRA continuation of the high deductible insurance coverage, funds in an Archer MSA may be used to pay those premiums. Funds may also be used to pay long-term care insurance and health care coverage while receiving unemployment insurance. [Pub. No. 969]

Q 9:309　Can employees use the funds in their MSA to pay for Medicare Part D prescription drug benefits?

No. The Centers for Medicare & Medicaid Services (CMS) issued guidance to employers and unions that may apply for the Part D retiree drug subsidy, reiterating that most account-based plans will not be eligible. According to the guidance, FSAs, HSAs, and Archer MSAs cannot be counted toward creditable coverage for beneficiaries. Account-based plans generally are those in which employers, unions, or employees contribute annual amounts to be used to pay for health care costs.

According to CMS, it is difficult to accurately determine creditable coverage for FSAs, in part, because employers would be unable to determine prospectively the actuarial value. Participants determine the amount to be contributed to FSAs and thus actuarial equivalence would not be possible. Similarly, creditable coverage could not accurately be determined for HSAs and MSAs. In addition, contributions to HSAs and MSAs are not permitted after an individual is eligible for Medicare. However, beneficiaries may withdraw funds from FSAs, HSAs, and MSAs to cover Part D cost-sharing amounts, and those funds would count toward an individual's out-of-pocket limit.

Q 9:310　How are employer and employee contributions to MSAs reported for employment tax purposes?

Employer contributions meeting the requirements for MSAs (generally, 65 percent of the deductible amount for individual coverage and 75 percent of the deductible amount for other coverage) are excluded from wages subject to FIT, FITW, FICA, and FUTA. Amounts in excess of this limit are treated as wages and subject to FIT, FITW, FICA, and FUTA. Employer contributions to a qualified MSA account that are excluded from wages are reported in Form W-2, Box 12, Code R.

Employee contributions under a payroll deduction arrangement (e.g., with aftertax income) are treated as wages and included in Boxes 1, 3, and 5 of Form W-2. Such employee contributions are not reported in Box 12. The employee will generally be permitted a deduction on his or her personal tax filing for the amount contributed to an MSA. [I.R.C. §§ 106(b), 3306(b)(17), 3401(a)(21); Notice 96-53, 1996-51 I.R.B. 5; Pub. No. 969]

Moving Expenses

Q 9:311 When are moving expense payments made by an employer not taxable to employees?

Nontaxable moving expense payments made by an employer are expenses relating to a move from one home to another of a newly hired or relocated employee. These may be provided without being treated as additional compensation as long as the costs are reasonable and those expenses would qualify as tax-deductible expenses for the employee if the employee paid those expenses. These basic rules are part of a change in the tax laws in 1994 that also implemented a more restrictive definition of moving expenses. Moving expense payments made to reimburse an employee (or paid to a third party) are excluded from the wages subject to FIT, FITW, FICA, and FUTA under I.R.C. Section 132 as "qualified moving expenses" when they meet the following two tests:

1. *Distance test.* The employee's commute to the new workplace from the old residence must be at least 50 miles further than the employee's commute from the old residence to the previous workplace. For example, an employee who lived 15 miles from his or her old workplace must have a commute of at least 65 miles from the old residence to the new workplace before relocation expense reimbursements for moving to a new residence are nontaxable.

2. *Time test.* The employee must work on a substantially full-time basis for at least 39 weeks in the general area of the new job in the 12 months immediately following the move. Exceptions apply when employment ends because of death, disability, involuntary termination of employment (except for willful misconduct), or transfer for the employer's benefit. The 39 weeks of employment during the 12-month period need not be with the same employer.

The two types of "qualifying moving expenses" are (1) transportation and in-transit storage of household goods for up to 30 days (a longer period applies for foreign moves); and (2) travel from the old residence to the new residence, including lodging, but not meals (only one trip per family member qualifies). [I.R.C. § 217(b); Treas. Reg. §§ 1.217-2(c), 1.217-2(d)]

Expenses that do not qualify as moving expenses include meals and temporary lodging at the new job location; travel expenses, meals, and lodging for premove house-hunting trips; expenses related to selling a home; and meal expenses during the move to the new job location. A special exception for certain meals and lodging expenses related to a move is available to certain federal employees. [Treas. Reg. § 1.217-2(b); 41 C.F.R. § 302-6.2]

In-transit storage expenses are storage costs that are incurred within 30 days after the goods and effects are moved from the old to the new location. For foreign moves, the cost of storage can include the period while the employee is out of the country. [Treas. Reg. § 1.217-2(b)(2)]

Q 9:312   What is a qualified moving expense reimbursement?

The term *qualified moving expense reimbursement* refers to any amount received (directly or indirectly) by an employee from an employer under an accountable plan as a payment for (or reimbursement of) expenses that would be deductible as moving expenses by the employee under I.R.C. Section 217 if directly paid by the individual. [I.R.C. §§ 82, 132(g), 217, 3121(a)(11), 3306(b)(9), 3401(a)(15)]

Q 9:313   How are qualified moving expense reimbursements treated for employment tax purposes?

Qualified moving expense reimbursements are treated as nontaxable fringe benefits when (1) they include any amount received, directly or indirectly, by an employee under an accountable plan from an employer as a payment for, or reimbursement of, expenses that would be deductible by the employee as moving expenses; and (2) the employer can reasonably assume that those expenses would be deductible by the employee if paid by the employee. Such expenses are excluded from the wages subject to withholding and employment tax. [Pub. No. 521]

Q 9:314   What are the substantiation requirements that apply to moving expense reimbursements?

The exclusion from taxable wages for moving expense reimbursements is conditioned on the reimbursements being made from an accountable plan. Reimbursements from a nonaccountable plan are included in wages subject to FIT, FITW, FICA, and FUTA. [I.R.C. § 132] (See Q 9:22 for more information concerning the substantiation requirements.)

Q 9:315   Are there any special rules for the moving expenses of military personnel?

Yes. In addition to the moving expenses that qualify under Treasury Regulations Section 1.217-2, members of the armed forces are entitled to the following excludable expense reimbursements: move-in housing allowances, certain temporary lodging allowances, and dislocation allowances. [Treas. Reg. § 1.61-2(b)(2)]

Q 9:316   What is the mileage rate for auto travel related to moving from an old residence to a new residence?

An individual may be reimbursed for the actual cost of travel related to qualified moving expenses (e.g., airfare). If that travel is by automobile, the employee may be reimbursed in 2017 at a rate of $0.17 per mile (down from $0.19 cents per mile in 2016) or, if a log is kept, the actual cost of the auto use (e.g., gas and oil). Only one trip per family member is reimbursable. In addition to the cents-per-mile rate, reimbursement is allowed for tolls and parking expenses while moving from the old residence to the new. [I.R.C. § 1.217-2(b)(2); Pub. No. 521]

Q 9:317 What are the reporting requirements for moving expense reimbursements?

Nontaxable payments by the employer to a third party for qualified moving expenses are not reported on Form W-2.

Nontaxable moving expense reimbursements are not included in Boxes 1, 3, or 5 of Form W-2. These amounts are reported in Box 12, with a Code P, if paid directly to the employee. Qualified expenses paid directly to a third party (i.e., payments made directly to the moving company) are not included in Box 12 or in Boxes 1, 3, or 5. Amounts that do not qualify as moving expenses are treated as additional compensation and included in Boxes 1, 3, and 5 of Form W-2, but not Box 12. An employer is no longer required to report moving expense reimbursements or direct payments made on the employee's behalf on Form 4782, Employee Moving Expenses Information; however, it is recommended that a similar statement be provided to assist employees in completing Form 3903, which is attached to their Forms 1040. [OBRA '93 § 13213; I.R.C. §§ 62(a)(15), 132(a)(6), 217]

Nondiscrimination Requirements

Q 9:318 Who is a highly compensated employee?

The term *highly compensated employee* (HCE) is used to define the "prohibited group" for certain discrimination testing of a qualified pension plan (e.g., a 401(k) plan) and some fringe benefits. When no other definition is provided by the I.R.C. for a specific application, the most common definition used is that in Section 414(q). Under Section 414(q), an HCE for a plan year beginning in 2007 is any employee who either: (1) owned more than 5 percent of the employer in the current or prior plan year or (2) earned more than $125,000 in 2016. [I.R.C. § 414(q)]

For purposes of determining whether an individual is an HCE under the 5 percent stock ownership threshold, the I.R.C. attributes stock owned by a spouse, child, parent, or grandchild to the individual. In addition, an employee's option to purchase stock of a company generally is treated as being owned by the employee for this purpose. [I.R.C. § 318] To determine whether an individual is an HCE under the compensation threshold, use compensation after 401(k) salary deferrals, Section 125 salary reductions, or elective contributions to a Section 457 or 403(b) plan or salary reductions to a transportation benefit plan.

The compensation threshold for determining an HCE looks to the prior year; thus, the $125,000 threshold for a plan year beginning in 2017 looks only at compensation paid in the 2016 plan year and not the 2017 plan year. The compensation threshold for 2017 is $125,000.

The following schedule reflects the determination of whether an individual is an HCE for the 2017 plan year. (The individual below does not own any interest in the employer.)

	2016	2017
Compensation	$125,000	120,000
HCE for year	Yes	Yes
HCE threshold for prior year	$125,000	120,000

Note that under this definition a new employee who owns 5 percent or less of the employer will never be highly compensated in his or her first year of employment. There is no prior year compensation with this employer.

Q 9:319   How does the top-paid election apply in determining HCE classification?

One of the options available to a plan sponsor in preparing the annual nondiscrimination tests for a pension plan and certain fringe benefits is the ability to elect to limit the number of HCEs that may be included in the nondiscrimination testing (i.e., the top-paid group election). This election to limit the number of HCEs included in the testing applies only to individuals who are classified as HCEs, based on their compensation (i.e., owning more than 5 percent of the employer). The election limits the number of HCEs to the highest paid 20 percent of employees who worked in the prior year. The application of the top-paid election can lead to more favorable testing results. Individuals who are more than 5 percent owners in the current and prior year are HCEs, regardless of their compensation in the prior year.

The number of employees included in the calculation of the top-paid 20 percent basically includes all individuals (i.e., not just participants) employed in the lookback year less three excluded groups: (1) individuals who have not been employed at least six months (or who normally work fewer than six months) by the last day of the plan year, (2) those who normally work fewer than $17\frac{1}{2}$ hours per week, and (3) employees who are younger than age 21. A plan may modify these thresholds to a shorter service or younger age if applied on a uniform basis. Note that this exclusion is only applied to determine the number of employees in the top-paid test group.

These exclusions are not affected by the plan's eligibility provisions, which may require a year of service and attainment of a specific age. This permits a plan to provide for immediate entry but apply the 20 percent top-paid election to only those individuals who were employed six months or more. [I.R.C. § 414(q)(3); Treas. Reg. § 1.414(q)-1T, A-9(b)(2); Notice 97-45, sec. VII, 1997-33 I.R.B. 7]

The employer calculates the 20 percent threshold of the employee group not excluded under one of the criteria identified above. If the result is not a whole number, any reasonable rounding may be used (e.g., round to nearest whole number or round up). Thus, 20 percent of 11 employees will result in three HCEs, if rounding up, or two HCEs, if rounding to the nearest whole number. However, 20 percent of nine employees is two HCEs under any reasonable approach. If the resulting number is less than the number of individuals who earned at least $120,000 in the prior year, the highest paid individuals are HCEs in the current year, along with any 5 percent owners.

Note that any change in employment (e.g., termination) or compensation in the current year is ignored.

Example. Applying the Top-Paid Test to Determine HCEs in 2017.

Dream Machine, Inc. employs ten workers, three of whom earned over $120,000 in 2016 and none of whom owned more than 5 percent of Dream Machine, Inc. in 2016 and 2017. We will assume that all ten have worked more than six months and are over age 21. Under the top-paid election, for the 2017 plan year only Shawn is an HCE. Harold (who is in the top-paid group) terminated prior to the end of the 2016 plan year.

	Plan Year 2015 Compensation	Plan Year 2016 Compensation	An HCE in 2017
Shawn	$140,000	$142,000	Yes
Harold	135,000	None	No
Jewel	132,000	121,000	No
7 Non-HCEs	57,000 each	49,000 each	N/A

In this example, ten employees make up the individuals who are included in the top-paid HCE test group. Applying the 20 percent threshold to ten employees limits the number of individuals who may be treated as HCEs in 2017 based on their compensation in 2016 to Shawn and Harold. However, Harold terminated in 2016 and, as a result, has no compensation in 2017. As a result, only Shawn is included in the test group as an HCE for 2017, because Harold is omitted from all testing because he had no income in 2017.

If the top-paid test had not been elected, Shawn and Jewel would have been HCEs for testing in 2017.

Q 9:320 Who are the "key" employees for purposes of the I.R.C.'s nondiscrimination tests?

The rules for determining who are the "key employees" changed in 2002, greatly simplifying the determination as to who is a key employee.

A key employee is any employee who meets one of three classifications during the plan year: (1) an officer with compensation in excess of $170,000, as adjusted for cost-of-living increases (COLI), (2) a 5 percent owner of the employer, or (3) a 1 percent owner who received compensation in excess of $150,000.

In calculating whether the employee meets one of the ownership thresholds, an individual is treated as owning stock owned by a spouse, parent, child, or grandchild. Compensation for purposes of classifying individuals as key employees is gross compensation (i.e., includes 401(k) salary deferrals, employee contributions to a transportation benefit plan, Section 125 salary reduction, and certain elective contributions to a Section 403(b) annuity plan or Section 457 plan). [Prop. Treas. Reg. §§ 1.416.1; T-7Q to 7-14Q; see I.R.C. §§ 318(a), 416(i)(1)]

The annual compensation thresholds are based on gross compensation paid to the employee (i.e., includes 401(k) salary deferrals and Section 125 salary reduction). The thresholds for key employees are shown in the following chart.

	Compensation Threshold		
	2015	*2016*	*2017*
(1) Highly compensated employee/officer	$170,000	$170,000	$175,000
(2) Ownership regardless of income	5%	5%	5%
(3) 1% owner with income over	$150,000	$150,000	$150,000

By statutory definition, government employers do not have key employees. Therefore, government group-term life insurance plans are deemed to have satisfied the nondiscrimination requirements of I.R.C. Section 79 that apply to key employees. [I.R.C. § 416(i)(1)]

Q 9:321   Who are considered highly compensated employees under the nondiscrimination tests that apply to fringe benefits?

Treasury Regulations Section 1.132-8(f) contains a special definition that applies in determining who the HCEs are under the fringe benefit rules. Basically, these rules follow the rules for pension plans. A former employee is an HCE if the employee was highly compensated any time after age 55 or at the time employment terminated. [Treas. Reg. § 1.132-8(f)] It is important to remember that the I.R.C. identifies nondiscrimination rules and definitions relevant to its specific sections. One cannot rely on the pension rules or the fringe benefit special definition to determine who is highly compensated if the I.R.C. specifies nondiscrimination rules for that section.

Q 9:322   Who is a control employee for purposes of determining the value of the personal use of a company vehicle?

A control employee is an employee who works (1) for a government employer and is either an elected official or earns more than a federal employee at Executive Level V, $151,700 for 2017; or (2) in the private sector and is one of the following: (a) a director of the corporation; (b) a corporate officer earning at least $105,000 in 2017; (c) a 1 percent owner of the employer; or (d) an employee who earns at least $ 215,000 in 2017 (indexed annually). [Treas. Reg. §§ 1.61-21(f)(5), 1.61-21(f)(6); Pub. No. 15-B]

A special rule is available when an employer applies the commuting valuation rules or the FAVR method. Both government and private sector employers may apply the definition of HCE, rather than that of a control employee, under the pension rules. [Treas. Reg. § 1.132-8(f)]

Nonqualified Deferred Compensation

Q 9:323   What is a nonqualified deferred compensation plan?

A nonqualified deferred compensation plan is designed to provide retirement and/or preretirement death benefits to individuals who are classified under DOL regulations as "management and highly compensated employees." (This is not the same classification as HCE for pension tax laws.) These plans are typically for executives and other highly paid employees. Retirement benefits from these plans are seldom paid through a trust or other financial vehicle that is exempt from the claims of the employer's creditors. As a result, assets reserved by the employer to pay these retirement benefits are generally subject to forfeiture should the company go bankrupt. In some cases, the employer may establish a trust (i.e., a rabbi trust) as a company asset to prefund these benefits. However, rabbi trusts are grantor trusts with the employer as grantor that are subject to the claims of the employer's creditors.

Significantly increased scrutiny has been directed towards the taxation of nonqualified deferred compensation with the addition of I.R.C. Section 409A. These rules are quite complicated and continue to be a source of confusion and debate among payroll practitioners. While not all regulations have been finalized under Section 409A, the issues are discussed in Q 9:324 et. seq.

This element of forfeiture in the event of bankruptcy is key to the federal income taxation of benefits under a nonqualified plan, but not necessarily to the FICA and FUTA treatment of such benefits. The I.R.C. treats such a possibility as a limitation on the employee's right to receive retirement benefits, and thus the value of the benefit is not subject to federal income taxation or federal income tax withholding as long as the risk of forfeiture exists.

However, when the employer transfers the funds out of the company (e.g., sets up a secular trust) and those funds are no longer subject to the claims of the employer's creditors, the vested value of those funds is treated as additional compensation and is subject to federal income taxes and federal income tax withholding (and FICA and FUTA taxes unless previously reported).

A nonqualified deferred compensation plan may not involve any employee election to defer compensation. Most nonqualified plans of large corporations are fully employer-paid.

Note that ERISA, the federal law regulating pension plans, requires that these plans not cover any rank-and-file employees. That is, they must discriminate in favor of the highly paid employees. Should such a plan cover an individual who is not found by the DOL to constitute management and HCEs, the plan will become subject to ERISA and basically be a disqualified pension plan. [ERISA § 4021(b)]

Q 9:324   How did the American Jobs Creation Act of 2004 affect nonqualified deferred compensation plans?

The American Jobs Creation Act of 2004 significantly restricts the historic tax advantages associated with nonqualified deferred compensation plans. Plans or arrangements that are subject to these rules as set forth in I.R.C. Section 409A were required to be fully compliant with the final regulations under Section 409A by January 1, 2009.

Section 409A specifically addresses when a service provider may make an election to defer payments under a deferred compensation plan or arrangement, when compensation under a deferred compensation plan or arrangement may be distributed, and how a service provider may delay the receipt of payments under a deferred compensation plan or arrangement.

Each deferred compensation plan or arrangement (including employment agreements, severance agreements, and other similar arrangements) must be in writing and fully compliant with Section 409A by January 1, 2009.

"Deferred compensation" means almost every type of plan or arrangement in which compensation is paid in a year subsequent to the year in which the services were performed by the individual. Compensation is deferred when the service provider first has a legally binding right to the payment of compensation. Because the definition of deferred compensation is very broad, it not only encompasses traditional nonqualified deferred compensation plans such as the deferral of salary or bonuses, but also payments under employment agreements, severance agreements, and other similar arrangements. Tax-qualified plans such as 401(k) plans and IRAs are exempt from Section 409A, as are bona fide vacation, sick leave, disability pay and death benefit plans.

Failure to comply with Section 409A will have severe consequences to the service provider. Those consequences include immediate taxation of all amounts deferred under the plan or arrangement, assessment of an interest penalty for the underpayment of taxes during the deferral period, and an additional 20 percent penalty tax. In addition, the employer will have additional tax reporting requirements under Section 409A.

Reporting requirements. Beginning in calendar year 2007, an employer was not required to report amounts deferred during the year under a nonqualified deferred compensation plan subject to Section 409A in Box 12 of Form W-2 using code Y.

Also beginning with calendar year 2007, a payer was not required to report amounts deferred during the year under a nonqualified deferred compensation plan subject to Section 409A in Box 15a of Form 1099-MISC. Section 3401(a) provides that for income tax withholding purposes the term "wages" includes any amount includible in gross income of an employee under Section 409A, and payment of such amount is treated as having been made in the taxable year in which the amount is includible in gross income.

Thus, an employer has to treat amounts includible in gross income under Section 409A as wages for income tax withholding purposes. An employer is required to report such amounts as wages paid on line 2 of Form 941, Employer's QUARTERLY Federal Tax Return, and in Box 1 of Form W-2. An employer must also report such amounts as Section 409A income in Box 12 of Form W-2 using code Z. Amounts includible in gross income under Section 409A are supplemental wages for purposes of determining the amount of income tax required to be deducted and withheld under Section 3402(a), regardless of whether the employer has paid the employee any regular wages during the calendar year of the payment. The amount required to be withheld is not increased on account of the additional income taxes imposed under Section 409A(a)(1)(B). (Employees should thus be aware that estimated tax payments may be required to avoid penalties under Section 6654.)

For nonemployees, Section 6041(g)(2) requires a payer to report to a nonemployee any amount that is includible in gross income under Section 409A that is not treated as wages under Section 3401(a). Thus, for calendar year 2007, a payer had to report amounts includible in gross income under Section 409A and not treated as wages under Section 3401(a) as nonemployee compensation in Box 7 of Form 1099-MISC. A payer must also report such amounts as Section 409A income in Box 15b of Form 1099-MISC.

Pension Protection Act of 2006 funding requirements. Restrictions on funding nonqualified deferred compensation plans were added by Section 116 of the Pension Protection Act, amending I.R.C. Section 409A, effective August 17, 2006. [Pub. L. No. 109-280, 120 Stat. 780] The restrictions apply when any one of three conditions is present to limit funding of the nonqualified plan, including a rabbi trust.

The first restricted period occurs when a plan sponsor, or member of the plan sponsor's controlled group, has a single employer-defined benefit plan that is "at risk," which, in general, is defined as 80 percent underfunded. The requirements to determine at-risk status are found in Section 430(i)(4) of PPA's minimum funding standards provisions that take effect in 2008. The other two restricted periods occur when the plan sponsor is in bankruptcy, or the defined benefit plan is terminated in a distress or involuntary termination.

Teachers. Taxation of teacher salaries will not be affected by rules under I.R.C. Section 409A. The IRS acted to clear up confusion relating to elections to annualize recurring part-year compensation by issuing a news release and a list of "Frequently Asked Questions" relating specifically to the type of deferred compensation faced by teachers when their pay is spread over a 12-month period.

Key points made by the IRS include that the final rules under Section 409A do not require school districts to offer teachers an annualized election. In addition, the IRS exempts recurring part-year compensation from proposed regulations to be issued under I.R.C. Sections 457(f) and 409A, as long as the compensation is not deferred beyond a certain limited period of time. Recurring part-year compensation arrangements are commonly used in public schools to pay employees who work for 10 months but are paid ratably over a 12-month period. The anticipated guidance will specify that compensation will not be considered deferred compensation for purposes of I.R.C. Sections 457(f) and 409A if the recurring part-year compensation arrangements do not permit deferral of payment beyond the 13th month following the beginning of the service period, and do not permit deferral of more than the Section 402(g) amount from one taxable year to the next taxable year.

Rulings and determination letters. The IRS issued a no-ruling/no determination letter policy in Revenue Procedure 2008-3, as it relates to I.R.C. Section 409A. Subsequently, this position was modified for questions relating to the tax consequences of Section 409A. Specifically, the IRS said the no-ruling/no determination letter policy in Revenue Procedure 2008-3 "unnecessarily restricts the ability of the Service to issue private letter rulings" with respect to certain other tax law provisions that do not directly involve the application of Section 409A. Other tax law provisions are, for example, estate and gift tax consequences of certain transfers of rights and issues relating to application of the FICA under nonqualified deferred compensation plans.

The IRS will continue its no-ruling policy on issues concerning the income tax consequences of establishing, operating, or participating in a nonqualified deferred compensation plan described in I.R.C. Section 409A. Specifically, it will not issue rulings with respect to the income and withholding tax consequences of establishing, operating, or participating in a nonqualified deferred compensation plan as defined in the final regulations; whether a plan is subject to a totalization agreement, or whether it is a broad-based foreign retirement plan as described in the final regulations; whether a plan is a bona fide vacation leave, sick leave, or compensatory time plan described in the final regulations; and whether a plan provides for the deferral of compensation, including whether an amount is a short-term deferral and whether certain stock rights, foreign plans, and separation pay plans are subject to I.R.C. Section 409A.

Under the Emergency Economic Stabilization Act of 2008, if the Treasury Department buys troubled assets directly and receives a meaningful equity or debt position in the financial institution resulting from the transaction, the institution must: (1) exclude incentives for senior executive officers to take "unnecessary and excessive risks that threaten the value of the financial institution" while the secretary holds an equity or debt position in the financial institution (the "authorities period"); (2) include a "clawback" provision for the financial institution to recover any bonus or incentive compensation paid to a senior executive officer based on earnings, gains, or other criteria that are proven later to be materially inaccurate; and (3) prohibit golden parachute payments to senior executive officers during the authorities period. [Pub. L. No. 110-343, 122 Stat. 3765]

Corrections. Notice 2007-100 [2007-52 I.R.B. 1243] provides guidance for correcting certain unintentional operational failures of nonqualified deferred compensation plan provisions subject to Section 409A; provided, however, that these unintentional operational failures are corrected in the same taxable year. This notice also provides transition relief through 2010 for operational failures involving amounts up to the limit on elective deferrals under I.R.C. Section 402(g) that are not corrected in the same taxable year by limiting the amount of income inclusion and additional taxes. The IRS has provided additional guidance for correcting failures under Section 409A in Notice 2010-80 with clarification on types of plans that are linked to a qualified plan or another nonqualified plan provided the linkage does not affect the time and form of payments under the plan, the types of plans that may include certain stock rights and correcting certain failures that relate to payments at separation of service that require certain release forms. This notice modifies certain provisions of Notice 2008-113 involving the amounts to be reported under Section 409A,

Foreign nonqualified deferred compensation. Also under the Emergency Economic Stabilization Act of 2008, I.R.C. Section 457A was added, requiring individuals to be taxed on a current basis on deferred compensation received from a "tax indifferent party," even if the promise to pay is unfunded and unsecured. Foreign corporations and partnerships comprised of foreign persons—for example, certain hedge funds or private equity funds—have no offsetting deduction to be deferred.

Foreign corporations and partnerships comprised of foreign persons—for example, certain hedge funds or private equity funds—have no offsetting deduction to be deferred. As a result, employees receiving deferred compensation from these tax indifferent parties benefit from the deferral, while these corporations and partnerships are indifferent to the timing of the payments.

Under I.R.C. Section 457A, any compensation that is deferred under a nonqualified deferred compensation plan is includible in gross income when there is no substantial risk of forfeiture. The provision applies to two classes of entities: any foreign corporation, unless substantially all of its income is "effectively connected" with a trade or business in the United States; or any partnership comprised of foreign persons that are not subject to: U.S. income tax, a comprehensive foreign income tax, or tax-exempt entities. The exception for partnerships subject to a comprehensive foreign income tax might apply if a comprehensive tax is imposed by an income tax treaty.

"Nonqualified deferred compensation plan," under the provision, has the same meaning under I.R.C. Section 409A(d), except that it includes any plan that provides a right to compensation based on the appreciation in value of a specified number of equity units. The provision does not apply to compensation that would have been deductible by a foreign corporation taxed under I.R.C. Section 882 had it been paid in cash on the date it was no longer subject to a substantial risk of forfeiture.

Also, this provision applies in addition to I.R.C. Section 409A, and any other I.R.C. provisions or tax law principles that apply to nonqualified deferred compensation, such as I.R.C. Section 83, which requires that substantial services must be performed before compensation is vested.

The provision is effective for amounts deferred that are attributable to services performed beginning January 1, 2009. For amounts to which the provision does not apply solely because they are attributable to service performed before January 1, 2009, to the extent it is not includible in gross income in a tax year beginning before 2018, applicable nonqualified deferred compensation will be includible in the later of the last taxable year beginning before 2018, or the taxable year in which there is no substantial risk of forfeiture (determined under Section 457A).

Guidance. The IRS issued interim guidance in question and answer format on identifying plans and plan sponsors covered under I.R.C. Section 457A and on determining whether the sponsor is a nonqualified entity. [Interim Guidance Under § 457A, Notice 2009-8, 2009-4 I.R.B. 347] Generally, the notice uses the Section 409A(d) definition of a nonqualified deferred compensation plan, with some modifications. Under I.R.C. Section 457A, the rights to compensation are subject to a substantial risk of forfeiture only if those rights "are conditioned upon the future performance of substantial services" by the person.

The IRS said Section 457A does not include short-term deferrals in the definition of deferred compensation. The notice in Q&A 4 defines "short-term deferrals" as "compensation that is paid no later than 12 months after the end of the service recipient's taxable year during which the right to the payment of the compensation is first no longer subject to a substantial risk of forfeiture."

The term "nonqualified entity" refers to any foreign corporation, except ones for which substantially all of their income is effectively derived from conduct of a trade or business in the United States or is subject to a comprehensive foreign income tax, the IRS said. A nonqualified entity can also mean any partnership except ones for which substantially all of their income is allocated to tax-exempt organizations or to foreign individuals for whom the income is not subject to a comprehensive foreign income tax.

Until the IRS issues further guidance, taxpayers may rely on the rules in Notice 2009-8 for purposes of I.R.C. Section 457A effective from October 3, 2008, the notice said.

Change of control: The IRS issued Notice 2009-49, which provides that purchases of equity interests in financial institutions by the Treasury Department will not be considered a change in control event under I.R.C. Section 409A. [Notice 2009-49, 2009-25 I.R.B. 1093] Under the Emergency Economic Stabilization Act of 2008 (EESA) [Pub. L. No. 110-343, 122 Stat. 3765], preferred stock, common stock, and warrants to purchase common stock or other types of equity may be purchased by or on behalf of the Treasury pursuant to the EESA Equity Acquisition Transaction program. Treating the government's investment as a change in control and, therefore, a permissible payment event, "would be inconsistent with the purposes of EESA and Section 409A, and would be contrary to the public interest," the notice said.

The notice also addressed EESA's effect on the final regulations under Section 409A. A nonqualified deferred compensation plan that fails in the plan document to explicitly provide that a Treasury EESA Equity Acquisition Transaction is not a change in control payment trigger will not fail to satisfy the plan document requirements of I.R.C. Section 409A(a), the notice said.

Q 9:325 How are nonqualified deferred compensation plans treated for FICA and FUTA tax purposes?

Employer contributions (and any employee salary deferrals) made to nonqualified deferred compensation plans are generally subject to FICA and FUTA taxes (but excluded from wages subject to FIT and FITW) when the services related to the plan's benefits are performed, or, if later, when the employee no longer has a substantial risk of forfeiting his or her right to the deferred compensation. This is typically when the employee vests in the benefits. Vested benefits that are subject to FICA and FUTA are not subject to FICA and FUTA when paid. The value of vested deferred compensation is taxable to an employee at the earlier of when amounts can be withdrawn, or the benefits are no longer subject to forfeiture should the company become bankrupt (i.e., they are constructively received). [Pub. No. 15-A]

In most cases where the benefits are subject to FICA or FUTA, only the Medicare portion of FICA taxes applies because the employee's compensation exceeds the Social Security and FUTA wage base. [I.R.C. §§ 3121(v)(2), 3306(r)(2)]

Q 9:326 What is the difference between a nonqualified deferred compensation plan and a disqualified pension plan?

A nonqualified deferred compensation plan is a plan for certain company executives or key management that has been designed to avoid the trust funding, vesting, minimum coverage, and nondiscrimination requirements of ERISA. When this is successfully done, the benefits can be discriminatory (i.e., be limited to a select group of management or HCEs). A qualified plan is a plan designed to comply with ERISA and must by law cover a broad classification of employees, use a trust to hold the funds, and satisfy minimum coverage and nondiscrimination requirements of the I.R.C. As long as such a plan meets these I.R.C. requirements, it is qualified. All employer contributions to a qualified plan are currently deductible and exempt from FIT and FITW (until paid) and are excluded from FICA and FUTA. Benefits are subject to FIT and FITW only when the benefits are paid. A special rule treats an employee's before-tax (federal income taxes) 401(k) contribution as wages for FICA and FUTA purposes when contributed as a salary deferral.

A disqualified "qualified" plan is a qualified plan that has failed to satisfy one or more of the requirements of the I.R.C. and has lost all of its tax-favored status. The value of retirement benefits under a disqualified plan is included in wages subject to FIT and FITW to the extent the benefits are funded and vested, even if benefits are not payable for several years. These "deemed distributions" are reported on Form 1099-R. A disqualified plan must continue to comply with all the vesting, funding, reporting, and coverage requirements of ERISA. Thus, when a nonqualified deferred compensation plan covers a rank-and-file employee, it becomes a disqualified plan subject to all the requirements of ERISA. [I.R.C. § 401(a); ERISA § 4021(b)(6)]

Q 9:327   What is a funded nonqualified deferred compensation plan?

From a technical standpoint, the term *funded plan* refers to an arrangement in which an employer irrevocably transfers the assets relating to the payment of the deferred compensation to a separate entity not subject to the claims of the employer's creditors (i.e., transferred to a secular trust). If at that time the funded benefits become vested, the employee is treated as receiving compensation that is subject to federal income taxes as a transfer of property. Then the value is included in wages subject to FIT, FITW, FICA, and FUTA if not previously reported. [I.R.C. § 83; Treas. Reg. §§ 1.83-3(e), 1.451-2] These funded amounts are treated as additional compensation and reported in Boxes 1, 3, 5, and 11 of Form W-2.

The tax treatment of benefits accrued in an unfunded plan differs from the tax treatment of benefits accrued in a funded plan. Benefits from an unfunded plan are not subject to federal income taxes until paid. Employees and employers frequently misclassify unfunded plans as funded plans when corporate assets (e.g., a life insurance policy or a rabbi trust) are merely earmarked to pay benefits but the assets are subject to the claims of creditors. From a technical standpoint, such a plan is deemed to be unfunded. An employer sometimes establishes a grantor trust, with the employer as grantor to prefund benefits. These arrangements are generally referred to as rabbi trusts and are not classified as "funded" for I.R.C. purposes. Earnings in grantor trust are taxable to the grantor (i.e., employer). In general, benefits under an unfunded nonqualified deferred compensation plan are subject to FICA and FUTA when the benefits vest, and FIT and FITW apply when the benefits are payable. Employers that fail to collect and report the FICA and FUTA taxes when benefits vest will cause the FICA and FUTA taxes to be underreported and potentially subject to penalties. Restrictions on funding nonqualified deferred compensation plans were added by Section 116 of the Pension Protection Act, amending I.R.C. Section 409A, effective August 17, 2006. [Pub. L. No. 109-280, 120 Stat. 780] The restrictions apply when any one of three conditions is present to limit funding of the nonqualified plan, including a rabbi trust. The first restricted period occurs when a plan sponsor, or member of the plan sponsor's controlled group, has a single employer-defined benefit plan that is "at risk," which, in general, is defined as 80 percent underfunded. The requirements to determine at-risk status are found in Section 430(i)(4) of PPA's minimum funding standards provisions that take effect in 2008. The other two restricted periods occur when the plan sponsor is in bankruptcy, or the defined benefit plan is terminated in a distress or involuntary termination.

Q 9:328 When are distributions from a nonqualified deferred compensation plan reported on Form SSA-131?

Form SSA-131, Employer Reporting of Special Wage Payments, is used to report wage payments from a nonqualified deferred compensation plan or a Section 457 plan to an individual who has attained age 62 by the end of the tax year, when deferrals vest and payments are made in the same year. [Pub. No. 957, Reporting Back Pay and Special Wage Payments to the Social Security Administration] Do not report amounts in Box 11 of the employee's Form W-2 that were reported on Form SSA-131. This form is used to notify the SSA of the participant's earnings attributable to a prior year.

Q 9:329 When are amounts distributed from a nonqualified deferred compensation plan reported on Form W-2 or 1099?

When a nonqualified deferred compensation plan fails to comply with the new rules under I.R.C. Section 409A, and an amount is required to be included in an individual participant's income, it must be reported on the individual's Form W-2 (or Form 1099) for the year in which the distribution amount is includible in income. In addition, the total amount of an employee's *deferrals* under a nonqualified deferred compensation plan is reported on Form W-2 (or 1099), even if the amounts are not included in the employee's income for that year. [I.R.C. § 6051(a)(13)]

Q 9:330 What are the most current employment tax rules that apply to nonqualified deferred compensation plans?

The American Jobs Creation Act of 2004 had a significant impact on nonqualified deferred compensation plans, and in particular, imposes new restrictions in the funding and distribution from such plans (see Q 9:323 et. seq.). Regulations issued in 1999 under Section 3121(v) address the FICA treatment of benefits earned under a nonqualified deferred compensation plan. These regulations clarify several of the most common questions relating to the FICA tax treatment of nonqualified deferred compensation plan benefits, such as (1) clarification of the treatment of benefits under a nonqualified deferred compensation plan classified as a "nonaccount" balance plan; (2) improvements to the "true-up" rules where an employer is permitted to apply an early inclusion date for the benefit; (3) expanded use of the "lag" method and the "estimated" method; and (4) certain employer-friendly transition rules. [Treas. Reg. § 31.3121(v)(2)-2]

Q 9:331 What types of nonqualified deferred compensation plans are subject to FICA and FUTA?

For FICA (and FUTA) purposes, nonqualified deferred compensation plans include (1) defined contribution-type supplemental employee retirement plans (SERPs), (2) defined benefit-type SERPs and excess benefit plans, and

(3) phantom stock plans (plans that pay benefits equal to the value of a specified number of shares of employer stock). The distinction between the type of plans is important to understanding the FICA and FUTA treatment of the benefit under the plan.

The current regulations apply two sets of valuation rules to these benefits based on whether the plan is classified as an account balance plan or a nonaccount balance plan. Account balance plans have three characteristics: (1) principal amounts are credited to the employee's individual account; (2) net income attributable to the principal amounts is credited (or debited) to the individual account; and (3) benefits payable to the employee are based solely on the balance credited to the individual account. That is, account balance plans are defined contribution SERPs, whereas nonaccount balance plans are defined benefit SERPs. Note that the term *deferred compensation* includes nonqualified plans that have no employee deferral and are solely paid by the employer. [Treas. Reg. § 31.3121(v)(2)]

In March 2007, the IRS ruled that accrual-basis taxpayers who meet certain tests may deduct FICA taxes on deferred compensation before the year in which the deferred compensation is actually paid. [Rev. Rul. 2007-12, 2007-11 I.R.B. 685.] The ruling reversed a 38-year-old ruling under which the IRS maintained that an accrual-basis taxpayer could not deduct otherwise-deductible payroll taxes until the year the deferred compensation itself was paid and deductible.

Under I.R.C. Section 404(a)(5), nonqualified deferred compensation is not deductible until the taxable year in which the compensation is includible in the employee's gross income (the matching rule). Employment taxes, however, are not subject to the same rules as the income tax. Under I.R.C. Section 3121(v)(2), deferred compensation is generally subject to FICA and FUTA taxes as of the later of the performance of services or the time when there is no longer a substantial risk of forfeiture of the right to the deferred compensation. This means that in the case of vested deferred compensation, payroll taxes are payable when the services are performed, even though the deferred compensation may be paid much later.

In Revenue Ruling 2007-12, the IRS ruled that the matching rule under I.R.C. Section 404 does not apply to an accrual-basis taxpayer's payroll tax liability. Provided the employer meets the standard timing rules under I.R.C. Section 461, the employer's payroll taxes will be deductible in the year services are performed. Under the timing rules, an amount is deductible when all the events have occurred that establish the fact of the liability, the amount of the liability is determinable with reasonable accuracy, and economic performance has occurred with respect to the liability.

The IRS did make clear in the ruling that changing the treatment of payroll tax liabilities would constitute a change in method of accounting. Taxpayers must obtain the consent of the IRS under I.R.C. Section 446(e) and Treasury Regulation § 1.446-1(e)(2)(i).

Q 9:332 How are the benefits under a nonqualified deferred compensation plan, an account balance plan, and a nonaccount balance plan valued for FICA and FUTA purposes?

Account balance plans. The value of a benefit under a nonqualified deferred compensation plan classified as an account balance plan is equal to the vested portion of the principal amount credited to the employee's account for the period. Where benefits under the plan are subject to a delayed vesting schedule, this value is included in wages, subject to FICA and FUTA, and increased or decreased by any income attributable to that amount through the date that amount must be taken into account as FICA wages (generally when the benefits vest). If FICA and FUTA are applied as benefits vest, the nonduplication rule will apply at the time benefits are paid. This will serve to avoid FICA and FUTA on income attributable to principal based on (1) the actual rate of return on a predetermined actual investment or (2) a reasonable rate of interest (if no predetermined actual investment has been specified). Where the nonduplication rule does not apply (i.e., the earnings on principal under the plan exceed these thresholds, or amounts were not reported when vested), the amount of income subject to the nonduplication rule is limited to amounts determined under the midterm AFR for the first day of the calendar year. Excess income over that amount is considered additional principal and is included in wages subject to FICA and FUTA each year. Where either the principal or the excess amounts are reported as they become vested, the accumulated value of benefits attributable to these amounts is not subject to FICA and FUTA when paid. [Treas. Reg. § 31.3121(v)(2)]

Nonaccount balance plans. For these plans, the participant does not receive an accounting of the funds accumulated to pay benefits (as with an account plan). Rather, the participant is awarded with the amount of a monthly retirement benefit paid at retirement (e.g., a monthly benefit of $100 payable beginning at age 65 was earned in 2001). FICA and FUTA apply to the current value of the accrual of benefit on the earlier of (1) the earliest date on which the value of the benefit under the plan is reasonably ascertainable or (2) an amount that is reasonably ascertainable when it can be determined using only interest, mortality, or cost-of-living assumptions. An amount is not reasonably ascertainable if additional assumptions are required to determine the value of the benefit (e.g., future pay or the time or form of benefit payments). This approach was taken by the IRS to avoid situations where the employer might overestimate its FICA and FUTA tax liability and then be required to file for a refund for open tax years. Note that FICA and FUTA apply not to $100 (the monthly benefit beginning at age 65) but to the present value of that benefit as of 2001, when it is first accrued.

The regulations allow an employer to calculate and pay FICA at an earlier date. This will result in a lower amount being subject to FICA. These regulations allow employers to apply a "true-up" at the time that the actual value can be ascertained. If there is an overpayment at that time, the employer may claim a refund or credit for open tax years. [Treas. Reg. § 31.3121(v)(2)]

Q 9:333   If amounts under a nonqualified deferred compensation plan cannot be readily ascertained, when are they subject to FICA and FUTA?

The value of the benefit deferred or accrued in the year that is no longer subject to substantial risk of forfeiture (i.e., becomes vested) is subject to FICA and FUTA. With some plan designs it may not be easy to ascertain the value subject to FICA and FUTA in the current year. The regulations provide alternatives if the employer cannot readily calculate the amount subject to FICA and FUTA for the year by December 31. Under an estimated method allowed in the regulations, employers may treat a reasonably estimated amount as wages paid on the last day of the calendar year. If the employer underestimates the amount deferred, the employer may treat the shortfall as wages subject to FICA and FUTA either in the first year or in the first quarter of the next year. If the amount is overestimated, the employer may claim a refund or credit of the FICA and FUTA.

The employer is also permitted to apply a lag method in determining the amount subject to FICA and FUTA. Under the lag method, the employer may calculate the end-of-year amount on any date in the first quarter of the next calendar year. The lag method could create higher FICA taxes for employees who terminate employment before other FICA wages in the lag year exceed the FICA wage base. [Treas. Reg. § 31.3121(v)(2)]

Q 9:334   What transition rules apply where an employer could not determine how to apply the old valuation rules for nonqualified plans?

The IRS developed a set of transition rules that apply to the value of benefits accrued prior to 1994. It should be noted that these transition rules were established prior to the establishment of Section 409A, and should be relied upon only where the current rules are not applicable. One transition rule applies for periods before 1994 where the employer acted in accordance with a reasonable, good-faith interpretation of I.R.C. Section 3121(v)(2). Under this rule, a vested benefit earned before 1994 that would have been required to be treated as FICA wages is treated as if it had been subject to FICA as determined under the final regulations. This means that the nonduplication rule will apply as if the benefits had been reported. For example, the employer was not able to determine the benefit that should have been treated as FICA wages under a nonaccount plan because it was not reasonably ascertainable under existing IRS guidance. The employer is treated as having reported the amount for FICA purposes and the accumulated value for the benefit will not be subject to FICA. The FUTA rules follow the same requirements.

A transition rule applies to amounts that were required to be taken into account in 1994 or 1995. An employer will be treated as taking the amounts into account under the final regulations to the extent the employer had reported the proper amounts before April 1, 2000. The amount taken into account before April 1, 2000, is not required to be increased by attributable income or interest.

That is, only the original principal at the date the benefit vested is required to be reported. [Treas. Reg. § 31.3121(v)(2)]

Outplacement Services

Q 9:335   What are outplacement services?

Outplacement services help an employee or former employee find a new job after a layoff, a reduction in force, or termination. These services may be provided by the employer, but are typically provided by outplacement agencies that are paid by the employer. The most common services include résumé preparation, interview training, and help in locating potential jobs. [Rev. Rul. 92-69, 1992-2 C.B. 51]

Q 9:336   How are outplacement services treated for payroll tax purposes?

When the employer provides outplacement services (such as career counseling, résumé assistance, or skills assessment), they qualify as a working condition fringe benefit for employees or former employees to help them find new employment if two conditions are met. First the employer receives a substantial business benefit from offering the services. This could be promoting a positive business image, maintaining employee morale or avoiding wrongful termination suits. The second requirement is that the outplacement services are distinct from the benefit of the payment of additional wages. If these conditions are met, the outplacement services qualify as a working condition benefit and are not taxable and not subject to FIT, FITW, FICA, and FUTA.

If the employer allows the employee to receive cash or taxable benefits in place of the outplacement services, then the outplacement services do not qualify as a working condition fringe benefit. Also, if there is a severance plan and employees have the option to take a reduced severance plan along with the outplacement services, the difference between the reduced severance plan and the unreduced severance pay is wages subject to FIT, FITW, FICA, or FUTA. and included in Boxes 1, 3, and 5 of the employee's Form W-2. [I.R.C. §§ 3121(a)(21), 3306(b)(16); Pub 15-B]

Pension and Profit Sharing Plans

Annuities and Pensions

Q 9:337   How are pensions and annuities treated for employment tax purposes?

A taxable distribution from a qualified plan (as opposed to employer payments) generally is subject to FITW under one of three methods: (1) a distribution that satisfies the definition of being an "eligible rollover distribution" is subject to a mandatory 20 percent federal income tax withholding on the taxable value of the distribution; (2) periodic distributions that are not classified as eligible "rollover distributions" are subject to FITW as if the payment was a payment of wages; and (3) nonperiodic distributions that are also not classified as a rollover distribution are subject to a flat 10 percent withholding unless the participant elects no federal income tax withholding. Under items (2) and (3), the participant or beneficiary may waive all federal income tax withholding. The amount that is to be withheld is based on the FMV of the assets distributed. Certain participant loans in default are treated as a distribution, but are exempted from a withholding requirement unless cash is also distributed. The I.R.C. provides a general exemption from any withholding on an eligible rollover distribution when the participant does not receive a total distribution of $200 or more in the calendar year. [I.R.C. §§ 3405(a)(1), 3405(b)(1); Rev. Proc. 92-93, 1992-2 C.B. 505; Treas. Reg. §§ 31.3405-1T, Q-6, 31.3405(c)-1, Q-14]

Taxable distributions from a qualified retirement plan are not subject to FICA or FUTA taxes. [I.R.C. §§ 3121(a)(5), 3306(b)(5)]

An "eligible rollover distribution" may escape current taxation and mandatory withholding when distributed as a direct rollover (a direct transfer to another plan or to an IRA). There is no withholding on any part of any plan distribution that is not expected to be includible in the recipient's gross income. For example, portions of distributions that consist of an employee's aftertax distributions or a participant loan that was a "deemed distribution" and was later repaid are not subject to federal income tax or withholding. There is generally no exemption from federal employment taxes for retirement benefits paid directly by the employer unless the benefits are paid from a nonqualified deferred compensation plan. However, ERISA, the federal law controlling retirement plans, limits such benefits to only the highest paid employees. [I.R.C. §§ 3405(a), 3405(e)(10); Treas. Reg. § 5.3405-1B; Rev. Rul. 65-276, 1965-2 C.B. 386]

ERISA requires the plan administrator to provide a written explanation to the recipient within a reasonable period of time before making an eligible rollover distribution that discusses the federal income tax treatment of the distribution. This notice must explain the rollover rules, special tax treatment for lump-sum distributions, direct rollover option, and mandatory 20 percent withholding rule if benefits are to be paid in cash. Notice 2000-11 [2000-6 I.R.B. 572] and Notice 2002-3 [2002-2 I.R.B. 1] contain a model notice that can be used to satisfy this requirement. Distributions from a qualified plan are reported on Form 1099-R. [Treas. Reg. 35.3405-1, D-3; I.R.C. §§ 6652(h), 6047(d), 6704]

Benefits Under a Qualified Plan

Q 9:338   What is the largest contribution that a participant's account can receive under a qualified plan?

For 2017, a participant in a profit sharing or other defined contribution plan cannot receive an allocation of any employer or employee contribution that in the aggregate exceeds the lesser of (1) $54,000 or (2) 100 percent of the individual's gross compensation. [I.R.C. § 415(c)] Note that there is a practical danger in allowing a participant to defer 100 percent of compensation because deferrals are subject to FICA, thus leaving an employee without funds to have FICA deducted without the employer altering the deferral amount. In addition, any deductions for other benefits (i.e., health care) could again leave the employee unable to pay what has been elected.

The maximum salary deferral that may be made in 2017 is $18,000. This $18,000 contribution limit is included in the overall $54,000 maximum limit. [I.R.C. § 402(g)] The maximum salary deferral for a SIMPLE Plan in 2017 is $12,500. The catch-up contribution for participants over the age of 50 may increase the maximum salary deferral by $6,000. These are referred to as *catch-up contributions*. This contribution is not part of the $54,000 or the $18,000 limits in 2017, nor is it subject to any I.R.C. limits that apply to other salary deferrals.

This limitation applies to all plans of any employers that constitute an employer group under common control (as determined under I.R.C. Section 414(b) or (c)) or are part of an affiliated service group under I.R.C. Section 414(m). [Treas. Reg. § 1.415-2(b)(1)]

The catch-up contribution is $6,000 for 2017 for SIMPLE plans. [I.R.C. § 414(v)(2)(B)(ii)(10)]

Combined defined benefit plans and qualified cash or deferred arrangements. Under the Pension Protection Act of 2006, a small employer (i.e., an employer with an average of at least two but not more than 500 employees) may establish a combined defined benefit Section 401(k) plan governed by one document and having specific accounting for the defined benefit and defined contribution portions of the trust. Generally, under the law, the defined benefit rules would apply to the defined benefit portion of the plan, and the defined contribution rules would apply to the defined contribution portion of the plan. [Pub. L. No. 109-280, 120 Stat. 780]

Also, the Worker, Retiree, and Employer Recovery Act of 2008 [Pub. L. No. 110-458, 122 Stat. 5092] states that an employer's deduction limitations for contributions to defined benefit and defined contribution plans are superseded by a combined plan limit if an employer maintains both kinds of plans. The employer's annual deductible contribution for combined plans is generally limited to the greater of (1) 25 percent of compensation or (2) the amount necessary to meet the minimum funding requirement of the defined benefit plan for the year. The law clarifies that in the case of a single-employer plan not covered by the Pension Benefit Guaranty Corporation, the combined plan limit is not less than the excess (if any) of the plan's funding target over the value of the plan's assets.

Q 9:339   Are retirement benefits provided under a qualified retirement plan taxable to the employee any time prior to being paid?

Generally, no. Although the doctrine of constructive receipt generally taxes the right to receive income, even if no election to receive the income is made, the doctrine of constructive receipt does not apply to a right to receive benefits from a tax-qualified plan when the individual has the right to receive a benefit but does not request payment. As a result, retirement benefits under a tax-qualified pension or profit sharing plan are not subject to FIT or FITW until paid as benefits. Employer contributions to tax-qualified pension, profit sharing, or stock bonus plans are excluded from an employee's taxable wages until paid as benefits and are never subject to FICA or FUTA. Salary deferrals (pretax employee contributions to a 401(k) plan) are subject to FICA and FUTA but FITW does apply when amounts are contributed.

To be treated as tax qualified, such plans must be funded, meet certain vesting and participation standards, satisfy special nondiscrimination rules, and comply with benefit distribution and other requirements contained in Section 401(a). But note that the unpaid balance of certain participant loans made from a plan becomes taxable when any of the I.R.C. or regulatory requirements applicable to such loans are not met. [I.R.C. §§ 72(p), 3121(a)(5)(A), 3121(a)(5)(F), 3306(b)(5)(A), 3306(b)(5)(F), 3401(a)(12)(A)]

Q 9:340   When are distributions from a qualified pension plan exempt from federal income tax withholding?

All "eligible rollover" distributions are subject to FITW of 20 percent. However, eligible rollover distributions from a qualified pension or profit sharing plan that are made as a direct transfer to another plan or IRA are not subject to FITW because there is no taxable distribution. Retirees who are receiving periodic benefits (e.g., monthly benefits) generally must be given a right to elect not to have withholding on the "periodic payments" at least once a year. The portion of any other distribution not classified as an eligible rollover distribution (e.g., hardship distribution) is subject to a 10 percent federal income tax withholding requirement that may be waived. In addition, certain distributions of employer stock from a qualified plan that include portions of net unrealized appreciation are also not subject to FITW. [Treas. Reg. § 31.3405(c)-1T]

Q 9:341   What is an "eligible rollover distribution" that is subject to a mandatory 20 percent withholding?

An "eligible rollover distribution" is any distribution from a qualified plan that can, under the I.R.C., be rolled over to another qualified plan or IRA. An eligible rollover distribution is generally any distribution of all or a portion of the balance to the credit of the employee in the plan. An eligible rollover distribution does not include the portion of any distribution that would not be included in the taxable income of the participant (e.g., the portion of a distribution including aftertax contributions). The plan administrator is required to notify participants when a distribution that they are eligible to receive is an eligible rollover distribution.

A distribution would not be classified as an eligible rollover distribution when it consists of any of the following:

1. A required minimum distribution made under Section 401(a)(9);

2. Any distribution that is one of a series of substantially equal periodic payments made over a period of at least 10 years or over the life expectancy of the participant (or of the life expectancy of the participant and a designated beneficiary);

3. A corrective distribution of excess contributions, excess deferrals, or excess annual additions under a qualified 401(k) plan; or

4. Any hardship distribution.

An eligible rollover distribution made to a participant can be rolled over to a plan or IRA. Such a distribution would be subject to withholding at 20 percent. In addition, a participant can avoid the 20 percent withholding by making a direct rollover—the plan administrator transfers the funds directly to an IRA or a plan.

Any distribution meeting the preceding requirements that also is being made subject to the minimum required distributions of the I.R.C. (e.g., after age 70 ½) may not be rolled over.

Q 9:342   What are the withholding rules that apply to pensions and other periodic distributions that are not rollover distributions?

A periodic distribution (e.g., retiree benefits) that is not an "eligible rollover distribution" is subject to FITW as if the amounts were paid to the participant or beneficiary as wages. A periodic distribution is not an eligible rollover distribution when it is either paid as a series of substantially equal payments made over the participant's life expectancy or, if less, for a period of at least 10 years. [I.R.C. § 3405(a)(1)] Withholding on a periodic distribution may be waived when the participant completes a Form W-4P. Distributions from qualified plans are not subject to FICA or FUTA.

Q 9:343   How can a retiree elect not to have federal taxes withheld?

A retiree who is receiving periodic distributions subject to FITW from a former employer's plan may complete Form W-4P to elect not to have federal income taxes withheld. This form can also be used to determine the amount of federal income taxes to be withheld.

Certain retirees cannot elect to waive withholding by the plan for the following periodic distributions: (1) payments mailed to individuals residing outside the United States, (2) payments to individuals who have not provided a residence address in the United States, and (3) payments to participants or beneficiaries who have not provided a Social Security number or have provided an invalid number. [Form W-4P instructions]

Q 9:344 What are the requirements that apply to recipients of pension and annuity payments who elect not to have withholding apply?

Recipients of pension and annuity payments can choose not to have withholding apply to their pensions or annuities when the distribution is classified as a "periodic distribution." The election remains in effect until the recipient revokes it. The payer must notify the recipient that this election is available. Note that certain payments from pension and profit sharing plans are subject to mandatory withholding if they satisfy the definition for being paid as an "eligible rollover" distribution. For example, a retiree who under the plan can make an annual election to determine the amount to receive each month is generally treated as receiving eligible rollover distributions subject to a mandatory 20 percent withholding on those distributions. [Pub. No. 15-A]

Q 9:345 How are annuity payments paid by an employer to a retired executive treated for employment tax purposes?

Governmental employers are permitted under law to pay retiree benefits directly to former employees. However, ERISA generally prohibits nongovernmental employers from paying retirement benefits directly to former employees (other than benefits for a select group of HCEs and management under a nonqualified deferred compensation plan). Such benefits must be provided through a trusted ERISA plan. An ERISA plan is required to provide for minimum funding, minimum coverage, and minimum vesting, and otherwise comply with I.R.C. Section 401(a). Thus, employers are generally prevented from providing retirement benefits on a pay-as-you-go basis to an individual other than an executive.

An employer may decide to award a pension benefit to a specific employee at the time of retirement by purchasing an annuity and transferring it to the employee. Severe penalties under ERISA apply if this becomes a pattern or is part of a "promise" made to a rank-and-file employee prior to retirement. Where an employer buys an annuity and transfers the annuity to the employee, the employee is treated as receiving wages equal to the value of the annuity on the date it is transferred. At the time of the transfer it is reported as taxable wages and fully subject to federal income tax withholding and FICA and FUTA taxes on the date it is transferred. [Treas. Reg. § 1.83-1]

Q 9:346   What are the distribution rules that apply to withholding on noncash assets distributed from a plan?

There is basically no exemption from FITW when noncash assets are distributed from a qualified plan. Withholding is calculated on the FMV of the assets distributed. Withholding is made from the cash portion of the distributions and, if necessary, the cash proceeds from the sale of any noncash assets distributed. The participant may avoid such a sale by providing cash to the plan administrator to satisfy the withholding obligation. The employer may use the most recent valuation of the noncash asset to determine the amount of the withholding. (The I.R.C. requires that a plan value all assets at least once a year.) [Treas. Reg. §§ 31.3405(c)-1, A(10), 35.3405-1, F-1 to F-4]

Special rules apply when the noncash assets are employer securities or if a portion of the distribution is attributable to a loan offset for a delinquent participant loan. A distribution that consists solely of employer securities is exempt from withholding. [I.R.C. § 3405(e)(8); Treas. Reg. § 31.3405(c)-1, Q-11] When a distribution of employer stock includes a distribution of at least $200 or other property, this exemption from withholding is lost, to the extent that other property is distributed. The value of such a distribution subject to withholding is based on the value of stock, property, and cash distributed, less the net unrealized appreciation (NUA) on the employer securities that are distributed. Basically, the NUA is the difference between the FMV of the employer securities at the date of distribution, less the cost that the plan paid for those securities. This treatment only applies when there is a distribution that is classified as a lump-sum distribution. Basically, the NUA is not taxed until the employer securities are sold, and then the NUA is taxed as a capital gain. [I.R.C. § 3405(e)(1)(B)(ii); Treas. Reg. § 31.3405(c)-1, Q-12; Notice 93-3, 1993-1 C.B. 293]

When a plan distribution consists of a nontransferable annuity contract, there is no withholding on that distribution on the date of transfer because it is not taxable at that time. Subsequent distributions from the annuity will be subject to a flat 10 percent withholding requirement when the annuity payments are made, subject to the waiver option described above.

Q 9:347   Are any taxable plan distributions not subject to federal income tax withholding?

Yes. There are five types of taxable distributions that are not subject to FITW: (1) certain distributions consisting solely of employer stock; (2) a "deemed distribution" of a participant loan prior to the date when a participant is entitled to any other plan distribution; (3) total eligible rollover distributions to a single participant that do not exceed $200 in a calendar year (distributions from all plans of the employer are aggregated in determining the threshold); (4) distributions that are not classified as a rollover distribution where the participant or beneficiary elects to forgo withholding by completing a Form W-4P; and (5) an eligible rollover distribution that is made as a direct rollover to another plan or IRA.

Q 9:348 What is the withholding treatment of a nonperiodic distribution that is also not an eligible rollover distribution?

Distributions that are classified as neither periodic distributions nor eligible rollover distributions are subject to a flat 10 percent withholding. [I.R.C. § 3405(b)(1)] These distributions include corrective distributions for (1) excess annual additions, (2) excess deferrals, (3) excess contributions, and (4) excess aggregate contributions. This withholding may be waived. [Notice 87-77, 1987-2 C.B. 385; Rev. Rul. 92-93, 1992-2 C.B. 45]

Q 9:349 What is the process for locating a missing beneficiary?

In terminated or abandoned plans, participants or beneficiaries that do not respond to requests to elect a benefit distribution form are considered to be missing participants or beneficiaries. DOL regulations provide a safe harbor for fiduciaries to distribute benefits. The rule includes a model notice that fiduciaries may use. The rule also provides a means for financial institutions holding assets of abandoned individual account plans to terminate the plans and distribute benefits to participants or beneficiaries, with limited liability. A model notice is also provided for this purpose.

The rule permits a "qualified termination administrator" (QTA) of an individual account plan that has been abandoned by its sponsoring employer to select itself to provide services to the plan in connection with the plan's termination and to pay itself fees for those services. The fiduciary safe harbor provides that both a fiduciary and a QTA will be deemed to have satisfied ERISA's prudence requirements under ERISA Section 404(a) ("prudent man" standard of care) if the conditions of the safe harbor are met with respect to the distribution of benefits on behalf of missing participants from terminated individual account plans. In general, a fiduciary or QTA qualifies for the safe harbor if a distribution is made to an individual retirement plan within the meaning of I.R.C. Section 7701(a)(37).

For missing nonspouse beneficiaries in terminated and abandoned individual account plans, such as 401(k) plans, the DOL has a similar rule promulgated in 2008.

It is suggested that an attorney or third-party administrator be consulted for assistance in all missing participant or beneficiary situations to ensure compliance.

Participant Loans

Q 9:350 What is the employment tax treatment of distributions that consist of plan loans?

Many qualified pension and profit sharing plans permit participants to borrow a portion of their account balance. These loans are not treated as a distribution at the time the loan is made as long as certain rules are met (e.g., the loan must be paid at least quarterly and the maximum amount of the loan is generally capped at the lesser of $50,000 or 50 percent of the participant's vested account balance). [I.R.C. § 72(p)(2)]

A distribution that includes a participant loan that has been fully repaid is treated as any other distribution (i.e., is fully taxable). When a distribution includes a participant loan that has not been fully repaid, the unpaid balance of the loan is offset against the full value of the participant's account and only the net difference is actually distributed. However, the full amount of the participant's account is treated as a taxable distribution and subject to withholding under the normal rules that apply to plan distributions.

When the requirements applicable to participant loans from a plan are not met, the loan is treated as a "deemed distribution" at the time any requirement is violated. At that time, the unpaid portion of the loan (i.e., the amount of deemed distribution) is taxed as if it had been distributed and theoretically subject to withholding. A delinquent participant loan is treated as a "deemed distribution" no later than the last day of the calendar quarter following the calendar-year quarter when the missed payment occurred. Technically, a flat 10 percent withholding applies to the amount of the deemed distribution, except where the participant elects to forgo the withholding. However, there is no withholding when there are no other assets distributed at the same time as the deemed distribution occurs (and hence there are no funds from which the withholding can be made). [Treas. Reg. § 1.402(c)-2, A-4(c); Prop. Treas. Reg. § 1.72(p)-1, Q-15]

Note that when a deemed distribution occurs, the participant is not relieved of a requirement to repay the loan and the trustee will need to take appropriate steps to collect the funds. When the participant repays the defaulted loan that has been treated as a deemed distribution, that amount becomes "basis" in the plan and is not subject to federal income taxation (or withholding) when it is included in a later distribution. Most plans provide that the amount of any unpaid loan is offset against the participant's benefits in the plan at the time that a participant is first eligible to receive a forced distribution. When a loan offset and a deemed distribution occur at the time a participant receives a distribution, the amount of the deemed distribution is treated as a distribution and subject to federal income tax withholding under the normal distribution rules that apply to the distribution that the individual is entitled to receive, but only to the extent that cash or other property is distributed. [Treas. Reg. § 31.3405(c)-1, A-11] In most cases, collecting on an unpaid loan is avoided when the plan requires payment through payroll deductions as a condition of receiving a participant loan.

A question frequently arises as to whether any interest must be accrued on the amount of the loan that is in default. The plan administrator must continue to accrue interest on the unpaid loan for recordkeeping purposes and determining the maximum amount of any future loan; however, there is no federal income tax impact to the participant as a result of this accrual. That is, the participant is not treated as having received additional income equal to the interest on the unpaid loan that is due but has not been paid each year.

In addition, the accrued amount of the unpaid interest on the delinquent loan is ignored when the participant receives a distribution that consists of all or a portion of the delinquent loan. If the participant pays the accrued interest before the distribution occurs, the amount of the paid interest is included in the distribution and is subject to federal income taxes and withholding under the normal rules that apply to plan distributions. [I.R.C. § 4975(d)(1)(D); Prop. Treas. Reg. § 1.72(p)-1, Q-19 to Q-21; Rev. Rul. 89-14, 1989-1 C.B. 633]

Q 9:351   How are deemed distributions reported?

Enter the appropriate amount in Boxes 1 and 2a on Form 1099-R. The plan reports the amount of a deemed distribution on a loan that is in default on Form 1099-R. Box 7 is completed as a premature distribution if the deemed distribution occurs prior to age 59½. Use Code L in Box 7 to identify a deemed distribution, but not for loan offsets that occur simultaneously with a deemed distribution (e.g., a distribution following termination of employment). Also enter Code 1 in Box 7 for deemed distributions before age 59½ and subject to the 10 percent early distribution tax, if prior to age 59½ and not subject to the additional tax, enter in Box 2.

As part of its continuing improvement process, the IRS released streamlined procedures for correcting plan errors using the Voluntary Correction Program (within the Employee Plans Compliance Resolution Program), so practitioners can use the VCP option to correct loan mistakes. This option reduces the penalty fee for correcting plan loan administrative errors.

Reporting of Plan Distributions

Q 9:352   Who is responsible for the withholding of federal income taxes and reporting of distributions from qualified plans?

The individual who is named as the "plan administrator" in the plan document is primarily responsible for required federal income tax withholding. The plan administrator may transfer this responsibility to the payer of the distribution (e.g., a bank trustee) when (1) the payer is directed by the plan administrator to withhold the tax and provides the appropriate information to determine the amount of the withholding, or (2) the payer is acting as an agent for the plan administrator. [I.R.C. § 3405(d)(2); Treas. Reg. § 35.3401-1, E-2, E-3]

Q 9:353   Who is the taxpayer for purposes of determining whether the $200,000 threshold for electronic reporting for plan distributions is met?

The plan is the taxpayer for benefits paid under the plan; and if total aggregate tax deposits for distributions from the plan in 1999 or any year thereafter exceed $200,000, the plan administrator must comply with the requirement to make electronic deposits for the calendar year. [I.R.C. § 6656; Notice 99-20, 1999-17 I.R.B. 16]

Q 9:354 What are the requirements that apply to depositing and reporting income taxes withheld from pension distributions?

Plan administrators of qualified plans report income tax withholding from pensions and annuities on Form 945, Annual Return of Withheld Federal Income Tax. Do not report these liabilities on Form 941. The plan administrator must furnish the recipients and the IRS with Form 1099-R, Distributions From Pensions, Annuities, Retirement or Profit-Sharing Plans, IRAs, Insurance Contracts, etc.

Plan administrators deposit withholding from pensions and annuities combined with any other nonpayroll withholding reported on Form 945 (e.g., backup withholding). Do not combine the Form 945 deposits with deposits for payroll taxes. Circular E and the separate Instructions for Form 945 include information on the deposit rules. Beginning January 1, 2011, all deposit withholding from pensions and annuities must be deposited electronically. Federal Tax Deposit Coupon 8109 has been eliminated. [Pub. No. 15-A]

FICA and FUTA Taxability of Pension Benefits

Q 9:355 When are pension benefits subject to FICA and FUTA?

Retirement benefits are exempt from FICA and FUTA when payment is made under one of the following conditions: (1) from a tax-exempt trust and plan described in Sections 401(a) and 501(a) (i.e., a qualified pension or profit sharing plan); (2) from a plan described in Section 403(b) or 403(a) (e.g., a tax-deferred annuity); (3) from a SEP or SIMPLE plan; (4) from an exempt government plan as described in Section 457; (5) from a nonqualified deferred compensation plan that previously reported the value of benefits as they became vested for FICA and FUTA purposes; or (6) disability-retirement benefits paid directly by an employer to a disabled retiree while the individual is receiving Social Security benefits (this last exemption only applies to FICA taxes). [I.R.C. §§ 3121(a)(5), 3121(a)(15), 3121(a)(16), 3306(b)(2), 3306(b)(5), 3306(b)(10), 3306(b)(15)]

Q 9:356 Are employee salary deferrals under a 401(k) plan or salary reduction to a SEP or SIMPLE plan subject to federal employment taxes?

Before-tax employee contributions made to a 401(k), SEP, or SIMPLE plan are generally referred to as "salary deferrals" and are not subject to federal income taxes or federal income tax withholding when contributed, but are subject to FICA and FUTA taxes. [I.R.C. §§ 3121(v)(1)(A), 3306(r)(1)(A)] State law generally follows federal law, with limited exceptions.

Hardship and Other Distributions

Q 9:357   How are hardship distributions from a 401(k) plan treated for federal employment tax purposes?

A *hardship distribution* is a distribution to a participant made before the time when retirement benefits would be paid (e.g., while the participant is still working for the plan sponsor). A hardship distribution is not treated as an eligible rollover distribution and is not subject to a mandatory 20 percent withholding. The term *hardship distribution* is most often associated with a participant's ability to withdraw salary deferrals while still employed due to his or her hardship (or his or her beneficiary's hardship, beginning January 1, 2007). These in-service distributions are subject to federal income taxes, but not FICA or FUTA taxes. In addition, if the individual has not attained age 59½, an additional 10 percent excise tax applies.

Hardship distributions from any plan account (e.g., a salary deferral account) are not treated as eligible rollover distributions. As a result, hardship withdrawals are a nonperiodic distribution subject to the 10 percent withholding that in most cases is waived. A safe harbor notice is supplied by the IRS for distributions that must be given to employees. [I.R.C. § 402(d); Notice 99-5, 1999-3 I.R.B. 10; Notice 2000-11, 2000-6 I.R.B. 572; Notice 2003-3, 2003-2 I.R.B. 258]

Q 9:358   What is the impact of the bankruptcy of the participant on a distribution?

The Prevention and Consumer Protection Act of 2005 [Pub. L. No. 109-8, 119 Stat. 23] expands the protection for tax-favored retirement plans for arrangements that arguably were not already protected under the Bankruptcy Code. The effective date of the law was October 17, 2005. The Consumer Bankruptcy Act provides for exemptions of property from a debtor's estate, to permit a debtor to specifically exclude retirement funds that are exempt from taxation under the following provisions of the I.R.C.: Section 401 (qualified plans), Section 403 (annuities), Section 408 (IRAs), Section 408A (Roth IRAs), Section 414 (hybrid plans), Section 457 (deferred compensation arrangements for government and tax-exempt organizations), and Section 501(a) (plans funded with employee contributions only).

The law therefore expands the protections afforded retirement savings of an individual filing for bankruptcy to include qualified plans that are not subject to ERISA (i.e., governmental and church plans), 403(b) annuities, and IRAs. A retirement fund is deemed to be tax exempt if there is a current IRS determination that it is exempt or if the fund is in substantial compliance and neither the IRS nor a court has made a determination to the contrary. Even if the retirement fund is not in "substantial compliance," the participant's interest will be excluded from the bankruptcy estate if "the debtor is not materially responsible for that failure." It should be noted that there is a $1 million cap on the value of the debtor's interest in an IRA subject to the new exemption, but the cap does not apply to amounts rolled over from a qualified plan or 403(b) annuity. The $1 million cap may be increased if the interests of justice so require.

The statute also amended Section 362(b) of the Bankruptcy Code to exempt the withholding of income from a debtor's wages to repay a plan loan from the automatic stay. Accordingly, the employer may continue to withhold the plan loan payments even though the employee is in bankruptcy. Furthermore, Section 523(a) of the Bankruptcy Code was amended to provide that plan loans cannot be discharged in bankruptcy. Further, Section 541(b) of the Bankruptcy Code, which provides exceptions to the definition of property of the estate, was amended to expand the list of excluded property to include contributions withheld from employees' wages for all employee welfare and pension benefit plans subject to ERISA or a government plan under I.R.C. Section 414(d); a deferred compensation plan of a state or local governmental unit under I.R.C. Section 457; a deferred compensation plan of a tax-exempt employer under I.R.C. Section 403(b); or a health insurance plan regulated by state law. The change does not appear to apply to church plans, other than health insurance plans regulated by state law.

Q 9:359   Are aftertax employee contributions to a qualified pension or profit sharing plan entitled to any special employment tax relief?

Some plans, generally those of government employers, require that the employee make aftertax contributions to a pension plan to be eligible to receive employer-funded benefits. Few other plans permit an employee to make aftertax contributions to a plan. For nongovernmental employers, these aftertax employee contributions generally must satisfy certain nondiscrimination requirements under Section 401(m), meaning that the HCE (as defined under Section 414(q)) cannot generally make aftertax contributions unless some non-HCEs make similar contributions. Aftertax contributions are made from wages that have been subject to FIT, FITW, FICA, and FUTA.

Distributions from a qualified plan that include a portion of amounts attributable to aftertax contributions (but not the earnings on those accounts) are exempt from FIT and FITW. The portion of a periodic distribution that consists of aftertax contributions is now determined under special rules that calculate the amount to exclude (e.g., an exclusion ratio). Earnings on these amounts are subject to FITW and to the normal withholding rules that apply to any plan distribution that is taxable.

Q 9:360   How do the withholding rules apply to minimum distributions required under Section 401(a)(9)?

Any required minimum distribution (e.g., the level payments that generally must begin upon attaining age 70½) is not an eligible rollover distribution; therefore, it is not subject to the 20 percent mandatory withholding, because these amounts cannot be rolled over. The amount of minimum distribution is subject to withholding based on being classified as a periodic distribution that is not eligible for rollover (i.e., taxed as wages paid to the participant or beneficiary). Any excess amount paid at the same time as the minimum required distribution would be subject to either 10 percent (which can be waived) or 20 percent (mandatory) withholding based on whether the excess amount satisfies the requirements for being classified as an eligible rollover distribution.

Q 9:361   May workers who have attained age 70 elect to defer receiving pension benefits until after they terminate their employment?

Generally, yes, as long as the older worker is not deemed to be a more than 5 percent owner of the plan sponsor and the plan document has been amended to permit the delayed starting date. Stock owned by lineal ascendants and descendents of the employee is treated as being owned by the employee. [I.R.C. § 318] Some employers will not amend their plans to follow this change in tax laws; it is not required. Without this amendment, a plan may continue to require that the payment of benefits begin at 70½, even if the plan participant is still employed by the plan sponsor. [Notice 97-75, 1997-15 I.R.B. 18]

Under the Worker, Retiree, and Employer Recovery Act of 2008 [Pub. L. No. 110-458, 122 Stat. 5092], no minimum distributions were required for 2009 from individual retirement plans and employer-provided qualified defined contribution plans. The required minimum distribution will occur in calendar year 2010. Thus, for an individual whose required beginning date is April 1, 2010, the required minimum distribution for 2010 will be required to be made no later than the last day of calendar year 2010. If the individual dies on or after April 1, 2010, the required minimum distribution for the individual's beneficiary will be determined using the rule for death on or after the individual's required beginning date.

ESOPs

Q 9:362   How are pass-through dividends from an employee stock ownership plan reported?

The tax laws permit an employee stock ownership plan (ESOP) to "pass through" dividends paid on employer stock held by the ESOP. The ESOP must meet certain requirements of I.R.C. Section 4975(e)(7). These pass-through dividends are paid to the participants based on the stock allocated in the plan, and are taxable to the participant and reported on Form 1099-DIV. [Form 1099-DIV instructions]

Q 9:363   May participants in an ESOP be permitted to elect to contribute pass-through dividends to a 401(k) plan as salary deferrals?

The IRS has ruled in several private letter rulings that ESOP participants may elect to defer pass-through dividends on employer stock held by an ESOP to a

401(k) component of the ESOP. These elective contributions are treated as salary deferrals. The elective contributions are exempt from FIT but are subject to FICA and FUTA. Amounts not deferred are reported on Form 1099-DIV. [Priv. Ltr. Rul. 9821064, May 22, 1998; Priv. Ltr. Rul. 9825034, Mar. 25, 1998]

401(k) Plans

Q 9:364   What is a 401(k) plan?

A 401(k) plan is a type of qualified plan (it generally must be part of a profit sharing plan) that permits employees to make before-tax contributions in the form of salary deferrals. Participants may revise or stop these contributions at any time during the plan year as permitted by the plan document. The I.R.C. restricts payment of these contributions to an employee prior to retirement, death, attainment of age 59½, or separation from service unless the distribution qualifies as a hardship distribution. [I.R.C. § 401(k)]

Q 9:365   When must an employer transfer the employee's contributions to a qualified 401(k) plan?

Employers are required to transfer employee contributions that have been collected from an employee's pay (e.g., 401(k) salary deferrals, aftertax employee contributions, salary deferrals to a salary reduction SEP, and salary deferrals to a 403(b) plan) no later than the *earlier* of (1) the 15th business day of the calendar month following the month when the contributions were collected from the employee or (2) as soon as it is practical to make the transfer.

Note that although the transfer to the plan could theoretically be delayed up until the 15th business day of the next month, the employer must transfer the funds on an earlier date *if it is possible to do so*. Thus, an employer that makes a payroll deposit on amounts withheld for federal employment taxes in one to three days would have no latitude in delaying deposits of 401(k) salary deferrals beyond three days, unless a unique problem exists. There is a procedure to obtain an additional 10 days for the transfer where unusual circumstances prohibit an earlier transfer (e.g., fire destroys the payroll system), but the procedures are not easy to comply with and may be too cumbersome for general usage. [29 C.F.R. § 2510.3-102]

The DOL treats any violations of this transfer requirement (generally, in three to five days) as a fiduciary breach under ERISA. The violation arises because the employer has retained plan assets for its use. The DOL has taken a hard line on meeting this requirement. It holds that if an employer transfers these employee contributions in one or two days for one payroll, it has demonstrated an ability to make such a deposit for all payrolls, and thus it must do so for all future deposits. Employers and plan fiduciaries that fail to meet this deadline will be subject to a penalty for a prohibited transaction and are subject to mandatory reporting of the violation and payment of an excise tax penalty.

Salary deferrals under a SIMPLE IRA plan are subject to a different transfer requirement. Transfers to a SIMPLE IRA must be made 30 days after the close of the month when the contributions were collected, unless it is possible to do so on an earlier date. Note that SIMPLE 401(k) plans are subject to the 15-business-day rule cited above. SIMPLE IRAs are not subject to ERISA. [I.R.C. § 408(p)(5)(A)]

Q 9:366   What are the penalties for failing to make timely 401(k) deposits?

Failing to make the timely transfer of salary deferrals to a 401(k) plan results in a reportable prohibited transaction and payment of an excise tax. It may also subject the employer to a DOL investigation. A prohibited transaction occurs on the earliest date when these contributions could have been transferred but remain in the custody of the employer. A prohibited transaction is required to be reported on Form 5500 and on Form 5330. An excise tax is paid with Form 5330 based on the "amount involved" in the prohibited transaction. Treasury regulations define the amount involved in a prohibited transaction to be the value of the use of the retained contributions by the employer, which is basically a specified interest rate applied to the undeposited taxes for the days that the funds are held after the earliest date the funds could have been transferred. The rate of interest is defined under I.R.C. Section 6621(a)(2) to be the federal short-term rate plus 3 percentage points. The excise tax is 15 percent of the interest for the period the funds were not deposited. Where the employer seeks self-correction for the violation under the DOL's DVCP (Delinquent Voluntary Compliance Program) program, the employer will be required to contribute lost earnings while it retained the funds. Note that the filing of Form 5330 will generally trigger a DOL investigation of the employer's deposits.

Q 9:367   What is the maximum salary deferral an employee can make to a 401(k) or 403(b) plan?

The annual limit on employee salary deferrals reached its statutory maximum of $18,000 for 2017; in the alternative, 100 percent of the individual's before-deferral pay if it is less than the statutory amount. This maximum limitation of $15,000 indexed for inflation, previously set to expire in 2011, was made permanent by the Pension Protection Act of 2006. [Pub. L. No. 109-280, 120 Stat. 780]

Note that other I.R.C. sections can act to reduce these limits. The $18,000 limit for 2017 is an individual limit for all deferrals to any plan in the calendar year.

In addition to this deferral limit, 401(k) and 403(b) plans can permit any participant who has attained age 50 by the end of the year to make an additional catch-up contribution to the plan. These "catch-up" contributions are not subject to any I.R.C. limitation.

Salary deferrals made to a 401(k) plan (but not the catch-up contributions) are included with the employer's other contributions made to the 401(k) and all other pension and profit sharing plans maintained by the employer in applying the Section 415 and tax-deduction limits.

Example. Charlotte, age 25, is employed at Flower Market, Inc. during the day. She also works for Bread Basket, Inc., a bakery, at night. Both companies sponsor a 401(k) plan in 2016.

	Flower Market	Bread Basket
Charlotte's compensation	$46,500	$33,300
401(k) salary deferral	9,500	9,500

Charlotte's total salary deferrals in calendar year 2017 are $19,000.

Charlotte is permitted to make only $18,000 of salary deferrals to all 401(k) plans she participates in during the 2017 calendar year, even if the employers are unrelated. Technically, both employer plans have an "operational failure" because Charlotte's total salary deferrals exceed $18,000 for 2017. Charlotte is required to report the excess contribution of $1,000 to one of her employers and receive a distribution of the $1,000 plus investment earnings. If she does not report the excess amount, the IRS will pick up the excess amount when the employee's Form 1040 is filed. If Charlotte were age 50, the additional contribution could have stayed in the plans as a catch-up contribution.

Another I.R.C. limitation applies to the deferral ratio test for HCEs as defined under Section 414(q)—the actual deferral percentage (ADP) test—which could reduce the maximum amount of salary deferrals made by an HCE. That test can result in the plan making a distribution of certain salary deferrals to the HCEs. (See Q 9:318 for the definition of an HCE.) [I.R.C. § 401(k)]

Q 9:368   How are excess deferrals reported on Form W-2?

The full amount of the employee's deferral is entered in Box 12 with a Code D and included in the amounts reported in Boxes 3 and 5 of Form W-2. The full amount of the deferral, including the excess deferral, is not reported in Box 1.

Individuals who have attained age 50 by December 31, 2017 can make a $6,000 catch-up contribution (this is a statutory amount not adjusted for inflation). Catch-up contributions are not subject to any I.R.C. limit applicable to qualified plans. As a result, excess deferrals for these individuals may be reclassified as catch-up contributions up to the current dollar limit. The amount of the catch-up is also reported in Box 12 with a Code D and in Boxes 3 and 5. No separate identification as to a catch-up contribution is required.

Q 9:369   How does a plan make corrective distributions for salary deferrals exceeding the calendar-year limit?

The I.R.C. limits the dollar amount of salary deferrals that may be made in a calendar year (e.g., $18,000 in 2017). Where those limits are exceeded, they are referred to as "excess deferrals" and must be distributed to the employee to avoid plan disqualification. The regulations permit a distribution of an excess deferral as soon as the violation is discovered. These excess deferrals must be distributed by April 1 of the year following the year of the deferral. The IRS may permit later distributions under one of its plan correction programs, referred to EPCRS.

Excess deferrals, in contrast to a typical plan distribution, are taxable in the year of deferral regardless of when returned to the participant; however, if the excess deferral is paid after April 15 of the next calendar year, excess deferrals are also taxable when distributed. The I.R.C. requires that certain investment earnings or losses on the excess deferrals also be distributed. These amounts may be determined in any reasonable way and are generally spelled out in the plan document. At one time, the regulations required a distribution of investment income or loss attributable to excess deferrals distributed after the end of the plan year in which the deferral was made. Updated regulations no longer require a plan to distribute investment earnings or losses after the close of the plan year that are associated with an excess deferral; however, a plan document drafted under the original proposed regulations will probably require a distribution of plan earnings accrued on the excess deferral after the end of the plan year. The I.R.C. requires that the plan be followed. [I.R.C. §§ 401(a), 402(g)]

Investment earnings distributed with an excess deferral are subject to federal income tax in the year of distribution and for withholding purposes are subject to the flat 10 percent withholding on non-rollover distributions, which may be waived. Plans must report both the excess deferral that is distributed and any earnings on the Form 1099-R for the year in which the distribution is made, regardless of when the distribution is subject to federal income taxes. Plan administrators complete Boxes 1 and 2(a) of Form 1099-R to report the total distribution and investment income if distributed during the calendar year of the deferral. There is no requirement to separate the two amounts to show that a portion is a deferral and a portion is investment income. If an investment loss is distributed during the year of deferral, this same procedure is followed (i.e., the loss and the excess deferral are netted and reported in Boxes 1 and 2a).

If the excess deferral is distributed after the calendar year, the administrator is required to use two 1099-R forms to designate in which year the excess deferral and the investment earnings are taxed: one for the excess deferral (taxable in the prior year) and one for any investment earnings that are distributed and taxed in the year of distribution. Report the taxable distributions in Boxes 1 and 2(a) of the separate form. If a loss is distributed with the excess deferral after the calendar year ends, use two 1099-R forms. Report the excess deferral in Boxes 1 and 2(a) on one form, which is taxable in the year of deferral. The loss is reported on the other form, in which Boxes 1 and 2(a) are left blank and the loss shown in brackets in Box 8, for which the employee may take a deduction in the year of distribution. In Box 7, apply the following coding for the distributions.

Coding for Box 7. Coding in Box 7 is used to identify the year in which the distribution is subject to federal income taxes and does not distinguish between types of distribution (e.g., excess deferral, excess contributions, or investment earnings). Select the correct code for Box 7 of the 1099-R form for the calendar year when the distribution was made. If taxable in the current year, use Code 8; if taxable in the immediately prior year, use P; and, if two years prior, use D.

> **Example.** A $25,000 deferral for 2017 resulted in an excess deferral of $7,000; the investment earnings attributable to the excess deferral, which the plan sponsor calculates is $195. If the excess deferral was distributed in 2017, with $195 of plan earnings, report the $7,000 excess deferral on a 2017 Form 1099-R coded P. The $195 of investment earnings is reported on a separate 2017 Form 1099-R with Code 8 in Box 7.

> If a $195 loss is distributed with the excess deferral prior to the end of the calendar year, report the full distribution on a single form. Place the full amount in Boxes 1 and 2(a) and code Box 7 with 8.

Q 9:370   How are employee contributions under a 401(k) plan treated for Form W-2 purposes?

Employee contributions made on a pretax basis to a 401(k) plan (i.e., salary deferrals) are not subject to federal income taxes when contributed but are subject to FUTA and FICA taxes. These contributions are included in Boxes 3 and 5 of the employee's Form W-2. The amount of the 401(k) salary deferrals is reported in Box 12 with a Code D. Aftertax contributions made to a pension or profit sharing plan are generally made with payroll deductions, after all federal employment taxes have been applied. As a result, these contributions have already been included in Boxes 1, 3, and 5 of Form W-2.

Q 9:371   Are distributions of excess contributions and excess aggregate contributions from a 401(k) plan subject to any federal income tax withholding?

Yes. Excess contributions (from a failed ADP test) and excess aggregate contributions (from a failed actual contribution percentage (ACP) test) distributed from a 401(k) or SARSEP are subject to 10 percent federal income tax withholding. There appears to be no way the participant may waive this withholding requirement. Most employers do not withhold, and the IRS does not enforce this requirement. [Form 1099-R instructions]

Q 9:372   What are the employment tax implications when the employer utilizes an automatic 401(k) or 403(b) salary deferral?

The term *automatic salary deferral* refers to a contribution strategy that is designed to improve participation in an employer's 401(k) or 403(b) plan. The strategy, also known as negative enrollment, involves an automatic reduction in the employee's compensation, with that amount being contributed to the company's 401(k) plan, unless the employee elects not to participate in the 401(k) plan. Thus, the employee is effectively enrolled in the plan at the time of employment even though actual participation may not occur until a later date. At the time the employee begins participating, the employee will have his or her compensation reduced and those contributions made as a salary deferral to the employer's plan. This contribution is exempt from federal income taxes but subject to FICA and FUTA taxes. The IRS confirmed that such an enrollment feature qualifies as an elective deferral as long as the employee could, at any time prior to or after the effective date of the salary deferral, stop or reduce the amount. Basically, a salary deferral under this type of enrollment is treated for employment tax purposes as an elected salary deferral.

Although the IRS has approved this enrollment technique, certain states prohibit any reduction in an employee's pay that is not specifically authorized by the employee. As a result, the automatic election will need to be tailored to avoid violating state labor laws. Although these programs were initially touted as a means to increase participation, some employers have abandoned these plans because they can result in many small accounts that are costly to administer.

The Pension Protection Act of 2006 added new I.R.C. Section 401(k)(13) in an attempt to increase defined contribution plan participation through automatic enrollment in 401(k) plans that provides a safe harbor; it also amended I.R.C. Sections 401(k), 401(m), 414, and 4979, and ERISA Sections 404(c) and 514 all for conforming provisions. [Pub. L. No. 109-280, 120 Stat. 780] Section 401(k)(13) created a safe harbor where plans are deemed to meet the nondiscrimination requirements and are exempt from top-heavy plan requirements. Requirements regarding default investments, as well as notices that must be provided, must be followed.

Such a qualified automatic enrollment plan feature must provide that, unless an employee elects otherwise, the employee is treated as making an election to make deferrals equal to a stated percentage of compensation not in excess of 10 percent and at least equal to 3 percent of compensation for the first year, 4 percent during the second year, 5 percent the third year, and 6 percent during the fourth year and thereafter. The plan sponsor must make matching contributions, distribute notices, and meet other specific requirements. Certain automatic investment options for participants in a safe harbor plan are set forth in regulations promulgated by the Department of Labor. [29 C.F.R. Section 2550.404c-5] Proposed regulations issued by IRS describe an "eligible automatic contribution arrangement" (EACA) that meets the requirements of the statute. [72 Fed. Reg. 63144-01, 2007 WL 3283615 (F.R.)] Further, an automatic contribution arrangement that meets safe harbor provisions for contributions, notices, and other requirements is called a "qualified automatic contribution arrangement."

Plans that have automatic enrollment but do not meet the safe harbor should generally establish the level of contribution at a reasonable level to avoid possible fiduciary issues. Although there is no regulatory guidance, practitioners generally believe that an initial 2 to 3 percent of pay deferral is reasonable. The employee must receive a notice of the availability to make an election to not participate, or to change level of participation, and have a reasonable period to revoke the election or reduce the amount of the contribution prior to the enrollment date. IRS guidance for non-safe-harbor plans also extends the ability to write a plan to make automatic elections for aftertax employee contributions when the requirements identified above are met. If both options are available, the employer must notify the employee how much of each contribution is before tax and how much is aftertax. These strategies work best when the employee is permitted to participate at or shortly after his or her date of hire.

The DOL issued regulations regarding the investment alternatives available for such safe-harbor plans. Plan fiduciaries should be made aware of these requirements. Generally, there are three types of investments: (1) a "life-cycle" or "targeted-retirement-date" fund or account, which is an investment fund, product, or model portfolio that applies generally accepted investment theories, diversified so as to minimize risk of large losses, and designed to provide varying degrees of long-term capital appreciation and capital preservation through a mix of equity and fixed income exposures based on the participant's age, target retirement date, or life expectancy; (2) a "balanced" fund, which is an investment fund, product, or model portfolio that applies generally accepted investment theories, diversified so as to minimize the risk of large losses, and designed to provide long-term appreciation and capital preservation through a mix of equity and fixed income exposures consistent with a target level of risk appropriate for participants of the plan as a whole; and (3) a "managed account" provided by an investment management service where an investment manager allocates the assets of a participant's individual account to achieve varying degrees of long-term appreciation and capital preservation through a mix of equity and fixed income exposures, offered through investment alternatives available under the plan, based on the participant's age, target retirement date, or life expectancy.

Expansion of availability. Three notices containing guidance on adding automatic enrollment and escalation features to Section 401(k) and SIMPLE IRAs were released in 2009. Notice 2009-65 provided two sample amendments that employers could use upon its release. [Adding Automatic Enrollment to Section 401(K) Plans—Sample Amendments, Notice 2009-65, 2009 WL 2844170 (I.R.S. Notice 2009)] With either of those plan amendments, modified or used verbatim, an employer could begin withholding a certain percentage of an employee's pay and contributing that amount to the employer's Section 401(k) plan on the employee's behalf, unless the employee chose to opt out of the arrangement.

One amendment would add a basic automatic contribution arrangement with an escalation provision. The other amendment would add an I.R.C. Section 414(w) eligible automatic contribution arrangement with an escalation provision to a plan to ensure that all covered employees are subject to the same salary deferral percentage. An employer would have to sign and date a document showing that it adopted the amendment and notify plan participants within a reasonable time before the escalation feature became effective.

By adopting either sample plan amendment and, if necessary, modifying the amendment to conform to the plan's terms and administrative procedures, employers would be in no jeopardy of losing their reliance on a favorable opinion, advisory, or determination letter from the IRS, the notice said.

Notice 2009-66 provided guidance in a question-and-answer format on how employers can add an automatic contribution feature to a SIMPLE IRA plan. [Automatic Enrollment In Simple IRAs, Notice 2009-66, 2009-39 I.R.B. 418] In one answer, the IRS said a SIMPLE IRA plan with an automatic contribution feature would permit default salary reduction contributions to be made only for employees who become eligible participants under the SIMPLE IRA "on or after the effective date of the automatic contribution arrangement and who do not make an affirmative election (including an affirmative election of zero)." Another answer in the notice said the Labor Department advised the IRS that regulations concerning qualified default investment alternatives and related fiduciary protections under ERISA Section 404(c) would apply to the investment of automatic contributions to SIMPLE IRA plans.

Notice 2009-67 provided sample language that sponsors could use to amend preapproved SIMPLE IRAs plan by adding an automatic contribution feature, provided the sponsors had a designated financial institution to administer their SIMPLE IRAs. [Adding Automatic Enrollment to Simple IRA PLANS—Sample Amendment, Notice 2009-67, 2009 WL 2844172 (I.R.S. Notice 2009)] Sponsors that used the sample amendment language to add automatic contribution features to their preapproved plans would have to provide a copy of the amendment to each employer that has adopted the SIMPLE IRA.

Revenue Ruling 2009-30 offered two examples of how automatic enrollment with automatic escalation would work in a Section 401(k) plan. [Rev. Rul. 2009-30, 2009-39 I.R.B. 391] In one example, the employer would add automatic contribution increases to a calendar year profit sharing plan that satisfied the IRS tax-qualification requirements under Section 401(a), 401(k), and 401(m) features. In that example, employers would not be required to maintain default contribution percentages that are uniform percentages of compensation for all eligible employees. The profit sharing plan would have provisions providing that default contributions and related matching contributions could be invested in qualified default investment alternatives.

A second example described an employer that maintained a calendar year profit sharing Section 401(k) plan amended to include qualified automatic contribution and eligible automatic contribution features. In that example, the default contribution percentage would satisfy IRS uniformity and minimum percentage requirements under safe harbor nondiscrimination rules for automatic enrollment and 90-day withdrawal rules for employees who elect to opt out.

Q 9:373   May a plan permit an employee to make "Roth" contributions to a 401(k) plan?

Yes. Beginning in 2006, a 403(b) or 401(k) plan could permit aftertax Roth contributions. Distributions from Roth plan contributions would be tax-free. The tax treatment and reporting of these contributions will be identified in guidance to be released prior to the effective date. [EGTRRA § 617, I.R.C. § 402A] Proposed rules released by the Treasury Department and the IRS in March 2005 state that the Roth contributions would be includible in employees' gross incomes, and the plans' distributions would be tax-free, according to the proposed rules. [Prop. Treas. Reg. § 1.401(k)-1(f)] The IRS and Treasury had issued final rules on 401(k)s on December 29, 2004, which reserved for a later amendment designated Roth contributions. The proposed rules also provide guidance on matching designated Roth contributions under Section 401(m).

Under I.R.C. Section 402A, a plan may permit an employee who makes elective contributions under a qualified cash or deferred arrangement to designate some or all of those contributions as Roth contributions. Although designated Roth contributions are elective under a qualified cash or deferred arrangement, they currently are includible in gross income. However, qualified distributions are excludable from gross income, according to the proposed rules.

The proposal defined designated Roth contributions as elective contributions under qualified cash or deferred arrangements that, to the extent permitted by the plan, are designated irrevocably by the employee at the time of the cash or deferred election as designated Roth contributions treated by the employer as includible in the employee's income at the time the employee would have received the contribution amounts in cash if the employee had not made the cash or deferred election; and maintained by the plan in a separate account.

The contributions and withdrawals of designated Roth contributions must be credited and debited to separate accounts maintained for employees who make the designations. Plan sponsors must also maintain records of the employee's investment contract for their Roth contribution accounts, according to the proposed regulations. Furthermore, gains, losses, and other credits or charges are to be allocated separately "on a reasonable and consistent basis to the designated Roth contribution account and other accounts under the plan," but forfeitures may not be allocated to the accounts. The separate accounting requirement applies at the time the contribution is made, according to the guidance, and must continue to apply until the Roth contribution account is completely distributed.

Other requirements set forth in the proposed regulations included amendments stipulating that contributions are subject to the nonforfeitability and distribution restrictions applicable to elective contributions and are taken into account under the ADP test of Section 401(k) in the same manner as pretax elective contributions. Further, contributions are subject to the minimum required distribution rules of I.R.C. Section 401(a)(9)(A) and (B) in the same manner as pretax elective contributions. Also, correction methods in the final regulations under Section 401(k) for plans that fail the ADP for a year would be amended to permit highly compensated employees with elective contributions for a year that includes both pretax elective contributions and designated Roth contributions to elect whether excess contributions are to be attributed to pretax elective contributions or designated Roth contributions.

Q 9:374   May a plan permit an employee to make IRA contributions to a plan?

Yes, beginning in 2003, a qualified pension or profit sharing plan may be drafted to permit employees to make IRA contributions to the plan. These contributions are to be maintained in a separate account, and the trustee must be a trustee that can hold IRA accounts (e.g., a bank). These contributions are generally exempt from any I.R.C. requirement that applies to employer contributions or employee salary deferrals under a 401(k) or 403(b) plan. Because of the trustee requirements, few employer plans will add this feature. Any employer contributions made as IRA contributions will be made with aftertax payroll deductions and are fully subject to federal income tax withholding and FICA and FUTA taxes. [EGTRRA § 602(b)]

Testing of 401(k) Plans

Q 9:375   What is an excess contribution under a 401(k) plan?

An excess contribution is that portion of a salary deferral contribution made to the account of an HCE that causes the plan to fail the ADP test. When the plan fails this test, the employer will generally distribute the excess portion to the HCE. However, some plans permit the employer to make additional fully vested contributions to the accounts of all or some of the non-HCEs (these are called qualified nonelective contributions or QNECs) to avoid having an excess contribution (see Qs 9:318–9:322).

Q 9:376   What is the ADP test?

The actual deferral percentage (ADP) test is a nondiscrimination test that compares the average salary deferral ratios of the HCEs to the average deferral ratios of the non-HCEs (NHCEs). The average for the HCEs cannot exceed the average for the NHCEs by more than a threshold percentage limit set by the I.R.C. (See Q 9:318 for a definition of HCE.) [I.R.C. § 401(k)(3)]

The ADP test requires that the average deferral ratio of the group of eligible HCEs be either: (1) not greater than 125 percent of the average deferral ratio (i.e., deferral divided by plan compensation) of the group of NHCEs (the "general ADP test") or (2) not greater than the average deferral ratio of the group of NHCEs by more than 2 percentage points and not more than double the average deferral ratio of the group of NHCEs. [I.R.C. § 401(k)(3)] (The second testing option is the "alternate ADP test.")

These limits are demonstrated in the following chart:

Average Deferral by non-HCEs	Maximum Average Permitted for HCEs	
0%	0%	
1%	2%	"2 times" portion of the alternate test is the limiting factor until non-HCE ratio exceeds 2%
2%	4%	
3%	5%	
4%	6%	
5%	7%	"2 plus" portion of the alternate test is the limiting factor until non-HCE ratio exceeds 8%
6%	8%	
7%	9%	
8%	10%	
9%	11.25%	
10%	12.5%	"1.25 times" test is the limiting factor
12%	15.00%	

The deferral ratio for any participant is the amount of his or her deferral divided by the plan's definition of compensation. It may be gross compensation or exclude certain components of compensation. All individuals who are eligible to make salary deferrals are included in the test.

Note that any employee who is eligible to make salary deferrals, but who does not elect to make such deferrals, is treated as having a deferral percentage of 0 percent and as benefiting under the plan.

Example. A 401(k) plan maintained by Vantage, Inc. tests the employee salary deferrals utilizing gross compensation. The plan could be tested using compensation after salary deferrals to a 401(k) and 403(b) plan and salary reductions to a cafeteria or transportation assistance plan. Charles's gross pay is $112,000, and in 2017 he makes a salary deferral of $14,000. His deferral ratio is 12.5 percent ($14,000 ÷ $112,000). If he made no salary deferrals, his deferral ratio would be 0 percent.

Q 9:377 How is each participant's deferral ratio calculated?

A participant's deferral ratio is determined by dividing his or her salary deferrals by his or her compensation as defined under the plan. The plan sponsor may amend the plan to test on gross compensation to test based on compensation after salary deferrals (to a 401(k) plan) and salary reduction contributions (to a cafeteria plan or a transportation benefit plan) for purposes of calculating each participant's deferral ratio. For 2014, no more than $260,000 of compensation can be counted in determining a deferral ratio. [Treas. Reg. § 1.401(k)-1(f)(5)(iii); I.R.C. § 414(s)]

Q 9:378 Are the ADP and ACP tests prepared on a current-year or prior-year basis?

Current-year deferrals, matching contributions, and compensation for the HCEs may be tested against the prior-year test results for the NHCEs; or a sponsor may test the deferral ratio, using compensation and deferrals, of both the HCEs and NHCEs on a current-year basis. The election as to which will apply must be made prior to the start of the plan year and must be reflected in the plan document.

Prior-year ADP testing is based on test results of the individuals who were NHCEs in the prior year. That is, there is no recalculation of the average ADP for the NHCE participants using current-year compensation and deferrals, even when an NHCE had a change of status in the current year (e.g., is now an HCE or terminated employment in the current or prior year). The average for the prior year is just brought forward. These situations were discussed in Notices 97-2 [1997-2 I.R.B. 22] and 98-1 [1998-3 I.R.B. 42].

A plan may switch to current-year testing at any time. A plan sponsor may elect to switch from current-year testing to prior-year testing only under one of the following conditions:

- The current-year testing method has been used for each of the five preceding plan years (or the number of plan years the plan has been in existence, if less than five), or
- The plan is the aggregation of two or more plans, and each of the plans meets the five-year (or since plan establishment) rule above, or
- When the plan was amended for the 2002 plan year, the document reflected the testing method used in the prior plan year.

In the case of plans that are part of certain corporate acquisitions or dispositions described under I.R.C. Section 410(b)(6)(C), an employer maintaining a plan using prior-year testing and current-year testing may change from current-year testing to prior-year testing during the transition period (generally ending on the last day of the plan year beginning after the merger or disposition). [Notice 98-1, 1998-3 I.R.B. 42]

Q 9:379   How does a new plan apply prior-year testing?

Plans classified as "first-year" 401(k) plans may prepare the ADP and ACP tests, assuming that the NHCE group has an average deferral ratio (or average contribution ratio) for the prior year of at least 3 percent. Thus the HCEs on average may defer at least 5 percent of salary regardless of what the NHCEs actually contribute in the first year. The statute applies a similar 3 percent contribution rule to the ACP test for the NHCEs in a first-year 401(m) plan. Basically, a "first-year" plan is a plan of an employer where the employer has not had another plan with a salary deferral feature for at least two years.

In the case of a merger, certain recalculations of the prior-year NHCE ADP and ACP test results are required using a weighted average formula. [Notice 98-1, 1998-3 I.R.B. 42]

Q 9:380   How is the ADP test prepared?

First, the deferral ratio of each eligible HCE (and each eligible NHCE, if using current-year testing) is calculated. Then the deferral ratios of the two groups are averaged. If the plan is being tested on a prior-year basis, merely apply the calculation of the prior-year NHCE average with no adjustments for status change (e.g., NHCE to HCE), compensation, employment termination, or new employees.

Example. The ADP Test (Current-Year Testing)

The plan shown below does not pass the ADP test and must be corrected. The plan document specifies that excess contributions are distributed.

HCEs	Before-Deferral Pay	Deferral	Deferral Ratio[1]	Average for Group	Theoretical Amount to be "Distributed"[2]
Alisa	$138,000	$13,110	9.5%	9.25%	($3,450)
Jack	$125,000	$11,250	9%		($3,125)

[1] Deferral ratio = deferral divided by before-deferral pay.

[2] This is the dollar amount of the distribution; this amount may be distributed on a different basis. It is taken from the HCE with the highest deferral percentage.

NHCEs	Before-Deferral Pay	Deferral	Deferral Ratio[1]	Average for Group
Jason	$18,000	$720	4%	
Jackie	$18,000	$900	5%	5%
Neal	$18,000	$1,080	6%	

[1] Deferral ratio = deferral divided by before-deferral pay.

The ADP test for this example fails because the 9.25 percent average for the HCEs exceeds by more than 2 percent the average for the NHCEs and also exceeds the NHCEs' average by more than 125 percent. See test table in Q 9:376. A distribution of $3,450 of Alisa's deferrals and $3,125 of Jack's deferrals would reduce the average for the HCEs to 7 percent so the plan will pass the ADP test. As an alternate method to pass the test, the employer may make a QNEC of 2.75 percent to the NHCEs to raise the average for NHCEs to 6 percent, which would be sufficient to pass.

Q 9:381   How are corrections to a failed ADP test made?

When the plan fails the ADP test, the plan document may permit up to three options to bring the plan into compliance. The plan document will control which options apply. These are (1) distribute "excess contributions" to the HCEs, (2) make additional fully vested contributions or QNECs to the accounts of the NHCEs, or (3) recharacterize the excess contributions as aftertax contributions. (The last alternative is seldom useful as these aftertax contributions have to be tested under ACP testing.)

Most plans require that the excess contributions (i.e., a portion of the salary deferrals) be distributed to one or more HCEs (plus certain income on the excess contributions) by the end of the plan year following the year of deferral. Note that the I.R.C. does not authorize a distribution of "excess contributions" during the plan year in which the deferral is made. The associated plan earnings (or loss) on excess contributions must also be distributed based on the requirements of the plan document.

If the excess contributions are distributed two and one-half months or more after the close of the plan year, the excess is taxed in the year of distribution and the employer will pay a 10 percent excise tax on the excess contributions that are distributed. Excess contributions distributed within two and one-half months after the end of the plan year are taxed to the individual based on when the deferrals could first have been made in the plan year (i.e., the first in, first out [FIFO] method), but the 10 percent excise tax does not apply.

If the distributions are not made by the end of the next plan year, the plan has a qualification failure and could be disqualified. However, this disqualification can be avoided through correction under the Employee Plans Compliance Resolution System (EPCRS), which includes a self-correction and two formal correction programs.

Q 9:382   How are excess contributions under a failed ADP test distributed?

The plan sponsor must follow a two-step process in making a distribution of an excess contribution. First, the amount is determined based on the HCEs with the highest deferred ratios (see Q 9:377). Then, that amount is withdrawn based on the HCEs with the largest dollar amount of deferral in the plan year.

Determining excess contributions. Excess contributions are the amount of deferrals that must be distributed to one or more HCEs to sufficiently decrease the deferral ratio of the group of HCEs to pass the ADP test. The excess amount is determined by applying a leveling procedure to the HCEs (if the plan covers more than one HCE). Under this procedure, the deferral ratio of the HCE with the highest deferral ratio is reduced until the average deferral ratio for the group of HCEs passes the ADP test, or the HCE's deferral percentage becomes equal to the ratio of the HCE who has the second-highest ratio (whichever comes first).

If the ADP test is not passed, then the ratio of the HCEs with the highest deferral ratio is lowered to the third-highest ratio for an HCE or until the test is satisfied. The procedure is repeated (lowering the ratio of these two HCEs until it reaches the ratio of the fourth-highest HCE, etc.), and so on, until the ADP test is passed. [Treas. Reg. § 1.401(k)-1(f)(2)]

Include in the test only individuals who could have participated in the plan year.

Making the distribution. The plan administrator determines the amount to be distributed as shown above. Then, if a correction is to be made by distribution of the excess contribution, that amount is withdrawn from the HCEs' deferral accounts under a different method. Distributions are taken from HCE accounts based on who deferred the largest dollar amount. That process starts with the HCEs who have the highest deferral amount, reducing those deferrals until they equal the next highest deferral amount for an HCE or the proper amount has been distributed. This leveling process continues until the excess contribution amount determined in the first part of the ADP testing has been distributed.

Q 9:383 How are excess contributions treated for federal employment tax purposes?

Corrective distributions of excess contributions arise when a plan initially fails the ADP test. When these amounts are made within two and one-half months after the close of the plan year, they are taxable to the employee on the earliest date the employee could have taken cash rather than make the elective deferrals for the plan year. Where the plan year is other than a calendar year, this treatment can affect a prior year's tax return. If the distribution is made more than two and one-half months after the plan year, it is taxable in the participant's tax year of distribution and the employer pays an excise tax. Investment earnings on the excess contributions that are distributed are taxed in the year when distributed. These distributions are reported on a Form 1099-R under Code P, D, or 8. [Treas. Reg. §§ 1.401(k)-1(f)(4)(v)(A), 1.401(k)-1(f)(4)(v)(B)]

Income attributable to excess contributions during the plan year in which the excess contributions were made must be distributed. For the period between the year-end and the date of distribution, the document may require a distribution of the related plan earnings. Basically, any reasonable method can be used in the plan document to determine the amount of income to be distributed;

however, the document will generally specify a method to be used. [Treas. Reg. §§ 1.401(k)-1(f)(4)(i) and 1.401(k)-1(f)(4)(ii)]

An exception to these taxation rules applies when the total excess contribution (and excess aggregate contribution) distributed to the participant for any plan year is less than $100 (excluding any income distributed). Then the distribution can be taxed in the year of distribution. [Treas. Reg. § 1.401(k)-1(f)(4)(v)(B)]

Q 9:384 Can a failed ADP test be corrected by making contributions to the NHCEs?

Yes. A 401(k) plan document may permit an employer to make QNECs to pass a failed ADP test and qualified matching contributions (QMACs) to pass a failed ACP test. These are fully vested contributions made by the employer and generally subject to the same pre-59 distribution restrictions that would apply to salary deferrals. [Treas. Reg. §§ 1.401(k)-1(g)(13), 1.401(m)-1(b)(4)(ii)(13)] In effect, the employer makes the employees' salary deferrals for NHCEs (QNECs) to bring up the average deferral percentage or makes additional matching contributions (QMACs) to increase the average contribution percentage for the group of NHCEs. The plan document will spell out how these contributions are to be made and to whom. There is no payroll tax reporting for either a QNEC or QMAC, as these are employer contributions. QNECs and QMACs are required to be immediately 100 percent vested and subject to withdrawal restrictions. These contributions must be deposited by the last day of the following plan year.

Example. Gold Lo's QNECs in Current Year to Fix Excess Contributions

In this example, the employer made a QNEC equal to 1 percent of each NHCE's pay (a total of $620). That contribution raised the average for the NHCEs to 5 percent, enabling the plan to pass the ADP test.

Highly Compensated Employees

	Pay	Deferral	Deferral Percentage	Average for Group
I	$120,000	$7,200	6%	7%
J	$120,000	$9,600	8%	

Non-Highly Compensated Employees

	Pay	Deferral	Initial Deferral Percentage	QNEC	QNEC and Deferral	Final Deferral Percentage	Average for Group
K	$30,000	$1,200	4%	$300	$1,000	5%	
L	$30,000	$2,400	8%	$300	$1,800	9%	5%
M	$2,000	0	0	$20	$10	1%	
				($620)			

IRS audit guidelines for 401(k) plans [Ann. 93-105, 1993-27 I.R.B. 15] previously stated that a plan document can provide for QNECs to only be made for a select group of NHCEs. In the example below, a QNEC could be given to the lowest-paid NHCE (generally referred to as a "bottoms-up" QNEC). That would raise the average deferral ratio for the NHCEs to enable the ADP test to be passed. For employers that wish to minimize the amount of QNECs needed, this technique could be attractive, but will require specific wording in the plan document.

In the legislative history of EGTRRA, Congress requested that the Secretary of the Treasury exercise his regulatory authority to eliminate situations where a high percentage of compensation QNEC is targeted to a small number of participants with low income in the affected year. The final regulations issued in 2005 do not eliminate the use of the targeted QNEC but restrict their usage. If a targeted QNEC has been selected as part of the plan's design, it may still be used without restriction until the effective date of the final regulations—which is for plan years starting on or after January 1, 2006. Once the final regulations are effective, targeted QNECs will be subject to new, more limiting rules that will require a broader number of NHCEs to receive the QNEC.

The IRS added administratively complex requirements to prevent targeting of a high percentage of compensation QNEC to a small number of individuals. The IRS would treat the plan as providing an impermissible targeted QNEC if targeted QNECs are provided in excess of the following IRS rules.

These targeted rules state that QNECs may be made up to 5 percent of compensation before being treated as targeted QNECs. QNECs that exceed 5 percent of compensation will be treated as targeted QNECs. To exceed a 5 percent QNEC to a NHCE and have it included in the ADP test, the QNEC may not be more than two times the plan's representative contribution rate. The plan's representative contribution rate is defined as the greater of:

1. The lowest applicable contribution rate of any eligible NHCE among a group of eligible NHCEs that consists of half of all the eligible NHCEs, or
2. The lowest applicable contribution rate of any eligible NHCE in the group of all eligible NHCEs for the plan year and who are employed by the employer on the last day of the year.

The definition of applicable contribution rate for an eligible NHCE is the sum of all of the QMACs and QNECs taken into account for ADP testing for that eligible NHCE for the plan year, divided by that eligible NHCE's compensation for the same period.

The regulations provide an exception for Davis-Bacon plans. Because Davis-Bacon plans make prevailing wage contributions to certain employees, the maximum percentage that may be used in testing is increased from 5 percent to 10 percent. This exception applies to both the ADP and ACP test.

The targeted QNECs rule would also apply to the ACP test. The 5 percent of compensation QNEC limit is applied separately to the ADP and ACP test.

Therefore, the employer may make a 5 percent of compensation QNEC for ADP test purposes and a 5 percent QNEC for ACP test purposes to the same NHCEs without regard to which or how many receive each 5 percent. The regulations restrict the ability to exceed 5 percent of compensation QNEC for ACP testing purposes by stating that QNECs are not to be taken into account in the ACP test to the extent such contributions exceed the product of that NHCE's compensation and the greater of 5 percent or 2 times the plan's representative contribution rate.

The plan's representative contribution rate is defined as the greater of:

1. The lowest applicable contribution rate of any eligible NHCE among a group of eligible NHCEs that consists of half of all the eligible NHCEs, or

2. The lowest applicable contribution rate of any eligible NHCE in the group of all eligible NHCEs for the plan year and who are employed by the employer on the last day of the year.

The definition of applicable contribution rate for an eligible NHCE is the sum of matching contributions taken into account for the employee for the plan year and the QNECs made for the employee for the plan year, divided by that eligible NHCE's compensation for the same period.

In the ACP test, the lowest contribution for NHCEs would be based on the sum of QNECs and those matching contributions that are taken into account for the ACP test, where in the ADP test, QNECs and QMACs were taken into account. QNECs taken into account in the parallel ADP test may not be used in this ACP test. Only employees actually deferring may be counted in the ACP test.

Q 9:385 Can a QNEC be made when the ADP test is prepared on a prior-year basis?

Yes. However, the regulations apply certain restrictions that make this option less useful. When an employer makes a QNEC to the NHCEs under prior-year testing, the mechanics of that test will result in a recalculation of the average deferral ratio of the NHCEs for the prior year. In making this calculation, the plan administrator will use the prior compensation and deferral for the group of individuals who were classified as NHCEs. Any change in status in the current year will be ignored (i.e., termination of employment or a change in status from an NHCE to an HCE in the current year). [Notice 98-1, 1998-3 I.R.B. 42]

Q 9:386 What is the ACP test for a 401(k) plan?

The actual contribution percentage (ACP) test is a test to demonstrate that the matching contributions (and any aftertax employee contributions) are not discriminating in favor of the HCEs. The test requires that the plan sponsor calculate the average contribution ratio for each eligible HCE and NHCE and average these amounts. Each eligible participant's contribution ratio is the sum of the matching contribution and any aftertax employee contribution divided by the individual's compensation as defined in the plan document.

Matching contributions and aftertax employee contributions must be tested under the ACP test. This testing is similar to the ADP testing discussed above. All participants who could have made salary deferrals and who are eligible to receive a match are included in the ACP testing. However, if the individual's ability to receive a match is conditioned on additional service or employment at the plan year-end and the individual does not meet these conditions, the individual is excluded from the ACP testing. When such a condition applies to receipt of the match, the group of participants eligible to receive matching contributions also must satisfy the Section 410(b) minimum coverage requirements. [Treas. Reg. § 1.401(m)-1(a)(2)] A plan sponsor may not exclude from the ACP test participants who are not eligible to receive a match simply because they choose not to make a deferral. Such participants have a contribution ratio of 0. [Treas. Reg. § 1.401(m)-1(f)(4)(i)]

Nondiscrimination rules and tax-exempt organizations. The IRS issued final regulations that address the basis on which employees of tax-exempt organizations or governmental entities can be excluded from Section 401(k) plan minimum coverage tests. [T.D. 9275, 71 Fed. Reg. 41,357] The regulation states that employees of state and local government entities who are ineligible to participate in an I.R.C. Section 401(k) plan because of Section 401(k)(4)(B)(ii), can be treated as excludable employees for the coverage tests if more 95 percent of the employer's eligible employees benefit under the plan for the year.

Employees of tax-exempt organizations that participate in a Section 403(b) plan may be excluded from the coverage rules of a Section 401(k) or (m) plan if no employee of an organization described in Section 403(b)(1)(A)(i) is eligible to participate and at least 95 percent of the employees of an employer benefit when those employees are not employed by tax-exempt organizations or governmental entities. This means that tax-exempt employers that offer both Section 403(b) plans and Section 401(k) plans do not have to cover employees under both plans to meet the coverage rules.

Note also that any aftertax employee contributions are tested under the ACP test, even if the plan is not a 401(k) plan. And remember that aftertax employee contributions are part of the employee's annual $53,000 contribution limit under I.R.C. Section 415(c) for 2016.

Like the ADP test, the ACP for the group of HCEs must (1) not be greater than 125 percent of the ACP (i.e., match plus aftertax employee contribution divided by plan compensation) of the group of NHCEs (the general test), or (2) not be greater than the ACP of the NHCEs by more than 2 percentage points and not be more than two times the average contribution percentage of the group of NHCEs (sometimes called the alternate test). [I.R.C. § 401(m)(3)(A)]

These limits are demonstrated in the chart below.

Average Percentage of Match and After-Tax Contributions for NHCEs	Maximum Percentage Permitted for HCEs	
0%	0%	
1%	2%	2 times
2%	4%	—
3%	5%	2 plus
4%	6%	
5%	7%	
6%	8%	
7%	9%	
8%	10%	—
9%	11.25%	1.25 times
10%	12.5%	
12%	15%	

Like the ADP test, the ACP test can be performed using the prior-year result of the ACP for the NHCEs.

Matches and aftertax employee contributions that cause the ACP test to fail are called "excess aggregate contributions." When a plan fails the ACP test, the employer has several options with respect to the excess aggregate contributions. To the extent that matching contributions are vested and make up the excess aggregate contributions and the plan specifies, they can be distributed (along with earnings) to the HCEs before the end of the next plan year. To the extent these matching contributions are not vested, they can be forfeited. In the alternative, the employer can make QMACs to the NHCEs in an amount sufficient to raise the ACP of the group of NHCEs to pass the ACP test. [Treas. Reg. § 1.401(m)-1(e)(1)(i)]

The method for first determining the amount of aggregate contribution and the procedure for distributing the excess aggregate contribution follows the steps outlined for ADP testing.

That is, the amount of the forfeiture or distribution of the excess aggregate contribution is based on the HCEs who have the largest contributions ratio. Then the distribution or forfeitures are applied starting with the HCEs with the largest amount of aftertax contributions and match.

Example. Preparing the ADP and ACP Tests

This plan matches 50 percent of the first 6 percent of pay that is deferred.

Highly Compensated Employees

	Pay	Deferral	Deferral Percentage	Average Ratio	Match	Contribution Ratio	Average
M	$200,000	$12000	6%		$6,000	3%	
N	$150,000	$9000	6.5%	6.33%	$4500	3%	3%
O	$120,000	$7,800	6.5%		$3,900	3%	

Non-Highly Compensated Employees

	Pay	Deferral	Deferral Percentage	Average Ratio	Match	Contribution Ratio	Average
P	$30,000	$900	3%		$450	1.5%	
Q	$30,000	$1,200	4%	4.33%	$600	2.0%	2.17%
R	$30,000	$1,800	6%		$900	3.0%	

The ACP test is passed in the example because the ACP for the HCEs does not exceed 2 percent more than the ACP for the NHCEs or two times the average contribution percentage for the NHCEs.

Q 9:387   What is the multiple-use test for 401(k) plans?

Prior to the 2002 plan year, a 401(k) had to satisfy the ADP and ACP testing and sometimes a multiple-use test. It has been eliminated for plan years after 2001. [I.R.C. § 401(m)(9)]

The multiple-use test was a special test that also applied when the ADP and ACP tests were satisfied by meeting the 2-plus/2-times percentage thresholds. That is, neither test could satisfy the 1.25 threshold. As noted earlier, a plan sponsor can satisfy the ADP test under the "alternate test" (the 2-plus/2-times rule) rather than the "general test" (the 1.25-times rule), and a plan sponsor can satisfy the ACP test under the "alternate test" (the 2-plus/2-times rule) rather than the "general test" (the 1.25-times rule). However, if both the ADP and ACP tests are met using the alternate test, the plan must also satisfy the "multiple-use" test. [Treas. Reg. §§ 1.401(m)(2)(a), 1.401-2(b)(2)]

Saver's Credit

Q 9:388   What is the "saver's credit" for employee contributions to IRAs and 401(k) and other employer-sponsored plans?

Certain participants in an employer-sponsored plan are eligible for a tax credit of up to 50 percent of their elective contributions to a 401(k), a 403(b) arrangement, or other employer plans. The credit is also available for contributions to an IRA. Only the first $1,000, $2,000 if filing jointly, that is contributed to a plan or IRA is eligible for the credit and the employee contribution eligible for the credit is reduced by certain distributions from a plan or IRA. The credit is equal to a percentage of the employee's contributions, with the percentage based on the individual's status for filing Form 1040 and his or her modified AGI.

Employee contributions to the following arrangements and plans are eligible for the credit: IRAs, Roth IRAs, 401(k) plan, 403(b) annuity, eligible deferred compensation arrangement of a state or local government, SIMPLE IRA, and SARSEP. Both deductible employee contributions (e.g., salary deferrals to a 401(k) plan) and voluntary aftertax employee contributions are eligible for the credit.

The AGI limit for the saver's credit was increased this year and is $31,000 for singles, $46,500 for heads of household, and $62,000 for married couples filing jointly. The amount of the employee contribution that is eligible for the credit is reduced by the following distributions in the tax year for which the credit is claimed and the two preceding tax years. In addition, distributions after the tax year for which the credit is claimed and up to the due date plus extensions for filing the individual's tax return on which the credit is claimed reduce the total contribution on which the credit is based. Distributions that do not reduce the credit include loans to a participant that are treated as a distribution (e.g., go into default); excess deferrals, excess contributions, and excess aggregate deferrals distributed from a 401(k) or 403(b) plan; dividends of IRA contributions that are returned before the due date of the taxpayer's return; and rollovers of IRAs to Roth IRAs. [I.R.C. § 25B]

There is no additional reporting by the employer. The employer merely reports the employee contribution as a salary deferral on Form W-2 with the correct dates in Box 12. The employee applies for the tax credit upon filing his or her Form 1040 at the end of the year.

403(b) Arrangements

Q 9:389   What is a 403(b) arrangement?

A 403(b) arrangement is a tax-favored savings program that may only be offered to employees of public schools and to certain tax-exempt charitable, religious, and educational organizations that are classified as Section 501(c)(3) organizations. A 403(b) arrangement is structured similarly to a 401(k) plan, in that it is generally funded by employee contributions via salary deferrals. However, 403(b) plans are not subject to the complex testing requirements that apply to 401(k) plans. The tax legislation passed in 2001 eliminated many of the differences between 403(b) and 401(k) plans.

Section 403(b) arrangements were historically structured with an insurance company; many now utilize mutual funds as investment vehicles. These arrangements, sometimes called "tax-deferred" annuities (even where annuity products are not utilized), must satisfy the requirements of I.R.C. Section 403(b), including the following:

1. The annuity contract may be purchased through a qualified annuity plan under Section 403(a).

2. The plan (other than church plans) must meet certain nondiscrimination requirements; in general, the 403(b) arrangement must be made available to all employees of the organization—no one can be excluded based on a minimum service or age request.

3. The employee's rights must be nonforfeitable; however, where the arrangement is funded with life insurance, certain forfeitures are permitted if the employee fails to pay premiums.

4. The plan must offer *all* employees the chance to defer at least $200 in compensation annually if one employee is given the opportunity.

5. The total elective deferral for each participant does not exceed certain limits.

Note that many 403(b) arrangements are structured through a custodial account using mutual funds as the investment medium.

A 501(c)(3) organization is any corporation that (1) is organized and updated exclusively for religious, charitable, scientific, public safety testing, literary, or educational purposes, or for the prevention of cruelty to children or animals; (2) is operated on a nonprofit basis; and (3) does not devote more than 20 percent of its activities to carry on propaganda or otherwise attempt to influence legislation or a political campaign on behalf of a single candidate for public office.

Regulations. After proposed regulations that were expected to be effective January 1, 2007 were delayed by Treasury and the IRS to January 1, 2008, final regulations were issued by the IRS, effective July 26, 2007, although they apply for taxable years beginning after December 31, 2008. [T.D. 9340, 72 Fed. Reg. 41128] There are transition rules for collectively bargained plans. The rules were the first changes since 1964.

The rules require the Section 403(b) contract to be a written plan that satisfies the tax exclusion requirements in form and operation. The IRS said a written plan helps to allocate responsibilities among the employer, the contract issuer, and others who implement the plan. The final rules clarify that the written plan does not have to be a single document, and can incorporate other documents by reference as long as those documents do not conflict. The preamble to the regulations noted that if the annuity contracts fall within the scope of a safe harbor under 29 C.F.R. § 2510.3-2(f), then the 403(b) plans are not covered under Title I of ERISA. Because the final regulations may cause some tax-exempt employers to fall outside of the safe harbor, DOL issued a Field Assistance Bulletin to coincide with the publication of this final rule, discussed below.

Written plan. The regulations require that a Section 403(b) contract be issued under a written plan that meets the requirements of Section 403(b) and the regulations in both form and operation. Requiring the plan to be in writing is important, the agencies said in the preamble, because certain requirements—such as the limits on elective deferrals or requirements for loans that are not taxable distributions—require more information about other contracts which participants may have, but about which issuers may have no information outside of representations from the employer or employee. Model plan provisions for public school employers will be published.

The regulations allow an exchange of one contract for another to be an investment change if the second contract has the same distribution restrictions and the employer enters into an agreement with the issuer of the other contract to share information. This information would cover such areas as severance of employment, hardship withdrawals, and plan loans.

Aftertax employee contributions are not subject to in-service distributions restrictions. Also, distributions on disability must be treated as an incidental benefit that must satisfy the incidental benefit requirements for qualified plans.

If one of an employee's contracts fails to meet any of the Section 403(b) requirements, then none of that employee's contracts qualify for tax deferral. If employers fail to operate under a written plan or are ineligible to offer 403(b) plans, then all of their contracts fail to qualify for tax deferral. However, an operational failure that is to one employee's contract will not affect the contracts of other employees that qualify in form and operation.

ERISA and DOL viewpoint. TSA programs, if established or maintained by an employer engaged in commerce or in any industry or activity affecting commerce, generally are "pension plans" within the meaning of ERISA Section 3(2) and covered by Title I pursuant to Section 4(a) of ERISA. The terms "establish" or "maintain" are not defined in ERISA, and uncertainty as to the application of ERISA to TSA programs funded entirely with employee contributions prompted the department in 1979 to issue a safe harbor regulation at 29 C.F.R. Section 2510.3-2(f).

The safe harbor at ERISA regulations Section 2510.3-2(f) states that a program for the purchase of annuity contracts or custodial accounts in accordance with provisions set forth in I.R.C. Section 403(b) and funded solely through salary reduction agreements or agreements to forego an increase in salary, are not "established or maintained" by an employer under ERISA Section 3(2), and, therefore, are not employee pension benefit plans subject to Title I, provided that certain factors are present.

Q 9:390   What contribution limits apply to 403(b) arrangements?

Beginning in 2002, a 403(b) arrangement was subject to two contribution limits. No more than $270,000 for 2017 of compensation may be used in determining each of these limitations. [I.R.C. §§ 401(a)(17), 415(c), 415(g)]

1. The maximum exclusion allowance was repealed after 2001 and has been replaced with the pension $54,000 (for 2017).

2. *Elective deferral limit.* Where the 403(b) arrangement provides for a salary reduction agreement, employees can defer the lesser of up to $18,000 for 2017, or 100 percent of pay. This limitation is reduced for any

current year amounts deferred under any 401(k) plan or a simplified employee pension plan that provides for salary reductions. [I.R.C. §§ 402(g)(3), 402(g)(4), 403(b)(1)(E)]

An employee who has attained age 50 in 2017 and is participating in a Section 403(b) plan can take advantage of the same "catch-up" provision for 401(k) plans; that is, such an employee can defer an additional $6,000.

The total employer and employee contributions to all defined contribution plans (of an employer), including the 403(b) arrangement, for any one employee cannot exceed the lesser of (1) 100 percent of the employee's annual compensation or (2) $54,000 for 2017.

Participants with at least 15 years of service with a public school system, hospital, home health service agency, church, or convention of churches are entitled to a higher elective deferral amount. The IRS provides a worksheet in Publication 571.

Q 9:391   What is the tax treatment of elective contributions to a 403(b) arrangement?

As long as the 403(b) arrangement meets the qualifications of Section 403(b), employer contributions (including employee elective deferrals) to the plan to purchase annuity contracts are not wages subject to federal income tax withholding up to the contribution limits. Distributions from the plan are fully subject to federal income taxes. Employee elective deferrals are subject to FICA and FUTA taxes when made. [I.R.C. §§ 401(a)(17), 415(c), 415(g); Treas. Reg. § 1.415-8]

When the employee's salary deferrals exceed the $18,000 (for 2017) limitation, the excess is treated as an excess deferral. The employee will include the excess amount as additional income on his or her personal income tax return, regardless of whether distributed by the employer. [I.R.C. §§ 3121(a)(5)(D), 3306(b)(5)(D)]

Payroll practitioners have growing concerns, especially those working in and for school districts, about the increased IRS focus on 403(b) plans. As the effective date of the new 403(b) regulations arrived (see Q 9:389), the IRS took the position that school districts have been the most frequent offenders of failing to observe the salary deferral limits. The IRS has stated what payroll practitioners have feared for years—that payments to administrators and other employees have been deferred past the applicable limits even where the employee was given a choice of either receiving the payment as wages or having it contributed to a 403(b) plan. Thus, for example, where a school district administrator is entitled upon retirement to a $30,000 lump-sum payment that consists of unused sick and vacation pay, the administrator may defer only an amount equal to the applicable deferral amount for the year. Accordingly, in 2017, the administrator would be allowed to defer $18,000, plus $6,000 if he or she had attained age 50; the remainder would have to be taken as taxable income.

The IRS believes that departing employees have often been allowed to "elect" to have the entire payment go into a 403(b) arrangement. The only way an amount above the deferral amount may be paid into a 403(b) arrangement is as an employer contribution; employer contributions may never be taken in cash. Payroll practitioners may conduct a self-audit by simply asking for the administrator's contract to ensure that the language utilized does not provide the employee with a choice. If a choice is present, the payroll practitioner must limit the amount payable into the 403(b) arrangement to the applicable deferral amount.

An additional deferral is, however, available for employees who have left employment for five years immediately following separation from service. Thus, an employee who has a lump-sum cash payment due in his or her final year of employment may, with the employer's agreement and cooperation, choose to defer for five years after employment ends.

Example. Shannon, the Dean at Bright Star School, is leaving after 45 years of employment. She is eligible to receive $87,000 as follows:

$42,000	Accrued sick leave not taken
$25,000	Accrued vacation pay not taken
$20,000	One-time retirement incentive

The contract between Dean Shannon and the school district states that she may take the amounts in cash or defer them to a 403(b) arrangement. The parties may agree that deferrals be made as follows:

2012	$18,000
2013	$17,000
2014	$17,000
2015	$12,000
2016	$15,000

In addition, employer contributions may continue for five years following separation from service. Thus, in the alternative, the contract could be written that Dean Shannon will receive an employer contribution of a set amount. The risk is that the agreement will attempt to allow Dean Shannon to defer, for example, $12,000 in 2017 from the total amount of $87,000 owed. If, however, Dean Shannon was deferring throughout the year from her pay, the maximum deferral may not be available. Thus, utilizing an employer contribution, Dean Shannon's contract could allow for the following:

2017	Employer contribution $36,000 (maximum total contribution of $54,000, less possible $18,000 deferral that could have been made by Dean Shannon)
2017	$36,000 employer contribution

In either case, the payroll practitioners must be careful both to set up the arrangement in accordance with the law, as well as keep track of subsequent annual payments or deferrals.

Q 9:392   Is an employee who makes salary deferral contributions to a 403(b) tax-deferred annuity designated as a pension participant for IRA purposes?

Yes. Employers will check the "Retirement plan" Box in Box 13 of any employee's W-2 Form if the employee makes a salary deferral or the employer makes a contribution to a 403(b) plan in the calendar year.

Q 9:393   How are distributions from a tax-deferred annuity treated for income tax withholding purposes?

Distributions from tax-deferred annuities are subject to federal income taxes when paid, but not FICA or FUTA taxes. Employee contributions to the 403(b) plan were subject to FICA and FUTA taxes at the time the contributions were made. There is mandatory withholding of federal income taxes on distributions made from a 403(b) arrangement. [I.R.C. §§ 401(a)(31), 402, 403(b), 3405; Treas. Reg. § 31.3405(c)-1T]

Q 9:394   What are the reporting requirements for a 403(b) arrangement?

Elective contributions and employer contributions to a Section 403(b) tax-deferred annuity are not wages subject to federal income tax. The employee's elective contributions are included on Form W-2 in Box 3 as Social Security wages and in Box 5 as Medicare wages. The elective deferrals must also be reported in Box 12 with Code E. The employer must check the "Retirement plan" box in Box 13.

Form 5500. The Department of Labor provided transition relief to administrators of 403(b) plans that make "good faith efforts" to comply with the new Form 5500 Annual Reporting Requirements, according to a field assistance bulletin. [Field Assistance Bulletin No. 2009-02, see http://www.dol.gov/ebsa/regs/fab2009-2.html] The relief includes easing "the requirement for large plans (100 or more participants) to include as part of their Form 5500, the report of an independent qualified public accountant." A waiver of this requirement is provided for small plans with fewer than 100 participants. The Department of Labor's transition relief for I.R.C. Section 403(b) plans to comply with the Form 5500 is not intended to be limited just to plan year 2009, but applies to future years beyond the 2009 plan year.

457 Plans

Q 9:395 What are government 457 plans?

Section 457 plans are nonqualified deferred compensation plans that are maintained by state and local government employers and tax-exempt organizations other than churches. These plans, although they are not qualified plans, are subject to many of the I.R.C. and some of the ERISA requirements that apply to qualified plans. Only governmental 457 plans are not subject to ERISA. The taxation of benefits accrued under 457 plans is subject to the requirements of I.R.C. Section 457(b). Such plans may be classified as "eligible" or "ineligible" plans, based on the level of benefits vested each year. Generally, the salary deferral to an eligible plan cannot exceed the lesser of the individual's compensation or $18,000 for 2017 without becoming an "ineligible" plan. This maximum limitation of $18,000 (indexed for inflation), previously set to expire in 2010, was made permanent by the Pension Protection Act of 2006. [Pub. L. No. 109-280] In many ways, a Section 457 plan can be structured to resemble a 401(k) plan, which cannot be adopted by governmental employers. Distributions from a governmental 457 plan, but not other 457 plans, can be rolled over to an IRA.

Benefits under an "eligible" 457 plan are generally subject to federal income taxes and federal income tax withholding when paid. FICA and FUTA taxes apply to the value of benefits when they are no longer subject to substantial risk of forfeiture (e.g., as they vest), and not when paid; however, benefits under an "ineligible" 457(f) plan are subject to federal income taxes, federal income tax withholding, and generally FICA and FUTA taxes when the benefits vest, even though no distributions may be available to pay these taxes at that time.

Nonqualified 457 plans are subject to the following requirements: (1) only eligible individuals who provide services (e.g., employees and independent contractors) may participate in the plan; (2) elective contributions by employees cannot exceed the lesser of the individual's annual compensation or $18,000 for 2017 (this limit is reduced dollar-for-dollar by any contributions made to a 401(k) plan but not a 403(b) arrangement), and a higher limit applies to "catch-up" contributions made in the three years prior to retirement; (3) only certain organizations can adopt a 457 plan; and (4) the employee contributions must be placed in trust but must remain subject to the employer's creditors. [I.R.C. §§ 457(b)–457(e), 457(g), 3121(a)(5)(E), 3121(v)(3), 3306(b)(5)(E); Treas. Reg. § 1.457-2]

Nonqualified 457 plans of a governmental employer are not subject to ERISA and, as a result, can cover any employees. However, 457 plans of a nongovernmental employer are subject to ERISA, which generally prohibits covering individuals who do not compose a select group of management. As a result, only highly paid or management employees may participate.

Payroll practitioners must also consider whether the nonqualified 457 plan is subject to the provisions of Section 409A. If so, a complete consideration of those rules must be undertaken to determine when income is reportable. Under the rules at Treasury Regulations Section 1.409A-1(b)(4)(i) relating to short-term deferrals, an I.R.C. Section 409A compensation deferral does not occur if the plan under which a payment is made does not provide for a deferred payment and the employee actually or constructively receives the payment on or before the first day of the applicable two and one-half month period. Under Section 1.409A-1(a)(4), the inclusion in income of an amount under Section 457(f) is treated as a payment of the amount for purposes of the Section 1.409A-1(b)(4) short-term deferral rule.

If the Section 409A standard on substantial risk of forfeiture is adopted for Section 457 plans, a substantial risk of forfeiture under Section 457(f)(1)(B) could not lapse later than the date the substantial risk of forfeiture lapsed under Section 409A and Section 1.409A-1(d).

In addition, Internal Revenue Service Notice 2009-8 provides guidance on coordination of I.R.C. Section 457A with Section 409A where both sections may apply to amounts deferred under the same arrangement. [Interim Guidance Under § 457A, Notice 2009-8, 2009-4 I.R.B. 347] The guidance specifically applies to the application of both sections' short-term deferral rules.

The notice also provides guidance in question and answer format on how to determine whether an entity is a foreign corporation, what is considered "substantially all" of a foreign corporation's or partnership's income, and provides examples clarifying some of the issues raised by the statute's use of definitions borrowed from Section 409A.

Q 9:396 How are an employee's pretax contributions to a government Section 457 plan reported?

Neither an employee's elective contribution nor a nonelective contribution (i.e., an employer's contribution) to an "eligible" Section 457 plan is treated as income for federal income tax purposes until paid as benefits if the contribution limits are not exceeded. If there is no risk of forfeiture (i.e., the account is vested), both the employer contribution and employee contribution are included in Boxes 3 and 5 of Form W-2, and the total is reported in Box 12 preceded by Code G. If the plan is an "ineligible" plan (meaning that benefits exceed the annual contribution limit) under I.R.C. Section 457(b), all employee and employer contributions are included in Boxes 1, 3, and 5 for the first year in which there is no substantial risk of forfeiture of the contributions—that is, when the contributions or benefits vest (which can be much earlier than the date the benefits are paid). [I.R.C. §§ 457(a), 457(f), 3121(a)(5)(E), 3121(v)(3), 3306(b)(5)(E); Treas. Reg. § 1.457-1; Pub. No. 957; Form SSA-131 instructions]

Employee and employer contributions that are in excess of the limits identified and are thus ineligible plans under I.R.C. Section 457(f) are included in the Box 12 amount and not excluded from federal income taxes. Do not include any 457(f) amount in Box 12.

Participation in a governmental 457 plan is not treated as active participation, and in Box 13 "Retirement plan" is not checked. Participation in any other plan of a governmental entity would require Box 13 to be checked.

Q 9:397   Must elective contributions to a Section 457 plan be deposited into a trust?

Note that when plan assets are transferred to a trust, the trust remains an asset of the employer and the assets of the trust are subject to the claims of creditors. [I.R.C. §§ 457(b)–457(e), 457(g); Treas. Reg. § 1.457-2]

Q 9:398   How are distributions from a Section 457 plan treated after 2001?

After 2001, distributions from a Section 457 plan are subject to many of the same rules that apply to a 401(k) plan. Where a distribution qualifies as an eligible rollover distribution, it is subject to mandatory 20 percent withholding. [I.R.C. § 457(e)(16)(A)]

In addition, an eligible rollover distribution from a government 457 plan may be rolled into an IRA, another 457 plan, or a qualified plan. [I.R.C. § 3401(a)(12)(E)]

Catch-Up Contributions

Q 9:399   What are "catch-up" contributions?

"Catch-up" contributions are additional pretax employee contributions that may be made by participants in 401(k), 403(b), and government 457 plans who have attained age 50 by December 31. The catch-up contribution is $6,000 for 2017. These contributions are not subject to any of the I.R.C. limitations that apply to employee or employer contributions made to 401(k) (or 403(b) or 457) plans. That is, although the salary deferral limit for a 401(k) plan is $18,000 in 2017, a participant meeting the age 50 requirement may also contribute an additional $6,000 in 2017.

Employee contributions must first be applied as non-catch-up contributions until either the $18,000 calendar limit for 2016, the 415 (the maximum contribution of an employee and employer cannot exceed 100 percent of pay), or the 401(k) limits (the annual actual deferral percentage test) are met. Then they are applied as a catch-up contribution. This will prevent an employer from shifting employee contributions to satisfy one of the top-heavy or nondiscrimination tests under the I.R.C.

Catch-up contributions are exempt from federal income tax withholding, but are subject to FICA and FUTA taxes. Report these elective contributions in Box 12 of the Form W-2 along with other salary deferrals to a 401(k), 403(b), SIMPLE, or SARSEP using the appropriate code (D, E, F, and D, respectively). There is no need to separately identify the catch-up from other salary deferrals. [Ann. 2001-93, 2001-44 I.R.B. 416]

IRA Contribution Programs

Q 9:400   Are employee contributions to an employer-sponsored IRA subject to employment taxes?

Yes. There is no current exclusion from any federal employment taxes for any employee contributions made to an employer-sponsored IRA, other than a SIMPLE IRA or SEP IRA program. That is, IRA contributions that are payroll deductions and made by an employer for an employee are subject to federal income taxes, federal income tax withholding, and FICA, and FUTA. The maximum IRA contribution outside a SARSEP or SIMPLE plan is $6,000 for 2017 (i.e., the calendar years). Employee contributions to IRAs through a payroll deduction election are made with aftertax contributions. Note, however, that SARSEP and SIMPLE plans adopted by the employer are funded through IRAs, and these plans permit employee contributions in excess of the $6,000 IRA limit and are exempt from income tax withholding because they are part of an employer-sponsored SIMPLE or SARSEP. Any employee (but not employer) contributions to these plans are subject to FICA and FUTA taxes.

Beginning in 2002, individuals who are age 50 or older may make additional contributions of $500 to an IRA. The catch-up for an IRA is $1,000 in 2017.

Leased Employees' Participation

Q 9:401   Are leased employees working on a full-time basis entitled to pension benefits under the worksite employer's plan?

Yes, only when the plan document at the worksite employer so specifies. However, nothing in the I.R.C. requires any mandatory private pension coverage for any worker. In certain circumstances, coverage may be dictated by a contract agreed to between the employer and leasing company. Whether or not an employee or leased employee is entitled to a pension benefit (including contributions under profit sharing and 401(k) plans), the level and type of benefits provided will be based on the terms of the plan document. Where the document specifically excludes a group of employees (e.g., leased employees), they are not entitled to benefits. When leased employees are included in a worksite employer's plan, all reporting for contributions and benefits follows the reporting applicable to plans covering common-law employees. When the leased employees participate in the 401(k) plan of the worksite employer rather than the plan of the leasing company, an issue frequently arises as to how to make (and report) the salary deferrals on compensation paid by the leasing company. There is no formal guidance; however, the preambles to the regulations discuss such contributions to SIMPLE IRAs. The IRS appears to recognize the fact that the leasing company reports the salary deferrals and related FICA and FUTA taxes but can transfer the amounts to the worksite employer's plan. An employer with a small number of leased employees may exclude in its pension or profit sharing plan all leased employees.

Note, however, that although no federal law requires that any workers, including leased employees, be covered under an employer's pension plan, excluding a group of otherwise eligible employees, or a group of employees, could cause the plan to lose its tax qualification. For purposes of meeting the I.R.C.'s minimum coverage and nondiscrimination requirements, a leased employee who has been employed for a year is generally treated as a common-law employee. Thus, failing to cover leased employees who otherwise satisfy all requirements for coverage could cause the plan to fail one of these tests and lose its tax qualification. The I.R.C. and regulations offer specific mathematical tests to demonstrate whether a plan's coverage of less than all the employees satisfies certain minimum coverage and nondiscrimination requirements. [I.R.C. §§ 401(a)(4), 410(b), 414(m), 414(n), 414(o)]

In IRS Notice 84-11, the I.R.C. "requires only that a leased employee be treated as an employee; it does not require that a leased employee be a participant in the recipient's qualified plan." [I.R.C. § 414(n)(1)(A); Bronk v. Mountain States Tel. & Tel., Inc., 1998 U.S. App. LEXIS 6901 (10th Cir. 1998)]

Picked-Up Contributions

Q 9:402   What are picked-up contributions?

The term "picked-up" contributions refers to a procedure that is utilized by many state or local government retirement plans that require an aftertax contribution by the employee as a condition for participation in the plan. A picked-up contribution occurs when the employer pays the employee's required contribution but does not treat the contribution as taxable wages of the employee. Thus, these might appear to be similar to 401(k) plans, which are not permitted for government employers. When the contributions qualify as a "picked up" contribution, they are not treated as elective contributions and are not subject to federal income tax or FICA or FUTA taxes. This exclusion from income taxation is only available for government employers and is generally exempt from any nondiscrimination requirements. That is, the government entity can pick and choose whose contributions are picked up. Most government employers obtain a private letter ruling from the IRS when they implement a pick-up procedure. This ruling will confirm that the picked-up contributions are not additional compensation subject to federal employment taxes. [I.R.C. §§ 414(h), 3121(v)(1)(B), 3306(r)(1)(B)]

A picked-up contribution qualifies for this treatment when two conditions are met: (1) the employer must specify that the contributions are being paid in lieu of the employee contributions (these contributions are treated as employee contributions under the plan for benefit eligibility) and (2) the employee cannot have the option to elect out of the picked-up program and receive the contribution amount as a cash payment (i.e., it cannot be a salary reduction). [Rev. Rul. 81-35, 1981-1 C.B. 255; Priv. Ltr. Rul. 9724028, June 13, 1997]

Contribution of Unused Sick Pay or Paid Time Off

Q 9:403   Can an employer contribute the value of unused sick pay to its retirement plan?

Yes. In two revenue rulings, IRS concluded that unused sick and vacation time off may be contributed to a retirement plan. The employer's plan called for forfeiture of unused sick and vacation time. In the first situation the employer amended the plan to allow this time to be contributed to the retirement plan. The employee did not have an option for a payment of that time. This contribution would be treated as an employer contribution without the tax implication to the employee. In the second situation the payout of unused sick and vacation time up to the limit was paid out by February 28 of the following year. The amount of unused sick and vacation time above the limit could by election be contributed to the retirement plan, provided the amount was within the contribution limit. In this case the amount contributed was the employee's contribution and was treated as any other employee contribution. [Rev. Rul. 2009-31, 2009-39 I.R.B. (Sept. 28, 2009)]; *also* Rev. Rul. 2009-32, 2009-39 I.R.B. (Sept. 28, 2009)]

The IRS held in a private letter ruling [Priv. Ltr. Rul. 200247050, Nov. 22, 2002], that an employer could contribute unused sick pay to its retirement plan. The retirement plan would have to be amended to permit such a contribution, and the provision must be carefully crafted to avoid plan disqualification where specific amounts are being contributed to an employee's account. Under this ruling, the contribution was treated as an employer contribution and not an employee deferral. The IRS also held that when constructive receipt did not cause the payment to be treated as taxable wages, the contribution also was not a 401(k) salary deferral contribution. That is, the employee cannot be permitted to choose whether to make the contribution or receive the amount in cash. The amount of the contribution was not subject to federal income taxes, federal income tax withholding, or FICA or FUTA taxes. No additional reporting on Form W-2 would be required.

The employer sponsored a pension plan and was amending the plan to accept this type of employer contribution. Under the employer's sick-leave policy, each eligible full-time employee accrued 12 paid sick days per calendar year. An employee's accrued, but unused, sick days for each calendar year were credited to the employee's sick-leave bank. Under a proposed change in the sick-pay plan, the employer would permit any NHCE to elect annually, prior to the start of the plan year, to have the value of any accumulated sick days in excess of 30 days contributed to the employee's account under the pension plan. Key to this election was the fact that employees did not have the option of receiving cash from the plan in lieu of the plan contribution. Thus, the election avoided current taxation under the constructive receipt rules. [Priv. Ltr. Rul. 9840006, Oct. 2, 1998]

Note that in this ruling only NHCEs were eligible to make this election. As a result, the contributions were generally exempt from having to satisfy certain nondiscrimination rules that apply to pension and profit sharing plans.

A different design could lead to extensive annual testing by the plan adminis-trator to ensure that the pension plan continues to qualify under the I.R.C.

The proposed regulations under Section 457 permit a contribution of accrued vacation and sick pay to be contributed to a governmental 457 plan. It is common for a school district, for example, to make an employer contribution of unused sick pay to a 403(b) plan upon a participant's retirement. As long as the appropriate language is utilized in the underlying collective bargaining agree-ment that ensures the contribution is from the employer, and not a deferral by the employee, the deferral limit does not apply, but rather the overall defined contribution limit for the year is applicable. Thus, amounts over the deferral limit may be accepted by the plan because the contributions are by the employer.

Restoration Contributions Made to Pension Plans

Q 9:404   Are restoration contributions to pension and profit sharing plans for investment losses in the plan included in the gross wages of the employee?

In most cases, no; however, any employer contemplating such a contribution should request a private ruling from the IRS on the taxability and deductibility of such a contribution. Neither the I.R.C. nor the federal tax regulations provide specific guidance on the status of restoration payments. As more litigation against 401(k) plans evolves, employers may seek to utilize this strategy for the purpose of a settlement, or to avoid a lawsuit.

The purpose of a restoration payment by the employer is to ensure that participants with a large plan investment loss recover a significant portion of their losses; the employer does this by making additional contributions to employees' accounts in a plan. Such a payment is typically designed to place participants in a position similar to where they would have been had the loss not occurred and is not treated as an employer contribution subject to the 2017 limit of $54,000. These contributions may be characterized as ordinary and necessary expenses of the employer and be fully deductible; however, the IRS has allowed this tax treatment only following a threatened or actual lawsuit over a plan loss. Where the restoration payment is treated as an employer contribution, the plan could violate Section 415(c) if it is too large or violates the nondiscrimination rules if it is paid unevenly to highly paid participants. Then the plan could lose its tax qualification. [Abbott v. Commissioner, 38 B.T.A. 1290 (1938); DeVito v. Commissioner, T.C. Memo. 1979-377; Priv. Ltr. Rul. 9807028, Feb. 13, 1998]

SEP Benefits

Q 9:405   What are simplified employee pension plans?

A simplified employee pension (SEP) is not a qualified plan; rather, it is an employer-sponsored program consisting of a series of IRAs to which the employer makes contributions for all eligible employees. Certain salary reduc-tion SEPs (SARSEPs) permit the employee to make before-tax salary reduction contributions. New SARSEPs cannot be implemented after December 31, 1996; however, SARSEPs established prior to that date may enroll new participants and continue to accept elective employee contributions. Note that the I.R.C. does impose certain limitations and requirements on when an employer with a SARSEP must permit employees to make elective contributions. These are identified in the SARSEP document. When the percentage of eligible participants making salary deferrals falls below 50 percent, no salary deferrals are permitted. [I.R.C. § 408(k)(6)]

The IRS has released an updated SARSEP document (Form 5305A-SEP). In most cases, SARSEP forms from a financial institution will be less restrictive than the Form 5305A-SEP. [Pub. No. 590]

Q 9:406   What are the eligibility requirements for SEP participation?

A SEP may be designed to limit participation to individuals who have worked in up to three out of the five prior calendar years and/or who have attained age 21. A SEP may also allow for immediate entry. Any employment in the calendar year satisfies this requirement. In addition, the plan can exclude individuals meeting this requirement from sharing in a contribution for the current year when their compensation is less than a minimum compensation threshold. The minimum amount of compensation for 2017 is $600. The SEP cannot restrict participation to individuals who have worked a minimum number of hours in the current plan year, nor can it exclude a participant from sharing in the employer allocation merely because he or she was not employed on the last day of the plan year. [I.R.C. § 408(k)]

Q 9:407   How are contributions to a SEP treated for employment tax purposes?

An employer's SEP contributions to an employee's IRA are excluded from the employee's gross income. These excluded amounts are not subject to Social Security, Medicare, and FUTA taxes, or federal income tax withholding. Any employee contributions paid under a salary reduction agreement (i.e., a SARSEP) are included in the employee's wages for purposes of FICA and FUTA taxes, but are not subject to federal income tax withholding. A distribution from a SEP is treated as a distribution from an IRA. [Pub. No. 590; I.R.C. §§ 402(g)(3)(B), 402(h), 3121(a)(5)(C), 3306(b)(5)(C)]

Q 9:408   What is the maximum contribution that can be made for an employee in a SEP or SARSEP?

The maximum combined employee and employer contribution to any SEP for a *single employee* is $54,000 for 2017 or, if less, 25 percent of each individual's compensation. Note that the 25 percent limit for SEPs is applied to each individual participant's contribution. For qualified plans (e.g., a 401(k) plan), the maximum contribution percentage is 100 percent. The salary deferral limit for each employee is the *lesser* of: (1) $18,000 for 2017; or (2) 25 percent of the employee's net annual compensation. An additional $6,000 catch-up contribution is also permitted for individuals age 50 by December 31, 2017. [I.R.C. § 402(h)] Property may not be contributed to a SEP. This maximum limitation of $15,000 adjusted for inflation, previously set to expire in 2010, was made permanent by the Pension Protection Act of 2006. [Pub. L. No. 109-280, 120 Stat. 780]

Only compensation of up to $265,000 may be included in this calculation for 2017.

Q 9:409 How are excess SEP and SARSEP contributions treated for employment tax purposes?

Contributions (i.e., total employee and employer) to a SEP or SARSEP that exceed the 25 percent of pay limit or the dollar limit ($18,000 for deferrals in 2017, or $54,000 for employee and employer contributions in 2017) are classified as excess contributions. Excess contributions are included in the gross wages of the employee and are fully subject to federal income tax, federal income tax withholding, and FICA and FUTA taxes. [I.R.C. § 402(h)(2)(B)]

Excess SEP contributions that are not withdrawn from the IRA by April 15 are subject to a 6 percent penalty assessed on the IRA holder (i.e., the participant). [I.R.C. § 4973(a)] Excess contributions may not be carried over and distributed in the next year. The employer is also subject to a 10 percent excise tax for the excess contribution treated as a nondeductible contribution. [I.R.C. § 404(h)(1)(C)]

Q 9:410 How are SEP and SARSEP contributions reported on Form W-2?

Basically, employer contributions to a SEP are not part of an employee's wages for all employment tax purposes. Salary deferrals to a SARSEP, like those to a 401(k) plan, are exempt from federal income taxes but are subject to FICA and FUTA taxes and are included in Boxes 3 and 5 of Form W-2. The total employee contribution (i.e., the elective contribution) is shown in Box 12 with Code F.

Q 9:411 Is participation in a SEP or SARSEP treated as participation in a qualified plan for IRA contribution restrictions?

Yes. Participation in a SEP or SARSEP is treated as active participation in a retirement plan of the employer, requiring that Box 13 be checked on Form W-2 for "Retirement plan." An employee who makes a salary deferral to either a SEP or SARSEP is treated as participating in a pension plan of the employer. As a result, the employer checks Box 13 on the employee's Form W-2 for "Retirement plan." [Treas. Reg. §§ 31.3121(a), 31.3306(b), 31.3401(a)(12)-1(d)]

SIMPLE Plans

Q 9:412   What is a SIMPLE retirement plan?

The term "SIMPLE plan" refers to two savings programs implemented with the Small Business Job Protection Act of 1996. SIMPLE stands for Savings Incentive Match Plan for Employees. These retirement plan programs were designed to reduce the administrative requirements for the employer and permit the employee to make annual salary deferrals of up to $12,500 for 2017. SIMPLE plans can be structured either through IRAs (SIMPLE IRAs) or a 401(k) qualified plan. Only the SIMPLE IRA is not required to file Form 5500. These plans are only available to small employers (generally, employers with no more than 100 employees who earned $5,000 or more in the two prior calendar years). A SIMPLE plan requires that the employer decide prior to the start of the plan year whether to match the employee's salary deferrals or to make a pro rata contribution (generally at 2 percent) to all employees who are eligible. Either type of employer contribution is fully vested, but no testing for discrimination is required as in a 401(k) plan. Employers electing to make the match are also required, under current law, to make any required top-heavy contributions (as defined under I.R.C. Section 416). [I.R.C. §§ 401(k)(11), 408(p)(1)]

Q 9:413   What is the elective contribution limit for SIMPLE plans?

The limit on salary deferrals will depend on whether the plan is a SIMPLE IRA or a SIMPLE 401(k). A SIMPLE IRA is subject to a lower contribution limit than a SIMPLE 401(k). An individual in a SIMPLE IRA may contribute the lesser of $12,500 for 2017 or 100 percent of the individual's wages (after payment of employment taxes). Participants age 50 by December 31, 2016 can match an additional catch-up contribution of $3,000 for 2017 to a SIMPLE IRA. A participant in a SIMPLE 401(k) plan may contribute the lesser of $12,500 for 2017 or 100 percent of the participant's compensation. Compensation is gross compensation before Section 125 salary reductions, employee contributions to a transportation benefit plan, and the SIMPLE contributions. [I.R.C. § 415(c)]

Q 9:414   How are employer contributions to a SIMPLE retirement account treated for employment tax purposes?

Employers that sponsor a SIMPLE plan must either make a pro rata contribution of 2 percent (this may be reduced with SIMPLE IRAs in some cases) to all employees who are eligible for the plan or a dollar-for-dollar match of up to 3 percent of compensation for all employees who make salary deferrals to the SIMPLE plan. These employer contributions are exempt from federal income tax and FICA and FUTA taxes. The benefits would be subject to federal income tax when paid and, if paid as an "eligible rollover distribution" from a SIMPLE 401(k) plan, mandatory federal income tax is withheld. [I.R.C. §§ 401(k)(11), 408(p)(1)]

Q 9:415   How are employee contributions to a SIMPLE plan treated for employment tax purposes?

Employee contributions to a SIMPLE 401(k) plan or SIMPLE IRA are exempt from federal income taxes but are subject to FICA and FUTA taxes. The employee elective contributions (salary deferrals) are included on the employee's Form W-2, Boxes 3 and 5. The employer will also report the amount of salary deferrals in Box 12 with a Code D for a participant in a SIMPLE 401(k) and Code S for a participant in a SIMPLE IRA.

Q 9:416   Are participants eligible to make salary deferrals to a SIMPLE plan treated as participating in a pension plan for the IRA contribution restriction?

Yes, but only if the employee makes a salary deferral or receives any employer contribution. Merely being eligible does not count as participating. Note that an employer may elect prior to the start of the plan year to make a 2 percent pro rata contribution to the SIMPLE IRA. In that case, the eligible employee who receives an allocation of that contribution is an active participant, regardless of whether he or she makes a salary deferral.

An individual who receives an allocation of any employer contribution under a SIMPLE IRA or SIMPLE 401(k) plan in the calendar year is classified as an active participant and "Retirement plan" under Box 13 of Form W-2 should be checked.

USERRA Plan Implications

Q 9:417   What is USERRA?

The Uniformed Services Employment and Reemployment Rights Act of 1994 (USERRA) requires employers with employees who have been called up for military duty to contribute "make-up" pension and profit sharing contributions when the worker returns to employment. The returning employee's contribution for a prior year when the employee was on military leave and had reduced, or no, compensation is referred to as the "make-up" contribution. The contribution amount made to the returning employee's account is based on the individual's compensation prior to the military leave and not on the amount paid during the leave.

For plan participation purposes, USERRA requires employers to treat these returning employees who were absent from work to serve in the military as if they had not been absent from work. The amount of any make-up pension or profit sharing contribution is based on the employee's earnings in the 12-month period immediately preceding the period of qualified military leave.

Where a 401(k) plan exists, employers must allow these returning employees to make the salary deferrals that could have been made if the individual had actually been employed during the period of military service. Such contributions would be matched at the rate available to active participants during the period of leave. These make-up salary deferrals are not included with the employee's current year 401(k) salary deferrals in meeting the annual deferral limit. A separate salary deferral limit will apply to the make-up and current-year salary deferral contribution. Thus, a returning employee under age 50 could contribute up to $36,000 in 2017 ($18,000 for 2017 and $18,000 for 2016) to a 401(k) plan. [38 U.S.C. §§ 4318, 414(u)]

Note. In 2006, the Heroes Earned Retirement Opportunities Act became effective to ease the rules for individual retirement account contributions by military personnel serving in combat areas. [Pub. L. No. 109-227, 120 Stat 385] The law allows typically nontaxable combat pay to count as taxable income for purposes of calculating allowable IRA contributions under I.R.C. Section 219.

Q 9:418 How does an employer report "make-up" pension contributions under the USERRA?

Salary deferrals to a 401(k) plan, SARSEP, or SIMPLE plan made under the USERRA requirements for a prior year are reported in Box 12 of Form W-2, using Codes D, H, or S, as appropriate. The employer must also note the year of the contribution. Some employers have had difficulty accommodating the USERRA reporting on Form W-2. Employers may provide a separate statement to their employees showing the employer (i.e., nonelective) USERRA make-up contributions or use Box 14. Report in Box 12 the type of plan, the amount of the contribution, and the calendar years to which the contribution relates. Thus, an employee making a salary deferral to a 401(k) plan of $8,800 for 2015 and $11,000 for 2016 in 2017 would use Box 12 of the 2017 Form W-2 coded as "D 2015 8,800, D 2016 11,000." [38 U.S.C. §§ 4303, 4318; Form W-2 instructions]

Rollovers

Q 9:419 What is an eligible rollover distribution?

The term *eligible rollover distribution* refers to the taxable portion (and after 2001, certain taxable and nontaxable amounts) of any distribution from a qualified plan, tax-deferred annuity (i.e., from a 403(b) plan), or governmental 457 plan (but not from an IRA) that may be rolled over to another plan or IRA if the participant so elected. Note that although distributions from an IRA may generally be rolled over, they are not classified under Code regulations as an eligible rollover distribution. Cash distributions of an eligible rollover distribution are subject to mandatory federal income tax withholding.

A distribution is an eligible rollover distribution when it is not one of the following: (1) one of a series of substantially equal periodic payments (at least annually) made for the life or life expectancy of the employee and the employee's beneficiary or for a specified period of 10 years or more; (2) required minimum distributions under Section 401(a)(9); (3) death benefit distributions that are not taxable under I.R.C. Section 101(a); (4) distributions of aftertax contributions and other distributions of funds that have been taxed to the employee (e.g., PS 58 costs); (5) certain corrective distributions from a 401(k) plan (i.e., made to satisfy the ADP or ACP tests or that exceed the deferral limit of $18,000 for 2017 and not eligible for an additional $6,000 catch up under Section 402(g)); (6) a distributed excess Section 415(c) violation (more than the 100 percent of pay or $54,000 for 2017 annual allocation limit [Treas. Reg. § 1.415-6(b)(6)(iv)]); (7) loans that have been treated as "deemed distributions" when made or when the loan fails to meet the conditions of I.R.C. Section 72(p) (certain "loan offsets" of terminated participants may qualify as eligible rollover distributions [Treas. Reg. § 1.402(c)-2, Q-9, ex. 1-4]); (8) certain dividends paid on employer securities held by an ESOP; and (9) the total value of life insurance coverage that was treated as taxable income by the participant. None of the distributions in this list can be rolled to another plan or an IRA, and none are subject to the mandatory 20 percent withholding, although other withholding requirements will apply. [Treas. Reg. § 1.72-16] Under prior law, only the IRA participant or his or her surviving spouse may roll over any distribution from the IRA or IRA annuity (to another IRA, etc.). The surviving spouse must have acquired his or her interest (in the IRA, etc.) as a result of the death of the employee-participant (an "inherited" IRA or IRA annuity). This meant that only the employee-participant, or, if he or she died, the surviving spouse, could roll over amounts from an IRA or IRA annuity. The Pension Protection Act of 2006 (PPA) added a provision that allows nonspouse beneficiaries to roll over to an IRA amounts inherited as a designated beneficiary. [Pub. L. No. 109-280, 120 Stat. 780] Note that beginning in 2002, any amounts distributed from an IRA that would be taxable if not rolled over may be rolled to an IRA, qualified plan, or governmental Section 457 plan.

Prior to the PPA, permissible rollovers to a Roth IRA were limited to "qualified rollover contributions" and subject to substantial restrictions unless coming from another Roth IRA. PPA changed the rule to allow for direct rollovers from eligible retirement plans to Roth IRAs. [Pub. L. No. 109-280, 120 Stat. 780]

Q 9:420 How must a mandatory distribution of more than $1,000 and less than $5,000 be rolled over, when a participant has not given the plan direction?

Section 401(a)(31)(B) (added by the Economic Growth and Tax Relief Reconciliation Act of 2001—EGTRRA) provides that mandatory distributions of more than $1,000 from a qualified plan must be paid in a direct rollover to an individual retirement plan if the former plan participant does not make an affirmative election to have the amount paid in a direct rollover to an eligible retirement plan or to receive the distribution directly. When a participant has not provided direction to a plan regarding disposition of a distribution, the plan is permitted to act on the participant's behalf in setting up a rollover vehicle for funds distributed by the plan.

The automatic rollover rules are effective for mandatory distributions made on or after March 28, 2005. A sample amendment and further guidance is given in IRS Notice 2005-3 [2005-1 C.B. 447]. Among other issues, the notice states that compliance also is required for small employers that have adopted master and prototype plans.

Active Participation for IRA Contributions

Q 9:421   When is an employee classified as an "active participant" in a retirement plan of the employer for Form W-2, Box 13 purposes?

Active participant status can affect whether an employee can or cannot make a fully deductible IRA contribution. In general, individuals are blocked from making fully deductible IRA contributions when their AGIs are above specific thresholds and/or their Form W-2 shows them to have been an active participant in a pension plan during the calendar year. Thresholds under the Taxpayer Relief Act of 1997 permit individuals who could not make deductible IRA contributions in prior years to make such contributions beginning in 1998.

An employee becomes an active participant (meaning that Box 13, "Retirement plan," is checked) for purposes of the W-2 filing when he or she actively participates in any one of the following plans: (1) a qualified pension, profit sharing, or stock bonus plan; (2) a qualified annuity plan; (3) a plan covering employees of the federal government, a state, or a political subdivision (or an agency or instrumentality thereof other than a governmental 457 plan); (4) a tax-deferred annuity for employees of certain tax-exempt organizations; (5) a simplified employee pension; or (6) a SIMPLE retirement account (SIMPLE IRA).

Defined benefit pension plans. These basic definitions apply regardless of whether the plan is a defined contribution plan or a defined benefit plan. With a defined benefit pension plan, an individual is deemed to be an active participant if the individual has been *covered* under the defined benefit plan at any time during the calendar year. An individual need not accrue a benefit or be vested to be classified as an active participant in this type of plan. Under these rules, an individual who participates in a defined benefit plan, for example, from June 1, 2015 to May 30, 2016 is an active participant for the 2016 and 2017 calendar years.

There are few exceptions to these rules for defined benefit plans. Individuals who elect not to be covered (which happens rarely), and who therefore do not accrue any benefits because they do not make a mandatory contribution, are treated as active participants if they have satisfied the other requirements of the plan. Individuals who are excluded from the plan because they are members of a class of employees that is not covered (e.g., hourly workers) are not treated as active participants. This could apply where a group of workers, such as salespeople, are not eligible to participate under the terms of the plan document. Individuals who have not met the age and service requirements (e.g., one year of service and age 21) are not treated as covered and are not active participants.

Defined contribution plans. The rules for determining active participation under a defined contribution plan are somewhat more complicated, with active participation under a 401(k) being the most difficult to ascertain.

An individual becomes an active participant in a defined contribution plan when any employer contributions (e.g., match or profit sharing) or forfeiture reallocations are allocated to the individual's account in the plan year that ends with or within the calendar year. For most plans, such allocations occur on the last day of the plan year. Thus, for example, an individual covered under a defined contribution plan for the plan year ending January 31, 2017 is an active participant for 2015 only if either a forfeiture or contribution is allocated for the plan year ending on January 31, 2017. [Notice 87-16, 1987-1 C.B. 446]

These rules vary slightly when determining active participation under a profit sharing plan. The employer generally has discretion over whether and when a contribution is to be made. An individual is an active participant in a profit sharing plan during the calendar year under one of two criteria: (1) a contribution or forfeiture reallocation is allocated to the individual's account in the plan year that ends in the calendar year, or (2) the employer makes all of its contributions, after the end of the plan year, in the calendar year of the W-2 filing. This second component of the active participant classification applies only when the employer makes no contribution during the plan year *and is not required to make a contribution.*

Thus, if the employee receives no allocation of the employer's profit sharing contribution, employee contributions, or a forfeiture reallocation by the end of the plan year, and the employer's contributions are "purely discretionary," the individual is not treated as an active participant for that plan year. However, if after the end of that plan year that employer decides to make its contribution, the individual is an active participant for the calendar year when the contribution was made, regardless of the plan year-end. Contributions are treated as discretionary when the employer is not obligated under the law or under the terms of the plan to make a contribution. This condition applies to most profit sharing plans.

Consider a profit sharing plan with the plan year of October 1, 2015 to September 30, 2016. If the employer makes any contribution during the plan year or if there is a reallocation of forfeiture for the plan year, the individual is an actual participant for the 2015 calendar year. However, if there are no contributions (employee or employer) during the plan year and no forfeiture reallocation, the individual is not an active participant in 2015. Should this employer decide to make a contribution on January 1, 2017 for the plan year ending September 30, 2016 (and no other contributions were made in 2016), the individual is an active participant only for the 2017 plan year.

An individual is not an active participant in a defined contribution plan merely because earnings (rather than contributions or forfeitures) are allocated during the plan year, and a participant who is not entitled to an allocation of contributions or forfeiture reallocation in the plan year because he or she did not satisfy a minimum service requirement (i.e., 1,000 hours or last-day-of-year requirement) is not an active participant.

401(k) plan. There is one variation in these basic rules for defined contribution plans when the employer's plan is a 401(k) plan. An individual who declines to make a deferral election in the plan year, and who receives no other contributions or forfeiture reallocations in the plan year, is not an active participant for the plan year.

Announcement 91-11 distinguishes between individuals who are covered under a defined benefit pension plan but accrue no benefit because they did not make a mandatory aftertax contribution, and participants in a 401(k) plan who do not elect to participate. Individuals in the defined benefit plan are treated as active participants; however, a 401(k) participant who elects to make no deferrals in the plan year is not an active participant as long as no other contributions or forfeitures are allocated, as discussed previously.

Note that an individual who elects to make no 401(k) deferrals will be treated as an active participant when the individual receives a forfeiture that is allocated in the plan year ending in the calendar year, even if it is only $0.01. Generally, electing not to make salary deferrals will not prevent the individual from being eligible for other employer contributions or forfeiture reallocations. [Tolley v. Commissioner, T.C. Memo. 1997-244]

Q 9:422   When are employees eligible to make an IRA contribution?

Individuals who are not classified as active participants in any qualified retirement plan of the employer may contribute and deduct from their personal income taxes up to $5,500 a calendar year to an IRA. In addition, an individual may make an IRA contribution for a nonworking spouse. For 2017, the limit is the lesser of taxable compensation or $5,500, subject to certain limitations. Individuals who are classified as an active participant in any qualified retirement plan of the employer may be subject to a limit on the deductible amount. In each of these instances, the amount is increased to $6,500 for a taxpayer who has attained age 50.

An individual who has been classified as an active participant may make a full $5,500 IRA contribution, but the amount of the deduction is capped (less than $5,500) (1) when the individual's AGI exceeds $72,000 for 2017 and (2) if the individual is married and filing a joint return and the AGI of the individual and his or her spouse exceeds $119,000 for 2017. Married individuals who file separately are treated as single individuals if they do not live together. The $5,500 deduction limit is reduced by 30 percent for each dollar of AGI above these limits. The calculation is separate for each individual based on his or her status of being an active participant. The 2016 limitations are as shown in the chart below. [I.R.C. § 219(g)(3)(B)]

Married Filing Jointly

	Begin Phaseout	*Complete Phaseout*
2017	$99,000	$119,000

*Unmarried Individuals and Married
Individuals Filing Separately and
Living Apart*

	Begin Phaseout	*Complete Phaseout*
2017	$62,000	$72,000

*Married Individuals Filing Separately
but Live Together.*

	Begin Phaseout	*Complete Phaseout*
2017	$0	$10,000

Example. Sarah and Henry, a married couple under the age of 50, want to maximize their deductible IRA contribution for 2017. Only Henry is an active participant in a qualified plan of his employer. The couple's AGI is $104,000. Using 2017 limits, the maximum tax-deductible IRA contribution that Henry may contribute is $3,500 (the maximum $5,500 deductible is reduced by $1,500: ($104,000 − $99,000) × 0.30). He can still contribute $5,500; $2,000 of that contribution will not be deductible. Sarah may contribute and have as a tax deduction the full $5,500.

Note that if the couple's AGI exceeded $119,000 for 2017, Sarah would have no deduction for an IRA contribution.

If either spouse is an active participant in a qualified plan and if the couple's AGI on a jointly filed return exceeds $196,000 (with a phaseout beginning at $186,000), the reduction in maximum deductible IRA is applied to the amount of contribution that is deductible for a nonworking spouse's IRA. The same 30 percent reduction calculation applies to a spousal IRA for AGI above $99,000. Participation is signified when Box 13, "Retirement plan," is checked on Form W-2. [I.R.C. § 219(g)(7)]

Note that the compensation cap on making deductible IRA contributions is defined in I.R.C. Section 219(g) as AGI. The IRS released in 1991 a revenue procedure that offers an alternative definition of compensation. It offers a safe harbor by basing the compensation cap on amounts reported for federal income tax purposes in Box 1 of Form W-2 less amounts reported in Box 11 as "compensation." [Rev. Proc. 91-18, 1991-1 C.B. 522]

Plans for Domestic Workers

Q 9:423   May an individual provide retirement benefits to a domestic worker?

Generally, yes. However, contributions to these plans will generally be subject to a 10 percent excise tax that applies to nondeductible contributions. Because no employee–employer relationship exists between the individual and the domestic worker, any contribution to a retirement plan is not deductible and thus subject to the excise tax on nondeductible contributions. However, beginning in 2002, such contributions may be made to a SIMPLE plan (IRA or 401(k) plan) without the contributions being subject to the excise tax. [I.R.C. § 4972(c)(6)(C)]

Early Distributions Tax—Pensions

Q 9:424   What is the early distribution penalty?

The early distribution penalty is an additional tax that applies to certain taxable distributions from qualified plans, IRAs, and I.R.C. Section 403(b) arrangements that are made before the participant attains age 59½. The penalty is in the form of an additional 10 percent income tax on the taxable amount of the distribution. The tax is paid by the participant receiving the distribution when he or she files his or her Form 1040. The party that makes the distribution is generally responsible for notifying the IRS that the distribution is an early distribution (i.e., Code 1 in Box 7 of Form 1099-R). Note that neither the employer nor the plan is responsible for withholding this 10 percent additional tax. [I.R.C. § 72(p); Form 1099-R instructions]

Exceptions to this additional tax include: (1) payments to an individual who has attained age 59½, (2) distributions to individuals who have been classified as disabled for Social Security purposes, (3) distributions from an employer's plan (i.e., not an IRA) to individuals who have separated from employment with the plan sponsor after reaching age 55, (4) corrective distributions under a 401(k) plan, (5) distributions to a beneficiary after the employee's death, (6) a series of substantially equal payments over the life of a participant, (7) a payment to satisfy a federal tax levy, and (8) certain dividends paid to ESOP participants. The exception for participants who are receiving distributions as a periodic payment requires that the amount of those payments be based on the participant's and beneficiary's life expectancy and continue for at least five years and until the individual attains age 59½. When a pre-59½ distribution is exempt from the 10 percent tax, enter Code 2 in Box 7 of Form 1099.

Scholarships and Fellowships

Q 9:425   How are scholarships and fellowships treated for employment tax purposes?

A qualified scholarship is any amount granted to pay for or reimburse an individual's expenses for (1) tuition and fees required to enroll in, or to attend, an educational institution; or (2) fees, books, supplies, and equipment that are required for courses at the educational institution. These amounts are generally not subject to employment taxes when they are awarded by an educational institution to an individual enrolled at the institution. Amounts the educational institution pays for the room and board of an employee (e.g., a teaching assistant) and any amounts paid for teaching, research, or other services required as a condition of receiving the scholarship are not considered a scholarship and are generally treated as additional compensation by the recipient. [I.R.C. §§ 117(a), 3121(a)(20), 3401(a)(19), 3306(b)(16)]

A qualified tuition reduction may be awarded to a graduate student who is teaching nongraduate courses without the amount being treated as compensation to the student. [Pub. No. 15-A]

The IRS has ruled that scholarships awarded to degree candidates under a program that requires 10 hours of community service per week in the school year (or 20 hours per week in the summer) qualify as a tax-free benefit under I.R.C. Section 117. This tax treatment was available because the IRS found that such services by the students did not constitute wages. There was no quid pro quo. [Priv. Ltr. Rul. 9645021, Nov. 8, 1996]

Employers that are not educational institutions may establish scholarship programs for the children and spouses of employees without the value of those benefits being treated as wages subject to federal income tax or FICA or FUTA taxes, though these are quite uncommon. [Rev. Proc. 76-47, 1976-2 C.B. 670; Tech. Adv. Mem. 9408001, Feb. 25, 1994]

A qualified scholarship under I.R.C. Section 117(a) is not subject to Social Security, Medicare, and federal unemployment taxes, or income tax withholding. For more information, see Publication 970, Tax Benefits for Education. Only amounts an employer pays as a qualified scholarship to a degree candidate may be excluded from the recipient's gross income. [I.R.C. §§ 117(a), 3121(a)(19), 3306(b), 3401(a)(19)]

Q 9:426 How are scholarships treated for federal employment tax purposes?

Scholarships received by individuals for tuition and related expenses (but not room and board or meals) are excludable from federal income taxes and FICA and FUTA taxes. The exclusion is lost where the scholarship is disguised compensation in payment for teaching or research services. Where a scholarship is provided in whole or part for services rendered, the grantor must make a good-faith effort to determine the amount to be treated as compensation (and subject to federal income tax withholding and FICA and FUTA taxes). The I.R.C. treats such compensation as earned on the date that the individual is notified of the scholarship, not the date the individual is enrolled. Amounts treated as compensation are included in Boxes 1, 3, and 5 of the employee's Form W-2. [I.R.C. §§ 3121(b)(10), 3306(c)(10)]

A special exception to the FICA and FUTA taxes is available for certain students attending an educational institution who are classified as "noncareer employees" of the institution. The exception is not available to graduate students or medical residents. [I.R.C. § 3306(c)(10); Rev. Proc. 98-16, 1998-1 C.B. 403]

Certain payments to a spouse of a student at an educational institution are also exempt from FUTA taxes. [I.R.C. § 3306(c)(10)(B)]

Severance Pay

Q 9:427   How is severance pay provided to a terminated employee treated for employment tax purposes?

Severance payments made to a terminated employee are treated as wages and are subject to FIT, FITW, FICA, and FUTA when paid. Severance payments are included in Boxes 1, 3, and 5 of the employee's Form W-2, and the withheld tax is included in Boxes 2, 4, and 6.

It does not matter whether the severance payments are from an employer plan requiring an employee to release the employer from certain liabilities associated with employment, or if the payments are made in a lump sum or paid over a period of months. [Treas. Reg. § 31.3401(a)-1(b)(4); Taggi v. United States, 35 F.3d 93 (2d Cir. 1994)] In a case, not appealed by the taxpayer, it was also held that supplemental unemployment benefits are also wages subject to withholding and employment tax if paid in a lump sum. [CSX Corp. v. United States, 518 F.3d 1328 (Fed. Cir. 2008)] However, see Q 9:432 for an update.

Q 9:428   Are severance awards subject to federal employment taxes?

The Eighth Circuit Court of Appeals ruled in 1998 that severance payment awards that arise from litigation over a wrongful termination or other employment practice are wages subject to FIT, FITW, FICA, and FUTA. A payment is excludable from treatment as wages only when the award is for personal injuries. Awards of damages for personal injuries are exempt under I.R.C. Section 104 only when the recovery is based on an emotional or physical injury. [Mayberry v. United States, 151 F.3d 855 (8th Cir. 1998)]

Similarly, the Sixth Circuit Court of Appeals ruled in 2006 that early retirement payments made to Michigan public school teachers who relinquished their tenure rights in exchange for such payments constitute wages under the Federal Insurance Contribution Act. [Appoloni v. United States, No. 04-2068 (6th Cir. 2006)] In this issue of first impression for the Sixth Circuit, the majority found that the early retirement payments were similar to severance payments, which have consistently been treated by courts as wages subject to FICA taxes. The majority rejected the argument that the early retirement benefits differed from severance packages because the teachers relinquished their tenure rights in exchange for benefits.

Q 9:429 Are separation payments to employees who voluntarily terminate employment subject to federal income tax withholding?

Yes. The IRS addressed this issue in a field service advice memorandum. [Field Serv. Adv. 199931012, Aug. 8, 1999] An employer's separation payments for voluntary departures of its employees were considered wages, even though the employer–employee relationship no longer existed. The payments were made by an employer under a program to reduce its workforce. Under the program, the employer offered separation payments to employees who voluntarily departed from their jobs. The payments were based on length of service and amount of pay. Some of the departing employees also received a special assistance payment, retraining assistance, services for career transition, and a transitional medical program. [Treas. Reg. § 31.3401(a)-1(a)(5)]

Q 9:430 Are payments made to cancel an employment contract subject to employment taxation?

Yes. The IRS held that amounts paid to employees as consideration to cancel employment contracts and relinquish contract rights are wages subject to FIT, FITW, FICA, and FUTA. [Rev. Rul. 2004-110, 2004-50 I.R.B. 960]

Q 9:431 Can employees make 401(k) contributions from their severance pay?

No. Only employees, not former employees, can participate in an employer's qualified plan. Therefore, severance pay paid to a terminated employee cannot be used to fund a 401(k) plan. If the individual has not been terminated and if the plan document permits, salary deferrals can be made to a 401(k) plan from compensation paid in anticipation of severance. Note that the plan document may require that severance payments be included in determining the amount of employer contribution that may be made to the plan. Also note that under legislation enacted in 2008, employees that are on leave for active duty in the U.S. Military may continue to participate in the 401(k) plan. [Pub. L. No. 110-245]

Q 9:432 Are there any recent court cases that might reopen the position that severance payments provided to laid off employees are exempt from FICA even if paid in a lump sum and not connected to state unemployment benefits?

On February 23, 2010, a Michigan Federal District Court in *United States v. Quality Stores, Inc.* rejected the reasoning in the *CSX* case (see Q 9:445), holding that severance payments that were not connected to the receipt of state unemployment benefits and that were, at least in part, paid in a lump sum, were not wages subject to Social Security and Medicare tax because they fell within the exclusion allowed for supplemental unemployment benefits under I.R.C. Section 3402(o)(2). This case restores the potential for FICA refunds for large companies that have made severance payments pursuant to layoffs, bankruptcy, or facility closings since 2006. [In re Quality Stores Inc., No. 1:09-cv-00044 (W.D. Mich., 2-23-10)]

The position taken in *Quality Stores* for the FICA exemption was the same that was advanced in the *CSX* case. The U.S. Court of Federal Claims upheld the position [CSX Corp. v. United States, 52 Fed. Cl. 208 (2002)]; however, on appeal, the Federal Circuit decided the case in the favor of the IRS. CSX did not request a rehearing, and on August 11, 2008, it was considered final that to be exempt from FICA, severance payments must meet the requirements of Revenue Ruling 90-72 and Revenue Ruling 56-249. [CSX Corp., 518 F.3d at 1339-40] The IRS then announced its intent to refuse all claims for FICA refund pursuant to the *CSX* case.

In contrast to the *CSX* case, which was decided by the Federal District, the *Quality Stores* case was decided by the U.S. District Court for the Western District of Michigan, meaning, at the time, it was precedential only in Michigan. On September 14, 2012, the Sixth Circuit affirmed the U.S. District Court for the Western District thereby providing opposing positions to the issue of whether these benefits were subject to FICA. On March 25, 2014, the United States Supreme Court decided the *Quality Stores* case. [United States v. Quality Stores, Inc., No. 12-1408 (U.S. Mar, 25, 2014)] According to the Court, wages for purposes of FICA tax are defined broadly to include all remuneration for employment. Severance payments are remuneration and fall within the definition of wages. Therefore, severance payments are taxable for FICA purposes.

Spousal Travel

Q 9:433 Is the value of spousal travel paid by the employer exempt from federal employment taxes?

Yes, when there is a business purpose for the spousal travel. An employer can provide tax-free payments of travel expenses for a spouse as a working condition fringe benefit when three conditions are met: (1) the employer does not treat the payment as wages; (2) the expenses would be deductible for the employer under I.R.C. Section 274(m)(3) as existing prior to the Omnibus Budget Reconciliation Act of 1993 (OBRA '93); and (3) the employee properly substantiates the spousal travel expenses as a valid business expense. [Treas. Reg. § 1.132-5(t)]

An employer's payment of nonbusiness travel expenses for a spouse is not deductible unless reported as gross income to the employee. Then it is deductible only as a compensation expense. I.R.C. Section 274(m) disallows any deduction for travel expenses (i.e., a noncompensation deduction) for a spouse, dependent, or guest who accompanies the taxpayer on business travel unless all of the following apply: (1) the spouse, dependent, or other individual is an employee of the taxpayer; (2) the travel of the spouse, dependent, or other individual is for a bona fide business purpose; and (3) such expenses would otherwise be deductible by the spouse, dependent, or other individual. Where such payment is deductible as a valid travel expense, no employment taxes apply. [I.R.C. § 274(m)(3)] Note that travel expenses of the employee's spouse or other companion that are deemed to be taxable wages are reported on the Form W-2 of the employee and not on a 1099 to the spouse.

An exception to the general rule allows reimbursements for a spouse's travel expenses associated with a qualified move to be excluded from an employee's gross income. [I.R.C. § 217(b)(1)]

An airline may provide seats on its planes to an employee (or spouse, parents, or dependents of an airline employee) as a tax-free no-additional-cost service. [I.R.C. § 132(b)]

Stock and Stock Options

Q 9:434   How is a stock option different from stock that is issued to the employee for services rendered?

When an employer issues its stock to an employee, the employee is treated as the beneficial owner of the stock and is then generally free to transfer or sell that stock unless restrictions are attached to the stock. Frequently, stock issued to an employee is subject to restrictions on when the stock may be transferred or sold. For example, stock in a nonpublic corporation will typically have a restriction that it may only be sold back to the corporation. This stock is referred to as "restricted stock." When severe restrictions apply on the employee's right to transfer the stock, these restrictions can reduce the value of the stock.

When the employer issues an employee an option to purchase the stock of the employer, the option generally involves a bargain element. That is, the employee will generally be given the right to purchase employer stock at a discount at some time in the future. The date when the employee is given the stock option is the grant date. When the employee exercises his or her right to purchase the stock (i.e., the exercise date), the employee surrenders the option and pays the difference between the FMV of the stock and the purchase price in the option. The difference between the FMV of the stock and the amount paid is treated as additional wages.

Q 9:435   How is employer-issued stock treated for federal employment tax purposes?

The value of an employer's stock issued to an employee for services rendered is treated as additional wages unless subject to substantial risk of forfeiture. The

FMV of such a transfer is subject to FITW, FICA, and FUTA on the date of transfer. Where the transfer is subject to substantial restrictions (e.g., a risk of forfeiture), the transfer will not be included in income until those restrictions lapse. An employee may, however, elect to treat the FMV of such restricted stock as current income with a timely filed Section 83(b) election. All federal employment taxes apply on the value of the transfer. Where an 83(b) election is made by the employee, the employer will apply federal employment tax, including federal income tax withholding based on that election. [I.R.C. §§ 31.3121(a)-1(e), 31.3306(b)-1(e), 31.3401(a)-1(a)(4)]

Q 9:436   What are employee stock options?

Stock options are a form of incentive payment entitling the employee to certain stock ownership rights issued by the employer. These options generally enable the employee to obtain an employer's stock (or a parent company or subsidiary's stock) at a discount. The value of the option granted to the employee is not treated as additional compensation at the time of issue (i.e., the grant date) unless the option has a "readily ascertainable" value.

If the nonqualified option has a readily ascertainable value at the date of grant, this value is treated as additional compensation on the date the option is granted. Few options actually have a readily ascertainable value, generally meaning there is an active public market for the option. Thus, options are rarely taxed at the time they are granted. Note that where the value of the stock that can be purchased with the option has an FMV on the date of grant, the FMV of the option cannot be determined by subtracting the option price from that value.

For nonqualified stock options, the employee is treated as receiving additional compensation at the exercise date, the date when the employee surrenders the option and obtains the stock. The amount of any additional compensation to the employee at the date of exercise will be equal to the difference between the FMV of the stock purchased on the exercise date less the amount paid (i.e., the option price).

For other types of options, qualified stock options (i.e., an employee stock purchase plan or incentive stock options), the employee is not taxed at the date of the grant of the option nor at the exercise date. The employee is taxed only when the stock purchased with the option is sold. This treatment is only available when the qualified stock option meets certain requirements (e.g., the incentive stock option and the stock purchased with the incentive stock option are held for the requisite time).

Q 9:437   How are qualified stock options issued to an employee treated for federal employment tax purposes?

The American Jobs Creation Act of 2004 clarified that remuneration received on account of the transfer of stock pursuant to exercise of an incentive stock option or under an employee stock purchase plan is excluded from FICA and FUTA tax.

Furthermore, income tax withholding is not required on a disqualifying disposition of stock, or when compensation is not recognized in connection with an employee stock purchase plan discount.

Prior to the American Jobs Creation Act of 2004 and resulting changes to the I.R.C., the most recent IRS position was stated in Notice 2002-47 [2002-28 I.R.B. 97]. Under this Notice, the IRS had announced a moratorium on its previously stated intention to subject statutory stock options to all federal employment taxes at the date the option is exercised.

The IRS had proposed new rules that would have treated as compensation and subject to FICA and FUTA taxes, certain gains on statutory stock options after 2002. Now, separate rules exist on the federal income tax treatment of statutory and nonstatutory stock options. Options that are not deemed to be statutory (e.g., incentive stock options) are by default nonstatutory. Two formal types of statutory stock option plans exist: (1) statutory incentive stock options (ISOs) and (2) employee stock purchase plans.

Incentive stock option plans. ISO plans that meet certain plan requirements are entitled to a special exemption from federal employment taxes. FIT, FITW, FICA, and FUTA are not imposed on ISOs when granted or exercised, nor when the shares purchased with the options are sold. Prior to Notice 2002-47, the IRS had proposed applying FICA and FUTA on the exercise of an ISO. [Notice 2001-73, 2001-49 I.R.B. 549] Note that an alternate minimum income tax that the employee pays applies to the difference between the price the employee paid and the FMV at the date the ISO is exercised continues to apply; however, no income tax withholding is required. When the stock purchased with the ISO is sold and certain holding requirements are met, the employee is taxed on the capital gain on the difference between the sales price and cash he or she paid; that gain is not subject to FITW, FICA, or FUTA. [Notice 2001-73, 2001-49 I.R.B. 549; Rev. Rul. 71-52, 1971-1 C.B. 278]

When stock purchased under an otherwise qualified ISO is sold before either the one-year holding period (the period between the exercise date and sale date) or the two-year holding period (the period between the grant date and sale date), the sale is treated as a disqualifying disposition. Then the employee loses the capital gain treatment and the employee is treated as having additional income based on the difference between the FMV and the price the employee paid at the date of exercise. This additional income is, however, not subject to FITW, FICA, or FUTA. The employer is required to report such a transaction on an employee's or former employee's W-2 as "other compensation." This reporting of a disqualifying disposition is required for the employer to receive a deduction for the amount reported as other compensation. [I.R.C. §§ 421, 422; Notice 87-49, 1987-2 C.B. 355; Notice 2002-47, 2002-28 I.R.B. 97; Rev. Rul. 71-52, 1971-1 C.B. 278; Treas. Reg. §§ 1.421-6, 1.422-5]

Nonstatutory stock options. The value of a nonstatutory stock option granted to employees is normally treated as additional wages when the option is exercised and is equal to the difference between the value of the stock received and the amount paid. This amount is not currently subject to FIT, FITW, FICA, or FUTA at the date of exercise. As noted earlier, if the stock option has a readily ascertainable value on the grant date, that value is treated as income at the date of grant. [Notice 2002-47, 2002-28 I.R.B. 97; I.R.C. § 83; Treas. Reg. § 1.83-7; Rev. Rul. 67-257, 1967-2 C.B. 359]

Employee stock purchase plans. An employee stock purchase plan is considered a statutory stock option and subject to the same federal employment tax treatment as an ISO.

An employee stock purchase plan is a program that gives employees the option to purchase the employer's stock at a discount under special tax benefits when the plan meets certain requirements and the employee holds the stock purchased under the plan for certain specified periods. The value of the option is not treated as wages on the date of grant unless it has a readily ascertainable value, which seldom applies. The difference in value between the value of the stock received and the price paid on the date of exercise is not additional wages subject to federal income tax withholding, nor to FICA and FUTA taxes. [Notice 2002-47, 2002-28 I.R.B. 97; Field Serv. Adv. 199926034 (Apr. 7, 1999); Sun Microsystems v. Commissioner, T.C. Memo. 1995-69]

If the stock purchased under an employee stock purchase plan is held for a period that equals or exceeds two years after the date of the grant *and* six months after the exercise, any gain on the stock when sold is treated as a capital gain. This favorable income tax treatment is lost if the holding periods are not met. A sale of the stock purchased under this option plan prior to the end of the two holding periods noted above results in the employee having the gain treated as additional compensation on the date of the sale; however, that value is subject to federal income tax withholding, but not FICA and FUTA taxes. [Notice 2002-47, 2002-28 I.R.B. 97]

Q 9:438   How are ISO transactions reported?

A disqualifying distribution is reported on Form W-2. The employer includes in Box 1, but not Boxes 3 and 5, the difference between what the employee paid for the stock and the FMV on the date of exercise; however, the amounts are not subject to FITW. [Notice 2002-31, 2002-1 C.B. 908]

An employer is required to furnish a statement to each employee who exercises an ISO on or before January 31 of the year following the year in which the ISO exercise occurs. The statement must contain the following information:

1. The employer's name, address, and taxpayer identification number;

2. The name, address, and taxpayer identification number of the person to whom the ISO shares were transferred;

3. The name and address of the corporation the stock of which is the ISO stock (if different from the employer);

4. The date the option was granted;

5. The date the shares were transferred pursuant to the exercise of the option;

6. The FMV of the stock on the date of exercise;

7. The number of shares transferred upon exercise of the option;

8. A statement that the option was an ISO; and

9. The total cost of the shares.

[I.R.C. § 6039(a)(1); Prop. Treas. Reg. § 1.6039-2(a)]

Beginning in 2001, the IRS requested reporting of the excess of the FMV of the stock over the exercise price of a nonstatutory stock option, at the time of the exercise of the option, in Box 12 of Form W-2 with Code V. This reporting was optional for the 2001 and 2002 Forms W-2. However, it is mandatory for 2003 and after. This reporting requirement does not apply to the exercise of a statutory stock option or the sale or disposition of stock acquired via the exercise of a statutory stock option. For more information, see IRS Publication 15-B.

Q 9:439   Does federal income tax withholding apply to a qualified stock option on the exercise date?

The IRS announced in 2002 in Notice 2002-47 that it would not assess FICA or FUTA, nor would it impose FITW on the grant or exercise of any qualified stock option (i.e., an ISO or employee stock purchase plan), or on the sale of any stock obtained through such option. [Notice 2002-47, 2002-28 I.R.B. 97]

Q 9:440   Are any nonstatutory stock options subject to employment taxes at the grant date?

No income is realized (and no federal employment taxes apply) at the grant of a nonstatutory stock option unless the nonstatutory stock option has a readily ascertainable value (e.g., the option is traded on a market) at the date of grant. When the stock option has a readily ascertainable value but is subject to substantial restrictions, the taxation of the grant is delayed until those restrictions lapse. Few stock options have a readily ascertainable value. [I.R.C. §§ 83(b), 83(e)]

Q 9:441   What is a Section 83(b) election?

A Section 83(b) election is a means for an employee to shift the timing of a taxable transfer of property to the employer. It is only available when the property (typically stock) is transferred subject to substantial restrictions (e.g., a vesting schedule) that may lapse (e.g., the transfer of stock that is subject to forfeiture). With the 83(b) election, the employee treats the transfer as being made prior to the period when the restrictions may lapse; the FMV of the transfer, less any amounts paid by the employee, is treated as compensation on the date of the election. Without the election, the employee would report the transfer as income on the date that the restriction is removed under Section

83(a). However, if the restriction does not lapse and the property is not transferred (e.g., it is forfeited), the employee cannot obtain a refund of the taxes paid at an earlier date.

The 83(b) election affects both the timing and the character of the gain to the employee and the timing of the deduction to the employer. In essence, the 83(b) election permits the employee to avoid ordinary income tax treatment on the appreciation in value from when the restricted property is granted until the date when the restrictions lapse. In addition, the holding period for capital gains purposes begins "on the date such property is transferred"—the date of the election. [Treas. Reg. § 1.83-4(a)] The employee's basis includes the amount paid plus the amount reported as compensation. At the time of the election, the employee is treated as receiving the property, with the FMV of the property, less any amounts paid by the employee subject to federal income tax and FICA and FUTA taxes.

The election must be made by the employee within 30 days after the date of the transfer as provided in Treasury Regulations § 1.83-2(c). The 83(b) election will normally generate a compensation deduction for the employer. A copy of the statement must be sent to the employer. [Treas. Reg. § 1.83-2(d)] The election is made by filing two copies of a written statement with the IRS Service Center where the taxpayer files his or her federal income tax return. One copy is to be filed at the time of the election and the other with the tax return for the tax year in which the property was transferred. [Treas. Reg. § 1.83-2(e)] Once made, the election is irrevocable unless the IRS consents to the revocation.

If property taxed to the employee under a Section 83(b) election is later forfeited, the employer recognizes income under the "tax benefit rule." [Treas. Reg. § 1.83-6(c)]

Q 9:442   What statutory requirements apply to a qualified employee stock purchase?

To receive favorable tax treatment, a qualified stock purchase plan must observe the requirements of I.R.C. Section 423. The requirements are met when:

1. The plan is only available to the employees of the employer, its parent, or subsidiary.
2. The stock offered must be stock of the employer, its parent, or subsidiary.
3. The plan must be approved by the stockholder within 12 months (before or after) of the date on which the plan is adopted.
4. More-than-5-percent stockholders are ineligible.
5. The plan must not discriminate in favor of highly paid employees (special rules apply under I.R.C. Section 423(b)(4)).
6. The purchase price of the stock under the option must be at least equal to 85 percent of the FMV of the stock on the date the option is offered.

7. The maximum annual value of the stock available to each employee does not exceed $25,000.

8. The purchase must not be transferable and generally must be exercised within a specified period following the grant.

9. The required holding period is met. To avoid disqualifying the stock from favorable tax treatment, the stock cannot be sold within 12 months of the exercise date and within 24 months of the grant date.

The discount associated with a stock purchase under a qualified stock purchase plan is not subject to federal income taxes on the date the stock is purchased. In general, if the stock purchased with the option is held for two years after the date of grant and one year after the exercise date, any gain is treated as a capital gain when the shares are sold. [I.R.C. §§ 421, 422, 423]

Q 9:443   What is the federal employment tax treatment of an employee stock purchase plan?

An option to purchase employer stock under an employee stock purchase plan is treated as a qualified stock option. There are no federal income tax consequences to employees when options are granted under a qualified employee stock purchase plan and, in general, any gain on the sale of stock acquired on exercise of an option under the plan is capital gain. Ordinary income can be triggered if the option price was less than 85 percent of the FMV of the stock at the time the option was granted (e.g., the plan does not satisfy Section 423) or if the stock is disposed of before meeting certain holding period requirements (disqualifying disposition). At the time of a disqualifying disposition, the favorable tax treatment is lost and the option is treated as a nonqualified option, the income that would have been reported at the exercise of the option is reported in Box 1 of Form W-2, but is not subject to FITW, FICA, or FUTA. [I.R.C. § 423]

Supplemental Unemployment Benefits

Q 9:444   What are supplemental unemployment benefits?

Supplemental unemployment benefits are paid to an employee via an employer plan when the employee loses his or her job. Such employer plans are common in the case of a layoff or plant shutdown. Supplemental unemployment benefits are designed to supplement state unemployment benefits and may be subject to special employment tax treatment. [I.R.C. § 3402(o)]

Q 9:445   How are supplemental unemployment benefits treated for employment tax purposes?

Supplemental unemployment benefits are always subject to federal income tax and federal income tax withholding. A case decided in 2008 [CSX Corp. v.

United States, 518 F.3d 1328 (Fed. Cir. 2008)] and not appealed has removed doubt as to whether benefits made under an employer's plan that are limited to receipt of state unemployment benefits are exempt from FICA and FUTA. Therefore, such payments were exempt from FITW, FICA, and FUTA when the following conditions are met:

1. The benefits are only paid to unemployed former employees who were laid off by the employer.
2. The amount of benefits is based on the employee's regular rate of pay (minus state unemployment benefits).
3. Eligibility for the plan is conditioned on meeting certain prescribed conditions after termination of employment, such as attaining eligibility for state unemployment benefits.
4. The duration of the benefits is based on funds available and the employee's seniority.
5. The benefits are not conditioned on providing any services.
6. No employee has any rights to benefits until qualified for state unemployment benefits.
7. The benefits are paid to supplement unemployment and are not paid in a lump sum. Under such conditions, these payments are designed to supplement state unemployment benefits and thus are exempt from FICA and FUTA taxes.

[I.R.C. § 3402(o); Rev. Rul. 90-72, 1990-2 C.B. 21]

Under some taxable plans, only a portion of the payment is included in the employee's gross wages. This occurs when employees receive certain amounts that represent a return of amounts previously subject to tax. This treatment may apply when benefits are paid from a union fund to members who paid special dues. It does not matter whether the separation is temporary or permanent. Supplemental unemployment benefits cannot be paid in a lump sum and qualify as wages. Federal income tax withholding on taxable supplemental unemployment benefits for taxable payments must be based on the employee's withholding certificate (Form W-4). See Publication 525, Taxable and Nontaxable Income, for more information about the taxability of supplemental unemployment benefits. [Pub. No. 15-A]

Tax-Deferred Annuities

Q 9:446   What are tax-deferred annuities?

A tax-deferred annuity (TDA) (sometimes referred to as a 403(b) plan or tax-sheltered annuity) is a savings plan that may only be offered to employees of public schools or employers that are qualified under Section 501(c)(3). (See Qs 9:389–9:394.)

Taxes (Employees' Share) Paid by Employer

Q 9:447   How does an employer gross up an employee's wages to match an aftertax payment dollar amount?

A gross-up of wages can occur when the employer wishes to pay the employee's taxes, or wants the net pay to reflect a sum certain amount. A situation may occur when imputed income or noncash benefits are prorated for an employee and the taxes are due before the taxes can be deducted from the employee's compensation. The IRS has described a procedure in Revenue Procedure 81-48 and Revenue Ruling 86-14 that may be used to determine the amount of taxes due without being subject to an underpayment penalty. [Rev. Proc. 81-48, 1981-2 C.B. 623; Rev. Rul. 86-14, 1986-1 C.B. 304]

The formula for determining the employee's gross earnings to provide a specific net payment is:

$$\frac{\text{desired net payment}}{1.00 - \text{"total tax rate" as a percentage}}$$

The "total tax rate" used under this formula is a combination of the individual's federal income tax rate for withholding (e.g., 25 percent supplemental rate) plus supplemental state withholding, Social Security (if required), and Medicare rates and any city or local tax.

When the employee's gross wages before the payment exceed the Social Security wage base, exclude the Social Security tax rate (6.2 percent) from the formula. If the employee's wages before the payment are near the Social Security wage base and the payment will cause the employee's wages to exceed the Social Security wage base, make the following adjustment: Exclude the Social Security rates from the formula, but after the calculations, add an amount that is the difference between the total Social Security taxes paid by the employee and 6.2 percent from the current wage base ($127,200 for 2017) or $7,886.40.

Example. Ramport Co. wants to make an $8,400 cash payment (after all taxes) to Geoff. Geoff's pay is currently substantially below the Social Security wage base, his federal income tax withholding is at 25 percent, and his state withholding is at 5 percent. Geoff's total tax for withholding purposes is 37.65 percent (25 percent + 5 percent + 6.2 percent + 1.45 percent) (i.e., federal wage withholding + state tax + Social Security + Medicare).

The formula to calculate the gross wages for Jason's cash payment is:

Step 1

100 − total tax percentage:

100 − (25 + 6.2 + 1.45 + 5) = 62.35

Step 2

Net amount ÷ tax or percentage

$8,400 ÷ 62.35% = $13,472.33 (gross pay)

Step 3

Calculate

$13,472.33 × 25% (FIT) = $3,368.08

$13,472.33 × 6.2% (Social Security) = $835.28

$13,472.33 × 1.45% (Medicare) = $195.35

$13,472.33 × 5% (SIT) = $673.62

$13,472.33 − $3,368.08 − $835.28 − $195.35 − $673.62 = $8,400

Example. If this amount would take Geoff over the Social Security wage base, an adjustment would be made to this calculation. Ramport Co. would determine the total Social Security taxes paid prior to this payment and subtract that amount from the total Social Security taxes payable for the year. The maximum Social Security payment, deducted from employee for 2017 is $7,886.40 (6.2 percent × $127,200). The difference would be added to the gross amount determined under the formula.

Q 9:448 What is the employment tax treatment when the employer pays the employee's federal and/or state income tax withholding and/or the employee's portion of Social Security and Medicare taxes?

In some cases, an employer's liability for withholding federal income and FICA taxes may arise when no further cash payments are to be paid. Then the employer will be required to pay the employee's portion of the federal income tax withholding and FICA and report those payments as additional wages, which will in turn create an additional liability for FITW and FICA. When the employer pays the employee's FITW and FICA on wages earned by the employee, those payments are themselves subject to FIT, FITW, FICA, and FUTA (this is commonly called a "gross-up" payment; see Q 9:447).

The amount of Social Security due on the taxes paid by the employer is determined based on whether the employee's wages after the employer's payment are above or below the current Social Security wage base.

Stated pay of $117,469.20 or less in 2017. For an employee with stated pay (before the employer's payment of the employee's portion of Social Security or Medicare taxes) of $117,469.20 (0.9235 × $127,200, the Social Security wage base for 2017) or less in 2017, for each dollar of wages paid, the employer reports $1.4848 in wages subject to FITW and FICA. The amount shown as FICA wages is $0.11 (7.65 percent × $1.4848). To figure the correct wages (wages plus employer-paid employee taxes) and withholding to report, divide the employee's actual wages by 0.6735. The result is the grossed-up wages to include in Box

1 and the Social Security and Medicare wages to include in Boxes 3 and 5 of Form W-2.

The correct Social Security tax to enter in Box 4 and Medicare tax to enter in Box 6 is calculated by multiplying the amounts in Boxes 3 and 5 by the withholding rates for those taxes. Those amounts are included in Boxes 4 and 6.

Stated pay of more than $117,469.20 in 2017. For an employee with stated pay of more than $117,469.20 in 2017, the additional wage payments are only subject to Medicare.

To figure the correct Medicare wages, divide the additional wage by 0.9855 $(1 − 0.0145)$. This is added to the employee's other Social Security and Medicare wages and wages subject to federal income tax withholding.

Although these Social Security and Medicare taxes are not actually withheld, employers report them as withheld on Form 941 and are responsible for paying equal amounts as the employer's share of the Social Security and Medicare taxes.

Q 9:449 Is there a special exception from treating employer payments for the employee's portion of FICA as wages?

Yes. A special exception applies to employer payments of Medicare and Social Security taxes for certain household and agricultural workers. If the employer pays a household or agricultural employee's Social Security and Medicare taxes, these payments must be included in the employee's wages; however, the wage increase attributable to these tax payments is equal to the taxes paid by the employer without gross up (see Q 9:447).

Tool Allowances

Q 9:450 How is a tool allowance treated for employment tax purposes?

Payments by an employer to reimburse employees for the use of their tools or equipment are not treated as wages and are not subject to FIT, FITW, FICA, and FUTA. The tool allowance must not be disguised compensation (i.e., the payment must be reasonable and reflect the fair rental value of similar tools). These allowances should be paid apart from the employee's wages, and are not reported on the employee's W-2. [Rev. Rul. 65-187, 1965-2 C.B. 382; Rev. Rul. 68-624, 1968-2 C.B. 424]

In 2008, the IRS issued a coordinated issue paper in which its Large and Mid-Size Business Division ruled that payments to employees for the use of tools and equipment under such plans that are not paid under an "accountable plan" are subject to federal income tax withholding and employment tax. [LMSB-04-0608-037, see 154 Cong. Rec. H6574-03, 2008 WL 2744068 (Cong. Rec.)] Such payments must be reported as wages or other compensation on the employee's

Form W-2, and are subject to withholding and federal employment tax. The IRS held that the plans meet none of the three requirements for exemption under I.R.C. Section 62: a business connection, proper substantiation, and return of excess payments. The guidance was issued after the IRS discovered what it called "evidence [of] a pattern of abuse."

The IRS released the guidance after examining situations where, as a condition of employment, workers were required to provide and maintain their own tools and equipment, which were stored at the business location or at the employee's home. In these situations, the employee's total hourly wage and compensation did not change, but was divided into two components, one treated as taxable and one treated as nontaxable. The worker received two checks, one from the employer for taxable wages, and one from the employer or tool plan administrator that was characterized as a "tool and equipment reimbursement" or "tool allowance" and treated as nontaxable. The latter payments were not reported on the Form W-2 or the Form 1099.

The IRS further noted that employers and tool plan administrators used various methods to determine reimbursement for employee tool expenses, generally basing the amount on the value or cost of the employee's complete inventory of tools. In many cases that inventory included previously purchased tools, with estimates of the value when receipts were not kept, and depreciation was not properly taken into account.

Q 9:451   Can an employer avoid income tax withholding or FICA by paying an equipment rental fee to an employee?

Yes, but only if the rental fee is paid under an accountable plan that matches the payment to the expenses incurred by an employee for providing the equipment. Where the payment amount is made without regard to the expenses actually incurred as an employee business expense, the payment is treated as additional wages and subject to all federal employment taxes. [Internal Legal Mem. 20000600] Treasury and the IRS in 2005 released a package of guidance concerning the application of the accountable plan rules to employee-owned tools. Revenue Ruling 2005-52 [2005-35 I.R.B. 423] holds that a tool allowance arrangement fails to meet the substantiation and the return of excess amounts requirements in I.R.C. Section 62(c) and does not qualify as an accountable plan. Notice 2005-59 provides information about criteria that the IRS will apply in selecting proposals for the industry issue resolution program.

The revenue ruling addresses where an employer operates an automobile repair and maintenance business. The employer hires service technicians and requires them to provide and maintain various tools needed to make repairs and maintain services. The employer pays each employee a "tool allowance" to cover the costs of acquiring and maintaining the tools.

The revenue ruling holds that the described arrangement is not an accountable plan and all tool allowances paid under the arrangement must be included in the employees' gross income, reported as wages on Forms W-2, and are subject to withholding and payment of federal employment taxes. It explained that an arrangement qualifies as an accountable plan if it satisfies all three requirements in the statute and regulations and that an arrangement that fails to meet one or more of the requirements is treated as a nonaccountable plan. The revenue ruling said the stated arrangement failed to meet both the substantiation and return of excess requirements and thus did not qualify as an accountable plan.

The IRS also provided guidance in a revenue ruling where a company contracting with cable providers for residential installations required the workers to provide their own tools. The employer took the projected tool reimbursement, divided by the projected total hours, to obtain a tool hourly rate. This amount was deducted from the contract hourly rate. The difference was treated as taxable wages, and the "tool rate" payment was treated as a reimbursement that is not taxable. The IRS ruled that the plan did not qualify because the business connection was not satisfied. The cable technician who was reimbursed for the tools was paid the equivalent to the cable technician who was not reimbursed for the tools. Therefore, the three requirements to substantiate the business expense—business connection, substantiation, and return excess amounts–were not satisfied. [Rev. Rul. 2012-25, I.R.B. 2012-37, 337, Sept. 10, 2012]

Transportation Fringe Benefits

Q 9:452 What is a qualified transportation fringe benefit?

The term *qualified transportation fringe benefits* generally refers to specific commuting benefits authorized under I.R.C. Section 132 that may be offered to employees without the value of the benefits being treated as additional compensation. The FMV of these commuting benefits is not considered wages subject to FIT, FITW, FICA, and FUTA as long as the value does not exceed certain limits, *de minimis* or meets the definition of qualified transportation benefits. Qualified transportation fringe benefits include (1) transportation in a commuter highway vehicle, (2) transit passes, (3) qualified parking and qualified bicycle commuting reimbursement. These benefits are excluded from gross income only if the payment, tokens, passes, or reimbursements are not disguised compensation otherwise payable to the employee. An employee may receive any combination of these four benefits on a tax-free basis as long as certain limits are met. [I.R.C. § 132(f)]

A qualified transportation fringe benefit includes cash reimbursement for transportation in a commuter highway vehicle and qualified parking. However, a qualified transportation fringe benefit does not include cash reimbursement for a transit pass if a voucher or similar item that may be exchanged only for a transit pass is readily available for direct distribution by the employer to the employer's employees. Thus, in circumstances where vouchers are readily available, an employer must provide vouchers to its employees for a transit pass benefit to be excludable from gross income and wages. If a qualified transportation fringe can be provided through cash reimbursement, the employer must use a bona fide reimbursement arrangement. To meet the requirements for such an arrangement, first the payment must be a reimbursement, and not an advance. Second, the employee must substantiate to the employer that an expense for a transit benefit was actually incurred.

After 2008, qualified transportation fringe benefits include any qualified bicycle commuting reimbursement. For any calendar year, the exclusion for qualified bicycle commuting reimbursement includes any employer reimbursement during the 15-month period beginning with the first day of the calendar year for reasonable expenses incurred by the employee during the calendar year. Reasonable expenses include the purchase of a bicycle and bicycle improvements, repair, and storage as long as the bicycle is regularly used for travel between the employee's residence and place of employment.

The calendar year exclusion from wages for qualified bicycle commuting benefits is $20 multiplied by the number of qualified bicycle commuting months during that year for qualified bicycle commuting reimbursement.

For any employee, a qualified bicycle commuting month is any month the employee regularly uses the bicycle for a substantial portion of the travel between the employee's residence and place of employment and does not receive transportation in a commuter highway vehicle, any transit pass, or qualified parking benefits. Qualified bicycle commuting reimbursements, unlike other qualified transportation benefits, cannot be offered under a pretax or salary deferral plan.

The IRS has described certain circumstances in which an employer may use smart cards, debit or credit cards, and other electronic media to provide employees with qualified transportation fringe benefits that are excludable from gross income. Although the ruling was originally effective January 1, 2008, its effective date was repeatedly delayed until January 1, 2012 to provide certain transit systems additional time to modify their technology and make it compatible with requirements for vouchers. [Rev. Proc. 2006-57; I.R.S. Notice 2010-94, 2010-52 I.R.B. 927] Despite the effective date, it may be relied on for prior transactions. The IRS previously indicated that if a debit card qualifies as a voucher, then cash reimbursement for transit pass expenses are precluded if the debit card is readily available. The IRS intends to issue future guidance clarifying the circumstances under which terminal-restricted debit cards will be considered readily available. Until then, the IRS will not challenge cash reimbursement arrangements if the only available voucher is a terminal-restricted debit card.

Q 9:453   May transportation benefits be offered under a cafeteria plan?

No. Qualified transportation fringe benefits are a *de minimis* fringe benefit that may not be offered as a tax-free benefit under Section 125 (i.e., a cafeteria plan). However, qualified transportation benefits may be available as part of a salary reduction program outside of a Section 125 plan. Any election between cash compensation and any qualified transportation benefit is subject to the following requirements: (1) the amount of the election (e.g., salary reduction election) is capped at the monthly limits that apply; (2) the employee's election is in writing (or a verifiable electronic format) and it identifies the amount of the election for each benefit and the period to which the election applies; and (3) the arrangement satisfies certain compensation reduction and benefit payment guidelines. The election may be for one month or longer and can thus be changed each month. The final regulations also permit the use of a negative election, which provides that the compensation reduction will be deemed to have been made in any open enrollment period unless the employee elects cash.

The employer must keep "appropriate records" of salary reduction elections.

The compensation reduction election must be made prior to the date when the employee earns the compensation. The election must specify how much of the election is attributed to each benefit available and unused reductions cannot be refunded. This rule is similar to certain rules that apply to cafeteria elections. However, unused amounts may be carried forward and used in a subsequent period, unlike amounts contributed to a cafeteria plan.

Transit pass benefits generally are provided through the employer's purchase of the pass, fare card, or tokens that are given to the employees. Reimbursements may be made for transit pass expenses paid by the employee only where a pass, fare card, token, or similar item is not readily available for purchase by the employer. A voucher (or fare card token) may be treated as not readily available if the employee cannot obtain it without "significant administrative cost." Guidance released in 2001 and effective 2002 defines when vouchers are readily available. Administrative costs cannot exceed 1 percent of the average monthly costs and cannot include the employer's internal costs. Any reimbursement is subject to substantiation that is reasonable and that the employer may establish. Substantiation of expenses is required except when the employer distributes transit passes in kind.

Example. Castle Pines Trails permits its employees, who are paid twice a month, to reduce their compensation by $30 each payday to purchase travel tokens for the local rail system. The $30 semimonthly salary reduction is not subject to federal income tax withholding or FICA or FUTA taxes.

Note that the amount of the employee's election that is exempt from federal employment taxation depends the monthly dollar limit established by the IRS each year. [Treas. Reg. § 1.132-9, Q-11, Q-12]

In January 2001, the IRS released regulations on the structure and operation of transportation benefits. These requirements clarify (1) the conditions under which tax-free transit passes or vouchers can be distributed, (2) additional restrictions on salary reduction transportation plans, and (3) when terminated employees are taxed on unused passes or vouchers. [Treas. Reg. § 1.132-9]

Q 9:454   Do the dollar limitations for the exclusion for a qualified transportation fringe benefit vary depending on the benefit?

Similar to how it was prior to March 2009, the amount of a qualified transportation fringe benefit that is tax-free depends on the type of transportation fringe benefit. The American Recovery and Reinvestment Act of 2009 had equalized the tax-free value of transportation fringe benefits for 2009 and 2010. [Pub. L. No. 111-5] The Tax Relief, Unemployment Insurance Reauthorization, and Job Creation Act of 2010 extended this provision for 2011. [Pub. L. No. 111-312] The American Taxpayer Relief Act of 2012 restored the parity for 2013 and retroactively for 2012. [Pub. L. No. 112-240]

In 2015, the maximum value of qualified transportation fringe benefits that may be provided by an employer to an employee and excluded from gross income was $250 per month for qualified parking; $130 per month for combined commuter highway vehicle transportation and transit passes; and $20 multiplied by the number of qualified bicycle commuting months that correspond to the expenses incurred. The PATH Act (Protecting Americans from Tax Hikes) provides for permanent benefit parity with parking and transit benefits retroactive to the beginning of 2015. The rate for 2017 is $255.

Note that the value of a transportation benefit is calculated on a monthly basis to determine whether the limitations are exceeded. The value of transportation in a commuter highway vehicle and qualified parking is based on the benefits provided in the monthly period. With transit passes, the limit is based on the transit passes provided in the monthly period for that month or any previous month. [Treas. Reg. § 1.132-9, Q-8, Q-9] The employer may advance up to three months of vouchers at a time. If the employee terminates employment during that period, then a pro rata portion of the advances, based on the period when the individual is not employed, is treated as wages subject to all taxes.

When benefits are offered as a salary reduction plan, these limitations apply to the amount of compensation reduction made in the monthly period.

In addition, the value of certain commuting expenses is partially excluded from gross income as a *de minimis* benefit, such as when an employer provides transportation (such as taxi fare) to employees other than control employees when travel would otherwise be unsafe. For example, cab fare given to an employee who worked late would qualify as a tax-free transportation fringe benefit when the security of employees after hours is in question. [Treas. Reg. §§ 1.132-6(d)(2)(iii), 1.132-9, Q-7, and Q-12; Rev. Proc. 95-53, 1955-2 C.B. 445]

Q 9:455   When does a vehicle qualify as a "commuter highway vehicle"?

A vehicle qualifies as a commuter highway vehicle if it meets all of the following requirements: (1) seats at least six adults not counting the driver, (2) is used at least 80 percent of the time for commuting, and (3) at least one-half of the riders are employees. The value of qualified transportation fringe benefits is applied pro rata on a monthly basis to employees receiving this benefit, for periods when the benefit is offered. Employers are required to make a good-faith effort to apply these rules. [I.R.C. § 132(f)(2); Treas. Reg. § 1.132-9, Q-2; Notice 94-3, 1994-3 C.B. 327, Q&A 3(b)]

Q 9:456   Must a transportation benefit plan be in writing?

No. [Treas. Reg. § 1.132-9, Q-6]

Q 9:457   Is the cost of security while traveling considered a qualified transportation fringe benefit?

The value of employer-provided security for traveling employees is excludable from gross income when certain conditions are met that qualify the benefit as a working condition benefit rather than a transportation fringe benefit. The employer generally must demonstrate a bona fide business security concern for each covered employee, or do a security study and apply the resulting recommendations to each affected employee. The regulations make it clear that there must be a specific basis for the concern (e.g., threatened kidnapping). [Treas. Reg. § 1.132-5(m)]

Q 9:458   What conditions permit the payment of employee parking as a tax-free fringe benefit?

The final regulations on transportation benefits state that the value of a parking benefit is determined under Treasury Regulations Section 1.61-21(b)(2). Payment or reimbursement of an employee's parking qualifies as a transportation fringe benefit if it is (1) at or near the employer's worksite; (2) at a "park-and-ride" facility for an employee using mass transit; or (3) at a location from which the employee commutes in a commuter highway vehicle or a carpool. The value of such benefits may not exceed $255 for 2017. The I.R.C. does not impose any nondiscrimination requirements on this benefit. For example, on-site parking may have reserved spaces without the value of the benefit being treated as additional income. The employer may either reimburse the employee for the parking or pay the expense directly. Where on-site parking is provided in a company-owned location, the value of reserved parking must be based on comparable parking charges; where those benefits exceed $255 for 2017, the excess is treated as additional compensation. [I.R.C. § 132(f); Treas. Reg. § 1.132-9, Q-4; Rev. Proc. 2003-85, 2003-49 I.R.B. 1184]

Q 9:459   May an employee receive transportation benefits from more than one employer?

Yes. The monthly limit on qualified transportation benefits is based on the value of benefits provided by an employer to its employee. Thus, an employee working for two unrelated employers could receive transit passes valued at $255 in one month in 2016 from one employer and also receive an additional amount from another unrelated employer. [Treas. Reg. § 1.132-9, Q-10]

Q 9:460 How does an employer calculate the value of on-site parking benefits?

Employers value parking benefits by determining the cost that an individual would incur in an arm's-length transaction to obtain parking at the same location. The employer can take into account the fact that the parking is unreserved in making this determination. The I.R.C. treats certain parking as having no value when (1) an individual other than an employee (e.g., a customer) may park in the location at no charge; (2) the parking is used by customers with no reserved spots, or (3) the employee is unable to use the parking spot for a full calendar month. The value of reserved parking will generally be more than unreserved parking in the same lot. [I.R.C. § 132(p); Treas. Reg. § 1.132-5(p)]

Q 9:461 How are excess qualified transportation fringe benefits treated for employment tax purposes?

The value of any qualified transportation fringe benefit provided directly by the employer or purchased under a salary reduction plan that exceeds the total of the monthly dollar limitations is treated as additional compensation subject to FIT, FITW, FICA, and FUTA. These excess amounts are included in Boxes 1, 3, and 5 of the employee's Form W-2. Qualified transportation fringe benefits are not reported on the employee's Form W-2. [I.R.C. §§ 61, 3121(a)(20), 3306(b)(16)]

Tuition Reduction Benefits

Q 9:462 May educational institutions offer tax-free tuition reduction benefits to their employees?

The I.R.C. permits educational institutions to offer tuition reduction benefits without the value of those benefits being taxable to certain employees. Tuition reductions (including cash grants) are given to employees of educational institutions for education below the graduate level, and are excludable from gross income without dollar limitation. A tuition reduction is also available to teaching assistants and research assistants as long as the reduction does not represent payment for services. This exclusion is available to current and retired employees of the educational institution, a widow or widower of an individual who died while an employee, as well as their spouses and dependent children. The exclusion also applies if, under a reciprocal agreement between the two institutions, the recipient attends a different educational institution than the one operated by the employer. These benefits must not discriminate in favor of highly compensated employees as identified under I.R.C. Section 414(q). [I.R.C. §§ 117(d), 3121(a)(19), 3306(b)(16), 3401(a)(19)]

Q 9:463　May tuition reduction benefits be offered to certain graduate students employed by the educational institution?

Yes. Employees of an educational institution may receive tuition reductions for courses at their employer's facilities or another institution without the reductions being treated as wages for federal income tax, federal income tax withholding, FICA, or FUTA. This benefit is only available to graduate students employed as teaching and research assistants for undergraduate courses (even though they are studying at the graduate level). [I.R.C. §§ 117(d), 132(h), 3121(a)(19), 3306(b)(16), 3401(a)(19)]

Uniform Allowances

Q 9:464　Are uniform allowances subject to employment taxes?

Uniform allowances that pay for the purchase or maintenance of an employee's uniform are not wages and are exempt from all employment taxes if two conditions are met: (1) the uniform must be required by the employer and (2) the uniform cannot be wearable as street clothes. Where an allowance for a uniform does not meet both of these requirements (e.g., the uniform can be worn after hours), the value of the allowance is additional compensation to the employee and included in Boxes 1, 3, and 5, and the value of the benefits is subject to FIT, FITW, FICA, and FUTA. Where the employer merely provides a flat-dollar allowance for a uniform meeting these requirements, the allowance is treated as additional compensation. The employee who receives such a taxable benefit may be entitled to a deduction for actual expenses to maintain the uniform on Form 1040. Some employers note the value of the allowance in Box 14 to assist in that substantiation. [I.R.C. § 62(c); Treas. Reg. §§ 1.62-2, 1.274-5T(f)(2), 31.3121(a)-3, 31.3306(b)-2, 31.3401(a)-4]

Workers' Compensation Benefits

Q 9:465　Are workers' compensation benefits subject to employment taxes?

No. Payments received under a state workers' compensation program are not wages subject to FITW, FICA, and FUTA. Benefits paid from certain public employer plans that are "in the nature of a workman's compensation act" are exempt from FITW and FUTA, but are subject to FICA. Where the employer agrees to pay additional wages to an individual receiving workers' compensation benefits, the additional wages are subject to all employment taxes (see

Qs 9:447–9:448). [Rev. Proc. 56-83, 1956-1 C.B. 79; I.R.C. §§ 104(a)(3), 3121(a)(2)(A), 3306(b)(2)(A)]

When employers pay employees all (or a part) of their compensation while the employees are receiving workers' compensation benefits, and require that the employees turn over their workers' compensation benefits to the employer, amounts paid in excess of the workers' compensation benefits are subject to FIT, FITW, FICA, and FUTA. [Rev. Rul. 56-83, 1956-1 C.B. 79]

W-2 Reporting for 2017

Q 9:466   How are fringe benefits reported on Form W-2 for 2017?

Item	2017 Calendar-Year Reporting
Adoption benefits	Include in Boxes 3 and 5 (less amounts forfeited under Section 125 cafeteria plan). Up to $13,570 of qualified expenses (less forfeited amounts) excluded from Box 1. Total amount in Box 12, Code T.
Agent reporting	Name of agent (with approved Form 2678) in Box C. Special rules if agent for two or more employers.
Clergy and religious worker	If exempt from Social Security and Medicare taxes, omit entry in Boxes 3 and 5.
Deceased employer wages	Accrued vacation pay and other compensation paid after date of death but in same calendar year, include in Boxes 3 and 5, not in Box 1. If paid in year following year of death, no W-2 reporting is required.
	Regardless of when wages are paid after death (in the same calendar year or the following year), report amounts paid after death in Box 3 of Form 1099-MISC. Use name and taxpayer identification of the recipient of payment.
Dependent care benefits	Report total dependent care benefits paid by employer or reimbursed through a Flexible Spending Account in Box 10. Amounts paid in excess of $5,000 are also reported in Boxes 1, 3, and 5.
Educational assistance	Up to $5,250 per year can be paid on an employment tax-exempt basis including graduate courses. Amounts received above $5,250 are reported in Boxes 1, 3, and 5. Employer may also report educational assistance amounts in Box 14.

Item	2017 Calendar-Year Reporting
Election workers	Payments of $600 or more to state, county, and municipal election workers reported on W-2. Payment of less than $600 not reported on W-2 unless Social Security and Medicare taxes are withheld.
Employee business expense reimbursements	Amounts paid under accountable plan not reported on Form W-2. Excess amounts under a per diem or mileage allowance plan or amounts paid from nonaccountable plan are reported in Boxes 1, 3, and 5. If paid in excess of federal rate, report per diem or mileage allowances treated as substantiated (i.e., nontaxable portion) in Box 12 with Code L.
Employee's taxes paid by employer	Except for certain payments to agricultural and household employees, report employer-paid Social Security (up to $7,886.40 in 2017) and Medicare taxes in Boxes 1, 3, and 5. If an employer pays a household or agricultural employee's FICA taxes, include the payment in the employee's wages. However, do not gross up the employer-paid taxes.
Fringe benefits (taxable)	Include taxable amounts in Box 1 and, if applicable, in Boxes 3 and 5. Employer may also include total value of fringe benefits in Box 14 or use a separate statement. If employer includes 100% of the lease value of an automobile in employee's gross income, must use Box 14 (or a separate statement) and report taxable amount in Boxes 1, 3, and 5.
Golden parachute payment	Include amounts in Boxes 1, 3, and 5. Report 20% excise tax on excess parachute payments that are withheld in Box 2. Also report excess parachute payments in Box 12 with Code K.
Government employers	When employee's wages are subject to Medicare tax for part of the year and subject to full Social Security and Medicare taxes for part of the year. Option 1: File single Form W-2 with Medicare only, and Medicare and Social Security wages combined (also on Form W-3, check the 941 box in Box (b)). Option 2: File two Form W-2s, one for wages only subject to Medicare taxes (check "Medicare government employee" box in Box b of Form W-3), and one for wages subject to Social Security and Medicare taxes. (Check "941" in Box b of Form W-3)

Item	_2017 Calendar-Year Reporting_
Group-term life insurance	Cost of coverage above $50,000 (using Table rates) reported in Boxes 1, 3, and 5 of Form W-2. Show total FMV less employee aftertax contributions in Box 12 with Code C. No federal income tax withholding is required. If benefits for former employee and no Social Security or Medicare taxes were withheld from employee's wages, report uncollected amounts with Code M (Social Security) and Code N (Medicare) in Box 12 of Form W-2.
Health savings accounts	Employer's contributions to employee's HSA is reported in Boxes 1, 3, 5 only if it is not reasonable to believe at the time of payment that the payment will be excludable from the employee's income. Report all employer contributions to an HSA in Box 12 with Code W. Report on Form 8889.
(Archer) Medical savings accounts	Employee contributions that are treated as wages are included in Boxes 1, 3, and 5. All employer payments reported in Box 12 of Form W-2 with Code R. Report on Form 8883.
Moving expenses	Qualified moving expenses paid to third party not reported in Boxes 1, 3, and 5. If paid directly to employee, reported in Box 12 with Code P. Taxable moving expenses are reported in Boxes 1, 3, and 5 of Form W-2.
Repayment of wages paid in error	If repayments are for prior tax year, file Form W-2c with the SSA to correct Social Security and Medicare taxes (omit reporting in Box 1 of Form W-2c).

Retirement Plans

Nonqualified deferred compensation plans (NQDCs)	The reporting of these was changed by Section 409A of the American Jobs Creation Act of 2004. Report yearly deferrals (plus earnings) under a Section 409A nonqualified deferred compensation plan in Box 12 with Code Y. (Note that Code Y reporting is indefinitely suspended **and not require**d.) Report income included under Section 409A in Box 1 and in Box 12 with Code Z.
	Report amounts that are no longer subject to risk of forfeiture in Boxes 3 and 5. Report in Box 11 any amount in Boxes 1, 3, or 5 that were earned in a previous year.

Item	*2017 Calendar-Year Reporting*
	Report distributions to an employee from a nonqualified plan or a nongovernmental Section 457(b) plan in Box 1. Report elective deferrals and employer contributions (including nonelective deferrals) to any governmental or nongovernmental Section 457(b) compensation plan in Box 12, Code G. Do not report either Section 457(b) or 457(f) amounts that are subject to a substantial risk of forfeiture. Distributions from Section 457 plans or nonqualified deferred compensation plans to beneficiaries of deceased employee are reported on Form 1099-R, not W-2. See coding for specific plans.
401(k) Plans	Report elective deferrals for employee in Boxes 3 and 5 and Box 12 with Code D and check Box 13, Retirement Plan.
403(b) Plans	Report elective deferrals for employees in Boxes 3 and 5 and Box 12 with Code E and check Box 13, Retirement Plan.
457 Plans	Report elective deferrals for employees in Boxes 3 and 5 (if applicable) and Box 12 with Code G.
501(c)(18)(D) Plans	Report elective deferrals in Boxes 3 and 5 (if applicable) and Box 12 with Code H. These amounts are also reported in Box 1, and employee deducts on Form 1040.
Employee aftertax contributions	Do not report in Box 12 employee aftertax contributions or 401(k) salary deferrals reclassified as aftertax contributions. May report in Box 14 of Form W-2.
Salary reduction SEP (SARSEP)	Report elective deferrals for employees in Boxes 3 and 5 and Box 12 with Code F and check Box 13, Retirement Plan.
SIMPLE retirement account	Amounts contributed by employee are not reported in Box 1, but are reported in Boxes 3 and 5. Report total amount in Box 12 with Code D (if part of a 401(k) plan) or S (for 408(p) salary reduction SIMPLE retirement account) and check Box 13, Retirement Plan.
Reporting of pension deferred compensation	If a participant is in a qualified plan, annuity plan, 403(b) arrangement, SEP, SIMPLE retirement account, 501(c)(18), or 457 plan, check "Retirement plan" in Box 13.

Item	_2017 Calendar-Year Reporting_
Scholarships and fellowship grants	Amounts paid as fellowship or grants for services provided (e.g., teaching, research, or other services under I.R.C. Section 117(c)) are reported in Box 1 and, if applicable, Boxes 3 and 5.
USERRA make-up amounts to pension plan	Employees returning from military service who receive prior year contributions are reported in Box 12, using the code for Box 12 that is applicable, showing date and amount (e.g., D 16 1375 for salary deferrals for 2016).
Tips	Show tips employee reported in Boxes 1, 3, 5, and 7. The totals in Boxes 3 and 7 should not exceed $127,200 in 2017. Allocated tips are reported in Box 8 but do not include amounts in Boxes 1, 3, 5, and 7.
Uncollected Social Security or RRTA tax on tips	Report uncollected amounts in Box 12, Code A (do not include amounts in Box 4).

Item	2012 Calendar Year Reporting
Scholarships and fellowship grants	Amounts paid as fellowship or grants for services provided (e.g., teaching, research, or other services under I.R.C. Section 117(c)) are reported in Box 1 and, if applicable, Boxes 3 and 5.
USERRA make-up amounts to pension plan	Employees returning from military service who receive prior year contributions are reported in Box 12, using the code for Box 12 that is applicable, showing date and amount (e.g., D 16-1375 for salary deferrals for 2016).
Tips	Show tips employee reported in Boxes 1, 3, 5, and 7. The totals in Boxes 3 and 7 should not exceed $122,200 in 2012. Allocated tips are reported in Box 8 but do not include amounts in Boxes 1, 3, 5, and 7.
Uncollected Social Security or RRTA tax on tips	Report uncollected amounts in Box 12, Code A (do not include amounts in Box 4).

Chapter 10

Sick Pay

This chapter addresses the federal income taxes, Federal Insurance Contributions Act (FICA) taxes, and federal unemployment taxes that apply to employer and third-party payer payments to employees during periods when they are sick or disabled. The discussion includes the withholding, deposit, and reporting rules that apply to sick pay, including special rules that split employment tax responsibilities among the employer, an agent for the employer, and a third-party payer. Also reviewed is the process by which employers and third-party payers report sick pay on Forms W-2, W-3, 940, and 941. Form 8922, Third-Party Sick Pay Recap, replaces the W-2 and W-3 Recap forms filed with 2017 W-2s. In addition, these forms should be sent to the IRS and not the Social Security Administration.

At the state and local levels, new sick pay is legislation increasing the requirements for employers in the areas of recording, reporting, and auditing have been implemented. In some cases, sick leave benefits have been granted to employees. The change in the legal landscape will require employers to implement or improve compliance oversight. A written leave plan could be instrumental for employers to meet many of the new requirements from states and local jurisdictions. On the federal level, President Obama has recommended financial support of state and local jurisdictions to pass mandatory sick leave. President Obama through Executive Order 13706 requires paid sick leave for federal contractors by 2017.

In General

Q 10:1   What does the term *sick pay* mean for employment tax purposes?

Sick pay generally refers to any amount paid under a plan established by the employer for salary continuation benefits during an employee's temporary absence from work as the result of injury, sickness, or disability. The benefits may be paid directly by the employer, through an agent of the employer, or by a third-party payer (e.g., an insurance company). Sick pay includes both short-term and long-term benefits and is separate and apart from employer payments for medical expenses and payments to employees unrelated to an absence from work. Sick pay may be paid as a company policy, or as part of an employment contract. [I.R.C. § 105]

Sick pay is generally treated as wages and subject to federal income tax withholding, FICA taxes, and Federal Unemployment Tax Act (FUTA) taxes. Special FICA and FUTA exceptions apply to payments made from a "plan" or "system" more than six calendar months after the employee's last day at work. A special FICA exception applies to payments when the individual is receiving retirement disability or is disabled and entitled to Social Security benefits. All or a portion of the sick pay from a plan or insurance contract contributed to by an employee may be exempt from all taxation. [I.R.C. § 104; IRS Reg. § 1.104-1]

Note. Sick or disability benefits paid six calendar months following the last day of the month the employee worked for the employer are exempt from FICA and FUTA taxes. The benefits paid previous to this date are subject to FICA and FUTA withholding and reporting.

Q 10:2   What is the difference in the requirements for withholding and payment of federal employment taxes between agency-paid and third-party-paid sick pay?

When an employer or an agent of an employer issues sick pay, withholding of federal income taxes and collection of FICA and FUTA taxes are mandatory in the six-month coverage period. The employer remains fully liable for the correct payment and reporting of all federal employment taxes. Federal income tax withholding is mandatory and is based on the Form W-4.

When sick pay is paid through an insurance contract (i.e., by a third party), the sick pay is generally subject to federal income taxes, FICA, and FUTA in the six-month coverage period. The reporting and payment of these taxes are generally the responsibility of the third-party payer (subject to certain exceptions); federal income tax withholding is optional, based on whether the employee completes a Form W-4S to request that the third party withhold federal income tax. [I.R.C. §§ 3121(a), 3306(b), 3401(a)]

Q 10:3   What is meant by a definite plan or a system maintained by the employer for the payment of sick pay?

A plan (sometimes referred to in the regulations as a definite plan or a system of payment) generally refers to a program established by an employer under which sick-pay benefits are available to employees generally or to a class or classes of employees. A definite plan or system of payment is not present if the benefits are provided on a discretionary or occasional basis with merely an intention to aid particular employees in time of need. Employers should generally avoid making discretionary or occasional benefits payments. The pattern of payment may, under the Employee Retirement Income Security Act of 1974 (ERISA), entitle other employees to receive unspecified payments in the future, although that is generally decided only in litigation, and is a difficult case for a plaintiff to prove. [I.R.C. § 105(e); ERISA § 3(1), Rev. Rul. 2005-24, 2005-16 I.R.B. 892]

A plan to pay sick-pay benefits is generally treated under ERISA as a welfare plan, granting certain protections of an employee's right to the payment and imposing reporting requirements on the employer. The existence of a plan or system is confirmed if it is in writing or is otherwise made known to employees. That communication can be made by posting a notice on a bulletin board or by an established practice of the employer. Most employers have written formalized policies regarding sick-pay eligibility and benefit payments. Other indications of the existence of a plan or system include, but are not limited to, references to the plan or system in the contract of employment, employer contributions to a plan, and segregated accounts for the payment of benefits. [ERISA § 3(1)]

Q 10:4   How are sick-pay benefits generally paid?

Most employers pay sick-pay benefits directly to the employee for short periods of absence that are the result of sickness or injury. Payments for longer periods of absence are frequently paid by an agent acting for the employer or a third party (e.g., an insurance company) and are generally paid as a percentage of regular earnings. An employer's agent is distinguished from a third-party payer in that a third party generally assumes full liability for all payments under the plan, including verification of eligibility and determining the benefits due under the plan. An agent merely acts for the employer, but the employer has the financial liability for making the correct tax deposits and filing the employment tax returns.

Unused sick pay may be paid at the termination of employment, if company policy or an employment contract so dictates. Sick pay paid under this system is subject to the same federal employment tax treatment as regular wages.

The liability for collecting the applicable employment taxes differs between a third-party payer and an agent of the employer. An employer is liable for the correct withholding and reporting of sick pay paid by its agent. With a third-party payer, the responsibility may be split, depending on the arrangement between the employer and the third-party insurance company. [Treas. Reg. § 31.3401(a)-1(b)(8)]

Q 10:5   May an employer appoint another party to collect federal income and FICA taxes from an employee's sick-pay benefits, as applicable?

Yes. An employer can appoint an agent to withhold and deposit wage and FICA taxes from sick-pay benefits, when applicable. The employer cannot, however, escape liability for collecting and depositing those taxes if the agent fails to perform its duties properly. (The agent also can incur liability for failing to withhold and deposit taxes.) The IRS will recognize an agent's being responsible for collecting and depositing the employer's required federal employment taxes attributable to sick pay when the employer files a Form 2678, Employer/Payer Appointment of Agent, with the IRS, which will then send a letter to the agent after the IRS approves the agent.

An agent duly appointed by more than one employer will file only one return, aggregating all taxes withheld by it on that return. [Rev. Proc.2013-39, 2013-52 I.R.B. 830] Moreover, if an agent pays wages to the same individual on behalf of more than one employer, the agent must compute the proper amount to withhold based on the aggregate wages paid to the individual. [Treas. Reg. § 31.3402(g)-3(a)] Although the agent deposits the appropriate tax amounts, each employer is ultimately liable for its pro rata portion of the withheld amounts, which is based on the percentage of total wages attributable to each employer. Additionally, each employer is liable for taxes not withheld and deposited and penalties and interest if the agent fails to file the appropriate returns. [Treas. Reg. § 31.3402(g)-3(b)]

Q 10:6   What is a third-party payer of sick pay?

The employer may contract with a third party to assume the liability for payment of sick pay and for the proper reporting and collection of federal employment taxes. These are typically made through an insurance contract that shifts to the insurance company the financial risk for payment of benefits and liability for FICA tax not withheld from sick payments.

Provided the third party gives timely notification of wages paid and taxes withheld, and supplies the annual statement by January 15 of the following year, a third party may transfer back to the employer the responsibility for payment of FUTA taxes and the employer's share of FICA taxes, and for filing the employee's Form W-2 for the sick-pay payments. [Treas. Reg. § 31.3401(a)-1(b)(8)]

Q 10:7   Who is responsible for federal employment taxes when sick-pay benefits are paid to a former employee by an "agent" of the employer?

When sick-pay benefits are made by an "agent" of the employer, the I.R.C. treats the employer for whom the employee was working at the time the employee became sick or disabled as the employer. The regulations apply a lookback rule when an employee on sick leave takes a job while receiving benefits; then the employer is the last employer for whom the employee worked before becoming sick or disabled if that employer made contributions to the sick-pay plan on behalf of the sick or disabled employee. [Treas. Reg. § 31.3401(a)-1(b)(8)]

Q 10:8 May a third-party payer rely on information provided by the employer in determining the proper taxes to collect?

Yes. Although the I.R.C. imposes certain withholding, deposit, and reporting requirements on a third-party payer, the third-party payer avoids penalties for violations when it relies on information provided by the employer to fulfill these responsibilities. For instance, the third-party payer may need information from the employer to determine what portions, if any, of the sick-pay benefits are not subject to FICA. Conversely, the employer may take into account payments made by the third party for FICA and FUTA purposes. Unless the parties have reason not to rely on the information provided, they may use, in their tax calculations, representations as to the following items:

1. The total wages paid by the employer to the employee during the calendar year (payments from the third party and employer are aggregated in determining the wage base for Social Security and FUTA taxes);

2. The last month in which the employee worked for the employer (payments made more than six calendar months after the employee's last day at work are excluded for FICA and FUTA purposes);

3. The amount (if any) of employee contributions to the sick-pay plan that were made with aftertax dollars (if a portion is paid by the employee with aftertax dollars, a portion of the payment is not subject to federal income tax withholding, FICA taxes, or FUTA taxes); and

4. The amount of wages paid by the third party and the FICA tax withheld.

The third party and employer cannot avoid penalties by relying on statements made by the *employee* regarding these items. [Temp. Treas. Reg. § 32.1(e); Pub. No. 15-A]

Federal Income Tax Withholding

Q 10:9 Are sick-pay benefits subject to federal income taxes?

Yes. In general, sick-pay benefits, whether for a prolonged period or for a short term, are subject to federal income tax withholding unless the benefits are attributable to aftertax employee contributions. The taxable payments may or may not be subject to federal income tax withholding, depending on whether the employer, an agent of the employer, or a third party pays the benefit. Payments are normally subject to federal income tax withholding when paid by the employer or an agent of the employer. Payments made directly by a third-party payer (e.g., an insurance company) that is not merely an administrator of the employer's sick-pay plan are not subject to federal income tax withholding provided the third party assumes an insurance risk pursuant to the sick-pay plan. The employee may request that the third party withhold federal income tax by filing a Form W-4S. Sick pay received from a disability insurance policy paid with aftertax employee contributions is exempt from federal income tax withholding; however, FICA and FUTA tax continues to apply during the six-month coverage period. If the premiums are paid with pretax salary reductions under I.R.C. Section 125, the benefits are fully subject to federal income tax withholding and to FICA, and FUTA tax during the six-month coverage period. (See exception at Q 10:10.) [I.R.C. § 3121(a)(2)(A); Treas. Reg. § 31.3401(a)-1(b)(8)]

Note. An employer-sponsored plan may provide cash benefits on account of a disability or loss of bodily function. If such payments are unrelated to the period of absence from work, they are exempt from federal income tax withholding, FICA, and FUTA taxes. A plan could, for example, provide a cash payment for loss of a finger, arm, or vision. [I.R.C. §§ 104(a)(3), 105(a); Treas. Reg. §§ 1.104-1(d), 1.105-1]

Q 10:10   Is there a plan option that can relieve employees of paying federal income tax on future sick-pay benefits?

Yes. The IRS clarified that if employees elect to have the employer-paid disability insurance premiums included in taxable wages subject to federal income tax, future sick-pay benefits paid under the employer's sick-pay plan will not be subject to federal income tax or federal income tax withholding.

For this exemption to apply, employees must make an irrevocable election at the beginning of the plan year to include employer-paid disability insurance premiums in their taxable wages for the tax year in which the election was made. This election is not available unless the employer pays 100 percent of the cost of the disability insurance. Note that the exemption applies only to federal income tax and federal income tax withholding. Social Security, Medicare and FUTA taxes continue to apply in the first six months of disability. [Treas. Reg. § 1.104-1(d); Rev. Rul. 2004-55, 2004-26 I.R.B. 1081]

Q 10:11   What are the federal income tax withholding requirements for sick-pay benefits?

The requirements for federal income tax withholding on sick-pay benefits and the methods for determining the amount to withhold differ depending on whether the benefits are paid by (1) the employer, (2) an agent of the employer, or (3) a third-party payer that bears an insurance risk for the sick-pay plan.

Employer or employer's agent. Sick-pay benefits paid by the employer or the employer's agent are subject to federal income tax withholding. An employer or agent of the employer paying sick-pay benefits generally determines the amount of federal income tax to be withheld based on the employee's Form W-4, Employee's Withholding Allowance Certificate. The employee *cannot* choose how much will be withheld by giving the employer or agent a Form W-4S, Request for Federal Income Tax Withholding From Sick Pay. The Internal

Revenue Code (I.R.C.) treats sick-pay benefits paid by an agent as supplemental wages in determining the amount of federal income tax withholding. If an agent does not make regular wage payments to an employee, the agent may choose to withhold income tax at a flat 25 percent (39.6 percent if supplemental wages for the year exceed $1 million) rate for 2016, rather than at the employee's wage withholding rate. [Treas. Reg. § 31.3401(a)-1(b)(8); Temp. Treas. Reg. § 32.1(e)(3); T.D. 9276]

Third party not an agent. Sick-pay benefits paid by a third party that bears an insurance risk pursuant to the sick-pay plan (e.g., an insurance company) are not subject to federal income tax withholding, but the employee may elect to have federal income tax withheld by filing Form W-4S with the third party.

A third party making payments of sick pay to an employee who has submitted a Form W-4S will determine the amount to withhold for federal income taxes under one of two methods: (1) whole-dollar withholding or (2) percentage method withholding. Under the whole-dollar method, the employee specifies on Form W-4S the amount of income tax that can be withheld. That amount cannot be less than $20 per weekly payment, $88 per monthly payment or $4 per day for employees paid on a daily basis.

If the requested withholding would reduce any net payment below $10, the third party should not withhold any income tax from that payment. If a particular sick-pay benefit payment is less than or greater than a regular payment, the amount withheld must be in the same proportion to the particular payment as the regular withholding is to a regular payment. Thus, for example, if $50 is withheld from a regular payment of $150, then $25 should be withheld from a partial payment of $100. The minimum withholding and net check thresholds continue to apply.

Under the percentage method, the payer may, at its option, permit the employee to elect to have federal income tax withholding computed as a percentage of the payments (at least 10 percent). In no case can less than $10 be withheld. [I.R.C. § 3402(o); Treas. Reg. § 31.3402(o)-3(c); Form W-4S; IRS Pub. 15-A]

Q 10:12   What is the purpose of Form W-4S?

Form W-4S, Request for Federal Income Tax Withholding from Sick Pay, is used by an employee receiving payments from a third party that is not an agent of the employer (e.g., an insurance company) bearing an insurance risk pursuant to the sick-pay plan to elect to have federal income tax withheld from sick payments. This payer is not required to withhold federal income tax unless the employee requests withholding using Form W-4S. If a Form W-4S is filed, the third party should withhold federal income tax on all payments of sick-pay benefits made eight or more days after receiving the form; the third party may, at its option, withhold federal income tax before eight days have passed. [Pub. No. 15-A]

Q 10:13 What sick-pay benefit payments are not subject to federal income tax withholding?

The I.R.C. exempts certain sick-pay benefit payments, whether paid by the employer or a third party, from being treated as wages subject to federal income tax withholding. They include the following:

1. Benefit payments received under a workers' compensation law or a statute in the nature of a workers' compensation act [I.R.C. §§ 104(a)(3), 3121(a)(2)(A)];

2. Benefit payments, or portions of payments, attributable to employee contributions made to a sick-pay plan with aftertax dollars (e.g., the employee paid for disability insurance with aftertax payroll deductions) [I.R.C. §§ 104(a)(3), 105(a), 3121(a)(2)(A)];

3. Accident or health insurance payments unrelated to absence from work, including payments for:

   a. Permanent loss of a member or function of the body,

   b. Permanent loss of the use of a member or function of the body, or

   c. Permanent disfigurement of the body, but only if the payments are based on the nature of the injury and not the period of time the employee is absent from work [I.R.C. § 105(c)]; and

4. Amounts received by an employee, spouse, or dependent under an accident or health plan as a reimbursement of medical expenses (special rules apply to reimbursements of medical expenses for domestic partners) [I.R.C. §§ 105(a), 105(c)].

See also exception at Q 10:10.

Q 10:14 May sick pay be treated as compensation for purposes of making tax-deferred contributions to qualified 401(k) or 403(b) retirement plans?

Generally, yes, although the definition of "compensation" in the applicable plan document should specifically define "sick pay" as eligible compensation. Sick pay that is paid at the termination of employment may also be deferred, subject to the underlying plan rules (see chapter 9).

FICA and FUTA Taxes

Q 10:15 Are sick-pay benefits subject to FICA and FUTA tax?

Generally, yes. If sick-pay benefits are subject to federal income tax withholding, they are usually subject to Social Security, Medicare, and FUTA taxes in the first six months following the first day of disability. Note that the same rule applies even if sick pay is deferred into a 401(k) or 403(b) plan.

Certain payments, whether paid by a third party, the employer, or an agent of the employer, are exempt from FICA and FUTA taxes. [I.R.C. § 3306(b)(2)] These include:

1. *Death or disability retirement.* Amounts paid under a definite plan or system (see Q 10:3) on or after the termination of the employment relationship because of death or disability retirement. Even if there is a definite plan or system, amounts paid to a former employee are subject to FICA and FUTA taxes if they would have been paid had the employment relationship not terminated because of the death or disability retirement of the former employee. For example, a payment to a disabled former employee for unused vacation time that would have been made whether or not the employee retired on disability is treated as wages for FICA and FUTA tax purposes. [I.R.C. §§ 3121(a)(13), 3306(b)(10); Treas. Reg. § 31.3402(O)-3(h)]

   Note. IRS regulations state that sick pay includes amounts paid under a plan unless all amounts paid under the plan are paid to individuals who separated from employment because of permanent and total disability. Because of this language of the regulations, it is prudent for employers to maintain a separate plan covering employees who separate from employment because of permanent disability so that the exemption from FICA and FUTA is clearly applicable in the first six-month coverage period.

2. *Estate or beneficiary payments.* Payments to the employee's estate or survivor after the calendar year of the employee's death (including accumulated sick leave). Such payments are reported on a Form 1099-MISC, not a Form W-2.

3. *Certain disabled individuals.* Payments to an employee when the employee is entitled to disability insurance benefits under Section 223(a) of the Social Security Act. This rule applies only if the employee became entitled to such benefits before the calendar year in which the payments are made and the employee performs no service for the employer during the period for which the payments are made. The exemption applies only to FICA taxes; FUTA taxes still apply. [I.R.C. § 3121(a)(15)]

4. *Payments that exceed the applicable wage base.* The Social Security tax wage base for 2017 is $127,200. There is no wage base for Medicare tax. The FUTA tax wage base is $7,000. Thus, for example, if an employee receives $119,000 in wages from an employer in 2017 and then receives $10,000 of sick pay, only the first $8,200 ($127,200 – $119,000) of the sick pay is subject to Social Security tax. All of the sick pay is subject to Medicare tax. None of the sick pay is subject to FUTA tax.

5. *Payments for long periods.* Payments made on account of sickness or accident disability that continue for more than six calendar months after the last calendar month in which the employee worked. If, for example, the employee's last day of work was February 17, 2017, payments of sick pay made after August 31, 2017 are not subject to FICA or FUTA taxes. If the employee returns to work for one day on June 9, 2017, the six-month period would begin again, and only those payments made after December

31, 2017 would be exempt. [I.R.C. §§ 3121(a)(4), 3306(b)(4); Treas. Reg. §§ 31.3121(a)(4)-1, 31.3306(a)(4)-1]

6. *Payments received under a workers' compensation law.* Under proposed regulations, the exception from FICA taxes would apply to payments to state and local government employees under a statute that is "in the nature of a workers' compensation act." [I.R.C. §§ 104(a)(1), 3121(a)(2)(A), 3306(b)(2)(A); REG-160315-03]

7. *Medical expenses.* Payments of medical and hospitalization expenses of employees, spouses, and dependents, and insurance premiums for such coverage, if paid under a definite plan or system of payment.

8. *Employee-paid disability insurance.* Payments, or parts of payments, attributable to employee contributions to a sick-pay plan (e.g., disability insurance) made with aftertax dollars. [I.R.C. § 104(a)(3)] Sick payments are exempt from FICA and FUTA taxes in the first six months of disability to the extent the employee made aftertax contributions to the cost of the insurance. For instance, if an employee pays 60 percent of the cost of the disability insurance, only 40 percent of the sick payments are subject to FICA and FUTA. Note that if the employee's contribution ratio changes, there is a three-year averaging required to determine the percentage of sick pay that is taxable. [IRS § 104(a)(1)] See Q 10:32 for more information.

9. *Accident or health insurance payments unrelated to absence from work.* These include payments for (a) permanent loss of a member or function of the body; (b) permanent loss of the use of a member or function of the body; or (c) permanent disfigurement of the body, but only if the payments are based on the nature of the injury and not the period the employee is absent from work. [I.R.C. § 105(c)]

Q 10:16 Who withholds and deposits FICA and FUTA taxes on sick-pay benefits?

The responsibility for withholding, depositing, and reporting FICA and FUTA taxes on sick-pay benefits will generally depend on who makes the payments to the employees.

Employer pays. If the employer pays the sick-pay benefits (as is the case in what is generally referred to as a self-insured plan), the employer is responsible for paying and withholding FICA tax from the sick pay. The employer must timely deposit FICA and FUTA tax; there are no special deposit rules for sick-pay benefits. [I.R.C. §§ 3121(a)(2)(A), 3306(b)(2)(A), 3306(b)(4)]

Agent of the employer pays. An entity acting as an agent of the employer that makes payments of sick-pay benefits is acting on behalf of the employer, and payments made by the agent are treated as paid by the employer. Thus, the responsibility for withholding and depositing remains with the employer. Under an exception to that rule, the employer and a third party may enter into an agreement that makes the third party an agent responsible for such actions. When such an agent becomes contractually responsible for the payment of employment taxes, it will use its own name and employer identification number (EIN) for the withholding, depositing, and reporting duties it has assumed. Although the agent may be contractually liable for such duties, the employer remains fully liable when the agent fails to meet the tax and reporting requirements. [Treas. Reg. § 31.3401(a)-1(b)(8)]

Nonagent third party pays. When a third party makes payments of sick-pay benefits other than as an agent of the employer (i.e., benefits are paid under an insurance contract), the third party is fully liable for withholding the *employee's portion* of the FICA taxes. The third party is also liable for the FUTA and the *employer's portion* of the FICA taxes, unless the third party transfers that liability back to the employer. A third party may transfer liability for employer FICA and FUTA taxes when the following three conditions are met:

1. It must withhold FICA tax from the sick-pay benefit payments paid to employees;

2. It must make timely deposits of the FICA tax withheld; and

3. It must notify the employer for whom the employee normally works of the payments on which tax was withheld. Such notification should be provided at the same time the third-party payer is required to deposit the tax withheld. For instance, if the third party is a monthly depositor, it must notify the employer by the 15th day of the month following the month in which the sick-pay benefit payment is made because that is the day by which the third-party payer is required to deposit the tax withheld. An annual statement of payments made and taxes withheld must be given to the employer no later than January 15 following the year in which the payments were made. [I.R.C. § 6051(f); Treas. Reg. § 31.6051-3(a); Temp. Treas. Reg. § 32.1(e)]

The third party does not withhold federal income tax unless requested by the employee (Form W-4S). If requested, the third party is liable for collecting and timely depositing those taxes.

Q 10:17   What employment tax liabilities and responsibilities can be transferred to the employer from a third-party payer that is not an agent of the employer?

Generally, when a third party satisfies the requirements for transferring liability for the employer's portion of the FICA and FUTA taxes (see Q 10:16), the following rules apply:

Deposits. The third party must make deposits of the withheld amounts of employee FICA taxes and any withheld federal income tax using its own name and EIN. The employer must make deposits of the FUTA and the employer's portion of the FICA using its own name and EIN. The employer's liability for such taxes begins upon timely receipt of the third party's notice of sick-pay payments made and taxes withheld.

Form 941. The third party and employer must each file Form 941, Employer's QUARTERLY Federal Tax Return. Line 8 of Form 941 contains a special adjusting entry for FICA taxes transferred to the employer or paid by the third party. Those entries are required because the total tax liability for FICA taxes is split between the third party and the employer: The third party is liable for the employee portion and the employer is liable for the employer portion of the tax on the sick pay. Therefore, each party reports a credit on line 8 for the portion deposited by the other party.

Employer filings. The employer must include third-party sick-pay benefit payments on lines 2, 5a, 5c, and if applicable, 5d of Form 941. The employer subtracts on line 8 the FICA tax withheld and deposited by the third-party payer.

Third-party filing. The third party must include on Form 941 the FICA tax withheld from employees' sick pay (and federal income tax withholding, if any). The third-party payer does not include on line 2 any sick-pay benefits it paid as a third party, but does include on line 3 any federal income tax withheld. On line 5a, the third party enters the total amount it paid subject to Social Security taxes. That amount includes both wages paid to its own employees and sick-pay benefits that it paid as a third party. The third-party payer completes line 5c in a similar manner. The third-party must include on line 5d any taxable wages subject to the Additional Medicare Tax withholding. For this purpose, wages paid by an employer and by the third party must be aggregated to determine whether the $200,000 withholding threshold has been met. On line 8, the third party subtracts the employer portion of the FICA taxes its client-employers are required to pay.

Q 10:18 Which party reports on Form 940 when the third party successfully transfers liability to the employer?

The employer must prepare Form 940, Employer's Annual Federal Unemployment (FUTA) Tax Return, for sick-pay benefits when the third-party payer has transferred liability for the tax to the employer. [Pub. No. 15-A]

Q 10:19 When is the third party responsible for collecting and reporting FUTA taxes and the employer's portion of FICA taxes for sick-pay benefits?

A third-party payer that does not satisfy the requirements for transferring liability for FUTA and the employer's portion of the FICA taxes (see Q 10:16) is responsible for reporting sick-pay benefits on its own Forms 940 and 941 or 944. [I.R.C. § 6051(f); Treas. Reg. § 31.6051-3(a); Pub. No. 15-A]

Q 10:20 How does a third-party payer determine its deposit schedule?

To determine the due date and amounts of its deposits of federal employment taxes, a third party should combine the liability for the wages paid to its own employees and the liability for payments it made to all employees of its client-employers. This does not include liability for the client-employers' portion of FICA and FUTA taxes that has been transferred to the client employers. [Pub. No. 15-A]

Q 10:21   Do special rules apply to payment of the employer's portion of FICA and FUTA taxes for multiemployer sick-pay plans?

Yes. A special rule applies to determine whether the third-party payer, the multiemployer plan, or the employer is responsible for the employer's portion of FICA and FUTA taxes. The rule applies to sick-pay benefit payments made to employees by a third-party insurer under an insurance contract with a multi-employer plan (sometimes referred to as a union plan) that was established under a collectively bargained agreement. If the third-party insurer making the payments complies with the withholding and timely deposit requirements of the I.R.C. and gives the plan (rather than the employer) the required timely notice, then the plan (and not the third-party insurer) must pay the employer's portion of the FICA and FUTA taxes. Similarly, if within six business days of the plan's receipt of notification, the plan gives notice to the employer for whom the employee normally works, the employer (and not the plan) must pay the employer's portion of the FICA taxes and FUTA taxes and file all related federal employment tax returns. [Temp. Treas. Reg. §§ 31.3401(d)-1(h), 31.6051-3(c); Pub. No. 15-A]

Q 10:22   What are the sick-pay benefit rules for amounts paid to state and local government employees under a statute "in the nature of a workers' compensation act"?

Under the general rules that apply to government employers, payments of sick-pay benefits are subject to FICA and FUTA taxes if the governmental employer is otherwise required to pay these taxes; however, exceptions apply. Police officers and firefighters sometimes receive payments for injuries received in the line of duty under a statute that is not the general workers' compensation law of a state. If the statute limits benefits to work-related injuries or sickness and does not base payments on the employee's age, length of service, or prior contributions, the statute is "in the nature of a workers' compensation act." Under the proposed regulations, payments under such a statute are not subject to federal income tax withholding, FICA, or FUTA. [Treas. Reg. §§ 1.104-1(b), 31.3121(a)(2)-1; IRS Reg. § 160315-03; Pub. No. 15-A]

Q 10:23   What is a Section 218 agreement?

Section 218 agreements prior to 1986 (for Medicare) and 1991 (for Social Security) permitted state or local government entities to cover an employee for FICA purposes who would not have otherwise been covered.

Example. State A entered into an agreement under Section 218 of the Social Security Act under which Social Security coverage is provided for many employees of State A, including all employees of Chatham Township on April 14, 2017. Wages paid to employees covered under the Section 218 agreement are subject to FICA taxes.

Charles, an employee of Chatham Township, was injured in a job-related accident on April 7, 2017. He received sick pay for eight months (April 2017 through November 2017) under a Chatham Township ordinance that provides benefits for city employees injured in work-related accidents. Chatham Township's ordinance is entirely separate and distinct from the general workers' compensation law of State A. Under the ordinance, an employee temporarily injured in the line of duty is entitled to sick pay for a period of up to 12 months. The payments are equal to 85 percent of the employee's regular salary payments during the last full month of employment before the job-related injury; they are not based on the employee's age or years of service or employee contributions. The payments are made by a third-party insurance company that is not an agent of Chatham Township. During the policy year of Charles's injury, Chatham Township paid 100 percent of the insurance premiums. Thus, the plan is not a "contributory plan."

The payments under Chatham Township's, ordinance are paid under a statute "in the nature of a workers' compensation act"; therefore, the payments are excludable from gross income and are not subject to federal income tax withholding. These payments are also excludable from FICA taxes because they are paid under an ordinance, which is in the nature of a workers' compensation act.

Forms W-2 and W-3

Q 10:24   What sick-pay benefits statement is required of the third-party payer and the employer?

The third party must furnish the employer with information concerning wage payments and federal income and FICA tax withheld so that the employer can make timely deposits of the FICA tax and timely report the wages and taxes on information returns and statements. In addition, the third-party payer is required to furnish an annual sick-pay benefit statement by January 15 of the year following the year in which the benefits were paid. The statement must show the following information about each employee who was paid sick pay:

1. The employee's name;

2. The Social Security number of the employee (if Social Security, Medicare, or federal income tax was withheld);

3. The sick pay paid to the employee;

4. Any federal income tax withheld;

5. Any employee Social Security tax withheld; and

6. Any employee Medicare tax withheld.

Upon receipt of that notice, the employer must generally prepare Forms W-2 for the sick-pay benefits. The employer may either combine the sick pay with other wages paid to the employees and prepare a single Form W-2, Wage and Tax Statement, for each employee or may prepare separate Forms W-2 for each employee, one reporting sick pay and the other reporting regular wages. A Form W-2 must be prepared even if all the sick pay is nontaxable. All Forms W-2 must be given to the employees by January 31 following the year the benefits were paid.

The employer-prepared Form W-2 filed for the sick-pay benefits must include the following information:

1. The employer's name, address, and EIN;
2. The employee's name, address, and Social Security number;
3. The sick pay included in federal taxable wages (Form W-2, Box 1);
4. Any federal income tax withheld from the sick pay by the third party (Form W-2, Box 2);
5. The sick pay subject to employee Social Security tax (Form W-2, Box 3);
6. The employee Social Security tax withheld from the sick pay (Form W-2, Box 4);
7. The amount of sick pay subject to Medicare tax (Form W-2, Box 5);
8. The employee Medicare tax (including Additional Medicare Tax, if applicable) withheld (Form W-2, Box 6); and
9. Any amount not subject to federal income tax withholding because the employee contributed with aftertax dollars to the sick-pay plan (Box 12, code J). [Pub. No. 15-A]

Q 10:25 Who is responsible for filing Forms W-2 and W-3 for sick-pay benefits?

The employer generally remains liable for the filing of Forms W-2, Wage and Tax Statements, and, if needed, W-3, Transmittal of Income and Tax Statements (used to provide a transmittal of Forms W-2 to the Social Security Administration). Unless the third party transfers the liability for reporting the sick pay to the employer, the third party is responsible. Where the third party transfers this responsibility to the employer, the employer is responsible.

Q 10:26 What are the W-2 filing requirements when a third-party payer is responsible for reporting?

The third-party payer must deposit FICA, FUTA, and withheld federal income and FICA taxes using its own name and EIN. Unless it transferred liability to the employer, it must give each employee to whom it paid sick-pay benefits a Form W-2 by January 31 following the year the sick payments were made. The Form W-2 must include the third party's name, address, and EIN, and the rest of the information contained in items 3 through 9 of the second list in Q 10:24. The third party should check the "Third-party sick pay" box in Box 13 of the 2016 Form W-2.

Note. When a third-party payer retains responsibility for reporting, the employer has no tax responsibilities for sick-pay benefits (e.g., withholding FICA or FUTA taxes and filing employment tax returns).

Q 10:27   What sick-pay reporting requirements apply to Forms W-2 and W-3 filed by the employer?

The employer reports sick-pay benefits under its name, EIN, and address. The taxable portion of the sick-pay payments is included in Boxes 1, 3, and 5, and the taxes withheld by the third party are included in Boxes 2, 4, and 6. Nontaxable sick pay (e.g., attributable to aftertax employee contributions) is shown in Box 12 using code J. Prior to 2014, the employer would also file a recap W-2 and recap W-3 forms with the Social Security Administration unless there was a binding agreement with the agent to act as the third party and employer's agent. For 2014 and beyond, a new Form 8922 is required to report third-party sick pay. The form is filed with the Internal Revenue Service.

Q 10:28   Is there an optional rule for preparation of Form W-2 when a third party makes the payment?

Yes. A third-party payer and an employer may choose to enter into a legally binding agreement designating the third party as the employer's agent for purposes of preparing Forms W-2 for sick-pay benefits. The agreement must specify what part, if any, of the payments under the sick-pay plan is excludable from the employees' gross incomes because it is attributable to their aftertax contributions to the plan. If the parties enter into an agreement, the third party prepares the actual Forms W-2, not recap Form 8922, for each employee who receives sick pay from the third party. If the optional rule is used, the third party does not provide the employer with a sick-pay statement (see Q 10:24) and the employer prepares the Form 8922 recap. Those recap forms are needed to reconcile the sick pay shown on the employer's Form 941 or 944. Note that Form 8922 third-party sick pay recap statements must be filed on paper and cannot be filed electronically. [Pub. No. 15-A; Form W-2 instructions]

Q 10:29   When are recap Forms 8922 required for sick pay?

A third-party payer that transfers FICA and FUTA liability to the employer (see Q 10:16) for sick-pay taxes must prepare Form 8922, Third-Party Sick Pay Recap. The form does not reflect sick pay paid to individual employees, but instead shows the combined amount of sick pay paid to all employees of all clients of the third party. The recap form provides a means of reconciling the wages shown on the third-party payer's Form 941 or 944 with its Forms W-2. Another change is that Form 8922 is not filed with the Social Security Administration but is filed with the Internal Revenue Service. The third-party payer fills out the recap Form 8922 as follows:

Filer's name, address

Other party's name

Other party's employer identification number

Filer is an:

Filer's employer identification number

Check the box for Employer or Insurer/Agent

Box b — The third party's EIN.

Box c — The third party's name and address.

Box e — "Third-Party Sick Pay Recap" in place of the employee's name.

Box 1 — Sick pay subject to federal income tax for all employees

Box 2 — Federal income tax withheld from the sick pay.

Box 3 — Sick pay subject to employee Social Security tax.

Box 4 — Social Security tax withheld from sick pay.

Box 5 — The sick pay subject to employee Medicare tax.

Box 6 — The employee Medicare tax (including Additional Medicare Tax, if applicable) withheld from the sick pay.

The third-party recap Form 8922 is filed with the Internal Revenue Service by February 28, 2018. The Forms W-2 and W-3 continue to be filed with the Social Security Administration, while the Forms 941 is filed with the Internal Revenue Service.

Note. The recap Form 8922 cannot be filed electronically. [Pub. No. 15-A]

Q 10:30 How can a correction be reported if there is an error on the Form 8922 already filed?

In the event that the Form 8922 you submitted to the Internal Revenue Service has an error, complete the entire Form 8922 again, not just the fields that need to be corrected. Enter an "x" in the box marked CORRECTED and submit the form to the Internal Revenue Service.

Third Party Sick Pay—Not as an Agent and Liability Transferred to Employer

	Employer Responsibilities	Third Party Responsibilities
Withhold Employee Taxes		
Income	No	Yes if W-4S is filed
Social Security	No	Yes
Medicare	No	Yes

Third Party Sick Pay—Not as an Agent and Liability
Transferred to Employer (*cont'd*)

Deposit Employee Taxes

Income	No	Yes, using Third Party EIN
Social Security	No	Yes, using Third Party EIN
Medicare	No	Yes, using Third Party EIN

Deposit Employer Taxes

Social Security	Yes, using employer EIN	No
Medicare	Yes, using employer EIN	No
FUTA	Yes, using employer EIN	No

Report Employee Wage and Taxes on Form 941

Income	Report Taxable Wages	Report Tax Withheld
Social Security	*Report Taxable Wages	*Report Taxable Wages
Medicare	*Report Taxable Wages	*Report Taxable Wages
	*Adjustment on Line 8 for employee taxes deposited by third party.	*Adjustment on Line 8 for employer taxes deposited by employer.

Report Employee Wage and Taxes on Form W-2

Income	Yes	No, File Form 8922
Social Security	Yes	No, File Form 8922
Medicare	Yes	No, File Form 8922

---

* See the instructions earlier if operating under the Optional rule for Form W-2.

Q 10:31   How are accrued sick-pay payments made to the estate of an employee after the calendar year of the employee's death treated for employment tax purposes?

Accrued sick-pay benefits paid to the employee's estate or survivor after the calendar year of the employee's death are not subject to Social Security, Medicare, or FUTA taxes. In addition, these wages are reported on a Form 1099-MISC, not a Form W-2.

Example. Taylor became entitled to sick pay on February 14, 2016 and died November 17, 2016. On January 24, 2017, Taylor's sick pay for the period from November 1 through November 30, 2016 was paid to his survivor. The payment is not subject to Social Security, Medicare, or FUTA taxes. [Pub. No. 15-A]

Employee-Paid Benefits

Q 10:32 How is the taxable portion of sick pay determined when the employee makes aftertax contributions to the plan?

In some plans, the payer of the sick-pay payments will separately identify which portion of the benefits is employee-paid (on an aftertax basis) and which portion is employer-paid (or paid by the employee on a before-tax basis). When a separation of taxable and nontaxable benefits exists, the employer can provide a pro rata separation under which the nontaxable portion of benefits is a pro rata portion of benefits paid to the employee. The employer can apply a three-year weighted average in determining the amounts paid by the employee and employer. The nontaxable portion is then equal to total employee contributions (paid on an aftertax basis) for the three-year period divided by the total employer and employee contributions for the three-year period ending on the last day of the calendar year prior to when benefits are first paid. When the employer does not have this information, a reasonable effort must be made to determine the amounts paid. [Treas. Reg. §§ 1.104-1(d), 1.105-1, 31.3121(a)(2)-1, 31.3306(b)(2)-1]

Example. Carol, an employee of Xavier Co., was seriously injured and lost an arm in a skiing accident on March 5, 2017; the accident was not job-related. Carol's last day of work was March 4, 2017.

Spartan Corp, Inc., an insurance company that was not an agent of Xavier Co., paid Carol $2,200 each month for eight months, beginning in April 2017. Carol submitted a Form W-4S to Spartan Corp, Inc., requesting that $225 be withheld from each payment for federal income tax. Carol received no payments from Xavier Co. from April 2017 through September 2017. In July 2017, Carol received a lump sum of $7,700 from Spartan Corp, Inc. as compensation for the loss of her arm. That payment was determined according to the type of injury and qualifies as a payment unrelated to absence from work (see Q 10:13). Carol intends to return to work in December 2017.

Total Benefit	Date Paid
Monthly benefits of $2,200	April 2017 to September 2017
Lump sum of $7,700	July 2017

For the policy year in which the skiing accident occurred, Carol paid a part of the premiums for her coverage, and Xavier Co. paid the remaining part. The plan was, therefore, a "contributory plan." During the three policy years before the calendar year of the accident, Xavier Co. paid 85 percent of the total of the net premiums for its employees' insurance coverage, and its employees paid 15 percent. No part of the premiums was paid with pretax dollars under a cafeteria plan.

Employee-Paid Portion Over 3 Years	
2016	15%
2015	15%
2014	15%

FICA taxes. No part of the $7,700 lump-sum payment for loss of the arm is included in wages for FICA tax purposes because the payment was determined according to the type of injury and qualifies as a payment unrelated to absence from work. Thus, for FICA tax purposes, taxable sick pay was $11,220 ($2,200 per month × 85% = $1,870 taxable portion per payment; $1,870 × 6 months = $11,220 total taxable sick pay). The six $2,200 checks received by Carol from April through September are included in the calculation. The checks received by Carol in October and November (the seventh and eight checks) was received more than six months after the month in which Carol last worked.

Exemption from FICA Taxes	
Lump sum for payment of loss of arm	$7,700
Monthly payments for October and November	4,400
Employee-paid portion from April 1 to September 30 (15%)	1,980

Of each $2,200 payment Carol received, 15 percent ($330) is not subject to FICA taxes because the plan is contributory, and Carol's aftertax contribution is considered to be 15 percent of the premiums during the three policy years before the calendar year of the accident. If Carol's contribution to the cost of the plan had been made with pretax dollars, the payment would be 100 percent taxable.

FUTA taxes. No part of the $7,700 lump-sum payment is included in wages for FUTA tax purposes. Of the $14,960 taxable sick pay (figured the same as the taxable sick pay for FICA tax purposes), only $7,000 is subject to the FUTA tax—the FUTA contribution base is $7,000.

Subject to FUTA Tax
First $7,000 of the $14,960 taxable portion

Income tax withholding. No part of the $7,700 lump-sum payment is subject to federal income tax withholding. Of each $2,200 payment, $1,870 ($2,200 × 85%) is subject to voluntary income tax withholding. In accordance with Carol's Form W-4S, $225 was withheld from each payment ($1,800 for the eight payments to be made during 2017).

Subject to Federal Income Tax Withholding
$14,960 at $1,870 a month

Liability transferred. For the first six months following the last month in which Carol worked, Spartan Corp, Inc. was liable for FICA and FUTA taxes on any payments that constituted taxable wages. Spartan Corp, Inc. could, however, have transferred the liability for the employer portion of the FICA (and for the FUTA tax) during the first six months by withholding FICA from Carol's sick pay benefits, timely depositing the FICA tax withheld, and notifying Xavier Co. of the payments. If Spartan Corp, Inc. transferred liability for the employer portion of the FICA tax to Xavier Co. and provided the company with a sick-pay statement, Spartan Corp, Inc. would not prepare a Form W-2 for Carol; however, Spartan Corp, Inc. would prepare recap Form 8922, reflecting the FICA tax withheld. Spartan Corp, Inc. and Xavier Co. must both prepare a Form 941 (or 944). Xavier Co. must also report the sick pay and withholding for Carol on Forms W-2, W-3, and 940.

Optional rule for Form W-2. As an alternative, the parties could have followed the optional rule for Form W-2 (see Q 10:28). Under that rule, Spartan Corp, Inc. would prepare Form W-2, even though liability for the employer FICA and FUTA was transferred to Xavier Co. Also, Spartan Corp, Inc. would not prepare a sick-pay statement, and Xavier Co., not Spartan Corp, Inc., would prepare the recap Form 8922 reflecting the sick pay shown on Xavier Co.'s Form 941 or 944.

Liability not transferred. If Spartan Corp, Inc. did not transfer liability for the employer portion of FICA or FUTA to Xavier Co., Spartan would prepare Forms W-2 and W-3 as well as Forms 941 or 944 and 940. Xavier Co. would not report the sick pay.

Payments received after six months. The payment received by Carol in September and October are not subject to FICA or FUTA taxes because the payments were received more than six months after the last day of the month in which Carol last worked (February 2017). Nonetheless, Spartan Corp, Inc. must continue to withhold federal income tax from each payment because Carol furnished Spartan Corp, Inc. a Form W-4S. Also, Spartan Corp, Inc. must prepare Forms W-2 and W-3, unless it has furnished Xavier Co. with a sick-pay statement. If the sick-pay statement was furnished, Xavier Co. must prepare Forms W-2 and W-3.

As explained previously, the taxable portion of the $2,200 monthly payments for sick pay was $1,870 per payment. Taxable sick pay for the second quarter of 2017 was $5,610 ($1,870 × 3 months), for the third quarter of 2017 was $5,610 ($1,870 × 3 months), and for the fourth quarter of 2017 was $3,740 ($1,870 × 2 month).

Third party transfers liability to employer. If the optional rule for Form W-2 is not used, Xavier Co. and Spartan Corp, Inc. must complete Forms 941, W-2, and W-3 as follows:

1. Employer Xavier Co. reports sick pay on Form 941 (for the four quarters of 2017) as follows:

   • Line 2—Includes $5,610 sick pay in wages for the second quarter ($1,870 × 3 payments received in quarter), $5,610 sick pay in wages for the third quarter ($1,870 × 3 payments received in quarter), and $3,740 sick pay in wages for the fourth quarter ($1,870 × 2).

   • Line 3—Does not include withholding from sick pay because the third-party payer (Spartan Corp, Inc.) withheld and deposited the income tax.

   • Line 5a—Includes in Social Security wages for the second and third quarters the following: $5,610 for the second quarter ($1,870 × 3 payments received in the quarter) and $5,610 for the third quarter ($1,870 × 3 payments received in quarter).

   • Line 5c—Includes in Medicare wages for the second and third quarters the following: $5,610 for the second quarter ($1,870 × 3 payments received in the quarter) and $5,610 for the third quarter ($1,870 × 3 payments received in quarter).

   • Line 8—Reports an adjustment (reduction) to Social Security and Medicare taxes for sick pay because Spartan Corp, Inc. withheld and deposited the employee's share of those taxes, second quarter $347.82 and third quarter $347.82. Xavier Co. enters the same on line 8.

2. By February 1, 2018, Xavier Co. issues a Form W-2 to Carol. The sick pay is reported on Form W-2 as follows:

   • Box 1—Includes the $14,960 sick pay in wages ($1,870 × 8 payments).

   • Box 2—Includes the $1,800 income tax withheld on sick pay ($225 × 8 payments).

   • Box 3—Includes the $11,220 sick pay in Social Security wages ($1,870 × 6 payments received in six months).

   • Box 4—Includes the $695.64 Social Security tax withheld on sick pay ($11,220 × 6.2%).

   • Box 5—Includes the $11,220 sick pay in Medicare wages ($1,870 × 6 payments received in six months).

   • Box 6—Includes the $162.69 Medicare tax withheld on sick pay ($11,220 × 1.45%).

3. Even though the preceding amounts were withheld by the third party (Spartan Corp, Inc.), Xavier Co. must include them on the Form W-2 issued to Carol. On Form W-3, Xavier Co. shows the income tax withheld by Spartan Corp, Inc. on Carol's sick pay in Box 14, "Income tax withheld by payer of third-party sick pay."

4. On Form 941 for the first, second, third, and fourth quarters of 2017, Spartan Corp, Inc. does not report the sick pay paid for its clients on line

2. Spartan Corp, Inc. includes on line 3 federal income tax withheld from sick pay for its clients. Spartan Corp, Inc. also includes the third-party sick pay on lines 5a and 5c. Because Spartan Corp, Inc. transferred the employer tax liability to its clients; it enters the employer's share of FICA taxes on third-party sick pay on line 8.

By February 28, 2018, Spartan Corp, Inc. files a Form 8922 to report the total amount of sick pay it paid employees of its clients in 2017. Spartan Corp, Inc. enters its EIN, name, and address in Boxes b and c of the recap Form W-2. Spartan Corp. Inc. prepares Form W-3 to report the W-2 summary for its employees and Form 8922 for the payments made to Xavier's employees.

Third party does not transfer liability to employer. Xavier Co. reports on Form 941 only the wages it paid to its employees. Xavier Co. does not include on lines 2, 5a, and 5c the sick pay Spartan Corp, Inc. paid the employees. Spartan Corp, Inc. includes on lines 2, 5a, and 5c of Form 941 the sick pay paid to insured employees. It also reports income tax withholding on the sick pay on line 3. Xavier Co. and Spartan Corp, Inc. must each issue a Form W-2 to each employee who received wages from Xavier Co. and sick pay from Spartan Corp, Inc. The employee's Form W-2 from Xavier Co. reflects only the paid wages and taxes withheld by Xavier Co. The Form W-2 from Spartan Corp, Inc. reflects only the sick pay paid and the taxes withheld by Spartan Corp, Inc.

State and Local Sick Pay Plan Requirements

Q 10:33 Are there additional requirements for states and localities to report sick pay?

Over the past few years, states and localities have dealt with the issue of paid sick leave. Through 2016 there are ten states and many more local jurisdictions have imposed new sick pay requirements on employers. The effect is that more employees will be eligible for sick pay and there will be an increase in the number of employees for whom payroll professionals have to follow these sick pay guidelines. In 2015, California was the second state, following Connecticut, to implement the sick pay leave for employees. California's law applies to all employers regardless of size and extends sick pay to employees working more than 30 days in the year, providing one hour of sick time for every 30 hours. The other states are Massachusetts, Oregon, and Vermont along with the District of Columbia, complete the list. Many local jurisdictions have also taken action to secure sick leave for employees. Local reforms have come from Spokane, St. Paul, Los Angeles, Chicago, Seattle, 14 localities in New Jersey, and New York City. At the other end, some states have voted to ban paid sick leave. To date 15 states (Alabama, Arizona, Florida, Georgia, Indiana, Kansas, Louisiana, Michigan, Minnesota, Mississippi, Missouri, North Carolina, Oklahoma, Oregon, and Tennessee) enacted legislation to prevent implementation of paid sick leave. The challenge for multistate employers is to find a way to manage the differences in laws. Some employers are opting to apply the highest common denominator to ensure compliance. With the increase of sick pay laws, employers and business associations have initiated lawsuits declaring that these laws are unenforceable. Employers have to be ready to comply with the law until there is some other definitive change. The impact of this trend may require employers to establish formal sick pay plans to ensure compliance with the new requirements.

State Disability Insurance Plans

Q 10:34 Are the federal employment tax and reporting requirements different when disability benefits are paid from a state fund?

The Internal Revenue Code makes no special provisions for sick-pay benefits that are paid under a state plan or system. Sick payments are taxable to the extent the employer is required to contribute toward the state disability insurance program. If, under the state plan, the employee is required to pay 100 percent of the state disability insurance, no portion of the sick pay is taxable (but it still must be reported on Form W-2, box 12, as code J, nontaxable sick pay).

Q 10:35 Which states have a disability insurance contribution requirement?

The following states have a disability insurance requirement:

- *California*. Employers generally elect disability insurance coverage under the state plan or a private plan. Under the state plan, employees are required to make contributions, but employers are not.
- *Hawaii*. Employers may obtain a policy for private disability insurance from a state-approved carrier or establish a self-insured plan if approved by the state. A state fund is available for the disabled unemployed and others. Employees and employers are required to make contributions.
- *New Jersey*. Employees are automatically covered by the state's disability insurance plan unless a private plan was elected by the employer and the majority of its employees. If employees are required to make contributions, the contributions cannot exceed the cost for the employee under the state plan.
- *New York*. Employers must choose between coverage under the state plan or a private plan. Employers and employees are required to make contributions.
- *Puerto Rico*. Employees are automatically covered by the state's disability insurance plan unless a private plan was elected by the employer and the majority of its employees. Employers and employees are required to make contributions.
- *Rhode Island*. The state disability fund must be used to cover employees. Employees are required to make contributions but employers are not.

6 11.1   Payroll Answer Book

Overview

Q 11.1   What are the general payroll recordkeeping requirements?

Chapter 11

Required Recordkeeping and Record Retention

Employers document compliance with federal, state, and local employment law through accurate payroll recordkeeping. A complete record of working hours, certain employee information, and pay must be kept for each and every employee.

It is important to note that the recordkeeping requirements vary under different laws and under the rules promulgated by different agencies. Penalties and other sanctions may also apply for failure to meet these recordkeeping requirements. For example, willful violation of the recordkeeping requirements under the Fair Labor Standards Act (FLSA) can result in criminal sanctions. This chapter explains the information employers are required to retain, the format for retaining it, and the statutory record retention period that applies under various payroll laws.

In addition to correctly maintaining records, it is important to have a process to properly destroy records at the end of the required time to retain. The disposal rule under the Fair and Accurate Credit Transaction Act (FACTA) identifies what employers are required to do to ensure the security of certain employee information.

Overview

Q 11:1   What are the general payroll recordkeeping requirements?

With limited exceptions, there is generally no required method or format of keeping records. However, both federal and state regulations essentially require employers to maintain a master file containing information such as employee data and various tax and payroll information for both pay period and calendar year. As a general matter, the information may be stored in a paper format, on microfilm, microfiche, CD-ROM, tape, diskette, or other magnetic format or electronically. Regardless of how such information is maintained, it is essential that it be complete and accurate. If stored off site, the records must generally be made available within 72 hours of receiving notice from any agency regulating payroll practices. When records are maintained on electronic/magnetic media, the employer must be prepared to produce written records from the stored data. This last requirement could become more difficult as computer systems are upgraded and files become unreadable. In 1996, the Internal Revenue Service (IRS) released a proposed procedure for maintaining electronically scanned records, in lieu of paper copies. This was last updated in 1998 by Internal Revenue Procedure 98-25 (see Qs 11:28–11:34). [Notice 96-9, 1996-1 C.B. 363; Rev. Proc. 97-22, 1997-13 I.R.B. 9]

Q 11:2   What basic payroll and employment information must be maintained?

Employers must generally keep the following payroll and employment tax-related information in their records:

1. The employee's full name, as it appears on his or her Social Security card, and date of employment;

2. The employee's identifying symbol or number if such a number is used in place of a name on any time, work, or payroll records;

3. The employee's complete address;

4. Date of birth, if the employee is under 19 years of age and proof of age, such as age certificates, where appropriate;

5. Sex and occupation in which employed;

6. Payment date and the starting and ending dates of the pay period;

7. Time of day and day of week on which the employee's workweek begins. (Note. A workweek is defined as 7 consecutive days, 168 hours);

8. Number of hours worked each workday (only for employees who are nonexempt under FLSA) and each workweek;

9. Regular rate of pay for weeks when overtime was worked and the basis for determining the rate and any records of any payments excluded from the overtime rate (e.g., $9 per hour, $440 per week);

10. All additions (such as a bonus) and deductions (e.g., insurance, taxes withheld, garnishments) per pay period;

11. Total earnings for straight time (base pay for all hours);

12. Total earnings for overtime (premium pay) for the work week;

13. Total wages paid for each pay period, including withholdings and Federal Insurance Contributions Act (FICA) and Federal Unemployment Tax Act (FUTA) taxes paid;

14. Copies of Forms W-2, W-4, W-4S, W-4P, 8233 and 8922;

15. Cancelled and void checks, stop payments and/or statements of direct deposit (electronic record of payments);

16. Substantiation of fringe benefits and authorization for deductions from employees' wages;

17. Substantiation of and authorizations for any reimbursements of or deductions from the employees' wages, such as expenses, advances, reimbursements, voluntary payroll deductions, garnishments, and wage assignments [29 C.F.R. § 516.6];

18. Dates of absence and records of sick pay;

19. Bank statements and bank reconciliations;

20. Federal, state, and local tax returns that relate to wages, wage expense, employment tax, or wage/tax credits;

21. General ledger, financial statements, and other documentation supporting business expenses, compensation, and tax expense or tax credits; and

22. The total amount an employee contributed to a charity, including a statement, if applicable that no goods or services were received in consideration of the contribution. [29 C.F.R. §§ 516.2, 516.5; FLSA § 11(c), 29 U.S.C. § 211(c); I.R.C. § 6001; Treas. Reg. §§ 31.6001-2, 31.6001-5; IRS Notice 2006-110, 2006-51 I.R.B. 1127; 2008 CFC Memorandum 2008-03]

Q 11:3   What are the basic payroll record retention requirements?

The FLSA has two basic recordkeeping requirements. It imposes a three-year requirement on employee payroll records (e.g., employee name, address, and occupation), weekly time summaries (including the straight time and overtime calculation), collective bargaining agreements, individual employment contracts, certificates and notices required by law, and the employer's sales and purchase records (e.g., total dollar volume of sales and business, and total volume of goods purchased or received, in such form as the employer maintains in the ordinary course of business). A two-year record retention requirement applies to basic time and earnings cards, work schedules, hourly and piece-rate pay schedules; additions or deductions from wages, and order and shipping records. (However, due to the statute of limitations under the FLSA, employers should consider keeping such time and earnings cards for at least three years, as well.) The employer must store the records in a format that allows the records to be available for Department of Labor (DOL) inspection within 72 hours. [29 C.F.R. §§ 516.2, 516.5; FLSA § 11(c), 29 U.S.C. § 211(c)]

The Internal Revenue Code (I.R.C.) imposes a basic four-year record retention requirement on records relating to an IRS filing. The period is measured from the due date of the return, or filing date if later, and applies to all records supporting that filing. With respect to employment tax returns and information statements that relate to federal individual tax returns (e.g., Forms 941 and W-2), the statute of limitations runs until April 15 of the year following the year to which the return relates. However, because the IRS can assess penalties over a three-year period following that date, and process collection for another 10 years after the assessment, and the taxpayer can claim a refund for up to three years following a collection, it is often advisable to retain these records for a dozen or more years after the filing. [Treas. Reg. §§ 31.6001-1(e)(2), 301.6502-1(a), 301.6511(a)-1(a); I.R.C. § 6501(b)(2)]

Q 11:4   What penalties can be imposed for improperly maintained records?

An employer can be subject to penalties and other fines for failing to maintain adequate records. Poor recordkeeping can be costly in establishing a defense when the DOL audits an employer or an employee files suit claiming an employer failed to comply with the FLSA (e.g., failed to pay a minimum wage or overtime). Failing to keep adequate records can also impact the defense to a workers' compensation claim. When the employer has incomplete records, a court or other fact-finder will rely on other evidence, including an employee's recollection of hours and earnings. [I.R.C. §§ 7203, 7204; 29 U.S.C. § 215(a)(5)]

The penalties vary under the numerous laws that can apply. A few of the more significant penalties imposed by federal laws include:

- *FLSA:* A fine of $10,000, imprisonment for up to six months, or both, may be imposed for failing to keep records documenting compliance with the Act. [29 U.S.C. §§ 215(a)(5), 216(a)]

- *I.R.C.:* A fine of $25,000 ($100,000 for corporations), one year imprisonment (or both), and the cost of prosecution may be imposed for willful failure to keep proper payroll records. [I.R.C. §§ 7203, 7204]

- *Immigration Reform and Control Act of 1986 (IRCA):* A fine of up to $1,100 can be imposed for each violation of failing to keep required records documenting the status of a worker. [Pub. L. No. 99-603, 100 Stat. 3359 (Nov. 6, 1986); 73 Fed. Reg. 10,130 (Feb. 26, 2008)]

FLSA Record Retention

Q 11:5   What are the basic record retention requirements under the FLSA for employment records?

In general, an employer must retain payroll records and other documents relevant to FLSA compliance for a minimum of three years. Certain documents that can be classified as "supplementary records" (e.g., time sheets) need only be retained for a period of two years. However, considering the three-year statute of limitations for willful violations under the FLSA, employers are well advised to maintain these records for three years, as well. It should also be noted that some states have a substantially longer statute of limitations for such claims (e.g., New York at six years); accordingly, employers should consider maintaining such records for at least the longest statute of limitations applicable to claims for unpaid wages in the states where they conduct business.

The following records are subject to a mandatory three-year retention requirement under the FLSA:

- Payroll records containing information required under the regulations for recordkeeping purposes and that are "basic" rather than substantiating—the original document and not the weekly summary.

- Sales and purchase records showing a record of (1) total dollar volume of sales or business, and (2) total volume of goods purchased or received during such periods (weekly, monthly, quarterly, etc.), in such form as the employer maintains in the ordinary course of business.

- Collective bargaining agreements that set terms under which certain facilities are provided to employees.

- Agreements that were used to base overtime pay on piece, hourly, or basic rates.

- Certificates and notices required under the regulations for recordkeeping purposes (e.g., certificates authorizing the employment of apprentices, learners, students, handicapped workers, homeworkers, and children under age 18).

- Employment contracts; union contracts involving exclusions from the regular rate.

- Contracts and memoranda that relate to "Belo-type" contracts that guarantee a flat weekly pay for fluctuating hours.

The following records are subject to a two-year retention requirement:

- Basic employment and earnings records that substantiate payroll and other "basic" records (e.g., timecards or timesheets that show the daily starting and stopping times for individual employees).

- Work schedules that establish the hours and days of employment for an individual employee. These schedules must be preserved for two years from their last effective date and are to be kept in the same form as they were actually used (i.e., not copies).

- Wage rate tables for hourly, daily, weekly, or other pay periods or for pay based on a piece rate. These also must be kept for two years from their last effective date.

- Order, shipping, and billing records that the employer retains or creates in the course of business. Either originals or copies may be kept.

- Records of additions to or deductions from wages paid.

[29 C.F.R. §§ 516.5, 516.6]

Q 11:6   What payroll records need to be retained for exempt employees?

FLSA record retention requirements for exempt employees are not as detailed as those for nonexempt employees. Exempt, or "white-collar," employees generally are not subject to the minimum wage and overtime provisions of the FLSA. As a result, employers are not required to retain records on the exempt employee's regular rate of pay, hours worked, wages, or deductions from wages. An employer must maintain sufficient records for exempt employees to reproduce each employee's earnings for each pay period and to prove that the employee is exempt from the FLSA's provisions. An employer must also maintain the following:

- Name in full, as used for Social Security recordkeeping purposes (along with the employee's identifying symbol or number if such is used in place of name on any time, work, or payroll records).
- Home address, including ZIP code.
- Date of birth, if under 19 years of age.
- Sex and occupation in which employed.
- Time of day and day of week on which employee's workweek begins.

[29 C.F.R. § 516.3]

Q 11:7   What employment records are required to be retained for employees receiving tips in their jobs?

In addition to payroll records required of any worker, an employer that uses tip credits to satisfy the tipped employee's minimum wage and overtime requirements must retain additional records for each tipped employee. These include the following:

1. Documentation on each employee's record demonstrating that minimum wages and overtime pay are partly based on tips;

2. Weekly or monthly summaries of the tips reported by the employee, to the employer, of tips received. These totals may be taken from IRS Form 4070, Employee's Report of Tips to Employer or equivalent form;

3. The tip credit the employer is taking for each pay period;

4. Hours worked each workday in any occupation in which the employee does not receive tips, and total daily or weekly straight-time payment made by the employer for such hours; and

5. Hours worked each workday in occupations in which the employee receives tips, and total daily or weekly straight-time earnings for such hours.

[29 C.F.R. § 516.28]

Q 11:8   What employment records are to be retained for employees who produce goods in their home?

An employer that uses the services of industrial homeworkers must keep the following additional information for each job or lot of work:

1. The date the work was given out to the worker, or started by the worker;

2. The amount of work given out or started;

3. The date the work was turned in;

4. The amount of work turned in;

5. A description of the articles worked on and what work was performed;

6. Piece rates paid;

7. Hours worked on each lot of work turned in; and

8. Wages paid for each lot of work turned in.

Other records include:

1. Name and address of the agent, distributor, or contractor that gives work to, or collects work from, each homeworker; and

2. Name and address of each homeworker to whom homework is distributed or from whom it is collected. [29 C.F.R. § 516.31]

Q 11:9   What additional records must be retained for employees receiving subminimum wages under a valid Department of Labor certificate?

The DOL will, in certain circumstances, permit an employer to pay learners, student-learners, messengers, and apprentices less than the minimum hourly wage. Satisfaction of the DOL requirements in a wage program is evidenced by a certificate issued to the employer by the DOL. A copy of the application and the DOL certificate must be retained for three years after any employee's last employment under the program. Each employee under such a program must be designated as a subminimum wage worker on the payroll records along with the employee's occupation and rate of pay. At the time the learner is hired, a statement is required that includes all related industry experience, including vocational training, during the preceding three years. The employer must also retain all the same records as required under the FLSA. [29 C.F.R. §§ 520.203, 520.412, 520.508]

IRS Employment Records

Q 11:10   What are an employer's federal recordkeeping requirements for employment tax payment and reporting purposes?

Employers must keep all records of employment taxes paid for at least four years. The four-year period is measured from the due date of the tax (or the date the tax is actually paid) for the return period to which the records relate. However, with respect to tax returns or information statements that relate to the employee's personal income tax return, records must be retained for at least four years from the later of the due date of the tax to which the return relates or the due date of the employee's tax return (April 15). For example, Forms 941 and W-2 generally are retained four years from April 15 following the year to which the return relates, whereas Form 940 is generally retained four years from January 31 following the year to which the return relates. The records should be sufficient to enable the IRS to review the payroll processing and reconstruct the filed reports. [Treas. Reg. §§ 31.6001-1(e)(2), 31.6001-4(a); I.R.C. § 6501]

Records should include, at a minimum, the following information:

- The employer's federal employer identification number (EIN);
- Amounts and dates of all wage, annuity, and pension payments;
- Amounts of tips reported;
- The fair market value of in-kind wages paid;
- Records of allocated tips;
- Dates of employment;
- Periods for which employees and recipients were paid while absent due to sickness or injury, and the amount and weekly rate of payments the employer or third-party payers made to them;
- Names, addresses, Social Security numbers, and occupations of employees and recipients;
- Any employee copies of Form W-2, Wage and Tax Statement, that were returned to the employer as undeliverable;
- Copies of employees' and recipients' income tax withholding allowance certificates (Form W-4, Employee's Withholding Allowance Certificate; Form W-4P, Withholding Certificate for Pension or Annuity Payments; Form W-4S, Request for Federal Income Tax Withholding from Sick Pay; and Form W-4V, Voluntary Withholding Request);
- Dates and amounts of tax deposits made;
- Record of taxes paid under FUTA;
- Copies of returns filed; and
- Records of fringe benefits provided, including any supporting documentation required to substantiate those benefits as being tax exempt. [Treas. Reg. §§ 31.6001-1(e)(2), 31.6001-4(a)]

In addition to the above, the employer should keep detailed records showing all earnings and deductions used in arriving at net pay, including any pretax deductions (e.g., Section 125 elective contributions, 401(k) salary deferrals).

Q 11:11   What are the IRS employment record retention requirements for employee benefit plans?

An employer should maintain records sufficient to document an employee's eligibility and coverage under any retirement plan in which the employee ever participated. For example, an employee with 20 years of employment may have been covered under several pension plans (or under several amendments to a single pension plan). That employee may contest a benefit earned 20 years earlier. The employer should be able to document any accrual of benefits by presenting not only work history (e.g., hours of service, wages, employee contributions) but also each plan and amendment.

When employees are required to contribute to a fringe benefit plan, the employer should maintain evidence of those contributions as well as the employee's authorization for the contributions.

Employers are required to file annual reports for most plans with the Department of Labor and/or the IRS. Where benefits are provided on a tax-exempt basis conditioned on requirements in the I.R.C. or Treasury Regulations, records must be retained sufficient to satisfy those conditions. For example, records are required for health insurance, cafeteria benefits, educational assistance, or dependent care assistance programs that exclude these amounts from income. The employer may also be required to retain records of benefit payments and contributions sufficient to support an unqualified external audit that is required by certain Employment Retirement Income Security Act (ERISA) provisions. [I.R.C. § 6039(D)(b); ERISA §§ 104, 105]

Q 11:12   What is the IRS retention period for information on allocated tips?

For IRS purposes, wage and tax payment records sufficient to substantiate the information that the employer used on its employment returns must be kept for at least three years after the due date of the return. This can be longer than the required record retention period pursuant to the FLSA.

Q 11:13   How long are FUTA tax records retained?

Records sufficient to support the payment of FUTA tax and information reported on Form 940 must be retained for at least four years after the due date of the Form 940 or the date the required FUTA tax was paid (generally, January 31 following the year the FUTA tax liability was incurred), whichever is later. States may impose a longer record retention period for these records (e.g., Tennessee imposes a seven-year retention period).

I-9 Record Retention

Q 11:14　What law requires Form I-9, Employment Eligibility Verification, to be completed?

The Immigration Reform and Control Act of 1986 (IRCA) prohibits employers from hiring persons who are not authorized to work in the United States. An employee documents a valid authorization to work in the United States by completing Form I-9, Employment Eligibility Verification; providing documentation identified in the Form I-9; and having a representative of the employer sign the form certifying compliance. IRCA also contains provisions to help protect the employee from discrimination based on his or her national origin or citizenship.

Q 11:15　What are the record retention requirements for Form I-9?

Form I-9, Employment Eligibility Verification, must be retained for at least three years after the date the employee was hired or one year after the date the employee terminates employment, whichever is later. Verification records issued by state employment agencies must also be retained. The employer is permitted to keep certain copies of any documentation provided by the employee as support for the Form I-9 (e.g., visa, naturalization papers, Social Security cards). However, it is important to note that an employer must be consistent in this practice; that is, it must keep such records for all employees, or none at all. I-9 records must generally be stored in a format that allows them to be reproduced for inspection within 72 hours. [8 C.F.R. § 274A(b)(2)]

Q 11:16　May Forms I-9 be stored electronically?

Yes. The Immigration and Nationality Act allows employers to retain the I-9 forms electronically. [Pub. L. No. 108-390, 118 Stat. 2242] The United States Immigration and Customs Enforcement published an interim rule that allows employers to sign and retain I-9 forms electronically. The rule does not require employers to use a particular system to store I-9 forms electronically, and it does not identify one specific method for acceptable electronic signatures. Rather, the rule sets forth minimum standards for employers. For example, all documents reproduced by the electronic retention system must have a high degree of legibility and readability when displayed on a video display terminal, or when printed on paper, microfilm, or microfiche. In general, the interim rule also requires an I-9 storage system to include:

- Reasonable controls to ensure the integrity, accuracy, and reliability of the system;
- Reasonable controls designed to prevent and detect unauthorized or accidental use;
- An inspection and quality assurance program; and
- A retrieval system that includes an indexing system permitting searches.

Note. Employers are still permitted to retain the forms on paper, microfilm, or microfiche.

[71 Fed. Reg. 34,510 (June 15, 2006)]

Other Federal and State Requirements

Q 11:17 What are the basic record retention requirements of the Civil Rights Act of 1964 (Title VII)?

The Civil Rights Act of 1964 (Title VII) generally prohibits an employer from discriminating against employees on the basis of race, color, sex, religion, or national origin. The Equal Employment Opportunity Commission, which has authority for administration of Title VII, requires that certain records on which personnel decisions are made be maintained for at least one year following the date of the decision. If a lawsuit, complaint, or charge is filed, all such documents must be maintained until final disposition. [29 C.F.R. §§ 1602.14, 1602.30, 1602.31, 1602.39, 1602.48]

State and local governments may impose additional recordkeeping requirements under state or local laws that prohibit similar discrimination.

Q 11:18 What employment records are required to be retained under the Family and Medical Leave Act?

The Family and Medical Leave Act (FMLA) generally requires that employers with 50 or more employees provide up to 12 weeks of unpaid leave for eligible employees (1) for the birth of a son or daughter, and care for the newborn; (2) for placement with the employee of a son or daughter for adoption or foster care; (3) to care for the employee's spouse, son, daughter, or parent with a serious health condition; and (4) because of a serious health condition that makes the employee unable to perform the functions of the employee's job. The leave must be requested, and certain documentation explaining and authenticating the leave must be provided. An employer is required to retain specific records on the employees who request and become eligible for FMLA leave.

For each employee who requests and becomes eligible for FMLA-approved leave, the employer must retain the following records in addition to the employee's normal records:

1. All additions to and deductions from wages relating to the leave and the total wages paid;

2. Where time off is taken in increments of less than one day, a record of leave hours;

3. The dates of FMLA leave taken (this leave must be distinguished from other leave to which the employee may be entitled);

4. The policies and procedures relating to the leave, including all notices;

5. Copies of written notices of an employee's request to take FMLA leave;

6. Any premium payments made for the employee's benefits while he or she is on leave; and

7. Records of any dispute between the employer and an eligible employee regarding designation of the leave as FMLA leave.

In general, these records must be retained for at least three years. It is important to note that the FMLA does not require that these records be kept in any particular order or form; however, regardless of order or form, they must be complete, accurate, readable, and retrievable. [29 U.S.C. § 2616(b); 29 C.F.R. § 825.500]

A special exception to these requirements is available for exempt employees. An employer can omit the hourly retention requirement for employees who are exempt from the FLSA overtime pay and minimum wage requirements when two conditions exist: (1) FMLA leave is available for any exempt worker who has been employed for 12 months and (2) intermittent FMLA leave is requested and the employer and employee agree in writing to the employee's normal work schedule during that period. The written agreement must be retained. [29 C.F.R. §§ 825.110(c), 825.500(f)]

Q 11:19   Does the Affordable Care Act (ACA) require any different record retention?

The reporting requirements for the tracking of employee hours under the Affordable Care Act (ACA) may impact your company's current guidelines for retaining time records for employees. Generally, an employer must keep time records for two years. Under the new health care law, employers must track and record employees' hours to determine if the employers have complied with the requirement of offering medical coverage under ACA. Employers are required to track the monthly status of all full-time employees, who are defined as working at least 30 hours. This information is required to determine if the employer is required to pay a "shared responsibility" assessment to the IRS. For seasonal employees and variable hour employees, the IRS has provided guidance for safe harbor methods that may be used to measure the stability and measurement periods. [IRS Notice 2012-58, 2012-41 I.R.B. 436]

An additional consideration is that the ACA requires an employer to support the information provided to substantiate that the benefits offered to employees comply with the outlined requirements. ERISA requires employers to be able to verify that all requirements have been met. The recordkeeping requirements for benefit plans are six years. This should be taken into consideration when defining your company's record retention guidelines.

Q 11:20   Do the same FLSA recordkeeping requirements apply to government contractors?

Yes. The basic employee and payroll requirements are the same as those under the FLSA (i.e., three years); however, an employer that is governed under the Walsh-Healey Public Contracts Act and the Davis-Bacon Act must also keep a log of occupational injuries and illnesses. Under the Walsh-Healey Public Contracts Act, certain required Occupational Safety and Health Act (OSHA) records must be kept for five years. Age certificates for minors (under age 19) are required to be kept for as long as the minor is employed. [41 C.F.R. § 50-201.502; 29 C.F.R. §§ 1904.2–1904.6]

Q 11:21   What are the record retention requirements of the Occupational Safety and Health Act?

OSHA generally requires that employers with 11 or more workers maintain a log and summary of occupational injuries and illnesses, and supplementary records of injuries or illnesses. The documents must be retained for five years after the end of the calendar year to which the records relate. [29 C.F.R. §§ 1904.2, 1904.6] OSHA also requires employers to maintain certain medical and exposure records relating to toxic substances or harmful physical agents. [29 C.F.R. § 1910.102]

Q 11:22   What records are required for state unemployment insurance laws?

There is little consistency among state unemployment insurance laws regarding the time period for preserving required records. However, the following information is generally applicable under most state statutes:

1. Employee name;
2. Employee Social Security number;
3. The dates of hire, separation, rehire, and reinstatement after a temporary layoff;
4. The amount of compensation paid in each payroll period (this could be cash as well as noncash items);
5. The dates the pay period covers (beginning and end dates);
6. A list of the paydays;
7. The date and reason for termination of employment; and
8. The amount of time lost during a payroll period because the employee was unavailable for work.

Note that additional records such as names of owners and percentage of ownership will likely be required in the event of a merger, acquisition, or restructuring and with respect to multiple business entities having common ownership. In addition, all opinion letters and other documentation supporting the request for a transfer of wages or experience is also essential for audit defense purposes.

Table 11-1 provides a record retention schedule.

Table 11-1.   Periods for Which State Unemployment Insurance Records Are Required to Be Retained

State	Number of Years	State	Number of Years
Alabama	5	Missouri	3
Alaska	5	Montana	5
Arizona	4	Nebraska	4
Arkansas	5	Nevada	4
California	4	New Hampshire	6
Colorado	5	New Jersey	5
Connecticut	4	New Mexico	3
Delaware	4	New York	5
District of Columbia	5	North Carolina	5
		North Dakota	5
Florida	5	Ohio	5
Georgia	7	Oklahoma	4
Hawaii	5	Oregon	5
Idaho	3	Pennsylvania	4
Illinois	5	Rhode Island	4
Indiana	5	South Carolina	4
Iowa	5	South Dakota	4
Kansas	5	Tennessee	7
Kentucky	6	Texas	4
Louisiana	5	Utah	3
Maine	4	Vermont	6
Maryland	5	Virginia	4
Massachusetts	4	Washington	4
Michigan	6	West Virginia	5
Minnesota	8	Wisconsin	5
Mississippi	5	Wyoming	4

Note. In some states the retention period begins at the end of the current calendar year. If the retention period is less than four years, the company should still retain the records for the four-year period to be in compliance with the retention period required under FUTA.

Source: 2017 Multistate Payroll Guide (CCH Incorporated, 2017).

Q 11:23   What records are required for state income tax withholding purposes?

Generally, the same records that are kept for federal income tax withholding purposes should also be retained for state income tax withholding purposes. For instance, records of wage payments by benefit type, withholding tax calculations, withholding allowance and exemption certificates, if applicable, deposit records, copies of income tax withholding returns (including Forms W-2), etc. (see Q 11:10). Because each state's income tax withholding requirements are unique, it is prudent to review each state income tax agency's recordkeeping requirements, which are generally provided together with the state's income tax withholding tables and/or withholding and tax reporting instruction guidelines.

Table 11-2.   Periods for Which State Income Tax Withholding Records Are Required to Be Retained

State	Number of Years	State	Number of Years
Alabama	3	Mississippi	3
Alaska	No income tax	Missouri	3
Arizona	4	Montana	5
Arkansas	4 (6 if computer generated)	Nebraska	3
		Nevada	No income tax
California	7	New Hampshire	No income tax
Colorado	4	New Jersey	5
Connecticut	4	New Mexico	7
Delaware	3	(no state law or regulations. State recommends 7 years; minimum IRS standard of 4 years should apply)	
District of Columbia	3		
Florida	No income tax		
Georgia	4		
Hawaii	3		
Idaho	4		
Illinois	3	New York	4
Indiana	4	North Carolina	3
Iowa	5	North Dakota	4
Kansas	3	(no state law or regulations. State tax commissioner may audit returns and make assessments up to 3 years after the due date of a return)	
Kentucky	4		
Louisiana	3		
Maine	6		
Maryland	3		
Massachusetts	4		
Michigan	6		
Minnesota	4		

Table 11-2.   Periods for Which State Income Tax Withholding
Records Are Required to Be Retained (*cont'd*)

State	Number of Years	State	Number of Years
Ohio	4	Texas	No income tax
Oklahoma (no specific statue, recommends 3-7 years)		Utah	3
		Vermont (no provision but if fraud is involved up to 6 years)	6
Oregon	5		
Pennsylvania (no provision)	4	Virginia	3
Rhode Island	3	Washington	No income tax
South Carolina	3	West Virginia	2
South Dakota	No income tax	Wisconsin	4
Tennessee	No income tax	Wyoming	No income tax

Q 11:24   What are the typical record retention requirements for state wage and hour laws?

In most cases, state statutes on record retention follow the requirements under the FLSA. Most states require that basic employee wage and hour records be retained for each nonexempt employee. This includes the following:

1. The employee's name;

2. The employee's complete address;

3. The employee's position;

4. The hours worked each day and week;

5. The amount of compensation paid to the employee each pay period;

6. The employee's rate of pay; and

7. The employee's age if the employee is a minor.

The most common retention period for state wage and hour laws is three years; however, some states have no stated provision. Regardless of what the stated retention period is in a particular state, it may be advisable to retain wage and hour records for the duration of the statute of limitations period applicable to wage and hour claims in a particular state (e.g., for six years in New York).

Q 11:25   What are the basic record retention requirements that apply to garnishments?

Records for garnishments that are the result of a federal income tax levy are required to be maintained for four years from the date of final withholding used to satisfy the levy.

Records for general creditor garnishments that are subject to FLSA minimum wage limitations are to be retained for three years. State laws generally impose additional requirements on record retention for creditor garnishments.

Records that document garnishments arising from child support orders should be retained for three years after the order has been released.

Q 11:26   What record retention rules apply to unclaimed wages?

Wages that are not claimed by the employee (e.g., an uncashed paycheck) must eventually be turned over to the state treasury under each state's abandoned property or escheat laws. State laws vary as to how long wages must remain unclaimed to be considered abandoned property and how long the records regarding these wages should be retained.

Q 11:27   Are the record retention requirements eliminated when the employer uses a third-party payroll service provider?

No. Employers are not relieved of their recordkeeping responsibilities when a third party processes the payroll. Information supplied by the third-party service provider, whether in paper or electronic form, should be obtained and retained by the employer. [Rev. Proc. 98-25, 1998-11 I.R.B. 7]

Machine-Sensible Records

Q 11:28   What are the current recordkeeping requirements that apply to automatic payroll processing?

I.R.C. Section 6001 identifies the basic recordkeeping requirements for most IRS reporting purposes. That section applies regardless of whether an employer's records are maintained on paper or in one of several computer or machine-readable formats (generally referred to by the IRS as "machine-sensible" formats). Revenue Procedure 98-25 [1998-11 I.R.B. 7] contains the current recordkeeping requirements for employment and payroll records that are maintained in an electronic or other nonpaper format. The records should be sufficient to support a detailed review of whether an individual is subject to a tax or to I.R.C. reporting. This revenue procedure updates Revenue Ruling 71-20 [1971-1 C.B. 392], which set out basic record retention requirements.

Revenue Procedure 98-25 also contains specific recordkeeping requirements for machine-sensible records maintained by the employer to meet the business-purpose requirements of I.R.C. Section 274(d), relating to the amount, time, place, and purpose of a business expense.

Employers subject to the recordkeeping requirements of Revenue Procedure 98-25 include any of the following:

1. *Any employer with assets of $10 million or more at the end of its taxable year.* Such an employer must also comply with the record retention requirements of Revenue Ruling 71-20. Note that the controlled group rules as determined under I.R.C. Section 1563 apply to aggregate members of a controlled group for meeting this asset threshold.

2. *Any employer with assets of less than $10 million at the end of its taxable year.* These employers are subject to the requirements of Revenue Ruling 71-20 and the provisions of Revenue Procedure 98-25 if any of the following conditions exist:

   a. All or any portion of the information required by I.R.C. Section 6001 is not in the employer's hard-copy books and records but is available only in machine-sensible records;

   b. Machine-sensible records were used for payroll computations that cannot be reasonably verified or recomputed without using a computer (e.g., certain withholding requirements); or

   c. The employer is notified by the District Director that machine-sensible records must be retained to meet the requirements of I.R.C. Section 6001.

3. *A controlled foreign corporation (CFC).* Revenue Procedure 98-25 applies to a domestic corporation that is 25 percent foreign-owned and a CFC if the foreign corporation was engaged in a trade or business within the United States at any time during a taxable year that the CFC maintains machine-sensible records within an automated data processing (ADP) system to satisfy the requirements of I.R.C. Sections 964(c), 982(d), 6038A(c)(4), and 6038C.

An employer that is otherwise required to maintain records under Revenue Procedure 98-25 but that uses the services of a third party (e.g., a payroll processing bureau) to provide services that result in machine-sensible records continues to be responsible for satisfying the requirements of the revenue procedure. [I.R.C. § 6001; Rev. Proc. 98-25, 1998-11 I.R.B. 7; Rev. Rul. 71-20, 1971-1 C.B. 392]

Q 11:29 What are the specific record retention requirements under Revenue Procedure 98-25 for machine-sensible records?

Revenue Procedure 98-25 [1998-11 I.R.B. 7] details specific requirements that apply to the recordkeeping requirements for records processed through Automatic Data Processing (ADP) systems. An ADP system consists of an accounting or financial system that processes all or part of an employer's transactions by other than manual methods. An ADP system includes, but is not limited to, a mainframe computer system, a stand-alone or networked micro-computer system, a database management system (DBMS), and a system that uses or incorporates electronic data interchange (EDI) technology, or an electronic storage system. [Rev. Proc. 98-25, 1998-11 I.R.B. 7]

The revenue procedure does not require retention of the program or system originally used to process the data as long as the data used in the process can be retrieved for review. That data must be in a format that will allow reprocessing to reproduce the same results. An employer is permitted to maintain employment records in any recognized electronic storage system, including electronic images of hard-copy documents and computerized books and records in computer output to laser disk (COLD), that are the same length as the underlying books and records to be viewed or reproduced without the use of the original program. This requirement is further discussed in Revenue Procedure 97-22. [1997-13 I.R.B. 9]

The revenue procedure contains specific information on the retention of machine-sensible records. In general, an employer that is subject to these requirements must retain machine-sensible records that are material to the administration of the I.R.C. At a minimum, this requirement applies until the expiration of the period of limitation for IRS assessment, including extensions, for each tax year, which in certain situations can extend for up to 15 years. [Treas. Reg. § 1.6001-1(e)]

An employer's machine-sensible records must be sufficient to support and verify entries made on tax filings and to confirm the correct tax liability. These records must be sufficient to enable reconciliation with the employer's books and any tax filing. Specifically, the employer must be able to identify the underlying source documents and the data must be capable of being processed.

An employer may elect to establish files solely for the use of the IRS. That is, it is not necessary to provide all of the employer's original records used to process payroll or prepare a tax filing. Where an election is made to create a separate file with limited records, the employer must provide documentation to show that the process used to create the IRS-specific file properly reflects the actual data used to prepare the original reports. The employer must establish audit trails between the retained records and the employer's books and between the retained records and the tax return.

Revenue Procedure 98-25 specifies that the employer must maintain and make available to the IRS, upon request, records that satisfy the following requirements:

1. Documentation of the business processes that created the retained records;
2. Documentation to satisfy a requirement to support and verify entries made on the employer's return;
3. Documentation to determine the correct tax liability; and
4. Evidence as to the authenticity and integrity of the employer's records.

That documentation must be sufficiently detailed to identify:

1. The functions being performed as they relate to the flow of data through the system;

2. The internal controls used to ensure accurate and reliable processing;

3. The internal controls used to prevent the unauthorized addition, alteration, or deletion of retained records; and

4. The charts of accounts and detailed account descriptions.

With respect to each file that is retained, the employer must maintain and must make available to the IRS upon request:

1. Documentation of record formats or layouts;

2. Field definitions (including the meaning of all codes used to represent information);

3. File descriptions (e.g., data field names);

4. Evidence that periodic checks of the retained records were performed;

5. Evidence that the retained records reconcile to the employer's books; and

6. Evidence that the retained records reconcile to the employer's tax return.

Note that when an employer sells or otherwise disposes of a subsidiary company, the employer is not relieved of its responsibilities under Revenue Procedure 98-25. [1998-11 I.R.B. 7]

Q 11:30 Does the IRS impose any specific records management practices for machine-sensible records?

No. The IRS does not dictate how the employer must implement records management practices; however, it makes recommendations about certain records management practices, including the labeling of records, providing a secure storage environment, creating backup copies, selecting an offsite storage location, and testing to confirm records integrity. The National Archives and Record Administration's (NARA) Standards for the Creation, Use, Preservation, and Disposition of Electronic Records [36 C.F.R. ch. XII, pt. 1234, subpt. C (1996)] is one example of a records management resource that an employer may choose to consult when formulating its records management practices. The NARA standard requires an annual reading of a statistical sampling of magnetic computer tape reels to identify any loss of data and to discover and correct the causes of data loss. In libraries with 1,800 or fewer storage units (e.g., magnetic tape reels), a 20 percent random sampling or a sample size of 50 units, whichever is larger, should be read. In libraries with more than 1,800 units, a sample of 384 units should be read. Although this NARA sampling standard is specifically for magnetic computer tape, the IRS recommends that all retained machine-sensible records be sampled and tested as described in the NARA standard. [36 C.F.R. § 1234.30(g)(4); Rev. Proc. 98-25, 1998-11 I.R.B. 7]

Note. In July 2013, the IRS sought comments regarding the Automatic Data Processing (ADP) system required under Rev. Proc. 98-25.

Q 11:31   Can an employer get confirmation that its retention of an abbreviated machine-sensible record will be acceptable to the IRS?

Yes. An employer that maintains machine-sensible records may enter into a record retention limitation agreement (RRLA) with the IRS. Such an agreement would provide for the establishment and maintenance of records. An employer wanting to enter into such an agreement must identify and describe the records that will not be retained and state why those records will not become material to the administration of any I.R.C. requirement. The District Director will notify the employer if the proposed agreement is acceptable.

Unless an RRLA otherwise specifies, the agreement shall not apply to accounting and tax records added by the employer that were not a part of the evaluation that led to the agreement. An RRLA does not apply to a subsidiary acquired subsequent to the completion of the agreement unless the agreement so specifies. [Rev. Proc. 98-25, 1998-11 I.R.B. 7]

Q 11:32   Are there special requirements for information related to tipped income?

Yes. The record retention requirements apply to data required from an employee to an employer reporting tipped income as required under Regulations Section 31.6053-1. The information is not required to be a facsimile of Form 4070 or any employer-designed form. The requirement is satisfied if the following is retained:

1. Name, address, and Social Security number of the employee;
2. Name and address of the employer;
3. The period to which and the date on which the statement is furnished. Beginning and ending dates unless reporting the calendar month, then month and year are required;
4. Total amount of tips received by employee during period reported.

Q 11:33   What are the consequences when some of an employer's machine-sensible records are lost?

An employer that loses some of its records (hard copy or machine-sensible data) from a particular storage unit generally will not be subject to penalties for not retaining its records, but only if it demonstrates to the satisfaction of the IRS that its data maintenance practices conform to the NARA sampling standard. [36 C.F.R. § 1234.30(g)(4)] Such an employer is not given relief from penalties if, as a result of the loss, the employer is unable to substantiate the information on its return as required by I.R.C. Section 6001. Ultimately, the employer is responsible for taking appropriate safeguards to ensure that adequate records are maintained. [I.R.C. § 6001; Rev. Proc. 98-25, 1998-11 I.R.B. 7]

Q 11:34　Must an employer that retains machine-sensible records also retain paper copies of records and reports?

Although the guidance provided under Revenue Procedure 98-25 [1998-11 I.R.B. 7] applies to the maintenance of records and data in an electronic format, employers are not relieved of their responsibility to retain hard-copy records that are created or received in the ordinary course of business as required by existing law and regulations. Hard-copy records may be retained in microfiche or microfilm format in conformity with Revenue Procedure 81-46. [1981-2 C.B. 621] Hard-copy records may also be retained in an electronic storage system in conformity with Revenue Procedure 97-22. [1997-13 I.R.B. 9] These records are not a substitute for the machine-sensible records that Revenue Procedure 98-25 requires to be retained.

An employer need not create or retain hard-copy records when one of the following situations exists:

1. The hard-copy records are merely computer printouts created only for validation, control, or other temporary purposes;

2. The hard-copy records are not produced in the ordinary course of transacting business (as may be the case when EDI technology is used); or

3. All the details relating to the transaction are subsequently received by the employer in an EDI transaction and are retained as machine-sensible records by the employer in conformity with Revenue Procedure 98-25. There is no requirement to create hardcopy printouts unless requested to do so by the IRS.

Failure to comply with these requirements can result in the imposition of civil penalties under I.R.C. Section 6662(a) and criminal penalties under I.R.C. Section 7203. [Rev. Proc. 98-25, 1998-11 I.R.B. 7]

Summary of Retention Requirements

Q 11:35　Given that all of the agencies have different retention requirements, is there an easy way to remember how long a record needs to be retained?

Yes. Table 11-3 provides a quick reference for the federal retention requirements. Note, however, that retention requirements may also be set by each state for income tax, unemployment, and other state-mandated programs. These dates may also be impacted if you are under audit or have not completed an audit cycle.

Table 11-3. Federal Record Retention Requirements

5 Years: OSHA Documents

- Log of all occupational illnesses accidents or fatalities.
- Other OSHA records.

Table 11-3. Federal Record Retention Requirements (*cont'd*)

4 Years: IRS, SSA, and FUTA Documents

- Duplicate copies of all tax returns and deposits.
- Returned copies of W-2s.
- All canceled and voided checks.
- Employee's name, address, occupation, and Social Security number.
- The amounts and dates of wages, annuities, pensions, tips, and any fair market value for wages-in-kind payments.
- Records of all allocated tips.
- The amount of wages that was subject to withholding.
- The amount of the taxes withheld and the date (if other than the normal payroll date).
- The W-4 for at least 4 years after the date the last tax return was filed using the information from the form. (Because Form W-5 was discontinued in 2010, it is no longer required to be retained.)
- Any agreements to withhold additional amounts.
- The dates when an employee received pay when absent due to an injury, including the amount and rate, even if the amount was paid by a third party.
- The dates when an employee received pay when absent and payments were made under a contingency plan, including amount and rate.
- Copies of all returns filed on magnetic media, such as Forms 940, 941, W-2, W-3, Schedule A, and Schedule B.

3 Years: FLSA and IRCA Documents

- Employee's name, address, occupation, date of birth, and gender.
- A record of hours worked for each day and week.
- The amount paid and the pay date.
- The amount earned at straight-time pay as well as overtime.
- Any additions and/or deductions made to the employee's pay.
- All collective bargaining agreements.
- Sales and purchase records.

Form I-9 must be retained for 3 years after the date of hire or 1 year after the date the employment is terminated, whichever is later. (If copies of Social Security cards, etc., were obtained by the employer, these are also subject to the same record retention requirements.)

3 Years: FMLA Documents

- Employee's name, address, occupation, rate of pay, and hours worked (both daily and weekly) per pay period.
- Any additions to and deductions from the employee's pay and the total compensation.

- FMLA leave dates and hours if taken in less than one day.
- Written notices from the employee notifying the employer of his or her intention to take FMLA leave.
- All notices provided to employees, general and specific.
- The policies and procedures for unpaid and paid leaves including the plan's descriptions.
- Any premium payments made for the employee's benefits.
- A record of any disputes.

2 Years: Supplemental Documents

- Time cards or reports showing times in and out.
- Wage and piece-rate tables.
- Schedules of work times.
- Records that show orders, shipping, and billing.
- Record of any additions to and deductions from the employee's wages.

**Table 11-4.   General State-by-State
Recordkeeping Requirements for Employee Records
(Specific Records to Be Retained for Each Worker Under State Law)**

Code:

—	State law does not cover this topic.
Yes	Record is required to be retained under state law.
No	No requirement is specified under state law.

State	Employee Name and Address	Employee Occupation Identified	Pay Rate per Pay Period	Wage per Week or Pay Period	Hours per Day or Week	Deductions per Pay Period	Conditions of Employment
AL	—	—	—	—	—	—	—
AK	Yes	Yes	Yes	Yes	Yes	No	No
AZ	Yes	No	Yes	Yes	Yes	No	No
AR	Yes	Yes	Yes	Yes	Yes	No	No
CA	Yes	Yes	Yes	Yes	Yes	No	No
CO	Yes	Yes	Yes	Yes	Yes	No	No
CT	Yes	Yes	Yes	Yes	Yes	Yes	No
DE	Yes	Yes	Yes	Yes	Yes	No	No
DC	Yes	Yes	Yes	Yes	Yes	Yes	No
FL	—	—	—				
GA	Yes	Yes	No	Yes	Yes	No	No
HI	Yes	Yes	Yes	Yes	Yes	Yes	Yes
ID	No	No	No	No	No	No	No
IL	Yes	Yes	Yes	Yes	Yes	Yes	No
IN	Yes	Yes	No	Yes	Yes	Yes	No

Table 11-4. General State-by-State
Recordkeeping Requirements for Employee Records
(Specific Records to Be Retained for Each Worker Under State Law) (cont'd)

State	Employee Name and Address	Employee Occupation Identified	Pay Rate per Pay Period	Wage per Week or Pay Period	Hours per Day or Week	Deductions per Pay Period	Conditions of Employment
IA	Yes	No	No	Yes	Yes	Yes	No
KS	Yes	Yes	Yes	Yes	Yes	Yes	No
KY	Yes	Yes	Yes	Yes	Yes	Yes	No
LA	Yes	Yes	No	Yes	Yes	No	No
ME	No	No	No	Yes	Yes	Yes	No
MD	Yes	Yes	Yes	Yes	Yes	No	No
MA	Yes	Yes	No	Yes	Yes	Yes	No
MI	Yes	Yes	Yes	Yes	Yes	Yes	No
MN	Yes	Yes	Yes	Yes	Yes	No	No
MS	—	—	—	—	—	—	—
MO	Yes	Yes	Yes	Yes	Yes	No	No
MT	Yes	Yes	Yes	Yes	Yes	Yes	No
NE	Yes	Yes	Yes	Yes	Yes	Yes	Yes
NV	No	No	No	Yes	Yes	Yes	No
NH	No	Yes	No	Yes	Yes	No	No
NJ	No	No	No	Yes	Yes	No	No
NM	No	No	No	Yes	Yes	No	No
NY	Yes	No	Yes	Yes	Yes	Yes	No
NC	Yes	Yes	Yes	Yes	Yes	Yes	Yes
ND	No, but employers must keep a register of names of employees	Yes	Yes	Yes	Yes	No	No
OH	Yes	Yes	Yes	Yes	Yes	No	No
OK	—	—	—	—	—	—	—
OR	Yes	Yes	Yes	Yes	Yes	Yes	No
PA	Yes	Yes	Yes	Yes	Yes	Yes	No
PR	Yes	No	No	Yes	Yes	No	No
RI	Yes	Yes	Yes	Yes	Yes	No	No
SC	Yes	No	No	Yes	No	Yes	No
SD	No	Yes (job classification)	Yes	Yes	No	No	Yes
TN	—	—	—	—	—	—	—
TX	—	—	—	—	—	—	—

Table 11-4. General State-by-State
Recordkeeping Requirements for Employee Records
(Specific Records to Be Retained for Each Worker Under State Law) (*cont'd*)

State	Employee Name and Address	Employee Occupation Identified	Pay Rate per Pay Period	Wage per Week or Pay Period	Hours per Day or Week	Deductions per Pay Period	Conditions of Employment
UT	Yes; date of birth is also required	No	No	Yes	Yes	No	No
VT	No; date of birth is required for all employees under 19	No	No	Yes	Yes	No	No
VA	—	—	—	—	—	—	—
WA	Yes	Yes	Yes	Yes	Yes	No	No
WV	Yes	Yes	Yes	Yes	Yes	Yes	No
WI	Yes; date of birth is also required	No	Yes	Yes	Yes	Yes	No
WY	Yes	Yes	Yes	Yes	Yes	No	No

Source: 2017 Multistate Payroll Guide (CCH Incorporated 2017).

Table 11-5. Specific Recordkeeping Requirements for Minors

State	Address	Hours per Day or Week	Time Starting, Ending Work/Meals	Wages	Other Requirements
AL	Yes	Yes	Yes	No	Names, dates of birth, proof of age, school of attendance, and dates of hire. Post notice of maximum hours minors are permitted to work. Keep required records on file for not less than 3 years.
AK	No	No	No	No	No

Table 11-5. Specific Recordkeeping Requirements for Minors (*cont'd*)

State	Address	Hours per Day or Week	Time Starting, Ending Work/Meals	Wages	Other Requirements
AZ	No	No	No	Industrial Commission may require employers to submit records of wages paid to minors if deemed necessary.	No
AR	Yes	Yes	Yes	Yes	Date of birth
CA	No	No	No	No	Names and ages
CO	No	No	No	No	Date of birth
CT	No	No	No	No	No
DE	No	No	No	No	No
DC	Yes	Yes	Yes	No	Post rules regarding the employment of minors. List of all employees under 18. Keep date of birth of all employees under 19.
FL	No	No	No	No	Post child labor laws. Required records shall be kept for the period of the minor's employment.
GA	No	No	No	No	No
HI	No	No	No	No	No
ID	Yes	No	No	No	Ages
IL	Yes	No	Yes	No	Post rules and list of ages.

Table 11-5. Specific Recordkeeping Requirements for Minors (*cont'd*)

State	Address	Hours per Day or Week	Time Starting, Ending Work/Meals	Wages	Other Requirements
IN	No	Yes	Yes	No	Post maximum number of hours that minors may work each day and the hours of beginning and ending each day.
IA	No	No	No	No	Names and ages of all minor employees.
KS	No	No	No	No	Post rules.
KY	Yes	No	Yes	No	Post rules and list of names and ages.
LA	No	No	No	No	Post rules.
ME	No	Yes, for each employee age 17 or younger	No	No	No
MD	No	No	No	No	Post rules.
MA	No	No	No	No	Names and ages. Keep complete list of minors employed under educational certificates.
MI	No	Yes	Yes	No	Post statutory sections. Keep records for at least 1 year. Employers of persons exempted from child labor laws must keep on file proof of employee's exempt status.
MN	No	No	No	No	Date of birth, as required by Department of Labor and Industry. Post summary of rules.

Table 11-5. Specific Recordkeeping Requirements for Minors (*cont'd*)

State	Address	Hours per Day or Week	Time Starting, Ending Work/Meals	Wages	Other Requirements
MS	No	No	No	No	Keep affidavit of parent or guardian and certificate issued by superintendent of school district stating minor's place and date of birth, last school attended and grade pursued, name of school, and name of teacher in charge.
MO	No	No	No	No	Post list of employed minors under 16 years old.
MT	—	—	—	—	Keep on file employment records that may aid in the enforcement of the child labor law by the Department of Labor and Industry.
NE	No	Yes	Yes	No	Keep separate lists of all employees ages 14 and 15.
NV	No	No	No	No	After termination of a minor's employment, employer must return the permit that excused the minor from school attendance to the authority that issued it.
NH	No	No	Yes	No	Post maximum hours per day.
NJ	Yes	Yes	Yes	Yes	Date of birth (keep 1 year). Post rules.
NM	No	No	No	No	Post list of employed minors who require labor permits.

Table 11-5. Specific Recordkeeping Requirements for Minors (*cont'd*)

State	Address	Hours per Day or Week	Time Starting, Ending Work/Meals	Wages	Other Requirements
NY	Yes, for 6 years	Yes, for 6 years	No	No	Post schedule of hours for minors, including starting and stopping times and the amount of time allowed for meals.
NC	Yes	Yes	Yes	Yes	Names, ages, and dates of birth if under 20.
ND	No	No	No	No	Post names of employed minors 14- to 15-years old, list of hours per day, start and stop times, and time for meals. Complete and maintain Employment and Age Certificate of minors.
OH	Yes	Yes	Yes	Yes	Keep (for 2 years) record of occupation, certificate or proof of age, and parent's or guardian's statement of consent. Post list of minors employed.
OK	No	Yes	Yes	No	Keep list of minors employed under employment certificates and records of times the establishment opens and closes.
OR	Yes	Yes, for 2 years	Yes	Yes, for 2 years	Name, date of birth, sex, and occupation in which employed. Records must be kept for 2 years. Post notice of maximum hours per week or day for minors employed.

Table 11-5. Specific Recordkeeping Requirements for Minors (*cont'd*)

State	Address	Hours per Day or Week	Time Starting, Ending Work/Meals	Wages	Other Requirements
PA	No	Yes	Yes	Yes	Post statutory sections, hours of labor, maximum hours per day, and start and stop hours. Submit a list (including name, age, place of residence, and name of parent or guardian) of employees ages 14 to 18 years old, on a semiannual basis.
RI	No	No	No	No	Post minimum rate of pay, number of required work hours on each day of the week, hours of commencing and stopping work, and copy of wage and recordkeeping laws for minors found at §§ 28-3-1–28-3-20.
SC	—	—	—	—	The Director of the Department of Labor, Licensing, and Regulation and its inspectors and agents may have access to all employment records as may aid in enforcement of S.C. child labor law.
SD	No	Yes	Yes	Yes	Keep list of minors 15 and under who work under employment certificates.

Table 11-5. Specific Recordkeeping Requirements for Minors (*cont'd*)

State	Address	Hours per Day or Week	Time Starting, Ending Work/Meals	Wages	Other Requirements
TN	No	No	Yes	No	Keep evidence of age and other documentation such as minor's employment application and records of all qualified exemptions from child labor laws (e.g., high school diploma). Post rules.
TX	No	No	No	No	No
UT	No	No	No	No	The Labor Commission and its authorized representatives may have access to such records as may aid in the enforcement of Utah's child labor law.
VT	No	No	Yes	No	Post permitted and prohibited occupations, number of hours of work permitted, hours of commencing and stopping work, and when time for meals begins and ends.
VA	No	No	Yes	No	Keep records for preceding 12 months for 36 months from the date of the minor's latest work period. Special requirements for minors under age 16 employed in agriculture.

Table 11-5. Specific Recordkeeping Requirements for Minors (cont'd)

State	Address	Hours per Day or Week	Time Starting, Ending Work/Meals	Wages	Other Requirements
WA	No	No	No	No	Parent/School Authorization form, proof of age, date of birth, home address, and telephone number. (Employer obtains minor work permit.) Although not a recordkeeping requirement, the Department of Labor & Industries may inquire into wages, hours, and conditions of labor at any time.
WV	No	No	No	No	Date of birth
WI	Yes	Yes	Yes (both)	No	Date of birth
WY	No	No	No	No	No

Source: 2017 Multistate Payroll Guide (CCH Incorporated, 2017).

Employee Privacy Concerns in Recordkeeping

Q 11:36   What employee privacy concerns should employers understand when gathering and maintaining employee information?

There is currently no federal privacy statute mandating that employers protect personal employee information such as addresses, dates of birth, account numbers, and Social Security numbers. Although employers often require such information to comply with various federal filing and other statutes, the Social Security Administration and other governmental agencies discourage employers from displaying such private information on any document, including badges and parking permits.

The Federal Trade Commission issued a "disposal rule," under the Fair and Accurate Credit Transaction Act of 2003, which may impact how employers destroy certain employee information. As of June 1, 2005, all businesses must take steps to safeguard and effectively destroy information that qualifies as a "credit report" under the Fair and Accurate Credit Transaction Act. For employers, credit reports will include criminal history checks, driver's history checks, credit checks, and certain other employee background checks. Among other things, the disposal rule requires employers to effectively and securely retain such records. It also requires employers to ensure that such records are properly and effectively destroyed.

Many states also have statutes that provide certain privacy rights to employees, and impact how employers must retain employee information. For example, Section 226 of California's Labor Law prohibits employers from displaying all but the last four digits of the employee's Social Security number on the wage statement. In addition, New York's Disposal of Personal Information Law requires employers to use specific procedures when purging employees' personal identifying information, including Social Security numbers.

Beyond the disposal rule for credit records, employers should take necessary steps to ensure controls are in place and back up of data and plan for proper disposal is required.

In short, more and more states—and the federal government—are putting restrictions on how employers must retain sensitive employee information (in particular, the Social Security number) and how they purge it. Employers should consult their attorney to determine what, if any, restrictions apply to them. See chapter 14 for more information about data privacy.

Disposal of Records

Q 11:37 What are the proper methods for disposal of records under · FACTA?

Under the Fair and Accurate Credit Transaction Act of 2003 (FACTA). employers must use reasonable methods to protect against unauthorized access to "consumer reports," which include certain employee records generated through the payroll department. The disposal rule requires reasonable and appropriate disposal practices to prevent unauthorized access to or use of information contained in a consumer report. The rules provide the following examples to dispose of such information:

1. Burn, pulverize, or shred papers so that the information cannot be read or reconstructed.
2. Destroy or erase electronic media so that the information cannot be read or reconstructed.

Q 11:38 What other requirements should an employer implement to comply with the disposal rule?

The disposal rule also requires an employer to implement and monitor the policies of a third party that the employer has engaged to destroy the employer's records. To meet this requirement, the employer should exercise due diligence by reviewing an independent audit of the third party's practices to ensure they are consistent with the disposal rule.

The rule does not provide any retention timelines but encourages employers to consider keeping records only as long as required. Employers are also encouraged to train employees who handle documents covered by the disposal rule on security policies and the process for destroying records.

Q 11:39   What are some of the best practices employers can implement to improve the security of employee records?

Employers can ensure compliance with the disposal rule by implementing the following practices:

1. Secure records in fireproof containers and limit physical access to files.
2. Have dedicated equipment, such as printers and fax machines.
3. Ensure staff knows the appropriate record retention dates and adheres to those dates.
4. Regularly review the policies and ensure compliance with the established guidelines.

Chapter 12

Mergers, Acquisitions, Divestitures, and Other Business Restructurings

Payroll professionals face numerous tax and legal challenges when companies change ownership, restructure, or acquire other companies. If payroll matters are mishandled or overlooked, the misjudgments can be very costly and difficult to correct. Payroll should play a key role in planning efforts from the very beginning and should be part of any core strategizing along with business, legal, human resources, tax, and other company representatives.

Undertakings, such as mergers, consolidations, acquisitions, terminations, divestitures, spin-offs, spin-outs, split-ups, demergers, to name just a few of the many transactions often referred to under the umbrella of mergers and acquisitions or M&A events, also cause payroll processing restructurings. But, not all of these events are treated the same. What is required of a payroll professional will depend upon the specifics of the transaction. Even the simple act of transferring employees between business entities or changing a company name can present additional considerations in administrating payroll. This chapter will help a professional identify the M&A event and its federal and state payroll tax requirements. It will also give a due diligence focus to important considerations in a successful transition of employees, including how to handle qualified plans, immigration concerns, and some labor and banking matters that arise.

When one company is merged into or consolidated with another company, usually all of its historical payroll details, including liabilities, flow into the surviving company. Mergers are not alone in this treatment. Other transactions may also provide for a carryover of payroll tax liabilities into restructured companies if considered one of the listed transactions covered by I.R.C. § 381(c) or when involving certain partnership restructurings, including restructurings of limited liability companies (LLCs) treated as partnerships. Other business events that fall under the broader "successor employer" rules allow companies to elect to transfer some compliance responsibilities related to transferred employees to the acquiring company. As a result, attention must be paid to the legal form of the transaction before determining the employment tax requirements and options that apply. Federal income, Social Security and Medicare (FICA), 0.9 percent Additional Medicare, as well as federal unemployment (FUTA) tax obligations and the need to obtain a new federal employer identification number (EIN), will differ depending upon the type of M&A event.

Once the type of transaction is identified and the potential requirements determined, the single most important task is to establish a payroll team as part of any "due diligence." Prior to the actual event, the due diligence team should be charged with finding, reviewing, and holding safe all the critical payroll data of the target company, as well as identifying the tasks important to assuring a safe payroll transition.

To assist in this process, a checklist is provided of frequently affected compensation benefits in an M&A event, such as sign-on and retention bonuses, severance pay, golden parachutes, accrued vacation and sick pay, accelerated deferred compensation, and stock option exercises. Action steps are outlined for Payroll and Human Resources.

Finally, the chapter includes a discussion of special recordkeeping needs and provides pointers on how to prevent and handle M&A-related inquiries from government agencies.

Overview

Q 12:1 What are the basic federal and state employment tax applications in the context of M&A events?

The first question a payroll professional should always ask when facing any kind of business restructuring is "what kind of transaction is it?" Federal and state employment tax requirements vary depending on the legal structure of the M&A event. No matter what the transaction is called, traditionally, M&A events fall into one of four categories: (1) statutory mergers or stock consolidations and other transactions that require the acquiring corporation to assume the acquired's payroll tax liabilities, (2) asset acquisitions, a catch-all category where the successor employer rules may attach, (3) transactions where the old employer continues to operate, such as when only stock is acquired or a name is changed, or (4) transactions disqualified under the successor employer rules, where transferred employees are considered to have two separate legal employers. Business changes that are in name only, and do not involve transfers of employees to new employers, may, nonetheless, require some form of reporting to governmental agencies. Changes of ownership, address and business location, as well as of company officers and their addresses may require updated filings with state and federal agencies.

Other transactions, such as de-mergers, spin-offs, spin-outs, and split-ups where a company splits into two or more new entities, if pursuant to a tax-free qualified event, may result in a mandatory carryover of payroll liabilities to the new company the same as required for a statutory merger or consolidation. Or if pursuant to a taxable transaction, the event might fall under the successor employer rules. Similar considerations exist for partnership restructurings, including limited liability companies (LLCs) treated as partnerships. LLCs electing corporate status on either Form 8832 to be a C corporation or Form 2553 to be an S corporation fall under the rules for corporations. Some LLCs that are owned by a single owner are disregarded for federal tax purposes, but are regarded for payroll tax purposes. Many requirements are still unclear when a transaction involves a federally disregarded entity that is nonetheless subject to payroll taxes at the entity level. (See Qs 12:80 and 12:81.) Newer legal structures, such as series limited liability companies or celled companies, may require payroll administrators to chart unknown applications since the entities are so new that compliance requirements have not yet been defined.

In a stock acquisition, only the shareholders change. The business usually continues to operate unimpeded by the acquisition, retaining the same employer status for federal, state, and local purposes that it held before the acquisition, as well as its federal employer identification number (EIN) and state tax identification numbers (referred to as tax IDs). In stock acquisitions, pre-deal wage amounts will be applied along with post-deal wage payments to meet the employees' federal Social Security and federal unemployment insurance (FUTA) thresholds, as well as usually the state unemployment and other payroll tax thresholds since the entity itself has not changed, only its ownership has. Even in stock acquisitions, some reporting requirements may apply. Changes of ownership and of company officers may require the filing of a state notice, and new owners can change company names also requiring agency notification.

In most asset acquisitions, if the successor employer satisfies the federal successorship rules, the successor employer in agreement with the predecessor may elect to include the predecessor's wages paid to employees who are retained in the new enterprise in determining whether they have met the Social Security and FUTA wage limits, and in order to consolidate wages at the end of the year in the employees' W-2. Many employers believe that buying assets of a target as opposed to acquiring its stock or entering into a structural reorganization, such as a merger, frees them from being liable for a predecessor's federal payroll tax liabilities. This is not entirely true. The recent Tax Court opinion in the case of *TFT Galveston Portfolio, Ltd.*, filed February 26, 2015, illustrates the way successor in interest liability attaches in a case involving federal employment taxes where the successor has acquired the assets of a predecessor. See Q 12:47 for more on successors in interest. Care needs to be taken in determining the legal structure of a transaction. Deals that look like asset purchases might not be what they appear to be, but instead such a deal may be a tax-free reorganization, where different rules apply. (See Q 12:8.)

Federal rules for statutory mergers or stock consolidations (collectively called the "statutory merger rules"), on the other hand, mandate consolidation of the wage bases for testing Social Security and FUTA limits as well as for W-2 reporting. This result stems from the fact that in these transactions, the survivor is not a new employer, but instead is considered to be the very same employer as the acquired corporation. Everything carries over to the survivor because in effect the survivor is the acquired employer. Social Security and FUTA consolidation may also apply to some corporate transactions covered under I.R.C. § 381, which requires the tax liabilities of the absorbed corporation to carry over to the survivor, even though this is not addressed in Rev. Proc. 2004-53, the primary procedure that covers payroll acquisitions. [2004-34 I.R.B. 320] (See Qs 12:5–12:8.) Similar considerations apply to certain partnership restructurings. (See Qs 12:75–12:79.)

In some M&A events, new federal EINs are required, but not always. Even where new federal EINs are required and under federal treatment the transaction results in a new employer, states do not always agree, particularly for state unemployment taxes when the state may see the new employer as essentially unchanged from the old one. For the most part, however, a state will require a new state tax identification number if there is a new federal EIN required. For payroll operations, where a new identification number is established, new filing protocols and system and operational changes will be needed which may take time to work through. For this and many other reasons, payroll representatives need to be positioned early in the planning for any of these events. In the case of statutory mergers or consolidations, the surviving company either retains or assumes all the payroll liabilities of the acquired company. In an asset acquisition, the predecessor usually retains the liabilities of its own payroll activities, but states do not always agree with that result as explained in Qs 12:93 and 12:108. Payroll data will need to be gathered from both the acquired and acquiring companies to assure compliance is met and that the liabilities taken on remain minimal.

Many states follow the federal rules in administrating state income tax (SIT) withholding. For purposes of state unemployment insurance (SUI) and other state payroll taxes, however, each state can set its own requirements restricted only by certain constraints under federal law. Four fundamental SUI tax questions arise in an M&A event: (1) whether wages paid by the predecessor carry over to meet the SUI wage limit of the successor employer; (2) whether a predecessor employer's SUI experience rating will be transferred to the successor employer; (3) what SUI rate will be assigned after the event; and (4) when will the new rate apply. The questions may sound simple, but in administrating SUI taxes, there are lots of complexities to consider on the part of both the company to be acquired or reorganized and the acquiring company. Are there wide disparities of SUI rates and experience between the companies? Does either company have a history of recent layoffs? Does either company have a joint SUI account? Will the transaction affect that joint structure? Does either company plan to make or has it made voluntary contributions? Will the transaction cause a change in tax rates and projections and, if so, how will this affect the transaction's cost and the companies' budgets? Will this cause a need for additional funding on the short term or for a longer period? Will planned layoffs be part of the restructuring that could affect future SUI rates? It is important to note that as the number of employees in a payroll grows whether through hiring, attrition, merger, or acquisition, the SUI cost also exponentially grows so if the end result is a much larger company, costs will grow. All of these points need to be considered in the early stages of a proposed transaction.

Critical to these determinations is whether the event will fall under a state's mandatory experience transfer rules. Some states apply an automatic wage base credit transfer; even more states require an experience transfer to occur before wage transfers take effect. Remember that when an employer is required to restart wages, the overall cost of SUI coverage for the year is increased since the SUI tax will be applied to a larger annual wage figure than the statutorily defined annual threshold. The same is true for federal Social Security and FUTA taxes when wages are required to restart. For this reason, many of the more complex deals are scheduled to be made effective on December 31 with the surviving company's wage bases starting anew on January 1. Planning around yearend dates makes it a lot easier for payroll administration as well.

Note. States are concerned in M&A events with the elimination of any employer and the loss of collection opportunities or where there may be manipulation to inappropriately lower UI tax rates. As a result, the states are quick to audit employers involved in M&A transactions. Where employers have employees located in many different states, there is potential for numerous audits and the level of audit profile in each one could be high.

Where companies have significant interstate operations, interstate SUI wage credits also need to be carefully considered. Generally, if an employee works entirely within one state, the employment is covered by that state's law. But if an employee works partly within and partly outside a state, then he or she must be allocated to the jurisdiction of the proper state based on certain factors. Once properly allocated, contributions are payable to that state based on the employee's entire services performed within and outside the state. When an employer is not able to determine a primary UI state, most states subscribe to the Interstate Reciprocal Coverage Arrangement (IRCA) to resolve where the claim lies. Under IRCA arrangements, the employer is usually required to request written approvals from the states where services are performed to report all wages to a designated state. The designated state is assigned under IRCA based upon where services are performed, the employee has a residence, or the employer maintains a place of business if the employee also performs some services in that state. Many businesses use these rules to unify their UI filings.

All states, except Louisiana, Minnesota and Montana allow employers to take credit for wages paid in other states. The Montana Department of Labor and Industry (DLI) finalized regulations effective January 1, 2014, that preclude UI wages and credits from being transferred from other states. In issuing the changes, the DLI stated that although less than 1 percent of employers reported out-of-state wages, it accounted for more than 25 percent of wage submission errors. In states following the trend to calculate UI taxes from reported employees' wages, there have been problems when the state is unaware of wages paid for services in other states where credits should apply. To address this issue, some states now require the reporting of all wages paid including wages for services outside the state. But, many employers have difficulty meeting this requirement. Mergers and successions compound these discrepancies.

The federal rules provide for interstate UI credit transfers through the IRCA. In U.S.C., Title 26, § 3304(a)(9)(B) reciprocal arrangements between states are respected for funding purposes when an applicant for UI benefits combines wages from multiple states to support his or her UI benefits from one state. But, not all states follow these rules. In some states, the UI commissioner may not enter into any reciprocal arrangement unless it contains provisions for reimbursements to the state's trust fund by the other state. These days, states are short of UI trust funds and transfers fail to occur. For an example of such a requirement, see Minnesota UI Code § 268.131.

When M&A events occur and employees are spread throughout the country, there is no guarantee that affected states will allow the continuation of any predecessor practices in the surviving company even if previously agreed to under an IRCA reciprocal arrangement and even if the arrangement has been settled through state audits. In addition, even the acquiring company might find its own such agreement revisited if the state finds the impact of the acquisition is significant enough to change its terms. If the target company has mobile employees performing services in many states but the target is only filing in one or two specific states, this could pose significant liability for any acquirer.

With changes in federal FUTA law under the Trade Adjustment Assistance Extension Act of 2011, employers that fail to monitor their employees' claims may not receive the benefit of a reversal of any claim charges to their UI account when benefits are improperly paid because the employer has a pattern of failures to respond to an agency's request for information on a claim. Nearly half of the states have amended laws to be in compliance with the new federal requirements. When employees have filed claims in states where they have worked and the target has failed to respond to agency queries, certainly more states will take notice these days.

The U.S. Department of Labor (USDOL) and state unemployment insurance (UI) agencies have jointly created the State Information Data Exchange System (SIDES) that offers secure, standardized eformats to supply the data needed to electronically respond to UI information requests. Use of SIDES reduces follow-up phone calls and streamlines UI response processes. Where employers or their third-party agents use SIDES, improper claims payments are prevented, and UI tax rates are kept as low as possible. If not already implemented, SIDES offers solutions to manage claim follow-ups in large payroll settings that have become unwieldy particularly after M&A events. For more information, see http://info.uisides.org/.

Practices need to be evaluated in each location where a target company has employees performing services to establish where those services should be reflected in the target's SUI returns and how to timely respond to an agency's questions about an employee claim. Critical focus then needs to be given to reconciling the target's practices with the acquirer's practices. Renewed written reciprocal applications with the states may be well advised if there is a variance between practices. In the past, these matters were not significant considerations in M&A transactions, but with many states with bankrupt UI trust funds, states are hesitant to continue to allow UI taxes to be paid to other states to cover employees also performing services within their boundaries and are quick to assess large figures where failures are found. A large M&A transaction will gain attention of state agencies and filing predicates will be explored. It is important to be on top of these matters before the agency makes contact.

Federal law (under the SUTA Dumping Prevention Act of 2004) requires that states amend their laws governing unemployment programs to prohibit practices known as "SUTA Dumping" and to impose penalties on employers and their tax advisors found engaging in such practices. All states have now enacted some form of conforming legislation. A critical component of the federal legislation requires mandatory experience transfers if, at the time of the transfer, both predecessor and successor employers are under substantially common ownership, management, or control.

SUTA Dumping is tax avoidance through SUI tax rate manipulation. It occurs when employers "dump" higher unemployment taxes by improperly claiming a lower experience rate, usually through some form of M&A event devised solely for the purpose of achieving the lower SUI tax rate. States scrutinize many M&A events in attempts to isolate potential SUTA Dumping schemes. Following federal requirements, states look for common ownership interests in the companies involved. Many states have developed mathematical tests to determine whether the SUTA Dumping laws apply. These tests are automatic to the filing of notice of the M&A event with the state agency. If the algebraic formulas applied to the companies' reserve accounts and rate and claim histories result in significantly lower SUI tax rates in the presence of a high unemployment claim history, SUTA Dumping violations are likely to be asserted by the state, along with penalty assessments. When such assessments are made, it is essential that the business be able to provide sufficient evidence of the business issues that drove the M&A events apart from the mere lowering of the SUI rate.

There are many different arrangements that potentially fall under the umbrella of SUTA Dumping. SUI tax rates are based primarily on the employer's own experience and can vary widely. There are several ways an employer can engage in SUTA Dumping, but one factor is common to every method—the employer "dumps" or abandons its history of employment (payroll) and unemployment benefit charges, known as the unemployment "experience." This practice avoids the tracking of experience, by shifting employees who should have subjected the employer to a higher SUI tax rate as the result of their actual layoff history to a lower SUI tax rate. Both FUTA and state laws provide for an "experience-rated" system of funding unemployment benefits. When the state's SUTA Dumping laws are triggered, a punitive SUI rate can be assigned to employers as well as specified civil and criminal penalties.

A few years ago, facing the worst decline in state revenues in at least 50 years as a direct result of the national economic downturn, many states stepped up enforcement. Even with recovery now underway, the health of each state's SUI funding is still of serious concern and states are still strongly focusing on collecting underpayments. Key audit issues still include "SUTA Dumping," employee misclassification matters, and failures to file and pay over SUI taxes for employees found to be performing services within a state's boundaries. Companies whose profile includes M&A events are more likely to incur audits than other companies. Liabilities are very high and companies acquiring targets are well advised to carefully review their target's practices in all SUI areas. The state agencies are also working with the Internal Revenue Service (IRS) in sharing information through the "Questionable Employment Tax Practices" (QETP) Program, where the IRS and state tax, unemployment and workforce agencies exchange audit reports and conduct joint examinations. For the states, special attention is being given to accountabilities of surviving, new, interim, and terminated employers under state personal income tax (PIT) withholding and state unemployment insurance (SUI) taxes, as well as under many other state employment laws triggered by M&A events.

M&A events need to be analyzed from a perspective of SUI tax cost, looking at whether the SUI cost will increase or decrease; whether the SUI rate will be that of the predecessor, the successor, a blended rate or a new employer rate; whether the experience of the target will be required to be transferred over; and whether the wage history will transfer. With the SUTA Dumping rules in place, there are fewer planning opportunities, but some planning to ensure a timely and seamless filing transition is necessary to avoid costly pitfalls and to take advantage of favorable elections where allowed.

Rarely will a state make a distinction between a merger or consolidation or asset acquisition in establishing the resulting SUI tax rate; most apply a single set of responsibilities to both types of transactions. If a successor employer has an existing experience rating in the state, it generally will retain the SUI tax rate in effect immediately before the transaction through the end of the year in which the transaction took place. Where the state's successor employer requirements are met and the predecessor employer's SUI experience rating is transferred to the successor employer, an experience rating for the successor employer for the year following the transaction is usually determined by referencing the previous experience ratings of both the successor and predecessor employers. Some states allow a retroactive lookback for SUI refund purposes.

In determining whether to transfer the predecessor employer's SUI experience rating to a successor employer, states generally consider (1) whether the successor employer has acquired all or part of a predecessor employer's business, (2) whether the successor employer is continuing the operation of the acquired business, and (3) whether the employees in the predecessor employer's operation were hired by the successor employer. Unlike the federal rules, these considerations are not limited to some form of asset acquisition, but may equally apply to a merger or other reorganization where employees are transferred to a new employer. Successor status is generally granted where there is a transfer of a trade or business and the buyer maintains the predecessor's operations. The transfer of one segment or department of the predecessor may also establish successor status ("partial transfers"). If the successor continues to use the same workforce, it is more likely that the successor can show that a transfer of business has occurred.

If the employer satisfies the states' SUI successorship rules and the predecessor employer's SUI experience rating is transferred (whether by mandate or application), the successor employer can generally count the wages paid to an employee by a predecessor employer in determining whether the SUI wage base has been met. If not, then the predecessor employer's SUI wage base usually will not carry over and a restart of the employees' SUI wages will be necessary.

For the most part, a transfer of experience is favorable to successors so that they do not need to restart SUI wage thresholds, usually required if experience does not transfer. But, where the transfer would cause a much higher rate experience to carry over, a different result might be desired. It is fairly important for those involved to be assured of the right way to structure a transaction to derive the desired result in the jurisdictions involved. Under both federal and state versions of SUTA Dumping legislation, timing is important as to when common ownership, management, or control exists that would require a mandatory transfer. A common practice is for the buyer to establish ahead of a sale a separate business unit intended for the business to be acquired that includes its executives to co-manage the unit with the seller. The seller earmarks employees to be transferred to include its executives to co-manage with the buyer. Common management under this practice was seen as existing until the date of the transaction when all employees are transferred to the buyer. This structure was thought to trigger a mandatory experience transfer.

Recently, a state court has challenged this set up. The Minnesota Court of Appeals held on June 10, 2013, that the Minnesota agency incorrectly transferred a predecessor employer rate and should have applied the lower new employer rate to a transaction structured in this way. The agency believed that a partial experience transfer was required because the unit transferred was under substantially common management or control at the time of the transfer. The court disagreed and held that transfer of experience only applies when there is the same common management or control both before the acquisition and on the date of the acquisition. So under these facts, no mandatory transfer was allowed since on the date of the acquisition, the common management was lost. [CMI v. DEED, 832 N.W.2d 298 (Minn. App. 2013)] How a state's courts interpret common ownership and control in determining when a mandatory experience transfer will be required will matter in your SUI planning. In addition, when facts are not clearly specified on registration forms, the agency's result may not be what an employer expected. Care needs to be taken to avoid a rush in agency applications and to give time to study how the transaction needs to be structured and explained to the jurisdictions involved.

Many states still consolidate income tax and unemployment tax filings. The combined filing requirements in these states give more credence to the state's singular set of SUI rules than to maintaining the SIT distinctions between statutory mergers and asset acquisitions found under the federal income tax withholding rules. Even where the state wage base for income tax purposes starts with the federal definition, filing requirements in the combined states may require separate quarterly and annual reconciliations from each company involved in the transaction. The jurisdictional conflicts in payroll administration, particularly in the context of an M&A event, result in employers having to weigh the pros and cons when attempting to consolidate the administration of multiple wage bases in compliance with both the state and federal tax rules. With states needing more frequent SUI wage reports, some previously combined states have eliminated consolidated SIT/SUI filings to allow for separate more frequent SUI filings. For example, for tax periods beginning on or after January 1, 2015, Maine's combined quarterly filing for income tax withholding and unemployment contributions (Form 941/C1-ME) has been eliminated and replaced with separate Forms 941ME (income tax withholding) and ME UC-1 (unemployment contributions report), to be filed with the different agencies that administer the taxes.

Early in the planning stages of any M&A event, the payroll professional will need to determine:

- Who is the successor and who is the predecessor?
- What is the deal: an asset acquisition (and whether it is partial or total acquisition of the predecessor), a merger or consolidation, a stock purchase, a series of events, a mere name change, or one of many other events?
- What is the timing: midyear, December 31 or January 1?
- What agencies are involved—where do the predecessor and successor employers currently file SIT and SUI returns, what are their tax identification numbers, and where are employees actually performing services?

- What are the plans for employee transfer and possible layoffs, as well as their timing?
- What are the compliance requirements over the transition period?

In every transaction, the payroll professional must understand the laws that come into play in each jurisdiction, be prepared to document ownership and management movements throughout the transaction, and acquire SUI transcripts of all employers to be able to prepare rate projections for post-acquisition review.

At the due diligence stage, a payroll professional must start to gather federal and state filings, agency notices and assessments, UI and other payroll tax rates, payroll policies and procedures, and compliance histories, such as records of other M&A events in the target's history. Look for high SUI rates, unpaid assessments, missed payroll runs where taxes and reporting were unaccounted, such as special bonuses or stock option exercises, as they will increase the risk in the transaction.

Next plan for payroll integration with SUI models. Strategize appropriate timing for any layoffs that might be necessary. Set a plan for integrating payroll wage bases that is mindful of timing of FICA, FUTA, SUI, 0.9 percent Medicare tax and other wage carryovers needed to maintain thresholds so that the combining will still allow for proper federal, state, and local filing calendars to be met.

Be sure to leave enough time to file all necessary paperwork on business changes with agencies, to register new accounts with agencies, and where needed to acquire new tax IDs before the first returns are due under the new structure.

A payroll professional should follow-up on SUI rate assignments after each transaction in order to timely file a protest if needed. It may be prudent to hire SUI experts for planning and post reviews.

Federal Payroll Rules for Statutory Mergers, Consolidations, and Other Section 381 Transactions Involving Corporations

Q 12:2   When a corporation is absorbed by another corporation as a result of a statutory merger or consolidation, is the surviving corporation considered the same federal taxpayer (employer) as the absorbed corporation?

Yes. When a corporation is absorbed by another corporation in a statutory merger or consolidation, the survivor is considered the same federal taxpayer (employer) as the absorbed corporation. In the context of a statutory merger or consolidation, there is no successor-employer relationship; there is only one continuing employer. As a result, the survivor is subject to liabilities imposed under federal income, Social Security and Medicare (FICA), and FUTA tax laws on premerger or preconsolidation compensation paid by the absorbed corporation as well as for compensation paid in the new structure. The required rollover of the absorbed corporation's payroll liabilities goes beyond those liabilities that arise in the year of the transaction to extend to all open payroll liabilities no matter when they may have arisen. Due diligence in these deals takes on a much more important role. [Rev. Proc. 2004-53, 2004-34 I.R.B. 320; Rev. Rul. 62-60, 1962-1 C.B. 186] There are also other transactions where federal tax laws require a carryover of certain tax benefits to the acquiring company apart from in the context of statutory mergers and consolidations that will result in similar treatment as for a merger or consolidation even though not addressed in Rev. Proc. 2004-53, the primary procedure that covers payroll acquisitions. See Q 12:6 below.

Since, under federal tax laws, the absorbed employer's payroll liabilities roll over to the survivor, for the year of the transaction, the wage bases for Social Security and FUTA purposes will not start over in the surviving company. Social Security taxes on wages are limited each year to a specific wage base amount. For 2017, the new Social Security limit increased to $127,200 above the 2016 threshold of $118,500. The premerger wages of an employee will need to be carried over to the surviving employer to assure when the specific threshold for the year is met for each employee. This task is not optional in a statutory merger or consolidation and is one of the key compliance differences between this form of transaction and an asset acquisition.

The Medicare wage base has no limiting threshold so Medicare withholding applies to all FICA wages taxable to the employee. On the other hand, the 0.9 percent Additional Medicare Tax withholding is a different tax from the Medicare tax and it does have a starting threshold, requiring withholding for high earners on compensation amounts that exceed $200,000 in a calendar year. [I.R.C. § 3102(f)(1)] The 0.9 percent Additional Medicare Tax requires tracking of wage amounts to ascertain when to begin to withhold at the increased rate. Unlike the Medicare tax that also has a portion taxable to the employer, the 0.9 percent Additional Medicare Tax is only withheld against the employee's earnings. All compensation that is generally subject to Medicare withholding is subject to the additional 0.9 percent withholding if compensation is paid to an employee in excess of $200,000 for the calendar year. In the context of a statutory merger or consolidation, it is now critical to also earmark and carryover Medicare wages paid by the predecessor to enable tracking of the point when paid compensation exceeds the $200,000 threshold for the year requiring the additional withholding. This task needs to be added to the payroll interface being built for handling the merger.

Wages subject to this new withholding requirement may be paid by third parties under arrangements with the target company. So those parties serving the predecessor's plans must be located and arrangements made to coordinate the aggregation of compensation amounts as part of the payroll tasks in the transaction.

For example, sick pay paid by an employer and by the third party need to be aggregated to determine whether the $200,000 withholding threshold has been met. The same rules that currently assign responsibility for sick pay reporting and payment of Medicare tax based on which party is treated as the employer (i.e., the employer, the employer's agent, or a third party that is not the employer's agent) apply also to the Additional Medicare Tax. For more information on sick pay, see Publication 15-A, *Employer's Supplemental Tax Guide*, and Notice 2016-55, 2016-40 I.R.B. 432. For the rules on aggregation of sick pay for 0.9 percent Medicare withholding, see FAQ #45 at http://www.irs.gov/Businesses/Small-Businesses-&-Self-Employed/Questions-and-Answers-for-the-Additional-Medicare-Tax#!

However, FAQ #50 found on the same IRS website gives a different result for agents appointed on a Form 2678, *Employer Appointment of Agent*. If an agent pays wages to an employee on behalf of an employer (under an approved Form 2678), then, for purposes of determining whether wages are paid in excess of the $200,000 withholding threshold, the agent is not required to combine the wages it pays with wages paid to that same employee: (1) directly by the employer, (2) by the same agent on behalf of a different employer, or (3) by another agent on behalf of the same employer. Wages paid on behalf of an employer by an agent appointed on an approved Form 2678 are not combined with these other wages in determining whether to withhold Additional Medicare Tax. So, under this FAQ, wages paid by the target's payroll agent appointed on a Form 2678 will not need to be located and aggregated with other wages.

Health care reforms have brought about many new compliance accountabilities that will need to be added to the payroll due diligence team's responsibilities in these transactions. Tasks that now need to be added include performing risk assessments for an employer's Affordable Care Act (ACA) shared responsibility payments (called ESRPs) that apply to an employer with 50 or more full-time equivalent employees (known as an Applicable Large Employer, or ALE) and ensuring that annual ACA information returns will be filed, reporting whether and what health insurance the employer offered employees (on Forms 1094-C and 1095-C). If any employer self-insures for the health care of its employees, reporting will need to made in Part III of each employee's Form 1095-C (or in certain cases on Forms 1095-B, necessitating filing of a 1094-B). Another task involves monitoring the coverage terms of health care plans to avoid penalties for ACA violations, such as those imposed under I.R.C. § 4980D on failures of a group health plan to meet special coverage requirements. The amount of the tax on any such failure is $100 for each day in the noncompliance period with respect to each individual to whom the failure relates. And, yet another may involve the payment of medical loss ratio (MLR) rebates to employees by employers that maintain group health insurance policies and that received the premium rebates from their insurance carriers for a previous year. When rebates are passed on to employees, it may change their W-2 calculations for the year if employees are part of a pretax deferral plan or their employer pays their premiums. It will be important to determine whether such amounts were paid out by a predecessor to assure correct W-2 forms. See Q 12:24 for additional W-2 responsibilities, including reporting the aggregate cost of employer-provided health care. In a statutory merger or consolidation, tracking these items is not optional.

A statutory merger or consolidation (also known as an "A" reorganization) under Internal Revenue Code (I.R.C.) § 368(a)(1)(A) occurs when one corporation acquires the assets and assumes the liabilities of another corporation and the acquired corporation goes out of existence by operation of law (a merger), or where two or more corporations consolidate into one new corporation and the old corporations cease to exist (a consolidation). In business terms, a merger is a combination of two companies into one larger company. Mergers are voluntary and can occur through a stock swap or cash payment or a combination of both. A merger can resemble a takeover but result in a new company name (often combining the names of the original companies) and in new branding. In some cases, terming the combination a "merger" rather than an acquisition is done purely for political or marketing reasons. So it is not always clear from a tax standpoint whether the statutory terms have been met.

See Qs 12:5–12:9 for technical information needed to identify an "A" reorganization and a listing of transactions falling under the "A" reorganization classification.

Q 12:3 Will considering the resulting corporation to be the same federal taxpayer (employer) as the absorbed corporation make a difference in a payroll professional's handling of the survivor's payroll?

Yes. Because the survivor is considered the same federal taxpayer (employer) as the absorbed corporation, the survivor is required in a statutory merger or consolidation to be accountable for the previous employer's federal tax responsibilities regarding payroll matters, no matter when they arose, as long as the matters are still open for IRS audit. In an asset acquisition, the payroll professional can elect to assume responsibilities for federal income tax, FICA, and FUTA compliance for the year of the transaction related to those employees it chooses to retain if the successor employer standards are met, or choose to walk away from the responsibilities. In statutory mergers and consolidations, the payroll professional is mandated to cover the compliance responsibilities of the absorbed company and assume all of the absorbed corporation's payroll liabilities as well even if from a period prior to the merger. This distinction will heighten the payroll professional's compliance tasks.

There are also other transactions where federal tax laws require a carryover of certain tax benefits to the acquiring company apart from in the context of statutory mergers and consolidations that will result in similar treatment as for a merger or consolidation even though not addressed in Rev. Proc. 2004-53, the primary procedure that covers payroll acquisitions. See Q 12:6 below.

Q 12:4   **In a statutory merger or consolidation (an "A" reorganization), is there ever a successor employer for federal tax purposes?**

Technically, no. The survivor is considered the same federal taxpayer (employer) as the absorbed corporation for purposes of federal income tax withholding, and FICA and FUTA taxes, rather than a successor. Under I.R.C. § 381(a) and Treas. Reg. § 1.381(a)-1, the taxable year of the absorbed corporation will end constructively on the effective date of the reorganization, and the successor will succeed to and take into account the absorbed company's tax items as of the close of the date of distribution or transfer.

That being the case, the survivor would never be considered a successor employer and, as a result, separate and unique federal payroll compliance requirements are outlined for statutory mergers and consolidations ("A" reorganizations) apart from the general rules established for successor employers (as will be discussed in the next section). [Rev. Proc. 2004-53, 2004-34 I.R.B. 320; Rev. Rul. 62-60, 1962-1 C.B. 186]

There are also other transactions where federal tax laws require a carryover of certain tax benefits to the acquiring company apart from in the context of statutory mergers and consolidations that will result in similar treatment as for a merger or consolidation even though not addressed in Rev. Proc. 2004-53, the primary procedure that covers payroll acquisitions. See Q 12:6 below.

Recent changes to regulations under I.R.C. § 381, effective for transactions occurring on or after November 12, 2014, modified the definition of the acquiring corporation in transactions that include mergers and consolidations as well as certain other transactions. Under the new provisions, only a single acquiring corporation may inherit the tax attributes of the transferor pursuant to a plan of reorganization. The acquiring corporation is the one that directly acquires the assets transferred by the transferor corporation, even if that corporation retains none of the transferred assets, for example, because the assets were immediately transferred to one of the acquirer's subsidiaries. The second asset transfer from the acquirer to its subsidiary would be looked at separately, apart from § 381(a). [Treas. Reg. § 1.381(a)-1(b)(2)] Under the older regulations, the subsidiary would have succeeded to the tax attributes directly under § 381(a). This new change may make a difference for payroll services since the payroll attributes might follow the assets to the subsidiary under different rules.

"Statutory Mergers and Consolidations" Defined as "A" Reorganizations and Other Section 381 Transactions Involving Corporations

Q 12:5   **What is a statutory merger or consolidation?**

To be a "statutory" merger or consolidation, the transaction must also be a tax-free reorganization under the terms of I.R.C. § 368(a)(1)(A), otherwise known as an "A reorganization."

Note. "A reorganizations" are fairly complex and generally beyond the scope of this text. However, some fundamentals are presented to assist in determining when to apply the payroll tax rules specific to a statutory merger or consolidation. I.R.C. § 368(a)(1) lists seven transactions that qualify as tax-free reorganizations in subparagraphs A through G. There are common requisites that apply to all reorganizations, but each also has separate requirements. The popular name given to each form of reorganization matches its alpha letter in section 368 of the Internal Revenue Code (I.R.C.). In this case, "A" refers to I.R.C. § 368(a)(1)(A), otherwise known as an "A reorganization."

Under the A reorganization requirements, whether a merger or a consolidation, the events must occur simultaneously and the transferors must go out of existence at the effective time of the transaction by operation of law. Their shareholders become shareholders in the survivor. In a merger, the surviving corporation acquires all the assets and assumes all the liabilities of the target corporation. In a statutory consolidation, two or more corporations combine into one new corporation that acquires all the assets and assumes all the liabilities of predecessors. Assets may also be distributed and liabilities discharged during the transaction. See Treas. Reg. § 1.368-2(b)(1)(ii).

A consolidation usually involves two or more corporations of about the same size that agree to go forward as a single new company rather than remain separately owned and operated. This kind of action is more precisely referred to as a "merger of equals." The companies' stocks are surrendered and new company stock is issued in its place. For example, both Daimler-Benz and Chrysler ceased to exist when the two firms merged, and a new company, DaimlerChrysler, was created. Another example was the 1999 merger of Glaxo Wellcome and SmithKline Beecham, both firms ceased to exist when they merged, and a new company, GlaxoSmithKline, was created.

In practice, actual mergers of equals do not happen very often. Even if they do, valuations are balanced out by cash or other distributions to shareholders. In these types of mergers, the assets and liabilities of the target corporation become the assets and liabilities of the surviving corporation. In essence, the absorbed corporation lives on in the new corporation formed by the merger or consolidation.

To fall under the "A" reorganization rules, the combining entities must be corporations under Treas. Reg. § 301.7701-2(b) and cannot be "disregarded" for federal tax purposes (although a "disregarded entity" that belongs to any combining corporation will be considered part of the parent and, as such, can be part of the transaction in the combining unit). See Treas. Reg. § 1.368-2(b)(1)(i)(B) and (C) and Qs 12:80–12:81. Final regulations released in 2006 now favorably allow a corporation to be merged into a disregarded entity of an acquiring corporation. [Treas. Reg. § 1.368-2(b)(1)(iii), Ex. 2]

The IRS is still struggling with the impact of having a disregarded entity in the mix of many different forms of mergers and where one exists, it is important to have legal counsel also look at the structure for payroll tax purposes. This is particularly true now that disregarded entities are required to make federal employment tax deposits and file federal employment tax returns for their own employees. See Treas. Reg. § 301.7701-2(c)(2)(iv) and the explanation in Q 12:9 below.

No limits have been placed on the type of consideration (i.e., monies and other property, collectively called "boot") shareholders of the acquired corporation can receive to maintain "A" reorganization status. However, the taxable "boot" restrictions will apply and, under these rules, any additional consideration can be taxable even it would be considered part of a tax-free reorganization. To be qualified, however, the transaction must have a business purpose, it must result in the continuity of a business enterprise, and it must allow for the continuity of proprietary (shareholder ownership) interests. [Treas. Reg. § 1.368-2(b)(1)(ii)] All of these terms have specific meanings, which have evolved into a fairly complex set of requirements that are way beyond the scope of this text and are better left with the merger specialists. It is important, however, that a payroll professional be aware that what a deal is called does not necessarily translate into what the deal actually is for tax purposes. An asset purchase deal may be labeled a merger when both companies agree that joining together is in the best interest of both of their companies and they want the world to understand the takeover is friendly. In essence, they agree to call it a merger even if it is not. See Qs 12:6–12:9 below. Payroll professionals should ask their legal counsels that consideration of payroll matters be made part of the legal opinions written in support of the transaction. Specifically, opinions should be express what the structure of the transaction is for payroll tax purposes and its effective date.

Note. An LLC with more than one member can be either a partnership or a corporation, including an S corporation. To be treated as a Subchapter C corporation, an LLC has to file a Form 8832, *Entity Classification Election*, and elect to be taxed as a corporation. If qualified, an LLC may also choose to be an S corporation by filing Form 2553, *Election by a Small Business Corporation* (under § 1362 of the Internal Revenue Code). Once electing corporate status, reorganization provisions of I.R.C. § 368 will apply the same as to other corporations.

If a single member LLC (SMLLC) does not elect to be a corporation, it will be considered a "disregarded entity." To be treated as a corporation, the SMLLC has to file the Form 8832 and elect to be classified as a C corporation or file Form 2553 and elect to be treated as an S corporation. Once electing corporate status, reorganization provisions of I.R.C. § 368 will apply the same as to other corporations.

For purposes of these provisions, a restructuring of an S Corporation may fall under the reorganization rules of I.R.C. § 368 the same as any corporation that is restructuring. [*See* Priv. Ltr. Rul. 201402002 (Jan. 15, 2014) and Priv. Ltr. Rul. 201115016 (Jan. 5, 2011)]

Many new regulations, rulings, and procedures have been released that set additional restrictions on international and cross-border transactions. It is important to note that a payroll specialist will need additional help from the tax counsel structuring the transaction to understand the nature of most international deals.

Q 12:6 If a transaction does not result in an "A" reorganization, what are the next steps in classifying the transaction for purposes of applying the right employment tax rules?

If a transaction does not result in a qualified "A" reorganization, the next step is to look for the correct classification of the transaction. In Rev. Rul. 62-60 in addressing statutory mergers and consolidations, the IRS concluded that "The effect of the foregoing is to impute the employment . . . to the resultant corporation in which the corporate life of the absorbed corporation is deemed to continue." There are other transactions involving corporations where federal tax laws require a carryover of certain tax benefits to the acquiring corporation that will result in similar treatment as for a merger or consolidation even though not addressed in Rev. Proc. 2004-53, the primary procedure that covers payroll acquisitions. In these other transactions, the acquired employer generally remains intact in the resultant corporation. In certain cases, the resulting organization continues to operate under the same federal EIN both before and after the transaction. Or, if a new company is formed, it acquires a new EIN, but still retains liability for all of the acquired company's payroll functions for all years still open for audit. At minimum, the acquired and its tax liabilities are deemed to continue in the survivor under I.R.C. § 381.

As was learned in Q 12:4, under I.R.C. § 381(a) and Treas. Reg. § 1.381(a)-1, a successor will succeed to and take into account the absorbed company's tax items as of the close of the date of distribution or transfer for mergers and consolidations. This same rule will also apply to a few other transactions named in § 381, including:

- Complete liquidation of a subsidiary corporation into its parent under § 332 where the result for payroll purposes is the same as in the context of a statutory merger;

- "C" reorganization under § 368(a)(1)(C) defined as an acquisition by one corporation of substantially all the properties of another corporation, in exchange "solely" for all or a part of its voting stock;

- Non-divisive "D" reorganization under § 368(a)(1)(D) where the target corporation transfers substantially all of its assets to the acquirer and liquidates, distributing the acquirer's stock to the target's shareholders. (see Q 12:7 below); and

- Mere changes in identity, form, or place of organization qualifying as an "F" reorganization under § 368(a)(1)(F).

Where any of the above transactions occur, as in the context of a statutory merger or consolidation, the resulting employer assumes all the payroll responsibilities of the acquired corporation and payroll professionals would look to consolidate payroll responsibilities of the absorbed company into the survivor.

Section 381 applies only to corporations, and the transaction must be one included in the list above for the carry over rules to apply. Even corporations when involved in transactions not included in the above list, such as a partial liquidation (not a total liquidation under § 332) or divisive reorganization (outside § 368(a)(1)(D)), will need to meet the requirements for successor employers (see Qs 12:36–12:44) in order for wage history on election to be carried over for FICA and FUTA purposes, as well as for an election to be made to combine the employee's Forms W-2. If a transaction in no way meets one of the above listed § 381 transactions or the corporate employers fail to satisfy the successor employer requirements, the surviving employer will need to treat the transferred employees as newly hired and restart wages for Social Security and FUTA tax purposes.

Contrast these rules to where one company acquires the stock of another corporation. In a stock acquisition, the acquired corporation continues to operate payroll as the same corporation under the same EIN. Nothing has actually changed other than the corporation has new shareholders. Sometimes names are changed and, since ownership has changed, for the most part these transactions will require updating registration information with all the agencies.

Partnership tax laws operate separately from the corporate requirements and offer similar tax benefit continuity rules that will also result in the continuation of the old partnership in a new structure. (See Rev. Rul. 54-31, 1954-1 C.B. 212.) These requirements are covered in Qs 12:75–12:79. Disregarded entities add further complexities to these transactions. (See Qs 12:80 and 12:81.)

Determining the tax characterization of the transaction enables application of the appropriate payroll tax rules. The sooner the transaction is characterized, the easier it will be for payroll staff to establish and manage the payroll tax compliance issues relating to the transaction. Payroll professionals are advised to seek expert guidance in this endeavor.

Q 12:7   Can a transaction be called a merger but, for federal tax purposes, actually be another type of transaction?

Yes. A purchase deal may be labeled a merger when both companies agree that joining together is in the best interest of both of their companies and they want the world to understand the takeover is friendly. In essence, they agree to call it a merger even if it is not. Calling the deal a merger does not mean that in fact it is one for tax purposes. Some transactions may appear to be statutory mergers, but fail on some point to meet the specific requirements of an "A" reorganization. As a result, the transaction might be considered one of the other types of tax-free reorganizations listed in § 368 or may fall outside of § 368 altogether.

For example, when a corporation acquires stock of a target corporation then converts the target into a disregarded single-owned limited liability company, the transaction will not qualify as a statutory merger or consolidation. The IRS sees this transaction as a single integrated acquisition of the assets of the target. [Treas. Reg. § 1.368-2(b)(1)(iii) Ex. 9]

It is not unusual for the IRS to use the "step transaction" doctrine to collapse a string of transactions into one substantive structure. The step transaction doctrine treats a series of formally separate steps as a single transaction if such steps are in substance integrated, interdependent, and focused toward a particular result. [T.D. 9396; T.D. 9361; Rev. Rul. 2004-83, 2004-32 I.R.B. 157; and Penrod v. Commissioner, 88 T.C. 1415 (1987)] Treas. Reg. § 1.368-1(a) provides that a transaction must be evaluated under all relevant provisions of law, including the step transaction doctrine, to determine whether it qualifies as a reorganization under I.R.C. § 368.

One of the more important focuses in recent years has been on the treatment of a forward triangular merger where a corporation merges into a wholly owned subsidiary of another corporation in exchange for the other corporation's stock. When this occurs, usually all the assets and liabilities of the original corporation are transferred to the subsidiary and it ceases to exist. Stopping here, it would appear that a statutory merger has taken place. But, in the process, shareholders exchange their old stock in the merged corporation for stock in the parent of the subsidiary. The transaction now qualifies as a forward triangular merger under I.R.C. § 368(a)(2)(D), as a non-divisive "D reorganization" intended to facilitate the acquisition of the target's assets rather than to divide an existing corporation. And, if the stock received in the exchange were voting stock, the transaction would also qualify as a "C reorganization" under I.R.C. § 368(a)(1)(C). In either case, I.R.C. § 381(a) will attach, tax attributes will carry over, and payroll professionals would look to consolidate payroll responsibilities of the absorbed company into the survivor just the same as if a statutory merger had occurred.

New Treas. Reg. § 1.381(a)-1(b)(2) has modified the definition of the acquiring corporation in transactions such as these. Only a single acquiring corporation may inherit the tax attributes of the transferor pursuant to a plan of reorganization. The acquiring corporation is the one that directly acquires the assets transferred by the transferor corporation, even if that corporation retains none of the transferred assets. This new regulation may have bearing on payroll processes if the assets are transferred from the acquiring corporation since payroll attributes may flow to the transferee under different tax rules.

In 2015, we saw the IRS attempting to wrap its hands around a string of transactions, querying when to collapse them into one, or when to deconstruct the string into several transactions, looking at each segment separately for purposes of the tax attribution rules, or when some segments should be segregated and others collapsed in the same transaction. Their efforts resulted in two published rulings. In Rev. Rul. 2015-9, 2015-21 I.R.B. 972, two exchanges of stock were followed by a reorganization under § 368(a)(1)(D) to which § 381 applied. A similar result occurred in Rev. Rul. 2015-10, 2015-21 I.R.B. 973, which involved the interests in a limited liability company that elected to be treated as a corporation being passed through the hands of a string of subsidiaries before resulting in a D reorganization.

Trying to follow payroll accountabilities through these strings of transactions proves to be a difficult task. Where a merger, or a C or D tax-free reorganization, occurs and the survivor then spins off the assets of the new business in a taxable transaction, the payroll carryover rules would apply to the survivor since a § 381 transaction makes the survivor responsible for all payroll matters of the acquired for all open tax years. But, possibly the successor employer rules would then attach to the ultimate asset acquirer. If the asset acquirer elects with the survivor to carry over wage bases of the transferred employees, the end result would be a division of current year's payroll accountabilities between the survivor and the asset acquirer, with the remaining payroll responsibilities of the acquired remaining with the survivor. But where the spinoff of the new business was through a tax-free transaction, perhaps the ultimate acquirer of the business would carry accountability for all of the acquired's payroll liabilities. Tax counsels should always be asked to include payroll accountabilities in the early stages of design of the transactions.

Fairly complex deals can be given simple labels for convenience. For example, it was announced in a simple statement that Schering-Plough Corporation merged with Merck in 2009. But, in actuality, the combination of Merck and Schering-Plough was a complex, multiple-step process. First, a wholly owned subsidiary of Schering-Plough merged into Schering-Plough. Then, in the second half of the transaction, this new merger product became the acquirer of a company formed in another merger of a different wholly owned subsidiary of Schering-Plough into Merck (creating New Merck). New Merck continued as the surviving company, but as a wholly owned subsidiary of the first merger. Consider what happens to the employees throughout this process and which entity will be handling wage withholding and reporting during the transition. Further consider what impact each of the steps in the multi-step process will have on unemployment insurance claims reserves and where their attributes may need to be considered to transfer for SUI tax purposes. See Q 12:105 and following.

When operating companies move into or out of bankruptcy, it is particularly difficult to determine what the transaction really is from a payroll perspective. [See Ralphs Grocery Co. & Subsidiaries f. k. a. Ralphs Supermarkets, Inc., & Subsidiaries v. Commissioner; Fred Meyer, Inc., & Subsidiaries v. Commissioner, U.S. Tax Court, T.C. Memo. 58,529(M) (Jan. 27, 2011) where litigation was necessary to determine that the transaction was not a tax-free reorganization and that the § 338 election to be an asset purchase was valid.]

Determining the tax characterization of the transaction enables application of the appropriate payroll tax rules. The sooner the transaction is characterized, the easier it will be for payroll staff to establish and manage the payroll tax compliance issues relating to the transaction. As most payroll professionals are not typically versed in such legal matters, it is essential to consult tax counsel to gain assurance on the appropriate tax characterization of the transactions to be addressed.

Q 12:8   Can a transaction be called an asset purchase, but actually be an "A" reorganization or other transaction that triggers the tax attribution rules, for example, through collapsing a multi-step acquisition?

Yes, as pointed out in Qs 12:6 and 12:7, many transactions can look like one form and actually be another. Payroll professionals, focusing on the end result of a transaction that involves asset transfers, can be surprised to learn that what to them was obviously an asset transfer was in fact a tax-free reorganization under section 368 that triggered the section 381 tax attribution rules. This could happen, for example, when subsequent to an A reorganization (merger), an acquiring corporation transfers all or part of the acquired assets to its 80 percent controlled subsidiary. This event will not disqualify the original "A" reorganization(merger of the acquired company with the acquiring corporation) that required the carrying over of the acquired's payroll liabilities. Depending on the terms of the later asset transfer, an allocation of the acquired's liabilities may transfer to the new subsidiary (if a tax-free spinoff) or may allow the use of the successor employer rules between the parent and its subsidiary with the end result of leaving the parent accountable for the payroll compliance of the acquired unrelated company not transferred to the subsidiary. Transactions that do not look like mergers can actually be "A" reorganization mergers.

The IRS has used the step transaction doctrine to grant "A" reorganization status when a subsidiary is merged into a target corporation with the target surviving (the acquisition merger), where the target is later merged into the parent (an upstream merger). This structure is a common way of acquiring a target company. If each leg of the transaction were viewed separately, the acquisition merger would be considered a stock purchase by the parent followed by a § 332 liquidation of the target into the parent. The IRS views such a structure collectively, using the step transaction doctrine to hold that the target was merged with the parent in an "A" reorganization.

See collapses resulting in "C" or "D" reorganizations above in Qs 12:6 and 12:7. "C" and "D" reorganizations are covered under section 381 and will result in a carryover of payroll liabilities to the surviving employer in the same manner an "A" reorganization merger or consolidation.

When one company takes over another and clearly establishes itself as the new owner, the deal can be publicly called an "acquisition" even though, from a legal or tax standpoint, it may in fact be a classic merger. When the deal is unfriendly—that is, when the target company does not want to be purchased—it is almost always labeled as an acquisition even if its legal structure is a merger. For the most part, as explained above in Q 12:7, whether an M&A event is announced as a merger or an acquisition really depends on whether the purchase is friendly or hostile and not what it really is from a legal perspective. Payroll professionals are well advised to seek a tax classification from their counsel as soon as possible to be able to outline the compliance needs of the transaction.

The characterization of the transaction as an "A" reorganization or as one of the other transactions covered under section 381 can have significant ramifications to a payroll professional who mistakenly believes a successor employer election is available and inappropriately chooses not to consolidate income tax, FICA, and FUTA liabilities. Determining the tax characterization of the transaction enables application of the appropriate payroll tax rules. The sooner the transaction is characterized, the easier it will be for Payroll to establish and manage the payroll tax compliance issues relating to the transaction. Payroll professionals are advised to seek expert guidance in this endeavor. Payroll professionals should ask of their legal counsels that consideration of payroll matters be made part of the legal opinions written in support of the transaction. Specifically, opinions should express what the structure of the transaction is for payroll tax purposes and its effective date.

Q 12:9   What transactions are considered statutory mergers or consolidations under I.R.C. § 368(a)(1)(A) or fall under § 381 tax attribution rules where payroll liabilities may be seen to carry over to the surviving company?

"A" reorganizations may take several different forms:

- An upstream merger where a subsidiary corporation merges into the parent, but caution is warranted. Liquidation rules under § 332 take precedence over application of an "A" reorganization. So if the terms of liquidation are met, such as when an 80 percent-owned subsidiary is merged into its parent, the transaction will not be an "A" reorganization.

- A downstream merger where the parent corporation merges into its subsidiary and transfers subsidiary stock to its own shareholders in exchange for its own shares. See Revenue Ruling 70-223, 1970-1 C.B. 79.

- A forward subsidiary merger where the target corporation merges into a subsidiary of the acquiring parent corporation.

- A reverse subsidiary merger where a subsidiary of the acquiring parent corporation merges into the target corporation, including a reverse triangular merger where the resulting company later merges into the acquiring corporation. However, the IRS has said that where an I.R.C. § 338(h)(10) election to treat the transaction as an asset purchase has been made, the IRS will not challenge an asset purchase election. [Treas. Reg. § 1.338(h)(10)-1; T.D. 9271, 2006-33 I.R.B. 224; Rev. Rul. 2001-46, 2001-2 C.B. 321] See Q 12:40 below for a discussion of payroll uncertainties when such elections are made.

Transactions named in I.R.C. § 381 where the result for payroll purposes is the same as in the context of a statutory merger include:

- Complete liquidation of a subsidiary corporation into its parent under § 332;

- "C" reorganization under § 368(a)(1)(C) defined as an acquisition by one corporation of substantially all the properties of another corporation, in exchange "solely" for all or a part of its voting stock;

- Non-divisive "D" reorganization under § 368(a)(1)(D) (see Q 12:6 above for definition of a D reorganization); and

- Mere changes in identity, form, or place of organization qualifying as an "F" reorganization under § 368(a)(1)(F).

As pointed out above in Q 12:7, a "forward triangular merger" may not qualify as an "A" reorganization, but instead may be a "D" reorganization under I.R.C. § 368(a)(2)(D) or possibly a "C" reorganization under § 368(a)(1)(C). See Treas. Reg. § 1.368-2(b)(2). In either case, I.R.C. § 381(a) will attach, tax attributes will carry over, and payroll professionals would look to consolidate payroll responsibilities of the absorbed company into the survivor.

Also consider similar rules that apply to certain partnership transactions covered in Qs 12:75–12:79 below.

Federal Income, FICA, and FUTA Tax Compliance for Statutory Mergers and Consolidations and Other Section 381 Transactions Involving Corporations

Note. Keep in mind as you read this section that the compliance may have broader application than just to those transactions directly addressed by the payroll authorities. Other substantive workings of the tax laws that come into play for particular transactions also require the survivor to carry over the tax attributes of the acquired under I.R.C. § 381 (see the list in Q 12:9 above).

Q 12:10   What guidance has the IRS issued regarding payroll tax compliance when employees are transferred pursuant to a statutory merger or consolidation?

Guidance for transactions after 2004 can be found in Revenue Procedure 2004-53 [2004-34 I.R.B. 320], amplifying Revenue Ruling 62-60, [1962-1 C.B. 186] and in the instructions for IRS Form 941, *Employer's QUARTERLY Federal Tax Return*, and for Schedule D (Form 941), *Report of Discrepancies Caused by Acquisitions, Statutory Mergers, or Consolidations*. Under these requirements, wages paid by the predecessor are treated as if paid by the successor for income and FICA tax purposes, for the purpose of applying the Social Security wage base for the year and identifying when to begin to withhold the 0.9 percent Additional Medicare Tax on compensation exceeding $200,000 annually. (See Q 12:2.)

For FUTA purposes, the primary guidelines for statutory mergers and consolidations are contained in instructions for Form 940, *Employer's Annual Federal Unemployment (FUTA) Tax Return* and I.R.C. § 3302(e) and related regulations. (See chapter 3 for a further discussion of contributions and credits and other issues related to FUTA. See chapter 4 for a general discussion of FICA.)

Form 941 Requirements for Surviving Corporations

Q 12:11   Must a surviving corporation in a statutory merger or consolidation file Schedule D (Form 941)?

Yes. Surviving employers involved in a statutory merger or consolidation must file Schedule D (Form 941) if the transaction will otherwise cause Forms 941 to be out of balance with Forms W-2. [Rev. Proc. 2004-53, 2004-34 I.R.B. 320] The primary tax compliance authority for statutory mergers is still found in Revenue Ruling 62-60 [1962-1 C.B. 186], which survives Revenue Procedure 2004-53. The only change in Revenue Procedure 2004-53 as it pertains to mergers is the allowance of the use of Schedule D to meet the notice of a statutory merger or consolidation required to be filed under Revenue Ruling 62-60.

Note. Schedule D follows Rev. Proc. 2004-53 and fails to address the other transactions with similar tax results to a statutory merger or consolidation covered by I.R.C. § 381 (see Q 12:9) or when involving partnership transactions that trigger the continuity rules (see Qs 12:75–12:79). To date, we do not have solid instructions for handling these transactions.

To provide employers with time to reconcile their respective Forms W-2 with Forms 941, Schedule D is filed independent of the Form 941 but by the due date of the Form 941 for the first quarter of the year following the year of the transaction. Where a final Form 941 may be due earlier, the Schedule D must be filed by the due date of the final return. If filed on paper, the Schedule D is to be filed separately from the Form 941 using the following address:

IRS Philadelphia Campus
Mail Stop 4-G08 151
2970 Market Street
Philadelphia, PA 19104

This is not the same address that is used for filing Form 941. (See instructions to Form 941 for those mailing addresses.) Schedule D can also be filed electronically with an electronic submission of Form 941. Electronic filing of Schedule D enables the IRS to process information on the form more efficiently and accurately.

After a statutory merger or consolidation, the wages paid and the taxes withheld by the acquired corporation are included on the Forms W-2 (Copy A) filed by the surviving corporation. This consolidated filing will cause a discrepancy between the amounts shown on the surviving corporation's Forms W-2 (Copy A) and Forms 941 in the totals of Social Security wages, Medicare wages, Social Security tips, and federal income tax withheld. Schedule D is used to explain the discrepancies between the consolidated totals on Form W-2 filed by the survivor and the combined totals on Forms 941 filed by both the survivor and the acquired corporations.

Q 12:12   What are the Form 941 requirements for a surviving corporation in a statutory merger under Revenue Ruling 62-60 (adopted by Revenue Procedure 2004-53) and instructions to Form 941?

The primary tax compliance authority for statutory mergers is still found in Revenue Ruling 62-60 [1962-1 C.B. 186], which survives Revenue Procedure 2004-53. Revenue Ruling 62-60 requires the survivor to file a single Form 941 for the quarter in which the merger takes place, consolidating the acquired corporation's liabilities with its own, and is silent as to any filing requirement on the part of the acquired corporation. Instructions to Form 941 are different for selling or transferring a business and state: "If you sell or transfer your business, you and the new owner must each file a Form 941 for the quarter in which the transfer occurred. Report only the wages you paid . . . When two businesses merge, the continuing firm must file a return for the quarter in which the change took place and the other firm should file a final return."

Form 941 also instructs on changing from one form of business to another—such as from a sole proprietorship to a partnership or corporation and considers such a change as a transfer. Note that characterizing the transaction as a "transfer" does not mean that the transaction qualifies for the successor employer election, since mergers and other transactions are included in the transfer category and could also include § 381 transactions as well those requiring partnership continuity. For transfers, the instructions caution that a new EIN might be required. Employers are instructed to attach a statement to the 941 that includes the new owner's name (or the new name of the business); whether the business is now a sole proprietorship, partnership, or corporation; the kind of change that occurred (a sale or transfer); the date of the change; and the name of the person keeping the payroll records and the address where those records will be kept.

When a revenue ruling varies from the official IRS instructions to Form 941, employers should follow the Form 941 instructions. The regulations specify that all Forms 941 are required to be filed in accordance with the related form instructions and regulations. [Treas. Reg. § 31.6011(a)-7] In this case, following form instructions makes sense if they support the filing by each corporation of Forms 941 to report the wages each separately has paid in the quarter of the merger. There are several pitfalls if Revenue Ruling 62-60 were to be followed even though it is still considered the primary authority.

Instructions to Schedule D require surviving corporations in a merger or consolidation to provide the date of the statutory merger or consolidation; the name, trade name (doing business as or d/b/a), and an explanation of any discrepancies between Forms W-2 (Copy A) and Forms 941 in the totals of Social Security wages, Medicare wages and tips, Social Security tips, federal income tax withheld, and (prior to 2011) advance EIC payments.

If the survivor files a consolidated Form 941 for the quarter in which the merger takes place, reporting both the survivor's and acquired's liabilities and, following instructions to the Schedule D, then files the Schedule D in the following year, two concerns may arise:

1. The IRS may not look for tax deposits made in the quarter of the merger under the acquired corporation's EIN to offset the consolidated liabilities filed on a Form 941 under the survivor's EIN. This could cause an unsettled 941 liability, and the survivor could receive an assessment in the amount of the acquired's deposits plus penalties and interest charges. The timing for filing Schedule D relates to the timing for balancing the totals on Forms W-2 with the totals on Forms 941; it does not consider the timing for balancing tax deposits with Forms 941.

2. The acquired corporation may also file a Form 941 reporting its own liabilities and offsetting deposits, creating a double reporting and wiping out the credit, or not file at all leaving the deposits as a credit to be refunded to the acquired corporation. Both frequently happen in M&A events, and in either case the survivor will be short deposit credits to offset liabilities if it includes the acquired corporation's Form 941 liabilities with its own.

Once filings occur that are out-of-balance with deposits, correcting them can be very difficult. Since lack of coordination on these matters can be costly to both parties, it is recommended that early on in the transaction planning, discussion be had as to what will be done to avoid double reporting or failing to report actual Form 941 liabilities. Instructions to Form 941 allow each employer to file a Form 941 for the quarter of the merger, reporting only the wages each employer paid. If done this way, both returns should be in balance with deposits. According to Revenue Procedure 2004-53 and the instructions for Schedule D, Schedule D can also be filed by the acquired corporation when it files a final Form 941. (See Qs 12:13–12:16 for further discussions on the uses of Schedule D by an acquired corporation and the need for the acquired corporation to file a final Form 941. See Qs 12:18–12:19 for details on what to include in Schedule D.) Consideration can also be given to making the M&A event effective at the end of or beginning of a quarter to avoid wages paid by both corporations in the same quarter.

Q 12:13   Must an acquired corporation in a statutory merger or consolidation or other tax-free transaction where payroll liabilities flow to the survivor file a final Form 941?

The better answer is yes. The regulations specify that all Forms 941 are required to be filed in accordance with the related form instructions and regulations. [Treas. Reg. § 31.6011(a)-7] Even though Revenue Ruling 62-60 [1962-1 C.B. 186] in addressing statutory mergers and consolidations is silent on the point and the regulations conflict somewhat with the instructions to Form 941, the acquired corporation should follow Form 941 instructions to file a final return. The conflict in the regulations results from the requirement that only employers that cease to pay wages are required to file a final Form 941 for the period, and in the case of a statutory merger or consolidation and in the other similar transactions where payroll liabilities carryover, the acquired corporation is considered the same taxpayer as the survivor, and technically does not cease to pay wages. [Rev. Rul. 62-60, 1962-1 C.B. 186; Treas. Reg. § 31.6011(a)-6]

Following Form 941 instructions, the acquired corporation is to file a final Form 941 for the quarter in which the transfer occurs. Filing of Schedule D by the acquired corporation along with the filing of a final Form 941 is highly recommended because it will help the IRS reconcile deposits and liabilities for the quarter in which the merger takes place (see Qs 12:12, and 12:18–12:19 for details on inclusions in Schedule D).

For the other transactions with similar tax results to a statutory merger or consolidation covered by I.R.C. § 381 (see Q 12:9) or when involving partnership transactions that trigger the continuity rules (see Qs 12:75–12:79), remember that Schedule D follows Rev. Proc. 2004-53 and fails to address them. To date, we do not have solid instructions for handling these transactions. However, following the literal terms of the Form 941 instructions for business transfers, which arguably include all of these transactions, will be critical to lowering associated tax risk. Any acquired business should file a final Form 941 for the quarter in which the transfer occurs if it will no longer be making any payrolls under the same EIN.

Form 941 instructs on changing from one form of business to another—such as from a sole proprietorship to a partnership or corporation—and considers such a change as a transfer. Note that characterizing the transaction as a "transfer" does not mean that the transaction qualifies for the successor employer election, since mergers and other transactions are also included in the transfer category and the category could include § 381 transactions as well those requiring partnership continuity. For transfers, the instructions caution that a new EIN might be required. Employers are instructed for sales and transfers to attach a statement to the 941 that includes the new owner's name (or the new name of the business); whether the business is now a sole proprietorship, partnership, or corporation; the kind of change that occurred (a sale or transfer); the date of the change; and the name of the person keeping the payroll records and the address where those records will be kept.

Q 12:14   **How does an acquired corporation in a statutory merger or consolidation or other tax-free transaction where payroll liabilities flow to the survivor file a final Form 941 and Schedule D?**

To tell the IRS that a particular Form 941 is a final return, check the box on line 15 and enter the date when wages were last paid. You are also instructed to attach a statement to your return showing the name of the person keeping the payroll records and the address where those records will be kept. For statutory mergers or consolidations, use Schedule D (Form 941) to provide: the date of the statutory merger or consolidation; the name, trade name (doing business as or d/b/a), address, and EIN of the acquired corporation and an indication that as filer you are the acquired corporation; the name, trade name (doing business as or d/b/a), address, and EIN of the surviving corporation; and an explanation of any discrepancies between W-2 (Copy A) and Form 941 in the totals of Social Security wages, Medicare wages and tips, Social Security tips, and federal income tax withheld. Part 3 of Schedule D is only required if you are involved in more than one transaction in the same year to help the IRS reconcile the different Schedules D that you are to file.

Where a final Form 941 is due, the Schedule D must be filed by the due date of the final return. If filed on paper, the Schedule D is to be filed separately from the Form 941 using the following address:

> IRS Philadelphia Campus
> Mail Stop 4-G08 151
> 2970 Market Street
> Philadelphia, PA 19104

This is different from the address where the Form 941 is filed. (See instructions to Form 941 for those mailing addresses.) Schedule D can also be filed electronically with an electronic submission of Form 941. Electronic filing of Schedule D enables the IRS to process information on the form more efficiently and accurately.

Remember that Schedule D follows Rev. Proc. 2004-53 and fails to address the other transactions with similar tax results to a statutory merger or consolidation covered by I.R.C. § 381 (see Q 12:9) or when involving partnership transactions that trigger the continuity rules (see Qs 12:75–12:79). To date, we do not have solid instructions for handling these transactions. However, following the literal terms of the Form 941 instructions for transfers will be critical to lowering associated tax risk. Any acquired corporation should file a final Form 941 for the quarter in which the transfer occurs if it will no longer be making payrolls under the same EIN. Form 941 instructs on changing from one form of business to another. Note that characterizing the transaction as a "transfer" does not mean that the transaction qualifies for the successor employer election, since mergers are included in the transfer category. Such transfers arguably could include § 381 transactions as well those requiring partnership continuity. Instructions tell employers to attach a statement to the 941 that includes the new owner's name (or the new name of the business); whether the business is now a sole proprietorship, partnership, or corporation; the kind of change that occurred (a sale or transfer); the date of the change; and the name of the person keeping the payroll records and the address where those records will be kept.

Q 12:15   What is the history behind Schedule D (Form 941)?

Prior to Revenue Procedure 2004-53 [2004-34 I.R.B. 320], with the increasing number of transactions generating a greater number of paper filings, the lack of uniformity among the attachments, coupled with the IRS's inability to electronically administer the submitted data, made it very difficult for the IRS to find and match the tax accounts of the companies involved in statutory mergers—even where the rules were followed. The IRS's inability to reconcile accounts resulted in many erroneous assessments, requiring employers to step in to balance their own accounts to resolve the assessments. In 2003, the IRS agreed to accept this quagmire as an issue to be addressed by its Industry Issue Resolution Program. The Industry Issue Resolution Program released Revenue Procedure 2004-53, which amplified Revenue Ruling 62-60 [1962-1 C.B. 186], and a new reconciliation schedule, Schedule D, Report of Discrepancies Caused by Acquisitions, Statutory Mergers, or Consolidations, which is to be filed in lieu of any attachments to Form 941. Schedule D applies to transactions after 2004. [I.R.S. News Release IR-2003-92 (July 24, 2003); I.R.S. News Release IR-2004-109 (Aug. 18, 2004)]

Matters to Be Resolved in Filing a Final Form 941 under Current Rules

Q 12:16   **Are there pragmatic solutions to the timing of the filing of a final Form 941 by an acquired corporation in a statutory merger or consolidation or other tax-free transaction where payroll liabilities flow to the survivor?**

When mergers occur toward the end of a quarter, many payroll departments do not receive notice of the merger's effective date in time to plan filing coordination between the two payroll areas. If the survivor prepares its return covering all or part of the acquired corporation's wages paid in the quarter of the merger and the acquired corporation also files for the same period covering the same wages, the duplication is a concern. Bringing all of these rules into alignment can be a struggle unless the "due diligence" team for the M&A event is charged with the responsibility of coordinating the payroll filings. It is possible that knowledge of the merger may come too late to mark the quarter's Form 941 as final. A correction to the line on the Form 941 designated to be completed if your business has closed or you have stopped paying wages is not available on Form 941-X, Adjusted Employer's QUARTERLY Federal Tax Return or Claim for Refund, making it difficult to inform the IRS of a final return filing after the return is filed. (See Form 941-X instructions.)

If knowledge of the merger takes place too late to mark the quarter's return as final, businesses can alternately have the acquired corporation prepare a "final" Form 941 for the next quarter showing zero liabilities and zero deposits, as well as a Schedule D. The survivor should also file a Schedule D by the due date of the Form 941 for the first quarter of the year following the year of the transaction unless a final Form 941 is due earlier, in which case the schedule should be filed by the due date of the final return. The ideal for the IRS is to receive two matching Schedules D: one from the survivor and one from the acquired corporation. The matching Schedules D increases the chances the IRS will appropriately reconcile the filings.

Like the federal rules, most states require that the acquired corporation and the survivor file separately for the quarter in which a merger occurs, each reconciling its income tax withholding liabilities for that quarter. Separate SUI wage statements are also required of each corporation. Because many payroll systems do not allow for multiple configurations of wage bases for different agency filings, it will be important not to carry over wage histories too early. To do so may preclude the acquired corporation from filing the quarterly federal and state returns reflecting the proper amount of liabilities and place the surviving corporation in a position of including the acquired's liabilities inappropriately in its returns.

Regardless of the solution chosen, the amounts of liabilities and deposits must be correct and the surviving and the acquired corporations must not duplicate each other's liabilities or deposits in their separate filings through wage transfers that include tax histories. These are tasks that need to be added to the due diligence payroll checklist for the transaction. Liabilities and amounts still due and owing that would generate penalties or interest charges must not be understated. The returns should be collectively in balance, enabling the IRS to balance the tax accounts appropriately from the returns.

Remember that Schedule D follows Rev. Proc. 2004-53 and fails to address the other transactions with similar tax results to a statutory merger or consolidation covered by I.R.C. § 381 (see Q 12:9) or when involving partnership transactions that trigger the continuity rules (see Qs 12:75–12:79). Similar concerns are found in these transactions, and to date we do not have solid instructions for handling them. Solutions discussed above might also solve concerns in these transactions.

Tax counsel should be sought in weighing any compliance determinations that are unclear.

Impact of Mid-Quarter Effective Dates

Q 12:17   What can be done to minimize the risk associated with out-of-balance Form 941 filings resulting from employee wage transfers?

To minimize this risk, many tax professionals strive to make a transaction's effective date either at quarter-end or on the very first day of a quarter. Quarter-end or first-day effective dates enable each corporation to avoid transferring employees to new payrolls until a payroll cycle is complete for the quarter. Transferring employees after quarter-end, but before the first payroll in the following quarter, allows the surviving employer to pay all the wages in the new quarter to the transferred employees. With this structure, both the surviving and the acquired corporations will file balanced Forms 941 in which tax deposits equal reported liabilities over the transition period. Moving payrolls (switching employers) between quarters allows tax activities to remain consistent for each employer during the transitional quarters. Balanced quarterly filings also allow for easier agency reconciliations of the related tax accounts with year-end filings. This translates into lower payroll tax liabilities.

Eliminating mid-quarter effective dates may have an even more positive effect on state and local payroll tax returns associated with mergers. Because most state and local filings must be split between the employers involved, each filing for their own payrolls, there is a variance between the federal consolidated filing and state segregated filing requirements that can be resolved by using a quarter-end effective date. (See Qs 12:93–12:114 for further information on state income and unemployment taxes.)

More about Schedule D (Form 941)

Q 12:18   What are the specific requirements of Schedule D (Form 941)?

Schedule D (Form 941) must be filed by both surviving and acquired corporations for those statutory mergers or consolidations that create discrepancies between Forms W-2 (Copy A) and Forms 941. Schedule D requires inclusion of the same information necessary under the provisions of Revenue Ruling 62-60 [1962-1 C.B. 186] as well as the disclosure of specific amounts of the following discrepancies between Forms 941 and Forms W-2: Social Security wages, Medicare wages and tips, Social Security tips, and federal income taxes withheld.

Included in Schedule D should be the date of the event, the tax year of the discrepancies, the type of event, and the name, trade name, address, telephone number, and EIN of both the filing employer and the other party. Always be sure the EIN on the Schedule D (Form 941) for both parties exactly matches the EIN the IRS assigned to the businesses. The filer needs to also indicate whether it is filing as the acquired or the surviving corporation.

Schedule D must be submitted by the due date of the Form 941 for the first quarter of the year after the calendar year in which the event took place, or by the due date of the final Form 941 if due at an earlier date. [Rev. Proc. 2004-53, 2004-34 I.R.B. 320, and Schedule D (Form 941)] Schedule D is not filed at the same place that Form 941 is filed. File Schedule D using the following address:

IRS Philadelphia Campus
Mail Stop 4-G08 151
2970 Market Street
Philadelphia, PA 19104

Remember that Schedule D follows Rev. Proc. 2004-53 and fails to address the other transactions with similar tax results to a statutory merger or consolidation covered by I.R.C. § 381 (see Q 12:9) or when involving partnership transactions that trigger the continuity rules (see Qs 12:75–12:79). To date, we do not have solid instructions for handling these transactions. See the suggestions above in Qs 12:12–12:16 that are rooted in following the instructions found in Form 941 for sales and transfers.

Q 12:19   What is the primary purpose of Schedule D (Form 941)?

Each year the IRS and the Social Security Administration (SSA) compare the total numbers of Social Security wages and tips, Medicare wages and tips, and federal income tax withheld on Forms 941 with those reported on Forms W-2, Wage and Tax Statement, to verify that they match and that no additional taxes are due. In performing this task, the IRS will use Schedule D information to link the acquired and surviving corporation's Form 941 information with the required consolidated Forms W-2, regarding Social Security wages and tips, Medicare wages and tips, and federal income tax withheld. [Rev. Proc. 2004-53, 2004-34 I.R.B. 320]

Schedule D was not modified to accommodate the 0.9 percent Additional Medicare Tax. In its current version, Schedule D already covers matters that are part of the IRS matching program. Current Form 941 instructions say "The IRS matches amounts reported on your four quarterly Forms 941 with Form W-2 amounts totaled on your yearly Form W-3, Transmittal of Wage and Tax Statements. If the amounts do not agree, you may be contacted by the IRS or the Social Security Administration (SSA). The following amounts are reconciled: Federal income tax withholding, Social security wages, Social security tips, and Medicare wages and tips."

Wages subject to withholding of the 0.9 percent Additional Medicare Tax are defined the same as Medicare wages, but withholding only attaches to the excess wages over $200,000. The Additional Medicare Tax wages are not required to be reported separately on the Form W-2 from Medicare wages. Both the subject wages and the additional 0.9 percent withholding are to be included in Boxes 5 and 6 along with the general Medicare wages and withholding. For this reason, Schedule D was not amended to accommodate matching of the new withholding.

Statutory Mergers and Consolidations: Employee Forms W-4

Remember that the requirements covered below may also have bearing on transactions with similar tax results to a statutory merger or consolidation covered by I.R.C. § 381 (see Q 12:9) or when involving partnership transactions that trigger the continuity rules (see Qs 12:75–12:79 below). When payroll liabilities are carried over from one company to another, all the compliance functions and responsibilities travel with them for all open tax years still subject to possible audit. The authorities in this section are older and for the most part relate only to statutory mergers and consolidations. They may or may not have bearing to other transactions under I.R.C. § 381 or when involving partnership transactions that trigger the continuity rules. Nonetheless, if you are involved in these other transactions where all payroll liabilities should be carried over for all open tax years, plans should be made to capture and preserve information from the acquired's files and accommodations should be made for their use in the survivor's payroll process. Tasks outlined below should be added to the due diligence payroll checklist for the transaction. Tax counsel should be sought in weighing any compliance determinations that are unclear.

Q 12:20　Does a surviving corporation need to receive new Forms W-4 from the acquired corporation's employees when there is a statutory merger or consolidation?

No. New forms would only be required if an acquired corporation's Form W-4, Employee's Withholding Allowance Certificate, was invalid or expired, or if a Form W-4 claiming exemption from withholding was valid only for a previous tax year. (See Q 12:21 for terms of invalidation and chapter 2 for general applications of Forms W-4.)

Because in a statutory merger the survivor is considered the same employer as the acquired corporation, the Forms W-4 received by the acquired corporation from its employees are valid in the hands of the surviving corporation. W-4s received by a surviving employer from an acquired employer can be used by the surviving employer to affect income tax withholding on wages it continues to pay to employees.

The W-4s may be transferred and stored electronically. [Rev. Proc. 2004-53, 2004-34 I.R.B. 320; Rev. Rul. 62-60, 1962-1 C.B. 186; Treas. Reg. § 31.3402(f)(5)-1(c); Ann. 99-6, 1999-4 I.R.B. 24] Remember that in the context of a merger or consolidation, since the surviving corporation has continuity with the acquired corporation, the survivor will be held liable for the acquired's previous acts or omissions. It will be imperative that a survivor captures and retains these forms to assure availability should a later audit occur.

Because in a statutory merger the survivor must rely on the acquired corporation to forward Forms W-4, plans should be made to capture and preserve the Forms W-4 from the acquired corporation's files and accommodations should be made for their use in the surviving corporation's payroll process. These are tasks that need to be added to the due diligence payroll checklist for the transaction.

Increasing use of employee self-service (ESS) modules, such as an employee interactive voice response (IVR) system that allows employees to make changes to their personal information and their federal, state, and local withholding allowance elections on Forms W-4, may make transfer of this information easier, but will present additional compliance concerns. Payroll professionals will need to be vigilant that the eservice system is compliant with IRS requirements for data gathering and recordkeeping, and with state and local tax requirements, assuring coverage of all the necessary agency's forms as well as whether eservice of the particular forms are allowed. [T.D. 8706; Treas. Reg. § 31.3402(f)(5)-1(c)] When inheriting a prior employer's process, the surviving corporation will need to examine these matters and others, such as how the system is updated and maintained, whether the system retains the full history of withholding allowance changes, and what are data retention periods.

Q 12:21   In the context of a statutory merger or consolidation, will the surviving corporation be held liable for relying on the Forms W-4 transferred from the acquired corporation that are considered invalid?

Yes. The surviving corporation will be held fully liable for its reliance on invalid Forms W-4 transferred from the acquired corporation. [Rev. Proc. 2004-53, 2004-23 I.R.B. 320; Rev. Rul. 62-60, 1962-1 C.B. 186] If an employee fails to give an employer a properly completed Form W-4, the employer must withhold as if the employee is single and with no withholding allowances. Any unauthorized change or addition to Form W-4 also invalidates the form, including striking out any certification language.

Because liability may potentially be transferred to the surviving corporation, the forms, wage bases, and any policies and procedures used in the administration of the forms should undergo strenuous due diligence reviews in the conversion process. See Q 12:20 above for a particular need to review employee self-service and employee interactive voice response eservicing modules.

Q 12:22   Will the surviving corporation be held liable for the acquired corporation's reliance on invalid Forms W-4 in periods prior to the merger that are still open for assessment?

Yes. Because, in the context of a statutory merger or consolidation, the surviving corporation is considered the same taxpayer as the acquired corporation, the surviving corporation will be held liable for the acquired corporation's reliance on invalid Forms W-4 in periods prior to the merger that are still open for assessment. [Rev. Proc. 2004-53, 2004-34 I.R.B. 320; Rev. Rul. 62-60, 1962-1 C.B. 186]

Because liability may potentially be transferred to the surviving corporation, the acquired corporation's forms, wage bases, and any policies and procedures used in the administration of the forms should undergo strenuous due diligence reviews in the conversion process. See Q 12:20 above for a particular need to review employee self-service and employee interactive voice response eservicing modules.

Q 12:23   Will the surviving corporation need to be concerned about lock-in-letters and other IRS or SSA correspondence concerning employees of the acquired corporation?

Employers may be directed (in a written notice or in future published guidance) to send certain Forms W-4 to the IRS. The IRS reviews employee withholding compliance through careful screenings of the employee's individual tax return (Form 1040) and submitted W-2. When there is serious underwithholding for a particular employee, the IRS may issue a notice (commonly referred to as a "lock-in-letter") to the employer specifying the maximum number of withholding allowances permitted for that employee. After the lock-in-letter takes effect, the employer must disregard any Form W-4 that claims more allowances or exempt status, until the IRS notifies the employer to withhold tax based on the new Form W-4. In the context of a statutory merger, because the surviving corporation is considered the same employer as the acquired employer, the surviving corporation will need to respond to any IRS direction, including lock-in-letters regarding employees submitting Forms W-4 to the acquired corporation. [Treas. Reg. § 31.3402(f)(2)-1(g)]

Because surviving corporations will be held accountable for an acquired corporation's lock-in letters, it will be important that any existing lock-in letters be found and transferred to the surviving corporation, as well as a procedure established to collect and send payroll-related mail to the acquired company during the transitional period so that any new lock-in letters received are addressed.

Caution is warranted as many states still require W-4 (or their state version) filings with the state even though the federal requirement has been withdrawn. See Q 12:98 for further discussion on this filing need. In this context, employers completing due diligence of a soon-to-be-acquired company should identify state requirements in all jurisdictions where the company operates.

Year-End Filing in Statutory Mergers and Consolidations: W-2

Remember that the requirements covered below may also have bearing on transactions with similar tax results to a statutory merger or consolidation covered by I.R.C. § 381 (see Q 12:9) or when involving partnership transactions that trigger the continuity rules (see Qs 12:75–12:79). When payroll liabilities for tax years still open to audits are required to be carried over from one company to another in any transaction, all the compliance functions and responsibilities associated with those liabilities travel with them. The authorities in this section are older and for the most part relate only to statutory mergers and consolidations. They may or may not have bearing to other transactions under I.R.C. § 381 or when involving partnership transactions that trigger the continuity rules. Nonetheless, plans should be made to capture and preserve information from the acquired's files anytime when the nature of the transaction would require the acquired's payroll liabilities for tax years still open to audit be carried over to a successor. Remember that all the compliance functions and responsibilities associated with those liabilities travel with them to the successor and would require the tasks outlined below to be added to the due diligence payroll checklist for the transaction. Tax counsel should be sought in weighing any compliance determinations that are unclear.

Q 12:24   In the context of a statutory merger or consolidation, is the surviving corporation required to file single, consolidated Forms W-2 for the absorbed employees, as well as other acquired corporation employees, reporting wages paid and taxes withheld by the acquired corporation along with any wages paid and taxes withheld by the surviving corporation in the year of the transaction?

Yes. For the year in which the merger took place, the surviving corporation must file Forms W-2, as the employer, under its EIN, covering all wages paid (including wages paid to employees who were not retained after the merger and who were only paid wages by the acquired corporation) and taxes withheld by both the acquired corporation and the surviving corporation. If the surviving corporation is filing fewer than 250 Forms W-2 with the SSA reporting wages paid to both the survivor's and the acquired's employees, paper Forms W-2 are allowed to be filed with a Form W-3, Transmittal of Wage and Tax Statements, listing the surviving corporation as the employer. If, on the other hand, the surviving corporation is filing 250 or more consolidated Forms W-2 electronically, a single electronic transmission is required from the surviving corporation (as the employer) reporting wages paid to both the survivor's and the acquired's employees. The acquired corporation is not required to file Forms W-2 for the year in which the merger took place. [Rev. Proc. 2004-53, 2004-34 I.R.B. 320; Rev. Rul. 62-60, 1962-1 C.B. 186; I.R.C. § 6051(a); Treas. Reg. §§ 31.6051-1(a), 31.6051-2] Electronic filing requirements are covered in the SSA's EFW2, Specifications for Filing Forms W-2 Electronically, issued for the tax year involved.

The Consolidated Appropriations Act of 2016 accelerated to January 31 the due date for Forms W-2, whether filing on paper or electronically, starting in 2017. In addition, the IRS has eliminated automatically obtaining a 30-day extension of the filing due date through a Form 8809. For filings due on or after January 1, 2017, you may request one 30-day extension to file Form W-2 by submitting a complete application on Form 8809, including a detailed explanation of why you need additional time and signed under penalties of perjury. The IRS has said it will grant the extension only in extraordinary circumstances or catastrophe. See 2017 General Instructions to Form W-2 and Form W-3. This acceleration of the general W-2 filing date will put pressure on employers struggling to gather all the data needed for correct W-2 forms after a merger or consolidation or any transaction that requires aggregation of data from many systems and locations.

The health care reforms have also brought more compliance accountabilities that need to be added to the payroll due diligence team's responsibilities in these transactions to assure correct W-2 forms are issued at yearend and other risks are appropriately weighted. Some of the many considerations include:

- **Performing risk assessments for the Employer's Shared Responsibility Payments (ESRP) and for other possible penalties that may arise under new health insurance mandates.** The ESRP will apply to applicable large employers with 50 or more full-time equivalent employees when full-time employees of the acquired company subscribe to health insurance from a qualified Exchange Program. Performing this assessment will entail a review of the target's health care plans and packages for meeting the terms of minimum essential coverage and the terms of offers of coverage to employees on a month-by-month basis since the ESRP applies month-to-month. The assessment should also include how employees were determined to be full-time, if there were any employees overlooked in the health care offerings, and whether any waiting period met requirements that would allow eliminating an employee from any offering during the period. Monitoring will also be necessary as to the coverage terms of health care plans to avoid other penalties for plan violations, such as those imposed under I.R.C. § 4980D on failures of a group health plan to meet special group coverage requirements. The amount of the tax on any failure is $100 for each day in the noncompliance period with respect to each individual to whom the group plan failure relates.

- **Reporting aggregate cost of health care coverage in Box 12 of the Form W-2, with Code DD.** IRS Notice 2012-9 requires surviving employers to report the aggregate reportable cost of health care coverage by both the survivor and the absorbed employer. Notice 2012-9 is the principal source on how to report, what coverage to include and how to determine the reportable cost of the coverage. [2012-4 I.R.B. 315] For employers with fewer than 250 employees, reporting the aggregate cost of health care remains optional until the IRS issues future guidance. For other employers that filed 250 or more W-2s in the previous year, reporting the cost of employer-provided health care for tax year 2012 and later years is mandatory. For more information, see http://www.irs.gov/uac/Form-W-2-Reporting-of-Employer-Sponsored-Health-Coverage.

- **Meeting ACA information reporting requirements under I.R.C. § 6055 and § 6056 on Forms 1094-C and 1095-C.** Applicable large employers with 50 or more full-time equivalent employees, insurance companies, sponsors of a self-insured health plan (including employers that self-insure), government agencies that administer government-sponsored health insurance programs, and other entities must now report numerous details on those individuals offered health insurance coverage as well as on the coverage offered. The ESRP and the new reporting requirements will pose risk and compliance concerns in M&A transactions. Beginning with tax year 2015 (reporting in 2016), applicable large employers began to report information about the employer and each full-time employee on Form 1095-C, and on the transmittal Form 1094-C. Self-insured employers, like insurance companies, report minimum essential coverage to insured persons on Form 1095-B as well as complete the transmittal on Form 1094-B. Employers that are both self-insured and an applicable large employer may instead report coverage in Part III of Form 1095-C.

- **Health Flexible Spending Account (FSA) and its limitations.** An employee salary deferral now has a limit for a Health FSA. Initially, it was set at $2,500. In 2015, the annual dollar limit on employee contributions was indexed for inflation and is set for $2,600 for 2017. There are legislative efforts being made to repeal this restriction that employers will need to keep up with. Misapplied thresholds can affect taxable wage amounts. Plans also need to stay current by adopting appropriate amendments to reflect the new limits each year the limit and other rules change. Other matters also need to be looked at for employees who participate in a general health FSA, such as whether restrictions have been appropriately applied when a Health FSA is combined with employer contributions to a Health Savings Account (HSA). Employers would need to set up a limited HSA-compatible FSA if they offer an HSA interface in their health plan offering.

- **MLR rebates.** Another concern involves the payment of medical loss ratio (MLR) rebates to employees by employers that maintain group health insurance policies and that received the premium rebates from their insurance carriers for a previous year. Where rebates are passed on to employees, it may change their W-2 calculations for the year if employees are part of a pretax deferral plan or their employer pays their premiums. It will be important to determine whether such amounts were paid out by a predecessor to assure correct W-2 forms. And, in a statutory merger or consolidation, or in any transaction where liabilities of the acquired carry over to the survivor, tracking these items will not be optional.

- **Other provisions.** In future years, other aspects of the Affordable Care Act will become effective and will have serious impact on payroll, such as what has become known as the Cadillac tax under I.R.C. § 4980I, now delayed until 2020, which will impose on affected employees a 40 percent excise tax on the cost of health care coverage valued over a certain amount. There will also be future guidance issued on other Affordable Care Act provisions, such as on implementation of I.R.C. § 105(h) that provides for nondiscrimination within health care plans, on revamping the cafeteria plan requirements under I.R.C. § 125 to meet the new health care provisions, and in the ever-expanding information reporting requirements associated with enforcement of the new rules.

In the last few years, employers have come to expect last-minute legislation and even significant court holdings that force retroactive adjustments in current and prior years' taxable wage amounts and that require amendments to be made to previous compliance filings. Events marked by late legislation include retroactive paired treatment of qualified transportation fringe benefits now made permanent by the PATH Act of 2015, which also extended a modified Work Opportunity Tax Credit retroactively to cover 2015 through 2019. The U.S. Supreme Court holding in *Windsor* [United States v. Windsor, 133 S. Ct. 2675 (2013)] required recognition of same-sex married spouses for health care and other benefit coverage, allowing reversal of taxable wages and income tax, FICA, and FUTA adjustments to be made to W-2 forms and other filings. Payroll professionals will need to be alert to these and newer events, add review of a target's practices to their due diligence task lists, and be prepared to include correct treatment in their W-2 and other filings, where required.

Q 12:25   Must the surviving corporation file Forms W-2 for the acquired corporation's employees that were terminated or who retired before the transaction's effective date, but who received wages in the year of the transaction?

Yes. In transactions where the surviving corporation is considered the same employer as the acquired corporation, the surviving corporation is responsible for filing all Forms W-2 as the employer under its EIN for all of the acquired corporation's employees, covering all wages paid during the year of the merger even if paid to terminated and retired employees before the date of the merger or other similar transaction. [Rev. Rul. 62-60, 1962-1 C.B. 186; Rev. Proc. 2004-53, 2004-34 I.R.B. 320] See Q 12:9 for a list of § 381 transactions and Qs 12:75–12:79 for explanation of when partnership transactions require continuity.

IRS Notice 2012-9 requires surviving employers to report the aggregate reportable cost of health care coverage by both employers for these employees (see Q 12:24). [2012-4 I.R.B. 315] But, an exception is provided for retirees and other former employees if W-2 reporting is not otherwise required. Reporting health care is also optional on Forms W-2 when furnished to employees who terminate before the end of a calendar year and request, in writing, their Forms W-2 before the end of that year. See Q 12:27 below on this early reporting requirement. For more items to be aware of in W-2 reporting for the acquired corporation's terminated employees, see the list above in Q 12:24.

Q 12:26   Is the surviving corporation required to file Forms W-2c to correct errors on the part of the acquired corporation on wages paid by the acquired corporation prior to a merger or other transaction that requires carryover of payroll liabilities to the survivor?

Yes. Because the surviving corporation is considered the same employer as the acquired corporation, the surviving corporation must file Forms W-2c, Corrected Wage and Tax Statement, to correct any errors reported on Forms W-2 filed by the acquired corporation for any previous period. Special instructions apply to employers correcting W-2s when the previous Form W-2 was filed by an acquired employer with a different identity. The SSA strongly recommends that employers contact the SSA to confirm that the original money amount(s) agrees with the employee's earnings record. Call the SSA at 1-800-772-6270 Monday through Friday, 7:00 a.m. to 7:00 p.m. Eastern Time and see the SSA's EFW2C, *Specifications for Filing Forms W-2c Electronically*, issued for the tax year involved. (See also chapter 4 for a further discussion on Form W-2 filing and correction requirements.)

In the last few years, employers have come to expect last-minute legislation and even significant court holdings that force retroactive adjustments in current and prior years' taxable wage amounts and that may require Forms W-2c. See Q 12:24 for examples of such events.

Q 12:27   In the context of a statutory merger or other transaction that requires carryover of payroll liabilities to the survivor, must accelerated Forms W-2 be furnished to terminated employees?

Yes, if the employee requests it. The rules for furnishing a Form W-2 to terminated employees apply to employees terminated in the context of statutory mergers (see Qs 4:83 and 12:54).

IRS Notice 2012-9 requires surviving employers to report the aggregate reportable cost of health care coverage by both employers for these employees. [2012-4 I.R.B. 315] However, Notice 2012-9 also provides an exception from reporting the cost of the health care for terminated employees who request early provision of Form W-2 under the acceleration rules. See Q 12:24 above for more on this new reporting requirement.

Q 12:28   In the context of a statutory merger, do the provisions of Forms W-2 that address when an employer goes out of business apply?

No. The provisions that address when an employer goes out of business would not apply in a statutory merger because the surviving corporation is considered to be the same employer as the acquired corporation and the business is considered to continue operations under the survivor employer (see Qs 4:84 and 12:55). This same result would apply in other similar transactions where the survivor is considered to be the same employer as the acquired, such as in § 381 transactions and certain partnership transactions requiring continuity. Some states override the federal continuity application and require that annual or quarterly reconciliations with wage details be submitted early by absorbed companies in a merger context as well as the early provision of Forms W-2 (see Q 12:101).

Q 12:29   In the context of a statutory merger or consolidation, does the Form W-2 electronic filing record contain a field into which the acquired corporation's EIN can be entered when the surviving corporation files Forms W-2 reporting taxes paid by the acquired corporation?

Yes. Per the electronic filing specifications issued by the SSA EFW2, the "Other EIN" field (locations 31-39 of the RE record) can be used in all M&A events in instances where taxes are legally filed under one EIN and Forms W-2 under another EIN. (This field is not the same as the one used for common pay agents or common paymasters (locations 7–25 of the RE record)). Because the other EIN field can only accommodate one EIN, it cannot be used when multiple transactions in a single year involve two or more companies.

FUTA and Form 940 for Statutory Mergers and Consolidations

Note that the matters covered below may also apply in the context of other transactions where payroll liabilities are transferred to an acquirer although reporting for transactions not directly addressed in instructions to Form 940 remain unclear. Neither Rev. Rul. 62-60 nor Form 940 instructions currently address application beyond traditional terms, such as where tax benefits flow to the acquirer under I.R.C. § 381 (see Q 12:9) or where partnership tax laws support continuity between old and new partnerships. (See Qs 12:75–12:79.)

Q 12:30 What are the filing requirements regarding federal unemployment insurance taxes (FUTA) in the context of a statutory merger or consolidation?

The surviving corporation must file one Form 940, Employer's Annual Federal Unemployment (FUTA) Tax Return, for the calendar year in which the merger took place covering the wages paid by both the surviving corporation and the acquired corporation. The acquired corporation is not required to file Form 940.

By virtue of being considered the same employer as the absorbed corporation in the context of a statutory merger or consolidation, the survivor can claim wages paid by the absorbed corporation as paid directly by the survivor for purposes of computing FUTA tax liability on a single Form 940, consolidating wages of both the acquired and surviving corporations paid throughout the year. [Rev. Rul. 62-60, 1962-1 C.B. 186; Form 940 instructions; I.R.C. § 3302(e)]

As will be discussed later in this chapter, the merger provision substantially varies from what is required when a "successor employer" carries over the FUTA wage base from a transferred employee (see Q 12:105). The successor employer's FUTA wages are generally offset by the predecessor's wages if both companies are covered employers. The successor's FUTA liability is lowered, but the successor may not claim credit for the predecessor's state unemployment credits or related installments in its Form 940 unless the predecessor is not required to file a Form 940 and, even then, the credit is only the portion that relates to employees later hired by the successor. FUTA wages paid by the predecessor and related state unemployment credits, as well as any installments, are generally claimed on the predecessor's own Form 940. [I.R.C. § 3302(e); Treas. Reg. §§ 31.3302(e)-1, 31.3306(b)(1)-1(b)] (See chapter 3 for a further discussion of contributions and credits and other FUTA matters.)

Even though the FUTA return is filed on a consolidated basis for a statutory merger or consolidation under the surviving company's EIN, it will be important to remember that unemployment records may still be associated at the state level with the old target company's state tax ID and EIN.

An employer is allowed a maximum credit of 5.4 percent for state unemployment contributions (including contributions made to the District of Columbia, Puerto Rico, and the U.S. Virgin Islands) against the FUTA tax of 6.0 percent unless the state is subject to credit reduction for failing to repay loans from the

Federal Unemployment Fund. All contributions must be made to the state by the due date of the federal Form 940 to receive the full state credit available. If payments are received after the 940 due date, employers are only allowed 90 percent of the state credit otherwise allowable. In a merger, the surviving corporation may claim state credits against FUTA liabilities for timely contributions made by the absorbed corporation. [I.R.C. § 3302(a)(3)]

Every year states certify SUI credits to the IRS for use in validating SUI credit claims on federal Form 940. This state/IRS verification is accomplished through the FUTA Certification Program explained in detail in IRS Publication 4485, *Guide for the Certification of State FUTA Credits*, found at https://www.irs.gov/pub/irs-pdf/p4485.pdf.

Each October, the IRS distributes the FUTA Identification Data file to the states via the IRS Secure Data Transfer System (STD). States are to return their certifications by January 31 of the following year. The IRS file includes information for each employer that claimed a credit or liability on Form 940 for unemployment tax paid to the state, including fields for the state tax ID transmitted when the IRS has the information. States are instructed to certify based on the federal EIN and use the state tax ID only as a research tool. If there is no certification data on the EIN provided, they are told to return the record as a Zero Certification, which is a discrepancy record where a Form 940 reported credits but the state agency reported no taxable wages or payments made to the state. The IRS later returns these discrepancies to the state agency for manual recertification.

On receipt of the states' certification files, the IRS runs them against the federal data to identify discrepancies. The Enterprise Computing Center–Memphis (MEM)and the IRS Cincinnati SBSE Campus sort the data into the following categories for taxpayer follow up: Zero Certification records, Potential Adjustment Registers (known as PARS), and listings requiring a 4010C Letter–Proposed Increase to Tax, or requiring a 4011C Letter–Proposed Decrease to Tax. Potential Adjustment Registers (PARS) are discrepancy records for which an automatic determination regarding a proposed increase or decrease tax adjustment cannot be made. PARS are sent to IRS tax examiners for a manual review and issuance of the appropriate letter. More information on this process is available in Pub. 4485.

Although the IRS has been working to improve the accuracy of this Program, on February 9, 2016, the Treasury Inspector General for Tax Administration (TIGTA) published an audit finding that the IRS needed to have better processes in place to administer its FUTA Certification Program and that the current process failed to ensure the accuracy of many state certifications before use in identifying discrepancy cases. In its audit report, TIGTA found that 94 percent of state agencies submitted data that contained formatting errors in key data fields used to identify FUTA discrepancy cases. [TIGTA Report Reference Number: 2016-40-009 (Feb. 9, 2016)] This report comes as no surprise to many, who have struggled to obtain proper credits for state payments once denied.

A few years ago, Schedule A of Form 940 was modified to no longer require employers to list their state tax IDs. Where more than one state tax ID is used to report credits throughout the year as can be the case in complex M&A transactions, Form 940 credit matching can pose difficult stumbling blocks. See Q 12:32 below for more Form 940 filing assistance.

After the SUTA Dumping rules were enacted, particularly where a substantial number of the new company's employees came from an acquired company with a high unemployment rate, some states refused to follow the federal filing requirements under the survivor's federal EIN. Instead, states required the continued use of the acquired company's old state tax ID originally associated with the acquired's federal EIN. Even though this concern has become less prevalent with the closer workings between federal and state agencies, payroll professionals are still advised to follow up with the state agencies as soon as possible to make sure the correct federal EIN is associated with the state account to avoid loss of FUTA credits for the unemployment taxes paid.

States do not operate in the blind on related federal EINs. The IRS sends a Quarterly Entity Update file to the states the month following the close of each quarter. The file contains data on newly assigned EINs or employers that have changed their name during the previous quarter. This is why it is so critical that the proper processing occur with the IRS as soon as possible where new EINs are needed in a transaction or where there is a company name change. See Qs 12:84–12:87 below for more information on processing new EINs and name changes.

Sometimes, when the state attempts to merge companies' claim histories, the state's records can become muddled, leaving the pre-merger SUI history under the acquired company's tax ID rather than transferring it or, worse, moving the acquirer's records to the acquired's account. For many states this is a manual process and errors happen. When a state takes a different position regarding where the credits are to be posted and which state tax IDs are to be used to file SUI returns or makes errors in postings, credit certifications sent by the state will be out of balance with the federal EIN used to file the consolidated Form 940. Moreover, since states can change their filing predicates retroactively, the employer may not even know at the point of filing the Form 940 that a conflict exists and that the IRS may not be able to validate the employer's SUI credits claimed on the federal Form 940. Where this is the case, the IRS will send letters proposing adjustments.

To respond to IRS letters and resolve any proposed assessment, you will need from each state a written proof of credit (known as a credit statement). To avoid the IRS letters, obtain SUI account transcripts for each EIN where credits are allowed (even where the account should be closed and the EIN no longer used) as soon as you know the agencies have made needed adjustments. From the transcripts, you should see whether proper transfers have occurred and where credits are posted. Work with the agencies to bring the accounts in balance under the proper EINs and be sure to obtain written credit statements, as you may need them.

On June 27, 2014, in a private letter, the IRS contemplated the difficulties in mergers with meeting the terms of the FUTA Certification Program. In the ruling, it was noted that many states allowed combining the accounts of separate employers for state unemployment insurance purposes if the employer entities (1) have common ownership, management, and control and (2) operate in the same line of business. The employer requesting the ruling indicated that most merged employer entities file combined quarterly unemployment tax returns. However, each separate employer retains its unique Federal Employer Identification Number (FEIN) and each employer files its own Form 940, Employer's Annual Federal Unemployment (FUTA) Tax Return, with the IRS. The use of two different reporting methods has created an issue with the FUTA Certification Program, because the certification information provided by the state to the IRS relating to the merged entity does not match the information reported by each separate employer entity to the IRS. In an effort to resolve the mismatch issue, the employer was considering providing a certification to the IRS for each separate employer entity, based on information provided to it by the merged entity regarding the employees and wages of each separate employer entity.

In responding to the employer, the IRS noted that employers may claim credits against their FUTA tax liabilities if their state's unemployment compensation law, and the administration of the state's unemployment compensation program, satisfy the federal requirements, and the employer made timely contributions to the state's fund. Currently, a maximum credit of 5.4 percent (reduced for certain states that did not repay money they borrowed from the federal government to pay unemployment benefits) is allowed against the 6.0 percent FUTA tax if the employer makes all payments to the state by the due date of the return. The IRS affirmed that the FUTA Certification Program is the method IRS uses to verify with the state that the credit an employer claims against FUTA tax on Form 940 actually was timely paid into the states' unemployment funds (not limited to 90 percent for late payment).

As explained in this private letter of general guidance, Treasury Regulation Section 31.3302(a)-3 indicates that each state must, among other things, provide to the IRS "a certificate of the proper officer of each state" showing for the taxpayer: (1) the total amount of contributions required to be paid under the State law with respect to such calendar year (exclusive of penalties and interest) which was actually paid on or before the date the federal return is required to be filed; and (2) the amounts and dates of such required payments (exclusive of penalties and interest) actually paid after the date the federal return is required to be filed. In the letter, the IRS confirmed that if employers report unemployment compensation information to a state on one aggregate form pursuant to state law, but the employers each report unemployment compensation information to the IRS separately for FUTA purposes, the information required by Treasury Regulation section 31.3302(a)-3 must be certified separately for purposes of the FUTA Certification Program and for purposes of obtaining the credit allowed under I.R.C. § 3302(a)(1). This letter was issued as non-binding general guidance, but it certainly explains the IRS's present position regarding the need to obtain separate state certifications to support state FUTA credits. [IRS Office of Chief Counsel, Information Letter No. 2014-0022, June 27, 2014; Treasury Inspector General for Tax Administration, Ref. No: 2016-40-009, Dec. 22, 2015]

Payroll professionals are well advised to seek from states written validations of all of their SUI credits that reflect the making of timely SUI payments for provision to the IRS to support the credits taken on the federal Form 940, particularly for years where M&A activities have occurred. When there is conflict in state records, the conflict will need to be resolved to ensure a clean Form 940 process. It is also wise to request state transcripts of all accounts affected prior to and after the transaction takes place.

See Q 12:32 below for more filing suggestions.

Q 12:31   What should be considered when combining FUTA wages of the acquired corporation and the surviving corporation in the context of a statutory merger or consolidation?

When combining the wages of the surviving corporation and the acquired corporation, do not use the state taxable SUI payroll figures. Many states have higher wage bases than the federal wage base of $7,000, and some redefine some aspects of what is to be included in the wage base so using the SUI payroll figures may result in an over- or understatement of taxable wages on Form 940.

Instructions to Form 940 say "When you figure the payments made to each employee in excess of the FUTA wage base [currently $7,000, but legislation is being considered to increase this amount], you may include the payments that the predecessor made to the employees who continue to work for you only if the predecessor was an employer for FUTA tax purposes resulting in the predecessor being required to file Form 940." Technically, in a merger remember that you are not a "successor employer" and unless you have acquired an entity truly exempt from FUTA, the absorbed employer's wages in the calendar year should always be part of the wage calculation.

Q 12:32   How should the state credit information of the acquired corporation and the surviving corporation be entered on the Form 940?

Technically, wages and credits should be merged between the survivor and the absorbed corporation. However, employers are no longer required to list their state reporting number(s) on Schedule A of Form 940, making it difficult to allow for any reconciliation in the context of merged or consolidated corporations. When an employer registers with each state and provides the state with the federal EIN specific to that employer, the state then assigns the employer a state reporting number unique to that federal EIN. SUI credit information is later provided by the state to the IRS through the FUTA Certification Program based upon the affiliated EIN. See more details in Q 12:30 above. To avoid 4010C proposed increases or 4011C proposed decreases to FUTA taxes, timely inform both the state and the IRS of any statutory merger or consolidation so that EINs and state reporting numbers can be appropriately associated. See the discussion above in Q 12:31 for additional actions you can take.

Mergers do not fall under the "successor employer" rules discussed below, so you should not check Box b, "Successor Employer" on Form 940. For statutory mergers and consolidations, it is recommended that a letter accompany the Form 940 that explains the transaction and provides the names, addresses, EINs, and state reporting numbers of the companies involved as well as individual contact information should there be questions. Where necessary, the letter should list all tax installments by EIN paid by both companies throughout the year so that proper credit of tax payments can be had and, where possible, include state certifications of the credits. See Q 12:30 above. Providing this statement as an attachment may preclude an electronic filing of the Form 940. If electronic filing is required, consider drafting a letter of instruction with this same information to send to the IRS Service Center where the Form 940 is being processed. A separate letter will not be used to process your return; however, once the Service Center receives it, the Service Center will assign a person to oversee the letter, validate your filing records, and respond to you.

Employers should obtain and attach state letters of certification in cases where there may be an excess or unrecognized credit in the return. Some employers request written state credit verifications from state agencies each year that they are involved in an M&A event that may result in the posting of credits of multiple companies to their Form 940. If it is necessary to include a written verification with a Form 940, request the verifications early, as some states are slow to respond to such requests.

As explained in Q 12:30, there is an annual interface between the IRS and state agencies to validate state credits on Form 940; late contributions and filings as well as failures to file are revealed in the process and could result in the loss of some state credit. A surviving employer should investigate the acquired corporation's SUI filing histories to avoid problems with its federal return and to identify when there is potential of loss of SUI credits.

The IRS provides a worksheet for calculating the SUI tax credit if some of the wages paid were excluded from unemployment tax or if any state unemployment taxes were paid late. The worksheet can be found in the Form 940 instructions and can be adapted for use in investigating the acquired company's filing history.

Q 12:33   What are the guidelines regarding crediting to the survivor any FUTA installments made by the absorbed corporation?

The Form 940 instructions are silent on how to transfer the acquired corporation's FUTA quarterly installments, if any, to the survivor's FUTA account. In practice, letters are often attached to the survivor's Form 940 explaining the merger (or other transaction that would allow credit of the acquired's installments) and requesting transfers of the acquired corporation's previous installments.

Special Recordkeeping and Due Diligence Needs in Statutory Mergers and Consolidations

Matters covered in this section may also be of concern in the context of other transactions where payroll liabilities are transferred to an acquirer, such as where tax benefits flow to the acquiring corporation under I.R.C. § 381 (see Q 12:9) or where partnership tax laws support continuity between old and new partnerships (see Qs 12:75–12:79) even though not directly addressed in cited authorities. Seek advice from your tax counsel if there is any doubt about the ramifications of your particular M&A event.

Q 12:34   Must the surviving corporation keep the acquired corporation's previous years' Forms W-4 and other employment tax records related to the acquired corporation's employment history and federal payroll tax filings?

Yes. Because the surviving corporation is the same employer as the acquired corporation, the surviving corporation is responsible for keeping the acquired corporation's employment tax records that relate to all open federal employment tax matters, including Forms W-4, Employee's Withholding Allowance Certificate.

Currently, Forms W-4 and all records relevant to the employment tax filing requirements are required to be kept for four years after the later of the due date for taxes for the return period covering the last return filed (usually you track based on April 15), relying on the form or the date the taxes were actually paid related to that period. [Treas. Reg. § 31.6001-1(e)(2), 31.6001-5(a)(1) to 31.6001-5(a)(17)] Many companies make it a practice to waive certain statutes of limitation in the context of federal corporate audits. Records should be kept for as long as the employer is still open for audit for any period, even beyond the four-year period.

Inherent in the recordkeeping requirement is the concept that the surviving corporation will be accountable for all payroll tax liabilities associated with the acquired corporation. Particular concern arises where there is a prior year error in the FICA or FUTA wage limit on the part of the acquired corporation, or where continuing compensation benefits were improperly accounted for by the acquired corporation. The surviving corporation will be liable for the acquired corporation's prior tax shortfalls and related penalties and interest, as well as for further underwithholding or improper accounting for continued payment of those benefits on its part.

Record maintenance also includes the acquired corporation's EIN; amounts and dates of all wage, annuity, and pension payments; amounts of reported tips; records of allocated tips; fair market value of in-kind wages; names, addresses, Social Security numbers, and occupations of all employees; Forms W-2 and W-2c; employee copies of W-2s and W-2cs returned undeliverable; dates of employment; payment periods and amounts and rate of payment for sick time; dates and amounts of tax deposits; EFTPS acknowledgments; copies of filed

941s and 940s; records of fringe benefits; copies of any requested filing waivers or filing extensions; copies of all agency correspondence; and assigned filing identifications such as IRS transmitter control code (TCC) numbers. [I.R.S. Pub. No. 15; Treas. Reg. §§ 31.6001-1 to 31.6001-5] (See chapter 11 for a further discussion on documents, recordkeeping methodology, and storage time periods.)

The surviving corporation must locate any files that may relate to M&A events prior to the one at issue in which the acquired corporation was involved as liabilities related to those files will also carry over.

Due diligence on the part of the surviving corporation would dictate an early review of all payroll records, early identification of all components of compensation in the payroll process, reviews of all compensation and other benefits plans by professionals, and the early application of risk management assessment in planning for the merger, as well as the early development of a plan for necessary recordkeeping continuance before critical documentation is lost in the merger process (see Q 12:71). Other tasks to considering adding to your checklist include:

- Establish a listing as early as possible of all jurisdictions requiring returns or other filings as far back in time as there are open audit periods, identifying due dates particularly over the transition period of the transaction, and whether efile is required as well as the media and formatting requirements used.

- From the list, gather as many details as possible and look to identify possible exposure points as well as compliance action items, such as coordinating payroll audits currently underway.

- Verify the payroll processing schedules, including tax calendars that show both tax deposit and filing timing as well as method identified.

- Obtain copies of all jurisdiction assessments open and still outstanding and locate historical files on closed matters.

- Obtain copies of all agency settlement and closing audit agreements.

- Establish a listing of all third-party processors involved in the payroll function, e.g., sick pay, severance pay, and nonqualified deferred compensation or stock option services.

- Develop a payroll system configuration so you know how processing works.

- Consider bank and general ledger reconciliations for all open audit years.

- Make sure you have copies of any disaster plans.

- Determine whether the accounts payable areas are properly identifying any fringe benefits or reimbursed expenses that are wages and passing information on to payroll and that such items are being included in payroll processing.

See Qs 12:100–12:113 for other items that need to be evaluated.

Obtaining agency transcripts takes time; however, such transcripts are an important part of this review process. Therefore, the target's federal, state, and local tax transcripts, including liability and deposit transcripts for federal Forms 940, 941, 945, and 1042 and SIT and SUI tax activities, as well as for SUI reserve and rate histories, should be requested for the current and previous three years early on in the process and reconciled against the target's filing activities and ledgers.

Common Pay Agents

Q 12:35   Will a prior appointment of an acquired corporation as a common pay agent under I.R.C. Section 3504 carry over to the surviving corporation in the context of a statutory merger or consolidation?

Possibly. In Private Letter Ruling 9843019 (July 23, 1998), the IRS held that the statutory merger of a common pay agent into a new company would not invalidate the agent appointment as long as the appointee employers remained the same entities after the reorganization under state law. The new surviving corporation, however, was advised to follow procedures outlined in Rev. Proc. 70-6 [1970-1 C.B. 420] to designate an authorized pay agent within the meaning of I.R.C. Section 3504. (See Qs 4:118 and 10:5 for more information on a common pay agent with an approved Form 2678, Employer/Payer Appointment of Agent.) Rev. Proc. 70-6 has now been replaced with Rev. Proc. 2013-39. [2013-52 I.R.B. 830] In addition, T.D. 9649 updated regulations for authorizing an agent using IRS Form 2678. Both the final regulations and the new revenue procedure clarify the rules for agents delegating obligations to reporting agents and subagents, but for the most part they conform the existing rules to the current usage of the relevant IRS forms and schedules.

Under Rev. Proc. 2013-39, an agent would file Form 2678 to revoke an authorization if there is no longer an agency relationship. Examples where revocation is warranted include an employer or agent going out of business, an employer no longer existing due to a merger or acquisition, an employer's being deceased, or an employer appointing another person on Form 2678 to act as its agent to perform the same acts the agent is authorized to perform.

Note that a Schedule R to Form 941 is required to be filed by the common pay agent. See also the instructions to Form 2678. Form 2678 now covers depository taxes reported on Form 945 such as backup and retirement plan withholding.

Federal Successor Employer Rules

The Criteria for Application of the Successor Employer Rules—Social Security and FUTA Wage Base Carryover

Q 12:36   What allows successor employers to carry over the Social Security and FUTA wage bases for transferred employees to avoid a restart of the tax liabilities?

I.R.C. § 3121(a)(1) for FICA and I.R.C. § 3306(b)(1) for FUTA allow an employer that meets the criteria of a "successor employer" to treat any compensation paid to an acquired employee by the predecessor during the calendar year of the transaction but prior to the acquisition as having been paid by the successor employer. Under this authority, the successor carries over the Social Security and FUTA wages of transferred employees to avoid a restart of the related tax liabilities. [Treas. Reg. §§ 31.3121(a)(1)-1(b), 31.3306(b)(1)-1(b)]

Q 12:37   May a successor employer use a predecessor employer's FUTA credits for state unemployment insurance contributions?

Yes, under certain circumstances. An employer that meets the criteria of a "successor employer" claims the credit against FUTA taxes for a predecessor's SUI contributions made in the year of the transaction in periods prior to the transaction as if the employer had been the predecessor. This is only applicable if the predecessor was not a covered employer for the calendar year in which the acquisition occurred—and then only to the extent that the credit related to employees immediately hired by the successor after the transaction. [I.R.C. § 3302(e); Treas. Reg. §§ 31.3301(e)-1(a) to 31.3301(e)-1(d)]

Q 12:38   When may a successor employer carry over a predecessor employer's Social Security and FUTA wages of acquired employees and related SUI credits?

A successor employer is defined as an employer that received a unit of another employer's trade or business or all or most of the property used in the trade or business of another employer. To qualify to carry over a predecessor's Social Security and FUTA wages of acquired employees, the successor employer must employ one or more individuals (the acquired employees) who were employed by the previous employer immediately after the acquisition. Employees being transferred need to be common law employees of the predecessor and be hired as common law employees of the successor. In addition, pursuant to these requirements, wages need to be paid to the acquired employees during the calendar year in which the acquisition occurs, both after and prior to the acquisition. [Treas. Reg. §§ 31.3121(a)(1)-1(b), 31.3306(b)(1)-1(b)]

See Q 12:49 below regarding the electing successor employer's additional responsibilities beginning in 2013 to carry over and track Medicare wages paid by the predecessor to enable the successor to identify the point at which paid compensation exceeds the annual $200,000 threshold so that the successor employer may begin withholding the 0.9 percent Additional Medicare Tax.

For FUTA purposes, a successor employer is instructed to check box b on Form 940 indicating successor employer status only if the employer is a successor employer as defined above and:

- Reporting wages paid before the employer acquired the business by a predecessor who was required to file a Form 940 because the predecessor was an employer for FUTA tax purposes, or

- Claiming a special credit for state unemployment tax paid before the employer acquired the business by a predecessor who was not required to file a Form 940 because the predecessor was not an employer for FUTA tax purposes.

Provisions for successor employers substantially vary from those that apply in the context of a statutory merger or consolidation. Even though a successor employer's FUTA wages are offset by the predecessor's wages, lowering the successor employer's FUTA liability, FUTA wages paid by the predecessor employer and related state unemployment credits are not combined on the acquirer's Form 940. Instead, the predecessor's wages and state credits are claimed on the predecessor's own Form 940. Contrast this to what is required for a statutory merger or consolidation, where FUTA wages paid by the acquired company and the surviving company are reported on the survivor's Form 940 and all state unemployment credits from payments made by both companies are also covered on the surviving company's Form 940. The acquired corporation does not file a 940 (see Q 12:30).

Generally, both the successor and the predecessor must be FUTA-covered employers under I.R.C. § 3306(a) for SUI contribution credits to apply. [Treas. Reg. § 31.3306(b)(1)-1(b)(1); Instructions to Form 940] However, in a successor employer setting, a special exception allows carryover of SUI contribution credits to a covered successor even if the predecessor was not considered a FUTA-covered employer and was not required to file a Form 940 for the calendar year in which the acquisition took place. This could happen if the predecessor did not have any employees for any portion of any day in 20 different calendar weeks in the current or preceding year, possible in an early year acquisition where the acquired entity ceases business after the acquisition or where the company was newly formed for the transaction. The 20 weeks need not be consecutive (see Q 3:7). [I.R.C. § 3306(a)(1); Treas. Reg. § 31.3306(a)-1]

When the exception applies, successors get credit for what they would have been entitled to if the predecessor were covered but only for those employees who worked for both companies. If the noncovered predecessor paid any wages to employees who were not also employed by the successor, the credit is limited to only the portion that applies to the employees that were hired by the successor. [I.R.C. § 3302(e); Treas. Reg. § 31.3302(e)-1; Rev. Rul. 54-313, 1954-2 C.B. 371; and Instructions to Form 940] (See chapter 3 and Qs 3:32 and 3:33 for a further discussion of SUI contributions and credits and other FUTA matters. See chapter 2 and Qs 2:13–2:49 for a further discussion of FICA.)

Apart from this special exception, instructions to Form 940 say "When you figure the payments made to each employee in excess of the FUTA wage base [currently $7,000, but proposed legislation would increase this amount], you may include the payments that the predecessor made to the employees who continue to work for you only if the predecessor was an employer for FUTA tax purposes resulting in the predecessor being required to file Form 940."

In figuring the payments made to each employee in excess of $7,000, instructions to Form 940 illustrate with the following example: During the calendar year, the predecessor employer paid $5,000 to Employee A. You acquired the predecessor's business. After the acquisition, you employed Employee A and paid Employee A an additional $3,000 in wages. None of the amounts paid to Employee A were payments exempt from FUTA tax.

$ 5,000 Wages paid by predecessor employer

+ 3,000 Wages paid by you

$ 8,000 Total payments to Employee A; include this amount in line 3 of Form 940.

$ 8,000 Total payments to Employee A

− 7,000 FUTA wage base

$ 1,000 Payments made to Employee A in excess of $7,000.

$ 1,000 Payments made to Employee A in excess of $7,000

+ 5,000 Taxable FUTA wages paid by predecessor employer

$ 6,000 You would include this amount on line 5 of Form 940.

Q 12:39　Are any employers expressly excluded from the successor employer rules?

Yes, the following are excluded:

- Employers in statutory mergers and consolidations fall under separate rules (see Qs 12:4–12:5) and are not considered successor employers for these purposes. Keep in mind that this excluded category may be broader than statutory mergers and consolidations that are directly addressed by the payroll authorities. Through substantive workings of the tax laws where a survivor is required to carry over the tax attributes of the acquired such as in the application of I.R.C. § 381 (see Qs 12:6– 12:9) or where partnership tax laws support continuity between old and new partnerships (see Qs 12:75–12:81), the successor employer elections may not apply.

- Employers that are exempt from FICA or FUTA, such as certain I.R.C. § 501(c)(3) organizations, churches and religious organizations, and federal, state, and local governments, as well as related agencies not allowed to elect or that do not elect coverage are excluded from the carryover rules. (See Qs 2:115–2:116 for exempt FICA employers and exempt services and

Q 3:8 for exempt FUTA employers; see Q 12:83 regarding the handling of waivers of FICA exemptions in an M&A event.)

For FUTA wage carryover, both successor and predecessor employers must be covered under the FUTA rules. [Treas. Reg. § 31.3306(b)(1)-1(b)] If either or both are not covered, the rules do not apply unless the special exception discussed in Q 12:38 above applies.

- Professional employer organizations (PEOs) that are considered co-employers (common law employers) as opposed to statutory employers (defined under I.R.C. § 3504) are not covered by these rules. But, see the discussion below on a new law establishing a category of PEOs that can be successor employers.

"Certified" PEOs as successor employers. The tax provision extender bill, Law 2014, HR 5771, was expanded to include a Division B with additional provisions unrelated to the extenders. [Section 206 of Title II, Division B, HR 5771] In new I.R.C. § 3511, created by this new law, is a new regulatory regime established for a "Certified Professional Employer Organization" that meets specific requirements:

1. Demonstrates that the PEO (and any owner, officer, and other persons as may be specified in regulations) meets requirements with respect to tax status, background, experience, business location, and annual financial audits,

2. Agrees that it will satisfy new requirements for a bond and independent financial review,

3. Agrees that it will satisfy certain reporting obligations,

4. Computes its taxable income using an accrual method of accounting unless the Secretary approves another method,

5. Agrees to verify on a periodic basis that it continues to meet the requirements of this subsection,

6. Agrees to notify the Secretary in writing within such time as the Secretary may prescribe of any change that materially affects the continuing accuracy of any agreement or information that was previously made or provided under this subsection, and

7. Pays an annual fee.

PEOs meeting these criteria will be treated as the employer (and no other person shall be treated as the employer) of any work site employee performing services for any customer of such organization, but only with respect to remuneration remitted by the qualified organization to a work site employee. A certified professional employer organization entering into a service contract with a customer with respect to a work site employee will be treated as a successor employer and the customer will be treated as a predecessor employer during the term of the service contract.

Since the enactment, the IRS has been working to determine the procedures and information system changes necessary to implement the new law.

See https://www.irs.gov/Businesses/Small-Businesses-&-Self-Employed/Voluntary-Certification-Program-for-Professional-Employer-Organizations.

Absent meeting this new criteria, caution is warranted. Employee leasing firms and other PEOs considered co-employers under I.R.C. § 3504 rather than statutory employers under I.R.C. § 3401(d)(1) are treated as having separate wage bases and are generally not considered to have acquired assets of the employer in the transition of the employees over to the leasing firm. [Field Serv. Adv. 200017041 (Mar. 3, 2000), and Field Serv. Adv. 200023006 (Feb. 2, 2000), considering an employee leasing company as a co-employer/common-law employer and disallowing FICA and FUTA carryover; but see United States v. Total Employment Co., 2004-1 U.S. Tax Ct. (CCH) § 50,177 (Feb. 12, 2004), holding that the leasing company was a statutory employer under I.R.C. § 3504, not a co-employer, but subject of the case was bankruptcy and accountability for wage withholding and not the application of the successor employer rules] Some states impose different rules for SUI purposes on PEOs and define them very broadly. In these cases, the federal application may vary from who is actually given the SUI wage credit at the state level. Some examples include Alaska [http://www.labor.state.ak.us/estax/forms/UI_Tax_Notice.pdf], Colorado [HB 1312, L. 2007], Montana [HB 72, L. 2007], New York [NY Labor Law § 923], North Dakota [SB 2036, L. 2007], and State of Washington [SB 5373, L. 2007].

Q 12:40 Will the method of acquisition of the predecessor's property be material?

Generally, no. The method of acquisition by an employer of another employer's property is immaterial. These rules differ from the ones that apply to statutory mergers.

For purposes of the successor employer rules, the acquisition can occur through a purchase or by any other transaction whereby substantially all the property either used in a trade or business of a predecessor or used in a separate unit of a trade or business of a predecessor is acquired by the successor. [Treas. Reg. §§ 31.3121(a)(1)-1(b)(3), 31.3306(b)(1)-1(b)(3)]

In Revenue Ruling 72-269, 1972-1 C.B. 313, the IRS concluded that an employer met the requirement to acquire substantially all the assets in a separate unit of a trade or business even though the employer merely gained the use of the property that was used by the previous employer in the essential operation of the facility. In this published ruling, it is important to note that the IRS thought it was immaterial that the successor did not acquire an ownership interest in the property. The test can be interpreted broadly to include mostly any transfer of property as long as the successor acquires use of the property that was used by the predecessor in the essential operation. For similar holdings, see Revenue Ruling 68-105, 1968-1 C.B. 418 and IRS Letter Ruling 201611007 dated (Mar. 24, 2016). The letter ruling is directed only to the taxpayer requesting it and may not be used or cited as precedent, but is a recent example of the IRS relying on the broad application of this test.

In certain stock purchases, an acquirer may make a tax election to treat the transaction as an asset purchase. Currently, there are two forms of such elections I.R.C. § 338. Section 338(g) offers an election that applies unilaterally on the part of the acquirer and under § 338(h)(10) an election is available if the target corporation is a subsidiary in a consolidated group and requires joint approval of both the acquirer and shareholders. The better-known election falls under I.R.C. § 338(h)(10), but in either case, the end result is that the acquirer may elect to treat an initial purchase of stock as an asset purchase. When a § 338 election has been made, questions arise as to whether the payroll treatment might fall under the successor employer rules, providing for another election to either consolidate certain payroll tax liabilities or choose to leave them separated between the two companies. [Treas. Reg. § 1.338(h)(10)-1; T.D. 9271, 2006-33 I.R.B. 224]

To date, payroll treatment in the context of this election is unclear. Generally, in § 338 elections, tax attributes that are not used by the end of the tax year do not carry over to the acquirer. And, more importantly, the predecessor's tax basis in the assets do not carry over to the acquirer. In a § 338(h)(10) election, in some cases certain tax attributes may end up with a corporate shareholder. In this regard, the transactions are unlike statutory mergers or consolidations, or other tax free reorganizations and in structure may fit better under the successor employer rules the same as other asset purchases.

In final regulations issued under I.R.C. § 338(h)(10), the IRS has agreed to allow a § 338(h)(10) election where acquisition of stock, viewed independently, constitutes a qualified stock purchase and, after the stock acquisition, the taxpayer merges or liquidates into another entity (or another member of the affiliated group that includes the taxpayer), whether or not under relevant provisions of law, including the step transaction doctrine, the acquisition of stock and the merger or liquidation qualify as a reorganization described in I.R.C. § 368(a). So, for example, if this election is made on the first leg of a reverse triangular merger where a subsidiary of the acquiring corporation merges into the target, followed by an upstream merger of the resulting company into the acquirer, the IRS has agreed not to challenge the asset election. Will making this election result in successor employer payroll treatment instead of treatment under the statutory merger requirements? Possibly, but the answer is unclear. [Treas. Reg. § 1.338(h)(10)-1(c)(2); Rev. Rul. 2001-46, 2001-2 C.B. 321]

A similar election to treat a transaction as an asset purchase is available under I.R.C. § 336(e). In final regulations, the IRS indicated that it would be appropriate in an I.R.C. § 336(e) election to substitute the application of current guidance under I.R.C. § 338(h)(10). [T.D. 9619, 2013-24 I.R.B. 1212] Under I.R.C. § 336(e), taxpayers may elect to treat the sale, exchange, or distribution of at least 80 percent of a target corporation's stock (a qualified stock disposition) as a deemed disposition of the target corporation's underlying assets. For an I.R.C. § 336(e) election, the payroll result is as unclear as in the case of a § 338(h)(10) election.

Both § 338 and § 336(e) elections are intended to give relief from potential multiple taxation of the same economic gain that can result when a transfer of appreciated corporate stock is taxed without providing a corresponding step up in the basis of the assets of the corporation. Whether this treatment would carry through to payroll, converting a stock transaction (where the resulting company would be treated as the same employer and all payroll tax liabilities from the acquired company would carry over to the resulting company) or a statutory merger (requiring similar compliance responsibilities) into an asset deal that would allow the successor employer election is an uncertainty.

Q 12:41   Are there limits on what is considered a unit of a trade or business for purposes of the successor employer tests?

Yes. There is a limit on a separate unit acquisition that the property be substantially all the property used in the performance of an essential operation of the trade or business or used in a relatively self-sustaining entity that forms part of the trade or business. [Treas. Reg. §§ 31.3121(a)(1)-1(b)(4), 31.3306(b)(1)-1(b)(4)]

Q 12:42   Does it matter whether the predecessor dissolves after the transaction?

No. As long as the successor employer tests have been met it does not matter whether the predecessor ceases business, dissolves, or remains dormant. [Rev. Rul. 55-585, 1955-2 C.B. 395]

Q 12:43   What transactions are covered by the successor employer rules?

Transactions covered by the successor employer rules are those in which the contributions of property meet the specifics of the successor employer test described in Q 12:38, to name a few:

- Direct asset purchases;
- I.R.C. § 351 contributions of assets to a new or already existing corporation in exchange for stock in the corporation;
- Property transferred to a partnership for an interest in the partnership, including limited liability companies (LLCs) when treated as partnerships for tax purposes; and
- Partnership formations, including formations of limited liability companies (LLCs) when treated as partnerships for tax purposes, through the contributions of property.

Note. See comments in Q 12:40 on unclear payroll treatment in cases of I.R.C. § 338(h)(10) and § 336(e) elections to treat stock purchases as asset acquisitions that are intended to give relief from a potential multiple taxation of the same economic gain that can result when a transfer of appreciated corporate stock is taxed without providing a corresponding step up in the basis of the assets of the corporation. Whether this treatment would carry through to payroll, converting a stock transaction or a statutory merger, where the resulting company would assume all payroll tax liabilities of the acquired company, into an asset deal that would allow the successor employer election is possible, but such treatment is uncertain.

Note. A multi-member LLC can be either a partnership or a corporation, including an S corporation. To be treated as a subchapter C corporation, an LLC has to file a Form 8832, Entity Classification Election, and elect to be taxed as a corporation. If qualified, an LLC may also choose to be an S corporation by filing Form 2553, Election by a Small Business Corporation (under I.R.C. § 1362). A multi-member LLC that does not elect to be treated as a corporation will be classified by the IRS as a partnership. Once electing corporate status, reorganization provisions of I.R.C. § 368 will apply the same as to other corporations.

A single member LLC (SMLLC) can be either a corporation or a single member "disregarded entity." To be treated as a corporation, the SMLLC has to file the Form 8832 and elect to be classified as a C corporation or file Form 2553 and elect to be treated as an S corporation. Once electing corporate status, reorganization provisions of I.R.C. § 368 will apply the same as to other corporations.

An SMLLC that does not elect to be a corporation will be classified by the IRS as a disregarded entity, which is taxed the same as a "doing business as" or DBA of a sole proprietor or as a division of its entity parent for federal income taxes.

It is only those LLCs that are treated as partnerships or elect to be treated as corporations for tax purposes under the rules above that will be clearly covered when involved in one of the above listed transactions. See the discussions on partnerships and disregarded entities at Qs 12:75–12:81 below.

For purposes of these provisions, a restructuring of an S Corporation may fall under the reorganization rules of I.R.C. § 368 the same as any corporation that is restructuring. [Priv. Ltr. Rul. 201115016 (Jan. 5, 2011)]

Q 12:44   **If employees worked for multiple related predecessor employers during the year at different times and all of the predecessors were acquired by a successor in a transaction that otherwise satisfied the successor employer rules, can all of the wages paid for the time worked in the different related predecessors be counted for purposes of the rollover?**

No. Only the wages paid by the company for which the employees immediately worked prior to the transaction may be counted for purposes of the wage limitations. [Rev. Rul. 56-678, 1956-2 C.B. 682] A successor may receive credit for wages paid to an employee by a predecessor only if immediately prior to the acquisition the employee was employed by the predecessor in the trade or business that was acquired by the successor and if immediately after the acquisition such employee is employed by the successor in the trade or business (whether or not in the same trade or business where the acquired property is used). [Treas. Reg. §§ 31.3121(a)(1)-1(b)(5), 31.3306(b)(1)-1(b)(5)]

Transactions Involving Common Paymasters and Common Pay Agents

Q 12:45　If employees worked for related predecessor employers during the year and one of the predecessors was a common paymaster for the period the employees worked, would wages paid in the concurrent employment period be counted for purposes of the rollover?

Yes. If the concurrent employment (dual employment) rules under I.R.C. § 3121(s) were met and the common paymaster was one of the predecessors, all the wages related to the concurrent employment would be part of the successor employer's rollover from the predecessor common paymaster. [Rev. Rul. 56-678, 1956-2 C.B. 682]

Q 12:46　When employees worked for several related employers at different times, but were all paid by a common pay agent appointed by each employer under a Form 2678, Employer/Payer Appointment of Agent, would the wages of the different employers paid by the pay agent be counted for purposes of wage rollover to a later successor acquiring the pay agent?

No. Only the wages paid by the company for which the employees worked immediately prior to the transaction may be counted for purposes of the wage limitations. An employer may designate an agent under I.R.C. § 3504 to withhold, report, and pay federal employment taxes. However, all provisions of law applicable with respect to employers remain applicable to the employer. [I.R.C. § 3504] Treas. Reg. § 31.3504-1(a) says that "if the agent is authorized by the Internal Revenue Service to perform such acts, all provisions of law (including penalties) and of the regulations applicable to an employer with respect to such acts shall be applicable to the agent. However, each employer for whom the agent acts shall remain subject to all provisions of law (including penalties) and of the regulations applicable to an employer with respect to such acts." As a result, the successor employer rules should apply directly to employers and not to their common pay agents. In this regard, the pay agent is an employer of its own employees and as such, it would be a predecessor when its employees are transferred to a successor, but it would not be a predecessor of employees of other employers.

Rev. Proc. 70-6 has now been replaced with Rev. Proc. 2013-39 [2013-52 I.R.B. 830], and T.D. 9649 (Dec. 11, 2013) updated regulations and procedures for authorizing an agent using IRS Form 2678. Both final regulations and the new revenue procedure clarify the rules for agents delegating obligations to reporting agents and subagents, but for the most part, they conform the existing rules to the current usage of the relevant IRS forms and schedules.

If the successor employer provisions were applied directly to the employers, ignoring the agent, the result would be the same as in Q 12:44. See Private Letter Ruling 9853048 (Oct. 2, 1998), which applied the fundamentals of the alternate procedure in Rev. Proc. 96-60 [1996-2 C.B. 399] in an I.R.C. § 355 reorganization to the actual employees of the agent as a predecessor, but not to employees of other employers in the corporate group. In the ruling, the taxpayer represented that the successor would become a newly authorized pay agent for the other corporations in the group. Revenue Procedure 2004-53 [2004-34 I.R.B. 320] superseded Revenue Procedure 96-60 [1996-2 C.B. 399]. Revenue Procedure 96-60 was relied on for several years as the authority for the special filing instructions for successor employers. In the context of this ruling, what was relied upon in Revenue Procedure 96-60 was not changed by Revenue Procedure 2004-53 and still has bearing to these facts.

Note that a Schedule R to Form 941 is required to be filed by common pay agents and completion of this schedule requires separate reporting of each employer's liabilities contained in the aggregate amounts on the Form 941. See also instructions to Form 2678. Form 2678 now covers depository taxes reported on Form 945 such as backup and retirement plan withholding.

Federal Income and FICA Tax Compliance under the Successor Employer Rules

Q 12:47 Who is a successor employer for filing purposes and what difference will being a successor employer make?

When the employer acquires substantially all the property used in a trade or business of another employer (predecessor) or used in a separate unit of a trade or business of a predecessor, and, in connection with or immediately after the acquisition (but in the same calendar year), employs individuals who were employed in the trade or business of the predecessor immediately prior to the acquisition, the employer will qualify as a successor employer. [Rev. Proc. 2004-53, 2004-34 I.R.B. 320]

Being a successor employer will make a difference in the preparation and filing of Forms 941, W-2, and W-3. Revenue Procedure 2004-53 [2004-34 I.R.B. 320] and the instructions to Schedule D of Form 941 address the employment tax filing options available to a successor employer. Revenue Procedure 2004-53 supersedes Revenue Procedure 96-60 [1996-2 C.B. 399], which was relied on for several years as the authority for the special filing instructions for successor employers. Revenue Procedure 2004-53 covers rules for filing Forms 941, W-2, W-3, and W-4 and contains the procedures for using Schedule D (Form 941). Many employers believe that buying assets of a target as opposed to acquiring its stock or entering into a structural reorganization, such as a merger, frees them from being liable for a predecessor's federal payroll tax liabilities. This is not entirely true.

The recent Tax Court opinion in the case of *TFT Galveston Portfolio, Ltd.*, filed February 26, 2015, illustrates the way successor in interest liability attaches in a case involving federal employment taxes where the successor has acquired the assets of a predecessor. I.R.C. § 6901 sets a procedure allowing the IRS to collect unpaid taxes owed by a property transferor from the party who receives the property. Just because the tax laws do not support automatic transfer of liability does not mean that the IRS is without tools to collect payroll taxes gone unpaid by a predecessor when a successor acquires its assets. *TFT Galveston Portfolio* dealt with liabilities related to misclassified employees that should have been treated as employees by the predecessors.

Even though a federal tax case, in dispute was whether the petitioner was in fact a successor in interest since under Texas law the petitioner did not assume the predecessor's liabilities and would not have seen a successor in interest. In this context, the IRS asserted that the court should establish a federal standard of successor in interest under federal common law and not look to Texas law. The Tax Court declined to do so. Because TFT Galveston Portfolio and its predecessors were all organized in Texas, the Tax Court chose to look to Texas law to determine whether TFT Galveston Portfolio was a successor in interest. Under Texas law "a person acquiring property may not be held responsible or liable for a liability or obligation of the transferring domestic entity that was not expressly assumed by the person."

There are many ways that states address successor liability. See Q 12:93 below for more on state successor liabilities. Texas has one way, and there are fundamentally three other ways by which state law may establish successors in interest: (1) when the transaction amounts to a de facto merger; (2) when the successor is a mere continuation of the seller company; and (3) when the transaction is entered into fraudulently to escape liability. State laws vary on approach. Looking to Texas law that applied in this case, since TFT Galveston Portfolio did not expressly assume the liabilities of the predecessors, it was not a successor in interest to the predecessor employers. The Tax Court said that their decision against applying federal successor standards and holding that TFT Galveston Portfolio was not a successor in interest did not by itself thwart the IRS's crucial function of collecting federal employment taxes. Using the successor in interest liability is only one procedure by which the IRS may collect taxes from a successor who received assets from a taxpayer who owed the taxes. The IRS conceded that they could have potentially applied transferee liability against the petitioner under I.R.C. § 6901 by issuing Notices of Determination Concerning Worker Classification to the predecessors, assessing the resulting liabilities, and then issuing a Notice of Transferee Liability to TFT Galveston Portfolio. Additionally, the IRS could have potentially attempted to collect directly from one of the predecessor's officers as a "responsible person" under I.R.C. § 6672. [TFT Galveston Portfolio, Ltd., as successor in interest for TFT #2, Ltd., et al. v. Commissioner, 144 T.C. 7 (2015)]

Q 12:48   What options are available to successor employers?

There are two options available for successors: (1) the standard procedure and (2) the alternate procedure.

The standard procedure applies when employees are transferred from one employer to another (even if the successor employer tests are not met) as long as the transfer is not pursuant to a statutory merger or consolidation. The predecessor performs all reporting duties for compensation it paid to the employees.

The alternate procedure applies if the successor employer tests are met as described in Q 12:49 below and both predecessor and successor agree to use the alternate procedure. The predecessor does not have to furnish Forms W-2 to any employees who are employed in the same calendar year by the successor. Where the alternative procedure is elected, the successor must provide the acquired employees with Forms W-2 that include all wages earned in the reporting year, including the wages paid by the predecessor. [Rev. Proc. 2004-53, 2004-34 I.R.B. 320]

Q 12:49   Are "successor employers" that elect to carryover Social Security wages required to consolidate Forms W-2 under the alternate procedure?

Not necessarily. Pursuant to Section 1.01 of Revenue Procedure 2004-53 [2004-34 I.R.B. 320], a successor employer is defined as an employer that received a unit of another employer's trade or business or all or most of the property used in the trade or business of another employer. To qualify, the successor employer must employ one or more individuals who were employed by the previous employer immediately after the acquisition. Pursuant to these requirements, wages need to be paid to the transferred employees during the calendar year in which the acquisition occurs, both after and prior to the acquisition. This is the very same definition as provided in Treas. Reg. § 31.3121(a)(1)-1(b), which defines who is allowed to carryover the Social Security wage base; however, the procedure does not dictate that the filing election be made once the carryover election has been made.

Using the same successor employer criteria as in the regulations ensures that the alternative filing options are only granted to successor employers that can carry over the Social Security wage limits of the acquired employees. However, there is no mandate that the successor employer use the alternative filing option when that successor employer carries over an acquired employee's Social Security wage base under the FICA regulations. Instead, Section 5.04 of Revenue Procedure 2004-53 [Rev. Proc. 96-60, § 5.04, 1996-2 C.B. 399], which specifically addresses the successor employer's alternative filing options, tells the reader to see Treasury Regulations § 31.3121(a)(1)-1 for separate instructions regarding the annual wage limitations. (The cross-reference seems to indicate that the workings of the FICA regulations are independent of the choices on filing Forms W-2 in the Revenue Procedure.)

Revenue Procedure 2004-53 grants successor employers more leeway in complying during a transitional period—unlike during a statutory merger, which has mandates. Although it would make sense when a successor employer carries over Social Security and FUTA wage limits of an acquired employee, that the wages paid by both the predecessor and the successor would be consolidated by the successor into a single Form W-2, there are times when consolidation is difficult to accomplish. The ability to select W-2 consolidation or not and still be able to carry over the Social Security wage limits is critically important to successor employers that can administer the carryover of that wage base, but, due to system constraints, cannot merge payroll databases to create a single Form W-2. (See the concern raised in Q 12:53 regarding the SSA's edit functions on W-2 submissions where carryover wage bases are applied but consolidated W-2s are not filed.)

Successor employers will need to consider their responsibilities to meet compliance under the health care reform provisions before electing to carry over Social Security thresholds.

Generally, Medicare wages have no limiting threshold. However, starting in 2013, an additional 0.9 percent Medicare withholding is required for high earners on compensation amounts that exceed $200,000. All compensation that is generally subject to Medicare withholding is subject to the additional 0.9 percent withholding if compensation is paid to an employee in excess of $200,000 for the calendar year. For electing successor employers, it will now be critical to also earmark and carryover Medicare wages paid by the predecessor to enable tracking of the point where paid compensation exceeds the $200,000 threshold for the year requiring the additional withholding. This task needs to be added to the payroll interface being built for handling the transaction by electing employers. The IRS has made clear the requirement to carry over wage bases to meet this responsibility by an electing successor employer and may require the carryover of these wages if any Social Security wages are also elected to be carried over even if the employer does not elect to consolidate wages for W-2 reporting. This reporting requirement might be difficult for some to meet and may even thwart some successors from electing to carryover the Social Security wage base altogether. Assuming liabilities for correctly withholding this tax is a serious consideration.

Wages subject to this new withholding requirement may be paid by third parties under arrangements with the target company. So those parties serving the predecessor's plans must be located and arrangements made to coordinate the aggregation of compensation amounts as part of the payroll tasks in the transaction.

For example, sick pay paid by an employer and by the third party needs to be aggregated to determine whether the $200,000 withholding threshold has been met. The same rules that currently assign responsibility for sick pay reporting and payment of Medicare tax based on which party is treated as the employer (i.e., the employer, the employer's agent, or a third party that is not the employer's agent) apply also to the Additional Medicare Tax. For more information on sick pay, see Publication 15-A, Employer's Supplemental Tax Guide, and Notice 2015-6, 2015-5 I.R.B. 412. For the rules on the aggregation of sick pay for the 0.9 percent Additional Medicare withholding, see FAQ #45 at http://www.irs.gov/Businesses/Small-Businesses-&-Self-Employed/Questions-and-Answers-for-the-Additional-Medicare-Tax#!.

However, FAQ #50 found on the same IRS website gives a different result for agents appointed on a Form 2678, Employer/Payer Appointment of Agent: "If an agent pays wages to an employee on behalf of an employer (under an approved Form 2678), then, for purposes of determining whether wages are paid in excess of the $200,000 withholding threshold, the agent is not required to combine the wages it pays with wages paid to that same employee: 1) directly by the employer, 2) by the same agent on behalf of a different employer, or 3) by another agent on behalf of the same employer. Wages paid on behalf of an employer by an agent appointed on an approved Form 2678 are not combined with these other wages in determining whether to withhold the Additional Medicare Tax." So under this FAQ, wages paid by the target's payroll agent appointed on a Form 2678 will not need to be located and aggregated with other wages.

See Q 12:60 for W-2 related considerations.

Standard Procedure

Standard Rules for Form 941

Q 12:50 What are a successor's and a predecessor's responsibilities regarding Form 941?

A predecessor employer that sells or transfers its business is required to separately file Form 941 for the quarter in which the transfer occurs, reporting only wages that it paid and taxes related to those wages. The successor is also required to separately file Form 941 reporting only the wages that it paid and taxes related to those wages. The instructions for Form 941 provide that changing from one form of business to another, such as from a sole proprietorship to a partnership or corporation, also constitutes a transfer of business. If a transfer occurs, the employer may need a new EIN. When a transfer occurs, the employer must attach a statement to its return that shows the new owner's name or the new name of the business, the type of new business structure (e.g., corporation, partnership, or sole proprietorship), the kind of change that occurred (such as a sale or transfer), the date of the change, and the name of the person keeping the payroll records and the address where the records will be kept. [Rev. Proc. 2004-53, 2004-34 I.R.B. 320; Form 941 instructions, Treas. Reg. § 31.6011(a)-7]

All employers that withhold income tax on wages or that must pay Social Security or Medicare taxes are required to file quarterly Forms 941; successors and predecessors are no different in this regard. Once an employer files a Form 941, the employer must continue to file it for each quarter thereafter, even if there are no taxes to report. [I.R.C. § 6011(a); Treas. Reg. §§ 31.6011(a)-4, 31.6011(a)-5] There is an exception for seasonal employers when they regularly have no liability because they pay no wages. [Treas. Reg. § 31.6011(a)-10; Form 941 instructions] (See chapter 4 for more specific rules on employer accountabilities in filing Forms 941.)

Q 12:51   If the predecessor goes out of business or stops paying wages after the transaction, will its responsibilities regarding Form 941 change?

Yes. If the predecessor goes out of business or stops paying wages, the predecessor is required to file a final Form 941. The box on Line 15 of Form 941 needs to be checked and the date the final wages were paid must be entered. Form 941 instructs employers going out of business to attach a statement to the final return showing the name of the person keeping payroll records and their location. [Treas. Reg. § 31.6011(a)-6; Rev. Proc. 2004-53, 2004-34 I.R.B. 320; Form 941 instructions] (See Q 12:55 for special Form W-2 filing requirements.)

Filing Forms W-2 under the Standard Procedure

Q 12:52   What are the general rules for successors and predecessors to file Forms W-2?

If the predecessor does not terminate its business, the predecessor and the successor must separately file their Forms W-2 with the SSA and furnish to their employees Forms W-2 reflecting wages each has respectively paid during the year of the acquisition pursuant to the general Form W-2 filing requirements. [Rev. Proc. 2004-53, 2004-34 I.R.B. 320; I.R.C. § 6051(a); Treas. Reg. §§ 31.6051-1(a), 31.6051-2] (See Qs 4:77–4:92 for a detailed discussion of Form W-2 filing requirements.)

IRS Notice 2012-9 requires successor and predecessor employers that do not elect the alternative method to each report their own employer-sponsored group health plan coverage on their respective W-2s. [2012-4 I.R.B. 315] However, the Notice provides an exception from this reporting provision for terminated employees who request early provision of Form W-2 under the acceleration rules. This informational reporting is required under I.R.C. § 6051(a)(14), enacted as part of the Patient Protection and Affordable Care Act of 2010 (the Affordable Care Act). [Pub. L. No. 111-148] However, the reporting is optional for employers with fewer than 250 employees until the IRS issues future guidance.

Similarly, each employer will need to include the wages subject to the Additional Medicare Tax as a subset of Medicare wages (the excess over $200,000) and related withholding in Lines 5 and 6 along with the general Medicare wages and withholding.

Q 12:53 Are there any special concerns if a successor carries over Social Security wages, but does not elect the alternative procedure or file consolidated W-2s?

Possibly. If a successor carries over FICA wages paid by a predecessor to avoid a restart of the Social Security wage limit for the transferred employees, but does not elect to file consolidated Forms W-2, successors will file W-2s with Social Security wages and related withholdings reported at lower amounts than would otherwise be expected if the transferred employees were treated as new hires. Even though the employer is not required to consolidate Forms W-2 when such an election is made to carry over FICA wage limits, in previous years safely navigating under the prior SSA edit programs used to review electronically filed W-2s proved problematic. The older SSA edit programs checked the total Medicare wages reported as paid in Box 5 of the W-2 and if equal to or more than the Social Security wage threshold for the year would have then validated whether Box 3 reported the full threshold for the year as Social Security wages. If not, the SSA edit program assumed an error in the W-2 report. The new SSA tests are no longer as specific.

Generally, Medicare wages have no wage base limit. However, an additional 0.9 percent Medicare tax withholding is required for high earners on compensation amounts that exceed $200,000. All compensation that is generally subject to Medicare withholding is subject to the additional 0.9 percent withholding if compensation is paid to an employee in excess of $200,000 for the calendar year. For electing successor employers, it will now be critical to also earmark and carryover Medicare wages paid by the predecessor to enable tracking of the point where paid compensation exceeds the $200,000 threshold for the year requiring the additional withholding. The IRS has made clear the requirement to carry over wage bases to meet this responsibility and may require the carryover of these wages if any Social Security wages are also elected to be carried over even if the employer does not elect to consolidate wages for W-2 reporting. For more information, see http://www.irs.gov/Businesses/Small-Businesses-&-Self-Employed/Questions-and-Answers-for-the-Additional-Medicare-Tax.

The SSA has now indicated that inclusion of wages and withholdings for the 0.9 percent Additional Medicare Tax in the same Boxes 5 and 6 on the W-2 as regular Medicare wages and withholding are being reported has thwarted the SSA's edit efforts.

For Tax Year 2015, the SSA has said it will reject either paper reports or electronic reports that contain any of the following conditions: Medicare wages and tips are less than the sum of Social Security wages and Social Security tips; Social Security tax is greater than zero and Social Security wages and Social Security tips are equal to zero; and/or Medicare tax is greater than zero and Medicare wages and tips are equal to zero. Find a list of possible W-2 errors at https://www.socialsecurity.gov/employer/onlineerror.htm. See also https://www.ssa.gov/employer/remindersChangesTY15.pdf and https://www.social security.gov/employer/bsohbnew.htm.

Although the SSA is in the final stage of finishing its effort to redesign its wage processing system, edit features could still change from one year to the next. Employers will need to check each year for list of SSA errors that could cause the SSA to reject a filing. And, even if an edit feature is not triggered by a successor employer's treatment of FICA wage carryovers, failure to trigger the edit feature will not guarantee that a later agency follow-up will not occur. Employers filing W-2s in this manner should be prepared to address possible notices or later follow-ups to explain what appears to be a Social Security withholding shortfall.

Q 12:54 Must a successor or predecessor furnish an accelerated W-2 to employees who are terminated before the close of the year?

Yes. The rules are the same for successor and predecessor employers. If an employee is terminated before the close of a calendar year and the employee requests a Form W-2 in writing, then the employee's W-2 statement must be given to the employee within 30 days of the later of the date of the written request or the last payment of wages if the 30-day period ends before January 31 of the following year when the W-2 would otherwise be due. [Treas. Reg. § 31.6051-1(d); Rev. Proc. 2004-53, 2004-34 I.R.B. 320] IRS Notice 2012-9 exempts from reporting any employer-sponsored group health plan coverage on Forms W-2 provided to employees who request their Forms W-2 early. Apart from this exception, all other reportable employee benefits must be provided on the W-2.

The filing of the W-2 with the SSA, on the other hand, is not accelerated. The W-2 is to be included with the regular filing of all W-2s for the employer, unless the employer is terminating its business (see Q 12:55). [Treas. Reg. § 31.6071(a)-1(a)(3)]

Some states have adopted the early provision of W-2s as part of necessary compliance with tax and Department of Labor standards. Many states have rules that vary from the federal rules, and certain states require provision of Forms W-2 to terminating employees on an even earlier date. (Arizona—15 days, Arkansas—immediately, California—within 30 days after the last payment of wages unless there is a reasonable expectation on the part of both the employer and the employee that the employee will resume working for the employer, District of Columbia, Virginia, West Virginia, Wisconsin—with payment of final wages.) Payroll professionals are cautioned to check their state laws to determine responsibilities in this area.

Q 12:55 Are there special expedited W-2 requirements for successor and predecessor employers that terminate or stop paying wages and are required to file a final Form 941?

Yes. Successor and predecessor employers must follow the same rules as other employers when businesses are terminated. An employer that is required to file a final Form 941 is also required to furnish employees with W-2s on or before the date that the final Form 941 is due. [Treas. Reg. § 31.6051-1(d)(1)(ii); Rev. Proc. 2004-53, 2004-34 I.R.B. 320, Instructions to Forms W-2 and W-3] In addition, those employers that terminate their businesses are required to file expedited Forms W-2 with the SSA on or before the last day of the month that follows the due date of the final Form 941. [Treas. Reg. § 31.6071(a)-1(a)(3)(ii); Rev. Proc. 2004-53, 2004-34 I.R.B. 320, Instructions to Forms W-2 and W-3] Under this provision, the W-2 provided to employees must include all employee benefits required to be reported on the W-2 in Boxes 12 and 13, apart from the exception for reporting employer-sponsored group health plan coverage under IRS Notice 2012-9. See Q 12:60 below.

Special extensions are provided to employers that are required to file the expedited W-2s electronically, or if they filed Forms W-2 electronically for the previous year. Employers terminating business who fall under this special rule may furnish Forms W-2 to their employees on or before the later of the date that the final Form 941 is due or October 31 of the year in which they file their final Form 941. This automatic extension of time to furnish Forms W-2 to employees does not relieve an employer of its obligation to furnish a Form W-2 within 30 days to any employee who makes such a request in writing under I.R.C. § 6051 or under a separate state requirement. Employers covered under this special rule can also receive an automatic extension to file with the SSA. The due date under the automatic extension is the later of the last day of the month that follows the due date of the final Form 941 or November 30. [Rev. Proc. 96-57, 1996-2 C.B. 389 and Instructions to Forms W-2 and W-3] This extension is separate and apart from an extension applied for on Form 8809, Application for Extension of Time to File Information Returns, at year end before the due date of Forms W-2.

Filers and transmitters required to file Forms W-2 on this expedited basis under Treas. Reg. § 31.6071(a)-1(a)(3)(ii) may receive an automatic extension of time to file Forms W-2 only under provisions of Revenue Procedure 96-57, 1996-2 C.B. 389. If these filers and transmitters need even more additional time, they may request an extension under the generally applicable procedures for obtaining additional extensions of time to file Form W-2 using Form 8809.

The due date for Forms W-2, whether filing on paper or electronically, is January 31, 2018 for tax year 2017. In addition, the IRS has eliminated automatically obtaining a 30-day extension of the filing due date through a Form 8809. For filings due on or after January 1, 2017, you may request one 30-day extension to file Form W-2 by submitting a complete application on Form 8809, including a detailed explanation of why you need additional time and signed under penalties of perjury. The IRS has said it will only grant the extension in extraordinary circumstances or catastrophe. See 2017 General Instructions to Form W-2 and Form W-3.

Forms W-4 under the Standard Procedure

Q 12:56   Must successors and predecessors treat Forms W-4 differently under the standard procedure?

No. The predecessor must keep the Forms W-4 in support of its withholding actions in reliance on the forms. [Rev. Proc. 2004-53, 2004-34 I.R.B. 320] Minimally, Forms W-4 and all records relevant to the employment tax filings must be kept for four years after the later of the due date for taxes for the return period covering the last return filed relying on the form or the date the taxes were actually paid related to that period. [Treas. Reg. §§ 31.6001-1(e)(2), 31.6001-5(a)(1) to 31.6001-5(a)(13)] Practically, however, records should be kept for as long as the predecessor is still open for audit for any period, even beyond the four-year period.

The transferred employees are treated as new hires by the successor employer, and must submit new Forms W-4. Under the standard procedure, where employees fail to provide new Forms W-4, successor employers would follow the general rules that apply in the absence of a Form W-4 (i.e., withhold on the employee's wages as if the employee were a single person with no withholding exemptions). [Treas. Reg. § 31.3402(f)(2)-1(a); Rev. Proc. 2004-53, 2004-34 I.R.B. 320]

Alternate Procedure

Alternate Requirements for Forms 941

Q 12:57   Under the alternate procedure, what are the responsibilities of the successor and predecessor employers regarding Form 941?

Under the alternate procedure, if employers sell or transfer their business, predecessors and the new successors must each file Forms 941 for the quarter in which the transfer occurs. Each must report only on the wages it paid. If the predecessor terminates its business or ceases to pay wages due to the transfer, the predecessor is required to mark its return as "final." [Rev. Proc. 2004-53, 2004-34 I.R.B. 320; Rev. Proc. 96-60, 1996-2 C.B. 399; Form 941 and Schedule D instructions] (See Q 12:51 for further information on filing a final Form 941. If the predecessor is required to file a final return, see Q 12:55 regarding the need to expedite Forms W-2 to the employee and the SSA.)

In addition, predecessors and successors must file Schedule D explaining the transaction and reconciling discrepancies between Forms 941 and W-2s caused by electing the alternate procedure. (See Q 12:59 for a discussion of the causes of the discrepancies and the specific filing requirements for Schedule D.)

To provide employers with time to reconcile their own W-2s with 941s, Schedule D is to be filed independent of the Form 941 but by the due date of the Form 941 for the first quarter of the year following the year of the transaction. Where a final Form 941 may be due earlier, the Schedule D must be filed by the due date of the final return. If filed on paper, the Schedule D is to be filed separately from the Form 941 using the following address:

IRS Philadelphia Campus
Mail Stop 4-G08 151
2970 Market Street
Philadelphia, PA 19104

This is a different address than where the Form 941 is to be filed. (See instructions to Form 941 for those mailing addresses.) Schedule D can also be filed electronically with an electronic submission of Form 941. Electronic filing of Schedule D enables IRS to process information on the form more efficiently and accurately.

(See Q 12:63 regarding the SSA EFW2 employer field for linking the predecessor's Forms 941 account with the successor's W-2s.)

Historical note: The older rules in Revenue Procedure 96-60 [1996-2 C.B. 399] were revamped through the IRS 2003 Industry Issue Resolution Program to provide for easier filings in M&A contexts. [I.R.S. News Release IR-2003-92 (July 24, 2003); I.R.S. News Release IR-2004-109 (Aug. 18, 2004)] As a result of this project, a new Schedule D (Form 941) replaced the older paper attachments and was implemented for use beginning in 2005. Revenue Procedure 2004-53 [2004-34 I.R.B. 320] supersedes the instructions in Revenue Procedure 96-60. The requirement that Schedule D be filed is a substantial change from the requirements before 2005 under Revenue Procedure 96-60. Under the old rules, the predecessor was required to attach a statement to its Form 941 filed for the quarter of the transfer that explained the discrepancy and included the name, address, and EIN of the successor, and a reference to Revenue Procedure 96-60. Similarly, the successor had to attach a statement to its Form 941 for the quarter of the transfer that explained the discrepancy and included the name, address, and EIN of the predecessor, and a reference to Revenue Procedure 96-60. The attached statements would enable the IRS to link the two companies' accounts to balance Forms 941 with related Forms W-2.

Q 12:58 Under the alternate procedure, if the successor and predecessor employer each file Forms 941 for the quarter of the transfer covering their own separate wages, but agree to allow the successor employer to file Forms W-2 for the transferred employees for the full year, will this cause each employer's Forms 941 to be out-of-balance with their Forms W-2?

Yes. If the requirements to classify the acquiring corporation as a successor employer are met, and both the successor and the predecessor employers collectively agree, the successor employer will furnish Forms W-2 to the transferred employees covering wage liabilities and related tax deposits that were posted to the predecessor employer's Forms 941. When each company is viewed individually, this will result in a variance in the amounts reported on each company's Forms 941 when compared to the Forms W-2 filed under each company's EIN. However, if both companies' Forms 941 and W-2s are viewed collectively, the tax accounts would be seen as being in balance. The overstatement in the predecessor's Forms 941, when compared to its W-2s, would offset the understatement in the successor's Forms 941 when compared to its W-2s. Schedule D was designed to assist the IRS in the reconciliation process.

Q 12:59 What are the specific requirements of Schedule D (Form 941) under the alternate procedure?

Schedule D (Form 941) must be filed by both the successor and the predecessor electing the alternate procedure. [Rev. Proc. 2004-53, 2004-34 I.R.B. 320] Schedule D requires: the date of the acquisition; the name, trade name (doing business as or d/b/a), address, and EIN of both the predecessor and the successor and an indication depending upon who is filing whether they are either the predecessor or successor; and an explanation of any discrepancies between W-2 (Copy A) and Form 941 in the totals of Social Security wages, Medicare wages and tips, Social Security tips, and federal income tax withheld. Part 3 of Schedule D is only required if you are involved in more than one transaction in the same year to help the IRS reconcile the different Schedules D that you are to file. Schedule D must be submitted by the due date of the Form 941 for the first quarter of the year after the calendar year in which the event took place, or by the due date of the final Form 941 if due at an earlier date. [Rev. Proc. 2004-53, 2004-34 I.R.B. 320, and Schedule D (Form 941)]

Schedule D is not filed at the same place that Form 941 is filed. File Schedule D using the following address:

IRS Philadelphia Campus
Mail Stop 4-G08 151
2970 Market Street
Philadelphia, PA 19104

Filing Forms W-2 under the Alternate Procedure

Q 12:60 What are the predecessor's and successor's requirements for filing Forms W-2 under the alternate procedure?

If the requirements to classify the acquiring corporation as a "successor employer," are met and both the successor and the predecessor employers agree, the successor will furnish Forms W-2 to the transferred employees. The W-2s for the transferred employees are to be included with the successor's Forms W-2 for its other employees (if any) and filed along with the successor employer's transmittal for the W-2s (Form W-3) if paper versions of Forms W-2 are used. The W-2s for transferred employees must include wages paid and taxes withheld by both the successor and the predecessor. If the total number of W-2s to be filed equals or exceeds 250—returns for transferred employees and those for its own employees—the W-2s must be filed with the SSA electronically. A single transmission is required from the successor as the employer. The transferred employees must be employed by the successor in the same calendar year for this rule to apply. [Rev. Proc. 2004-53, 2004-34 I.R.B. 320; I.R.C. § 6051(a); Treas. Reg. §§ 31.6051-1(a), 31.6051-2; SSA EFW2 instructions for the tax year involved]

If the rule applies and both employers agree to follow it, the predecessor will be relieved from filing W-2s for the transferred employees. The predecessor will, however, be responsible for providing to employees, and filing with the SSA, any Forms W-2 for those employees who were not employed by the successor, including employees who either retired or were terminated before the effective date of the transaction. [Rev. Proc. 2004-53, 2004-34 I.R.B. 320] (See Qs 4:77–4:92 for further information on Form W-2 filing requirements.)

The alternate procedure under Revenue Procedure 2004-53 is not mandated even if FICA and FUTA wage bases are carried over to the successor under the provisions of the Treasury Regulations. [Rev. Proc. 2004-53, 2004-34 I.R.B. 320; Treas. Reg. §§ 31.3121(a)(1)-1(b), 31.3306(b)(1)-1(b)] (See Q 12:53 for concerns regarding SSA edit functions if carryovers are made and W-2s are not consolidated.)

Successor employers must consider their responsibility to meet the compliance accountabilities under the new health care reform provisions before electing to consolidate wages for W-2 purposes. Some considerations include:

- The 0.9 percent Additional Medicare Tax must be withheld for high earners on compensation amounts that exceed $200,000. All compensation that is generally subject to Medicare withholding is subject to the additional 0.9 percent withholding if compensation is paid to an employee in excess of $200,000 for the calendar year. For electing successor employers, it will now be critical to also earmark and carryover Medicare wages paid by the predecessor to enable tracking of the point where paid compensation exceeds the $200,000 threshold for the year requiring the additional withholding. This task needs to be added to the payroll interface being built for handling the transaction by electing employers. The IRS has made clear the requirement to carry over wage bases to meet this responsibility by an electing successor employer and may require the carryover of these wages if any Social Security wages are also elected to be carried over even if the employer does not elect to consolidate wages for W-2 reporting. This reporting requirement might be difficult for some to meet and may even thwart some successors from electing to carryover the Social Security wage base altogether. Assuming liabilities for correctly withholding this tax is a serious consideration.

- Wages subject to the Additional Medicare Tax withholding requirement may be paid by third parties under arrangements with the target company, such as sick pay and payments under deferred compensation arrangements. So those parties serving the predecessor's plans must be located and arrangements made to coordinate the aggregation of compensation amounts as part of the payroll tasks in the transaction.

Sick pay paid by an employer and by the third party need to be aggregated to determine whether the $200,000 withholding threshold has been met. The same rules that currently assign responsibility for sick pay reporting and payment of Medicare tax based on which party is treated as the employer (i.e., the employer, the employer's agent, or a third party that is not the employer's agent) apply also to the Additional Medicare Tax. For more information on sick pay, see Publication 15-A, Employer's Supplemental Tax Guide, and Notice 2015-6, 2015-5 I.R.B. For the rules on aggregation of sick pay for the 0.9 percent Medicare withholding, see FAQ #45 at http://www.irs.gov/Businesses/Small-Businesses-&-Self-Employed/Questions-and-Answers-for-the-Additional-Medicare-Tax#!.

However, FAQ #50 on the above IRS website gives a different result for agents appointed on a Form 2678, Employer/Payer Appointment of Agent: "If an agent pays wages to an employee on behalf of an employer (under an approved Form 2678), then, for purposes of determining whether wages are paid in excess of the $200,000 withholding threshold, the agent is not required to combine the wages it pays with wages paid to that same employee: 1) directly by the employer, 2) by the same agent on behalf of a different employer, or 3) by another agent on behalf of the same employer. Wages paid on behalf of an employer by an agent appointed on an approved Form 2678 are not combined with these other wages in determining whether to withhold Additional Medicare Tax." So under this FAQ, wages paid by the target's payroll agent appointed on a Form 2678 will not need to be located and aggregated with other wages.

- Reporting aggregate cost of health care coverage will require gathering data about a predecessor's health care coverage of the transferred employees. IRS Notice 2012-9 requires successor employers electing to issue one Form W-2 reflecting wages paid to a transferred employee during the calendar year by both the predecessor and the successor to also report the aggregate reportable cost of health care coverage by both employers to that transferred employee. [2012-4 I.R.B. 315] Notice 2012-9 provides guidance on informational reporting to employees of the cost of their employer-sponsored group health plan coverage and is now the principal source on how to report, what coverage to include, and how to determine the reportable cost of the coverage. However, the reporting is optional for employers with fewer than 250 employees until the IRS issues future guidance. For more information, see http://www.irs.gov/uac/Form-W-2-Reporting-of-Employer-Sponsored-Health-Coverage.

- Information reporting requirements under I.R.C. § 6055 and § 6056 have expanded reporting on an employee's health care coverage and, in turn, data gathering requirements on a predecessor's health care coverage of transferred employees. Applicable large employers, insurance companies, sponsors of a self-insured health plan (including self-insured employers), government agencies that administer government-sponsored health insurance programs, and other entities must now report numerous details on those individuals offered health insurance coverage as well as on the coverage offered. The ESRP and the new reporting requirements will pose risk and compliance concerns in M&A transactions. Since 2015 (reporting in 2016), applicable large employers with 50 or more full-time equivalent employees began to report information about offerings of health coverage to each full-time employee on Form 1095-C, as well as the transmittal Form

1094-C. Self-insured employers, like insurance companies, report information about a policy's minimum essential coverage to insured persons on Form 1095-B and the transmittal Form 1094-B. Employers that are both self-insured and meet the terms of an applicable large employer may report about their coverage in Part III of Form 1095-C.

- Another concern involves the payment of medical loss ratio (MLR) rebates to employees by employers that maintain group health insurance policies and that received the premium rebates from their insurance carriers for a previous year. Where rebates are passed on to employees, it may change their W-2 calculations for the year if employees are part of a pretax deferral plan or their employer pays their premiums. It will be important to determine whether such amounts were paid out by a predecessor to assure correct W-2 forms.

- In future years, other aspects of the Affordable Care Act will become effective and will have serious impact on payroll, such as what has become known as the Cadillac tax under I.R.C. § 4980I, now delayed until 2020,which will impose on affected employees a 40-percent excise tax on the cost of health care coverage valued over a certain amount. There will also be future guidance issued on other Affordable Care Act provisions such as on implementation of I.R.C. § 105(h), which provides for nondiscrimination within health care plans, and the revamping of the cafeteria plan requirements under I.R.C. § 125 to meet the new health care provisions, as well as the ever-expanding information reporting requirements associated with enforcement of the new rules. Momentum continues to grow to repeal the Cadillac Tax by Congress and President Donald Trump.

In the last few years, employers have come to expect last-minute legislation and even significant court holdings that force retroactive adjustments in current and prior years' taxable wage amounts and that require amendments to be made to previous compliance filings. See Q 12:24 for examples of such events.

Q 12:61   Under the alternate procedure, must the successor employer include all reportable information required on a transferred employee's Form W-2 for the year, whether paid or accounted for by the predecessor, including information on deferrals to retirement plans, compensation from other benefit plans, allocated tips, uncollected employee tax on tips, dependent care benefits, and so on?

Yes. Where the alternate procedure is to be used, the successor employer must collect and report on Form W-2 any amount required to be reported by the predecessor employer for a transferred employee for the tax year involved. [Rev. Proc. 2004-53, 2004-34 I.R.B. 320] See information about the health care reporting requirements in Q 12:60 above.

Q 12:62 **Under the alternate procedure, is the successor employer required to file Forms W-2 for any employees of the predecessor employer that were terminated or who retired before the effective date of the transfer to the successor, but who received wages in the year of the transaction?**

No. Successor employers are only required to file Forms W-2 for employees transferred from the predecessor employer. The predecessor employer will remain responsible for providing any Forms W-2 for those employees who were not employed by the successor employer immediately after the asset acquisition, including employees who either retired or were terminated before the effective date of the transaction. Moreover, if the predecessor employer goes out of business or stops paying wages, the rules requiring expedited Forms W-2 will apply (see Q 12:55). [Rev. Proc. 2004-53, 2004-34 I.R.B. 320]

Q 12:63 **Under the alternate procedure, when the successor employer electronically files Forms W-2 reporting taxes paid by the predecessor, is there a field in the SSA's record layout to provide the predecessor's EIN?**

Yes. Per the electronic filing specifications issued by the SSA EFW2, the "Other EIN" field (locations 31-39 of the RE record) can be used in all M&A events in instances where taxes are legally filed under one EIN and Forms W-2 under another EIN. (This field is not the same as the one used for common pay agents or common paymasters (locations 7–25 of the RE record)). Using this field enables the agencies to balance the predecessor employer's Form 941 withholding accounts against the successor employer's totals reported in Forms W-2. Because this field can only accommodate one EIN, it cannot be used when multiple transactions in a single year involve two or more companies.

Q 12:64 **Are there special expedited W-2 requirements for predecessor employers that terminate or that stop paying wages and are required to file a final Form 941?**

Yes. Predecessor employers must follow the same rules as other employers when businesses are terminated. An employer that is required to file a final Form 941 is also required to furnish employees with W-2s on or before the date that the final Form 941 is due. [Treas. Reg. § 31.6051-1(d)(1)(ii); Rev. Proc. 2004-53, 2004-34 I.R.B. 320, Instructions to Forms W-2 and W-3] Those employers that terminate their businesses are also required to file expedited Forms W-2 with the SSA on or before the last day of the month that follows the due date of the final Form 941. [Treas. Reg. § 31.6071(a)-1(a)(3)(ii); Rev. Proc. 2004-53, 2004-34 I.R.B. 320, Instructions to Forms W-2 and W-3] Under this provision, the W-2 provided to employees must include all employee benefits required to be reported on the W-2 in Boxes 12 and 13, apart from the exception for reporting employer-sponsored group health plan coverage under IRS Notice 2012-9. See Q 12:60 above.

Special extensions are provided to employers that are required to file the expedited W-2s electronically, or if they filed Forms W-2 electronically for the previous year. Employers terminating business who fall under this special rule may furnish Forms W-2 to their employees on or before the later of the date that the final Form 941 is due or October 31 of the year in which they file their final Form 941. This automatic extension of time to furnish Forms W-2 to employees does not relieve an employer of its obligation to furnish a Form W-2 within 30 days to any employee who makes such a request in writing under I.R.C. Section 6051 or under a separate state requirement. Employers covered under this special rule can also receive an automatic extension to file with the SSA. The due date under the automatic extension is the later of the last day of the month that follows the due date of the final Form 941 or November 30. [Rev. Proc. 96-57, 1996-2 C.B. 389 and Instructions to Forms W-2 and W-3] This extension is separate and apart from the 30-day extension from a Form 8809, Application for Extension of Time To File Information Returns, sent in at year end before the due date of Forms W-2 if accepted by the IRS.

Filers and transmitters required to file Forms W-2 on this expedited basis under Treas. Reg. § 31.6071(a)-1(a)(3)(ii) may receive an automatic extension of time to file Forms W-2 only under provisions of Revenue Procedure 96-57, 1996-2 C.B. 389. If these filers and transmitters need even more additional time, they may request an extension under the generally applicable procedures for obtaining additional extensions of time to file Form W-2 using Form 8809.

The Consolidated Appropriations Act of 2016 accelerated to January 31 the due date for Forms W-2, whether filing on paper or electronically, starting in 2018 for tax year 2017. In addition, the IRS has eliminated automatically obtaining a 30-day extension of the filing due date through a Form 8809. For filings due on or after January 1, 2018, you may request one 30-day extension to file Form W-2 by submitting a complete application on Form 8809, including a detailed explanation of why you need additional time and signed under penalties of perjury. The IRS has said it will only grant the extension in extraordinary circumstances or catastrophe. See 2017 General Instructions to Form W-2 and Form W-3.

Forms W-4 under the Alternate Procedure

Q 12:65   Under the alternate procedure, must the successor employer solicit new Forms W-4 from the transferred employees?

No. New Forms W-4 would be required only if the current forms were invalid or had expired (e.g., in the case of a Form W-4 claiming exemption from withholding). (See chapter 2 for a detailed discussion.)

The predecessor employer must transfer to the successor employer all current Forms W-4 provided by the transferred employees that are effective for the current year. Unless the employee submits a revised form, the transferred Forms W-4 are equally valid in the hands of the successor employer, and can be stored and transferred electronically. [Rev. Proc. 2004-53, 2004-34 I.R.B. 320; Treas. Reg. § 31.3402(f)(5)-1(c)]

Because W-4s are considered valid in the hands of the successor employer, where plans are to elect the alternate procedure the successor must consider the capture of the forms from the predecessor's files. (See Q 12:66 regarding the option to obtain new forms.) [Form W-4 instructions; Pub. No. 15]

Increasing use of employee self-service (ESS) modules, such as an employee interactive voice response (IVR) system that allows employees to make changes to their personal information and their federal, state and local withholding allowance elections on Forms W-4, may make transfer of this information easier, but will present additional compliance concerns. Payroll professionals will need to be vigilant that the eservice system is compliant with IRS requirements on data gathering and recordkeeping. [T.D. 8706 and Treas. Reg. § 31.3402(f)(5)-1(c)] Use of the process for state and local purposes may raise further considerations that the proper certificates are supported and that the jurisdiction allows eservicing of the forms. When inheriting Forms W-4 from a predecessor's process, these matters will need to be examined.

Q 12:66   What can be done if the predecessor employer cannot electronically transfer the Forms W-4 to the successor employer because their systems are incompatible?

A successor employer can choose to acquire and maintain the predecessor employer's system or to require the transferred employees to provide new forms, electronically or on paper. [Rev. Proc. 2004-53, 2004-34 I.R.B. 320] (See chapter 2 for a discussion of soliciting electronic or paper Form W-4.) See note on employee self-service modules in Q 12:65 above.

Q 12:67   Under the alternate procedure, will the successor employer be held liable for relying on invalid Forms W-4 transferred from the acquired corporation?

Yes. The successor employer will be fully liable in its reliance on the predecessor employer's forms in operating its own payroll process if the forms are considered invalid so they should be reviewed. (See Q 2:70 for a discussion of invalid Form W-4.)

Q 12:68   Under the alternate procedure, will the successor employer be held liable for the predecessor employer's reliance on invalid Forms W-4 in periods prior to the transfer that are still open for assessment?

No. Each employer is accountable for its own payroll process in the context of applying the successor employer rules for income tax withholding purposes. Successor employers should be cautioned, however, that an IRS audit may involve reviews of Forms W-2 that a successor employer filed on a consolidated basis that included wages and taxes paid by the predecessor. If errors in a predecessor's practice cause an out-of-balance position with the IRS records, the successor employer could be held responsible for penalties for filing an incorrect Form W-2 and may be held liable for Form 941 shortfalls of related paid taxes. Such liability will be imposed on the successor employer unless the successor can show the error was committed by the predecessor.

In addition, if the predecessor employer made an error computing the FICA or FUTA threshold, which causes the transferred wage base to be overstated, the successor employer may be held liable for underwithholding on its part on future wages paid and for not paying FICA and FUTA taxes on the shortfall caused in the successor employer's processing of taxes based on the predecessor's overstatement of wages.

Because potential liability may be transferred to the successor employer, the forms, wage bases, and any policies and procedures used to administer them should be subjected to strenuous due diligence reviews in the conversion process to minimize related acquisition risks.

Q 12:69   Will the successor employer need to be concerned about lock-in-letters and other IRS correspondence concerning employees of the predecessor employer?

Yes. Forms W-4 may still be subject to IRS review. Employers may be directed (in a written notice or in future published guidance) to send certain Forms W-4 to the IRS. The IRS reviews employee withholding compliance through careful screenings of the employee's individual tax return (Form 1040) and submitted W-2. When there is serious underwithholding for a particular employee, the IRS may issue a lock-in-letter to the employer specifying the maximum number of withholding allowances permitted for that employee. After the lock-in-letter takes effect, the employer must disregard any Form W-4 that claims more allowances or exempt status until the IRS notifies the employer to withhold tax based on the new Form W-4. In the context of a successor employer electing the alternative procedure, because the successor is required to obtain the W-4 from the predecessor for transferred employees and file a consolidated W-2 based on wages paid by the predecessor, the successor will need to respond to any IRS direction, including lock-in-letters regarding transferred employees even if the Forms W-4 were originally submitted to the acquired corporation. A Form W-4 electing to reduce the number of allowances thus increasing withholding is permitted. [Treas. Reg. § 31.3402(f)(2)-1(g)]

Some states require filings of certain Forms W-4 (or their state version) even though the federal requirement has long been withdrawn. See Q 12:98 for further discussion on this filing need. In this context, employers completing due diligence of a soon-to-be-acquired company should identify state requirements in all jurisdictions where the company operates.

Managing Liability and Special Recordkeeping under the Alternative Procedure

Q 12:70   **Under the alternate procedure, could the successor employer be liable for any of the predecessor's federal employment tax history on the transferred employees, such as for FICA taxes on tips, requiring special review in the transaction?**

Yes. Because the successor employer will include the predecessor's wages with its wages in the transferred employees' Forms W-2, the successor employer will need to understand and be accountable for data from the predecessor employer included in the Forms W-2. Additionally, successor employers should proceed cautiously when employees participated in similar benefit plans with annual thresholds (e.g., I.R.C. § 401(k) deferrals or flexible benefit or other cafeteria plans) with the predecessor, as well as in validating FICA and FUTA wage bases provided by the predecessor. The successor employer should exercise due diligence early in the transaction by identifying and reviewing all components of compensation paid to the transferred employees in the year of the transfer and then having professional reviews of all compensation and other benefit plans involving the transferred employees in the year of the transfer to ensure the accuracy of information reported in the employees' W-2s.

A June 4, 1993 IRS Field Service Advice Memo (released Apr. 30, 1998) concluded that for purposes of assessment of underreported FICA taxes on tips, the liability usually falls on the employer at the time of the "notice and demand." Liability for employment taxes is based on whether the tips were reported and, if not reported, requires that tips be treated as wages subject to FICA on the date the IRS serves "notice and demand." [I.R.C. § 3121(q)] However, where a corporate reorganization results in a different employer at the point of the "notice and demand" without knowledge of the underreported tips, one of the following four situations could result:

1. The IRS can determine that the predecessor is the employer for purposes of the "notice and demand" following an asset sale;

2. If the reorganization was a statutory merger, where the survivor is considered the same employer as the acquired corporation, the survivor could be considered the employer for purposes of the "notice and demand";

3. If the acquisition was through the purchase of stock, the current employer could be considered the employer for purposes of the "notice and demand," as the entity is the same taxpayer; or

4. In certain cases when the transaction is complex, liability can be split.

This Field Service Advice Memo is consistent in other aspects of payroll liability management in the context of an M&A event. Under the successor employer rules, a successor employer should not be held liable for a predecessor's actions prior to the acquisition unless it has agreed to assume the liability. [Rev. Proc. 2004-53, 2004-34 I.R.B. 320] However, see Q 12:47 above on federal approach to successor in interest liabilities that currently relies on state successor in interest laws. The IRS has many tools to collect unpaid taxes on the part of a predecessor.

Q 12:71   Under the alternate procedure, is the successor employer responsible for maintaining Forms W-4 and other employment tax records on the transferred employees from the predecessor's employment history?

Yes, if relevant to tax filings on the part of the successor employer for the year of the transaction. The successor employer is accountable for the Forms W-4 transferred to it from the predecessor employer under the alternate procedure if the successor relies on the W-4 to calculate withholdings. In addition, because the successor employer will include the predecessor's wages with its wages in the transferred employees' Forms W-2, the successor must keep all records necessary to substantiate the W-2 calculations. (See chapter 11 for a further discussion on documents, recordkeeping methodology, and storage time periods.) [Pub. No. 15; Treas. Reg. §§ 31.6001-2 to 31.6001-5] See also cautions in Q 12:69 above.

Successor Employer Rules for FUTA and Form 940

Q 12:72   What FUTA tax requirements affect successor employers?

Treasury Regulations §§ 31.3306(b)(1)-1(b) and 31.3302(e)-1 address the carryover rules for FUTA purposes. It is possible for a successor employer to carry over employees' FUTA taxable wage bases of acquired employees. To do so, the successor must meet the following requirements:

- The successor employer must acquire substantially all property used in a trade or business of another employer (predecessor), or used in a separate unit of a trade or business of a predecessor; and

- In connection with or immediately after the acquisition (but in the same calendar year), the successor employer must employ individuals who, immediately prior to the acquisition, were employed in the trade or business of the predecessor and wages must be paid to the transferred employees during the calendar year in which the acquisition occurs both prior to and after the acquisition.

Further, both employers must be covered by FUTA. [I.R.C. §§ 3306(b)(1), 3302(e); Treas. Reg. §§ 31.3306(b)(1)-1(b), 31.3302(e)-1; Form 940 instructions]

SUI credit transfers are limited to circumstances where the predecessor is not required to file a Form 940 and, where allowed, are restricted to only the ratable portion of the credit that relates to predecessor wages paid to employees also hired by the successor employer (see Qs 12:36–12:44 for a further discussion of details). If the predecessor employer files a Form 940, the successor can nonetheless count the wages that the predecessor employer paid to the transferred employees in calculating the wage limitations for FUTA purposes. This offset lowers the successor's FUTA liability. The Form 940 instructions include special calculations on how to offset a transferred employee's wages by the wages paid by the predecessor employer and special instructions requiring employers to mark Box b, *Successor Employer,* where any of these rules attach.

Comparatively speaking, the provisions for successor employers substantially vary from those that apply in the context of a statutory merger or consolidation. The successor employer's FUTA wages are offset by the predecessor's wages, lowering the successor employer's FUTA liability. However, the successor employer may not claim credit for the predecessor's state unemployment credits on its Form 940 unless the predecessor is not a covered employer required to file a Form 940. Generally, FUTA wages paid by the predecessor employer and related state unemployment credits are claimed on the predecessor's Form 940. Contrast this with a statutory merger or consolidation where all FUTA wages, whether paid by the acquired company or the surviving company, are reported on the survivor's Form 940 and all state unemployment credits from payments made by both companies are also covered on the surviving company's Form 940. The acquired corporation does not file a 940 (see Q 12:30).

Instructions to Form 940 say "when you figure the payments made to each employee in excess of the FUTA wage base [currently $7,000, but legislation is being considered to increase this amount], you may include the payments that the predecessor made to the employees who continue to work for you only if the predecessor was an employer for FUTA tax purposes resulting in the predecessor being required to file Form 940."

The instructions are illustrated with an example: "During the calendar year, the predecessor employer paid $5,000 to Employee A. You acquired the predecessor's business. After the acquisition, you employed Employee A and paid Employee A an additional $3,000 in wages. None of the amounts paid to Employee A were payments exempt from FUTA tax.

$5,000 Wages paid by predecessor employer

+ 3,000 Wages paid by you

$8,000 Total payments to Employee A; include this amount in line 3 of Form 940.

$ 8,000 Total payments to Employee A

− 7,000 FUTA wage base

$ 1,000 Payments made to Employee A in excess of $7,000.

$1,000 Payments made to Employee A in excess of $7,000

+ 5,000 Taxable FUTA wages paid by predecessor employer

$6,000 You would include this amount on line 5 of Form 940.

It is important to remember that unemployment records in complex M&A events, even when falling under the successor employer rules, can get lost in the transfers at the state level. Every year, states certify SUI credits to the IRS for use in validating SUI credit claims on federal Form 940. An employer gets a credit for amounts it pays to a state (including the District of Columbia, Puerto Rico, and the U.S. Virgin Islands) unemployment fund by the Form 940 due date. The FUTA tax will be higher if either the survivor or the acquired corporation failed to pay the state unemployment tax on a timely basis. Under I.R.C. § 3302(a)(3), the credit for contributions paid after the due date for the return is limited to 90 percent of the amount which would have been allowable had the contributions been timely.

This state/IRS verification is accomplished through the FUTA Certification Program under which states transmit records of activities in the SUI account maintained under each employer's account directly to the IRS. The operations of this Program are explained in detail in IRS Publication 4485, Guide for the Certification of State FUTA Credits, found at https://www.irs.gov/pub/irs-pdf/p4485.pdf. State credit certification is tied to the federal EIN and not always to the state tax ID. See an explanation of the process in Q 12:30. A few years ago the federal Form 940 was modified to no longer require employers to list their state tax IDs on Form 940. Form 940 credit matching can pose difficult stumbling blocks for companies with complex acquisitions.

After the SUTA Dumping rules were enacted, particularly where a substantial number of the new company's employees came from an acquired company with a high unemployment rate, some states refused to follow the federal filing requirements under the survivor's federal EIN. Instead, states required the continued use of the acquired company's old state tax ID originally associated with the acquired's federal EIN. Even though this concern has become less prevalent with the closer workings between federal and state agencies, payroll professionals are still advised to follow up with the state agencies as soon as possible to make sure the correct federal EIN is associated with the state account to avoid loss of FUTA credits for the unemployment taxes paid.

States do not operate in the blind on related federal EINs. The IRS sends a Quarterly Entity Update file to the states the month following the close of each quarter. The file contains data on newly assigned EINs or employers who have changed their name during the previous quarter. This is why it is so critical that as soon as possible where new EINs are needed in a transaction or where there is a company name change that the proper processing occur with the IRS. See Qs 12:84–12:87 for more information on processing new EINs and name changes.

When the IRS cannot validate the state SUI credits, the employer will receive a 4010C Letter proposing to increase taxes, or a 4011C Letter proposing to decrease taxes, depending on which employer the credits are attributed to.

To respond to IRS letters and resolve any proposed assessment, you will need from each state a written proof of credit (known as a credit statement). To avoid the letters, obtain SUI account transcripts for each EIN where credits are allowed (even where the account should be closed and the EIN no longer used) as soon as you know the agencies have made needed adjustments. From the transcripts, you should see whether proper transfers have occurred and where credits are posted. Work with the agencies to bring the accounts in balance under the proper EINs, and be sure to obtain written credit statements as you may need them.

See Q 12:30 above on a recent IRS private information letter issued as non-binding general guidance that explains the IRS's present position regarding the need to obtain separate state certifications to support state FUTA credits. [IRS Office of Chief Counsel, Information Letter No. 2014-0022, June 27, 2014] Q 12:30 also discusses the February 9, 2016 Treasury Inspector General for Tax Administration (TIGTA) published audit finding that the IRS needed to have better processes in place to administer its FUTA Certification Program.

Payroll professionals are well advised to seek from states written validations of all of their SUI credits that reflect the making of timely SUI payments for provision to the IRS to support the credits taken on the federal Form 940, particularly for years where M&A activities have occurred. When there is a conflict in state records, the conflict will need to be resolved to ensure a clean Form 940 process. It is also wise to request of the state transcripts of all accounts affected prior to and after the transaction takes place.

Transactions Outside the Successor Employer and Statutory Merger Rules

Q 12:73   Are there any other exceptions that would allow FICA and FUTA wage base carryovers when the test of successor employer is not met or absent a statutory merger or consolidation?

Yes, there are a few, but apart from these exceptions, when an employee is employed by two unrelated successive employers during a tax year, the second employer is required to withhold FICA and FUTA taxes, without regard to the taxes withheld by any prior employer. [I.R.C. §§ 3121(a)(1), 3306(b)(1)] There is no credit or refund available to the employers for the excess withholding on wages over the FICA or FUTA wage base.

In a stock acquisition, only the shareholders change. The business usually continues to operate unimpeded by the acquisition, retaining the same employer status for federal, state, and local purposes that it held before the acquisition, as well as its federal employer identification number (EIN) and state tax identification numbers (referred to as tax IDs). In stock acquisitions, pre-deal wage amounts will be applied along with post-deal wage payments to meet the employees' federal Social Security and federal unemployment insurance (FUTA) thresholds, as well as usually the state unemployment and other payroll tax thresholds since the entity itself has not changed, only its ownership has. Even in stock acquisitions, some reporting requirements may apply. Changes of ownership and of company officers may require the filing of a state notice, and new owners can change company names also requiring agency notification.

Keep in mind as you read this section that compliance for statutory mergers and consolidations where broader liabilities attach without the successor employer elections may actually apply to other transactions not directly addressed by the payroll authorities: Revenue Procedure 2004-53 [2004-34 I.R.B. 320], amplifying Revenue Ruling 62-60 [1962-1 C.B. 186], and in the instructions for IRS Form 941, Schedule D (Form 941), and Form 940. This expansion occurs through the substantive workings of the tax laws that come into play for particular transactions that would require the survivor to carry over the tax attributes of the acquired such as when I.R.C. § 381 (see Q 12:6 above) might attach to the transaction or where partnership tax laws support continuity between old and new partnerships discussed in Qs 12:75–12:79 below.

In these transactions involving employee transfers to what appears to be a new entity, but for tax purposes is actually the old entity with a changed name, identity, form, or place of organization, the new entity is treated as the same entity as the old and usually retains the same federal EIN. Where any of these events occur, as in the context of a statutory merger or consolidation, the resulting employer assumes all the payroll responsibilities of the acquired corporation and payroll professionals would look to consolidate payroll responsibilities of the absorbed company into the survivor. See Qs 12:2–12:35, which address statutory mergers and consolidations, for concerns that could also arise in these transactions and their recommended solutions. Partnership tax laws offer similar tax benefit continuity rules that will also result in the continuation of the old partnership in a new structure. See Rev. Rul. 54-31, 1954-1 C.B. 212. These requirements are covered in Qs 12:75–12:79 below.

Disregarded entities add further complexities to these transactions. See Qs 12:80–12:81 below. In Private Letter Ruling 201115016 (Jan. 5, 2011), I.R.C. § 368(a)(1)(F) applied to a transaction in which an S corporation became a QSub, a disregarded entity of a newly formed S corporation. The new S corporation and the QSub were treated as a single S corporation because the Qsub was considered a disregarded entity and ignored for purposes of the transaction. Although not entirely clear from the ruling, it appears that the wage history and EIN of the old S corporation could carry over to the new QSub now required to maintain payroll at the QSub level. Under Treas. Reg. § 1.1361-4(a)(7), a QSub is treated as a separate corporation for purposes of employment tax and related reporting requirements (effective for wages paid on or after January 1, 2009).

In Revenue Ruling 2008-18, in the context of an I.R.C. § 368(a)(1)(F) reorganization, the IRS takes into consideration that a resulting QSub will be treated as a separate corporation for certain federal tax purposes, and requires the QSub to retain its old EIN to use when it is treated as a separate corporation for federal tax purposes. The ruling holds that it would not be appropriate for the newly acquiring corporation in a reorganization under § 368(a)(1)(F) to use the EIN of the transferor corporation that becomes a QSub, but the Qsub would keep the old EIN as a separate employer. [Rev. Rul. 2008-18, 2008-13 I.R.B. 674]

Note. The following are recommendations for employers:

- Notify the IRS immediately if you change your business name or address.
- Write to the IRS office where you file your returns to notify the IRS of any name change.
- Get IRS Pub. 1635, Understanding Your EIN, to see if you need to apply for a new EIN.
- Complete and mail IRS Form 8822-B, Change of Address or Responsible Party—Business, for any address change.

Q 12:74   Can employees claim a credit or refund of the excess Social Security withholding on their wages over $127,200 for 2017 when the Social Security wage base restarts with a new employer and will employees be required to pay any 0.9 percent Additional Medicare Tax not withheld due to a change of employer after meeting the $200,000 threshold with a previous employer?

Yes. If Social Security taxes are withheld on wages over $127,200 for 2017 (up from $118,500 for 2016) because employees had multiple employers, employees may claim a credit or refund on their federal income tax returns pursuant to instructions for the return (Form 1040). [I.R.C. §§ 6413(c), 31(b)] In a memorandum from IRS Chief Counsel's Office, clarifications were given on when corrections of employee FICA overwithholdings can occur in federal agency setting, but memorandum makes certain positions known that affect all employers. [Office of Chief Counsel 2011-25015 (June 24, 2011)] The memorandum holds that:

- An employer cannot file a refund claim for the employer's portion of FICA without first complying with employee notification procedures regarding the employee's rights and responsibilities as outlined in instructions to IRS Form 941-X, Adjusted Employer's Quarterly Federal Tax Return or Claim for Refund. This includes making refunds or reimbursements to employees of overwithheld FICA, or soliciting employee permission to make the reclaim for them, as well as other required employee certifications if involving prior years.
- Employers cannot leave employees on their own to reclaim overwithheld FICA taxes on their Forms 1040.
- Overwithholding on the part of a single employer needs to be refunded by that employer and cannot be refunded through a Form 1040 tax return claim on the part of the employee.
- A shared service center (appointed use of a paying agent, usually on Form 2678) may not reclaim overwithholding if it occurs between two legal employers even though they deposit and file Form 941 under one EIN. Remember, a Form 2678 appointed paying agent is required to file Schedule R, containing separate reporting of liabilities of each legal employer.

Under Treas. Reg. § 31.3102-4, employers are instructed to disregard any compensation paid to the employee by another employer when determining whether the $200,000 threshold has been met that requires 0.9 percent withholding of the Additional Medicare Tax on any excess wages. To the extent the employer does not collect Additional Medicare Tax imposed on the employee under I.R.C. § 3101(b)(2), the employee is liable to pay the tax with his or her Form 1040 due for the tax year.

However, in the context of statutory mergers or consolidations and where successor employers elect to carry over Social Security wages, it is now critical to carry over Medicare wages paid by the predecessor to enable tracking of the point when paid compensation exceeds the $200,000 threshold for the year requiring the additional withholding. Employers will carry liabilities for failing to withhold where required unless they can demonstrate that the employee has paid the taxes. See Q 12:2 on mergers and Q 12:49 on successor employers.

For employers involved in M&A events, this information could impact decisions particularly when made regarding choices to transfer employees and prepare a single W-2 under the alternative method.

Partnerships and Disregarded Entities

Q 12:75   When a partnership is formed through the contribution of a business to the partnership, will successor employer rules apply to employees transferred with the business?

Yes, if the asset transfer otherwise meets the successor employer criteria (see Qs 12:36–12:44). The method of acquisition of the property is immaterial. For purposes of the successor employer rules, the acquisition can occur through a purchase or by any other transaction whereby substantially all the property used in a trade or business of a predecessor or used in a separate unit of a trade or business of a predecessor is acquired by the successor employer. This provision includes partnership contributions, as long as all other successor employer provisions are met. [Treas. Reg. §§ 31.3121(a)(1)-1(b)(3), 31.3306(b)(1)-1(b)(3). See Private Letter Ruling 9315007 for examples of the application of these criteria in a partnership context.] This rule only applies to employees who are transferred and rehired. Partners are technically not employees so the partners are subject to a different tax treatment.

The rules are given broad application since the term "partnership" has broad meaning. A partnership includes a limited partnership, syndicate, group, pool, joint venture, or other unincorporated organization, through or by which any business, financial operation, or venture is carried on. An unincorporated organization with two or more members is generally classified as a partnership for federal tax purposes if its members carry on a trade, business, financial operation, or venture and divide its profits. The successor employer rules will apply if the terms are otherwise met when these business entities acquire substantially all property used in a trade or business of another employer (predecessor), or used in a separate unit of a trade or business of a predecessor.

Special rules for husbands and wives in joint ventures. Many small businesses are operated by husband and wife, without incorporating or creating a formal partnership agreement. A husband and wife business may be a partnership, whether or not a formal partnership agreement is made. However, the Small Business and Work Opportunity Tax Act of 2007, § 8215, provides that a qualified joint venture conducted by a husband and wife who file a joint return is not rated as a partnership for federal tax purposes. [Pub. L. No. 110-28] If a husband and wife materially participate as the only members of a jointly owned and operated business, and file a joint federal income tax return (Form 1040), they can elect for the business to be taxed as a qualified joint venture instead of a partnership. To make the election, all items of income, gain, loss, deduction, and credit must be divided between the spouses, in accordance with each spouse's interest in the venture, and reported on separate Schedules C or F as sole proprietors.

Spouses who meet these qualifications and require EINs actually submit separate Forms SS-4, each as sole proprietor to obtain two separate EINs, and they may not apply for a joint EIN as a "Qualified Joint Venture." In this context, it is thought that the successor employer rules will apply if the terms are otherwise met when the business acquires substantially all property used in a trade or business of another employer (predecessor), or used in a separate unit of a trade or business of a predecessor. Each spouse should be considered to carry the payroll responsibilities for any transferred employees in proportion to each spouse's interest in the venture in the same manner as other liabilities are allocated. [Pub. No. 1635]

Q 12:76 If a partnership has a change in ownership where partners die, retire, or leave for other reasons will this cause the partnership to be considered a new entity for payroll purposes?

Generally, no. When a partner leaves, his or her departure will generally not terminate a partnership even if his or her interest is eventually liquidated by the partnership. Unless the partnership terminates under I.R.C. § 708, the taxable year of a partnership does not close as the result of the death of a partner, the entry of a new partner, the liquidation of a partner's interest in the partnership, or the sale or exchange of a partner's interest in the partnership. [I.R.C. § 706(c)] An existing partnership is considered continuing unless it is terminated in one of two statutorily defined ways and even facing one of them, there are many exceptions. [I.R.C. § 708] See Q 12:77 below.

One cause of termination occurs when a partnership's operations are discontinued and no part of any business, financial operation, or venture of the partnership continues to be carried on by any of its partners. Since the business continues to operate when a partner leaves, the partnership will not be terminated under this provision. Even upon the death of one partner in a two-member partnership, the partnership will not be terminated if the estate or other successor in interest of the deceased partner continues to share in the profits or losses of the partnership. Special rules apply where the partnership pays retiring partners. [I.R.C. § 708(b)(1)(A); Treas. Reg. § 1.708-1(b)]

Under the second method of determining termination of a partnership, a change in membership must affect over 50 percent of the interest in the partnership through a sale or exchange within a 12-month period. This is known as a technical termination. The partnership is seen as liquidated, contributing all assets and transferring all liabilities to the new partnership in exchange for interests in the new partnership, then distributing the interests in the new partnership to its partners. Even when a leaving partner's interest is more than 50 percent of the business, there is a way around the technical termination if the leaving partner's interest is not in fact sold, but instead liquidated back into the partnership. A liquidation by the partnership is not a sale or exchange for purposes of this termination. [I.R.C. § 708(b)(1)(B); Treas. Reg. § 1.708-1(b)(1)(ii)]

See Q 12:77 for a discussion of another carve out from sale or exchange treatment for contributed property; Q 12:78 for mergers, consolidations, and divisions of partnerships as exceptions to the termination rules; and Q 12:81 for possible conversion of an LLC from a partnership to disregarded single member LLC when the loss of a member results in a single member LLC.

Q 12:77 When will a new partnership be allowed to keep the same EIN, to continue the Social Security and FUTA wage bases, as well as be held responsible for all prior payroll compliance of a terminated partnership?

A partnership is considered to continue even if within a new partnership unless it is terminated in one of two statutorily defined ways. [I.R.C. § 708] There are many ways around the termination events. One way, liquidating a partner's interest, is discussed above in Q 12:76, but there are others. Under the continuity rules that are triggered when a termination is not considered to occur, because there is technically no change of employers, the successor employer rules will not apply and the transaction becomes more like a statutory merger where all the payroll liabilities of the old partnership pour into the resulting partnership. [Rev. Rul. 54-31, 1954-1 C.B. 212; Treas. Reg. §§ 31.3121(a)(1)-1(b)(3), 31.3306(b)(1)-1(b)(3); Rev. Rul. 95-37, 1995-1 C.B. 130; Rev. Rul. 84-52, 1984-1 C.B. 157; and Priv. Ltr. Rul. 199916010 (Jan. 11, 1999)]

If either termination event occurs, the partnership's payroll attributes will not automatically carry over to a new successor. So where a partnership is terminated, the successor employer rules may apply. Trying to follow all the possibilities in these configuration can be mind boggling, particularly in large transactions involving many legal entities where some partnerships are considered terminated while others are not. Getting tax counsel involved to assist in sorting payroll administration matters early in the transaction will be important to a successful transition. Planning strategies for moving payrolls will be critical.

The key to determining if payroll matters of an old partnership will carry over to the new partnership is to first examine whether a terminating event has occurred. If not, then continuity is triggered. Even though Rev. Rul. 54-31, 1954-1 C.B. 212, dates back to 1954, it is still authority in the context of payroll administration in these events and under its terms if continuity continues, FICA and FUTA liabilities and wage bases carry over.

One way for an existing partnership to terminate is when operations are discontinued and no part of any business, financial operation, or venture of the partnership continues to be carried on by any of its partners in a partnership. See Q 12:76 above. [I.R.C. § 708(b)(1)(A); Treas. Reg. § 1.708-1(b)]

A second way a partnership is considered to terminate is when 50 percent or more of the total interest in partnership capital and profits is sold or exchanged within a period of 12 consecutive months. This is known as a technical termination. The partnership is seen as liquidated, contributing all assets and transferring all liabilities to the new partnership in exchange for interests in the new partnership, then distributing the interests in the new partnership to its partners. Sales or exchanges include those made to another member of the partnership. Gifts (including assignment to a successor in interest), bequests, inheritance, and the liquidation of a partnership interest, however, are not considered sales or exchanges for this purpose, and neither is the contribution of property to a partnership. For purposes of this test, 50 percent or more of the total interest in partnership capital and profits is defined in the regulations to mean 50 percent or more of the total interest in partnership capital plus 50 percent or more of the total interest in partnership profits. [I.R.C. § 708(b)(1)(B); Treas. Reg. § 1.708-1(b)]

The 50 percent or more test is mutually exclusive from the discontinuance of business test. If either is met, the partnership is terminated unless an exception applies. If neither of these conditions for terminating the partnership is met or if one of the caveats applies, the partnership will be treated as continuing to exist. [I.R.C. § 708(a)] Contribution of property, like partnership liquidations discussed in Q 12:76 above, will preclude termination of a partnership even though 50 percent or more of the total interest in the partnership has been disposed of.

Since contributions of property are not considered sales or exchanges of interests in a partnership, where a new partnership is created in the transaction through contributions of interests in the old partnership, the new partnership generally is allowed to keep the same EIN and continuity of payroll compliance continues. This result happens as long as any new purchasers and the old partners immediately contribute the properties to the new partnership. [I.R.C. § 708(b)(1)(B); Treas. Reg. § 301.6109-1; Rev. Rul. 95-37, 1995-1 C.B. 130; Pub. No. 1635] The end result is much like a mere name change. Payroll continues to operate as if there has been no transaction, and the EIN is retained; but if a name change occurs, agencies will need to be informed. See Rev. Rul. 54-31, 1954-1 C.B. 212 and Q 12:73 above.

If one of the two termination events actually occurs, there are two exceptions that will nonetheless preclude termination and allow continuity: I.R.C.

§ 708(b)(2)(A) covering mergers and consolidations and I.R.C. § 708(b)(2)(B) covering divisions of a partnership into two or more partnerships. In each case, resulting partnerships are considered a continuation of the prior partnership if terms of the exception are met.

If two or more partnerships merge or consolidate into one partnership, the resulting partnership is considered a continuation of the merging or consolidating partnership if members of the old partnership own an interest of more than 50 percent in the capital and profits of the resulting partnership.

If the resulting partnership is a continuation of more than one merging or consolidating partnership because members in more than one partnership end up owning more than 50 percent in the capital and profits of the resulting partnership, the resulting partnership will be considered the continuation solely of that partnership which is credited with the contribution of assets having the greatest fair market value (net of liabilities) to the resulting partnership. Any other merging or consolidating partnerships are considered terminated. If no members of merging or consolidating partnerships hold more than 50 percent interest in the resulting partnership, all of the merged or consolidated partnerships are considered terminated. [Treas. Reg. § 1.708-1(c)] See Q 12:78 for more on partnership mergers.

Because trying to follow all the possibilities in a merger configuration can be mind boggling, getting tax counsel involved to assist in sorting payroll administration matters early on in the transaction will be important to a successful transition.

The complexity of partnership restructurings is demonstrated in a recent IRS private ruling where the IRS held that there was a continuation of the old partnership even though a new EIN was required of the new partnership solely because there were contributions of property. In the private letter ruling, the original partnership merged with an existing disregarded entity held by the new partnership, while at the same time the partners contributed their interests in the original partnership in exchange for interests in the new partnership. This resulted in the partners holding the same interests in the new partnership as they held in the original partnership, and the original partnership becoming a disregarded entity held by the new partnership.

To get to this conclusion, IRS Counsel looked at many authorities, including some very old rulings to resolve treatment of the transaction. I.R.C. § 708(b)(1)(A) provides that a partnership terminates if no part of any business of the partnership continues to be carried on by any of its partners in a partnership. In Rev. Rul. 66-264, 1966-2 C.B. 248, a partnership did not terminate when three partners of a five-partner partnership purchased the partnership's assets at a judicial sale, and then continued the partnership's business through a new three-person partnership. In the recent ruling, Counsel considered these authorities and felt that as long as the historic partners of a partnership continue the old partnership's business through a new partnership, the old partnership should not be treated as terminating under § 708(b)(1)(A).

As pointed out above, I.R.C. § 708(b)(1)(B) provides that a partnership terminates if within a 12-month period, there is a sale or exchange of 50 percent or more of the total interest in partnership capital and profits. However, Treas. Reg. § 1.708-1(b)(2) further provides that the contribution of property to a partnership does not constitute a sale or exchange. Applying these points to the facts above, IRS Counsel concluded that the transfer of the partnership interests in the original partnership to the new partnership through a disregarded entity was not treated as a sale or exchange of partnership interests in the original partnership so there was no termination of the original partnership under I.R.C. § 708(b)(1)(B). Counsel pointed out that a similar conclusion was reached by the IRS in Priv. Ltr. Rul. 9834039 (Mar. 18, 1997). See Q 12:80 below on disregarded entities.

What makes this ruling more interesting is that the resulting partnership was considered a continuation of the original partnership (not really a merger since I.R.C. § 708(b)(2)(A) was not relied upon), even though the resulting partnership already existed and carried a different EIN. [Priv. Ltr. Rul. 201315026 (Mar. 14, 2013); Treas. Reg. §§ 31.3121(a)(1)-1(b)(3), 31.3306(b)(1)-1(b)(3); Rev. Rul. 95-37, 1995-1 C.B. 130; Rev. Rul. 84-52, 1984-1 C.B. 157; Priv. Ltr. Rul. 199916010 (Jan. 11, 1999)]

For payroll purposes, applying continuity in this context makes the tax treatment more like a "merger" where all the predecessor's liabilities pour into the surviving company (merged with existing payroll liabilities of the survivor). See Rev. Rul. 54-31, 1954-1 C.B. 212 and Q 12:78 below for more on how this happens.

There are challenges even among tax professionals on the treatment of many partnership transactions. The IRS has been asked to provide more guidance when contribution of interests in an existing partnership is made to a newly formed partnership where partners in the new partnership include partners of the existing partnership. Treatment becomes an issue when less than 50 percent of the partners' interests in the new partnership are held by partners in the existing partnership. At issue is whether the existing partnership becomes a disregarded entity as a single owned entity of the newly formed partnership, or whether the existing partnership terminates under § 708(b)(1)(A), or whether the newly-formed partnership is considered a continuation of the existing partnership.

You can see some of the confusion through a read of Private Letter Ruling 201528007 (Apr. 7, 2015), where the IRS held that an LLC would terminate as a partnership under I.R.C. § 708(b)(1)(A) as a result of the transaction. The IRS looked at composite result to terminate the partnership, focusing at the end that the partnership would have a single owner (and be disregarded). Several competing concepts are integrated in this ruling.

The American Institute of Certified Public Accountants (AICPA), in a public letter to IRS dated May 1, 2015, made in response to the IRS request for comments on its 2015-2016 Guidance Priority List (Notice 2015-27, 2015-13 I.R.B. 816), asked the IRS to clarify these transactions and, in particular, to clarify the manner in which employment tax returns for a newly formed partnership and an existing partnership should be filed in situations where the newly formed partnership is treated as a continuation of the existing partnership by identifying the correct employer identification number (EIN) to be used for compliance—whether the EIN of the existing partnership should be used or a new EIN would be required of the newly formed partnership.

Where the partnership is actually terminated by a sale or exchange of a 50 percent or more interest and the business continues in the new structure, the following is deemed to occur: the partnership contributes all of its assets and liabilities to a new partnership in exchange for an interest in the new partnership; and, immediately thereafter, the terminated partnership distributes interests in the new partnership to the purchasing partner and the other remaining partners in proportion to their respective interests in the terminated partnership. [I.R.C. § 708(b); Treas. Reg. § 1.708-1(b)(4)]

When a partnership is actually terminated, there is no continuity. Because the manner in which the property is contributed is immaterial for purposes of the successor employer rules, as long as the other aspects of the requirements are met, the compliance rules for successor employers should apply to the transfer of employees from the terminated partnership to the resulting partnership. [Treas. Reg. §§ 31.3121(a)(1)-1(b)(3), 31.3306(b)(1)-1(b)(3); Rev. Rul. 95-37, 1995-1 C.B. 130; Rev. Rul. 84-52, 1984-1 C.B. 157; Priv. Ltr. Rul. 199916010 (Jan. 11, 1999)]

Even though terminated, a partnership will be considered to continue as the same employer for assessment purposes where the business, financial operation, or venture of the partnership wholly fails to be carried on by any of the partners. [I.R.C. § 708(a), (b); Treas. Reg. § 1.708-1(b)(2); Rev. Rul. 62-60, 1962-1 C.B. 186; Rev. Rul. 54-31, 1954-1 C.B. 212]

Q 12:78 If a partnership is merged or consolidated with another partnership, will the successor employer rules apply to allow for election to carryover the Social Security and FUTA wage bases for employees transferred to the merged survivor?

Possibly, depending on the transaction. The election under the successor employer rules to carry over the Social Security and FUTA wage bases for employees transferred to the surviving partnership (or to leave wage bases behind for compliance by the old partnership) will apply where the absorbed partnership is considered terminated.

However, the successor employer election will not apply if the transaction is covered under the partnership continuity rules under which the absorbed partnership is not considered terminated. When continuity applies, there is no change of employers. The old partnership is not terminated, but is seen as continuing to survive in the new partnership. Like the rules for statutory mergers and consolidations of corporations, when the partnership continuity rules apply, it is mandated that the Social Security and FUTA wage bases for all employees continue in the merged survivor. You may not elect to segregate compliance and leave the wage bases behind.

Note. Where the transaction falls under the partnership continuity rules, see discussions in Qs 12:2–12:35 relating to statutory merger and consolidation requirements, as the concerns and solutions will be similar.

If two or more partnerships merge or consolidate into one partnership, the resulting partnership is considered a continuation of the merging or consolidating partnership if the members now own an interest of more than 50 percent in the capital and profits of the resulting partnership. If the resulting partnership can be considered a continuation of more than one of the merging or consolidating partnerships under this test, the resulting partnership will be considered the continuation solely of that partnership which is credited with the contribution of assets having the greatest fair market value (net of liabilities) to the resulting partnership. Any other merging or consolidating partnerships shall be considered as terminated. To take this one step further, if none of the merging or consolidating partnerships had members with an interest of more than 50 percent in the capital and profits of the resulting partnership, all of the merged or consolidated partnerships are considered terminated, and a new partnership results. [I.R.C. § 708(b)(2)(A); Treas. Reg. § 1.708-1(c)]

When continuity rules apply, because there is technically no change of employers, the successor employer rules will not apply. Where a partnership is terminated and the continuity rules do not apply, the successor employer rules will apply. Trying to follow all the possibilities in a merger configuration can be mind boggling, particularly where some partnerships are considered terminated while others are not. Getting tax counsel involved to assist in sorting payroll administration matters early on in the transaction will be important to a successful transition. Planning strategies for moving payrolls will be critical.

In the case of a division of a partnership into two or more partnerships, the resulting partnerships (other than any resulting partnership the members of which had an interest of 50 percent or less in the capital and profits of the prior partnership) are considered a continuation of the prior partnership. [I.R.C. § 708(b)(2)(B); Treas. Reg. § 1.708-1(d)] Working with tax counsel to plan strategies for moving payrolls will be critical here too.

In cases where the resulting partnership is a continuation of a previous partnership, the payroll issues that may arise should be similar to those in the case of a statutory merger or consolidation (see Qs 12:2–12:35). [Rev. Rul. 54-31, 1954-1 C.B. 212; Treas. Reg. §§ 31.3121(a)(1)-1(b)(3) 31.3121(a)(1)-1(b)(3), 31.3306(b)(1)-1(b)(3); Rev. Rul. 95-37, 1995-1 C.B. 130; Rev. Rul. 84-52, 1984-1 C.B. 157; Priv. Ltr. Rul. 199916010 (Jan. 11, 1999)]

See the discussion in Q 12:77 on tax professional challenges in these transactions. Caution is also warranted as the partnership taxation can vary if the transaction is based on state law treatment that is not respected for federal tax purposes. [See the federal defaults in place for working outside applicable jurisdictional law in Treas. Reg. § 1.708-1(c)(3). See also Rev. Rul. 2004-43,

2004-18 I.R.B. 842] Payroll professionals would be wise to consult tax counsel on the tax consequences of partnership restructuring.

Q 12:79   Will the successor employer rules apply to a partnership conversion into an LLC?

No. If the conversion does not result in a termination under I.R.C. § 708 and continuity applies, the successor employer elections will not apply. Successor employer rules only attach if the partnership is terminated under I.R.C. § 708 and the resulting LLC is considered a new partnership (a rare occurrence in a conversion). Commonly, in a conversion to an LLC, continuity is carried over because there is no termination. The limited liability company (LLC) is treated as the same employer as the old partnership and payroll treatment is similar to a statutory merger covered in Qs 12:2–12:35 above. The LLC will most likely retain the same federal EIN. [Rev. Rul. 54-31, 1954-1 C.B. 212; Rev. Rul. 95-37, 1995-1 C.B. 130] (See Qs 12:84–12:87 for a discussion of when new federal EINs are needed.)

LLCs are generally treated as partnerships for federal tax purposes, unless they elect to be treated as a corporation or they are disregarded as a single-owned LLC. So conversion of a partnership to an LLC is usually the same as a conversion of a partnership to another partnership. In Private Letter Ruling 199916010, the IRS held that the new LLC was the same employer, although it was considered necessary for it to receive a new federal EIN. Special payroll rules would result in a different determination if the resulting LLC had only one member and were considered a disregarded entity. See Q 12:87 below.

Q 12:80   What is a disregarded entity?

A disregarded entity is a business entity disregarded as an entity separate from its owner for federal tax purposes. The entity, when disregarded, is considered a branch or division of its parent. [Treas. Reg. § 301.7701-2(a)] Examples include a domestic single member LLC that does not elect to be classified as a corporation and a qualified subchapter S subsidiary (QSub) under I.R.C. § 1361(b)(3)(B). (See Q 12:81 for a discussion of who is responsible for employment tax obligations related to a disregarded entity.)

Disregarded entities are derived from federal "Check-the-Box" regulations that allow an unincorporated entity to elect how the entity will be treated for federal tax purposes. These regulations apply to domestic entities formed on or after January 1, 1997. Under these rules, where the entity fails to choose, defaults apply to characterize the entity. Three preliminary requirements must be met before default treatment can apply:

- The entity must be a separate entity for federal tax purposes.
- The entity must be a business entity.
- The entity must not be properly classified as a corporation or trust under Treas. Reg. § 301.7701-4 or otherwise as an entity subject to special treatment under the Internal Revenue Code regarding the entity's

classification. Corporations are defined to be business entities organized under a federal or state statute or a statute of a federally recognized Indian tribe, if the statute describes the entity as: incorporated or as a corporation, a corporate body, or body politic. Under state statutes, corporations also include a joint-stock company or joint-stock association. Other entities are also expressly defined as corporations such as an insurance company, state-chartered bank, an entity that is wholly owned by a state or a political subdivision, to name a few. [Treas. Reg. § 301.7701-2(a)]

A newly formed domestic organization not already defined as a type of business entity will default to either a partnership if the organization has two or more owners or a "disregarded entity" if it has a single owner.

Foreign entities are also covered under these rules, but are automatically treated as corporations if they are included on the "per se" list in Treas. Reg. § 301.7701-2(b)(8)(i). For example, "P.L.C." in U.K., "Ag" in German-speaking countries, "S.A." in French- and Spanish-speaking countries are generally considered corporations for U.S. tax purposes (but you will need to check the per se list by country to be certain of the characterization). If the entity is not on the "per se" list or classified as a corporation under complex tests outlined in Treas. Reg. § 301.7701, the entity defaults the same as under the domestic rules to a partnership if there are two or more owners or to a "disregarded entity" if a single owner. The default rules will not apply unless at least one of the organization's members has personal liability for the debts of the organization. A foreign entity is classified as a corporation only if all members have limited liability. So if it has a single owner, it is disregarded only if the owner does not have limited liability.

For payroll purposes, the more common entities that default to disregarded status are single-owned limited liability companies (LLCs) and Subchapter S subsidiaries (QSub). There is no need to file an election for classification in a default status. But entities can elect out of the default status by filing Form 8832, Entity Classification Election, or Form 2553, Election by a Small Business Corporation, to be classified as either a subchapter C or S corporation. When an entity "checks the box" on Form 8832 to be treated as a corporation or qualifies and designates S corporation status on Form 2553, it is also a corporation for payroll reporting purposes.

Q 12:81   Are there special payroll rules that make the application of the successor employer rules to disregarded entities more difficult?

Yes. For wages paid on or after January 1, 2009, a disregarded entity is treated as a separate corporate entity for purposes of employment taxes and related reporting requirements. In T.D. 9553 filed with the Federal Register on October 25, 2011, the IRS replaced the temporary regulations with a final version with no substantial changes to the payroll components of Treas. Reg. § 301. 7701-2. Under the temporary and now final regulations, the election process offered by Notice 99-6 [1999-1 C.B. 321] discussed further below under "Some history and unanswered questions" was eliminated and disregarded entities are treated as separate from their owners for federal employment tax and related reporting purposes. A disregarded entity continues to be disregarded for other federal tax purposes.

Under the final regulations, a disregarded entity is regarded and liable for employment taxes on wages paid to its employees and also responsible for satisfying other employment tax obligations such as making timely deposits of employment taxes, filing returns, and providing wage statements to employees on Forms W-2. The owner of the disregarded entity would no longer be liable for employment taxes or satisfying other employment tax obligations with respect to the employees of the disregarded entity. The IRS and the Treasury Department believe that recognizing disregarded entities as employers for federal employment taxes will improve administration of the federal tax laws and simplify federal tax compliance with respect to reporting, payment, and collection of employment taxes. Since most states recognize disregarded entities as employers for reporting, payment, and collection of state employment taxes, treating a disregarded entity as a separate corporate entity for employment compliance purposes will more closely align federal and state reporting, payment and collection of employment taxes.

Splitting of Payroll and 1099 functions. While Treas. Reg. § 301.7701-2(c)(2)(iv) treats disregarded entities as separate corporations for employment tax purposes, the regulation failed to directly address disregarded entities for backup withholding and related information reporting purposes. The absence of language in the regulation caused some confusion as to the responsible party for filing information returns for reportable payments and related backup withholding requirements. In 2011, the IRS issued proposed and temporary regulations to clarify treatment. In the preamble to the proposed regulations, the IRS considered this provision not to be a change in the existing rules. New Treas. Reg. § 301.7701-2T expressly provides that the owner of a disregarded business entity, apart from a Qsub, is subject to the withholding and reporting requirements imposed under I.R.C. § 3406 (backup withholding). [T.D. 9554, 2011-50 I.R.B. 843] It is important to note that the amended regulations speak to § 3406, the backup withholding provisions, and not all Form 1099 reportable payments are subject to the backup withholding rules under I.R.C. § 3406. But, the direction this is taking is now clearer. Employment taxes are only employment taxes. Owners of disregarded entities should consider themselves responsible for meeting other tax reporting and withholding compliance requirements. Following the logic of T.D. 9554, owners of disregarded entities are more than likely also responsible for compliance with withholding at source rules under I.R.C. § 1441 and § 1442 (for payments subject to Chapter 3 withholding and reporting on Form 1042 and 1042-S) and I.R.C. § 1471 and § 1472 (Chapter 4 FATCA provisions). However, there is no express guidance on point.

QSub has special rules. Except to the extent provided by the Secretary, QSubs are not disregarded for purposes of information returns. [I.R.C. § 1361(b)(3)(E)] In addition, an individual owner (or sole proprietorship) of a disregarded entity continues to be treated as self-employed for purposes of taxes under the Self-Employment Contributions Act (SECA) (§ 1401 et. seq.) [T.D.

9356, 8-15-07; Treas. Reg. § 301.7701-2(c)(2); T.D. 9553, 10-25-2011, replacing the temporary regulations with a final version with no substantial changes to the payroll components of Treas. Reg. § 301.7701-2]

See Private Letter Ruling 201115016 (Jan. 5, 2011) for an example of application of I.R.C. § 368(a)(1)(F) to a transaction in which an S corporation became a QSub, a disregarded entity of a newly formed S corporation, and qualified as a Type F reorganization. The new S corporation and the QSub were treated as a single S corporation because the Qsub was considered a disregarded entity and ignored for purposes of the transaction. Although not entirely clear from the ruling, it appears that the wage history and EIN of the old S corporation could carry over to the new QSub now required to maintain payroll at the QSub level.

Under Treas. Reg. § 1.1361-4(a)(7), a QSub is treated as a separate corporation for purposes of employment tax and related reporting requirements (effective for wages paid on or after January 1, 2009), and under Treasury Regulations § 1.1361-4(a)(8), a QSub is treated as a separate corporation for purposes of certain excise taxes (effective for liabilities imposed and actions first required or permitted in periods beginning on or after January 1, 2008). In Revenue Ruling 2008-18, in the context of an I.R.C. § 368(a)(1)(F) reorganization, the IRS takes into consideration that a resulting QSub will be treated as a separate corporation for certain federal tax purposes, and requires the QSub to retain its old EIN to use when it is treated as a separate corporation for federal tax purposes. The ruling holds that it would not be appropriate for the newly acquiring corporation in a reorganization under I.R.C. § 368(a)(1)(F) to use the EIN of the transferor corporation that becomes a QSub, but the Qsub would keep the old EIN as a separate employer. [Rev. Rul. 2008-18, 2008-13 I.R.B. 674]

EINS for newly created disregarded entities. Form SS-4 is needed to request an EIN for employment tax requirements for a Single Member LLC that is a disregarded entity.

Disregarded entities owned by tax-exempt organizations. Even though a disregarded entity is treated as a separate corporate entity for purposes of employment taxes, a disregarded entity owned solely by an I.R.C. § 501(c)(3) organization will not be subject to FUTA tax on wages it pays its employees.

Disregarded entities formed when a partner drops out of a two-partner partnership or a member leaves a two-member LLC. The IRS has now instructed that when a former partnership (or LLC) becomes a disregarded entity, the former partnership's (LLC's) EIN must continue to be used on the filings of the disregarded entity's employment tax returns and a name change, where needed, must be submitted to agencies. In coming to this conclusion, IRS Counsel has relied upon T.D. 9356, which provides that the disregarded entity reports its employment tax obligations, not the owner. [Treas. Reg. § 301.7701-2(c)(2)(iv)(B)]

The IRS has also formalized some audit instructions for handling the bridge period when disregarded entities have been formed through the loss of a partner or member and there is tax history and open audit periods in the former partnership. For tax examination purposes, all business activity after the partnership becomes a disregarded entity of a sole proprietorship is to be reported on Schedule C of the sole proprietor, except with respect to employment tax or excise tax, as covered above. Any former partnership's employment tax returns filed under the former partnership's old EIN are still valid employment tax returns. IRS examiners are being instructed to ask for statute extensions in these cases to be given time to figure the matters out. Any consent to an extension is to be signed by the sole proprietor or if the sole owner is an entity, its officers. Examiners are also being instructed that any assessment and other notices should be issued to the owner of the disregarded entity because the partnership ceased to exist when its membership was reduced to one member. [CCA 201351018 (Aug. 16, 2013)]

Conversion of a disregarded entity into a regarded entity. Treas. Reg. § 301.7701-3(f)(2) provides that a single member entity disregarded as an entity separate from its owner is classified as a partnership when the entity adds more than one member. [Rev. Rul. 99-5, 1999-1 C.B. 434]

When an individual contributes cash to a single-owned LLC in exchange for a 50 percent ownership interest in the LLC, the disregarded LLC is converted to a recognized partnership. The existing member of the LLC is treated as contributing all of the assets of the LLC to the partnership in exchange for a 50 percent partnership interest. Contribution of assets, along with employees to the new partnership might fall under the successor employer rules if all of the requirements are considered met. A new EIN will be required of the partnership.

For Qsubs, I.R.C. § 1361(b)(3)(C)(i) provides that if a QSub ceases to meet the requirements of I.R.C. § 1361(b)(3)(B), the corporation is to be treated as a new Corporation acquiring all of its assets (and assuming all of its liabilities) immediately before the cessation from the S corporation in exchange for its stock. Treas. Reg. § 1.1361-5(a)(1)(iii) provides that the termination of a QSub election is effective at the close of the day on which an event occurs that renders the subsidiary ineligible for QSub status. Different rules apply should the parent's S Corporation election terminate. [*See also* Treas. Reg. § 1.1361-5(b)(1)(i)] The liability carryover rule is similar to that which applies to corporate statutory consolidations and for payroll purposes, the rules for statutory mergers discussed above at Qs 12:2–12:35 should be consulted.

See CCA 201326014 (Mar. 4, 2013), for insight into both single-owned LLC and Qsub conversions.

Some history and unanswered questions. Disregarded entities and their owners were allowed to use the procedures permitted by Notice 99-6 for wages paid prior to January 1, 2009. Under Notice 99-6, absent the election, payroll was to be processed at the parent level and, with the election, payroll was processed at the disregarded entity level. Employment taxes for employees of a disregarded entity were to be reported and paid in one of the following two ways:

1. By its parent, as if the employees were employed directly by the parent using the parent's name and EIN for all federal payroll tax compliance purposes; or

2. By the entity as a separate entity under state law, in which case it would use its own name and have a separate EIN for all federal payroll tax compliance purposes.

For periods prior to 2009, Notice 99-6 states that ultimate liability for employment taxes remained with the owner of the disregarded entity regardless of which alternative was chosen.

In the transitional period prior to 2009, some applications were unclear in an M&A context. If the disregarded entity chose under Notice 99-6 to be separate for payroll tax compliance purposes and that entity later underwent some M&A event, it was unclear whether the elected entity status would apply for purposes of the application of the successor employer rules, or whether the parent became the focus of the tests. For example, if a corporate subsidiary converts to a single member LLC that is disregarded for federal tax purposes but elects to have a separate payroll on conversion, will the transaction be considered a statutory upstream merger, as the LLC is disregarded and treated as a branch of the parent triggering the merger rules for payroll purposes, or will the transaction be considered an asset contribution in formation of a partnership requiring the application of the successor employer rules as the LLC will have a separate payroll process? Even after 2008, will the successor employer rules attach substantively to the parent or to the disregarded entity? In addition, regulations under I.R.C. § 338 will allow an election under I.R.C. § 338(h)(10) to avoid statutory merger treatment, but provided that any resulting disregarded entity is looked through. This leaves challenges since a disregarded entity is respected for payroll taxes and although unclear, the payroll may remain with the disregarded entity under merger treatment. See Q 12:80 above for the payroll ramifications.

Some questions also arise as to the federal tax treatment of transactions under new state laws allowing conversions of LLCs into corporations, and vice versa, and treating the resultant entity as the same entity regarding assets and liabilities. [See Cal. Corp. Code §§ 1150 et seq., and Del. Gen. Corp. Law §§ 265, 266; Del. Code tit. 6, §§ 18-214, 18-216, for examples.]

Unanswered employment tax questions for Series LLCs, protected cell companies, segregated account companies or segregated portfolio companies (cell companies).

A number of states have enacted statutes providing for the creation of entities that may be established in series, including limited liability companies (series LLCs). Although a series of LLCs generally is not treated as separate entities for state law purposes and, thus, the series cannot have its own members, each series has "associated" with it specified members from the underlying LLCs and associated assets, assets, rights, obligations, and investment objectives or business purposes. A member's association with one or more particular series is comparable to direct ownership by the members in such series, in that their rights, duties, and powers with respect to the series are direct and specifically identified. If the conditions enumerated in the relevant statute are satisfied, the debts, liabilities, and obligations of one series generally are enforceable only against the assets of that series and not against assets of other series. Series statutes generally provide that:

- Each unit has its own owners (members) and may be managed separately from the master LLC and other units.

- Each unit must maintain separate books and records.

- As with a regularly formed LLC, the owners (members) of each unit are not financially responsible for the unit's debts and obligations.

- A unit may conduct part of the business of the master LLC, or may conduct a wholly different business.

- Each unit has its own assets and liabilities.

- The members of each unit are treated under the laws of the state where the master LLC is formed as owning an interest in only that unit, and have no rights as members of one unit in the assets or income of any other unit.

- Each unit is liable only for its own debts and obligations.

- In general, creditors of one unit may only make claims against the assets of that unit.

The IRS is looking at many issues involving series limited liability companies and has indicated that it will eventually release detailed guidance, particularly on foreign series LLCs. Proposed regulations released in September, 2010, conclude a series is a separate entity for federal taxes, but do not address ownership issues or tax reporting issues.

Some states have already addressed these issues. Although California law does not allow for a series LLC to be formed in California, it has chosen to recognize them if they are organized under a state statute that addresses the bullets above. A series LLC that is formed under the laws of another state may register as a foreign LLC with the California Secretary of State and transact business in California. In this case, the California Franchise Tax Board (FTB) will respect each unit as a separate entity for filing and tax purposes. The same filing guidelines and estimated taxes that apply to a regular LLC will apply to each unit of a series LLC. If the LLC has elected to be taxed as a corporation, the FTB will follow corporation filing guidelines and estimated tax requirements, and will be subject to the minimum franchise tax. In this regard, the unit would be a payer for payroll taxes, information reporting, and withholding purposes. Unlike the California FTB, the Texas Comptroller has chosen to treat a series LLC as a single entity for purposes of reporting its activities for the Texas franchise tax. It must pay one filing fee, register as a single entity with the Texas Secretary of State, file one franchise tax report, and file one public information report under a single Texas taxpayer identification number. See FAQs on the Texas Franchise Tax Rule 3.581 at http://www.window.state.tx.us/taxinfo/franchise/faq_tax_ent.html#tax_ent19.

Similar to series LLCs, protected cell companies, another new business structure in the market place, also present similar classification issues. Certain jurisdictions have enacted statutes providing for entities similar to the series LLC. For example, certain statutes provide for the chartering of a legal entity (or the establishment of cells) under a structure commonly known as a protected cell company, segregated account company, or segregated portfolio company (cell company). There is little specific guidance regarding whether for federal tax purposes a series (or cell) is treated as an entity separate from other series or the series LLC (or other cells or the cell company, as the case may be), or whether the company and all of its series (or cells) should be treated as a single entity.

For federal and state purposes, classification of these entities for payroll tax purposes is presently unclear on many points and if questions arise, it is best to seek counsel advice on their treatment. [NPRM REG-119921-09 (Sept. 14, 2010); Notice 2008-19, 2008-5 I.R.B. 366]

See also Q 12:87 below for further considerations on EIN use.

Section 530 Relief—Safe Harbor for Independent Contractor Status

Q 12:82   Can certain M&A events cause the loss of a safe harbor (Section 530 relief) that minimizes uncertainty regarding the proper treatment of independent contractors?

Yes. Section 530 relief is specific to taxpayers. [*See* provisions of § 530 of the Revenue Act of 1978, Pub. L. No. 95-600, 92 Stat. 2763, *as amended by* Small Business Job Protection Act of 1996 (Pub. L. No. 104-188), 110 Stat. 1755 (Aug. 20, 1996), and Rev. Proc. 85-18, 1985-1 C.B. 518.]

When an M&A event occurs, the benefit of Section 530 relief could be lost if the taxpayer no longer exists and a new company is considered formed. In a statutory merger or other transaction where the surviving taxpayer is considered the same taxpayer as the acquired taxpayer, it is possible that relief may be preserved. Caution and planning are advised in the context of any business restructuring if Section 530 relief is valued. (See Qs 6:45–6:56 for further discussion of Section 530 relief.)

Possible reform in the works. At the time of this writing, there have been several bills introduced in the U.S. legislature that would repeal Section 530 relief. Readers are advised to check for possible law changes.

FICA Exemptions for Nonprofit Organizations in M&A Events

Q 12:83   Does a new I.R.C. § 501(c)(3) organization established to acquire all the activities, operations, and employees of another I.R.C. § 501(c)(3) organization need to file a new waiver under I.R.C. § 508 to obtain Social Security coverage for its employees, even though the old organization had effective waivers covering the employees to be transferred?

Yes. If an organization is considered new for purposes of I.R.C. § 501(c)(3) status, it is also new for purposes of the waiver of exemption for Social Security coverage. [GCM 38740 (June 3, 1981); Rev. Rul. 77-159, 1977-1 C.B. 303; Rev. Rul. 71-276, 1971-1 C.B. 289]

On the other hand, in a merger or consolidation where one entity survives and absorbs the other, the old waiver remains in effect after the merger. The surviving organization is not considered a new entity. [GCM 37601 (July 10, 1977)]

In the context of successor employer transfers, the activity in which the I.R.C. § 501(c)(3) organization is engaged is considered to be its trade or business for purposes of determining whether transferred property was used in the trade or business of the predecessor and for purposes of determining whether the employment by the predecessor and successor employers of an individual whose services were retained by the successor constitute employment in the trade or business. If an organization subject to FICA by virtue of the waiver acquires all the property of another such organization, also subject to FICA by virtue of a waiver, and retains the services of an employee of the predecessor, the wages paid by the predecessor to that employee can be attributed to the successor employer for purposes of the annual wage limitation. [Treas. Reg. § 31.3121(a)(1)-1(b)(6)]

In addition, it is important to be aware that a restructuring of state and local governments or other public agencies, including teaching hospitals, and state schools, colleges and universities covered by Section 218 Agreements may modify the existing Social Security coverage of their employees. Depending on the type of restructuring (called, for Section 218 purposes, a "predecessor-successor" situation), an entity may be required to go through the process of obtaining new coverage.

Federal Employer Identification Numbers

Q 12:84   When are new federal EINs needed in the context of an M&A event?

New EINs are required when new entities are considered to be formed. Once an entity has an EIN, it normally keeps it even if classification changes. [Treas.]

In some cases, most specifically in the context of a merger or consolidation, activities and payments before the M&A event are required to be combined under the new EIN/name with activities and payments after the event. In other cases, consolidation is optional where the successor employer rules attach as discussed above. Sometimes, consolidation is not allowed and pre-M&A event payments must be reported under the old name/EIN and post-M&A events are reported under the new name/EIN. So it is important to know specifically what the M&A event is for tax purposes, in order to know your options and how payroll compliance is to be handled.

In the context of an M&A event, new federal EINs ARE needed for:

- Corporate subsidiaries that currently use the parent's EIN or are newly created.
- Corporation that becomes a partnership, LLC, or a sole proprietorship.
- A sole proprietor who incorporates.
- A new corporation that is created after a statutory merger.
- Corporations with new corporate charters, even if created as part of a statutory consolidation or after a statutory merger or as a subsidiary. In a reincorporation that does not involve an F reorganization, the new entity must acquire a new EIN and discontinue use of the old EIN. Entities that terminate and reopen with a new corporate charter are also required to obtain new EINs.
- Disregarded entities that pay wages or file excise taxes. [T.D. 9356, Aug. 15, 2007; Treas. Reg. § 301.7701-2(c)(2)]
- Bankruptcy filings under Chapter 7 (liquidation) or 11 (reorganization). Corporations in bankruptcy usually do not require new EINs unless a liquidating trust is established for a corporation that is in bankruptcy where an EIN for that trust is required.
- New incorporations.
- New partnerships, including sole proprietors who take in partners and operate as a partnership.
- One partner takes over and operates business as a sole proprietorship.
- Corporations that become partnerships.
- Partnerships that incorporate.
- Partnership that is terminated without continuity under I.R.C. § 708 (for example, if no part of any business, financial operation, or venture of the partnership continues to be carried on by any of its partners in a partnership or if within a 12-month period there is a sale or exchange of at least 50 percent of the total interest in partnership capital and profits to another partner) and a new partnership is begun. The new partnership will need a new EIN. However, where a partnership is terminated and the purchaser and remaining partners immediately contribute the properties to a new partnership, the old partnership EIN may be retained.

[Treas. Reg. § 301.6109-1; Pub. No. 1635 and Pub. No. 4485]

SS-4 EIN application considerations in M&A transactions.

- **Avoid special characters in an entity's legal name.** The only special characters IRS systems can accept in a business name are: 1. alpha (A-Z), 2. numeric (0-9), 3. hyphen (-), and 4. ampersand (&). If the legal name of a business includes any characters other than those listed above, it may cause difficulties in tax filings. Even titles on Form SS-4 must conform to these restrictions. If a legal name contains a symbol or character such as a "plus" symbol (+) or a period (.), such as Jones.com, it could be submitted on Form SS-4 as Jones Dot Com or Jones Com. Later when returns are filed on a different basis, there is a risk of the tax return not being processed because the taxpayer's name and taxpayer identification number (TIN, which is an SSN, ITIN, or EIN) cannot be matched in the IRS business files, a step required for every return to be processed. Other symbols are also troublesome, such as a backward (\) or forward (/) slash or an apostrophe.

- **Avoid using individual nominees to complete SS-4.** It has often been the practice in M&A transactions that the legal counsel instrumental in setting up any new legal entity also files the paperwork for a new EIN. This practice has now been seriously curtailed by new IRS requirements regarding the use of nominee individuals in applying for EINs. Use of a nominee temporarily authorized to act on behalf of the entity during the formation process to endorse an EIN application is seen as preventing the IRS from gathering appropriate information on entity ownership, and per the IRS has been found to facilitate tax non-compliance by entities and their owners. Under the new procedure, the IRS does not authorize the use of nominees to obtain EINs.

- **Third Party Designee (TPD) may be used if cannot be avoided.** If a third party is making the application for an EIN, the taxpayer must authorize the third party to apply for and receive the EIN. A Third Party Designee (TPD) must complete his or her identifying information at the bottom of the Form SS-4. However, the SS-4 must be signed by the taxpayer for the TPD authorization to be valid. For corporations, the president, vice president, or other principal officer must sign the application. For partnerships and LLCs, a responsible and duly authorized member or officer having knowledge of the partnership's affairs must sign the application if the Third Party Designee section is completed. An application that includes a TPD must be either mailed or faxed to the IRS and this will show receipt of the EIN. Use of the faster online EIN service is not available for TPD applications. Moreover, the designee's authority terminates at the time the EIN is assigned and released to the designee. IRS instructions say to complete the TPD section only if you want to authorize the named individual to receive the EIN and answer questions about the completion of Form SS-4.

- **Make sure the correct responsible party is disclosed on the SS-4 and that the party's TIN is included.** All EIN applications (mail, fax, phone, electronic) must disclose the name and TIN of the true principal officer, general partner, owner, or other responsible party for the entity. A TIN is required even if the responsible party is a non-U.S. resident alien who has never been assigned a TIN (in such cases, a Form W-7 ITIN application must be attached to the SS-4). An SS-4 will be rejected if the responsible party's taxpayer identification number has been omitted unless the EIN is only needed to make an entity classification election and the entity is a foreign entity with no effectively connected income from sources within the United States.

A "responsible party" must be named in the SS-4 and is the party who controls, manages, or directs the applicant entity and the disposition of its funds and assets. If there is more than one responsible party, the entity may list whichever party the entity wants the IRS to recognize as the responsible party. For entities with shares or interests traded on a public exchange, or which are registered with the Securities and Exchange Commission, "responsible party" is (a) the principal officer, if the business is a corporation, (b) a general partner, if a partnership, (c) the owner of an entity that is disregarded as separate from its owner (disregarded entities owned by a corporation enter the corporation's name and EIN), or (d) a grantor, owner, or trustor, if a trust. For all other entities, "responsible party" is the person who has a level of control over, or entitlement to, the funds or assets in the entity that, as a practical matter, enables the individual, directly or indirectly, to control, manage, or direct the entity and the disposition of its funds and assets. The ability to fund the entity or the entitlement to the property of the entity alone, however, without any corresponding authority to control, manage, or direct the entity (such as in the case of a minor child beneficiary), does not cause the individual to be a responsible party.

- **The IRS now limits EIN issuance to one per responsible party per day**. Do not forget and attempt to process multiple applications at the same time. Some may be rejected.

- **Pick an appropriate responsible party and keep the IRS current on the responsible party for the EIN as it will affect processing of tax filings**. Any entity that in the past applied for an EIN listing a nominee as the "principal officer," etc., and listing the nominee's TIN as that of the principal officer as well as an entity that listed a responsible party who is now no longer the true responsible party will need to update the responsible party information by filing Form 8822-B, *Change of Address or Responsible Party-Business*, to notify the IRS of the new responsible party. Any entity with an EIN is now required to report a change in its "responsible party" by: (a) completing Form 8822-B as appropriate, including entering the new responsible party's name on line 8 and the new responsible party's SSN, ITIN, or EIN on line 9; and (b) filing the completed form with the IRS within 60 days of the change. [Treas. Reg. § 301.6109-1(d)(2)(ii)] There are currently no directly applicable penalties for failure to update this information; however, the IRS looks at who the responsible party is in some cases to verify signatures on tax filings and on penalty abatement requests, as well as for other tax reasons so keeping the IRS current on the responsible party for the entity will be critical to lowering tax risk. [See CCA 201520011, Apr. 24, 2015.]

- **Use the IRS free online EIN application portal**. SS-4 applications submitted by mail take four to six weeks to process. Applications submitted by fax will be processed quicker, but are hard to track. IRS says EINs are issued within four business days of faxing. The fastest way to obtain an EIN is through use of the online service. The IRS says that the Internet is the preferred method to use when applying for an EIN. Find the portal on the IRS website at www.irs.gov (using keyword "EIN"). The information submitted is validated during the online session. Once the application is completed, an EIN is immediately issued. Online filing is only available for entities whose principal business, office or agency, or legal residence (in the case of an individual), is located in the United States or U.S. Territories and where the principal officer, general partner, grantor, owner, or trustor already has a valid TIN. Online filing is not available to Third Party Designees.

- **Give filing SS-4 applications high priority**. EINs are necessary in order to set up accounts in EFTPS now mandated for all federal payroll tax deposits. And, remember that a federal EIN must first be obtained before state tax identification numbers may be acquired. Most states will not accept payroll tax returns on an "applied for" basis. Timing is critical and where it is known that a new EIN will be needed, making the application for it as soon as legally possible should be on a high priority.

When new EINs are provided to new employers, the initial federal deposit frequency is monthly until a total undeposited liability of $100,000 or more is reached in which case, the next day deposit rule attaches and the frequency then becomes semiweekly.

Q 12:85 When are new federal EINs not needed in the context of an M&A event?

New federal EINs **ARE NOT** needed and federal payroll tax compliance can continue under the same EIN for:

- Multiple divisions or branches of a taxpayer (the taxpayer's EIN is used).

- Individuals (sole proprietors) keep the same EIN when the trade name is changed without a change of ownership. Remember that only one EIN is allowed regardless of the number of businesses the individual owns.

- Survivors of statutory mergers (the existing EIN of the survivor before the merger is used).

- Corporations or partnerships that declare bankruptcy unless a liquidating trust is formed in which case, the trust needs to obtain an EIN.

- Businesses that change names, for example, when a corporate charter is amended to show a name change only, the corporate structure is not changing and so the EIN remains the same.

- Businesses that change or add locations.

- Election to be taxed as an S Corporation by filing Form 2553. Original EIN is retained.

- A corporation that is sold and the assets, liabilities, and charters are obtained by the buyer.

- A partnership that would otherwise terminate under I.R.C. § 708(b)(1)(B) because 50 percent or more of the interest in the partnership has been sold or exchanged within a 12-month period, but the purchaser and remaining partners immediately contribute the properties to a new partnership or where the leaving partner's share is liquidated by the partnership allowing continuity. See Q 12:77. Note that in cases of qualifying partnership consolidations or divisions, even though continuity is retained, new EINs are frequently necessary for newly created surviving partnerships.

- Partnership-to-partnership conversions with continuity under § 708, including a conversion of a partnership to a regarded LLC or a conversion of a general partnership to a limited partnership as long as the partnership does not terminate and continuity is retained. [Rev. Rul. 95-37, 1995-1 C.B. 130; Rev. Rul. 84-52, 1984-1 C.B. 157]

- Corporate reorganizations where only the identity, form, or place of organization changes (i.e., an F reorganization). If a corporation reincorporates in an F reorganization, the new entity must continue to use the EIN of the old entity.

- A QSub (Qualified Subchapter S subsidiary) will be treated as a separate corporation for certain federal tax purposes in an I.R.C. § 368(a)(1)(F) reorganization. However, Revenue Ruling 2008-18 [2008-13 I.R.B. 674] requires the QSub to retain and use its own EIN when it is treated as a separate corporation for federal tax purposes. The ruling holds that it would not be appropriate for the acquiring corporation in a reorganization under I.R.C. § 368(a)(1)(F) to retain the EIN of the transferor corporation that later becomes a QSub.

[Pub. No. 1635; Pub. No. 4485]

Name and address changes. Even if a new EIN is not required, if a company changes its name, it is important to correct IRS and other tax agencies' records to reflect the change. Filings and tax deposits made under names and EINS that do not match tax agency records are often mishandled by the agency, incorrectly posted, and sometimes even returned without processing. It is important that payroll professionals keep addresses and business information current with the IRS for any EIN issued. If it is necessary to update business address information, complete Form 8822-B, Change of Address or Responsible Person—Business, and mail it to the IRS at the address listed on the form.

For company name changes, write to the IRS Service Center where the Form 941 is filed to notify the IRS of the change. Make sure the request is signed by an officer or person otherwise authorized to sign a tax return for your company. Additionally, partnerships and corporations must include a copy of the Articles of Amendment that were filed with the state that authorized the name change.

Currently, the IRS can only maintain one address for each EIN. Remember that when filing the Form 8822-B, the address also changes the information for the firm's corporate tax and other returns such as Forms 1099 and 1042/1042-S operations. Where a single address becomes a concern, consider centralizing the IRS mail receipt process and using that address for everyone concerned. If a business is centralized, it should ensure that it has in place a process to keep current the contact information for those in the firm that will need to know about the receipt of IRS correspondence related to their unit's activities.

Keep the IRS current on responsible party for the EIN as it will affect processing of tax filings. See Q 12:84 for the reasoning.

Q 12:86   Which EIN survives when there is a statutory merger or consolidation or a reincorporation?

The guidelines are as follows:

- In the event of a merger between two existing corporations, the EIN assigned to the survivor should be used; discontinue use of the other EIN.

- In the event of a consolidation of two existing corporations, the newly created survivor must acquire a new EIN and discontinue use of all other EINs.

- If a corporation reincorporates in an F reorganization, the new entity must continue to use the EIN of the old entity. But see, Revenue Ruling 2008-18 discussed in Q 12:85 above, involving a QSub where the IRS comes to a different conclusion when the need for separate treatment is apparent.

- In a reincorporation that does not involve an F reorganization, the new entity must acquire a new EIN and discontinue use of the old EIN.

[*See* GCM 35094 (Oct. 27, 1972), for further thoughts on these guidelines, and I.R.S. Pub. No. 1635, Understanding Your EIN.]

Remember that where continuity carries over between employers, even if the payroll professional is required to obtain a new EIN for the resulting entity, you will still need to consolidate predecessor payroll liabilities and processes with those of the successor entity. This will be true in the cases of statutory mergers and consolidations and other transactions where tax benefits carry over under I.R.C. § 381, as well as partnership restructurings that do not result in a termination under I.R.C. § 708. See Q 12:6 and Qs 12:75–12:81 above.

Q 12:87   Will involvement of a disregarded entity affect the outcome of whether a new federal EIN will be needed? Can a new federal EIN be acquired for an entity for administrative purposes even if not technically needed?

Yes to both questions as long as the entity does not already have an EIN. The IRS's current policy is not to issue a new federal EIN to a company that already has one. Disregarded entities (see Q 12:80 above) must use their own EIN for employment and excise tax purposes so will be required to acquire one; but they must use the owner's EIN for all other purposes. [Treas. Reg. § 301.6109-1(h)(2)] LLCs are partnerships for tax purposes unless disregarded or electing corporate status. There are different sets of EIN rules on mergers of partnerships with other partnerships or if they convert to another legal entity, requiring the resulting entity to keep the EIN of the consolidated or older partnership. But these rules may have a different result if involving a disregarded entity.

In a *merger of a disregarded entity into an acquiring corporation,* the merger does not qualify as a statutory merger under I.R.C. § 368(a)(1)(A) because, technically, the assets of the disregarded entity's owner (other than those held in the disregarded entity) are not transferred to the acquiring corporation and the owner does not cease to exist as a result of the state or federal law. The IRS has released proposed regulations to say that the transaction can qualify for tax-free treatment for federal income tax purposes as a C, D, or F reorganization if it meets all applicable requirements. This may allow the use of the acquiring corporate entity's EIN, but rules are not clear at this point.

The same is true of *a merger of a target corporation into a disregarded entity. This transaction also* does not qualify as a statutory merger because the owner of the disregarded entity, the only potential party to a reorganization, is not a party under state or federal law to the merger transaction. However, the transaction can qualify for tax-free treatment for federal income tax purposes as a C, D, or F reorganization if those terms are met. Again, this may result in a different EIN treatment than the general rules described above. More than likely, the use of the disregarded entity's EIN will continue at least for payroll purposes, but rules are not clear at this point either.

If an entity becomes disregarded in restructuring, it should be able to keep its old EIN from prior to the transaction for payroll purposes, but the IRS has to clarify that point. We also need to contend with the possibilities that Form 1042 and 1099, as well as related backup withholding activities discussed further below in Q 12:88, may still be required at the owner level. These matters can be very confusing.

In Private Letter Ruling 199916010 (Jan. 11, 1999), where two partnerships merged, the resulting partnership was considered to be the same employer for FICA and FUTA purposes as one of the merging partnerships. Nonetheless, the resulting partnership requested a new EIN and was granted it. Although the ruling was unclear on the need for the new EIN, it is assumed that the new EIN was acquired to support state treatment of the surviving partnership as a new entity for unemployment tax purposes. This ruling is important in that it does support a separation from the substantive tax result and the need for an EIN for administrative purposes. Caution is warranted in acquiring a new EIN where technically not otherwise required since the state tax identification number should relate to the same federal EIN used to file Form 940 for FUTA tax purposes. When this is not the case, the state unemployment tax credit may not match to offset FUTA liabilities thereby creating a certification issue. See Q 12:32.

What if the state does not want to change the EIN it has on file even though federally required? What if the state declines to issue a new state tax identification number for state compliance purposes? It is not always clear when to continue to use an existing EIN or to acquire a new one and each case will need to be viewed independently. See Q 12:117 below for further considerations regarding state IDs.

Once a transaction is locked in, payroll professionals should form a task team to begin to evaluate all federal, state, and local tax compliance in the companies involved and determine how they will be consolidated and under which EIN the consolidation is appropriate. It will be important to collaborate with accounts payable, treasury, and tax and legal representatives in this process who may also have other activities under EINs to be considered.

Filing Forms 1099 Series in an M&A Event

Q 12:88   Can a successor file the predecessor's Forms 1099, 1098, 5498, and W-2G series (the "Forms 1099 series") or Forms 1042-S?

Yes. A successor business (corporation, partnership, or sole proprietor) and a predecessor business (corporation, partnership, or sole proprietor) may agree that the successor business will assume all or part of the predecessor's information reporting responsibilities. This allows the successor business to file one Form 1099, 1098, 5498, or W-2G for each recipient by combining the predecessor's and successor's reportable amounts, including any withholding. Similar provisions are set up for filing Forms 1042S, Foreign Person's U.S. Source Income Subject to Withholding, on a combined basis. For this purpose, "business" includes a corporation, a partnership, or a sole proprietorship. Under this provision, the successor employer can file one Form 1099 for each recipient, combining the predecessor's and the successor's reportable amounts, including any backup withholding under I.R.C. § 3406, pension withholding under I.R.C. § 3405, withholding on gambling winnings under I.R.C. § 3402(q) or § 3402(r), and withholding at source rules under I.R.C. § 1441, § 1442, § 1471, or § 1472, as applicable. If the requirements are met, the predecessor business is relieved from filing any Forms 1099 or 1042-S. [General Instructions to the Forms 1099 series; Rev. Proc. 99-50, 1999-2 C.B. 757]

Q 12:89   What conditions must be met for a successor to file the predecessor's Forms 1099 and 1042-S?

For a successor business to file the predecessor's Forms 1099 and 1042-S, the following conditions must be met:

1. The successor business must have acquired from the predecessor business substantially all the property used in the trade or business of the predecessor, including when one or more corporations are absorbed by another corporation pursuant to a merger agreement, or used in a separate unit of a trade or business of the predecessor.

2. The predecessor must report amounts, including any withholding, on information returns for the year of the acquisition for the period before the acquisition.

3. The predecessor business is not required to report amounts, including withholding, on information returns for the year of the acquisition for the period after the acquisition.

4. The predecessor and the successor must have agreed on the specific forms for combined reporting and that the successor business must assume the entire obligation for filing the forms.

Even if both the successor business and the predecessor business agree that the successor will file the predecessor's forms, the predecessor is not relieved of its obligations until the successor satisfies its obligations under the agreement and other provisions of Revenue Procedure 99-50 [1999-2 C.B. 757] (see Q 12:90). The agreement may cover all Forms 1099 that the predecessor is accountable for, or may limit the reportable forms to specific forms or to forms to be filed by specific reporting entities, including branches, units, and locations that file separate information returns, or to forms to be filed in compatible systems. [Rev. Proc. 99-50, 1999-2 C.B. 757; General Instructions to the Forms 1099 series]

Q 12:90　How is the IRS informed that the predecessor business and the successor business intend to combine their reporting?

The successor business must file a statement with the IRS indicating which forms are being filed on a combined basis under Revenue Procedure 99-50. [1999-2 C.B. 757] The statement is needed to assist the IRS in reconciling the withholding discrepancy that arises when the amounts of withholding on the combined Forms 1099 exceed the Form 945, Annual Return of Withheld Federal Income Tax, or amounts of withholding on the combined Forms 1042-S exceed the Form 1042 filed by the successor. The statement must also include the predecessor and successor's names, addresses, EINs, telephone numbers; the name of the person who prepared the statement; and separately list the amount of federal income tax withheld by the predecessor business and successor business for each type of form that will be filed on a combined basis.

The statement is to be sent separately from Form 945 and Forms 1099 series by the forms' due date to the Internal Revenue Service, Information Returns Branch, 230 Murall Drive, Mail Stop 4360, Kearneysville, WV 25430. The address and complete instructions can be found in the General Instructions to the Forms 1099 series. For Forms 1042 and 1042-S, the statement needs to be attached to Form 1042 and filed with the form pursuant to the Form 1042 filing instructions. [Rev. Proc. 99-50, 1999-2 C.B. 757; General Instructions to Forms 1099 series and 1042/1042S]

Q 12:91　What payments can be combined in the 1099 series?

Along with payments to foreign persons reported on Form 1042S under I.R.C. §§ 1441, 1442, and 1461, use the combined reporting procedure for all Forms 1098, 1099, 3921, 3922, 5498, and W-2G covered by the annual General Instructions for Certain Information Returns (Forms 1097, 1098, 1099, 3921,

3922, 5498, and W-2G) ("General Instructions"). The following payments under the noted I.R.C. sections are reported in the 1099 series, and others added to this list if covered by the General Instructions for the year can be filed on a combined basis:

- Section 220(h) medical savings accounts;
- Section 408(i) individual retirement accounts;
- Section 539(d) qualified state tuition programs;
- Section 530(h) education individual retirement accounts;
- Section 6039 reporting stock transfers in context of employee stock options or purchase plans;
- Section 6041 miscellaneous payments;
- Section 6041A remunerations for services and direct sales;
- Section 6042 dividends;
- Section 6043 liquidating transactions;
- Section 6044 patronage dividends;
- Section 6045 brokers' returns (with individual transactions separately reported);
- Section 6047 trust and annuity plans;
- Section 6049 interest;
- Section 6050A fishing boat operators;
- Section 6050B unemployment compensation;
- Section 6050D energy grants and financing;
- Section 6050E state and local income tax refunds;
- Section 6050J foreclosures and abandonments;
- Section 6050N royalties;
- Section 6050P cancellation of indebtedness;
- Section 6050Q long-term care benefits;
- Section 6050R purchases of fish; and
- Section 6050W merchant card and third-party network payments.

Q 12:92   Are the requirements for combined filing of information reports the same whether the successor business is derived from a statutory merger or consolidation or from another form of acquisition?

Yes. [Rev. Proc. 99-50, 1999-2 C.B. 757]

State Issues for M&As

State Income Taxes

Q 12:93   Do states generally follow the federal rules in an M&A context for purposes of managing employer liabilities and defining taxable wage inclusions, as well as Form W-2 reporting?

Yes. States with personal income taxes have income tax codes that are based on some version of the federal Internal Revenue Code, so their tax determinations begin with the federal adjusted gross income and require state adjustments to that amount to derive the state's taxable income. In this way, federal reported wages are included in the state income tax base. To maintain consistency, most but not all states with income taxes also adopt the federal definitions of "wages" and "employer," and require state withholding be attached to the federal wage base. Through this process, states inherit the federal rules that impact wages in the context of an M&A event, particularly regarding managing employer liabilities, defining taxable wage inclusions, and year-end Form W-2 reporting. For examples, see Illinois (35 Ill. Comp. Stat. 5/102 and 701) and Connecticut (Conn. Gen. Stat. § 12-701).

However, when it comes to actual filing requirements for periodic and annual withholding reconciliations, the state conventions can vary substantially from those that apply to the federal Form 941. In addition, state requirements for unemployment taxes, disability taxes, employment training taxes, and other payroll taxes, as well as workers' compensation coverage and other wage based matters are not required and for the most part do not follow the federal rules.

Many states, concerned about collecting required taxes in the event of an M&A event, have statutes in place that provide for unique ways of capturing successor liability. For example, in Connecticut, for sales of businesses or sales of stock of goods, the purchaser is required to withhold a sufficient portion of the purchase price to cover the amount of Connecticut income tax withholding, plus any interest and penalties on such taxes due and unpaid by the seller as of the time of the sale. Failure to withhold a portion of the purchase price, as required, will result in the purchaser being personally liable for the payment of the amounts required to be withheld, to the extent of the purchase price. To avoid successor liability, the purchaser must request a clearance certificate from the Connecticut Department of Revenue before purchasing the existing business or stock of goods. The request may be made in conjunction with the request for a clearance certificate for sales and use taxes or admissions and dues tax. The tax clearance certificate is Form AU-712WTH, Tax Clearance Certificate for Connecticut Income Tax Withholding. [Conn. Gen. Stat. § 12-424, Conn. Gen. Stat. § 12-15(b)(6), Conn. Gen. Stat. § 12-546, and Conn. Gen. Stat. § 12-707, as amended by 2011 Conn. Pub. Acts 61, § 58]

In West Virginia, the statute on its face does not require that consideration pass in order to be held liable as a successor for personal income withholding and other taxes. In an Office of Tax Appeals case, one distributor stopped business and another started one in the same area with the other's left-over product. The relevant statute imposes liability on any successor in business where the predecessor either sells out its business, sells out its stock of goods, or ceases doing business if the successor acquires or succeeds to substantially all of the predecessor's business assets. In the facts of the appeal, the second distributor acquired substantially all of the business assets, including the customer lists and delivery routes of the first, and essentially was seen as holding itself out as an extension of the first company. The Office of Appeals held that terms of the statute were met even though no cash changed hands. [Decision Nos. 11-091 W, 11-092 C, and 11-093 X, West Virginia Office of Tax Appeals, May 22, 2012]

In California, if you acquire the assets of a business, you also acquire the payer's withholding tax liability under California law. [RT&C § 18669] A successor of business assets can be held personally liable for the amount of withholding taxes, interest, and penalties if not paid by the payer. It does not matter how the assets were acquired, whether purchased, transferred, inherited, or distributed in liquidation. The obligation to pay required withholding tax transfers with the assets. However, the successor's liability is limited to the fair market value of the assets acquired.

As a successor in California, you are required to hold back in trust a sufficient part of the purchase price or set aside money or property to cover the amount of the taxes required to be withheld and any interest or penalties associated with the withholding tax obligation(s) that are due or unpaid by the business entity (payer).

A successor can submit a written request to the Franchise Tax Board (FTB) for the amount of withholding taxes, interest, or penalties due. The FTB has 60 days to issue a certificate or statement showing the amount due. The successor is then required to pay any required withholding taxes and any interest or penalties due or unpaid within 30 days after the FTB issues a statement showing the amount due or on the day the business or assets are acquired, whichever occurs later. If a written request for a certificate is not made by the successor, the amount of withholding taxes, interest, or penalties due or unpaid is due the day the business or assets are acquired. If payment is not made by the due date, a 10 percent penalty, based on the payable amount, can be assessed. But, if the FTB does not issue a certificate or statement within the 60-day period after a successor submits a request, the FTB is deemed to have issued a certificate stating no withholding taxes, interest, or penalties are due.

The successor of a California business, successor representative, escrow officer, or title officer may submit a written request for a bulk sale certificate, but it must include the following information: name of successor, complete successor's mailing address, escrow company's name, complete escrow company's address, phone, and fax, escrow officer's name, escrow number, sales price, estimated closing date, name of business being transferred, physical address of business, liquor license number (if any), payer name, complete payer physical address, and state tax account number. For more information, call 888-792-4900 or 916-845-4900.

Whether or not the FTB issues a certificate or statement within the 60-day period or collects amounts due from a successor, the payer still remains liable for the amount due, less any amounts collected from any successor(s).

If the matter involves a wage and hour violation by a predecessor, imposing employer liabilities on a successor may seem harsh, but many states' laws address wage and hour and other labor violations on change of the ownership of the violator. A California appellate court recently held that a car wash with a clean employer record was nonetheless liable for a previous owner's wage and hour violations in *People ex rel. Harris v. Sunset Car Wash LLC*, No. B233915 (Cal. Ct. App. May 16, 2012). The ruling came under California Labor Code § 2066 which has since been repealed effective 2014, but worth noting that such laws still exist in many states.

In Nebraska, whether you purchase an existing business or its assets, the buyer may be held liable for any unpaid taxes at the time of sale. Contract statements that the business has cleared encumbrances do not protect the buyer. Nebraska requires verification that there is no tax due through a certificate of clearance from the Department of Revenue, which is obtained by filing Form 36 pursuant to its instructions. Owed taxes, penalties, and interest are required to be held back from sales proceeds to avoid personal liability as a successor or transferee for any taxes due (including employee income tax withholding). [Neb. Rev. Stat. §§ 77-2707; 77-27,110]

In New Mexico, tangible and intangible property used in any business remains subject to liability for payment of the tax due on account of that business, even though the business changes hands. The successor is required to place into a trust account sufficient funds to cover any outstanding tax liability until the Department of Taxation either issues a clearance certificate or makes a demand or assessment for the outstanding liability. [NMSA 1978, § 7-1-61 (B) (1997)] New Mexico has eight indicia used to determine whether a business is a successor: (1) Has a sale and purchase of a major part of the materials, supplies, equipment, merchandise or other inventory of a business enterprise occurred between a transferor and a transferee in a single or limited number of transactions? (2) Was a transfer not in the ordinary course of the transferor's business? (3) Was a substantial part of both equipment and inventories transferred? (4) Was a substantial portion of the business enterprise that had been conducted by the transferor continued by the transferee? (5) By express or implied agreement, did the transferor's goodwill follow the transfer of the business properties? (6) Were uncompleted sales, service, or lease contracts of the transferor honored by the transferee? (7) Was unpaid indebtedness to suppliers, utility companies, service contractors, landlords or employees of the transferor paid by the transferee? (8) Was there an agreement precluding the transferor from engaging in a competing business to that which was transferred? Any one of these factors will allow a presumption of liability as a successor in business. [Regulation 3.1.10.16 (B) NMAC]

These are only a few examples of how states protect their rights to taxes due in an M&A event. Research on the legalities of successor liability in each state where a target company has a business presence is wise and appropriate steps should be taken to request appropriate certifications where allowed. Sole reliance placed on contract representations may be unwise in many cases without serious due diligence in locating any possible outstanding tax or other debts. See Q 12:47 above for discussion of the federal reliance on state successor in interest liability laws to collect federal payroll taxes of a predecessor.

Quarterly or Other Periodic Filings

Q 12:94   Are there differences between federal Form 941 requirements and the state requirements for quarterly or other periodic income tax withholding returns in the context of an M&A event?

Yes. Unlike the federal filing rules, states generally do not differentiate between compliance requirements for a surviving employer in a statutory merger and those for a successor employer in an asset acquisition or other M&A event. More specifically, unlike the federal rules for filing Form 941 in a statutory merger, the surviving employer may not consolidate the state employment tax liabilities of the acquired corporation into one quarterly report for the period that includes the effective date of the M&A event. Employers that deposit withholding taxes in any quarter must file the state's quarterly report, covering wage liabilities for taxes withheld from payments it made regardless of the context of the M&A event. Every state that requires income tax withholding on wages generally has a periodic filing requirement to report wages and related liabilities and to reconcile related tax deposits with those liabilities. Each employer must report the wages it paid, the related tax liabilities for those wages, and the taxes it actually withheld and deposited during the reporting period on the state's periodical reconciliation. The frequency of filings can be monthly, quarterly, or annually, depending on the size and frequency of the payroll and the required frequency of related tax deposits.

For example, in Wisconsin, when two companies merge mid-year, each company has a withholding reporting requirement so long as each withholding account is active. Each company is required to submit its own Form WT-7 annual reconciliation and wage statements. The department will not accept a combined Form WT-7 or combined Forms W-2 from companies that merged mid-year. See Tax Bulletin No. 177, Wisconsin Department of Revenue, October 2012. For other examples of periodical and annual filings, see the employer guides for California, Connecticut, Michigan, Minnesota, and New York.

Under state M&A rules, the predecessor/acquired corporation generally files a quarterly or other periodic withholding return for the filing period of the M&A event for withholdings on wages it pays to its employees during the filing period, including the wages paid to transferred employees up to the effective date of the M&A event when the employees are transferred. In turn, the successor/ surviving corporation files a quarterly or other periodic return for the wages paid and taxes withheld for its employees, if any, from the beginning of the quarter to the end, including the wages paid to the transferred employees from the effective date of the M&A event (the date of the employees' transfer) to the end of the quarter. Handling returns in this manner allows for balancing of deposits and liabilities in company's tax account with the agencies involved.

See Q 12:97 for caution regarding payrolls that are consolidated mid-quarter.

Q 12:95   Are there accelerated filing requirements for acquired companies that no longer have employees and cease to pay wages?

Yes. Similar to the federal requirement to file a final Form 941, predecessor employers that are no longer in business or that no longer pay wages are usually required to mark the return for the quarter of the M&A event (or the last quarter in which it actually pays wages, if different) as "final." Special rules usually accelerate the annual reconciliation filing to within a short period after the final quarterly return is filed, as well as require that employees receive their W-2s or other wage report earlier than usual. In California, employers are required to file the final Form DE-9 and DE-9C (Quarterly Returns) within 10 days of going out of business, regardless of the typical due dates. [See California Employer Guide (DE-44).] For other examples, see the instructions to IL-941 (Illinois) and M-941 (Massachusetts) and Q 12:101.

Comparable rules exist in every state. When payroll administrators are involved in transactions where employers will cease to operate, it is wise to check out final filing requirements for reconciliatory filings as well as W-2s in all jurisdictions where that company operates.

Q 12:96   In the context of a statutory merger, what issues arise when states require filings by each company in the transaction?

Instructions to Form 941 allow each employer to file a Form 941 for the quarter of the merger, reporting only the wages each employer paid. Similarly, most states also require filings by each employer to reflect the wages that each employer paid. If done this way, both the acquired and surviving employers' sets of federal and state returns for the quarter of the merger should be in balance with related tax deposits. (See Qs 12:11–12:16 for further discussions on filing Forms 941 and Schedule D and the need for the acquired corporation to file a final Form 941. See Qs 12:18–12:19 for details on what to include in Schedule D.)

Even so, caution is warranted if employees' wage histories are consolidated early in the quarter of the transaction to enable, for example, a carryover of the 401(k) contribution amounts to establish a correct Section 401(k) deferral or to avoid resetting the Social Security wage base limits or to allow for the 0.9 percent Additional Medicare Tax withholding on wages exceeding $200,000 for wages paid in the quarter of the merger after its effective date. Attempts to consolidate wage histories mid-quarter for these purposes may preclude access to the absorbed company's and surviving company's segregated wage histories needed to file the correct state returns at quarter-end.

Q 12:97 What concerns arise when payroll databases are combined to support a consolidated payroll in mid-quarter where successor employer rules require segregated federal and state quarter-end tax returns?

Mid-quarter movements of wage histories from one employer to another may thwart the correct development of segregated returns for federal purposes in a "successor employer" transaction, and for all state quarterly returns for which wage histories cannot be combined.

Most payrolls operate on system platforms that allow for housing of a singular database (i.e., one database that supports both the payroll and tax functions and that holds all wage payment and tax and other withholding history). When tax returns are prepared, tax programs are run against the singular payroll database. If that database is combined with other payroll databases from other companies within a quarterly filing period without careful planning for when and how the tax programs are to be run, the consolidation may preclude correct segregated tax filings at quarter-end.

Care must be taken in planning to meet all payroll tax filing responsibilities when developing any strategy to consolidate or maintain segregation of payroll databases in a mid-quarter filing period. Quarter-end effective dates for M&As will eliminate the risk that a mid-period change presents. (See Q 12:17 for a discussion of other concerns associated with mid-quarter changes.)

Where mid-quarter consolidations of wage histories are unavoidable, consider a partial movement of wage thresholds for Social Security and § 401(k) deferrals, and to effect 0.9 percent Additional Medicare Tax withholding on wages over $200,000 or for other plan purposes and hold back on full consolidation until after returns are developed at quarter-end. Remember also that segregated state annual reconciliations will be required and that some may require employee wage details specific to the company that paid them. Be sure to preserve that capability where required. See Qs 12:100–12:102 for a discussion on annual reconciliations.

Forms W-4

Q 12:98 When states allow reliance on the federal Form W-4 for state withholding purposes, will states generally follow the federal requirement allowing the survivor/successor employer to rely on the predecessor's Forms W-4 (or the state's version) in the context of a statutory merger or consolidation or when a successor employer elects the alternate procedure?

Generally, yes. However, each state's current practices should be verified. States rarely outline the W-4 requirements in the context of an M&A event. However, because states follow federal rules for most income tax matters, states that allow reliance on federal Forms W-4 will likely respect the acquired company's forms in the hands of the survivor/successor where the federal rules would allow reliance.

The following states allow use of the federal Form W-4 for state purposes: Arkansas, California, Colorado, Delaware, Georgia, Idaho, Massachusetts, Minnesota, Montana, Nebraska, New Jersey, New Mexico, New York, North Dakota, Oklahoma, Oregon, Rhode Island, South Carolina, Utah, Vermont, West Virginia, and Wisconsin. Many of these states also have their own versions and recommend their use to more closely conform state wage withholding to the employee's actual state tax liability. Rules are less certain where the state's own version of the form is transferred (see Q 12:99).

Other employee withholding forms. Almost every state has other employee forms, for example, those used to claim exemption from withholding based on state reciprocity and those used to claim nonresident status. These forms may be necessary in order to continue the same withholding treatment on transferred employees as they experienced in the predecessor's payroll operations, and need to be gathered up early in the transfer process. For example, see Delaware W-4NR Non-Resident; New York, IT-2104.1 Non-Resident, IT-2104-E Exempt, IT-2104-IND Exempt Native American, and IT-2104-MS Military; and Wisconsin WT-4A Resident (allowance adjustment), W-220 Non-Resident (IL,IN,KY,MI), W-222 Non-Resident (MN), and WT-4B Exempt. Since these forms are complex and often incomplete, they should be sampled and reviewed and, where many are missing or the quality is poor, consideration should be given to resoliciting the forms from all affected employees as the forms are critical in supporting withholding positions in the context of a payroll audit. In recent years, many states have chosen to accelerate their audits of companies involved in M&A events right after the transaction period closes; accordingly, ensuring that these forms are on file will be important.

Caution is warranted as many states still require certain filings of copies of employee withholding certificates with the state even though the federal requirement has been withdrawn for W-4 forms. For example, the California Franchise Tax Board (FTB) mostly follows the federal rules, however, employers still must send a copy of either Form W-4 or Form DE 4 to the FTB (not the Employment Development Department) if any of the following conditions exists: (1) the employee claims 10 or more exemptions; (2) the employee claims exemption from state or federal income tax withholding and the employee's usual weekly wages will exceed $200; (3) the employee makes major changes to Form W-4 or Form DE 4, such as crossing out words or writing more than is asked; or (4) the employee admits that the Form W-4 is false. In this context, California may expect employers involved in M&A events to be accountable for this filing on behalf of the acquired corporations in a statutory merger context or on the part of the successor employer for the quarter of transition as specified in Revenue Procedure 2004-53. [2004-34 I.R.B. 320; I.R.S. News Release IR-2005-45 (Apr. 13, 2005)]

As another example, Minnesota employers are to file copies of withholding allowance certificates (Minnesota Form W-4MN or federal Form W-4) with the Minnesota Department of Revenue if the employee claims more than 10 withholding allowances, or the employee claims exemption from withholding and his or her wages normally exceed $200 per week unless he or she has completed Form MWR; and/or the employer believes an employee is not entitled to the number of allowances claimed. Minnesota law imposes a penalty of $50 per form not filed when required. [Employer Instructions to W-4MN.]

In these contexts, employers completing due diligence of a soon-to-be-acquired company should identify state requirements in all jurisdictions where the company operates.

Q 12:99　Will states with their own versions of a Form W-4 generally allow the survivor/successor employer to rely on the predecessor's state version in the context of a statutory merger or consolidation or when a successor employer elects the alternate procedure?

In the context of M&A events, there is always a struggle about when, or even if, it is necessary to solicit new documents of any kind from the employees affected by the event. There is always the concern that any new solicitations may cause even more anxiety among the employees who are already tense about their livelihood. So, the question arises as to whether new state W-4s are really needed. Most states that require use of their own versions of Form W-4 do not instruct employers on whether reliance can be placed on forms of a predecessor employer in the hands of a successor employer. In order to understand when it may be possible to make a case for not resoliciting wage forms, it is important to first understand where the state stands regarding reliance on use of the federal form and why the state may vary from that reliance. The reason that states require use of their own versions of Form W-4 is generally both to set the particular state's income tax calculations or wage base apart from the federal rules and to derive withholdings that come close to offsetting the employee's true state income tax liabilities.

States that require use of their own versions of W-4 include: Alabama, Arizona, Connecticut, District of Columbia, Hawaii, Illinois, Indiana, Iowa, Kansas, Kentucky, Louisiana, Maine, Maryland, Michigan, Mississippi, Missouri, North Carolina, Ohio, Virginia, and Puerto Rico. Some states have their own forms even though they respect the federal Form W-4: Arkansas, California, Georgia, Massachusetts, Minnesota, New Jersey, New York, Rhode Island, Vermont, West Virginia, and Wisconsin. Their instructions generally say to use the state form if the withholding allowances or additional dollar amounts to be withheld are different for state purposes than claimed on the federal form.

Illinois requires the use of its own IL-W-4 and exploring the form's requirements shows the concerns that can arise when a state's unique wage form is to be transferred in an M&A event. The instructions to this form state that "even if [employee] claimed exemption from withholding on Form W-4, . . . [employee] may be required to have Illinois income tax withheld from pay." Employers are instructed that if the Form IL-W-4 is not completed, the employer is required to withhold Illinois income tax without allowing any exemptions. Illinois makes it clear that the state does not rely on the federal Form W-4. Although Form IL-W-4 does not address the requirements in the context of an M&A event, Illinois has the authority to instruct an employer to disregard forms (see instructions to Form IL-W-4 and IL DOR Pub. 130 and Pub. 131).

Although Illinois requires use of its Form IL-W-4, much of the state's other compliance functions rely heavily on the federal rules. Employers must withhold Illinois income tax when they are required to withhold federal income tax from compensation paid in Illinois. Wages are defined following the federal requirements. Before February 1 of each year, employers must give their employees three copies of federal Form W-2. Only employers with 250 or more employees must transmit W-2 and W-2c returns using the Social Security Administration's (SSA) EFW2 and EFW2c format. Any employer that is mandated to electronically file with the SSA must also register and electronically transmit to Illinois any W-2 and W-2c returns. [IL DOR Pub. 110, Pub. 130] In this regard, Illinois relies on the federal wage withholding and W-2 filing requirements and appears to adopt the federal positions required of those filings, including those under the successor employer or statutory merger rules. Illinois does not require employee wage details to be submitted with its IL-941 quarterly reconciliation and appears to rely on the federal W-2 filings for reconciling wages both as to the employer and employee. [IL 941 and instructions] Starting with tax year 2014, Forms W-2 are required to be filed with Illinois by February 15, unlike the federal returns that are due March 31 when filed electronically.

Even with the heavy federal reliance on data, Illinois, like many states, is still unclear as to whether it will allow reliance on another company's Form IL-W-4 transferred to a successor employer under the alternate procedure or to a survivor in the context of a statutory merger.

When a state requires use of its own form, like Illinois, and it was shown in a due diligence review that the predecessor has not consistently used the state form, a new solicitation may be wise. Some companies make it a standard practice to re-solicit in every acquisition involving states that require use of their own form, or when the state puts heavy reliance on unique forms to claim, for example, state reciprocity or nonresidence. If an employer has a history of not taking the state seriously as to the use of its form, and, if required, not providing the annual employee notices to their employees reminding them to update their state forms, a state may express concern over an acquiring corporation's continued reliance on the forms available. Each state's current practices should be confirmed when there is a planned M&A event.

Note. These states also have other employee forms used to claim exemption from withholding based on state reciprocity and those used to claim nonresident status. These forms may be necessary in order to continue the same withholding treatment on transferred employees as they experienced in the predecessor's payroll operations, and need to be gathered early in the transfer process. Since these forms are complex and often incomplete, they should be sampled and reviewed and, if many are missing or poor in quality, consideration should be given to re-soliciting the forms from all affected employees as they are critical in supporting withholding positions in the context of a payroll audit. In recent years, many states have chosen to accelerate their audits of companies involved in M&A events right after the transaction period closes; accordingly, ensuring that these forms are on file will be important.

Annual Reconciliations

Q 12:100   In the context of an M&A event, are there special considerations in filing year-end reconciliations of state income tax withholdings?

Yes. Where acquired companies have paid wages, withheld state income taxes, and filed quarterly or other periodical withholding statements, the acquired companies will need to file annual state reconciliations in states that require such year-end filings. This is required even if the wages are consolidated with the successor employer for W-2 purposes. For the most part, annual reconciliations are required on a separate basis by each employer in an M&A event, even if, for federal purposes, the predecessor employer has appropriately transferred the data to a successor to generate the consolidated Forms W-2 for both employers as a result of either a statutory merger or under the alternate procedure in an asset acquisition. Successors and predecessors must file annual reconciliations in balance with their quarterly (or other periodic) returns filed throughout the year. To be in balance with the periodic returns, and to avoid double reporting of liabilities also covered in the predecessor's annual reconciliation, the successor employer must not include wages paid by the predecessor employer in the portion of the year prior to the M&A event; those liabilities and related withholdings should be reported in the predecessor's annual reconciliation. (See Q 12:101.)

States trying to get ahead of increases in fraud in filing tax returns, and ahead of the 2017 federal government W-2 acceleration, have already accelerated to January 31 the due dates of many annual reconciliations along with the state versions of Form W-2. This push up of the general filing date has put pressure on employers struggling to gather all the data needed for correct W-2 forms after M&A events that require aggregation of data from many systems and locations. Plan ahead to meet the dates as extensions are becoming harder to obtain.

Be sure to follow the agency's instructions in closing accounts when paying final wages. File all returns required being sure to mark the forms as final. Remember to follow up and request copies of final account transcripts. Failure to stay on top of old accounts and forgetting to close them with the final returns may mean large assessments and an expensive protest process. A company learned this lesson in Indiana when it received an assessment of over $125,000 from the Indiana Department of Workforce Development on what it thought was a closed account. But for a favorable Indiana unemployment insurance appeals decision that lowered the assessment to $200 after a lengthy protest, the company's failure to file a final return and wage report when it ceased operations could have been an expensive lesson to learn. [TPUSA, Inc. v.

Unemployment Ins. Appeals of the Indiana Department of Workforce Development, 988 N.E.2d 284 (Ind. App. 2013)]

Q 12:101   Are there accelerated filing requirements for state annual reconciliations and/or Forms W-2 when a predecessor ceases to pay wages or goes out of business as a result of an M&A event?

Yes. Many states have special accelerated annual reconciliation filing requirements when a predecessor employer ceases to pay wages or goes out of business as a result of an M&A event with filing timings that vary from the federal rules on business termination. For example, in California, employers are required to file the final Forms DE-9 and DE-9C (Quarterly Returns) including the required employee wage records within 10 days of going out of business, regardless of the usual due dates (see the California Employer Guide (Form DE-44)).

Some states require that Forms W-2 be provided to terminating employees on an even earlier date than the federal date. For example, Arizona requires W-2 provision to a terminating employee within 15 days of termination and Arkansas requires the W-2 to be provided to the employee immediately upon termination. California requires the W-2 to be reported within 30 days after the last payment of wages unless there is a reasonable expectation on the part of both the employer and the employee that the employee will resume working for the employer and Wisconsin requires the W-2 when the final paycheck is due.

Payroll professionals are cautioned to check their local state laws to determine responsibilities in this area.

Conflicts Between Federal and State Reporting of Employee Wages (Forms W-2 vs. State Quarterly or Annual Reconciliations)

Q 12:102   In the context of an M&A event, are there differences between federal and state requirements for reporting employee wages (i.e., Forms W-2 or other employee-specific state wage reports)?

Yes. Many payroll professionals erroneously think that when W-2s can be consolidated for federal purposes, every other tax filing can also be consolidated. Payroll professionals must be careful not to confuse the allowances for federal consolidated Form W-2 filings with the allowances for other filings requiring wage details (e.g., when required to be submitted along with annual reconciliations, or with quarterly SUI returns) (see 12:97 and 12:100).

Under the federal rules, year-end wages on Forms W-2 can be consolidated between predecessor employers and successor employers under the alternate procedure or in a statutory merger. For federal purposes, there are no requirements for filing an employer annual reconciliation of Forms W-2 with Forms 941. If filing electronically, the employer header (the code RE employer Record of the SSA EFW2) or, if filing paper forms, the Form W-3, Transmittal of Wage and Tax Statements) only take into consideration the totals in the W-2s, not the Form 941 data. Schedule D (Form 941), however, does require employers to reconcile 941 data with Forms W-2 when involved in M&A events where Forms 941 would otherwise be out of balance with the totals on Forms W-2.

For state purposes, there is no Schedule D (Form 941) to bring M&A transactions into balance when W-2s are filed on a consolidated basis. States eliminate the need to file some version of Schedule D by requiring reconciliations to be filed by every employer that has withheld income taxes and filed a periodical statement during the tax year, that is, states for the most part disallow a consolidated annual reconciliation after an M&A event. Each employer must account for the employee-specific wages it paid when employee wages are posted to records. In some states, these reconciliations are attached to periodic or annual filings for state income tax withholdings (PIT returns) and are used to reconcile state income taxes deposited in an employer's tax account with the tax withheld that employees report on their state income tax returns.

Caution. When wage details must be reported on a separate basis by the employers that actually paid the wages (rather than consolidated wages reported by a successor employer), payroll professionals must take into consideration the timing of the wage consolidations to avoid thwarting their ability to later prepare the other returns. In addition, where states have combined their PIT and SUI filing functions, the unique wage base requirements and the needed processing applications heighten the focus on timing in consolidating payrolls.

States trying to get ahead of increases in fraud in filing tax returns, and ahead of the 2017 federal government W-2 acceleration, have already accelerated to January 31 the due dates of many annual reconciliations along with the state versions of Form W-2. This push up of the general filing date has put pressure on employers struggling to gather all the data needed for correct W-2 forms after M&A events that require aggregation of data from many systems and locations. Plan ahead to meet the dates, as extensions are becoming harder to obtain.

Q 12:103   Are there specific states where filing considerations are more heightened in an M&A event?

Yes. Many states still consolidate income tax and unemployment tax filings. The combined filing requirements in these states give more credence to the state's singular set of SUI rules than to maintaining the SIT distinctions between statutory mergers and asset acquisitions found under the federal income tax withholding rules. Even where the state wage base for income tax purposes starts with the federal definition, filing requirements in the combined states may require separate quarterly and annual reconciliations from each company involved in the transaction.

The jurisdictional conflicts in payroll administration, particularly in the context of an M&A event, result in employers having to weigh the pros and cons when attempting to consolidate the administration of multiple wage bases in compliance with both the state and federal tax rules. With states needing more frequent SUI wage reports, some previously combined states have eliminated consolidated SIT/SUI filings to allow for separate more frequent SUI filings. For example, for tax periods beginning on or after January 1, 2015, Maine's combined quarterly filing for income tax withholding and unemployment contributions (Form 941/C1-ME) has been eliminated and replaced with separate Forms 941ME (income tax withholding) and ME UC-1 (unemployment contributions report), to be filed with the different agencies that administer the taxes.

Where states keep the functions segregated, the income tax compliance functions can follow the federal requirements, eliminating the need for separate work to accommodate a different state income tax filing base. UI filings with wage details are usually filed quarterly and once those requirements are met, the companies' wage histories can be safely consolidated. On the other hand, where states combine income tax and UI filings, particularly where wage details are required at year end on a separate company basis, there is less flexibility on the part of employers in accommodating the different wage bases involved in the transaction and employers are forced to weigh the advantages and disadvantages when attempting to consolidate multiple wage bases to comply with the many sets of tax rules.

Some states—New York and New Jersey, for example—require wage details at year-end. In New York, employers are required to quarterly report their payroll and pay unemployment insurance contributions using Form NYS-45, *Quarterly Combined Withholding, Wage Reporting, and Unemployment Insurance Return*, and Form NYS-45-ATT, *Quarterly Combined Withholding, Wage Reporting, And Unemployment Insurance Return - Attachment*, if applicable, showing the name, Social Security number, and gross wages paid to each employee performing services in employment. New York also requires employers to report annual wage and withholding information on the final quarterly combined withholding, wage reporting, and unemployment insurance return filed for the year by January 31. New Jersey requires state versions of Forms W-2 to be filed directly with the state in balance with the year-end withholding reconciliation Form NJ-W-3. Quarterly Forms NJ927 and NJ927W and wage reports (Form WR-30) for unemployment insurance and other payroll taxes are filed electronically, online or through the State's Secure File Transfer Program (SFTP). However, annual wage statements (W-2s) are also required electronically by February 28. When wage details are required at year end on an unconsolidated basis, difficulties can arise in developing the report if payrolls have been consolidated.

Employers facing filing difficulties in any state are advised to first contact the state to determine what, if any, alternatives the state will accept. If filing considerations cannot be reconciled, consolidated W-2s may need to be reevaluated.

Q 12:104   In the context of an M&A event, what are the advantages of quarter-end or first-day-of-the-quarter effective dates of transactions?

Quarter-end or first-day-of-the-quarter effective dates of transactions allow each employer to delay transferring employees to new payrolls until a payroll cycle is complete for the quarter. Transferring employees after quarter-end but before the first payroll period in the following quarter (i.e., between quarters) allows the survivor to pay all the wages in the new quarter to the transferred employees, enabling both the survivor and the acquired corporation to file balanced periodic returns (i.e., tax deposits will equal reported liabilities) and attach the necessary employee-specific wage details to the correct employer's return during the transition period. (Balanced quarterly filings allow for easier agency reconciliations of the related tax accounts with year-end filings, resulting in lower payroll tax liabilities.) Also, tax activities remain consistent for each employer during the transitional quarters and tax filings are made easier.

Quarter-end effective dates can aid in resolving the variance between the federal consolidated filing and state segregated filing requirements, as most state and local filings must be divided between the employers involved with each filing for its own payrolls.

State Unemployment Insurance (SUI)

Q 12:105   What are the fundamental issues regarding state unemployment insurance in the context of an M&A event?

A few years ago, facing the worst decline in state revenues in at least 50 years as a direct result of the national economic downturn, many states stepped up enforcement. Even with recovery now underway, the health of each state's SUI funding is still of serious concern and states are still strongly focusing on collecting underpayments. Key audit issues still include "SUTA Dumping" and employee misclassification matters. Companies whose profile includes M&A events are more likely to incur audits than other companies. Liabilities are very high and companies acquiring targets are well advised to carefully review their target's practices in both areas. The state agencies are working with the IRS in sharing information through the "Questionable Employment Tax Practices" (QETP) Program, in which the IRS and state tax, unemployment, and workforce agencies exchange audit reports and conduct joint examinations.

For SUI purposes, each state can set many of its own requirements constrained only by the federal FUTA regime. The fundamental issues regarding SUI in the context of an M&A event are:

1. Whether a prior employer's UI experience will transfer to the new employer;
2. What the UI rate will be after the event and when it will apply;
3. Whether the wage limit carries over to the new employer;
4. Whether the M&A event could be seen by a state agency as an attempt to SUTA dump even though unintended; and

5. Whether and under what circumstances successor employers can be held liable for payment of the predecessor's unpaid unemployment taxes and penalties.

The questions may sound simple, but in administrating SUI taxes, there are lots of complexities to consider on the part of both the company to be acquired or reorganized and the acquiring company. Are there wide disparities of SUI rates and experience between the companies? Does either company have a history of recent layoffs? Does either company have a joint SUI account? Will the transaction affect that joint structure? Does either company plan to make or has it made voluntary contributions? Will the transaction cause a change in tax rates and projections and, if so, how will this affect the transaction's cost and the companies' budgets? Will this cause a need for additional funding in the short term or for a longer period? Will planned layoffs be part of the restructuring that could affect future SUI rates? It is important to note that as the number of employees in a payroll grows whether through hiring, attrition, merger, or acquisition, the SUI cost also exponentially grows so if the end result is a much larger company, costs will grow. All of these points need to be considered in the early stages of a proposed transaction.

The federal SUTA Dumping Prevention Act of 2004 requires states to amend their laws governing unemployment programs to prohibit SUTA Dumping or face financial penalties. [Pub. L. No. 108-295] At this point, all 50 states have enacted some form of legislation to prevent SUTA Dumping. SUTA Dumping is a form of tax avoidance or tax rate manipulation through which employers "dump" higher unemployment taxes by attempting to improperly claim a lower experience rate usually through some form of M&A event. States scrutinize many M&A events in attempts to isolate any SUTA Dumping possibility. In general, states look for common ownership interests in the companies involved. Many states use mathematical tests to determine whether their SUTA Dumping laws apply and the business intent of the transaction does not enter the equation. These tests are automatic to the filing of notice of the M&A event with the agency. If the algebraic formulas applied to the companies' reserve accounts and rate and claim histories result in significantly lower ratings in the presence of a high unemployment claim history, SUTA Dumping will be assumed and the state will attempt to impose the fairly high penalties.

New SUTA Dumping legislation has armed states with stiff penalties to curb the abuse. The increased state scrutiny brings new concerns to those involved in M&A events. To avoid higher tax rates, some companies apply for multiple SUI account numbers and shuffle employees around to the account number with the lowest unemployment insurance rate each year. There are two primary types of SUTA Dumping and many variations:

1. Purchased shell transactions. A new company buys an existing business that has a low SUI tax rate. The low tax rate is transferred to the new company under state laws dealing with employer succession and transfer of experience. Once the experience is transferred and the lower rate established, the new company begins operations.

2. Affiliated shell transactions. An existing company forms a new company, obtains a UI account, reports wages for a small number of individuals, and pays state UI taxes on those wages until the new company earns a minimum tax rate. Then the original company transfers its employees to the new company with the low tax rate allowing it to effectively "dump" its higher tax rate.

The federal SUTA Dumping Prevention Act of 2004 requires the unemployment compensation law of every state to provide for:

- Mandatory transfers. If an employer transfers its business to another employer, and both employers are under substantially common ownership, then the unemployment experience attributable to the transferred business is to be transferred to (and combined with the unemployment experience attributable to) the employer to whom such business is transferred,

- Prohibited transfers. Unemployment experience shall not, by virtue of the transfer of a business, be transferred to the person acquiring such business if:

  — A person is not otherwise an employer at the time of such acquisition, and

  — The state agency finds that the person acquired the business solely or primarily for the purpose of obtaining a lower rate of contributions.

- Penalties. "Meaningful civil and criminal penalties" are to be imposed with respect to violators and those who advise violators.

The majority of states follow the model penalty provisions published by the U.S. Department of Labor (DOL) which has recommended that the employer be assessed the higher of the maximum contribution rate under state law or 2 percent for four years. The state agencies actively pursue and prosecute employers that participate in SUTA Dumping and other tax manipulation schemes and have the authority to subpoena records and individuals in their investigations. For example, as a result of the California EDD's efforts to fight SUTA Dumping, the EDD says that it has worked numerous rate manipulation cases over the past years, collected hundreds of millions in liability charges, including penalty and interest, and has over $200 million in prospective collections.

Algebraic SUTA Dumping tests. The DOL funded a cooperative agreement with the North Carolina Employment Security Agency to develop an automated SUTA Dumping Detection System (SDDS). Forty-three states chose the SDDS option to detect SUTA dumpers. By 2007, nearly every one of these states had implemented the SDDS software and initiated active SUTA dumping detection measures. The remaining states chose to implement other systems or augment existing systems to satisfy the requirements of the Act.

The impact for employers involved in M&A transactions. For maintenance purposes, most state agencies require some form of change of ownership filing, usually within 30 to 90 days of the effective date of the transaction, but experienced employers know to file early to avoid the problems that can arise if the agency is not on board as to the right tax account and tax identification number to use and to work through new rate applications and timing.

A common M&A fact pattern that can lead to trouble. One of the most significant SUTA Dumping snares can occur in a very innocent business setting. When assets are purchased, it is not unusual for a new company to be created as a subsidiary to acquire the assets. Employees are then transferred into the new company from the target and possibly from the acquirer. In the rush to get the deal done, notices of change of ownership are filed late with the state SUI agency without a great deal of thought put to them and state tax identification numbers are not obtained in time for the first payroll tax filing. In this chain of events, which happens frequently in M&A settings, it is not unusual for the new employer to innocently begin to use the state's start up (new employer) rate to process SUI wages and supply the new company's federal EIN. The state, in later sorting through the filing and the employee transfers, sees threads of common ownership and applies its SUTA Dumping standard, finds higher rate histories in the target and acquiring companies, and then calculates a much higher SUI experience rate retroactively to the new company as well as attempts to impose all the SUTA Dumping penalties. When the employer chooses to move forward with the new employer rate and the state later denies it, claiming SUTA Dumping constraints, the end result can be disastrous for an employer.

The state SUTA Dumping program will identify this accident as SUTA Dumping even though unintentional, looking only to the high difference between the experience rate of the prior employers of the transferred employees and the state's new employer rate now in use. It is the mathematics that counts, not the intent. These events are very hard to defend and reverse once they occur. Remember that unlike the IRS, states do not always issue a new employer account number when there is a change in business ownership, particularly where there is common ownership between the successor and the acquired company and the successor hires a significant portion of the target's employees. In these cases, the target's rate history may be mandatorily transferred to the new company. States make their determination from the change of ownership filing and other information that they ascertain as to the appropriate unemployment insurance (SUI) rate to apply to the new structure. Failure to file the state's change of ownership form can cause the state to apply an inappropriate SUI rate and may trigger the state's SUTA Dumping applications.

What to do. States are looking for employers moving large numbers of employees to another company with a lower tax rate than the rate at the company that they are moving from. They will spot employers with negative account balances that stop paying wages and query where the employees were transferred. Think ahead and spot the pitfalls in any planned M&A event. Check the SUI claims statistics and obtain current and historical rate information for every company involved in transferring employees in the M&A event. Also obtain reserve account histories and SUI liability and deposit transcripts for the prior three years. Root out if there are any defenses available to the high rate or ability to appeal the applied rate. Do everything possible to strengthen the negative reserve accounts and improve the ratio of claims of those companies with high SUI rates. Avoid layoffs prior to the event and consider voluntary contributions to improve the reserves. File change of ownership notices discussed in Q 12:115 below and, where needed, request new state Tax IDs from the state agencies as far ahead of the first payroll under the structure as possible. Do not be shy about calling the agencies and discussing the proper rates that should be applied to the new payrolls and document your conversations. In large transactions with many employee transfers scheduled, consider hiring an SUI advisor to plan the events with an eye to managing SUI expenses.

See the discussion below in Qs 12:107 to 12:109 on SUTA Dumping and mandatory rate transfers.

Q 12:106 What rules do states apply when determining successor employer status?

Most states apply a single set of responsibilities to determine successor employer status. If a successor employer already has an experience rating in the state, the employer generally will retain its own tax rate in effect immediately before the transaction through the end of the year of the transaction. If the successor employer does not have an experience rating, the successor may use the state's new employer rate or, if lower, it can generally assume the predecessor employer's rate for the remainder of the year, but caution is warranted. See Q 12:109 below.

Critical to this determination is whether the event will fall under a state's mandatory experience transfer rules. Some states apply an automatic wage base credit transfer; even more states require an experience transfer to occur before wage transfers take effect. Remember that when an employer is required to restart wages, the overall cost of SUI coverage for the year is increased since the SUI tax will be applied to a larger annual wage figure than the statutorily defined annual threshold. The same is true for federal Social Security and FUTA taxes where wages are required to restart. For this reason, many of the more complex deals are scheduled to be made effective on December 31 with the surviving company's wage bases starting anew on January 1. Planning around yearend dates makes it a lot easier for payroll administration.

Where the predecessor's UI experience is subject to a mandatory transfer to the successor employer, the successor's new UI contribution rate is usually determined by examining the combined experience history of both the successor employer and the predecessor employer. Many states make the rate change effective within the year of transaction, but some allow application in the year following the transaction year, including the new rate in the company's rate notice sent out when new rates are announced for all employers. If the combined rate is determined to be lower, the economic benefit sometimes may only be derived through refund filings.

Where the predecessor's UI experience is voluntarily transferred to the successor employer, the successor's new UI contribution rate for the year following the transaction is also determined by examining the combined experience history of both the successor employer and the predecessor employer. However, where the election to transfer the UI experience is not made (such as when the new employer's rate or successor employer's existing rate is lower than a projected combined rate), the successor rate will either continue or, if applicable, the new employer rate will be applied. But see the discussion in Q 12:105 above and Q 12:109 below on SUTA Dumping and mandatory rate transfers.

Q 12:107 How do states determine whether to transfer a predecessor's SUI experience to a successor employer?

In determining whether to transfer a predecessor's SUI experience to a successor employer, states generally consider:

- Whether the successor has acquired all or part of a predecessor's business;
- Whether the successor is continuing the operation of the predecessor's business; and
- Whether the successor has hired any of the predecessor's employees.

Experience transfers can be either voluntary (in the case of a partial acquisition) or mandatory (in the case of a complete acquisition). For consideration of mandatory transfer requirement in the context of substantially common ownership, management or control, see Q 12:109 below. For information on voluntary transfers, see Qs 12:110–12:111 below.

Unlike the federal rules, these considerations are not limited to a form of asset acquisition. They may apply equally to a merger or other reorganization where employees are transferred to a new employer. Employers can gain "successor" status through buying another business, foreclosure, lease, bankruptcy, merger, or by many other means.

If the employer satisfies the particular SUI successor rules, and the predecessor's UI experience is transferred to the successor employer (whether by mandate or by application), the successor can generally count the wages paid to an employee by a predecessor in determining whether the UI wage base has been met. It is important to note that when voluntary elections are not made, the predecessor's SUI wage base usually will not carry over, which may necessitate that employees' SUI wages be restarted.

Tax professionals planning any M&A activity must consider the impact on the respective SUI experience accounts in the states involved and plan for the mandatory transfer or, in the case of a partial acquisition, determine ahead of time whether to effect the voluntary election to carry over the predecessor's UI history. (See Qs 3:66–3:79 for a general discussion of SUI.)

Q 12:108 Can a new successor employer be held liable for payment of the predecessor's unpaid unemployment taxes?

Yes. In most states, if an employer acquires a business that has employees, the new employer can be held liable for the previous owner's unemployment tax liabilities. Some states, such as California, hold the new employer liable unless the new employer acquires a release from the state agency and places an amount in escrow from the acquisition to cover the outstanding amounts owed. [C.U.I.C. § 1733] (See California Form DE 3409A, Information Sheet: Requirements for Obtaining Certificate of Release of Buyer When a Business Is Sold; Form DE 2220, Certificate of Release of Buyer; and instructions in Form DE-44 publication.) Other states, such as Michigan, require the purchaser or seller to request, before the transfer of the business, a "clearance of account" for any amounts owing to the unemployment agency and require the seller to provide SUI information to the buyer regarding matters of rate and experience. (See Michigan Form UC 1027, Business Transferor's Notice to Transferee of Unemployment Tax Liability and Rate.)

State audit potential. When M&A events occur, states become concerned with the elimination of any employer and the loss of collection opportunities or where there may be manipulation to inappropriately lower UI tax rates. Thus, states may be quick to audit employers involved in M&A transactions, especially when employers have employees located in many different states.

When companies have significant interstate operations, interstate SUI wage credits also need to be carefully considered. Generally, if an employee works entirely within one state, the employment is covered by that state's law. But if an employee works partly within and partly outside a state, then he or she must be allocated to the jurisdiction of the proper state based on certain factors. Once properly allocated, contributions are payable to that state based on the employee's entire services performed within and outside the state. Where an employer is not able to determine a primary UI state, most states subscribe to the Interstate Reciprocal Coverage Arrangement (IRCA) to resolve where the claim lies. Under IRCA arrangements, the employer is usually required to request written approvals from the states where services are performed to report all wages to a designated state. The designated state is assigned under IRCA based upon where services are performed, where the employee has a residence, or where the employer maintains a place of business if the employee also performs some services in that state. Many businesses use these rules to unify their UI filings.

All states except Louisiana, Minnesota and Montana allow employers to take credit for wages paid in other states. The Montana Department of Labor and Industry (DLI) finalized regulations effective January 1, 2014, that preclude UI wages and credits from being transferred from other states. In issuing the changes, the DLI stated that although less than 1 percent of employers reported out of state wages, it accounted for more than 25 percent of wage submission errors. In states following the trend to calculate UI taxes from reported employees' wages, there have been difficulties reported when the state is unaware of wages paid for services in other states where credits should apply. Some states are now requiring the reporting of all wages paid even for services outside their state boundaries, a requirement that many employers have difficulty meeting. Mergers and successions compound these discrepancies. Ohio and Texas now provide an indicator to be used when wages include out-of-state wages. Massachusetts, New Mexico, and Washington State require reporting of all wages paid including out-of-state wages, and require a separate claim form for claims related to out-of-state wages. States are taking various positions in reporting of out-of-state wages. Arkansas requires all wages to be reported. Michigan, Ohio, and Texas require summaries of out-of-state wages for affected employees. Florida and Iowa require detailed out-of-state wage reporting for each employee that includes listing each state where the employee performed services.

The federal rules provide for interstate UI credit transfers through the IRCA. In U.S.C., Title 26, § 3304(a)(9)(B), reciprocal arrangements between states are respected for funding purposes when an applicant for UI benefits combines wages from multiple states to support his or her UI benefits from one state. But, not all states follow these rules.

In some states, the commissioner may not enter into any reciprocal arrangement unless it contains provisions for reimbursements to the state's trust fund by the other state. These days, states are short UI trust funds and transfers fail to occur. For an example of such a requirement, see Minnesota U.I. Code § 268.131.

When M&A events occur and employees are spread throughout the country, there is no guarantee that affected states will allow the continuation of predecessor practices in the surviving company even if previously agreed to under an IRCA reciprocal arrangement and even if the arrangement has been settled through a state audit. In addition, even the acquiring company might find its own such agreement revisited if the state sees the impact of the acquisition as significant enough to change its terms. If the target company has mobile employees performing services in many states but the target is only filing in one or two specific states, this could pose significant liability for any acquirer. Practices need to be evaluated as to where a target to be acquired is currently filing SUI returns and paying related taxes in relationship to where employees are actually performing services; and those practices need to be reconciled with the successor's practices. Renewed written applications with the states are well advised.

In the past, these matters were not significant considerations in M&A transactions, but with many states with bankrupt UI trust funds, states are hesitant to continue to allow UI taxes to be paid to other states to cover employees also performing services within their boundaries and are quick to assess large figures where failures are found. A large M&A transaction will gain attention of state agencies and filing predicates will be explored. It will be important to be aware of these matters before the agency makes contact.

With changes in federal FUTA law under the Trade Adjustment Assistance Extension Act of 2011, employers that fail to monitor their employees' claims may not receive the benefit of a reversal of any claim charges to their UI account when benefits are improperly paid because the employer has a pattern of failures to respond to an agency's request for information on a claim. Nearly half of the states have amended laws to be in compliance with the new federal requirements and many have added more stringent penalties for failing to respond to an agency's request for information on a claim. Where employees have filed claims in states where they have worked and the target has failed to respond to agency queries, penalties may be outstanding and audit profile of the target and any M&A event involving that target will increase.

The U.S. Department of Labor (USDOL) and state unemployment insurance (UI) agencies have jointly created the State Information Data Exchange System (SIDES) that offers secure, standardized eformats to supply the data needed for electronically responding to UI information requests. Use of SIDES reduces follow-up phone calls and streamlines UI response processes. Where employers or their third-party agents use SIDES, improper claims payments are prevented, and UI tax rates are kept as low as possible. If not already implemented, SIDES offers solutions to managing claim follow ups in large payroll settings that have become unwieldy particularly after M&A events. For more information, see http://info.uisides.org/.

Practices need to be evaluated in each location where a target company has employees performing services, establishing where those services are reflected in the target's SUI returns and related practices regarding timely responding to an agency's questions about an employee claim. Critical focus then needs to be given to reconciling the target's practices with the acquirer's practices. Renewed written reciprocal applications with the states may be well advised if there is a variance between practices. It is important to be on top of these matters before the agency makes contact.

Q 12:109   When do states generally require a mandatory transfer of UI experience?

The transfer of unemployment experience to adjust SUI rates can only occur when there is a change in ownership of a business. States allow transfers of UI experience from predecessors to successors under differing conditions. Where the acquisition is of substantially all the assets or of the entire business and the successor continues the business operation, the state will usually require a mandatory transfer of the predecessor's complete unemployment tax experience (or history) to the successor employer.

The successor employer, upon inheriting a predecessor's UI experience—including prior benefit payments, charges against the business, and tax payments—also inherits the components of the predecessor's tax rate. If the predecessor recently laid off a number of employees, the tax rate will include charges for benefits being paid to those former employees. Additionally, where benefits are continuing, the continuing charges will usually be against the successor employer's account. When the experience transfer is complete, successors are allowed carryover of the SUI wage bases so as not to restart SUI contributions on the predecessor's employees. (See Q 3:41 for a general discussion of transfers of experience.)

Federal law (under the SUTA Dumping Prevention Act of 2004) requires that states amend their laws governing unemployment programs to prohibit practices known as "SUTA Dumping" and to impose penalties on employers and their tax advisors found engaging in such practices. All states have now enacted some form of conforming legislation. A critical component of the federal legislation requires mandatory experience transfers if at the time of the transfer, both predecessor and successor employers are under substantially common ownership, management, or control.

For the most part, a transfer of experience is favorable to successors so that they do not need to restart SUI wage thresholds, usually required if experience does not transfer. But, where the transfer would cause a much higher rate experience to carry over, a different result might be desired. It is fairly important for those involved to be assured of the right way to structure a transaction to derive the desired result in the jurisdictions involved. Under both federal and state versions of SUTA Dumping legislation, timing is important as to when common ownership, management, or control exists that would require a mandatory transfer. A common practice is for the buyer to establish ahead of a sale a separate business unit intended for the business to be acquired that includes its executives to co-manage the unit with the seller. The seller earmarks employees to be transferred to include its executives to co-manage with the buyer. Common management under this practice was seen as existing until the date of the transaction when all employees are transferred to the buyer. This structure was thought to trigger a mandatory experience transfer.

Recently, a state court has challenged this setup. The Minnesota Court of Appeals held on June 10, 2013, that the Minnesota agency incorrectly transferred a predecessor employer rate and should have applied the lower new employer rate to a transaction structured in this way. The agency believed that a partial experience transfer was required because the unit transferred was under substantially common management or control at the time of the transfer. The court disagreed and held that transfer of experience only applies when there is the same common management or control both before the acquisition and on the date of the acquisition. So under these facts, no mandatory transfer was allowed since on the date of the acquisition, the common management was lost. [Continental Hydraulics Inc. v. DEED, No. A12-1654 (June 10, 2013)]

How a state's courts interpret common ownership and control in determining when a mandatory experience transfer will be required will matter in your SUI planning. In addition, when registration forms are completed but facts are not clearly specified, the agency's result may not be what an employer expected. Avoid rushing agency applications. Give yourself time to understand the transaction and work with your counsel on how to explain it to the jurisdictions involved.

Q 12:110   When do states generally allow a voluntary transfer of UI experience?

When only a portion of the business is acquired, many states will allow a partial transfer of the predecessor's UI experience on a voluntary basis. The percentage of the business that needs to be acquired that would trigger a voluntary transfer, or that would distinguish a voluntary transfer from a mandatory transfer, varies from state to state. For example, in Michigan, if less than 75 percent of the assets of an existing business are acquired, the acquirer can request a voluntary transfer. If 75 percent or more of the assets are acquired, the transfer becomes mandatory.

Q 12:111   How and when must requests for voluntary transfers of UI experience be made?

Typically, an employer files an application requesting a transfer of the UI experience rating when involving a voluntary transfer event and the rate and reserve account history of the transferee/employer is favorable. For the most part, requests for voluntary transfers must be made within a fixed period after the transfer of assets, usually within 30–90 days from the effective date of the M&A event or from the quarter close that included the event. In Michigan, for example, the request must be made by both employers within 30 days of the close of the quarter in which the assets were transferred. Transfers of UI experience are usually proportional to the payrolls associated with the assets transferred.

Q 12:112   How do states determine a successor's new tax rate?

States determine tax rates by using one of the following four methods or formulas:

1. The reserve ratio formula;

2. The benefit ratio formula;

3. The benefit wage ratio formula (Delaware and Oklahoma); or

4. Alaska's stabilization method.

The transfer of UI experience from the predecessor to the successor, whether voluntary or mandatory, will necessitate that a percentage of the predecessor's payroll, benefit charges, and tax payments be moved to the successor's account. New tax rates for the successor employer are derived by using one of the previously noted four methods from the transferred information from the predecessor combined with the existing experience, if any, of the successor. The predecessor's experience is reduced by the amounts transferred and, if it still has a payroll, a new tax rate is also generally assigned to the predecessor employer. (See Qs 3:68–3:75 for a detailed discussion of the rate methods and formulas.)

Employers must be sure to understand when the new rates will actually begin to apply and where refunds may be necessary to effectuate the economic benefit of the reduced rates. One of the most significant sources of agency notices after an M&A event is due to the misapplied timing of the new rates.

Twenty-seven states (almost all that use the reserve ratio formula) allow voluntary contributions to reduce tax rates. Employers wanting to make a contribution must first determine if the contribution amount will be less than the increased tax amount using the higher rate. States set timing on when voluntary contributions are allowed. M&A events can make it hard to determine what the actual rates will be, making contribution calculations harder. Making voluntary contributions can be helpful to lower ultimate costs, but may require complex calculations and assumptions to be made in the context of M&A transactions. This is yet another consideration for bringing in UI experts to help you plan strategies around M&A events.

Histories of such contributions, related calculations, and resulting rates are important information to gather from target companies.

Q 12:113   After SUTA dumping laws, do any states allow for reserve account transfers on a completely optional basis?

No. Before SUTA dumping laws were in place, California and Texas were the only states that made rate experience transfers completely optional. Under the older versions of the laws, if no transfer was requested, SUI wage bases for transferred employees would not carry over from the predecessor employer and would restart with the successor employer. Both states have now changed their laws and adopted the federal measures in HB 3250. California's SUTA Dumping law now specifies a mandatory transfer of the reserve account whenever an employer transfers its business to another employer if they are under common ownership, management, or control. The new law also provides that if the acquisition was for the purpose of getting a lower UI rate, the transfer will be denied. [C.U.I.C. § 977(c)] The Texas legislature passed § 204.083 of the Texas Labor Code to mandate the transfer of compensation experience in acquisitions of all or part of an experience-rated organization, trade, or business in which there is substantially common management or control or substantially common ownership.

In California, the request is still made for voluntary transfers using Form DE 4453, Application for Transfer of Reserve Account. In partial transfers, Form DE 4453 must be filed within 90 days of the date of acquisition. There are no provisions for an extension of time to file the form. For total transfers, the successor employer has three years from the date of the acquisition in which to file the transfer application. New employers should consider filing Form DE 4453 only if the rate derived from the transfer would be lower than California's new hire rate. If California accepts an application from a new employer, the rate will be retroactive to the quarter in which the acquisition occurred—if the application is filed within 90 days of the date of acquisition. For existing employers that file the application within 90 days of the date of acquisition, the rate will be retroactive to the quarter following the quarter in which the acquisition occurred. (See Information Sheet: California System of Experience Rating (Form DE-231Z).)

In Texas, employers must notify the Texas Workforce Commission (TWC) of any changes in business status, including those arising in the context of an acquisition, sale, or merger. For discontinued businesses, the Status Change Form (C3SCF) must be filed. In the case of the acquisition of a business in Texas or the modification of information regarding an account, the Amended Status Report (C-1AM) must be filed. Both forms require the inclusion of details on the successor employer's and predecessor employer's TWC accounts, including the account numbers and names and addresses, as well as an indication as to whether the asset acquisition was total or partial. From its assessment of these forms, the TWC decides on the employment tax rate in the event of a merger, acquisition, or other change in ownership. (For more information on the requirements for a change of business status in Texas, go to http://www.twc. state.tx.us.)

Employee Contributions to State Unemployment Insurance, Disability Insurance, and Other State Benefit Programs

Q 12:114   When employees are required to contribute to state unemployment insurance and other state benefits (such as disability), will the respective wage bases carry over to successor employers?

Possibly. Five states, California, Hawaii, New Jersey, New York, and Rhode Island, as well as Puerto Rico provide some form of disability benefits to employees. Three of these states, California, New Jersey, and Rhode Island have paid family leave plans as part of their disability programs. Washington State has now delayed paid family leave legislation indefinitely.

In Hawaii, New Jersey, New York, and Puerto Rico, employers are required to pay a payroll tax to support the state's disability program. In all five states and Puerto Rico, employers also withhold some percentage of employee wages up to a specified wage base. The programs operate much like UI. In some states, employers may also be required to withhold from employees' wages to fund UI insurance, health care, and workforce development. For example, in California, New Jersey, and Pennsylvania, employers must deposit and report several additional withholding taxes along with the employer's withheld income taxes and UI contributions in a single filing. In states where the UI wage bases are carried over to successor employers, questions arise about whether the wage bases for the employees' contributions to these other programs also carry over. For Alaska, New Jersey, and Pennsylvania, where the withholding relates to employee supplements of UI contributions, it appears that the wage base would carry over, so long as the SUI wage base carries over to the successor employer (predecessor UI experience is transferred to the successor).

If in doubt and it is certain that for state purposes the new employer is a different employer with a different state tax identification number, restarting the withholding base would be prudent. For states in which employees have experienced withholding from their wages from two separate employers, particularly when restarting the withholding wage base, two W-2s must be produced to ensure that employees can claim credits for any overwithholding on their tax returns and receive refunds. For example, in New Jersey in order to claim any credit for overwithholding that may occur because the employee worked for different employers during the year, the employee must file Form NJ-2450 with his or her NJ-1040 return. The agency instructs that if the required information from the W-2 forms is not available to substantiate the claim, the claim for credit will be denied.

State "Changes of Status" and Other Notice Requirements

Q 12:115   Must an employer notify the state in the event of an M&A event?

Yes. Employers are generally required to provide notices of all events that change an employer status from that originally included in registrations with a state's employment and income tax agency. This includes notices of termination, as well as, notices of change. Such notices can be required within 30 to 90 days (depending on the state) from the effective date of any transaction. Reportable changes include name changes and most ownership changes. Each state has a form that must be used when there is a change of status. Payroll professionals are advised to locate the forms and related instructions for every tax jurisdiction where the transaction will affect employment. Many states have recently consolidated business registrations in a single location for all their agencies (many online) making this process much simpler than in prior years. When consolidation has not occurred, for states that separate income tax administration from the state employment tax administration, there may be several required filings (one for each agency).

If the transaction results in a new employer, along with the notices of change or termination of an old employer, the new employer must file original employer registrations with the proper state authorities, within the specified time periods, and obtain the appropriate state tax identification numbers prior to the first payroll for which withholding deposits must be made. The original employer registrations must be filed in addition to filing with the State Secretary's Office (e.g., Form DE 24 in California; Forms 1897 and AL-1 in Massachusetts; Form NJ-REG—C-L in New Jersey; Forms AI-15 and DTF-95 in New York; Forms C3SCF and C-1AM in Texas; and Forms UC-2B, UC-920, and REV-1706 in Pennsylvania). Many states now provide this service online. See cautions in Q 12:105 above.

There are other state filing concerns as well. For example, when any person or entity carrying on a trade or business decides to use a name that does not include the owner's last name or portray the nature of the business, or is not the entity's legal name, a fictitious business name (FBN) statement must be filed. This process is also known as registering a "Doing Business As" (DBA) or "Trade Name." The business usually registers with the Registrar-Recorder/County Clerk's office in the county where the business will be primarily located. The filing of a fictitious business name certificate is designed to make available to the public the identities of persons doing business under the name and is almost always required in the following circumstances when: a sole proprietorship uses a name that does not contain the owner's last name; a partnership or other association uses a name that does not include the surname of the general partner or if it uses a name that suggests the existence of additional owners, such as "Company," "& Company," "& Son," "& Sons," "& Associates," "Brothers"; a partnership, corporation, or LLC doing business under a name not stated in its articles of incorporation or articles of organization; or a name does not describe the nature of the business. In M&A events, where logos, brand names, or other business references change, or where an acquisition involves an entity described above, new filings may be needed.

Q 12:116 Are there concerns if the transaction's legally specified effective date varies from the operational dates when payrolls are transferred?

Yes. The legally specified effective date of a transaction must generally be disclosed in amendments to the registration required by an employer due to an M&A event. The reported effective date may have an impact on employment tax compliance accountabilities. Efforts must be made to avoid discrepancies between the legally specified effective date of the transaction and the dates the employee transfers will actually occur. A discrepancy between the effective date of the legal contracts and the date when payrolls are actually consolidated can cause uncertainty in the state employer registration process and difficulties in a tax agency's efforts to balance the related tax deposits from wage withholdings with reported liabilities. A discrepancy between the information that an employer files with the Secretary of State regarding the transaction or on its registration form and what it files with tax authorities may result in the state being unable to consolidate tax accounts the way an employer has consolidated its payroll. If this were to happen, an employer could expect to incur increased liabilities from the transaction and to receive numerous notices and assessments that may be difficult to resolve.

As Q 12:109 cautions above, when registration forms are completed with unclear facts or incorrect descriptions, the agency's result may not be what an employer expects. Avoid rushing agency applications. Give yourself time to understand the transaction and work with your counsel on how to explain it to the jurisdictions involved.

State Tax Identification Numbers

Q 12:117 What are state practices regarding state tax identification numbers in an M&A context?

An employer that changes the type of business entity (e.g., sole proprietorship to partnership or corporation, or partnership to corporation) or in any other case where a new federal EIN is required, the employer will for the most part also need to obtain new state tax identification numbers. See Q 12:84 for a listing of when new federal EINs are required. Generally, an employer that acquires the business of another employer must NOT use the state identification number issued to the former employer, or deposit with reporting forms with the former employer's name or identification number preprinted on them. The new employer must apply for his or her own state identification number, and even if the federal ID number does not change, change of ownership reports may still be necessary with the state. See Q 12:115.

When an employer registers with a state, the company's federal EIN is provided to the state in the application process. The state then assigns the employer a state reporting number with ties to the federal EIN. The IRS no longer asks for the state reporting numbers on the Form 940, Employer's Annual Federal Unemployment (FUTA) Tax Return, because the states provide the state reporting numbers to the IRS along with the assigned federal EINs in their records. The IRS uses the state information to validate state UI credits as well as timeliness of UI payments in validating the Form 940 claims. This bonded relationship between the federal EIN and state identification numbers issued for SUI purposes is an important focus for employers since the syncing of the numbers has a direct bearing on the level of tax risk an employer may carry in sustaining the state tax credits claimed on its Form 940 FUTA return.

States do not operate in the blind on related federal EINs. The IRS sends a Quarterly Entity Update file to the states the month following the close of each quarter. The file contains data on newly assigned EINs or employers that have changed their name during the previous quarter. This is why it is so critical that, as soon as possible where new EINs are required in a transaction or where there is a company name change, the proper processing occur with the IRS. See Qs 12:84–12:87 for more information on processing new EINs and name changes.

All states require employers to supply their federal EINs when requesting a new state tax identification number (tax ID). However, states do not always follow the lead of the federal government in requiring a new state tax ID when, for federal purposes, a new EIN is required. When there is an ownership change, but one or more of the business owners of the old employer remain as an owner of the new employer, many states will require the new employer to retain the old employer's tax ID and will merely reassign any new federal EIN to the old account. This has been noted most frequently where states have found SUTA Dumping occurrences. In other cases void of a SUTA Dumping profile, states have allowed, and in fact encouraged, employers to retain the old employer's tax ID. When new employers retain old employers' tax IDs for SUI purposes, the SUI account history of the old employer usually carries over to the new employer.

Hopefully, under the coordinated FUTA Certification Program, the state syncs the state tax ID with the same federal EIN under which Form 940 will be filed. Under this program, states transmit records of activities in the SUI account maintained under each employer's state-issued tax ID account directly to the IRS. However, state credit certification is tied to the federal EIN and not necessarily to the state tax ID. The operations of this program are explained in detail in IRS Publication 4485, Guide for the Certification of State FUTA Credits, found at https://www.irs.gov/pub/irs-pdf/p4485.pdf. See an explanation of the process in Q 12:30. Q 12:30 also discusses the February 9, 2016 Treasury Inspector General for Tax Administration (TIGTA) published audit finding that the IRS needed to have better processes in place to administer its FUTA Certification Program. Employers need to be astute to the inter-workings of the agencies in this regard and make sure that correct federal EINs are provided to the state as part of the notices of restructuring covered in Q 12:115, or when applying for new state tax ID.

Under the older Federal-State Internet Employer Identification Number service, states were able to obtain new federal EINs for employers directly from the IRS. In the past, many states used this service to obtain federal EINs (sometimes without the employers' knowledge) to expedite state tax IDs when there was no federal EIN supplied to them or the one supplied conflicted with their records. With the substantial changes to the SS-4, Application for Employer Identification Number (EIN), regarding disclosure and maintenance of information on a responsible party for the entity applying for the EIN, it is unclear at this point whether this program continues to operate. Employers acquiring new state tax IDs are advised to check the state issuing document to be assured that the federal EIN listed with the new state tax ID is the same one that was submitted and that the federal EIN is the one actually being used for federal purposes. [I.R.S. News Release IR-2004-77 (June 7, 2004), and see Q 12:84 for when new EINs are needed in restructurings.]

When states have separate agencies for PIT and SUI purposes, the different agencies can require separate state tax IDs. Massachusetts uses the federal EIN for PIT purposes, but requires a separate tax ID for SUI purposes. The more recent trend is for states to merge services and require one ID. California assigns one number for both purposes. New York and New Jersey use the federal EIN for both purposes. Kentucky now has a unique business identification number for use in filing through the electronic business portal. (See Q 12:103 for a list of the states that combine PIT and SUI for compliance purposes.)

Generally, states preclude the issuance of a new tax ID when on the application for the tax ID, the new company lists a federal EIN that the state already has associated with another taxpayer on an active SUI account. This limitation stems from federal and state agreements in the context of participation in the federal and state matching program regarding SUI credits on FUTA returns. (See Q 12:87 for a ruling where a partnership received a new EIN even though not technically required to satisfy a state need for a new federal EIN.)

State tax ID concerns have arisen in the past when a newly formed, federally disregarded entity was treated as a division of the parent and the new entity used the parent's existing federal EIN for processing payroll. States see many federally disregarded entities separately from the parent, requiring separate state tax IDs for SUI purposes. This conflict made it difficult in some states for the new entity to obtain a separate state tax ID. (See Q 12:81, which covers the final federal provisions that after 2008 require disregarded entities to be treated as corporate entities for processing payroll and to have their own federal EINs.)

Prior to the issuance of final regulations covering a disregarded entity's payroll compliance under Treas. Reg. § 301.7701-2, because disregarded entities were treated for federal purposes as a mere division of the parent, the disregarded entity could use the parent's federal EIN for managing its federal payroll taxes on a combined basis with the parent. For state purposes, the disregarded entity had substance as separate tax entity. Some states saw the need to require a new federal EIN from the entity before granting a new state tax ID, at least for UI purposes. They declined the parent's EIN if the parent was also operating in the state (because the parent's EIN was already assigned to its own SUI account). States took this position mostly because of internal system constraints, even though the disregarded entity and its parent planned to file a single consolidated federal Form 940. For the most part, states have now worked through their understandings of disregarded entities and this situation rarely poses concern today particularly after the federal rules changed in 2009. For example, prior to 2009, in Wisconsin the disregarded entity's owner was required to withhold, deposit, and furnish reports of Wisconsin income taxes withheld for services performed by employees of the LLC or the owner. After 2008, a disregarded entity is automatically considered an "employer" for purposes of Wisconsin compliance and needs to obtain its own business identification number. [Wis. Stats. § 71.63(3) c] (See Qs 12:80–12:81 for additional information on disregarded entities in an M&A context.)

Another transaction that at one point posed some concern at the state level prior to the new state UI laws requiring mandatory experience carryover involved a restructuring of a partnership and its resulting conversion into a single owned LLC disregarded for federal tax, but not disregarded for state UI purposes. In some of these conversions, the new LLC would then attempt to elect to use the state's new company experience rating as a new employer, requiring the need for the state to issue a new tax ID to the LLC as a new entity. For federal purposes, when a partnership is converted to a disregarded LLC, for payroll and excise tax continuity, the LLC would be required to keep the same federal EIN as the old partnership. States facing the dilemma of the new tax ID request on the part of the LLC would usually decline to issue one since there already was a state tax ID issued to the old partnership tied to the same federal EIN. To resolve the conflict even before the SUTA Dumping laws, many states declined to allow the new employer rate and following the federal lead, required UI experience continuity with the old partnership (similar to the rationale on the federal level that allows the LLC to keep the old partnership's EIN). Under this approach, the new LLC kept the old state tax IDs and maintained the old partnership's SUI account and rate. After the advent of the SUTA Dumping provisions, conflict over this issue is mostly resolved since the provisions would more than likely mandate an experience rate carryover. See Q 12:87.

Q 12:118   If a transaction occurs quickly and there is no time to obtain new state identification numbers, may returns be filed on an "applied for" basis?

Most tax agencies highly discourage filing returns on an "applied for" basis. Some refuse to accept them. Current standards dictate that filings be electronic (in most agencies and for most functions). Therefore, if paper returns are filed and manual checks produced for deposits on an "applied for" basis, posting the data in the state's electronic process without a tax ID may be virtually impossible for a state. Returns that are filed without tax IDs are extremely likely to be processed incorrectly, or not processed at all. In the state's eyes, if a return is filed without a tax ID, it is likely that the entity has not filed the state's required registration paperwork. In addition, many state agencies can no longer legally hold taxpayer funds in an omnibus account awaiting posting. States have escheatment issues. To address these issues, states are enacting policies to return filings and checks to the sender with instructions to refile with a correct tax ID. This means penalties and interest to affected employers.

Many states' SUI systems are designed to process employee wage reports only when submitted with an associated SUI tax ID. Some states have released related procedures that provide for penalties where filings are made without the employer's tax ID. For example, in Florida and Massachusetts, filings without a valid state tax ID can be rejected, returned to employers, and treated as unfiled.

Employers that must file without a state tax ID are advised to use the federal EIN as opposed to filing with no number. Even then, some agencies will return the filings, lose them, or fail to post them. See Q 12:105 for other matters that can go wrong when returns are filed without a state tax ID and only a new federal EIN prior to the agency's review of any reserve experience.

Once it has been determined that a new entity will be created that will pay wages, the first item on a payroll professional's "to-do" list is to file the state change of status and new registration forms and obtain new tax IDs when required. This will greatly reduce the levels of agency notices and related penalties and interest charges for late filings and tax payments traditionally associated with M&A transactions.

Other Concerns

Direct Deposit

Q 12:119 What must employers know regarding direct deposit of employees' pay in the case of an M&A conversion?

Per federal regulations, employers' access to the banking "access device" is restricted, although they are authorized to deposit funds into employees' accounts. Whenever an employer changes its identity, new bank authorizations must be issued. Because new bank authorizations can take some time, the earlier the employer contacts the bank, the sooner the new employer will be equipped to handle the new payroll deposits. [12 C.F.R. § 205.5]

Immigration

Q 12:120 Can a new employer honor Forms I-9 of the predecessor's employees and continue to respect the nonimmigrant classifications of a sponsor predecessor?

Since M&A transactions vary widely in complexity and timing, answers to these questions may require the advice of specialized counsel. Forms I-9 are deemed to be liabilities of the hiring employer, and employees working under nonimmigrant classifications that permit employment only for the "sponsoring" employer are deemed liabilities of the sponsoring employer. Examples of nonimmigrant classifications include H-1b and L-1. Concern about the effects of mergers or acquisitions extends to "sponsorship" for aliens for temporary or permanent employment if the pending classification depends upon a specific job for a specific employer. If the "sponsoring employer" changes, the process may terminate at that point even if inadvertently.

In an M&A context, if immigration-related liabilities of the acquired entity do not pass to the acquiring entity, the acquiring entity is deemed to be a new (as opposed to continuing) employer. Only if the acquiring entity is a "successor in interest" is the acquired entity permitted to act as a continuing employer and assume the acquired entity's I-9 records (and employees) as its own.

Under federal statues, a "successor in interest" is an employer that is related to the original employer, or is a successor of or a reorganized version of the original employer. Successors in interest include acquiring entities that continue to employ some of the acquired entity's entire workforce in cases involving a corporate reorganization, merger, or sale of stock or assets. [8 C.F.R. § 274a. 2(b)(1)(viii)(A)(7)] Per M-274 Handbook for Employers (dated January 22, 2017), a related, successor, or reorganized employer is defined to include the same employer at another location and an employer that continues to employ any employee of another employer's workforce, where both employers belong to the same multi-employer association and the employee continues to work in the same bargaining unit under the same collective bargaining agreement. For these purposes, any agent designated to complete and maintain Forms I-9 must enter the employee's date of hire and/or termination each time the employee is hired and/or terminated by an employer of the multi-employer association.

The April, 2013 version of the Handbook deleted the part of the statutory reference to "an employer that continues to employ some or all of a previous employer's workforce in cases involving a corporate reorganization, merger, or sale of stock or assets" in the listing of who can be a related, successor, or reorganized employer. The USCIS website, however, continues to carry this reference of who is a related, successor, or reorganized employer: "This includes the same employer at another location or an employer who continues to employ some or all of a previous employer's workforce in cases involving a corporate reorganization, merger, or sale of stock or assets." See http://www.uscis.gov/i-9-central/complete-correct-form-i-9/complete-section-1-employee-information-and-verification/continuing-employment. Although unclear, it appears the Handbook may have accidentally omitted this key phrasing since the provision still survives in the definition in the statute cited above and the provision is still contained on the agency's website in discussion of mergers.

Although the requirements sound much like those that come into play for federal and state tax purposes, facts may have different legal consequences and the laws may be interpreted differently for immigration purposes. To the extent that an M&A deal is complex, the successor in interest analysis can be equally complex. If immigration-related "interests" (liabilities) have not passed to the acquiring entity in the course of a merger or acquisition, the acquiring entity is not a successor in interest, but rather a new employer that must obtain and complete new Forms I-9 from all of the acquired entity's (and any other new) employees. As an additional complication under this scenario, the acquiring employer will be unable to obtain and complete new Forms I-9 for any of the acquired company's employment-specific nonimmigrant employees unless it has petitioned timely to "sponsor" them itself and has received approval from USCIS to be their new employer.

In case of an interruption in employment, employers should determine whether the employee is continuing in his or her employment and has a reasonable expectation of employment at all times. Continuing employment with a related, successor, or reorganized employer will be considered "continuing employment" for these purposes provided that the employer obtains and maintains, from the previous employer, records and Forms I-9 where applicable.

The Handbook does make it clear that a related, successor, or reorganized employer may also choose to treat the employees as new hires and complete new Forms I-9 for each of them. To not do so under the continued employment exception, the employer must also show that the employee continuing in his or her employment had a reasonable expectation of employment at all times. Suggestions on meeting this burden are included in the Handbook.

For employees who have not been continuously employed and/or did not have a reasonable expectation of employment at all times, a "hire" is considered to have taken place upon their return to work. If this occurs within three years from the initial hire, then the procedures for rehires may be followed. Otherwise, a new Form I-9 must be completed.

Mergers and acquisitions are complicated processes. Employers may find it difficult to determine whether employees acquired during a merger or acquisition are continuing in their employment or whether they are considered a new hire for Form I-9 purposes. For this reason, the U.S. Department of Homeland Security (DHS) strongly recommends that any business confronted with this question consult with its legal counsel. See USCIS E-Verify Supplemental Guide for Federal Contractors (dated September 2012), E-Verify Employer Agents (dated December 2016), and E-Verify User Manual (dated August 2016).

Q 12:121   Are there any special considerations regarding E-Verify in an M&A context?

Serious considerations arise in an M&A context where the employer participates in the federal E-Verify program or operates in a state with special rules (see Qs 1:8–1:9). For example, employers are generally precluded from reinitiating E-Verify on existing employees. In the case of continuous employment of an employee in a merger or acquisition in which an employer can choose to re-solicit I-9 forms, is the employer allowed to re-E-Verify these employees since technically they are existing employees?

This question is answered as follows on USCIS website at http://www.uscis.gov/e-verify/questions-and-answers/if-employer-acquires-new-employees-through-merger-or-acquisition-and-chooses-treat-those-employees-new-hires-may-company-create-case-e-verify-those-employees.

"Q. If an employer acquires new employees through a merger or acquisition and chooses to treat those employees as new hires, may the company create a case in E-Verify for those employees? A. Yes, employers who acquire another company or merge with another company may choose to treat employees who continue being employed with the related, successor, or reorganized employer as new hires, and complete new Forms I-9 and create cases in E-Verify for all of these employees. Enter the date of acquisition or merger as the date the employee began employment in Section 2 of the new Form I-9. If you choose to complete new Form I-9 and create a case in E-Verify, in order to avoid the appearance of discrimination, you must do so for all acquired employees, without regard to actual or perceived citizenship status or national origin."

For federal contractors, there are additional timelines to consider. In USCIS E-Verify Supplemental Guide for Federal Contractors (dated September, 2012) it says that "if you are a federal contractor with the Federal Acquisition Regulation (FAR) E-Verify clause and the merger or acquisition took place prior to the federal contract award date, your acquired employees are considered existing employees. Federal contractors with the FAR E-Verify clause have special rules relating to the verification of existing employees . . . Employers who are already using E-Verify as required by the FAR E-Verify clause, which then merge with or acquire another company, must comply with the timelines listed below for verifying employees gained through merger or acquisition.

- If you have chosen to verify your entire workforce, you will have 180 days from the effective date of the merger or acquisition to create an E-Verify case for each of the non-exempt employees acquired through a merger with or acquisition of the other company; OR

- If you are not verifying your entire workforce, you will have 90 days from the effective date of the merger or acquisition to create an E-Verify case for each of the non-exempt employees assigned to the contract who joined the company due to a merger with or acquisition of the other company.

Regardless of the timeline for creating cases for acquired employees, you must create cases for each newly hired employee who joins the company outside of the merger or acquisition process no later than the third business day after the employee begins work for pay."

These timelines are specified only for federal contractors and do not apply to other employers.

See Q 12:120 above. These and other open questions on the use of E-Verify remain unanswered even at the federal level in the context of M&A events.

New Hire Reporting

Q 12:122   What are the new hire reporting requirements in the context of an M&A event?

If an employer acquires an ongoing business and employs any of the former owner's employees, the employees are considered new hires and must be reported for new hire purposes. States use new hire information to prepare child support notices. It is important that the state records include the name and address of the current employer for each employee in the national registry. The resubmission of new hire information allows this to happen. Some states also require new hire reporting of independent contractors so successors are cautioned to validate service contract relationships of predecessors and to ascertain whether the predecessors operated in any states requiring new hire contractor reporting. (See Qs 7:43–7:53 for a detailed discussion of new-hire reporting.).

Child Support and Other Garnishments

Q 12:123   Is the successor employer required to honor the family support orders of the predecessor employer?

Generally, yes. Due diligence actions in all M&A events should assure that all Income Withholding Orders (IWOs) of an acquired company are passed over to the acquirer. A company that acquires another company also assumes all the legal responsibilities with it, including withholding from wages under family support orders (e.g., child support, alimony) and will need to follow pre-existing orders. To avoid duplicate orders, the new employer should notify the issuing enforcement agency of the acquisition and its intent to continue withholding. Depending on state law, the issuing agency may then release a new order. Lapses of withholding should be avoided.

Q 12:124   Are there special considerations regarding tax and other garnishments?

There are other types of garnishments orders, such as under bankruptcy, or through other agencies, such as for student loans, or rendered through court judgments for general creditors. Garnishment orders usually require some form of notice when employment ends. If the federal tax identification number is eliminated, the new employer generally is required to contact the agency or creditor and let them know of the change. If employee is no longer working for the new company, most garnishments require notification of the termination and information on the new employer. In the context of an IRS tax levy, if the employee continues with the predecessor, no action is required and the levy continues in force, but if the employee is transferred to the successor, the IRS requires that you notify it, and the IRS normally sends a new levy notice to the new employer. IRS Form 668-W is used to notify the IRS.

In the context of an M&A event, all such orders should be carefully sought out and reviewed. Caution is warranted as missing even one withholding can bring on liabilities on the part of the employer for unpaid balances, fines, and even possibly court costs.

Family and Medical Leave Act

Q 12:125   Does FMLA have rules for successors in interest that provide for the carryover of an acquired company's responsibilities regarding commitments and the continuation of eligibility time and leaves already in process?

Yes. The Family and Medical Leave Act (FMLA), in determining whether an employer is covered because it is a successor in interest to a covered employer, considers the factors used under Title VII of the Civil Rights Act and the Vietnam Era Veterans' Adjustment Act. These factors require a facts and circumstances look at the relationship between the successor and predecessor employers. The factors considered in determining whether a successor in interest relationship exists include whether there is a substantial continuity of the same business operation; use of the same plant or facilities; continuity of the workforce; similarity of jobs and working conditions; similarity of supervisory personnel; similarity of machinery, equipment, and production methods; similarity of products and services; and the ability of the predecessor employer to provide relief after the acquisition. Where the determination is one of a successor in interest, the transferred employees are treated as continuing covered employment with the predecessor and the successor employer is required to honor the predecessor's FMLA practices regarding eligibility, leaves in process, and health insurance. [29 C.F.R. § 825.107] (See Qs 9:181–9:194 for a further discussion of the FMLA provisions.)

In 2013, a U.S. district court judge in Phoenix granted a consent judgment, requiring that an Arizona delivery driver be offered reinstatement, back pay, and reimbursement of medical expenses under FMLA. The U.S. Department of Labor's Wage and Hour Division's investigation determined that a successor company had a legal obligation to allow the employee to complete his leave that started with a predecessor company and then restore him to an equivalent position as required by the Act. [Solis v. D.S. Waters of America, Inc., d/b/a Sparkletts, DOL Release No. 13-0572-SAN, Case No. 2:11cv2075 (D. Ariz. Apr. 17, 2013)]

Mass Layoffs

Q 12:126   Is an employer required to give employees advance notice of facility or plant closings or mass layoffs associated with the restructuring of the business?

Yes. Many times when companies restructure, they take the opportunity to lay off workers. This happens for many reasons such as duplicated positions, closing unneeded branches, downsizing the new operation, just to name a few. Provisions of federal WARN (Workers Adjustment and Retraining Notifications) provides protection to employees, their families, and communities by requiring employers to give 60 days' advance notice of facility or plant closings and mass layoffs with 100 or more full-time employees who have been employed for at least six months of the previous 12 months. In some states, the threshold is lower. [29 U.S.C. § 2101; 29 C.F.R. § 639.3] These requirements apply even in the context of a company's involvement in a merger or acquisition or other restructuring as there is no exception for these events. The penalties are high if the requirements are overlooked.

Almost every state also has WARN provisions that can impose even more stringent standards. For example, in California, the requirement applies to employers with 75 or more full-or part-time employees. [Cal. Lab. Code §§ 1400(a), 1400(h)]

Under the federal WARN provisions, employers with 50 or more employees during a 30-day period must provide advance notice of a facility or plant closing. And, if an employer plans to lay off 50 to 499 of its full-time employees and that constitutes one-third or more of the full-time workforce at a single site, the employer must provide advance notice of the layoff. Employers with 500 or more full-time employees are required to provide advance notice of layoffs of any size regardless of the percentage of the workforce involved. [29 U.S.C. § 2101; 29 C.F.R. § 639.3]

In comparison, California employers are required to provide advance notice of plant closing, layoffs, or relocations of 50 or more employees within a 30-day period regardless of the percentage of workforce involved. To be covered, a relocation of employees must be to a facility 100 miles away from the current location. [Cal. Lab. Code §§ 1400(c), 1400(d)]

Employers that violate the advance notice requirements can be federally liable to each employee for an amount equal to back pay and benefits for the period of the violation up to 60 days, but no more than half the number of days the employee was employed by the employer. [12 U.S.C. § 2104(a); 29 U.S.C. § 2102, 29 C.F.R. §§ 639.5, 639.9]

States can have even stiffer penalties. For example, California will impose a civil penalty of $500 a day for each day of the violation, along with certain more specific refinements of employee back pay and benefit amounts. [Cal. Lab. Code §§ 1400(d), 1400(g), 1401, 1402 and 1403].

Some states also require layoff notification to the state's UI coordinator. As an example, an Ohio employer that lays off or separates within any seven-day period 50 or more individuals because of lack of work is required to furnish notice to the Ohio Unemployment Compensation Technical Services of the dates of layoff or separation and the approximate number of individuals being laid off or separated. The notice needs to be furnished at least three working days before the date of the first day of the layoff or separation. In addition, at the time of the layoff or separation, the employer is to furnish to the individual and to the Director information necessary to determine the individual's eligibility for unemployment compensation. [This provision is part of Ohio's unemployment compensation law, which is found in the O.R.C. under Title 41, Chapter 4141, § 4141.28.]

Qualified Retirement Plans

Q 12:127   Are there special federal filing requirements when an employer's restructuring involves the merger, consolidation, spin-off, termination, or transfer of assets or liabilities from a pension plan, profit sharing plan, or other deferred compensation plan?

Yes, however, which employer should file Forms 5310, Application for Determination for Terminating Plan; or Forms 5310-A, Notice of Plan Merger or Consolidation, Spin-off, or Transfer of Plan Assets or Liabilities; Notice of Qualified Separate Lines of Business, and how the forms should be completed are beyond the scope of this text. Payroll professionals must be aware that compensation is closely aligned with the employer that pays it in the context of qualified plan participation. Any movement of employees participating in a qualified retirement plan to another employer or in the context of a restructuring and any payment of substantial compensation apart from regular, planned-for compensation to any plan participant can dramatically affect the plan. Therefore, payroll professionals involved in M&A activities should be closely aligned with their counterparts in human resources or plan administration regarding the deployment of the strategy's impact on the related benefit plans. Even a decision to continue a transferred employee's deferral into a 401(k) plan should first be reviewed by those accountable for the plan.

The exclusive benefit rule of I.R.C. § 401(a) is considered to be violated if the sponsorship of a qualified retirement plan is transferred from an employer to an unrelated taxpayer and the transfer of the sponsorship of the plan is not in connection with a transfer of business assets, operations, or employees from the employer to the unrelated taxpayer. An employer can transfer sponsorship for an underfunded defined benefit plan to a subsidiary without violating the exclusive benefits rule due to the subsidiary being part of the employer corporation's controlled group. However, once the employer corporation later sells the stock of that subsidiary to an unrelated corporation, it would violate I.R.C. § 401(a) when the subsidiary falls out of the employer's controlled group. [Rev. Rul. 2008-45, 2008-34 I.R.B. 403] The lesson from this ruling is that care needs to be taken not to shift liabilities for a qualified plan with other liabilities to a transitional entity as part of an M&A strategy.

Federal Notices and Other Agency Inquiries in Context of Change of Ownership

Q 12:128   What can be done if the SSA finds that the successor's Forms W-2 are not in balance with Forms 941 and that more taxes are due or that the acquired company has failed to file Forms W-2 to cover represented wage liabilities reported in Forms 941?

As the SSA processes W-2 reports, it maintains a record of total Social Security and Medicare wages and tips processed for each employer. These totals are then compared with the totals of employment tax records filed by the employer with IRS on Forms 941. Employers whose reports to the IRS and SSA do not balance are contacted for an explanation of the discrepancy and asked for additional wage evidence. The IRS contacts employers that reported more wages to the SSA than to the IRS. The SSA contacts employers that reported more wages to the IRS than to the SSA. Failure to resolve these discrepancies may result in an IRS assessment of penalties for filing incorrect reports.

Usually within an 18-month period after the final Forms W-2 are filed, the SSA, with the help of the IRS, will begin balancing the employer's Forms W-2 with Forms 941. If a discrepancy is found, the SSA will send the employer an initial notice and questionnaire alerting the employer to a discrepancy and requesting the earnings data needed to resolve the case. If the SSA does not receive a response after 45 days, the employer is sent a follow-up letter. When no response is received after the second notice, the IRS is responsible for contacting the employer and may impose penalties, if necessary. The initial SSA notice (and follow-up letter) gives employers an opportunity to clear up any discrepancies before they become potential IRS assessments. On receipt of an SSA letter, the employer must first review its payroll records and ascertain the source of the discrepancy. Next, the employer must explain in correspondence to the SSA the reason for the discrepancy and, where required, prepare amended filings. It is important in responding to the SSA that you use the questionnaire provided to you in the notice. Copies of the different SSA notices where the SSA has no record of an employer's report of wages or where there is a discrepancy between the IRS data and the SSA data can be found at http://www.ssa.gov/employer/recon/recon.htm.

If an employer receives a query from the SSA, the employer can sometimes resolve the matter by explaining (1) that the out of balance was due to merger or asset acquisition and, pursuant to IRS authority, W-2s were consolidated under the successor's EIN; (2) the predecessor's name, address, and EIN; and (3) it should balance both companies' records together. If this resolves the concern, the SSA will more than likely pass this information on to the IRS, which may then preclude any further federal agency notices to the employers. Where the accounts are still out of balance when compared together, the employer will need to assist the agency in resolving the discrepancies.

The SSA does not currently have access to the IRS records that may contain Schedule D (Form 941) resolving the discrepancies (see Qs 12:11–12:19 and 12:57–12:59). Therefore, the notice from the SSA may reflect the fact that it is not aware of the M&A event and does not see the account relationship between the employers. However, employers must address the issue outlined in the notice (follow-up letter) to prevent it from escalating. It is important to note that Schedule D was designed specifically to assist the IRS in M&A event-related balancing of Forms 941 and Forms W-2. Evidence of a timely submission of a Schedule D to the IRS and a copy of the filing should be a sufficient response to an initial notice from the SSA as long as it resolves the out-of-balance positions. Where agency records vary from the Schedule D numbers, which can happen on occasion, employers will need to do more and perhaps file W-2c corrections, amended 941 returns, and a new Schedule D with the IRS. Remember that there is also a field in the EFW2 employer record for an employer to enter another EIN if related 941s were not all filed with the EIN of the employer that submitted the W-2s. Because the SSA will reference that EIN when consolidating Form 941 accounts for comparison, it is critical that the field be used wherever possible (see Qs 12:24 and 12:63). The SSA suggests that if you have additional questions, to call 1-800-772-6270 (TTY 1-800-325-0778) between 7:00 a.m. and 7:00 p.m. Eastern time, Monday through Friday.

Q 12:129   What happens if employers do not take steps to resolve discrepancies outlined by the SSA?

If employers fail to resolve matters with the SSA, the SSA will refer the matter to a special unit in the IRS that handles the SSA Combined Annual Wage Reporting (CAWR) program to work the discrepancy and assess penalties. In September, 2015, the Treasury Inspector General for Tax Administration (TIGTA) released an audit report on the CAWR program's handling of discrepancy cases. The report concluded that employers that did not comply with SSA requests to provide wage documents were not always appropriately assessed penalties. The IRS agreed to TIGTA's findings and will be stepping up enforcement and improving its case tracking system. [TIGTA Audit Report No. 2015-40-090 (Sept. 22, 2015)] Overlooked reporting in M&A events are a leading cause of discrepancies. We can expect to see more agency challenges and fewer matters overlooked.

The IRS takes employment tax failures very seriously and uses its arsenal of steep penalties to enforce the rules. Many employers that receive a notice from the IRS mistakenly assume that the matter will eventually become a nonissue because the employers know they paid the taxes and filed the W-2s. This will not be obvious to the IRS and employers are advised to quickly address any notice received to avoid high penalties.

When the SSA refers the discrepancy to the IRS CAWR unit, the IRS will view the predecessor as remitting payroll taxes and filing Forms 941, but failing to file Forms W-2 that match its larger Forms 941 totals. The difference is known as "excess 941 liabilities." The IRS CAWR unit will send the employer Letter 0098C, Wage Discrepancy per SSA; Information/Verification Requested, that reports a comparison of the amounts recorded by the SSA as submitted on W-2s with the amounts recorded on Forms 941. The letter requests copies of Forms W-2 and proposes a potential penalty assessment if the discrepancy is not resolved. W-2s are necessary to ensure that the employees are given the appropriate wage credits in support of their SSA benefits and to ensure that employees have the right information to file their tax returns.

The successor, on the other hand, will receive an IRS notice informing it of increases made to its Form 941 tax liabilities for the excess of reported W-2 liabilities over the total reported Form 941 liabilities, also known as the "excess W-2 liabilities." The successor will be seen as filing Forms W-2 in excess of the amounts reported on Forms 941. The IRS views this difference as actual 941 unpaid liabilities and will make adjustments to filed Forms 941 to account for the difference. These adjustments are accompanied by penalties up to 15 percent of the unpaid liabilities under I.R.C. Section 6656 for insufficient tax deposits to cover the adjusted return. Other penalties for filing incomplete returns or failing to pay the taxes actually due when the return is filed may also be assessed.

Q 12:130   What kinds of processing errors can cause information to be out of balance?

Double reporting of Forms W-2 can frequently occur when two unrelated employers are struggling to consolidate payrolls while dealing with the time constraints of an M&A event. When the predecessor (or third-party service provider) files W-2s, and the W-2s are also consolidated with the successor's W-2s and filed, the agencies' records reflect duplicate wages. In most payroll processes, the employee statement process is usually separate from the agency filing process, which is how one set of W-2s can be handled correctly and the other set incorrectly. For some, the tasks are handled by different service providers that are not in sync with each other. This is not uncommon in e-services today. Where two copies are provided to employees, the employees are quick to catch the errors before the agency filings. However, when employees receive one copy and the duplicate payroll data is stored in a data warehouse (e.g., to support a predecessor employer's state filing), the duplicate data can accidentally be filed when the filing programs are processed. Therefore, it is important that payroll professionals, particularly those involved in M&A activities, ensure the quality control of all data output before any filings. Samples must be taken and validated against other control records.

When double reporting occurs, the SSA will typically require that the predecessor submit Forms W-2c to correct the problem. By the time the SSA has sent notices to employers, it will have already run the two sets of W-2s through its edit process and employee wage history files. Edits in the SSA system will, in most cases, preclude the double posting of reports in the same amount (although the amounts will rarely be the same because the successor will have also continued to pay wages to the employees). Problems arise where the two amounts reported are equal and the SSA has eliminated one of the duplicate records when the employer later files a W-2c to eliminate the original filing.

Because one record was already removed by the SSA, a W-2c would eliminate the remaining record. Employers with these types of corrections need to work closely with their SSA-assigned agency liaison officer in correcting the records.

The SSA also will have transmitted the duplicate W-2 information to the IRS for Form 1040 matching very close to the time that it processes the reports for its files. Where the wage reports differ, the IRS will look for the totals of both reports in the employee's tax return. The IRS has an edit process similar to that of the SSA that it uses to search for amounts that have been reported twice (which can cause the same problems for the IRS as it does for the SSA). Corrections to W-2s (via Forms W-2c) must be made quickly to preclude the IRS's desk audit activities regarding the employee for understating wages, because, without the W-2c correction, the IRS will be looking for both sets of wages in the employee's return. The employer will need to work closely with both the SSA and the IRS to ensure that the W-2c corrections were successful.

Other common errors include duplication of 941 liabilities when the employees were transferred in mid-quarter with full histories of the wages paid by the predecessor employer earlier in the quarter. Problems arise when the successor reports the full quarter wages and the predecessor reports the partial quarter wages. When this occurs in the context of the successor employer rules, if the successor actually pays the liability difference when the return is filed (and many employers automatically do), the successor may be due a refund. Many times, the successor is unaware of the problem until it begins to receive the SSA out-of-balance notices or IRS threats to assess intentional disregard penalties for failure to file enough W-2s to cover the posted 941 amounts. If the employer does not react quickly, the lag period between when the Form 941 was originally filed incorrectly and the date the employer receives out-of-balance notices might give rise to a statute of limitation issue regarding claiming the refund. When this has happened in the past, the IRS will make the adjustment to eliminate the intentional disregard penalty. However, it will not grant the refund (providing another reason why employers should react quickly on receiving any agency out-of-balance notice).

There have been instances where each company assumes that the other company has filed the Forms W-2 and neither company files them (in which case, original W-2s must be filed). Although this rarely happens on a large scale, it can happen when a separate business unit, for some reason, was left out of the consolidation process.

One of the more frequent causes of out-of-balance positions relates to mismanaged third-party sick pay. Where an acquired company has a relationship with the third-party insurance company that delivers W-2 information at year-end to the old address, the information is often overlooked and fails to be included in the consolidated W-2 process. Surviving companies are well advised to seek in the early stages of the discussion, the details of all third-party managed employee benefits that could affect the W-2 process.

Q 12:131　What is the best course of action when state agencies discover discrepancies in filings related to M&A events?

During an M&A event (especially a large transaction), many "tracers" (or state agency notices) can be expected. Not every agency will have processed the change of status filing, not every jurisdiction will have assigned tax IDs for new companies, and there will be mix-ups in new SUI rates. Seasoned employers will increase staff temporarily or establish compliance teams and set new short-term expectations of staff accountability until the end of the transition period (usually 12 to 18 months for large transactions). However, when the number of tracers received by an employer results in significant unexpected workloads, something may be wrong.

State agencies, particularly SUI agencies, are known to detect and react to discrepancies faster than federal agencies. This is because the SUI agencies usually receive employee wage details before other agencies. The causes of the discrepancies are much the same as discussed previously (see Q 12:130), including double reporting where the M&A event happens in mid-quarter and the wages are transferred with the SUI histories for the full quarter causing both employers to report for the same period. SUI notices regarding wage discrepancies are early warnings that something may have gone wrong and should be taken seriously. Some notices merely point out a failure to file under a tax ID where a return was expected. These notices indicate potential registration problems with the agencies that must be addressed to avoid larger concerns or processing that went awry in the conversion.

Many employers simply pay the SUI assessments because they are usually small or mostly relate to the timing of application of new SUI rates caused by the M&A event. Employers are advised to scrutinize each assessment and understand it before paying it. When a processing error is very probable, payroll professionals should work diligently to identify the error and begin the amendment of returns before the agencies accelerate the liability risks with penalties and interest charges. Reasonable cause to avert penalties is always easier to establish when the employer has taken the initiative to correct its errors.

Compensation Benefits

Q 12:132　Which compensation benefits require unique compliance treatment in an M&A event?

Employers facing an M&A event are advised to make a complete list of all compensation benefits that will require special payroll processing as well as other matters that could increase liability risk or that will need to be tracked to assure compliance is met, particularly during the event's transitional period. Such benefits and tasks could include the following:

- Sign-on and retention bonuses.
- Unscheduled bonuses.

- Severance pay.
- Golden parachute payments.
- COBRA payments.
- Accrued vacation and sick pay.
- Accelerated vesting of deferred compensation.
- Accelerated vesting of qualified and nonqualified stock options and related earn-out payments.
- More frequent exercises of qualified and nonqualified stock options.
- Accelerated vesting of restricted stock or other equity-based benefits and related earn-out payments.
- Accelerated payouts of nonqualified deferred compensation.
- Lump-sum payments from qualified plans.
- Lump-sum payments from supplemental retirement plans.
- Earn-out payments in lieu of other actual benefits.
- Payments related to covenants not to compete and noncompete agreements.
- Increased numbers of employee settlements, including attorney fees.
- Payments in lieu of work placement services.
- Payments for work placement services.
- Forgiven employee loans.
- Relocation expenses, including moving expense reimbursement and temporary housing costs.
- Travel advances still outstanding for terminated sales staff.
- Payments including reimbursements that do not meet the accountable plan rules and therefore require wage treatment (e.g., for unreturned company equipment such as laptops or tools or for use of the company credit card). Look at Accounts Payable and HR areas to determine if wage or other employment interfaces exist and if items that should be are properly treated and reported as wages are so treated whenever they arise.
- The treatment of other fringe benefit plans, including cafeteria plans and flexible spending arrangements (FSAs) that might affect wages and W-2 reporting such as those for: medical expense reimbursement; adoption assistance; dependent care; merchandise and service discounts; educational assistance; scholarships; relocation; expatriation totalization and gross-up; health, life and other insurance coverage; parking; company cars; transit passes; longevity, safety and other awards.
- Third-party sick pay arrangements and all third-party arrangements for administration of employee benefit or wage matters.
- Open and closed settlements for any employment reason such as employment discrimination, sexual harassment, as well as any pending litigation.

Section 409A, added to the Internal Revenue Code as part of the American Jobs Creation Act of 2004, provides that all amounts deferred under a broadly defined nonqualified deferred compensation plan are currently includible in gross income to the extent not subject to a substantial risk of forfeiture and not previously included in gross income, unless certain requirements are met. If deferred compensation arrangements fail to comply with the § 409A requirements, interest at the underpayment rate plus 1 percent will be imposed on the underpayments that would have occurred had the compensation been includible in income when first deferred, or if later, when not subject to a substantial risk of forfeiture. Terms of M&A transactions many times can trigger acceleration of deferred arrangements and sometimes, because of the far-reaching aspects of § 409A, the application may not be apparent until such an event exposes the arrangement for payment consideration. In this regard, it is imperative that a benefit counsel review the planned payouts for purposes of § 409A and earmark those arrangements requiring special income reporting on Form W-2 (use of Code Z in Box 12) (or if involving a director or other contractor, on Form 1099-MISC, Box 15b).

Deferred amounts including earnings were to be reported on Form W-2 using Code Y (Box 15a on Form 1099-MISC for directors and other contractors); however, in IRS Notice 2008-115, 2008-52 I.R.B. 1367, as modified by Notice 2010-6, 2010-3 I.R.B. 275, the IRS announced that until further guidance is released, deferred amounts are not required to be reported.

The new health care reforms have brought many new compliance accountabilities that will need to be added to the payroll due diligence team's responsibilities in these transactions to assure continuity and compliance. A few of considerations include:

- Tracking the wage threshold and managing correct withholding of the 0.9 percent Additional Medicare Tax on wage amounts exceeding $200,000, as well as consolidating these amounts on W-2 forms.

- Reporting aggregate cost of health care coverage on W-2 forms.

- Performing risk assessments for the Employer's Shared Responsibility Payments (ESRP). ESRP is one of the enforcement tools in the health care legislation. It was postponed from 2014 to 2015, for larger employers with 100 or more full-time equivalent employees and to 2016 for mid-size employers with 50 to 99 full-time equivalent employees. The ESRP and related new reporting requirements will pose risk and compliance concerns in M&A transactions.

- Meeting information reporting requirements under I.R.C. § 6055 and § 6056 on Forms 1094-C, 1095-C, and possibly 1094-B and 1095-B for employers who are self-insured and cannot report on Part III of Form 1095-C. The new reporting requirements will pose risk and compliance concerns in M&A transactions.

- Complying with Flexible Health Spending Accounts limitations. An employee salary deferral now has a limit for a Health FSA. The 2017 annual dollar limit on employee contributions increases to $2,600 from $2,550 in 2016. Misapplied thresholds can affect taxable wage amounts. Plans also need to stay current by adopting appropriate amendments to reflect the new limits each year the limit and other rules change. Other matters also need to be examined for employees that participate in a general health FSA. There are restrictions when a Health FSA is combined with employer contributions to a Health Savings Account (HSAs). Employers would need to set up a limited HSA-compatible FSA if they offer an HSA interface in their health plan offering. See CCA 2014-13005 released February 12, 2014, for details on how this works.

- Handling the payment of medical loss ratio (MLR) rebates to employees by employers that maintain group health insurance policies and that received the premium rebates from their insurance carriers for a previous year.

- Monitoring the coverage terms of health care plans to avoid penalties for violations, such as those imposed under I.R.C. § 4980D on failures of a group health plan to meet special coverage requirements. The amount of the tax on any failure is $100 for each day in the noncompliance period with respect to each individual to whom the failure relates.

- Implementing other aspects of the Affordable Care Act will become effective in future years and will have serious impact on payroll, such as what has become known as the Cadillac tax under I.R.C. § 4980I, now delayed until 2020, which will impose on affected employees a 40 percent excise tax on the cost of health care coverage valued over a certain amount. There will also be future guidance issued on other Affordable Care Act provisions as well, such as on implementation of I.R.C. § 105(h) that provides for nondiscrimination within health care plans, revamping the cafeteria plan requirements under I.R.C. § 125 to meet the new health care provisions, and ever expanding information reporting requirements associated with enforcement of the new rules. These too will need to be monitored for accountability in M&A events.

- Complying with last-minute legislation and even significant court holdings regarding health care reform.

Q 12:133   What are the key compensation and benefit plans and contracts that may require special compliance treatment in planning for an M&A event?

The following plans and contracts are a few of those that require special consideration due to the impact of changes in control due to an M&A event:

- All qualified retirement plans, including 401(k) cash or deferred plans; Section 401(a) defined benefit and profit sharing plans; ESOPs; Section 457 plans, Section 403(a) annuities, and Section 403(b) salary reduction agreements (for nonprofits); SIMPLE 401(k) and IRA plans; deductible voluntary employee contribution (DEC) plans, simplified employee pensions (SEPs), and salary reduction SEPs (SARSEPs) concerning payroll requirements and other compliance responsibilities associated with lump-sum payments, matching and timing of contributions, funding needs, M&A impact on meeting testing requirements, outstanding employee loans, ESOP loans, adequacy of third-party service, integration, or sever-ance of member companies in multiemployer plans.

- All nonqualified deferred compensation plans, including supplemental employee retirement plans (SERPs) and supplemental retirement options (SROs), as well as sales incentive plans in terms of who is covered, funding matters, accelerated vesting, and other contractual promises in the context of the plans.

- Group life, health, short- and long-term disability, accident, long-term care and other insurance plans or employer self-insurance plans. Pay particular attention to those administered by third parties such as third-party sick pay where W-2 reportable wages and payroll tax liabilities are subject to a special arrangement.

- Health and welfare plans, such as cafeteria plans or other flexible benefit plans for health care, dependent care, and legal services regarding em-ployee commitments.

- COBRA service plans, in terms of coverage and cost.

- Vacation, sick pay, or severance plans, in terms of accruals and cost, levels of vesting, and employee commitments.

- Executive insurance plans, such as split-dollar life arrangements.

- All employee contracts, in terms of whether changes in company control will trigger vesting of certain guaranteed severance or other payments or accelerate vesting of others, terms of termination, discharge of employee loans and other promised benefits (such as continued health insurance).

- Qualified and nonqualified stock options and restricted stock or other equity incentive plans, in terms of accelerated vesting, assumption or substitution restrictions, or cash earn-outs.

- Bonus plans, in terms of accelerated vesting or other contractual promises.

- All union plans or other collective bargaining agreements, in terms of successor accountability for employer contributions or withdrawal from the plans.

- Other fringe benefit plan compliance, including cafeteria plans and flexible spending arrangements (FSAs) that might affect wages and W-2 reporting such as those for: medical expense reimbursement; adoption assistance; dependent care; merchandise and service discounts; educational assis-tance; scholarships; relocation; expatriation totalization and gross-up; parking; company cars; transit passes; longevity, safety and other awards to name a few of many fringe possibilities.

- Accountable plans for business expense reimbursement to employees, members of the board of directors or contractors.

See also Q 12:132 above on the cautions as to I.R.C. § 409A compliance and chapter 9 for a detailed discussion of compensation benefits.

Administration and M&A Events

Q 12:134   What activities should be included on the payroll and employment tax checklist in anticipation of an M&A event?

Payroll staff, in anticipation of an acquisition or reorganization, should include the following on its M&A checklist:

- Establish a task force to develop a work plan and related timeline that includes individuals from payroll administration and key payroll tax and operations functions, human resources, treasury, accounts payable, information or system services, as well as legal and tax counsel.

- Review the proposed structure of the transaction from legal, technical, cost, and liability perspectives and, if needed, obtain opinions from counsel on the tax classification (i.e., statutory merger, asset acquisition, etc.) that focus on payroll compliance needs.

- Analyze payroll system capacities, plan for the continued maintenance of critical, ongoing payroll functions throughout the transition, and test data from programs that will be involved in the payroll processing of special compensation arising due to the transaction event (e.g., golden parachute payments and earn-out payments on stock options).

- Identify service providers involved in current payroll compliance functions and enlist their support in establishing necessary payroll interfaces.

- Assign responsibilities for employee communications and outline the needed announcements and related timing.

- Identify responsibilities for the pools of employees to be retained, severed, or transferred, including where FICA, FUTA, and SUI wage carryovers are needed.

- Make a complete list of all compensation benefits that may require special payroll processing (see Q 12:132 and Q 12:133).

- Make sure that those responsible are reviewing benefits plans (see Q 12:132 and Q 12:133) and employee contracts and that the requirements for the employees involved are outlined.

- Set the timelines and allocate resources to handle the special payroll processing.

- Begin work-ups on terminations to avoid last-minute processing problems.

- Consider funding needs to cover the special payments, taxes on in-kind benefits, or tax gross-ups.

- Identify all third-party service providers or administrators of any benefits that could involve W-2 reporting or handling of payroll taxes and work with them to outline a course of action.

When a company is acquiring another company or operation, the aforementioned points must be considered from the standpoint of gaining knowledge of the target's liabilities in its payroll activities and assuring the continuation of a healthy payroll process during the transition. In addition, a payroll strategy for implementing an acquisition should also include the following tasks:

- Determine the overall structure of the target company's payroll process, including programs and departments involved, and whether common pay agents or common paymasters are part of the process, or whether the target uses a third party to process payroll, and which systems (and types) are deployed.

- Locate and plan for preservation of the target company's payroll and payroll tax records for the current year and previous years—including current and past employee payroll records, time cards and paystubs, and employees' Forms I-9 and W-4; all federal, state, and local versions of employees' Forms W-2 and related agency W-2 or other employee wage-detail filings or transmissions; all quarterly, annual, and/or other with-holding tax reconciliations or other tax filings—to ensure compliance with recordkeeping responsibilities under federal and state DOL standards.

- If the employer has claimed Form 941 exemptions or credits, for example, under the HIRE Act or regarding COBRA premium recovery, or taken advantage under any other recent enactments to encourage increased hiring and to preserve jobs that require detailed recordkeeping and in some cases certifications from state agencies and employees, such as Forms W-11, these records and certifications will be important to find and preserve.

- Obtain a complete listing of all payroll tax jurisdictions where filings are made or have been made in the last four years, and the related tax calendars that show the frequency of filings and deposits.

- Validate tax deposit mechanisms and obtain tax deposit records, wherever possible, for the past four years.

- Consider requesting tax transcripts from all tax authorities to ensure that liabilities have been appropriately identified and that filings and deposits have been appropriately made.

- Obtain a complete list of the ongoing day-to-day payroll activities, the parties responsible for performing those activities, and key due dates for filings and deposits, particularly over the transition period, to ensure that no task is overlooked.

- Validate the existing garnishment process and obtain a list of ongoing garnishments, particularly those that involve child support payments that must be continued after the acquisition.

- Determine whether there exist ex-pat or in-pat programs and establish the related payroll practices for global payrolls.

- Resolve to work with target company's payroll staff to facilitate a smooth transition.

- Consider post acquisition, merger, or other reorganization integration needs including whether the two companies' payroll systems interface and whether bridge programming may be needed.

- Determine whether the two companies use similar accrual methods for key payroll items, such as vacation or sick pay, including whether the timing methods for establishing tax liabilities for compensation items (e.g., compensation related to the exercise of a stock option) of the two companies are the same.

- Consider whether it will be possible to integrate benefit plans and, if so, which plans.

- Look at whether the two companies have similar compensation incentives (e.g., based on performance or on time served) and review for possible I.R.C. § 409A impact. See Q 12:132 above.

- Make sure you have plans to integrate current and prior year compensation data and payroll tax liabilities, as well as qualified and nonqualified plan histories managed by third-party service providers and administrators, such as that involving third-party sick pay and nonqualified deferred compensation (maintained through trustees).

- Contemplate whether there are fundamental differences in corporate culture of the two companies regarding payrolls that could affect the integration strategy.

Taking the time to ensure that the required planning activities are implemented prior to the M&A event can help to ensure that the transition between the predecessor and successor employers is smooth, employees are not adversely affected by the merger, and the corporations involved are not subject to expensive and burdensome penalties and enforcement actions by the various state and federal agencies that become involved in such transitions. Advance planning can help to ensure a positive result.

Chapter 13

Global Payroll

Launching and managing payrolls internationally is challenging to most organizations and especially for those with limited exposure to the complexities of payroll requirements at international locations. Many organizations find themselves in a situation where Operations has a desire or need to set up locations internationally but then the administrative team (usually Human Resources and Payroll) has the task of setting up payroll for a variety of employee types in locations where the organization has limited experience. In other cases, a division may be divested from a global parent organization with limited support from the parent's centralized functions of finance, accounting, human resources, and payroll. This new organization not only has to find the resources to fill these roles, but it immediately has local employee populations all over the world which need these services. Typically, the new organization can purchase these services through the parent for a transition period through a Transition Services Agreement (TSA), which lasts from a few months to one year. In any event, these organizations have the same challenges: How do we launch and manage payrolls in multiple international locations in a compliant, efficient, and controlled manner?

Companies are also looking to increase their visibility of local operations and improve their compliance worldwide. With the advent of the Sarbanes-Oxley Act of 2002 (SOX), Global Privacy Directives, U.S. Department of the Treasury's Office of Foreign Assets Control (OFAC), UK Bribery Act, Foreign Corrupt Practices Act (FCPA), and increased penalties for executives who sign organizational documents, companies are more sensitive than ever to ensure proper controls are in place worldwide. Finance, HR, and Payroll professionals are now being challenged to ensure international locations follow similar processes and protocols as those in the United States thereby reducing risk and increasing compliance on a global level.

This chapter will help payroll professionals determine the types of questions that should be asked when launching and managing payrolls in international locations. While this section gives some specific examples that support the explanations, each country has its own unique payroll requirements, which may change from year to year.

Note. This chapter provides points of reference from a U.S. Payroll Professional's perspective.

Overview

Q 13:1 When determining what kind of workers to hire overseas, what type of analysis should be performed?

As in the employee versus independent contractor issue (see chapter 6), the first step in determining what type of working arrangement is most appropriate for each international location is to understand the goals of the organization. Some organizations are committed to opening an office in another country for sales or operational purposes. In this case, the company may want to employ a local consultant to help with the local set-up, and to perform initial market research and limited operations. Often, this consultant is converted to an employee once the entity is established. Other times, a specialized consultant, an international start-up organization, or a local accounting firm is hired to perform the set-up activities and help the organization hire its first few employees. This type of consultant will move on to another organization once the set-up is complete. The accounting firm is usually retained after the initial set-up to provide ongoing accounting and local legal services.

If a company is not sure it wants to enter a market, it may hire a contractor for a time period to gather market research. This arrangement works well for many companies, but if this person will be working for the company more than three to six months, and/or is performing activities that can be construed as creating a permanent establishment for the organization, then the company should review the situation with its legal counsel. Each country has its own nuances on what creates a permanent establishment and what constitutes an employment situation. If it is determined that the person appears to be an employee in the eyes of the local government, the next step is to ascertain if a legal entity is required for operational and/or payroll purposes.

Expatriates

Q 13:2   Who are expatriates?

Expatriates are generally defined as individuals who are working away from their home country for typically a period of one to five years and will return to their home country once their assignment is completed. Expatriate assignments may be short-term, long-term, or rotators, and may be home-based, headquarters-based, or host-based. Expatriates are often eligible for certain benefits and incur additional deductions, including but not limited to: cost of living adjustments (COLA), housing allowances, transportation allowances, tuition reimbursement for children, hypothetical taxes, housing norms, transportation norms, tax preparation assistance, etc. These packages are typically structured to ensure that employees have the same standard of living in their new "host" location as they had in their home location. Depending on the combination of locations, these benefits/deductions vary. For example, an expatriate moving from the United States to Canada would have a lower COLA than an expatriate moving from the United States to Japan, since it is more expensive to live in Japan than Canada.

Q 13:3   How does an expatriate differ from a local hire?

Although an expatriate and a local hire are both employees of the same company, an expatriate is typically not a citizen of the country where he or she is working, the host country, while a local hire is usually a citizen of the country or has a permit to work locally where he or she is employed. The expatriate will hold a work visa and often will have additional benefits and deductions to his or her pay. These additional compensation items, often referred to as *above base compensation*, are utilized to equalize the employee to his or her home country, with the intent that he or she would have a similar lifestyle in the host location as enjoyed at home (similar housing, diet, schooling for children, tax burden, etc.). In many cases, an expatriate will have both home and host country tax liabilities while on an international assignment. An expatriate is also expected to return to his or her home country once the assignment has ended, which is typically no more than five years. If an expatriate extends his or her stay beyond five years, the host country, from a taxation perspective, may start considering the expatriate a local and therefore require him or her to pay into local social insurance programs, etc. If this employee is in a European country, for example, Belgium, this change in status can significantly increase the cost to the employer in Belgium. When the employee was an expatriate, the Belgium office did not have to pay the employer's portion of the social tax if a totalization agreement was in place with the home country. The switch to a local status will require the employer in

Belgium to pay the employer's portion of the social tax in Belgium and discontinue the employer's match of the social tax in the home country, which will most likely be at a lower rate (as it would, for example, in the United States).

It also will be important to look at treaties between the home and host locations to avoid double taxation.

Generally, the distinction between an expatriate and a local hire is clear, but there are cases where the distinction is blurred especially in Europe with the advent of the European Union (EU). In the EU, individuals can move freely among participating nations and accept employment as locals, receiving local pay and benefits. These employees are treated no differently than the local nationals in that country and are typically not considered expatriates.

The distinction between an expatriate and a local is important for purposes of benefits and taxation. See Q 13:52 below.

Q 13:4   Does a typical expatriate have a different compensation package than an employee working in his or her home country?

Yes, most long-term expatriates, who are abroad typically for more than a year and less than five years, are offered an assignment-related compensation package for their time worked abroad. This package often is based on the concept of tax equalization, which means that employees should pay no more in taxes at their host location than they would have paid if they stayed in their home country. Companies also apply this concept to living costs, so employees should have the same purchasing power to buy equivalent goods at the host location and not be out of pocket. These two concepts generate above base compensation elements, including cost of living allowance (COLA), housing allowance, transportation allowance, hypothetical taxes, hardship allowances, housing norms, etc. Not all expatriates will receive the same types or amounts of allowances, since above base compensation elements are often based on family size, expatriate policy type, and country combinations. Additionally, companies often pay for benefits in kind, which, basically, are company-paid expenses. See Q 13:5 for more information on benefits in kind.

Q 13:5   What are benefits in kind?

Benefits in kind for expatriates are payments made by the company on behalf of the employees, such as for their children's tuition, housing, host taxes, training, or property management. These benefits may have tax ramifications in the home and host countries. The value of the benefits needs to be added to earnings and are often grossed-up by the employer. See Q 13:10 for more details.

Q 13:6   Why would a company compute a hypothetical tax for an expatriate?

A hypothetical tax is computed when a tax equalization program is implemented. Typically, an expatriate will continue to receive his or her basic compensation package, including salary, bonus, and pension deductions and employer's pension match. From this core data, plus personal information such as the employee's size of family and work state (if the home country is the United States), the employee's hypothetical tax (often referred to as hypo tax) will be calculated. This amount is the tax the employee would have paid had he or she stayed home and not taken the expatriate assignment. The hypothetical tax is usually expressed as a percent of salary although in some cases, the hypo tax may appear as a flat number per pay cycle. There often is one percentage calculated for base salary and another for bonuses. A unique property of hypothetical tax is that, although it is withheld from the employee, it is NOT paid to the home government.

If the employee's home country is the United States, the employee should have waived withholding for federal taxes by completing a Form 673, Statement for Claiming Exemption From Withholding on Foreign Earned Income Eligible for the Exclusion(s) Provided by Section 911. As a long-term expatriate, the employee will be paying taxes in a foreign location and those tax credits will be utilized to offset the employee's U.S. tax liability. In many cases, this tax credit will completely offset any U.S. tax owed by the individual. If the employee is going to a lower tax jurisdiction, like Hong Kong, a calculation near the end of the year should be performed by the U.S. tax provider to determine if any actual tax should be paid to the U.S. government since there will not be enough offsetting credit. This calculation will help ensure the employee has paid in enough U.S. tax over the year with the goal of being penalty-proof.

Q 13:7   Is hypothetical tax withheld from an expatriate's pay?

Yes, the hypo tax is actually the employee's contribution to the taxes the employer is paying on the employee's behalf in the host location. So, for example, if the expatriate is working in Germany, the company is paying the employee's German tax liability and grossing it up in the host location. (In essence, this is a benefit in kind because the company is paying it on the employee's behalf, which requires the gross-up.) So, assume the hypo tax is $2,625 for a month. This is the amount the employee would have paid to the U.S. government had he stayed at home. The $2,625 will be withheld from the employee each pay cycle and used to offset the German host tax (often referred to as shadow payroll calculations) paid by the company, which has a higher tax rate and is grossed up. A typical month may see a German host tax converted to USD with a cost of $5,200, assuming no benefits in kind were processed. The company will expense the differential of $2,575 which will be booked to the expatriate's cost center and included in the company's cost of the assignment.

Q 13:8   What are allowances and norms?

Allowances and norms are additional payments and deductions provided to expatriates to give them purchasing power parity. The theory is that expatriates should be able to buy the same types and amounts of goods in the host country, as they were able to purchase at home. This parity is accomplished through different types of allowances, with the most typical being a cost of living allowance (COLA), which is calculated based upon the cost of a basket of goods in the home country versus buying that same basket of goods in the host country. (For example, it is less expensive to buy hamburgers in Cleveland, Ohio than in Tokyo, Japan.) COLA takes into account an employee's income, family size, and home and host location. Other common allowances include housing, transportation, and hardship. Housing allowances are paid in lieu of the company paying the rent on behalf of the employee in the host. The transportation allowance helps offset the increased cost of automobile ownership or commuting expenses in the host location. Hardship allowances are paid for employees who work in difficult locations as an added incentive to take the assignment. In very rare cases, a company will impose a negative COLA, resulting in a reduced income when an employee goes from a higher cost country to a lower cost country.

Companies need to ensure that they balance the costs of assignment by reducing the employees' compensation with what they would have paid if they were in the home country. For example, norms are deductions withheld from the employees' pay that are equivalent expense to maintain a house or car in the home country. Therefore, if the company is paying for a housing allowance equivalent to $5,000 in the host country, the company may reduce the employee's income by $2,000, which is the amount the employee would have paid in rent at home. The same concept applies for cars or transportation. In some cases, companies net the allowances and norms, so the employee basically gets a reduced allowance. So, in the above example, the expatriate will receive a housing allowance of $3,000. Or if the employee is still maintaining a house in the home country, the company may elect not to charge a housing norm. In other cases, companies as a policy, will not charge norms as an incentive for employees to take expatriate assignments.

Q 13:9   What are totalization agreements, and how do they affect expatriate home and host taxes?

Totalization agreements exempt expatriates from having to pay into the social insurance programs at the host location as long as they continue to pay into their home social programs. Countries must have treaties in place that allow for these exemptions. The United States has 25 totalization agreements in place today, with new ones continually being negotiated. The expatriate must complete a Certificate of Coverage (COC) at time of expatriation. Typically, tax providers or relocation companies will provide this service for the expatriate as part of their outbound briefings. The premise behind these agreements is that the expatriate will not benefit from government-sponsored pensions, long-term disability, unemployment programs, etc., since the expatriate is in the host location for less than five years. The European Economic Area has a similar program, which requires employees to have an A1 for working in participating countries.

In practice, if the expatriate has a COC or an A1 in place, the company will continue to withhold his home social insurance, but does not have to withhold social insurance in the host location. It is best to have tax advice regarding COCs and A1s, because not all social insurances are exempt, as many countries statutorily withhold benefits, including health care, that the expatriate may need when living in the host location.

Example: If an expatriate is from the U.S., is working in the UK, is on a tax equalization program, and has completed a COC:

- The expatriate would remain on U.S. payroll and the company would withhold Social Security, Medicare, and FUTA.

- The company would calculate PAYE (which is the UK wage tax) on a shadow payroll for the expatriate, but would exempt the employee from National Insurance (NI) in the UK.

For a list of totalization agreements, refer to https://www.irs.gov/individuals/international-taxpayers/totalization-agreements.

Q 13:10   Does the host country and/or the home country tax benefits in kind?

Payments for benefits in kind must be included in the tax calculation at the host country and also at the home country if the home country taxes worldwide income for social insurance purposes (e.g., United States, South Africa, and Switzerland). Benefits in kind are often included through off-cycle processing, as they need to be grossed up; otherwise, the employee will end up bearing the increased cost of these taxes.

Because the determination of taxability is different in each country and is also determined based on the expatriate program (short-term, long-term, commuters, local plus, etc.), best practice is to create a tax grid for each payroll of all compensation elements to ensure that the payroll team at the host and home (if applicable) knows how to tax each element. A basic excel sheet with multiple columns is sufficient if it details the taxability for each program (and by each tax) for each compensation element. Tax providers can help a company refine the matrix, which will ultimately support how they calculate the taxes in the tax return. If done properly, adhering to a tax matrix should also reduce costs of ensuring that all benefits were included in each payroll cycle, as it details what should be included and what is taxable. Additionally, a tax matrix will increase the accuracy of withholdings each pay cycle, thus reducing the probability of overpayment and underpayment of taxes at year end. In some countries, overpaid taxes are difficult to reclaim (in China, for example), while the underpayment of taxes can lead to a penalty in most countries. An example of how to create a tax matrix is provided below.

Compensation Element	Income Tax Taxable (Yes/No/Deductible)	Social Security Taxable (Yes/No/Deductible)
Salary	Yes	Yes
Salary Adjustment	Yes	Yes
Bonus	Yes	Yes
Annual Vacation Travel Allowance	Yes	Yes
Foreign Service Premium	Yes	Yes
Hypothetical Income Tax (Salary)	Deductible	Deductible
Hypothetical Income Tax (Bonus)	Deductible	Deductible
Transportation Norm	Deductible	Deductible
Co. Paid Utilities	Yes	Yes
Co Paid Housing	Yes	Yes
Life Insurance	No	No
Tax Preparation Fees	Yes	Yes
Company Car/Car Allowance	Yes	Yes
Relocation Allowance	Yes	Yes
Storage	No	No
Cross Cultural Training	No	No
Destination Assistance	Yes	Yes
Familiarization Trip Expense	Yes	Yes
Transfer of Household Goods Expenses	No	No
Misc. Relocation Expenses	Yes	Yes
Temporary Living Expenses	No	No
Tax Equalization	Yes	Yes
Life Insurance Co Paid	No	No
Additional Life Insurance (EE Paid)	No	No
Additional AD&D (EE Paid)	No	No

Note: This is an example for education purposes only. Each company has its own relocation policy and internal risk tolerance related to tax policy. Some companies are more aggressive and others more conservative on the interpretation of tax law in the host location.

Q 13:11   What would be included on a compensation worksheet for an expatriate?

Below is an example of an expatriate compensation worksheet for a U.S. employee who is working abroad for a couple of years. Please note that this is

NOT how the employee's pay stub would appear because the Medicare and Social Security calculations will differ. However, the salary, COLA, car allowance, hypo tax, 401k, and medical should be the same.

Compensation Package

Salary	$10,000.00
COLA	$2,800.00
Car Allowance	$500.00
Housing Norm	($1,500.00)
Hypo Tax (Fed & State)	($2,625.00)
Hypo Medicare	($145.00)
Hypo Social Security	($620.00)
401k	($750.00)
Medical	($250.00)
Net Pay:	**$7,410.00**

Q 13:12   Are there any special considerations for U.S. Medicare and Social Security taxes for expatriates?

Yes, if the company is using the concept of hypo tax for federal and state tax purposes, the company may elect to use a hypo tax calculation for Medicare and Social Security taxes. In the example in Q 13:11 above, the employee is bearing the Medicare and Social Security on his or her base salary, just as the employee would have if he or she stayed home (without any allowances, norms, or COLA as a local). This would be considered a hypo tax, the approximation of the real taxes on his or her home compensation. In reality, though, the U.S. government will require companies to increase Medicare and Social Security by the allowances and decrease the calculation by the hypo tax and norms. Therefore, companies handle this calculation in one of three ways:

1. Employee Bears the Additional Tax on Full Assignment Costs: In this case, the employer calculates the Medicare and Social Security on the salary plus the COLA, allowances, and benefits in kind, minus the hypo taxes and norms. The employee then pays the additional tax calculated on the allowances, assuming the allowances plus the benefits in kind are greater than the norms, thereby creating additional positive income. For example, COLA of $4,000 plus transportation allowance of $1,000 (plus hypo taxes of $3,000) would create income of $2,000. The employee would bear the cost of the FICA on the $2,000. In general, companies see this calculation method as unfair, because the employee is paying additional Medicare and Social Security taxes because he or she took the assignment at the request of his or her employer.

2. <u>Employee Bears the Additional Tax (But Not for Benefits in Kind)</u>: In this scenario, the employee will pay actual Social Security and Medicare taxes on his or her total base compensation package (salary plus allowances and COLA, minus hypo taxes and norms). Benefits in kind are run on off-cycles and grossed up and so do not affect the employee. At the end of the year, most expatriates will max out Social Security, and companies will true up the employee for the extra Medicare taxes he or she paid throughout the year.

3. <u>Employee Pays Hypo Tax and Employer Pays Actual Tax</u>: In this case, the employee will receive the net pay as illustrated in the example above. The employer then performs a separate calculation for actual Social Security and Medicare tax to pay to the U.S. government for both the base compensation package and benefits in kind.

Legal Requirements

Q 13:13   Can international payrolls be managed centrally or regionally versus locally?

Payrolls can be managed locally, regionally, or centrally depending on how the organization is structured. There are pros and cons to each approach, usually dependent on how many employees are working in each country, available system structures, internal resources, turnover, employment complexities, and available expertise. System structures for local payroll vary, with sophisticated systems like SAP and Oracle for large commoditized markets including the United States, Canada, UK, and France, specialized software like DATEV in Germany, and excel spreadsheet for small markets like Nigeria. It is important to understand local data security requirements and restrictions prior to determining the best methodology for managing international payroll (see Q 13:58). Language, culture, and time zones may also impact the decision of how to manage global payroll. If all employees are required to speak English, for example, it might be more feasible to have a central approach for small populations. But if the employee populations are in the Middle East, where the work week differs from that in the United States, or there are larger populations, as in Asia, a regional or local approach may be more appropriate.

Q 13:14   What are the options for managing international payrolls?

Companies have several options for managing their payrolls in each country, including supporting local in-house payroll systems and teams, outsourcing to local payroll providers in each country, outsourcing to a regional or global payroll provider, or outsourcing to a global Business Process Outsourcer (BPO). Generally, the option selected is based upon several factors: number of employees in the country, local and international system structures, control requirements by headquarters, internal resources, outsourcing experience, employment complexities, and payroll expertise.

The first factor is the number of employees in the country. If the location has a small population, generally fewer than 50 employees, the location typically does not have a local in-house payroll expert. These small offices are usually dedicated to marketing and sales, purchasing, customer support, engineering, or another function that has minimal administrative support. Along with limited expertise, the organization may not want someone local to be privy to everyone's salary and benefits information. With this size population, it is not unusual for companies to outsource to a local, regional, or global payroll provider (if there are other locations in other countries) and manage the payroll either regionally or centrally.

The second factor is internal system structure. Many larger organizations have internal Enterprise Resource Planning (ERP) systems (software), Human Capital Management (HCM) systems, or local payroll systems, which can be deployed for large local populations, usually for 1,500 or more employees in a given country. Typically, the cost benefit analysis indicates that a deployment of a system for local payroll calculations for fewer than 1,500 employees is not cost effective unless other long-term benefits, such as control or data integration, outweigh the implementation costs. Many of the ERP systems have payroll packages for the major labor markets where companies have large employee populations, such as Canada, the UK, and Germany. One downside to an ERP is that it may not cover more exotic locations like Angola, Cambodia, Dominican Republic, Kenya, Moldova, and Suriname; however, payroll functionality for new countries is added each year.

The third factor is control requirements by headquarters. For many companies, payroll is one of the most closely monitored functions to ensure local compliance, appropriate pay methodologies for base salary, benefits, bonuses, commissions, accuracy of tax calculations, and timeliness of payments to both employees and government organizations. When control requirements are analyzed in conjunction with the size of employee population, these organizations tend to outsource their payrolls to a provider, manage them centrally for smaller populations, or utilize an ERP, HCM system, or local payroll system to calculate payroll internally for larger local employee populations or those with complex requirements.

The fourth and fifth factors tend to be linked together. Many organizations do not have the internal resources that are knowledgeable about the different payroll requirements in each country. This is often the case when a company has a small number of employees in many countries or when a company has been recently divested and has not built up internal human resource and payroll resources yet. In both cases, the few internal human resource and/or payroll people in the organization usually outsource the local payrolls to a local or global provider and utilize their limited resources to manage those providers.

It is important to remember, that even if a payroll is outsourced, someone in the company has to still have enough payroll expertise to manage the vendor. Although country specific knowledge on each payroll is not required, it is very helpful to have someone with basic payroll knowledge to ensure the outsourcer(s) is/are managing the payrolls in an accurate, timely, and compliant manner.

Q 13:15   Is a legal entity necessary to pay employees in each country?

A legal entity is not required to run payroll in all countries. Once an organization determines that the workers are employees (rather than independent contractors), the first step in the legal process is to determine if the activities the employee will be performing constitute a permanent establishment of the organization in the location. If the answer is no, then the next step is to determine if a legal entity is required to run payroll. If the answer is no, often a local payroll ID can be established based upon the entity set-up in the headquartered country. Examples of countries that do not require an entity for payroll include France, Germany, Sweden, Netherlands, and the United Kingdom.

If a legal entity is required, employees cannot be paid via a company payroll until the entity establishment paperwork has been completed. Be aware, entity set-up can be a long and laborious process that can take from one month (at the earliest) to six months, depending on the country. Also, once the entity paperwork is received, it is often necessary to setup company payroll IDs with the local statutory agencies, which will take additional time. Companies need to plan appropriately to ensure they have enough time to setup an entity, payroll registration, and bank accounts if necessary, prior to hiring employees and running payroll.

Q 13:16   What type of registrations are needed for a new payroll set-up?

Each country has its own requirements for corporate registrations. Often these will include a local tax or payroll ID, social insurance registration, workers' compensation insurance, and pension. Some of the statutory registrations are handled though government agencies. Others are similar to workers' compensation in the United States where the programs are compulsory, but the organization can pick the agent providing the insurance or benefit. Also, varying degrees of the benefit may be selected, with a minimum being statutorily required and a higher level of benefits being the industry norm. This is often the case with medical, pensions, life insurance, and accident insurance. Benefit requirements may also depend on the size of payroll, where organizations with small employee populations will not be required to provide a pension program, meal tickets, etc.

Also note that many of the benefits that in the United States are paid for separately are actually included in the social contributions via payroll deductions and employer matches. A pension is typically part of the social scheme, so it is not tied to a company, but to an individual. Similarly, in Hong Kong and Singapore, the MPF (Mandatory Provident Fund) and CPF (Central Provident Fund) respectively follow the employee, although it is compulsory for companies to have the plan and contribute to it. In the UK, employees' pensions are portable so pensions can remain with employees when they change jobs.

Pensions in many countries are compulsory and are managed by the government, unlike the 401(k) benefits in the United States.

Q 13:17   If an organization does not have a legal entity and will not have one in the near future, are there any other options for payroll for an individual in another country?

If an organization does not have a local legal entity, but needs to have an employee work in the foreign location immediately, the organization can consider using a Professional Employer Organization (PEO). Generally, the PEO in a foreign location will "hire" the employee onto its own staff and charge the organization a percentage of the *total* employer's cost for payroll, benefits management, and other services. PEOs usually charge a percentage of an employer's cost, which typically includes salary, benefits, statutory employer matches, etc. These costs can run from 10 percent to 25 percent of the employer's cost and, in some cases, VAT (value added tax) may be charged on top of the fees. Although PEOs are very common in certain countries, such as the United States, India, Mexico, Canada, and many countries in Europe, in other countries, PEOs may face restrictions on their scope or may not be an option at all. Not all countries require local entities to process payroll. In some cases, such as in Germany, France, and the Netherlands, a company can register for payroll without an entity and simply tie the registration to the foreign office. This will allow the company to employ people locally without having to go the expensive route of utilizing a PEO. Of course, if the company wishes to have another company bear the local risk of employment, manage benefits, and process payroll, then a PEO may still be the better option.

Q 13:18   What is the cost of using a PEO?

The cost of a PEO typically ranges from 10 percent to 25 percent of the employer's cost. In some less mature markets, the fees can reach as high as 35 percent of employer's cost. When getting an estimate of the cost, it is important to understand what is included in the fee. For example, the fee may be a higher percent if the PEO will provide the employee with benefits. Also, because, in essence, these organizations are "leasing" the employee back to the organization, value added taxes (VATs) or local sales tax may apply. This may make the cost of a PEO quite prohibitive for a highly compensated individual.

Example. John Smith has a base salary of $10,000 per month. The cost of a PEO paying him would be figured as follows:

Base Salary	$10,000
Bonus	$ 2,000
Benefits	$ 1,000
Employer's Taxes	$ 2,000
Total Package	$15,000
PEO Fees (20%)	$ 3,000
VAT (10%)	**$ 1,800** (VAT is 10% of $15,000 + $3,000)
Total Monthly Cost	$19,800

When obtaining pricing from a PEO, it is important to have the PEO provide an example of costs to ensure there is an understanding of the total fee structure. The VAT does not apply in all situations, so it is important to determine its applicability when negotiating these contracts. As the PEO market becomes more mature, more global PEOs are now offering flat fees, similar to the type of fee arrangement in the United States, rather than charging a percentage of employer's cost. When negotiating with a PEO, ask if a flat fee is available as it is often a less expensive option. A PEO is a great option for companies with small populations that are not sure if they want a full entity set-up in the early days or need an employment vehicle while an entity is being established.

Q 13:19 **Is there any special new hire paperwork that needs to be reviewed prior to starting someone on payroll?**

Many countries treat new hires differently than the United States. Besides the employment contract, many new hires are required to submit copies of their tax ID cards, passports, health declaration forms, dependent forms, etc. This information is required for payroll tax calculation, registration with the local social insurance agencies, and for local payroll compliance documents. New employees in China, for example, would need to provide a copy of their Employment Record Booklet. In Italy, France, and Greece a copy of the employment contract is required. In New Zealand, the Kiwi Saver Plan document is required. In some countries, these "new hire" requirements may need to be updated on an annual basis.

Employment Contracts

Q 13:20 **Are employment contracts necessary for employees in foreign locations to run payroll?**

Although in the United States, Human Resources is more involved than Payroll with employment contracts, in other countries employment contracts are often mandatory for payroll purposes. The employment contract typically outlines local statutory requirements, collective agreements, full compensation, termination clauses, and benefits for the individual. Often these contracts are bilingual with the local language and the language of the organization's headquarters presented side by side. In many countries, these contracts need to be registered with the local social insurance agencies before the employee can start work. Similarly, when an employee leaves a company, this contract must be deregistered with the social agencies. If the social registration is handled by a payroll provider, hefty new hire and termination fees may be quoted because of the laborious and often manual requirements of these processes.

Q 13:21   Can an employee start anytime after an employment contract is signed?

Most countries require a long notice period for a person leaving his or her job, sometimes up to two months, depending on the country and the level of employee. Typically, higher-level employees have longer notice periods. Therefore, there may be several weeks to months before the new employee can start. Once the employee signs the employment contract, it is essential to have Payroll notified that a new employee will be joining the company. If the contract needs to be registered with the social security agencies, this process may take several days. An employee should not start work until these registrations are complete. Unlike U.S. requirements, the social programs in many countries cover medical and life insurance in addition to retirement benefits.

Note. If there is a gap in employment, the employee may not be covered by insurance during this period. This means the employee will not have the equivalent of health, life, or disability insurance, and pension. Many companies will "hire" an employee and pay him or her as a contractor until an entity is completed, bank accounts are set-up, etc. During this period, the employee is not paying into the social insurance schemas, which creates the gap. This may put the company at risk if the employee has an accident or health issue during this gap. Also, in some countries, the government will accept retroactive payments into an employee's social insurance accounts to eliminate the gap, but others will not

Q 13:22   Does a typical employment contract spell out the terms of payment?

Yes, the employment contract stipulates how the employee will be paid, and, frequently, which collective agreement will be utilized. For example, in Belgium an employee is paid 13.92 payments per year. In the employment contract, a company should stipulate that the employee will receive total compensation of 100,000 EUR paid out over 13.92 payments. If the company states the base compensation is 100,000 EUR, it is often inferred by the employees that they will receive 100,000/12 = 8,333.33 per month with two additional payments of (.92) = 7,666.66 for vacation payment in the summer and (1) = 8,333.33 in December for the Christmas payment. The total cash compensation would then be 116,000 EUR instead of the intended 100,000 EUR. The concept of stipulating the exact terms should extend to other payments and deductions as well, including COLA, transportation allowances, housing allowances, etc. It is also important to indicate if the company is bearing the tax by grossing-up the additional payments/benefits or if the employee is expected to bear the tax.

Q 13:23   What is a collective agreement and how does it affect payroll?

A collective agreement is similar to a union agreement in the United States although it is often defined at a national level. Therefore, the government designates what types of employees fall under which collective agreements that, in turn, determine minimum wages, benefits levels, taxability, pay cycles, and in some cases vacation entitlement. Although technically, collective agreements are between the employer and employees, the government sets the terms. National collective agreements are popular in European and Latin American countries and often cover most levels of employees in an organization. Collective agreements are regularly updated by local governments adjusting taxability, payroll timing, vacation days, etc. In 2012, Argentina went through a series of updates to the local collective agreements in the oil and gas industry that required local employers to retro calculate certain payments multiple times during the year. Therefore, it is important for a company to ensure it has the latest information on any collective agreements affecting the company for compliance purposes. From a payroll perspective, one of the more important aspects in the collective agreement is the determination of the pay cycle for the employee population with 12, 13, and 14 cycles being the most common. It is important for Human Resources to ensure that Payroll is aware when new employee types are added to the organization because they may be assigned to a different collective agreement, which, in turn, may affect the timing of their payroll and calculations of certain pay elements.

Time Reporting

Q 13:24   Is capturing time required?

Capturing time is required for some countries regardless of whether the employee is salaried or hourly. This will be dictated by local practice and organization requirements. In some countries, time is tracked to ensure that overtime does not exceed local statutory limits. Interestingly, time collection is often necessary for ancillary benefits, like vacation day calculation and meal tickets, versus actual payroll calculation to determine compensation. Meal tickets are discussed in more detail in Q 13:36.

Payment of Wages

Q 13:25   Which payroll cycles are the most common worldwide?

Payroll cycles tend to vary by country with the most common being 12, 13, 14, 24, 26, and 52 cycles per year. It is typical in Europe to pay monthly, with an extra cycle in the summer, usually June or July for vacation pay and in December for Christmas pay. Although this practice may seem strange to payroll professionals in the United States, what actually happens is that taxes are withheld at a higher rate for the 12 equal installments to cover the full compensation for the year. Then the two extra payments appear to be "tax free" to the individuals when they are paid. These extra payments result in a forced savings program to offset vacation and Christmas expenses. In some countries, these extra cycles are paid separately from normal payroll processing, and in others they are paid with the normal pay in those two months and often appear as bonuses.

In Asia and the Middle East, pay cycles are typically monthly. In Australia, New Zealand, Canada, the United States, and many Latin American countries, the pay cycle is more commonly 24 (semimonthly) or 26 (biweekly), with the exception of retail and some manufacturing companies, which are often weekly. Interestingly, in some Latin American countries, companies process payroll only once a month, and the first payment (around the 15th of the month) is an advance against the balance, which will be paid at the end of the month when the payroll is finalized. Often the advance is not actually calculated for taxes (similar to a regular payroll cycle), but rather is just a portion of expected net pay to be delivered mid-month. For example, if an employee is paid 10,000 Brazilian Reais per month, he or she would receive 4,000 Reais on the 15th of the month as an advance. On the last day of the month the remainder would be paid (6,000 Reais) minus the taxes on the full 10,000 Reais and all other deductions.

In some countries, pay dates and pay cycles are dictated by local law. In Israel, for example, an employer is required to pay its employees between the 1st and 7th of each month. In the Philippines, an employer must pay its employees within 10 days after the work is performed. Therefore, in the Philippines a monthly payroll would not be acceptable. When determining the pay cycle and pay dates for a country, it is important to ensure the local entity is in compliance with local law.

Q 13:26 What are the most popular pay dates for monthly payroll?

Pay dates most commonly occur on the 15th, 25th, 27th, or last working day of the month. These pay dates cover the current month, therefore, for the working time of March 1st through March 31st, the pay date would be March 25th. Normally, when payroll is set for a few days before the end of the month, the company is not concerned about paying for time not worked, usually because employees are required to give long leave notices and vacation accruals are very high. An advantage of a pay date a few days before the last day of the month is the extra time it allows Accounting to close the books for that month.

Q 13:27 Are off-cycle payments common internationally?

Off-cycle payments, do occur internationally but are much rarer than in the United States for organized and efficient payroll departments. Generally, these "off-cycle" payments are, in fact, regularly scheduled events for expected bonuses. There are several countries where off-cycle payments are exceptionally difficult to manage, including France and Italy, where payrolls are only run once a month because the tax calculations are so complex. Typically, if an off-cycle payment is critical enough to be required, an estimated advance is given and then reconciled through the next pay run in those countries. A typical example of an off-cycle in Europe would be a payment of a stock option exercise. In this case, the gross amount minus estimated tax rate will be paid to the employee as an "advance." Then the gross amount will be processed through the next payroll cycle, and the advance will be subtracted from the net. Generally, companies utilize a high estimate for the taxes in the stock option exercise calculation to avoid underwithholding on the advance payment. Basi-cally, the employee will receive a little extra net pay in the month that the stock option was processed through payroll.

Another common reason to pay off-cycle in Europe and Latin America is for terminations. Many countries have requirements to pay terminated employees all compensation due within a very short time frame, often 48 hours after termination. This requires HR to be heavily involved in the termination process, as often a labor lawyer will need to review the employment contract to accurately determine the final calculations. Payroll also needs to be involved to ensure the final net pay is delivered into the terminated employee's bank account within the time frame specified, which means an off-cycle payment may be required. Note that most countries do not use "checks" for final payments after a termination. Practically all of the termination paperwork needs to be performed before the employee is notified of his or her change in status. If several people are being terminated, it is best to do these terminations in one batch to alleviate off-cycle costs.

Off-cycles processing is a key indicator of how well a payroll department is functioning. If the company is processing lots of off-cycles that are not statuto-rily required, then, typically, there are processes in place that are not capturing payroll information in an accurate and timely manner. This might be the outcome of inadequate HR infrastructure, which could be a result of poor systems, policies, processes, inexperience, or a combination of the aforementioned. Or similar issues may plague the payroll department itself. It is important to review the reasons behind off-cycles, as they are often inefficient, costly, and time-intensive for payroll professionals to execute.

Q 13:28   Is the typical workweek Monday through Friday?

Each organization may have its own unique working pattern for its employees. For example, some retailers have MTWTF and SS patterns to accommodate their sales personnel, although most corporations have a Monday through Friday workweek. On an international level, some countries have different working patterns. In the Middle East and South East Asia, where a large percentage of the population is Muslim, the standard workweek is Sunday through Thursday. Other locations, like Algeria, work Saturday through Wednesday, with Thursday and Friday being the "weekend." This includes local business, banks, etc., so if the payroll is being managed at one of these locations, payroll calendars must be modified to ensure that payroll is delivered on time, taking into account what days are considered weekends not only for the company, but also for the banks processing net pays.

Q 13:29   Is the payment of overtime mandatory?

Similar to the United States, employers must pay overtime to certain types of employees. The overtime rate of pay may also be determined by the type of work performed and when it is performed. Some countries have very complex rules on how overtime pay is calculated, including overtime rates that increase based on the number of hours worked in a given time period.

Example: If an employee works 10 hours of overtime during a two-week period, he may only be paid time and a half on the 10 hours. But if he works an additional 2 hours for a total of 12 hours, the whole 12 hours of his overtime will be calculated at 2 times his base rate instead of 10 at 1.5 and 2 at 2.0. Another complication arises in countries where there is a limit as to how much overtime an employee can work during a given time period. In such countries, companies must track each employee's total overtime to ensure they do not exceed the local limit on overtime hours.

In many countries, there are very strict rules about when overtime must be paid, often precluding a company from processing a monthly payroll. For example, if overtime has to be paid within the month it was earned, the payroll processing time is too tight to allow a monthly payroll. In these cases, companies will opt for 24 or 26 pay periods per year.

Q 13:30   Are employees typically paid in cash, check, or bank transfer?

A few manufacturers in remote locations or organizations working in war zones may pay in cash; however, the majority of worldwide locations pay employees via bank transfer, a fact that frequently surprises United States and Canadian payroll professionals who are still producing paper checks. The concept of a "check" is quite uncommon in many countries, as the local populations are more familiar with the debit card process for paying bills. Electronic wage payments ease delivery, as there is no need to manage stale, lost, or stolen checks. Therefore, it is imperative to obtain accurate banking details from employees, especially at time of hire.

Q 13:31   How much time should be allotted in a payroll schedule to move money to the payroll provider, employees, and local governments?

Moving funds internationally is not an overnight process. Depending on the country, funds can take two to ten business days to arrive. To add to the complication of funds transfers, each country has its own set of holidays and potential work schedules. In the Middle East, most banks are open during the standard workweek of Sunday to Thursday versus Monday through Friday. In China, the banks and businesses can close for up to two weeks for Chinese New Year. Another complication is that banks are constantly merging. With a merger, often the Society for Worldwide Interbank Financial Telecommunication (SWIFT) and routing codes change, without notification to the sender. A SWIFT or Bank Identifier Code (BIC) is an 8- or 11-digit code that is a unique identifier for a financial institution. (SWIFT codes can be validated at www.swift.com.) SWIFT codes are often required to transfer funds between two international banks. Therefore, repetitive wires that have been working for years may suddenly stop functioning. The sending bank will receive a rejection from the receiving bank. The employees may need to contact their bank for new banking details.

Certain countries take longer to receive funds as the money may need to move through an intermediary bank such as Citibank or Standard Chartered Bank. This adds time and complexity, but may be necessary depending on the recipient country. Korea and Taiwan have some of the longest lead times while European countries tend to have the shortest. The sophistication of the sending and receiving bank also affects the timeliness of payments. The more sophisticated the bank, the more likely the funds will be received in a timely manner. Additionally, some countries have currency restrictions and you may only be able to send USD, which will be converted by the banks locally. This is common in several Latin American, African, and Asian countries. This situation can also cause crediting delays locally. Companies need to be careful not to overfund a payroll, because many countries, like Argentina and China have restrictions on moving money out of the country. In some countries, inter-country payments may be settled overnight, or processed within 48 hours through an ACH-like process. In other countries, an inter-country transfer can take three to five business days. For example, in the U.K., funds need to be released on a Wednesday to meet a Friday pay date. In Japan, five business days are needed to transfer funds from one Japanese bank account to another. Generally, there is a faster option in each country, which is a wire transfer. By using a wire transfer, the money can typically be sent within the same country the same day or by the next day, but there is a very high cost to these transactions. Wires can cost the equivalent of $15 to $40 U.S. dollars versus an in-country transfer (ACH, BACs, etc.), which costs the equivalent of just a few cents. Also note that other countries have banking institutions that are the equivalent to credit unions in the United States. If a company is transferring net pay to employees who have accounts at credit unions, building societies, etc., those payments may take an extra day to clear.

In Europe, the Single Euro Payments Area (SEPA) was rolled out to 35 countries. Additional countries and territories are being added to the overall SEPA program, widening the network of participating organizations. The goal of SEPA is to allow companies and individuals to make electronic payments across the Euro area as easily as domestic payments are handled inter-country, utilizing a single bank account and a single set of banking instructions. All SEPA transactions have to be routed using only the International Bank Account Number (IBAN) and will no longer need the Society for Worldwide Interbank Financial Telecommunication (SWIFT) or Business Identifier Codes (BIC) codes for identification of the recipient's account.

Another difference in international banking is some countries do not allow "direct debit" by a payroll provider from a client account. It is very common in the United States for a payroll provider to debit the funds from the client's account for payroll distribution to employees and governments. In other countries, this is not common and, in some countries, it is illegal. In those cases, the client either needs to send the funds directly to the payroll provider or set up a zero-based payroll account, which the payroll provider has access to in order to distribute payroll funds each cycle.

Office of Foreign Assets Control (OFAC) screening may also cause delays in the funding process, especially to Middle Eastern and Asian locations. OFAC is covered in more detail in Q 13:57.

Q 13:32   How are pay slips delivered in other countries?

Pay slips are generally delivered either online, via physical mail, or at the work location. Many countries have poor local mail systems; therefore, most companies with paper pay slips opt to distribute them at work. Each country has a set of requirements for the format of pay slips and the information required to appear on the document.

In France, for example, local pay slips can be more than two pages long because they detail all the social insurance payments. These pay slips are considered a legal document. One of the items that appear on this pay slip is vacation accrued. When the employee leaves the company, that accrued vacation is due to the employee. If a company does not keep its time records up to date correctly and does not have them synchronized with the payroll system, the accrued vacation numbers will not be accurate and may be too high. This leads to a situation where the employee can demand a payout based upon the accrual number on his or her pay slip versus what was actually owed to the employee.

Some countries have unique processes around the pay slips, including Mexico, where employees need to sign their pay slip each cycle. Others cannot be delivered online, although more countries are going to an online format as the local mail systems are unreliable. Even for countries requiring the "official" pay slips to be paper, companies are providing base data online for reference only. Now many Human Capital Management (HCM) systems will take an interface directly from the payroll provider and provide pay slip detail in the employee portal for employees to view, creating a closed loop from payroll changes to payroll results. It is very important to understand pay slip regulations in each country to ensure the organization is in compliance.

Q 13:33   How is change data passed to payroll internationally?

Payroll change data is typically passed to local payroll in a country or to providers via an interface from an HCM system, upload of an Excel spreadsheet, or manual entry directly into the payroll system. Larger companies, which have international HCM systems containing accurate data, will utilize this system to pass information to local payroll systems and/or vendors. The initial interface build can be laborious as each country has a unique set of requirements to process payroll. Once the interface is in place, it is very important for the data in the HCM system to be accurate and updated to maintain a compliant payroll. With the advent of SAS HCM providers, standard interfaces to payroll providers are being created that do not need to be customized. This will save companies the expense of building a unique interface and the time and energy of maintaining that interface, as updates are the responsibility of the payroll provider. Although interface certifications reduce cost by providing the base configuration, companies will still need to expend resources to set up and test these interfaces on a country-by-country basis. Data needs to be synced, files need to be timed, and HR processes need to be in place for an integration to work properly.

If the changes are passed via a spreadsheet internally or manually keyed into a payroll provider's system, it is important to protect the data for data privacy purposes. Most companies consider all data related to payroll as confidential, therefore falling under the highest category of data protection. There are a variety of ways to handle the protection via encryption, internal email protocol, document management systems, payroll management systems with encrypted transfer methodologies, and/or a combination of the above. Note that some payroll requirements will still need to be provided manually, including copies of passports, employment contracts, etc. which should be loaded up to a secure site for transfer.

Q 13:34 Are there cases where countries will automatically increase local pay?

Although this is a rare practice, there are some countries that will automatically increase all employees' base salary by a fixed percentage each year. This percentage is determined by the government and processed via payroll around the same time each year. Belgium is known for including these annual increases automatically as part of the payroll run in the designated month. Conversely, Belgium will decrease salaries if negative indexation occurs (i.e., no inflation for the prior year) and companies have the choice to reduce salaries. This situation occurred as recently as 2010. The issue here is to ensure the organization's HCM system is in sync with the payroll system; otherwise, the payroll system will have a slightly higher or lower salary than the HCM system. Many organizations incorporate the mandatory increase into their salary planning process to ensure equity in the salary increase process across all their countries.

Benefits

Q 13:35 How do employers' costs differ in other countries?

Most countries have social programs that are matched by the employer, similar to Medicare and Social Security in the United States. Many also have social programs that are 100 percent funded by the employer, similar to FUTA. Unlike in the United States (except in 2011 and 2012), the employers' portion often is not equal to the employees' share. Mostly, the employer's share is higher, but it can be lower than the portion the employee pays. Also, the range of social programs in other countries is typically much greater than in the United States. These social programs may include government-sponsored pension, housing, maternity benefits, paternity benefits, life insurance, accident insurance, employment insurance, medical benefits, short-term disability, long-term disability, and training programs.

It is very important for an HR professional to understand the local statutory social programs before determining if additional benefit programs are necessary. In many European countries, much of the medical, life, accident, and other insurances are covered by statutory social programs, so additional benefits are not necessary. In these countries, the social program costs can exceed 35 percent of the employee's base pay. Although this may seem very high when compared to the FICA match of 7.65 percent an employer pays in the United States, companies in other countries do not have to pay for medical insurance, life insurance, pension, etc., which can easily add up to the differential of 27.35 percent or more.

In some countries, these social programs are a set percentage or flat amount for each employee on the payroll. In other countries, the employer can pick and choose the type of pension, medical, and other insurance programs, etc., it wishes to provide to its employees. These programs are still statutory and have lower limits, but companies can opt to provide richer benefits to its employees. In some countries, it is required for the employer to set up the program and not merely enroll in a government-sponsored program. Therefore, it is still mandatory to have the program, which must meet certain limits, but the onus is on the company to set up the plan. A good example is the Mandatory Provident Fund (MPF) in Hong Kong. It is the company's responsibility to ensure the MPF is set up and funded for every payroll processed, although the employer can pick the program and the company to manage the MPF.

Q 13:36   What are meal tickets and how are they managed?

In many European countries, the practice of providing meal tickets to employees is quite common. A meal ticket is a voucher, generally free of tax, for a specified amount depending on the country and program, that employees can use to purchase lunch for days they are at work. For example, typical meal tickets are worth 5 to 7 EUR a day, with the employer paying usually 50 to 100 percent of the ticket and the employee pays the remaining portion through a payroll deduction. Employees are only eligible for meal tickets for days worked; no meal tickets are provided for days off for vacation, sickness, holiday, etc. Attendance data needs to be provided to Payroll for calculation of the meal ticket deduction each pay cycle based on days worked. A third-party meal ticket vendor is usually hired to manage the actual tickets themselves. This vendor provides the meal tickets to the company for distribution to the employees.

Q 13:37   What other benefits affect payroll?

Common payroll payments and deductions in Asia include housing allowances and meal allowances, which although they do not change the total compensation package, will reduce the taxable income to the employee (similar to a 401(k) program in the United States). Each country sets differing limits on the amount that can be excluded from taxable wages, but housing and meal allowances are both quite common in Asia. Other common payment types in Asia are birthday, child birth, marriage, seasonal, and condolence bonuses. In Europe, cell phones and car usage are closely monitored. If an employee utilizes a cell phone or car for personal use, the value of this personal usage must be returned to the company or treated as taxable compensation. The return of the value of the personal use is usually facilitated through a deduction or negative payment via payroll. The payment or deduction for personal/company usage is usually based upon an approved expense report.

Q 13:38   How are stock options and equity payments handled worldwide?

Equity plans are very popular at U.S.-based companies and many try to deploy their equity plans across all countries. Each country has a unique way of handling equity plans that may affect payroll and how these plans are paid out. Once the plan is created for each country, payroll should be involved to determine what taxes need to be withheld and how the payments will flow through payroll. Many companies use a third party to calculate equity disbursements. These third parties will sometime just handle the calculations and other times they will handle the calculations and make the payments. Often these payments are in U.S. dollars (USD) which complicates the transactions. When the third party is just handling the calculations, payroll will need to be sure the payment is tagged as a stock option exercise to ensure proper taxability and pay the option with the next payroll run. The proper designation as a stock option exercise is especially important in countries where social taxes are not withheld from stock option exercise payments. France is a country where, depending on the stock plan, no social taxes are withheld from a stock option payment. The amount is merely recorded as income for year-end purposes.

When a third party is calculating and paying the employee, the third party generally withholds a percentage to cover taxes. Since this can be very tricky internationally, it is suggested that the third party use a higher withholding percentage to ensure that when the payment is passed through payroll for the "true-up" of taxes, the employee has paid enough withholding tax and does not inadvertently end up with a negative paycheck and owing money to the company.

Another situation to watch out for is when the stock option disbursement calculation is done in USD and then the employees are paid in USD. Payroll needs to convert this amount into local currency prior to submission to the payroll provider/system to ensure the right amount is used for tax calculation.

Lastly, in some countries there is a requirement to pass through the increased value of a stock option for tax purposes, even if it has not been exercised. Depending on the country, this amount needs to be passed through on a periodic basis so Payroll can include it in employees' income for tax withholding purposes. Of particular interest are Restricted Stock Options and/or Restricted Stock Units (RSUs). It is important to inform Payroll when stock or units are sold to cover the incremental taxes because this information needs to be included in the employee's compensation.

Time Off

Q 13:39   How are vacation days managed internationally?

The first difference an organization will notice is that other countries typically grant more vacation days to their employees overall and at time of hire. In Europe, 20 to 25 days of vacation at hire date is not uncommon. Also, employees tend to take their vacation time in larger blocks or all at once. Two- to four-week vacations, especially in the summer months, are not unusual. This actually can cause operational issues for an organization during the months of July and August. In some countries, the payroll providers will shut down in August and just run an "estimated" payroll. In Canada it is mandatory for employees to take two weeks' worth of vacation, or the company must pay the employee for days not used. Accruals for vacation balances in Canada are often part of the payroll register. Note that the concept of Paid Time Off (PTO) which is a combination of sick days, vacation and personal time is not common in other countries.

From a payroll perspective, vacation days have some special properties. In some countries, employees are paid a higher rate for the days they take vacation. Additionally, some companies pay 13.92, 14, or 15 cycles, which means that one of those "extra" cycles is paid in the summer to cover holiday expenses. This practice can be seen in some collective agreements in Europe. Note that the cost for meal tickets is not deducted for days an employee is on vacation. Additionally, vacation time is a statutory reporting requirement on some countries' pay slips.

Q 13:40   How are holidays managed internationally?

Similar to vacation days, it is typical for other countries to have more standard holidays than the United States. In some cases, these holidays can span several weeks like Ramadan and Chinese New Year. Other holidays are similar to Memorial Day and only extend over a three-day weekend. It is also common for holidays to appear in the middle of the week, instead of having an "observance day" like Presidents' Day in the United States, where the actual day may fall on a Thursday, but it is always observed on a Monday. Many of the holidays are based on religious calendars and these dates can fluctuate from year to year. In some countries, a reigning figure, such as a king or queen, may also declare holidays as significant events occur. This is true in the United Arab Emirates, where the king may have an extra holiday or two added each year or in the UK when holidays are declared to commemorate weddings or other major royal events. In other countries, holidays are based on whether a natural occurrence appears, such as the full moon being visible.

The biggest concern about holidays is ensuring the payroll is delivered on time and the banks are open to distribute and receive the funds. Banks are generally closed on every major country holiday and often for minor holidays as well. This would be the equivalent to the U.S. holidays of Martin Luther King, Jr.'s Birthday or Presidents' Day when many organizations are still open for business, but the banks are closed. In some countries, like the UK, banks also have "bank holidays" which may not be tied to any specific country holiday, but the bank will be closed, usually for a three-day weekend. The bank closure dates normally will be published the year prior to their occurrence so these dates can be incorporated into the payroll calendar. It is very important when setting a payroll calendar for each country or region to take holidays into account, especially when the holiday lasts for several days.

Q 13:41   What type of employee leaves are common internationally?

Employee leave types range from the typical: maternity, paternity, short-term disability, long-term disability, bereavement, medical, jury, and personal to the unique; volunteer, menstrual, child rearing, and nursing. Each country has its own set of "common" leave types, which can be very different than the standard leave types in the United States. The leave types may be valued differently as full pay, partial pay, or no pay. Many companies will offer additional leave options above statutory levels to match local labor market conditions.

Q 13:42   How is maternity leave handled in other countries?

Maternity pay and leave is handled in a variety of ways. In some countries, it is similar to the United States in that there is an unpaid maternity leave for a maximum number of weeks. Certain countries will pay the employee on maternity leave from social funds for the weeks that the employee is off from work. This is handled in one of two ways. Either the government pays the employee directly or it issues a social insurance credit to the employer that offsets the wages paid to the employee. In some countries, companies will provide a benefit of fully paid maternity leave for a given number of weeks if it is common practice in that marketplace.

Q 13:43   Do other countries provide paternity leave?

Paternity leave is also handled in a variety of ways. In some countries, there is no provision at all; the employee simply takes vacation time. While in other countries, it is a leave/benefit option for the employee. Paternity leave is typically shorter than maternity leave. Fewer countries offer time off for paternity leave, although the company may have its own plan to pay the employee for these days out of the office.

Taxes

Q 13:44   Do all countries have a tax system?

There are some countries that do not tax employee wages. These are generally in the Middle East, including the United Arab Emirates (UAE) and Qatar (although in Qatar there is an employer social security tax, but no employee social tax deduction). Employees in these countries tend to have compensation plans that are relatively straightforward with some basic sever-ance type programs, but minimal to zero social programs. Increasingly, Middle East countries are adding social programs, which will require withholding from payroll. Some Middle Eastern Countries have created a social insurance zone, where employees from one Middle Eastern country working in another Middle Eastern country pay social taxes of their home country. So if an Oman national were working in the UAE, Oman social taxes would be withheld from his pay and paid over to the Oman authorities. Although wage tax still is not common in any of these countries, new regulations regarding funding to employees have been instituted to ensure that workers are paid properly and on time. The UAE was the first country to formalize this practice, through its Wage Protection System (WPS), which commenced in late 2009. Saudi Arabia started a WPS in 2013, and Qatar followed in 2015. In Qatar, employers are required to pay employees in Qatar Riyal (QAR) and into local Qatari bank accounts.

Q 13:45   Does the taxability of compensation differ from country to country?

Taxability does vary from country to country on payments and deductions. For example, the amount of taxable compensation may be reduced by deduc-tions for meal tickets, meal allowances, housing allowances, and pension funds.

It is very important to understand each payment and how it is taxed locally to ensure that the correct information is given to the local payroll team. For example, in many countries, a commission may be taxed differently than a bonus based on employment contracts or collective agreements. Therefore, these payments need to be differentiated for the payroll team to tax appropriately. Also, in some countries, certain benefits are not taxable such as a rent paid by the company directly in China, although rent paid by the company directly is taxable in the UK. It is not uncommon for a company to hire a local (labor) attorney or a tax accountant to review its payroll elements to determine the taxability and timing of each payment. Both social and wage taxes need to be scrutinized for each payment. In some cases, a payment may be taxable at the federal level, but not for social insurance taxes.

Payments are not the only elements that need to be reviewed, as benefits are often taxable depending on the type and limit. Similar to the United States, many countries have a limit on what level of benefits are considered nontaxable (e.g., life insurance) versus taxable. Some of these fringe benefits will appear in the payroll each cycle and others will be reviewed annually by the company as a separate procedure, which is the common practice in the UK and Australia.

There can be severe corporate penalties if a company does not report these benefits properly for tax purposes.

Q 13:46   Do all countries withhold taxes?

Some countries withhold tax very similarly to the United States. There are wage taxes, which are equivalent to the U.S. federal taxes, and social tax components. Other countries only withhold for social tax and the employees are responsible for paying their own wage taxes when they file their personal tax returns. Sometimes withholding is based upon citizenship/work permit status. In some countries, employers are required only to withhold wage taxes on expatriates or others who are not local residents. This ensures the government will receive all the wage taxes due before the person leaves the country. France, Singapore, and Hong Kong do not withhold federal wage taxes on local employees, but do withhold funds for other programs like pension and social taxes. This is not to be confused with the Middle East, where some countries, like the UAE, do not tax employee wages at all. Employees in France, Singapore, and Hong Kong pay their own federal taxes to the government on a periodic basis versus through a deduction from payroll.

Q 13:47   Do other countries have regional taxes similar to state taxation in the United States?

Unlike the United States, very few countries have the concept of "state/ province/canton" taxes and filings. If there is a "state-like" component to the taxing structure, it is usually paid and filed as a part of the federal wage taxes. A few exceptions are Canada and Japan. The United States continues to be one of the most complex payroll countries in the world due to the state and local components of the U.S. payroll withholding and taxing structure.

Q 13:48   How do other countries calculate the amount of tax due for employees?

In the United States, tax calculations are based on very few factors, mainly state, filing status, and number of exemptions. In other countries, a variety of other personal details are needed to ensure payroll calculations and local compliance paperwork is processed correctly. Some of these include children's ages, citizenship, work permit status, union, collective agreement, age, nationality, and profession. Often additional paperwork is necessary to establish the correct withholding for benefits and for compliance with governmental requirements. Some of these include copies of work permits, wage tax cards, passports, national IDs, marriage certificates, birth certificates, and transportation tickets.

Q 13:49 When are withholding taxes paid to local governments?

Determining when withholding taxes are to be paid is typically not as complex as in the United States. Unlike the United States, where the frequency of tax withholding is based upon the size of payroll, many countries have a consistent date, usually in the month following the pay date. Most taxes are typically due on a designated day between the 10th to the 15th of the following month. In others, taxes are paid at the end of the month or even quarterly.

Social taxes are another process altogether. In Europe, there are countries which require social taxes to be paid in advance and then these taxes are reconciled every quarter. Belgium has followed this procedure for years and creates estimated social tax payments for each month and then reconciles them each quarter. Germany also switched to paying social insurance in advance. In France, some social taxes are paid monthly, while others are paid quarterly. In Asia, some social programs are deducted from the employee each pay cycle, but paid annually. Therefore, it is important to understand when all the different types of taxes are collected and paid.

Q 13:50 What are the typical types of tax filings an organization should expect at an international location?

Similar to the United States, most countries have filing requirements for both federal and social taxes. If a regional tax, similar to "state," is calculated, it is typically filed alongside the federal paperwork, although "state taxes" are relatively uncommon in other countries. Most filings have a monthly and annual component. Some require returns for individuals, similar to the W-2 process in the United States.

Q 13:51 For tax purposes, does it raise a red flag to have employees and contractors work in the same country?

If an organization has employees and contractors, it must be sure it understands local law regarding withholding. In the United States, companies issue Forms 1099 to contractors who are paid more than $600. In other countries, it may be mandatory to withhold taxes on all payments made to contractors and on professional payments. For example, in Spain, a local Spanish legal entity would be required to withhold taxes on the fees paid to outside legal counsel and pay these taxes to the government on the entity's behalf. This is common in many countries in Europe, Africa, and Asia. Often, these withholding amounts are a flat percentage of the bill, often 5 to 35 percent of the total invoice. Note that these withholding rates can change rapidly and may be dependent on the type of entity that is set up in the country.

Q 13:52   What complexities do long-term expatriate taxes present to payroll?

Expatriates who are on assignment for more than six months typically have a requirement to pay taxes in the host country. The amount that is taxable in the host country depends on the host country, the type of compensation, and when the compensation is earned. Typically, all payments made directly to the employee are considered taxable income regardless of where the funds are actually distributed. It is important that the host payroll is provided with the expatriate's full compensation package including any additional expatriate benefits paid on his or her behalf such as the cost of living adjustments, allowances, rent, children's tuition, and car leases. These expenses are often referred to as benefits in kind (see Q 13:5).

Most companies utilize a tax provider, usually from an international accounting firm, to help determine the most tax efficient package for the employee and company. This may include paying rent on behalf of the employee as some countries will consider this benefit tax free since the employee is only on assignment in the host country for a finite amount of time. Tax providers often are utilized to compile the personal tax returns for the expatriate in the home and host country as applicable. This process will help determine if all the compensation elements were taxed properly and improve the process with the payroll providers for the following year. Companies typically pay for the employee's tax return preparation in both the home and host locations. This ensures that the company's policies are being followed and that the funds are collected from the employee, if applicable, after the tax equalization calculation is finalized.

Complexities for U.S. expatriates. Expatriates with U.S. citizenship are required to file a U.S. tax return since taxes are imposed by the United States on worldwide income, regardless of how long a U.S. citizen works outside the United States. This concept is very different from the rest of the world. Very few countries other than the United States, Switzerland, and South Africa tax worldwide income that is earned outside the home country. If expatriates do not have foreign tax credits to offset their U.S. tax liability, they may owe taxes in the United States. Best practice is for the tax provider to perform a calculation late in the year to determine if any U.S. tax is due. Then a catch-up payment can be made in November or December so it is in the correct tax year and the employee is penalty-proof. Also, if U.S. outbound expatriates are on a tax equalization approach, their entire compensation plus expatriate benefits should be provided to the U.S. payroll to calculate their Social Security and Medicare taxes.

Complexities for expatriates on a host compensation package: The situation becomes difficult when an "expatriate" is placed on a host compensation package. All ties to the home payroll are severed and the employee is treated like a local in the host location. The employee may receive some additional benefits through payroll, but generally there is little difference between this individual and other locals. In this case, is the employee still an expatriate? From a payroll perspective, the employee is considered a local for most or all calculations. In some countries, a company may be required to withhold wage taxes from a foreigner depending on his or her work permit. This ensures the country receives all the appropriate wage taxes if the foreigner/expatriate decides to leave the country. In this case, the expatriate would be treated differently from a local on the host payroll at least in regards to the federal tax withholding calculation. Additionally, some companies will provide tax return preparation services and other miscellaneous benefits to these individuals.

From a corporate perspective, employees may still be considered expatriates when they carry work permits that will expire at some future date and may be a part of the corporate rotation/training program. If they are outbound U.S. citizens, they will need to file U.S. tax returns, even if they have no income in the United States since the United States imposes tax on worldwide income. Companies may give U.S. expatriates some assistance with their U.S. tax return, even if they are on a host compensation package.

Q 13:53   Do organizations have any obligation to help local employees with their personal tax returns?

In some countries, employees at a certain level are not required to submit a tax return. Any adjustments to taxes are handled through payroll by the employer. For example, in Japan, at the end of the year, employees are required to submit additional data to determine if a refund is due to the employee. That refund is then passed through payroll as a refund to taxes owed. In Korea, this adjustment is processed as a part of payroll in January of the following year. In many countries, all taxes are submitted via payroll and no personal adjustments (i.e., tax returns) are required.

Q 13:54   What is an "offshore" payroll and when do companies use this mechanism?

Offshore payrolls are typically created by companies with employees who rotate between multiple tax jurisdictions but are never physically in a location long enough to incur a tax liability. These employees are generally hired by an offshore legal entity or Global Employment Company (GEC), usually based in Bermuda, Singapore, Cyprus, or some other tax-friendly country. Non-U.S. employees who have no residence and spend more than 183 days out of their home country and less than 183 days in any particular tax jurisdiction, in essence, have no tax liability. This is common in the oil and gas industry where employees move from oil rig to oil rig every few weeks.

Employees who are U.S. citizens will be taxed in the United States even if they do not reside in the United States and are outside the United States for more than 183 days, as the U.S. government imposes income taxes on worldwide income of U.S. citizens and residents. If U.S. employees do not incur taxes at any foreign jurisdictions, they will have no offsetting tax credits and their full income will be taxable in the United States (minus the normal deductions allowed to them). If employees with U.S. citizenship or resident alien status are hired by a non-U.S. company, the employees will be responsible for paying their own taxes to the U.S. government. This situation is unique to a few countries in the world as most do not tax on worldwide income for their nationals who are living abroad. The most notable exceptions to this policy are the United States, South Africa, and Switzerland. Note that if a foreign subsidiary of a U.S. company hires a U.S. citizen, the company needs to calculate and withhold Medicare and Social Security for that U.S. citizen on the foreign payroll. This requirement was instituted for organizations that were purposely creating offshore entities to hire U.S. employees to evade paying U.S. employer taxes.

Year-End Processing

Q 13:55　Are all year-end timings the same?

Most countries operate on a calendar-year basis, so they have the same December 31 year-end as the United States. But there are some jurisdictions (mostly old British colonies) that have a different year end—usually around March 31. These include the UK, Hong Kong, and India. Australia's tax year is July to June, and various African countries have different year ends. In these countries, the year-end filings then occur in the spring/summer versus early in the year.

Also, some countries, such as China and Poland, have no year end at all. In China, payroll closes each month; therefore, an organization cannot adjust a payment/deduction in the current month to offset an error in an earlier month, as each month consists of a full payroll cycle/year. All tax tables are driven on a monthly amount.

Accountability

Q 13:56　Will payroll providers worldwide follow Sarbanes-Oxley?

The Sarbanes-Oxley Act of 2002 (SOX) requires public companies in the United States to certify their internal control procedures for their corporate affairs, formerly handled through an SAS70 Type II audit. Today service companies will certify under SSAE 16, which is an updated standard for compliance and has a slightly different methodology than the previous SAS70 Type II audits. The most reviewed areas for a company are its Information Technology, Financial, and Accounting processes. Since payroll typically touches each of these areas, it is an important function reviewed during the SOX certification process.

Most countries do not have legislation similar to SOX, although a few are starting to pass legislation to create similar requirements. Some of the larger payroll companies are slowly certifying their international locations for SSAE 16, mainly in the major European Markets. But overall, it is rare to find a payroll provider outside the United States that is SSAE 16 certified because it is costly to obtain and maintain that status.

Although local providers outside the United States are often not SSAE 16 certified, companies can still ensure they have the proper controls over their payroll by performing due diligence on the payroll provider's IT structure and internal controls prior to signing a contract. Many companies use the same audit procedure they use for their own internal compliance as the basis for their due diligence questionnaires.

Q 13:57 What is OFAC, and how does it relate to international payroll processing?

Compliance with the Office of Foreign Assets Control (OFAC) is being scrutinized more aggressively by the U.S. government in recent years. OFAC is a division of the U.S. Department of the Treasury that administers and enforces economic and trade sanctions based on U.S. foreign policy and national security goals against targeted foreign countries, regimes, terrorists, narcotics traffickers, and other threats to the national security, foreign policy, or economy of the United States. All U.S. persons must comply with OFAC regulations. Therefore, compliance is required by all U.S. citizens and permanent resident aliens, regardless of where they are located, all persons and entities within the United States, and all U.S. incorporated entities and their foreign branches.

OFAC maintains a list of known individuals, countries, and entities that are involved in terrorism, narcotics trafficking, and other activities that pose a threat to the national security, foreign policy, or economy of the United States. It is the responsibility of all U.S. citizens and corporations to ensure that they are not doing business with or sending money to anyone who appears on this list. In addition, OFAC also continually updates its stance on what functions may be performed in which countries worldwide. In some cases, a country is completely on the unapproved list, and no business of any nature can be performed there (e.g., Democratic Republic of Congo (DRC) and the Sudan). In other countries, there may be limitations on functions and financial transactions that may be performed in that country. For more information on OFAC, go to https://www.treasury.gov/about/organizational-structure/offices/Pages/Office-of-Foreign-Assets-Control.aspx. The reason OFAC affects Payroll is that every U.S. company must ensure that its employees have cleared the OFAC list, thereby proving that its employees are not involved in an OFAC-restricted activity (such as terrorism, child trafficking, narcotics, etc.). If companies have international locations and have limited visibility as to who is on their payroll, they could have an OFAC violation due to an employee's nationality (e.g., Liberian), prior affiliation with certain targeted groups, or participation in activities that violate OFAC. If a company pays an entity or person on the OFAC list, the fine can be up to $200,000 per occurrence. It is important to have an OFAC program in place to prove compliance with sanctions if an audit or violation occurs. If a company can prove it is diligent in its OFAC efforts and inadvertently violates one of the sanctions, then a lesser penalty may be applied. It is important to periodically run employees through an OFAC checking system, starting at time of hire and periodically throughout the year to ensure there are no changes to an employee's status.

Each company should have an OFAC program in-house to ensure compliance. A couple of key components of the program include:

1. Designate a Compliance Officer.
2. Create an OFAC Program and specify what risks are being mitigated.
3. Develop procedures:
   a. Document process;
   b. Determine timing of review of employees, vendors, locations, banking institutions, and other defined risks;
   c. Implement a OFAC screening technology;
   d. Determine data collection protocols;
   e. Create escalation paths for issue resolution.
4. Create a documented solution through:
   a. Periodic internal audits;
   b. Oversight programs;
   c. Records of executed protocols.
5. Review the overall program at least annually.

When reviewing the employee list against the OFAC sanctions list, it is important to have more information than just the employee's name and nationality. Some first and last names may be very common and frequently occurring in certain regions of the world, which may make it appear as if the employee is on the OFAC list. Typically, a birth date or passport number may clear the employee if a name match is found. OFAC requirements and regulations are increasing each year, so it is important to keep up to date on the changes imposed by this government organization to ensure compliance. (See chapter 5 for more information concerning OFAC considerations for direct deposit.)

Q 13:58   What do companies need to know about data privacy?

Data Privacy is ever changing on a global basis and each country has its own set of rules and regulations regarding data privacy and data protection. In general, most countries require employers to disclose how they use their employees' data, which is often outlined in the employee's employment contract. All companies are required to protect this data against theft and misuse, although misuse by corporate entities is rare. An example of misuse would be if a company sold its employees' data to a third party for marketing purposes. (See chapter 14.)

Theft or system breach is a more common issue, for example, when data is inadvertently lost (i.e., when an unencrypted laptop is stolen or a thumb drive is lost) or a system is hacked. In these cases, a company is required to notify affected employees as soon as reasonably possible and in some countries the company is required to also notify government agencies that monitor data protection. Often these companies will put credit monitoring in place for the affected employees in case the data is maliciously used. If a company is outsourcing its payrolls, it is important to understand the outsourcer's data protection program and specifically ask about encryption programs, data security facilities (T3 or T4 is preferable), and data management protocols.

Some countries, such as Denmark, used to require that, at a minimum, a copy of payroll data must be available in-country. In 2015, this requirement changed to allow information to be held outside Denmark, but readily accessible. It is acceptable if a copy is available in a consolidation or HCM system housed outside the payroll country as long as the data also is present in the payroll country. Additionally, countries are always looking at whether data can legally reside outside their borders. The Chinese government, for example, has been considering for the last few years whether to allow employee data to be available outside its borders. A law passed in Russia in 2014 requires personal data to be maintained in Russia and restricts how it can be utilized abroad. In January of 2016, Japan moved to the My Number system. Japanese people will be issued a 12-digit code that will be used to track social security and taxes. Although this new system will help with government efficiency, it comes with many privacy restrictions, which companies will need to monitor. Countries continue to review their privacy standards on personal data and are constantly refining their requirements.

In the past, U.S. companies could help protect themselves by becoming Safe Harbor Certified. This process allowed U.S. companies to self-certify that they protect their European employees' data in compliance with the EU Data Privacy Directive. But in October of 2015, the Court of Justice of the European Union ruled that Safe Harbor was no longer valid because U.S. government agencies, like the NSA, have access to personal information of European people without their explicit consent if the data is on U.S. soil. Many companies are using Standard Contractual Clauses to ensure data controllers and data processors are in sync with the current requirements. These require Data Transfer Agreements (DTAs) to be filed with each payroll processor in each European country. In July 2016, the EU and the U.S. ratified a framework called the EU-US Privacy Shield. This is a new program to replace Safe Harbor with tougher requirements.

Q 13:59   What is Privacy Shield, and how does it differ from Safe Harbor?

Privacy Shield replaces Safe Harbor as the certified means of transferring data between the European Union and the United States. There are some key differences between Safe Harbor and Privacy Shield. These include:

1. *Stronger company obligations:* There will be greater transparency, oversight, and sanctions for companies that do not conform.

2. *Multiple redress options for individuals:* Companies must respond to an employee complaint regarding data privacy within 45 days. Individuals have alternative dispute resolution, may work with the Data Protection Agency if the complaint is not resolved, and, as last resort, can go to a Privacy Shield Panel for arbitration.

3. _Restriction of U.S. government access:_ The U.S. government has agreed to limitations on mass surveillance and guidelines for access to personal data.

4. _Monitoring of the privacy shield program:_ The European Union and the United States will participate in annual summits and review of the current program, and will publish public reports on the status of the program.

U.S. companies will be required to self-certify annually, display publicly their privacy policies on their websites, reply to privacy complaints, and comply with European Data Protection Authorities.

Q 13:60   Why is compliance with local country laws so important?

Although this seems like an obvious question, many companies try to "slide" by on local payroll compliance. Some companies treat employees like contractors (i.e., paying them in cash, but in every other respect treating them like employees). Often companies make it a requirement in the employment contract (another employee-like instrument) that the employee is responsible for his or her own taxes. This creates an untenable situation, because if the local government discovers the situation, which it often does when the employee files his or her taxes or tax returns, the government will come after the company for the employer's match to the social security taxes and often impose extreme penalties. In addition, the company may lose business permits in that country, which will completely stop all commercial trade until the matter is resolved.

Compliance also ensures employees are paid properly by the company standards and local statutory standards. By following approved procedures, the company will have visibility into the local payroll operation to ensure the proper payments and deductions are made. In addition, all compliance paperwork must be filed with the local government and the company must retain a copy for audit documentation. This is especially important if a payroll provider is used. The company should insist on having copies of all filings after every payroll cycle to ensure compliance and to keep for audit and emergency purposes.

Q 13:61   Does a company need a local bank account?

This answer varies from country to country and may depend on the type of entity that is set up. Many countries do not require a company to have a local bank account. In these cases, a company can directly pay its employees from its own international bank account, or send funds to its local payroll provider for disbursements. Sending funds to the local payroll provider is often the easiest and least expensive means of disbursing payroll funds to employees and government agencies. The local provider will then manage all the tax and deduction due dates for the payroll. These dates can vary, as some taxes and deductions (i.e., pension, health benefits, etc.) are paid each cycle, month, quarter, and year.

In other cases, the company must open a local bank account. Typically, this is a requirement for investment entities, where a company must prove how much money it is investing in a local country and the easiest way to "invest" is by sending payroll funds through the company's local bank account. Investment entities are very common in China. Often the payroll cost is the largest expense for international start-ups. In other cases, a local bank account is required to make tax payments. For example, in Japan, a company can directly pay its employees from an international account, but must make local tax payments from an in-country bank account. Finally, some countries require all payments to be made through a local bank account, as is the case in Brazil and Russia.

Q 13:62   What are international data retention requirements?

As with any question, data retention is country specific. In general, most companies only think about how long they need to keep data to be compliant. But an interesting twist on the international scene is that many countries require employers to delete employee information after a certain time frame. This is especially true for employees that leave the company. Therefore, companies may be required to keep records for seven years, but for anyone who is terminated, the company may only be able to keep data for two years after an employee leaves. This significantly complicates issues as a company may want to keep a pay register for seven years, but may be in violation of a country's retention policy if someone terminated after the first year. So in the fourth year, the company needs to delete that unique person's information. Therefore, it is important that each company understands the local data retention policies and applies them appropriately.

Q 13:63   Does integrating an HCM system make payroll seamless?

Although HCM system integrations do help improve the process of data exchange, payrolls do not just run themselves. Often the HCM system is just one component of many inputs, generally providing indicative data (name, address, job title, salary, and sometimes banking detail). It is becoming more common for payments and deductions (e.g., bonuses, commissions, health care deductions, etc.) to come through the HCM system with time and labor inputs. Additionally, some companies pay expense reports through payroll, which often will be sent via an interface from a separate expense reporting system.

Therefore, it is important to review the internal HCM system structure to see what can be automated. In many cases, the HCM system may not be set up to send full new hire information for every country (i.e., it does not carry country-specific fields, such as federal deductions and state deductions in the United States, for each country) and cannot pass to the payroll provider copies of documents such as wage tax cards and employment contracts, which are required to register a new employee on payroll in many countries. Additionally, many countries have odd multiple cycles (for example, Belgium has 13.92) and terminations, which require off-cycles. Stock options stock payouts, and expenses often have to be processed separately. All of these inputs complicate the payroll process, and they are not always easy to automate, especially through one system.

HCM systems are improving every year, and many are even building in local country requirements to pass the appropriate data to local payroll providers. It is important to look at the cost benefit of each country to determine if an interface is viable. Many companies are not integrating payrolls into their HCM systems if there are less than 20 to 50 employees on the payroll. Additionally, data integrity and timeliness is of the utmost importance if the two systems are linked. HR must input accurate, validated data on time, each cycle to maintain a compliant payroll.

Q 13:64   How should an organization prepare for creating a Request for Proposal (RFP) for global payroll outsourcing?

When an organization is ready to consider outsourcing its global payroll, there are a series of steps that should be completed to execute a successful RFP. The organization should:

1. *Understand its needs*: Is the company looking for a local-to-local approach, a consolidated approach, or a payroll system managed in-house? Are there local language requirements? What are the company's reporting needs? What are the interface needs, HCM system, Accounting? Why is the company considering outsourcing (e.g., cost, compliance, visibility)?

2. *Understand how it is currently organized*: How is payroll handled today? Are there several providers, or one provider, or is payroll executed in-house? What are the current costs of doing payroll today? How does HR input changes into payroll? How does Finance receive cost reports? A spreadsheet detailing all these specifics including headcount, providers, costs, requirements, statistics on off cycles, turnover, interfaces, etc., is a great tool to understand the current payroll environment.

3. *Determine what the future state will be*: Does the company want a local, regional, or global platform? Does the company want in-country support? Should the process be centralized or decentralized? How will HR interface with the process? Will there be an accounting feed? Will there be an HCM system interface? Will the payroll be supported on a global, regional, or local basis?

4. *Enlist the support of senior management*: Ensure that the project has senior management support not only for the RFP process, but also for implementation and ongoing process improvement. This will be especially important during the implementation process, when local country management may need some encouragement to participate.

5. *Determine if there are any ancillary projects that will impact the global payroll outsourcing project*: Is there an HCM system, accounting transition, or other implementation that is going on simultaneously that may impact timing and providing resources for the global payroll project?

6. *Determine the availability of internal resources*: Does the company have enough experienced resources to implement a global solution in the time frame established?

7. *Review budget*: Is there budget set aside for implementation and ongoing costs? Who in the organization owns the financial responsibility (budget)? Will a portion be rebilled to local offices? Will the cost be borne by the head office or local offices?

8. *Determine timing*: When do all of the countries need to be rolled out? Are there current contracts for providers that would need to be cancelled? Are there competing projects or does one project have to be completed prior to payroll going live (i.e., does the HCM system need to go live in a given location before payroll can be implemented)?

9. *Obtain buy-in*: Has the concept been socialized with local management, senior management, HR, Payroll, and Finance? What are their concerns? Will they be addressed by the solution selected?

Once the above steps are completed, it is important to perform due diligence on the global payroll providers in the market to see which ones will meet the organization's needs/constraints as determined above. There are many methods of ascertaining if a global payroll provider is right for your organization. A company can meet many of these providers at trade shows, learn more on their websites, informally ask industry colleagues about their experiences, and/or submit an RFI. Also, sometimes it is easiest just to call the provider and ask some questions. Often the provider will set up a demonstration of its services as an online, one-hour meeting. This is probably the best way to get a feel about the provider and if it might fit with your organization. The next step would be to write the RFP and submit it to the providers. Give the providers enough time to ask questions and respond. A better proposal is produced if the provider has the option of talking to the subject matter experts at the company. Since global payroll is relatively a new outsourced service, procurement often does not know enough to answer questions fully for a well-prepared proposal to be presented. Once the completed RFPs are gathered, a committee should review the documents to select the provider that best fits the needs detailed above.

Q 13:65   What are the common metrics for international payroll?

When looking to improve payroll processes, it is important to measure each aspect of the process. Typically, organizations will create a series of metrics, often called Service Level Agreements (SLAs) or Key Performance Indicators (KPIs) to determine how well the department is functioning. For payroll, these often fall into broad categories including:

1. *Timeliness:* Were all inputs and outputs completed in accordance with the payroll calendar? These may include: input of payroll changes, calculation turnaround, approvals of payroll, approvals of funding, pay slip release dates, GL/Accounting report submission, statutory filings, other report submission, and payment of employees, government agencies, and benefit providers.

2. *Accuracy:* Were inputs and outputs accurate? Many companies only measure outputs, but, in reality, they need to review the inputs to ensure there is a high degree of accuracy and clarity prior to submitting changes

to payroll. Accuracy also includes the concept of completeness. Highlighting situations when incomplete data is provided, which is often the case in submitting new hire or termination forms, is important to improving the overall process. This concept is very critical if data is being interfaced into payroll from an Enterprise Resource Planning (ERP) or HCM system. If the interface data is corrupted or inaccurate, it can affect large employee populations. On the output side, it is important to check for accuracy of payroll registers, banking files, accounting files, benefit interfaces, and compliance paperwork.

3. *Responsiveness:* How long does it take to get a question answered or an issue resolved? This metric is usually broken into two components: Time to respond to the initial inquiry and then time to answer the question/solve the issue. Usual initial response times are 24 to 48 hours during the business week for base inquiries. Critical escalations may have response requirements of hours or minutes. The second metric is more difficult to quantify as a KPI, but is often used more as a measurement to reduce cycle time or number of queries. A good example is answering employee questions on benefits. By instituting a benefits portal and self-service, the cycle time and number of queries can be significantly reduced. Note that some inquiries may take several weeks if they include interacting with government officials in certain countries.

4. *Cost per pay:* What is the cost per person per payroll? This is an interesting metric as it should include all costs, internal and external if a payroll provider is utilized. As departments become more efficient, receive better input from HR, interface more systems, and reduce the number of payroll cycles, this cost should decrease.

5. *Cycle time:* How long does each component of the payroll process take? This is an important measurement to see if complexity can be driven out of the payroll process, improving the overall efficiency, accuracy, and visibility of the payroll inputs and outputs.

6. *Number of cycles:* This measurement is important for companies that often have off-cycle processing. In some cases, off cycles cannot be avoided as they are statutorily required for terminations or for handling bonuses or stock options. But it is often the case that off cycles are processed because of poor change, time, and HR data, creating situations where off cycles are used as a crutch and become a "normal" part of payroll operations. Off cycles are very expensive in terms of internal labor and provider costs and should be minimized wherever possible.

A baseline needs to be established for each of these metrics, preferably before it is outsourced. Typical measurements are numbers of hours, days, transactions, employees, and pay slips. It is good to have goals defined for each metric; for example, 99 percent accuracy and 48-hour turnaround on inquiries. To be truly effective, SLAs should be reviewed on a monthly or quarterly basis.

Often SLAs minimums are reached each cycle, but the process itself is full of "hidden factories." So ultimately the payroll goes out accurately and on time, but the calculations might be run three or four times or the reports are hand manipulated. This is where KPIs can be used to help the collective team concentration on improving overall efficiency. KPIs generally do not have penalties associated with them; they are only used to do root cause analysis and continuous improvement.

Q 13:66   What are typical vendor contract terms?

First of all, it is important to have a contract with the payroll provider. So many companies utilize accounting firms for accounting services and payroll is just an extra service on an engagement letter. Only after a company has an issue does the importance of a contract become clear. When contracting for global payroll, there are several areas that need to be addressed in every contract: basic services covered (often detailed in a Statement of Work), ownership of liabilities, data and compliance for each party, fees, insurance, data privacy, termination clauses, and SLAs. Most contracts will have a term of one to three years, with a few contracts having a five-year term. When contracting with a new supplier, it is better to limit the term until the relationship develops to a point that a three- or five-year contract is palatable. The shorter-term contracts will allow an organization to test the water without incurring long-term risk. When a relationship is going well, a second three-year contract will often include pricing concessions for signing for a longer term.

Q 13:67   What types of risk mitigation activities should be considered?

While all payrolls create a certain amount of risk for an organization, international payroll brings an additional set of complications. The following factors should be considered when assessing risk:

1. *Location:* Countries vary as to the inherent risks involved. When opening an office in a less developed part of the world, additional factors will contribute to the risk of paying employees accurately and on time, guaranteeing that compliance is being met and ensuring the payroll operations and funding are secure. Some locations will have political strife, where labor unions are striking (Argentina) or the local government is not stable (Egypt). These countries may have situations where the country is completely shut down, under martial law, or simply does not have power. In other cases, data protection is minimal as there are no Tier 3 sites in country, or in some cases payroll is calculated by hand because local systems do not exist (or are very poor). There may be situations in which filings are manual and may require multiple trips to the tax authorities to physically hand over paperwork. This may be further complicated by manual filings needing to be presented to multiple offices in different geographic locations. In some cases, compliance paperwork must be "chopped" with the company seal and counter stamped with the government agency when funds are remitted.

2. *Weather:* Tsunamis, earthquakes, power outages, wind storms, hurricanes, blizzards, and flooding are all potential risks to getting payroll out on time. In some severe incidences, local in-house teams or payroll

providers are rendered inoperable as their offices are shut down or destroyed.

3. *In-house issues:* A payroll team can become incapacitated if a payroll technology shuts down or fails during an upgrade or the network is not operating optimally. Similarly, the organization is at risk if a payroll professional leaves the company, or becomes ill and this person is the only expert in country as the population is too small to warrant a full-time back-up.

4. *Payroll provider issues:* These often include: A local payroll provider has turnover of its payroll professionals, becomes insolvent, provides poor or no services, has infrastructure failure (technology, power, physical location, etc.), does not file taxes on time, and/or does not makes the appropriate payments.

5. *Funding:* The funding of the payroll is often the most critical and risky component of the payroll process. Banking files can be created improperly, causing employees to be paid incorrect amounts or not paid at all. Banks can lose transactions especially if there are complicated wire instructions. Taxes can be paid to the wrong account as many taxing authorities truncate the notes on a wire transfer that indicate the clients' payroll account numbers. Banks close often, lose power, and change SWIFT codes as they merge. It is critical to monitor every step of the payroll process and periodically confirm that employees and statutory agencies are paid.

6. *Business continuity plan (BCP):* With all of the above potential issues, it is critical to have a business continuity plan for the organization. BCPs include communication trees, incident escalation, and alternative methodologies to ensure payroll goes out on time, accurately. A couple of examples include:

   (a) *Local payroll/local provider not able to calculate payroll:* Remove all one-time payments and estimate taxes from the prior period's pay register. Process the estimated net amounts and send funds to the employees and government agencies via a local or international bank. Reconcile the following month when the location is back online. If a location is high risk, a company may elect to have a back-up provider or in-house capability in case the primary processor is unable to perform. This back-up can be offsite, in another country (depending on data privacy concerns), or with another payroll provider.

   (b) *Bank is unavailable:* Local banks can become unavailable due to local country strife or sanctions from the government or other banking institutions. It is prudent to have all employees' local and international banking details, so employees can be issued payment from an international versus local bank account if necessary. This requires the organization to have all the SWIFT or International Bank Account Number (IBAN) details for every employee, not just local banking details.

7. *Disaster recovery:* This varies from the BCP because it often relates to IT infrastructure. It is important to know: What is the process and protocol for bringing systems back online? Is there a back-up facility? Are there failover protocols? Are these tested on a regular basis? Disaster recovery is particularly important for companies that have large payroll systems that are managed internally. Even with the advent of cloud computing, it is imperative for companies to understand the disaster recovery capability of all of its suppliers that are part of the payroll process.

There are multiple ways to reduce risk, through thorough vetting of local situations, insurance, disaster recovery testing, and BCP planning. Each payroll will have its own level of risk based upon size of payroll, complexity, and location. It is up to each organization to determine that level of acceptable risk and the necessary protocols for mitigation.

Q 13:68   What countries are automating their local payroll processes?

Several countries have made considerable progress in automating their statutory filing processes in the last 24 months. Most notably, the United Kingdom, France, Brazil, and Australia have made significant strides:

1. *United Kingdom's RTI:* The UK was one of the first to automate information on employees with its move to Real Time Information (RTI) in 2014. This requires companies to file PAYE (tax information) every time employees are paid rather than once a year. Employers also will no longer be required to submit P14s, P35s, P38As, and P45s to the HRMC.

2. *Australia's Superstream:* This automated program requires employers to make payments automatically into the Superannuation (pension) schemes for employees. In Australia, employees may select from a variety of Superannuation programs, which all had different mechanisms for payment. With the advent of Superstream, all Superannuation payments go through the same standard interface. The program started with the largest employers in November 2014, and all companies, including the smallest, needed to comply by June 30, 2016. Employees are required to provide the details of their Superannuation program to their employer. These items include: their SMSF's Australian Business Number (ABN), the SMSF's bank details (BSB and account number), and an electronic service address, which each employee must set up themselves. The electronic service address allows the program to send messages to the employee regarding contributions.

3. *Brazil's e- Social:* This program does not change the obligations of companies in Brazil, but rather automates and streamlines how employee data is sent to the government. This includes payroll, social security, tax obligations, and other labor-related information. It will gradually replace withholding forms like CAGED, RAIS, SEFIP, and GFIP. The overall goals are to simplify the compliance process and improve the accuracy of data submitted. The date for companies to comply with this new program has

been extended several times. The latest date requiring all organizations to comply is January 1, 2018.

4. *France's DNS:* Similar to e-Social in Brazil, France's Declaration Sociale Nominative (DNS) is a program to streamline the filing of specific forms with the government. In this case, the forms are related to hires, various leaves, and changes to pay. Some examples include the requirement to send data within three days of a medical, maternity, paternity, or other leave to the government. Additionally, any bonuses or premiums paid to employees must be sent with the effective dates. Another twist included in this program requires employees on parental leave or sabbatical leave to receive pay slips. Companies were required to comply with this program by January 2016.

More and more countries are automating their data collection processes. The above locations are the pioneers in improving the efficiency of the process for submitting critical information for statutory filings. Over the next several years, it is anticipated that other countries will follow these examples to improve the overall reporting structures.

Q 13:69   How has the change in HR focus affected integration needs between HCM systems and payroll?

Companies are continually looking at ways to streamline processes, improve overall efficacy, and reduce the cost of their internal administration. With the advent of global Human Capital Management (HCM) systems, companies are trying to integrate human resources data into payroll systems on a global basis. This leads to myriad challenges, as each location has differing rules, data requirements, and internal procedures. However, for the companies that have tackled this journey, the benefits of reduced errors, improved data for analytics, and enhanced employee experiences are providing a hefty payback.

To understand how automation is creating value for organizations, it is important to understand the key components that are driving the need for automation. They are:

- HR departments have shifted focus from compliance and administration to improving employee engagement, thus ensuring that the company can hire and retain the talent it needs to remain competitive. This is coupled with the trend that employees are demanding better tools to manage their digital corporate lives. These include one portal for all their needs, including pay results, and more real-time changes to payroll.

- HR data is now used for predictive analysis rather than just for headcount or compliance reporting. Therefore, it is important to have payroll data available in the HCM to support this new requirement. HR managers are using combined data not just for head count reports, but also to *predict* when an employee is going to leave, what training is needed based on increase productivity, who needs career progression management, and cost.

- More and more government agencies are moving toward automated reporting. Ten years ago, automated filings were relatively unheard of outside the United States. In the last five years, countries like the UK, France, Brazil, Japan, Australia, Mexico, and others are requiring companies to file *in real time* changes to their employee populations in addition to filings. This trend is continuing to unfold as more countries automate governmental processes.

In combining HR needs with employee experience expectations and the latest government requirements, HCM systems and payroll providers are often caught in a technology squeeze. Therefore, it is vital for organizations to increase the velocity of their integration strategy to meet the needs of their employees, while keeping up with the government automation requirements to remain globally compliant.

Chapter 14

Data Privacy

Over the last several decades, there has been an explosion in the amount of data that individuals and organizations create, store on computers, and share via the Internet, Intranets, and even through the airwaves using mobile devices. In the context of payroll administration and processing, employees are required to provide personal information to their employers so the employees can be paid properly and have their wages and withheld taxes correctly reported to the government.

With the increase of personally identifiable information (PII) passing through many entities involved with payroll administration, including trusted third-party service providers, greater vigilance is required to ensure protection of that PII. This is especially true given the high-profile news media stories reporting significant data breach events throughout 2016. In December 2016, the European Court of Justice deemed the Safe Harbor framework used for the past 15 years to be invalid. The European Commission and the U.S. Department of Commerce have come forth with a new agreement, EU-U.S. Privacy Shield, which addresses the court's concerns. In addition, the European Union promulgated the Global Protection Data Regulation, which provides a standard across the EU to protect personal data for EU citizens. The two initiatives will have a significant impact on U.S. companies that deal within the EU.

This chapter addresses how to determine which data needs to be protected, the steps a payroll department can implement to lessen the chances of the data being compromised, what to do if the data is breached, how to educate employees about data privacy, and the special issues a payroll department may encounter when it deals with third-party service providers or global payroll.

Payroll and Data Privacy

Q 14:1   Why should Payroll be concerned about data privacy matters?

Payroll leaders and their extended teams within all organizations should be quite concerned about data privacy matters because some of the most sought after employee data, such as names and Social Security numbers, by identity thieves reside within payroll administration records and systems. Identity thieves use this information, along with other personally identifiable information (PII), to fraudulently open lines of credit and bank accounts and then subsequently make illegal purchases of goods and services in the name of their victims, your employees. These acts of identity theft can devastate the credit history and ratings of your employees for an extended length of time until they eventually "clear their name" with creditors and credit reporting agencies that think that your employee(s) made these purchases and decided not to pay the bills associated with them.

Also, there is a growing body of federal and state laws and regulations that now require companies to take preventative measures to protect the PII of employees and consumers. Global employers must also be aware of their entire workforce footprint and abide by country-specific data protection laws governing consumer and employee data. If employers do not adequately protect PII and comply with data protection laws pertaining to their workforce and it becomes compromised due to negligence or simple non-compliance, government regulators can and will sanction the employers. Such actions can lead to legal liability, shareholder discontent, and the tarnishing of a company's reputation in the eyes of workers, government officials, and the general public. Employers can also be subjected to government audits for extended durations of time to validate the future roll-out and effectiveness of an employer's long-term data protection program efforts. Employers may also be subject to litigation from employees, vendors, and other interested parties.

Q 14:2 Does Payroll have to create and publish a written policy around data privacy?

It is highly recommended that Payroll create and publish a written policy around data privacy and security for the payroll administration team, business partners, service providers, and the physical environment for all parties. To achieve this, start out by exploring if your organization has a data privacy and protection team that manages the life cycle of data privacy policies for your entire enterprise. If dedicated privacy, security, and risk management teams exist within your organization, engage them for assistance and guidance to help develop your own payroll specific policies. If your organization does not have a dedicated privacy team, reach out to the leadership team within your HR, Finance, Treasury, Legal, Compliance, Risk Management, and IT departments to initiate a dialogue about the development and execution of your specific data privacy and security policy in the context of mitigating data breach risk within the payroll department. You may be able to leverage existing programs within your organization.

Q 14:3 What is personally identifiable information (PII)?

Personally identifiable information (PII) may be defined differently by federal and state laws. The information reporting and sharing between employers and government entities requires employers to understand how these agencies define these terms. The definition of PII and Sensitive PII also is important when developing a data protection strategy.

The following agencies have defined PII and/or Sensitive PII in similar ways. These definitions are good benchmarks for your organization to follow within the United States:

Department of Homeland Security: The Department of Homeland Security (DHS) defines PII as "any information that permits the identity of an individual to be directly or indirectly inferred, including any information which is linked or linkable to that individual regardless of whether the individual is a U.S. citizen, lawful permanent resident, visitor to the United States, or employee or contractor to the Department."

DHS defines Sensitive PII as "personally identifiable information, which if lost, compromised, or disclosed without authorization, could result in substantial harm, embarrassment, inconvenience, or unfairness to an individual." Some data elements such as Social Security numbers (SSNs), driver's licenses, and passport numbers are considered sensitive PII on their own, while other data elements such as citizenship, medical information, or account passwords in conjunction with identification with an individual also become sensitive PII.

Office of Management & Budget: The federal Office of Management & Budget (OMB) defines PII as "information which can be used to distinguish or trace an individual's identity, such as their name, SSN, biometric records, etc. alone or when combined with other personal or identifying information which is linked or linkable to a specific individual, such as date and place of birth, mother's maiden name, etc. . . . ."

OMB Memorandum M-07-16, Safeguarding Against and Responding to the Breach of Personally Identifiable Information gives further guidance. [http://www.whitehouse.gov/sites/default/files/omb/memoranda/fy2007/m07-16.pdf]

California: One of the first states to adopt data privacy legislation, the law was enacted in 2002 and provides the definition of personal information as "an individual's first name or first initial and last name in combination with any one or more of the following data elements, when either the name or the data elements are not encrypted: (1) Social security number. (2) Driver's license number or California Identification Card number. (3) Medical information. (4) Health insurance information. (5) Account number, credit or debit card number, in combination with any required security code, access code, or password that would permit access to an individual's financial account. Or User name or email address, in combination with a password or security question and answer that would permit access to an online account. [Cal. Civil Code § 1789.84].

California also adopted requirements around breach notification to include what information must be provided to those individuals subject to the breach and if the party making the notification was the cause of the breach, identity theft protection must be offered. California has also added encrypted data, even if an encryption key or security credential was also required.

Massachusetts: In Massachusetts, personal information is defined as "a Massachusetts resident's first name and last name or first initial and last name in combination with any one or more of the following data elements that relate to such resident: (a) Social Security number; (b) driver's license number or state-issued identification card number; or (c) financial account number, or credit or debit card number, with or without any required security code, access code, personal identification number or password, that would permit access to a resident's financial account; provided, however, that 'personal information' does not include information that is lawfully obtained from publicly available information, or from federal, state or local government records lawfully made available to the general public." [940 C.M.R. § 27.02]

Q 14:4   What examples of PII and Sensitive PII would payroll professionals typically handle within their organizations?

Payroll professionals typically handle employee Sensitive PII, including a combination of the following: full name, Social Security number or other tax identification number, home address, bank account information, date of birth, "work status" resulting from a Form I-9 process, and wage garnishments including child support.

Q 14:5   What other departments might handle or receive sensitive PII data from Payroll?

The payroll department might need to share employees' PII with other departments such as:

- Compensation department when submitting corrections to salary information

- Corporate Tax to complete a worksite report
- Accounts Payable to create a paper or electronic payment of an employee's garnishment
- Remote hiring managers so they can collect and forward information to HR and Payroll for further processing
- Benefits to provide information to send to vendors.

Q 14:6 Must Payroll send PII to government agencies?

Yes. Payroll is often required by law to send employees' personally identifiable information to the state and federal governments, such as immigration and work authorization agencies, unemployment insurance agencies, and tax authorities. These government entities may correspond with your department regarding employee-level issues with PII data.

Q 14:7 Who should have access to PII in the payroll department?

Access to PII should be restricted to members of the payroll department. Even within the payroll department, access should only be granted if it is necessary to fulfill a work assignment. For example, every member of the payroll department may not need access to the wage garnishment files.

Q 14:8 What are the basics to secure PII data?

PII in paper format should always be safely stored and locked away when not in use in an office. When PII data is stored electronically or is in transit from one computer system to another, the PII data should be encrypted to ensure it is secured from unauthorized access or use.

Q 14:9 What steps can be taken by Payroll to help secure all PII?

The payroll department can engage in the following activities to help secure all PII:

- Be aware of the types of PII that are created and managed within the payroll department on a daily basis.
- Only collect the PII that you need for all of your payroll processes—nothing more.
- Identify the various data flows of PII into and out of the payroll department.
- Determine who should have access to the payroll department's PII and limit the access to those people.
- Ensure that there is a process to identify people who have left the company to terminate their access to PII.

- Physically secure PII in electronic and paper formats from unauthorized individuals, departments, or vendors.
- Move physical PII offsite to a secure location.
- Manage the "life cycle" of all PII within the payroll processes.
- Properly identify and manage third-party contractors and vendors who are authorized to access, process, and store the payroll department's PII.
- Document the payroll department's PII protection policies and data flows.

Data Classification and Flow Mapping

Q 14:10   Why is it important to classify and map payroll data flows?

It is important to classify payroll data, such as employee address, bank account information, date of birth, Social Security number, state driver's license or identification number, and date of hire as these are key data elements when combined can be deemed PII within the payroll processes. Once these data elements are identified, you can determine which data flows must be protected and map them from point A to point B. Mapping then leads to determining who has and needs access to the payroll processes related to these data flows of PII. Then, the payroll department will have a clearer picture of its PII landscape to create processes and procedures to protect PII.

For example, if bank account information is part of the payroll process, then where those elements are found and who requires access to the data will be part of the process of mapping. A question to be asked is how the records that contain the bank account information are entered into the HR/ERP system. Is the information keyed in by a data management team or uploaded from a self-service portal into the system? Access to these fields or modules of the software is also critical. Then, how the information is transmitted to the bank must be mapped. In this scenario, the information is mapped to an ACH file that is sent to the bank first as a prenote and then with the actual payroll file each payroll. This data is also mapped to the pay advice slip for each employee, usually with the last four digits of the bank account number.

Q 14:11   What are the first steps to take in establishing a data protection program?

To initiate a data protection program within a payroll department, the first task is to take a comprehensive inventory of where all of the types of employee data is received by the department, generated by the payroll system and other software, shared with internal stakeholders, as well as, shared with or generated by external third-party providers. The types of software to be reviewed include time systems, the general ledger (GL), and ancillary applications (e.g., bonus or commissions calculated on a database and shared drives). Once this cache of data is identified, determine how the data passes into payroll, what data is created in payroll and what data is transmitted to other departments and third parties. All of this information should be well documented. Some examples of data that is transmitted or sent to the payroll department are exception timesheets and Forms W-4. Data that is created within the payroll department are the exception reports for data rejects and commission payments that are loaded. An example of data transmitted to another department is the general ledger file.

Q 14:12 How would a payroll department classify its various data elements?

To classify a data element, identify every place that element can be found and reflect that in your data flow document. For example, with bank account information for direct deposit, there is the source of receiving the account information, either a document submitted by the employee or the transfer of the data via a self-service portal. Then there is the ACH file and finally the file that creates the print file. The final stage is the data that flows through to the general ledger (GL), either by employee-level detail or by total.

Once Payroll inventories all of its employee data flows and sources, it is important to evaluate the various sets of employee data that are combined and stored together to determine if the data is considered to be PII. For example, if employees' full names and their Social Security numbers (SSNs) are a core set of combined data that is regularly stored together and used in payroll-related data processing, most of your employee data will be considered PII and need to be protected.

Note. It is considered a best practice to use an employee identification number system that does not use SSNs. Many payroll software applications will issue either a sequential or random number as employees are on-boarded.

Q 14:13 Do I need to include employee data that is in a paper format in the data inventory and data flow mapping process?

Yes. All data, regardless of how and where it flows into or out of the payroll environment, either via electronic or paper format, must be inventoried and mapped to build a comprehensive and effective data protection program.

Q 14:14 Must Payroll also include the data flows to internal and external partners, third-party vendors, and end users of employee data in this data inventory and data mapping process?

Yes. Payroll organizations should indeed map out all of their data flows of employee data within and beyond their entity and include all external partners, third-party vendors, and even government entities (such as the IRS, SSA, and state tax authorities), which are traditionally the end users of the employee data generated from the payroll process.

Q 14:15   How far beyond the payroll department do I need to follow the employee data flow mapping chain to support our specific data protection program?

It is advisable to map your employee data flows from all the sources where it enters the payroll department and where it exits from it. When utilizing any type of third-party service or software provider (internal and external partners), have a detailed dialogue with them about how they are also mapping and protecting the data you receive from or send to them. It is also critical that you make your external third-party contractors and vendors accountable to protect your employee data as they are your proxies in the eyes of government regulators. (See Q 14:67.) Although the various government entities to which you pass data essentially become the responsible parties of it when the data reaches them, it is a good idea to learn about their internal data protection policies, procedures, protocols, and technologies. The end point of the data flow is where the data is transferred to a repository and the data is no longer handled unless required at some later time.

Q 14:16   Should our department notate the actual frequencies and times of our data flows?

Yes. If the payroll department has regular data flows of employee PII that are transmitted in and out of the department on specific days, it is a good idea to notate the actual frequencies if it is reasonable to do. The more frequent the occurrence of PII data, the higher the risk of a breach.

Q 14:17   What is the best way to document the employee data flows of a payroll organization?

A spreadsheet is one effective way to document all of the employee data flows of a payroll department. Another option is to create a database. If your organization has a dedicated data privacy or security team, the team may have templates and tools to help effectively document the entire employee data environment. This may include the use of Privacy Impact Assessments (PIAs).

Q 14:18   What is a privacy impact assessment (PIA)?

A privacy impact assessment (PIA) is a process that allows organizations to specifically document how PII is being collected, used, shared, and stored within in a specific data program or system through a series of targeted questions. It is a tool that allows specific program/system managers or owners to easily demonstrate that they have indeed contemplated known data privacy and protection best practices into the development, deployment, and life cycle of a given program/system. This would include payroll administration systems.

Q 14:19   How often should the payroll department update its employee data flow/mapping document as well as classify its data?

The payroll department should consider its employee data flow and mapping document as a living reference tool that will constantly change and should therefore be updated as soon as new employee data flows and systems are discovered, launched, or planned. This means that corresponding data will need to be classified too.

Q 14:20   How should the payroll department handle data privacy and protection considerations when merging with or acquiring a new entity?

If possible, the payroll department should initiate a dialogue with its internal legal, compliance, and/or risk management team(s) about the specific merger or acquisition event prior to its conclusion on a variety of payroll administration matters—including the status of the data privacy and protection posture of the other entity. In fact, your organization should be proactively assessing data privacy and protection risk for that entire entity beyond the payroll department. If a pre-M&A discussion is not possible, be sure to engage the other entity's payroll team as soon as possible to begin to assess all of their payroll policies, programs, systems, and vendors in the context of PII protection and their compliance/risk status. Then, prioritize the major privacy deficiencies found and address them according to your existing privacy policies and programs. As well, you may find that the entity you are merging with or acquiring may have some excellent privacy policies and programs that can be incorporated into your entire organization. See chapter 12 for more information about the payroll ramifications of a merger, acquisition, or divestiture.

Data Governance

Q 14:21   What is data governance?

According to a definition found on the Data Governance Institute's website, "Data Governance is a system of decision rights and accountabilities for information-related processes, executed according to agreed-upon models which describe who can take what actions with what information, and when, under what circumstances, using what methods." [http://www.data governance.com/adg_data_governance_definition]

Q 14:22   What is the significance of data governance with regard to data privacy and security?

Many payroll departments are already practicing data governance through their daily employee data management, operations, and processes. However, the deployment of data protection compliance measures can be one component of data governance programs that could significantly be lacking within many payroll departments. This is because of the absence of actual proactive privacy awareness and education within many entities during a time when new technologies make it very easy to create, move, process, and store employee data that can be easily lost or stolen. As a result, many global public policy makers and regulators have been establishing new rules about how entities protect data deemed PII, including employee data. These rules include fines and other sanctions for noncompliance.

Q 14:23   How can data governance practices within the payroll department be incorporated to account for data privacy and security matters to protect employee data?

By using your data flows and data process inventory documents, your department can begin to establish operational rules governing who has the right and responsibility to create, access, manage, process, share, preserve, and destroy various classes of employee data within your sphere of control and influence. This exercise should be performed with all of your third-party service providers and software vendors. Finally, consider all of the internal corporate governance rules that apply to your payroll department, as well as, the external legal and regulatory requirements established by government entities based on your national or global footprint.

Q 14:24   Before embarking on establishing a data governance program, should Payroll engage and discuss this with other departments in the company?

Yes. Your company may have an existing comprehensive data governance program for other departments, divisions, or groups within your company. Payroll may be able to leverage other internal data governance policies, procedures, and controls. There may be a dedicated team that oversees and manages the data governance program for the company. It may be beneficial to have the payroll department represented on any internal data governance risk management committees that already exist.

Q 14:25   Should the topic of data governance strategy be discussed with contractors, partners, and third-party vendors that perform payroll administration work for the payroll department before doing business with them?

Yes, it is important to inquire about and understand the data governance strategy of all of the external partners, including how they would protect your employee data on or off-site. Any of your external vendors should be able to provide the SSAE-16 (which is the successor to SAS 70) audit report that outlines the vendors' controls and how employee data is protected. This allows your payroll department to make an informed decision about working with the vendors in light of how they approach data privacy, security, and governance. Vendors that operate globally may have instituted the more stringent European rules across the globe.

Physical Security

Q 14:26   Is a payroll department required to be located in a space separated from other departments?

While there is no rule that establishes guidelines on the physical space for a payroll department, the sensitive nature of the information processed and stored within it warrants taking steps to ensure the data is secure. From the salary information of employees including senior management to court documents for child support, it would be disastrous if any of this information became public. Another risk of having personal information be accessible to those not authorized to see it is the company's legal implications of failing to perform due diligence and having the proper controls in place. A third consideration is the threat of identity theft and fraud when information is inadvertently available to other employees or third parties.

Having a separate, secure space for the payroll department is the first step in securing the data managed by the payroll team.

Q 14:27   Should security of the payroll department require locks for doors and/or other security access devices?

To obtain the most secure, controlled physical environment, a locked office would be preferable with security access that tracks with a date stamp who enters and leaves the office. Even within the payroll department, any check printers should be secure along with the MICR toner, check stock, and signature stamp if one is used. Desks and filing cabinets should have locks as well.

Q 14:28   What is a best practice for a payroll department to improve its physical security in order to protect employee data?

Surprisingly, many payroll departments within various companies are not physically separated from other departments such as accounting, accounts payable, HR, finance, legal, or shared services. By providing the payroll department with a separate and secure area within its physical location, employee data protection can be significantly improved because many data breaches are a result of internal physical data theft.

Q 14:29   What is a "clean desk" policy and how does it help protect employee data within the payroll organization?

A "clean desk" policy means employees should not leave their work materials out in public view whenever they are away from their desk and, at the end of each work day, all paperwork should be securely stored away. At the conclusion of each day, by securely storing work-related documents and reports, especially ones that contain employee data (PII), an organization can significantly reduce the risk of data theft, potential data misuse, and possible legal liability and reputational risk as a result of such a theft. In addition, computers should be locked and password protected when an employee leaves his or her desk. The clean desk policy also pertains to closing/hiding screen displays or windows on their monitors before stepping away from their desks.

Q 14:30   **Is it appropriate to convene meetings within the payroll administration office with individuals who are not members or official contractors of the payroll department?**

It depends. If you have a secure department and non-payroll attendees have to be escorted to a meeting space that is not in the middle of your payroll team's work environment, then there is less concern. If you do not have a separate space for conducting meetings, it is less desirable to convene them within the confines of the payroll administration office. It is best to avoid the risk of unauthorized access or viewing of payroll records and employee PII. If members of the payroll team must meet with colleagues of their entity and third-party vendors to discuss a variety of project or service issues, the payroll person should find an onsite meeting room in another department.

Q 14:31   **Is it wise for Payroll to use the network copiers, printers, and/or multi-function peripherals (MFPs) that are utilized by other department in the company?**

Payroll should not utilize network copiers, printers, and/or MFPs that are located outside their separate physical location because most of today's copiers/MFPs contain hard drives that image everything that is copied and/or scanned and your payroll print job will frequently include employee data (PII) that can easily be picked up by accident (or on purpose) by other employees who are not members of the payroll department and therefore are not authorized to have access to this type of sensitive data. There should be a defined disposal or retirement policy for these types of devices to mitigate any future data breach event(s) for your organization. Be sure to discuss with your IT, compliance, and/or information security department how to do this properly.

Q 14:32   **How should Payroll dispose of reports containing employee data (PII)?**

Many organizations have strategically placed security container bins for the purpose of collecting and later destroying various internal non-public business documents that are placed within them. In many cases, a third-party professional document destruction firm is under contract with your organization to empty these bins and destroy their contents. The payroll department should try to secure one of these bins for its own use if such a service exists. Otherwise, a document destruction service should be explored. Payroll documents and reports should never be disposed of within the normal trash collection service of your physical site as this could result in a highly publicized data breach event.

Q 14:33   **Are there additional considerations when payroll checks are printed on site?**

If Payroll prints checks and advices in-house, there are several considerations to ensure this sensitive data is protected. When possible use a dedicated printer for printing paychecks. (This is another reason why the payroll department should have its own secure space as the first line of physical security.)

If a dedicated printer is not possible, ensure that the MICR toner and signature plate are kept in a secured place with a log for when they are signed out. There should also be a log for the check stock and each pay run should be logged in with start and finish numbers, voided checks, and the other procedures that are currently in place to avoid theft and fraud. An additional security concern is the check stock itself. As thieves have become more savvy, there are many more security features to be incorporated into check stock that should be explored to prevent the checks from easily being duplicated. In many cases, the signature is embedded in the software to address concerns about printing on unintended documents.

In addition, it is advisable to only have one or two staff members who have the responsibility of printing payroll checks.

Data Life Cycle Management

Q 14:34   **What is data life cycle management?**

Data life cycle management is the responsibility for end-to-end management of all data that moves in, through, and out of the payroll department. The sensitive nature, on an employee and company level, requires Payroll to establish the program around protecting the data and ensuring the appropriate personnel and controls are in place.

Q 14:35   **Why is it important for the payroll department to be concerned about data life cycle management in terms of the payroll administration process?**

The payroll department is responsible for generating a tremendous amount of data related to paying workers and paying taxes, as well as information reporting to various government entities. Most of the data associated with these processes includes employee PII. In addition, the payroll department receives many inbound electronic and paper data flows containing PII from a variety of sources. This means that payroll departments must have a documented process and strategy to safely and securely create, share, retain, and eventually destroy this data in whatever form it may be in. In many instances, federal and state laws, as well as internal information governance programs, may set a length of time that employers are required to retain the data.

Q 14:36   How does data privacy compliance and risk management play into the data life cycle within the payroll department?

Whether currently in use or in storage by electronic or physical paper format, the payroll department must be sensitive to how its data is accessed, used, and retained before it is eventually destroyed when it is no longer needed. If the organization does not have a strong sense of the life cycle of its data, it can put itself at greater risk for misuse or unauthorized access that could lead to a reportable data breach.

Q 14:37   Why is data retention an important consideration with regard to data privacy and security?

Since a great deal of payroll data must be retained for specific durations of time due to statutory and regulatory requirements, it is possible that electronic or paper employee information kept longer than legally necessary can actually increase the risk and potential liability for employers. This is because retaining data longer than necessary can increase your exposure to data breach events that could harm your employees, result in adverse government actions including financial penalties, or expose your company to negative press in the news media that can tarnish your organization's reputation with customers, as well as increase the risk of legal liability. Sometimes it is necessary to retain documents beyond what is legally required, such as for retiree benefit calculations.

Q 14:38   What are suggestions for implementing a data life cycle management program and strategy in the payroll department?

The first step to implement a data life cycle management program is to determine if any documentation exists from internal teams of document managers, information management experts, and IT professionals within your company. These internal sources can also help address data privacy and security concerns related to your managing the life cycle of all of your data. If internal resources are not available, seek external information to get started.

Technology Considerations

Q 14:39   Are there specific methods for transmission of employee data that are recommended for organizations that manage various types of PII?

There are many solutions deployed by organizations to manage, store, and transmit their data. However, when storing or transmitting sensitive PII such as employee data, it is always advisable to use the latest data encryption technologies available to protect the data. To determine and utilize the best data encryption solution for your specific environment, have an open dialogue with your internal IT department, external technology partners, as well as service providers on best practices related to your current data transport and encryption methods. Ensure that you discuss how data should be protected when transmitting to and from the various government entities that are typically the end users of your employee data in many cases.

Q 14:40   What are the potential data protection vulnerabilities in utilizing a variety of hardware and software technologies to conduct and manage various payroll processes with the payroll department?

The payroll department should take a complete inventory of its computers, fax machines, laptops, media storage devices, mobile devices, printers, servers, scanners, telephone systems, and all software applications—including business collaboration systems. From this inventory, list the various processes and/or tasks (large or small) that each device and software performs to complete your payroll processes. (As an added benefit, the inventory exercise will even help identify many of the inbound and outbound employee data flows.) It is beneficial to include your IT department when conducting the inventory process because IT may be able to identify hardware and software that Payroll may not be aware exists as part of the payroll process, such as automated schedulers that run specific jobs based on a schedule. This partnership with IT may add value toward helping identify vulnerabilities and demonstrate that Payroll is being proactive.

Q 14:41   Should the payroll administration organization have a written technology use policy for its extended team?

Yes. It is strongly advisable for the payroll department to have a clear and concise written policy about how it uses various technologies that are available to team members within the payroll administration environment. This will significantly help mitigate the risk of unauthorized access to your department's data.

Q 14:42   How can the payroll management team go about instituting a written technology use policy within the payroll department?

The best place to start to develop a departmental technology use policy is to reach out to your HR and IT departments to determine if there are already written policies available that must be complied with by all employees within your company. If such a company-wide policy exists, this can be the baseline document to model your department's version.

Q 14:43   If the company already has a good and solid technology use policy for all employees, why does the payroll department need a separate one?

The payroll department is a very PII-rich environment due to the amount of employee data that it creates, processes, manages, shares, retains, and protects. Although your company-wide technology use policy is likely very adequate for most business environments, there are some specific policies about technology use in the payroll administration environment that may not have been contemplated.

A potential concern arises when Payroll uses software that is dated, or platforms that are not supported, which increases the possibility of a breach. Examples include outdated versions of browsers and Java. Because employee portals rely on the Internet, ensuring that your platform is continually updated is very important from a security perspective.

Q 14:44   What topics should be addressed in a policy and procedures document?

In composing and publishing technology deployment/access/use/security/retirement policies and procedures that must be put into practice by the payroll department, the IT department can be a resource to help advise Payroll about creating the policies and procedures. Topics to be addressed in policy and procedure documents include:

- Access and identity management for hardware and software use
- Authorized only applications (apps) and software installations for the payroll environment
- Bring your own device to work (BYOD)
- Data encryption technology deployment and use (for everything)
- Document management and storage software
- Employee communications with the payroll team (email/fax/portals)
- Hardware technology retirement procedures and protocols for anything with a hard drive or memory
- Inbound/outbound email use
- Inbound/outbound fax machine use
- Internet use in the payroll department (personal and professional)
- Laptop, mobile device, and storage device use (in and outside the office)
- Local drives on a computer
- Mobile/remote access
- Password policy use for all hardware and software
- Peer-to-peer file sharing
- Printer use
- Scanner use

- Servers, payroll and nonpayroll
- Shared drives on a server
- Teleworkers
- Wireless devices and networks (internal and external).

Q 14:45   What kind of specific technology use policies should the payroll department deploy that may not be a part of a company-wide technology use policy document?

The following is a list of recommended technology use policies for the payroll department to consider beyond any typical company-wide policies to help minimize unauthorized access to your employee data:

- Your Internet use policy should explicitly state that payroll department employees should not conduct personal Internet activities on computers that run payroll administration software or systems. This includes visiting websites of any sort that could potentially download any type of malware or viruses on to your computers (e.g., gaming sites, peer-to-peer file sharing sites, music downloading sites, instant messaging sites, etc.).

- The practice of using USB drives to move files from one computer to another within the department should be avoided as this can be an easy way to spread computer malware and viruses.

- The downloading of any type of software onto payroll department computers is prohibited unless the employee has approval from the IT department to avoid any type of unintentional vulnerabilities to your payroll processing environment.

- A "strong" password protection policy must be in place for all payroll team members to access all computers and payroll systems. The password should be at least eight characters in length with both upper- and lower-case letters along with numbers and/or special characters. The password must be changed every one to three months. Team members are not allowed to share passwords.

- All laptops, smartphones, and other mobile devices must be secured with passwords and have installed encryption software if the devices are used for or connected to payroll systems. Through an app, VPN technology can be used to increase the security around passwords.

- The payroll team must be educated about physically protecting laptops and mobile devices outside of the payroll department, especially when the employee is on business travel.

- Passwords must be required to access computers that are running but not in use after being idle for several moments. This is to protect against unauthorized access to your systems if team members walk away from their computers for long or short periods of time.

- Employees who bring their own devices (BYOD) to work for personal use are not permitted to sync them to computers in the payroll department that are used for payroll processing.

- Payroll team members who telework from home or other remote locations must be educated about the proper use of accessing your entity's computer network and the use of personal or public Wi-Fi systems. Employees should not allow family members to use the work computer and personal programs should not be loaded onto the computer. Your IT department should be able to guide payroll team members about how to secure their Internet connections at home, especially if home Wi-Fi systems are used.

- Temporary contractors must be proactively educated about the company's technology use policies and the policies must be enforced.

Q 14:46   How often should the technology inventory document and the policies and procedures document be updated for the payroll department?

The inventory document and policies and procedures should be viewed as "living documents," which should be regularly updated based on the changes and deployment of technologies used within your payroll department. Assign a member of your team with the responsibility of keeping these documents current and perhaps enlist another team member as a back-up person to manage the documents. Payroll should also monitor company-wide technology deployments and evaluate their potential impact(s) to your payroll administration environment.

Q 14:47   How is it best to keep up with the knowledge of potential payroll department data protection vulnerabilities to minimize risk of data breach when technology is changing so quickly?

Regular communication and meetings with the IT department should help Payroll stay abreast of the newest technologies that may be deployed within the work environment. Before launching any new technology or cloud services software on the company's computer network, Payroll should include IT early in the process because IT may be a critical part of any successful deployment.

Q 14:48   What criteria for sending and receiving information can be implemented to ensure data privacy compliance?

At a minimum, all payroll data containing PII that is electronically sent or received should be encrypted. Your internal IT and/or information security department can help Payroll establish the correct methods, standards, and technology to secure your data whenever it is in electronic storage or transit. Likewise, the best protocol(s) should be determined for transmitting data files. A good practice is to validate the controls that are in place on the recipient side of any data sharing to ensure only authorized individuals are receiving and handling the data. There should be a log or audit trail detailing when the files are received and where the files are to be located and stored. On the recipient side, ensure that Payroll knows who will have access to data. Access should be limited and there should be security measures to protect the data, such as encryption and passwords to protect data when it is not in use.

Q 14:49 Should the payroll department allow its employees to bring their own devices into the work environment to perform their work on company networks?

Before considering bring your own device (BYOD) in the payroll environment, the head of the payroll department should have a discussion with the company's IT department and the cyber security team about their opinions about this technology topic and trend. Since the payroll administration environment handles a tremendous amount of PII and Payroll can never be sure how someone uses his or her personal devices outside of the work environment, it is advisable that members of the payroll department only use company-issued devices.

Q 14:50 What considerations are necessary when there is a third-party provider of software or complete outsourcing?

When communicating to third-party providers, you should always transmit PII in an encrypted format that is password protected. You should also ensure that communications between employees at your payroll service provider are protected.

Breach of Data

Q 14:51 What protocols can Payroll establish to prevent data breach?

Immediate policies can be quickly implemented to protect sensitive data related to computer, laptop, and mobile device use within the payroll department. For example, limit web surfing on company computers to only known and reputable sites to minimize exposure to computer viruses. Prohibit the use of USB thumb drives as the possibility of loss or theft would be a breach if the disk contained PII or sensitive PII. Establish the department protocol to use a shared secured network for data—including business collaboration platforms. With guidelines on what data should be on shared drives, ensure that your team, in coordination with IT, keeps anti-virus software up-to-date on all computers. Also, ensure that effective security and file encryption software is loaded on all equipment including mobile and remote log-in devices. In many cases, the company does not own the software and must manage the supplier. The use of unknown public Wi-Fi services and unauthorized file sharing and storage sites outside your organization with payroll department computers and devices should also be avoided, especially as the workforce has become more mobile and telecommuting has become commonplace. If you are not already using the VPN token encrypted method for accessing the network, consider that option. In fact, your department telecommuters should ensure they secure their own home Wi-Fi systems too if used to access your organization's network remotely. There should also be a policy for laptops taken home or given to remote workers to ensure data won't be compromised if the laptop is stolen. Use of public Wi-Fi networks should be discouraged. If employees are allowed to take computers home, guidelines for accessing the Internet and shared devices should be communicated and a sign-off for team members should be implemented. Clarify what data can be communicated on spreadsheets to other departments. For example, in order for the General Ledger team to accrue the payroll liability for a particular period does not require the individual names of the employee on that payroll, only the totals. For example, when the General Ledger team has to accrue the payroll liability for a particular period, only the totals are required not the individual names. Also, requests for lists of employees with their social security numbers should be avoided and other identifiers such as employee ids should be used instead.

Q 14:52   Are there any laws that employers must comply with when there is a breach of the security of employees' personal data?

At the state level in the United States, there are many breach notification and data protection laws that require employers to report the loss or theft of PII if the data was not encrypted or if the password associated with an encrypted file of PII is known to be compromised. In fact, 47 of the 50 states and the District of Colombia, Puerto Rico, Guam, and the Virgin Islands have passed some form of data breach security laws since California established its first data breach law back in 2003. [Senate Bill 1386] Alabama, New Mexico, and South Dakota are the three states that do not have breach notification laws. The format of the notification, timing, and parties to be notified vary from state to state. It is important for the payroll department to work with legal counsel in the event of a breach to ensure that the proper notification occurs.

In 2016, several states updated their data breach security, and court cases have brought the issue to a new level of attention. Rhode Island revised its privacy law; the revised law will take effect on June 26, 2016, one year from the passage. The law was amended to expand the definition of PI to include SSNs, health insurance and medical information, and much more. In addition to expanding the definition of what is covered under the law, features of the revised privacy law include:

- New required notification. Some 15 states require notification to the State Regulator if the breach may cause harm to the individual, while some require notification if there is a breach.
- Clarification of the definition of a security breach.
- Implementation of a risk-based security program that gives employers the option of managing information security in a manner similar to HIPAA standards.

Washington State amended its privacy law to address several issues related to prior legislation. Among other things, these changes:

- Expand notification requirements to include what information must be provided to consumers and provide that notification must be within 45 days of the breach unless there is no harm to the consumer

- Define encryption and extend the law to encrypted data when a person has access to such data through key or password

- Expand law to cover hard copy data that contains personal information

- Provide the Attorney General with the authority to enforce the law.

- While employers felt there was a safe harbor when data was encrypted, Tennessee enacted legislation that encrypted as well as unencrypted data are subject to data breach notification. Encrypted data is no longer per se exempt from notification requirements. California has also included encrypted data in their data privacy law.

In Tennessee, although employers felt there was a safe harbor when data was encrypted, the state enacted legislation stating that encrypted as well as unencrypted data are subject to data breach notification. Encrypted data per se is no longer exempt from notification requirements.

Massachusetts has taken a comprehensive approach that covers many aspects of data security and what employers would be responsible for managing:

> Every person that owns or licenses personal information about a resident of the Commonwealth shall develop, implement, and maintain a comprehensive information security program that is written in one or more readily accessible parts and contains administrative, techni-cal, and physical safeguards that are appropriate to develop, implement, and maintain a comprehensive information security program that is written in one or more readily accessible parts and contains adminis-trative, technical, and physical safeguards that are appropriate to (a) the size, scope and type of business of the person obligated to safeguard the personal information under such comprehensive information security program; (b) the amount of resources available to such person; (c) the amount of stored data; and (d) the need for security and confidentiality of both consumer and employee information.

The Massachusetts law also requires a business to do the following:

- Designate one or more employees to maintain the entity's information security program

- Identify and assess reasonable and foreseeable internal and external security risks to personal information

- Implement employee training and security policies and procedures

- Establish controls to detect and prevent potential "security system" failures

- Develop security policies for employees to follow related to accessing, storing, and transporting sensitive personal data outside of the workplace, including disciplinary actions for non-compliance of these policies

- Implement a policy and strategy for preventing former employees from accessing personal information maintained by the company

- Take "reasonable steps" to engage with third-party service providers that can abide by a company's security measures to ensure protection of personal information

- Contractually obligate third-party service providers, such as payroll service companies, to implement and maintain security measure to ensure the protection of personal information (emphasis added)

- Employ physical protective measures of records containing personal information on or off the business site

- Regularly monitor security measures to ensure unauthorized access and/or use of personal information and any upgrades of information safeguards to limit risks

- Conduct formal reviews of security programs annually or when there is a significant change to business practices related to the security of personal information

- Instill a formal process to document changes to improve the security measures deployed to protect personal information after a breach incident.

The Massachusetts law also contains almost a full page of *Computer System Security Requirements* that businesses must comply with and their IT or cyber security teams would need to fully implement. These requirements address topics such as encryption, password deployment, and the protection of personal information.

Businesses that fail to comply with this law can be subjected to penalties of up to $5,000 per Massachusetts resident impacted by a data breach. A key and important caveat to this law is that it applies to businesses both in and out of state who own or license personal information for Massachusetts's residents. Lastly, businesses must require that their third-party service providers or vendors contractually agree to comply with this law.

[201 C.M.R. 17.00, Standards for the Protection of Personal Information of Residents of the Commonwealth]

For information about the entire state data breach law landscape, visit the National Conference of State Legislatures website (http://www.ncsl.org/issues-research/telecom/security-breach-notification-laws.aspx).

Q 14:53 How does Payroll determine the impact of a data breach?

The first step in capturing the impact of a data breach is to determine if it relates to an unauthorized access or entry into an actual computer network where the payroll data is stored or a single computer device such as a lost or stolen laptop computer, other mobile device, or back-up storage hard drive. If it is a lost or stolen device that is password protected with encrypted payroll files, Payroll should be less concerned. However, if the lost or stolen device had no basic data protections, Payroll will likely need to report it as a breach if it contained PII. It is also important to ensure that when an employee retires, terminates, or transfers from Payroll that the security profile is updated. It is good practice to review the security profile every two to three months to ensure that the necessary changes have been made.

Computer network breaches discovered by the IT department as a result of an unauthorized access to the entity's network require a deeper investigation by cyber security experts. By having computer forensics performed on the impacted data environment, the breadth and depth of the breach can be fully determined. This is critical because Payroll does not want to publicly report a data breach impacting a large percentage of the workforce when, in reality, only a small percentage of employee records were actually viewed and downloaded (stolen) by an unauthorized person or entity.

Q 14:54   When would a payroll department be required to report a data breach of employee PII?

Depending on the level, size, and circumstances of unauthorized access or data breach, many states in the United States have laws about notifying the individuals potentially impacted. This may require a notification in writing to employees and may require actually alerting the news media. As well, many laws require that a breach event be reported to a state government entity, such as the state Attorney General's office or another regulatory body in charge of data protection. If there is a likelihood of a significant data breach, immediately engage your senior management, internal/external legal counsel, and IT, cyber security, data privacy and risk management teams.

Illinois provides several options for notifying an Illinois resident. These include: (a) electronic notice; (b) written notice; (c) substitute notice, if there would be a prohibitive cost or if more than 500,00 people are impacted, which may include email, conspicuous posting, and major statewide media; or (d) method provided within company policy. [815 ILCS 530/ Personal Information Protection Act]

California requires the impacted individuals to be contacted immediately, except in situations where the delay is required due to a criminal investigation that would be impeded by the notification. [Civil Code § 1798.80–1798.84]

Q 14:55   How can the payroll department begin to incorporate data protection best practices within its daily operations?

Before a payroll department begins to incorporate data protection best practices, Payroll should determine if there are corporate standards that every department should be following. If the accounting, human resources, information technology, finance, treasury, legal, risk management, or shared services organizations of your company already have a data protection program in place, the program may be easily replicated for deployment within the payroll department. If the payroll department wants to be proactive, it can learn and understand what other companies are doing to protect their payroll data.

If any prior breaches of data within your company have occurred, learn from the mistakes and ensure the necessary changes have been implemented to prevent them from reoccurring in the future. Review incidents that have been published in the news and determine that the payroll department has the best controls in place to prevent such incidents from happening within your company. In all cases, document what are considered the best practices and refine and review them on a periodic basis.

Q 14:56   What are the considerations if there is a breach by a third party who receives or sends data to the payroll department?

In many companies, there are third-party providers for stock transactions, health benefits, 401(k) plans, etc. that send files and communications back and forth. The company should require each vendor to provide a copy of its written guidelines, policies, and procedures that relate to the protection of the company's data and its criteria and process for notifying customers of a data breach. If successfully stipulated within your service contract, the company should be made aware of breaches by the vendor company even if the breach is related to another customer.

The payroll department should ensure that data is transmitted in a secure manner, which might involve measures such as using encrypted files or placing data on FTP-type servers.

Awareness and Education

Q 14:57   How should the payroll department staff be educated about data privacy?

Building data privacy awareness requires an ongoing commitment from management and engaging other departments within the company. The best way to build privacy awareness and education for the payroll department is to discuss these topics during regular staff meetings. Also, Payroll may reach out to HR, IT, the legal department, and risk management teams about existing data protection training materials and programs that already exist within the company and share them with the payroll staff. Some of the materials may even be in the form of a video tutorial accessible via the Internet or Intranet. If there are no materials within your company, then some other options are to locate them in the public domain. Many government entities throughout the world provide some excellent resources to help build public awareness about data privacy matters for the individual and organizations.

Q 14:58   **What are the key topics to cover with the payroll staff to ensure that the data privacy and data protection guidelines are understood and followed?**

The members of the payroll department should understand the basic topics regarding data privacy. For example, a first step would be to define data privacy and data protection. Ensure that everyone is clear on the meaning and understanding of these terms. Provide examples of the types of data that the payroll department handles and where the data comes from and is sent to once it leaves the payroll department. Discuss policies and protocols around how information requests from other departments or third-party vendors must be screened to ensure that personally identifiable information (PII) is not sent to those who really do not need access to that specific information.

In recent months, there have been examples of requests for data that appear to be from a company executive or from another legitimate source but are really a scam. Data requests should be in writing, and a verbal confirmation should be obtained before releasing any sensitive information.

Example. The General Ledger (GL) team has to update the GL with relocation expenses paid by the company. Payroll has a list of all the employees who received those reimbursements. Payroll does not want to send the spreadsheet with names and amounts when the GL team may only require the totals.

Another focus for data privacy and protection is on the physical protection of employee data within the payroll department and the degree of vulnerability around the physical security of employee data. These areas must be examined and recommendations made to improve or mitigate the findings.

Another topic is data flows within your organization and how your third-party consultants or service providers should be protecting your employee data.

It is a good idea to document the material covered in these team sessions so the information can then be leveraged to support existing risk and vendor management programs, as well as, new and emerging privacy awareness and education programs.

Q 14:59   **What are sources for finding materials for requirements about data privacy and data protection?**

In addition to resources within your company through HR, IT, risk management, or internal audit departments or a data privacy and security team, there are external organizations that can be a source for you. Examples of such sources are:

- The International Association of Privacy Professionals (IAPP) (https://www.privacyassociation.org/)
- The Federal Trade Commission (http://business.ftc.gov/privacy-and-security)

- The National Cyber Security Alliance (NCSA) (http://www.staysafe online.org/data-privacy-day/business-resources/)

- The American Payroll Association (APA) Strategic Payroll Leadership Task Force with subcommittees that focus on best practices, emerging technologies, global issues and outsourcing practices that could provide assistance (http://www.americanpayroll.org/community/bio/?pid = 50)

- The American Institute of CPAs (AICPA) website on privacy and data protection matters (http://www.aicpa.org/INTERESTAREAS/ INFORMATIONTECHNOLOGY/RESOURCES/PRIVACY/Pages/default.aspx).

In addition, there are specific industry or market segments that have their own industry or professional associations. Many of these organizations may have their own data privacy and security-oriented resources for their members that you can tap into to address various nuances of specific industries, professions, or trades.

Q 14:60   Should Payroll have a written policy about receiving PII from employees and giving PII to employees?

Yes. Payroll should have a written policy highlighting protocols for receiving communications from employees that contain their PII, as well as how to provide information to employees in a secure way. This policy should be communicated to the teams and reviewed to make changes as required.

Q 14:61   To whom should Payroll work with internally to help write, finalize, and disseminate the payroll department communications policy to employees?

Your payroll leader should initially reach out to your organization's Corporate Communications and HR to discuss how to best compose and share your payroll communications policy with employees. It would also be an excellent idea to have a dialogue with the data privacy and security team members about your policy as they may have some input to ensure that you minimize the risk around communications of PII to and from the payroll department. These teams can also help to successfully educate your workforce about these payroll department communication policies.

Q 14:62   What topics should the payroll department communication policies for employees specifically address?

The topics that should be addressed in a payroll department communications policy should include the following:

- *Email communications:* What to include and not include within emails between employees and the payroll department related to PII.

- *Fax communications:* Share specific fax numbers assigned to specific paper-based machines that operate or can only be accessed in physically secured areas of the payroll department.

Note. Fax service technology that allows employees to fax information directly into a payroll department controlled email account needs further data privacy and security evaluation.

- *Employee self-service use:* Tips for employees on how and where to securely access and send to the payroll department through your entity's employee self-service systems payroll PII, such as Forms W-2, paycheck deposit advice, electronic Forms I-9, Forms W-4, and other "employee on-boarding" forms.

- *Telephone communications:* Protocols should be developed concerning telephone calls between employees and the payroll department as well as voicemail use.

Note. Employees should never leave voicemail messages with the payroll department that include their PII. The protocol should include verification of the identity of the employee.

- *Physical inter-office mail:* Policies related to forwarding employee PII to the payroll department should be well thought out and shared with your team. Some companies distribute Forms W-2 to their employees via email. It is important to have the necessary controls in place to ensure that the intended party receives the email.

Note. It is generally not advisable to send unsecured paper documents with employee PII within your company.

- *Discussing employee information with third parties:* The payroll department should work with the HR department to determine the circumstances when the payroll staff can discuss employee PII with external third parties (e.g., collection agencies, contractors, employees' family members, financial institutions, government entities, etc.).

Q 14:63 What is the best way to disseminate the communication and information exchange policies with employees to promote data privacy and security?

Work with your HR counterparts to incorporate your policy into any existing employee handbook that is shared during the new hire on-boarding process. If you have a company Intranet website, you may have a specific area within it that provides information to employees on a variety of subjects related to internal communications, policies, and operations related to your entity.

Q 14:64 How does the payroll department ensure that its HR and payroll employee self-service system protects employee PII?

A dialogue about data privacy and security matters with your third-party provider should have occurred prior to signing a service contract including the self-service functionality. If data privacy and security issues related to employee provided PII to the system was not addressed, initiate a discussion about it and ensure that the matter is revisited when renewing the service contract.

Data Privacy and Other Laws

Q 14:65   Since payroll departments handle employee PII, interact with financial institutions through the use of direct deposit and/or payroll cards, and make employment tax deposits to various financial institutions, is Payroll subject to the "privacy rule" provision of Gramm-Leach-Bliley (GLB) Act?

No. Generally, the GLB "privacy rule" only applies to U.S.-based financial institutions (FIs). The basic tenet of GLB is that it requires financial institutions to provide notice to their customers about their specific consumer data-sharing practices with affiliates and third-party partners and provides them with some "opt-out" rights related to these business practices related to information sharing. FIs must also protect the consumer data that they collect.

Q 14:66   Is the execution of effective data privacy and protection practices within the payroll department relevant to the Sarbanes-Oxley (SOX) compliance responsibilities of a publicly traded U.S. company?

Yes. Section 404 of SOX requires publicly traded companies to establish data access, retrieval, and storage controls to data systems, including those related to payroll administration. This means that your company must have strong identity management policies and programs with regard to accessing employee data within payroll systems. In addition, to ensure the integrity of payroll data, the protection of this data from unauthorized access and misuse is critical. Lack of "controls" associated with the protection of data from a potential "breach" may also lead to broader questions during an audit about the effectiveness of your entire Section 404 SOX compliance program.

Third-Party Service Providers

Q 14:67   What is the responsibility of a third-party service provider to ensure a client's data is protected?

When an employer engages a third-party service provider to perform payroll or tax services, there must be controls in place to ensure that PII data is secure. The employer is always ultimately responsible for the security of the data but it is important to ask the questions before the company signs the contract.

Q 14:68   What controls should the service provider have in place to ensure the company's data is secure?

The controls that will ensure that PII data is protected will be similar to the controls that would be in place in your payroll organization. The guidelines on what is considered PII data, the access to that data, and how the data moves within the company as well as to the service provider must be in place and communicated to the service provider. In addition, the service provider should tell Payroll who in the vendor's company will have access to which data. Files that have secure data should be encrypted. The vendor will engage proactively to employ adequate data protection policies, best practices, and standards when managing, processing, and storing PII related to their payroll data. However, in the eyes of various governments and regulators throughout the globe, your company is ultimately responsible for the protection of its employee and customer PII regardless of outsourced service provider relationships that the company chooses to have. With this in mind, it is critical that the payroll department incorporate clear and strong data protection clauses within its service provider contract agreements to ensure that the vendor fully adheres to the company's established data protection compliance policies, procedures, and protocols.

Q 14:69   What information should be covered in the data privacy policies and procedures of a third-party provider?

Payroll should provide the business requirements around privacy and other considerations to be included in a contract for a service provider or software vendor. When evaluating a third-party provider, its data privacy program should include the following areas:

- An understanding of your company's PII and sensitive PII
- Security around software and hardware and the vulnerability for a security breach
- The protocol to access secure data regarding your account
- Physical security of the data
- Security around your data and the data of other clients to ensure there is no leakage
- Confirmation of the use of subcontractors and their specific data protection practices
- Data ownership, retention, and destruction policies at the conclusion of the contract
- A disaster recovery and business continuity program
- The ability to initiate spot audits and site visits at vendor and subcontractor locations
- Guidelines on record retention and destruction of client records.

Q 14:70   How does Payroll validate if the third-party provider follows Payroll's stated data privacy and security controls, policies, and procedures?

The first document Payroll should request is its own internal document regarding the company's own data privacy and security practices. Then Payroll should request the similar data privacy and security practices of the third-party provider. By obtaining a copy of the vendor's own stated data protection practices, Payroll can then review them and compare and contrast them to those of its own organization. Optimally, Payroll will also want to request and review copies of the vendor's SSAE 16 audit reports too. SSAE 16 replaces the SAS 70 audits that clients relied upon to demonstrate that the third-party vendor has sufficient controls in place through documentation and practice to protect their clients' information.

Q 14:71   What is an SSAE 16 audit report?

SSAE 16 stands for "Statements on Standards of Attestation Engagements - Number 16." SSAE 16 and other SSAEs are issued by senior technical bodies within the American Institute of CPAs (AICPA) to make recommendations about attestation standards related to specific business and financial practices. SSAE 16 "addresses examination engagements undertaken by a service auditor to report on controls at organizations that provide services to user entities when those controls are likely to be relevant to user entities' internal control over financial reporting."

Q 14:72   Should Payroll physically visit the third-party vendor's site where payroll processes are conducted and employee data is stored?

Yes, where feasible. Conduct your full due diligence and request a physical site security review visit of the third-party vendor's facilities where it processes and stores your payroll data. It is advisable that IT managers also visit the facilities and ask relevant questions related to the best practices and technology used at the site to protect data. Where it is not feasible to conduct an onsite visit, ensure that you have a clear idea of the trail of your data within the vendor's organization, including the personnel who will have access to your company's information.

Q 14:73   Should a third-party vendor contract include the right to a regularly scheduled audit of the payroll vendor's data protection and security practices?

Yes. Payroll should include a mandatory clause in its vendor contract that stipulates that Payroll may audit the vendor's service practices, including those related to data privacy and security. If the vendor objects, DO NOT sign a contract with the vendor.

Data Breach Notification

Q 14:74   Should the vendor contract include a "breach notification" clause?

Absolutely! If the third-party vendor experiences a reportable breach that impacts your employee PII, Payroll will need to know about the breach because the vendor is essentially your proxy. This means that in the context of a data breach, your company is still legally responsible for the breach even though it may not have occurred in the physical location of your organization. Since most states have data security protection, your company will probably have some reporting obligation. Ultimately, government regulators could fine and sanction your company for a breach originating from your vendor's site or systems.

Q 14:75   Should a company have a dialogue with a vendor about a specific "disaster" plan and strategy related to any potential data breach events?

Yes. In fact, it is important that Payroll know its company's own data breach response plan in case the PII of your employees ever becomes compromised as a result of any internal or external breach. Payroll should also be clear about how its vendors handle breach events and how they can assist when and if a breach arises in the future. Both the vendor and the company should have a documented breach reaction strategy. Specific internal stakeholders to assist with any potential data breach should include your legal, HR, privacy, security, PR, and government affairs and relations teams. Other external consultants may need to be called in with regard to computer forensics to determine when and if a breach occurred and the scope of the event.

Q 14:76   Should Payroll have a strategy to "off-board" third-party payroll service and software vendors in the event Payroll wants to migrate to a new vendor?

It is critical that Payroll always have an "off-boarding" strategy with its significant core payroll administration vendors in the event they fail to live up to the contract. This means that Payroll should incorporate language in the initial contract with the vendor about who owns the data at the end of the contract, how Payroll can access and obtain the data at the end of the contract, and define the data use and destruction policies after the client relationship has ended. For example, the contract should be very clear about the fact that the vendor may not keep the data and use it for other commercial or non-commercial use during or after the conclusion of the contract.

Q 14:77   Do offshore payroll-service providers need to be managed any differently?

Offshore service providers should be managed in the same manner as onshore service providers with respect to data protection expectations, roles, and responsibilities. Depending on where the service provider's offshore payroll processes operate, your payroll department will need to ensure that it adheres to specific data protection practices based on the local laws and regulations of the country where the processing occurs, particularly if you are involved with a country in the EU. In addition, the specific laws and regulations of the country where the employee data originates need to be considered. Again, this should be addressed within the service provider contract.

Q 14:78   How should a payroll department address the issue of subcontractors with regard to the various third-party service providers it may engage to perform employee data management, processing, storage, and transport as it pertains to data privacy and security?

The payroll department should have an honest dialogue about the role of any subcontractors who may perform work on behalf of their third-party service providers that allows them access to your company's employee data. It should be made clear in the service agreement contract that all subcontractors must abide by the agreed-upon data privacy and security practices and protocols.

Q 14:79   Is the procedure any different for offshore work performed by your own entity's employees?

If your organization is global, it is advisable to have a clear and comprehensive data privacy and protection policy that all company employees must follow regardless of where work is performed in the world. Again, companies must be sensitive to country-specific data protection laws and regulations too.

Q 14:80   What data privacy considerations should be considered with regard to third-party contractors, service providers, or vendors that support the payroll department seasonally or with multi-year contractual agreements?

Even when Payroll brings in seasonal workers year after year, it is still important that HR or a temporary service agency properly screen these individuals by running background checks to ensure they have no known criminal history or financial problems that could potentially create a greater risk of a data theft. Seasonal workers should also be trained about your specific data privacy and protection best practices and procedures.

Cloud Computing

Q 14:81 How does a payroll department use cloud computing?

For many years, many individuals have been utilizing cloud computing services such as Internet (web-based) email where a company hosts the service on its computers (servers) and it is then accessed at will (24/7) by customers via a standard web browser. Now, there are countless software-as-a-service (SaaS) applications that individuals and small businesses can access in the same manner on the Internet in the "cloud." These SaaS solutions include those related to business accounting and personal finance, customer relationship management (CRM), file and photo sharing, back-up storage, personal and business social networking, gaming, and even tax preparation to name a few.

Large and mid-sized entities are now starting to deploy cloud-based SaaS solutions designed for their specific enterprise needs to manage and operate core front and back office business processes, even on a global scale. Some of the benefits of moving to the "cloud" are cost savings related to moving away from customized software upgrades and server ownership costs (maintenance and upgrades), subscription-based pricing models (per user), software updates managed by the SaaS vendor, and customers/users access applications via the Internet using a web browser. However, some of the prominent concerns of cloud computing (SaaS) solutions include ensuring consistent and real 24/7 access to applications and data, data privacy and security compliance, and data migration and ownership issues if the data processing, managing, or storage is moved.

Q 14:82 What are the primary data privacy and protection considerations for selecting a cloud computing provider?

When selecting a cloud computing provider, its capability to offer the level of security and controls that the internal IT organization maintains should be evaluated. This is the case even if the employee data is processed, managed, and stored in the United States. Your cloud solution provider must maintain the proper level of security for its applications and storage, whether it is onshore or offshore.

Q 14:83 What is required from the cloud service provider regarding the physical location where the data will be stored?

A comprehensive dialogue with your cloud computing provider should be held to discuss the exact physical locations of where your data will be processed, managed, and stored. The locations where your company data will be physically backed up for disaster recovery purposes should be disclosed. The reason for this is to be able to validate the existence and compliance of laws and regulations governing the protection of employee data and the movement of this data to and from countries and/or across continents. Companies with a global footprint have additional complexities to address as there are cross-border considerations.

Q 14:84   Which other internal departments and stakeholders should be included in the selection process for a cloud computing provider for our specific payroll administration environment and footprint?

The payroll organization should engage representatives from HR, Accounting, Finance, IT, Legal, and Risk Management to serve as advisors during your cloud computing provider selection process. Each representative may have requirements for scope and specifications of your future cloud solution including data privacy and security issues. There may be additional services under consideration such as HR (employee management), finance, etc. that could seamlessly connect with each other and add value and cost savings to the entire company. One single cloud provider could offer services beyond payroll administration.

Q 14:85   What criteria can be utilized to measure and validate solution providers, ensuring that Payroll is protecting its employee data wherever it is processed, managed, and stored?

Most IT departments have standards for data encryption, data protocols, storage mediums, and network administration. It is important to establish service level agreements (SLAs) with vendors that reflect the key requirements. The company's internal data privacy and security experts must be engaged to validate that the cloud provider can adequately protect your employee data. The experts can provide guidance to establish the appropriate service level agreements related to data privacy and security, including data encryption practices and standards.

Q 14:86   What is the best means to ensure that a cloud provider is adequately keeping up with changes, especially to federal and state regulations, to protect employee data?

Your internal data privacy and security experts can render advice about setting data protection expectations for the cloud solutions provider. In addition, legal counsel should be consulted about this matter when a cloud provider's service contract is being prepared or modified.

Q 14:87   What are key considerations for cloud provider's service contracts?

The following are some of the key and often overlooked aspects of cloud computing service provider contracts that Payroll and its extended internal team should address with legal counsel:

- A commitment to stay abreast and comply with all country and regional specific laws and regulations governing the processing, management, storage, and transport of employee or company data, including data privacy and security measures.

- Full disclosure and knowledge of any use of subcontractors and their country of operations to fulfill the obligations of the contract and assurances that these entities will also follow all of the provisions of the contract, including data privacy and security measures. Consider the issue of indemnification for provider's employees and contractors.

- Actual ownership rights of your company's employee data that is being processed within your cloud provider's data environment during and after your contract ends.

- Payroll's retrieval of all of its employee data at the conclusion of a contract for potential data migration to another (future) payroll system and data retention and destruction policies of your service provider with regard to your data.

- The restriction that the cloud provider can only manage, process, transport, and store your employee data for your company's intended use for specific services to be performed (i.e., pay workers, pay taxes, e-file information returns, new-hire reporting, I-9 work authorization verification, electronic payments, etc.) and for no other purpose that may relate to the provider or related companies or parent company.

- Security regarding employees' background checks and proper training for current and former employees.

- Provisions in the contract that allow for spot audits of your cloud provider and/or its subcontractors.

- The right to examine annual and quarterly external audit reports from reputable third parties related to risk management and system controls. [SSAE-16, superseded SAS 70 reports]

- Reports of data breach(es) that the vendor has committed in the past five years.

Global Payroll Data Protection

Q 14:88   Is the data protection and security compliance landscape the same in every country or region of the world?

No, the legal and regulatory landscape for data privacy and security is vastly different in various countries and regions of the world.

Q 14:89   What are the primary differences between data protection laws and mindsets in the United States compared to countries within, for example, the European Union?

European Union (EU) member nations consider privacy as a "fundamental human right" and developed what is called the EU Data Protection Directive (aka 95/96/EC or "the Directive"), which is a comprehensive law governing data privacy within the private and public sectors. [http://ec.europa.eu/justice/data-protection/index_en.htm] The United States has taken the approach of promoting data privacy and protection for its citizens by regulating data collection and use by industry/sector (e.g., financial services and health care) as well as through self-regulatory bodies, entities, or groups. Forty-seven out of 50 states, as well as the District of Columbia, Virgin Islands, Guam, and Puerto Rico, have implemented some sort of data breach law, with some states starting to pass legislation to address minimum data security standards within organizations. Alabama, New Mexico, and South Dakota are the three states that do not have data privacy requirements.

Q 14:90   How can data privacy and security compliance concerns be addressed within all of the countries where employees work and are paid?

Your central payroll organization and management team will have to first define the data elements that must be protected for each of the nations where the company pays employees. Payroll must also be aware of the employee data flows (including contractors and third-party vendors) from each regional payroll site and research the data privacy and data transfer laws of each country. Also note that there may be additional considerations when workers are represented by labor or trade unions because Works Councils within the EU have a tremendous amount of input and control concerning how their data can be collected and handled by employers. This means Payroll should work closely with the country-specific or regional HR teams to understand how to effectively interact with the foreign workforce on data privacy, transport, protection, and use matters.

Q 14:91   Who can assist the payroll department to address the company's global data protection strategy?

Payroll will want to leverage HR counterparts, IT, legal department and risk management team(s) and seek their country-specific guidance on employee data collection, privacy, transport and use matters related to payroll processing. If the company is a large global entity, it may even have dedicated data privacy and security teams that can help guide Payroll through this process to ensure that the company complies with country-specific laws governing employee data.

Q 14:92   Can the payroll department freely move employee payroll data to and from the United States for processing?

No. There are many country-specific laws that regulate how and where employee data can be transported and used for business processes like payroll administration. For example, the EU does not deem the United States' data protection laws as "adequate" for allowing the transfer of personal data (including for payroll processing) of EU member country citizens to the United States. However, the EU and the United States established what is called the "Safe Harbor Framework" agreement in 2000 that created a legal path for U.S. entities to self-certify and publicly declare that they comply with the EU privacy protection "Directive." With this in mind, payroll departments proactively engaged their legal departments and regional HR organizations about their entity's participation in the "Safe Harbor" program and would indeed satisfy the requirements of country-specific data protection laws and regulations related to employee data. It was advisable to engage EU unions and/or work councils on this matter, too, even if you participated in the Safe Harbor program. This process worked for the past 15 years.

The European Court of Justice ruled that the Safe Harbor agreement, in place for the past 15 years, is invalid. There are over 4,000 U.S. companies that transact business in the European Union and are impacted by this ruling. The Court does not believe, in light of the NSA-Snowden leak, that there is sufficient assurance of the protection of data that crosses the borders. To address this immediate gap, the United States Department of Commerce met with the European Commission and developed a new agreement.

On February 2, 2016, the U.S. Department of Commerce reached an agreement with the European Commission, entitled the EU-U.S. Privacy Shield, to create a new framework to replace the now defunct Safe Harbor agreement. The European Commission formally approved the agreement on July 8, 2016. The substance of the agreement includes:

- Stronger obligation on the part of the United States to protect the PI of EU citizens
- Increased monitoring and enforcement of covered activities
- Provision that there will be no mass surveillance of EU citizens
- Increased controls for data of EU citizens passed to third parties.

For countries outside the European Union, you must do your research about the data privacy laws related to your global footprint.

Q 14:93   Are there any current provisions that would allow a U.S. entity to transfer EU employee data to the United States to perform various data management and processing tasks including payroll administration?

Yes. As the Safe Harbor Framework ends and a new era of the Privacy Shield begins, companies will have to determine how the increased requirements for data oversight and monitoring will be implemented. Under the Safe Harbor

Framework there was a legal path for U.S. entities to self-certify and publicly declare that they comply with the EU privacy protection "Directive." With the new Privacy Shield, companies will have to wait and see what practices may continue and what may become new requirements.

Q 14:94   What is required to "self certify" with the U.S. Department of Commerce in order to comply with the new Privacy Shield program?

The requirements are similar to the former Safe Harbor self-certification, although the Department of Commerce is to be more active in the oversight. To successfully enter the Privacy Shield program, an entity must fulfill the following requirements:

• Read the EU-U.S. Safe Harbor privacy principles, 15 FAQs, and enforcement documents

• Develop a privacy policy statement that complies with the Safe Harbor program

• Establish an independent recourse mechanism within the entity (e.g., private dispute resolution mechanism or direct accountability to European data protection regulators)

• Ensure that recourse mechanism options are free of charge to individuals making a complaint

• Ensure that a verification mechanism is in place within the entity

• Agree to investigate complaints within 45 days

• Designate a specific contact within the entity with regard to the Privacy Shield program

• Fill out and submit the self-certification form.

Q 14:95   Following the implementation of the Privacy Shield, are there any other regulations in the European Union that may affect U.S. companies?

Yes. In addition to the agreement between the United States and the EU, the EU has approved the General Data Protection Regulation (GDPR), effective in 2018, which creates a standard throughout the EU that covers businesses selling goods and services in Europe, particularly around the process or storage of personal data of EU citizens.

Q 14:96   What are the elements of the new law?

The elements of the new law are as follows:

1. Expanded trade: The law applies to EU companies and those that process EU subject data.

2. Accountability: Both processor and controller have responsibility regarding privacy assurance.

3. A data protection officer must be appointed, particularly if dealing with employee data.

4. Consent to use of data must be explicit, subject to request or rescind.

5. Notification must be made within 72 hours of discovery.

6. Penalties can be up to 4 percent of the worldwide revenue.

The impact on Brexit on the data privacy landscape is yet to be seen.

Q 14:97   What rules are in place for countries in the Asia Pacific (APAC) region?

The APAC region does not have a single, comprehensive plan such as EMEA, and there are no regional guidelines on data privacy. There is, however, the APEC Cross Border Privacy Rules System, which is modeled on the EU process. Some of the early adopters were Australia, the Netherlands, Hong Kong, and Japan. Below is a sampling of various approaches in the region.

China has taken a layered approach to cyber security, making use of three regulations; the National Security Law, the Cyber Security Law, and the Counter-Terrorism Law. With the explosive growth in the region, China is looking for a more comprehensive approach in the future. There is no single body overseeing data privacy.

The most comprehensive rules are in South Korea, which has implemented the Personal Information Protection Act and the IT Network Act, imposing extensive registration and disclosure requirements. The country has recently added punitive damages.

Japan, one of the early adopters of privacy regulation, has passed new legislation that provides extensive reforms to address recent high-profile data breaches.

The Philippines National Policy Commission published final regulations on implementing the Data Privacy Act of 2012. One important provision is that when data is collected in a foreign jurisdiction for processing in the Philippines, these regulations will still apply. With a number of outsourcing functions in the Philippines, this may provide some reassurance that there are data protections in place.

Singapore has implemented the Personal Data Protection Act, which carries stiff penalties of up to S$1 million (USD800,000) for data protection offenses.

Q 14:98   How can the payroll department keep track of new or updated data protection laws and regulations throughout the world that could have an impact on the global payroll operations?

The company's internal data privacy or security department may already be keeping track of data protection laws and regulations that impact your entire organization on a global scale. If these teams don't exist within the company, seek legal counsel about how best to track the laws and regulations as there are implications related to them beyond the payroll department. If your company has a global vendor, it may offer that service as a part of its contract or as an available service for an additional fee.

Q 14:99 How does Payroll effectively manage the company's global payroll administration process if it is decentralized by country or region with multiple payroll teams and third-party processors?

When a global payroll administration process is decentralized, each country- or region-specific team may have to independently institute a data protection program to fully manage the company's risk. However, much of the data protection policies, procedures, best practices, and educational materials centrally developed can be leveraged and then modified as appropriate based on local laws and regulations related to data protection. One strategy is to build a network of privacy champions within all of your global payroll teams to help promote your data privacy and protection policies related to employee-oriented PII.

Q 14:100 How does the payroll organization effectively manage data privacy and security risk for employee data (PII) on a global scale?

A global organization with a large footprint may have global data privacy, security, and risk management teams already working on data protection projects. If not, the entire organization will need to address global data protection matters beyond the payroll department. Therefore, the payroll department should not try to tackle global data protection compliance on its own without consulting with senior management about developing a comprehensive strategy.

If your organization has any presence in the European Union, explore the European Commission website that focuses on the "Protection of Personal Data" (http://ec.europa.eu/justice/data-protection/index_en.htm).

If your organization has a presence in Canada and Payroll will be processing personal data, consult The Office of the Privacy Commissioner of Canada (OPC) and some of their privacy educational resources (http://www.priv.gc.ca/index_e.asp) and the Personal Information Protection and Electronic Documents Act (PIPEDA) (http://www.priv.gc.ca/leg_c/leg_c_p_e.asp).

If your organization conducts business in the Asia-Pacific region, Payroll will also want to explore and understand the new *Asia-Pacific Economic Cooperation* (APEC) *Cross-Border Privacy Rules* (CBPRs), which were issued by the *APEC Electronic Commerce Steering Group* (http://www.apec.org/Groups/Committee-on-Trade-and-Investment/Electronic-Commerce-Steering-Group.aspx). CBPRs are a "voluntary, certification-based system promotes a consistent baseline set of data privacy practices for companies doing business in participating APEC economies."

Appendix A

Directory of State Labor Departments

ALABAMA
Dept. of Labor
649 Monroe Street
Montgomery, AL 36131
334-242-8888
www.labor.alabama.gov

ALASKA
Dept. of Labor & Workforce Development
Div. of Labor Standards and Safety
Wage and Hour Administration
1111 W. 8th Street, Rm. 302
P.O. Box 111149
Juneau, AK 99811-1149
907-465-4842
email: Juneau.LSS-WH@alaska.gov;
http://labor.state.ak.us/lss/whhome.htm

ARIZONA
Industrial Commission
Labor Dept.
800 W. Washington Street
Phoenix, AZ 85007
602-542-4515;
2675 E. Broadway Blvd.
Tucson, AZ 85716
520-628-5459
www.azica.gov

ARKANSAS
Dept. of Labor
10421 W. Markham Street
Little Rock, AR 72205
501-682-4500
email: asklabor@arkansas.gov;
www.labor.ar.gov/

CALIFORNIA	Dept. of Industrial Relations Div. of Labor Standards Enforcement 455 Golden Gate Avenue San Francisco, CA 94102 415-703-5300 (Office Line) www.dir.ca.gov
COLORADO	Dept. of Labor & Employment Div. of Labor 633 17th Street, Ste. 200 Denver, CO 80202-3611 303-318-8441 email: cdle_labor_standards@state.co.us; www.colorado.gov/CDLE/labor
CONNECTICUT	Dept. of Labor Div. of Wage and Workplace Standards 200 Folly Brook Boulevard Wethersfield, CT 06109 860-263-6790 email: dol.webhelp@ct.gov; http://www.ctdol.state.ct.us/wgwkstnd/
DELAWARE	Dept. of Labor Div. of Industrial Affairs 4425 N. Market Street, 3rd Fl. Wilmington, DE 19802 302-761-8200 http://dia.delawareworks.com/
DISTRICT OF COLUMBIA	Dept. of Employment Services 4058 Minnesota Avenue, N.E. Washington, DC 20019 202-724-7000 email: does@dc.gov; http://does.dc.gov/page/employers
FLORIDA	Dept. of Economic Opportunity 107 E. Madison Street Caldwell Bldg. Tallahassee, FL 32399-4120 850-245-7105 www.floridajobs.org

GEORGIA
Dept. of Labor
148 Andrew Young International Boulevard, N.E.,
Ste. 600
Atlanta, GA 30303
404-232-7300
http://dol.georgia.gov/employers

HAWAII
Dept. of Labor & Industrial Relations
Wage Standards Div.
830 Punchbowl Street, Rm. 321
Honolulu, HI 96813
808-586-8777
email: dlir.wages@hawaii.gov;
http://labor.hawaii.gov/

IDAHO
Dept. of Labor
317 W. Main Street
Boise, ID 83735
208-332-3570
http://labor.idaho.gov

ILLINOIS
Dept. of Labor
Fair Labor Standards Div.
160 N. LaSalle C-1300
Chicago, IL 60601
900 S. Spring Street
Springfield, IL 62704
312-793-2804;
800-478-3998 (Minimum Wage/Overtime Hotline)
www.illinois.gov/idol/Pages/default.aspx

INDIANA
Dept. of Labor
Gov't Center—South
402 W. Washington Street, Rm. W195
Indianapolis, IN 46204
317-232-2655
www.in.gov/dol

IOWA
Workforce Development
Div. of Labor Services—Wage
1000 E. Grand Avenue
Des Moines, IA 50319-0209
515-242-2182
www.iowadivisionoflabor.gov

KANSAS	Dept. of Labor Employment Standards 401 S.W. Topeka Boulevard Topeka, KS 66603-3182 785-296-5000, ext. 1068 www.dol.ks.gov
KENTUCKY	Dept. of Workplace Standards Division of Employment Standards Apprenticeship and Mediation 1047 U.S. Highway 127 S., Ste. 4 Frankfort, KY 40601 502-564-3534 email: labor.desam@ky.gov; www.labor.ky.gov/dows/Pages/Department-of-Workplace-Standards.aspx
LOUISIANA	Workforce Commission 1001 N. 23rd Street P.O. Box 94094 Baton Rouge, LA 70804-9094 225-342-3111 www.laworks.net
MAINE	Dept. of Labor Bureau of Labor Standards 45 State House Station Augusta, ME 04333-0045 207-623-7900 email: mdol@maine.gov; www.maine.gov/labor/bls
MARYLAND	Dept. of Labor, Licensing, and Regulation Div. of Labor and Industry 1100 N. Eutaw Street, Rm. 600 Baltimore, MD 21201 410-767-2241; 410-767-2342 (Prevailing Wage) email: dldlilaborindustry-dllr@maryland.gov; www.dllr.state.md.us/labor/
MASSACHUSETTS	Office of Labor and Workforce Development Dept. of Labor Standards 19 Staniford St., 2nd Fl. Boston, MA 02114 617-626-6975 (General information); 617-626-6952 (Minimum wage) email: DLSFeedback@state.ma.us; www.mass.gov/lwd/labor-standards

MICHIGAN	Dept. of Licensing and Regulatory Affairs Wage and Hour Program 530 W. Allegan St., 2nd Fl., Lansing, MI 48913 P.O. Box 30476 Lansing, MI 48909-7976 855-464-9243; 517-284-7800 email: whinfo@michigan.gov; www.michigan.gov/lara
MINNESOTA	Dept. of Labor & Industry Labor Standards Unit 443 Lafayette Road N. St. Paul, MN 55155 651-284-5070; 800-342-5354 email: dli.laborstandards@state.mn.us; www.dli.mn.gov/main.asp
MISSISSIPPI	Dept. of Employment Security Office of the Governor 1235 Echelon Parkway P.O. Box 1699 Jackson, MS 39215-1699 601-321-6000 email: comments@mdes.ms.gov; www.mdes.ms.gov/
MISSOURI	Dept. of Labor and Industrial Relations Division of Labor Standards 3315 W. Truman Boulevard, Rm. 205 P.O. Box 449 Jefferson City, MO 65102-0449 573-751-3403 email: laborstandards@labor.mo.gov; http://labor.mo.gov/dls
MONTANA	Dept. of Labor & Industry Employment Relations Div. Labor Standards Bureau Wage and Hour Unit Beck Bldg. 1805 Prospect Avenue Helena, MT 59601 Mailing address: P.O. Box 201503 Helena, MT 59620-1503 406-444-5600 http://erd.dli.mt.gov/labor-standards/ wage-and-hour-payment-act

NEBRASKA	Dept. of Labor Labor Standards 550 S. 16th Street P.O. Box 94600 Lincoln, NE 68509-4600 402-471-9000 email: ndol.lmi_ne@nebraska.gov; http://dol.nebraska.gov
NEVADA	Dept. of Business & Industry Office of the Labor Commissioner 555 E. Washington Avenue, Ste. 4100 Las Vegas, NV 89101 702-486-2650 email: mail1@laborcommissioner.com; http://labor.nv.gov/Employer/ Employer_Information
NEW HAMPSHIRE	Dept. of Labor State Office Park Spaulding Building 95 Pleasant Street Concord, NH 03301 603-271-3176 www.nh.gov/labor
NEW JERSEY	Dept. of Labor and Workforce Development Div. of Wage and Hour Compliance P.O. Box 389 Trenton, NJ 08625-0389 609-292-2305 email: Wage.Hour@dol.nj.gov; http://lwd.state.nj.us/labor/wagehour/ wagehour_index.html
NEW MEXICO	Department of Workforce Solutions Wage and Hour Bureau 121 Tijeras N.E., Ste. 3000 Albuquerque, NM 87102 505-841-4400 www.dws.state.nm.us/Labor-Relations/ Labor-Information/Wage-and-Hour

NEW YORK	Dept. of Labor Div. of Labor Standards W. Averell Harriman State Office Campus, Bldg. 12 Albany, NY 12240 888-469-7365; 518-457-9000 email: labor.sm.ls.ask@labor.ny.gov; www.labor.ny.gov
NORTH CAROLINA	Dept. of Labor Wage and Hour Bureau 1101 Mail Service Center Raleigh, NC 27699-1101 919-807-2796; 800-NC-LABOR (625-2267) email: DOL.Webmaster@labor.nc.gov; www.nclabor.com
NORTH DAKOTA	Dept. of Labor and Human Rights State Capitol Bldg. 600 E. Boulevard Avenue, Dept. 406 Bismarck, ND 58505-0340 701-328-2660; 800-582-8032 (in-state toll free) email: labor@nd.gov; www.nd.gov/labor/
OHIO	Dept. of Commerce Div. of Industrial Compliance and Labor Bureau of Wage and Hour Administration 6606 Tussing Road P.O. Box 4009 Reynoldsburg, OH 43068-9009 614-644-2239 email: IC@com.state.oh.us; www.com.ohio.gov/dico/
OKLAHOMA	Dept. of Labor Wage and Hour Unit 3017 N. Stiles Street, Ste. 100 Oklahoma City, OK 73105 405-521-6100; 888-269-5353 www.ok.gov/odol
OREGON	Bureau of Labor & Industries Wage and Hour Div. 800 N.E. Oregon Street, Ste. 1045 Portland, OR 97232 971-673-0844 email: whdscreener@boli.state.or.us; www.oregon.gov/BOLI/pages/index.aspx

PENNSYLVANIA	Dept. of Labor & Industry Bureau of Labor Law Compliance 1301 Labor and Industry Bldg. 7th and Forster Streets Harrisburg, PA 17121 717-787-4763; 800-932-0665 www.dli.pa.gov/
RHODE ISLAND	Dept. of Labor and Training Workforce Regulation and Safety Div. Labor Standards Unit 1511 Pontiac Avenue Cranston, RI 02920 401-462-8550 www.dlt.ri.gov/ls/
SOUTH CAROLINA	Dept. of Labor, Licensing & Regulation Synergy Business Park, Kingstree Bldg. 110 Centerview Drive Columbia, SC 29210 Mailing address: P.O. Box 11329 Columbia, SC 29211 803-896-7756; 803-896-4300 www.llr.state.sc.us
SOUTH DAKOTA	Dept. of Labor and Regulation Div. of Labor and Management Wage and Hour Office 123 W. Missouri Avenue Pierre, SD 57501 605-773-3101 http://dlr.sd.gov
TENNESSEE	Dept. of Labor and Workforce Development 220 French Landing Drive Nashville, TN 37243 844-224-5818 http://tn.gov/workforce
TEXAS	Texas Workforce Commission Labor Law Dept. 101 E. 15th St., Rm. 651 Austin, TX 78778-0001 800-832-9243 (within Texas only); 512-475-2670 www.twc.state.tx.us/businesses/employment-law-discrimination-wages-child-labor

UTAH	Labor Commission Antidiscrimination and Labor Div. 160 East 300 South, 3rd Fl. P.O. Box 146640 Salt Lake City, UT 84114-6640 801-530-6801; 800-222-1238 (in-state) email: discrimination@utah.gov; http://laborcommission.utah.gov
VERMONT	Dept. of Labor 5 Green Mountain Drive P.O. Box 488 Montpelier, VT 05601-0488 802-828-4000; 802-828-0267 (Wage and Hour Laws) http://labor.vermont.gov/
VIRGINIA	Dept. of Labor & Industry Main St. Centre Bldg. 600 E. Main St., Ste. 207 Richmond, VA 23219-4101 804-371-2327 email: laborlaw@doli.virginia.gov; www.doli.virginia.gov
WASHINGTON	Dept. of Labor & Industries P.O. Box 44000 Olympia, WA 98504-4000 360-902-5316; 866-219-7321 www.lni.wa.gov/workplacerights/
WEST VIRGINIA	Dept. of Commerce Div. of Labor State Capitol Complex, Bldg. #6, Rm. B749 Charleston, WV 25305 304-558-7890; 304-356-3929 www.wvlabor.com/newwebsite/Pages/Index.html
WISCONSIN	Dept. of Workforce Development Equal Rights Division 201 E. Washington Avenue, Rm. A100 Madison, WI 53708 Mailing address: P.O. Box 8928 Madison, WI 53708 608-266-6860 http://dwd.wisconsin.gov/er

WYOMING   Dept. of Workforce Services
Labor Standards
1510 E. Pershing Boulevard, West Wing, Rm. 150
Cheyenne, WY 82002
307-777-7261
www.wyomingworkforce.org/businesses/labor/

Appendix B

Directory of State Agencies Dealing with Income Tax Withholding

ALABAMA Dept. of Revenue
Individual and Corporate Tax Div.
Withholding Tax Section
Gordon Persons Bldg., Rm. 4326
50 N. Ripley Street
Montgomery, AL 36104
Mailing address: P.O. Box 327480
Montgomery, AL 36132-7480
334-242-1300
www.revenue.alabama.gov/Withholding/
index.cfm

ARIZONA Dept. of Revenue
1600 W. Monroe St.
Phoenix, AZ 85007-2650
Withholding Tax Returns and Payments:
P.O. Box 29009
Phoenix, AZ 85038-9009
602-255-2060; 800-843-7196 (in state)
www.azdor.gov/Business/WithholdingTax.aspx

ARKANSAS Dept. of Finance and Administration
Withholding Tax Branch
Ledbetter Bldg.
1816 W. 7th Street, Rm. 1380
Little Rock, AR 72201
Mailing address: P.O. Box 9941
Little Rock, AR 72203
501-682-7290
email: withholding@dfa.arkansas.gov;
www.dfa.arkansas.gov/offices/incometax/
withholding/Pages/default.aspx

CALIFORNIA Employment Development Dept.
800 Capitol Mall, MIC 83
Sacramento, CA 95814
Mailing address: P.O. Box 826880
Sacramento, CA 94280-0001
888-745-3886
www.edd.ca.gov/Payroll_Taxes/

COLORADO Dept. of Revenue
Div. of Taxation
1375 Sherman Street
Denver, CO 80261
303-238-7378
www.colorado.gov/revenue

CONNECTICUT Dept. of Revenue Services
450 Columbus Boulevard
Hartford, CT 06103
860-297-5962; 800-382-9463 (in state)
http://www.ct.gov/drs/cwp/
view.asp?a=1454&q=510148

DELAWARE Div. of Revenue
820 N. French Street
Wilmington, DE 19801
302-577-8779
email: michael.x.smith@state.de.us;
www.revenue.delaware.gov/services/
BusServices.shtml

DISTRICT OF COLUMBIA Office of Tax and Revenue
1101 4th Street, S.W., Ste. W270
Washington, DC 20024
202-727-4829
http://otr.cfo.dc.gov/

GEORGIA Dept. of Revenue
Taxpayer Services Div.
1800 Century Boulevard, N.E.
Atlanta, GA 30345
Mailing address: P.O. Box 49432
Atlanta, GA 30359
877-423-6711
email: taxpayer.services@dor.ga.gov;
http://dor.georgia.gov/withholding-0

HAWAII	Dept. of Taxation Taxpayer Services Branch P.O. Box 3827 Honolulu, HI 96812-3827 808-587-4242 http://tax.hawaii.gov/forms/a1_b1_5whhold/
IDAHO	State Tax Commission 800 E. Park Boulevard, Plaza IV Boise, ID 83712-7742 Mailing address: P.O. Box 36 Boise, ID 83722-0410 208-334-7660 (Boise area); 800-972-7660 email: taxrep@tax.idaho.gov; http://tax.idaho.gov/i-1026.cfm
ILLINOIS	Dept. of Revenue Willard Ice Building 101 W. Jefferson Street Springfield, IL 62702 Mailing address: P.O. Box 19052 Springfield, IL 62794-9052 Business Hot Line: 217-524-4772 217-782-3336; 800-732-8866 www.revenue.state.il.us/Businesses/ TaxInformation/Payroll/index.htm
INDIANA	Dept. of Revenue Withholding Tax P.O. Box 7222 Indianapolis, IN 46207-7222 317-233-4016; 317-615-2581 (to order forms) email: businesstaxassistance@dor.in.gov; www.in.gov/dor/index.htm
IOWA	Dept. of Revenue Withholding Correspondence P.O. Box 10465 Des Moines, IA 50306-0465 515-281-3114; 800-367-3388 email: idr@iowa.gov; https://tax.iowa.gov/withholding-tax- information-0

KANSAS

Dept. of Revenue
Taxpayer Assistance Center
Withholding Tax
Docking State Office Bldg.
915 S.W. Harrison Street, Rm. 150
Topeka, KS 66612-1588
785-368-8222
email: kdor_tax@ks.gov;
www.ksrevenue.org/withholdingtt.html

KENTUCKY

Dept. of Revenue
Withholding Tax Branch
P.O. Box 181, Station 57
Frankfort, KY 40602-0181
502-564-7287
http://revenue.ky.gov/Business/Pages/Employer-
Payroll-Withholding.aspx

LOUISIANA

Dept. of Revenue
Withholding Tax
617 N. Third Street
Baton Rouge, LA 70802
Mailing address: P.O. Box 201
Baton Rouge, LA 70821-0201
225-219-7462
http://www.revenue.louisiana.gov/
WithholdingTax

MAINE

Revenue Services
Withholding Tax
Taxpayer Service Center
51 Commerce Drive
Augusta, ME 04330
Mailing address: P.O. Box 1060
Augusta, ME 04332-1060
207-626-8475
email: withholding.tax@maine.gov;
www.maine.gov/revenue/incomeestate/with/
withuc.htm

MARYLAND	Comptroller of Maryland Revenue Administration Center 110 Carroll Street Annapolis, MD 21411-0001 410-260-7980; 800-638-2937 email: taxhelp@comp.state.md.us; http://taxes.marylandtaxes.com/Business_Taxes/ Business_Tax_Types/Income_Tax/Employer_ Withholding/
MASSACHUSETTS	Dept. of Revenue 100 Cambridge Street Boston, MA 02114 Mailing address: P.O. Box 7010 Boston, MA 02204 617-887-6367; 800-392-6089 www.mass.gov/dor/all-taxes/income/ withholding/
MICHIGAN	Dept. of Treasury Sales, Use, and Withholding Taxes Div. 430 W. Allegan Street Lansing, MI 48922 517-636-6925 www.michigan.gov/treasury
MINNESOTA	Dept. of Revenue Income Tax and Withholding Div. Mail Station 6501 St. Paul, MN 55146-6501 651-282-9999; 800-657-3594 www.revenue.state.mn.us/businesses/ withholding/Pages/File-and-Pay.aspx
MISSISSIPPI	Dept. of Revenue Withholding Tax Div. South Pointe Bldg. Plaza 500 Clinton Center Dr. Clinton, MS 39056 Attention: Withholding P.O. Box 1033 Jackson, MS 39215-1033 601-923-7088 www.dor.ms.gov/Business/Pages/ Withholding-Tax.aspx

MISSOURI

Dept. of Revenue
Employer Withholding Tax
Harry S. Truman State Office Bldg.
301 W. High Street, Rm. 102
Jefferson City, MO 65101
Mailing address: P.O. Box 3375
Jefferson City, MO 65105-3375
573-751-8750
For forms: 800-877-6881
email: withholding@dor.mo.gov;
http://dor.mo.gov/business/withhold/

MONTANA

Dept. of Revenue
Withholding
Sam W. Mitchell Bldg.
125 N. Roberts, 3rd Fl.
Helena, MT 59604-5805
Mailing address: P.O. Box 5835
Helena, MT 59604-5835
406-444-6900 (in Helena); 866-859-2254
http://revenue.mt.gov/home/businesses/
wage_withholding

NEBRASKA

Dept. of Revenue
Taxpayer Assistance
301 Centennial Mall S.
Lincoln, NE 68508
Mailing address: P.O. Box 94818
Lincoln, NE 68509-4818
402-471-5729; 800-742-7474 (toll free in NE and IA)
www.revenue.nebraska.gov/withhold.html

NEW JERSEY

Dept. of the Treasury
Div. of Taxation
P.O. Box 269
Trenton, NJ 08695-0269
609-292-6400; 800-323-4400 (Automated Tax
Information System for NJ, NY, PA, DE, MD);
609-826-4400 (from anywhere)
www.state.nj.us/treasury/taxation/freqqite.shtml

NEW MEXICO	Taxation and Revenue Dept.
	1100 S. St. Francis Drive
	Sante Fe, NM 87504
	Mailing address: P.O. Box 630
	Santa Fe, NM 87504-0630
	505-827-0700
	http://www.tax.newmexico.gov/Businesses/
	wage-witholding-tax.aspx
NEW YORK	Dept. of Taxation and Finance
	Withholding Tax Information
	W.A. Harriman Campus
	Albany, NY 12227
	518-457-5431 (ordering forms)
	518-485-6654 (Withholding Tax Information
	Center)
	www.tax.ny.gov/bus/wt/wtidx.htm
NORTH CAROLINA	Dept. of Revenue
	Income Tax Withholding Section
	501 N. Wilmington Street
	Raleigh, NC 27604
	Mailing address: P.O. Box 25000
	Raleigh, NC 27640-0640
	877-252-3052
	www.dor.state.nc.us/taxes/wh_tax/index.html
NORTH DAKOTA	Office of State Tax Commissioner
	600 E. Boulevard Avenue, Dept. 127
	Bismarck, ND 58505-0599
	701-328-1248; 877-328-7088
	email: withhold@nd.gov;
	www.nd.gov/tax/withholding/
OHIO	Dept. of Taxation
	Employment Tax Division
	4485 Northland Ridge Boulevard
	Columbus, OH 43229
	888-405-4039
	www.tax.ohio.gov/employer_withholding.aspx

OKLAHOMA	Tax Commission Connors Bldg. 2501 N. Lincoln Blvd. Oklahoma City, OK 73194 405-521-3160 email: otcmaster@tax.ok.gov; www.ok.gov/tax/Businesses/Tax_Types/ Withholding/
OREGON	Dept. of Revenue Payroll Withholding and Transit Taxes 955 Center Street N.E. Salem, OR 97301-2555 503-378-4988; 800-356-4222; 503-945-8091 (withholding program representative) email: payroll.help.dor@oregon.gov; www.oregon.gov/DOR/programs/businesses/ Pages/payroll-withholding.aspx
PENNSYLVANIA	Dept. of Revenue Bureau of Business Trust Fund Taxes Employer Tax Div. P.O. Box 280904 Harrisburg, PA 17128-0904 717-787-1064; 888-PATAXES (728-2937) http://www.revenue.pa.gov/ GeneralTaxInformation/ Tax%20Types%20and%20Information/Pages/ Employer-Withholding.aspx
RHODE ISLAND	Div. of Taxation One Capitol Hill Providence, RI 02908 401-574-8829 email: Leo.Lebeuf@tax.ri.gov; www.tax.ri.gov
SOUTH CAROLINA	Dept. of Revenue Withholding Section 300A Outlet Pointe Blvd. Columbia, SC 29210 Mailing address: S.C. Dept. of Revenue Withholding Section Columbia, SC 29214-0004 844-898-8542 (option 4) https://dor.sc.gov/tax/withholding

UTAH

State Tax Commission
210 North 1950 West
Salt Lake City, UT 84134-0266
801-297-2200; 800-662-4335
email: taxmaster@utah.gov;
http://tax.utah.gov/withholding

VERMONT

Dept. of Taxes
133 State Street, 2nd Floor
Montpelier, VT 05603
Mailing address: P.O. Box 1779
Montpelier, VT 05601-0547
802-828-2551
email: tax.business@vermont.gov;
http://tax.vermont.gov/business-and-corp/
withholding-tax

VIRGINIA

Dept. of Taxation
Customer Services
P.O. Box 1115
Richmond, VA 23218-1115
804-367-8037
email: TaxBusQuestions@tax.virginia.gov;
www.tax.virginia.gov/content/withholding-tax

WEST VIRGINIA

State Tax Dept.
Taxpayer Services Div.
1001 Lee Street E
Charleston, WV 25337-3784
1206 Quarrier Street
Charleston, WV 25301
Mailing address: P.O. Box 3784
Charleston, WV 25337-3784
304-558-3333; 800-982-8297
email: TaxHelp@WV.Gov;
http://tax.wv.gov/Business/Withholding/Pages/
WithholdingTaxForms.aspx

WISCONSIN

Dept. of Revenue
P.O. Box 8902 or 8949
Madison, WI 53708
608-266-2776
email: DORSalesanduse@wisconsin.gov;
www.revenue.wi.gov/Pages/withholding/

UTAH	State Tax Commission
	210 North 1950 West
	Salt Lake City, UT 84134-0266
	801-297-2200; 800-662-4335
	email: taxmaster@utah.gov;
	http://tax.utah.gov/withholding
VERMONT	Dept. of Taxes
	133 State Street, 2nd Floor
	Montpelier, VT 05603
	Mailing address: P.O. Box 1779
	Montpelier, VT 05601-0547
	802-828-2551
	email: tax.business@vermont.gov;
	http://tax.vermont.gov/business-and-corp/withholding-tax
VIRGINIA	Dept. of Taxation
	Customer Services
	P.O. Box 1115
	Richmond, VA 23218-1115
	804-367-8037
	email: TaxBusQuestions@tax.virginia.gov;
	www.tax.virginia.gov/content/withholding-tax
WEST VIRGINIA	State Tax Dept.
	Taxpayer Services Div.
	1001 Lee Street E
	Charleston, WV 25337-8784
	1206 Quarrier Street
	Charleston, WV 25301
	Mailing address: P.O. Box 3784
	Charleston, WV 25337-8784
	304-558-3333; 800-982-8297
	email: TaxHelp@WV.Gov;
	http://tax.wv.gov/Business/Withholding/Pages/WithholdingTaxForms.aspx
WISCONSIN	Dept. of Revenue
	P.O. Box 8902 or 8949
	Madison, WI 53708
	608-266-2776
	email: DORSalesandUse@wisconsin.gov;
	www.revenue.wi.gov/Pages/withholding/

Appendix C

State Employment Security Agencies Dealing with State Unemployment Insurance Tax Programs

ALABAMA   Dept. of Labor
649 Monroe Street
Montgomery, AL 36131
334-242-8025
http://labor.alabama.gov

ALASKA   Dept. of Labor and Workforce Development
Employment Security Tax
1111 W. 8th Street, Rm. 203
P.O. Box 115509
Juneau, AK 99811-5509
907-465-2757; 888-448-3527
email: esd.tax@alaska.gov;
http://www.labor.alaska.gov/estax

ARIZONA   Dept. of Economic Security
Division of Employment & Rehabilitation Services
Unemployment Insurance Tax
4000 N. Central Ave., Ste. 500
Phoenix, AZ 85012
Mailing address: P.O. Box 6028
Phoenix, AZ 85005-6028
602-771-6601
https://des.az.gov/services/employment/
unemployment-employer

ARKANSAS
Dept. of Workforce Services
Unemployment Insurance Dept.
2 Capitol Mall
Little Rock, AR 72201
Mailing address: P.O. Box 2981
Little Rock, AR 72203
501-682-3798
email: ADWS.Info@arkansas.gov;
http://dws.arkansas.gov/

CALIFORNIA
Employment Development Dept.
800 Capitol Mall, MIC 83
Sacramento, CA 95814
Mailing address:
P.O. Box 826880—UIPCD,
MIC 40
Sacramento, CA 94280-0001
866-333-4606 (Automated Self-Service);
800-300-5616 (Customer Service Representative)
www.edd.ca.gov

COLORADO
Dept. of Labor and Employment
Div. of Unemployment Insurance
633 17th Street, Ste. 201
Denver, CO 80202-3660
Mailing address: UI Employer Services
P.O. Box 8789
Denver, CO 80201-8789
303-318-9100; 800-480-8299
email: cdle_employer_services@state.co.us;
https://www.colorado.gov/cdle/unemployment/

CONNECTICUT
Dept. of Labor
Unemployment Insurance Tax Div.
Employer Status Unit
200 Folly Brook Boulevard
Wethersfield, CT 06109
860-263-6000
email: dol.webhelp@ct.gov;
www.ctdol.state.ct.us

DELAWARE	Dept. of Labor Div. of Unemployment Insurance Employer Contributions P.O. Box 9953 Wilmington, DE 19809 302-761-8484 http://ui.delawareworks.com
DISTRICT OF COLUMBIA	Dept. of Employment Services Tax Division 4058 Minnesota Avenue, N.E., 4th Fl. Washington, DC 20019 202-698-7550 http://does.dc.gov
FLORIDA	Dept. of Revenue Taxpayer Services 5050 W. Tennessee St., Mail Stop 3-2000 Tallahassee, FL 32399-0100 800-352-3671 http://dor.myflorida.com/dor/taxes/ reemployment.html
GEORGIA	Dept. of Labor Unemployment Insurance and Regional Operations Division 148 Andrew Young International Boulevard, N.E. Atlanta, GA 30303-1751 404-232-3320 855-436-7365 (Employer Hotline) http://dol.georgia.gov/
HAWAII	Dept. of Labor and Industrial Relations Unemployment Insurance Div. 830 Punchbowl Street, Rm. 437 Honolulu, HI 96813-5080 808-586-8915 http://labor.hawaii.gov/ui/
IDAHO	Dept. of Labor 317 W. Main Street Boise, ID 83735-0760 800-448-2977; 208-332-3576 http://labor.idaho.gov/dnn/idl/Businesses/ eservices.aspx

ILLINOIS   Dept. of Employment Security
33 S. State Street, 10th Fl.
Chicago, IL 60603
800-247-4984
www.ides.illinois.gov/Pages/default.aspx

INDIANA   Dept. of Workforce Development
UI Tax Administration
10 N. Senate Avenue
Indianapolis, IN 46204
800-437-9136
www.in.gov/dwd

IOWA   Iowa Workforce Development
Unemployment Insurance Tax Bureau
1000 E. Grand Avenue
Des Moines, IA 50319
800-562-4692
email: iwduitax@iwd.iowa.gov;
www.iowaworkforcedevelopment.gov

KANSAS   Dept. of Labor
Division of Employment Security
Contributions Unit
401 S.W. Topeka Boulevard
Topeka, KS 66603-3182
785-296-5000
www.dol.ks.gov

KENTUCKY   Kentucky Career Center
275 E. Main Street, 2nd Fl.
Frankfort, KY 40621
502-564-2900
http://kcc.ky.gov

LOUISIANA   Workforce Commission
Unemployment Insurance Tax Liability and
Adjudication
1001 N. 23rd Street
Baton Rouge, LA 70802
Mailing address: P.O. Box 94186
Baton Rouge, LA 70804-9186
866-783-5567
www.laworks.net/UnemploymentInsurance/UI_
Employers.asp

MAINE	Dept. of Labor Bureau of Unemployment Compensation Employer Services Division (UI Taxes) 47S State House Station Augusta, ME 04333-0047 207-621-5120 www.maine.gov/labor/unemployment/
MARYLAND	Dept. of Labor, Licensing & Regulation Div. of Unemployment Insurance Contributions Division 1100 N. Eutaw Street, Rm. 414 Baltimore, MD 21201 410-767-2412 800-492-5524 email: dluiemployerassistance-dllr@maryland.gov; www.dllr.state.md.us
MASSACHUSETTS	Labor and Workforce Development Charles F. Hurley Bldg. 19 Staniford Street Boston, MA 02114 617-626-5075 www.mass.gov/lwd
MICHIGAN	Unemployment Insurance Agency—Tax Office 3024 W. Grand Boulevard, Ste. 11-500 Detroit, MI 48202 855-484-2636 (in-state employers); 313-456-2180 (out-of-state employers) email: OEO@michigan.gov; www.michigan.gov/uia
MINNESOTA	Dept. of Employment and Economic Development Unemployment Insurance Program 1st National Bank Building, Ste. E200 332 Minnesota Street St. Paul, MN 55101-1351 651-296-6141 http://www.uimn.org/uimn/employers

MISSISSIPPI Dept. of Employment Security
Office of the Governor
1235 Echelon Parkway
P.O. Box 1699
Jackson, MS 39215-1699
601-321-6000
email: tax@mdes.ms.gov;
http://www.mdes.ms.gov/employers/
unemployment-tax/

MISSOURI Dept. of Labor and Industrial Relations
Div. of Employment Security
Main address and magnetic media reports:
421 E. Dunklin Street
P.O. Box 59
Jefferson City, MO 65104-0059
Quarterly wage reports:
P.O. Box 888
Jefferson City, MO 65102-0888
573-751-3215
email: esemptax@labor.mo.gov;
http://labor.mo.gov/Employers

MONTANA Dept. of Labor and Industry
Walt Sullivan Building
1315 Lockey Avenue
Helena, MT 59601-5178
Unemployment Insurance Contributions Bureau
P.O. Box 6339
Helena, MT 59604-6339
406-444-3834
www.dli.mt.gov/employers

NEBRASKA Dept. of Labor
Office of Unemployment Insurance Tax
550 S. 16th Street
P.O. Box 94600
Lincoln, NE 68509-4600
402-471-9898
email: NDOL.UICContact@nebraska.gov;
http://dol.nebraska.gov

NEVADA   Dept. of Employment, Training & Rehabilitation
Employment Security Div.
Contributions Section
500 E. Third Street
Carson City, NV 89713-0030
775-684-6310
www.detr.state.nv.us/esd.htm

NEW HAMPSHIRE   New Hampshire Employment Security
45 S. Fruit Street
Concord, NH 03301
603-228-4042
www.nhes.nh.gov

NEW JERSEY   Dept. of Labor and Workforce Development
Div. of Employer Accounts
135 E. State Street, 9th Fl.
Trenton, NJ 08625
Mailing address: P.O. Box 913
Trenton, NJ 08625-0913
609-633-6400 (Employer Status);
609-984-7988 (electronic media filing)
http://lwd.dol.state.nj.us/labor/ea/ea_index.html

NEW MEXICO   Dept. of Workforce Solutions
Unemployment Insurance Bureau
Tax Section
P.O. Box 2281
401 Broadway, N.E.
Albuquerque, NM 87103
877-664-6984
www.dws.state.nm.us

NEW YORK   Dept. of Labor
Unemployment Insurance Div.
Liability and Determination Section
W.A. Harriman Campus, Bldg. 12, Rm. 356
Albany, NY 12240-0322
888-899-8810
email: labor.sm.ui.division@labor.ny.gov;
https://www.labor.ny.gov/home

NORTH CAROLINA   Division of Employment Security
Unemployment Insurance
700 Wade Avenue
Raleigh, NC 27605
Mailing address:
P.O. Box 25903
Raleigh, NC 27611-5903
919-707-1150
email: des.tax.customerservice@nccommerce.com;
https://des.nc.gov/des

NORTH DAKOTA   Job Service North Dakota
Unemployment Insurance
1000 E. Divide Avenue
P.O. Box 5507
Bismarck, ND 58506-5507
701-328-2814
http://www.jobsnd.com/unemployment-business

OHIO   Dept. of Job & Family Services
Office of Unemployment Insurance Operations
Contribution Section
4020 E. 5th Avenue
Columbus, OH 43211-1811
Mailing Address:
P.O. Box 182404
Columbus, OH 43218-2404
614-466-2319
http://jfs.ohio.gov/ouc/uctax/index.stm

OKLAHOMA   Employment Security Commission
Unemployment Insurance Division
Attn: Status Department
P.O. Box 52003
Oklahoma City, OK 73152-2003
405-557-5452 (EZ Tax Express Help Desk);
405-557-7222 (Employer tax rate questions);
405-557-5330 (Employer taxes compliance)
www.ok.gov/oesc_web

OREGON

Employment Dept.
Unemployment Insurance Tax Division
875 Union St., N.E.
Salem, OR 97311
Mailing address: P.O. Box 14800
Salem, OR 97309-0920 (to file Form WR
with payment, all paper reports, and all
Form OTC payments)
503-947-1544
email: OED_Taxinfo_User@oregon.gov;
www.oregon.gov/employ/businesses/tax/Pages/
Payroll-Taxes.aspx

PENNSYLVANIA

Dept. of Labor and Industry
Office of UC Tax Services
651 Boas Street, Rm. 1700
Harrisburg, PA 17121
866-403-6163; 717-787-7679 (Harrisburg area)
email: UIEMPCHARGE@pa.gov;
www.uc.pa.gov/employers-uc-services-uc-tax/
Pages/default.aspx

RHODE ISLAND

Div. of Taxation
Employer Tax Section
One Capitol Hill
Providence, RI 02908
401-574-8700 (Tax Administration)
www.uitax.ri.gov

SOUTH CAROLINA

Dept. of Employment and Workforce
1550 Gadsden Street
Columbia, SC 29202
Mailing address: P.O. Box 995
Columbia, SC 29202
803-737-2400, Option 3
email: uitax@dew.sc.gov;
http://dew.sc.gov

SOUTH DAKOTA

Dept. of Labor and Regulation
Unemployment Insurance Div., Tax Unit
420 S. Roosevelt Street
P.O. Box 4730
Aberdeen, SD 57402-4730
605-626-2312
http://dlr.sd.gov/ui

TENNESSEE	Dept. of Labor & Workforce Development Employment Security Div. 220 French Landing Drive Nashville, TN 37243 844-224-5818 (in state); 615-741-2346 (out of state) Dept. of Labor & Workforce Development Employer Accounts Operations P.O. Box 101 Nashville, TN 37202-0101 (to file quarterly reports) http://www.tn.gov/workforce/topic/unemployment-insurance-tax
TEXAS	Tax Dept. Workforce Commission 101 E. 15th Street Austin, TX 78778-0001 512-463-2699; 866-274-1722 email: tax@twc.state.tx.us; http://www.texasworkforce.org/businesses/unemployment-tax
UTAH	Dept. of Workforce Services Unemployment Insurance Div. 140 East 300 South, 3rd Fl. P.O. Box 45288 Salt Lake City, UT 84145-0288 801-526-9235; 800-222-2857 (toll free) email: dws-ui-contrib@utah.gov; https://jobs.utah.gov/ui/employer/employerhome.aspx
VERMONT	Dept. of Labor Administrative Office 5 Green Mountain Drive P.O. Box 488 Montpelier, VT 05601-0488 802-828-4344 (Unemployment Employer Services) email: labor-uiandwages@vermont.gov; http://labor.vermont.gov

VIRGINIA   Employment Commission
703 E. Main Street
Richmond, VA 23219
Mailing address: P.O. Box 1358
Richmond, VA 23218-1358
804-786-3061
email: employer.accounts@vec.virginia.gov;
www.vec.virginia.gov

WASHINGTON   Employment Security Dept.
212 Maple Park Avenue, S.E.
Olympia, WA 98501-2347
Mailing address: P.O. Box 9046
Olympia, WA 98507-9046
888-836-1900
email: employeraccounts@esd.wa.gov;
https://esd.wa.gov/employer-taxes

WEST VIRGINIA   WorkForce West Virginia
Unemployment Compensation Division
Unemployment Compensation Contribution
Accounting Section
Central Administrative Office
112 California Avenue
Charleston, WV 25305-0112
304-558-2677
http://workforcewv.org/unemployment/
employers.html

WISCONSIN   Dept. of Workforce Development
Unemployment Insurance Div.,
Bureau of Tax and Accounting
201 E. Washington Avenue
Madison, WI 53703
Mailing address: P.O. Box 7905
Madison, WI 53707
608-232-0633 (Madison); 414-438-7705
(Milwaukee); 800-247-1744 (toll free)
email: taxnet@dwd.wisconsin.gov;
http://dwd.wisconsin.gov/uitax

WYOMING

Dept. of Workforce Services
Unemployment Insurance
100 W. Midwest Avenue
Casper, WY 82601
Mailing address: P.O. Box 2760
Casper, WY 82602-2760
307-235-3264
email: shelli.stewart@wyo.gov;
http://wyomingworkforce.org/businesses/ui/

Index

[References are to Question Numbers and Appendixes. Entries containing numbers are alphabetized as though spelled out (e.g., W-3 precedes W-2).]

G

O